Administrative Law

Theory and Fundamentals

AN INTEGRATED APPROACH

ILAN WURMAN

SANDRA DAY O'CONNOR COLLEGE OF LAW
ARIZONA STATE UNIVERSITY

DOCTRINE AND PRACTICE SERIES™

FOUNDATION
PRESS

© 2021 LEG, Inc. d/b/a West Academic
  444 Cedar Street, Suite 700
  St. Paul, MN 55101
  1-877-888-1330

Printed in the United States of America

ISBN: 978-1-64708-426-4

To all my teachers—past, present, and future.

Preface

This casebook, while also giving much play to functionalism, assumes a formalist approach to administrative law that largely, although not entirely, defends the constitutionality of the modern administrative state. The theory driving the casebook is that there are "exclusive" powers that only Congress, the President, and the courts can respectively exercise, but also "nonexclusive" powers that can be exercised by more than one branch. The overarching claim is that much of what the administrative state does is in this latter category, although some, to be sure, is not.

In a time when the modern Supreme Court appears on the verge of rethinking many administrative law doctrines, a casebook like this that focuses not only on fundamentals, but also on theory, is terribly needed. The book has many innovations, but one that highlights its approach is the extensive discussion of the 1852 steamboat legislation and the 1887 Interstate Commerce Act, the full texts of which are supplied in appendices. Another is the inclusion of sections on "Debating Deference," "Debating Delegation," "Debating Presidential Control," "Debating the Due Process Revolution," and "Debating Universal Injunctions," which comprise excerpts from the secondary literature debating the theory, values, and policy merits of the various doctrines.

Organizationally, the book begins with a historical introduction and constitutional overview, before turning to rulemaking, adjudication, and judicial review of the same. The second half then returns to constitutional questions, with dedicated chapters on legislative, executive, and judicial power, before concluding with reviewability.

The book discusses Article III and due process in the same chapter, with due process following Article III. The history and theory of private rights and public rights makes this organization logical. The material on agency action "committed to agency discretion by law," 5 U.S.C. § 701(a), possibly for the first time, is included with material on judicial review of agency action. Many exercises of discretion are reviewable, and the question thus becomes whether such exercises are reviewable under § 706 or not per § 701. These materials also fit together because they involve distinguishing different kinds of agency action, whereas other reviewability doctrines apply irrespective of the kind of agency action at hand. The casebook further reworks reviewability by placing the zone-of-interests test where it belongs: not as part of prudential standing, but instead as part of the materials on causes of action.

There is much intellectual ferment in administrative law. My hope is that this casebook can help students, professors, and scholars navigate both the steady, and the shifting, currents.

ILAN WURMAN

February 5, 2021
Arizona State University

Acknowledgments

The idea for this casebook, and the ideas in it, have been shaped by many academic exchanges in writing and in person. Here I wish specifically to mention Kristin Hickman, Gary Lawson, and Richard Pierce, whose own casebooks on administrative law inspired many of my choices here in terms of both inclusion and, of course, deviation. I also thanks Alanna Ostby and Katherine Johnson, both star students at Arizona State University, for their research assistance.

Finally, I would like to acknowledge the following authors and publishers who gave me permission to reprint their work:

James Landis, The Administrative Process, © Yale University Press, 1938, reprinted with permission of Yale University Press

Gillian E. Metzger, The Administrative State Under Siege, © Harvard Law Review, 2017, vol. 131, p. 1

Cass R. Sunstein, Beyond Marbury: The Executive's Power to Say What the Law Is, © The Yale Law Journal, 2006, vol. 115, p. 2580

Richard J. Pierce, Jr., Two Problems in Administrative Law: Political Polarity on the District of Columbia Circuit and Judicial Deterrence of Agency Rulemaking, © Duke Law Journal, 1988, p. 300, 308–09

Russell L. Weaver & Linda D. Jellum, Chenery II and the Development of Federal Administrative Law, 58 Admin. L. Rev. 815, 824–27 (2006). ©2006 by the American Bar Association. Reprinted with permission. All rights reserved. This information or any or portion thereof may not be copied or disseminated in any form or by any means or stored in an electronic database or retrieval system without the express written consent of the American Bar Association.

Christopher J. Walker & Melissa F. Wasserman, The New World of Agency Adjudication, 107 Cal. L. Rev. 141 (2019). © 2019 by California Law Review, Inc.

Michael Asimow, Administrative Conference of the United States, Adjudication Outside the Administrative Procedure Act, Sept. 16, 2016.

Brett M. Kavanaugh, Fixing Statutory Interpretation, © Harvard Law Review, 2016, vol. 129, p. 2118, 2136–38.

Jerry L. Mashaw, Greed, Chaos, and Governance, © Yale University Press, 1997, pp. 136, 139–41, 146–48, 152–54, reprinted with permission of Yale University Press

David Schoenbrod, Power Without Responsibility, © Yale University Press, 1993, pp. 9–11, 99, 119–21, reprinted with permission of Yale University Press

Peter H. Schuck, Delegation and Democracy, 20 Cardozo L. Rev. 775 (1999)

Joseph Postell, Bureaucracy in America, © University of Missouri Press, 2016, pp. 42–49, reprinted with permission of the University of Missouri Press

Elena Kagan, Presidential Administration, © Harvard Law Review, 2001, vol. 114, p. 2246

Martin S. Flaherty, The Most Dangerous Branch, © The Yale Law Journal, 1996, vol. 105, p. 1725

Peter L. Strauss, The Place of Agencies in Government, © Columbia Law Review, 1984, vol. 84, pp. 573, 575–80. This article originally appears at 84 Colum. L. Rev. 573 (1984). Reprinted with permission.

Charles A. Reich, Individual Rights and Social Welfare: The Emerging Legal Issues, © The Yale Law Journal, 1965, vol. 74, pp. 1245, 1252–53

Stephen F. Williams, Liberty and Property: The Problem of Government Benefits, © Journal of Legal Studies, 1983, vol. 12, pp. 3, 11–13

Henry J. Friendly, "Some Kind of Hearing", © The University of Pennsylvania Law Review, 1975, vol. 123 pp. 1267, 1287–91

Jerry L. Mashaw, The Management Side of Due Process, © Cornell Law Review, 1974, vol. 59, p. 772

Samuel L. Bray, Multiple Chancellors: Reforming the National Injunction, © Harvard Law Review, 2017, vol. 131, p. 417

Amanda Frost, In Defense of Nationwide Injunctions, © New York University Law Review, 2018, vol. 93, p. 1065

Table of Contents

Table of Cases

Principal cases are in bold.

Administrative Law

Theory and Fundamentals

AN INTEGRATED APPROACH

CHAPTER ONE

Introduction and Overview

A. Introduction

1. Why Another Casebook?

It is an exciting time to be a student of administrative law: the Supreme Court in the past few years has started to rethink doctrines that for decades have been the cornerstone of the subject. The rise of textualism, originalism, and formalism (to the extent they are different; perhaps they are not, at least not in separation of powers cases), now ascendant on the Supreme Court, has led to a veritable reconsideration of the very foundations of administrative law among both courts and scholars. It has also led to reaffirmations of the administrative state on the part of many with both old and new arguments. Yet most existing casebooks on administrative law, whose first editions were written decades ago, do not fully bring to the fore the nature of the modern debate.

For example, most casebooks spend almost no time on the early history of administration. Not many historical overviews carefully analyze the nature and contours of the steamboat legislation in the mid-nineteenth century or the legislation creating the Interstate Commerce Commission in 1887. Yet these two pieces of legislation are considered to be significant historical precedents for modern administration and often justify modern administrative activity for those who look to historical practice as a guide. It therefore matters a great deal that there is a robust debate over what these precedents establish. To that end, not only does the introductory chapter focus on these statutes in more depth than they have traditionally been accorded, but for the first time among case-books two appendices (C and D) reproduce the 1852 steamboat legislation and the 1887 Interstate Commerce Act in full.

To be sure, this casebook is still a casebook—it focuses mostly on courts, and mostly on the modern doctrine. But it aims to equip the student with the historical and theoretical materials necessary for understanding the full nature, extent, and implications of the modern debate. If modern scholars and judges are seeking to rethink administrative law—or perhaps to rethink defenses of it—they must understand this theoretical and historical material, too. This casebook thus summarizes the relevant history, and also excerpts from relevant theorists like Woodrow Wilson, Frank Goodnow, and James Landis, more than conventional casebooks.

This casebook, in short, takes the new formalism seriously, and it thus speaks to the concerns of the modern Supreme Court. But, unlike most formalist accounts of the administrative state, the one presented in this casebook largely accepts the constitutionality of the administrative state, even as it doubts several of the existing doctrines. This casebook therefore ought to be of interest not only to formalists, but also to skeptics of formalism who nevertheless want to understand and teach an approach that appeals to the modern Court.

Perhaps most importantly—and what most distinguishes this casebook from others—is that it is driven by a particular theory of administrative power (it canvasses several competing views, of course). The book explores the competing theories of the nondelegation doctrine, the meaning of "the executive power," and the requirements of Article III. As already hinted, many formalists believe that the administrative state is unconstitutional. They argue that the administrative state unconstitutionally exercises combined legislative, executive, and judicial powers. One account of formalism in the administrative law literature maintains that "[u]nder a pure formalist approach, most, if not all, of the administrative state is unconstitutional" because agency "rulemaking and adjudication"—the core functions of modern administrative agencies—are "inconsistent with the formalist model." Peter B. McCutchen, *Mistakes, Precedent, and the Rise of the Administrative State: Toward a Constitutional Theory of the Second Best*, 80 Cornell L. Rev. 1, 11 (1994). Many functionalists, on the other hand, accept the constitutionality of the administrative state on any number of theories. Some argue that broad delegations of power to agencies have been with us from the beginning (Mashaw 2012); that there is a distinction between executive power and "administrative" power (Lessig & Sunstein 1994); that it is impossible to distinguish between legislative, executive, and judicial power (Magill 2001 among many others); or that delegations of power to agencies are inevitable even if originally unconstitutional (Metzger 2017).

As one reads the cases and the history, however, none of the accounts described above seems quite right. There are many textual, structural, and theoretical justifications for much, even if not all, modern administration under a formalist model. But it is not true that the broad scope and nature of modern delegations have been with us from the beginning. And, although administrative power is hard to characterize, it is not impossible to do so. The idea of this casebook is that there are *exclusive* powers—exclusively legislative power that only Congress may exercise, exclusively executive power that only the President may exercise (or supervise), and exclusively judicial power that only the courts may exercise. But many powers are "nonexclusive," in the sense that they partake in multiple qualities and can be exercised by more than one branch of government. Not every agency adjudication is an exercise of *the* federal judicial power, although the federal courts could hear such cases themselves if Congress assigned them to the courts. And most (if not all) regulations could be enacted by Congress, and hence are partly legislative in nature; but many also implement the details of a statutory scheme, and surely it is acceptable for agencies to promulgate them. The making of such a regulation, in other words, is the exercise of a nonexclusive power. Keeping the distinction between exclusive and nonexclusive powers in mind clarifies the theory of administrative law, and allows us better to analyze many separation of powers cases. That is the theoretical approach underpinning much of the materials that follow.

Beyond focusing more on "theory" than conventional casebooks, this casebook also focuses more on "fundamentals." The aim is to be digestible and clear about black-letter law. Having written semi-academic, semi-commercial books on constitutional law, I aim to maintain a similar tone, style, and pacing here. Administrative law is complicated as it is, particularly in light of its many contradictions and tensions. There is no reason why a casebook can't be explicit in explaining to the student the black-letter doctrines, the tensions and problems with the black-letter doctrines, and possible solutions. For example, it is notoriously difficult to synthesize the cases surrounding the permissibility of Article I legislative courts and adjudicatory administrative agencies as opposed to using Article III courts vested with the federal judicial power. The relevant section of this casebook offers a synthesis of these cases. Some scholars may disagree with that synthesis, and of course the casebook highlights other possibilities, but at least the student will have some framing for digesting and remembering the key cases.

Another important way in which this casebook innovates from others is that it equips the student throughout with tools of statutory interpretation. As any student of administrative law knows (or will come to know), everything starts with a statute. Numerous administrative law doctrines require us to interpret those statutes. Yet few if any administrative law casebooks teach students about statutory interpretation. The student has to pick up on the relevant tools and rules for herself. At least two administrative law casebooks offer large introductory chapters to statutory interpretation. Unlike all of these other casebooks, this one teaches the tools of statutory interpretation throughout, as they arise in particular cases. Conveniently, many of the tools and rules of statutory interpretation will be discussed in two early cases (*Franklin v. Massachusetts*, p. 16, and *National Petroleum Refiners*, p. 87), equipping the student to handle most issues of statutory interpretation in the remainder of the text.

As a general matter, this casebook also covers fewer cases but with longer excerpts that raise more issues. It accounts for the possibility that some professors will not have the time to assign all of these cases but will want their students to be familiar with them. Thus, after many cases, the first note will provide a summary of the holding that will help students digest the material and will sometimes allow instructors to assign the note without having the students read the entire case.

Finally, this casebook also innovates in its organization. As most scholars of administrative law recognize, teaching administrative law is something of a "catch 22." It is hard to know whether one should start with what agencies actually do, i.e., rulemaking and adjudication, or start with the constitutional issues of legislative delegation, executive control, and judicial power. Most casebooks start with the constitutional issues. However, to understand these issues, one really must understand what agencies actually do. On the flip side, as soon as one starts to examine what agencies do, the constitutional questions immediately come to mind. This casebook seeks to resolve this problem by having an introductory section on what administrative law actually is and the constitutional questions that arise (Chapter 1.A.2), an extensive section on the history of administration that highlights the constitutional questions that arise from this history (Chapter 1.B), and then a section specifically on modern-day constitutional concerns that introduces the problem of delegation of legislative power (Chapter 1.C).

After this introduction and overview, the casebook starts in the first half with what agencies do and the statutory constraints on them—rulemaking, adjudication, and judicial review of the same. Some casebooks start with adjudication, and save judicial review for the very end of the course. This casebook starts with rulemaking, as regulations are more familiar to students and these days they are often logically prior to adjudications. It then discusses judicial review (or the "scope of review") right after adjudications. After all, the substantive standards of review—the grounds on which courts may overturn agency actions—themselves create and are part of the statutory constraints on what agencies do. In the second half, the casebook takes a deeper dive into the constitutional questions surrounding legislative, executive, and judicial power, and due process considerations. It then concludes, as is typical, with reviewability doctrines such as causes of action, statutory preclusion of review, the timing of review, and standing.

Some more specific organizational innovations include the following:

First, some administrative law books have entire chapters devoted to the Freedom of Information Act; many others omit the subject altogether. This book takes an intermediate approach: it deals with FOIA in an "interlude" section following the discussions of disclosing data and ex parte contacts in the context of informal rulemaking. This material is placed here because FOIA is usually the mechanism by which practitioners and public interest groups find out that an agency has been withholding data or engaging in undisclosed ex parte contacts. A brief detour into FOIA law is therefore an option for professors and students interested in that subject.

Second, following the relevant material are short sections—"Debating Deference," "Debating Delegation," "Debating Presidential Control," "Debating the Due Process Revolution," and "Debating Universal Injunctions"—with excerpts from the secondary literature debating the various doctrines. These short excerpts will allow students to take a deeper dive into the theoretical, normative, and policy debates over the various constitutional doctrines.

Third, the organization of Chapter 7 is also important, and diverges from most (perhaps all) other casebooks on administrative law: it discusses Article III and due process together, beginning with Article III and concluding with due process. This ordering is critical because one cannot make sense of the evolution of modern procedural due process law without understanding the distinction between private rights and public rights and understanding the role judicial courts and processes play in due process of law. It turns out that the due process materials, which are traditionally located in the chapter on statutory procedural constraints on agency adjudications, make much more sense when they directly follow the Article III materials.

Finally, and perhaps most significantly, this casebook reworks the material on reviewability in several important ways. The material on agency action "committed to agency discretion by law," APA § 701(a), is typically, perhaps universally, included with the materials on reviewability, such as finality, ripeness, and exhaustion. This casebook places this material much more suitably right after judicial review of agency policymaking, fact-finding, and legal interpretation. This is more suitable because many kinds of agency discretion are reviewable, whether under the abuse of discretion standard of APA § 706(a)(2)(A), or under the arbitrary-and-capricious standard of that same provision. The question thus becomes when is there discretion of the type reviewable under § 706, and when is there discretion of the type not reviewable per § 701. One can make sense of these materials only if they are addressed together. These materials also fit together because they involve distinguishing different *kinds* of agency actions, whereas the doctrines of finality, ripeness, exhaustion, standing, and causes of action apply across the board and can preclude judicial review irrespective of the kind of agency action at hand.

The second key change regarding reviewability is the placement of the so-called "statutory standing" or "zone of interests" cases. These are traditionally understood to be part of prudential standing limits, and thus are generally included after "constitutional standing" in a dedicated section on "standing." But, in reality, the zone-of-interests cases are really about *causes of action*—they are about whether particular people have been conferred legal rights, and therefore rights of action, under administrative statutes. The Supreme Court occasionally describes the zone-of-interests test as involving causes of action, and the best current scholarly research confirms the connection between the so-called statutory standing cases and causes of action. Therefore, Chapter 8 begins with non-APA causes of action, then discusses the "APA cause of action," where the instructor and student will find the traditional materials on statutory preclusion of review, as well as the material typically covered under the "statutory standing" heading; and only then it will proceed to constitutional standing and finally to the timing of judicial review.

As to timing, this chapter will address finality and exhaustion together, but ripeness is now part of a dedicated section on preenforcement injunctions. As this section will make clear, modern ripeness doctrine is really just a part of this broader doctrine on equitable relief. The Supreme Court does not always understand many of the preenforcement injunction cases in terms of equity—usually it analyzes them as statutory preclusion cases—but equity is the better lens through which to view them.

2.   An Overview of Administrative Law

Administrative law is concerned with administrative agencies and their work. The task of these agencies is principally to "administer," or "implement," the policies of the national government. Usually these policies are established at only the most general level by Congress, leaving much for agencies to decide through regulations, although sometimes Congress legislates quite specifically and agencies have to carry out Congress's specific instructions. Within the realm of discretion, the President often directs what kinds of policies the agencies should adopt, although to what extent the President should have a role is contested (see Chapter 6). Federal administrative agencies, at the most fundamental level, are there to assist the President, or perhaps to assist Congress, in clarifying, sometimes in establishing, and then in implementing these policies of the national government.

The Administrative Procedure Act (APA), a statute with which we shall become intimately familiar, defines an agency as "each authority of the Government of the United States, whether or not it is within or subject to review by another agency," but excluding Congress, the courts, the national territories and the government of the District of Columbia, military authority in the field in times of war, and courts martial and military commissions. Although this definition would seem to include the President, the Supreme Court has assumed that the APA does not apply to the President.

 Defined Term

THE APA: The Administrative Procedure Act (APA) is often said to be a kind of "constitution" for the administrative state. Enacted in 1946, it largely provides procedural constraints, but also some substantive constraints, on how agencies operate.

By this definition, there are legions of such agencies at the federal level: at the "cabinet" level, all of the cabinet departments such as the Department of Education and the Department of Labor, all subcabinet authorities such as the Occupational Safety and Health Administration (OSHA, under the Department of Labor), freestanding agencies like the Environmental Protection Agency (EPA), and also "independent agencies" like the Federal Trade Commission (FTC), Federal Communications Commission (FCC), and the Securities and Exchange Commission (SEC) are "agencies." In fact, one might say that any governmental actor with substantial decision-making "authority" that is not also named in the Constitution itself—that is, any such actor other than Congress, the President and Vice President, or the federal courts—is an "agency." Because the Constitution does not directly create any administrative agency, each agency is established by Congress in what is termed an agency's "organic statute"—the statute that gives the agency authority, empowers it to do things, and constrains it in particular ways.

Defined Term

AGENCY: Different statutes define the term "agency" differently for their own purposes. For purposes of this course, you should be most familiar with the term as defined in the Administrative Procedure Act.

This raises the question of *where* administrative agencies are located within our constitutional structure. The answer, for the most part, is that they are located within the executive branch. "Administration," as it was historically understood, was synonymous with "execution," although some scholars claim that "administration"

Defined Term

ORGANIC STATUTE: An agency's organic statute is the statute that establishes it and gives it authority. The specific requirements of an agency's particular organic statute usually take precedence over the more general requirements of the APA that apply to all agencies.

is something different than pure "execution" of law. But whatever else public administration might entail, it is certainly intimately connected with execution of the law—the execution of Congress's explicit instructions and also its more general policy decisions. In short, as part of the executive branch, agencies are essentially the President's assistants in executing the law, although, again, many agencies are, and many scholars argue they ought to be, independent of presidential influence.

The most obvious category of agencies that scholars claim should be independent of presidential influence are the so-called "independent agencies." We shall see (in Chapter 6) what exactly makes these agencies independent, but the bottom line is that they tend to be headed by multiple commissioners of both political parties, and their authorizing statutes declare that the President can only fire these commissioners "for cause." Although no one has ever truly litigated what might constitute "cause,"

 CROSS REFERENCE In Chapter 6, we will explore "independent agencies" in more detail. For now, it is helpful to know simply that what makes such agencies "independent" is the President is restricted in the ability to remove their commissioners. Usually such agencies are composed of multiple commissioners with a bipartisan makeup.

it is generally believed that the President cannot remove commissioners of independent agencies for mere disagreements over policy. These for-cause removal provisions are what make these agencies "independent" of the President. This insulation naturally raises the question of where exactly within the constitutional structure do these particular agencies fit. Are they a part of the executive branch, or apart from it? If they are not fully within the executive branch, and they are not part of Congress or the courts, are they a "fourth branch" of government? Is that constitutional? We shall come back to this question in more detail in Chapter 6 and elsewhere in this course.

Now that we have a basic understanding of what agencies are, and at the most general level what they do (administer or implement national policies), we can consider more specifically *how* agencies administer and implement the policies of the national government. There are three principal functions that agencies exercise. First, they implement Congress's law and an agency's own regulations through traditional "enforcement" activities. This is what traditionally comes to mind when students think of "executing the law." Agencies conduct investigations, issue subpoenas, engage in administrative searches, and sometimes even use SWAT teams; they then bring enforcement actions in the federal courts, and sometimes in front of an adjudicatory body within the agency itself. Some administrative law casebooks include this material; most don't, and this one does not include material on enforcement activity either. It is the stuff of criminal procedure and federal jurisdiction courses, and is of less interest to students of administrative law.

Second, agencies implement Congress's statutes and also their own regulations through *adjudication*—deciding through some kind of proceeding to take a course of action based on the existence of certain facts in light of statutory or regulatory requirements. Should a highway go through a historic public park? That depends on a variety of statutory factors. Are you eligible for federal student loans, for a passport, or for social security disability benefits? That depends again on a variety of statutory criteria and whether you meet those criteria. Someone has to decide what those criteria are and whether you meet them; agencies do this through "adjudication," which can be anything from an informal meeting with an agency official to proceedings in front of an Administrative Law Judge with lawyers and cross-examination.

> **CROSS REFERENCE** We will discuss the technical definition of the term "adjudication" in more detail in Chapter 2. Under the APA, adjudications are essentially any agency action that isn't a "rulemaking."

Third and finally, agencies implement Congress's statutes through rulemaking, that is, by issuing their own regulations (also called "rules"). Sometimes an agency doesn't need to issue regulations at all; sometimes it can just apply Congress's statutes directly in adjudications. But regulations can be very helpful; they often specify in much more detail how an agency intends to implement Congress's law and what the agency understands Congress's law to require. These regulations can then come into play in adjudications and enforcement actions, but they also do work on their own because most regulated entities will conform to the regulations to which they are subject.

> **Defined Term** **RULEMAKING, RULE, REGULATION:** The terms rulemaking, rule, and regulation are often interchangeable. Rulemaking is the process by which a regulation, also called a "rule," is made.

Administrative law, then, is concerned principally with these latter two modes of implementing national law and policy: it is concerned with how agencies make regulations, and how they engage in adjudications. In particular, administrative law is concerned with the *legal constraints* on how agencies undertake these activities. That's the "law" in "administrative law." First, there are statutory constraints. Most importantly, the Administrative Procedure Act sets out a whole host of procedural rules for how an agency can adjudicate and how it can make regulations. It also sets limits on the *substance* of what agencies can do through its judicial review requirements. For example, the APA allows courts to set aside an agency's factual findings if not supported by "substantial evidence," and to set aside an agency's action more broadly if it is "arbitrary and capricious." These judicial review provisions thus set limits on the substance of how agencies exercise their discretion. Second, administrative law is also concerned with certain constitutional constraints, and particularly due process constraints. For example, when an agency adjudication might take away your social security benefits, are you entitled to a hearing? A pre-termination or post-termination hearing? Do you get a lawyer?

In addition to the statutory and constitutional constraints on how agencies exercise their functions, administrative law is concerned with the relationship of agencies to the three constitutional actors named in the first three articles of the United States Constitution: Congress, the President, and the federal courts. When agencies make regulations, doesn't that look like they're exercising legislative power? In other words, does there come a point where Congress impermissibly delegates too much power? And if most of what agencies do is ultimately executive power, doesn't that mean the President gets to direct agencies as the person in whom the "executive power" of the United States is vested? And what about agency adjudications; how do they relate to the federal judicial power? Are there certain things an agency cannot hear because only federal courts can hear them?

THE CONSTITUTIONAL PLACE OF AGENCIES
What is the relation of administrative agencies to Congress, to the President, and to the courts? Are regulations laws, or something else? What's the difference between a court adjudication and an agency adjudication? We will revisit these questions throughout the materials.

This casebook therefore deals with both aspects of administrative law and organizes them as follows. The remainder of this chapter will go over the definition of an "agency" and our first few rules of statutory interpretation; the history of administrative law and administrative agencies; and will introduce the student to the constitutional issues surrounding the administrative state. Have agencies been with us since the beginning? What do we make of the Congress's steamboat legislation in the mid-nineteenth century, and the

Interstate Commerce Act of 1887, by which Congress is sometimes thought to have created the first modern administrative agency, the Interstate Commerce Commission? The student will also have the option of reading some excerpts from early administrative theorists like Woodrow Wilson, Frank Goodnow, and James Landis. Section 1.B will go through this history from the beginning of the Republic to today, flagging the implications for the constitutional debates. Section 1.C then presents one modern case that raises these constitutional issues in the present-day, to introduce the reader to what agencies do and whether and why what they do might (or might not) sometimes be constitutionally problematic.

After this introductory material, we dive into the meat of the course. The first half of the casebook starts with the *statutory* constraints on how agencies make regulations and engage in adjudications. We start with regulations in Chapter 2 because this is more familiar to students, and often adjudications involve regulations. The focus here is *procedural* constraints in the Administrative Procedure Act. Chapter 3 then turns to the procedural rules and constraints on how agencies adjudicate. Chapter 4 then turns to the *substantive* limits on agency adjudications and rulemakings imposed by the judicial review provisions of the Administrative Procedure Act. Chapter 4 thus goes through judicial review of agency fact-finding, judicial review of agency reasoning, and judicial review of agency legal determinations. Judicial review within these categories occurs both when agencies make regulations and also when they adjudicate.

The second half then turns back to and takes a deeper dive into the constitutional issues. This second half also includes the important constitutional constraint of due process, which easily could be taught along with the statutory constraints on agency adjudications. Chapter 5 examines the relationship of agencies to Congress and the legislative power. The key doctrine here is the nondelegation doctrine—the rule that Congress can't delegate its legislative power to agencies. The nondelegation doctrine raises other interesting separation of powers issues, like the validity of a legislative veto and judicial deference to agency "interpretations" of law. Chapter 6 then turns to the role of the President in appointments, removals, and the direction of administrative agencies. Here we explore the constitutional issues surrounding "independent agencies." Chapter 7 then turns to the relationship of agency adjudications to Article III courts and the federal judicial power, and finally to due process. This material is notoriously difficult, and is also the subject of courses in federal jurisdiction.

The final chapter is on reviewability. To get judicial review of the substance or procedure of an agency rulemaking or adjudication, or of the constitutionality of an agency's (or Congress's) action, you need to get into court in the first place. Whether an agency action is judicially reviewable might depend on the finality of the agency action, whether administrative remedies have been exhausted, the ripeness of the case for review, whether a plaintiff even has a cause of action, and whether a plaintiff has constitutional standing. Much of this material is also the subject of a federal jurisdiction course.

3. Course Themes

Throughout the course and these readings, the student may find it helpful to keep certain themes in mind. Here are three important ones. First is the theme of "expertise" versus "accountability." Why do we, or should we, allow agencies to make important policy decisions and to implement the law? Is it because they are "experts" in particular fields? Does this mean their decisions should be insulated from political influence? That administrative policy should not change whenever there is a new presidential administration? On the other hand, agency officials and bureaucrats are unelected. Is it not more important that policy decisions be made by elected officials accountable to the people? Doesn't that mean the President should direct all administrative policy? And is there even such a thing as value-neutral expertise uncolored by political considerations?

EXPERTISE VS. ACCOUNTABILITY
Why should agencies and bureaucrats have power? Is it because they are technical experts? Does it matter that they are unelected? How should we balance expertise and political accountability?

Second is the theme of "efficiency" versus the "separation of powers" and "checks and balances." People often complain that nothing ever gets done in Washington because of "gridlock." Two different houses of Congress and also the President all have to agree on something to make it into a law. This is a slow and tedious

EFFICIENCY VS. SEPARATED POWERS
Are agencies more efficient at making rules than Congress? Is that desirable?

process. On the other hand, legislating in only the broadest terms and leaving it to agencies to fill in the details can be much more efficient. This raises the question of how much efficiency do we want versus how many procedural safeguards we might want to impose on agencies.

Third and finally is the theme which has already been touched upon: where exactly do agencies fit in the constitutional scheme of things? The constitutionality of the administrative state can only be assessed by carefully considering (1) the nature of administrative power, i.e. what administrative agencies do; and (2) the requirements of the U.S. Constitution. There is robust debate on both questions, and the debate courses through all of these materials. The student should keep them always at the fore.

Perhaps most importantly, it is worth reminding the reader of the *importance* of administrative law. Administrative agencies touch everything in modern life. They often determine what kind of drugs you can buy, how many passengers are allowed on airplanes, what kind of disclosures you have to make to your investors, who gets licenses to broadcast on the airwaves, what safety standards your car must meet, how many pollutants a factory can emit, whether you can build a house on a wetland, and licenses for certain occupations. The bottom line is that administrative law has huge implications for the economy, for liberty, and for social justice. It may be one of the most important and useful—and, fortunately, fun—fields in the entirety of the law.

4.   What Is an Agency?

Let us wrap up this introductory section with a definition of "agencies," which will also allow us to introduce our first few rules of statutory interpretation.

Agencies, in short, can be generally defined as the various departments and entities within the executive branch of government, with varying degrees of insulation from the President, that help the President (or Congress) implement the nation's laws and policies. The Paperwork Reduction Act defines agency as "any executive department, military department, Government corporation, Government controlled corporation, or other establishment in the executive branch of the Government (including the Executive Office of the President), or any independent regulatory agency," excluding some specific agencies that are not subject to the requirements of that act and excluding the government of the District of Columbia and the national territories. 44 U.S.C. § 3502. The Freedom of Information Act (FOIA), which amended the APA, similarly defines "agency" as "any executive department, military department, Government corporation, Government controlled corporation, or other establishment in the executive branch of the Government (including the Executive Office of the President), or any independent regulatory agency." 5 U.S.C. § 552(f).

The APA itself, 5 U.S.C. § 551(1), offers the following more technical definition of "agency":

> "[A]gency" means each authority of the Government of the United States, whether or not it is within or subject to review by another agency, but does not include—
>
> (A) the Congress;
>
> (B) the courts of the United States;
>
> (C) the governments of the territories or possessions of the United States;
>
> (D) the government of the District of Columbia;
>
> or except as to the requirements of section 552 of this title [having to do with releasing information to the public, for example in the Federal Register]—
>
> (E) agencies composed of representatives of the parties or of representatives of organizations of the parties to the disputes determined by them;
>
> (F) courts martial and military commissions;
>
> (G) military authority exercised in the field in time of war or in occupied territory; or
>
> (H) functions conferred by [various sections of the U.S. code involving mortgage insurance and public airports].

Defined Term

FEDERAL REGISTER: A compilation of all agency proceedings. Agencies publish final regulations and notices of proposed rulemakings in the federal register, among other notices.

Under this definition, an agency is any "authority" of the government, not including Congress, the courts, the national territories or the District of Columbia, and military authorities under specified circumstances. An agency is therefore any authority of the government within the executive branch. The courts have sometimes had to decide what exactly constitutes an "authority" of the government for purposes of the definition of "agency," and they have generally concluded that the entity in question must exercise "substantial independent authority." Citizens for Responsibility and Ethics in Washington v. Office of Admin., 566 F.3d 219, 220 (D.C. Cir. 2009). Thus the courts have held that the Office of Administration, which provides budgeting and administrative support for the Executive Office of the President, is not an agency because it "performs only operational and administrative tasks in support of the President and his staff," id.; the staff of the Executive Residence is not an agency, Sweetland v. Walters, 60 F.3d 852 (D.C. Cir. 1995) (per curiam); and the Council of Economic Advisors and the National Security Council are not agencies because they have no substantive role apart from that of the President, Rushforth v. Council of Econ. Advisers, 762 F.2d 1038 (D.C. Cir. 1985) (CEA); Armstrong v. Exec. Office of the President, 90 F.3d 553, 565 (D.C. Cir. 1996) (NSC).

The APA does not specify whether the President is included within this definition; nor does the definition exclude the President. The Supreme Court addressed this question in Franklin v. Massachusetts, 505 U.S. 788 (1992). At issue in *Franklin* was how the Census Bureau, the Secretary of Commerce, and the President administered congressional statutes requiring the executive branch to undertake the decennial census. The Secretary of Commerce decided to include overseas federal employees in the census count, including nearly a million military servicemembers, and to allocate them to their "home of record states." Massachusetts lost representation by including these overseas servicemembers according to that formula, and so sued the administration. Massachusetts argued that the inclusion of overseas employees and the formula by which they were allocated was "arbitrary and capricious" because many overseas employees chose a particular home-of-record state merely because that state had a low tax burden.

The Supreme Court therefore had to decide *whose* decision was being reviewed under this standard. It concluded that, because the President still had discretion in implementing the apportionment before final transmittal to

Congress, the relevant action was the President's. But, in a brief paragraph, 505 U.S. at 800–01, the Supreme Court concluded that the President was not included under the APA's definition of "agency":

> The APA defines "agency" as "each authority of the Government of the United States, whether or not it is within or subject to review by another agency, but does not include—(A) the Congress; (B) the courts of the United States; (C) the governments of the territories or possessions of the United States; (D) the government of the District of Columbia." 5 U.S.C. §§ 701(b)(1), 551(1). The President is not explicitly excluded from the APA's purview, but he is not explicitly included, either. Out of respect for the separation of powers and the unique constitutional position of the President, we find that textual silence is not enough to subject the President to the provisions of the APA. We would require an express statement by Congress before assuming it intended the President's performance of his statutory duties to be reviewed for abuse of discretion. As the APA does not expressly allow review of the President's actions, we must presume that his actions are not subject to its requirements. Although the President's actions may still be reviewed for constitutionality, we hold that they are not reviewable for abuse of discretion under the APA.

That's it. The Court's analysis raises interesting questions of statutory interpretation, which will provide us with our first lessons and rules of statutory interpretation.

STATUTORY INTERPRETATION LESSONS 1–5

Lesson 1: Ordinary Meaning. Take a look again at the APA's definition of agency. It says that an agency is each "authority" of the government of the United States. Isn't the President obviously an "authority" of the federal government? Of course she is. Thus, it would seem that the President is included within the definition of agency, at least if we're using the ordinary meaning of the words in the statute. Normally, that's what we do, at least as a first cut—statutes are intended to *instruct* people and officials about what they can and can't do, and so we usually give their words their ordinary meaning, that is, the meaning those words would have had to the legislators who drafted them and to the public and legal officials who must follow them.

William Blackstone explained this "ordinary meaning rule," if you will, in his famous *Commentaries*: "Words [in a statute] are generally to be understood in their usual and most known signification; not so much regarding the propriety of grammar, as their general and popular use." 1 William Blackstone, Commentaries on the Laws of England 59 (15th ed. 1809). Joseph Story, in discussing constitutional interpretation in America, wrote that "[t]he first and fundamental rule in the interpretation of all instruments is, to construe them according to the sense of the terms, and the intention of the parties." 1 Joseph Story, Commentaries on the Constitution of the United States § 400 (1833). As the Supreme Court has said in several cases, "Statutory construction must begin with the language employed by Congress and the assumption that the ordinary meaning of that language accurately expresses the legislative purpose." Gross v. FBL Fin. Servs., Inc., 557 U.S. 167, 175 (2009).

Lesson 2: Plain Meaning Rule. The ordinary meaning rule—the idea that we interpret words, at least as a first cut, with their ordinary meanings—should not be confused with the "plain meaning rule." The plain meaning rule has more to do with what judges ought to do once they've ascertained the ordinary meaning of a statute. The rule maintains that, if the ordinary meaning of the words is "plain"—evident or clear or obvious—then we stick with that meaning. If the meaning is plain, judges don't have to look to other methods of interpretation, and in particular they should not resort to "legislative history" (more on legislative history on p. 100).

The plain meaning rule also has a long pedigree. Justice Story described it as follows: "Where the words are plain and clear, and the sense distinct and perfect arising on them, there is generally no necessity to have recourse to other means of interpretation." 1 Joseph Story, Commentaries on the Constitution of the United States § 401 (1833). The Supreme Court dutifully repeats—although it does not always follow—this rule: "If the statutory language is plain, we must enforce it according to its terms." King v. Burwell, 135 S. Ct. 2480, 2489 (2015).

The plain meaning rule, however, is contested. Many judges believe that they should always look to legislative history or statutory titles and preambles as evidence of meaning, even if the meaning of a statute otherwise appears plain. After all, in light of the legislative history or other statutory cues, like a statute's title or preamble, the meaning might not be so obvious after all. It may appear that the legislature intended to do something quite different from what the plain meaning of a statute might suggest. Usually "textualists," those who think the purpose of statutory interpretation is discerning the public *meaning* of the statutory texts, like the plain meaning rule. On the other hand "intentionalists," those who think the purpose of statutory interpretation is figuring out the actual intent of the enacting legislature, by whatever means available, tend to disregard the plain meaning rule.

But the lines are not always drawn so cleanly. In *Yates v. United States,* the Supreme Court decided 5–4 that the word "tangible object" did not include a red grouper fish. 574 U.S. 528 (2015). The statute was enacted in the aftermath of various national accounting scandals and prohibited the alteration or destruction of "any record, document, or tangible object with the intent to impede, obstruct, or influence" an investigation. Justices Ginsburg, Breyer, and Sotomayor were joined by Chief Justice Roberts in rejecting the "ordinary meaning" of "tangible object," noting that a term's apparent plain meaning might actually be contradicted by the statutory context and background in which it is used. Relying on the caption of the relevant statutory section, the plurality argued that "tangible object" refers to things like "records," but not to all *things* simpliciter. Justice Alito was also persuaded by the section title to limit the reach of the term "tangible object." In dissent, Justices Kagan, Scalia, Kennedy, and Thomas agreed that context matters to textual interpretation, but argued that the Court has never "relied on a title to override the law's clear terms."

Lesson 3: Expressio Unius. Back to the APA. So far, the ordinary and plain meaning rules suggest that the President, as an authority of the government, is an "agency" within the meaning of the APA. Consider now the list of exclusions from this definition. The APA specifically excludes Congress, the courts, and the government of the territories, for example. But it does not exclude the President. What inference can you draw from this fact? Doesn't the enumeration of authorities excluded from the definition of the APA, and the omission of the President from this enumeration, suggest that the President is not similarly excluded from the definition of "agency"?

Indeed, there is a prominent canon of statutory interpretation to this effect, *expressio unius est exclusio alterius*—the inclusion of a particular item in a list implies the exclusion of other, similar items, not included. The classic example is if a parent tells a child that the child can have a cookie for dessert, that doesn't mean the child can *also* have ice cream. The granting of permission for one specific item implies the exclusion of other, similar items. In the APA, the enumeration of specific exemptions implies that other "authorities of the government" not included within these exemptions are excluded from being exempt. The President is not on the list of exempt authorities, and therefore seems included within the definition of "agency."

Lesson 4: Clear Statement Rules. Thus far, the tools of statutory interpretation seem to suggest that the President is, in fact, an "agency" within the meaning of the APA. Why did the Court conclude otherwise? The Court held: "Out of respect for the separation of powers and the unique constitutional position of the President, we find that textual silence is not enough to subject the President to the provisions of the APA. We would require an express statement by Congress before assuming it intended the President's performance of his statutory duties to be reviewed for abuse of discretion." This is an example of a "clear statement" requirement. The Court won't presume Congress intended to accomplish something, even if the ordinary meaning and ordinary tools of statutory interpretation suggest that Congress did; rather, the Court will require a *clear statement* before so presuming.

Why? Here, the Court notes that it won't presume Congress intended to allow the courts to review the President's actions for an abuse of discretion out of respect for the separation of powers. In other words, there was a constitutional value at stake; if Congress wants to trench on that value, perhaps it can do so, but it must do so *clearly*. Another example of a clear statement rule is the "presumption against preemption." The idea here is that federalism is a constitutional value, and so as a general matter the courts will not presume Congress intended for a particular federal law to preempt related state laws (unless, of course, there is an irreconcilable conflict between the federal and state laws). Congress can, however, specifically declare that it intends to preempt state laws.

Lesson 5: Constitutional Avoidance. Clear statement rules should not be confused with canons of constitutional avoidance. Clear statement rules suggest that Congress *can* take a certain action, but to do so it must speak clearly and explicitly. In the presumption against preemption, Congress *can* preempt state law, assuming of course Congress is legislating within its enumerated powers. Constitutional avoidance stands for a different proposition: the courts will refuse to give a statute its most probable meaning *if* that reading of the statute might raise constitutional concerns. The courts, in other words, will *avoid* a potential constitutional problem by giving the statute some other reasonable, or at least a possible, interpretation, even if that wouldn't otherwise be the best interpretation. The idea here is that even if Congress wanted to do something, and did it explicitly, it might still not be able to because doing so would raise constitutional concerns.

The constitutional avoidance canon is a pretty ingrained part of statutory interpretation, but its use is contested. Historically, the constitutional avoidance canon worked a bit differently—the court would have to *decide* that a statute violated the Constitution, and then would "avoid" striking down the statute by giving the statute some narrowing construction to save its constitutionality. Blodgett v. Holden, 275 U.S. 142, 148 (1927); Clark v. Martinez, 543 U.S. 371, 395 (2005) (Thomas, J., dissenting); Anita S. Krishnakumar, *Passive Avoidance,* 71 Stan. L. Rev. 513, 523 (2019). Under the modern doctrine, the court must only have a "serious doubt" about the constitutionality of Congress's action, it need not actually *decide* that Congress's law would otherwise be unconstitutional. See, e.g., Nielsen v. Preap, 139 S. Ct. 954, 971 (2019) ("when a serious doubt is raised about the constitutionality of an act of Congress, this Court will first ascertain whether a construction of the statute is fairly possible by which the question may be avoided") (cleaned up). Not only does the Court not have to decide the constitutional question, critics have argued that the Court sometimes warps the meaning of the statute in order to save it from the mere doubt about the constitutionality. This effectively gives courts some power to revise congressional statutes without actually having to decide the constitutional issue, i.e. without having to decide that they *must* rewrite them to save them. Eric S. Fish, *Constitutional Avoidance As Interpretation and As Remedy,* 114 Mich. L. Rev. 1275, 1283–84 (2016); Krishnakumar, supra, at 531.

In *Franklin*, what was the Court really deploying: a clear statement rule, or constitutional avoidance? It's not entirely clear. Did the Court have doubts about the constitutionality of Congress applying various APA requirements to the President, or would it have been fine with applying those requirements so long as Congress does so explicitly? What do you think: Would it be unconstitutional to permit courts to decide for themselves whether the President is not exercising her discretion properly? Is exercising the discretion within the bounds of a statute, as part of implementing a statute, part of "the executive power" of the United States? Would allowing courts to police the President's exercise of this discretion be impermissibly granting part of this "executive power" to the courts? On the other hand, the President can only execute the laws that Congress enacts, and, for the most part, only with the officers and prescriptions that Congress establishes. If Congress directs that the President must exercise discretion under a statute "reasonably," can the courts not review the President's exercise of discretion?

B. A Brief History of Administrative Law

The history of administrative law can be subdivided in various ways, but is typically subdivided into the first hundred years (1789–1887); 1887 through the progressive era; the New Deal era and the enactment of the Administrative Procedure Act; and the 1960s/70s. This chapter divides the history along those lines, and then discusses some modern developments in administrative law.

1.   Agencies, the Constitution, and the Early Republic

With the definitions of "agency" in mind, it is quite obvious to see that administrative agencies have been with us from the beginning. That is because the Constitution expressly contemplates such administrative agencies. The President is vested with "the executive power" (Article II, § 1), but it was commonly understood that the President could not possibly hope to execute the law alone. The President would need assistants. Thus, Article II, § 2, para. 1 provides in the so-called "Opinions Clause" that the President "may require the Opinion, in writing, of the principal Officer in each of the executive Departments, upon any Subject relating to the Duties of their respective Offices." The Constitution therefore contemplated that there would be executive departments under the President. And Article II, § 2, para. 2 provides for the appointment by and with advice and consent of the Senate of all "[o]fficers of the United States, whose Appointments are not herein otherwise provided for, and which shall be established by Law," suggesting that Congress may establish offices. This paragraph also gives Congress the power to "vest the Appointment of such inferior Officers, as they think proper, in the President alone, in the Courts of Law, or in the Heads of Departments." This suggests once again that there are to be "departments" under the President, and even "inferior officers" under the heads of these departments. Finally, the Necessary and Proper Clause grants Congress the power "to make all laws which shall be necessary and proper for carrying into execution" not only Congress's enumerated powers, but also "all other powers vested by this Constitution in . . . any department or officer" of the United States, including the executive branch. Art. I, § 8, cl. 18. The Constitution, in short, contemplates the existence of an administrative state of some kind.

The First Congress got busy creating the first executive departments. In 1789, it enacted statutes establishing the Department of Foreign Affairs (which soon became the Department of State), the War Department, and the Treasury

Department. 1 Stat. 28 (1789) (Foreign Affairs); 1 Stat. 49 (1789) (War); 1 Stat. 65 (1789) (Treasury). Congress did not assign the duties of the Foreign Affairs and War Departments with great specificity, noting only that the principal officers of those departments should conduct their duties under instructions from the President of the United States. The Foreign Affairs statute provided that the Secretary shall

 IN QUIRY What role should history play in constitutional interpretation today? What do these historical precedents tell us about the constitutionality of the modern administrative state?

> perform and execute such duties as shall from time to time be enjoined on or intrusted to him by the President of the United States, agreeable to the Constitution, relative to correspondences, commissions or instructions to or with public ministers or consuls, from the United States, or to negotiations with public ministers from foreign states or princes, or to memorials or other applications from foreign public ministers or other foreigners, or to such other matters respecting foreign affairs, as the President of the United States shall assign to the said department; and furthermore, that the said principal officer shall conduct the business of the said department in such manner as the President of the United States shall from time to time order or instruct.

The War Department statute was structured similarly, and the duties of that department would be "relative to military commissions, or to the land or naval forces, ships, or warlike stores of the United States, or to such other matters respecting military or naval affairs," and "relative to the granting of lands to persons entitled thereto, for military services rendered to the United States, or relative to Indian affairs."

The Treasury statute was much more detailed. The statute not only provided for a "Secretary of the Treasury," but also "a Comptroller, an Auditor, a Treasurer, a Register, and an Assistant to the Secretary of the Treasury." The Secretary's duties were numerous:

> [I]t shall be the duty of the Secretary of the Treasury to digest and prepare plans for the improvement and management of the revenue, and for the support of public credit; to prepare and report estimates

of the public revenue, and the public expenditures; to superintend the collection of the revenue; to decide on the forms of keeping and stating accounts and making returns, and to grant under the limitations herein established, or to be hereafter provided, all warrants for monies to be issued from the Treasury, in pursuance of appropriations by law; to execute such services relative to the sale of the lands belonging to the United States, as may be by law required of him; to make report, and give information to either branch of the legislature, in person or in writing (as he may be required), respecting all matters referred to him by the Senate or House of Representatives, or which shall appertain to his office; and generally to perform all such services relative to the finances, as he shall be directed to perform.

The Comptroller's duties were also listed in great detail. The Comptroller was "to superintend the adjustment and preservation of the public accounts; to examine all accounts settled by the Auditor, and certify the balances arising thereon to the Register," and "to countersign all warrants drawn by the Secretary of the Treasury, which shall be warranted by law." He was to "provide for the regular and punctual payment of all monies which may be collected," and was in charge of directing "prosecutions for all delinquencies of officers of the revenue, and for debts that are, or shall be due to the United States." The Treasurer, among other duties, was to receive and keep the monies of the United States, and to disburse the same upon warrants drawn by the Secretary of the Treasury, countersigned by the Comptroller, recorded by the Register, and not otherwise." And the Register, among other duties, was "to keep all accounts of the receipts and expenditures of the public money, and of all debts due to or from the United States."

From the beginning, then, these departments did a lot of "administering." To provide a more concrete example, one of the earliest statutes declared in a single sentence "[t]hat the Military Pensions which have been granted and paid by the states respectively, in pursuance of the Acts of the United States Congress assembled, to the Invalids who were wounded and disabled during the late war, shall be continued and paid by the United States from the fourth day of March last, for the space of one year, under such regulations as the President of the United States may direct." 1 Stat. 95 (1789). It was left up to George Washington and his secretary of war, Henry Knox, to implement and administer this statutory requirement. Their regulation, preserved in the Library of

Congress, is reproduced in Image 1. The statute required that the payments be made to the invalid veterans within the span of one year; Washington and Knox settled on two equal installments three months apart. And to ensure the recipient was entitled to these payments, the regulation required that anyone claiming a pension had to provide an affidavit attesting to their service and injury during the Revolutionary War as well as the returns from the states that had previously made such payments. Finally, the regulation specified that representatives of the invalids had to provide a specific power of attorney form, and that executors of estates had to supply evidence of their office.

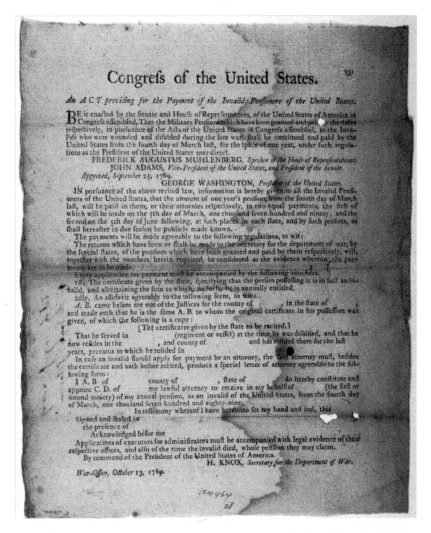

The Invalid Pensioner Statute and Accompanying Regulations

FOR DISCUSSION

We will return throughout these materials to the example of President Washington and Secretary Knox's regulation under this early statute involving invalid pensioners. How does this regulation compare to modern-day regulations? Does this early regulation supply support for the constitutionality of modern regulations? Is this early regulation different in kind from some modern regulations?

There was lots of other administration going around, much of it discussed in Leonard White's The Federalists: A Study in Administrative History (1956). The first collection act of 1789 directed that shipowners had to keep manifests of their goods. 1 Stat. 29, 36. That was it. It was left up to Secretary of Treasury Alexander Hamilton to create the forms and procedures to implement this legislative command, which included the precise form to be used by shipowners for the manifest of imported goods and merchandise, the precise form of the certification of the manifests to be made by customs officials, and the form to be used to report on spirits brought by the vessel, as well as other details of administration. Interestingly, Congress subsequently adopted these procedures in the collection act of 1799. 1 Stat. 627, 644–45. This points to an important theme that will play out throughout these materials: some powers or activities can be exercised by more than one branch. Congress can of course legislate in as much detail as it wants, but some details Congress may decide for itself or may leave to the executive agencies to fill in.

One of the more important series of administrative legislation in this early period included statutes regulating steamboats. See generally Jerry L. Mashaw, Creating the Administrative Constitution: The Lost One Hundred Years of Administrative Law 187–208 (2012). Steamboats were a relatively new technology, and there were lots of accidents, particularly steamboat explosions. Nearly 300 people reportedly were killed by such explosions from 1825–30. In 1838, Congress finally enacted the Steamboat Inspection Act of 1838, which required compliance with safety regulations if the owner or master of the vessel wanted to renew a federal coasting trade license. The law also required semi-annual inspections of boilers, to be made by competent inspectors appointed by federal district judges on petition. The masters and owners had to employ competent engineers or be subject to liability for resulting damages, and if the masters and owners were themselves negligent in some manner leading to death, they were liable to manslaughter prosecutions.

As Jerry Mashaw explains, supra at 190, this Act "was very far from a modern regulatory statute." There was no agency charged with enforcing its requirements "or with authority to further specify the vague statutory standards." It would appear that this scheme was rather ineffective, as steamboat engines kept exploding.

Thus Congress amended the Act in 1852. 10 Stat. 61. The 1852 statute reflected much "scientific consensus" on steamboat engines, such as the maximum operating load of boiler pressure. Mashaw, supra at 192. Indeed, Section 3 of the act provided:

> That every vessel so propelled by steam, and carrying passengers, shall have not less than three double-acting forcing pumps, with chamber at least four inches in diameter, two to be worked by hand and one by steam, if steam can be employed, otherwise by hand; one whereof shall be placed near the stern, one near the stem, and one amidship; each having a suitable, well-fitted hose, of at least two thirds the length of the vessel, kept at all times in perfect order and ready for immediate use; each of which pumps shall also be supplied with water by a pipe connected therewith, and passing through the side of the vessel, so low as to be at all times in the water when she is afloat: *Provided,* That, in steamers not exceeding two hundred tons measurement, two of said pumps may be dispensed with; and in steamers of over two hundred tons, and not exceeding five hundred tons measurement, one of said pumps may be dispensed with.

The succeeding sections of the act (for the full text of the Act, see Appendix C) further required specific lifeboats and life preservers; suitable escape routes from the lower decks; and specific packaging for a variety of flammable materials. The statute also specified what maximum pressure of what types of boilers the inspectors should allow, although the inspectors had discretion to depart from such requirements. The statute specified the precise form of the certificate that was to be issued by the inspectors. What is particularly interesting

CROSS REFERENCE In Chapter Five, we will explore the "non-delegation doctrine": the principle that Congress cannot give away its legislative power to agencies. The modern test is the "intelligible principle test": Has Congress laid down sufficient standards in the statute to guide the agency's exercise of discretion?

What kind of power do these early statutes delegate? Are they delegating legislative power?

here is how specific this statute was. Congress created boards of inspectors and a board of supervising inspectors to carry out the inspections of the ships, but the safety and technical requirements themselves were specified in quite great detail in this statute. Congress of course did not have any independent technical expertise in these matters, but it knew how to incorporate the scientific consensus into the statute that it enacted.

To be sure, the statute also granted significant discretion to the inspectors. The statute did not specify the method by which the boilers would be tested. The act allowed a board of inspectors to license an engineer if "they are satisfied that his character, habits of life, knowledge, and experience in the duties of an engineer, are all such as to authorize the belief that the applicant is a suitable and safe person to be intrusted with the powers and duties of such a station," without specifying exactly how the inspectors were to arrive at this determination. In section 10, the statute prohibited carrying passengers in excess of the limit determined by the inspectors to be safe, without specifying exactly how these determinations were to be made. Section 18 authorized the supervising inspectors collectively to establish "rules and regulations for their own conduct" and for the conduct of the several boards within the respective districts. And perhaps most significantly, section 29 provided, "That it shall be the duty of the supervising inspectors to establish such rules and regulations to be obeyed by all such vessels in passing each other, as they shall from time to time deem necessary for safety."

The upshot of all this is that administrative agencies have been with us from the beginning. Congress often legislated in incredible detail, incorporating specific scientific standards directly into law, leaving little discretion to executive officials in administering the law. But Congress sometimes did grant quite broad discretion over at least some issues. Congress sometimes granted broad discretion to executive officers to make rules of conduct for themselves and their agencies; and, in the 1852 Steamboat Act, gave administrative officials broad discretion to make rules respecting the passing of ships as may be necessary for "safety," and these rules were binding on private individuals.

2.   1887–1930s

The year 1887 is often heralded as the beginning of the modern administrative state, and further as the beginning of modern federal intervention in the national economy. It was in 1887 that Congress enacted the Interstate

Commerce Act, 24 Stat. 379, creating the Interstate Commerce Commission (ICC), after over a decade of debate over national railroad policy. The standard picture of the ICC is that it is the first example of a modern "independent" agency, and that it exercised broad discretion to regulate railroads and adjudicate disputes.

The Interstate Commerce Act is reproduced in full in Appendix D. At first glance, the authority of the ICC does seem quite broad. The act provided that "[a]ll charges made for any service rendered or to be rendered in the transportation of passengers or property as aforesaid, or in connection therewith, or for the receiving, delivering, storage, or handling of such property, shall be reasonable and just; and every unjust and unreasonable charge for such service is prohibited and declared to be unlawful." § 1. If this were all the statute said, and if the ICC had the power to adjudicate disputes under this "reasonable and just" standard, it would indeed have been a sweeping delegation of power akin to delegations found in many modern statutes.

The statute, however, does not lend itself to such an interpretation—at least not entirely. As students of this time period know, the key railroad policy disputes of the era were over whether railroads could issue rebates to certain favored customers; whether they could charge less for long-hauls as opposed to short-hauls; and whether the railroads could fix prices and enter into combinations to avoid what they viewed as ruinous competition. Stephen Skowronek, Building a New American State: The Expansion of National Administrative Capacities 1877–1920, at 123–50 (1982); Robert L. Rabin, *Federal Regulation in Historical Perspective*, 38 Stan. L. Rev. 1189, 1197–1200, 1206–07 (1986). Congress legislated on each issue in the Interstate Commerce Act. The Act prohibited (in section 2) "any special rate, rebate, drawback, or other device" that led to different compensation to the railroad from different parties for "contemporaneous service in the transportation of a like kind of traffic under substantially similar circumstances and conditions." It forbade (in section 4) railroads "to charge or receive any greater compensation in the aggregate for the transportation of passengers or of like kind of property, under substantially similar circumstances and conditions, for a shorter than for a longer distance over the same line, in the same direction, the shorter being included within the longer distance." Finally, the Act (in section 5) made it "unlawful for any common carrier subject to the provisions of this act to enter into any contract, agreement, or combination with any other common carrier or carriers for the pooling of freights of different and competing railroads, or to divide between them the aggregate or net proceeds of the earnings of such railroads, or any portion thereof."

In other words, the statute very specifically resolved all the politically controversial issues: it prohibited rebates, prohibited discrimination in long-haul and short-haul rates, and prohibited combinations. James Landis wrote that "[d]etailed regulative provisions encumber the Interstate Commerce Act," and the Act "has ceased to have the appearance of a constituent document and resembles rather a regulative code." James Landis, The Administrative Process 68 (1938).

On the other hand, the statute did grant quite a bit of discretion to the ICC in at least one important instance: section 4 permitted the Commission to allow in its discretion, in "special cases," different rates for long and short hauls after conducting an investigation. This is, indeed, quite broad discretion, but over a rather narrow issue. The general policy was established by statute, and the Commission had power to waive that legal requirement in special cases after an investigation. The legacy of the ICC as a watershed agency with broad regulatory powers is therefore decidedly mixed.

In a different respect, the ICC was indeed a watershed. The ICC was the first "independent" regulatory agency. The ICC was to comprise five commissioners, appointed by the President by and with advice and consent of the Senate, for staggered six-year terms and no more than three of the five commissioners could be from the same political party. Further, Congress specified that the President could remove a commissioner only "for inefficiency, neglect of duty, or malfeasance in office." § 11. The ICC had all the hallmarks of a modern independent regulatory agency: a multimember, bipartisan board with some degree of insulation from the President.

We have now considered the relationship of the ICC to Congress and to the President, to legislative power and executive power. What about the relationship of the ICC to courts and the federal judicial power? Here the Interstate Commerce Act also innovated, but its innovations were somewhat narrow. Complainants under the law had the option of bringing an action in federal court or in front of the Commission itself, but had to choose one or the other. § 9. If a complainant chose to proceed in front of the Commission, the Commission had power to subpoena witnesses and documents and, with the assistance of the federal courts, to compel obedience. § 12. The Commission then had the power to make findings of fact and to make conclusions as to what remedy, if any, was warranted. §§ 13–14. If a defendant refused to comply with the order, however, the Commission had no choice but to seek relief in federal court. The federal courts would decide the matter for themselves, but the findings and reports of the Commission in the matter would be "prima facie evidence as to each and every fact found." § 14; *see also id.* § 15 ("and on such hearing the report of said Commission shall be prima facie evidence of the matters therein stated").

In sum, it would appear that the Interstate Commerce Act was, indeed, a turning point. The ICC was what today would be described as an independent regulatory agency, and it had broad discretion to make policy in certain narrow areas (like exemptions from the short-haul/long-haul rule) and it could investigate complaints and issue findings. But most of the controversial political questions were decided by Congress itself in detail, and ultimately the Commission had

FOR DISCUSSION

What do you think: Was the Interstate Commerce Commission a turning point in the history of administrative law? What kind of support might the ICC provide for modern regulatory agencies?

to rely on the federal courts to enforce its findings and conclusions, and those courts would decide the matters at hand for themselves. It was innovative in many respects, but in important ways it was not particularly new at all.

Interestingly, relatively recent scholarship has tried to locate the emergence of the modern administrative state prior to the creation of the ICC and with the creation of the Bureau of Animal Industry (BAI) within the federal Department of Agriculture in 1884. See Alan L. Olmstead & Paul W. Rhode, Arresting Contagion: Science, Policy, and Conflicts over Animal Disease Control (2015). Although this is an interesting thesis, the author of this casebook, anyhow, is not convinced that the BAI was any kind of watershed. The agency had such little authority that when a major outbreak of contagious bovine pleuropneumonia (CBPP) broke out in 1884, it could do little more than request state cooperation. It was not until 1886 that Congress enacted a statute authorizing the agency to purchase diseased cattle and to compensate owners. And it was not until 1887 that Congress allowed it to create and enforce interstate quarantines. See Olmstead & Rhode, at 63–76. At each step of the way, Congress made the critical policy decisions, leaving the agency negligible discretion.

Standing alone, then, perhaps neither the ICC nor the BAI would justify treating the 1880s as some kind of watershed decade in administrative law. But 1887 is prominent for another reason: it is the year in which Woodrow Wilson published his widely influential "The Study of Administration," establishing a theory of administrative government that continues to have influence today.

As you read the following excerpts from Wilson's famous article, consider the following three questions.

Questions to Consider While Reading the Article

(1) What did Wilson think about the Constitution's tripartite separation of powers?

(2) What did he say about the relationship between "politics" and "administration"?

(3) Finally, why did he believe administration by experts was necessary in his time?

As we shall see throughout these materials, such questions—and what Wilson had to say about them—are still very much pertinent in our own time.

Woodrow Wilson, The Study of Administration

Political Science Quarterly, Vol. 2, No. 2, June 1887

I suppose that no practical science is ever studied where there is no need to know it. The very fact, therefore, that the eminently practical science of administration is finding its way into college courses in this country would prove that this country needs to know more about administration, were such proof of the fact required to make out a case. . . . It is the object of administrative study to discover, first, what government can properly and successfully do, and, secondly, how it can do these proper things with the utmost possible efficiency and at the least possible cost either of money or of energy. On both these points there is obviously much need of light among us; and only careful study can supply that light.

* * *

I.

The science of administration is the latest fruit of that study of the science of politics which was begun some twenty-two hundred years ago. It is a birth of our own century, almost of our own generation. Why was it so late in coming? Why did it wait till this too busy century of ours to demand attention for itself? Administration is the most obvious part of government; it is government in action; it is the executive, the operative, the most visible side of government, and is of course as old as government itself. It is government in action, and one might very naturally expect to find that government in action had arrested the attention and provoked the scrutiny of writers of politics very early in the history of systematic thought. But such was not the case. No one wrote systematically of administration as a branch of the science of government until the present century had passed its first youth and had begun to put forth its characteristic flower of systematic knowledge. Up to our own day all the political writers whom we now read had thought, argued, dogmatized only about the *constitution* of government; about the nature of the state, the essence and seat of sovereignty, popular power and kingly prerogative; about the greatest meanings lying at the heart of government, and the high ends set before the purpose of government by man's nature and man's aims.

The central field of controversy was that great field of theory in which monarchy rode tilt against democracy, in which oligarchy would have built for itself strongholds of privilege, and in which tyranny sought opportunity to make good its claim to receive submission from all competitors. Amidst this high warfare of principles, administration could command no pause for its own consideration. The question was always: Who shall make law, and what shall that law be? The other question, how law should be administered with enlightenment, with equity, with speed, and without friction, was put aside as "practical detail" which clerks could arrange after doctors had agreed upon principles. . . .

The trouble in early times was almost altogether about the constitution of government; and consequently that was what engrossed men's thoughts. There was little or no trouble about administration,—at least little that was heeded by administrators. The functions of government were simple, because life itself was simple. Government went about imperatively and compelled men, without thought of consulting their wishes. There was no complex system of public revenues and public debts to puzzle financiers; there were, consequently, no financiers to be puzzled. No one who possessed power was long at a loss how to use it. The great and only question was: Who shall possess it? Populations were of manageable numbers; property was of simple sorts. There were plenty of farms, but no stocks and bonds: more cattle than vested interests.

I have said that all this was true of "early times"; but it was substantially true also of comparatively late times. One does not have to look back of the last century for the beginnings of the present complexities of trade and perplexities of commercial speculation, nor for the portentous birth of national debts. Good Queen Bess, doubtless, thought that the monopolies of the sixteenth century were hard enough to handle without burning her hands; but they are not remembered in the presence of the giant monopolies of the nineteenth century. When Blackstone lamented that corporations had no bodies to be kicked and no souls to be damned, he was anticipating the proper time for such regrets by full a century. The perennial discords between master and workmen which now so often disturb industrial society began before the Black Death and the Statute of Laborers; but never before our own day did they assume such ominous proportions as they wear now. In brief, if difficulties of governmental action are to be seen gathering in other centuries, they are to be seen culminating in our own.

This is the reason why administrative tasks have nowadays to be so studiously and systematically adjusted to carefully tested standards of policy, the reason why we are having now what we never had before, a science of administration. The weightier debates of constitutional principle are even yet by no means concluded; but they are no longer of more immediate practical moment than questions of administration. It is getting to be harder to *run* a constitution than to frame one. . . .

There is scarcely a single duty of government which was once simple which is not now complex; government once had but a few masters; it now has scores of masters. Majorities formerly only underwent government; they now conduct government. Where government once might follow the whims of a court, it must now follow the views of a nation. And those views are steadily widening to new conceptions of state duty; so that, at the same time that the functions of government are every day becoming more complex and difficult, they are also vastly multiplying in number. Administration is everywhere putting its hands to new undertakings. The utility, cheapness, and success of the government's postal service, for instance, point towards the early establishment of governmental control of the telegraph system. . . . Seeing every day new things which the state ought to do, the next thing is to see clearly how it ought to do them. This is why there should be a science of administration . . . .

[The science of administration] has been developed by French and German professors, and is consequently in all parts adapted to the needs of a compact state, and made to fit highly centralized forms of government; whereas, to answer our purposes, it must be adapted, not to a simple and compact, but to a complex and multiform state, and made to fit highly decentralized forms of government. If we would employ it, we must Americanize it, and that not formally, in language merely, but radically, in thought, principle, and aim as well. It must learn our constitutions by heart; must get the bureaucratic fever out of its veins; must inhale much free American air.

[In many omitted paragraphs, Wilson argues that the Germans and the French were able to perfect administrative government under the rule of enlightened despots, while the English and Americans were more concerned with constitutional struggles.—Ed.]

Of course all reasonable preference would declare for this English and American course of politics rather than for that of any European country. We should not like to have had Prussia's history for the sake of having Prussia's administrative skill; and Prussia's particular system of administration would quite suffocate us. It is better to be untrained and free than to be servile and systematic. Still there is no denying that it would be better yet to be both free in spirit and proficient in practice. . . .

  * * *

So much, then, for the history of the study of administration, and the peculiarly difficult conditions under which, entering upon it when we do, we must undertake it. What, now, is the subject-matter of this study, and what are its characteristic objects?

II.

The field of administration is a field of business. It is removed from the hurry and strife of politics; it at most points stands apart even from the debatable ground of constitutional study. . . .

[W]e must regard civil-service reform in its present stages as but a prelude to a fuller administrative reform. . . . It is clearing the moral atmosphere of official life by establishing the sanctity of public office as a public trust, and, by making the service unpartisan, it is opening the way for making it businesslike. . . .

Let me expand a little what I have said of the province of administration. Most important to be observed is the truth already so much and so fortunately insisted upon by our civil-service reformers; namely, that administration lies outside the proper sphere of *politics*. Administrative questions are not political questions. Although politics sets the tasks for administration, it should not be suffered to manipulate its offices.

This is distinction of high authority; eminent German writers insist upon it as of course. . . . "Politics is thus the special province of the statesman, administration of the technical officials." . . . But we do not require German authority for this position; this discrimination between administration and politics is now, happily, too obvious to need further discussion. . . .

A clear view of the difference between the province of constitutional law and the province of administrative function ought to leave no room for misconception; and it is possible to name some roughly definite criteria upon which such a view can be built. Public administration is detailed and systematic execution of public law. Every particular application of general law is an act of administration. The assessment and raising of taxes, for instance, the hanging of a criminal, the transportation and delivery of the mails, the equipment and recruiting of the army and navy, *etc.*, are all obviously acts of administration; but the general laws which direct these things to be done are as obviously outside of and above administration. The broad plans of governmental action are not administrative; the detailed execution of such plans is administrative. Constitutions, therefore, properly concern themselves only with those instrumentalities of government which are to control general law. Our federal constitution observes this principle in saying nothing of even the greatest of the purely executive offices, and speaking only of that President of the Union who was to share the legislative and policy-making functions of government, only of those judges of highest jurisdiction who were to interpret and guard its principles, and not of those who were merely to give utterance to them. . . .

There is, indeed, one point at which administrative studies trench on constitutional ground—or at least upon what seems constitutional ground. The study of administration, philosophically viewed, is closely connected with the study of the proper distribution of constitutional authority. To be efficient it must discover the simplest arrangements by which responsibility can be unmistakably fixed upon officials; the best way of dividing authority without hampering it, and responsibility without obscuring it. And this question of the distribution of authority, when taken into the sphere of the higher, the originating functions of government, is obviously a central constitutional question. If administrative study can discover the best principles upon which to base such distribution, it will have done constitutional study an invaluable service. . . .

And let me say that large powers and unhampered discretion seem to me the indispensable conditions of responsibility. Public attention must be easily directed, in each case of good or bad administration, to just the man deserving of praise or blame. There is no danger in power, if only it be not irresponsible. If it be divided, dealt out in shares to many, it is obscured; and if it be obscured, it is made irresponsible. But if it be centred in heads of the service and in heads of branches of the service, it is easily watched and brought to book. If to keep his office a man must achieve open and honest success, and if at the same time he feels himself intrusted with large freedom of discretion, the greater his power the less likely is he to abuse it, the more is he nerved and sobered and elevated by it. The less his power, the more safely obscure and unnoticed does he feel his position to be, and the more readily does he relapse into remissness. . . .

NOTES AND QUESTIONS

1. Administration versus law-execution? In Part I of his famous essay, Wilson gives two reasons why there hasn't been much study of administration in the United States. The first is that Americans have been traditionally concerned with questions of "constitutional" government, that is, of constitutional structure. Who shall make the law, and what shall the law be, were the principal inquiries. Is Wilson here understating the importance of administration to constitutional structure? Was there no question of *who* should *execute* the law, and *how* the law should be executed? Indeed, the Framers appear to have been aware of the importance of administration. In *Federalist No. 68,*

Alexander Hamilton wrote that "we may safely pronounce, that the true test of a good government is its aptitude and tendency to produce a good administration." John Adams, in his *Thoughts on Government,* also wrote, "Nothing is more certain, from the history of nations and nature of man, than that some forms of government are better fitted for being well administered than others." Julian Mortenson has written that a central concern of the Framers was the utter lack of "execution" and central "administration" under the Articles of Confederation, whereby the Confederation Congress had to depend on the states themselves to execute the national law. Julian Davis Mortenson, *The Executive Power Clause,* 168 U. Pa. L. Rev. 1269 (2020). The question for the Framers was how to craft an executive with sufficient powers and energy to execute the laws without also risking tyranny; thus Hamilton, in *Federalist No. 77,* argued that the President under the U.S. Constitution would have "all the requisites to energy," but only "as far as republican principles will admit." Was Wilson simply wrong about the Framers' concern over administration, or was Wilson using "administration" in a sense different from the way the founding generation used the term?

HISTORICAL PERSPECTIVE Today, many scholars believe there is a distinction between "administration" and "executive power" or "law execution." Reading this material, did the Founding generation distinguish between the two concepts? Should that matter for constitutional interpretation today?

2. *Complexity of modern society.* The second reason Wilson gives for the absence of a science of administration is the complexity of modern society. Administration in the olden days—when "[p]opulations were of manageable numbers; property was of simple sorts," and "[t]here were plenty of farms, but no stocks and bonds: more cattle than vested interests"—was simple because the problems of society were simple. If society was complex in Wilson's time, one can only imagine what he would have thought of our own time—in the world of the Internet and social media, where trading in financial markets can be done by algorithms and in cryptocurrency. But do you agree that complexity in society justifies a "science of administration"? Complexity is still to this day invoked by supporters of the administrative state; complex problems require bureaucratic experts to solve. In Mistretta v. United States, 488 U.S. 361 (1989), the Supreme Court justified broad delegations from Congress to agencies on the ground that "in our increasingly complex society, replete with

ever-changing and more technical problems, Congress simply cannot do its job absent an ability to delegate power under broad general directives." In *Mistretta*, the Court confronted Congress's delegation of authority to the U.S. Sentencing Commission to create sentencing guidelines. Is society too complex for legislatures to decide on the criminal punishments for criminal offenses?

EXPERTISE VS. ACCOUNTABILITY
Why give power to agencies? Is society too complex for Congress to resolve technical policy questions? Will agencies be more efficient and expert at solving modern problems?

---

3. Is "administration" apolitical? Wilson argues that administration is independent of politics. "The field of administration is a field of business. It is removed from the hurry and strife of politics," he writes. Do you agree? Once the policy is decided upon by the principals—Congress, or perhaps We the People speaking through Congress—is there no politics left in administering what the people have willed?

4. The separation of powers. What does Wilson say of the separation of powers? He writes "that large powers and unhampered discretion" are "indispensable conditions of responsibility." If power is "divided, dealt out in shares to many, it is obscured; and if it be obscured, it is made irresponsible." Do you agree? Is this a rejection of eighteenth-century separation of powers theory that divided power better secures liberty? Some modern-day scholars have similarly argued that high-level agency officials must combine legislative, executive, and judicial powers if they are to discharge their trusts expertly and accountably. Gillian Metzger has argued, "[T]he constitutional imperatives to ensure that delegated authority is faithfully executed and to supervise delegated power entail that high-level agency officials be able to review applications of that authority by lower-level agency staff. Or in other words, these legislative, judicial, and executive functions must be combined not just in executive branch agencies, but more particularly in the heads of departments charged with overseeing their respective department's activities." Gillian E. Metzger, *Foreword: 1930s Redux: The Administrative State Under Siege*, 131 Harv. L. Rev. 1, 92 (2017).

Note how the themes from Wilson—societal complexity, the separation of politics from administration, and the rejection of eighteenth-century theories of separation of powers—repeat more explicitly in Frank Goodnow's famous short work from 1900. Goodnow was a law professor at Columbia University and is considered one of the fathers of American administrative law.

Frank J. Goodnow, Politics and Administration

(1900)

. . . . At the time of our early constitutions, including the national Constitution, were framed, this principle of the separation of powers with its corollary, the separation of authorities, was universally accepted in this country. . . . This principle of the separation of powers and authorities has proven, however, to be unworkable as a legal principle. . . . No political organization, based on the general theory of a differentiation of governmental functions, has ever been established which assigns the function of expressing the will of the state exclusively to any one of the organs for which it makes provision.

Thus, the organ of government whose main function is the execution of the will of the state is often, and indeed usually, intrusted with the expression of that will in its details. These details, however, when expressed, must conform with the general principles laid down by the organ whose main duty is that of expression. That is, the authority called executive has, in almost all cases, considerable ordinance or legislative power.

On the other hand, the organ whose main duty is to express the will of the state, i.e. the legislature, has usually the power to control in one way or another the execution of the state will by that organ to which such execution is in the main intrusted. That is, while the two primary functions of government are susceptible of differentiation, the organs of government to which the discharge of these functions is intrusted cannot be clearly defined. . . . Again, as a result, either of the provisions of the constitution or of the delegation of the power by the legislature, the chief executive or subordinate executive authorities may, through the issue of ordinances, express the will of the state as to details where it is inconvenient for the legislature to act.

The same is true of the execution of the will of the state. If we analyze the organization of any concrete government, we shall find that there are three kinds of authorities which are engaged in the execution of the state will. These are, in the first place, the authorities which apply the law in concrete cases where controversies arise owing to the failure of private individuals or public authorities to observe the rights of others. Such authorities are known as judicial authorities. They are, in the second place, the authorities which have the general supervision of the execution of the state will, and which are commonly referred to as executive authorities. They are, finally, the authorities which are attending to the scientific, technical, and, so to speak, commercial activities of the government, and which are in all countries, where such activities have attained prominence, known as administrative authorities. . . .

Enough has been said, it is believed, to show that there are two distinct functions of government, and that their differentiation results in a differentiation, though less complete, of the organs of government provided by the formal governmental system. These two functions of government may for purposes of convenience be designated respectively as Politics and Administration. Politics has to do with policies or expressions of the state will. Administration has to do with the execution of these policies. . . .

The attempt was made at the time of the formation of our governmental system, as has been pointed out, to incorporate into it the principle of the separation of powers. What had been a somewhat nebulous theory of political science thus became a rigid legal doctrine. What had been a somewhat attractive political theory in its nebulous form became at once an unworkable and unapplicable rule of law.

To avoid the inconvenience resulting from the attempt made to apply it logically to our governmental system, the judges of the United States have been accustomed to call "administrative" any power which was not in their eyes exclusively and unqualifiedly legislative, executive, or judicial, and to permit such a power to be exercised by any authority.

While this habit on the part of the judges makes the selection of the word "administration" somewhat unfortunate; at the same time it is indicative of the fact to which attention has been more than once directed, that although the differentiation of two functions of government is clear, the assignment of such functions to separate authorities is impossible. . . .

* * *

The function of politics, it has been shown, consists in the expression of the will of the state. Its discharge may not, however, be intrusted exclusively to any authority or any set of authorities in the government. Nor on the other hand may any authority or set of authorities be confined exclusively to its discharge. The principle of the separation of powers in its extreme form cannot, therefore, be made the basis of any concrete political organization. For this principle demands that there shall be separate authorities of the government, each of which shall be confined to the discharge of one of the functions of government which are differentiated. Actual political necessity however requires that there shall be harmony between the expression and execution of the state will.

Lack of harmony between the law and its execution results in political paralysis. A rule of conduct, i.e. an expression of the state will, practically amounts to nothing if it is not executed. . . . [I]n order that this harmony between the expression and the execution of the state will may be obtained, the independence either of the body which expresses the state will or of the body which executes it must be sacrificed. . . .

The American political system is largely based on the fundamental principle of the separation of governmental powers. It has been impossible for the necessary control of politics over administration to develop within the formal governmental system on account of the independent position assigned by the constitutional law to executive and administrative officers. The control has therefore developed in the party system. . . .

   * * *

It has been said that the function of politics, while having to do primarily with the expression of the will of the state, has also to do secondarily with its execution. For there must be harmony between the expression and the execution of the state will, *i.e.* between the making and enforcement of the law. It has also been said, that in a popular government the body which expresses the state will or makes the law, must have some control over the body which executes such state will or law. Finally, it has been shown that such necessary control may be found either in the formal governmental system, or outside of that system and in the political party.

Whether this control be found in or outside of the governmental system, its existence is necessitated by the fact, that without it orderly and progressive government is impossible. It should, therefore, extend so far as is necessary to produce that harmony between the expression and the execution of the state will which has been shown to be so necessary. If, however, it is extended beyond this limit, it at once loses its *raison d'être*. This control may be made use of, for example, to perpetuate the existence of a particular party organization, instead of serving as a means to aid in bringing it about that a given expression of the state will shall become an actual rule of conduct. If such use is made of this control, it becomes a means whereby the spontaneous expression by the people of the popular will is actually prevented. . . .

Too greatly extending this necessary control, therefore, really defeats the purpose for which it is formed. Not only is this the case, but as will be pointed out later, too greatly extending this control tends to hamper the efficient discharge of the function of administration. . . . While, therefore, in the interest of securing the execution of the state will, politics should have a control over administration, in the interest both of popular government and efficient administration, that control should not be permitted to extend beyond the limits necessary in order that the legitimate purpose of its existence be fulfilled. . . .

* * *

It may be said, therefore, that English speaking people have come to the conclusion that the danger of permitting distinctly political bodies to exercise a control over the administration of justice is so great, that the authorities entrusted with this branch of the execution of the state will should be vested with very great independence, even at the risk of depriving the expressed will of the state of its quality of being actually a rule of conduct. . . .

What has been said must not be understood as meaning that the administrative system should be as completely removed from political control as the courts. Such a claim could not be for a moment admitted. For the execution of law, the expressed will of the state, depends in a large degree upon the active initiative of the administrative authorities. They should be subjected to political control to the end that they take such initiative. Such is not the case with the courts, which are called upon merely to execute the law on the application of individuals. . . .

The undue extension of politics over the administration of government may be prevented, indeed has been in the past prevented, by recognizing a degree of independence in the administrative as in the judicial authorities. . . .

* * *

. . . . In order to determine the exact limits to which this most necessary [political] control [over administration] should extend, it becomes necessary to analyze this function of administration. . . . The proper determination of the value of property for the purpose of taxation thus requires of those who assess it considerable knowledge of property values. The approval of plans of buildings should be made by those acquainted with building processes. Therefore these matters are, as a general thing, not classed as part of the administration of justice, but rather as a part of the administration of government. . . .

In order, finally, that the general work of government may go on, the governmental organization must have at its disposal wide information and varied knowledge. . . . [M]uch of this information can be obtained only as the result of a series of observations, lasting through a long period of time. The authorities of the government which acquire this information must be absolutely impartial and as free from prejudice as possible, if it is to be hoped to get at the truth. Their work is, therefore, quite similar to the *quasi*-judicial work already described. . . .

As regards the executive function, as it has been called, there can be no question of the necessity of subjecting it to the control of the body intrusted ultimately with the expression of the state will. . . . No such close connection, however, exists between the function of politics and the other branches of the administration of government. No control of a political character can bring it about that administrative officers will discharge better their *quasi*-judicial duties, for example, any more than such a control can bring it about that judges will make better decisions.

No control which a political body can have over a body instrusted with the acquisition of facts and the gathering of information can result in the gathering of more facts or the acquisition of more exact information. . . . [A] close connection between politics and work of an administrative character is liable, in the case of the work done by the administration in the investigation of facts and the gathering of information, to pollute the sources of truth, in that it may give a bias to the investigator. . . . Political control over administrative functions is liable finally to produce inefficient administration in that it makes administrative officers feel that what is demanded of them is not so much work that will improve their own department, as compliance with the behests of the political party.

Up to within comparatively few years, . . . [t]he distinctly administrative functions were naturally confused with the executive function. It was regarded as proper to attempt to exercise the same control over administrative matters as was exercised, and properly exercised, over the executive function. . . .

The fact is, then, that there is a large part of administration which is unconnected with politics, which should therefore be relieved very largely, if not altogether, from the control of political bodies. It is unconnected with politics because it embraces fields of semi-scientific, *quasi*-judicial and *quasi*-business or commercial activity—work which has little if any influence on the expression of the true state will. For the most advantageous discharge of this branch of the function of administration there should be organized a force of governmental agents absolutely free from the influence of politics. Such a force should be free from the influence of politics because of the fact that their mission is the exercise of foresight and discretion, the pursuit of truth, the gathering of information, the maintenance of a strictly impartial attitude toward the individuals with whom they have dealings, and the provision of the most efficient possible administrative organization. . . . Their work is no more political in character than is that of judges . . . .

The governmental authorities intrusted with the discharge of the administrative function should not only, like judges, be free from the influence of politics; they should also, again like judges, have considerable permanence of tenure. They should have permanence of tenure because the excellence of their work is often conditioned by the fact that they are expert, and expertness comes largely from long practice. Reasonable permanence of tenure is absolutely necessary for the semi-scientific, *quasi*-judicial, and technical branches of the administrative service. . . .

Care should be taken, however, that permanence of tenure be not given to those distinctly executive officers to whom is entrusted the general execution of the law. If permanence of tenure is provided for such officers, the government, as a whole, will tend to lose its popular character, since the execution of law has an important influence on the expression of the will of the state. An unenforced law is not really a rule of conduct, and the enforcement of law is in the hands of such officers. . . .

In the semi-scientific, *quasi*-judicial, clerical, and ministerial divisions of the administrative system provision should be made for permanence of tenure, if efficient and impartial administration is to be expected, and if questions of policy are to be determined in accordance with the popular will. In its higher divisions, that is, those where the incumbents of offices have a determining influence on questions of policy, and particularly in case of the executive head, permanence of tenure should be avoided. Provision should in these cases be made for political control if it is hoped to secure the decision of questions of policy by bodies representative of the people. . . . Safety lies alone in frankly recognizing both that there should be a control over the general execution of the law and that there is a part of the work of administration into which politics should not enter. Only in this way may really popular government and efficient administration be obtained.

NOTES AND QUESTIONS

1.   *The role of political parties.* Goodnow's work is a bit hard to parse, but the thrust of his argument is that there is a distinction between "administrative" functions and "executive" functions, and that the former should be free from political influence while the latter should be controlled by "politics," i.e. the legislative body responsible for expressing the will of the state. Note how different Goodnow's framework is from that underlying the U.S. Constitution. According to the Framers' separation-of-powers theory, administration and execution are synonymous, and the executive power tasked with this function must be independent of the legislative body—although, of course, the executive can only enforce laws that Congress enacts and must do so faithfully. Goodnow argues that the making and enforcing of the laws must both be under the influence of politics, or the general will of the state, and in the American system this harmony is supplied extra-constitutionally by political parties. (Note how this argument anticipates by over a century the famous article by Daryl J. Levinson & Richard H. Pildes, *Separation of Parties, Not Powers*, 119 Harv. L. Rev. 1 (2006).) Do you agree with Goodnow's rejection of the separation of powers and the necessity of harmony between the law-making authority and the authority tasked with law-execution?

2.   *Administration versus execution.* For that matter, do you agree with Goodnow that there is in fact a distinction between "administrative" functions and "executive" functions? What exactly is the distinction that he draws? Do you understand from his text what kinds of officers are administrative and should have permanence in tenure, and those who are executive and shouldn't? The distinction seems to be based on the nature of some duties being scientific and technical, and the nature of others involving policy choices. Is this a valuable distinction?

3.   The New Deal and the APA

Between the establishment of the Interstate Commerce Commission in 1887 and the New Deal, Congress established a handful of new agencies, particularly relating to antitrust. For example, Congress enacted the Sherman Antitrust Act in 1890, the Clayton Act in 1914, and created the Federal Trade Commission to assist in enforcing these laws in the Federal Trade Commission Act of 1914. Congress also enacted the first national food and drug law, the Pure Food and Drug Act of 1906, assigning the task of administering the law to the Bureau of Chemistry in the U.S. Department of Agriculture, and to a newly established Food and Drug Administration in 1927.

In the New Deal era, there was a burgeoning of federal legislation over the national economy and a corresponding burgeoning of administrative agencies to help administer these national programs. What resulted was a veritable "alphabet soup" of administrative agencies: among those that still exist today, these included the FAA (Federal Aviation Administration), FDIC (Federal Deposit Insurance Corporation), FHA (Federal Housing Administration), NLRB (National Labor Relations Board), SEC (Securities and Exchange Commission), SSA (Social Security Administration), and TVA (Tennessee Valley Authority), among others.

With over 200 agencies, each created by its own statute—called an organic statute—members of the public and elected officials began increasingly to demand uniformity in the procedures used by agencies. In 1950, the Supreme Court explained that one purpose of the Administrative Procedure Act, enacted unanimously by Congress in 1946, was "to introduce greater uniformity of procedure and standardization of administrative practice among the diverse agencies whose customs had departed widely from each other." Wong Yang Sung v. McGrath, 339 U.S. 33, 41 (1950). Another was "to curtail and change the practice of embodying in one person or agency the duties of prosecutor and judge." Id. Numerous reports by the Attorney General, Secretary of Labor, and the President's Committee on Administrative Management had voiced such concerns in the 1930s and early 1940s over the "commingling of functions of investigation or advocacy with the function of deciding." Rep. Atty. Gen. Comm. Ad. Proc. 56 (1941), S. Doc. No. 8, 77th Cong., 1st Sess. 56 (1941). Thus the Attorney General's report recommended an "internal division of labor" within an agency. Id.

The Administrative Procedure Act—which forms the core of Chapters 2–4 in this casebook—thus provided that when an agency "adjudicated" cases, typically it had to give interested parties notice and opportunity to submit evidence, and the initial agency adjudicator could not "be responsible to or subject to the supervision or direction of an employee or agent engaged in the performance of investigative or prosecuting functions for an agency." 5 U.S.C. § 554(d)(2). The agency then had to engage in a trial-like adjudication. Id. § 556(c). If an agency official subordinate to the head of the agency conducted the trial, that official's decision would become final without further agency action, but the agency itself could review and revise any such decision. Id. § 557(b), (c). Note that it was widely understood that agencies would follow these requirements of what has been called "formal adjudication."

HISTORICAL PERSPECTIVE Why did Congress think the APA was necessary? As you read the modern material, do you think the APA needs to be updated?

For reasons that shall be explained in Chapter 3.B.2, agencies no longer have to engage in such a formal process. Instead, most agency action takes the form of "informal" adjudication. The APA, interestingly, does not have many specific requirements for informal adjudications. This is arguably a major "hole" in the APA, and has led to numerous calls to reform and amend the APA to adopt best practices for these types of adjudications. Michael Asimow, Administrative Conference of the United States, Adjudication Outside the Administrative Procedure Act, Sept. 16, 2016; Michael Asimow, *The Spreading Umbrella: Extending the APA's Adjudication Provisions to All Evidentiary Hearings Required by Statute*, 56 Admin L. Rev. 1003 (2004).

Additionally, the APA allowed for "rulemaking," both informal and formal. Some have argued that this was a major victory for the administrative state. See, e.g., Martin Shapiro, *APA: Past, Present, Future*, 72 Va. L. Rev. 447, 453 (1986). Until then (and actually until a few decades after the APA's enactment), most agencies proceeded via adjudication. The APA, however, also allowed them to make "rules" or "regulations," the stuff of much agency action today. The procedures for rulemaking are discussed in Chapter 2.

It is worth repeating that the APA was enacted unanimously. This of course raises the question, how was it that such a law could garner unanimity given the many strong and competing views on administrative power? It has often been suggested that this unanimity was achieved through the use of only vague outlines and general principles. The APA is often thought to be a kind of "constitution" for the administrative state, rather than a particularly specific statute. Throughout the course, consider whether the APA can be interpreted with its original meaning—indeed, does the APA even have much of an original meaning?—and whether some amount of administrative "common law" fleshing out the provisions of the APA is inevitable.

The following excerpt is from James Landis's *The Administrative Process*, written in 1938 as all of these developments were coming to fruition.

Questions to Consider While Reading the Article

(1)   What course themes do you detect in Landis's writing?

James Landis, The Administrative Process

Yale University Press, 1938

The last century has witnessed the rise of a new instrument of government, the administrative tribunal. In its mature form it is difficult to find its parallels in our earlier political history; its development seems indigenous. The rapidity of its growth, the significance of its powers, and the implications of its being, are such as to require notice of the extent to which this new "administrative law" is weaving itself more and more into our governmental fabric.

In terms of political theory, the administrative process springs from the inadequacy of a simple tripartite form of government to deal with modern problems. It represents a striving to adapt governmental technique, that still divides under three rubrics, to modern needs and, at the same time, to preserve those elements of responsibility and those conditions of balance that have distinguished Anglo-American government.

Separation of powers as a political maxim is old; but as a principle of government, sanctified by being elevated to the constitutional level and embroidered by pontifical moral phrases, it has a distinctly American flavor. Our British cousins discover it now and then as they find that its preachment fits some practical or political need. But it was left to us to hallow the tripartite ideal of government, wherein all power delegated by the people was in the purported interests of liberty divided neatly between legislative, executive, and judicial. It was left to us, moreover, not merely to make of this division a convenient way of thinking about government, of considering the desirability of checking and balancing a particular power that might be vested in some official or some body, but also by judicial introspection to distinguish minutely and definitively between these powers. . . .

The insistence upon the compartmentalization of power along triadic lines gave way in the nineteenth century to the exigencies of governance. Without too much political theory but with a keen sense of the practicalities of the situation, agencies were created whose functions embraced the three aspects of government. Rule-making, enforcement, and the disposition of competing claims made by contending parties, were all intrusted to them. As the years passed, the process grew. These agencies, tribunals, and rule-making boards were for the sake of convenience distinguished from the existing governmental bureaucracies by terming them "administrative." The law the courts permitted them to make was named "administrative law," so that now the process in all its component parts can be appropriately termed "the administrative process." . . .

* * *

At the turn of nineteenth century the functions of government were limited essentially to the prevention of disorder, protection from foreign invasion, the enlargement of national boundaries, the stimulation of international trade, and the creation of a scheme of officials to settle civil disputes. . . .

The rise of industrialism and the rise of democracy, however, brought new and difficult problems to government. A world that scarcely a hundred years ago could listen to Wordsworth's denunciation of railroads because their building despoiled the beauty of his northern landscapes is different, very different, from one that in 1938 has to determine lanes and flight levels for air traffic.

While it was true that advances in transportation, communication, and mass production were in themselves disturbing elements, the profound problems were the social and economic questions that flowed from the era of mechanical invention. To their solution some contribution derived from the rise of humanitarianism. But the driving force was the recognition by the governing classes of our civilization of their growing dependence upon the promotion of the welfare of the governed. . . .

More important than the immediate powers that in 1887 were vested in the Interstate Commerce Commission was the creation of the Commission itself. A government had to be provided to direct and control an industry, and governance as a practical matter implied not merely legislative power or simply executive power, but whatever power might be required to achieve the desired results. . . . The dominant theme in the administrative structure is thus determined not primarily by political conceptualism but rather by concern for an industry whose economic health has become a responsibility of government. . . . [A]s responsibility for the efficient functioning of the railroads is assumed in greater degree by the nation, the Commission possesses less the appearance of a tribunal and more that of a committee charged with the task of achieving the best possible operation of the railroads. . . .

As particular industries, due to lack of effective economic restraints, posited problems of abusive tactics with which traditional legal devices had failed to cope, this new method of control made its appearance. Banking, insurance, utilities, shipping, communications—industries with sicknesses stemming from misdirection as to objective or from failure adequately to meet public needs—all came under the fostering guardianship of the state. The mode of the exercise of that guardianship was the administrative process. . . .

Viewed from this standpoint, it is obvious that the resort to the administrative process is not, as some suppose, simply an extension of executive power. Confused observers have sought to liken this development to a pervasive use of executive power. But the administrative differs not only with regard to the scope of its powers; it differs most radically in regard to the responsibility it possesses for their exercise. In the grant to it of that full ambit of authority necessary for it in order to plan, to promote, and to police, it presents an assemblage of rights normally exercisable by government as a whole.

* * *

If the administrative process is to fill the need for expertness, obviously, as regulation increases, the number of our administrative authorities must increase. . . . Efficiency in the processes of governmental regulation is best served by the creation of more rather than less agencies. And it is efficiency that is the desperate need. . . . The demand for expertness, for a continuity of concern, naturally leads to the creation of authorities limited in their sphere of action to the new tasks that government may conclude to undertake. . . . By creating a new [Securities and Exchange] Commission . . . it was possible to have individuals in charge whose single concern was the problem of securities regulation. . . .Placing responsibility directly upon a specific group means that a finger can be publicly pointed at a particular man or men who are charged with the solution of a particular question. . . .

Admittedly, the judicial process suffers from several basic and more or less unchangeable characteristics. One of these is its inability to maintain a long-time, uninterrupted interest in a relatively narrow and carefully defined area of economic and social activity. . . . Then, too, it seemed desirable to have some uniformity in approach, a uniformity that under the judicial process could only be attained by the time-consuming and expensive device of appeals to the court of last resort.

To these considerations must be added . . . others. The first is the recognition that there are certain fields where the making of law springs less from generalizations and principles drawn from the majestic authority of textbooks and cases, than from a "practical" judgment which is based upon all the available considerations and which has in mind the most desirable and pragmatic method of solving that particular problem. . . .

One other significant distinction between the administrative and the judicial processes is the power of "independent" investigation possessed by the former. . . .

* * *

A marked tendency of modern legislation is to deal with regulatory problems by setting forth less frequently in the legislation itself the particular rules that shall control. . . . The chief virtue of this modern tendency toward delegation is that it is conducive to flexibility—a prime quality of good administration. The administrative is always in session. Its processes operate with comparative rapidity.

* * *

In discussing the functioning of the administrative as related to the sanctions that it employs, I have noted the rise of the independent, regulatory administrative agency. The reasons for favoring this form seem simple enough—a desire to have the fashioning of industrial policy removed to a degree from political influence. At the same time, there seems to have been a hope that the independent agency would make for more professionalism than that which characterized the normal executive department. Policies would thus be more permanent and could be fashioned with greater foresight than might attend their shaping under conditions where the dominance of executive power was pronounced. Again, the idea of the independent Commission seems naturally to have evolved from the very concept of administrative power. That power embraces functions exercisable by all three branches of government. To have taken these functions and to have placed them in the hands of any one of the three branches of government would have seemed incongruous. The natural solution was to place them beyond the immediate control of any one of the three branches, yet subject to checks by each of them.

NOTES AND QUESTIONS

1. Themes. Landis touched on all the standard themes of separation of powers, delegation, agency independence, expertise, efficiency, and flexibility. Note also that Landis agreed with Wilson that the growth of administrative agencies was connected with the increasing complexity of society and the desire for governmental management of some of that complexity. The idea of the administrative process was to have a body of neutral experts who could dedicate themselves to the problems of a particular industry. One anecdote, not excerpted above, relates to that observation. Landis remarked (p. 75): "One of the ablest administrators that it was my good fortune to know, I believe, never read, at least more than casually, the statutes that he translated into reality. He assumed that they gave him power to deal with the broad

COURSE THEME What course themes did you detect in Landis's book? Are Landis's concerns still relevant today?

problems of an industry and, upon that understanding, he sought his own solutions." What are the benefits of such an approach to administrative government? What are the costs? How would you balance them?

4.   Consumers, the Environment, and Public Choice

The 1960s and 70s witnessed a flurry of new administrative agencies, created to implement Lyndon Johnson's "Great Society" programs and various environmental and consumer protection legislation. The Environmental Protection Agency was created to help implement the National Environmental Policy Act of 1969, the Clean Air Act of 1970, the Clean Water Act of 1972, and the Endangered Species Act of 1973; the Occupational Safety and Health Administration was created to implement the Occupational Safety and Health Act of 1970; and the Consumer Product Safety Commission was created to implement the Consumer Product Safety Act of 1972, to name only some of the more prominent examples.

At the same time all this new legislation reflected faith in government to solve problems, many academics, and judges influenced by those academics, began to argue that agencies were not particularly trustworthy stewards of the public interest. Many "public choice" scholars argued that what often motivates private actors in a free market—namely, profit-maximization—also motivates government bureaucrats. Thus bureaucrats would seek to expand their budgets and the reach of their power, without necessarily consulting the public interest.

Defined Term

PUBLIC CHOICE THEORY: This theory posits that government actors are motivated by the same motivations that private actors have—self-interest and profit maximization. This theory suggests that bureaucrats will try to expand their jurisdictions and budgets, and may not always look out for the interest of the public.

Additionally, many academics and politicians argued that agencies were "captured" by the industries they were supposed to regulate—presumably because many regulators also hoped to enjoy future careers in the private sector, or simply because it was easier to rely on industry knowledge and expertise.

Thomas Merrill has explained the shifting public conception of the administrative state as follows:

During the period from roughly 1967 to 1983, the public interest theory gave way to a different paradigm of the administrative state. The rationalist ideal of the preceding period was displaced by what might be called a populist ideal. The public interest conception pointed toward government by supposedly nonpolitical agency experts, who could gather the information and develop solutions to complex problems that could be imposed on a centralized basis. The new populist mood that emerged around 1967 did not question the need for governmental solutions to social and economic problems. But it was deeply disturbed by the notion that those solutions should emerge from insulated agency experts.

The primary pathology of agency government emphasized during the era was that agencies were likely to become "captured" by the business organizations that they are charged with regulating. Other pathologies were cited as well. For example, agencies were commonly regarded as mindless "bureaucracies" more concerned with expanding their budgets and making life comfortable for tenured civil servants than with attending to the needs of the beneficiaries of regulation.

Thomas W. Merrill, *Capture Theory and the Courts: 1967–1983*, 72 Chi-Kent L. Rev. 1039, 1050 (1997).

In this era, courts began to review agency procedures more aggressively, and often required agencies to use additional procedures above and beyond those required by the APA—until the Supreme Court put a stop to that practice in the famous *Vermont Yankee* case in 1978 (see p. 119). The courts expanded the availability of judicial review, allowing affected parties to challenge regulations even if the agencies had not taken any enforcement actions against those parties (see Abbott Laboratories v. Gardner, 387 U.S. 136 (1967), p. 1045). And the courts solidified so-called "hard look" review of an agency' reasoning in the 1983 *State Farm* case (see p. 285).

Many of these doctrines still exist in the law today, although not all do and others have transformed. As explained, the Supreme Court in Vermont Yankee Nuclear Power Corp. v. Natural Resources Defense Council, Inc., 435 U.S. 519 (1978) put a stop to judicially created agency procedures. And more generally in United States v. Florida East Coast Railway, 410 U.S. 224 (1973), the Court interpreted the APA in such a way that agencies would no longer have to engage in excessively formal and procedure-laden proceedings to engage in rulemaking (see p. 109). "Hard look" doctrine is probably not what it used to be, with courts generally deferring to an agency as long as the agency "shows its work." And in 1984, in the seminal Chevron USA, Inc. v. Natural Resources Defense Council, Inc., 467 U.S. 837 (1984), the Supreme Court confirmed that courts should defer to an agency's reasonable "interpretation" of its own organic statute (see p. 353).

Administrative law doctrine, in short, still exists in a kind of hybrid state, deriving largely from this era of expanded judicial review and then the subsequent reining in of the judicial role. Much administrative law doctrine developed in an era of trust in expert and apolitical administrative agencies, but much also developed in an era of distrust.

5.   Modern Developments

Administrative law has not changed all that much since the 1967–1984 period described in the previous subsection. But there have been some developments. Of particular interest is the debate that began in the 1980s, which continues to this day, over how much control presidents should have in directing the rulemaking activities of agencies. In the decades immediately following the APA, the conventional wisdom was that if Congress assigned a statute to an agency to implement, it was largely left to that agency to decide how to do the implementing. In the 1990s and early 2000s, some scholars began to argue, as now-Justice Elena Kagan famously did in her article *Presidential Administration*, 114 Harv. L. Rev. 2246 (2001), that presidents should direct and control the rulemaking activities of at least those agencies properly within the "executive" branch, i.e., those that weren't considered "independent" agencies. Indeed starting even earlier in 1981 with Executive Order 12,291, issued by President Reagan and which President Clinton amended in Executive Order 12,866, presidents of both parties have centralized review of agency rulemaking in an Office of Information and Regulatory Affairs ("OIRA"), whose director ultimately reports to the President. And today, many formalist and originalist scholars argue that the President should have full control over all administrative agencies because, they argue, the Constitution recognizes no distinction between independent and non-independent agencies—they are all within the "executive" branch of government, controlled by a unitary President.

There have also been calls to reform the APA. As already suggested previously, much agency adjudication is "informal," and the APA does not actually have much to say about what procedures to follow in many kinds of informal adjudications. Additionally, agencies routinely use exemptions from the rulemaking process to achieve big shifts in regulatory law by issuing various "guidance" documents. Some have proposed to subject such guidance to the rulemaking process by amending the APA, and Presidents George W. Bush and Donald J. Trump at various times have sought to centralize review within OIRA of at least major guidance documents.

Finally, some scholars have called attention to the increasing privatization of administrative functions. Many prisons are run by private contractors today, to name but one example. And the case you will read in the next section involved a delegation of authority to a private entity—Amtrak—to engage in regulatory activity. What are the implications of delegations of authority to private parties, or to public-private partnerships? Should administrative law change in some ways in light of these modern-day practices? See generally Jon D. Michaels, Constitutional Coup: Privatization's Threat to the American Republic (2017); Jon D. Michaels, *Privatization's Pretensions*, 77 U. Chi. L. Rev. 717 (2010).

C. Constitutional Questions

This section introduces the student to the variety of constitutional questions that arise in the study of administrative law. It begins with one case excerpt that gives a good indication of what agencies actually do, and why that might raise constitutional questions. It then offers glimpses of some leading literature on these questions today.

Dep't of Transportation v. Ass'n of American Railroads

575 U.S. 43 (2015)

JUSTICE KENNEDY delivered the opinion of the Court.

In 1970, Congress created the National Railroad Passenger Corporation, most often known as Amtrak. Later, Congress granted Amtrak and the Federal Railroad Administration (FRA) joint authority to issue "metrics and standards" that address the performance and scheduling of passenger railroad services. Alleging that the metrics and standards have substantial and adverse effects upon its members' freight services, respondent—the Association of American Railroads—filed this suit to challenge their validity. The defendants below, petitioners here, are the Department of Transportation, the FRA, and two individuals sued in their official capacity.

Respondent alleges the metrics and standards must be invalidated on the ground that Amtrak is a private entity and it was therefore unconstitutional for Congress to allow and direct it to exercise joint authority in their issuance. This argument rests on the Fifth Amendment Due Process Clause and the constitutional provisions regarding separation of powers. The District Court rejected both of respondent's claims. The Court of Appeals for the District of Columbia Circuit reversed, finding that, for purposes of this dispute, Amtrak is a private entity and that Congress violated nondelegation principles in its grant of joint authority to Amtrak and the FRA. On that premise the Court of Appeals invalidated the metrics and standards.

Having granted the petition for writ of certiorari, 573 U. S. ___ (2014), this Court now holds that, for purposes of determining the validity of the metrics and standards, Amtrak is a governmental entity. Although Amtrak's actions here were governmental, substantial questions respecting the lawfulness of the metrics and standards—including questions implicating the Constitution's structural separation of powers and the Appointments Clause, U.S. Const., Art. II, § 2, cl. 2—may still remain in the case. As those matters have not yet been passed upon by the Court of Appeals, this case is remanded.

I

A

Amtrak is a corporation established and authorized by a detailed federal statute enacted by Congress for no less a purpose than to preserve passenger services and routes on our Nation's railroads. Congress recognized that Amtrak, of necessity, must rely for most of its operations on track systems owned by the freight railroads. So, as a condition of relief from their common-carrier duties, Congress required freight railroads to allow Amtrak to use their tracks and facilities at rates agreed to by the parties—or in the event of disagreement to be set by the Interstate Commerce Commission (ICC). The Surface Transportation Board (STB) now occupies the dispute-resolution role originally assigned to the ICC. Since 1973, Amtrak has received a statutory preference over freight transportation in using rail lines, junctions, and crossings.

The metrics and standards at issue here are the result of a further and more recent enactment. Concerned by poor service, unreliability, and delays resulting from freight traffic congestion, Congress passed the Passenger Rail Investment and Improvement Act (PRIIA) in 2008. Section 207(a) of the PRIIA provides for the creation of the metrics and standards:

> "Within 180 days after the date of enactment of this Act, the Federal Railroad Administration and Amtrak shall jointly, in consultation with the Surface Transportation Board, rail carriers over whose rail lines Amtrak trains operate, States, Amtrak employees, nonprofit employee organizations representing Amtrak employees, and groups representing Amtrak passengers, as appropriate, develop new or improve existing metrics and minimum standards for measuring the performance and service quality of intercity passenger train operations, including cost recovery, on-time performance and minutes of delay, ridership, on-board services, stations, facilities, equipment, and other services."

Section 207(d) of the PRIIA further provides:

> "If the development of the metrics and standards is not completed within the 180-day period required by subsection (a), any party involved in the development of those standards may petition the Surface Transportation Board to appoint an arbitrator to assist the parties in resolving their disputes through binding arbitration."

The PRIIA specifies that the metrics and standards created under § 207(a) are to be used for a variety of purposes. Section 207(b) requires the FRA to "publish a quarterly report on the performance and service quality of intercity passenger train operations" addressing the specific elements to be measured by the metrics and standards. Section 207(c) provides that, "[t]o the extent practicable, Amtrak and its host rail carriers shall incorporate the metrics and standards developed under subsection (a) into their access and service agreements." And § 222(a) obliges Amtrak, within one year after the metrics and standards are established, to "develop and implement a plan to improve on-board service pursuant to the metrics and standards for such service developed under [§ 207(a)]."

Under § 213(a) of the PRIIA, the metrics and standards also may play a role in prompting investigations by the STB and in subsequent enforcement actions. For instance, "[i]f the on-time performance of any intercity passenger train averages less than 80 percent for any 2 consecutive calendar quarters," the STB may initiate an investigation "to determine whether and to what extent delays . . . are due to causes that could reasonably be addressed . . . by Amtrak or other intercity passenger rail operators." While conducting an investigation under § 213(a), the STB "has authority to review the accuracy of the train performance data and the extent to which scheduling and congestion contribute to delays" and shall "obtain information from all parties involved and identify reasonable measures and make recommendations to improve the service, quality, and on-time performance of the train." Following an investigation, the STB may award damages if it "determines that delays or failures to achieve minimum standards . . . are attributable to a rail carrier's failure to provide preference to Amtrak over freight transportation." The STB is further empowered to "order the host rail carrier to remit" damages "to Amtrak or to an entity for which Amtrak operates intercity passenger rail service."

B.

In March 2009, Amtrak and the FRA published a notice in the Federal Register inviting comments on a draft version of the metrics and standards. The final version of the metrics and standards was issued jointly by Amtrak and the FRA in May 2010. The metrics and standards address, among other matters, Amtrak's financial performance, its scores on consumer satisfaction surveys, and the percentage of passenger-trips to and from underserved communities.

Of most importance for this case, the metrics and standards also address Amtrak's on-time performance and train delays caused by host railroads. The standards associated with the on-time performance metrics require on-time performance by Amtrak trains at least 80% to 95% of the time for each route, depending on the route and year. With respect to "host-responsible delays"—that is to say, delays attributed to the railroads along which Amtrak trains travel—the metrics and standards provide that "[d]elays must not be more than 900 minutes per 10,000 Train-Miles." Amtrak conductors determine responsibility for particular delays.

In the District Court for the District of Columbia, respondent alleged injury to its members from being required to modify their rail operations, which mostly involve freight traffic, to satisfy the metrics and standards. Respondent claimed that § 207 "violates the nondelegation doctrine and the separation of powers principle by placing legislative and rulemaking authority in the hands of a private entity [Amtrak] that participates in the very industry it is supposed to regulate." Respondent also asserted that § 207 violates the Fifth Amendment Due Process Clause by "[v]esting the coercive power of the government" in Amtrak, an "interested private part[y]." In its prayer for relief respondent sought, among other remedies, a declaration of § 207's unconstitutionality and invalidation of the metrics and standards.

The District Court granted summary judgment to petitioners on both claims. Without deciding whether Amtrak must be deemed private or governmental, it rejected respondent's nondelegation argument on the ground that the FRA, the STB, and the political branches exercised sufficient control over promulgation and enforcement of the metrics and standards so that § 207 is constitutional.

The Court of Appeals for the District of Columbia Circuit reversed the judgment of the District Court as to the nondelegation and separation of powers claim, reasoning in central part that because "Amtrak is a private corporation with respect to Congress's power to delegate . . . authority," it cannot constitutionally be granted the "regulatory power prescribed in § 207." The Court of Appeals did not reach respondent's due process claim.

II

* * *

Given the combination of these unique features and its significant ties to the Government, Amtrak is not an autonomous private enterprise. Among other important considerations, its priorities, operations, and decisions are extensively supervised and substantially funded by the political branches. A majority of its Board is appointed by the President and confirmed by the Senate and is understood by the Executive to be removable by the President at will. Amtrak was created by the Government, is controlled by the Government, and operates for the Government's benefit. Thus, in its joint issuance of the metrics and standards with the FRA, Amtrak acted as a governmental entity for purposes of the Constitution's separation of powers provisions. And that exercise of governmental power must be consistent with the design and requirements of the Constitution, including those provisions relating to the separation of powers.

Respondent urges that Amtrak cannot be deemed a governmental entity in this respect. Like the Court of Appeals, it relies principally on the statutory directives that Amtrak "shall be operated and managed as a for profit corporation" and "is not a department, agency, or instrumentality of the United States Government." §§ 24301(a)(2)–(3). In light of that statutory language, respondent asserts, Amtrak cannot exercise the joint authority entrusted to it and the FRA by § 207(a).

On that point this Court's decision in *Lebron v. National Railroad Passenger Corp.*, 513 U. S. 374 (1995), provides necessary instruction. In *Lebron*, Amtrak prohibited an artist from installing a politically controversial display in New York City's Penn Station. The artist sued Amtrak, alleging a violation of his First Amendment rights. In response Amtrak asserted that it was not a governmental entity, explaining that "its charter's disclaimer of agency status prevent[ed] it from being considered a Government entity." The Court rejected this contention, holding "it is not for Congress to make the final determination of Amtrak's status as a Government entity for purposes of determining the constitutional rights of citizens affected by its actions." To hold otherwise would allow the Government "to evade the most solemn obligations imposed in the Constitution by simply resorting to the corporate form." Noting that Amtrak "is established and organized under federal law for the very purpose of pursuing federal governmental objectives, under the direction and control of federal governmental appointees," and that the Government exerts its control over Amtrak "not as a creditor but as a policymaker," the Court held Amtrak "is an agency or instrumentality of the United States for the purpose of individual rights guaranteed against the Government by the Constitution."

* * *

III

Because the Court of Appeals' decision was based on the flawed premise that Amtrak should be treated as a private entity, that opinion is now vacated. On remand, the Court of Appeals, after identifying the issues that are properly preserved and before it, will then have the instruction of the analysis set forth here. . . .

Justice Thomas, concurring in the judgment.

We have come to a strange place in our separation-of-powers jurisprudence. Confronted with a statute that authorizes a putatively private market participant to work hand-in-hand with an executive agency to craft rules that have the force and effect of law, our primary question—indeed, the primary question the parties ask us to answer—is whether that market participant is subject to an adequate measure of control by the Federal Government. We never even glance at the Constitution to see what it says about how this authority must be exercised and by whom.

I agree with the Court that the proper disposition in this case is to vacate the decision below and to remand for further consideration of respondent's constitutional challenge to the metrics and standards. I cannot join the majority's analysis, however, because it fails to fully correct the errors that require us to vacate the Court of Appeals' decision. I write separately to describe the framework that I believe should guide our resolution of delegation challenges and to highlight serious constitutional defects in the Passenger Rail Investment and Improvement Act of 2008 (PRIIA) that are properly presented for the lower courts' review on remand.

I

The Constitution does not vest the Federal Government with an undifferentiated "governmental power." Instead, the Constitution identifies three types of governmental power and, in the Vesting Clauses, commits them to three branches of Government. Those Clauses provide that "[a]ll legislative Powers herein granted shall be vested in a Congress of the United States," Art. I, § 1, "[t]he executive Power shall be vested in a President of the United States," Art. II, § 1, cl. 1, and "[t]he judicial Power of the United States, shall be vested in one supreme Court, and in such inferior Courts as the Congress may from time to time ordain and establish," Art. III, § 1.

These grants are exclusive. When the Government is called upon to perform a function that requires an exercise of legislative, executive, or judicial power, only the vested recipient of that power can perform it.

In addition to allocating power among the different branches, the Constitution identifies certain restrictions on the *manner* in which those powers are to be exercised. Article I requires, among other things, that "[e]very Bill which shall have passed the House of Representatives and the Senate, shall, before it become a Law, be presented to the President of the United States; If he approve he shall sign it, but if not he shall return it . . . ." Art. I, § 7, cl. 2. And although the Constitution is less specific about how the President shall exercise power, it is clear that he may carry out his duty to take care that the laws be faithfully executed with the aid of subordinates. *Myers* v. *United States,* 272 U. S. 52, 117 (1926) [see Chapter 6—Ed.].

When the Court speaks of Congress improperly delegating power, what it means is Congress' authorizing an entity to exercise power in a manner inconsistent with the Constitution. For example, Congress improperly "delegates" legislative power when it authorizes an entity other than itself to make a determination that requires an exercise of legislative power. It also improperly "delegates" legislative power to itself when it authorizes itself to act without bicameralism and presentment. See, e.g., *INS* v. *Chadha,* 462 U. S. 919 (1983) [see Chapter 5—Ed.]. And Congress improperly "delegates"—or, more precisely, authorizes the exercise of—executive power when it authorizes individuals or groups outside of the President's control to perform a function that requires the exercise of that power.

In order to be able to adhere to the provisions of the Constitution that allocate and constrain the exercise of these powers, we must first understand their boundaries. Here, I do not purport to offer a comprehensive description of these powers. My purpose is to identify principles relevant to today's dispute, with an eye to offering guidance to the lower courts on remand. At issue in this case is the proper division between legislative and executive powers. An examination of the history of those powers reveals how far our modern separation-of-powers jurisprudence has departed from the original meaning of the Constitution.

II

The allocation of powers in the Constitution is absolute, but it does not follow that there is no overlap between the three categories of governmental power. Certain functions may be performed by two or more branches without either exceeding its enumerated powers under the Constitution. Resolution of claims against the Government is the classic example. At least when Congress waives its sovereign immunity, such claims may be heard by an Article III court, which adjudicates such claims by an exercise of judicial power. But Congress may also provide for an executive agency to adjudicate such claims by an exercise of executive power. Or Congress may resolve the claims itself, legislating by special Act. The question is whether the particular function requires the exercise of a certain type of power; if it does, then only the branch in which that power is vested can perform it. For example, although this Court has long recognized that it does not necessarily violate the Constitution for Congress to authorize another branch to make a determination that it could make itself, there are certain core functions that require the exercise of legislative power and that only Congress can perform. *Wayman* v. *Southard*, 10 Wheat. 1, 43 (1825) (distinguishing between those functions Congress must perform itself and those it may leave to another branch).

The function at issue here is the formulation of generally applicable rules of private conduct. Under the original understanding of the Constitution, that function requires the exercise of legislative power. By corollary, the discretion inherent in executive power does *not* comprehend the discretion to formulate generally applicable rules of private conduct.

[In omitted paragraphs, JUSTICE THOMAS goes through numerous early sources, from Bracton to Locke, for the proposition that "the Executive may not formulate generally applicable rules of private conduct."—Ed.]

William Blackstone, in his Commentaries, likewise maintained that the English Constitution required that no subject be deprived of core private rights except in accordance with the law of the land. He defined a "law" as a generally applicable "rule of civil conduct prescribed by the supreme power in a state, commanding what is right and prohibiting what is wrong." And he defined a tyrannical government as one in which "the right both of *making* and of *enforcing* the laws, is vested in one and the same man, or one and the same body of men," for "wherever these two powers are united together, there can be no public liberty." . . .

* * *

III

Even with these sound historical principles in mind, classifying governmental power is an elusive venture. But it is no less important for its difficulty. The "check" the judiciary provides to maintain our separation of powers is enforcement of the rule of law through judicial review. We may not—without imperiling the delicate balance of our constitutional system—forgo our judicial duty to ascertain the meaning of the Vesting Clauses and to adhere to that meaning as the law.

We have been willing to check the improper allocation of executive power, although probably not as often as we should. Our record with regard to legislative power has been far worse.

We have held that the Constitution categorically forbids Congress to delegate its legislative power to any other body, but it has become increasingly clear to me that the test we have applied to distinguish legislative from executive power largely abdicates our duty to enforce that prohibition. Implicitly recognizing that the power to fashion legally binding rules is legislative, we have nevertheless classified rulemaking as executive (or judicial) power when the authorizing statute sets out "an intelligible principle" to guide the rulemaker's discretion. Although the Court may never have intended the boundless standard the "intelligible principle" test has become, it is evident that it does not adequately reinforce the Constitution's allocation of legislative power. I would return to the original understanding of the federal legislative power and require that the Federal Government create generally applicable rules of private conduct only through the constitutionally prescribed legislative process.

A

The Court first announced the intelligible principle test in *J. W. Hampton, Jr., & Co.* v. *United States,* 276 U. S. 394 (1928). That case involved a challenge to a tariff assessed on a shipment of barium dioxide. The rate of the tariff had been set by proclamation of the President, pursuant to the so-called flexible tariff provision of the Tariff Act of 1922. That provision authorized the President to increase or decrease a duty set by the statute if he determined that the duty did not " 'equalize . . . differences in costs of production [of the item to which the duty applied] in the United States and the principal competing country.' " The importer of the barium dioxide challenged the provision as an unconstitutional delegation of legislative power to the President. Agreeing that Congress could not delegate legislative power, the Court nevertheless upheld the Act as constitutional, setting forth the now-famous formulation: "If Congress shall lay down by legislative act an intelligible principle to which the person or body authorized to fix such rates is directed to conform, such legislative action is not a forbidden delegation of legislative power." . . .

* * *

C

Today, the Court has abandoned all pretense of enforcing a qualitative distinction between legislative and executive power. To the extent that the "intelligible principle" test was ever an adequate means of enforcing that distinction, it has been decoupled from the historical understanding of the legislative and executive powers and thus does not keep executive "lawmaking" within the bounds of inherent executive discretion. Perhaps we were led astray by the optical illusion caused by different branches carrying out the same functions, believing that the separation of powers would be substantially honored so long as the encroachment were not too great. Or perhaps we deliberately departed from the separation, bowing to the exigencies of modern Government that were so often cited in cases upholding challenged delegations of rulemaking authority. See, e.g., *Mistretta* [*v. United States,* 488 U. S. 361, 372 (1989)]("[O]ur jurisprudence has been driven by a practical understanding that in our increasingly complex society, replete with ever changing and more technical problems, Congress simply cannot do its job absent an ability to delegate power under broad general directives").

For whatever reason, the intelligible principle test now requires nothing more than a minimal degree of specificity in the instructions Congress gives to the Executive when it authorizes the Executive to make rules having the force and effect of law. And because the Court has " 'almost never felt qualified to second-guess Congress regarding the permissible degree of policy judgment that can be left to those executing or applying the law,' " the level of specificity it has required has been very minimal indeed. Under the guise of the intelligible-principle test, the Court has allowed the Executive to go beyond the safe realm of factual investigation to make political judgments about what is "unfair" or "unnecessary" [and what is in the "public interest"—Ed.]. It has permitted the Executive to make trade-offs between competing policy goals. It has even permitted the Executive to decide which policy goals it wants to pursue. And it has given sanction to the Executive to craft significant rules of private conduct. See, e.g., *Whitman* [*v. American Trucking,* 531 U.S. 457, 472–476 (2001)] (approving delegation to EPA to set national standards for air quality). . . .

We should return to the original meaning of the Constitution: The Government may create generally applicable rules of private conduct only through the proper exercise of legislative power. I accept that this would inhibit the Government from acting with the speed and efficiency Congress has sometimes found desirable. In anticipating that result and accepting it, I am in good company. John Locke, for example, acknowledged that a legislative body "is usually too numerous, and so too slow for the dispatch requisite to execution." But he saw that as a benefit for legislation, for he believed that the creation of rules of private conduct should be an irregular and infrequent occurrence. The Framers, it appears, were inclined to agree. As Alexander Hamilton explained in another context, "It may perhaps be said that the power of preventing bad laws includes that of preventing good ones . . . . But this objection will have little weight with those who can properly estimate the mischiefs of that inconstancy and mutability in the laws, which form the greatest blemish in the character and genius of our governments." I am comfortable joining his conclusion that "[t]he injury which may possibly be done by defeating a few good laws will be amply compensated by the advantage of preventing a number of bad ones."

IV

* * *

B

The first step in the Court of Appeals' analysis on remand should be to classify the power that § 207 purports to authorize Amtrak to exercise. The second step should be to determine whether the Constitution's requirements for the exercise of that power have been satisfied.

Under the original understanding of the legislative and executive power, Amtrak's role in the creation of metrics and standards requires an exercise of legislative power because it allows Amtrak to decide the applicability of standards that provide content to generally applicable rules of private conduct. Specifically, the metrics and standards alter the railroads' common-carrier obligations under 49 U. S. C. § 11101. Host railroads may enter into contracts with Amtrak under §§ 10908 and 24308 to fulfill their common-carrier obligations. The metrics and standards shape the types of contracts that satisfy the common-carrier obligations because § 207 provides that "Amtrak and its host rail carriers *shall*" include the metrics and standards in their contracts "[t]o the extent practicable." PRIIA § 207(c). As Justice Alito explains, it matters little that the railroads may avoid incorporating the metrics and standards by arguing that incorporation is impracticable; the point is that they have a legal duty to try—a duty the substance of which is defined by the metrics and standards. And that duty is backed up by the Surface Transportation Board's coercive power to impose "reasonable terms" on host railroads when they fail to come to an agreement with Amtrak. § 24308(a)(2)(A)(ii). Presumably, when it is "practicable" to incorporate the metrics and standards, the Board is better positioned to deem such terms "reasonable" and to force them upon the railroads. . . .

Section 207 therefore violates the Constitution. Article I, § 1, vests the legislative power in Congress, and Amtrak is not Congress. The procedures that § 207 sets forth for enacting the metrics and standards also do not comply with bicameralism and presentment. Art. I, § 7. For these reasons, the metrics and standards promulgated under this provision are invalid. . . .

* * *

In this case, Congress has permitted a corporation subject only to limited control by the President to create legally binding rules. These rules give content to private railroads' statutory duty to share their private infrastructure with Amtrak. This arrangement raises serious constitutional questions to which the majority's holding that Amtrak is a governmental entity is all but a non sequitur. These concerns merit close consideration by the courts below and by this Court if the case reaches us again. We have too long abrogated our duty to enforce the separation of powers required by our Constitution. We have overseen and sanctioned the growth of an administrative system that concentrates the power to make laws and the power to enforce them in the hands of a vast and unaccountable administrative apparatus that finds no comfortable home in our constitutional structure. The end result may be trains that run on time (although I doubt it), but the cost is to our Constitution and the individual liberty it protects.

Notes and Questions

1. The Vesting Clauses. In the Amtrak case, Justice Thomas argues that the PRIIA is unconstitutional even if Amtrak is declared to be a governmental entity because Congress has unlawfully delegated its legislative power to Amtrak and the FRA in the statute. Justice Thomas argues that Congress cannot constitutionally delegate its power. Why? To what provisions of the Constitution does he point? There is no nondelegation clause in the Constitution.

The answer, of course, is the Vesting Clauses. These do not explicitly specify, however, that the legislative, executive, and judicial powers cannot be delegated. Is the reason the Court has said Congress cannot delegate its power structural? Is the whole point of assigning certain kinds of power in the Constitution to certain types of entities that those entities may be particularly well suited for those powers? Did the Founders want a deliberative body to make laws, a single individual to oversee the execution of the laws, and judges with lifetime tenure and salary protections to adjudicate cases involving life, liberty, and property? We shall discuss delegation in more depth in a future chapter. For now, for some competing literature, see Julian Davis Mortenson & Nicholas Bagley, *Delegation at the Founding,* 120 Colum. L. Rev. 277 (2021) (arguing there was no nondelegation doctrine at the Founding); Ilan Wurman, *Nondelegation at the Founding,* 130 Yale L.J. ___ (2021) (arguing that there probably was a nondelegation doctrine at the Founding); Thomas W. Merrill, *Rethinking Article I: From Nondelegation to Exclusive Delegation,* 104 Colum. L. Rev. 2097 (2004) (arguing that Congress is better at deciding who should resolve policy questions than resolving policy questions for itself).

COMPARATIVE PERSPECTIVE In his *Amtrak* dissent, Justice Thomas takes an "originalist" approach to constitutional interpretation. What role should the Founders' understanding of the separation of powers play in today's judicial decisions?

2. ***Nonexclusive powers.*** Does Thomas say that *all* power is either legislative, executive, or judicial and must be exercised by the corresponding branch? Or are there some kinds of powers or activities that may be exercised by more than one branch? What example does Thomas give? Consider as another example the regulations promulgated by Henry Knox and George Washington implementing the invalid pensioner statute. Could Congress have adopted those regulations itself? If either branch could do it, how exactly should we characterize that activity? As legislative or executive? Both? Neither? Is it a "blended" power? Is the issue, then, to identify what exactly constitutes the "core" of legislative power, or power that is *exclusively* legislative, and ensure that only Congress exercises that power, whatever it is?

COURSE THEME

NONEXCLUSIVE POWER

What is the nature of administrative power? What does Justice Thomas say about exclusive powers? Is all power exclusive to one branch or another?

3. *The nondelegation principle.* Black-letter doctrine agrees with Justice Thomas at least this much: Congress *cannot* constitutionally delegate its legislative power. So what is Thomas's point? That the existing intelligible principle test has not successfully stopped delegations of legislative power? What kind of delegations does Thomas say the Court has upheld under this intelligible principle standard?

4. *Private rights and private conduct.* What is Justice Thomas's alternative test for what constitutes legislative power and unlawful delegations of such power? He seems to say that any generally applicable rule that affects private rights or private conduct is the "core" of the legislative power, as opposed to rules that merely regulate official conduct. Can that test possibly be right? Think back to two examples from the Steamboat Act of 1852. Congress authorized the imposition of passenger limits on steamboats, and also authorized the creation of rules for the passing of ships, but left it up to the inspectors to devise the relevant limits and the relevant rules. Don't those rules affect private rights and private conduct? If the FAA imposes rules for passenger limits on airplanes, doesn't that affect private rights and conduct? Is that the kind of thing we really expect Congress to do?

5. *"Important subjects."* Maybe there is another test that's neither as broad as the intelligible principle standard, nor as narrow as Justice Thomas's proposed private-conduct test. In one of the nation's first nondelegation cases, Chief Justice Marshall wrote,

> It will not be contended that Congress can delegate to the courts or to any other tribunals powers which are strictly and exclusively legislative. But Congress may certainly delegate to others powers which the legislature may rightfully exercise itself. . . . The line has not been exactly drawn which separates those important subjects which must be entirely regulated by the legislature itself from those of less interest in which a general provision may be made and power given to those who are to act under such general provisions to fill up the details.

Wayman v. Southard, 23 U.S. 1, 42–43 (1825). Here Marshall is agreeing with Justice Thomas that there are some things that Congress might do itself if it wanted, but which it could also delegate. As for the "exclusively" legislative power, that is the power to decide the "important subjects," as opposed to those of "less interest."

Does this distinction make sense? Are there some decisions that are so important that we expect them to be decided by the people's representatives? What are those important subjects? It seems to your author, anyway, that whatever the answer is, it probably should allow the FAA (and the steamboat inspectors) to establish passenger limits. Consider that in the case of steamboats, Congress decided a series of very important questions: that steamboats *ought* to be regulated; the purpose for which they ought to be regulated (safety); and Congress even authorized the specific means to be used (passenger limits and passing rules). Isn't that enough? Rules affecting private conduct may certainly be more important than rules affecting official conduct only, but perhaps if Congress answers those other questions it's acceptable for an agency to make at least some rules affecting private conduct.

6. *The separation of powers.* The other structural consideration perhaps supporting a nondelegation doctrine is that if Congress delegates its power, that in effect authorizes the executive branch to combine powers that ought to be separate. To be sure, there is no separation of powers clause in the Constitution, but the constitutional drafters certainly believed that the separation of powers was essential for the preservation of liberty. James Madison argued that the combination of legislative, executive, and judicial powers in single hands was the very definition of tyranny. The Federalist No. 47, at 301 (James Madison) (Clinton Rossiter ed., 1961). Delegation thus raises a corollary constitutional concern, namely the undermining of the separation of powers. Consider the following statement from Chief Justice John Roberts:

> Although modern administrative agencies fit most comfortably within the Executive Branch, as a practical matter they exercise legislative power, by promulgating regulations with the force of law; executive power, by policing compliance with those regulations; and judicial power, by adjudicating enforcement actions and imposing sanctions on those found to have violated their rules. The accumulation of these powers in the same hands is not an occasional or isolated exception

to the constitutional plan; it is a central feature of modern American government.

City of Arlington v. FCC, 569 U.S. 290, 312–13 (2013) (Roberts, C.J., dissenting). Chief Justice Roberts was perhaps a bit imprecise; after all, not every regulation is legislative power, and not all adjudications are exercises of judicial power (see Chapter 7). But does he have a point anyway?

Thus far, we have discussed the potential constitutional concerns with the administrative state, and particularly with the potential problems that arise from broad delegations of power from Congress to agencies. We shall return to these issues in more detail in Chapters 6–8. But now, let us examine some constitutional *defenses* of modern administration. In the following excerpt, Professor Gillian Metzger argues not only that the administrative state is constitutionally sound, but that it is in fact constitutionally required in light of the numerous delegations of power from Congress and the President's duty to take care that the laws be faithfully executed. What are the implications of her claim?

Gillian E. Metzger, The Administrative State Under Siege

131 Harv. L. Rev. 1, 87–95 (2017)

. . . . Far from representing a constitutional threat, the administrative state thus plays a critical role in both cabining and effectuating executive power. Returning to the 1930s debates helps identify important constitutional functions that the administrative state performs. But the point can be taken even further: The modern national administrative state is now constitutionally obligatory, rendered necessary by the reality of delegation. . . .

Congressional delegations of authority to the executive branch date back to the nation's earliest days of existence, and have been upheld by courts for nearly as long. The 1930s witnessed the only times that the Supreme Court has held a delegation unconstitutional, with delegation representing a central bone of contention in the constitutional battle over the New Deal. The centrality of delegation to that battle should not be surprising. Reflecting the constitutional principle that administrative agencies can only exercise authority delegated to them, delegation represents the foundation on which the administrative state rests. In Professor Louis Jaffe's famous words, delegation is "the dynamo of modern government." The New Deal delegations sustained by the Court were notably open-ended, including instructions for agencies to regulate in the "public interest." But over the ensuing eight decades the scope of delegations has expanded significantly further. Today, Congress has delegated substantial policymaking authority to the executive branch across a wide array of contexts.

Many anti-administrativists maintain that the Court's multiple decisions sustaining broad delegations represent a fundamental deviation from the Constitution's separation of powers structure. These critiques rest on contested views about the meaning of "legislative" and "executive" power—contested even among anti-administrativists themselves. An additional reason for skepticism is the difficulty anti-administrativists face in constructing a plausible test for constitutionally permissible delegations. Justice Thomas's effort to prohibit any delegation of policymaking authority in setting general rules is practically infeasible and at odds with longstanding practice. But more functionalist assessments, focused on determining when a delegation goes too far, are similarly unworkable. As Justice Scalia argued, once "the debate over unconstitutional delegation becomes a debate not over a point of principle but over a question of degree," it becomes hard to conclude that courts are competent or "qualified to second-guess Congress."

Yet whatever their views on current nondelegation doctrine, both anti-administrativists and supporters of administrative government should agree that the phenomenon of broad delegation is not at risk of judicial invalidation. Justice Thomas aside, little support exists on the Court for invalidating delegations to the executive branch on constitutional grounds. More support exists for a variety of moves seen as curtailing the scope of delegated power, such as interpreting delegations narrowly or rejecting deference to agency determinations of the scope of their delegated authority. All of these moves, however, accept the basic phenomenon of broad delegation and seek to tame its perceived capacity for abuse. The relevant constitutional question then becomes what the separation of powers requires in a world of substantial delegation of policymaking authority to the executive branch. It is in this context that the administrative state is constitutionally obligatory.

Put differently, the modern national administrative state is the constitutionally mandated consequence of delegation. To see why, begin with the Constitution's requirement that the President shall "take Care that the Laws be faithfully executed." It follows that the administrative capacity the President needs in order to satisfy the take care duty is also required. So far, few would disagree. What does that administrative capacity entail in the context of broad delegations? For starters, it means sufficient bureaucratic apparatus and supervisory mechanisms to adequately oversee execution of these delegated powers. It also requires sufficient administrative resources and personnel, in particular adequate executive branch expertise and specialization, to be able to faithfully execute these delegated responsibilities in contexts of tremendous uncertainty and complexity. Arguably, this means that professional and expert government employees are now constitutionally required as well, and perhaps also the civil service, insofar as such career staff are necessary to ensure expertise and institutional stability in agencies.

Simply from the proposition that delegated power must be faithfully executed, then, the outlines of a constitutionally mandated administrative state begin to emerge. . . . Having chosen to delegate broad responsibilities to the executive branch, Congress has a duty to provide the resources necessary for the executive branch to adequately fulfill its constitutional functions. To be clear, such a duty is unlikely to be judicially enforceable. Judicially manageable standards for determining what counts as adequate supervision, staffing, and resources to fulfill delegated responsibilities will often be lacking, and a severe risk exists that courts would intrude on the constitutional responsibilities of the other branches were they to seek to play an enforcement role. Yet that the duty is dependent on the political branches for its realization does not affect its constitutional basis.

The constitutional consequences of delegation can be pushed further, to include a requirement of some internal administrative constraints of the kind described above. Such a requirement would rest on the danger that broad delegations to the executive branch may create an imbalance of power among the branches and breed presidential unilateralism. Moreover, external checks by Congress and the courts may be limited in practice. Thus, arguably, an additional constitutional string on delegations to the executive branch is that such delegations must be structured so as to limit the potential for aggrandizement and preserve checks and balances on governmental power. But even if delegation necessitates some internal constraint, it is harder (but not impossible) to claim that a specific checking measure is required. Moreover, even deriving a general requirement of internal constraint is debatable, given the constitutional value also attached to effective governance and to presidential oversight and supervisory control over the executive branch. Hence, the fact that internal constraints play an important constitutional function in implementing the separation of powers is not enough, on its own, to conclude that such structural measures are constitutionally mandated. . . .

In the end, however, the most important point is that the phenomenon of delegation represents such a fundamental and necessary feature of contemporary government that it is mandatory in practice. And from delegation key features of the administrative state follow. . . .

Recognizing the implications of delegation has particular relevance for current constitutional attacks on the administrative state. Many of the features of the administrative state that anti-administrativists condemn—the combination of legislative, executive, and judicial powers; administrative adjudication of private rights; and judicial deference to administrative statutory interpretations—arguably follow simply from the phenomenon of delegation.

Take first the combination of powers: Adequately supervising executive branch personnel to ensure they faithfully execute their delegated responsibilities means agency officials must specify what those responsibilities are for agency staff—and the broader the delegation, the more specification is required. This entails interpreting statutes delegating authority to determine what they require and allow, as well as developing and adopting policy that conforms to those delegations. Moreover, faithfully executing delegated authority also entails applying these policies and requirements to specific actions and contexts within their ambit. Such actions of interpretation and application can be viewed as simply different dimensions of executing the law, or as combined exercises of legislative, adjudicatory, and executive powers. The broader the delegation, as Chief Justice Roberts suggested, the more the latter appears descriptively accurate. Either way, the important point is that these actions become constitutionally necessary activities for executive branch officials to perform as a result of delegation. Furthermore, the constitutional imperatives to ensure that delegated authority is faithfully executed and to supervise delegated power entail that high-level agency officials be able to review applications of that authority by lower-level agency staff. Or in other words, these legislative, judicial, and executive functions must be combined not just in executive branch agencies, but more particularly in the heads of departments charged with overseeing their respective department's activities. . . .

[T]he constitutional requirement to ensure that delegated authority is faithfully executed does entail action applying that authority. That means agency staff will need to engage in actions that qualify as adjudication in the constitutional sense—applying general rules to specific cases. And insofar as an agency is therefore depriving an individual of property or liberty in a manner that would trigger due process, it may be required to provide notice and an opportunity to be heard before acting. Hence, some form of administrative adjudication may follow as a constitutionally necessary consequence of delegation.

This leaves the question of judicial deference, increasingly the flashpoint for anti-administrativist attacks. Although some anti-administrativists maintain that judicial deference is prohibited by Article III, giving due weight to delegation complicates such a claim. As Professor Henry Monaghan elaborated before *Chevron* was decided, judicial deference can be viewed as simply an acknowledgement of the scope of authority delegated to the executive branch. Unless such delegations are unconstitutional, the constitutional separation of powers system requires that the courts honor congressional policy choices. And honoring congressional choices to delegate means deferring to agency judgments within the sphere of the agency's constitutionally delegated authority. . . .

NOTES AND QUESTIONS

1. The centrality of delegation. Far from being constitutionally suspect, Metzger argues, the administrative state is constitutionally obligatory as a consequence of delegation. But does Metzger's account beg the question? Is delegation itself constitutional? Although the excerpt above left out some of the relevant discussion, Metzger ultimately concludes that "the phenomenon of delegation represents such a fundamental and necessary feature of contemporary government that it is mandatory in

DELEGATION: This is the term used to describe anytime Congress enacts a law that authorizes agencies to take certain actions. Every statute *delegates* some authority to the executive.

practice." Is Metzger's point that even if delegation, for whatever reason, is contrary to the "original meaning" of the Constitution, it's here to stay and constitutional theory must adjust to that reality?

This is related to other attempts to advocate a constitutional theory of the "second best." See Peter B. McCutchen, *Mistakes, Precedent, and the Rise of the Administrative State: Toward a Constitutional Theory of the Second Best*, 80 Cornell L. Rev. 1 (1994). McCutchen argues that broad delegations of power are inevitable even if unconstitutional, and so the Court should allow *other* innovations that might otherwise be unconstitutional in order to rebalance power among the three branches. McCutchen argues, for example, that the Court should allow Congress to veto administrative regulations so that Congress might retain some power on the backend. Id. at 3. (For more on the legislative veto and its unconstitutionality, see Chapter 5.)

In a different article, your author engaged in a similar thought experiment, which he'd probably reject today: if administrative law doctrine recognized that Congress in fact delegates legislative (and judicial) power, then that might open up a set of formalist separation of powers tools to give each constitutional branch of government more control over the function of administration (rulemaking, enforcement, adjudication) corresponding to that branch's constitutional function. Ilan Wurman, *Constitutional Administration*, 69 Stan. L. Rev. 359 (2017). The point of all three articles seems to be that the delegation of power in the modern world is inevitable, although the precise consequences that follow are different from each author's perspective. Do you agree that delegation is inevitable?

2. *The consequences of delegation.* What consequences follow from the inevitability of delegation, according to Metzger? She suggests that to ensure the faithful execution of delegated authority, a sufficient body of administrative experts is necessary. But, to ensure accountability in the exercise of this delegated authority, high-level agency heads must exercise combined rulemaking, enforcement, and adjudicatory functions. (Recall that Woodrow Wilson made the same point, see p. 37.) On the other hand, delegation to the executive in general also creates a risk of presidential aggrandizement, suggesting that perhaps a civil service and independent agencies insulated from presidential control are necessary to counterbalance this threat. Is there some tension between these last two implications, or can they be reconciled?

 TEST YOUR KNOWLEDGE: To assess your understanding of the material in this chapter, **click here** to take a quiz.

CHAPTER TWO

Rulemaking

A. Preliminary Matters

1. The Rulemaking-Adjudication Distinction

Today, students associate administrative agencies most often with "regulations." In administrative-law-speak regulations are also called "rules," and the making of a regulation is called a rulemaking. The APA defines a "rule" as "the whole or a part of an agency statement of general or particular applicability and future effect designed to implement, interpret, or prescribe law or policy or describing the organization, procedure, or practice requirements of an agency . . . ." 5 U.S.C. § 551(4). In contrast, the APA defines "adjudication" as any "agency process for the formulation of an order," id. § 551(7), and "order" as "the whole or a part of a final disposition, whether affirmative, negative, injunctive, or declaratory in form, of an agency in a matter other than rule making but including licensing," id. § 551(6). In other words, adjudications are more or less any agency action that is not a rulemaking; and note that licensing decisions are always considered adjudications. Note also the expansive definition of a rule as any "agency statement." If an agency announces a new policy in a press release, that, too, is a "rule." Sugar Cane Growers Co-op. of Fla. v. Veneman, 289 F.3d 89, 95–96 (D.C. Cir. 2002) (a press release announcing changes to submission procedures, payments, and sanctions to a program by which farmers bid for government sugar supplies was a "rule").

> **PRACTICE POINTER** Under the APA, many agency actions are "rules" even if they do not look like formal regulations. For example, a press release that announces a new policy is a "rule." Such actions can therefore be challenged under the APA's provisions dealing with rules.

According to the APA's definition of rule, the key feature of a rule is that it has future effect. In contrast, when an agency "adjudicates" a case, it has present effect, by which is meant the agency is applying some existing law or rule to an existing set of facts. Rules are supposed to create new legal obligations in the future. Also according to the APA's definition, a rule does not have to be of "general applicability." It can also be of "particular" applicability, meaning that a rulemaking can apply to a small subset of individuals. Most rules are generally applicable, however, in that they apply to a wide range of actors and individuals. But a rule, just like a law, can be written in general language but in actuality have an effect on only a small number of people. Thus a rule under the APA can also be of "particular applicability."

Some scholars have criticized the APA's definition of a rule. Then-law professor Antonin Scalia, for example, wrote that the definition of rule is "absurd" because everything an agency does has only "future effect." Thus, he wrote in 1978, the APA's definition means "that an EPA directive that a particular company must, in order to comply with existing law and regulations, install particular emission-control equipment at a particular factory is a rule rather than an order" (because it has a "future effect") and "that the proceeding looking to its issuance is rulemaking rather than adjudication," which is "contrary to the common understanding of what constitutes rulemaking." Antonin Scalia, Vermont Yankee: *The APA, The D.C. Circuit, and the Supreme Court*, 1978 Sup. Ct. Rev. 345, 383; see also Ronald M. Levin, *The Case for (Finally) Fixing the APA's Definition of "Rule"*, 56 Admin. L. Rev. 1077, 1078 (2004) (making the same kind of argument).

These arguments, however, seem to make a mountain out of a molehill; they depend on an overly rigid reading of "future effect." On Professor Scalia's reading, every court order has "future effect" because it in fact only operates on individuals in the future. But that's a truism. Everything under the sun has future effect in this sense; courts don't enter time machines and change things that happened in the past. That's not what "future effect" means, however. It means only that the rule is *prospective*. Before an agency can come and apply that rule to a particular party, it must announce the rule. The party then has the opportunity to order its affairs accordingly. The agency may still seek to "enforce" the rule through an "adjudication" if the agency believes the party is still not complying with the law. The party will then take additional actions "in the future" to comply, but that's not what we mean by "future effect." All that is meant by that term is the rule was announced and commenced *in futuro*—prospectively. The adjudication then applies this now-existing rule to a set of now-existing facts, and in that sense has a more "present" or "immediate" effect, not a "future" effect. (Note that it is a different question entirely whether rulemakings and adjudications can have *retroactive* effect—that is, whether they may change the past legal consequences for acts done in the past. The definition of "rule" suggests an easy answer for rulemakings: they cannot alter the legal consequences for past acts. Whether an adjudication can be retroactive is a trickier question, which we address in Chapter 3.A.1 in the discussion of the *Chenery II* case.)

Justice Oliver Wendell Holmes and the legal scholar Thomas Cooley both offered classic restatements of the distinction between rules and adjudications, or between legislative and judicial acts. As Holmes explained, "A judicial inquiry investigates, declares, and enforces liabilities as they stand on present or past facts and under laws supposed already to exist." On the other hand, "[l]egislation . . . looks to the future and changes existing conditions by making a new rule, to be applied thereafter to all or some part of those subject to its power." Prentis v. Atl. Coast Line Co., 211 U.S. 210, 226 (1908). And Cooley wrote, citing an earlier case, that what "distinguishes a judicial from a legislative act is[ ] that the one is a determination of what the existing law is in relation to some existing thing already done or happened, while the other is a predetermination of what the law shall be for the regulation of all future cases falling under its provisions." Thomas M. Cooley, A Treatise on the Constitutional Limitations which Rest upon the Legislative Power of the States of the American Union 91 (1868).

FOR DISCUSSION Can you describe the difference between "future effect," "present effect," and "retroactive effect"?

Those statements sound essentially right. However, because of the criticisms of the term future effect discussed above—because some believe that everything an agency does has only future effect—Ronald Levin and others have argued that the real difference between a rule and an adjudication is the generality of the agency action. Levin, supra, at 1079 ("A proper definition of 'rule' would turn on *generality*, not *prospectivity*."). Indeed, Executive Order 12,866, issued by President Clinton, and which requires centralized executive branch review of important rules, defines a rule or regulation as "an agency statement of general applicability and future effect, which the agency intends to have the force and effect of law, that is designed to implement, interpret, or prescribe law or policy . . . ." § 3(D). This definition drops the "or particular" part of the APA's definition of rule (although it does keep the future effect language).

The argument that the distinction between a rule and an adjudication turns on generality stems from a pair of famous due process cases often taught as part of a procedural due process unit (see Chapter 7). In these cases, the Supreme Court held that if only a select few individuals are affected by a rule—and the rule would lead to a deprivation of liberty or property (the due process clause only applies if there are deprivations of life, liberty, and property)—then those individuals may have a right to individualized hearings. In Londoner v. Denver, 210 U.S. 373 (1908), the Court required the city of Denver to provide an opportunity for taxpayers to be heard before a tax could be imposed on select landowners to pay for the paving of streets abutting their properties. In Bi-Metallic Investment Co. v. State Board of Equalization, 239 U.S. 441 (1915), the Colorado State Board of Equalization ordered an increase in the valuation of all taxable property in Denver by 40 percent; here in contrast the Court did not require a hearing, holding that "[w]here a rule of conduct applies to more than a few people, it is impracticable that everyone should have a direct voice in its adoption." The Court distinguished *Londoner* by noting that that case had involved "[a] relatively small number of persons . . . who were exceptionally affected, in each case upon individual grounds."

> **CROSS REFERENCE** The *Londoner/Bi-Metallic* distinction will become important for due process, which Chapter 7 explores. Courts often look to this pair of cases to determine whether an agency action looks more like a regulation or an adjudication, and therefore whether "procedural due process" is necessary.

Courts often rely on this pair of cases to determine whether an agency action is better characterized as a "rule" or an "adjudication." If only a small number of persons are affected, each on individual grounds, the agency action is more likely to be considered an "adjudication" that must follow the procedures for adjudications under the APA. If a broader number of people are affected on less individualized grounds, it is more likely to be a "rule" subject to the APA procedures for rulemakings.

This distinction seems problematic, however. A legislature may pass a law that is general in form but only affects a small number of individuals. A legislature can enact a law that imposes a tax on anyone with more than $50 billion in assets. It can enact a law that places construction restrictions on oceanfront properties in a certain location—and perhaps that law only affects one property. In these instances, do the few individuals affected get individualized hearings? Has the legislature "adjudicated" their cases? Of course not. These laws, although affecting a small number of people and therefore quite specific or "particular" in their applicability, are still laws. Why? Because they are *prospective*. They establish *new* laws or rules for future conduct. Although some scholars have argued that "due process of law" historically required laws to be general and not "partial," your author has elsewhere demonstrated that those claims are likely incorrect. See Ilan Wurman, The Second Founding: An Introduction to the Fourteenth Amendment 31–33 (2020). In truth, there appears to be no limitation on how particular a law can be. It merely must commence *in futuro*.

2.   The Overarching Framework of the APA

This chapter will deal with rulemakings. Before diving in to the procedural requirements for specific types of rules, it is helpful to understand the overarching framework of the APA. The APA recognizes three different categories of rules: rules that must go through "formal rulemaking"; rules that must go through "informal," notice-and-comment rulemaking; and rules that are exempt from most procedural requirements. The APA does not itself use the terms "formal" and "informal," but those are what

 Defined Term

FORMAL RULEMAKING: Some statutes require agencies to engage in rulemaking "on the record after opportunity for agency hearing." This triggers the procedural, trial-like requirements of APA §§ 556–57.

practitioners, scholars, and judges have come to use to describe these tiers of procedures. And, it is always worth emphasizing, recall that the APA's procedures are just *default requirements*—Congress may always authorize different procedures for any type of rule in the organic statutes authorizing particular agencies.

Defined Term

INFORMAL RULEMAKING: The far more common type of rulemaking today, informal rulemaking is actually quite formal but it requires less procedure than formal rulemaking. The informal rulemaking process is the notice-and-comment process of APA § 553.

As we shall see, formal rulemakings are almost never done anymore. These require the trial-type proceedings of APA §§ 556–57 and can take years to complete. In one famous example, it took the Food and Drug Administration 12 years to issue a rule under formal rulemaking procedures on the question whether to be classified as "peanut butter" a product had to contain 87.5% or rather 90% peanuts. Although this example is routinely cited in opposition to burdensome formal rulemaking, the story has recently been challenged. One scholar writes that the actual proceedings were relatively quick, with the hearing itself lasting only thirty days. The long delay can instead be attributed to the FDA's failure to eliminate duplicative evidence and failure to allow cross examination only on disputed facts, and to the relative unimportance of the case. Aaron L. Nielson, *In Defense of Formal Rulemaking*, 75 Ohio St. L.J. 237, 247–50 (2014).

 **HISTORICAL PERSPECTIVE** Agencies used to engage in formal rulemaking much more often. Today they almost entirely engage in informal rulemaking. What are the advantages of the two different kinds of rulemakings?

In any event, the "myth" of burdensome formal rulemaking—and, to be sure, formal rulemaking *is* very burdensome, at least compared to the nowadays much more common informal notice-and-comment process—stuck, and today agencies rarely engage in formal rulemaking. Many agencies used to believe that they had to undertake such formal proceedings if their statutes required them to make rules only after a "hearing." That all changed with *United States v. Florida East Coast Railway Co.* (see p. 109), which interpreted "hearing" to refer also to informal notice-and-comment procedures, and not just to formal rulemaking procedures.

Most rulemaking today is done under APA § 553, which sets out the procedures for informal, notice-and-comment rulemaking. To promulgate a rule under this process, the agency must 1) issue a notice of proposed rulemaking describing the "terms or substance" of the proposed rule; 2) allow the public a period of time to comment on the rule; and 3) incorporate in the final rule a "concise general statement" of the rule's "basis and purpose." Crucially, however, there is a category of rules that are exempt even from these procedures. The APA provides that unless "notice or hearing is required by statute," the requirements of APA § 553 don't apply "to interpretative rules, general statements of policy, or rules of agency organization, procedure, or practice." 5 U.S.C.

§ 553(b)(A). These procedural requirements also don't apply if the agency has "good cause" to avoid the notice-and-comment procedures, id. § 553(b)(B), and they don't apply to rules involving certain subject matters, namely military and foreign affairs and matters "relating to agency management or personnel or to public property, loans, grants, benefits, or contracts," id. § 553(a)(1)–(2). Take a look at APA § 553 in the Appendix and see if you can piece all of that together.

One important note of terminology: Rules that must go through notice-and-comment rulemaking are often called "legislative" rules, and those that are exempt because they are interpretative, procedural, or mere statements of policy are often called "nonlegislative" rules. This terminology is confusing; by "legislative," the doctrine does not mean to imply that such rules are legislative *for purposes of the nondelegation doctrine*. A rule can be "legislative" such that it must go through notice-and-comment procedures, but the making of that rule may not be an exercise of the "legislative power" that Congress cannot delegate.

Defined Term

LEGISLATIVE RULE: A legislative rule is not to be confused with legislative power. For purposes of the APA, a legislative rule is a rule that must go through the notice-and-comment process because it creates new underlying rights or obligations.

Defined Term

NONLEGISLATIVE RULE: A nonlegislative rule is exempt from the notice-and-comment process because the rule is a procedural rule, an interpretative rule, or a policy statement. The varieties of nonlegislative rules are discussed in more detail later in this chapter.

Some courts and scholars call these rules "substantive" rules rather than "legislative." Unfortunately this, too, is a bit confusing because "procedural" rules are often distinguished from "substantive" rules, but procedural rules are merely one category of exempt rules. Hence there is some confusion because "substantive" rules might refer to *any* rule that is not exempt from the APA's requirements, or merely to rules that are not procedural. But as we shall see, it is possible to have a rule that doesn't involve procedure—and is therefore

Defined Term

SUBSTANTIVE RULE: A legislative rule is also often called a substantive rule. This terminology is confusing, however, because the term "substantive rule" is often used to distinguish a rule from a "procedural rule," which is one type of nonlegislative rule.

"substantive" as opposed to procedural—but that rule is perhaps a statement of policy and therefore would still be nonlegislative and hence exempt from the procedural requirements. If that's confusing, it should be; it will make more sense as you read about nonlegislative rules.

For present purposes, you should note both that there is some terminological confusion, and that courts and scholars use both "legislative" and "substantive" rules to describe those rules that must go through notice-and-comment procedures. This casebook shall therefore use these terms interchangeably as well, but it will only use the term "substantive" when doing so is consistent with the particular case at hand. Otherwise, the casebook opts for "legislative" and "nonlegislative," or even better, non-exempt rules and exempt rules.

3.　Power to Issue Rules

Before we can get to the procedural requirements for the different types of rulemakings and all the related issues, we must ask whether an agency even has the power to make legislative (or substantive) rules in the first place. An agency may have some inherent executive power to conduct informal adjudications and also to make some types of rules and regulations in order to enforce the law. As for informal adjudications, every time the executive branch enforces the law by making some decision about what the law requires given a set of facts, it has "adjudicated." Adjudicating in this informal sense of applying law to facts in order to enforce the law is an inherent part of "the executive power" exercised by the President and by agencies.

As for making regulations, early on Alexander Hamilton routinely instructed the customs collectors about points of law through general instructions, or circulars. As Hamilton argued in one of these letters, "The power of *superintending* the collection of the revenue, as incident to the duty of doing it, comprises, in my opinion, among a variety of particulars not necessary to be specified, the right of *settling*, for the government of the officers employed in the collection of the several branches of the revenue, the *construction* of the laws relating to the revenue, in all cases of doubt." Leonard D. White, The Federalists: A Study in Administrative History 204–05 (1948) (quoting Revenue Circular from Alexander Hamilton to the Treasury Department (July 20, 1792), in 3 The Works of Alexander Hamilton 557, 557–59 (John C. Hamilton ed., 1850)). And the executive authority, according to William Blackstone, had a prerogative or executive power to issue "proclamations" as to the "manner, time, and circumstances" of putting existing laws into execution. 1 William Blackstone, Commentaries on the Laws of England *261 (1st ed. 1765–69); Ilan Wurman, *In Search of Prerogative*, 70 Duke L.J. 93 (2020); Ilan Wurman, *The Specification Power*, 168 U. Pa. L. Rev. 689, 721 (2020).

In a nutshell, it seems likely that agencies have an inherent power to issue interpretative rules or to adopt policy statements binding on the agencies them-selves. Such rules, at least in theory as we shall see, merely interpret ex-isting legal authorities or control official conduct. "Legislative" or "substantive" rules, on the other hand, create new legal obligations binding on private individuals. As the next case explains, whether an agency has the power to issue such substantive, legislative rules depends on the powers that Congress has conferred upon it. That makes some sense on a the-ory of exclusive and nonexclusive powers. The power to interpret law as an incident to enforcing the law, and to apply law to existing facts, is simply ex-ecutive power. Congress need not authorize the Executive to engage in such actions. But the power to make "legislative rules" is a *nonexclusive* power—Congress can make such rules, but perhaps so can the Executive. But if the Executive is to make such rules, it can only do so if Congress has *delegated* to it the power to do so and to share in this power.

PRACTICE POINTER Recall that in adminis-trative law, everything starts with a statute. An agency has no power to act unless Congress has delegated it power in a statute. That includes, as the next case shows, the power to issue legislative rules.

National Petroleum Refiners Ass'n v. FTC

482 F.2d 672 (D.C. Cir 1973)

J. Skelly Wright, Circuit Judge

This case presents an important question concerning the powers and pro-cedures of the Federal Trade Commission. We are asked to determine whether the Commission, under its governing statute, the Trade Commission Act, and specifically 15 U.S.C. § 46(g), is empowered to promulgate substantive rules of business conduct or, as it terms them, "Trade Regulation Rules." The effect of these rules would be to give greater specificity and clarity to the broad stan-dard of illegality—"unfair methods of competition in commerce, and unfair or deceptive acts or practices in commerce"—which the agency is empowered to prevent. 15 U.S.C. § 45(a). Once promulgated, the rules would be used by the agency in adjudicatory proceedings aimed at producing cease and desist orders against violations of the statutory standard. The central question in such adjudicatory proceedings would be whether the particular defendant's conduct violated the rule in question.

The case is here on appeal from a District Court ruling that the Commission lacks authority under its governing statute to issue rules of this sort. . . . Specifically at issue in the District Court was the Commission's rule declaring that failure to post octane rating numbers on gasoline pumps at service stations was an unfair method of competition and an unfair or deceptive act or practice. The plaintiffs in the District Court, appellees here, are two trade associations and 34 gasoline refining companies. Plaintiffs attacked the rule on several grounds, but the District Court disposed of the case solely on the question of the Commission's statutory authority to issue such rules. That is the only question presented for our consideration on appeal. We reverse . . . .

I

Our duty here is not simply to make a policy judgment as to what mode of procedure—adjudication alone or a mixed system of rule-making and adjudication, as the Commission proposes—best accommodates the need for effective enforcement of the Commission's mandate with maximum solicitude for the interests of parties whose activities might be within the scope of the statutory standard of illegality. The Federal Trade Commission is a creation of Congress, not a creation of judges' contemporary notions of what is wise policy. The extent of its powers can be decided only by considering the powers Congress specifically granted it in the light of the statutory language and background. . . .

As always, we must begin with the words of the statute creating the Commission and delineating its powers. Section 5 directs the Commission to "prevent persons, partnerships, or corporations * * * from using unfair methods of competition in commerce and unfair or deceptive acts or practices in commerce." Section 5(b) of the Trade Commission Act specifies that the Commission is to accomplish this goal by means of issuance of a complaint, a hearing, findings as to the facts, and issuance of a cease and desist order. The Commission's assertion that it is empowered by Section 6(g) to issue substantive rules defining the statutory standard of illegality in advance of specific adjudications does not in any formal sense circumvent this method of enforcement. For after the rules are issued, their mode of enforcement remains what it has always been under Section 5: the sequence of complaint, hearing, findings, and issuance of a cease and desist order. What rule-making does do, functionally, is to narrow the inquiry conducted in proceedings under Section 5(b). It is the legality of this practice which we must judge.

Appellees argue that since Section 5 mentions only adjudication as the means of enforcing the statutory standard, any supplemental means of putting flesh on that standard, such as rulemaking, is contrary to the overt legislative design. But Section 5(b) does not use limiting language suggesting that adjudication alone is the only proper means of elaborating the statutory standard. It merely makes clear that a Commission decision, after complaint and hearing, followed by a cease and desist order, is the way to force an offender to halt his illegal activities. Nor are we persuaded by appellees' argument that, despite the absence of limiting language in Section 5 regarding the role of adjudication in defining the meaning of the statutory standard, we should apply the maxim of statutory construction *expressio unius est exclusio alterius* and conclude that adjudication is the *only* means of defining the statutory standard. This maxim is increasingly considered unreliable, for it stands on the faulty premise that all possible alternative or supplemental provisions were necessarily considered and rejected by the legislative draftsmen. Here we have particularly good reason on the face of the statute to reject such arguments. For the Trade Commission Act includes a provision which specifically provides for rule-making by the Commission to implement its adjudicatory functions under Section 5 of the Act. Section 6(g) of the Act, 15 U.S.C. § 46(g), states that the Commission may "[f]rom time to time * * * classify corporations and * * * make rules and regulations for the purpose of carrying out the provisions of sections 41 to 46 and 47 to 58 of this title."

According to appellees, however, this rule-making power is limited to specifying the details of the Commission's nonadjudicatory, investigative and informative functions spelled out in the other provisions of Section 6[1] and

---

1   [In a footnote, the court here quotes Section 6 of the Trade Commission Act in full. We shall not do so here, but this section of the act gives the commission power to conduct investigations (subsection a), to require corporations to make reports (subsection b), to investigate compliance with antitrust decrees (subsection c), to investigate antitrust violations (subsection d), to make recommendations for alleviating antitrust violations (subsection e), to publicize reports (subsection f), and to investigate foreign trade conditions (subsection h). In subsection g, which is titled "classification of corporations; regulations," the commission is given the power "[f]rom time to time to classify corporations and to make rules and regulations for the purpose of carrying out

should not be read to encompass substantive rulemaking in implementation of Section 5 adjudications. We disagree for the simple reason that Section 6(g) clearly states that the Commission "may" make rules and regulations for the purpose of carrying out the provisions of Section 5 and it has been so applied. For example, the Commission has issued rules specifying in greater detail than the statute the mode of Commission procedure under Section 5 in matters involving service of process, requirements as to the filing of answers, and other litigation details necessarily involved in the Commission's work of prosecuting its complaints under Section 5. Such rulemaking by the Commission has been upheld. . . .

Of course, it is at least arguable that these cases go no farther than to justify utilizing Section 6(g) to promulgate procedural, as opposed to substantive, rules for administration of the Section 5 adjudication and enforcement powers. But we see no reason to import such a restriction on the "rules and regulations" permitted by Section 6(g). On the contrary, as we shall see, judicial precedents concerning rule-making by other agencies and the background and purpose of the Federal Trade Commission Act lead us liberally to construe the term "rules and regulations." The substantive rule here unquestionably implements the statutory plan. Section 5 adjudications—trial type proceedings—will still be necessary to obtain cease and desist orders against offenders, but Section 5 enforcement through adjudication will be expedited, simplified, and thus "carried out" by use of this substantive rule. And the overt language of both Section 5 and Section 6, read together, supports its use in Section 5 proceedings.

II

* * *

Thus there is little question that the availability of substantive rule-making gives any agency an invaluable resource-saving flexibility in carrying out its task of regulating parties subject to its statutory mandate. More than merely expediting the agency's job, use of substantive rule-making is increasingly felt to yield significant benefits to those the agency regulates. Increasingly, courts are recognizing that use of rule-making to make innovations in agency policy may actually be fairer to regulated parties than total reliance on case-by-case adjudication.

---

the provisions of sections 41 to 46 and 47 to 58 of this title. Note that Section 5 of the Act, to which the court next refers, corresponds to section 45 of the title referenced here (title 15 of the U.S. Code).—Ed.]

* * *

This judicial trend favoring rule-making over adjudication for development of new agency policy does not, of course, directly dispose of the question before us. . . . [But] [t]o us, these cases suggest that contemporary considerations of practicality and fairness—specifically the advisability of utilizing the Administrative Procedure Act's rule-making procedures to provide an agency about to embark on legal innovation with all relevant arguments and information—certainly support the Commission's position here. . . . [U]tilizing rule-making procedures opens up the process of agency policy innovation to a broad range of criticism, advice and data that is ordinarily less likely to be forthcoming in adjudication. Moreover, the availability of notice before promulgation and wide public participation in rule-making avoids the problem of singling out a single defendant among a group of competitors for initial imposition of a new and inevitably costly legal obligation.

Such benefits are especially obvious in cases involving initiation of rules of the sort the FTC has promulgated here. The Commission's statement on basis and purpose indicated that the decision to impose the obligation of octane rating disclosure on gasoline dealers entailed careful consideration of automobile engine requirements, automobile dealers' practices in instructing purchasers how to care for their engines, consumer gasoline purchasing habits, and costs to gasoline dealers. In addition, the Commission had to choose exactly what kind of disclosure was the fairest. In short, a vast amount of data had to be compiled and analyzed, and the Commission, armed with these data, had to weigh the conflicting policies of increasingly knowledgeable consumer decision-making against alleged costs to gasoline dealers which might be passed on to the consumer. True, the decision to impose a bright-line standard of behavior might have been evolved by the Commission in a single or a succession of adjudicatory proceedings, much as the Supreme Court has imposed *per se* rules of business behavior in antitrust cases. But evolution of bright-line rules is often a slow process and may involve the distinct disadvantage of acting without the broad range of data and argument from all those potentially affected that may be flushed out through use of legislative-type rule-making procedures. And utilizing rule-making in advance of adjudication here minimizes the unfairness of using a purely case-by-case approach requiring "compliance by one manufacturer while his competitors [engaging in similar practices] remain free to violate the Act." . . . [I]t is hard to escape noting that the policy innovation involved in this case underscores the need for increased reliance on rule-making rather than adjudication alone.

III

Appellees contend, however, that these cases and the general practice of agencies and courts in underwriting the broad use of rule-making are irrelevant to the FTC. They argue that the Trade Commission is somehow *sui generis*, that it is best characterized as a prosecuting rather than a regulatory agency, and that substantive rule-making power should be less readily implied from a general grant of rule-making authority where the agency does not stand astride an industry with pervasive license-granting, rate-setting, or clearance functions. . . . [A] more compelling argument [however] can be made that the FTC's duty to prevent "unfair methods of competition" and "unfair or deceptive acts or practices" is just as potentially pervasive, in the sense of affecting commercial practices, as the regulatory schemes of agencies utilizing rate-making, licensing, and similar means of regulation. . . .

And the Commission has this regulatory effect irrespective of whether it chooses to elaborate the vague but comprehensive statutory standards through rule-making or through case-by-case adjudication. Businesses whose practices appear clearly covered by the Trade Commission's adjudicatory decisions against similarly situated parties presumably will comply with the Commission's holding rather than await a Commission action against them individually; we must presume that in many cases where a guideline is laid down in an individual case it is, like many common law rules, generally obeyed by those similarly situated. Moreover, there are ample indications in the Commission's legislative history that the agency, by gathering information on business practices, issuing periodic reports, and moving against those practices which appear "unfair," was meant to have just this sort of regulatory impact, despite the purely prosecutorial mode of proceeding provided in Section 5 of the Act. Not only is the Commission's regulatory power much broader than appellees would have us believe; there is simply no compelling evidence in the Act's legislative history or in the language of the statute itself which would limit the exercise of that power to the prosecutorial function or prevent the Commission from making that function more effective by rule-making.

IV

Although we believe there are thus persuasive considerations for accepting the FTC's view that the plain meaning of the statute supports substantive rule-making, the question is not necessarily closed. For appellees' contention—that the phrase "rules and regulations for the purpose of carrying out" Section 5 refers only to rules of procedure and practice for carrying out the Commission's adjudicatory responsibility—is not implausible. The opinion of the District Court argues forcefully that, in spite of the clear and unlimited language of Section 6(g) granting rule-making authority to the Commission, the Congress that enacted Section 5 and Section 6(g) gave clear indications of its intent to reject substantive rule-making, that the FTC's own behavior in the years since that time supports a narrow interpretation of its mandate to promulgate "rules and regulations," and that where Congress desired to give the FTC substantive rule-making authority in discrete areas it did so in subsequent years in unambiguous terms. Our own conclusion, based on an independent review of this history, is different. We believe that, while the legislative history of Section 5 and Section 6(g) is ambiguous, it certainly does not compel the conclusion that the Commission was not meant to exercise the power to make substantive rules with binding effect in Section 5(a) adjudications. We also believe that the plain language of Section 6(g), read in light of the broad, clearly agreed-upon concerns that motivated passage of the Trade Commission Act, confirms the framers' intent to allow exercise of the power claimed here. We do not find the District Court's reliance on the agency's long-standing practice, until 1962, of not utilizing rule-making or the District Court's reliance on enactment of specific grants of rule-making power in narrow areas sufficiently persuasive to override our view, and the Commission's view, that rule-making is not only consistent with the original framers' broad purposes, but appears to be a particularly apt means of carrying them out.

In analyzing the origins of the Federal Trade Commission Act of 1914, and Section 5 and 6(g) in particular, both parties would have us focus heavily on the floor debates and committee reports that accompanied the legislation on its tortuous path toward enactment. Certainly these materials are relevant to our inquiry and cannot be ignored. But our examination of the comments made by legislators that allegedly bear directly on the question whether the Commission was initially meant to exercise substantive, legislative-type rule-making power has led us to the conclusion, familiar in cases dealing with strongly contested questions of statutory interpretation, that the *specific* intent of Congress here cannot be stated with any assurance. The materials cited to us indicate that the question before us—whether the Commission can elaborate the meaning of Section 5's standard of illegality through rule-making as well as through case-by-case adjudication—was not confronted straightforwardly and decisively. Given this conclusion, which we elaborate in detail in the appendix to this opinion, we are hardly at liberty to override the plain, expansive language of Section 6(g) . . . .

Moreover, while we believe the historical evidence is indecisive of the question before us, we are convinced that the broad, undisputed policies which clearly motivated the framers of the Federal Trade Commission Act of 1914 would indeed be furthered by our view as to the proper scope of the Commission's rule-making authority. . . . [T]he proponents of the agency all unquestionably shared deep objections to the existing structure of judicial monopolization of cases involving unfair, anticompetitive business practices. Those who believed from the start in a commission with independent enforcement powers, as the Commission was finally given in the 1914 legislation, and those who believed the Commission should have lesser powers, agreed that entrusting enforcement of congressional policy to prevent undue incursions on competition exclusively to the courts was a serious mistake. The courts were said to lack sufficient expertise in matters of economic complexity, their decisions were said to be wanting in the clarity planners of complicated business transactions and innovations required, and finally and most importantly, the courts lacked both the resources and the skill to proceed with speed and expedition in the trial and disposition of complicated cases involving economic questions. This concern over judicial delay, inefficiency and uncertainty was echoed time and again throughout the 1914 debates over the form a commission would take.

In determining the legislative intent, our duty is to favor an interpretation which would render the statutory design effective in terms of the policies behind its enactment and to avoid an interpretation which would make such policies more difficult of fulfillment, particularly where, as here, that interpretation is consistent with the plain language of the statute. . . . In short, where a statute is said to be susceptible of more than one meaning, we must not only consult its language; we must also relate the interpretation we provide to the felt and openly articulated concerns motivating the law's framers. In this way we may be sure we are construing the statute rather than constructing a new one. . . .

There is little disagreement that the Commission will be able to proceed more expeditiously, give greater certainty to businesses subject to the Act, and deploy its internal resources more efficiently with a mixed system of rule-making and adjudication than with adjudication alone. With the issues in Section 5 proceedings reduced by the existence of a rule delineating what is a violation of the statute or what presumptions the Commission proposes to rely upon, proceedings will be speeded up. For example, in an adjudication proceeding based on a violation of the octane rating rule at issue here, the central question to be decided will be whether or not pumps owned by a given refiner are properly marked. Without the rule, the Commission might well be obliged to prove and argue that the absence of the rating markers in each particular case was likely to have injurious and unfair effects on consumers or competition. Since this laborious process might well have to be repeated every time the Commission chose to proceed subsequently against another defendant on the same ground, the difference in administrative efficiency between the two kinds of proceedings is obvious. Furthermore, rules, as contrasted with the holdings reached by case-by-case adjudication, are more specific as to their scope, and industry compliance is more likely simply because each company is on clearer notice whether or not specific rules apply to it.

Moreover, when delay in agency proceedings is minimized by using rules, those violating the statutory standard lose an opportunity to turn litigation into a profitable and lengthy game of postponing the effect of the rule on their current practice. As a result, substantive rules will protect the companies which willingly comply with the law against what amounts to the unfair competition of those who would profit from delayed enforcement as to them. . . . But the important point here is not that rule-making is assuredly going to solve the Commission's problems. It is rather than recognition and use of rule-making by the Commission is convincingly linked to the goals of agency expedition, efficiency, and certainty of regulatory standards that loomed in the background of the 1914 passage of the Federal Trade Commission Act.

This relationship between rule-making's probable benefits and the broad concerns evident when the FTC was created, together with the express language of Section 6(g), help persuade us that any purported ambiguity of the statute be resolved in favor of the Commission's claim. . . .

* * *

VI

Our conclusion as to the scope of Section 6(g) is not disturbed by the fact that the agency itself did not assert the power to promulgate substantive rules until 1962 and indeed indicated intermittently before that time that it lacked such power. . . . The various statements made by Commission representatives questioning its authority to promulgate rules which are to be used with binding effect on subsequent adjudications are not determinative of the question before us. True, the accustomed judicial practice is to give "great weight" to an agency's construction of its own enabling legislation, particularly when such a construction stretches back, as here, to a time close to the agency's origin. The argument for judicial deference is not so strong where, as here, the question does not require special agency competence or expertise, requiring the agency, for example, to make a complex judgment involving its areas of expertise, competition and impact of business practices on consumer behavior. Here, the question is simply one of statutory interpretation concerning the procedures and setting in which the Commission may elaborate its statutory standard. Since this sort of question calls largely for the exercise of historical analysis and logical and analogical reasoning, it is the everyday staple of judges as well as agencies. Thus we feel confident in making our own judgment as to the proper construction of Section 6(g). We are, of course, reassured by the fact that the Commission itself, as distinguished from its former spokesmen, has come to the same conclusion. . . .

A more troubling obstacle to the Commission's position here is the argument that Congress was made fully aware of the formerly restrictive view of the Commission's power and passed a series of laws granting limited substantive rule-making authority to the Commission in discrete areas allegedly on the premise that the 1914 debate withheld such authority. . . . The view that the Commission lacked substantive rule-making power has been clearly brought to the attention of Congress and, rather than simply failing to act on the question, Congress, in expanding the agency's powers in several discrete areas of marketing regulation, affirmatively enacted limited grants of substantive rule-making authority . . . . Thus it is argued that Congress would not have granted the agency such powers unless it had felt that otherwise the agency lacked rule-making authority.

Conceding the greater force of this argument than one premised on congressional inaction, we believe it must not be accepted blindly. In such circumstances, it is equally possible that Congress granted the power out of uncertainty, understandable caution, and a desire to avoid litigation. . . . Where there is solid reason, as there plainly is here, to believe that Congress, in fact, has not wholeheartedly accepted the agency's viewpoint and instead enacted legislation out of caution and to eliminate the kind of disputes that invariably attend statutory ambiguity, we believe that relying on the *de facto* ratification argument is unwise. In such circumstances, we must perform our customary task of coming to an independent judgment as to the statute's meaning, confident that if Congress believes that its creature, the Commission, thus exercises too much power, it will repeal the grant. . . .

NOTES AND QUESTIONS

1. Statutory interpretation. Who had the better interpretation of the statute here—the D.C. Circuit and the FTC, or the District Court, the petitioners, and the FTC in its first few decades? There are interpretive clues going in both directions; following these notes and questions is a more extended discussion of the various tools of statutory interpretation that the court's opinion deploys. After exploring them, think about how you would have resolved the case.

2. Judicial deference to agency legal interpretations. The D.C. Circuit issued its opinion in this case in 1973. In 1984, the Supreme Court decided Chevron v. Natural Resources Defense Council, 467 U.S. 837 (1984), about which we will have much more to say in Chapter 4. That case established the proposition that if a statute that the agency is tasked with administering is ambiguous, the courts should *defer* to the agency's interpretation of that statute so long as its interpretation is reasonable. How would the D.C. Circuit have decided *National Petroleum Refiners* under the *Chevron* test?

 Chevron deference, discussed in detail in Chapter 4, stands for the proposition that courts should defer to an agency's reasonable interpretation of its organic statute, even if that interpretation is not the one the court would have arrived at on its own.

Does the court's interpretive analysis suggest that the statute is ambiguous, and therefore the agency's interpretation that the statute gives it rulemaking authority is reasonable? Would that have been an easier way to decide this case?

COMPARATIVE PERSPECTIVE

Much has changed in administrative law over the last several decades. Would *National Petroleum Refiners* be decided the same way today in light of subsequent Supreme Court cases maintaining that courts should defer to an agency's reasonable interpretation of its organic statute?

In a recent case involving the Patent Trial and Appeal Board (PTAB), the Supreme Court rejected an argument that the U.S. Patent and Trademark Office (USPTO) had authority to make only procedural rules involving *inter partes* review of patents. The Court upheld the USPTO's rule establishing that the PTAB was to construe the terms of patents according to their "broadest reasonable construction." In so holding, the Court appears to have relied on "*Chevron* deference," deferring to the USPTO's reasonable interpretation of its own rulemaking authority. Cuozzo Speed Techs., LLC v. Lee, 136 S. Ct. 2131, 2142–44 (2016); cf. City of Arlington v. FCC, 569 U.S. 290 (2013) (applying *Chevron* deference to the FCC's interpretation of the scope of its own rulemaking authority).

3.　Policy benefits of rulemaking. The court's opinion relies heavily on policy arguments about the benefits of rulemaking. What are the benefits the court mentions? The scholarship has generally identified the following four benefits of rulemaking: (1) the rulemaking process affords more notice and warning to the parties subject to the rule because the legal obligations are known in advance; (2) the process is more politically accountable because notice and comment rulemaking allows for broad public participation, and also for the involvement of political actors; (3) rules can be of higher quality (as the court's opinion in this case particularly emphasizes) because the agency must consider a wealth of data and arguments that might not be available to it in an adjudication; and (4) rulemaking is more efficient because it obviates the need for constant case-by-case adjudication on particular issues.

Is there an argument that adjudications might actually be both of higher quality and more efficient? As is the case with laws, the more general the law the harder it is to capture or anticipate specific circumstances that might warrant deviations from the particular legal requirement. Doesn't adjudication allow agencies to tailor their position to the nuances and idiosyncrasies of particular contexts? Doesn't that make adjudications more efficient, too? For a sample of the literature discussing and debating the advantages and disadvantages of rulemaking and adjudications, see Chapter 3.A.2.

4.   *Due process?* Might there be due process reasons to support rulemaking? Consider the breadth of the statutory standard with which the FTC was tasked with administering; the statute prohibited "using unfair methods of competition in commerce and unfair or deceptive acts or practices in commerce." What exactly is an "unfair" method of competition? Might it be problematic to enforce this standard directly against a private party in an adjudication and impose fines or other punishments without the benefits of a clarifying regula-

tion? This was at issue in *Chenery II*, a famous administrative law case upholding the power of the Securities and Exchange Commission to adjudicate and enforce a broad statutory standard directly, without the benefits of clarifying regulations. For more on *Chenery II*, see pp. 237–252.

 CROSS REFERENCE How broad is the term "unfair methods of competition"? Is it so broad that it might be unconstitutional to delegate to an agency the power to decide what an unfair method of competition is? Chapter 5 will discuss the nondelegation doctrine in more detail.

STATUTORY INTERPRETATION LESSONS 6–11

Lesson 6: Purpose. The court in *National Petroleum Refiners* relied heavily on the underlying purposes of the statute as supporting its interpretation that the FTC had rulemaking authority. The court held that "[o]ur duty is to favor an interpretation which would render the statutory design effective in terms of the policies behind its enactment and to avoid an interpretation which would make such policies more difficult of fulfillment," and that the probable benefits of rulemaking "persuade us that any purposed ambiguity of the statute" should "be resolved in favor of the Commission's claim." The use of purpose in this manner is a classic tool of statutory interpretation: if the words of a statute are ambiguous and one meaning would be consistent with the known statutory purposes and the other would be inconsistent with those purposes, courts will often conclude that the "correct" meaning of the statute is the one consistent with the purpose. This rule of interpretation is not to be confused with using the purpose of the statute to *override* the plain meaning of the text. That method of interpretation—giving legal effect to the "spirit" of the law—is associated with the famous case Church of the Holy Trinity v. U.S., 143 U.S. 457 (1892). Using purpose in that manner is far more controversial than using it to choose among legitimate possible meanings of an ambiguous statute.

Lesson 7: Legislative History. The use of statutory purpose to decide between two ambiguous meanings of a statute should not be confused with the use of legislative history, which refers to the legislative process by which a statute was enacted and the various oral and written statements other than the statute itself that were produced by that process. The classic examples of legislative history are written statements in committee reports or oral statements made by leading proponents and opponents of a bill on the floor of the House or Senate. Legislative history used to be widely used in statutory interpretation, but it has become more disfavored today. Using legislative history is liable to the famous criticism by Judge Harold Leventhal: it's like looking over the crowd at a cocktail party and picking out your friends. Adam M. Samaha, *Looking Over A Crowd—Do More Interpretive Sources Mean More Discretion?*, 92 N.Y.U. L. Rev. 554, 556 (2017) (citing sources). That is, the legislative history will sometimes (maybe often) be unreliable because there are competing statements in all directions, and the legislative history is often used selectively as a result. Additionally, some scholars and judges have argued that legislative history was simply not *the law* enacted pursuant to the Article I, Section 7 requirements of bicameralism and presentment. See, e.g., John F. Manning, *The New Purposivism*, 2011 Sup. Ct. Rev. 113, 167–68 (2011) ("Simply put, if the statute and the legislative history genuinely conflict, Article I, Section 7 of the Constitution itself gives the text a greater claim to authoritativeness."); Antonin Scalia, A Matter of Interpretation: Federal Courts and the Law 35 (1997) (similar). Still, like purpose, legislative history can sometimes help clarify the meaning of a legitimately ambiguous statute, and its use in statutory interpretation remains contested to this day.

Lesson 8: Context and Structural Arguments. It is often observed that "text" only has meaning in "context." Here, arguably supporting the petitioners' position was the context in which the statute's rulemaking authority was found. As explained in the footnote, the rulemaking power was found in Section 6 of the act, which entirely involved the adjudicatory and enforcement functions of the Commission. That Section empowered the FTC to investigate corporations, require reports, investigate antitrust violations and compliance, to make reports, and to investigate foreign conditions and make reports. In between two of these specific authorities is found the authority in question: the Commission shall have the power "[f]rom time to time to classify corporations and to make rules and regulations for the purpose of carrying out the provisions of sections 41 to 46 and 47 to 58 of this title." Section 45 of this title is Section 5 of the act, which created the prohibition on unfair and deceptive trade practices. Thus it would seem that the language of this rulemaking authority allows the Commission to make "regulations for the purpose of carrying out" this broad statutory prohibition, including by making clarifying regulations. Yet the provision is found in the context of a whole set of authorities involving the adjudicatory and investigatory authorities of the Commission. This is at least some suggestion that perhaps the intended meaning was to give rulemaking authority only respecting these various adjudicatory and investigatory functions. Using context in this manner is a type of "structural argument"—arguing for a specific meaning based on the structure of the document as a whole and the location of the specific terms or provisions within the document.

Lessons 9 & 10: Ejusdem Generis and Noscitur a Sociis. Related to the context lesson, although not directly relevant to *National Petroleum Refiners,* are two linguistic canons of interpretation: the *ejusdem generis* and the *noscitur a sociis* canons. *Ejusdem generis* is the canon of construction whereby a general word in a list of words typically refers to the same kinds of things as the more specific words in the list. In *Yates v. United States,* discussed in statutory interpretation lesson 2, at issue was the meaning of "tangible object" in the statutory prohibition on knowingly altering, destroying, mutilating, concealing, covering up, or falsifying "any record, document, or tangible object with the intent to impede, obstruct, or influence" a federal investigation. 574 U.S. 528, 135 S. Ct. 1074 (2015). The question was whether "tangible object" included a red grouper fish. Of course a fish is a tangible object. But the Court used the *ejusdem generis* canon to hold that "or tangible object" is limited to the same kinds of things as are referred to by the more specific terms "record" and "document," namely objects "used to record or preserve information." The idea of the canon is "to ensure that a general word will not render specific words meaningless." CSX Transp., Inc. v. Alabama Dept. of Revenue, 562 U.S. 277, 295 (2011).

The closely related *noscitur a sociis* canon provides that "a word is known by the company it keeps," i.e. the words with which it is most closely associated. *Yates,* supra, at 1085. In *Yates,* the Court used the *noscitur a sociis* canon along with the *ejusdem generis* canon to conclude that "any tangible object" referred only to that subset of tangible objections "used to record or preserve information." In that case, then, the *ejusdem generis* canon was itself a subset of the *noscitur a sociis canon.* Although the two canons often do independent work, they also often work in tandem.

The use of these canons in *Yates* was not uncontroversial, however. The four dissenting Justices argued that these canons are useful for *resolving* ambiguity, but cannot be used to *create* ambiguity. *Yates,* 135 S. Ct. at 1097

(2015) (Kagan, J., dissenting) ("As an initial matter, this Court uses *noscitur a sociis* and *ejusdem generis* to resolve ambiguity, not create it."). This is an important statement of the "plain meaning" principle (see statutory interpretation lesson 2). Justices Kagan, Scalia, Kennedy, and Thomas (note the eclectic set of Justices) would only have used the linguistic canons if the ordinary meaning of the provision was not otherwise clear. One possible counter to the dissenters is that the linguistic canons are useful precisely because they convey how we ordinarily speak. When Congress speaks through statutes, it presumably uses many of the same linguistic conventions that ordinary speakers do in everyday language. What do you make of this debate? Do you think Congress intended the Sarbanes-Oxley law—enacted after the Enron accounting scandal of 2002—to apply to a fisherman who threw overboard red grouper fish to avoid being caught fishing oversized groupers? Do you think Congress had any discernable intent on this or like questions one way or another?

Note again that these canons did not directly play a role in *National Petroleum Refiners*. Would the matter have been different had the FTC Act authorized the agency "to conduct investigations, require corporations to make reports, investigate compliance with antitrust decrees, investigate antitrust violations, make recommendations for alleviating antitrust violations, publicize reports, investigate foreign trade conditions, and from time to time to classify corporations and to make rules and regulations for the purpose of carrying out the provisions of sections 41 to 46 and 47 to 58 of this title"? How would you have ruled if that were the statute?

Lesson 11: Longstanding and Contemporaneous Interpretation. Also supporting petitioners' argument was the fact that the FTC had for decades interpreted its statute as not including the authority to promulgate rules fleshing out the substantive standard of Section 5. The court explained that "the agency itself did not assert the power to promulgate substantive rules until 1962 and indeed indicated intermittently before that time that it lacked such power," and that "the accustomed judicial practice is to give 'great weight' to an agency's construction of its own enabling legislation, particularly when such a construction stretches back, as here, to a time close to the agency's origin." The names for these two canons are *contemporanea exposition* and *interpres consuetudo*. The former idea is that an executive branch agency tasked with administering the statute near in time to its creation is more likely to know Congress's likely intended meaning. The latter idea is that if this interpretation is longstanding, that is further evidence of its correctness. Here, these canons provide some pretty powerful evidence that the FTC may not have the rulemaking authority in question. Were you persuaded by the court's discounting of the FTC's previous longstanding and contemporaneous interpretation?

Although we have not yet encountered *Chevron* deference, it is important to see the difference between these canons and that doctrine. Modern judicial deference doctrine (see Chapter 4) requires courts to defer to *any* reasonable agency interpretation of its statute, which allows the agency to choose among reasonable interpretations and therefore to change its mind about which interpretation to adopt. The two canons described here are different: an agency interpretation is entitled to great weight *if* it is contemporaneous with the enactment of the statute, and particularly if that interpretation is longstanding. See generally Aditya Bamzai, *The Origins of Judicial Deference to Executive Interpretation*, 126 Yale L.J. 908 (2017).

4.   The Use of Rulemaking in Adjudicatory Frameworks

In *National Petroleum Refiners*, we considered whether an agency had the statutory authority to create legislative rules in the first place. The next case considers a slightly different question: where a statute requires a hearing, but also grants rulemaking authority, are there certain kinds of things that cannot be subject to a rulemaking at all, and must be decided through an adjudication?

Heckler v. Campbell

461 U.S. 458 (1983)

JUSTICE POWELL delivered the opinion of the Court.

The issue is whether the Secretary of Health and Human Services may rely on published medical-vocational guidelines to determine a claimant's right to Social Security disability benefits.

I

The Social Security Act defines "disability" in terms of the effect a physical or mental impairment has on a person's ability to function in the work place. It provides disability benefits only to persons who are unable "to engage in any substantial gainful activity by reason of any medically determinable physical or mental impairment." 42 U.S.C. § 423(d)(1)(A). And it specifies that a person must "not only [be] unable to do his previous work but [must be unable], considering his age, education, and work experience, [to] engage in any other kind of substantial gainful work which exists in the national economy, regardless of whether such work exists in the immediate area in which he lives, or whether a specific job vacancy exists for him, or whether he would be hired if he applied for work." 42 U.S.C. § 423(d)(2)(A).

In 1978, the Secretary of Health and Human Services promulgated regulations implementing this definition. The regulations recognize that certain impairments are so severe that they prevent a person from pursuing any gainful work. A claimant who establishes that he suffers from one of these impairments will be considered disabled without further inquiry. If a claimant suffers from a less severe impairment, the Secretary must determine whether the claimant retains the ability to perform either his former work or some less demanding employment. If a claimant can pursue his former occupation, he is not entitled to disability benefits. See § 404.1520(e). If he cannot, the Secretary must determine whether the claimant retains the capacity to pursue less demanding work. See § 404.1520(f)(1).

The regulations divide this last inquiry into two stages. First, the Secretary must assess each claimant's present job qualifications. The regulations direct the Secretary to consider the factors Congress has identified as relevant: physical ability, age, education and work experience. Second, she must consider whether jobs exist in the national economy that a person having the claimant's qualifications could perform.

Prior to 1978, the Secretary relied on vocational experts to establish the existence of suitable jobs in the national economy. After a claimant's limitations and abilities had been determined at a hearing, a vocational expert ordinarily would testify whether work existed that the claimant could perform. Although this testimony often was based on standardized guides, vocational experts frequently were criticized for their inconsistent treatment of similarly situated claimants. To improve both the uniformity and efficiency of this determination, the Secretary promulgated medical-vocational guidelines as part of the 1978 regulations.

These guidelines relieve the Secretary of the need to rely on vocational experts by establishing through rulemaking the types and numbers of jobs that exist in the national economy. They consist of a matrix of the four factors identified by Congress—physical ability, age, education, and work experience—and set forth rules that identify whether jobs requiring specific combinations of these factors exist in significant numbers in the national economy. Where a claimant's qualifications correspond to the job requirements identified by a rule, the guidelines direct a conclusion as to whether work exists that the claimant could perform. If such work exists, the claimant is not considered disabled.

II

In 1979, Carmen Campbell applied for disability benefits because a back condition and hypertension prevented her from continuing her work as a hotel maid. After her application was denied, she requested a hearing *de novo* before an Administrative Law Judge. He determined that her back problem was not severe enough to find her disabled without further inquiry, and accordingly considered whether she retained the ability to perform either her past work or some less strenuous job. He concluded that even though Campbell's back condition prevented her from returning to her work as a maid, she retained the physical capacity to do light work. In accordance with the regulations, he found that Campbell was 52-years old, that her previous employment consisted of unskilled jobs and that she had a limited education. He noted that Campbell, who had been born in Panama, experienced difficulty in speaking and writing English. She was able, however, to understand and read English fairly well. Relying on the medical-vocational guidelines, the Administrative Law Judge found that a significant number of jobs existed that a person of Campbell's qualifications could perform. Accordingly, he concluded that she was not disabled.

This determination was upheld by both the Social Security Appeals Council, and the District Court for the Eastern District of New York. The Court of Appeals for the Second Circuit reversed. It accepted the Administrative Law Judge's determination that Campbell retained the ability to do light work. And it did not suggest that he had classified Campbell's age, education, or work experience incorrectly. . . .

The court found that the medical-vocational guidelines did not provide the specific evidence that it previously had required. It explained that in the absence of such a showing, "the claimant is deprived of any real chance to present evidence showing that she cannot in fact perform the types of jobs that are administratively noticed by the guidelines." The court concluded that because the Secretary had failed to introduce evidence that specific alternative jobs existed, the determination that Campbell was not disabled was not supported by substantial evidence. . . . We now reverse.

III

The Secretary argues that the Court of Appeals' holding effectively prevents the use of the medical-vocational guidelines. By requiring her to identify specific alternative jobs in every disability hearing, the court has rendered the guidelines useless. An examination of both the language of the Social Security Act and its legislative history clearly demonstrates that the Secretary may proceed by regulation to determine whether substantial gainful work exists in the national economy. . . .

A

. . . . The court's requirement that additional evidence be introduced on this issue prevents the Secretary from putting the guidelines to their intended use and implicitly calls their validity into question. Accordingly, we think the decision below requires us to consider whether the Secretary may rely on medical-vocational guidelines in appropriate cases.

The Social Security Act directs the Secretary to "adopt reasonable and proper rules and regulations to regulate and provide for the nature and extent of the proofs and evidence and the method of taking and furnishing the same" in disability cases. 42 U.S.C. § 405(a). As we previously have recognized, Congress has "conferred on the Secretary exceptionally broad authority to prescribe standards for applying certain sections of the [Social Security] Act." Where, as here, the statute expressly entrusts the Secretary with the responsibility for implementing a provision by regulation, our review is limited to determining whether the regulations promulgated exceeded the Secretary's statutory authority and whether they are arbitrary and capricious.

We do not think that the Secretary's reliance on medical-vocational guidelines is inconsistent with the Social Security Act. It is true that the statutory scheme contemplates that disability hearings will be individualized determinations based on evidence adduced at a hearing. See 42 U.S.C. § 423(d)(2)(A) (specifying consideration of each individual's condition); 42 U.S.C. § 405(b) (disability determination to be based on evidence adduced at hearing). But this does not bar the Secretary from relying on rulemaking to resolve certain classes of issues. The Court has recognized that even where an agency's enabling statute expressly requires it to hold a hearing, the agency may rely on its rulemaking authority to determine issues that do not require case-by-case consideration. A contrary holding would require the agency continually to relitigate issues that may be established fairly and efficiently in a single rulemaking proceeding.

. . . . As noted above, in determining whether a claimant can perform less strenuous work, the Secretary must make two determinations. She must assess each claimant's individual abilities and then determine whether jobs exist that a person having the claimant's qualifications could perform. The first inquiry involves a determination of historic facts, and the regulations properly require the Secretary to make these findings on the basis of evidence adduced at a hearing. We note that the regulations afford claimants ample opportunity both to present evidence relating to their own abilities and to offer evidence that the guidelines do not apply to them. The second inquiry requires the Secretary to determine an issue that is not unique to each claimant—the types and numbers of jobs that exist in the national economy. This type of general factual issue may be resolved as fairly through rulemaking as by introducing the testimony of vocational experts at each disability hearing.

As the Secretary has argued, the use of published guidelines brings with it a uniformity that previously had been perceived as lacking. To require the Secretary to relitigate the existence of jobs in the national economy at each hearing would hinder needlessly an already overburdened agency. We conclude that the Secretary's use of medical-vocational guidelines does not conflict with the statute, nor can we say on the record before us that they are arbitrary and capricious. . . .

[A concurring opinion by JUSTICE BRENNAN and a partial dissent by JUSTICE MARSHALL are omitted.—Ed.]

NOTES AND QUESTIONS

1. Summary. *Heckler v. Campbell* involves the question whether there are certain types of issues that must be determined in case-by-case adjudication. The Court held, in a nutshell, that "even where an agency's enabling statute expressly requires it to hold a hearing, the agency may rely on its rulemaking authority to determine issues that do not require case-by-case consideration."

In this case, what kinds of issues did not require such case-by-case consideration, and what issues did? Do you agree with the Court's resolution?

The Supreme Court has reiterated the rule of *Heckler* on other occasions. In 1991, the Court explained, "even if a statutory scheme requires individualized determinations, the decisionmaker has the authority to rely on rulemaking to resolve certain issues of general applicability unless Congress clearly expresses an intent to withhold that authority." Am. Hosp. Ass'n v. NLRB, 499 U.S. 606, 612 (1991). Of course, the agency must also have rulemaking authority somewhere in the organic statute, otherwise it cannot make rules at all. See *Nat'l Petroleum Refiners,* supra p. 87.

2.   *Are rules ever required?* What about the converse question: are there certain types of issues that *must* be resolved by regulation, and not case-by-case adjudication? What if a statutory standard is so broad and vague—might an agency have to issue clarifying regulations to put parties on fair notice? Are there due process concerns with applying vague standards directly to individuals? In SEC v. Chenery Corp., 332 U.S. 194 (1947), the Supreme Court held that an agency may go from a broad statutory standard directly to an adjudication. For more on that case and the surrounding issues, see pp. 237–252.

B.   Formal Rulemaking

As explained in the introduction to this Chapter, there are three categories of procedures that rules might have to go through under the APA. An organic statute may require the use of the formal rulemaking proceedings of APA §§ 556–57. That is because § 553, which sets out the procedures for informal rulemaking, provides in § 553(c) that "[w]hen rules are required by statute to be made on the record after opportunity for an agency hearing, sections 556 and 557 of this title apply instead of this subsection." Assuming the organic statute in question does not trigger §§ 556–57, the informal rulemaking procedures of § 553 apply with a few exceptions. "Nonlegislative" rules are exempt from notice-and-comment rulemaking, rules that relate to certain subject-matter (like military and foreign affairs) are similarly exempt, and the agency may assert "good cause" not to go through the notice-and-comment process for other rules that might otherwise have to go through the process. This is merely a default arrangement, however; an organic statute might provide differently. Section 553 itself provides that even nonlegislative rules must go through the informal rulemaking process "when notice or hearing is required by statute."

Up until 1978, many agencies believed that when their statutes required rulemaking to be made after a "hearing," that triggered the formal rulemaking procedures of §§ 556–57. These were incredibly laborious; as mentioned, it may have taken one agency over a decade to promulgate a rule as to the amount of peanuts that must be present in a product to count as "peanut butter," although some have questioned the reasons for this unusual delay. Whether or not the peanut butter rulemaking was representative of formal rulemakings generally, there is no question that such formal proceedings are quite burdensome. It is perhaps with that problem in mind that the Supreme Court decided the following case.

United States v. Florida East Coast Ry. Co.

410 U.S. 224 (1978)

MR. JUSTICE REHNQUIST delivered the opinion of the Court.

Appellees, two railroad companies, brought this action in the District Court for the Middle District of Florida to set aside the incentive per diem rates established by appellant Interstate Commerce Commission in a rule-making proceeding. They challenged the order of the Commission on both substantive and procedural grounds. The District Court sustained appellees' position that the Commission had failed to comply with the applicable provisions of the Administrative Procedure Act, 5 U.S.C. § 551 et seq., and therefore set aside the order without dealing with the railroads' other contentions. The District Court held that the language of § 1(14)(a) of the Interstate Commerce Act required the Commission in a proceeding such as this to act in accordance with the Administrative Procedure Act, 5 U.S.C. § 556(d), and that the Commission's determination to receive submissions from the appellees only in written form was a violation of that section because the respondents were 'prejudiced' by that determination within the meaning of that section.

. . . . [W]e . . . requested the parties to brief the question of whether the Commission's proceeding was governed by 5 U.S.C. § 553, or by 556 and 557, of the Administrative Procedure Act. We here decide that the Commission's proceeding was governed only by § 553 of that Act, and that appellees received the 'hearing' required by § 1(14)(a) of the Interstate Commerce Act. We, therefore, reverse the judgment of the District Court and remand the case to that court for further consideration of appellees' other contentions that were raised there, but which we do not decide.

I. BACKGROUND OF CHRONIC FREIGHT CAR SHORTAGES

This case arises from the factual background of a chronic freight-car shortage on the Nation's railroads, . . . Congressional concern for the problem was manifested in the enactment in 1966 of an amendment to § 1(14)(a) of the Interstate Commerce Act, enlarging the Commission's authority to prescribe per diem charges for the use by one railroad of freight cars owned by another. . . .

The Commission in 1966 commenced an investigation, Ex parte No. 252, Incentive Per Diem Charges, 'to determine whether information presently available warranted the establishment of an incentive element increase, on an interim basis, to apply pending further study and investigation.' Statements of position were received from the Commission staff and a number of railroads. Hearings were conducted at which witnesses were examined. In October 1967, the Commission rendered a decision discontinuing the earlier proceeding, but announcing a program of further investigation into the general subject.

In December 1967, the Commission initiated the rulemaking procedure giving rise to the order that appellees here challenge. It directed Class I and Class II line-haul railroads to compile and report detailed information with respect to freight-car demand and supply at numerous sample stations for selected days of the week during 12 four-week periods, beginning January 29, 1968.

Some of the affected railroads voiced questions about the proposed study or requested modification in the study procedures outlined by the Commission in its notice of proposed rulemaking. In response to petitions setting forth these carriers' views, the Commission staff held an informal conference in April 1968, at which the objections and proposed modifications were discussed. Twenty railroads, including appellee Seaboard, were represented at this conference, at which the Commission's staff sought to answer questions about reporting methods to accommodate individual circumstances of particular railroads. The conference adjourned on a note that undoubtedly left the impression that hearings would be held at some future date. A detailed report of the conference was sent to all parties to the proceeding before the Commission.

The results of the information thus collected were analyzed and presented to Congress by the Commission during a hearing before the Subcommittee on

Surface Transportation of the Senate Committee on Commerce in May 1969. Members of the Subcommittee expressed dissatisfaction with the Commission's slow pace in exercising the authority that had been conferred upon it by the 1966 Amendments to the Interstate Commerce Act. . . . [B]ut Commission counsel expressed doubt respecting the Commission's statutory power to act without additional hearings. . . . .

The Commission, now apparently imbued with a new sense of mission, issued in December 1969 an interim report announcing its tentative decision to adopt incentive per diem charges on standard boxcars based on the information compiled by the railroads. The substantive decision reached by the Commission was that so-called 'incentive' per diem charges should be paid by any railroad using on its lines a standard boxcar owned by another railroad. Before the enactment of the 1966 amendment to the Interstate Commerce Act, it was generally thought that the Commission's authority to fix per diem payments for freight car use was limited to setting an amount that reflected fair return on investment for the owning railroad, without any regard being had for the desirability of prompt return to the owning line or for the encouragement of additional purchases of freight cars by the railroads as a method of investing capital. The Commission concluded, however, that in view of the 1966 amendment it could impose additional 'incentive' per diem charges to spur prompt return of existing cars and to make acquisition of new cars financially attractive to the railroads. It did so by means of a proposed schedule that established such charges on an across-the-board basis for all common carriers by railroads subject to the Interstate Commerce Act. Embodied in the report was a proposed rule adopting the Commission's tentative conclusions and a notice to the railroads to file statements of position within 60 days . . . .

Both appellee railroads filed statements objecting to the Commission's proposal and requesting an oral hearing, as did numerous other railroads. In April 1970, the Commission, without having held further 'hearings,' issued a supplemental report making some modifications in the tentative conclusions earlier reached, but overruling *in toto* the requests of appellees.

The District Court held that in so doing the Commission violated § 556(d) of the Administrative Procedure Act, and it was on this basis that it set aside the order of the Commission.

II. APPLICABILITY OF ADMINISTRATIVE PROCEDURE ACT

In *United States v. Allegheny-Ludlum Steel Corp.*, we held that the language of § 1(14)(a) of the Interstate Commerce Act authorizing the Commission to act 'after hearing' was not the equivalent of a requirement that a rule be made 'on the record after opportunity for an agency hearing' as the latter term is used in § 553(c) of the Administrative Procedure Act. Since the 1966 amendment to § 1(14)(a), under which the Commission was here proceeding, does not by its terms add to the hearing requirement contained in the earlier language, the same result should obtain here unless that amendment contains language that is tantamount to such a requirement. . . . We know of no reason to think that an administrative agency in reaching a decision cannot accord consideration to factors such as those set forth in the 1966 amendment by means other than a trial-type hearing or the presentation of oral argument by the affected parties. Congress by that amendment specified necessary components of the ultimate decision, but it did not specify the method by which the Commission should acquire information about those components.

Both of the district courts that reviewed this order of the Commission concluded that its proceedings were governed by the stricter requirements of §§ 556 and 557 of the Administrative Procedure Act, rather than by the provisions of § 553 alone. The conclusion of the District Court for the Middle District of Florida, which we here review, was based on the assumption that the language in § 1(14)(a) of the Interstate Commerce Act requiring rulemaking under that section to be done 'after hearing' was the equivalent of a statutory requirement that the rule 'be made on the record after opportunity for an agency hearing.' Such an assumption is inconsistent with our decision in *Allegheny-Ludlum*.

The District Court for the Eastern District of New York reached the same conclusion by a somewhat different line of reasoning. That court felt that because § 1(14)(a) of the Interstate Commerce Act had required a 'hearing,' and because that section was originally enacted in 1917, Congress was probably thinking in terms of a 'hearing' such as that described in the opinion of this Court in [a] roughly contemporaneous case . . . .

Insofar as this conclusion is grounded on the belief that the language 'after hearing' of § 1(14)(a), without more, would trigger the applicability of §§ 556 and 557, it, too, is contrary to our decision in *Allegheny-Ludlum*. The District Court observed that it was 'rather hard to believe that the last sentence of § 553(c) was directed only to the few legislative spots where the words 'on the record' or their equivalent had found their way into the statute book.' This is, however, the language which Congress used, and since there are statutes on the books that do use these very words, adherence to that language cannot be said to render the provision nugatory or ineffectual. We recognized in *Allegheny-Ludlum* that the actual words 'on the record' and 'after . . . hearing' used in § 553 were not words of art, and that other statutory language having the same meaning could trigger the provisions of §§ 556 and 557 in rulemaking proceedings. But we adhere to our conclusion, expressed in that case, that the phrase 'after hearing' in § 1(14)(a) of the Interstate Commerce Act does not have such an effect.

III. 'HEARING' REQUIREMENT OF § 1(14)(A) OF THE INTERSTATE COMMERCE ACT

Inextricably intertwined with the hearing requirement of the Administrative Procedure Act in this case is the meaning to be given to the language 'after hearing' in § 1(14)(a) of the Interstate Commerce Act. Appellees, both here and in the court below, contend that the Commission procedure here fell short of that mandated by the 'hearing' requirement of § 1(14)(a), even though it may have satisfied § 553 of the Administrative Procedure Act. . . .

The term 'hearing' in its legal context undoubtedly has a host of meanings. Its meaning undoubtedly will vary, depending on whether it is used in the context of a rulemaking-type proceeding or in the context of a proceeding devoted to the adjudication of particular disputed facts. . . .

Under these circumstances, confronted with a grant of substantive authority made after the Administrative Procedure Act was enacted, we think that reference to that Act, in which Congress devoted itself exclusively to questions such as the nature and scope of hearings, is a satisfactory basis for determining what is meant by the term 'hearing' used in another statute. Turning to that Act, we are convinced that the term 'hearing' as used therein does not necessarily embrace either the right to present evidence orally and to cross-examine opposing witnesses, or the right to present oral argument to the agency's decisionmaker.

Section 553 excepts from its requirements rulemaking devoted to 'interpretative rules, general statements of policy, or rules of agency organization, procedure, or practice,' and rulemaking 'when the agency for good cause finds . . . that notice and public procedure thereon are impracticable, unnecessary, or contrary to the public interest.' This exception does not apply, however, 'when notice or hearing is required by statute'; in those cases, even though interpretative rulemaking be involved, the requirements of § 553 apply. But since these requirements themselves do not mandate any oral presentation, it cannot be doubted that a statute that requires a 'hearing' prior to rulemaking may in some circumstances be satisfied by procedures that meet only the standards of § 553. . . .

Similarly, even where the statute requires that the rulemaking procedure take place 'on the record after opportunity for an agency hearing,' thus triggering the applicability of § 556, subsection (d) provides that the agency may proceed by the submission of all or part of the evidence in written form if a party will not be 'prejudiced thereby.' Again, the Act makes it plain that a specific statutory mandate that the proceedings take place on the record after hearing may be satisfied in some circumstances by evidentiary submission in written form only.

We think this treatment of the term 'hearing' in the Administrative Procedure Act affords sufficient basis for concluding that the requirement of a 'hearing' contained in § 1(14)(a); in a situation where the Commission was acting under the 1966 statutory rulemaking authority that Congress had conferred upon it, did not by its own force require the Commission either to hear oral testimony, to permit cross-examination of Commission witnesses, or to hear oral argument. Here, the Commission promulgated a tentative draft of an order, and accorded all interested parties 60 days in which to file statements of position, submissions of evidence, and other relevant observations. The parties had fair notice of exactly what the Commission proposed to do, and were given an opportunity to comment, to object, or to make some other form of written submission. The final order of the Commission indicates that it gave consideration to the statements of the two appellees here. Given the 'open-ended' nature of the proceedings, and the Commission's announced willingness to consider proposals for modification after operating experience had been acquired, we think the hearing requirement of § 1(14)(a) of the Act was met. . . .

[A dissent by JUSTICES DOUGLAS and STEWARD is omitted.—Ed.]

NOTES AND QUESTIONS

1. The Court's textual analysis. In *Florida East Coast Railway*, the Supreme Court held that an agency that had to promulgate a rule after a "hearing" did not have to engage in the formal, trial-like process established by §§ 556–57 of the APA. It arrived at this conclusion through a textual analysis. According to § 553(c) of the APA, the formal proceedings are only triggered if the organic statute requires rules "to be made on the record after opportunity for an agency hearing." But there are many types of "hearings." First, §§ 556–57 themselves provide that in some cases a hearing can be made on a written record. § 556(d). Second, § 553 provides that nonlegislative rules have to go through the *informal* notice-and-comment process of that section if the organic statute requires "notice or hearing." This suggests that, according to the APA, a "hearing" can refer to the informal rulemaking process.

Thus, after *Florida East Coast Railway*, formal rulemaking is required only if the organic statute provides that a rule must be made "on the record after opportunity for agency hearing," or if the statute uses words that convey a similar, unmistakable congressional intent to require formal rulemaking procedures. As a result of this case, agencies rarely undertake formal rulemaking procedures—indeed, the informal notice-and-comment process is now the staple of regulatory agencies and administrative law courses.

2. Formal adjudications. Although formal rulemakings are rare, it is important to recognize that formal adjudications are still relatively common. Particularly where due process issues are at play—where an administrative agency brings an enforcement action against a private individual and his or her liberty or property interests are at risk—agencies tend to proceed with the full, trial-like hearings required by APA §§ 556–57. These formal adjudications will be discussed in more detail in Chapter 3.B.1.

3. The original understanding? It is hard to argue with the Supreme Court's textual analysis of the Administrative Procedure Act. But what about the original understanding of the drafters in 1946 and the drafters of the various organic statutes prior to 1978 (the year *Florida East Coast Railway* was decided)? One of the key differences under the APA between formal and informal proceedings is that formal proceedings create a closed record. "The transcript of testimony and exhibits, together with all papers and requests filed in the proceeding, constitutes the exclusive record for decision" in formal proceedings. § 556(e). Thus, the real question is whether Congress intended an agency to conduct a rulemaking on a "record." The Attorney General's Manual on the Administrative Procedure Act, which the Department of Justice wrote in 1947 and which the Court considers to be good evidence of the contemporaneous understanding of the APA (see statutory interpretation Lesson 11), suggests that only where an organic statute both requires a hearing and an agency decision to be made "on the record," the formal procedures apply. U.S. Dep't of Justice, Att'y General's Manual on the Admin. Proc. Act 34–35 (1947).

Nothing in *Florida East Coast Railway* is inconsistent with this contemporaneous interpretation: nothing in the statute seemed to require a decision on a closed record. The only problem was that Congress and the agency for many years *thought* a closed record was in fact required. The Attorney General's Manual, when discussing rate-making by agencies, explained that rate-making statutes "rarely specify in terms that the agency action must be taken on the basis of the 'record' developed in the hearing," but "the agencies themselves and the courts have long assumed that the agency's action must be based upon the evidence adduced at the hearing." Id. at 33. More still, as one of the district courts recognized in the *Florida East Coast Railway* saga, section 1(14)(a) of the Interstate Commerce Act was enacted in 1917, and "Congress was probably thinking in terms of a 'hearing' such as that described in the opinion of [the Supreme] Court in [a] roughly contemporaneous case," where a "hearing" was held to require that "[a]ll parties must be fully apprised of the evidence submitted or to be considered, and must be given opportunity to cross-examine witnesses, to inspect documents and to offer evidence in explanation or rebuttal." *Florida East Coast Railway*, 410 U.S. at 237 (quoting ICC v. Louisville & Nashville R. Co., 227 U.S. 88, 93 (1913)). Does this change your view of the case? Consider that question as you read the following statutory interpretation lesson.

STATUTORY INTERPRETATION LESSON 12

Lesson 12: The Reenactment Rule. The Reenactment Rule is an interpretive canon that courts do not deploy too often. The rule provides that when Congress reenacts statutory language without significant changes, it is presumed to accept any important prior judicial or even executive interpretations of that language. In *Florida East Coast Railway,* this canon would have worked against the Supreme Court's majority opinion. When Congress amended the agency's rate-making authority in 1966 to authorize the per diem charges, it presumably accepted the background executive interpretations of the statute as requiring formal rulemaking proceedings. Indeed when Congress enacted the relevant statutory language *for the first time* in 1917, presumably it understood that the language would be interpreted as a prominent Supreme Court case had interpreted such language only a few years earlier. Although there is no specific name for this presumption, one might just call it the "enactment rule," to relate it to the "reenactment" rule.

Still, this rule should not be deployed too rigorously—indeed the Supreme Court rarely mentions it, and it implicitly rejected it in *Florida East Coast Railway.* It is surely a fiction to imagine that Congress is always aware even of important prior judicial constructions of particular language. Perhaps the ordinary language and the intratextual analysis in *Florida East Coast Railway* are surer guides to statutory meaning. Nevertheless, the Reenactment Rule is another tool in the interpretive toolkit, and may sometimes be profitably used alongside the longstanding and contemporaneous interpretation canons.

C. Informal Rulemaking

We now come to the bread and butter of modern agencies: informal, or notice-and-comment, rulemaking. Under § 553 of the APA, there are three requirements for informal rulemaking: (1) the agency must publish a "[g]eneral notice of proposed rule making" that includes "the terms or substance of the proposed rule or a description of the subjects and issues involved," § 553(b)(3), called the Notice of Proposed Rulemaking (usually "NOPR" or "NPRM" for short); (2) the agency must "give interested persons an opportunity to participate in the rule making through submission of written data, views, or arguments with or without opportunity for oral presentation," § 553(c); and (3) "[a]fter consideration of the relevant matter presented" in the public comments, "the agency shall incorporate in the rules adopted a concise general statement of their basis and purpose," id.

The first set of issues that arise has to do with how the first and second requirements relate to each other—the requirements for notice of the proposed rule and an opportunity for interested persons to participate. For example, how different from the proposed rule is the final rule allowed to be? On the one hand, we want agencies to learn from the comments made over the public comment period; but on the other, if the new rule diverges too much, other parties may not have been put on sufficient notice that the agency might adopt a rule of the kind that was ultimately adopted. Another issue has to do with disclosure: Must the agency disclose data on which it relies to give the public time to comment on that data? Must the agency disclose *ex parte* contacts with industry insiders, or with political officials?

The second set of issues is about the second requirement standing alone: how much time must an agency allow for public comment? The APA does not specify a length of time. The third set of issues has to do with how the second and third requirements—the opportunity to participate and an explanation of the agency's ultimate choice—relate to each other: what comments must the agency address when making and justifying its final rule?

We shall come to these issues shortly. But first, we encounter the following seminal administrative law case, *Vermont Yankee*. The question in that case was whether courts had the power to *add* to the procedural requirements of the APA. The Supreme Court, as you shall see, said no. But courts routinely interpret the three requirements for informal rulemaking in a way that might seem to add procedural requirements. For example, the courts have held that an opportunity to participate requires the agency to offer a "meaningful" opportunity for comment. Is that adding to the requirements of the APA, or merely interpreting existing requirements? Keep such questions in mind as you read the case.

 **COURSE THEME**

APA TEXTUALISM VS. ADMINISTRATIVE COMMON LAW
How much of administrative law is based on "administrative common law"? How many doctrines can be explained by the text of the APA itself?

---

1. Vermont Yankee

Vermont Yankee Nuclear Power Corp. v. NRDC

435 U.S. 519 (1978)

MR. JUSTICE REHNQUIST delivered the opinion of the Court.

In 1946, Congress enacted the Administrative Procedure Act, which as we have noted elsewhere was not only "a new, basic and comprehensive regulation of procedures in many agencies," but was also a legislative enactment which settled "long-continued and hard-fought contentions, and enacts a formula upon which opposing social and political forces have come to rest." Section 4 of the Act, 5 U.S.C. § 553, dealing with rulemaking, requires in subsection (b) that "notice of proposed rule making shall be published in the Federal Register . . .," describes the contents of that notice, and goes on to require in subsection (c) that after the notice the agency "shall give interested persons an opportunity to participate in the rule making through submission of written data, views, or arguments with or without opportunity for oral presentation. After consideration of the relevant matter presented, the agency shall incorporate in the rules adopted a concise general statement of their basis and purpose." Interpreting this provision of the Act . . . we held that generally speaking this section of the Act established the maximum procedural requirements which Congress was willing to have the courts impose upon agencies in conducting rulemaking procedures. Agencies are free to grant additional procedural rights in the exercise of their discretion, but reviewing courts are generally not free to impose them if the agencies have not chosen to grant them. This is not to say necessarily that there are no circumstances which would ever justify a court in overturning agency action because of a failure to employ procedures beyond those required by the statute. But such circumstances, if they exist, are extremely rare.

Even apart from the Administrative Procedure Act this Court has for more than four decades emphasized that the formulation of procedures was basically to be left within the discretion of the agencies to which Congress had confided the responsibility for substantive judgments. In *FCC v. Schreiber,* 381 U.S. 279, 290 (1965), the Court explicated this principle, describing it as "an outgrowth of the congressional determination that administrative agencies and administrators will be familiar with the industries which they regulate and will be in a better position than federal courts or Congress itself to design procedural rules adapted to the peculiarities of the industry and the tasks of the agency involved." . . .

It is in the light of this background of statutory and decisional law that we granted certiorari to review two judgments of the Court of Appeals for the District of Columbia Circuit because of our concern that they had seriously misread or misapplied this statutory and decisional law cautioning reviewing courts against engrafting their own notions of proper procedures upon agencies entrusted with substantive functions by Congress. We conclude that the Court of Appeals has done just that in these cases, and we therefore remand them to it for further proceedings. . . .

I

A

Under the Atomic Energy Act of 1954, 42 U.S.C. § 2011 *et seq.*, the Atomic Energy Commission was given broad regulatory authority over the development of nuclear energy. Under the terms of the Act, a utility seeking to construct and operate a nuclear power plant must obtain a separate permit or license at both the construction and the operation stage of the project. In order to obtain the construction permit, the utility must file a preliminary safety analysis report, an environmental report, and certain information regarding the antitrust implications of the proposed project. This application then undergoes exhaustive review by the Commission's staff and by the Advisory Committee on Reactor Safeguards (ACRS), a group of distinguished experts in the field of atomic energy. Both groups submit to the Commission their own evaluations, which then become part of the record of the utility's application. The Commission staff also undertakes the review required by the National Environmental Policy Act of 1969 (NEPA), and prepares a draft environmental impact statement, which, after being circulated for comment, is revised and becomes a final environmental impact statement. Thereupon a three-member Atomic Safety and Licensing Board conducts a public adjudicatory hearing, and reaches a decision which can be appealed to the Atomic Safety and Licensing Appeal Board, and currently, in the Commission's discretion, to the Commission itself. The final agency decision may be appealed to the courts of appeals. The same sort of process occurs when the utility applies for a license to operate the plant, except that a hearing need only be held in contested cases and may be limited to the matters in controversy.

These cases arise from two separate decisions of the Court of Appeals for the District of Columbia Circuit. In the first, the court remanded a decision of the Commission to grant a license to petitioner Vermont Yankee Nuclear Power Corp. to operate a nuclear power plant. . . .

B

In December 1967, after the mandatory adjudicatory hearing and necessary review, the Commission granted petitioner Vermont Yankee a permit to build a nuclear power plant in Vernon, Vt. Thereafter, Vermont Yankee applied for an operating license. Respondent Natural Resources Defense Council (NRDC) objected to the granting of a license, however, and therefore a hearing on the application commenced on August 10, 1971. Excluded from consideration at the hearings, over NRDC's objection, was the issue of the environmental effects of operations to reprocess fuel or dispose of wastes resulting from the reprocessing operations. This ruling was affirmed by the Appeal Board in June 1972.

In November 1972, however, the Commission, making specific reference to the Appeal Board's decision with respect to the Vermont Yankee license, instituted rulemaking proceedings "that would specifically deal with the question of consideration of environmental effects associated with the uranium fuel cycle in the individual cost-benefit analyses for light water cooled nuclear power reactors." The notice of proposed rulemaking offered two alternatives, both predicated on a report prepared by the Commission's staff entitled Environmental Survey of the Nuclear Fuel Cycle. The first would have required no quantitative evaluation of the environmental hazards of fuel reprocessing or disposal because the Environmental Survey had found them to be slight. The second would have specified numerical values for the environmental impact of this part of the fuel cycle, which values would then be incorporated into a table, along with the other relevant factors, to determine the overall cost-benefit balance for each operating license.

Much of the controversy in this case revolves around the procedures used in the rulemaking hearing which commenced in February 1973. In a supplemental notice of hearing the Commission indicated that while discovery or cross-examination would not be utilized, the Environmental Survey would be available to the public before the hearing along with the extensive background documents cited therein. All participants would be given a reasonable opportunity to present their position and could be represented by counsel if they so desired. Written and, time permitting, oral statements would be received and incorporated into the record. All persons giving oral statements would be subject to questioning by the Commission. At the conclusion of the hearing, a transcript would be made available to the public and the record would remain open for 30 days to allow the filing of supplemental written statements. More than 40 individuals and organizations representing a wide variety of interests submitted written comments. On January 17, 1973, the Licensing Board held a planning session to schedule the appearance of witnesses and to discuss methods for compiling a record. The hearing was held on February 1 and 2, with participation by a number of groups, including the Commission's staff, the United States Environmental Protection Agency, a manufacturer of reactor equipment, a trade association from the nuclear industry, a group of electric utility companies, and a group called Consolidated National Intervenors which represented 79 groups and individuals including respondent NRDC.

After the hearing, the Commission's staff filed a supplemental document for the purpose of clarifying and revising the Environmental Survey. Then the Licensing Board forwarded its report to the Commission without rendering any decision. The Licensing Board identified as the principal procedural question the propriety of declining to use full formal adjudicatory procedures. The major substantive issue was the technical adequacy of the Environmental Survey.

In April 1974, the Commission issued a rule which adopted the second of the two proposed alternatives described above. The Commission also approved the procedures used at the hearing, and indicated that the record, including the Environmental Survey, provided an "adequate data base for the regulation adopted." Finally, the Commission ruled that to the extent the rule differed from the Appeal Board decisions in Vermont Yankee "those decisions have no further precedential significance," but that since "the environmental effects of the uranium fuel cycle have been shown to be relatively insignificant, . . . it is unnecessary to apply the amendment to applicant's environmental reports submitted prior to its effective date or to Final Environmental Statements for which Draft Environmental Statements have been circulated for comment prior to the effective date."

Respondents appealed from both the Commission's adoption of the rule and its decision to grant Vermont Yankee's license to the Court of Appeals for the District of Columbia Circuit.

* * *

D

With respect to the challenge of Vermont Yankee's license, the court first ruled that in the absence of effective rulemaking proceedings, the Commission must deal with the environmental impact of fuel reprocessing and disposal in individual licensing proceedings. The court then examined the rulemaking proceedings and, despite the fact that it appeared that the agency employed all the procedures required by 5 U.S.C. § 553 and more, the court determined the proceedings to be inadequate and overturned the rule. Accordingly, the Commission's determination with respect to Vermont Yankee's license was also remanded for further proceedings. . . .

II

* * *

B

We next turn to the invalidation of the fuel cycle rule. But before determining whether the Court of Appeals reached a permissible result, we must determine exactly what result it did reach, and in this case that is no mean feat. Vermont Yankee argues that the court invalidated the rule because of the inadequacy of the procedures employed in the proceedings. Respondents, on the other hand, labeling petitioner's view of the decision a "straw man," argue to this Court that the court merely held that the record was inadequate to enable the reviewing court to determine whether the agency had fulfilled its statutory obligation. . . .

After a thorough examination of the opinion itself, we conclude that while the matter is not entirely free from doubt, the majority of the Court of Appeals struck down the rule because of the perceived inadequacies of the procedures employed in the rulemaking proceedings. The court first determined the intervenors' primary argument to be "that the decision to preclude 'discovery or cross-examination' denied them a meaningful opportunity to participate in the proceedings as guaranteed by due process." The court then went on to frame the issue for decision thus: "Thus, we are called upon to decide whether the procedures provided by the agency were sufficient to ventilate the issues."

The court conceded that absent extraordinary circumstances it is improper for a reviewing court to prescribe the procedural format an agency must follow, but it likewise clearly thought it entirely appropriate to "scrutinize the record as a whole to insure that genuine opportunities to participate in a meaningful way were provided . . . ." The court also refrained from actually ordering the agency to follow any specific procedures, but there is little doubt in our minds that the ineluctable mandate of the court's decision is that the procedures afforded during the hearings were inadequate. This conclusion is particularly buttressed by the fact that after the court examined the record, particularly the testimony of Dr. Pittman, and declared it insufficient, the court proceeded to discuss at some length the necessity for further procedural devices or a more "sensitive" application of those devices employed during the proceedings. The exploration of the record and the statement regarding its insufficiency might initially lead one to conclude that the court was only examining the sufficiency of the evidence, but the remaining portions of the opinion dispel any doubt that this was certainly not the sole or even the principal basis of the decision. Accordingly, we feel compelled to address the opinion on its own terms, and we conclude that it was wrong.

In prior opinions we have intimated that even in a rulemaking proceeding when an agency is making a "quasi-judicial" determination by which a very small number of persons are "exceptionally affected, in each case upon individual grounds," in some circumstances additional procedures may be required in order to afford the aggrieved individuals due process. . . .

But this much is absolutely clear. Absent constitutional constraints or extremely compelling circumstances the "administrative agencies 'should be free to fashion their own rules of procedure and to pursue methods of inquiry capable of permitting them to discharge their multitudinous duties.' " . . . And the basic reason for this decision was the Court of Appeals' serious departure from the very basic tenet of administrative law that agencies should be free to fashion their own rules of procedure.

We have continually repeated this theme through the years . . . .

Respondent NRDC argues that § 4 of the Administrative Procedure Act, 5 U.S.C. § 553, merely establishes lower procedural bounds and that a court may routinely require more than the minimum when an agency's proposed rule addresses complex or technical factual issues or "Issues of Great Public Import." [In omitted paragraphs, the Court here goes through some of the legislative history and the contemporaneous Attorney General's manual on the APA— Ed.] In short, all of this leaves little doubt that Congress intended that the discretion of the *agencies* and not that of the courts be exercised in determining when extra procedural devices should be employed.

There are compelling reasons for construing § 4 in this manner. In the first place, if courts continually review agency proceedings to determine whether the agency employed procedures which were, in the court's opinion, perfectly tailored to reach what the court perceives to be the "best" or "correct" result, judicial review would be totally unpredictable. And the agencies, operating under this vague injunction to employ the "best" procedures and facing the threat of reversal if they did not, would undoubtedly adopt full adjudicatory procedures in every instance. Not only would this totally disrupt the statutory scheme, through which Congress enacted "a formula upon which opposing social and political forces have come to rest," but all the inherent advantages of informal rulemaking would be totally lost.

Secondly, it is obvious that the court in these cases reviewed the agency's choice of procedures on the basis of the record actually produced at the hearing, and not on the basis of the information available to the agency when it made the decision to structure the proceedings in a certain way. This sort of Monday morning quarterbacking not only encourages but almost compels the agency to conduct all rulemaking proceedings with the full panoply of procedural devices normally associated only with adjudicatory hearings.

Finally, and perhaps most importantly, this sort of review fundamentally misconceives the nature of the standard for judicial review of an agency rule. The court below uncritically assumed that additional procedures will automatically result in a more adequate record because it will give interested parties more of an opportunity to participate in and contribute to the proceedings. But informal rulemaking need not be based solely on the transcript of a hearing held before an agency. Indeed, the agency need not even hold a formal hearing. Thus, the adequacy of the "record" in this type of proceeding is not correlated directly to the type of procedural devices employed, but rather turns on whether the agency has followed the statutory mandate of the Administrative Procedure Act or other relevant statutes. If the agency is compelled to support the rule which it ultimately adopts with the type of record produced only after a full adjudicatory hearing, it simply will have no choice but to conduct a full adjudicatory hearing prior to promulgating every rule. In sum, this sort of unwarranted judicial examination of perceived procedural shortcomings of a rulemaking proceeding can do nothing but seriously interfere with that process prescribed by Congress. . . .

In short, nothing in the APA, NEPA, the circumstances of this case, the nature of the issues being considered, past agency practice, or the statutory mandate under which the Commission operates permitted the court to review and overturn the rulemaking proceeding on the basis of the procedural devices employed (or not employed) by the Commission so long as the Commission employed at least the statutory *minima,* a matter about which there is no doubt in this case. . . .

NOTES AND QUESTIONS

1. *The procedure-substance debate.* Why did things get the way they were such that the Supreme Court felt that it had to issue its opinion in *Vermont Yankee*? Recall from the introductory materials that in the 1960s and 1970s, there was a renewed faith in government to supply solutions to environmental and other problems, but also tremendous skepticism of the ability of government agencies to provide those solutions. Courts in those decades therefore sought to police the work of agencies more rigorously than courts had been doing in the first few decades post-APA.

A court that sought to supply more rigorous review of agency actions had two choices: it could more rigorously review the *substance* of an agency's decision, or it could more rigorously review the *procedure* an agency uses. In a famous debate between two stalwarts of the D.C. Circuit—the circuit that hears most administrative law cases—Judge Bazelon argued that the courts should focus on policing the procedures an agency uses while Judge Leventhal argued the

COMPARATIVE PERSPECTIVE How involved should judges be in reviewing the technical substance of an agency's work? Should judges only ensure procedural quality and fairness? What are the comparative advantages of agencies and judges, respectively?

courts should focus on the substance. Judge Bazelon argued, "Because substantive review of mathematical and scientific evidence by technically illiterate judges is dangerously unreliable, I continue to believe we will do more to improve administrative decision-making by concentrating our efforts on strengthening administrative procedures." Ethyl Corp. v. Envtl. Prot. Agency, 541 F.2d 1, 67 (D.C. Cir. 1976) (Bazelon, J., concurring). Judge Leventhal argued, in contrast, that "[o]ur present system of review assumes judges will acquire whatever technical knowledge is necessary as background for decision of the legal questions." Id. at 68–69 (Leventhal, J., concurring).

For the most part, Judge Bazelon won the debate, at least until the 1980s. (We will see how courts began in the 1980s to review substantive agency decisions more rigorously in Chapter 4.) As a result, the D.C. Circuit had been requiring agencies to add procedures that the court believed were necessary to ensure fair, equitable, and rational decisions, even if those procedures were nowhere required by the text of any statute. Thus the Supreme Court's pronouncement in *Vermont Yankee* putting a stop to that process—at least where there is no plausible textual hook in the procedural provisions of the APA or an organic statute.

2. *Hybrid rulemaking and the APA as default rule.* Now is a good time to remind the student that the APA's procedures are merely a default rule. An organic statute may require more or less procedures than the APA. Many statutes require what has been termed as "hybrid" rulemaking—a process much more robust than the informal rulemaking process, but much less rigorous than formal rulemaking proceedings. Aaron L. Nielson, *In Defense of Formal Rulemaking*, 75 Ohio St. L.J. 237, 256 (2014); Henry H. Perritt, Jr., *Negotiated Rulemaking Before Federal Agencies: Evaluation of Recommendations by the Administrative Conference of the United States*, 74 Geo. L.J. 1625, 1696 (1986). Note, too, that an agency might bind *itself* to additional procedures. See Chapter 3.C.

3. *Deference to scientific judgments.* The nuclear power saga continued. After *Vermont Yankee*, the agency promulgated a slightly revised rule, one that again assumed minimal environmental risk from buried waste depositories. The D.C. Circuit again vacated the rulemaking. And the Supreme Court again—unanimously—reversed. The Court held, "When examining this kind of scientific determination, as opposed to simple findings of fact, a reviewing court must generally be at its most deferential." Baltimore Gas & Elec. Co. v. Nat. Res. Def. Council, Inc., 462 U.S. 87, 103 (1983). Litigators defending or attacking a scientific determination of an agency would do well to remember the *Baltimore Gas* case.

2.   Notice Requirement

As explained previously, a key issue involving informal rulemakings is the interaction of the notice requirement and the opportunity for participation. How different can the final rule be from the proposed rule? On the one hand, we want agencies to learn from the comment process and thus we expect the final rule to be different from the proposed rule at least some of the time. On the other, if the final rule is too different, some interested parties might plausibly argue that they did not have a chance to comment on the substance of the final rule. The next case is representative of how courts have resolved this tension.

Shell Oil Co. v. EPA

950 F. 2d 741 (D.C. Cir. 1991)

Per Curiam:

In these consolidated cases, petitioners challenge both the substance of several rules promulgated by the Environmental Protection Agency pursuant to the Resource Conservation and Recovery Act of 1976 and its compliance with the Administrative Procedure Act's rulemaking requirements.

Consolidated petitioners challenge two rules that categorize substances as hazardous wastes until a contrary showing has been made: the "mixture" rule, which classifies as a hazardous waste any mixture of a "listed" hazardous waste with any other solid waste, and the "derived-from" rule, which so classifies any residue derived from the treatment of hazardous waste. They argue that the EPA failed to provide adequate notice and opportunity for comment when it promulgated the mixture and derived-from rules, and that the rules exceed the EPA's statutory authority. . . .

We agree with petitioners that the EPA failed to give sufficient notice and opportunity for comment in promulgating the "mixture" and "derived-from" rules . . . .

I. BACKGROUND

The EPA promulgated the disputed rules in order to implement the Resource Conservation and Recovery Act ("RCRA"). RCRA created a "cradle-to-grave" system for tracking wastes from their generation to disposal. The statute consists of two main parts: one governs the management of non-hazardous solid waste; the other, hazardous waste.

As enacted, Subtitle C of RCRA required the EPA to establish a comprehensive national system for safely treating, storing, and disposing of hazardous wastes. It defined "hazardous waste," in part, as a "solid waste" which may "pose a substantial present or potential hazard to human health or the environment when improperly treated, stored, transported, or disposed of, or otherwise managed." 42 U.S.C. § 6903(5). It gave the EPA until April 21, 1978 to develop and promulgate criteria for identifying characteristics of hazardous waste and to list particular wastes as hazardous. It further required the EPA to promulgate regulations "as may be necessary to protect human health and the environment" respecting the practices of generators, transporters, and those who own or operate hazardous waste treatment, storage, or disposal facilities. RCRA prohibited treatment, storage, or disposal of hazardous waste without a permit and required the EPA to promulgate standards governing permits for facilities performing such functions.

On February 17, 1977, the EPA published a Notice of Intent to Develop Rulemaking, 42 Fed.Reg. 9,803 (1977); and on May 2, 1977, it published an Advance Notice of Proposed Rulemaking, 42 Fed.Reg. 22,332 (1977), which set forth detailed questions on each of the subsections of Subtitle C. In addition, it circulated for comment several drafts of regulations, met with experts and representatives of interested groups, and held public hearings. This process culminated in the publication, on December 18, 1978, of proposed regulations covering most of the statutorily required standards. *See* 43 Fed.Reg. 58,946–59,022 (1978).

This proposal elicited voluminous comment, and the EPA held five large public hearings. The EPA failed to issue final regulations by the April 1978 statutory deadline; several parties sued the Agency to compel it to do so. Although the district court initially ordered the EPA to promulgate the regulations by December 31, 1979, the complexity of the task led the court to modify the order to require, instead, that the EPA use its best efforts to issue them by April 1980.

The EPA published its "[r]evisions to final rule and interim final rule" on May 19, 1980. 45 Fed.Reg. 33,066 (1980). It noted that time pressures had had an effect on the new regulations: Because of limited information, the Agency was unable to avoid underregulation and overregulation. It complained that the demands of developing a national, comprehensive system of hazardous-waste management made precise tailoring to individual cases impossible.

More than fifty petitions were brought to challenge these final rules. In 1982, we deferred briefing on these challenges to allow the parties to pursue settlement discussions and ordered the EPA to file monthly status reports. We did not stay the rules, however, which have remained in effect. Most of the issues have been resolved by settlement, by subsequent statutory or regulatory revision, or by the failure of petitioners to pursue them. The issues presented here are those that the EPA identified in January 1987 as unlikely to be settled, and that were subject to the briefing schedule established by this court on June 12, 1989.

Consolidated petitioners assert that the regulations proposed on December 18, 1978 did not foreshadow the inclusion of the mixture and derived-from rules in the final rule's definition of "hazardous waste." Thus, they assert, they were deprived of adequate notice and opportunity for comment. They also claim that the EPA exceeded its statutory authority by including the two rules in the final definition of hazardous waste. . . .

II. DISCUSSION

A. Principles Governing Judicial Review

The Administrative Procedure Act ("APA") governs judicial review of final regulations promulgated under RCRA. In issuing regulations, the EPA must observe the notice-and-comment procedures of the APA, and the public-participation directive of RCRA. The relationship between the proposed regulation and the final rule determines the adequacy of notice. A difference between the two will not invalidate the notice so long as the final rule is a "logical outgrowth" of the one proposed. If the deviation from the proposal is too sharp, the affected parties will not have had adequate notice and opportunity for comment. . . .

B. The Mixture and Derived-From Rules

The mixture and derived-from rules are to be found in the definition of "hazardous waste" that appears in the final rules. That definition includes as hazardous all wastes resulting from mixing hazardous and other wastes and from treating, storing, or disposing of hazardous wastes, until such time as the wastes are proven nonhazardous. Petitioners protest that these provisions had no counterpart in, and were not a logical outgrowth of, the proposed regulations; thus, the promulgation of the rules violated the notice-and-comment requirements of RCRA and the APA. We agree. . . .

2. *The Proposed Regulations*

In its proposed regulations, the EPA . . . set forth the following scheme for identifying and listing hazardous wastes: . . . A solid waste, or source or class of solid waste, will be listed as a hazardous waste . . . if the Administrator determines that the solid waste . . . [p]ossesses any of the characteristics defined in § 250.13 . . . . Although the EPA initially identified nine possible characteristics as potentially hazardous, it decided to rely on only four of them—ignitability, corrosivity, reactivity, and toxicity—in its proposed section 250.13, because only these could be tested reliably and inexpensively. Because solid wastes that present a hazard but do not display one of these four characteristics remained subject to RCRA, the EPA proposed to list such wastes specifically, and to treat any waste once listed as hazardous until a person managing the waste filed a delisting petition and demonstrated to the EPA that the waste did not pose a hazard.

3. *The Final Rules*

The final rules defined a hazardous waste more broadly than did the proposed regulations. Under the final rules, a hazardous waste is a solid waste that is not specifically excluded from regulation and meets any one of the following criteria:

(i)   It is listed in Subpart D and has not been excluded from the lists in Subpart D under §§ 260.20 and 260.22 of this Chapter.

(ii) It is a mixture of solid waste and one or more hazardous wastes listed in Subpart D and has not been excluded from this paragraph under §§ 260.20 and 260.22 of this Chapter.

(iii) It exhibits any of the characteristics of hazardous waste identified in Subpart C.

In addition, a solid waste generated from the treatment, storage, or disposal of a hazardous waste is considered a hazardous waste.

In establishing criteria for identifying and listing hazardous wastes in its final rules, the EPA relied heavily on the dangers that such wastes pose. Thus the EPA compiled a list of toxic constituents as a starting point and required that a waste be listed as hazardous if it (1) exhibits one of the four characteristics of hazardous waste identified in Subpart C of the regulations ("hazardous characteristics"), (2) meets certain toxicity criteria, or (3) contains any of the toxic constituents listed in Appendix VIII . . . .

4. *The Mixture Rule*

The mixture rule requires that a waste be treated as hazardous if "[i]t is a mixture of solid waste and one or more hazardous wastes listed in Subpart D and has not been excluded from this paragraph under §§ 260.20 and 260.22 of this Chapter." Once classified as hazardous, then, a mixture must be so treated until delisted.

The EPA acknowledged at the outset that the mixture rule was "a new provision," and that it had no "direct counterpart in the proposed regulations." Nevertheless, it added the rule "for purposes of clarification and in response to questions raised during the comment period concerning waste mixtures and when hazardous wastes become subject to and cease to be subject to the Subtitle C hazardous waste management system."

Although admitting that it had failed to say so in the proposed regulations, the EPA stated that it had "intended" to treat waste mixtures containing Subpart D wastes as hazardous. It then presented the mixture rule as necessary to close "a major loophole in the Subtitle C management system." Otherwise, generators of hazardous waste "could evade [those] requirements simply by commingling [Subpart D] wastes with nonhazardous solid waste" to create a waste that did not demonstrate any of the four testable characteristics but that posed a hazard for another reason. The Agency explained that although the mixture rule might include waste with concentrations of Subpart D wastes too low to pose a hazard, the delisting process and the possibility of segregating waste to avoid the problem mitigated the burden of the rule. . . .

While the EPA admits that the mixture rule lacks a clear antecedent in the proposed regulations, it nonetheless argues that the rule merely clarifies the intent behind the proposal that listed wastes remain hazardous until delisted: As industry could not have reasonably assumed that a generator could bring a listed waste outside the generic listing description simply by mixing it with a nonhazardous waste, the rule cannot be seen as a "bolt from the blue."

5. *The Derived-From Rule*

The derived-from rule provides that "[a]ny solid waste generated from the treatment, storage or disposal of a hazardous waste, including any sludge, spill residue, ash, emission control dust or leachate (but not including precipitation run-off), is a hazardous waste." Subpart D wastes continue to be regulated as hazardous until delisted; a solid waste derived from Subpart C wastes may emerge from regulation if it does not itself display a hazardous characteristic.

The EPA's justifications for the derived-from rule resemble those for the mixture rule. Arguing that the products of treatment, storage, or disposal of listed hazardous wastes usually continue to pose hazards, the EPA defends the rule as "the best regulatory approach we can devise," given the fact that "[w]e are not now in a position to prescribe waste-specific treatment standards which would identify those processes which do and do not render wastes or treatment residues nonhazardous." . . .

6. *Adequacy of Notice*

Although the EPA acknowledges that neither of the two rules was to be found among the proposed regulations, it nevertheless argues that they were foreseeable—and, therefore, the notice adequate—because certain of the comments received in response to the rulemaking appeared to anticipate both the mixture and the derived-from rules. We are unimpressed by the scanty evidence marshaled in support of this position.

The only comment actually cited by the EPA was made by the Manufacturing Chemists Association, which stated that under the proposed regulations, "a listed waste is a hazardous waste regardless of quantity or concentration," and that "[i]t is not reasonable to classify *all* waste streams which contain *any* concentration of one of the specific wastes as hazardous." This comment, we note, addresses the initial classification of a waste as hazardous rather than the problem of how to deal with residues resulting from the treatment of wastes, or with their subsequent mixture with other, nonhazardous materials.

The EPA also draws attention to a response it made before the close of the comment period to a question posed by the American Mining Congress in which the Agency indicated that the delisting procedure would permit generators to remove wastes from the RCRA system. This, apparently, is supposed to have alerted interested parties that delisting would be the only means of exit from regulation. But examination of the precise words that the EPA used reveals a different message. The EPA stated that "[de]listing provides a means on a case by case basis for [the generator of a given waste] to demonstrate that that waste does not belong in the system at all." This response concerned the exclusion from regulation of wastes included by initial regulatory error, not the deregulation of wastes that have ceased to be hazardous.

The EPA's remaining evidence of implied notice is equally unimpressive. It consists of generalized references to comments urging that wastes be evaluated only according to the four easily testable characteristics, and requests that the regulations specifically address the disposition of incinerator ash.

An agency, of course, may promulgate final rules that differ from the proposed regulations. To avoid "the absurdity that . . . the agency can learn from the comments on its proposals only at the peril of starting a new procedural round of commentary," we have held that final rules need only be a "logical outgrowth" of the proposed regulations. But an unexpressed intention cannot convert a final rule into a "logical outgrowth" that the public should have anticipated. Interested parties cannot be expected to divine the EPA's unspoken thoughts. The reasons given by the EPA in support of its contention that interested parties should have anticipated the new rules are simply too insubstantial to justify a finding of implicit notice.

While it is true that such parties might have anticipated the potential for avoiding regulation by simply mixing hazardous and nonhazardous wastes, it was the business of the EPA, and not the public, to foresee that possibility and to address it in its proposed regulations. Moreover, while a comment may evidence a recognition of a problem, it can tell us nothing of how, or even whether, the agency will choose to address it. The comments the EPA cites strike us as sparse and ambiguous at best. Some address similar concerns, but none squarely anticipates the rules.

Even if the mixture and derived-from rules had been widely anticipated, comments by members of the public would not in themselves constitute adequate notice. Under the standards of the APA, "notice necessarily must come—if at all—from the Agency." . . . [H]ere, the ambiguous comments and weak signals from the agency gave petitioners no such opportunity to anticipate and criticize the rules or to offer alternatives. Under these circumstances, the mixture and derived-from rules exceed the limits of a "logical outgrowth."

The EPA's argument also fails to take into account a marked shift in emphasis between the proposed regulations and the final rules. . . . [T]he proposed regulations imposed, as a generator's principal responsibility, the duty to test wastes for hazardous characteristics and suggested that if the required tests failed to reveal a hazard, the waste would not need to be managed as hazardous.

The final rules, however, place a heavy emphasis on listing. . . . A system that would rely primarily on lists of wastes and waste-producing processes might imply inclusion of a waste until it is formally removed from the list. The proposed regulations, however, did not suggest such a system. Rather, their emphasis on characteristics suggested that if a waste did not exhibit the nine characteristics originally proposed, it need not be regulated as hazardous. We conclude, therefore, that the mixture rule was neither implicit in nor a "logical outgrowth" of the proposed regulations.

Similarly, while the derived-from rule may well have been the best regulatory approach the EPA could devise, it was not a logical outgrowth of the proposed regulations. The derived-from rule is not implicit in a system based upon testing wastes for specified hazardous characteristics—the system presented in the proposed regulations. To the contrary, the derived-from rule becomes counterintuitive as applied to processes designed to render wastes nonhazardous. Rather than presuming that these processes will achieve their goals, the derived-from rule assumes their failure. . . .

Because the EPA has not provided adequate notice and opportunity for comment, we conclude that the mixture and derived-from rules must be set aside and remanded to the EPA. In light of the dangers that may be posed by a discontinuity in the regulation of hazardous wastes, however, the agency may wish to consider reenacting the rules, in whole or part, on an interim basis under the "good cause" exemption of 5 U.S.C. § 553(b)(3)(B) pending full notice and opportunity for comment. . . .

Notes and Questions

1. The "logical outgrowth" test. As should be reasonably clear from the opinion, the key test is whether the final rule is a "logical outgrowth" of the proposed rule. Courts have tried to give meat to this standard with various formulations. The final rule cannot "constitute a change in the basic approach of the Proposed Rule." Veterans Justice Grp., LLC v. Sec'y of Veterans Affairs, 818 F.3d 1336, 1345 (Fed. Cir. 2016). In *Veterans Justice,* the agency had had prior regulations allowing veterans who are entitled to certain compensation to establish the "effective date" of their claim by filing an "informal claim," as long as they file the proper paperwork for a "formal claim" within one year. The agency proposed to eliminate that system and to establish the effective date with an "incomplete" claim, which meant the online filling out of an application but without submitting it; this process would have excluded the traditional paper-filing of informal claims. After receiving negative comments, the agency backtracked and opted for an "intent to file" process, by which the effective date would be determined *either* by filling out (but not submitting) an online application, or by submitting a standard paper form, or by communicating orally to certain agency officials. The court held that surely this was a logical outgrowth because the agency may *reconsider* its proposed rule in light of negative comments and decide not to take that course of action.

In another case, the D.C. Circuit held that "[a] final rule is a logical outgrowth if affected parties should have anticipated that the relevant modification was possible." Allina Health Servs. v. Sebelius, 746 F.3d 1102, 1107 (D.C. Cir. 2014). In *Allina Health,* the Department of Health and Human Services (HHS) proposed to "clarify" in a rule that patients with a certain kind of insurance would be counted under Medicaid for purposes of reimbursements, as opposed to under Medicare. Apparently the Department had for some time prior to the proposed rule classified those patients under the Medicaid reimbursement formula—hence the agency simply wanted to "clarify." In the final rule, however, the agency chose the opposite—and would now classify those same patients under the Medicare formula. The D.C. Circuit invalidated the rule. The hospitals challenging the rule had argued that "nothing in the text of the notice" suggested "that the Secretary was thinking of reconsidering a longstanding practice." The court agreed: "The hospitals should not be held to have anticipated that the Secretary's 'proposal to clarify' could have meant that the Secretary was open to reconsidering existing policy. The word 'clarify' does not suggest that a potential underlying major issue is open for discussion." Id. at 1108.

2. Supplemental notices. In a slightly more famous case, the D.C. Circuit noted that many times an agency will *renotice* a proposed rule if the agency is considering a major change from the initial proposed rule. The court explained the supplemental notice rule as follows:

PRACTICE POINTER To avoid judicial invalidation under the "logical outgrowth" test, agencies will often issue supplementary notices of proposed rulemaking if the initial comments have led the agency to consider a different approach for which the initial notice might not have given sufficient warning.

> An agency adopting final rules that differ from its proposed rules is required to renotice when the changes are so major that the original notice did not adequately frame the subjects for discussion. The purpose of the new notice is to allow interested parties a fair opportunity to comment upon the final rules in their altered form. The agency need not renotice changes that follow logically from or that reasonably develop the rules it proposed originally.

Connecticut Light & Power Co. v. NRC, 673 F.2d 525, 533 (D.C. Cir. 1982).

In *Connecticut Light & Power*, the Nuclear Regulatory Commission (NRC) proposed and adopted a fire protection program for nuclear power plants. One part of the rule dealt with "duplicate shutdown capacity"—the ability of duplicate systems to take over in the event of a primary system shut down by fire. In the proposed rule, the agency proposed the "postulated hazards" approach to protect this duplicate shutdown capacity, an approach that depended on a number of factors such as "the likely area within which a fire might spread, the fire extinguishing system used in the area, the accessibility of the area to fire fighters and equipment, the relative fire danger in the area, the availability of alternative methods for shutting down the reactor unit safely, and the fire retardant capacity of protective devices such as fire retardant coatings." Id. at 528–29.

The final rule, however, opted for three other, more specific methods to protect duplicate shutdown capacity: "separation of the redundant system by a barrier able to withstand fire for at least three hours; separation of the redundant system by a distance of twenty feet containing no intervening combustible material, together with fire detectors and an automatic fire suppression system; and enclosure of the redundant system in a fire barrier able to withstand fire for one hour, coupled with fire detectors and an automatic fire suppression system." Id. at 529.

The court held that it was a close call whether this final rule was a logical outgrowth of the proposed rule. It was ultimately persuaded to uphold the rule, however, because there was also an "exemption" procedure that allowed a company to "prove that another method works as well as one of the three stipulated by the NRC, in light of the identified fire hazards at its plant." Id. at 534. Thus, the final rule was a logical outgrowth because the "postulated hazards" approach could still be used by a plant that demonstrated its likely effectiveness. "Certainly, a rule that continues to allow a proposed approach as an alternative to other stipulated methods may be regarded as the logical successor to the proposed approach." Id.

Although the court in *Connecticut Light & Power* upheld the final rule, it should not surprise you that agencies routinely issue supplemental NPRMs, or SNPRMs (supplemental notices), to avoid litigating the logical outgrowth issue.

3.   Opportunity to Comment

As explained previously, the key informal rulemaking issues that arise in administrative law involve the relationship of the notice requirement to the public participation requirement, and the public participation requirement to the final justification for the rule in the statement of basis and purpose (to which we come shortly). There is not much litigation involving the opportunity to comment itself. Note that there is no time minimum provided in the APA. Executive Order 12,866, promulgated by President Clinton, and which still largely governs administrative rulemakings within executive branch agencies, provided that agencies should accord the public a "meaningful opportunity to comment on any proposed regulation, which in most cases should include a comment period of not less than 60 days." § 6(a). Courts do require a "meaningful" opportunity to comment, but they rarely second-guess an agency's decision on the length of the comment period.

■ *Problem 2.1*

In the early 1980s, under President Reagan, the EPA and the Army Corps of Engineers promulgated a rule defining the "waters of the United States" for purposes of the Clean Water Act to be only interstate waters (the "WOTUS" rule). In 2015, under President Obama, these agencies promulgated a different WOTUS rule redefining the waters of the United States to include seasonal streams, wetlands, and tributaries, that affected interstate waters, even if the additional streams were not themselves interstate waters in any sense. This rule would have greatly expanded the jurisdiction of the EPA under the Clean Water Act.

In February 2018, under President Trump, the EPA proposed a "Suspension Rule," which proposed to delay the 2015 WOTUS Rule for two years and reinstate the 1980s rule, until the agency could engage in further rulemaking of its own. The agency only accorded the public a 10-day comment period and limited comments to the *delay itself*—not to the merits of either the 1980s rule or the 2015 rule.

Did the agency give a meaningful opportunity to comment? How would you rule on the issue? See S.C. Coastal Conservation League v. Pruitt, 318 F. Supp. 3d 959 (D.S.C. 2018).

4.   Concise Statement of Basis and Purpose

In *Shell Oil*, we considered the relationship of the final rule to the proposed rule in light of the comments received. We now move on to the statement of basis and purpose itself, and particularly its relationship to the public comment period. To what comments must an agency respond, and what kind of explanations must it give, in its statement of basis and purpose?

United States v. Nova Scotia Food Products Corp.

568 F.2d 240 (2d Cir. 1977)

GURFEIN, CIRCUIT JUDGE:

This . . . is an appeal from a judgment of the District Court for the Eastern District of New York . . . enjoining the appellants, after a hearing, from processing hot smoked whitefish except in accordance with time-temperature-salinity (T-T-S) regulations . . . . Appellant Nova Scotia receives frozen or iced whitefish in interstate commerce which it processes by brining, smoking and cooking. The fish are then sold as smoked whitefish.

The regulations cited above require that hot-process smoked fish be heated by a controlled heat process that provides a monitoring system positioned in as many strategic locations in the oven as necessary to assure a continuous temperature through each fish of not less than 180°F. for a minimum of 30 minutes for fish which have been brined to contain 3.5% Water phase salt or at 150°F. for a minimum of 30 minutes if the salinity was at 5% Water phase. Since each fish must meet these requirements, it is necessary to heat an entire batch of fish to even higher temperatures so that the lowest temperature for any fish will meet the minimum requirements.

Government inspection of appellants' plant established without question that the minimum T-T-S requirements were not being met. There is no substantial claim that the plant was processing whitefish under "insanitary conditions" in any other material respect. Appellants, on their part, do not defend on the ground that they were in compliance, but rather that the requirements could not be met if a marketable whitefish was to be produced. They defend upon the grounds that the regulation is invalid . . . because there was no adequate statement setting forth the basis of the regulation. We . . . find serious inadequacies in the procedure followed in the promulgation of the regulation and hold it to be invalid as applied to the appellants herein.

The hazard which the FDA sought to minimize was the outgrowth and toxin formation of Clostridium botulinum Type E spores of the bacteria which sometimes inhabit fish. There had been an occurrence of several cases of botulism traced to consumption of fish from inland waters in 1960 and 1963 which stimulated considerable bacteriological research. These bacteria can be present in the soil and water of various regions. They can invade fish in their natural habitat and can be further disseminated in the course of evisceration and preparation of the fish for cooking. A failure to destroy such spores through an adequate brining, thermal, and refrigeration process was found to be dangerous to public health.

The Commissioner of Food and Drugs ("Commissioner"), employing informal "notice-and-comment" procedures . . . issued a proposal for the control of C. botulinum bacteria Type E in fish. . . . Responding to the Commissioner's invitation in the notice of proposed rulemaking, members of the industry, including appellants and the intervenor-appellant, submitted comments on the proposed regulation.

The Commissioner thereafter issued the final regulations in which he adopted certain suggestions made in the comments, including a suggestion by the National Fisheries Institute, Inc. ("the Institute"), the intervenor herein. The original proposal provided that the fish would have to be cooked to a temperature of 180°F. for at least 30 minutes, if the fish have been brined to contain 3.5% Water phase salt, with no alternative. In the final regulation, an alternative suggested by the intervenor "that the parameter of 150°F. for 30 minutes and 5% Salt in the water phase be established as an alternate procedure to that stated in the proposed regulation for an interim period until specific parameters can be established" was accepted, but as a permanent part of the regulation rather than for an interim period.

The intervenor suggested that "specific parameters" be established. This referred to particular processing parameters for different species of fish on a "species by species" basis. Such "species by species" determination was proposed not only by the intervenor but also by the Bureau of Commercial Fisheries of the Department of the Interior. That Bureau objected to the general application of the T-T-S requirement proposed by the FDA on the ground that application of the regulation to all species of fish being smoked was not commercially feasible, and that the regulation should therefore specify time-temperature-salinity requirements, as developed by research and study, on a species-by-species basis. The Bureau suggested that "wholesomeness considerations could be more practically and adequately realized by reducing processing temperature and using suitable concentrations of nitrite and salt." The Commissioner took cognizance of the suggestion, but decided, nevertheless, to impose the T-T-S requirement on all species of fish (except chub, which were regulated by 21 C.F.R. 172.177 (1977) (dealing with food additives)).

He did acknowledge, however, in his "basis and purpose" statement required by the Administrative Procedure Act ("APA"), that "adequate times, temperatures and salt concentrations have not been demonstrated for each individual species of fish presently smoked." The Commissioner concluded, nevertheless, that "the processing requirements of the proposed regulations are the safest now known to prevent the outgrowth and toxin formation of C. botulinum Type E." He determined that "the conditions of current good manufacturing practice for this industry should be established without further delay."

The Commissioner did not answer the suggestion by the Bureau of Fisheries that nitrite and salt as additives could safely lower the high temperature otherwise required, a solution which the FDA had accepted in the case of chub. Nor did the Commissioner respond to the claim of Nova Scotia . . . that "(t)he proposed process requirements suggested by the FDA for hot processed smoked fish are neither commercially feasible nor based on sound scientific evidence obtained with the variety of smoked fish products to be included under this regulation."

Nova Scotia, in its own comment, wrote to the Commissioner that "the heating of certain types of fish to high temperatures will completely destroy the product." It suggested, as an alternative, that "specific processing procedures could be established for each species after adequate work and experimention (sic) has been done but not before." We have noted above that the response given by the Commissioner was in general terms. He did not specifically aver that the T-T-S requirements as applied to whitefish were, in fact, commercially feasible. . . .

      * * *

The key issues were (1) whether, in the light of the rather scant history of botulism in whitefish, that species should have been considered separately rather than included in a general regulation which failed to distinguish species from species; (2) whether the application of the proposed T-T-S requirements to smoked whitefish made the whitefish commercially unsaleable; and (3) whether the agency recognized that prospect, but nevertheless decided that the public health needs should prevail even if that meant commercial death for the whitefish industry. The procedural issue [is] whether, in the light of these key questions, the agency procedure was inadequate because . . . it failed utterly to address itself to the pertinent question of commercial feasibility. . . .

Between 1899 and 1964 there were only eight cases of botulism reported as attributable to hot-smoked whitefish. In all eight instances, vacuum-packed whitefish was involved. All of the eight cases occurred in 1960 and 1963. The industry has abandoned vacuum-packing, and there has not been a single case of botulism associated with commercially prepared whitefish since 1963, though 2,750,000 pounds of whitefish are processed annually. Thus, in the seven-year period from 1964 through 1970, 17.25 million pounds of whitefish have been commercially processed in the United States without a single reported case of botulism. The evidence also disclosed that defendant Nova Scotia has been in business some 56 years, and that there has never been a case of botulism illness from the whitefish processed by it. . . .

Appellants additionally attack the "concise general statement" required by APA, 5 U.S.C. § 553, as inadequate. We think that, in the circumstances, it was less than adequate. It is not in keeping with the rational process to leave vital questions, raised by comments which are of cogent materiality, completely unanswered. The agencies certainly have a good deal of discretion in expressing the basis of a rule, but the agencies do not have quite the prerogative of obscurantism reserved to legislatures. . . .

The test of adequacy of the "concise general statement" was expressed by Judge McGowan in the following terms:

> We do not expect the agency to discuss every item of fact or opinion included in the submissions made to it in informal rulemaking. We do expect that, if the judicial review which Congress has thought it important to provide is to be meaningful, the 'concise general statement of . . . basis and purpose' mandated by Section 4 will enable us to see what major issues of policy were ventilated by the informal proceedings and why the agency reacted to them as it did.

Automotive Parts & Accessories Ass'n v. Boyd, 407 F.2d 330, 338 (D.C. Cir. 1968). . . .

The Secretary was squarely faced with the question whether it was necessary to formulate a rule with specific parameters that applied to all species of fish, and particularly whether lower temperatures with the addition of nitrite and salt would not be sufficient. Though this alternative was suggested by an agency of the federal government, its suggestion, though acknowledged, was never answered.

Moreover, the comment that to apply the proposed T-T-S requirements to whitefish would destroy the commercial product was neither discussed nor answered. We think that to sanction silence in the face of such vital questions would be to make the statutory requirement of a "concise general statement" less than an adequate safeguard against arbitrary decision-making.

We cannot improve on the statement of the District of Columbia Circuit in Industrial Union Dep't, AFL-CIO v. Hodgson, 499 F.2d 467, 475 (D.C. Cir. 1974):

> What we are entitled to at all events is a careful identification by the Secretary, when his proposed standards are challenged, of the reasons why he chooses to follow one course rather than another. Where that choice purports to be based on the existence of certain determinable facts, the Secretary must, in form as well as in substance, find those facts from evidence in the record. By the same token, when the Secretary is obliged to make policy judgments where no factual certainties exist or where facts alone do not provide the answer, he should so state and go on to identify the considerations he found to be persuasive.

One may recognize that even commercial infeasibility cannot stand in the way of an overwhelming public interest. Yet the administrative process should disclose, at least, whether the proposed regulation is considered to be commercially feasible, or whether other considerations prevail even if commercial infeasibility is acknowledged. This kind of forthright disclosure and basic statement was lacking in the formulation of the T-T-S standard made applicable to whitefish. It is easy enough for an administrator to ban everything. In the regulation of food processing, the worldwide need for food also must be taken into account in formulating measures taken for the protection of health. In the light of the history of smoked whitefish to which we have referred, we find no articulate balancing here sufficient to make the procedure followed less than arbitrary. . . .

We hold in this enforcement proceeding, therefore, that the regulation, as it affects non-vacuum-packed hot-smoked whitefish, was promulgated in an arbitrary manner and is invalid. . . .

Notes and Questions

1.   Summary. Agencies are often inundated with comments over the course of a rulemaking. Must the agency respond to *every* comment? If not, to which ones must it respond? The APA says the agency must consider "relevant" comments. The *Nova Scotia* court held that the agency must respond to comments of "cogent materiality." How do we know if a comment is of cogent materiality? Was *Nova Scotia* an easy case in this regard?

2.   Arbitrary and capricious review. The court in *Nova Scotia* seems to combine two different administrative law tests. We have not yet learned about judicial review of the scope and substance of agency actions, but to enforce the APA's

> **CROSS REFERENCE** We will encounter "arbitrary and capricious" review of agency actions in Chapter 4. Section 706(a)(2) of the APA provides that a reviewing court shall "set aside agency action . . . found to be . . . arbitrary, capricious, an abuse of discretion, or otherwise not in accordance with law."
>
> Was the agency in *Nova Scotia* arbitrary and capricious in addition to violating the provision of § 553 that requires agencies to consider "relevant" comments?

mandate to set aside agency actions that are "arbitrary and capricious" the courts require agencies to develop a reviewable administrative record and to "show their work." In the words of the Supreme Court,

> To make this finding [whether the agency has been arbitrary and capricious] the court must consider whether the decision was based on a consideration of the relevant factors and whether there has been a clear error of judgment. Although this inquiry into the facts is to be searching and careful, the ultimate standard of review is a narrow one. The court is not empowered to substitute its judgment for that of the agency.

Citizens to Pres. Overton Park, Inc. v. Volpe, 401 U.S. 402, 416 (1971) (citations omitted). Over a decade later, the Court elaborated:

> The scope of review under the "arbitrary and capricious" standard is narrow and a court is not to substitute its judgment for that of the agency. Nevertheless, the agency must examine the relevant data and articulate a satisfactory explanation for its action including a "rational connection between the facts found and the choice made." In

reviewing that explanation, we must "consider whether the decision was based on a consideration of the relevant factors and whether there has been a clear error of judgment." Normally, an agency rule would be arbitrary and capricious if the agency has relied on factors which Congress has not intended it to consider, entirely failed to consider an important aspect of the problem, offered an explanation for its decision that runs counter to the evidence before the agency, or is so implausible that it could not be ascribed to a difference in view or the product of agency expertise.

Motor Vehicle Mfrs. Ass'n of U.S., Inc. v. State Farm Mut. Auto. Ins. Co., 463 U.S. 29, 43 (1983).

We will revisit both *Overton Park* and *State Farm* in the chapter on judicial review. But for now, does it appear to you that the various tests described in this chapter are simply manifestations of the broader *Overton Park/State Farm* standard? Are they simply offshoots of arbitrary-and-capricious review? After all, if the agency has to show its work, i.e., show that it considered the relevant factors, considered the relevant evidence, and gave explanations for its decisions, then surely it must also respond to relevant comments—after all, that's what the APA requires.

5. Disclosing Data

Taking into consideration the three requirements of the informal rulemaking process—the notice, the opportunity to comment, and the concise statement of basis and purpose—we now address the following two questions. First, does the agency have to disclose the data on which it relies in coming to a decision? Second, does the agency have to disclose ex parte contacts?

This section addresses the first of these questions. In a case called *Portland Cement*, the D.C. Circuit held that "[i]t is not consonant with the purpose of a rule-making proceeding to promulgate rules on the basis of inadequate data, or on data that, critical degree, is known only to the agency." Portland Cement Ass'n v. Ruckelshaus, 486 F.2d 375, 393 (D.C. Cir. 1973). The requirement to disclose data on which the agency relies in coming up with a proposed rule is still good law and is routinely invoked.

The APA, however, does not obviously require the disclosure of data; so long as the agency gives notice of the proposed rule and allows the public a chance to comment on it—and for private groups to provide their own data if they wish—then the requirements of the APA have arguably been met. Indeed, do participants in the rulemaking process really have any grounds to complain if an agency relies on information that it alone possesses, so long as they had an opportunity to provide their own comments and the agency had to respond to them? In the following case, the D.C. Circuit

FOR DISCUSSION Does the APA require the disclosure of data? What arguments can you make for and against? *Should* agencies be required to disclose data on which they rely?

reaffirmed the rule to require disclosure of data, but then-Judge Kavanaugh noted the potential inconsistency of this rule with the strictures of *Vermont Yankee*.

American Radio Relay League, Inc. v. FCC

524 F.3d 227 (D.C. Cir. 2008)

ROGERS, CIRCUIT JUDGE:

The American Radio Relay League, Inc., petitions on behalf of licensed amateur radio operators for review of two orders of the Federal Communications Commission promulgating a rule to regulate the use of the radio spectrum by Access Broadband over Power Line ("Access BPL") operators. The Commission concluded that existing safeguards combined with new protective measures required by the rule will prevent harmful interference to licensees from Access BPL radio emissions. The League challenges this conclusion, contending that the Commission has abandoned decades of precedent requiring shut-down and other protections for licensees and that the rule is substantively and procedurally flawed. We grant the petition in part and remand the rule to the Commission. The Commission failed to satisfy the notice and comment requirements of the Administrative Procedure Act ("APA") by redacting studies on which it relied in promulgating the rule and failed to provide a reasoned explanation for its choice of the extrapolation factor for measuring Access BPL emissions.

I

Under section 301 of the Communications Act, the owners and operators of "any apparatus for the transmission of energy or communications or signals by radio" are required to obtain a license as a condition of operation and they may not use or operate any such apparatus, for instance, "when interference is caused by such use or operation with the transmission of such energy, communications, or signals." 47 U.S.C. § 301. Section 302 of the Act authorizes the Commission, "consistent with the public interest, convenience, and necessity," to promulgate regulations for manufacture and use governing "the interference potential of devices which in their operation are capable of emitting radio frequency energy . . . in sufficient degree to cause harmful interference to radio communications." Id. § 302a(a). The Commission's rules, specifically Part 15, define "harmful interference" as "[a]ny emission, radiation or induction that endangers the functioning of a radio navigation service or of other safety services or seriously degrades, obstructs or repeatedly interrupts a radiocommunications service." . . .

The Commission, upon concluding that "the introduction of new high-speed [Access] BPL technologies warrants a systematic review of the Part 15 rules in order to facilitate the deployment of this new technology, promote consistency in the rules and ensure the ongoing protection of the licensed radio services," issued a notice of inquiry. Therein it stated that in the process of Access BPL transmission, devices installed along electric power lines transmit radio frequency energy over the 1.7–80 MHz spectrum, creating potential to interfere with the ability of nearby radio operators to send and receive signals on the same frequencies. Licensed radio operators on this part of the spectrum include public safety and federal government agencies, aeronautical navigation, maritime, radio-astronomy, citizen band radio, and amateur radio operators. Subsequently, in announcing a proposed rule, the Commission stated that its policy was to "promote and foster the development of [the] new technology [Access BPL] with its concomitant benefits while at the same time ensuring that existing licensed operations are protected from harmful interference."

In the final rule the Commission defined Access BPL and set technical and administrative requirements to protect licensed radio operators from harmful interference. To protect licensed operators, the rule requires Access BPL manufacturers and operators to comply with certification requirements and emission limits, and establishes a nationwide database of Access BPL operations in order to facilitate identification of a source of interference and its resolution. Access BPL operations also must have the capability, from a central location, to reduce or "notch" operating power, to avoid or adjust frequencies, and to shut down segments of their operations entirely when necessary to resolve licensees' complaints of "harmful interference." To protect government, aeronautical, and public safety operations, Access BPL operators must avoid certain frequencies and certain geographic areas, notify and consult with public safety users before beginning operations, and resolve public safety users' complaints of harmful interference within 24 hours. The Commission retained the existing extrapolation factor of 40 decibels ("dB") per decade for frequencies below 30 MHz to measure Access BPL emissions and any resulting interference.

The Commission acknowledged that "some cases of harmful interference may be possible from Access BPL emissions at levels up to the Part 15 limits" but it was satisfied that "the benefits of Access BPL service warrant acceptance of a small and manageable degree of interference risk." The Commission concluded that the risk of such harmful interference was "low." Regarding mobile operations, such as amateur radios in automobiles, the Commission concluded that the requirement that Access BPL operators "notch" their emitted power to a level at least 20 dB below emission limits on a frequency band would be "generally . . . sufficient to resolve any harmful interference that might occur to mobile operations." The Commission referenced its findings that "[only] low signal levels [are] allowed under the Part 15 emission limits" and that "a mobile transceiver can readily be re-positioned to provide some separation from the Access BPL operation."

In reaching its "low"-likelihood conclusion, the Commission stated that "[t]he record and our investigations indicate that [Access] BPL network systems can generally be configured and managed to minimize and/or eliminate . . . harmful interference potential [to licensed radio services]." The Commission also relied on "information provided by our field tests," "our own field measurements of Access BPL installations," and "our own field testing." Following issuance of the *NOI,* the League sought disclosure under the Freedom of Information Act ("FOIA") of the Commission's studies related to Access BPL systems. The Commission denied that request except as to one document that it placed in the record in the fall of 2003. When the League filed a second FOIA request citing the *Order,* the Commission released five studies in redacted form and made them part of the record in December 2004 after the rule was promulgated. The Commission stated that "[t]hese documents comprise internally-generated information upon which the Commission relied, in part, in reaching its determination." . . .

II

. . . . The League contends that . . . because "[t]he lynchpin" of the rule "is a series of studies conducted by the [Commission's] engineers" that have never been made available in unredacted form, their non-disclosure violates the APA's notice and comment requirements. . . .

The APA requires an agency to publish "notice" of "either the terms or substance of the proposed rule or a description of the subjects and issues involved," in order to "give interested persons an opportunity to participate in the rule making through submission of written data, views, or arguments," and then, "[a]fter consideration of the relevant matter presented, the agency shall incorporate in the rules adopted a concise general statement of their basis and purpose." 5 U.S.C. § 553(b)–(c). Longstanding precedent instructs that "[n]otice is sufficient 'if it affords interested parties a reasonable opportunity to participate in the rulemaking process,' and if the parties have not been 'deprived of the opportunity to present relevant information by lack of notice that the issue was there.' "

Under APA notice and comment requirements, "[a]mong the information that must be revealed for public evaluation are the 'technical studies and data' upon which the agency relies [in its rulemaking]." Construing section 553 of the APA, the court explained long ago that "[i]n order to allow for useful criticism, it is especially important for the agency to identify and make available *technical studies and data* that it has employed in reaching the decisions to propose particular rules." *Conn. Light & Power Co. v. Nuclear Regulatory Comm'n,* 673 F.2d 525, 530 (D.C. Cir. 1982) (emphasis added). More particularly, "[d]isclosure of *staff reports* allows the parties to focus on the information relied on by the agency and to point out where that information is erroneous or where the agency may be drawing improper conclusions from it."

. . . . Enforcing the APA's notice and comment requirements ensures that an agency does not "fail[ ] to reveal portions of the technical basis for a proposed rule in time to allow for meaningful commentary" so that "a genuine interchange" occurs rather than "allow[ing] an agency to play hunt the peanut with technical information, hiding or disguising the information that it employs." *Conn. Light & Power Co.*, 673 F.2d at 530–31. . . .

At issue are five scientific studies consisting of empirical data gathered from field tests performed by the Office of Engineering and Technology. . . .

It would appear to be a fairly obvious proposition that studies upon which an agency relies in promulgating a rule must be made available during the rulemaking in order to afford interested persons meaningful notice and an opportunity for comment. "It is not consonant with the purpose of a rule-making proceeding to promulgate rules on the basis of inadequate data, or on data that, [to a] critical degree, is known only to the agency." *Portland Cement Ass'n*, 486 F.2d at 393. Where, as here, an agency's determination "is based upon 'a complex mix of controversial and uncommented upon data and calculations,' " there is no APA precedent allowing an agency to cherry-pick a study on which it has chosen to rely in part. . . .

The narrowness of our holding under section 553 of the APA is manifest. The redacted studies consist of staff-prepared scientific data that the Commission's partial reliance made "critical factual material." The Commission has chosen to rely on the data in those studies and to place the redacted studies in the rulemaking record. Individual pages relied upon by the Commission reveal that the unredacted portions are likely to contain evidence that could call into question the Commission's decision to promulgate the rule. Under the circumstances, the Commission can point to no authority allowing it to rely on the studies in a rulemaking but hide from the public parts of the studies that may contain contrary evidence, inconvenient qualifications, or relevant explanations of the methodology employed. The Commission has not suggested that any other confidentiality considerations would be implicated were the unredacted studies made public for notice and comment. The Commission also has not suggested that the redacted portions of the studies contain only "supplementary information" merely "clarify[ing], expand[ing], or amend[ing] other data that has been offered for comment." Of course, it is within the Commission's prerogative to credit only certain parts of the studies. But what it did here was redact parts of those studies that are inextricably bound to the studies as a whole and thus to the data upon which the Commission has stated it relied, parts that explain the otherwise unidentified methodology underlying data cited by the Commission for its conclusions, and parts that signal caution about that data.

This is a critical distinction and no precedent sanctions such a "hide and seek" application of the APA's notice and comment requirements.

As our colleague notes, in *Vermont Yankee Nuclear Power Corp. v. Natural Resources Defense Council*, 435 U.S. 519, 98 S. Ct. 1197, 55 L.Ed.2d 460 (1978), the Supreme Court has limited the extent that a court may order additional agency procedures, but the procedures invalidated in *Vermont Yankee* were not anchored to any statutory provision. By contrast, the court does not impose any new procedures for the regulatory process, but merely applies settled law to the facts. The Commission made the choice to engage in notice-and-comment rulemaking and to rely on parts of its redacted studies as a basis for the rule. The court, consequently, is not imposing new procedures but enforcing the agency's procedural choice by ensuring that it conforms to APA requirements. It is one thing for the Commission to give notice and make available for comment the studies on which it relied in formulating the rule while explaining its non-reliance on certain parts. It is quite another thing to provide notice and an opportunity for comment on only those parts of the studies that the Commission likes best. . . .

Tatel, Circuit Judge, concurring:

I write separately to emphasize that in my view, the disclosure ordered by the court . . . is particularly important because the Commission's failure to turn over the unredacted studies undermines this court's ability to perform the review function APA section 706 demands. That provision requires us to set aside arbitrary and capricious agency action after reviewing "the whole record," 5 U.S.C. § 706, and the "whole record" in this case includes the complete content of the staff reports the Commission relied upon in promulgating the challenged rule.

We described the APA's "whole record" requirement . . . . [a discussion of previous cases is omitted—Ed.] A similar situation confronts us here. Given that the Commission relied on the studies at issue, there can be no doubt that they form part of the administrative record—a proposition unaffected by the Commission's claim that it chose not to rely on various parts of the studies. Nor is there any doubt that, as our case law makes clear, the APA means exactly what it says: an agency must make the "*whole* record" available, especially where, as here, the undisclosed portions might very well undercut the agency's ultimate decision.

This conclusion makes sense given that in the context of the APA, arbitrary and capricious review and the substantial evidence test " 'are one and the same' insofar as the requisite degree of evidentiary support is concerned." Because "[t]he substantiality of evidence must take into account whatever in the record fairly detracts from its weight," for petitioners to mount a substantial evidence challenge, and for us to resolve it in any meaningful sense, agencies must disclose information that appears to "fairly detract [ ] from [the] weight" of the evidence. . . . Contrary to the Commission's claim that petitioner's substantial evidence argument would compel the agency to "make available for public comment every internal document in its entirety that the agency's staff prepares relating to a rule making proceeding," APA section 706 requires disclosure only of staff studies relied upon by the agency and thus contained in the record. Agencies retain discretion to craft staff reports and studies as they see fit, or to exclude such studies from the record altogether simply by declining to rely on them. Under the Commission's view, however, an agency could redact from studies on which it expressly relies *any* evidence that "fairly detracts" from a proposed rule, thereby evading its obligation to account for contrary record evidence. . . .

This is hardly a novel conclusion. In previous informal rulemaking cases, we ordered additional agency disclosures to facilitate meaningful arbitrary and capricious review of agency action. . . .

Kavanaugh, Circuit Judge, concurring in part, concurring in the judgment in part, and dissenting in part.

To expand consumer access to broadband Internet services, increase competition against DSL and cable modem providers, and lower prices for consumers, the FCC adopted a rule to facilitate the use of electric power lines for broadband Internet access. The petitioner, an organization of amateur radio operators, has challenged this "Access Broadband Over Power Line Systems" rule. I agree with the majority opinion that the FCC's rule complies with the Communications Act.

Applying the Administrative Procedure Act and our *Portland Cement* line of decisions, however, the majority opinion remands for the FCC to release redacted portions of certain FCC staff documents analyzing field tests of broadband over power lines. In light of our precedents, I concur in the judgment on this point; but I write separately because of concerns about our case law in this area. . . .

In issuing its rule, the FCC relied on various technical studies, including an NTIA report; the various interference studies filed in the record, including petitioner's studies; and the unredacted portions of certain internal FCC staff studies. The FCC publicly disclosed all those materials. But the Commission did not release certain redacted portions of the internal staff studies on which it relied. Citing § 553 of the APA, petitioner says the FCC must release the redacted portions of the staff studies so that interested parties can comment on them and so the FCC, in turn, can consider those comments.

Petitioner's argument would be unavailing if analyzed solely under the text of APA § 553. The APA requires only that an agency provide public notice and a comment period before the agency issues a rule. *See* 5 U.S.C. § 553. The notice must include "the terms *or* substance of the proposed rule or a description of the subjects and issues involved." § 553(b)(3) (emphasis added). After issuing a notice and allowing time for interested persons to comment, the agency must issue a "concise general statement" of the rule's "basis and purpose" along with the final rule. § 553(c). One searches the text of APA § 553 in vain for a requirement that an agency disclose other agency information as part of the notice or later in the rulemaking process.

But beginning with the *Portland Cement* case in 1973—which was decided in an era when this Court created several procedural requirements not rooted in the text of the APA—our precedents have required agencies to disclose, in time to allow for meaningful comment, technical data or studies on which they relied in formulating proposed rules. . . .

I write separately to underscore that *Portland Cement* stands on a shaky legal foundation (even though it may make sense as a policy matter in some cases). Put bluntly, the *Portland Cement* doctrine cannot be squared with the text of § 553 of the APA. And *Portland Cement*'s lack of roots in the statutory text creates a serious jurisprudential problem because the Supreme Court later rejected this kind of freeform interpretation of the APA. In its landmark *Vermont Yankee* decision, which came a few years after *Portland Cement*, the Supreme Court forcefully stated that the text of the APA binds courts: Section 553 of the APA "established the *maximum procedural requirements* which Congress was willing to have the courts impose upon agencies in conducting rulemaking procedures." *Vermont Yankee Nuclear Power Corp. v. Natural Res. Def. Council, Inc.,* 435 U.S. 519, 524, 98 S. Ct. 1197, 55 L.Ed.2d 460 (1978) (emphasis added); *see also* Antonin Scalia, Vermont Yankee: *The APA, the D.C. Circuit, and the Supreme Court,* 1978 Sup. Ct. Rev. 345, 395–96 (*Vermont Yankee* was "a major watershed. It has put to rest the notion that the courts have a continuing 'common-law' authority to impose procedures not required by the Constitution in the areas covered by the APA.").

Because there is "nothing in the bare text of § 553 that could remotely give rise" to the *Portland Cement* requirement, some commentators argue that *Portland Cement* is "a violation of the basic principle of *Vermont Yankee* that Congress and the agencies, but not the courts, have the power to decide on proper agency procedures." At the very least, others say, the Supreme Court's decision in *Vermont Yankee* raises "a question concerning the continuing vitality of the *Portland Cement* requirement that an agency provide public notice of the data on which it proposes to rely in a rulemaking."

I do not believe *Portland Cement* is consistent with the text of the APA or Vermont Yankee. In the wake of *Vermont Yankee,* however, this Court has repeatedly continued to apply *Portland Cement* (albeit without analyzing the tension between *Vermont Yankee* and *Portland Cement*). In these circumstances, this three-judge panel must accept *Portland Cement* as binding precedent and must require the FCC to disclose the redacted portions of its staff studies. . . .

The two issues on which I write separately prompt a broader observation. In appropriate cases or controversies, courts of course must be vigilant in ensuring that agencies adhere to the plain text of statutes imposing substantive and procedural obligations. . . . Over time, those twin lines of decisions have gradually transformed rulemaking—whether regulatory or deregulatory rulemaking—from the simple and speedy practice contemplated by the APA into a laborious, seemingly never-ending process. The judicially created obstacle course can hinder Executive Branch agencies from rapidly and effectively responding to changing or emerging issues within their authority, such as consumer access to broadband, or effectuating policy or philosophical changes in the Executive's approach to the subject matter at hand. The trend has not been good as a jurisprudential matter, and it continues to have significant practical consequences for the operation of the Federal Government and those affected by federal regulation and deregulation.

Notes and Questions

1. ***Three views of data disclosure.*** The three opinions in the *American Radio Relay League* case take three different approaches to the question of disclosing data. Judge Rogers' opinion argues that disclosure is the only way for the public meaningfully to participate in the notice-and-comment process. This can be seen as judicial glosses on the notice and public participation requirements of the APA. Take a look at the text of APA § 553. Do you agree that the requirement to disclose data is a valid interpretation of the statutory provisions requiring notice and opportunity to comment?

Judge Kavanaugh, in contrast, argues that nothing in the text requires the disclosure of data. Put another way, so long as the proposed rule is in fact published and the public does in fact have an opportunity to comment, nothing should preclude the agency also from relying on other data in its possession even if it does not disclose that data. Is this view more persuasive than Judge Rogers'? Doesn't it seem counterintuitive to require agencies to undergo notice and comment and at the same time to make decisions on the basis of data and information completely apart from that process?

Judge Tatel takes a different tack. Although we have not yet encountered the material on judicial review, the APA requires courts to set aside agency actions that are "arbitrary and capricious," and this review must be made on the "whole record." Because the agency has "relied" on the studies, Tatel argues, they form a part of the "record." Is that persuasive? Or is it question-begging? Ask yourself the following: If an agency official is influenced by something she saw on the nightly news the day before, must she disclose that as part of the "record"? What if she had a fleeting thought about the matter as she was going about her daily business? What if a friend made a comment to her about a tangentially related matter but which subtly affected her views on the rulemaking? Don't these hypotheticals tend to show that what constitutes the "whole record" is *not* everything the agency relies upon, but merely the *record required by law*? And here, the required record is nothing but the rulemaking record?

Maybe Judge Tatel could have made a slightly different argument. As we shall see when we encounter the "arbitrary and capricious" standard of APA § 706(2)(a) in the context of informal adjudications, courts have interpreted that standard to require agencies to create an administrative record sufficient for the courts to review under this standard. If an agency does not disclose the data on which it relies, how can a court determine if the agency action is arbitrary or not? Is this a more promising argument for requiring the disclosure of data?

2. ***Distinguishing closed, "on the record" proceedings.*** Another issue related to Judge Tatel's opinion is the distinction between informal rulemakings and adjudications and formal rulemakings and adjudications. You may recall that a key distinction between the two types of proceedings is that formal rulemakings and adjudications have to be made on a *closed* record. The implications is that an agency, in informal proceedings, can make its policy decisions on the basis of whatever knowledge and experience is available to it—whether or not there has been public comment on any specific knowledge or experience. As the Attorney General Manual on the Administrative Procedure Act explained, in the informal as opposed to formal rulemaking process, "an agency is free to formulate rules upon the basis of materials in its files and the knowledge and experience of the agency, in addition to the materials adduced in public rule making proceedings." U.S. Dep't of Justice, Att'y General's Manual on the Admin. Proc. Act 31–32 (1947). Is this contemporaneous evidence that an agency may rely on data and anything else in its files for that matter in formulating a rule, so long as it *also* considers the relevant comments it receives through the notice-and-comment process?

3. ***What is "reliance"?*** Despite the potential inconsistency with the text of the APA, it is still black-letter law that agencies must disclose data on which they "rely." This raises the question: what is *reliance*? If the agency conducts a nonpublic study which militates against a particular rule, but the agency chooses to ignore the study for whatever reason, has the agency "relied" on that study if it goes ahead with the rule? It's hard to say. Perhaps *American Radio Relay League* is an easy case: the agency disclosed the good parts of studies on which it relied, but withheld the bad parts.

4. ***Regulatory Accountability Act.*** There have been proposals to amend the APA to require the disclosure of technical data on which the agency relies. The Regulatory Accountability Act of 2017 (Senate Bill 951) is one example. It is important to note, additionally and as

 PRACTICE POINTER It is worth recalling the role of Congress in both organic statutes and the APA. Can you recommend any legislation for amending the APA? Should the APA explicitly require the disclosure of data?

always, that there are already organic statutes out there that deviate from the requirements of the APA. The Clean Air Act of 1970 specifically requires the EPA to docket factual data and methodologies it uses when promulgating rules. 42 U.S.C. § 7607(d)(3).

6. Ex Parte Communications

Another issue that arises under the three informal rulemaking components is the question of *ex parte* contacts—off-the-record contacts between the agency and interested private parties and/or political officials elsewhere in the Executive Branch or in Congress. Does the agency have to disclose such contacts as part of the APA's notice requirement? The following leading case was decided under amendments to the Clean Air Act, but applies just as well to the APA. As you read the case, ask yourself what you make of the fact that agencies must disclose data on which they rely, but not ex parte communications. Are these inconsistent? Would a better rule be that agencies have to disclose both, or disclose neither?

Defined Term

EX PARTE CONTACTS: These are off-the-record contacts between the agency and an interested party or official.

Sierra Club v. Costle

657 F.2d 298 (D.C. Cir. 1981)

Wald, Circuit Judge:

This case concerns the extent to which new coal-fired steam generators that produce electricity must control their emissions of sulfur dioxide and particulate matter into the air. In June of 1979 EPA [the Environmental Protection Agency] revised the regulations called "new source performance standards" ("NSPS" or "standards") governing emission control by coal burning power plants. On this appeal we consider challenges to the revised NSPS brought by environmental groups which contend that the standards are too lax and by electric utilities which contend that the standards are too rigorous. Together these petitioners present an array of statutory, substantive, and procedural grounds for overturning the challenged standards. For the reasons stated below, we hold that EPA did not exceed its statutory authority under the Clean Air Act in promulgating the NSPS, and we decline to set aside the standards. . . .

The Clean Air Act provides for direct federal regulation of emissions from new stationary sources of air pollution by authorizing EPA to set performance standards for significant sources of air pollution which may be reasonably anticipated to endanger public health or welfare. In June 1979 EPA promulgated the NSPS involved in this case. The new standards increase pollution controls for new coal-fired electric power plants by tightening restrictions on emissions of sulfur dioxide and particulate matter. Sulfur dioxide emissions are limited to a maximum of 1.2 lbs./MBtu (or 520 ng/j) and a 90 percent reduction of potential uncontrolled sulfur dioxide emissions is required except when emissions to the atmosphere are less than 0.60 lbs./MBtu (or 260 ng/j). When sulfur dioxide emissions are less than 0.60 lbs./MBtu potential emissions must be reduced by no less than 70 percent. In addition, emissions of particulate matter are limited to 0.03 lbs./MBtu (or 13 ng/j).

* * *

EPA proposed and ultimately adopted a 1.2 lbs./MBtu ceiling for total sulfur dioxide emissions which is applicable regardless of the percentage of sulfur dioxide reduction attained. The 1.2 lbs./MBtu standard is identical to the emission ceiling required by the former standard. The achievability of the standard is undisputed.

EDF [Environmental Defense Fund] challenges this part of the final NSPS on procedural grounds, contending that although there may be evidence supporting the 1.2 lbs./MBtu standard, EPA should have and would have adopted a stricter standard if it had not engaged in post-comment period irregularities and succumbed to political pressures. EDF raises its procedural objections in the context of its view that a more stringent emission ceiling would have been better than the 1.2 lbs./MBtu limit because it would decrease total emissions significantly without impeding the production or use of coal. Although the substantive validity of the 1.2 lbs./MBtu standard is not before the court, it is not possible to evaluate EDF's procedural argument without first examining the evolution of the standard and EPA's explanation for adopting the emission ceiling.

A. EPA's Rationale for the Emission Ceiling

EPA explained in the preamble to the proposed rule that two primary factors were considered in selecting the 1.2 lbs./MBtu ceiling: FGD ["flue gas desulfurization"] performance, and the impact of the ceiling on high sulfur coal reserves. EPA further explained that it had considered whether to propose a 1.2 lbs./MBtu limitation with and without three exemptions per month. EPA's modeling analysis showed that under either option there would be no significant differences in total national production and there would be sufficient reserves available to satisfy national demand for coal. However, EPA predicted that on a regional basis a 1.2 lbs./MBtu ceiling without exemptions would adversely affect the Midwest. Consequently, EPA proposed that the emission limitation should have three exemptions but solicited comments on the level of the emission limit and the appropriateness of the 3 day exemption.

Following the September 1978 proposal the joint interagency working group investigated options lower than the 1.2 lbs./MBtu ceiling, according to EPA, in order "to take full advantage of the cost effectiveness benefits of a joint coal washing/scrubbing strategy on high-sulfur coal." The joint working group reasoned that since coal washing is relatively inexpensive, an emission ceiling which would require 90 percent scrubbing in addition to coal washing "could substantially reduce emissions in the East and Midwest at a relatively low cost." Since coal washing is a widespread practice, it was thought that the 1.2 lbs./MBtu proposal would not have a seriously detrimental impact upon Eastern coal production. During phase two EPA analyzed 10 different full control and partial control options with its econometric model. These various options included emission ceilings at the 1.2 lbs./MBtu, 0.80 lbs./MBtu and the 0.55 lbs./MBtu levels. The modeling results, published before the close of the public comment period in December 1978, confirmed the joint working group's conclusion that the 1.2 lbs./MBtu standard should be lowered. The results of the phase two modeling exercise were cited by internal EPA memoranda in January and March 1979 as a basis for lowering the 1.2 lbs./MBtu standard. After the phase two modeling, however, EPA undertook "a more detailed analysis of regional coal production impacts," using BOM [Bureau of Mines] seam by seam data on the sulfur content of the reserves and the coal washing potential for those reserves. This analysis identified the amount of reserves that would require more than 90 percent scrubbing of washed coal to meet alternative ceilings.

As a result of concerns expressed on the record by NCA [National Coal Association] and others about the impacts of more rigorous emission ceilings, EPA called a meeting of principal participants in the rulemaking for April 5, 1979. At the meeting EPA presented its new analysis which showed that a 0.55 lbs./MBtu limit would require more than 90 percent scrubbing on 5 to 10 percent of Northern Appalachian reserves and 12 to 25 percent of Eastern Midwest reserves. A 0.80 ceiling would require more than 90 percent scrubbing on less than 5 percent of the reserves in each of these regions. NCA presented its own analysis on the sulfur content and washability of reserves held by its member companies, "a very small portion of the total reserves but including reserves which are planned to be developed in the near future." The NCA data confirmed the EPA analysis within 5 percentage points. At the same meeting the Administrator "reviewed his assessment of state of the art coal cleaning technology" and accepted NCA's recommendation that common practice, i.e., crushing to 11/2 inch top size rather than to smaller sizes with separation at 1.6 specific gravity, be used as the standard when evaluating the impact of coal washing.

After the April 5 meeting EPA also "concluded that the actual buying practices of utilities rather than the mere technical usability of coals should be considered." This exercise was expected to identify high sulfur coals that utilities would not use in order to avoid the risk of failing to satisfy the standard. EPA assumed that utilities would only purchase coal that would provide about a 10 percent margin below the emission limit in order to minimize risk, and, further that utilities would only purchase coal that would meet the emission limit (with the 10 percent margin) with no more than a 90 percent overall reduction in potential emissions. EPA claimed that these assumptions reflected utility preference for buying washed coal for which only 85 percent scrubbing is needed to meet both the percent reduction and the emission limitation, as compared to the previous assumption that utilities would perform 90 percent scrubbing on washed coal (resulting in more than 90 percent reduction in overall emissions). The agency's analysis, according to EPA, showed that up to 22 percent of high sulfur coal reserves in the Eastern Midwest and parts of the Northern Appalachian coal regions would require more than 90 percent reduction if emissions were held to a 1.0 lbs./MBtu standard. Thus, although acknowledging that stricter controls were technically feasible, EPA chose to retain the 1.2 lbs./MBtu standard because "conservatism in utility perceptions of scrubber performance could create a significant disincentive against the use of these coals and disrupt the coal markets in these regions." EPA concluded that "a more stringent emission limit would be counter to one of the basic purposes of the 1977 Amendments, that is, encouraging the use of higher sulfur coals."

B. EDF's Procedural Attack

EDF alleges that as a result of an "ex parte blitz" by coal industry advocates conducted after the close of the comment period, EPA backed away from adopting the .55 lbs./MBtu limit, and instead adopted the higher 1.2 lbs./MBtu restriction. EDF asserts that even before the comment period had ended EPA had already narrowed its focus to include only options which provided for the .55 lbs./MBtu ceiling. EDF also claims that as of March 9, 1979, the three proposals which EPA had under active consideration all included the more stringent .55 lbs./MBtu ceiling, and the earlier 1.2 lbs./MBtu ceiling had been discarded. Whether or not EDF's scenario is credible, it is true that EPA did circulate a draft NSPS with an emissions ceiling below the 1.2 lbs./MBtu level for interagency comment during February, 1978. Following a "leak" of this proposal, EDF says, the so-called "ex parte blitz" began. "Scores" of pro-industry "ex parte" comments were received by EPA in the post-comment period, states EDF, and various meetings with coal industry advocates including Senator Robert Byrd of West Virginia took place during that period. These communications, EDF asserts, were unlawful and prejudicial to its position.

In order for this court to assess these claims, we must identify the particular actions and incidents which gave rise to EDF's complaints. Aside from a passing reference to a telephone call from an EPA official to the Chief Executive Officer of NCA, EDF's procedural objections stem from either (1) comments filed after the close of the official comment period, or (2) meetings between EPA officials and various government and private parties interested in the outcome of the final rule, all of which took place after the close of the comment period.

* * *

2. Meetings

EDF objects to nine different meetings. A chronological list and synopsis of the challenged meetings follows:

1. March 14, 1979. This was a one and a half hour briefing at the White House for high-level officials from the Department of Energy (DOE), the Council of Economic Advisers (CEA), the White House staff, the Department of Interior, the Council on Environmental Quality (CEQ), the Office of

Management and Budget (OMB), and the National Park Service. The meeting was reported in a May 9, 1979 memorandum from EPA to Senator Muskie's staff, responding to the Senator's request for a monthly report of contacts between EPA staff and other federal officials concerning the NSPS. A summary of the meeting and the materials distributed were docketed on May 30, 1979. EDF also obtained, after promulgation of the final rule, a copy of the memorandum to Senator Muskie in response to its Freedom of Information Act ("FOIA") request.

2.   April 5, 1979. This . . . meeting was attended by representatives of EPA, DOE, NCA, EDF, Congressman Paul Simon's office, ICF, Inc. (who performed the microanalysis), and Hunton & Williams (who represented the Electric Utilities). The participants were notified in advance of the agenda for the meeting. Materials relating to EPA's and NCA's presentations during the meeting were distributed and copies were later put into the docket along with detailed minutes of the meeting. Follow-up calls and letters between NCA and EPA came on April 20, 23, and 29, commenting or elaborating upon the April 5 data. All of these follow-up contacts were recorded in the docket.

3.   April 23, 1979. This was a 30–45 minute meeting held at then Senate Majority Leader Robert Byrd's request, in his office, attended by EPA Administrator Douglas Costle, Chief Presidential Assistant Stuart Eizenstat, and NCA officials. A summary of this meeting was put in the docket on May 1, 1979, and copies of the summary were sent to EDF and to other parties. In its denial of the petition for reconsideration, EPA was adamant that no new information was transmitted to EPA at this meeting.

4.   April 27, 1979. This was a briefing on dry scrubbing technology conducted by EPA for representatives of the Office of Science and Technology Policy, the Council on Wage and Price Stability, DOE, the President's domestic policy staff, OMB, and various offices within EPA. A description of this briefing and copies of the material distributed were docketed on May 1, 1979.

5.   April 30, 1979. At 10:00 a.m., a one hour White House briefing was held for the President, the White House staff, and high ranking members of the Executive Branch "concerning the issues and options presented by the rulemaking." This meeting was noted on an EPA official's personal calendar which EDF obtained after promulgation in response to its FOIA request, but was never noted in the rulemaking docket.

6. April 30, 1979. At 2:30 p.m., a technical briefing on dry scrubbing technology at the White House was conducted by EPA for the White House staff. A short memorandum describing this briefing was docketed on May 30, 1979.

7. May 1, 1979. Another White House briefing was held on the subject of FGD technology. A description of the meeting and materials distributed were docketed on May 30, 1979.

8. May 1, 1979 EPA conducted a one hour briefing of staff members of the Senate Committee on Environmental and Public Works concerning EPA's analysis of the effect of alternative emission ceilings on coal reserves. The briefing was "substantially the same as the briefing given to Senator Byrd on May 2, 1980." No persons other than Committee staff members and EPA officials attended the briefing. This meeting, like the one at 10:00 a. m. on April 30, was never entered on the rulemaking docket but was listed on an EPA official's calendar obtained by EDF in response to its FOIA request. This EPA official has since stated that it was an oversight not to have a memorandum of this briefing prepared for the docket.

9. May 2, 1979. This was a brief meeting between Senator Byrd, EPA, DOE and NCA officials held ostensibly for Senator Byrd to hear EPA's comments on the NCA data. A 49 word, not very informative, memorandum describing the meeting was entered on the docket on June 1, 1979.

On June 16, 1980, responding to motions filed by EDF, this court ordered EPA to file affidavits providing additional information regarding five of these nine meetings (March 14, April 23, April 27, April 30, and May 2, 1979). After EPA complied with the order, EDF argued that the other meetings held on April 30 and May 1 were still undocumented, whereupon EPA voluntarily filed an affidavit describing them.

EDF believes that the communications just outlined, when taken as a whole, were so extensive and had such a serious impact on the NSPS rulemaking, that they violated EDF's rights to due process in the proceeding, and that these "ex parte" contacts were procedural errors of such magnitude that this court must reverse. EDF does not specify which particular features in each of the above-enumerated communications violated due process or constituted errors under the statute; indeed, EDF nowhere lists the communications in a form designed to clarify why any particular communication was unlawful. Instead,

EDF labels all post-comment communications with EPA from whatever source and in whatever form as "ex parte," and claims that "this court has repeatedly stated that ex parte contacts of substance violate due process."

At the outset, we decline to begin our task of reviewing EPA's procedures by labeling all post-comment communications with the agency as "ex parte." Such an approach essentially begs the question whether these particular communications in an informal rulemaking proceeding were unlawful. Instead of beginning with a conclusion that these communications were "ex parte," we must evaluate the various communications in terms of their timing, source, mode, content, and the extent of their disclosure on the docket, in order to discover whether any of them violated the procedural requirements of the Clean Air Act, or of due process.

C. Standard for Judicial Review of EPA Procedures

. . . . Our authority to reverse informal administrative rulemaking for procedural reasons is also informed by *Vermont Yankee Nuclear Power Corp. v. Natural Resources Defense Council, Inc.* In its unanimous opinion, the Supreme Court unambiguously cautioned this court against imposing its own notions of proper procedures upon an administrative agency entrusted with substantive functions by Congress. The Court declared that so long as an agency abided by the minimum procedural requirements laid down by statute, this court was not free to impose additional procedural rights if the agency did not choose to grant them. Except in "extremely rare" circumstances, the Court stated, there is no justification for a reviewing court to overturn agency action because of the failure to employ procedures beyond those required by Congress. . . .

Bearing this caveat in mind, we now set out the procedural requirements which Congress mandated for this rulemaking. . . .

D. Statutory Provisions Concerning Procedure

The procedural provisions of the Clean Air Act specifying the creation and content of the administrative rulemaking record are contained in section 307. . . . [T]he 1977 Amendments required the agency to establish a "rulemaking docket" for each proposed rule which would form the basis of the record for judicial review. The docket must contain, inter alia, (1) "notice of the proposed rulemaking . . . accompanied by a statement of its basis and purpose," and a specification of the public comment period; (2) "all written comments and documentary information on the proposed rule received from any person . . . during the comment period; the transcript of public hearings, if any; and all documents . . . which become available after the proposed rule has been published and which the Administrator determines are of central relevance to the rulemaking. . . .", (3) drafts of proposed rules submitted for interagency review, and all documents accompanying them and responding to them; and (4) the promulgated rule and the various accompanying agency documents which explain and justify it.

In contrast to other recent statutes, there is no mention of any restrictions upon "ex parte" contacts. However, the statute apparently did envision that participants would normally submit comments, documentary material, and oral presentations during a prescribed comment period. . . . We now hold that EPA's procedures during the post-comment period were lawful . . . .

E. Validity of EPA's Procedures During the Post-Comment Period

The post-comment period communications about which EDF complains vary widely in their content and mode; some are written documents or letters, others are oral conversations and briefings, while still others are meetings where alleged political arm-twisting took place. For analytical purposes we have grouped the communications into categories and shall discuss each of them separately. As a general matter, however, we note at the outset that nothing in the statute prohibits EPA from admitting all post-comment communications into the record; nothing expressly requires it, either. Most likely the drafters envisioned promulgation of a rule soon after the close of the public comment period, and did not envision a months-long hiatus where continued outside communications with the agency would continue unabated. We must therefore attempt to glean the law for this case by inference from the procedural framework provided in the statute.

* * *

2. Meetings Held With Individuals Outside EPA

The statute does not explicitly treat the issue of post-comment period meetings with individuals outside EPA. Oral face-to-face discussions are not prohibited anywhere, anytime, in the Act. The absence of such prohibition may have arisen from the nature of the informal rulemaking procedures Congress had in mind. Where agency action resembles judicial action, where it involves formal rulemaking, adjudication, or quasi-adjudication among "conflicting private claims to a valuable privilege," the insulation of the decisionmaker from ex parte contacts is justified by basic notions of due process to the parties involved. But where agency action involves informal rulemaking of a policymaking sort, the concept of ex parte contacts is of more questionable utility.

Under our system of government, the very legitimacy of general policymaking performed by unelected administrators depends in no small part upon the openness, accessibility, and amenability of these officials to the needs and ideas of the public from whom their ultimate authority derives, and upon whom their commands must fall. . . . Furthermore, the importance to effective regulation of continuing contact with a regulated industry, other affected groups, and the public cannot be underestimated. Informal contacts may enable the agency to win needed support for its program, reduce future enforcement requirements by helping those regulated to anticipate and shape their plans for the future, and spur the provision of information which the agency needs. The possibility of course exists that in permitting ex parte communications with rulemakers we create the danger of "one administrative record for the public and this court and another for the Commission." Under the Clean Air Act procedures, however, . . . EPA must justify its rulemaking solely on the basis of the record it compiles and makes public. . . .

It still can be argued, however, that if oral communications are to be freely permitted after the close of the comment period, then at least some adequate summary of them must be made in order to preserve the integrity of the rulemaking docket, which under the statute must be the sole repository of material upon which EPA intends to rely. . . .

Turning to the particular oral communications in this case, we find that only two of the nine contested meetings were undocketed by EPA. The agency has maintained that, as to the May 1 meeting where Senate staff people were briefed on EPA's analysis concerning the impact of alternative emissions ceilings upon coal reserves, its failure to place a summary of the briefing in the docket was an oversight. We find no evidence that this oversight was anything but an honest inadvertence; furthermore, a briefing of this sort by EPA which simply provides background information about an upcoming rule is not the type of oral communication which would require a docket entry under the statute.

The other undocketed meeting occurred at the White House and involved the President and his White House staff. . . .

We have already held that a blanket prohibition against meetings during the post-comment period with individuals outside EPA is unwarranted, and this perforce applies to meetings with White House officials. We have not yet addressed, however, the issue whether such oral communications with White House staff, or the President himself, must be docketed on the rulemaking record, and we now turn to that issue. The facts, as noted earlier, present us with a single undocketed meeting held on April 30, 1979, at 10:00 a.m., attended by the President, White House staff, other high ranking members of the Executive Branch, as well as EPA officials, and which concerned the issues and options presented by the rulemaking. . . .

The court recognizes the basic need of the President and his White House staff to monitor the consistency of executive agency regulations with Administration policy. He and his White House advisers surely must be briefed fully and frequently about rules in the making, and their contributions to policymaking considered. The executive power under our Constitution, after all, is not shared it rests exclusively with the President. The idea of a "plural executive," or a President with a council of state, was considered and rejected by the Constitutional Convention. Instead the Founders chose to risk the potential for tyranny inherent in placing power in one person, in order to gain the advantages of accountability fixed on a single source. To ensure the President's control and supervision over the Executive Branch, the Constitution and its judicial gloss vests him with the powers of appointment and removal, the power to demand written opinions from executive officers, and the right to invoke executive privilege to protect consultative privacy. In the particular case of EPA, Presidential authority is clear since it has never been considered an "independent agency," but always part of the Executive Branch.

The authority of the President to control and supervise executive policymaking is derived from the Constitution; the desirability of such control is demonstrable from the practical realities of administrative rulemaking. Regulations such as those involved here demand a careful weighing of cost, environmental, and energy considerations. They also have broad implications for national economic policy. Our form of government simply could not function effectively or rationally if key executive policymakers were isolated from each other and from the Chief Executive. Single mission agencies do not always have the answers to complex regulatory problems. An overworked administrator exposed on a 24-hour basis to a dedicated but zealous staff needs to know the arguments and ideas of policymakers in other agencies as well as in the White House.

 CROSS REFERENCE We will encounter the material on presidential direction and control of administration in Chapter 6. Does your view of executive power under the Constitution affect your view of the permissibility of ex parte contacts with executive branch officers?

We recognize, however, that there may be instances where the docketing of conversations between the President or his staff and other Executive Branch officers or rulemakers may be necessary to ensure due process. This may be true, for example, where such conversations directly concern the outcome of adjudications or quasi-adjudicatory proceedings; there is no inherent executive power to control the rights of individuals in such settings. Docketing may also be necessary in some circumstances where a statute like this one specifically requires that essential "information or data" upon which a rule is based be docketed. But in the absence of any further Congressional requirements, we hold that it was not unlawful in this case for EPA not to docket a face-to-face policy session involving the President and EPA officials during the post-comment period, since EPA makes no effort to base the rule on any "information or data" arising from that meeting. Where the President himself is directly involved in oral communications with Executive Branch officials, Article II considerations combined with the strictures of *Vermont Yankee* require that courts tread with extraordinary caution in mandating disclosure beyond that already required by statute.

The purposes of full-record review which underlie the need for disclosing ex parte conversations in some settings do not require that courts know the details of every White House contact, including a Presidential one, in this informal rulemaking setting. After all, any rule issued here with or without White House assistance must have the requisite factual support in the rulemaking record, and under this particular statute the Administrator may not base the rule in whole or in part on any "information or data" which is not in the record, no matter what the source. . . . Of course, it is always possible that undisclosed Presidential prodding may direct an outcome that is factually based on the record, but different from the outcome that would have obtained in the absence of Presidential involvement. In such a case, it would be true that the political process did affect the outcome in a way the courts could not police. But we do not believe that Congress intended that the courts convert informal rulemaking into a rarified technocratic process, unaffected by political considerations or the presence of Presidential power. In sum, we find that the existence of intra-Executive Branch meetings during the post-comment period, and the failure to docket one such meeting involving the President, violated neither the procedures mandated by the Clean Air Act nor due process. . . .

Finally, EDF challenges the rulemaking on the basis of alleged Congressional pressure, citing principally two meetings with Senator Byrd. EDF asserts that under the controlling case law the political interference demonstrated in this case represents a separate and independent ground for invalidating this rulemaking. . . .

D.C. Federation thus requires that . . . the content of the pressure upon the Secretary is designed to force him to decide upon factors not made relevant by Congress in the applicable statute [and] . . . the Secretary's determination must be affected by those extraneous considerations.

In the case before us, there is no persuasive evidence that either criterion is satisfied. Senator Byrd requested a meeting in order to express "strongly" his already well-known views that the SO_2 standards' impact on coal reserves was a matter of concern to him. EPA initiated a second responsive meeting to report its reaction to the reserve data submitted by the NCA. In neither meeting is there any allegation that EPA made any commitments to Senator Byrd. The meetings did underscore Senator Byrd's deep concerns for EPA, but there is no evidence he attempted actively to use "extraneous" pressures to further his position. Americans rightly expect their elected representatives to voice their grievances and preferences concerning the administration of our laws. We believe it entirely proper for Congressional representatives vigorously to represent the interests of their constituents before administrative agencies engaged in informal, general policy rulemaking, so long as individual Congressmen do not frustrate the intent of Congress as a whole as expressed in statute, nor undermine applicable rules of procedure. Where Congressmen keep their comments focused on the substance of the proposed rule[,] and we have no substantial evidence to cause us to believe Senator Byrd did not do so here[,] administrative agencies are expected to balance Congressional pressure with the pressures emanating from all other sources. To hold otherwise would deprive the agencies of legitimate sources of information and call into question the validity of nearly every controversial rulemaking.

In sum, we conclude that EPA's adoption of the 1.2 lbs./MBtu emissions ceiling was free from procedural error. The post-comment period contacts here violated neither the statute nor the integrity of the proceeding. . . .

COURSE THEME

POLITICAL INFLUENCE
What role should political officials play in regulatory decision-making? Do we want agencies to freely communicate with members of Congress and the executive branch, or do we want agencies to be more insulated from political influence?

NOTES AND QUESTIONS

1. *Exception: competing private claims to valuable privileges.* Are ex parte contacts never prohibited unless the organic statute (or the APA) expressly forbids them? In *Costle,* the court cited to a case involving "conflicting private claims to a valuable privilege." Sangamon Val. Television Corp. v. United States, 269 F.2d 221, 224 (D.C. Cir. 1959). *Sangamon* involved the allocation of TV channels among communities and TV content producers. One producer met privately with a number of commissioners in their private offices, took them to lunch at various times, and wrote them letters—none of which made it onto the rulemaking docket. The D.C. Circuit required the Commission to reopen proceedings. In another FCC case, the D.C. Circuit admonished the agency of "the inconsistency of secrecy with fundamental notions of fairness implicit in due process and with the ideal of reasoned decisionmaking on the merits which undergirds all of our administrative law." Home Box Office, Inc. v. FCC, 567 F.2d 9, 56 (D.C. Cir. 1977). Yet are these decisions consistent with *Vermont Yankee,* absent a statutory bar on ex parte contacts?

In Action for Children's Television v. FCC, 564 F.2d 458 (D.C. Cir. 1977), the D.C. Circuit addressed the FCC's refusal to make changes to requirements for children's TV programming. The court refused to require the FCC to reopen its proceedings despite ex parte contacts, noting "the absence of support for" requiring disclosure "in the Administrative Procedure Act." The court limited the reach of *Sangamon* and *Home Box Office* to cases involving "conflicting private claims to a valuable privilege." The court observed the slippery slope in requiring disclosure of such ex parte contacts: "why not go further to require the decisionmaker to summarize and make available for public comment every status inquiry from a Congressman or any germane material say a newspaper editorial that he or she reads or their evening-hour ruminations?" Do you agree with the court's concern?

2. **Ex parte** *contacts in formal proceedings.* The APA doesn't prohibit ex parte contacts in the informal rulemaking context, but it *does* prohibit ex parte contacts during formal rulemakings and during adjudicatory proceedings. See 5 U.S.C. § 554(d)(1) (adjudications); id. § 557(d)(1)(A) (formal rulemakings and adjudications).

3. **The Attorney General Manual.** Is the bottom line here that so long as the statutory procedural requirements have been met, there are no grounds to complain? Put differently, if the agency disclosed the proposed rule, allowed the public to comment on them, responded to the relevant comments, and issued a final rule consistent with the statutory requirements, of what is there to complain? Indeed, recall the following explanation of informal rulemaking proceedings from the Attorney General's Manual: "an agency is free to formulate rules upon the basis of materials in its files and the knowledge and experience of the agency, in addition to the materials adduced in public rule making proceedings." U.S. Dep't of Justice, Att'y General's Manual on the Admin. Proc. Act 31–32 (1947).

Summarizing these cases, it would appear that absent a statutory prohibition, ex parte contacts are permitted unless there are due process concerns, or if those contacts led an agency to take an action inconsistent with statutory requirements.

7.   Interlude: Freedom of Information Act (FOIA)

It is now worth taking a short detour into the Freedom of Information Act (FOIA). Although FOIA has much broader implications than just for rulemaking, and is sometimes discussed in casebooks in an independent chapter (or not at all), FOIA is particularly relevant to rulemaking. After all, how do private parties learn that an agency has relied on data that it has failed to disclose? How do they learn that an agency has engaged in ex parte contacts that it has failed to disclose? The answer is often FOIA.

In brief, FOIA requires that "each agency, upon any request for records which (i) reasonably describes such records and (ii) is made in accordance with published rules stating the time, place, fees (if any), and procedures to be followed, shall make the records promptly available to any person." 5 U.S.C. § 552(a)(3)(A). The law, however, exempts several categories of records: (1) classified information; (2) those "related solely to the internal personnel rules and practices of an agency"; (3) those specifically exempted by statute; (4) trade secrets or other confidential commercial information; (5) internal administration communications that are privileged, particularly under the "deliberative process privilege"; (6) "personnel and medical files and similar files the disclosure of which would constitute a clearly unwarranted invasion of personal privacy"; (7) "records or information compiled for law enforcement purposes" that meet certain other conditions; (8) reports of agencies involved in regulating financial institutions; and (9) "geological and geophysical information and data, including maps, concerning wells." Id. § (b)(1)–(9). The law allows a federal court to compel the production of "agency records improperly withheld." Id. § (a)(4)(B).

There are numerous provisions involving the time in which an agency must respond, tolling the time, and seeking extensions of time; as well as provisions involving fees and exemptions from fees. A practicing administrative law attorney will have to become familiar with all of these rules. But for our purposes, the key questions are (1) what kinds of documents and information fall within the meaning of "agency records" subject to disclosure; and (2) the scope of the various exemptions from disclosure. The remainder of this section goes briefly through these two issues.

a.   What Are Agency Records?

FOIA does not define what are agency records, but the Supreme Court has elaborated upon this question in a series of opinions.

Defined Term

AGENCY RECORDS: The Freedom of Information Act allows courts to compel the production of "agency records improperly withheld." FOIA does not further define "agency records," but several court cases have expanded on the term.

In Kissinger v. Reporters Committee for Freedom of Press, 445 U.S. 136 (1980), the Supreme Court held that the President and his "immediate personal staff" whose role "is to advise and assist the President" were not an "agency" subject to FOIA. The Court next held that the *location* of records within an agency building does not automatically make them the "agency records" of that agency. At issue were notes of Henry Kissinger's telephone conversations from when he had been an Assistant to the President and therefore were not subject to FOIA. The Court held that when Kissinger became Secretary of State and brought with him to his State Department office his prior telephone notes, those notes did not thereby become *State Department* records subject to FOIA.

In Forsham v. Harris, 445 U.S. 169 (1980), the Supreme Court held "that written data generated, owned, and possessed by a privately controlled organization receiving federal study grants are not 'agency records' within the meaning of the Act when copies of those data have not been obtained by" the federal agency. This was so even though the agency—the Department of Health, Education, and Welfare—denied a new drug application in part on the basis of reports issued by the private organization in question, the University Group Diabetes Program (UGDP). The UGDP, of course, had relied on the data in its possession to create those reports. The Court reasoned "that an agency must first either create or obtain a record as a prerequisite to its becoming an 'agency record' within the meaning of the FOIA." The Court went on to say that "[t]he Freedom of Information Act deals with 'agency records,' not information in the abstract," and it does not matter "that HEW has a right of access to the data, and a right if it so chooses to obtain permanent custody of the UGDP records," because "FOIA applies to records which have been in fact obtained, and not to records which merely could have been obtained."

In United States Dep't of Justice v. Tax Analysts, 492 U.S. 136 (1989), the Supreme Court formulated a two-part test from *Kissinger* and *Forsham*: First, an agency must "either create or obtain" the requested materials; second, the "agency must be in control of the requested materials at the time the FOIA request is made." As to the first requirement, the Court observed that "[i]n performing their official duties, agencies routinely avail themselves of studies, trade journal reports, and other materials produced outside the agencies both by private and governmental organizations." As a result, "[t]o restrict the term 'agency records' to materials generated internally would frustrate Congress' desire to put within public reach the information available to an agency in its decision-making processes." Elaborating on the second requirement, the Court noted that "control" means "the materials have come into the agency's possession in the legitimate conduct of its official duties"—and not merely through an employee's personal possession, as in *Kissinger*. The Court applied this two-part test in *Tax Analysts* to hold that all federal district court tax decisions in the possession of the Department of Justice were agency records. This was so because the Department obtained them from the district courts as part of its official duties—to decide whether to appeal, for example. And, of course, those decisions weren't merely the personal possessions of employees, but rather were controlled by the agency itself.

Try applying the above analysis to the following problems.

■ *Problem 2.2*

In order to carry out its statutory responsibilities, the Secret Service monitors and controls access to the White House Complex. It accomplishes this task through an electronic system known as the White House Access Control System (WHACS). WHACS has two principal components: the Worker and Visitor Entrance System (WAVES) and the Access Control Records System (ACR). The information contained in WHACS records is provided to and used by the Secret Service for two limited purposes: to perform a background check on the visitor, and to verify the visitor's admissibility at the time of the visit. The ACR system records where in the building a visitor "swipes" the security badge. The data is produced by the Secret Service and is generally deleted within a few months. The data covers visitors to the President and his close advisers, but also to other agencies subject to FOIA that are housed in the White House Complex. Are the visitor logs "agency records" within the meaning of FOIA? (See Judicial Watch v. Secret Service, 726 F.3d 208 (D.C. Cir. 2013).)

■ *Problem 2.3*

After a FOIA request was brought for agency records, the Office of Science and Technology Policy (OSTP) refused to search the private e-mail account maintained by its director, which account was maintained by a private organization, for records that might be responsive to the FOIA request. The OSTP argued that such records were "beyond the reach of FOIA" because they were in an "account" that "is under the control of" a private organization. Did the agency "improperly withhold" "agency records" in violation of FOIA? (See Competitive Enterprise Institute v. Office of Science & Technology Policy, 827 F.3d 145 (D.C. Cir. 2016)).

■   *Problem 2.4*

In 1981, the Bureau of National Affairs (BNA) filed a FOIA request with the Department of Justice (DOJ or the Justice Department) for all records of appointments and meetings between William Baxter, then Assistant Attorney General for Antitrust, and all parties outside the Justice Department. Baxter's appointment materials included two types of documents. The first consisted of two sets of desk appointment calendars maintained for Baxter in 1981 and 1982. One set of calendars was maintained by Baxter himself; the other was kept by his personal secretary. According to Baxter, the calendar entries "generally reflect[ed] the location of a meeting or appointment, the people expected to be present, and on occasion, the general purpose of the meeting or appointment." Top level assistants occasionally had access to the calendars so that they would know how to contact Baxter. The calendars included personal appointments wholly unrelated to the business of the Antitrust Division and did not always reflect changes in appointments or cancellations of meetings. The other set of documents sought by BNA are the daily agendas which Mr. Baxter's secretary prepared and distributed to top staff within the Antitrust Division so that they would know his schedule on a given day. The staff usually destroyed these agendas at the end of each day, but Baxter's secretary retained copies for her own files. Which, if any, of the above documents are "agency records" subject to FOIA? (See The Bureau of National Affairs, Inc. v. United States Department of Justice, 742 F.2d 1484 (D.C. Cir. 1984).)

---

b.   Exemptions

As described previously, FOIA exempts several categories of records: (1) classified information; (2) those "related solely to the internal personnel rules and practices of an agency"; (3) those specifically exempted by statute; (4) trade secrets or other confidential commercial information; (5) internal administration communications that are privileged, particularly under the "deliberative process privilege"; (6) "personnel and medical files and similar files the disclosure

of which would constitute a clearly unwarranted invasion of personal privacy";
(7) "records or information compiled for law enforcement purposes" that meet
certain other conditions; (8) records "contained in or related to examination,
operating, or condition reports prepared by, on behalf of, or for the use of an
agency responsible for the regulation or supervision of financial institutions";
and (9) "geological and geophysical information and data, including maps,
concerning wells." 5 U.S.C. § 552(b)(1)–(9). The last two exemptions are rarely
litigated, but the following seven exemptions require more attention.

Exemption 1. One of the more regularly invoked exemptions is the first,
involving classified information. Yet courts rarely second-guess national security classifications, which are done by executive order pursuant to statute. As
long as the proper classification process was followed, courts are unlikely to
question an agency's invocation of this exemption.

Exemption 2. The second exemption involving records related solely to
"internal personnel rules and practices of an agency." In Department of Air
Force v. Rose, 425 U.S. 352 (1976), the Supreme Court rejected application of
this exemption to case summaries of honor and ethics hearings at the United
States Air Force Academy. Although such summaries do appear to relate to the
"internal personnel rules and practices of an agency," the Court explained that
the exemption was intended to apply to matters concerning employee relations
and human resources—not to matters of more general public interest such as
the records of disciplinary proceedings at the military academies. The Supreme
Court cautioned, however, that such disclosure under Exemption 2 was proper
"where disclosure" does not "risk circumvention of agency regulation."

In subsequent cases, this caution took on a life of its own, and various
courts of appeals held that Exemption 2 shielded material where disclosure
would circumvent an agency's regulations or effectiveness—even to the point
of withholding law enforcement surveillance training manuals. Crooker v.
Bureau of Alcohol, Tobacco & Firearms, 670 F.2d 1051 (D.C. Cir. 1981) (en
banc). In Milner v. Department of Navy, 562 U.S. 562 (2011), the Supreme
Court put a stop to the invocation of Exemption 2 under such circumstances.
In *Milner*, the Navy had invoked this exemption to withhold "data and maps
used to help store explosives at a naval base in Washington State." The Court
reiterated that such data and maps *are* agency records, and they are not exempt
under the second exemption because they did not "concern the conditions of

employment in federal agencies—such matters as hiring and firing, work rules and discipline, compensation and benefits."

Exemption 3. This exemption applies where a statute specifically prohibits disclosure of certain information. The statute was amended in 1976 to make clear that the exemption only applies where "such statute (A) requires that the matters be withheld from the public in such a manner as to leave no discretion on the issue, or (B) establishes particular criteria for withholding or refers to particular types of matters to be withheld." 5 U.S.C. § 552(b)(3)(A)(i)–(ii). The amended language was a rejection of a prior Supreme Court case that had held certain material exempt merely because the statute gave the agency broad discretion whether to withhold information from the public. The amended language makes clear that discretion is not enough. The statute itself must make the determination that certain information must be withheld—or it must establish the relevant criteria for the agency to make such decisions.

Exemption 4. Rule 4 exempts "trade secrets and commercial or financial information obtained from a person and privileged or confidential." Until 2019, a number of lower courts had held that release of private information was forbidden by FOIA only if it would lead to "substantial competitive harm" to the business that provided it. In Food Marketing Institute v. Argus Leader Media, 139 S. Ct. 2356 (2019), the Supreme Court held that even confidential information that does not lead to such harm is exempt from disclosure because nothing in the statute limited the exemption to cases of competitive harm. That case arose when a newspaper sought records in possession of the United States Department of Agriculture about the national food stamps program, SNAP. The paper asked for the names and addresses of all retail stores that participate in SNAP and each store's annual SNAP redemption data from 2005 to 2010. The Court held that information is usually "confidential" if (1) the "it is customarily kept private, or at least closely held, by the person imparting" the information, and (2) "if the party receiving it provides some assurance that it will remain secret." The Court held that the first requirement *has* to be met. It did not answer the question whether the second condition must also be met because in that case the USDA in any event provided such assurances to the stores.

Exemption 5. This exemption protects from disclosure "inter-agency or intra-agency memorandums or letters that would not be available by law to a party other than an agency in litigation with the agency, provided that the deliberative process privilege shall not apply to records created 25 years or more before the date on which the records were requested." The Supreme Court has held that to qualify for Exemption 5, "a document must . . . satisfy two conditions: its source must be a Government agency, and it must fall within the ambit of a privilege against discovery under judicial standards that would govern litigation against the agency that holds it." Dep't of Interior v. Klamath Water Users Protective Ass'n, 532 U.S. 1, 8 (2001). Such privileges include the attorney-client privilege and, importantly, the "deliberative process privilege." This privilege covers "documents reflecting advisory opinions, recommendations and deliberations comprising part of a process by which governmental decisions and policies are formulated." The privilege "rests on the obvious realization that officials will not communicate candidly among themselves if each remark is a potential item of discovery and front page news, and its object is to enhance the quality of agency decisions by protecting open and frank discussion among those who make them within the Government." This privilege applies to consultants outside of the Government, too, when they communicate with the agency and such consultations are a part of the agency's deliberative process and the consulting party has no independent motive or interest of its own. In *Klamath Water Users,* the Supreme Court rejected the contention that an agency's communications with Indian Tribes was protected under this exemption. The Tribes were not "consultants," and in fact the Tribes in question had interest adverse to others water claimants and its communications represented *its* own views, not those of the agency.

Exemption 6. This exemption protects from disclosure "personnel and medical files and similar files the disclosure of which would constitute a clearly unwarranted invasion of personal privacy." Note that not *all* personnel, medical, and similar files are protected, but rather only those whose disclosure "would constitute a clearly unwarranted invasion of personal privacy." The Supreme Court has therefore held that the public interest in disclosure—specifically the extent to which disclosure would contribute to the "public understanding of the operations or activities of the government"—must be weighed against the privacy interest. U.S. Dep't of Def. v. Fed. Labor Relations Auth., 510 U.S. 487, 495 (1994). Apply these definitions and principles to the following problems:

■ *Problem 2.5*

For purposes of FOIA and the APA, "person" is defined as any "individual, partnership, corporation, association, or public or private organization other than an agency." 5 U.S.C. § 551(2). In light of this definition of "person," does a corporation have "personal privacy" rights protected under Exemption 6? Assuming the corporation's information is not protected as confidential under Exemption 4, might it nevertheless be protected under Exemption 6? See FCC v. AT&T, Inc., 562 U.S. 397 (2011).

■ *Problem 2.6*

In 1981, the Secretary of State obtained an assurance from the Haitian Government that it would not subject to prosecution for illegal departure undocumented Haitians interdicted by the United States and returned to Haiti. Personnel of petitioner State Department monitored Haiti's compliance with the assurance by conducting interviews with a representative sample of unsuccessful emigrants. Michael Ray, a lawyer for an undocumented Haitian national currently in immigration proceedings, is seeking to prove that his client is entitled to political asylum in the United States because Haitians who immigrate illegally face a well-founded fear of persecution upon returning home to Haiti. He filed FOIA requests seeking the records of government interviews with returning Haitians. The government produced the records with the names of the returned immigrants redacted. Ray then sought the unredacted interview transcripts. Is he entitled to them, or are they protected under Exemption 6? See U.S. Dep't of State v. Ray, 502 U.S. 164 (1991).

Exemption 7. This Exemption, which has been amended several times, involves law enforcement records. The statutory requirements for withholding are very specific. "[R]ecords or information compiled for law enforcement purposes" are exempt, "but only to the extent that the production of such law enforcement records or information":

(A) could reasonably be expected to interfere with enforcement proceedings,

(B) would deprive a person of a right to a fair trial or an impartial adjudication,

(C) could reasonably be expected to constitute an unwarranted invasion of personal privacy,

(D) could reasonably be expected to disclose the identity of a confidential source, including a State, local, or foreign agency or authority or any private institution which furnished information on a confidential basis, and, in the case of a record or information compiled by criminal law enforcement authority in the course of a criminal investigation or by an agency conducting a lawful national security intelligence investigation, information furnished by a confidential source,

(E) would disclose techniques and procedures for law enforcement investigations or prosecutions, or would disclose guidelines for law enforcement investigations or prosecutions if such disclosure could reasonably be expected to risk circumvention of the law, or

(F) could reasonably be expected to endanger the life or physical safety of any individual.

5 U.S.C. § 551(b)(7).

D. Exemptions from Rulemaking Requirements

The APA specifies a number of rules that need not go through notice-and-comment. These are typically divided into three kinds of exemptions. The first involves certain subject matter. Section 553 does not apply to a rule involving the "military or foreign affairs function of the United States," or "a matter relating to agency management or personnel or to public property, loans, grants, benefits, or contracts." APA § 553(a). The second is the "good cause exemption": the rulemaking requirements do not apply "when the agency for good cause finds (and incorporates the finding and a brief statement of reasons therefor in the

PRACTICE POINTER It is worth remembering as you read the following materials that the subject matter exemptions and the good cause exemption apply even if a rule is a "legislative rule."

rules issued) that notice and public procedure thereon are impracticable, unnecessary, or contrary to the public interest." Id. § 553(b). Third and finally, section 553 does not apply "to interpretative rules, general statements of policy, or rules of agency organization, procedure, or practice." Id. Note that even if the agency promulgates a rule exempt from notice and comment, the agency must still publish the rule in the Federal Register. Id. § 552(a)(1)(C), (D). The following materials address each type of exemption.

1.   Subject Matter Exemptions

The subject matter exemptions are not too often litigated, but sometimes cases do arise. In *Rajah v. Mukasey,* the Attorney General had instituted a program after the terrorist attacks of 9/11 requiring "the collection of data from aliens upon entry and periodic registration of certain aliens present in the United States." 544 F.3d 427, 433 (2d Cir. 2008). In a regulation promulgated via notice-and-comment, the Attorney General established the framework for registration. In a second regulation promulgated *without* notice-and-comment, the Attorney General specified which groups of aliens must register. The Second Circuit held that the rule "fell within the APA's foreign affairs exemption." The court observed,

> There are at least three definitely undesirable international consequences that would follow from notice and comment rulemaking. First, sensitive foreign intelligence might be revealed in the course of explaining why some of a particular nation's citizens are regarded as a threat. Second, relations with other countries might be impaired if the government were to conduct and resolve a public debate over why some citizens of particular countries were a potential danger to our security. Third, the process would be slow and cumbersome, diminishing our ability to collect intelligence regarding, and enhance defenses in anticipation of, a potential attack by foreign terrorists.

Id. at 437. Does the exemption require that the consequences of going through notice-and-comment would be undesirable? Or was the court just adding some color? And what about the first regulation—would that have been exempt, too?

In *United States v. Ventura-Melendez,* the court held that a rule that "created a temporary security zone comprised of a combined area of ocean and land adjacent to a bombing range at a military installation" was exempt under the subject matter exemption for military matters. 321 F.3d 230, 233 (1st Cir. 2003). As a result, the court upheld convictions of private individuals who unlawfully entered the security zone. This suggests that the military exemption applies to private conduct of civilians, too, even in areas near military installations. Did the court interpret the exemption too broadly, or was the rule at issue obviously exempt?

2. Good Cause Exemption

A far more commonly litigated matter is the good cause exemption. Indeed, the good cause exemption, although it was intended to be used rarely, is invoked exceedingly often. One government study found that between 2003 and 2010, 35 percent out of 568 major rules, and 44 percent of some 30,000 nonmajor rules, were promulgated without notice-and-comment; the good cause exemption was asserted for 77 percent of the major rules and 61 percent of the nonmajor rules for which the agencies forwent notice-and-comment. Government Accountability Office, Federal Rulemaking: Agencies Could Take Additional Steps to Respond to Public Comments, GAO 13–21, at abstract (Dec. 2012). As

PRACTICE POINTER If you are a lawyer for an agency, what exemptions would you invoke? Good cause is the most commonly invoked, but are agencies overusing it?

you read the next case, ask yourself whether the exemption is invoked more than it should be.

Mack Trucks, Inc. v. EPA

682 F.3d 87 (D.C. Cir. 2012)

BROWN, CIRCUIT JUDGE:

In January 2012, EPA promulgated an interim final rule (IFR) to permit manufacturers of heavy-duty diesel engines to pay nonconformance penalties (NCPs) in exchange for the right to sell noncompliant engines. EPA took this action without providing formal notice or an opportunity for comment, invoking the "good cause" exception provided in the Administrative Procedure Act (APA). Because we find that none of the statutory criteria for "good cause" are satisfied, we vacate the IFR.

I

In 2001, pursuant to Section 202 of the Clean Air Act ("the Act"), EPA enacted a rule requiring a 95 percent reduction in the emissions of nitrogen oxide from heavy-duty diesel engines. By delaying the effective date until 2010, EPA gave industry nine years to innovate the necessary new technologies. . . . During those nine years, most manufacturers of heavy-duty diesel engines, including Petitioners, invested hundreds of millions of dollars to develop a technology called "selective catalytic reduction." This technology converts nitrogen oxide into nitrogen and water by using a special after-treatment system and a diesel-based chemical agent. With selective catalytic reduction, manufacturers have managed to meet the 2010 NO_x standard.

One manufacturer, Navistar, took a different approach. For its domestic sales, Navistar opted for a form of "exhaust gas recirculation," but this technology proved less successful; Navistar's engines do not meet the 2010 NO_x standard. All else being equal, Navistar would therefore be unable to sell these engines in the United States—unless, of course, it adopted a different, compliant technology. But for the last few years, Navistar has been able to lawfully forestall that result and continue selling its noncompliant engines by using banked emission credits. Simply put, it bet on finding a way to make exhaust gas recirculation a feasible and compliant technology before its finite supply of credits ran out.

Navistar's day of reckoning is fast approaching: its supply of credits is dwindling and its engines remain noncompliant. In October 2011, Navistar informed EPA that it would run out of credits sometime in 2012. EPA, estimating that Navistar "might have as little as three to four months" of available credits before it "would be forced to stop introducing its engines into commerce," leapt into action. Without formal notice and comment, EPA hurriedly promulgated the IFR on January 31, 2012, pursuant to its authority under 42 U.S.C. § 7525(g), to make NCPs available to Navistar.

To issue NCPs under its regulations, EPA must first find that a new emissions standard is "more stringent" or "more difficult to achieve" than a prior standard, that "substantial work will be required to meet the standard for which the NCP is offered," and that "there is likely to be a technological laggard." EPA found these criteria were met. The 2010 NO_x standard permits a significantly smaller amount of emissions than the prior standard, so the first criterion is easily satisfied. As for the second, EPA simply said that, because compliant engines (like Petitioners') use new technologies to be compliant, "[i]t is therefore logical to conclude . . . that substantial work was required to meet the emission standard." Finally, EPA determined that there was likely to be a technological laggard because "an engine manufacturer [Navistar] . . . has not yet met the requirements for technological reasons" and because "it is a reasonable possibility that this manufacturer may not be able to comply for technological reasons."

Having determined that NCPs are appropriate, EPA proceeded to set the amount of the penalty and establish the "upper limit" of emissions permitted even by a penalty-paying manufacturer. The IFR provides that manufacturers may sell heavy-duty diesel engines in model years 2012 and 2013 as long as they pay a penalty of $1,919 per engine and as long as the engines emit fewer than 0.50 grams of nitrogen oxide per horsepower-hour. This "upper limit" thus permits emissions of up to two-and-a-half times the 0.20 grams permitted under the 2010 NO_X standard with which Navistar is meant to comply and with which Petitioners do comply.

EPA explained its decision to forego notice and comment procedures by invoking the "good cause" exception of the APA, which provides that an agency may dispense with formal notice and comment procedures if the agency "for good cause finds . . . that notice and public procedure thereon are impracticable, unnecessary, or contrary to the public interest," 5 U.S.C. § 553(b)(B). EPA cited four factors to show the existence of good cause: (1) notice and comment would mean "the possibility of an engine manufacturer [Navistar] . . . being unable to certify a complete product line of engines for model year 2012 and/or 2013," (2) EPA was only "amending limited provisions in existing NCP regulations," (3) the IFR's "duration is limited," and (4) "there is no risk to the public interest in allowing manufacturers to certify using NCPs before the point at which EPA could make them available through a full notice-and-comment rulemaking."

Petitioners each requested administrative stays of the IFR, protesting that EPA lacked good cause within the meaning of the APA. . . .

* * *

III

Petitioners argue first that Section 206 of the Act requires notice and comment; alternatively, they claim EPA lacked good cause in any event. The

APA provides that, "[e]xcept when notice or hearing is required by statute," an agency is relieved of its obligation to provide notice and an opportunity to comment "when the agency for good cause finds (and incorporates the finding and a brief statement of reasons therefor in the rules issued) that notice and public procedure thereon are impracticable, unnecessary, or contrary to the public interest." 5 U.S.C. § 553(b)(B).

A

Is notice or hearing expressly required by statute? Section 206(g)(1) of the Act, 42 U.S.C. § 7525(g)(1), says that NCPs shall be provided "under regulations promulgated by the Administrator after notice and opportunity for public hearing." According to Petitioners, this is an express requirement of notice and comment that bars EPA from even invoking the good cause exception in this case. Read alone, this language seems to support their argument. But we cannot read one subsection in isolation. The rest of Section 206(g) clearly reveals, as EPA points out, that this requirement applies *only* to the very first NCP rule—which set out the regulatory criteria governing future NCPs—not for each and every NCP subsequently promulgated. . . .

Subsection (g)(2), the very next paragraph, says that "no [NCP] may be issued under paragraph (1) . . . if the degree by which the manufacturer fails to meet any standard . . . exceeds the percentage determined under regulations promulgated by the Administrator to be practicable. *Such regulations . . .* shall be promulgated not later than one year after August 7, 1977." 42 U.S.C. § 7525(g)(2) (emphasis added). The regulations to which subsection (g)(2) refers are clearly the regulations promulgated under subsection (g)(1). Subsection (g)(2) explains they are of a guiding nature and, importantly, that they must be issued by certain a date in 1977. This language cannot possibly be read to describe each and every NCP. Petitioners' interpretation of subsection (g)(1), suggesting that it does refer to every NCP, would render subsection (g)(2) not just superfluous, but impossible—a result we must avoid. Subsection (g)(3) makes the flaw in Petitioners' interpretation even clearer: "The regulations promulgated under paragraph (1) shall, not later than one year after August 7, 1977, provide for nonconformance penalties in amounts determined under a formula established by the Administrator." 42 U.S.C. § 7525(g)(3). Once again, this provision and its deadline reveal that subsection (g)(1) refers to a one-time promulgation of a formula that governs future penalty applications. Reading Section 206(g) as a whole, it is clear nothing in that provision requires EPA to provide notice and comment every time it applies the original formula to the establishment of specific penalties.

Contrary to Petitioners' fears, the Act's lack of a notice and comment requirement does not mean that *no* procedures are statutorily required when NCPs are issued. The APA's general rule requiring notice and comment—absent identified exceptions—still obviously applies. Indeed, EPA has always argued that the IFR is justified under the good cause exception, not that it is justified because notice and comment is never required.

B

Because the Act does not contain any notice-and-comment requirement applicable to the IFR, EPA may invoke the APA's good cause exception. We must therefore determine whether notice and comment were "impracticable, unnecessary, or contrary to the public interest." 5 U.S.C. § 553(b)(B). . . .

We have repeatedly made clear that the good cause exception "is to be narrowly construed and only reluctantly countenanced." *Util. Solid Waste Activities Grp.* [*v. EPA*], 236 F.3d[749,] 754 [(D.C. Cir. 2001)]; [omitted citations—Ed.]; *see also Jifry* [*v. FAA*], 370 F.3d [1174,] 1179 [(D.C. Cir. 2004)] ("The exception excuses notice and comment in emergency situations, or where delay could result in serious harm."); *Am. Fed. of Gov't Emps. v. Block*, 655 F.2d 1153, 1156 (D.C. Cir. 1981) ("As the legislative history of the APA makes clear, moreover, the exceptions at issue here are not 'escape clauses' that may be arbitrarily utilized at the agency's whim. Rather, use of these exceptions by administrative agencies should be limited to emergency situations. . . .").

First, an agency may invoke the impracticability of notice and comment. 5 U.S.C. § 553(b)(B). Our inquiry into impracticability "is inevitably fact- or context-dependent," *Mid-Tex Electric Coop. v. FERC*, 822 F.2d 1123, 1132 (D.C. Cir. 1987). For the sake of comparison, we have suggested agency action could be sustained on this basis if, for example, air travel security agencies would be unable to address threats posing "a possible imminent hazard to aircraft, persons, and property within the United States," *Jifry*, 370 F.3d at 1179, or if "a safety investigation shows that a new safety rule must be put in place immediately," *Util. Solid Waste Activities Grp.*, 236 F.3d at 755 (ultimately finding that not to be the case and rejecting the agency's argument), or if a rule was of "life-saving importance" to mine workers in the event of a mine explosion, *Council of the*

S. Mountains, Inc. v. Donovan, 653 F.2d 573, 581 (D.C. Cir. 1981) (describing that circumstance as "a special, possibly unique, case").

By contrast, the context of this case reveals that the only purpose of the IFR is, as Petitioners put it, "to rescue a lone manufacturer from the folly of its own choices." . . . The IFR does not stave off any imminent threat to the environment or safety or national security. It does not remedy any real emergency at all, save the "emergency" facing Navistar's bottom line. Indeed, all EPA points to is "the serious harm to Navistar and its employees" and "the ripple effect on its customers and suppliers," but the same could be said for any manufacturer facing a standard with which its product does not comply.

EPA claims the harm to Navistar and the resulting up- and down-stream impacts should still be enough under our precedents. The only case on which it relies, however, is one in which an entire industry and its customers were imperiled. *See Am. Fed. of Gov't Emps.*, 655 F.2d at 1157. Navistar's plight is not even remotely close to such a weighty, systemic interest, especially since it is a consequence brought about by Navistar's own choice to continue to pursue a technology which, so far, is noncompliant. At bottom, EPA's approach would give agencies "good cause" under the APA every time a manufacturer in a regulated field felt a new regulation imposed some degree of economic hardship, even if the company could have avoided that hardship had it made different business choices. This is both nonsensical and in direct tension with our long-standing position that the exception should be "narrowly construed and only reluctantly countenanced." *Util. Solid Waste Activities Grp.*, 236 F.3d at 754.

Second, an agency may claim notice and comment were "unnecessary." 5 U.S.C. § 553(b)(B). This prong of the good cause inquiry is "confined to those situations in which the administrative rule is a routine determination, insignificant in nature and impact, and inconsequential to the industry and to the public." *Util. Solid Waste Activities Grp.*, 236 F.3d at 755. This case does not present such a situation. Just as in *Utility Solid Waste*, the IFR is a rule "about which these members of the public [the petitioners] were greatly interested," so notice and comment were not "unnecessary." *Id.* EPA argues that since the IFR is just an interim rule, good cause is satisfied because "the interim status of the challenged rule is a significant factor" in determining whether notice and comment are unnecessary. But we held, in the very case on which EPA relies, that "the limited nature of the rule cannot in itself justify a failure to follow notice and comment procedures." *Mid-Tex Electric Coop.*, 822 F.2d at

CHAPTER Two | RULEMAKING

1132. And for good reason: if a rule's interim nature were enough to satisfy the element of good cause, then "agencies could issue interim rules of limited effect for any plausible reason, irrespective of the degree of urgency" and "the good cause exception would soon swallow the notice and comment rule." *Tenn. Gas Pipeline* [*Co. v. FERC*], 969 F.2d [1141,] 1145 [(D.C. Cir. 1992)]. . . .

Finally, an agency may invoke the good cause exception if providing notice and comment would be contrary to the public interest. 5 U.S.C. § 553(b)(B). In the IFR, EPA says it has good cause since "there is no risk to the public interest in allowing manufacturers to [use] NCPs before the point at which EPA could make them available through a full notice-and-comment rulemaking," but this misstates the statutory criterion. The question is not whether *dispensing* with notice and comment would be contrary to the public interest, but whether *providing* notice and comment would be contrary to the public interest. By improperly framing the question in this way, the IFR inverts the presumption, apparently suggesting that notice and comment is usually unnecessary. We cannot permit this subtle malformation of the APA. The public interest prong of the good cause exception is met only in the rare circumstance when ordinary procedures—generally presumed to serve the public interest—would in fact harm that interest. It is appropriately invoked when the timing and disclosure requirements of the usual procedures would defeat the purpose of the proposal—if, for example, "announcement of a proposed rule would enable the sort of financial manipulation the rule sought to prevent." *Util. Solid Waste Activities Grp.*, 236 F.3d at 755. In such a circumstance, notice and comment could be dispensed with "in order to prevent the amended rule from being evaded." *Id.* . . .

IV

Because EPA lacked good cause to dispense with required notice and comment procedures, we conclude the IFR must be vacated without reaching Petitioners' alternative arguments. We are aware EPA is currently in the process of promulgating a final rule—with the benefit of notice and comment—on this precise issue. However, we strongly reject EPA's claim that the challenged errors are harmless simply because of the pendency of a properly-noticed final rule. Were that true, agencies would have no use for the APA when promulgating any interim rules. So long as the agency eventually opened a final rule for comment, every error in every interim rule—no matter how egregious—could be excused as a harmless error. . . .

Notes and Questions

1. *The APA is a default rule.* In Part III.A of its opinion, the court examines whether *all* rules under the relevant provision of the Clean Air Act must go through notice-and-comment rulemaking. Recall that even under the APA, the exemptions from notice-and-comment rulemaking don't apply if the organic statute requires a "hearing" for those rules. The APA, as the court here explains, is just a default and a gap-filling statute.

2. *Statutory interpretation.* In concluding that the organic statute did not specifically require any particular procedures—and thus the APA by default applied—the court had to do some statutory interpretation. The court observed that the initial regulation providing for nonconformance penalties (NCPs) did indeed have to be promulgated after notice-and-comment according to subsection (g)(1) of the statute; but "such regulations," according to subsection (g)(2), had to be promulgated within a year after enactment of this provision of the Clean Air Act—many decades prior to the 2012 rulemaking at issue here. Thus, the court concluded that *this* rulemaking was not subject to the notice-and-comment requirement of subsection (g)(1) because if subsection (g)(1) referred to every NCP rulemaking, then subsection (g)(2) would be "impossible," since obviously not all such rulemakings would be made within a year of enactment. This is a standard move in statutory interpretation whereby a court will read the statute, if possible, so as to render each provision effective. Although there is no one label for this move, it really can be described simply as interpreting a provision in context and within the overall structure of the Act. See Statutory Interpretation Lesson 8.

3. *The Attorney General's Manual.* The Attorney General's Manual on the Administrative Procedure Act from 1947 is often considered as contemporaneous evidence of the meaning of the APA. See Statutory Interpretation Lesson 11. According to the manual, for purposes of the good cause exception, "impracticable" means that "due and timely execution of [an agency's] functions would be impeded by" the procedures; "unnecessary" means the rule is "a minor

PRACTICE POINTER It is often useful to turn to the 1947 Attorney General's Manual on the Administrative Procedure Act. Created shortly after the APA's enactment, it helps to explain the meaning and reasoning behind a lot of the APA's provisions.

rule or amendment in which the public is not particularly interested"; and "contrary to the public interest" means "the interest of the public would be defeated by any requirement of advance notice." U.S. Dep't of Justice, Att'y General's Manual on the Admin. Proc. Act 30–31 (1947).

4. *Interim rules and direct final rules.* The rule at issue in *Mack Trucks* was an "interim final rule." When an agency promulgates such a rule, it takes effect immediately, but the agency then promises to take comments on the interim final rule and subsequently promulgate a "final final rule," if you will. The APA does not recognize this category of rulemaking; therefore, the authority to issue the interim rule without no-

> **Defined Term**
>
> **INTERIM FINAL RULE:** A rule that will take immediate effect, but the agency will go through the notice-and-comment process to consider revisions before the ultimate rule is adopted.

tice-and-comment must derive from the APA good cause exemption. And if the rule is exempt under that exemption, the agency need not actually consider comments and promulgate a subsequent, final final rule. As a result, many agencies leave interim final rules in place indefinitely.

> **Defined Term**
>
> **DIRECT FINAL RULEMAKING:** A rulemaking without notice and comment that will become final unless an adverse comment is received.

Interim final rules are not to be confused with "direct final rulemaking." Another innovation of the last few decades, a direct final rulemaking is proposed and will become final *unless* the agency receives any adverse comments on it. If it receives even one material, adverse comment, the agency withdraws the rule and proceeds through the notice-and-comment process. Does the APA authorize this kind of rulemaking? One scholar has argued yes—if no one lodges an adverse comment, then presumably the rule is one in which the public is not particularly interested, and therefore exempt under the "unnecessary" prong of the good cause

> **IN QUIRY**
>
> As previously explained, the APA is often understood to be a kind of "constitution" for the administrative state. But the APA has lots of gaps between which agencies can innovate. Nowhere does the APA contemplate direct final rulemaking. What do you make of the agencies' innovation?

exemption. Ronald M. Levin, *Direct Final Rulemaking*, 64 Geo. Wash. L. Rev. 1, 11 (1995).

5. ***Remedy for improper interim rules.*** In the final paragraph of the excerpted opinion, the court noted that the EPA was going through notice-and-comment rulemaking in order to make the rule final. Does that cure the error in the case at hand? The courts typically hold that if an agency improperly relies on the good cause exemption, it cannot cure the error in the case at bar through post-promulgation notice. See, e.g., United States v. Dean, 604 F.3d 1275, 1280 (11th Cir. 2010); U.S. Steel Corp. v. EPA, 595 F.2d 207, 214–15 (5th Cir. 1979). The agency can, however, promulgate the same rule properly and bring enforcement actions in *future* cases, but even here the courts typically require the agency to show that it has kept an "open mind" about the comments received and the content of the final rule. Advocates for Highway & Auto Safety v. FHA, 28 F.3d 1288 (D.C. Cir. 1994).

■ *Problem 2.7*

The CDC publishes a notice in the Federal Register during the coronavirus pandemic of 2020/21. The notice "announces the issuance of an Order to temporarily halt residential evictions to prevent the further spread of COVID-19." The agency explains in the notice: "In the context of a pandemic, eviction moratoria—like quarantine, isolation, and social distancing—can be an effective public health measure utilized to prevent the spread of communicable disease. Eviction moratoria facilitate self-isolation by people who become ill or who are at risk for severe illness from COVID-19 due to an underlying medical condition."

The Order then provides: "Under this Order, a landlord, owner of a residential property, or other person with a legal right to pursue eviction or possessory action, shall not evict any covered person from any residential property in any jurisdiction to which this Order applies during the effective period of the Order. . . . This Order does not relieve any individual of any obligation to pay rent, make a housing payment, or comply with any other obligation that the individual may have under a tenancy, lease, or similar contract."

The agency did not engage in the notice-and-comment process prior to issuing the Order. Is the agency's action lawful?

3. Procedural Rules

As noted, section 553 does not apply "to interpretative rules, general statements of policy, or rules of agency organization, procedure, or practice." As a general matter, these categories of rules—interpretative rules, policy statements, and procedural rules—are collectively called "nonlegislative" rules. These are distinguished from "legislative rules," which do have to go through notice-and-comment rulemaking. Legislative rules are often said to have the "force of law." They create *new* legal rights and obligations on private parties. The octane rating rule from *National Petroleum Refiners* is an example. The hazardous waste rules in *Shell Oil* are another. And the rule in *Mack Trucks* was also legislative in this sense, which is why the good cause exemption had to be invoked as opposed to one of the nonlegislative rule categories. A nonlegislative rule, in contrast, does not have the force and effect of law—that is, it does not affect underlying rights or obligations—for one of three reasons. It could be because the rule is actually about procedure and not about substantive obligations at all. It could be because the rule is merely an interpretation of some *other* rule that already creates or determines one's underlying rights or obligations. Or it could be a mere "statement of policy," that is, it does not affect underlying rights and obligations because the agency has left itself discretion over how to handle some particular issue in the future, or because the "rule" merely identifies how the agency is going to exercise its discretion.

The first category of nonlegislative rules that we will discuss are procedural rules. In other areas of law, courts have had to grapple with the distinction between procedural and substantive rules. In Erie Railroad Co. v. Tompkins, 304 U.S. 64 (1938), the Supreme Court held that a federal court sitting in diversity must apply the substantive law of the relevant state, but the procedural law of the federal courts. Similarly, applying conflict-of-laws principles, courts often apply the substantive law of other states or countries but not the procedural laws of those other states or countries.

Yet this distinction is notoriously difficult to apply because procedure often affects substantive outcomes. If there is no remedy, is there a right? If a state legislature passed a law requiring plaintiffs to prove civil claims beyond a reasonable doubt, as opposed to the preponderance of the evidence standard, is that procedural or substantive? If as a result of a new procedural rule, 99 percent of substantive outcomes would be different, does that rule not change the underlying substantive right?

These issues were ventilated in the following influential opinion, although it was subsequently vacated as moot.

Air Transp. Ass'n of Am. v. Dep't of Transp.

900 F.2d 369, 371–84 (D.C. Cir. 1990), *vacated*, 498 U.S. 1077 (1991), *and vacated*, 933 F.2d 1043 (D.C. Cir. 1991)

Harry T. Edwards, Circuit Judge:

The issue in this case is whether respondent governmental agencies (collectively "Federal Aviation Administration" or "FAA") were obliged to engage in notice and comment procedures before promulgating a body of regulations governing the adjudication of administrative civil penalty actions. The FAA issued the Penalty Rules pursuant to a temporary enabling statute intended to augment the agency's authority to enforce compliance with aviation safety standards. Petitioner Air Transport Association of America ("Air Transport") contends that the FAA's failure to comply with the notice and comment requirements of the Administrative Procedure Act renders the Penalty Rules invalid. The FAA maintains that it was justified in dispensing with notice and comment under the "rules of agency organization, procedure, or practice" and "good cause" exceptions to section 553. . . .

It is well established that the exemption under section 553(b)(A), for "rules of agency organization, procedure, or practice," does *not* apply to agency action that "substantially alter[s] the rights or interests of regulated" parties. *American Hosp. Ass'n v. Bowen*, 834 F.2d 1037, 1041 (D.C.Cir.1987). The Penalty Rules fall outside the scope of the exception because they substantially affect civil penalty defendants' "right to avail [themselves] of an administrative adjudication." . . .

In December of 1987, Congress enacted a series of amendments to the Federal Aviation Act relating to civil penalties. Among other things, these amendments raised to $10,000 the maximum penalty for a single violation of aviation safety standards . . . .

At the same time, however, Congress remained attentive to the adjudicative rights of civil penalty defendants. Congress provided that the FAA could assess a civil penalty "only after notice and opportunity for a hearing on the record in accordance with section 554 of [the APA]." . . .

Approximately nine months after enactment . . . , the FAA promulgated the Penalty Rules. Effective immediately upon their issuance, the Penalty Rules established a schedule of civil penalties, including fines of up to $10,000 for violations of the safety standards of the Federal Aviation Act and related regulations. The Penalty Rules also established a comprehensive adjudicatory scheme providing for formal notice, settlement procedures, discovery, an adversary hearing before an ALJ and an administrative appeal. In explaining why it dispensed with prepromulgation notice and comment, the FAA emphasized the procedural character of the Penalty Rules . . . .

In its report to Congress, the FAA vigorously defended the Penalty Rules. Others . . . were less enthusiastic, criticizing what they perceived to be the Rules' systematic procedural bias in favor of the FAA. . . .

Section 553 of the APA obliges an agency to provide notice and an opportunity to comment before promulgating a final rule. . . .

Section 553's notice and comment requirements are essential to the scheme of administrative governance established by the APA. . . . For these reasons, we have consistently afforded a narrow cast to the exceptions to section 553, permitting an agency to forgo notice and comment only when the subject matter or the circumstances of the rulemaking divest the public of any legitimate stake in influencing the outcome. In the instant case, because the Penalty Rules substantially affected civil penalty defendants' right to avail themselves of an administrative adjudication, we cannot accept the FAA's contention that the Rules could be promulgated without notice and comment. . . .

Our cases construing section 553(b)(A) have long emphasized that a rule does not fall within the scope of the exception merely because it is capable of bearing the label "procedural." . . .

Rather than focus on whether a particular rule is "procedural" or "substantive," these decisions employ a functional analysis. Section 553(b)(A) has been described as essentially a "housekeeping" measure, *Chrysler Corp. v. Brown*, 441 U.S. 281, 310 (1979), "[t]he distinctive purpose of . . . [which] is to ensure 'that agencies retain latitude in organizing their *internal* operations,'" *American Hosp. Ass'n v. Bowen*, 834 F.2d 1037, 1047 (D.C. Cir. 1987) (quoting *Batterton*, 648

F.2d at 707) (emphasis added). Where nominally "procedural" rules "encode[ ] a substantive value judgment" or "substantially alter the rights or interests of regulated" parties, however, the rules must be preceded by notice and comment. *Id.* at 1047, 1041.

The Penalty Rules fall outside the scope of section 553(b)(A) because they substantially affect a civil penalty defendant's *right to an administrative adjudication.* . . .

[I]napposite are various decisions in which we have applied section 553(b)(A) to rules that regulate such matters as the timing of applications for benefits, or the timing of the agency's processing of such applications. . . . They were all cases, in short, in which "the need for public participation" in the rulemaking process was "too small to warrant it." The Penalty Rules, in contrast, affect the entire range of adjudicatory rights . . . —matters far too important to be withdrawn from public deliberation. . . .

Silberman, Circuit Judge, dissenting:

. . . . Lines between substance and procedure in various areas of the law are difficult to draw and therefore often perplex scholars and judges. But Congress, when it passed the Administrative Procedure Act, made that difference critical, and we are therefore obliged to implement a viable distinction between "procedural" rules and those that are substantive. . . .

If we assume a spectrum of rules running from the most substantive to the most procedural, I would describe the former as those that regulate "primary conduct" . . . and the latter are those furthest away from primary conduct. In other words, if a given regulation purports to direct, control, or condition the behavior of those institutions or individuals subject to regulation by the authorizing statute it is not procedural, it is substantive. At the other end of the spectrum are those rules, such as the ones before us in this case, which deal with enforcement or adjudication of claims of violations of the substantive norm but which do not *purport* to affect the substantive norm. These kinds of rules are, in my view, clearly procedural.

Rules are no less procedural because they are thought to be important or affect outcomes. . . .

It is in this context that in *Batterton v. Marshall,* 648 F.2d 694 (D.C. Cir. 1980), we said that substantive rules are those that affect the "rights and interests of parties." In *Batterton,* Maryland challenged the Department of Labor's adoption of a new method of calculating local unemployment rates, which in turn determined the amount of CETA job training funds each state and locality would receive. We categorized those new rules as substantive because they altered the criteria by which Government benefits would be distributed rather than simply change the manner in which claimants for benefits communicated to the agency the nature of their substantive claim. Similarly, in *Reeder v. FCC,* 865 F.2d 1298 (D.C. Cir. 1989), a radio station objected to the FCC's adoption of rules governing counterproposals to the agency's allotment of new FM channels throughout the United States. We decided that the procedural exemption was inapplicable because the FCC had altered its decisionmaking criteria for new station allotments.

In contrast, in *Neighborhood TV Co., Inc v. FCC,* 742 F.2d 629 (D.C. Cir. 1984), we concluded that FCC rules that froze contested applications for "translators" (devices which amplify and rebroadcast television signals) and then processed rural applications before urban ones were procedural because the rules did not alter the standards by which those applications would be judged. . . .

Of course, procedure impacts outcomes and thus can virtually always be described as affecting substance, but to pursue that line of analysis results in the obliteration of the distinction that Congress demanded. We avoided that snare only recently in *American Hosp. Ass'n v. Bowen,* 834 F.2d 1037, 1047 (D.C. Cir. 1987), where we held, over a strong dissent in many respects redolent of the majority opinion here, that HHS rules that set forth the enforcement priorities for peer review organizations (acting as agents to ensure medically reasonable and necessary hospital health care), as well as some adjudicatory procedures similar to those contained in the rules before us, did not have to be published for comment. Although it was argued that the procedures would affect hospital behavior by discouraging activity in the zone of an enforcement priority, we nevertheless held that the rules did not "encode [ ] a substantive value judgment or put[ ] a stamp of approval or disapproval on a given type of behavior." We recognized that hospital costs would be affected by the enforcement scheme, but that was not enough to bring the rules out of the procedural safe harbor. The case at bar involves rules that are, *a fortiori,* procedural because, unlike in *American Hospital Ass'n,* it is not even argued here that primary behavior—the safety efforts of the airlines—is even affected by the adjudicatory rules. . . .

NOTES AND QUESTIONS

1.   Two alternative tests. The majority and dissent adopt two different tests for what makes a rule substantive versus procedural. The dissent's approach is a bit easier to understand. Substantive rules change underlying rights and obligations. Whether or not a right can be vindicated in light of the available procedures, or whether a violation of underlying prohibitions on conduct can be proved, the question is simply whether as a matter of *law* there is a right or an obligation. Procedural rules do not actually affect these rights and obligations, except insofar as sometimes those rights may not be vindicated, or the available procedures may sweep up innocent people and fail to punish some guilty ones. The majority opinion, on the other hand, opted for a more functional test. How important is the regulation, and how substantially does it affect the *interests* of private parties? On this approach, it would seem that any regulation establishing adjudicatory proceedings for the first time would be "substantive." But can that possibly be right? Is there any-thing *more* procedural than the adjudicatory proceedings that will be used to vindicate rights or punish violations of underlying legal obligations?

 The second half of the casebook, about the separation of powers, will heavily feature debates between "formalism" and "functionalism." For now, it is helpful to know that formalists prefer clear legal rules, often derived from original meaning. Functionalists prefer multi-part tests that perhaps more accurately capture the realities of modern governance.

Surveying the legal tests propounded by other court decisions, it seems that the dissent has the better of the argument—at least as a first cut. In one case, the D.C. Circuit held that an "agency's abolition of face-to-face [meetings] did not alter the substantive criteria by which it would approve or deny proposed labels; it simply changed the procedures it would follow in applying those substantive standards." James V. Hurson Assocs., Inc. v. Glickman, 229 F.3d 277, 281 (D.C. Cir. 2000). In contrast, where OSHA issued a "directive" providing that certain employers would be inspected unless they adopted "a comprehensive safety and health program designed to meet standards that in some respects exceed those required by law," the court held that rule substantive because it was no different than "a plainly substantive rule mandating a comprehensive safety program." Chamber of Commerce of U.S. v. U.S. Dep't of Labor, 174 F.3d 206, 208, 212 (D.C. Cir. 1999).

There is little doubt, however, that procedures can affect outcomes. A trial by jury is very different from a trial by star chamber. The right to counsel and cross-examination at a live hearing will likely affect outcomes as well in comparison to a paper hearing. If a procedure is so skewed in favor of one particular outcome such that it *effectively* denies vindication of a substantive right, does there come a point when we say that the substantive right itself is diminished? And if so, is the procedural rule substantive? How rare will be the situation in which such procedural rules so affect outcomes that they should be deemed substantive?

FOR DISCUSSION

What is the relationship between procedure and substance? Is the line between the two easy to maintain? Doesn't procedure affect substantive outcomes?

4. Interpretative Rules

The next two categories of non-legislative rules are interpretative (or interpretive) rules, and statements of policy. Many casebooks treat these two exemptions together. And one legal scholar, in a prominent article, has argued that the two types of rules should be treated together under the label "guidance." Ronald M. Levin, *Rulemaking and the Guidance Exemption*, 70 Admin. L. Rev. 263 (2018). The D.C. Circuit still treats the two rules differently, however, and the APA itself appears to treat them differently, too. Your present author also believes the two to be distinct. Therefore, we begin with interpretative rules, and in the next section proceed to statements of policy.

Defined Term

INTERPRETATIVE RULE: Under the APA, an "interpretative" rule is a type of exempt nonlegislative rule. Many cases simplify the word to "interpretive." The exact definition is hard to pin down, but typically courts hold that an interpretive rule is merely interpreting some preexisting legal authority, as opposed to creating new substantive legal obligations.

Defined Term

GUIDANCE: Interpretative rules and policy statements are often considered collectively as agency "guidance."

American Mining Congress v. Mine Safety & Health Administration

995 F.2d 1106 (D.C. Cir. 1993)

STEPHEN F. WILLIAMS, CIRCUIT JUDGE:

This case presents a single issue: whether Program Policy Letters of the Mine Safety and Health Administration, stating the agency's position that certain x-ray readings qualify as "diagnose[s]" of lung disease within the meaning of agency reporting regulations, are interpretive rules under the Administrative Procedure Act. We hold that they are.

The Federal Mine Safety and Health Act, 30 U.S.C. § 801 *et seq.*, extensively regulates health and safety conditions in the nation's mines and empowers the Secretary of Labor to enforce the statute and relevant regulations. In addition, the Act requires "every operator of a . . . mine . . . [to] establish and maintain such records, make such reports, and provide such information, as the Secretary . . . may reasonably require from time to time to enable him to perform his functions." *Id.* at § 813(h). The Act makes a general grant of authority to the Secretary to issue "such regulations as . . . [he] deems appropriate to carry out" any of its provisions. *Id.* at § 957.

Pursuant to its statutory authority, the Mine Safety and Health Administration (acting on behalf of the Secretary of Labor) maintains regulations known as "Part 50" regulations, which cover the "Notification, Investigation, Reports and Records of Accidents, Injuries, Illnesses, Employment, and Coal Production in Mines." See 30 CFR Part 50. These were adopted via notice-and-comment rulemaking. Subpart C deals with the "Reporting of Accidents, Injuries, and Illnesses" and requires mine operators to report to the MSHA within ten days "each accident, occupational injury, or occupational illness" that occurs at a mine. Of central importance here, the regulation also says that whenever any of certain occupational illnesses are "*diagnosed*," the operator must similarly report the diagnosis within ten days. Among the occupational illnesses covered are "[s]ilicosis, asbestosis, coal worker's pneumoconiosis, and other pneumoconioses." An operator's failure to report may lead to citation and penalty.

As the statute and formal regulations contain ambiguities, the MSHA from time to time issues Program Policy Letters ("PPLs") intended to coordinate and convey agency policies, guidelines, and interpretations to agency employees and interested members of the public. One subject on which it has done so—apparently in response to inquiries from mine operators about whether certain x-ray results needed to be reported as "diagnos[es]"—has been the meaning of the term diagnosis for purposes of Part 50.

The first of the PPLs at issue here, PPL No. 91–III–2 (effective September 6, 1991), stated that any chest x-ray of a miner who had a history of exposure to pneumonoconiosis-causing dust that rated 1/0 or higher on the International Labor Office (ILO) classification system would be considered a "diagnosis that the x-rayed miner has silicosis or one of the other pneumonoconioses" for the purposes of the Part 50 reporting requirements. (The ILO classification system uses a 12-step scale to measure the concentration of opacities (i.e., areas of darkness or shading) on chest x-rays. A 1/0 rating is the fourth most severe of the ratings.) The 1991 PPL also set up a procedure whereby, if a mine operator had a chest x-ray initially evaluated by a relatively unskilled reader, the operator could seek a reading by a more skilled one; if the latter rated the x-ray below 1/0, the MSHA would delete the "diagnosis" from its files. We explain the multiple-reader rules further in the context of the third PPL, where they took their final form (so far).

The second letter, PPL No. P92–III–2 (effective May 6, 1992), superseded the 1991 PPL but largely repeated its view about a Part 50 diagnosis. In addition, the May 1992 PPL stated the MSHA's position that mere diagnosis of an occupational disease or illness within the meaning of Part 50 did not automatically entitle a miner to benefits for disability or impairment under a workers' compensation scheme. The PPL also said that the MSHA did not intend for an operator's mandatory reporting of an x-ray reading to be equated with an admission of liability for the reported disease.

The final PPL under dispute, PPL No. P92–III–2 (effective August 1, 1992), replaced the May 1992 PPL and again restated the MSHA's basic view that a chest x-ray rating above 1/0 on the ILO scale constituted a "diagnosis" of silicosis or some other pneumoconiosis. The August 1992 PPL also modified the MSHA's position on additional readings. Specifically, when the first reader is not a "B" reader (i.e., one certified by the National Institute of Occupational Safety and Health to perform ILO ratings), and the operator seeks a reading from a "B" reader, the MSHA will stay enforcement for failure to report the first reading. If the "B" reader concurs with the initial determination that the x-ray should be scored a 1/0 or higher, the mine operator must report the "diagnosis". If the "B" reader scores the x-ray below 1/0, the MSHA will continue to stay enforcement if the operator gets a third reading, again from a "B" reader; the MSHA then will accept the majority opinion of the three readers.

The MSHA did not follow the notice and comment requirements of 5 U.S.C. § 553 in issuing any of the three PPLs. In defending its omission of notice and comment, the agency relies solely on the interpretive rule exemption of § 553(b)(3)(A). . . .

The distinction between those agency pronouncements subject to APA notice-and-comment requirements and those that are exempt has been aptly described as "enshrouded in considerable smog," *General Motors Corporation v. Ruckelshaus,* 742 F.2d 1561, 1565 (D.C. Cir. 1984) (en banc) (quoting *Noel v. Chapman,* 508 F.2d 1023, 1030 (2d Cir.1975)); see also *American Hospital Association v. Bowen,* 834 F.2d 1037, 1046 (D.C. Cir. 1987) (calling the line between interpretive and legislative rules "fuzzy"); *Community Nutrition Institute v. Young,* 818 F.2d 943, 946 (D.C. Cir. 1987) (quoting authorities describing the present distinction between legislative rules and policy statements as "tenuous," "blurred" and "baffling").

Given the confusion, it makes some sense to go back to the origins of the distinction in the legislative history of the Administrative Procedure Act. Here the key document is the *Attorney General's Manual on the Administrative Procedure Act* (1947), which offers "the following working definitions":

> *Substantive rules*—rules, other than organizational or procedural under section 3(a)(1) and (2), issued by an agency pursuant to statutory authority and which implement the statute, as, for example, the proxy rules issued by the Securities and Exchange Commission pursuant to section 14 of the Securities Exchange Act of 1934 (15 U.S.C. 78n). Such rules have the force and effect of law.

> *Interpretative rules*—rules or statements issued by an agency to advise the public of the agency's construction of the statutes and rules which it administers. . . .

> *General statements of policy*—statements issued by an agency to advise the public prospectively of the manner in which the agency proposes to exercise a discretionary power.

. . . . Our own decisions have often used similar language, inquiring whether the disputed rule has "the force of law." We have said that a rule has such force only if Congress has delegated legislative power to the agency and if the agency intended to exercise that power in promulgating the rule.

On its face, the "intent to exercise" language may seem to lead only to more smog, but in fact there are a substantial number of instances where such "intent" can be found with some confidence. The first and clearest case is where, in the absence of a legislative rule by the agency, the legislative basis for agency enforcement would be inadequate. The example used by the Attorney General's Manual fits exactly—the SEC's proxy authority under § 14 of the Securities Exchange Act of 1934, 15 U.S.C. § 78n. Section 14(b), for example, forbids certain persons, "to give, or to refrain from giving a proxy" "in contravention of such rules and regulations as the Commission may prescribe." 15 U.S.C. § 78n(b). The statute itself forbids *nothing* except acts or omissions to be spelled out by the Commission in "rules or regulations." The present case is similar, as to Part 50 itself, in that § 813(h) merely requires an operator to maintain "such records . . . as the Secretary . . . may reasonably require from time to time." 30 U.S.C. § 813(h). Although the Secretary might conceivably create some "require[ments]" ad hoc, clearly some agency creation of a duty is a necessary predicate to any enforcement against an operator for failure to keep records. . . .

Second, an agency seems likely to have intended a rule to be legislative if it has the rule published in the Code of Federal Regulations; 44 U.S.C. § 1510 limits publication in that code to rules "having general applicability and legal effect."

Third, " '[i]f a second rule repudiates or is irreconcilable with [a prior legislative rule], the second rule must be an amendment of the first; and, of course, an amendment to a legislative rule must itself be legislative.' "

There are variations on these themes. For example, in *Chamber of Commerce v. OSHA*, 636 F.2d 464 (D.C. Cir. 1980), the agency had on a prior occasion claimed that a certain statutory term, correctly understood, itself imposed a specific requirement on affected businesses. We found that interpretation substantively invalid . . . . The agency then issued a purported interpretive rule to fill the gap (without notice and comment), and we struck it down as an invalid exercise of the agency's legislative powers.

We reviewed a similar juxtaposition of different agency modes in *Fertilizer Institute v. EPA*, 935 F.2d 1303, 1308 (D.C. Cir. 1991). There a statute created a duty to report any "release" of a "reportable quantity" or "RQ" of certain hazardous materials, specifying the RQs but authorizing the EPA to change them by regulation. In the preamble to a legislative rule exercising its authority to amend the RQs, the EPA also expatiated on the meaning of the statutory term "release"—improperly broadening it, as petitioners claimed and as we ultimately found. But we rejected a claim that the agency's attempted exposition of the term "release" was not an interpretation and therefore required notice and comment.

In *United States v. Picciotto*, 875 F.2d 345 (D.C. Cir. 1989), the Park Service had issued an indisputably legislative rule containing an "open-ended" provision stating that a "permit may contain additional reasonable conditions." Then, in a rule issued without notice and comment, it established some such conditions. We struck down the disputed condition, as it was not an interpretation of the prior regulation but an exercise of the legislative authority reserved by the prior legislative rule.

This focus on whether the agency *needs* to exercise legislative power (to provide a basis for enforcement actions or agency decisions conferring benefits) helps explain some distinctions that may, out of context, appear rather metaphysical. For example, in *Fertilizer Institute* we drew a distinction between instances where an agency merely "declare[s] its understanding of what a statute requires" (interpretive), and ones where an agency "go[es] beyond the text of a statute" (legislative). See also *Chamber of Commerce*, 636 F.2d at 469 (distinguishing between "constru[ing]" a statutory provision and "supplement[ing]" it). The difficulty with the distinction is that almost every rule may seem to do both. But if the dividing line is the necessity for agency legislative action, then a rule supplying that action will be legislative no matter how grounded in the agency's "understanding of what the statute requires," and an interpretation that spells out the scope of an agency's or regulated entity's pre-existing duty (such as EPA's interpretation of "release" in *Fertilizer Institute*), will be interpretive . . . .

Similarly, we have distinguished between cases where a rule is "based on specific statutory provisions" (interpretive), and where one is instead "based on an agency's power to exercise its judgment as to how best to implement a general statutory mandate" (legislative). *United Technologies Corp. v. EPA*, 821 F.2d 714, 719–20 (D.C. Cir. 1987). A statute or legislative rule that actually establishes a duty or a right is likely to be relatively specific (and the agency's refinement will be interpretive), whereas an agency's authority to create rights and duties will typically be relatively broad (and the agency's actual establishment of rights and duties will be legislative). But the legislative or interpretive status of the agency rules turns not in some general sense on the narrowness or breadth of the statutory (or regulatory) term in question, but on the prior existence or non-existence of legal duties and rights. . . .

In an occasional case we have appeared to stress whether the disputed rule is one with "binding effect"—"binding" in the sense that the rule does not " 'genuinely leave[ ] the agency . . . free to exercise discretion.' " That inquiry arose in a quite different context, that of distinguishing *policy statements*, rather than interpretive rules, from legislative norms. . . .

But while a good rule of thumb is that a norm is less likely to be a general policy statement when it purports (or, even better, has proven) to restrict agency discretion, restricting discretion tells one little about whether a rule is interpretive. . . .

[T]he ability to promulgate such rules, without notice and comment, does not appear more hazardous to affected parties than the likely alternative. Where a statute or legislative rule has created a legal basis for enforcement, an agency can simply let its interpretation evolve ad hoc in the process of enforcement or other applications (e.g., grants). The protection that Congress sought to secure by requiring notice and comment for legislative rules is not advanced by reading the exemption for "interpretive rule" so narrowly as to drive agencies into pure ad hocery—an ad hocery, moreover, that affords less notice, or less convenient notice, to affected parties.

Accordingly, insofar as our cases can be reconciled at all, we think it almost exclusively on the basis of whether the purported interpretive rule has "legal effect," which in turn is best ascertained by asking (1) whether in the absence of the rule there would not be an adequate legislative basis for enforcement action or other agency action to confer benefits or ensure the performance of duties, (2) whether the agency has published the rule in the Code of Federal Regulations, (3) whether the agency has explicitly invoked its general legislative authority, or (4) whether the rule effectively amends a prior legislative rule. If the answer to any of these questions is affirmative, we have a legislative, not an interpretive rule.

Here we conclude that the August 1992 PPL is an interpretive rule. The Part 50 regulations themselves require the reporting of diagnoses of the specified diseases, so there is no legislative gap that required the PPL as a predicate to enforcement action. Nor did the agency purport to act legislatively, either by including the letter in the Code of Federal Regulations, or by invoking its general legislative authority under 30 U.S.C. § 811(a). The remaining possibility therefore is that the August 1992 PPL is a de facto amendment of prior legislative rules, namely the Part 50 regulations.

A rule does not, in this inquiry, become an amendment merely because it supplies crisper and more detailed lines than the authority being interpreted. If that were so, no rule could pass as an interpretation of a legislative rule unless it were confined to parroting the rule or replacing the original vagueness with another.

Although petitioners cite some definitions of "diagnosis" suggesting that with pneumoconiosis and silicosis, a diagnosis requires more than a chest x-ray—specifically, additional diagnostic tools as tissue examination or at least an occupational history—MSHA points to some administrative rules that make x-rays at the level specified here the basis for a finding of pneumoconiosis. A finding of a disease is surely equivalent, in normal terminology, to a diagnosis, and thus the PPLs certainly offer no interpretation that repudiates or is irreconcilable with an existing legislative rule.

We stress that deciding whether an interpretation is an amendment of a legislative rule is different from deciding the substantive validity of that interpretation. An interpretive rule may be sufficiently within the language of a legislative rule to be a genuine interpretation and not an amendment, while at the same time being an incorrect interpretation of the agency's statutory authority. Here, petitioners have made no attack on the PPLs' substantive validity. Nothing that we say upholding the agency's decision to act without notice and comment bars any such substantive claims.

Notes and Questions

1. *Clarifying the "adequate basis to enforce" standard.* American Mining Congress is a leading case on the distinction between interpretative and legislative

rules, although not every scholar agrees with that characterization of the case. The key part of the test is this: "whether in the absence of the rule there would not be an adequate legislative basis for enforcement action or other agency action to confer benefits or ensure the performance of duties." The question, in other words, is whether the rule itself creates a *new* legal obligation—in which case it's not merely interpreting some prior authority—or whether there was already some legal obligation out there that this new rule merely clarifies. As the court noted, an interpretative rule "supplies crisper and more detailed lines than the authority being interpreted."

Unfortunately, this test has some potential to confuse. Recall what you have already learned about an agency's choice to proceed via adjudications or rulemakings. In the *National Petroleum Refiners* case, supra p. 87, the FTC had for decades proceeded directly from the broad statutory standard (prohibiting "unfair and deceptive trade acts and practices") to adjudications and enforcement actions. It was only several decades later that the agency sought to promulgate a legislative rule, such as the Octane Rule, to help implement the statute. But if the agency could have proceeded directly from the broad standard directly to an adjudication—and if it could have held in that adjudication that the failure to disclose octane ratings conspicuously on gas pumps was unfair and deceptive—wasn't there already an adequate basis to enforce the statute? Put another way, even extraordinarily broad statutory standards give the agency an adequate basis to "enforce" the statute, at least via adjudication.

The way out of this conundrum is to understand that when an agency implements a broad statutory standard, there may be an adequate basis to "enforce" it, but the agency is not actually *interpreting* the statute—it is implementing or supplementing it. Some standards are so broad that they authorize the agency to make regulations implementing them, but those regulations don't in any ordinary sense "interpret" the statutory terms. As the D.C. Circuit held in another case, quoting an administrative law scholar,

> if the relevant statute or regulation "consists of vague or vacuous terms—such as 'fair and equitable,' 'just and reasonable,' 'in the public interest,' and the like—the process of announcing propositions that specify applications of those terms is not ordinarily one of interpretation, because those terms in themselves do not supply substance from which the propositions can be derived."

Catholic Health Initiatives v. Sebelius, 617 F.3d 490, 495 (D.C. Cir. 2010) (quoting Robert A. Anthony, *"Interpretive" Rules, "Legislative" Rules and "Spurious" Rules: Lifting the Smog,* 8 Admin. L.J. Am. U. 1, 6 (1994)). And as your present author has written, broad statutory terms call for legislative specification, not interpretation. Ilan Wurman, *The Specification Power,* 168 U. Pa. L. Rev. 689 (2020).

The best way to understand the "adequate basis to enforce" test is simply to ask whether the "interpretive" rule is actually plausibly interpreting some statute or some other regulation, or is instead imposing a new legal obligation. As the D.C. Circuit said in yet another case, "An interpretative rule . . . typically reflects an agency's construction of a statute that has been entrusted to the agency to administer," or some other substantive regulation. Syncor Int'l Corp. v. Shalala, 127 F.3d 90, 94 (D.C. Cir. 1997). Thus, "[t]he distinction between an interpretative rule and substantive rule . . . likely turns on how tightly the agency's interpretation is drawn linguistically from the actual language of the statute" (or other substantive rule being interpreted). Id. (quoting Paralyzed Veterans of Am. v. D.C. Arena L.P., 117 F.3d 579, 588 (D.C. Cir. 1997)).

Does this suggest that Judge Williams was wrong where, in the last paragraph of his opinion, he decoupled the procedural question from the merits question? He said: "We stress that deciding whether an interpretation is an amendment of a legislative rule is different from deciding the substantive validity of that interpretation. An interpretive rule may be sufficiently within the language of a legislative rule to be a genuine interpretation and not an amendment, while at the same time being an incorrect interpretation of the agency's statutory authority." The court, in other words, held that a rule could be "interpretative" for purposes of the APA, but it could also be an *incorrect* interpretation on the merits. Is this distinction tenable? If an interpretative rule is *erroneous,* doesn't that mean by definition that the rule is not actually an interpretation of some prior authority, but an attempt to impose a *new* legal obligation instead?

IN QUIRY — What is the relationship between the procedural question (whether a rule is interpretive) and the merits (whether the interpretation is a correct interpretation of the prior authority)? Can the two questions be separated? Or are they related?

Consider this in the context of the x-ray rule. Suppose the policy required all x-rays to be forwarded on as "diagnoses," even if no reader had taken a look at them. In that case, the x-ray would not actually be a "diagnosis" in the sense of a conclusion from some medical data. And if it isn't a diagnosis, then wouldn't the attempt to require the disclosure of such x-rays actually be an attempt to create a *new* legal obligation? In which case, it would be a legislative rule. So can the merits question really be separated from the procedural question?

Perhaps a better approach would simply be to answer the question on the merits. If the rule is a good and proper interpretation of some prior authority, then no notice-and-comment is necessary and, as a proper interpretation on the merits, it will be upheld. On the other hand, if it is a bad interpretation, then it is in actuality an attempt to impose new legal requirements, which must go through notice-and-comment. Thus the "interpretation" must be invalidated on the merits but, if the agency wishes to proceed with the rule, it can always promulgate it as a *legislative* rule using notice-and-comment—that is, as a *new* substantive requirement. Whether such a legislative rule is authorized will depend on the delegation of authority in the statute.

This approach has another virtue. We should find it acceptable that an agency forgo notice and comment for an interpretative rule because at least the courts will get to review such legal "interpretations." Put another way, to the extent the rule is truly interpretative such that no public comment is necessary, at least the agency's interpretation is judicially reviewable on the merits. To be sure, under current law, agency interpretations get some amount of deference. See Chapter 4.C. But this review is much less deferential than review of the merits of an agency's regulatory policy choices. See Chapter 4.A. Although courts don't have much of a say in policing an agency's policy choices, at least the *public* does through the notice-and-comment process.

2. ***Example:*** **Hoctor v. U.S. Dep't of Agriculture.** *Hoctor* involved the Animal Welfare Act, which "is primarily designed to assure the humane treatment of animals." 82 F.3d 165, 167 (7th Cir. 1996). The Act allows the Secretary of Agriculture "to promulgate such rules, regulations, and orders as he may deem necessary in order to effectuate the purposes of [the Act]." In pursuance of this authority, the Department promulgated a "structural strength" regulation providing that any facility housing animals "must be constructed of such material and of such strength as appropriate for the animals involved," and "shall be structurally sound and shall be maintained in good repair to protect the animals from injury and to contain the animals." Hoctor kept "big cats," including lions and tigers, on his farm; in consultation with a Department inspector, Hoctor built a perimeter fence six feet high.

The year after, however, the Department "issued an internal memorandum addressed to its force of inspectors in which it said that all 'dangerous animals,' defined as including, among members of the cat family, lions, tigers, and leopards, must be inside a perimeter fence at least eight feet high." The Department did not go through notice-and-comment, relying instead on the interpretive rule exemption. The Seventh Circuit rejected that view. Even if the agency has authority to promulgate such a rule, it must do so through notice-and-comment because the eight-foot rule, as opposed to nine feet or seven feet, simply can't be derived from any *interpretation* of the statute or regulation. The court reasoned:

> [Even] if the eight-foot rule were deemed one of those minimum standards that the Department is required by statute to create, it could not possibly be thought an interpretive rule. For what would it be interpreting? When Congress authorizes an agency to create standards, it is delegating legislative authority, rather than itself setting forth a standard which the agency might then particularize through interpretation. Put differently, when a statute does not impose a duty on the persons subject to it but instead authorizes . . . an agency to impose a duty, the formulation of that duty becomes a legislative task entrusted to the agency. Provided that a rule promulgated pursuant to such a delegation is intended to bind, and not merely to be a tentative statement of the agency's view, . . . the rule would be the clearest possible example of a legislative rule, as to which the notice and comment procedure not followed here is mandatory, as distinct from an interpretive rule; for there would be nothing to interpret.

Id. at 169–70. Do you agree with this reasoning? Doesn't it rely on the *merits* of the agency's interpretation? No reasonable person could "interpret" the existing regulation or statute to require the eight-foot fence; therefore, if the agency is to impose such a requirement, it must do so through notice-and-comment rulemaking.

3.   The other factors from **American Mining Congress.** In addition to the adequate basis to enforce test, the other factors the court announced in *American Mining Congress* relevant to the analysis are (1) whether the rule is published in the Code of Federal Regulation, (2) whether the agency invoked its general rulemaking authority, and (3) whether the rule amends or repeals a prior legislative rule. Judge Williams' opinion stated that if any of these factors is met, then we have a legislative rule. And that will usually be true—but not always. Each of these factors is somewhat question-begging. For example, 44 U.S.C. § 1510 limits publication in the CFR to

 CODE OF FEDERAL REGULATIONS: Something of a hybrid between the federal register and the U.S. Code, the CFR compiles final agency regulations, and sometimes includes interpretative rules.

rules of general applicability and "legal effect." But the agency has to decide in the first place whether it has to publish the rule in the CFR, and thus has to determine whether the rule has "legal effect." Indeed, in Health Ins. Ass'n of Am., Inc. v. Shalala, 23 F.3d 412, 423 (D.C. Cir. 1994), Judge Williams found a rule to be interpretative even though the agency published it in the CFR.

Similarly, if the agency is invoking its general rulemaking authority, then it certainly believes it is promulgating a legislative rule. But of course the agency in the first place has to make the determination that the rule is legislative such that it must invoke its rulemaking authority. (If the rule is interpretative, then no invocation of general authority is necessary because interpreting law as an incident to enforcing the law is part of "the executive power" to carry laws into execution. Agencies only need to invoke their general legislative authority to make new, binding legal requirements, that is, to make "legislative rules.")

Finally, although a rule amending or repealing a prior legislative rule would surely itself be a legislative rule, there is still a question as to whether that initial rule that is being amended is in fact legislative. In each of these situations, something else must be the determining factor in whether a rule is interpretative or legislative. That key factor is the adequate basis to enforce test—which is another way of asking whether the rule is creating a new legal obligation, or merely clarifying some existing legal obligation.

5. Policy Statements

The next cases deal with statements of policy. Courts routinely cite cases involving interpretative rules and policy statements interchangeably, and the scholarly commentary widely believes the distinction between these two kinds of nonlegislative rules to be fuzzy. The D.C. Circuit, however, continues to maintain that there is a distinction between the two types of rules. To be sure, there will be commonality. As nonlegislative rules, both interpretative rules and policy statements do not create or alter any underlying private rights or obligations. But the reason this is so is different for each type of rule.

Pacific Gas & Electric Co. v. Federal Power Commission

506 F.2d 33 (D.C. Cir. 1974)

MacKinnon, Circuit Judge:

Petitioners assert that we have jurisdiction under section 19(b) of the Natural Gas Act to review Order No. 467, which the Federal Power Commission issued on January 8, 1973. Order No. 467 is a 'Statement of Policy' on 'priorities-of-deliveries by jurisdictional pipelines during periods of curtailment' which the Commission indicated it proposes to implement in all matters arising under the Act. The petitioning customers of pipeline companies, whose deliveries are subject to curtailment during natural gas shortages, contend that Order No. 467 is procedurally defective for failure to comply with the Administrative Procedure Act . . . . We hold that as a general statement of policy, Order No. 467 is exempt from the rulemaking requirements of the Administrative Procedure Act. . . .

I. BACKGROUND

This country appears to be experiencing a natural gas shortage which necessitates the curtailment of supplies to certain customers during peak demand periods. The problem confronting many pipeline companies is whether to curtail on the basis of existing contractual commitments or on the basis of the most efficient end use of the gas. In some instances the pipeline companies are concerned that withholding gas due under existing contracts may subject them to civil liability.

Recognizing these uncertainties and mindful of the desirability of providing uniform curtailment regulation, the FPC in 1971 issued a Statement of General Policy in the form of Order No. 431 directing jurisdictional pipeline companies which expected periods of shortages to file tariff sheets containing a curtailment plan. Order No. 431 hinted that curtailment priorities should be based on the end use of the gas and stated that curtailment plans approved by the Commission 'will control in all respects notwithstanding inconsistent provisions in (prior) sales contracts . . . .' In response to Order No. 431, numerous pipeline companies which had not already done so submitted a variety of curtailment plans for the Commission's approval. As could be expected, the curtailment plans reflected a wide range of views as to the proper priorities for delivery. Some plans were based on end use; others, on contract entitlements. The industry was forced to speculate as to which priorities would later be found to be just and reasonable by the Commission, and the absence of any stated Commission policy hindered effective long range planning by pipelines, distributors and consumers.

Sensing a need for guidance and uniformity in the curtailment area, on January 8, 1973 the Commission promulgated Order No. 467, the order presently under review, which is reprinted in the Appendix to this opinion. Entitled 'Statement of Policy,' Order No. 467 was issued without prior notice or opportunity for comment. The statement sets forth the Commission's view of a proper priority schedule and expresses the Commission's policy that the national interest would be best served by assigning curtailment priorities on the basis of end use rather than on the basis of prior contractual commitments. Order No. 467 further states the Commission's intent to follow this priority schedule unless a particular pipeline company demonstrates that a different curtailment plan is more in the public interest. On January 15, 1973 the Commission issued Order No. 467–A, which corrected an inadvertent omission in Order No. 467 of procedures to provide for emergency situations that may occur during curtailment periods.

The Commission immediately received numerous petitions for rehearing, reconsideration, modification or clarification of Orders Nos. 467 and 467–A, and several parties requested permission to intervene. Most of the petitioners were customers of pipeline companies subject to curtailment, particularly electric generating companies to whom Order No. 467 had assigned a low priority. Few pipeline companies objected to Order No. 467, apparently because the pipelines sell all the gas they can during periods of shortage and consequently are not overly concerned with which customers receive it. On March 2, 1973 the Commission issued Order No. 467–B, which affirmed the policy expressed in Order No. 467, amended that order in some minor instances and otherwise denied the petitions for rehearing and intervention.

Petitioners seek review of Order No. 467 in this court . . . and [argue] that Order No. 467 is in effect a substantive rule which the Commission should have promulgated after a rulemaking proceeding under the Administrative Procedure Act (APA) . . . .

II. STATEMENTS OF POLICY

. . . . The Commission maintains that Order No. 467 was exempt from the rulemaking requirements because it is a 'general statement of policy' within the meaning of section 553(b)(A) [of the APA]. . . .

Professor Davis has described the distinction between substantive rules and general statements of policy as a 'fuzzy product.' Unfortunately the issues in this case compel us to attempt to define the fuzzy perimeters of a general statement of policy.

An administrative agency has available two methods for formulating policy that will have the force of law. An agency may establish binding policy through rulemaking procedures by which it promulgates substantive rules, or through adjudications which constitute binding precedents. A general statement of policy is the outcome of neither a rulemaking nor an adjudication; it is neither a rule nor a precedent but is merely an announcement to the public of the policy which the agency hopes to implement in future rulemakings or adjudications. A general statement of policy, like a press release, presages an upcoming rulemaking or announces the course which the agency intends to follow in future adjudications.

As an informational device, the general statement of policy serves several beneficial functions. By providing a formal method by which an agency can express its views, the general statement of policy encourages public dissemination of the agency's policies prior to their actual application in particular situations. Thus the agency's initial views do not remain secret but are disclosed well in advance of their actual application. Additionally, the publication of a general statement of policy facilitates long range planning within the regulated industry and promotes uniformity in areas of national concern.

The critical distinction between a substantive rule and a general statement of policy is the different practical effect that these two types of pronouncements have in subsequent administrative proceedings. A properly adopted substantive rule establishes a standard of conduct which has the force of law. In subsequent administrative proceedings involving a substantive rule, the issues are whether the adjudicated facts conform to the rule and whether the rule should be waived or applied in that particular instance. The underlying policy embodied in the rule is not generally subject to challenge before the agency.

A general statement of policy, on the other hand, does not establish a 'binding norm.' It is not finally determinative of the issues or rights to which it is addressed. The agency cannot apply or rely upon a general statement of policy as law because a general statement of policy only announces what the agency seeks to establish as policy. A policy statement announces the agency's tentative intentions for the future. When the agency applies the policy in a particular situation, it must be prepared to support the policy just as if the policy statement had never been issued. An agency cannot escape its responsibility to present evidence and reasoning supporting its substantive rules by announcing binding precedent in the form of a general statement of policy.

Often the agency's own characterization of a particular order provides some indication of the nature of the announcement. The agency's express purpose may be to establish a binding rule of law not subject to challenge in particular cases. On the other hand the agency may intend merely to publish a policy guideline that is subject to complete attack before it is finally applied in future cases. When the agency states that in subsequent proceedings it will thoroughly consider not only the policy's applicability to the facts of a given case but also the underlying validity of the policy itself, then the agency intends to treat the order as a general statement of policy. . . .

Applying these general principles to the problem at hand, we conclude that Order No. 467 is a general statement of policy. Order No. 467 is entitled and consistently referred to by the Commission as a general statement of policy. Recognizing the 'need for Commission guidance in curtailment planning,' the Commission announced in Order No. 467 the curtailment policy which it 'proposes to implement,' the 'plan preferred by the Commission' which 'will serve as a guide in other proceedings.' Thus, the stated purpose of Order No. 467 was not to provide an inflexible, binding rule but to give advance notice of the general policy with respect to curtailment priorities that the Commission prefers.

Order No. 467 does not establish a curtailment plan for any particular pipeline. The effect of the order is to inform the public of the types of plans which will receive initial and tentative FPC approval, but there is no assurance that any such plan will be finally approved. As the Commission stated:

> When applied in specific cases, opportunity will be afforded interested parties to challenge or support this policy through factual or legal presentation as may be appropriate in the circumstances presented.

> (Order No. 467 is) not finally determinative of the rights and duties of a given pipeline, its customers or ultimate consumers; it expressly envisions further proceedings.

> . . . . Not only will petitioners have an opportunity to challenge the merits of the proposed plan, they will also have an opportunity to demonstrate that the plan is inappropriate in particular circumstances. . . .

> We, of course, recognize that extraordinary circumstances may preclude the strict adherence to the priorities established and, consequently, we will permit those persons who allege that their circumstances require such extraordinary treatment to file petitions for relief under Section 1.7(b) of our Rules of Practice and Procedure. Barring such circumstances, our review of those curtailment proceedings and our knowledge of the industry convinces us that the priorities-of-delivery set forth below should be applied to all jurisdictional pipeline companies during periods of curtailment.

> This does not mean that the parties may not propose or the commission may not adopt variations on the Sec. 2.78(a) plan, but there must be evidence in the record to support any such variations. . . .

Thus it is apparent from Order No. 467 itself that there is no final, inflexible impact upon the petitioners. And since the statement will be applied prospectively, the courts are in a position to police the Commission's application of the policy and to insure that the Commission gives no greater effect to Order No. 467 than the order is entitled to as a general statement of policy.

The FPC of course was under no compulsion to issue Order No. 467. The Commission issued the policy statement because the curtailment plans being submitted reflected sharp differences in philosophy which necessitated Commission guidance in the curtailment area. In the absence of such a policy statement, the Commission could have proceeded on an ad hoc basis and tentatively approved curtailment plans filed under section 4 of the Act which the Commission found to be just and reasonable. In following such a course the only difference from the present situation would be that the Commission would be acting under a secret policy rather than under the publicized guidelines of Order No. 467. The argument that an agency must follow rulemaking procedures when it elects to formulate policy by a substantive rule has no application in this case. Order No. 467 does not establish a substantive rule. Although the Commission is free to initiate a rulemaking proceeding to establish a binding substantive rule, the Commission apparently intends to establish its curtailment policies by proceeding through individual adjudications. Order No. 467 merely announces the general policy which the Commission hopes to establish in subsequent proceedings. . . .

We conclude that Order No. 467 is a general statement of policy and that it was therefore unnecessary for the Commission to conduct rulemaking proceedings under the Administrative Procedure Act.

Community Nutrition Institute v. Young

818 F.2d 943 (D.C. Cir. 1987)

PER CURIAM:

This case makes its second appearance before this court. It presents a challenge by a consortium of organizations and private citizens (collectively referred to as CNI) to the Food and Drug Administration's regulation of certain unavoidable contaminants in food, most particularly, aflatoxins in corn. Pursuant to its statutory mandate to limit the amount of "poisonous or deleterious substances" in food, *see* 21 U.S.C. § 346, FDA establishes "action levels" informing food producers of the allowable levels of unavoidable contaminants such as aflatoxins. Producers who sell products that are contaminated above the action level, which for aflatoxins in corn is currently set at 20 parts per billion, are subject to enforcement proceedings initiated by FDA. . . .

Under the APA, agency rules may be issued only after the familiar notice-and-comment procedures enumerated in the statute are completed. *See* 5 U.S.C. § 553. It is undisputed that the action level at issue here was promulgated *sans* those procedures. FDA, however, argues that notice-and-comment require-ments do not apply by virtue of subsection (b)(3)(A) of section 553, which carves out an exception for "interpretative rules [and] general statements of policy." According to the FDA, action levels represent nothing more than nonbinding statements of agency enforcement policy. CNI, on the other hand, argues that the action levels restrict enforcement discretion to such a degree as to consti-tute legislative rules.

The distinction between legislative rules and interpretative rules or policy statements has been described at various times as "tenuous," "fuzzy," "blurred," and, perhaps most picturesquely, "enshrouded in considerable smog." As Profes-sor Davis puts it, "the problem is baffling." By virtue of Congress' silence with respect to this matter, it has fallen to the courts to discern the line through the painstaking exercise of, hopefully, sound judgment.

Despite the difficulty of the terrain, prior cases do provide some useful guideposts. Judge McGowan identified "two criteria" that courts have used in their efforts to fathom the interpretative/legislative distinction:

> First, courts have said that, unless a pronouncement acts pro-spectively, it is a binding norm. Thus . . . a statement of policy may not have a present effect: "a 'general statement of policy' is one that does not impose any rights and obligations". . . .

> The second criterion is whether a purported policy statement genuinely leaves the agency and its decisionmakers free to exercise discretion.

[*American Bus Ass'n v. U.S.,*] 627 F.2d [525,] 529 [(D.C. Cir. 1980)] (quoting *Texaco v. FPC,* 412 F.2d 740, 744 (3d Cir.1969)). . . .

Applying these principles to the case at hand, we are persuaded that the FDA action levels are legislative rules and thus subject to the notice-and-com-ment requirements of section 553. While FDA now characterizes the action levels as policy statements, a variety of factors, when considered in light of the criteria set out in *American Bus,* indicate otherwise.

First. The language employed by FDA in creating and describing action levels suggests that those levels both have a present effect and are binding. Specifically, the agency's regulations on action levels explain an action level in the following way:

[A]n action level for an added poisonous or deleterious substance
. . . may be established to define the level of contamination at which
food *will be deemed to be adulterated.* An action level may *prohibit any
detectable amount of substance in food.*

21 C.F.R. § 109.4 (1986) (emphasis added). This language, speaking as
it does of an action level "defin[ing]" the acceptable level and "prohibit[ing]"
substances, clearly reflects an interpretation of action levels as presently binding
norms. This type of mandatory, definitive language is a powerful, even potentially dispositive, factor suggesting that action levels are substantive rules. . . .

Second. This view of action levels—as having a present, binding effect—
is confirmed by the fact that FDA considers it necessary for food producers
to secure *exceptions* to the action levels. A specific regulatory provision allows
FDA to "exempt from regulatory action and permit the marketing of any food
that is unlawfully contaminated with a poisonous or deleterious substance" if
certain conditions exist. *Id.* § 109.8(a). This language implies that in the absence of an exemption, food with aflatoxin contamination over the action level
is "unlawful." This putatively unlawful status can derive only from the action
level, which, again, indicates that the action level is a presently binding norm.
If, as the agency would have it, action levels did indeed "not bind courts, food
producers or FDA," it would scarcely be necessary to require that "exceptions"
be obtained.

Third. On several occasions, in authorizing blending of adulterated with
unadulterated corn, the FDA has made statements indicating that action levels establish a binding norm. . . . [I]n a formal notice published in the Federal
Register of a decision to permit blending and interstate shipment, FDA wrote:

Any food that contains aflatoxin in excess of 20 ppb . . . *is considered
by FDA to be adulterated* under section 402(a)(1) of the Federal Food,
Drug, and Cosmetic Act (21 U.S.C. 342(a)(1)), and *therefore may not
be shipped in interstate commerce.*

46 Fed. Reg. 7447 (1981) (emphasis added). . . . The agency's own words
strongly suggest that action levels are not musings about what the FDA might
do in the future but rather that they set a precise level of aflatoxin contamination that FDA has presently deemed permissible. Action levels inform food
producers what this level is; indeed, that is their very purpose.

We are not unmindful that in a suit to enjoin shipment of allegedly contaminated corn, it appears that FDA would be obliged to prove that the corn is "adulterated," within the meaning of the FDC Act, rather than merely prove non-compliance with the action level. The action level thus does not bind food producers in the sense that producers are automatically subject to enforcement proceedings for violating the action level. This factor, accordingly, points in favor of the agency's characterization. But the fact that action levels do not completely bind food producers as would a more classic legislative rule (where the only issue before the court would be if the agency rule were in fact violated) is not determinative of the issue. For here, we are convinced that FDA has bound itself. As FDA conceded at oral argument, it would be daunting indeed to try to convince a court that the agency could appropriately prosecute a producer for shipping corn with less than 20 ppb aflatoxin. And this type of cabining of an agency's prosecutorial discretion can in fact rise to the level of a substantive, legislative rule. . . .

In sum, consideration of a variety of factors leads us to conclude that the FDA's action levels are not within the section 553(b)(3)(A) exception to notice-and-comment requirements. Since all agree that those procedures were not followed, the action level at issue here cannot stand. . . .

We add one additional caveat. Our holding today in no way indicates that agencies develop written guidelines to aid their exercise of discretion only at the peril of having a court transmogrify those guidelines into binding norms. We recognize that such guidelines have the not inconsiderable benefits of apprising the regulated community of the agency's intentions as well as informing the exercise of discretion by agents and officers in the field. It is beyond question that many such statements are non-binding in nature and would thus be characterized by a court as interpretative rules or policy statements. We are persuaded that courts will appropriately reach an opposite conclusion only where, as here, the *agency* itself has given its rules substantive effect.

In sum, our holding today is narrow. We conclude that in the circumstances of this case, FDA by virtue of its own course of conduct has chosen to limit its discretion and promulgated action levels which it gives a present, binding effect. Having accorded such substantive significance to action levels, FDA is compelled by the APA to utilize notice-and-comment procedures in promulgating them. . . .

[An opinion concurring in part and dissenting in part is omitted.—Ed.]

NOTES AND QUESTIONS

1.   *What is the test?* What is the test for what makes a rule a policy statement? In both *PG&E* and *CNI*, the court used language about rights and obligations as well as discretion: First, "a 'general statement of policy' is one that does not impose any rights and obligations," and "[t]he second criterion is whether a purported policy statement genuinely leaves the agency and its decisionmakers free to exercise discretion." In a part of the opinion omitted from the excerpt, the court in *CNI* went on to say that the two inquiries overlap. But can the first part of the test possibly be correct? Whether a rule affects rights and obligations is the test for distinguishing any legislative rule from any nonlegislative rule. Thus, if the rule doesn't alter or impose rights and obligations, it is most certainly nonlegislative, but we still don't know if that's because the rule is a policy statement or because it is a procedural or interpretative rule.

As the AG Manual suggests, the real question in distinguishing a policy statement from both a legislative rule and other nonlegislative rules seems to be entirely about *discretion*—is the rule discretionary, or has the agency bound itself (or others)? An agency can bind itself to follow a certain procedure, or even to a certain interpretation of some prior regulation, and therefore the rule would not be a "policy statement" but it would still be an exempt nonlegislative rule. Thus the question is whether the "statement" leaves genuine discretion, or actually seems to change the underlying *legal rules* at play, whether those legal rules are procedural or substantive. The test, at least as a first cut, is whether the agency has purported to bind itself or instead has genuinely left itself discretion.

Even this formulation of the test, however, requires some qualification. Suppose an agency has bound itself, for example, by stating that it will prosecute every offense under its statute no matter how minor. The agency is purporting to bind itself here, and therefore it would appear that its statement is not merely a matter of "policy." But can't the agency always reverse itself, and in that sense it retains discretion? Is a rule that it will prosecute all offenses actually a legislative rule? Does it alter any rights or obligations? It doesn't seem to. Go back to the AG's Manual, quoted in the *American Mining Congress* case: a statement of policy is a statement made "to advise the public prospectively of the manner in which the agency proposes to exercise a discretionary power." Can't an agency bind itself to exercise a discretionary power in some way, and therefore the binding effects test also cannot be the right test?

To illustrate with a current example, consider the various executive orders involving racial equity promulgated in the first weeks of the Biden Administration. One such order requires agencies to assess existing regulations to determine if they create barriers to equity. Assume for a moment the APA applied to the President. These executive orders would be "rules," but they would not be procedural rules or interpretative rules. But these rules also do not create any underlying legal obligations. They are policy statements: they tell the agency heads how to exercise their discretion in a particular way, without altering any underlying legal rules. The executive order is most definitely *binding* on these agencies. But it binds them only to exercise their discretion in a certain way, and that does not change any underlying legal rights. Suppose an agency subsequently promulgates a rule that says, to the extent permissible by law, the agency will choose among competing potential regulations that which advances racial equity the most. Such a rule would certainly be binding on the agency, but the rule would still be a policy statement: it is all about how the agency will exercise its discretion. No underlying right or obligation is altered until the subsequent legislative rule, taking racial equity into account, is actually promulgated.

We might summarize as follows. If the agency has genuinely left itself discretion—it has merely announced its tentative intentions—then that is *sufficient* to determine that its rule is a nonbinding policy statement. But that condition, although sufficient, is not necessary. Even if the agency does purport to bind itself, the rule can *still* be a mere statement of policy if the agency has bound itself merely to exercise discretion in a way that does not actually alter any underlying substantive rights or obligations. In the *CNI* case, the agency bound itself to enforce a ceiling on aflatoxins, and that choice *also* altered the obligations of the private parties subject to the aflatoxin rule. In contrast, a rule that binds the agency to prosecute every instance of a certain type of offense, or that binds the agency always to choose among the rulemaking options that which most advances racial equity, is a rule that is binding on the agency but which does not alter any legal rights or obligations. Such a rule would also be an exempt policy statement.

2. *Policy statements versus interpretative rules.* Perhaps it's helpful to consider how policy statements are different from interpretative rules. Interpretative rules actually *interpret* something that's already out there—some language in a statute or regulation. Does a policy statement do that? Typically not. Usually a policy statement tells us something about how an agency is going to enforce some rule that we already know about. The D.C. Circuit explained in one case,

> An agency policy statement does not seek to impose or elaborate or interpret a legal norm. It merely represents an agency position with respect to how it will treat—typically enforce—the governing legal norm. By issuing a policy statement, an agency simply lets the public know its current enforcement or adjudicatory approach. The agency retains the discretion and the authority to change its position—even abruptly—in any specific case because a change in its policy does not affect the legal norm.

Syncor Int'l Corp. v. Shalala, 127 F.3d 90, 94 (D.C. Cir. 1997). In contrast, an interpretative rule actually *interprets* something.

It is, however, theoretically possible to have a policy statement *about* an interpretation. After all, doesn't interpretation sometimes entail discretion? Thus, it would still be a policy statement to say, "It is our policy to interpret the relevant statutory term in the following way, although we reserve the right to interpret the term differently if we determine that this interpretation is inappropriate in any given circumstances." Do you see how policy statements and interpretative rules are different?

3. *Do exceptions matter?* Is the existence of an "exception" or "exemption" to a general rule sufficient to confer discretion? That's what the court seems to assume in *PG&E*, but to reject in *CNI*. In *PG&E*, the court quoted the following language from the policy:

> We, of course, recognize that extraordinary circumstances may preclude the strict adherence to the priorities established and, consequently, we will permit those persons who allege that their circumstances require such extraordinary treatment to file petitions for relief under Section 1.7(b) of our Rules of Practice and Procedure. Barring such circumstances, our review of those curtailment proceedings and our knowledge of the industry convinces us that the priorities-of-delivery set forth below should be applied to all

jurisdictional pipeline companies during periods of curtailment. This does not mean that the parties may not propose or the commission may not adopt variations on the Sec. 2.78(a) plan, but there must be evidence in the record to support any such variations.

Is this really "discretion"? Imagine if Congress passed a law that declared, "The legal rule shall be x. But if you can demonstrate circumstances a, b, and c, then the agency has authority to do y instead." Does the mere existence of two possible legal outcomes mean there is discretion, or are both possible outcomes simply part of the overall legal rule?

Put differently, many statutes and legal rules take the form, "If a, then x; if b, then y; if c, then z." The mere fact of multiple possible outcomes does not mean the agency has "discretion" in enforcing the law. A truly discretionary rule would take the following, quite different, form: "If a, then usually but not necessarily x; if b, then usually but not necessarily y; if c, then usually but not necessarily z."

Which of these forms did the rule in *PG&E* take? Compare that to the rule in *CNI*. There, the court held that the mere possibility of establishing an exception to the general rule that a certain amount of aflatoxin in corn would be deemed an adulteration was not sufficient to confer "discretion." Indeed, the court held, the need to seek an exception suggests the bindingness of the general rule itself.

4. ***Post promulgation practices?*** Does whether a rule genuinely leaves discretion depend on how it is actually implemented on the ground? Or is that determined on the face of the statement/rule? Usually both kinds of evidence are available. Indeed, pre-enforcement judicial review may not even be available for policy statements because they may not be considered final agency actions (see Chapter 4.E). As a result, there is usually some record of how the agency has treated the statement/rule in practice.

5. ***Don't we want policy statements to be binding?*** The court in *PG&E* rightly noted that the whole point of policy statements is that they be somewhat binding; the whole point is for the regulated entity to know more or less what the agency is going to do. After all, the agency otherwise can proceed "ad hoc," adjudication by adjudication. Isn't it better to have official guidance? On the other hand, can't an agency achieve that guidance by promulgating the rule via notice-and-comment rulemaking? So if we want the policy statement to be at least somewhat binding, how binding can it be without being *so* binding that it doesn't leave genuine discretion? How do we know when we've reached that threshold? In one case, the Fifth Circuit explained that although we want a policy statement to guide officials, the better questions are whether the statement "affords an opportunity for individualized determinations" or "is so restrictive . . . that it effectively removes most, if not all," of the agency's discretion. Professionals and Patients for Customized Care v. Shalala, 56 F.3d 592, 597, 600 (1995). Is that helpful? Is the answer that policy statements can in fact be binding, as long as they merely announce how an agency is going to exercise its discretion, and do not actually impose or alter any underlying rights or obligations?

6. *Prosecutorial discretion.* Consider the case of prosecutorial discretion, which is widely understood to be a true example of "policy" discretion. Prosecutorial discretion does not change any underlying legal rules. It may be the policy of the present administration to de-prioritize prosecuting a certain kind of crime, but if someone nevertheless commits that crime, there's always

> **PRACTICE POINTER**
>
> Prosecutorial discretion—the decision whether to prosecute specific individuals and whether to give higher or lower enforcement priority to certain categories of crimes—is a classic example of an executive "policy" decision that indicates how the executive is to exercise its discretion. Can the example of prosecutorial discretion help you determine whether an agency has promulgated a policy statement?

a risk that the law will be applied against the offender, who will then have to suffer the consequences. Contrast that with a blanket statement from the administration to the effect that "the administration, in its discretion, will no longer bring any prosecutions for violating law *x*." Isn't that tantamount to *changing the law?* Consider these questions as you read the next case.

Texas v. United States

809 F.3d 134 (5th Cir. 2015)

JERRY E. SMITH, CIRCUIT JUDGE:

The United States appeals a preliminary injunction, pending trial, forbidding implementation of the Deferred Action for Parents of Americans and Lawful Permanent Residents program ("DAPA"). . . . Reviewing the district court's order for abuse of discretion, we affirm the preliminary injunction because the states . . . have established a substantial likelihood of success on the merits of their procedural and substantive APA claims; and they have satisfied the other elements required for an injunction.

I.

A.

In June 2012, the Department of Homeland Security ("DHS") implemented the Deferred Action for Childhood Arrivals program ("DACA"). In the DACA Memo to agency heads, the DHS Secretary "set[ ] forth how, in the exercise of . . . prosecutorial discretion, [DHS] should enforce the Nation's immigration laws against certain young people" and listed five "criteria [that] should be satisfied before an individual is considered for an exercise of prosecutorial discretion." The Secretary further instructed that "[n]o individual should receive deferred action . . . unless they [*sic*] first pass a background check and requests for relief . . . are to be decided on a case by case basis." Although stating that "[f]or individuals who are granted deferred action . . . , [U.S. Citizenship and Immigration Services ('USCIS')] shall accept applications to determine whether these individuals qualify for work authorization," the DACA Memo purported to "confer[ ] no substantive right, immigration status or pathway to citizenship." At least 1.2 million persons qualify for DACA, and approximately 636,000 applications were approved through 2014.

In November 2014, by what is termed the "DAPA Memo," DHS expanded DACA by making millions more persons eligible for the program and extending "[t]he period for which DACA and the accompanying employment authorization is granted . . . to three-year increments, rather than the current two-year increments." The Secretary also "direct[ed] USCIS to establish a process, similar to DACA," known as DAPA, which applies to "individuals who . . . have, [as of November 20, 2014], a son or daughter who is a U.S. citizen or lawful permanent resident" and meet five additional criteria. The Secretary stated that, although "[d]eferred action does not confer any form of legal status in this country, much less citizenship[,] it [does] mean[ ] that, for a specified period of time, an individual is permitted to be *lawfully present* in the United States." Of the approximately 11.3 million illegal aliens in the United States, 4.3 million would be eligible for lawful presence pursuant to DAPA.

"Lawful presence" is not an enforceable right to remain in the United States and can be revoked at any time, but that classification nevertheless has significant legal consequences. Unlawfully present aliens are generally not eligible to receive federal public benefits, *see* 8 U.S.C. § 1611, or state and local public benefits unless the state otherwise provides, *see* 8 U.S.C. § 1621. But as the government admits in its opening brief, persons granted lawful presence pursuant to DAPA are no longer "bar[red] . . . from receiving social security retirement benefits, social security disability benefits, or health insurance under Part A of the Medicare program." That follows from § 1611(b)(2)–(3), which provides that the exclusion of benefits in § 1611(a) "shall not apply to any benefit[s] payable under title[s] II [and XVIII] of the Social Security Act . . . to an alien who is *lawfully present* in the United States as determined by the Attorney General. . . ." (emphasis added). A lawfully present alien is still required to satisfy independent qualification criteria before receiving those benefits, but the grant of lawful presence removes the categorical bar and thereby makes otherwise ineligible persons eligible to qualify.

"Each person who applies for deferred action pursuant to the [DAPA] criteria . . . shall also be eligible to apply for work authorization for the [renewable three-year] period of deferred action." DAPA Memo at 4. The United States concedes that "[a]n alien with work authorization may obtain a Social Security Number," "accrue quarters of covered employment," and "correct wage records to add prior covered employment within approximately three years of the year in which the wages were earned or in limited circumstances thereafter." The district court determined—and the government does not dispute—"that DAPA recipients would be eligible for earned income tax credits once they received a Social Security number." . . .

B.

The states . . . asserted that DAPA violated the procedural requirements of the APA as a substantive rule that did not undergo the requisite notice-and-comment rulemaking. *See* 5 U.S.C. § 553. . . .

II.

"We review a preliminary injunction for abuse of discretion." A preliminary injunction should issue only if the states, as movants, establish

(1) a substantial likelihood of success on the merits, (2) a substantial threat of irreparable injury if the injunction is not issued, (3) that the threatened injury if the injunction is denied outweighs any harm that will result if the injunction is granted, and (4) that the grant of an injunction will not disserve the public interest.

"As to each element of the district court's preliminary-injunction analysis . . . findings of fact are subject to a clearly-erroneous standard of review, while conclusions of law are subject to broad review and will be reversed if incorrect."

* * *

VI.

. . . [W]e address whether Texas has established a substantial likelihood of success on its claim that DAPA must be submitted for notice and comment. The United States urges that DAPA is exempt as an "interpretative rule[ ], general statement[ ] of policy, or rule[ ] of agency organization, procedure, or practice." 5 U.S.C. § 553(b)(A). "In contrast, if a rule is 'substantive,' the exemption is inapplicable, and the full panoply of notice-and-comment requirements must be adhered to scrupulously. The 'APA's notice and comment exemptions must be narrowly construed.' "

A.

The government advances the notion that DAPA is exempt from notice and comment as a policy statement. We evaluate two criteria to distinguish policy statements from substantive rules: whether the rule (1) "impose[s] any rights and obligations" and (2) "genuinely leaves the agency and its decision-makers free to exercise discretion." There is some overlap in the analysis of those prongs "because '[i]f a statement denies the decisionmaker discretion in the area of its coverage . . . then the statement is binding, and creates rights or obligations.' " "While mindful but suspicious of the agency's own characterization, we . . . focus[ ] primarily on whether the rule has binding effect on agency discretion or severely restricts it." "[A]n agency pronouncement will be considered binding as a practical matter if it either appears on its face to be binding, or is applied by the agency in a way that indicates it is binding."

Although the DAPA Memo facially purports to confer discretion, the district court determined that "[n]othing about DAPA 'genuinely leaves the agency and its [employees] free to exercise discretion,' " a factual finding that we review for clear error. That finding was partly informed by analysis of the implementation of DACA, the precursor to DAPA.

Like the DAPA Memo, the DACA Memo instructed agencies to review applications on a case-by-case basis and exercise discretion, but the district court found that those statements were "merely pretext" because only about 5% of the 723,000 applications accepted for evaluation had been denied, and "[d]espite a request by the [district] [c]ourt, the [g]overnment's counsel did not provide the number, if any, of requests that were denied [for discretionary reasons] even though the applicant met the DACA criteria. . . ." The finding of pretext was also based on a declaration by Kenneth Palinkas, the president of the union representing the USCIS employees processing the DACA applications, that "DHS management has taken multiple steps to ensure that DACA applications are simply rubberstamped if the applicants meet the necessary criteria"; DACA's Operating Procedures, which "contain[ ] nearly 150 pages of specific instructions for granting or denying deferred action"; and some mandatory language in the DAPA Memo itself. In denying the government's motion for a stay of the injunction, the district court further noted that the President had made public statements suggesting that in reviewing applications pursuant to DAPA, DHS officials who "don't follow the policy" will face "consequences," and "they've got a problem."

The DACA and DAPA Memos purport to grant discretion, but a rule can be binding if it is "applied by the agency in a way that indicates it is binding," and there was evidence from DACA's implementation that DAPA's discretionary language was pretextual. For a number of reasons, any extrapolation from DACA must be done carefully. . . .

But despite those differences, there are important similarities: The Secretary "direct[ed] USCIS to *establish a process, similar to DACA*, for exercising prosecutorial discretion," *id.* (emphasis added), and there was evidence that the DACA application process *itself* did not allow for discretion, regardless of the rates of approval and denial. . . .

[T]he district court found pretext for additional reasons. . . . Certain denials of DAPA must be sent to a supervisor for approval[, and] there is no option for granting DAPA to an individual who does not meet each criterion." The finding was also based on the declaration from Palinkas that, as with DACA, the DAPA application process itself would preclude discretion: "[R]outing

DAPA applications through service centers instead of field offices . . . created an application process that bypasses traditional in-person investigatory interviews with trained USCIS adjudications officers" and "prevents officers from conducting case-by-case investigations, undermines officers' abilities to detect fraud and national-security risks, and ensures that applications will be rubber-stamped." . . .

Reviewing for clear error, we conclude that the states have established a substantial likelihood that DAPA would not genuinely leave the agency and its employees free to exercise discretion. . . .

King, Circuit Judge, dissenting:

Although there are approximately 11.3 million removable aliens in this country today, for the last several years Congress has provided the Department of Homeland Security (DHS) with only enough resources to remove approximately 400,000 of those aliens per year. Recognizing DHS's congressionally granted prosecutorial discretion to set removal enforcement priorities, Congress has exhorted DHS to use those resources to "mak[e] our country safer." In response, DHS has focused on removing "those who represent threats to national security, public safety, and border security." The DAPA Memorandum at issue here focuses on a subset of removable aliens who are unlikely to be removed unless and until more resources are made available by Congress: those who are the parents of United States citizens or legal permanent residents, who have resided in the United States for at least the last five years, who lack a criminal record, and who are not otherwise removal priorities as determined by DHS. The DAPA Memorandum has three primary objectives for these aliens: (1) to permit them to be lawfully employed and thereby enhance their ability to be self-sufficient, a goal of United States immigration law since this country's earliest immigration statutes; (2) to encourage them to come out of the shadows and to identify themselves and where they live, DHS's prime law enforcement objective; and (3) to maintain flexibility so that if Congress is able to make more resources for removal available, DHS will be able to respond.

Plaintiffs do not challenge DHS's ability to allow the aliens subject to the DAPA Memorandum—up to 4.3 million, some estimate—to remain in this country indefinitely. Indeed, Plaintiffs admit that such removal decisions are well within DHS's prosecutorial discretion. . . . Deferred action decisions, such as those contemplated by the DAPA Memorandum, are quintessential exercises of prosecutorial discretion. As the Supreme Court put it sixteen years ago, "[a]t each stage [of the removal process] the Executive has discretion to abandon the endeavor, [including by] engaging in a regular practice (which had come to be known as 'deferred action') of exercising that discretion for humanitarian reasons or simply for its own convenience." . . .

If the Memorandum is implemented in the truly discretionary, case-by-case manner it contemplates, it is not subject to the APA's notice-and-comment requirements, and the injunction cannot stand. Although the very face of the Memorandum makes clear that it must be applied with such discretion, the district court concluded on its own—prior to DAPA's implementation, based on improper burden-shifting, and without seeing the need even to hold an evidentiary hearing—that the Memorandum is a sham, a mere "pretext" for the Executive's plan "not [to] enforce the immigration laws as to over four million illegal aliens." That conclusion is clearly erroneous. . . .

It is important to recognize at the outset the backdrop upon which the Memorandum was written. As noted above, given the resource constraints faced by DHS, the agency is faced with important prioritization decisions as to which aliens should be the subject of removal proceedings. Congress has made clear that those decisions are to be made by DHS, not by Congress itself—and certainly not by the courts. Indeed, Congress has delegated to the Secretary of Homeland Security the authority to "[e]stablish[ ] national immigration enforcement policies and priorities," 6 U.S.C. § 202(5) . . . .

. . . [C]onsistent with his congressionally granted authority to set enforcement priorities, the Secretary contends that he has chosen—through the DACA and DAPA Memoranda—to divert some of DHS's resources away from the lowest priority aliens to better enforce the immigration laws against the highest priority aliens. . . . Although these programs will likely apply to a large number of individuals, that result is the inevitable upshot of decades of congressional appropriations decisions, which require DHS (whether by policy or by practice) to de-prioritize millions of removable aliens each year due to these resource constraints. . . .

* * *

IV. APA Procedural Claim

Our precedent is clear: "As long as the agency remains free to consider the individual facts in the various cases that arise, then the agency action in question has not established a binding norm," and thus need not go through the procedures of notice-and-comment. . . .

In determining whether the DAPA Memorandum constitutes a substantive rule, we must begin with the words of the Memorandum itself. The Memorandum states that it reflects "new policies," and "guidance for case-by-case use of deferred action." . . .

The discretionary nature of the DAPA Memorandum is further supported by the policy's substance. Although some of the Memorandum's criteria can be routinely applied, many will require agents to make discretionary judgments as to the application of the respective criteria to the facts of a particular case. For example, agents must determine whether an applicant "pose[s] a danger to national security," whether the applicant is "a threat to . . . border security" or "public safety," and whether the applicant has "significantly abused the visa or visa waiver programs." Such criteria cannot be mechanically applied, but rather entail a degree of judgment; in other words, they are "imprecise and discretionary—not exact and certain." . . .

Most strikingly, the last criterion contained in the DAPA Memorandum is entirely open-ended, stating that deferred action should be granted only if the applicant "present[s] no other factors that, in the exercise of discretion, makes the grant of deferred action inappropriate." The Memorandum does not elaborate on what such "other factors" should be considered—leaving this analysis entirely to the judgment of the agents processing the applications. . . .

Moreover, even absent the DAPA Memorandum, DHS would have the authority to take the action of which Plaintiffs complain—i.e., by granting deferred action on an *ad hoc* basis. Accordingly, based on its language and substance, the Memorandum does not constitute a binding substantive rule subject to the requirements of notice-and-comment. . . .

It is true that the plain language of the Memorandum—which, in the majority's words, "facially purports to confer discretion"—may not be conclusive if rebutted by "what the agency does in fact." Here, however, there is no such evidence of what the agency has done "in fact," as DAPA has yet to be implemented. . . .

Lacking any probative evidence as to *DAPA*'s implementation, the district court relied most heavily on evidence of *DACA*'s implementation—concluding unequivocally that DAPA will be "implemented exactly like DACA." . . .

More importantly, the fact that the *administration* of the two programs may be similar is not evidence that the *substantive review* under both programs will be the same. . . . Review under the DACA Memorandum does not, for example, require reference to the various discretionary factors contained in the Enforcement Priorities Memorandum, nor does DACA contain DAPA's criterion that the applicant "present no other factors that, in the exercise of discretion, makes the grant of deferred action inappropriate." . . .

Based on the record as it currently stands, the district court's conclusion that DAPA applications will not be reviewed on a discretionary, case-by-case basis cannot withstand even the most deferential scrutiny. . . .

NOTES AND QUESTIONS

1.   *Doctrinal confusion.* Note again the use of the rights and obligations language and the overlap of this factor with the genuine discretion factor. As explained in an earlier note, the latter factor is more useful. The question is whether a rule genuinely leaves discretion, or rather whether it affects underlying legal rules (whether procedural or substantive).

2.   *Post promulgation practices revisited.* Does the discretionary nature of a rule depend on how that rule is enforced on the ground? DAPA had not yet been implemented; the majority based its opinion on the similarities between DAPA and DACA, which had been implemented. If 5% of cases are treated differently from what the policy otherwise suggests, is the agency exercising genuine discretion? What if it only deviates from the policy in a single case? The D.C. Circuit has held that a single deviation does not a policy statement make. U.S. Tel. Ass'n v. FCC, 28 F.3d 1232, 1235 (D.C. Cir. 1994) ("[T]he Commission exercised discretion in only one out of over 300 cases, which is little support for the Commission's assertion that it intended not to be bound . . . .").

3. *Relying on multiple factors.* In the DACA and DAPA memos, not all children who arrived in the United States unlawfully, and not all parents with U.S. citizen children, would be entitled to protection against the enforcement of the immigration laws; but those who met a number of additional factors were so entitled. According to the court, the memos explained that "five criteria should be satisfied before an individual is considered for an exercise of prosecutorial discretion." Just as with "exemptions," discussed in a prior note, the mere fact that there are different legal outcomes under different sets of circumstances does not make a rule discretionary. It simply changes the scope of the various rules themselves. Thus, the question is whether an immigration official has genuine discretion *when* an otherwise eligible DACA or DAPA recipient satisfies those five additional criteria. If there's no discretion even when those five criteria are satisfied, then it's not a policy statement.

A very different case was presented in Professionals and Patients for Customized Care v. Shalala, 56 F.3d 592 (5th Cir. 1995). There, the FDA promulgated a rule, in the form of a policy statement, addressing when the FDA might bring enforcement actions against compounding pharmacies for improperly "manufacturing" drugs. The policy statement identified nine factors that the FDA "will consider" in determining whether to bring an enforcement action, but the FDA explained that the "list of factors is not intended to be exhaustive and other factors may be appropriate for consideration in a particular case." The court agreed this was a policy statement. Do you see the difference? In the DAPA case, the rule took the form: "if these five criteria are met, then they are candidates for not enforcing the immigration laws"—and most of the time that's exactly what happened. In *Customized Care,* the rule took the form: "if some number of these nine non-exhaustive factors are present, the agency may bring an enforcement action." It is certainly arguable that the former rule does not genuinely to leave discretion but the latter does. Do you agree?

4. *Deference mistakes.* It's important when reading cases to consider the standard of review and the deference given the lower courts. In *Texas v. US,* the standard of review was highly deferential. The question was whether there would be a *likelihood* of success on the merits, and in answering that question the appeals court also reviewed the lower court's factual findings about the practical bindingness of the rule for "clear error." It would be a mistake to conflate this decision with an ultimate decision on the merits; the opinion must always be taken with a grain of salt in light of the highly deferential review standard before analogizing DAPA to future policy statements. See generally Jonathan

S. Masur & Lisa Larrimore Ouellette, *Deference Mistakes*, 82 U. Chi. L. Rev. 643 (2015).

■ *Problem 2.8*

Title 13 of the U.S. Code deals entirely with the decennial census. It provides that "[t]he Secretary [of Commerce] shall prepare [census] questionnaires, and shall determine the inquiries, and the number, form, and subdivisions thereof, for the statistics, surveys, and censuses provided for in this title." The Secretary announces that it will be the policy of the administration to add a citizenship question to the census questionnaire.

Some experts argue that this will lead to lower survey responses by non-citizens, and thereby affect the number of seats in the US House of Representatives to which various states would otherwise be entitled according to their respective populations, as well as the amount of various federal grants and loans these states might otherwise receive.

The Secretary does not make this decision after notice-and-comment rulemaking. Is the Secretary's decision subject to procedural challenge under the APA?

 TEST YOUR KNOWLEDGE: To assess your understanding of the material in this chapter, **click here** to take a quiz.

CHAPTER THREE

Adjudication

This chapter examines the procedural constraints on agency adjudications generally. The focus will be largely, though not exclusively, on the statutory procedural constraints on how agencies must engage in adjudications. When those adjudications might result in deprivations of liberty or property, the due process clause also applies and may supply its own procedural requirements. These will be discussed in Chapter 7 along with Article III constraints.

A. The Choice of Rulemaking or Adjudication

1. The *Chenery II* Principle

Before we examine procedural constraints, we revisit the power of agencies to choose between rulemakings and adjudications. In the following famous case, *Chenery II*, the question was whether there are certain matters that an agency *must* decide by promulgating a rule instead of proceeding by adjudication. (Recall that in *Heckler v. Campbell*, p. 103, the question was whether there were certain matters that had to be determined by adjudication.)

To put the issue more concretely, *Chenery II* involves the question of *retroactivity*, which was briefly introduced in the discussion of the rulemaking-adjudication distinction. Rulemakings must have future effect under the APA's definition of rule. At a minimum, this seems to mean that *at least under the APA*—perhaps an organic statute might provide differently—rules cannot be "retroactive," in the sense of "altering the *past* legal consequences of past actions." Bowen v. Georgetown Univ. Hosp., 488 U.S. 204, 219 (1988) (Scalia, J., concurring). The classic example of a retroactive law is an ex post facto law. Suppose there was no legal prohibition on jaywalking yesterday, and you jaywalked. Can a legislature or an agency pass a law or rule making jaywalking a crime and punish you for having jaywalked *yesterday*? The answer is no—that would be altering the *past* legal consequences for *past* actions. Of course, many laws change the *present* legal consequences for past actions. Suppose a manufacturer builds a plant legally under existing law, but that plant is later declared to be a nuisance. The manufacturer must close up shop at great loss, but the point is there is no alteration of *past* legal consequences.

At least as a general matter, then, legislatures typically do not, and typically cannot, enact retroactive laws, although to be sure this prohibition is not quite universal. What about courts? Can they act retroactively? It is often believed that, at least in civil cases, they can and do. When a common law court "makes" law, that is, when it announces a new legal principle in an existing case between two private parties, and perhaps orders one party to pay another, hasn't the court acted retroactively? Maybe. But we generally accept courts acting in this manner because their "new" rules are usually not so "new" at all—they are simply extensions of existing common-law principles of, say, tort or contract to new factual situations. Thus when courts act "retroactively" their actions can actually be understood either as (1) clarifying existing law, (2) applying existing law to new circumstances, or (3) extending the law in a minor and reasonably foreseeable way. Hence it was often theorized, at least before the legal realist era, that common-law judges "found" or "discovered" the law rather than "made" the law.

Additionally, we accept some degree of retroactivity in this sense because common-law judges *have* to decide existing disputes between two private parties. These cases have to be resolved *somehow*. As then-Judge Gorsuch wrote in one opinion, "You might wonder why the due process and equal protection concerns that counsel in favor of prospectivity in legislation don't operate similarly when it comes to judicial decisions. The answer, we think, lies in the fact that for civil society to function the people need courts to provide backward-looking resolutions for their disputes." De Niz Robles v. Lynch, 803 F.3d 1165, 1170 (10th Cir. 2015). This is certainly true. But note that if there is *no law* on the question, then there is actually no need to provide any backward-looking resolution at all. If there is no law, if there's no actual legal claim, then the plaintiff loses, full stop. These backward-looking resolutions of which Judge Gorsuch spoke

IN QUIRY Do common-law courts act retroactively? How similar is an agency to a court when it adjudicates cases?

are only necessary when there is already some existing law on the question giving the plaintiff a colorable legal claim. In that sense, then, the court is not really making new law at all—it's clarifying, applying, or reasonably extending existing law.

With this background on retroactivity in legislative and judicial activity in mind, consider now the following case, which explores the issue of retroactivity of an agency's adjudication.

SEC v. Chenery Corp. ("Chenery II")

332 U.S. 194 (1947)

MR. JUSTICE MURPHY delivered the opinion of the Court.

This case is here for the second time. In *SEC v. Chenery Corporation*, 318 U.S. 80 [*Chenery I*], we held that an order of the Securities and Exchange Commission could not be sustained on the grounds upon which that agency acted. We therefore directed that the case be remanded to the Commission for such further proceedings as might be appropriate. On remand, the Commission reexamined the problem, recast its rationale and reached the same result. The issue now is whether the Commission's action is proper in light of the principles established in our prior decision.

When the case was first here, we emphasized a simple but fundamental rule of administrative law. That rule is to the effect that a reviewing court, in dealing with a determination or judgment which an administrative agency alone is authorized to make, must judge the propriety of such action solely by the grounds invoked by the agency. If those grounds are inadequate or improper, the court is powerless to affirm the administrative action by substituting what it considers to be a more adequate or proper basis. To do so would propel the court into the domain which Congress has set aside exclusively for the administrative agency.

We also emphasized in our prior decision an important corollary of the foregoing rule. If the administrative action is to be tested by the basis upon which it purports to rest, that basis must be set forth with such clarity as to be understandable. It will not do for a court to be compelled to guess at the theory underlying the agency's action . . . .

Applying this rule and its corollary, the Court was unable to sustain the Commission's original action. The Commission had been dealing with the reorganization of the Federal Water Service Corporation (Federal), a holding company registered under the Public Utility Holding Company Act of 1935. During the period when successive reorganization plans proposed by the management were before the Commission, the officers, directors and controlling stockholders of Federal purchased a substantial amount of Federal's preferred stock on the over-the-counter market. Under the fourth reorganization plan, this preferred stock was to be converted into common stock of a new corporation; on the basis of the purchases of preferred stock, the management would have received more than 10% of this new common stock. It was frankly admitted that the management's purpose in buying the preferred stock was to protect its interest in the new company. It was also plain that there was no fraud or lack of disclosure in making these purchases.

But the Commission would not approve the fourth plan so long as the preferred stock purchased by the management was to be treated on a parity with the other preferred stock. It felt that the officers and directors of a holding company in process of reorganization under the Act were fiduciaries and were under a duty not to trade in the securities of that company during the reorganization period. And so the plan was amended to provide that the preferred stock acquired by the management, unlike that held by others, was not to be converted into the new common stock; instead, it was to be surrendered at cost plus dividends accumulated since the purchase dates. As amended, the plan was approved by the Commission over the management's objections.

The Court interpreted the Commission's order approving this amended plan as grounded solely upon judicial authority. The Commission appeared to have treated the preferred stock acquired by the management in accordance with what it thought were standards theretofore recognized by courts. If it intended to create new standards growing out of its experience in effectuating the legislative policy, it failed to express itself with sufficient clarity and precision to be so understood. Hence the order was judged by the only standards clearly invoked by the Commission. On that basis, the order could not stand. The opinion pointed out that courts do not impose upon officers and directors of a corporation any fiduciary duty to its stockholders which precludes them merely because they are officers and directors, from buying and selling the corporation's stock. Nor was it felt that the cases upon which the Commission relied established any principles of law or equity which in themselves would be sufficient to justify this order.

The opinion further noted that neither Congress nor the Commission had promulgated any general rule proscribing such action as the purchase of preferred stock by Federal's management. And the only judge-made rule of equity which might have justified the Commission's order related to fraud or mismanagement of the reorganization by the officers and directors, matters which were admittedly absent in this situation. . . .

The latest order of the Commission definitely avoids the fatal error of relying on judicial precedents which do not sustain it. This time, after a thorough reexamination of the problem in light of the purposes and standards of the Holding Company Act, the Commission has concluded that the proposed transaction is inconsistent with the standards of §§ 7 and 11 of the Act. It has drawn heavily upon its accumulated experience in dealing with utility reorganizations. And it has expressed its reasons with a clarity and thoroughness that admit of no doubt as to the underlying basis of its order.

The argument is pressed upon us, however, that the Commission was foreclosed from taking such a step following our prior decision. . . . Under this view, the Commission would be free only to promulgate a general rule outlawing such profits in future utility reorganizations; but such a rule would have to be prospective in nature and have no retroactive effect upon the instant situation.

We reject this contention, for it grows out of a misapprehension of our prior decision and of the Commission's statutory duties. We held no more and no less than that the Commission's first order was unsupportable for the reasons supplied by that agency. But when the case left this Court, the problem whether Federal's management should be treated equally with other preferred stockholders still lacked a final and complete answer. It was clear that the Commission could not give a negative answer by resort to prior judicial declarations. And it was also clear that the Commission was not bound by settled judicial precedents in a situation of this nature. Still unsettled, however, was the answer the Commission might give were it to bring to bear on the facts the proper administrative and statutory considerations, a function which belongs exclusively to the Commission in the first instance. The administrative process had taken an erroneous rather than a final turn. Hence we carefully refrained from expressing any views as to the propriety of an order rooted in the proper and relevant considerations. . . .

The absence of a general rule or regulation governing management trading during reorganization did not affect the Commission's duties in relation to the particular proposal before it. The Commission was asked to grant or deny effectiveness to a proposed amendment to Federal's reorganization plan whereby the management would be accorded parity treatment on its holdings. It could do that only in the form of an order, entered after a due consideration of the particular facts in light of the relevant and proper standards. That was true regardless of whether those standards previously had been spelled out in a general rule or regulation. Indeed, if the Commission rightly felt that the proposed amendment was inconsistent with those standards, an order giving effect to the amendment merely because there was no general rule or regulation covering the matter would be unjustified. . . .

To hold that the Commission had no alternative in this proceeding but to approve the proposed transaction, while formulating any general rules it might desire for use in future cases of this nature, would be to stultify the administrative process. That we refuse to do.

Since the Commission, unlike a court, does have the ability to make new law prospectively through the exercise of its rule-making powers, it has less reason to rely upon ad hoc adjudication to formulate new standards of conduct within the framework of the Holding Company Act. The function of filling in the interstices of the Act should be performed, as much as possible, through this quasi-legislative promulgation of rules to be applied in the future. But any rigid requirement to that effect would make the administrative process inflexible and incapable of dealing with many of the specialized problems which arise. Not every principle essential to the effective administration of a statute can or should be cast immediately into the mold of a general rule. Some principles must await their own development, while others must be adjusted to meet particular, unforeseeable situations. In performing its important functions in these respects, therefore, an administrative agency must be equipped to act either by general rule or by individual order. To insist upon one form of action to the exclusion of the other is to exalt form over necessity.

In other words, problems may arise in a case which the administrative agency could not reasonably foresee, problems which must be solved despite the absence of a relevant general rule. Or the agency may not have had sufficient experience with a particular problem to warrant rigidifying its tentative judgment into a hard and fast rule. Or the problem may be so specialized and varying in nature as to be impossible of capture within the boundaries of a general rule. In those situations, the agency must retain power to deal with the problems on a case-to-case basis if the administrative process is to be effective. There is thus a very definite place for the case-by-case evolution of statutory standards. And the choice made between proceeding by general rule or by individual, ad hoc litigation is one that lies primarily in the informed discretion of the administrative agency.

Hence we refuse to say that the Commission, which had not previously been confronted with the problem of management trading during reorganization, was forbidden from utilizing this particular proceeding for announcing and applying a new standard of conduct. That such action might have a retroactive effect was not necessarily fatal to its validity. Every case of first impression has a retroactive effect, whether the new principle is announced by a court or by an administrative agency. But such retroactivity must be balanced against the mischief of producing a result which is contrary to a statutory design or to legal and equitable principles. If that mischief is greater than the ill effect of the retroactive application of a new standard, it is not the type of retroactivity which is condemned by law.

And so in this case, the fact that the Commission's order might retroactively prevent Federal's management from securing the profits and control which were the objects of the preferred stock purchases may well be outweighed by the dangers inherent in such purchases from the statutory standpoint. If that is true, the argument of retroactivity becomes nothing more than a claim that the Commission lacks power to enforce the standards of the Act in this proceeding. Such a claim deserves rejection.

The problem in this case thus resolves itself into a determination of whether the Commission's action in denying effectiveness to the proposed amendment to the Federal reorganization plan can be justified on the basis upon which it clearly rests. . . .

The Commission concluded that it could not find that the reorganization plan, if amended as proposed, would be 'fair and equitable to the persons affected (thereby)' within the meaning of § 11(e) of the Act, under which the reorganization was taking place. Its view was that the amended plan would involve the issuance of securities on terms 'detrimental to the public interest or the interest of investors' contrary to §§ 7(d)(6) and 7(e), and would result in an 'unfair or inequitable distribution of voting power' among the Federal security holders within the meaning of § 7(e). It was led to this result 'not by proof that the interveners (Federal's management) committed acts of conscious wrongdoing but by the character of the conflicting interests created by the interveners' program of stock purchases carried out while plans for reorganization were under consideration.' . . .

Drawing upon its experience, the Commission indicated that all these normal and special powers of the holding company management during the course of a § 11(e) reorganization placed in the management's command 'a formidable battery of devices that would enable it, if it should choose to use them selfishly, to affect in material degree the ultimate allocation of new securities among the various existing classes, to influence the market for its own gain and to manipulate or obstruct the reorganization required by the mandate of the statute.' . . .

The Commission further felt that its answer should be the same even where proof of intentional wrongdoing on the management's part is lacking. Assuming a conflict of interests, the Commission thought that the absence of actual misconduct is immaterial; injury to the public investors and to the corporation may result just as readily. . . .

We are unable to say in this case that the Commission erred in reaching the result it did. The facts being undisputed, we are free to disturb the Commission's conclusion only if it lacks any rational and statutory foundation. In that connection, the Commission has made a thorough examination of the problem, utilizing statutory standards and its own accumulated experience with reorganization matters. In essence, it has made what we indicated in our prior opinion would be an informed, expert judgment on the problem. . . .

The Commission's conclusion here rests squarely in that area where administrative judgments are entitled to the greatest amount of weight by appellate courts. It is the product of administrative experience, appreciation of the complexities of the problem, realization of the statutory policies, and responsible treatment of the uncontested facts. It is the type of judgment which administrative agencies are best equipped to make and which justifies the use of the administrative process. Whether we agree or disagree with the result reached, it is an allowable judgment which we cannot disturb.

JUSTICE JACKSON, joined by JUSTICE FRANKFURTER, dissenting.

The Court by this present decision sustains the identical administrative order which only recently it held invalid. . . . I feel constrained to disagree with the reasoning offered to rationalize this shift. It makes judicial review of administrative orders a hopeless formality for the litigant, even where granted to him by Congress. It reduces the judicial process in such cases to a mere feint. While the opinion does not have the adherence of a majority of the full Court, if its pronouncements should become governing principles they would, in practice, put most administrative orders over and above the law.

The essential facts are few and are not in dispute. This corporation filed with the Securities and Exchange Commission a voluntary plan of reorganization. While the reorganization proceedings were pending sixteen officers and directors bought on the open market about 7 1/2% of the corporation's preferred stock. Both the Commission and the Court admit that these purchases were not forbidden by any law, judicial precedent, regulation or rule of the Commission. Nevertheless, the Commission has ordered these individuals to surrender their shares to the corporation at cost, plus 4% interest, and the Court now approves that order.

It is helpful, before considering whether this order is authorized by law, to reflect on what it is and what it is not. It is not conceivably a discharge of the Commission's duty to determine whether a proposed plan of reorganization would be 'fair and equitable.' It has nothing to do with the corporate structure, or the classes and amounts of stock, or voting rights or dividend preferences. It does not remotely affect the impersonal financial or legal factors of the plan. It is a personal deprivation denying particular persons the right to continue to own their stock and to exercise its privileges. Other persons who bought at the same time and price in the open market would be allowed to keep and convert their stock. Thus, the order is in no sense an exercise of the function of control over the terms and relations of the corporate securities.

Neither is the order one merely to regulate the future use of property. It literally takes valuable property away from its lawful owners for the benefit of other private parties without full compensation and the Court expressly approves the taking. . . . No such power has ever been confirmed in any administrative body.

The reversal of the position of this Court is due to a fundamental change in prevailing philosophy. . . . The difference between the first and the latest decision of the Court is thus simply the difference between holding that administrative orders must have a basis in law and a holding that absence of a legal basis is no ground on which courts may annul them.

As there admittedly is no law or regulation to support this order we peruse the Court's opinion diligently to find on what grounds it is now held that the Court of Appeals, on pain of being reversed for error, was required to stamp this order with its approval. We find but one. That is the principle of judicial deference to administrative experience. That argument is five times stressed in as many different contexts . . . .

If it is of no consequence that no rule of law be existent to support an administrative order, and the Court of Appeals is obliged to defer to administrative experience and to sustain a Commission's power merely because it has been asserted and exercised, of what use is it to print a record or briefs in the case, or to hear argument? Administrative experience always is present, at least to the degree that it is here, and would always dictate a like deference by this Court to an assertion of administrative power. . . .

I suggest that administrative experience is of weight in judicial review only to this point—it is a persuasive reason for deference to the Commission in the exercise of its discretionary powers under and within the law. It cannot be invoked to support action outside of the law. And what action is, and what is not within the law must be determined by courts, when authorized to review, no matter how much deference is due to the agency's fact finding. Surely an administrative agency is not a law unto itself, but the Court does not really face up to the fact that this is the justification it is offering for sustaining the Commission action.

Even if the Commission had, as the Court says, utilized this case to announce a new legal standard of conduct, there would be hurdles to be cleared, but we need not dwell on them now. Because to promulgate a general rule of law, either by regulation or by case law, is something the Commission expressly declined to do. It did not previously promulgate, and it does not by this order profess to promulgate, any rule or regulation to prohibit such purchases absolutely or under stated conditions. On the other hand, its position is that no such rule or standard would be fair and equitable in all cases.

Whether, as matter of policy, corporate managers during reorganization should be prohibited from buying or selling its stock, is not a question for us to decide. But it is for us to decide whether, so long as no law or regulation prohibits them from buying, their purchases may be forfeited, or not, in the discretion of the Commission. If such a power exists in words of the statute or in their implication, it would be possible to point it out and thus end the case. Instead, the Court admits that there was no law prohibiting these purchases when they were made, or at any time thereafter. And, except for this decision, there is none now.

The truth is that in this decision the Court approves the Commission's assertion of power to govern the matter without law, power to force surrender of stock so purchased whenever it will, and power also to overlook such acquisitions if it so chooses. The reasons which will lead it to take one course as against the other remain locked in its own breast, and it has not and apparently does not intend to commit them to any rule or regulation. This administrative authoritarianism, this power to decide without law, is what the Court seems to approve in so many words . . . . This seems to me to undervalue and to belittle the place of law, even in the system of administrative justice. It calls to mind Mr. Justice Cardozo's statement that 'Law as a guide to conduct is reduced to the level of mere futility if it is unknown and unknowable.'

The Court's averment . . . is the first instance in which the administrative process is sustained by reliance on that disregard of law which enemies of the process have always alleged to be its principal evil. It is the first encouragement this Court has given to conscious lawlessness as a permissible rule of administrative action. This decision is an ominous one to those who believe that men should be governed by laws that they may ascertain and abide by, and which will guide the action of those in authority as well as of those who are subject to authority.

I have long urged, and still believe, that the administrative process deserves fostering in our system as an expeditious and nontechnical method of applying law in specialized fields. I can not agree that it be used, and I think its continued effectiveness is endangered when it is used, as a method of dispensing with law in those fields.

Notes and Questions

1.   *The* Chenery I *principle*. *Chenery II* has come to stand for a number of classic administrative law principles. The first was articulated in the prior case, *Chenery I*, where the Court, as the majority in *Chenery II* explained it, emphasized the "simple but fundamental rule of administrative law," namely "that a reviewing court, in dealing with a determination or judgment which an administrative agency alone is authorized to make, must judge the propriety of such action solely by the grounds invoked by the agency." This is a very different principle from the one used in ordinary appeals; appellate courts routinely uphold district court judgments on any ground supported by the record. It cannot be overstated how fundamental a principle this is in administrative law: a court must review the agency action *on its own terms*. A corollary of this principle was also articulated in *Chenery II*: the basis of the administrative action "must be set forth with such clarity as to be understandable." As a result of these principles, often courts will remand to an agency for more complete or alternative explanations of agency decisions.

> **COMPARATIVE PERSPECTIVE**
>
> The *Chenery I* principle is fundamental in administrative law. An agency's action must be justified on the record that was before it. Contrast that with the "rational basis" test in constitutional law, where courts will come up with any rational basis supporting certain types of congressional laws. Contrast the *Chenery I* rule also with the ordinary appellate rule that an appellate court can uphold a district court decision on any available grounds, and not merely on the ground on which the district court decided the case.

Note that *Chenery I* was decided in 1943, before the APA was enacted. Is there a statutory basis for *Chenery I*? Is it consistent with *Vermont Yankee*? In formal rulemakings (and formal adjudications), the proceedings are always on a "closed" record. See APA § 706(2)(E). For notice-and-comment rulemaking, perhaps the statutory basis is the requirement for a concise statement of basis and purpose. But what about for other types of administrative action? Is the answer to be found in APA § 559, which provides that the APA does not "limit or repeal additional requirements imposed by statute or otherwise recognized by law"? Is administrative common law prior to 1946 preserved by § 559? Does it make sense to preserve administrative common law as of 1946, but allow no further common-law development after?

**2. *What does* Chenery II *stand for?* ** *Chenery II* itself has come to stand for the proposition that the agency may articulate new legal requirements over the course of an adjudication and apply those new requirements retroactively to the case at hand. Note that although this case is often described as standing for the proposition that an agency may engage in "rulemaking via adjudication," strictly speaking that is an incorrect reading of the case. As the dissent noted, the Commission did not intend to formalize its ruling into a rule of any kind. Like a court case, it might be useful precedent in a future adjudication, and presumably future parties will conform their behavior to this particular ruling.

But, as the dissent noted, the SEC "does not by this order profess to promulgate[ ] any rule or regulation to prohibit such purchases absolutely or under stated conditions," and in fact "its position is that no such rule or standard would be fair and equitable in all cases." The most accurate description of the case, in other words, is that it permits an agency to create new legal obligations in an adjudication—even if the statute itself does not give any indication of such an obligation—and apply them retroactively in that same adjudication.

**3. *Due process and specificity.* ** Do you agree that it was appropriate for the agency to formulate new legal obligations and apply them retroactively? What do you make of the dissent's point that there was simply no law to apply? Is there a due process problem? A nondelegation problem? Are the two connected? Perhaps the statute, as broad as it is, has an intelligible principle to guide the agency and so it does not violate the nondelegation doctrine, but perhaps the statute is too broad to apply *directly* to private individuals. Could due process require more specificity than the nondelegation doctrine? Put another way, even if there is no nondelegation problem

IN QUIRY What is the connection between nondelegation and due process? How much specificity is required to put private parties on notice of their legal obligations?

with the broad statute, might the agency have to promulgate a more specific regulation before applying the statute to private parties to avoid a due process problem?

**4. *Deference to legal interpretations.* ** The issue of deference to agency legal interpretations arises in *Chenery II.* Chapter 4 will examine the modern cases requiring courts to give deference to reasonable agency interpretations of the statutes they administer. In dissent in *Chenery II,* however, Justices Jackson and Frankfurter argued that courts ought to defer to administrative expertise only insofar as their actions were within the law, and it was up to the courts themselves to determine what the bounds of the law were. Do you agree?

5.   **Subsequent cases.** The Court reaffirmed the holding of *Chenery II* in NLRB v. Bell Aerospace Co., 416 U.S. 267, 294 (1974) ("The views expressed in *Chenery II* . . . make plain that the Board is not precluded from announcing new principles in an adjudicative proceeding and that the choice between rulemaking and adjudication lies in the first instance within the Board's discretion."). To be clear about the issue, note that *no one questions the ability of an agency to promulgate new rules or articulate new principles through adjudications* (indeed, formal rulemakings undergo the adjudicatory-like proceedings of APA §§ 556–57). That perhaps is the ultimate takeaway of *Chenery II*. But the more contested question in that case was whether those new principles may be applied *retroactively* to the party before the agency, particularly where that party might be deprived of some liberty or property interest.

6.   **Retroactive rulemakings?** If agencies can apply new principles retroactively in adjudications, why can they not make regulations via rulemaking and apply those retroactively? The distinction between the two situations is hard to see. Recall, however, that the APA defines a "rule" as a statement of particular or general applicability *and future effect*. 5 U.S.C. § 551(1)(4). The Supreme Court has thus held that rulemakings cannot apply retroactively unless the statute specifically authorizes otherwise, although the majority opinion relied on general administrative law principles and not the text of the APA. Bowen v. Georgetown Univ. Hosp., 488 U.S. 204 (1988); see also id. at 216 (Scalia, J., concurring) (relying on the text of the APA).

 CROSS REFERENCE Recall the APA's definition of a rule. If by definition a rule can only have future effect, can a rule ever be applied retroactively?

7.   **Changes to prior agency policies and legal regularity.** *Chenery II* involved a new rule implementing broad and open-ended statutory provisions (the reorganization had to be "fair and equitable to the persons affected," and not "detrimental to the public interest or the interest of investors"). What if an agency, in the course of an adjudication, *changes* prior policies on which private parties have relied? Courts have been much more reluctant to allow agencies to act retroactively in such circumstances. In *De Niz Robles v. Lynch,* the Board of Immigration Appeals changed its policy in an adjudication, and the Tenth

Circuit held that this change could only apply to immigration petitions filed after that decision. 803 F.3d 1165 (10th Cir. 2015).

In *FCC v. Fox Television*, 567 U.S. 239 (2012), the Supreme Court, without mentioning the words "retroactive" or "retroactivity," reversed an agency decision retroactively applying a new rule prohibiting fleeting expletives on television. Fox Television had not policed its use of fleeting expletives because it had depended on a prior agency policy permitting such expletives. The Court invalidated the agency's attempted retroactive application of the new rule on the ground that the agency did not give "fair notice" to Fox.

The D.C. Circuit has relied many times on this distinction between new applications of law, and the substitution of new law for old law, in adjudications. As the court explained in one of the leading cases:

> [T]here has emerged a basic distinction between (1) new applications of law, clarifications, and additions, and (2) substitution of new law for old law that was reasonably clear. In the latter situation, which may give rise to questions of fairness, it may be necessary to deny retroactive effect to a rule announced in an agency adjudication in order to protect the settled expectations of those who had relied on the preexisting rule. By contrast, retroactivity in the former case is natural, normal, and necessary, a corollary of an agency's authority to develop policy through case-by-case adjudication rather than rulemaking. Thus, we have repeatedly held that retroactivity is appropriate when the agency's ruling represents a new policy for a new situation, rather than being a departure from a clear prior policy.

Williams Nat. Gas Co. v. FERC, 3 F.3d 1544, 1554 (D.C. Cir. 1993) (cleaned up).

These cases—involving retroactive application of new rules—are distinct from cases involving the ability of the agency to make the new rule in the first place. Administrative law also imposes certain procedural restrictions on when an agency can change its rules and precedents. Once an agency has developed a clear line of precedent over the course of several adjudications, it has to stick to those precedents where they apply. It can change course, but it must realize that it is doing so and explain the reasons for the change. In Shaw's Supermarkets, Inc. v. NLRB, 884 F.2d 34 (1st Cir. 1989), then-Judge Breyer reversed an agency decision adverse to an employer, where the agency on many similar occasions had ruled in favor of the employer. The agency was free "to depart from" its prior precedent "as long as it focuses upon the issue and explains why change is reasonable." But otherwise it had to follow the precedents because if it did not, then "those subject to the agency's authority cannot use its precedent as a guide for their conduct; nor will that precedent check arbitrary agency action." This presumption of "legal regularity" will be relevant in the next chapter where we discuss judicial review of agency policy changes.

8. *Impact on future parties.* When an agency announces a rule through an adjudication, many parties that will come to be affected by the agency's rule in future cases will not have had an opportunity to be heard in the initial adjudication that led to the formulation of the rule. In one interesting case, the Fifth Circuit reversed an agency order that had relied on a rule announced in a prior adjudication when the party adverse to the agency, Shell Oil, argued that the factual circumstances surrounding its oil wells were different from those surrounding the oil wells at issue in the previous adjudication. Shell Oil Co. v. FERC, 707 F.2d 230, 234 (5th Cir. 1983). The court recognized the ability of the agency to choose between rulemaking and adjudication and to announce new rules via adjudication, but argued that each agency action must be supported by "substantial evidence." (For more on the substantial evidence standard, see Chapter 4.A.) Thus, the court remanded for the agency to consider the factual arguments the Shell Oil had made for why the rule would be unreasonable as applied to its circumstances.

The above case raises the more general issue of the advantages and disadvantages of adjudications and rulemakings. Adjudications are typically conducted on closed records, and much depends on the parties before it and the arguments they happen to make. We now turn to a more general discussion of the advantages and disadvantages of these two modes of agency action.

2.   The Advantages of Each

The D.C. Circuit in the *National Petroleum Refiners* case (see supra p. 87) discussed the advantages of rulemakings. Consider now the following scholarly defenses of both rulemaking and adjudication.

FOR DISCUSSION

As you read the following excerpts, do you agree that agencies should engage in rulemaking as much as possible, or adjudications?

Richard J. Pierce, Jr., *Two Problems in Administrative Law: Political Polarity on the District of Columbia Circuit and Judicial Deterrence of Agency Rulemaking,* **1988 Duke L.J. 300, 308–09 (1988).** Judges and academics long ago reached rare consensus on the desirability of agency policymaking through the process of informal rulemaking. Justices Harlan and Douglas attempted to convince a majority of their colleagues to compel agencies to make policy decisions exclusively through the rulemaking process. The Supreme Court wisely abandoned that effort in recognition that it is impossible for agencies to make *all* policy decisions generically in advance, and that agencies are best positioned to determine the circumstances in which the many advantages of rulemaking must be sacrificed for the flexibility of ad hoc policymaking through adjudication.

Still, courts consistently recognize the advantages of rulemaking and frequently strive to encourage agencies to make policy primarily through the rulemaking process. Many of the landmark decisions in administrative law are explicable in part by reference to the nearly unanimous judicial preference for policymaking through rulemaking. Judges and scholars have identified eight significant advantages inherent in the rulemaking process as a means of making policy decisions.

Rulemaking yields higher-quality policy decisions than adjudication because it invites broad participation in the policymaking process by all affected entities and groups, and because it encourages the agency to focus on the broad effects of its policy rather than the often idiosyncratic adjudicative facts of a specific dispute. Rulemaking enhances efficiency in three ways. It avoids the needless cost and delay of finding legislative facts through trial-type procedures; it eliminates the need to relitigate policy issues in the context of disputes with no material differences in adjudicative facts; and, it yields much clearer 'rules' than can be extracted from a decision resolving a specific dispute. Rulemaking also provides greater fairness in three ways. It provides affected parties with clearer notice of what conduct is permissible and impermissible; it avoids the widely disparate temporal impact of agency policy decisions made and implemented through ad hoc adjudication; and, it allows all potentially affected segments of the public to participate in the process of determining the rules that will govern their conduct and affect their lives.

Russell L. Weaver & Linda D. Jellum, *Chenery II and the Development of Federal Administrative Law,* **58 Admin. L. Rev. 815, 824–27 (2006).** The short answer to the question of whether the Court in *Chenery II* could have or should have held that agencies are only allowed to articulate policy legislatively and not adjudicatively is "No." "[C]ourts are poorly situated to distinguish between circumstances appropriate for rulemaking and circumstances appropriate for [adjudication]." Moreover, requiring agencies to articulate policy only via legislative procedures would be both impractical and unworkable. Such a holding would cripple the regulatory process. If the Court had adopted that requirement in *Chenery II*, there would have been unexpected consequences including futility and administrative inflexibility.

First, such a requirement would promote futility. Agencies can neither conceive of every possible rule in advance, nor draft all regulations to ensure that they are not overbroad, vague, or ambiguous. Language is inherently imprecise. As with any code, inevitably there will be gaps and omissions. Courts and agencies must fill those gaps. At times, the only way those gaps will become apparent is in the context of an adjudication, and the way those gaps may best be addressed is with the benefit of a full factual record. Fundamentally, regulatory drafters are not prescient, and they cannot always anticipate and address all potential ensuing possibilities.

A different holding in *Chenery II* might also have resulted in less desirable rules. A holding requiring agencies to create advance rules might have forced agencies to commit themselves to specific rules with particular courses of action without knowing all the facts in advance. As a result, agencies would be forced to produce extremely detailed regulations anticipating and addressing every potential situation that might arise. If agencies were to overlook any potential problem, they would be precluded from addressing the problem adjudicatively.

Third, requiring agencies to develop all rules legislatively would deprive the agency of the ability to make tailored decisions in incremental fashion. Adjudication allows agency officials to "extend policy no further than needed to dispose of the issues at hand." If agencies could only issue rules legislatively, then they would always have to craft rules in a factual vacuum.

Additional concerns would arise in a non-*Chenery II* world. When existing statutes or regulations fail to address a problem adequately, agency personnel must do so. When there is time, they can do so by informal rule. But there is not always enough time, and informal procedures are not cheap. Notice and comment rulemaking has become both a time-consuming and expensive process. If an interpretive problem arises in a case, it may be impossible or impractical to use informal processes. Moreover, adjudicative "rules," unlike legislative rules, can be applied retroactively, so that a new rule can be applied in the case under consideration.

B. Formal Adjudications

The procedural constraints on agency adjudications are statutory, rooted in the APA and organic statutes, as well as constitutional, rooted in due process. This section explores what the APA has to say about procedures in agency adjudications. Due process constraints will be discussed in Chapter 7.

1. Statutory Overview

The same procedures the APA provides for formal rulemaking are used in formal adjudications. Section 554 of the APA applies to "every case of adjudication required by statute to be determined on the record after opportunity for an agency hearing," with certain enumerated exceptions. 5 U.S.C. § 554(a). The remainder of the section then entitles interested parties to notice, to submit facts and arguments, and to "hearing and decision on notice and in accordance with sections 556 and 557 of this title." Id. § 554(b)–(c). Section 554 also prohibits ex parte contacts and requires that the adjudicatory personnel be separate from the investigatory and prosecutorial agency personnel. Id. § 554(d).

Section 556 then provides that the agency itself, or an administrative law judge (ALJ), will preside over a trial-like hearing and take evidence. 5 U.S.C. § 556(b). The presiding ALJ or agency official is then authorized to conduct a hearing by administering oaths, issuing subpoenas, ruling on offers of proof, providing for depositions, holding settlement conferences, compelling attendance at hearings, and, finally, by making a recommended decision. Id. § 556(c). A party is entitled to present his or her case or defense "by oral or documentary evidence, to submit rebuttal evidence, and to conduct such cross-examination as may be required for a full and true disclosure of the facts." Id. § 556(d). (In a formal *rulemaking* and a narrow subset of other matters, this provision then allows the agency to provide for the submission of evidence in written form only.)

This section then provides that the burden of proof is on the proponent of the agency order (so, usually the agency has the burden of proof). Id. § 556(d). Importantly, the rules of evidence do not strictly apply, "but the agency as a matter of policy shall provide for the exclusion of irrelevant, immaterial, or unduly repetitious evidence." Id. The agency rule or order must be supported by "reliable, probative, and substantial evidence" on review of the "whole record" or those parts of the record cited by the parties. Id. The transcripts, exhibits, and filings produced in this proceeding are the exclusive record for the agency's ultimate decision in accordance with section 557. Id. § 556(e).

Section 557 then provides how an agency decision becomes final. If the agency itself is not presiding over the trial, then the decision of the ALJ or presiding officer becomes final if there is no appeal of the initial decision. If there is an appeal, the agency may make its own decision as though it were the initial decisionmaker; that is, it may disregard the initial decision of the ALJ. 5 U.S.C. § 557(b). The parties, however, are entitled to make arguments in favor of or in opposition to the initial decision. Id. § 557(c). Ex parte communications are again prohibited. Id. § 557(d). The crucial takeaway from this section is that the agency is not required to adhere to the underlying decision of the ALJ; it may entirely dispense with the decision of the officer who presided at the hearing. Do you think that is a good idea? Why or why not?

In case it is useful, here is a recent chart summarizing the key provisions of formal adjudication:

Table 1. Classic APA-Governed Formal Adjudication

	Statutory Requirement	APA Provision
1.	Notice of Legal Authority and Matters of Fact and Law Asserted	§ 554(b)
2.	Oral Evidentiary Hearing Before the Agency or Administrative Law Judge Who Must Be Impartial	§ 556(b)
3.	Limitations on Adjudicator's Ex Parte Communications with Parties and Within Agency	§§ 554(d), 557(d)(1)
4.	Availability of Legal or Other Authorized Representation	§ 555(b)
5.	Burden of Proof on Order's Proponent	§ 556(d)
6.	Party Entitled to Present Oral or Documentary Evidence	§ 556(d)
7.	Party Entitled to Cross-Examine Witnessess if Required for Full Disclosure of Facts	§ 556(d)
8.	Decision Limited to Bases Included in Hearing Record	§ 556(d)
9.	Party Entitled to Transcript of Evidence from Exclusive Record for Decision	§ 556(e)
10.	Decision Includes Reasons for All Material Findings and Conclusions	§ 557(c)(3)(A)
11.	Agency Head Final Decisionmaking Authority and De Novo Review of ALJ Decisions	§ 557(b)

Christopher J. Walker & Melissa F. Wasserman, *The New World of Agency Adjudication*, 107 Cal. L. Rev. 141 (2019).

2. The Prevalence of Formal Adjudications

Formal adjudications are only required in those cases which by statute have "to be determined on the record after opportunity for an agency hearing." You will recall that formal rulemaking is similarly triggered when such rulemaking must be made "on the record after opportunity for an agency hearing." In *Florida East Coast Railway,* supra p. 109, the Supreme Court held that agencies do not have to engage in formal rulemaking unless the statute uses that precise language or evinces in other clear language the unmistakable intent to require formal rulemaking. What about formal adjudications? Must Congress use the same "magic words" or something similarly unequivocal to trigger formal adjudications?

The Supreme Court has never weighed in, although one would think that the same rule of *Florida East Coast Railway* applies to formal adjudications as well. That was initially the position of the D.C. Circuit. United States Lines, Inc. v. Federal Maritime Commission, 584 F.2d 519 (DC. Cir. 1978). The First and Ninth Circuits, however, initially suggested the adjudications, which tend to require specific factual findings and less commonly involve general policy considerations, are more likely to require the formal proceedings of the APA. Marathon Oil Co. v. EPA, 564 F.2d 1253 (9th Cir. 1977); Seacoast Anti-Pollution League v. Costle, 572 F.2d 872 (1st Cir. 1978).

 CROSS REFERENCE Recall that in *Florida East Coast Railway* the Supreme Court held that agencies need not engage in formal rulemaking merely because a statute requires a "hearing" first. But note also that in a later chapter we will encounter *Chevron v. NRDC*, which requires courts to defer to an agency's reasonable interpretation of its organic statute. How would you resolve cases in which an adjudication required a "hearing," in light of these two precedents?

Since these cases were decided, however, the Supreme Court decided the prominent administrative law case Chevron USA, Inc. v. Natural Resources Defense Council, 467 U.S. 837 (1984), with which we shall become intimately familiar in the next chapter. This case held that courts should defer to reasonable agency interpretations of an agency's own governing statute. In other words, courts grant some amount of deference to agency legal interpretations. The question whether a statute requires a formal hearing or not is a legal question of statutory interpretation. In 1989, the D.C. Circuit held that it will defer to an agency's reasonable interpretation of its own hearing requirements, and therefore an agency's own understanding of whether formal adjudication is required. Chemical Waste Mgm't, Inc. v. EPA, 873 F.2d 1477 (1989). Other circuits have since followed suit. See, e.g., Dominion Energy Brayton Point, LLC v. Johnson, 443 F.3d 12 (1st Cir. 2006).

Intriguingly, there have been calls as of late for the Supreme Court to overturn so-called *Chevron* deference and to reassert the authority of courts to decide for themselves all questions of law. We will explore this debate in the next chapter as well. But for now, ask yourself: if the Supreme Court were to overturn *Chevron*, where does that leave the law on formal adjudications? Would you apply the rule of *Florida East Coast Railway*, or do you think adjudications are sufficiently distinct to warrant different treatment, as in *Marathon Oil* and *Seacoast*? Is this a question that will have to be answered on a statute-by-statute basis?

3.   The Process of Formal Adjudications

Although agencies get deference for their legal interpretations of whether their governing statutes require formal adjudications, such adjudications are far more common than formal rulemakings. Whenever the Federal Trade Commission brings an antitrust case in front of an FTC Administrative Law Judge, or whenever the Securities and Exchange Commission brings a securities fraud case in front of an SEC Administrative Law Judge, that proceeding is typically a formal adjudication. Of course, each statute is idiosyncratic and may have specific requirements for those types of cases. Still, formal adjudications are more common, and it is worthwhile addressing some issues that relate to these adjudications under the APA. Here we briefly address two overarching issues: (1) the costs and benefits of an agency adjudication as compared to a federal court, in terms of agency bias and expertise; and (2) the importance of an "exclusive record" in a formal adjudication, and the related issues of ex parte contacts and official notice. This latter issue relates to ex parte contacts, the use of experts, the taking of official notice, and political influence.

1. Agency bias and expertise. The first preliminary and foundational question related to administrative adjudications is why we might prefer to have administrative agencies adjudicate cases in the first places instead of a federal court. Under our traditional separation of powers framework, we typically expect an executive branch agency or official—say, a federal prosecutor—to bring an action in federal court. But agencies also adjudicate statutory violations for themselves all the time; for example, the FTC frequently decides whether a firm's activities constitute an "unfair" trade practice. The FTC also has jurisdiction to decide (under that same standard) whether firms have engaged in antitrust violations. Putting aside the question of whether such adjudications violate the requirements of Article III—that is, putting aside the question of whether agencies are exercising the federal judicial power in these cases, which we take up in Chapter 7—what are the costs and benefits of agency adjudications compared to federal courts? More specifically, do we worry about an agency's *bias* in serving both as a policymaker, an investigator, and an adjudicator? Or is an agency's "bias" really a reflection of its expertise, which we want the agency to deploy?

Many of these questions have long been considered settled, but in recent years there have been renewed attacks on agencies that have adjudicated cases in front of their own ALJs, whose decisions are reviewed by the top agency officials themselves. For example, the Securities and Exchange Commission has the option to bring many kinds of actions charging violations of the securities law in federal court *or* in front of an agency ALJ. In 2013, the agency announced, pursuant to new statutory authority in the Dodd-Frank Act of 2010, that it would hear more such cases in front of its own ALJs. Many critics argued that the SEC's win rate was much higher in front of its own ALJs than in front of federal district judges. When it comes to antitrust violations, the Department of Justice can bring an action in federal district court, or the FTC can bring an action in front of its own ALJs. In 2020, at least one company has sued the FTC, arguing that by pursuing actions in its own agency proceedings the FTC was impermissibly biased and violated due process norms.

EXPERTISE VS. ACCOUNTABILITY

Administrative law judges are supposed to be experts in their particular fields. But what about the separation of powers and political accountability? If an agency were bringing an enforcement action against you, would you rather an ALJ hear the case, or a federal judge? What are the trade-offs between efficiency and expertise on the one hand, and accountability and the separation of powers on the other?

It is well-established, however, that administrative law principles accept, and even embrace, some degree of bias in agency adjudications. The whole point is the agency is an expert in the matter. Thus, it's even acceptable for the agency officials to express an opinion on the matter at hand prior to an adjudication of the actual facts. In FTC v. Cement Institute, 333 U.S. 683 (1948), the FTC brought an antitrust enforcement action against several cement companies before an agency adjudicator. On appeal, the companies argued that the Commission was impermissibly biased because the Commission "had previously prejudged issues," pointing to reports the Commission made to Congress in which some commissioners had argued that the pricing system in the cement industry violated the antitrust laws. It should be noted, though, that notwithstanding these prior expressions of opinions, the agency adjudicator still took tens of thousands of pages of oral testimony and exhibits and engaged with thousands of pages of briefing.

The Supreme Court held that "the fact that the Commission had entertained such views as the result of its prior ex parte investigations did not necessarily mean that the minds of its members were irrevocably closed on the subject." Id. at 701. But more importantly, we would *expect* the agency to have developed opinions on such practices already—the whole point is the commissioners are supposed to develop expertise. If the previously expressed opinions disqualified the commissioners, then "experience acquired from their work as commissioners would be a handicap instead of an advantage." Id. at 702. Finally, many judges, too, express opinions about certain kinds of conduct in prior cases; that doesn't mean judges are required to recuse themselves in future, similar cases. For similar reasons, the Supreme Court in Withrow v. Larkin, 421 U.S. 35 (1975), held that it was not an unconstitutional violation of due process for a state administrative board to both investigate a matter initially and then to adjudicate the matter. "The contention that the combination of investigative and adjudicative functions necessarily creates an unconstitutional risk of bias in administrative adjudication," the Court held, "must overcome a presumption of honesty and integrity in those serving as adjudicators." Id. at 47. Such a combination of functions would violate due process only if it "poses such a risk of actual bias or prejudgment that the practice must be forbidden if the guarantee of due process is to be adequately implemented." Id.

Fast-forwarding to the present day, a director of the SEC's Enforcement Division defended the practice of trying cases in front of the agency's own ALJs. Administrative proceedings "can be much quicker than district court actions," providing parties quick relief. ALJs are also "sophisticated fact-finder," much more sophisticated than juries. See Oversight of the SEC's Division of

Enforcement: Hearing Before the H. Subcomm. on Capital Markets and Government Sponsored Enterprises, 114th Cong. 8–10 (2015). Does that reassure you? What if you're on the receiving end of the SEC's enforcement actions?

2. *The exclusive record.* APA § 556(e) provides that "[t]he transcript of testimony and exhibits, together with all papers and request filed in the proceedings, constitutes the exclusive record for decision." Relatedly, § 554(d) provides that the presiding adjudicator may not "consult a person or party on a fact in issue, unless on notice and opportunity for all parties to participate." The adjudicator may, however, take "official notice of a material fact not appearing in the evidence in the record," but "a party is entitled, on timely request, to an opportunity to show the contrary." Id. § 556(e). These related provisions all ensure that the agency decision will be made on the record before it, and all the parties will have had an opportunity to address that record.

(a) *Ex parte contacts.* In Ludwig v. Astrue, 681 F.3d 1047 (9th Cir. 2011), an ALJ heard evidence in a formal proceeding to determine eligibility for social security disability benefits. Ludwig presented evidence of chronic and severe knee and back pain and other medical issues, but there was significant contradictory evidence. For example, there was evidence that Ludwig routinely walked for exercise, cut wood, and stood for several hours a day in his previous job. He had also told previ-

 Recall that *ex parte* contacts need not be disclosed in informal rulemakings.

ous healthcare providers that he could press "1,000 pounds." In addition to this record evidence, though, an FBI agent told the ALJ after Ludwig's hearing that Ludwig was faking his injury. The FBI agent told the ALJ that he had observed Ludwig "in the parking lot walking with normal gait and station," and that he was exaggerating his limp when he was walking in the courthouse. The ALJ immediately disclosed the ex parte communication to Ludwig's counsel, but did not give an opportunity to cross-examine the FBI agent on the record.

The Court of Appeals ruled—albeit on the basis of the due process clause, and not on the basis of APA §§ 554 and 556—that it was error not to give Ludwig's counsel an opportunity to cross-examine the FBI agent on the record, especially because the ALJ gave some weight to the FBI agent's statement in the ultimate decision. Nevertheless, the court upheld that ALJ's decision on a "harmless error" analysis. The court concluded that the contradictions in the evidence "were dramatic," and held, "Considering the record as a whole, and the ALJ's explanation of his decision, we are convinced that Ludwig has not demonstrated that the decision would have been any different without the ex parte communication."

In an earlier case involving a strike of national air traffic controllers in the early 1980s, the D.C. Circuit held that "improper ex parte communications, even when undisclosed during agency proceedings, do not necessarily void an agency decision." In considering whether to void an adjudication "blemished by ex parte communications" or that has been "irrevocably tainted," the courts should look to the following factors: "the gravity of the ex parte communications; whether the contacts may have influenced the agency's ultimate decision; whether the party making the improper contacts benefited from the agency's ultimate decision; whether the contents of the communications were unknown to opposing parties, who therefore had no opportunity to respond; and whether vacation of the agency's decision and remand for new proceedings would serve a useful purpose." Prof'l Air Traffic Controllers Org. (PATCO) v. Fed. Labor Relations Auth., 685 F.2d 547, 564–65 (D.C. Cir. 1982).

(b) Reliance on agency experts. In Seacoast Anti-Pollution League v. Costle, 572 F.2d 872 (1st Cir. 1978), the EPA conducted an adjudication to determine whether to grant an exemption from the Clean Water Act to permit a company to discharge hot water, a pollutant, into an estuary which runs into the Gulf of Maine. After a hearing the EPA denied the exemption; but on appeal of the decision, the EPA Administrator empaneled several in-house agency experts, who convinced the Administrator to approve the exemption. How would you have ruled on this matter? Was relying on experts at the appeal stage improperly adding to the exclusive record? The Court of Appeals held that the Administrator was allowed to rely on the agency's own knowledge and expertise in coming to a decision. What the Administrator could *not* do, however, is rely on new *facts* introduced by the experts on appeal. The court concluded that that's what had happened—the panel of experts had relied on "scientific literature" on the "thermal sensitivity of members of the local biota" in approving the discharge exemption, even though that literature was not introduced or discussed at the initial hearing. The court remanded to the agency to give it an opportunity to rely only on the exclusive trial record, or to hold a hearing where the parties would have an opportunity to address the experts on this new evidence.

(c) Taking official notice. In Castillo-Villagra v. INS, 972 F.2d 1017 (9th Cir. 1992), at issue was the political asylum request of individuals from Nicaragua who were opposed to the Sandinista regime. The Board of Immigration Appeals, in upholding the denial of asylum, took official notice of the existence of the new anti-Sandinista regime that then-controlled Nicaragua. The Court of Appeals held that it was perfectly appropriate for the agency to take official notice of the existence of the new regime; but the court then remanded to give an opportunity for the asylum applicants to argue whether and how the existence of the anti-Sandinista regime might affect their fear of returning to Nicaragua.

Do you agree with the court's ruling? The APA only provides that when there is an official notice, "a party is entitled, on timely request, to an opportunity to show the contrary." Technically, there was no real dispute that an anti-Sandinista regime controlled Nicaragua. But doesn't it make eminent sense to allow a party to argue about the *implications* of that fact for which official notice is taken? The Ninth Circuit decided the case, again, on due process grounds. We take up due process considerations in another chapter. But due process aside, doesn't the Ninth Circuit's ruling at least consist with the spirit of the exclusive record requirement? Or would requiring the agency under the APA to give an opportunity for argument about the implications of an officially noticed fact be a violation of *Vermont Yankee*?

(d) Political influence. Recall that in the *Sierra Club v. Costle* case, involving informal rulemaking, the D.C. Circuit held that it was permissible for an agency to discuss the content of a potential rulemaking with congressional and other executive-branch officials. In short, so long as the agency's ultimate regulation comports with the statute, the agency took into account public comments, and the agency's policy choice is not arbitrary and capricious, there are no grounds to complain of ex parte political influence. Indeed, when making policy, we'd expect the agency to take into account the views of our elected policymakers.

But what about in the context of a formal adjudication? Can Congress and the President try to influence a formal adjudicatory proceeding? The difference between formal adjudications and informal rulemakings is that the former have to be made on an exclusive record and ex parte contacts are prohibited. Thus, in Pillsbury Co. v. FTC, 354 F.2d 952 (5th Cir. 1966), the court required the recusal of FTC commissioners in a pending adjudication because they had been hauled before a congressional committee where various senators referenced the pending case over one hundred times in discharging their views about the agency's approach to the relevant statutory standard. Do you agree? Shouldn't Congress be able to hold hearings as usual and conduct oversight, even if the issue is a formal adjudication? Perhaps the answer is that members of Congress can speak *generally* about the policy matters at hand, and the agency's *general* approach to formal adjudications writ large, but cannot reference or attempt to influence specific cases.

COURSE THEME

POLITICAL INFLUENCE
Recall earlier discussions of whether it is desirable that political officials should influence agency policymaking. Is the answer different when political officials try to interfere with particular adjudications?

Similarly, in Portland Audubon Society v. The Endangered Species Committee, 984 F.3d 1534 (9th Cir. 1993), the President and his aides had attempted to influence the decision of an agency committee charged with granting exemptions to the requirements of the Endangered Species Act, specifically requesting that an exemption be granted for thirteen timber sales affecting the northern spotted owl. The court reversed the agency's exemption ruling. It held that although the president may of course supervise executive branch officials, the president could not seek to interfere in particular formal adjudications, noting that "the general principle that the President may not interfere with quasi-adjudicatory agency actions is well settled." Id. at 1547.

Do you agree? In Myers v. United States, 272 U.S. 52 (1926), discussed in detail in Chapter 6, the Supreme Court held that because the president possesses "the executive power" and has the duty to "take care that the laws be faithfully executed," the president must be able to oversee, direct, and also remove at least those officers appointed by and with the advice and consent of the Senate. The Court recognized, however, that adjudications might be different, permitting *only* removal of officers, but not direct interference. Id. at 135 ("[T]here may be duties of a quasi judicial character imposed on executive officers and members of executive tribunals whose decisions after hearing affect interests of individuals, the discharge of which the President cannot in a particular case properly influence or control. But even in such a case he may consider the decision after its rendition as a reason for removing the officer, on the ground that the discretion regularly entrusted to that officer by statute has not been on the whole intelligently or wisely exercised. Otherwise he does not discharge his own constitutional duty of seeing that the laws be faithfully executed.").

Did *Myers* take an overly cramped view of presidential power? If the executive power is the power to execute the law, why can't the President decide on his or her own in any particular case whether the given facts satisfy the relevant statutory criteria? If the President is wrong on the facts or the law the courts will overturn the decision. See generally Saikrishna Prakash, *The Essential Meaning of Executive Power*, 2003 Ill. L. Rev. 701 (arguing that the President can personally execute the law). On the other hand, is the duty of faithful execution only a duty of supervision, and is the implication that the President cannot execute the law personally unless Congress entrusts particular tasks to the President specifically? See generally Gillian E. Metzger, *The Constitutional Duty to Supervise*, 124 Yale L.J. 1836, 1875–76 (2015) (arguing the President only has the power to supervise law execution, not to personally execute the laws). This discussion is taken up in more depth in Chapter 6.

> **CROSS REFERENCE** The role of political influence on administrative agencies is intimately connected with considerations of executive power, which are addressed in Chapter 6.

C. Informal Adjudications

Recall that most agency actions are adjudications. Whenever an agency or officer applies the law to a set of facts and makes a conclusion, that is an "adjudication." When a Customs and Border Patrol agent seizes goods at an airport, that is an adjudication. When a passport is denied, that is an adjudication. Under the APA, recall, an adjudication is basically any agency action that is not a rulemaking. The previous section explored the requirements of formal adjudication. What about the requirements for informal adjudication, by far the most common type of agency action? In contrast to the dedicated provisions for informal rulemaking, the APA has no specific provisions for informal adjudications. Does the APA not, then, require any particular procedures for such adjudications? The Supreme Court has found some procedural requirements in the next two cases.

Citizens to Preserve Overton Park, Inc. v. Volpe

401 U.S. 402 (1971)

Opinion of the Court by MR. JUSTICE MARSHALL, announced by MR. JUSTICE STEWART.

The growing public concern about the quality of our natural environment has prompted Congress in recent years to enact legislation designed to curb the accelerating destruction of our country's natural beauty. We are concerned in this case with § 4(f) of the Department of Transportation Act of 1966, as amended, and § 18(a) of the Federal-Aid Highway Act of 1968, 23 U.S.C. § 138. These statutes prohibit the Secretary of Transportation from authorizing the use of federal funds to finance the construction of highways through public parks if a 'feasible and prudent' alternative route exists. If no such route is available, the statutes allow him to approve construction through parks only if there has been 'all possible planning to minimize harm' to the park.

Petitioners, private citizens as well as local and national conservation organizations, contend that the Secretary has violated these statutes by authorizing the expenditure of federal funds for the construction of a six-lane interstate highway through a public park in Memphis, Tennessee. . . .

Overton Park is 342-acre city park located near the center of Memphis. The park contains a zoo, a nine-hole municipal golf course, an outdoor theater, nature trails, a bridle path, an art academy, picnic areas, and 170 acres of forest. The proposed highway, which is to be a six-lane, high-speed, expressway, will sever the zoo from the rest of the park. Although the roadway will be depressed below ground level except where it crosses a small creek, 26 acres of the park will be destroyed. The highway is to be a segment of Interstate Highway I-40, part of the National System of Interstate and Defense Highways. I-40 will provide Memphis with a major east-west expressway which will allow easier access to downtown Memphis from the residential areas on the eastern edge of the city.

Although the route through the park was approved by the Bureau of Public Roads in 1956 and by the Federal Highway Administrator in 1966, the enactment of § 4(f) of the Department of Transportation Act prevented distribution of federal funds for the section of the highway designated to go through Overton Park until the Secretary of Transportation determined whether the requirements of § 4(f) had been met. . . . In April 1968, the Secretary announced that he concurred in the judgment of local officials that I-40 should be built through the park. . . . Final approval for the project—the route as well as the design—was not announced until November 1969, after Congress had reiterated in § 138 of the Federal-Aid Highway Act that highway construction through public parks was to be restricted. Neither announcement approving the route and design of I-40 was accompanied by a statement of the Secretary's factual findings. He did not indicate why he believed there were no feasible and prudent alternative routes or why design changes could not be made to reduce the harm to the park. . . .

In the District Court, respondents introduced affidavits, prepared specifically for this litigation, which indicated that the Secretary had made the decision and that the decision was supportable. . . .

We agree that formal findings were not required. But we do not believe that in this case judicial review based solely on litigation affidavits was adequate. . . .

Review under the substantial-evidence test is authorized only when the agency action is taken pursuant to a rulemaking provision of the Administrative Procedure Act itself, 5 U.S.C. § 553, or when the agency action is based on a public adjudicatory hearing. See 5 U.S.C. §§ 556, 557. The Secretary's decision to allow the expenditure of federal funds to build I-40 through Overton Park was plainly not an exercise of a rulemaking function. And the only hearing that is required by either the Administrative Procedure Act or the statutes regulating the distribution of federal funds for highway construction is a public hearing conducted by local officials for the purpose of informing the community about the proposed project and eliciting community views on the design and route. . . .

Even though there is no de novo review in this case and the Secretary's approval of the route of I-40 does not have ultimately to meet the substantial-evidence test, the generally applicable standards of § 706 require the reviewing court to engage in a substantial inquiry. . . .

Section 706(2)(A) requires a finding that the actual choice made was not 'arbitrary, capricious, an abuse of discretion, or otherwise not in accordance with law.' 5 U.S.C. § 706(2)(A). To make this finding the court must consider whether the decision was based on a consideration of the relevant factors and whether there has been a clear error of judgment. Although this inquiry into the facts is to be searching and careful, the ultimate standard of review is a narrow one. The court is not empowered to substitute its judgment for that of the agency.

The final inquiry is whether the Secretary's action followed the necessary procedural requirements. Here the only procedural error alleged is the failure of the Secretary to make formal findings and state his reason for allowing the highway to be built through the park.

Undoubtedly, review of the Secretary's action is hampered by his failure to make such findings, but the absence of formal findings does not necessarily require that the case be remanded to the Secretary. Neither the Department of Transportation Act nor the Federal-Aid Highway Act requires such formal findings. Moreover, the Administrative Procedure Act requirements that there be formal findings in certain rulemaking and adjudicatory proceedings do not apply to the Secretary's action here. . . .

Here . . . there is an administrative record that allows the full, prompt review of the Secretary's action that is sought without additional delay which would result from having a remand to the Secretary.

That administrative record is not, however, before us. The lower courts based their review on the litigation affidavits that were presented. These affidavits were merely 'post hoc' rationalizations, which have traditionally been found to be an inadequate basis for review. And they clearly do not constitute the 'whole record' compiled by the agency: the basis for review required by § 706 of the Administrative Procedure Act.

Thus it is necessary to remand this case to the District Court for plenary review of the Secretary's decision. That review is to be based on the full administrative record that was before the Secretary at the time he made his decision. But since the bare record may not disclose the factors that were considered or the Secretary's construction of the evidence it may be necessary for the District Court to require some explanation in order to determine if the Secretary acted within the scope of his authority and if the Secretary's action was justifiable under the applicable standard.

The court may require the administrative officials who participated in the decision to give testimony explaining their action. Of course, such inquiry into the mental processes of administrative decisionmakers is usually to be avoided. And where there are administrative findings that were made at the same time as the decision . . . there must be a strong showing of bad faith or improper behavior before such inquiry may be made. But here there are no such formal findings and it may be that the only way there can be effective judicial review is by examining the decisionmakers themselves.

The District Court is not, however, required to make such an inquiry. It may be that the Secretary can prepare formal findings . . . that will provide an adequate explanation for his action. Such an explanation will, to some extent, be a 'post hoc rationalization' and thus must be viewed critically. If the District Court decides that additional explanation is necessary, that court should consider which method will prove the most expeditious so that full review may be had as soon as possible.

NOTES AND QUESTIONS

1. *The arbitrary and capricious standard.* The Court's opinion in *Overton Park* is not written with the utmost clarity. Nevertheless, the opinion is important for establishing, or confirming, two administrative law principles. The first is the general substantive standard of review under APA § 706(a)(2), which requires courts to set aside agency action that is "arbitrary, capricious, an abuse of discretion, or otherwise not in accordance with law." In *Overton Park,* the Court summarized existing case law and described the substantive standard of review as follows: "To make this finding the court must consider whether the decision was based on a consideration of the relevant factors and whether there has been a clear error of judgment. Although this inquiry into the facts is to be searching and careful, the ultimate standard of review is a narrow one. The court is not empowered to substitute its judgment for that of the agency." We shall encounter this standard again in Chapter 4, which examines judicial review of agency action under these standards.

 CROSS REFERENCE *Overton Park* is also a seminal case on the arbitrary and capricious standard of APA § 706.

2. *The requirement for a sufficient record.* For present purposes, *Overton Park* has come to stand for the proposition that if courts are to engage in their statutorily mandated "arbitrary and capricious" review under APA § 706(a)(2), then the agency must present the courts with an administrative record sufficient for the courts actually to engage in this inquiry. This has been held to mean that an agency must undertake sufficient procedures to produce a record by which the courts can evaluate the agency's action under the arbitrary-and-capricious standard.

3. *Deposing agency heads?* The Court in *Overton Park* seems to have held that a court could compel the testimony of an agency official if the administrative record is insufficient for the court to be able to conduct its review, or if the record evinces bad faith. For obvious reasons, this approach is disfavored. Yet in recent years the Court's dictum took on renewed prominence in the case involving whether the Commerce Department could add a citizenship question to the 2020 census. Plaintiffs argued that the Department's rationales for adding a citizenship question were mere pretext, and that the real motive for asking the question was to reduce the response rate of lawfully present non-citizens. The district court ordered a deposition of the Secretary of Commerce, but the Supreme Court stayed that order. In its final opinion the Court held that this request for additional discovery was improper. Dep't of Comm. v. New York, 139 S. Ct. 2551 (2019).

4. *The* Vermont Yankee *connection.* Does the requirement to produce an adequate record violate the principle of *Vermont Yankee?* The Supreme Court addressed that question in the next case, which also seems to have established, in passing, a set of minimum procedural requirements.

Pensions Benefit Guaranty Corp. v. LTV Corp.

496 U.S. 633 (1990)

Justice Blackmun delivered the opinion of the Court.

In this case we must determine whether the decision of the Pension Benefit Guaranty Corporation (PBGC) to restore certain pension plans under § 4047 of the Employee Retirement Income Security Act of 1974 (ERISA), was, as the Court of Appeals concluded, arbitrary and capricious or contrary to law, within the meaning of the Administrative Procedure Act (APA), 5 U.S.C. § 706.

Petitioner PBGC is a wholly owned United States Government corporation, see 29 U.S.C. § 1302, modeled after the Federal Deposit Insurance Corporation. . . . The PBGC administers and enforces Title IV of ERISA. Title IV includes a mandatory Government insurance program that protects the pension benefits of over 30 million private-sector American workers who participate in plans covered by the Title. In enacting Title IV, Congress sought to ensure that employees and their beneficiaries would not be completely "deprived of anticipated retirement benefits by the termination of pension plans before sufficient funds have been accumulated in the plans."

When a plan covered under Title IV terminates with insufficient assets to satisfy its pension obligations to the employees, the PBGC becomes trustee of the plan, taking over the plan's assets and liabilities. The PBGC then uses the plan's assets to cover what it can of the benefit obligations. The PBGC then must add its own funds to ensure payment of most of the remaining "nonforfeitable" benefits, i.e., those benefits to which participants have earned entitlement under the plan terms as of the date of termination. ERISA does place limits on the benefits PBGC may guarantee upon plan termination, however, even if an employee is entitled to greater benefits under the terms of the plan. . . .

The cost of the PBGC insurance is borne primarily by employers that maintain ongoing pension plans. Sections 4006 and 4007 of ERISA require these employers to pay annual premiums. . . .

This case arose after respondent The LTV Corporation (LTV Corp.) and many of its subsidiaries, including LTV Steel Company Inc. (LTV Steel), (collectively LTV), in July 1986 filed petitions for reorganization under Chapter 11 of the Bankruptcy Code. At that time, LTV Steel was the sponsor of three defined benefit pension plans (Plans) covered by Title IV of ERISA. Two of the Plans were the products of collective-bargaining negotiations with the United Steelworkers of America (Steelworkers). The third was for nonunion salaried employees. Chronically underfunded, the Plans, by late 1986, had unfunded liabilities for promised benefits of almost $2.3 billion. Approximately $2.1 billion of this amount was covered by PBGC insurance.

It is undisputed that one of LTV Corp.'s principal goals in filing the Chapter 11 petitions was the restructuring of LTV Steel's pension obligations, a goal which could be accomplished if the Plans were terminated and responsibility for the unfunded liabilities was placed on the PBGC. LTV Steel then could negotiate with its employees for new pension arrangements. LTV, however, could not voluntarily terminate the Plans because two of them had been negotiated in collective bargaining. LTV therefore sought to have the PBGC terminate the Plans.

To that end, LTV advised the PBGC in 1986 that it could not continue to provide complete funding for the Plans. PBGC estimated that, without continued funding, the Plans' $2.1 billion underfunding could increase by as much as $65 million by December 1987 and by another $63 million by December 1988, unless the Plans were terminated. Moreover, extensive plant shutdowns were anticipated. These shutdowns, if they occurred before the Plans were terminated, would have required the payment of significant "shutdown benefits." The PBGC estimated that such benefits could increase the Plans' liabilities by as much as $300 million to $700 million, of which up to $500 million would be covered by PBGC insurance. Confronted with this information, the PBGC, invoking § 4042(a)(4) of ERISA, 29 U.S.C. § 1342(a)(4), determined that the Plans should be terminated in order to protect the insurance program from the unreasonable risk of large losses, and commenced termination proceedings in the District Court. With LTV's consent, the Plans were terminated effective January 13, 1987.

Because the Plans' participants lost some benefits as a result of the termination, the Steelworkers filed an adversary action against LTV in the Bankruptcy Court, challenging the termination and seeking an order directing LTV to make up the lost benefits. This action was settled, with LTV and the Steelworkers negotiating an interim collective-bargaining agreement that included new pension arrangements intended to make up benefits that plan participants lost as a result of the termination. . . . Retired participants were thereby placed in substantially the same positions they would have occupied had the old Plans never been terminated. . . . With respect to shutdown benefits, LTV stated in Bankruptcy Court that the new benefits totaled "75% of benefits lost as a result of plan termination." With respect to some other kinds of benefits for active participants, the new arrangements provided 100% or more of the lost benefits.

The PBGC objected to these new pension agreements, characterizing them as "follow-on" plans. It defines a follow-on plan as a new benefit arrangement designed to wrap around the insurance benefits provided by the PBGC in such a way as to provide both retirees and active participants substantially the same benefits as they would have received had no termination occurred. The PBGC's policy against follow-on plans stems from the agency's belief that such plans are "abusive" of the insurance program and result in the PBGC's subsidizing an employer's ongoing pension program in a way not contemplated by Title IV. . . .

The Director issued a notice of restoration on September 22, 1987, indicating the PBGC's intent to restore the terminated Plans. The PBGC notice explained that the restoration decision was based on (1) LTV's establishment of "a retirement program that results in an abuse of the pension plan termination insurance system established by Title IV of ERISA," and (2) LTV's "improved financial circumstances." Restoration meant that the Plans were ongoing, and that LTV again would be responsible for administering and funding them.

LTV refused to comply with the restoration decision. This prompted the PBGC to initiate an enforcement action in the District Court. . . .

* * *

Finally, we consider the Court of Appeals' ruling that the agency procedures were inadequate in this particular case. . . . [T]he court held that the PBGC's decision was arbitrary and capricious because the "PBGC neither apprised LTV of the material on which it was to base its decision, gave LTV an adequate opportunity to offer contrary evidence, proceeded in accordance with ascertainable standards . . . , nor provided [LTV] a statement showing its reasoning in applying those standards." The court suggested that on remand the agency was required to do each of these things.

The PBGC argues that this holding conflicts with *Vermont Yankee Nuclear Power Corp. v. Natural Resources Defense Council, Inc.*, 435 U.S. 519 (1978), where, the PBGC contends, this Court made clear that when the Due Process Clause is not implicated and an agency's governing statute contains no specific procedural mandates, the APA establishes the maximum procedural requirements a reviewing court may impose on agencies. . . .

Respondents counter by arguing that courts, under some circumstances, do require agencies to undertake additional procedures. As support for this proposition, they rely on *Citizens to Preserve Overton Park, Inc. v. Volpe*, 401 U.S. 402 (1971). In *Overton Park*, the Court concluded that the Secretary of Transportation's "*post hoc* rationalizations" regarding a decision to authorize the construction of a highway did not provide "an [a]dequate basis for [judicial] review" for purposes of the APA, 5 U.S.C. § 706. Accordingly, the Court directed the District Court on remand to consider evidence that shed light on the Secretary's reasoning at the time he made the decision. Of particular relevance for present purposes, the Court in *Overton Park* intimated that one recourse for the District Court might be a remand to the agency for a fuller explanation of the agency's reasoning at the time of the agency action. Subsequent cases have made clear that remanding to the agency in fact is the preferred course. Respondents contend that the instant case is controlled by *Overton Park* rather than *Vermont Yankee*, and that the Court of Appeals' ruling was thus correct.

We believe that respondents' argument is wide of the mark. We begin by noting that although one initially might feel that there is some tension between *Vermont Yankee* and *Overton Park*, the two cases are not necessarily inconsistent. *Vermont Yankee* stands for the general proposition that courts are not free to impose upon agencies specific procedural requirements that have no basis in the APA. At most, *Overton Park* suggests that § 706(2)(A), which directs a court to ensure that an agency action is not arbitrary and capricious or otherwise contrary to law, imposes a general "procedural" requirement of sorts by mandating that an agency take whatever steps it needs to provide an explanation that will enable the court to evaluate the agency's rationale at the time of decision.

Here, unlike in *Overton Park*, the Court of Appeals did not suggest that the administrative record was inadequate to enable the court to fulfill its duties under § 706. Rather, to support its ruling, the court focused on "fundamental fairness" to LTV. With the possible exception of the absence of "ascertainable standards"—by which we are not exactly sure what the Court of Appeals meant—the procedural inadequacies cited by the court all relate to LTV's role in the PBGC's decisionmaking process. But the court did not point to any provision in ERISA or the APA which gives LTV the procedural rights the court identified. Thus, the court's holding runs afoul of *Vermont Yankee* and finds no support in *Overton Park*. . . .

The determination in this case . . . was lawfully made by informal adjudication, the minimal requirements for which are set forth in the APA, 5 U.S.C. § 555, and do not include such elements. A failure to provide them where the Due Process Clause itself does not require them (which has not been asserted here) is therefore not unlawful. . . .

Notes and Questions

1.   Vermont Yankee. The Court in *LTV Corp.* confirmed that *Overton Park* has come to stand for the proposition that APA § 706 imposes procedural requirements on agencies engaged in informal adjudications: if courts are to undertake their statutorily mandated review, there must be an adequate administrative record for the court to examine. Thus, *Overton Park* is consistent with *Vermont Yankee*.

2.   *What's the procedural minimum?* The exact minimum procedural requirements, however, were unclear, and still remain unclear. The Court in *LTV Corp.* stated that the minimum procedures are set forth in APA § 555. Sandwiched between the formal adjudication sections—554, and 556–57—APA § 555 deals with "ancillary matters." The most important of these is § 555(b), which provides that "[a] person compelled to appear in person before an agency" is entitled to legal representation. It then provides that a *party* to "an agency proceeding" is "entitled to appear in person." The next sentence adds that "an interested person" who is not a party may also "appear before an agency," but only "[s]o far as the orderly conduct of public business permits." Section 555(c) provides that if a person is "compelled to submit data or evidence," he is entitled to retain a copy. Section 555(e) provides that when an agency *denies* a petition or application, "the notice shall be accompanied by a brief statement of the grounds for denial." Section 555, in other words, does not establish much procedure at all, and does not cover the entire universe of informal adjudications.

In reality, then, the procedures used for informal adjudications vary widely. As one scholar put it, the APA "fails to regulate in any significant way the vast and rapidly increasing number of more or less formal evidentiary adjudicatory hearings required by federal statutes that are not conducted by ALJs [Administrative Law Judges] and yet are functionally indistinguishable from the hearings that are conducted by ALJs." Michael Asimow, *The Spreading Umbrella: Extending the APA's Adjudication Provisions to All Evidentiary Hearings Required by Statute*, 56 Admin L. Rev. 1003, 1020 (2004).

In September 2016, Professor Michael Asimow published a report for the Administrative Conference of the United States, an independent agency that studies the administrative process, on informal adjudications. Professor Asimow catalogued 20 "best practices" for such adjudications, and tracked whether nine different agencies that he studied used those practices:

TABLE 3: TYPE B AGENCIES AND BEST PRACTICE PROPOSALS

The following table indicates whether each agency I studied embodied the best practices recommended in this report in its generally available written procedural documents (procedural regulations, manuals, or other sources of procedure law).

TYPE B SCHEMES⇒	USDA PACA	CBCA	DOE	EEOC	EPA EAB	EOIR	MSPB	PTAB & TTAB	PRRB	BVA
RECOMMENDATIONS⇓										
INTEGRITY OF PRCSS										
a. Exclusive Record	N	Y	Y	Y	Y	Y	Y	Y	Y	N
b. Bias	Y	N	N	Y	Y	Y-N[127]	Y	N	Y	N
c. Ex Parte Comm.	N	Y	Y	N	Y	Y-N	Y	Y-N[128]	Y	N
d. Sep. of Func.	N	N/A[129]	Y-N	N/A	Y	Y-N	N/A	Y-N	N/A	N
PREHEARING										
a. Written Notice	Y	Y	Y	Y	Y	Y	Y	Y	Y	Y
b. Lay Representation	Y	N	Y	Y	Y	Y	Y	N	Y	Y
c. ADR	Y	Y	Y	Y	Y	N	Y	N	Y	N
d. Pretrial Conf.	N	Y	Y	N	Y	Y	Y	Y	Y	N
e. Electronic Filing	N	Y	Y	N	Y	N	Y	Y	Y	N
f. Discovery	Y	Y	Y	Y	Y	Y	Y	Y	Y	N
g. Subpoena Power	Y	Y	Y	N	Y	Y	Y	Y	Y	N
h. Open Hearings	N	Y	N	N	Y	Y	Y	N	N	N
HEARING										
a. Use of AJs	Y	Y	Y	Y	Y	Y	Y	Y	N	Y
b. Videoconference	Y	N	Y	N	N	Y	Y	N	Y	Y
c. Written-only Opp.	Y	Y	Y	Y	Y	N	Y	Y	Y	Y
d. Evidence Rules	N	Y	Y	Y	Y	N	N	Y	Y	N
e. Rebuttal Opp.	Y	Y	Y	Y	Y	Y	Y	Y	Y	Y
POST-HEARING										
a. Written Opinion	Y	Y	Y	Y	Y	Y	Y	Y	Y	Y
b. Reconsideration	Y	N	Y	Y	Y	Y	Y	N	Y	N
PROCEDURAL REGS										
a. Complete Statement	Y	Y	Y	N	Y	N	Y	Y	N	N
NUMBER OF YESSES	13	15	17.5	12	19	13.5	18	13	16	7

Michael Asimow, Administrative Conference of the United States, Adjudication Outside the Administrative Procedure Act, Sept. 16, 2016, at 33.

These best practices included the use of an exclusive record and a prohibition on ex parte contacts, the use of written opinions, and the existence of a complete statement of the relevant procedural regulations in the Federal Register. As you can see from the table, almost every agency Asimow studied used at least 12 of the best practices. Do you think it might be time to amend the APA to establish a set of procedures for informal agency adjudications?

Is it time to amend the APA? Is "informal adjudication" a category missing from the current APA framework?

3. *Informal adjudication as executive power?* Maybe there is another explanation for why the APA does not seem to address informal adjudications with any specificity. It may be because informal adjudications are just a catch-all category for any and all remaining executive actions that agencies undertake. Recall that the APA defines an adjudication as anything that is not a rulemaking (and including licensing). Thus the following activities are all examples of adjudications: (1) a Postal Service employee decides whether a

letter has enough postage; (2) a Forest Service ranger approves (or denies) an application for a camping permit; (3) a Custom's officer classifies a day planner not as a duty-free good, but rather as a bound diary subject to tariff; (4) the FCC grants a license to a wireless communications provider to use a specified portion of the electromagnetic spectrum; (5) an administrative judge working for the Veterans' Administration (VA) Board of Veterans' Appeals affirms an initial decision denying retroactive payment of disability benefits; (6) a Social Security employee working in a field office grants an initial claim for Social Security disability benefits; and (7) an administrative law judge working in SSA's Office of Disability Adjudication and Review affirms an initial denial of a claim for Social Security disability benefits. Only the last example is a formal adjudication with a full, trial-like hearing. The first six are all "informal." Of these, only the fifth example—the Board of Veterans' Appeals affirming an initial decision denying retroactive payment of benefits—is there an opportunity for a hearing. See Emily Bremer, *The Rediscovered Stages of Agency Adjudication* (forthcoming).

Bremer, supra, argues that most informal adjudication is simply best conceptualized as "executive power," and there is no reason to specify any particular procedures for the wide ranging and varying activities that fall within this umbrella. The APA is only concerned with the process for *specific types of executive action.* First, it is concerned with those that lead to the creation of rules and regulations. This is the domain of notice-and-comment rulemaking or the formal rulemaking proceedings. Second, it is concerned with the process for determining private rights and benefits *when such matters are genuinely contested.* APA § 555 might apply in those circumstances. Only when contestation remains was the formal adjudication process to be deployed. In other words, informal and formal adjudications are not really two separate *categories* of adjudications; they're two different *stages* of the same adjudication. Might that explain why there is no specific provision in the APA dealing with informal adjudications?

D. The *Accardi* Principle

In the previous section, we discussed the statutory procedural constraints on agency adjudications in the APA. It is worth recalling that there are many other sources of procedural constraints, particularly the organic statute itself, which may deviate from the APA's default rules. There are also other statutes that impose specialized procedures on agencies, like the Paperwork Reduction

Act or the Freedom of Information Act. Here, we briefly discuss one further source of procedural constraints on agency adjudications: agency regulations. That is, an agency, by regulation, might choose to constrain itself to particular procedures above and beyond the minimum required by the APA. In short, an agency must follow its own established procedures—indeed it must do so whether it is engaged in rulemaking or adjudication. This general rule, sometimes called "the *Accardi* principle," comes from the following landmark administrative law case.

United States *ex rel.* Accardi v. Shaugnessy

347 U.S. 260 (1954)

Mr. Justice Clark delivered the opinion of the Court.

This is a habeas corpus action in which the petitioner attacks the validity of the denial of his application for suspension of deportation under the provisions of § 19(c) of the Immigration Act of 1917. Admittedly deportable, the petitioner alleged, among other things, that the denial of his application by the Board of Immigration Appeals was prejudged through the issuance by the Attorney General in 1952, prior to the Board's decision, of a confidential list of 'unsavory characters' including petitioner's name, which made it impossible for him 'to secure fair consideration of this case.' . . . In 1948 [petitioner] applied for suspension of deportation pursuant to § 19(c) of the Immigration Act of 1917. . . .

Hearings on the deportation charge and the application for suspension of deportation were held before officers of the Immigration and Naturalization Service at various times from 1948 to 1952. A hearing officer ultimately found petitioner deportable and recommended a denial of discretionary relief. On July 7, 1952, the Acting Commissioner of Immigration adopted the officer's findings and recommendation. Almost nine months later, on April 3, 1953, the Board of Immigration Appeals affirmed the decision of the hearing officer. A warrant of deportation was issued the same day and arrangements were made for actual deportation to take place on April 24, 1953.

The scene of action then shifted to the United States District Court for the Southern District of New York. . . . [O]n May 15, his wife commenced this action by filing a petition for a second writ of habeas corpus. New grounds were alleged, on information and belief, for attacking the administrative refusal to suspend deportation. The principal ground is that on October 2, 1952—after the Acting Commissioner's decision in the case but before the decision of the Board of Immigration Appeals—the Attorney General announced at a press conference that he planned to deport certain 'unsavory characters'; on or about that date the Attorney General prepared a confidential list of one hundred individuals, including petitioner, whose deportation he wished; the list was circulated by the Department of Justice among all employees in the Immigration Service and on the Board of Immigration Appeals; and that issuance of the list and related publicity amounted to public prejudgment by the Attorney General so that fair consideration of petitioner's case by the Board of Immigration Appeals was made impossible. . . .

The crucial question is whether the alleged conduct of the Attorney General deprived petitioner of any of the rights guaranteed him by the statute or by the regulations issued pursuant thereto.

Regulations with the force and effect of law supplement the bare bones of § 19(c). The regulations prescribe the procedure to be followed in processing an alien's application for suspension of deportation. Until the 1952 revision of the regulations, the procedure called for decisions at three separate administrative levels below the Attorney General—hearing officer, Commissioner, and the Board of Immigration Appeals. The Board is appointed by the Attorney General, serves at his pleasure, and operates under regulations providing that: 'in considering and determining . . . appeals, the Board of Immigration Appeals shall exercise such discretion and power conferred upon the Attorney General by law as is appropriate and necessary for the disposition of the case. The decision of the Board . . . shall be final except in those cases reviewed by the Attorney General. . . .' 8 CFR s 90.3(c) (1949). And the Board was required to refer to the Attorney General for review all cases which:

'(a)   The Attorney General directs the Board to refer to him.

'(b)   The chairman or a majority of the Board believes should be referred to the Attorney General for review of its decision.

'(c)   The Commissioner requests be referred to the Attorney General by the Board and it agrees.' 8 CFR s 90.12 (1949).

The regulations just quoted pinpoint the decisive fact in this case: the Board was required, as it still is, to exercise its own judgment when considering appeals. The clear import of broad provisions for a final review by the Attorney General himself would be meaningless if the Board were not expected to render a decision in accord with its own collective belief. In unequivocal terms the regulations delegate to the Board discretionary authority as broad as the statute confers on the Attorney General; the scope of the Attorney General's discretion became the yardstick of the Board's. And if the word 'discretion' means anything in a statutory or administrative grant of power, it means that the recipient must exercise his authority according to his own understanding and conscience. This applies with equal force to the Board and the Attorney General. In short, as long as the regulations remain operative, the Attorney General denies himself the right to sidestep the Board or dictate its decision in any manner. . . .

It is important to emphasize that we are not here reviewing and reversing the manner in which discretion was exercised. If such were the case we would be discussing the evidence in the record supporting or undermining the alien's claim to discretionary relief. Rather, we object to the Board's alleged failure to exercise its own discretion, contrary to existing valid regulations. . . .

MR. JUSTICE JACKSON, whom MR. JUSTICE REED, MR. JUSTICE BURTON, and MR. JUSTICE MINTON join, dissenting.

We feel constrained to dissent from the legal doctrine being announced. The doctrine seems proof of the adage that hard cases make bad law.

Peculiarities which distinguish this administrative decision from others we have held judicially reviewable must be borne in mind. . . . Petitioner admittedly is in this country illegally and does not question his deportability or the validity of the order to deport him. The hearings in question relate only to whether carrying out an entirely legal deportation order is to be suspended.

Congress vested in the Attorney General, and in him alone, discretion as to whether to suspend deportation under certain circumstances. We think a refusal to exercise that discretion is not reviewable on habeas corpus, first, because the nature of the power and discretion vested in the Attorney General is analogous to the power of pardon or commutation of a sentence, which we trust no one thinks is subject to judicial control; and second, because no legal right exists in petitioner by virtue of constitution, statute or common law to have a lawful order of deportation suspended. Even if petitioner proves himself eligible for suspension, that gives him no right to it as a matter of law but merely establishes a condition precedent to exercise of discretion by the Attorney General. Habeas corpus is to enforce legal rights, not to transfer to the courts control of executive discretion.

The ground for judicial interference here seems to be that the Board of Immigration Appeals did find, or may have found, against suspension on instructions from the Attorney General. Even so, this Board is neither a judicial body nor an independent agency. It is created by the Attorney General as part of his office, he names its members, and they are responsible only to him. It operates under his supervision and direction, and its every decision is subject to his unlimited review and revision. The refusal to suspend deportation, no matter which subordinate officer actually makes it, is in law the Attorney General's decision. We do not think its validity can be impeached by showing that he over-influenced members of his own staff whose opinion in any event would be only advisory. . . .

We would affirm and leave the responsibility for suspension or execution of this deportation squarely on the Attorney General, where Congress has put it.

NOTES AND QUESTIONS

1.   The Accardi *principle.* The *Accardi* case stands for the proposition, often described as the *Accardi* principle, that an agency must follow its own promulgated regulations. Although not necessarily limited to procedural regulations, the doctrine is usually invoked when the issue is procedural. See Thomas W. Merrill, *The* Accardi *Principle,* 74 Geo. Wash. L. Rev. 569, 588–89 (2006). The case should always be read in light of the dissent. The Court was not purporting to tell the Attorney General how to exercise his discretion ultimately. The Court only held that, if the Attorney General precommits in advance to following a certain procedure in exercising that discretion, he must follow that procedure. Merrill has explained that *Accardi* can "be seen as finding that the presence of a claim of agency rule violation provides a basis for judicial review when otherwise it would not exist." Merill, supra, at 591.

2. *Basis for the principle.* What is the basis for the *Accardi* principle? Is it administrative common law? Does it sound in due process considerations? Are there separation of powers implications? The Supreme Court has not been consistent about the rationale. See generally Merrill, supra. Is there a connection to the anti-retroactivity cases, discussed in the notes to the *Chenery II* case? Is it just a matter of protecting the expectation interests of regulated parties? It might be a little bit of all of these things. The D.C. Circuit has most recently rooted the doctrine in the "binding" nature of regulations. But recall that a binding regulation may not go through notice-and-comment, because a procedural regulation can "bind" the agency but the APA exempts procedural rules from the notice-and-comment process. See Vietnam Veterans of Am. v. Sec'y of the Navy, 843 F.2d 528 (D.C. Cir. 1988).

3. *Standard of review.* We will encounter judicial review in the next chapter, which will go over the various standards of review courts apply when reviewing various kinds of agency actions. What happens when an agency fails to follow its own procedural rule, violating the *Accardi* principle? As a general matter, the courts will not set aside the agency action if the error is "harmless." Mazaleski v. Treusdell, 562 F.2d 701, 719 n. 41 (D.C. Cir. 1977). The standard is not entirely clear, but the D.C. Circuit has said that a plaintiff must show the procedural violation caused "substantial prejudice." Steenholdt v. FAA, 314 F.3d 633, 640 (D.C. Cir. 2003).

TEST YOUR KNOWLEDGE: To assess your understanding of the material in this chapter, **click here** to take a quiz.

CHAPTER FOUR

Judicial Review of Agency Action

This chapter deals with judicial review of agency actions, and particularly with the scope of judicial review of the *substance* or the *merits* of what agencies do. Because agency actions can be set aside for violating the substantive judicial review standards, these standards effectively serve as statutory constraints on what an agency can do. For example, as you will learn, an agency action can be set aside if its factual findings are not supported by substantial evidence; this means that when an agency engages in fact-finding, it must support its findings by substantial evidence.

Take a look at APA § 706, comprising the judicial review provisions, in the appendix. It begins with a provision for reviewing agency interpretations of law: "To the extent necessary to decision and when presented, the reviewing court shall decide all relevant questions of law, interpret constitutional and statutory provisions, and determine the meaning or applicability of the terms of an agency action." 5 U.S.C. § 706. It then provides that the "reviewing court shall" compel agency action unlawfully withheld, id. § 706(1), and, importantly for our purposes, the reviewing court shall "set aside agency action, findings, and conclusions found to be arbitrary, capricious, an abuse of discretion, or otherwise not in accordance with law," id. § 706(2)(a). This section then allows courts to set aside agency actions that are unconstitutional, in excess of statutory authority, or which violate any legal procedural requirements. Many of these overlap, and for our purposes they are less important for the study of administrative law. The next important provision requires courts to "set aside agency action, findings, and conclusions found to be . . . unsupported by substantial evidence in a case subject to sections 556 and 557 of this title or otherwise reviewed on the record of an agency hearing provided by statute." Id. § 706(2)(E).

These judicial review provisions, in short, determine how an agency is to support its factual findings, in what kind of reasoning it must engage when making policy choices, and how it can go about interpreting its organic statute.

<table>
<tr><td>

PRACTICE POINTER

OVERVIEW: Judicial review is often separated into review of questions of fact, review of questions of law, and review of an agency's reasoning.

</td></tr>
</table>

There is no one right order in which to examine these judicial review provisions—those respecting legal questions, agency reasoning (under the "arbitrary and capricious" standard), or factual findings. The following sections begin with agency reasoning, proceed to agency fact-finding, and conclude with agency legal interpretations. It does so mostly out of convenience: there is far more material under the umbrella of agency legal interpretations, which can easily take several class sessions to cover. Fewer class sessions are required to cover the relevant materials on agency reasoning and fact-finding. Additionally, however, the modern doctrine regarding agency legal interpretations developed after the Court decided the leading cases involving agency reasoning, raising important questions about the relationship between the two sets of doctrine. It is thus helpful to take the agency reasoning cases and the legal interpretation cases chronologically.

Sections A–C of this Chapter cover judicial review of agency reasoning, fact-finding, and legal interpretations. Section D then deals with situations in which agencies enjoy significant discretion, and particularly with the meaning of § 701(a)(2), which precludes judicial review of "agency action committed to agency discretion by law." This final bit of material is usually included in a chapter on "reviewability" and access to judicial review, but it is best considered here where the nature of the agency discretion that is not subject to review can be compared to the kind of discretion that is subject to review.

A. Judicial Review of Agency Reasoning

The reader may recall that the Supreme Court in *Overton Park* elaborated upon the "arbitrary and capricious" standard of APA § 706:

> Section 706(2)(A) requires a finding that the actual choice made was not 'arbitrary, capricious, an abuse of discretion, or otherwise not in accordance with law.' 5 U.S.C. § 706(2)(A). To make this finding the court must consider whether the decision was based on a consideration

of the relevant factors and whether there has been a clear error of judgment. Although this inquiry into the facts is to be searching and careful, the ultimate standard of review is a narrow one. The court is not empowered to substitute its judgment for that of the agency.

Citizens to Preserve Overton Park, Inc. v. Volpe, 401 U.S. 402, 416 (1971). The Supreme Court had to apply this test in the following landmark case, which is often described as establishing "hard look" review of agency reasoning under the arbitrary and capricious standard (although the Court does not use that term in its opinion).

Motor Vehicle Manufacturers Ass'n of U.S., Inc. v. State Farm Mutual Automobile Insurance Co.

463 U.S. 29 (1983)

Justice White delivered the opinion of the Court.

The development of the automobile gave Americans unprecedented freedom to travel, but exacted a high price for enhanced mobility. Since 1929, motor vehicles have been the leading cause of accidental deaths and injuries in the United States. In 1982, 46,300 Americans died in motor vehicle accidents and hundreds of thousands more were maimed and injured. While a consensus exists that the current loss of life on our highways is unacceptably high, improving safety does not admit to easy solution. In 1966, Congress decided that at least part of the answer lies in improving the design and safety features of the vehicle itself. But much of the technology for building safer cars was undeveloped or untested. Before changes in automobile design could be mandated, the effectiveness of these changes had to be studied, their costs examined, and public acceptance considered. This task called for considerable expertise and Congress responded by enacting the National Traffic and Motor Vehicle Safety Act of 1966 (Act), 15 U.S.C. §§ 1381 *et seq.* The Act, created for the purpose of "reduc[ing] traffic accidents and deaths and injuries to persons resulting from traffic accidents," 15 U.S.C. § 1381, directs the Secretary of Transportation or his delegate to issue motor vehicle safety standards that "shall be practicable, shall meet the need for motor vehicle safety, and shall be stated in objective terms." 15 U.S.C. § 1392(a). In issuing these standards, the Secretary is directed to consider "relevant available motor vehicle safety data," whether the proposed standard "is reasonable, practicable and appropriate" for the particular type of motor vehicle, and the "extent to which such standards will contribute to carrying out the purposes" of the Act. 15 U.S.C. § 1392(f)(1), (3), (4).

The Act also authorizes judicial review under the provisions of the Administrative Procedure Act (APA), 5 U.S.C. § 706 (1976), of all "orders establishing, amending, or revoking a Federal motor vehicle safety standard," 15 U.S.C. § 1392(b). Under this authority, we review today whether NHTSA acted arbitrarily and capriciously in revoking the requirement in Motor Vehicle Safety Standard 208 that new motor vehicles produced after September 1982 be equipped with passive restraints to protect the safety of the occupants of the vehicle in the event of a collision. Briefly summarized, we hold that the agency failed to present an adequate basis and explanation for rescinding the passive restraint requirement and that the agency must either consider the matter further or adhere to or amend Standard 208 along lines which its analysis supports.

I

The regulation whose rescission is at issue bears a complex and convoluted history. Over the course of approximately 60 rulemaking notices, the requirement has been imposed, amended, rescinded, reimposed, and now rescinded again.

As originally issued by the Department of Transportation in 1967, Standard 208 simply required the installation of seatbelts in all automobiles. 32 Fed. Reg. 2408, 2415 (Feb. 3, 1967). It soon became apparent that the level of seatbelt use was too low to reduce traffic injuries to an acceptable level. The Department therefore began consideration of "passive occupant restraint systems"—devices that do not depend for their effectiveness upon any action taken by the occupant except that necessary to operate the vehicle. Two types of automatic crash protection emerged: automatic seatbelts and airbags. The automatic seatbelt is a traditional safety belt, which when fastened to the interior of the door remains attached without impeding entry or exit from the vehicle, and deploys automatically without any action on the part of the passenger. The airbag is an inflatable device concealed in the dashboard and steering column. It automatically inflates when a sensor indicates that deceleration forces from an accident have exceeded a preset minimum, then rapidly deflates to dissipate those forces. The life-saving potential of these devices was immediately recognized, and in 1977, after substantial on-the-road experience with both devices, it was estimated by NHTSA that passive restraints could prevent approximately 12,000 deaths and over 100,000 serious injuries annually. 42 Fed. Reg. 34,298.

In 1969, the Department formally proposed a standard requiring the installation of passive restraints, thereby commencing a lengthy series of proceedings. In 1970, the agency revised Standard 208 to include passive protection requirements, and in 1972, the agency amended the standard to require full passive protection for all front seat occupants of vehicles manufactured after August 15, 1975. In the interim, vehicles built between August 1973 and August 1975 were to carry either passive restraints or lap and shoulder belts coupled with an "ignition interlock" that would prevent starting the vehicle if the belts were not connected. . . .

In preparing for the upcoming model year, most car makers chose the "ignition interlock" option, a decision which was highly unpopular, and led Congress to amend the Act to prohibit a motor vehicle safety standard from requiring or permitting compliance by means of an ignition interlock or a continuous buzzer designed to indicate that safety belts were not in use. . . .

The effective date for mandatory passive restraint systems was extended for a year until August 31, 1976. But in June 1976, Secretary of Transportation William Coleman initiated a new rulemaking on the issue, 41 Fed. Reg. 24,070 (June 9, 1976). After hearing testimony and reviewing written comments, Coleman extended the optional alternatives indefinitely and suspended the passive restraint requirement. Although he found passive restraints technologically and economically feasible, the Secretary based his decision on the expectation that there would be widespread public resistance to the new systems. He instead proposed a demonstration project involving up to 500,000 cars installed with passive restraints, in order to smooth the way for public acceptance of mandatory passive restraints at a later date.

Coleman's successor as Secretary of Transportation disagreed. Within months of assuming office, Secretary Brock Adams decided that the demonstration project was unnecessary. He issued a new mandatory passive restraint regulation, known as Modified Standard 208. The Modified Standard mandated the phasing in of passive restraints beginning with large cars in model year 1982 and extending to all cars by model year 1984. The two principal systems that would satisfy the Standard were airbags and passive belts; the choice of which system to install was left to the manufacturers. . . .

Over the next several years, the automobile industry geared up to comply with Modified Standard 208. . . .

In February 1981, however, Secretary of Transportation Andrew Lewis reopened the rulemaking due to changed economic circumstances and, in particular, the difficulties of the automobile industry. 46 Fed. Reg. 12,033 (Feb. 12, 1981). Two months later, the agency ordered a one-year delay in the application of the standard to large cars, extending the deadline to September 1982, and at the same time, proposed the possible rescission of the entire standard. After receiving written comments and holding public hearings, NHTSA issued a final rule (Notice 25) that rescinded the passive restraint requirement contained in Modified Standard 208.

II

In a statement explaining the rescission, NHTSA maintained that it was no longer able to find, as it had in 1977, that the automatic restraint requirement would produce significant safety benefits. This judgment reflected not a change of opinion on the effectiveness of the technology, but a change in plans by the automobile industry. In 1977, the agency had assumed that airbags would be installed in 60% of all new cars and automatic seatbelts in 40%. By 1981 it became apparent that automobile manufacturers planned to install the automatic seatbelts in approximately 99% of the new cars. For this reason, the life-saving potential of airbags would not be realized. Moreover, it now appeared that the overwhelming majority of passive belts planned to be installed by manufacturers could be detached easily and left that way permanently. Passive belts, once detached, then required "the same type of affirmative action that is the stumbling block to obtaining high usage levels of manual belts." For this reason, the agency concluded that there was no longer a basis for reliably predicting that the standard would lead to any significant increased usage of restraints at all.

In view of the possibly minimal safety benefits, the automatic restraint requirement no longer was reasonable or practicable in the agency's view. The requirement would require approximately $1 billion to implement and the agency did not believe it would be reasonable to impose such substantial costs on manufacturers and consumers without more adequate assurance that sufficient safety benefits would accrue. In addition, NHTSA concluded that automatic restraints might have an adverse effect on the public's attitude toward safety. Given the high expense and limited benefits of detachable belts, NHTSA feared that many consumers would regard the standard as an instance of ineffective regulation, adversely affecting the public's view of safety regulation and, in particular, "poisoning popular sentiment toward efforts to improve occupant restraint systems in the future." . . .

III

Unlike the Court of Appeals, we do not find the appropriate scope of judicial review to be the "most troublesome question" in the case. Both the Motor Vehicle Safety Act and the 1974 Amendments concerning occupant crash protection standards indicate that motor vehicle safety standards are to be promulgated under the informal rulemaking procedures of § 553 of the Administrative Procedure Act. The agency's action in promulgating such standards therefore may be set aside if found to be "arbitrary, capricious, an abuse of discretion, or otherwise not in accordance with law." 5 U.S.C. § 706(2)(A). *Citizens to Preserve Overton Park v. Volpe*, 401 U.S. 402, 414 (1971); *Bowman Transportation, Inc. v. Arkansas-Best Freight System, Inc.*, 419 U.S. 281 (1974). We believe that the rescission or modification of an occupant protection standard is subject to the same test. Section 103(b) of the Motor Vehicle Safety Act, 15 U.S.C. § 1392(b), states that the procedural and judicial review provisions of the Administrative Procedure Act "shall apply to all orders establishing, amending, or revoking a Federal motor vehicle safety standard," and suggests no difference in the scope of judicial review depending upon the nature of the agency's action.

Petitioner Motor Vehicle Manufacturers Association (MVMA) disagrees, contending that the rescission of an agency rule should be judged by the same standard a court would use to judge an agency's refusal to promulgate a rule in the first place—a standard Petitioner believes considerably narrower than the traditional arbitrary and capricious test and "close to the borderline of nonreviewability." We reject this view. The Motor Vehicle Safety Act expressly equates orders "revoking" and "establishing" safety standards; neither that Act nor the APA suggests that revocations are to be treated as refusals to promulgate standards. Petitioner's view would render meaningless Congress' authorization for judicial review of orders revoking safety rules. Moreover, the revocation of an extant regulation is substantially different than a failure to act. Revocation constitutes a reversal of the agency's former views as to the proper course. A "settled course of behavior embodies the agency's informed judgment that, by pursuing that course, it will carry out the policies committed to it by Congress. There is, then, at least a presumption that those policies will be carried out best if the settled rule is adhered to." *Atchison, T. & S.F.R. Co. v. Wichita Bd. of Trade*, 412 U.S. 800, 807–08 (1973). Accordingly, an agency changing its course by rescinding a rule is obligated to supply a reasoned analysis for the change beyond that which may be required when an agency does not act in the first instance.

In so holding, we fully recognize that "regulatory agencies do not establish rules of conduct to last forever," and that an agency must be given ample latitude to "adapt their rules and policies to the demands of changing circumstances." But the forces of change do not always or necessarily point in the direction of deregulation. In the abstract, there is no more reason to presume that changing circumstances require the rescission of prior action, instead of a revision in or even the extension of current regulation. If Congress established a presumption from which judicial review should start, that presumption—contrary to petitioners' views—is not *against* safety regulation, but *against* changes in current policy that are not justified by the rulemaking record. While the removal of a regulation may not entail the monetary expenditures and other costs of enacting a new standard, and accordingly, it may be easier for an agency to justify a deregulatory action, the direction in which an agency chooses to move does not alter the standard of judicial review established by law.

The Department of Transportation accepts the applicability of the "arbitrary and capricious" standard. It argues that under this standard, a reviewing court may not set aside an agency rule that is rational, based on consideration of the relevant factors and within the scope of the authority delegated to the agency by the statute. We do not disagree with this formulation. The scope of review under the "arbitrary and capricious" standard is narrow and a court is not to substitute its judgment for that of the agency. Nevertheless, the agency must examine the relevant data and articulate a satisfactory explanation for its action including a "rational connection between the facts found and the choice made." *Burlington Truck Lines v. United States*, 371 U.S. 156, 168 (1962). In reviewing that explanation, we must "consider whether the decision was based on a consideration of the relevant factors and whether there has been a clear error of judgment." *Bowman Transp. Inc. v. Arkansas-Best Freight System, supra,* 419 U.S., at 285, 95 S. Ct., at 442; *Citizens to Preserve Overton Park v. Volpe, supra,* 401 U.S., at 416, 91 S. Ct., at 823. Normally, an agency rule would be arbitrary and capricious if the agency has relied on factors which Congress has not intended it to consider, entirely failed to consider an important aspect of the problem, offered an explanation for its decision that runs counter to the evidence before the agency, or is so implausible that it could not be ascribed to a difference in view or the product of agency expertise. . . .

* * *

V

The ultimate question before us is whether NHTSA's rescission of the passive restraint requirement of Standard 208 was arbitrary and capricious. We conclude, as did the Court of Appeals, that it was. We also conclude, but for somewhat different reasons, that further consideration of the issue by the agency is therefore required. We deal separately with the rescission as it applies to airbags and as it applies to seatbelts.

A

The first and most obvious reason for finding the rescission arbitrary and capricious is that NHTSA apparently gave no consideration whatever to modifying the Standard to require that airbag technology be utilized. Standard 208 sought to achieve automatic crash protection by requiring automobile manufacturers to install either of two passive restraint devices: airbags or automatic seatbelts. There was no suggestion in the long rulemaking process that led to Standard 208 that if only one of these options were feasible, no passive restraint standard should be promulgated. Indeed, the agency's original proposed standard contemplated the installation of inflatable restraints in all cars. Automatic belts were added as a means of complying with the standard because they were believed to be as effective as airbags in achieving the goal of occupant crash protection. At that time, the passive belt approved by the agency could not be detached. Only later, at a manufacturer's behest, did the agency approve of the detachability feature—and only after assurances that the feature would not compromise the safety benefits of the restraint. Although it was then foreseen that 60% of the new cars would contain airbags and 40% would have automatic seatbelts, the ratio between the two was not significant as long as the passive belt would also assure greater passenger safety.

The agency has now determined that the detachable automatic belts will not attain anticipated safety benefits because so many individuals will detach the mechanism. Even if this conclusion were acceptable in its entirety, standing alone it would not justify any more than an amendment of Standard 208 to disallow compliance by means of the one technology which will not provide effective passenger protection. It does not cast doubt on the need for a passive restraint standard or upon the efficacy of airbag technology. In its most recent rule-making, the agency again acknowledged the life-saving potential of the airbag . . . .

Given the effectiveness ascribed to airbag technology by the agency, the mandate of the Safety Act to achieve traffic safety would suggest that the logical response to the faults of detachable seatbelts would be to require the installation of airbags. At the very least this alternative way of achieving the objectives of the Act should have been addressed and adequate reasons given for its abandonment. But the agency not only did not require compliance through airbags, it did not even consider the possibility in its 1981 rulemaking. Not one sentence of its rulemaking statement discusses the airbags-only option. . . .

We have frequently reiterated that an agency must cogently explain why it has exercised its discretion in a given manner; and we reaffirm this principle again today.

The automobile industry has opted for the passive belt over the airbag, but surely it is not enough that the regulated industry has eschewed a given safety device. For nearly a decade, the automobile industry waged the regulatory equivalent of war against the airbag and lost—the inflatable restraint was proven sufficiently effective. Now the automobile industry has decided to employ a seatbelt system which will not meet the safety objectives of Standard 208. This hardly constitutes cause to revoke the standard itself. Indeed, the Motor Vehicle Safety Act was necessary because the industry was not sufficiently responsive to safety concerns. The Act intended that safety standards not depend on current technology and could be "technology-forcing" in the sense of inducing the development of superior safety design. If, under the statute, the agency should not defer to the industry's failure to develop safer cars, which it surely should not do, *a fortiori* it may not revoke a safety standard which can be satisfied by current technology simply because the industry has opted for an ineffective seatbelt design. . . .

We do not require . . . an agency to consider all policy alternatives in reaching decision. It is true that a rulemaking "cannot be found wanting simply because the agency failed to include every alternative device and thought conceivable by the mind of man . . . regardless of how uncommon or unknown that alternative may have been. . . ." But the airbag is more than a policy alternative to the passive restraint standard; it is a technological alternative within the ambit of the existing standard. We hold only that given the judgment made in 1977 that airbags are an effective and cost-beneficial life-saving technology, the mandatory passive-restraint rule may not be abandoned without any consideration whatsoever of an airbags-only requirement.

B

Although the issue is closer, we also find that the agency was too quick to dismiss the safety benefits of automatic seatbelts. NHTSA's critical finding was that, in light of the industry's plans to install readily detachable passive belts, it could not reliably predict "even a 5 percentage point increase as the minimum level of expected usage increase." The Court of Appeals rejected this finding because there is "not one iota" of evidence that Modified Standard 208 will fail to increase nationwide seatbelt use by at least 13 percentage points, the level of increased usage necessary for the standard to justify its cost. Given the lack of probative evidence, the court held that "only a well-justified refusal to seek more evidence could render rescission non-arbitrary."

Petitioners object to this conclusion. In their view, "substantial uncertainty" that a regulation will accomplish its intended purpose is sufficient reason, without more, to rescind a regulation. We agree with petitioners that just as an agency reasonably may decline to issue a safety standard if it is uncertain about its efficacy, an agency may also revoke a standard on the basis of serious uncertainties if supported by the record and reasonably explained. Rescission of the passive restraint requirement would not be arbitrary and capricious simply because there was no evidence in direct support of the agency's conclusion. It is not infrequent that the available data does not settle a regulatory issue and the agency must then exercise its judgment in moving from the facts and probabilities on the record to a policy conclusion. Recognizing that policymaking in a complex society must account for uncertainty, however, does not imply that it is sufficient for an agency to merely recite the terms "substantial uncertainty" as a justification for its actions. The agency must explain the evidence which is available, and must offer a "rational connection between the facts found and the choice made." Generally, one aspect of that explanation would be a justification for rescinding the regulation before engaging in a search for further evidence.

In this case, the agency's explanation for rescission of the passive restraint requirement is *not* sufficient to enable us to conclude that the rescission was the product of reasoned decisionmaking. To reach this conclusion, we do not upset the agency's view of the facts, but we do appreciate the limitations of this record in supporting the agency's decision. We start with the accepted ground that if used, seatbelts unquestionably would save many thousands of lives and would prevent tens of thousands of crippling injuries. . . . We move next to the fact that there is no direct evidence in support of the agency's finding that detachable automatic belts cannot be predicted to yield a substantial increase in usage. The empirical evidence on the record, consisting of surveys of drivers of automobiles equipped with passive belts, reveals more than a doubling of the usage rate experienced with manual belts. Much of the agency's rulemaking statement—and much of the controversy in this case—centers on the conclusions that should be drawn from these studies. The agency maintained that the doubling of seatbelt usage in these studies could not be extrapolated to an across-the-board mandatory standard because the passive seatbelts were guarded by ignition interlocks and purchasers of the tested cars are somewhat atypical. Respondents insist these studies demonstrate that Modified Standard 208 will substantially increase seatbelt usage. We believe that it is within the agency's discretion to pass upon the generalizability of these field studies. This is precisely the type of issue which rests within the expertise of NHTSA, and upon which a reviewing court must be most hesitant to intrude.

But accepting the agency's view of the field tests on passive restraints indicates only that there is no reliable real-world experience that usage rates will substantially increase. To be sure, NHTSA opines that "it cannot reliably predict even a 5 percentage point increase as the minimum level of increased usage." But this and other statements that passive belts will not yield substantial increases in seatbelt usage apparently take no account of the critical difference between detachable automatic belts and current manual belts. A detached passive belt does require an affirmative act to reconnect it, but—unlike a manual seat belt—the passive belt, once reattached, will continue to function automatically unless again disconnected. Thus, inertia—a factor which the agency's own studies have found significant in explaining the current low usage rates for seatbelts—works in *favor* of, not *against*, use of the protective device. Since 20 to 50% of motorists currently wear seatbelts on some occasions, there would seem to be grounds to believe that seatbelt use by occasional users will be substantially increased by the detachable passive belts. Whether this is in fact the case is a matter for the agency to decide, but it must bring its expertise to bear on the question. . . .

The agency also failed to articulate a basis for not requiring nondetachable belts under Standard 208. It is argued that the concern of the agency with the easy detachability of the currently favored design would be readily solved by a continuous passive belt, which allows the occupant to "spool out" the belt and create the necessary slack for easy extrication from the vehicle. The agency did not separately consider the continuous belt option, but treated it together with the ignition interlock device . . . .

By failing to analyze the continuous seatbelts in its own right, the agency has failed to offer the rational connection between facts and judgment required to pass muster under the arbitrary and capricious standard. . . . In 1978, when General Motors obtained the agency's approval to install a continuous passive belt, it assured the agency that nondetachable belts with spool releases were as safe as detachable belts with buckle releases. NHTSA was satisfied that this belt design assured easy extricability . . . . While the agency is entitled to change its view on the acceptability of continuous passive belts, it is obligated to explain its reasons for doing so. . . .

JUSTICE REHNQUIST, with whom THE CHIEF JUSTICE, JUSTICE POWELL, and JUSTICE O'CONNOR join, concurring in part and dissenting in part.

I join parts I, II, III, IV, and V-A of the Court's opinion. In particular, I agree that, since the airbag and continuous spool automatic seatbelt were explicitly approved in the standard the agency was rescinding, the agency should explain why it declined to leave those requirements intact. In this case, the agency gave no explanation at all. Of course, if the agency can provide a rational explanation, it may adhere to its decision to rescind the entire standard.

I do not believe, however, that NHTSA's view of detachable automatic seatbelts was arbitrary and capricious. The agency adequately explained its decision to rescind the standard insofar as it was satisfied by detachable belts. . . .

The Court rejects the agency's explanation for its conclusion that there is substantial uncertainty whether requiring installation of detachable automatic belts would substantially increase seatbelt usage. The agency chose not to rely on a study showing a substantial increase in seatbelt usage in cars equipped with automatic seatbelts *and* an ignition interlock to prevent the car from being operated when the belts were not in place *and* which were voluntarily purchased with this equipment by consumers. It is reasonable for the agency to decide that this study does not support any conclusion concerning the effect of automatic seatbelts that are installed in all cars whether the consumer wants them or not and are not linked to an ignition interlock system. . . .

It seems to me that the agency's explanation, while by no means a model, is adequate. The agency acknowledged that there would probably be some increase in belt usage, but concluded that the increase would be small and not worth the cost of mandatory detachable automatic belts. The agency's obligation is to articulate a "rational connection between the facts found and the choice made." I believe it has met this standard. . . .

The agency's changed view of the standard seems to be related to the election of a new President of a different political party. It is readily apparent that the responsible members of one administration may consider public resistance and uncertainties to be more important than do their counterparts in a previous administration. A change in administration brought about by the people casting their votes is a perfectly reasonable basis for an executive agency's reappraisal of the costs and benefits of its programs and regulations. As long as the agency remains within the bounds established by Congress, it is entitled to assess administrative records and evaluate priorities in light of the philosophy of the administration.

Notes and Questions

1. *The standard of review.* In *State Farm*, there is an initial dispute about the standard of review: is the Court to review a rescission of a prior rule as deferentially as it reviews the refusal to promulgate a rule in the first place? Relying on the organic statute, the Court holds that the standard of review is the same as when reviewing a new rule. Would this have been the case if the Court had only the text of the APA on which to rely? Take a look at § 706 and see if you think the standard of review would be the same. (The Court answers this question in the *Fox Television* case, infra.)

2. *Rule rescissions.* *State Farm* stands for the proposition that an agency must justify a rescission or change of a rule just as it must justify the initial rule. The agency must show that it has considered the relevant factors, and must offer a "satisfactory explanation for its action including a 'rational connection between the facts found and the choice made.' " Are there special considerations that must be considered when changing or rescinding a previous rule? What might those be? (The Court answers this question more specifically also in the *Fox Television* case, infra.)

    3.   *What alternatives must the agency consider?* The Court was unanimous in its holding that the agency was arbitrary and capricious for failing even to consider the possibility of simply mandating airbags, instead of giving the manufacturers a choice between airbags and automatic (but detachable) seatbelts. Why did the agency have to address this possibility, but not others? The Court recognizes that an agency does not have to address every possible alternative conceivable to the human mind; but it must at least address those alternatives "within the ambit of the existing standard." Is this a tenable distinction? Does the *Nova Scotia* case offer some support for the Court's holding? There, the agency did not have to address all possibilities, but it did have to address those of "cogent materiality" that were raised by the comments. Is *Nova Scotia* an example of arbitrary-and-capricious review as applied to the procedural requirements of § 553?

    4.   *The available data.* The Court split 5–4 regarding the agency's decision to abandon the seatbelt option altogether. The majority thought the agency was unjustified in thinking that seatbelts wouldn't reduce deaths and injuries even if they were detachable; the minority observed that the agency's decision was rational in light of the studies and data it had before it—namely that there was some increase in seatbelt use *in combination with* ignition interlocks (and when used by study participants). With which position do you agree? Does the agency have to decide based on the data it has, or must it go out and conduct studies?

    5.   *Evolution of "hard look" review.* *State Farm* is often taken for the proposition that courts should take a "hard look" at an agency's reasoning and policy decisions. Originally the idea was that courts should ensure that the *agency* took a hard look at the problem. Greater Boston Television Corp. v. FCC, 444 F.2d 841, 851 (D.C. Cir. 1970):

    The function of the court is to assure that the agency has given reasoned consideration to all the material facts and issues. . . . Its supervisory function calls on the court to intervene not merely in case of procedural inadequacies, or bypassing of the mandate in the legislative charter, but more broadly if the court becomes aware, especially from a combination of danger signals, that the agency has not really taken a 'hard look' at the salient problems, and has not genuinely engaged in reasoned decision-making. If the agency has not shirked this fundamental task, however, the court exercises restraint and affirms the agency's action even though the court would on its own account have made different findings or adopted different standards.

Today it is fair to say that "hard look" review stands for the proposition that either the agency must take a hard look at the problems, or the court must take a hard look at the agency's reasoning process. Is this a "procedural" or a "substantive" standard of review? So long as the agency has addressed all the issues reasonably, the court lets the agency decision stand. How "hard" of a look is this, really, if the court merely ensures that the agency has addressed itself to all the relevant problems?

HISTORICAL PERSPECTIVE The meaning of "hard look" review has changed over time. Originally courts would ensure that an agency would take a hard look at the problem, but many subsequently interpreted hard-look review to mean the courts should take a hard look at the agency's work. Today, courts mostly ensure that agencies consider the relevant factors.

6. *The role of political influence.* The dissenters seemed to think that the agency's change of policy regarding the seatbelt requirement had to do with a change of administration and a change of governing philosophy. In other words, the agency looked at the exact same factors as did the agency when making the initial decision, but the new leadership simply came to a different conclusion about the costs and benefits. Is that acceptable? Do we want agency decisions to be liable to easy reversal with a new administration? Should elections have dramatic consequences for administrative policies? Or do we prefer administrative regularity and predictability, based on neutral expertise? Which of these worlds does the APA assume exists? Is that the world we in fact inhabit? Consider these questions in light of the next case.

POLITICAL INFLUENCE
What role should changes in presidential administration have in the regulatory environment? Should new administrations be able to quickly change regulations? Or do we value regularity and consistency in administrative rules?

FCC v. Fox Television Stations, Inc.

556 U.S. 502 (2009)

JUSTICE SCALIA delivered the opinion of the Court, except as to Part III-E.

Federal law prohibits the broadcasting of "any . . . indecent . . . language," 18 U.S.C. § 1464, which includes expletives referring to sexual or excretory activity or organs, see *FCC v. Pacifica Foundation*, 438 U.S. 726 (1978). This case concerns the adequacy of the Federal Communications Commission's explanation of its decision that this sometimes forbids the broadcasting of indecent expletives even when the offensive words are not repeated.

I. Statutory and Regulatory Background

. . . . The Commission first invoked the statutory ban on indecent broadcasts in 1975, declaring a daytime broadcast of George Carlin's "Filthy Words" monologue actionably indecent. At that time, the Commission announced the definition of indecent speech that it uses to this day, prohibiting "language that describes, in terms patently offensive as measured by contemporary community standards for the broadcast medium, sexual or excretory activities and organs, at times of the day when there is a reasonable risk that children may be in the audience." . . .

In the ensuing years, the Commission took a cautious, but gradually expanding, approach to enforcing the statutory prohibition against indecent broadcasts. Shortly after *Pacifica*, the Commission expressed its "inten[tion] strictly to observe the narrowness of the *Pacifica* holding," which "relied in part on the repetitive occurrence of the 'indecent' words" contained in Carlin's monologue. When the full Commission next considered its indecency standard, however, it repudiated the view that its enforcement power was limited to "deliberate, repetitive use of the seven words actually contained in the George Carlin monologue." . . .

Although the Commission had expanded its enforcement beyond the "repetitive use of specific words or phrases," it preserved a distinction between literal and nonliteral (or "expletive") uses of evocative language. The Commission explained that each literal "description or depiction of sexual or excretory functions must be examined in context to determine whether it is patently offensive," but that "deliberate and repetitive use . . . is a requisite to a finding of indecency" when a complaint focuses solely on the use of nonliteral expletives. . . .

In 2004, the Commission took one step further by declaring for the first time that a nonliteral (expletive) use of the F– and S–Words could be actionably indecent, even when the word is used only once. The first order to this effect dealt with an NBC broadcast of the Golden Globe Awards, in which the performer Bono commented, " '[T]his is really, really, f***ing brilliant.' " . . .

The Commission first declared that Bono's use of the F–Word fell within its indecency definition, even though the word was used as an intensifier rather than a literal descriptor. "[G]iven the core meaning of the 'F–Word,' " it said, "any use of that word . . . inherently has a sexual connotation." The Commission determined, moreover, that the broadcast was "patently offensive" because the F–Word "is one of the most vulgar, graphic and explicit descriptions of sexual activity in the English language," because "[i]ts use invariably invokes a coarse sexual image," and because Bono's use of the word was entirely "shocking and gratuitous."

The Commission observed that categorically exempting such language from enforcement actions would "likely lead to more widespread use." Commission action was necessary to "safeguard the well-being of the nation's children from the most objectionable, most offensive language." The order noted that technological advances have made it far easier to delete ("bleep out") a "single and gratuitous use of a vulgar expletive," without adulterating the content of a broadcast.

The order acknowledged that "prior Commission and staff action [has] indicated that isolated or fleeting broadcasts of the 'F–Word' . . . are not indecent or would not be acted upon." It explicitly ruled that "any such interpretation is no longer good law." It "clarif[ied] . . . that the mere fact that specific words or phrases are not sustained or repeated does not mandate a finding that material that is otherwise patently offensive to the broadcast medium is not indecent." Because, however, "existing precedent would have permitted this broadcast," the Commission determined that "NBC and its affiliates necessarily did not have the requisite notice to justify a penalty."

II. The Present Case

This case concerns utterances in two live broadcasts aired by Fox Television Stations, Inc., and its affiliates prior to the Commission's *Golden Globes Order.* The first occurred during the 2002 Billboard Music Awards, when the singer Cher exclaimed, "I've also had critics for the last 40 years saying that I was on my way out every year. Right. So f*** 'em." The second involved a segment of the 2003 Billboard Music Awards, during the presentation of an award by Nicole Richie and Paris Hilton, principals in a Fox television series called "The Simple Life." Ms. Hilton began their interchange by reminding Ms. Richie to "watch the bad language," but Ms. Richie proceeded to ask the audience, "Why do they even call it 'The Simple Life?' Have you ever tried to get cow s*** out of a Prada purse? It's not so f***ing simple." Following each of these broadcasts, the Commission received numerous complaints from parents whose children were exposed to the language.

On March 15, 2006, the Commission released "Notices of Apparent Liability" for a number of broadcasts that the Commission deemed actionably indecent, including the two described above. . . .

The [Commission] order . . . made clear [that] the *Golden Globes Order* eliminated any doubt that fleeting expletives could be actionably indecent, and the Commission disavowed the bureau-level decisions and its own dicta that had said otherwise. Under the new policy, a lack of repetition "weigh[s] against a finding of indecency," but is not a safe harbor. . . .

The Court of Appeals reversed the agency's orders, finding the Commission's reasoning inadequate under the Administrative Procedure Act. . . .

III. Analysis

A. Governing Principles

The Administrative Procedure Act, which sets forth the full extent of judicial authority to review executive agency action for procedural correctness, permits (insofar as relevant here) the setting aside of agency action that is "arbitrary" or "capricious," 5 U.S.C. § 706(2)(A). Under what we have called this "narrow" standard of review, we insist that an agency "examine the relevant data and articulate a satisfactory explanation for its action." *Motor Vehicle Mfrs. Assn. of United States, Inc. v. State Farm Mut. Automobile Ins. Co.*, 463 U.S. 29, 43 (1983). We have made clear, however, that "a court is not to substitute its judgment for that of the agency" . . . .

In overturning the Commission's judgment, the Court of Appeals here relied in part on Circuit precedent requiring a more substantial explanation for agency action that changes prior policy. The Second Circuit has interpreted the Administrative Procedure Act and our opinion in *State Farm* as requiring agencies to make clear " 'why the original reasons for adopting the [displaced] rule or policy are no longer dispositive' " as well as " 'why the new rule effectuates the statute as well as or better than the old rule.' " The Court of Appeals for the District of Columbia Circuit has similarly indicated that a court's standard of review is "heightened somewhat" when an agency reverses course.

We find no basis in the Administrative Procedure Act or in our opinions for a requirement that all agency change be subjected to more searching review. The Act mentions no such heightened standard. And our opinion in *State Farm* neither held nor implied that every agency action representing a policy change must be justified by reasons more substantial than those required to adopt a policy in the first instance. That case, which involved the rescission of a prior regulation, said only that such action requires "a reasoned analysis for the change beyond that which may be required when an agency *does not act* in the first instance." Treating failures to act and rescissions of prior action differently for purposes of the standard of review makes good sense, and has basis in the text of the statute, which likewise treats the two separately. It instructs a reviewing court to "compel agency action unlawfully withheld or unreasonably delayed," 5 U.S.C. § 706(1), and to "hold unlawful and set aside agency action, findings, and conclusions found to be [among other things] . . . arbitrary [or] capricious," § 706(2)(A). The statute makes no distinction, however, between initial agency action and subsequent agency action undoing or revising that action.

To be sure, the requirement that an agency provide reasoned explanation for its action would ordinarily demand that it display awareness that it *is* changing position. An agency may not, for example, depart from a prior policy *sub silentio* or simply disregard rules that are still on the books. And of course the agency must show that there are good reasons for the new policy.

But it need not demonstrate to a court's satisfaction that the reasons for the new policy are *better* than the reasons for the old one; it suffices that the new policy is permissible under the statute, that there are good reasons for it, and that the agency *believes* it to be better, which the conscious change of course adequately indicates. This means that the agency need not always provide a more detailed justification than what would suffice for a new policy created on a blank slate. Sometimes it must—when, for example, its new policy rests upon factual findings that contradict those which underlay its prior policy; or when its prior policy has engendered serious reliance interests that must be taken into account. It would be arbitrary or capricious to ignore such matters. In such cases it is not that further justification is demanded by the mere fact of policy change; but that a reasoned explanation is needed for disregarding facts and circumstances that underlay or were engendered by the prior policy. . . .

B. Application to This Case

Judged under the above described standards, the Commission's new enforcement policy and its order finding the broadcasts actionably indecent were neither arbitrary nor capricious. First, the Commission forthrightly acknowledged that its recent actions have broken new ground, taking account of inconsistent "prior Commission and staff action" and explicitly disavowing them as "no longer good law." To be sure, the (superfluous) explanation in its *Remand Order* of why the Cher broadcast would even have violated its earlier policy may not be entirely convincing. But that unnecessary detour is irrelevant. There is no doubt that the Commission knew it was making a change. That is why it declined to assess penalties; and it relied on the *Golden Globes Order* as removing any lingering doubt.

Moreover, the agency's reasons for expanding the scope of its enforcement activity were entirely rational. It was certainly reasonable to determine that it made no sense to distinguish between literal and nonliteral uses of offensive words, requiring repetitive use to render only the latter indecent. . . . It is surely rational (if not inescapable) to believe that a safe harbor for single words would "likely lead to more widespread use of the offensive language," *Golden Globes Order*. . . .

The Commission could rationally decide it needed to step away from its old regime where nonrepetitive use of an expletive was *per se* nonactionable . . . . The fact that technological advances have made it easier for broadcasters to bleep out offending words further supports the Commission's stepped-up enforcement policy. . . .

* * *

E. The Dissents' Arguments

Justice Breyer purports to "begin with applicable law," but in fact begins by stacking the deck. He claims that the FCC's status as an "independent" agency sheltered from political oversight requires courts to be "all the more" vigilant in ensuring "that major policy decisions be based upon articulable reasons." Not so. The independent agencies are sheltered not from politics but from the President, and it has often been observed that their freedom from Presidential oversight (and protection) has simply been replaced by increased subservience to congressional direction. Indeed, the precise policy change at issue here was spurred by significant political pressure from Congress. . . .

Regardless, it is assuredly not "applicable law" that rulemaking by independent regulatory agencies is subject to heightened scrutiny. The Administrative Procedure Act, which provides judicial review, makes no distinction between independent and other agencies, neither in its definition of agency, 5 U.S.C. § 701(b)(1), nor in the standards for reviewing agency action, § 706. . . .

Justice Breyer looks over the vast field of particular factual scenarios unaddressed by the FCC's 35-page *Remand Order* and finds one that is fatal: the plight of the small local broadcaster who cannot afford the new technology that enables the screening of live broadcasts for indecent utterances. The Commission has failed to address the fate of this unfortunate, who will, he believes, be subject to sanction.

We doubt, to begin with, that small-town broadcasters run a heightened risk of liability for indecent utterances. In programming that they originate, their down-home local guests probably employ vulgarity less than big-city folks; and small-town stations generally cannot afford or cannot attract foul-mouthed glitteratae from Hollywood. Their main exposure with regard to self-originated programming is live coverage of news and public affairs. But the *Remand Order* went out of its way to note that the case at hand did not involve "breaking news coverage," and that "it may be inequitable to hold a licensee responsible for airing offensive speech during live coverage of a public event." As for the programming that small stations receive on a network "feed": This *will* be cleansed by the expensive technology small stations (by Justice Breyer's hypothesis) cannot afford.

But never mind the detail of whether small broadcasters are uniquely subject to a great risk of punishment for fleeting expletives. The fundamental fallacy of Justice Breyer's small-broadcaster gloomy scenario is its demonstrably false assumption that the *Remand Order* makes no provision for the avoidance of unfairness—that the single-utterance prohibition will be invoked uniformly, in all situations. The *Remand Order* made very clear that this is not the case. It said that in determining "what, if any, remedy is appropriate" the Commission would consider the facts of each individual case, such as the "possibility of human error in using delay equipment." Thus, the fact that the agency believed that Fox (a large broadcaster that used suggestive scripting and a deficient delay system to air a prime-time awards show aimed at millions of children) "fail[ed] to exercise 'reasonable judgment, responsibility and sensitivity,' " says little about how the Commission would treat smaller broadcasters who cannot afford screening equipment. . . .

There was, in sum, no need for the Commission to compose a special treatise on local broadcasters. . . .

[A concurring opinion of Justice Thomas is omitted.—Ed.]

Justice Kennedy, concurring in part and concurring in the judgment.

. . . . This separate writing is to underscore certain background principles for the conclusion that an agency's decision to change course may be arbitrary and capricious if the agency sets a new course that reverses an earlier determination but does not provide a reasoned explanation for doing so. . . .

The question in each case is whether the agency's reasons for the change, when viewed in light of the data available to it, and when informed by the experience and expertise of the agency, suffice to demonstrate that the new policy rests upon principles that are rational, neutral, and in accord with the agency's proper understanding of its authority. . . .

These requirements stem from the administrative agency's unique constitutional position. The dynamics of the three branches of Government are well understood as a general matter. But the role and position of the agency, and the exact locus of its powers, present questions that are delicate, subtle, and complex. The Federal Government could not perform its duties in a responsible and effective way without administrative agencies. Yet the amorphous character of the administrative agency in the constitutional system escapes simple explanation.

If agencies were permitted unbridled discretion, their actions might violate important constitutional principles of separation of powers and checks and balances. . . .

Congress passed the Administrative Procedure Act (APA) to ensure that agencies follow constraints even as they exercise their powers. One of these constraints is the duty of agencies to find and formulate policies that can be justified by neutral principles and a reasoned explanation. To achieve that end, Congress confined agencies' discretion and subjected their decisions to judicial review. If an agency takes action not based on neutral and rational principles, the APA grants federal courts power to set aside the agency's action as "arbitrary" or "capricious." 5 U.S.C. § 706(2)(A); *Citizens to Preserve Overton Park, Inc. v. Volpe*, 401 U.S. 402, 416 (1971). For these reasons, agencies under the APA are subject to a "searching and careful" review by the courts.

Where there is a policy change the record may be much more developed because the agency based its prior policy on factual findings. In that instance, an agency's decision to change course may be arbitrary and capricious if the agency ignores or countermands its earlier factual findings without reasoned explanation for doing so. An agency cannot simply disregard contrary or inconvenient factual determinations that it made in the past, any more than it can ignore inconvenient facts when it writes on a blank slate. . . .

The present case does not raise the concerns addressed in *State Farm*. . . . The FCC did not base its prior policy on factual findings. . . . The Court's careful and complete analysis—both with respect to the procedural history of the FCC's indecency policies, and the reasons the agency has given to support them—is quite sufficient to sustain the FCC's change of course against respondents' claim that the agency acted in an arbitrary or capricious fashion. . . .

[Dissenting opinions by JUSTICE STEVENS and JUSTICE GINSBURG are omitted.—Ed.]

JUSTICE BREYER, with whom JUSTICE STEVENS, JUSTICE SOUTER, and JUSTICE GINSBURG join, dissenting.

In my view, the Federal Communications Commission failed adequately to explain *why* it *changed* its indecency policy from a policy permitting a single "fleeting use" of an expletive, to a policy that made no such exception. Its explanation fails to discuss two critical factors, at least one of which directly underlay its original policy decision. Its explanation instead discussed several factors well known to it the first time around, which by themselves provide no significant justification for a *change* of policy. . . .

I

I begin with applicable law. That law grants those in charge of independent administrative agencies broad authority to determine relevant policy. But it does not permit them to make policy choices for purely political reasons nor to rest them primarily upon unexplained policy preferences. Federal Communications Commissioners have fixed terms of office; they are not directly responsible to the voters; and they enjoy an independence expressly designed to insulate them, to a degree, from " 'the exercise of political oversight.' " That insulation helps to secure important governmental objectives, such as the constitutionally related objective of maintaining broadcast regulation that does not bend too readily before the political winds. But that agency's comparative freedom from ballot-box control makes it all the more important that courts review its decisionmaking to assure compliance with applicable provisions of the law—including law requiring that major policy decisions be based upon articulable reasons.

The statutory provision applicable here is the Administrative Procedure Act's (APA) prohibition of agency action that is "arbitrary, capricious, [or] an abuse of discretion," 5 U.S.C. § 706(2)(A). This legal requirement helps assure agency decisionmaking based upon more than the personal preferences of the decisionmakers. Courts have applied the provision sparingly, granting agencies broad policymaking leeway. But they have also made clear that agency discretion is not " 'unbounded.' " . . .

The law has also recognized that it is not so much a particular set of substantive commands but rather it is a *process*, a process of learning through reasoned argument, that is the antithesis of the "arbitrary." This means agencies must follow a "logical and rational" decisionmaking "process." An agency's policy decisions must reflect the reasoned exercise of expert judgment. And, as this Court has specified, in determining whether an agency's policy choice was "arbitrary," a reviewing court "must consider whether the decision was based on a consideration of the relevant factors and whether there has been a clear error of judgment." *Overton Park, supra*, at 416. . . .

To explain a change requires more than setting forth reasons why the new policy is a good one. It also requires the agency to answer the question, "Why did you change?" And a rational answer to this question typically requires a more complete explanation than would prove satisfactory were change itself not at issue. An (imaginary) administrator explaining why he chose a policy that requires driving on the right side, rather than the left side, of the road might say, "Well, one side seemed as good as the other, so I flipped a coin." But even assuming the rationality of that explanation for an *initial* choice, that explanation is not at all rational if offered to explain why the administrator *changed* driving practice, from right side to left side, 25 years later. . . .

[In *State Farm,*] the Court described the need for explanation in terms that apply, not simply to pure *rescissions* of earlier rules, but rather to changes of policy as it more broadly defined them. It said that the law required an explanation for such a *change* because the earlier policy, representing a " 'settled course of behavior[,] embodies the agency's informed judgment that, by pursuing that course, it will carry out the policies . . . best if the settled rule is adhered to.' " *State Farm, supra*, at 41–42. Thus, the agency must explain *why* it has come to the conclusion that it should now change direction. Why does it now reject the considerations that led it to adopt that initial policy? What has changed in the world that offers justification for the change? What other good reasons are there for departing from the earlier policy?

Contrary to the majority's characterization of this dissent, it would not (and *State Farm* does not) require a "*heightened standard*" of review. Rather, the law requires application of the *same standard* of review to different circumstances, namely, circumstances characterized by the fact that *change* is at issue. It requires the agency to focus upon the fact of change where change is relevant, just as it must focus upon any other relevant circumstance. It requires the agency here to focus upon the reasons that led the agency to adopt the initial policy, and to explain why it now comes to a new judgment.

I recognize that *sometimes* the ultimate explanation for a change may have to be, "We now weigh the relevant considerations differently." But at other times, an agency can and should say more. Where, for example, the agency rested its previous policy on particular factual findings, or where an agency rested its prior policy on its view of the governing law, or where an agency rested its previous policy on, say, a special need to coordinate with another agency, one would normally expect the agency to focus upon those earlier views of fact, of law, or of policy and explain why they are no longer controlling. Regardless, to say that the agency here must answer the question "why change" is not to require the agency to provide a justification that is "*better* than the reasons for the old [policy]." It is only to recognize the obvious fact that *change* is sometimes (not always) a relevant background feature that sometimes (not always) requires focus (upon prior justifications) and explanation lest the adoption of the new policy (in that circumstance) be "arbitrary, capricious, an abuse of discretion." . . .

II

We here must apply the general standards set forth in *State Farm* and *Overton Park* to an agency decision that changes a 25-year-old "fleeting expletive" policy from (1) the old policy that would normally permit broadcasters to transmit a single, fleeting use of an expletive to (2) a new policy that would threaten broadcasters with large fines for transmitting even a single use (including its use by a member of the public) of such an expletive, alone with nothing more. . . .

The FCC failed . . . to consider two critically important aspects of the problem that underlay its initial policy judgment (one of which directly, the other of which indirectly). First, the FCC said next to nothing about the relation between the change it made in its prior "fleeting expletive" policy and the First-Amendment-related need to avoid "censorship," a matter as closely related to broadcasting regulation as is health to that of the environment. . . .

[In omitted paragraphs, JUSTICE BREYER discussed the First Amendment implications of the FCC's order.—Ed.]

Second, the FCC failed to consider the potential impact of its new policy upon local broadcasting coverage. This "aspect of the problem" is particularly important because the FCC explicitly took account of potential broadcasting impact. Indeed, in setting forth "bleeping" technology changes (presumably lowering bleeping costs) as justifying the policy change, it implicitly reasoned that lower costs, making it easier for broadcasters to install bleeping equipment, made it less likely that the new policy would lead broadcasters to reduce coverage, say, by canceling coverage of public events.

What then did the FCC say about the likelihood that smaller independent broadcasters, including many public service broadcasters, still would not be able to afford "bleeping" technology and, as a consequence, would reduce local coverage, indeed cancel coverage, of many public events? It said nothing at all. . . .

What did the FCC say in response to this claim? What did it say about the likely impact of the new policy on the coverage that its new policy is most likely to affect, coverage of *local* live events—city council meetings, local sports events, community arts productions, and the like? It said nothing at all. . . .

I cannot agree with the plurality . . . that the new policy obviously provides smaller independent broadcasters with adequate assurance that they will not be fined. The new policy removes the "fleeting expletive" exception, an exception that assured smaller independent stations that they would not be fined should someone swear at a public event. In its place, it puts a policy that places all broadcasters at risk when they broadcast fleeting expletives, including expletives uttered at public events. . . . [I]t says *nothing* about a station's *inability to afford* delay equipment (a matter that in individual cases could itself prove debatable). All the FCC had to do was to *consider* this matter and either grant an exemption or explain why it did not grant an exemption. But it did not. . . .

Had the FCC used traditional administrative notice-and-comment procedures, 5 U.S.C. § 553, the two failures I have just discussed would clearly require a court to vacate the resulting agency decision. See *ACLU v. FCC*, 823 F.2d 1554, 1581 (D.C. Cir. 1987) ("Notice and comment rulemaking procedures obligate the FCC to respond to *all* significant comments, for the opportunity to comment is meaningless unless the agency responds to significant points raised by the public"). Here the agency did not make new policy through the medium of notice-and-comment proceedings. But the same failures here— where the policy is important, the significance of the issues clear, the failures near complete—should lead us to the same conclusion. The agency's failure to discuss these two "important aspect[s] of the problem" means that the resulting decision is " 'arbitrary, capricious, an abuse of discretion' " requiring us to remand the matter to the agency.

III

The three reasons the FCC did set forth in support of its change of policy cannot make up for the failures I have discussed. Consider each of them. First, as I have pointed out, the FCC based its decision in part upon the fact that "bleeping/delay systems" technology has advanced. I have already set forth my reasons for believing that that fact, without more, cannot provide a sufficient justification for its policy change.

Second, the FCC says that the expletives here in question always invoke a coarse excretory or sexual image; hence it makes no sense to distinguish between whether one uses the relevant terms as an expletive or as a literal description. The problem with this answer is that it does not help to justify the *change* in policy. The FCC was aware of the coarseness of the "image" the first time around. . . .

Third, the FCC said that "perhaps" its "most importan[t]" justification for the new policy lay in the fact that its new "contextual" approach to fleeting expletives is better and more "[c]onsistent with" the agency's "general approach to indecency" than was its previous "categorica[l]" approach, which offered broadcasters virtual immunity for the broadcast of fleeting expletives. This justification, however, offers no support for the change without an understanding of *why, i.e., in what way,* the FCC considered the new approach better or more consistent with the agency's general approach. . . .

In fact, the FCC found that the new policy was better in part because . . . its former policy of "granting an automatic exemption for 'isolated or fleeting' expletives unfairly forces viewers (including children) to take 'the first blow.'" The difficulty with this argument, however, is that it does not explain the *change.* The FCC has long used the theory of the "first blow" to justify its regulation of broadcast indecency. . . . So, to repeat the question: What, in respect to the "first blow," has changed? . . .

* * *

For these reasons I would find the FCC's decision "arbitrary, capricious, an abuse of discretion," 5 U.S.C. § 706(2)(A), requiring remand of this case to the FCC. . . .

NOTES AND QUESTIONS

1. *What's the disagreement?* At least on the face of the opinions, Justices Scalia and Breyer do not seem to disagree on the standard of review. What, then, do they disagree about? Is this a lower-order, factual dispute? Or is Justice Breyer in fact applying a different standard, even if he says he's not?

2. *Legal regularity.* An earlier note in the chapter on adjudications introduced the concept of legal regularity. As explained, in Shaw's Supermarkets, Inc. v. NLRB, 884 F.2d 34 (1st Cir. 1989), then-Judge Breyer reversed an agency decision adverse to an employer, where the agency on many similar occasions had ruled in favor of the employer. The agency was free "to depart from" its prior precedent "as long as it focuses upon the issue and explains why change is reasonable." But otherwise it had to follow the precedents because if it did not, then "those subject to the agency's authority cannot use its precedent as a guide for their conduct; nor will that precedent check arbitrary agency action." Is *Fox Television* of a piece with *Shaw's Supermarkets*?

3. *Political influence revisited.* Consider the political context of the change of policy. The change occurred in the early years of the socially conservative George W. Bush administration. Might that explain the change of agency policy? If so, is that acceptable? To ask the question more concretely, what is the relationship of administrative expertise and the administrative process to the President's exercise of executive power? If a statute leaves discretion to choose among multiple policy options, do we prefer a system in which the default rule is that the agency must maintain its initial policy decision, or a system in which the new President may choose one of the other options more consistent with his or her own policy priorities? If the statute does not direct one option over another, wouldn't we expect that the election of a more socially conservative administration would mean that the laws are to be executed more consistently with socially conservative priorities? Isn't exercising discretion where the law does not direct one particular answer part of "the executive power" to carry laws into execution? On the other hand, isn't Justice Kennedy correct that the whole point of judicial review under

 CROSS REFERENCE The role of political influence features in many facets of administrative law, including in the rules regarding *ex parte* contacts.

the APA is that agencies are supposed to base their decisions on *neutral* and rational arguments, and not political arguments?

This tension between administrative expertise and executive discretion has been central to judicial review of administrative action at least since the 1970s. Recall in *Sierra Club v. Costle* the D.C. Circuit observed,

The court recognizes the basic need of the President and his White House staff to monitor the consistency of executive agency regulations with Administration policy. He and his White House advisers surely must be briefed fully and frequently about rules in the making, and their contributions to policymaking considered. The executive power under our Constitution, after all, is not shared it rests exclusively with the President. . . . The authority of the President to control and supervise executive policymaking is derived from the Constitution; the desirability of such control is demonstrable from the practical realities of administrative rulemaking. Regulations such as those involved here demand a careful weighing of cost, environmental, and energy considerations. They also have broad implications for national economic policy. Our form of government simply could not function effectively or rationally if key executive policymakers were isolated from each other and from the Chief Executive.

657 F.2d 298, 405–06 (D.C. Cir. 1981). And in *State Farm,* four justices agreed that "[a] change in administration brought about by the people casting their votes is a perfectly reasonable basis for an executive agency's reappraisal of the costs and benefits of its programs and regulations. As long as the agency remains within the bounds established by Congress, it is entitled to assess administrative records and evaluate priorities in light of the philosophy of the administration." 463 U.S. 29, 59 (1983) (Rehnquist, J., concurring in part and dissenting in part).

On the other hand, as Justice Kennedy observed in *Fox Television,* the whole premise of arbitrary and capricious review under the APA is that courts would ensure that agencies exercise their discretion in neutral, expert manners. "If an agency takes action not based on neutral and rational principles," Kennedy wrote, "the APA grants federal courts power to set aside the agency's action as 'arbitrary' or 'capricious.' " There is therefore a critical tension in administrative law between the theory behind the administrative process the led to the enactment of the APA, and the modern realization that political influence is both inevitable and perhaps desirable. Thus, courts will often allow agencies to act in a "pretextual" manner—in a manner clearly influenced by political considerations—so long as it couches its arguments in neutral terms based on the statutory factors and the relevant data and evidence. Dep't of Commerce v. New York, 139 S. Ct. 2551, 2573 (2019); Jagers v. Fed. Crop Ins. Corp., 758

F.3d 1179, 1185–86 (10th Cir. 2014); Sierra Club v. Costle, 657 F.2d 298, 408 (D.C. Cir. 1981). For a small sample of the literature on the influence of politics and the tension between expertise and political accountability, see Kathryn A. Watts, *Proposing a Place for Politics in Arbitrary and Capricious Review*, 119 Yale. L.J. 2 (2009); Jodi L Short, *The Political Turn in American Administrative Law: Power, Rationality, and Reasons*, 61 Duke L.J. 1811 (2012); Michael A. Livermore & Daniel Richardson, *Administrative Law in an Era of Partisan Volatility*, 69 Emory L.J. 1 (2019).

The only time in which the Supreme Court has overturned an agency decision on the grounds of pretext was in the so-called "Census Case," involving the Trump Administration's attempt to add a citizenship question to the 2020 census; the question had been on every decennial census since 1790 up until 1950, when it dropped out. In Department of Commerce v. New York, 139 S. Ct. 2551 (2019), the majority invalidated the addition of the citizenship question—even though the Constitution and statute permitted such a question—because the agency had failed to give any neutral, rational reason for its change of policy. The majority concluded that the Commerce Secretary's reasons, based on enforcement of the Voting Rights Act, was entirely pretextual, and the real motivation was political. Although the true motivation was never stated, perhaps the majority believed the motivation was to suppress survey responses in states with more non-citizens, which tended to lean more heavily toward the opposition political party, and thereby reduce the representation of those states in Congress. Four justices dissented, arguing there was no basis in the APA for striking down the agency's decision so long as it was permissible under the statute and justified by the reasons given, even if those reasons were purely pretextual. Who was right?

*4. **Comparison to** Chevron **deference.*** Consider also the parallel to *Chevron* deference. We will encounter this in Section C of this chapter. For now, it is sufficient to understand that *Chevron* deference is the principle of administrative law by which courts defer to reasonable agency interpretations of the statutes they administer, even if those interpretations are not the "best" readings of the statute and even if the agency had for a long time adopted a different interpretation. The idea is that agencies are entirely free to change their interpretations at will, so long as the new interpretations are reasonable. Yet if we find it acceptable for agencies to change their legal interpretations more or less freely, why not their discretionary policies, too? In fact, why wasn't *Fox Television* a

Chevron case? Wasn't the agency changing its interpretation of the statute? Or was the statute clear, but merely left discretion to the agency to choose among competing policies—and hence the *State Farm* standard applied?

5. *Adjudication versus rulemaking.* Justice Breyer pointed out that, had the issue of small-town broadcasters been raised in a comment to a rulemaking, the agency would have had to address it. That's certainly true. But here the agency engaged in an adjudication. And that adjudication involved a big broadcaster. The issue of small-town broadcasters may not have even come up. Does the agency need to conceive of all possible objections to its rule in an adjudication, even if not raised by the parties? Is this adjudication an example of why rulemakings are more desirable—they can bring in broader perspectives?

DHS v. Regents of the University of California

140 S. Ct. 1891 (2020)

ROBERTS, C.J.

In the summer of 2012, the Department of Homeland Security (DHS) announced an immigration program known as Deferred Action for Childhood Arrivals, or DACA. That program allows certain unauthorized aliens who entered the United States as children to apply for a two-year forbearance of removal. Those granted such relief are also eligible for work authorization and various federal benefits. Some 700,000 aliens have availed themselves of this opportunity.

Five years later, the Attorney General advised DHS to rescind DACA, based on his conclusion that it was unlawful. The Department's Acting Secretary issued a memorandum terminating the program on that basis. The termination was challenged by affected individuals and third parties who alleged, among other things, that the Acting Secretary had violated the Administrative Procedure Act (APA) by failing to adequately address important factors bearing on her decision. For the reasons that follow, we conclude that the Acting Secretary did violate the APA, and that the rescission must be vacated. . . .

[The Fifth Circuit] [in the related Deferred Action for Parents of Americans and Lawful Permanent Residents, or DAPA, case, see supra p. 225—Ed.] concluded the States were likely to succeed on their procedural claim that the

DAPA Memorandum was a substantive rule that was required to undergo notice and comment. It then held that the APA required DAPA to be set aside because the program was "manifestly contrary" to the INA [Immigration and Nationality Act], which "expressly and carefully provides legal designations allowing defined classes" to "receive the benefits" associated with "lawful presence" and to qualify for work authorization. . . . This Court affirmed the Fifth Circuit's judgment by an equally divided vote, which meant that no opinion was issued. . . .

Then, in June 2017, following a change in Presidential administrations, DHS rescinded the DAPA Memorandum. In explaining that decision, DHS cited the preliminary injunction and ongoing litigation in Texas, the fact that DAPA had never taken effect, and the new administration's immigration enforcement priorities.

Three months later, in September 2017, Attorney General Jefferson B. Sessions III sent a letter to Acting Secretary of Homeland Security Elaine C. Duke, "advis[ing]" that DHS "should rescind" DACA as well. Citing the Fifth Circuit's opinion and this Court's equally divided affirmance, the Attorney General concluded that DACA shared the "same legal . . . defects that the courts recognized as to DAPA" and was "likely" to meet a similar fate. "In light of the costs and burdens" that a rescission would "impose[ ] on DHS," the Attorney General urged DHS to "consider an orderly and efficient wind-down process."

The next day, Duke acted on the Attorney General's advice. In her decision memorandum, Duke summarized the history of the DACA and DAPA programs, the Fifth Circuit opinion and ensuing affirmance, and the contents of the Attorney General's letter. "Taking into consideration the Supreme Court's and the Fifth Circuit's rulings" and the "letter from the Attorney General," she concluded that the "DACA program should be terminated." . . .

[The District Court] that Acting Secretary Duke's "conclusory statements were insufficient to explain the change in [the agency's] view of DACA's lawfulness." The District Court stayed its order for 90 days to permit DHS to "reissue a memorandum rescinding DACA, this time providing a fuller explanation for the determination that the program lacks statutory and constitutional authority."

Two months later, Duke's successor, Secretary Kirstjen M. Nielsen, responded via memorandum. She explained that, "[h]aving considered the Duke memorandum," she "decline[d] to disturb" the rescission. Secretary Nielsen went on to articulate her "understanding" of Duke's memorandum, identifying three reasons why, in Nielsen's estimation, "the decision to rescind the DACA policy was, and remains, sound." First, she reiterated that, "as the Attorney General concluded, the DACA policy was contrary to law." Second, she added that, regardless, the agency had "serious doubts about [DACA's] legality" and, for law enforcement reasons, wanted to avoid "legally questionable" policies. Third, she identified multiple policy reasons for rescinding DACA, including (1) the belief that any class-based immigration relief should come from Congress, not through executive non-enforcement; (2) DHS's preference for exercising prosecutorial discretion on "a truly individualized, case-by-case basis"; and (3) the importance of "project[ing] a message" that immigration laws would be enforced against all classes and categories of aliens. In her final paragraph, Secretary Nielsen acknowledged the "asserted reliance interests" in DACA's continuation but concluded that they did not "outweigh the questionable legality of the DACA policy and the other reasons" for the rescission discussed in her memorandum. . . .

The dispute before the Court is not whether DHS may rescind DACA. All parties agree that it may. The dispute is instead primarily about the procedure the agency followed in doing so. . . . Under this "narrow standard of review, . . . a court is not to substitute its judgment for that of the agency," *FCC* v. *Fox Television Stations, Inc.*, 556 U. S. 502, 513 (2009), but instead to assess only whether the decision was "based on a consideration of the relevant factors and whether there has been a clear error of judgment," *Citizens to Preserve Overton Park, Inc.* v. *Volpe*, 401 U. S. 402, 416 (1971). . . .

It is a "foundational principle of administrative law" that judicial review of agency action is limited to "the grounds that the agency invoked when it took the action." . . .

The District Court's remand thus presented DHS with a choice: rest on the Duke Memorandum while elaborating on its prior reasoning, or issue a new rescission bolstered by new reasons absent from the Duke Memorandum. Secretary Nielsen took the first path. Rather than making a new decision, she "decline[d] to disturb the Duke memorandum's rescission" and instead "provide[d] further explanation" for that action. . . . Contrary to the position of JUSTICE KAVANAUGH . . . the Nielsen Memorandum was by its own terms not a new rule implementing a new policy.

Because Secretary Nielsen chose to elaborate on the reasons for the initial rescission rather than take new administrative action, she was limited to the agency's original reasons. . . .

Respondents maintain that this explanation is deficient for three reasons. Their first and second arguments work in tandem, claiming that the Duke Memorandum does not adequately explain the conclusion that DACA is unlawful, and that this conclusion is, in any event, wrong. While those arguments carried the day in the lower courts, in our view they overlook an important constraint on Acting Secretary Duke's decisionmaking authority—she was *bound* by the Attorney General's legal determination.

The same statutory provision that establishes the Secretary of Homeland Security's authority to administer and enforce immigration laws limits that authority, specifying that, with respect to "all questions of law," the determinations of the Attorney General "shall be controlling." . . .

Because of these gaps in respondents' briefing, we do not evaluate the claims challenging the explanation and correctness of the illegality conclusion. Instead we focus our attention on respondents' third argument—that Acting Secretary Duke "failed to consider . . . important aspect[s] of the problem" before her. *Motor Vehicle Mfrs. Assn. of United States, Inc. v. State Farm Mut. Automobile Ins. Co.*, 463 U. S. 29, 43 (1983).

Whether DACA is illegal is, of course, a legal determination, and therefore a question for the Attorney General. But deciding how best to address a finding of illegality moving forward can involve important policy choices, especially when the finding concerns a program with the breadth of DACA. Those policy choices are for DHS. . . .

But Duke did not appear to appreciate the full scope of her discretion, which picked up where the Attorney General's legal reasoning left off. The Attorney General concluded that "the DACA policy has the same legal . . . defects that the courts recognized as to DAPA." So, to understand those defects, we look to the Fifth Circuit, the highest court to offer a reasoned opinion on the legality of DAPA. That court described the "core" issue before it as the "Secretary's decision" to grant "eligibility for benefits"—including work authorization, Social Security, and Medicare—to unauthorized aliens on "a class-wide basis." . . .

But there is more to DAPA (and DACA) than such benefits. The defining feature of deferred action is the decision to defer removal (and to notify the affected alien of that decision). And the Fifth Circuit was careful to distinguish that forbearance component from eligibility for benefits. As it explained, the "challenged portion of DAPA's deferred-action program" was the decision to make DAPA recipients eligible for benefits. The other "[p]art of DAPA," the court noted, "involve[d] the Secretary's decision—at least temporarily—not to enforce the immigration laws as to a class of what he deem[ed] to be low-priority illegal aliens." Borrowing from this Court's prior description of deferred action, the Fifth Circuit observed that "the states do not challenge the Secretary's decision to 'decline to institute proceedings, terminate proceedings, or decline to execute a final order of deportation.' " And the Fifth Circuit underscored that nothing in its decision or the preliminary injunction "requires the Secretary to remove any alien or to alter" the Secretary's class-based "enforcement priorities." In other words, the Secretary's forbearance authority was unimpaired. . . .

In short, the Attorney General neither addressed the forbearance policy at the heart of DACA nor compelled DHS to abandon that policy. Thus, removing benefits eligibility while continuing forbearance remained squarely within the discretion of Acting Secretary Duke . . . . Duke's memo offers no reason for terminating forbearance. She instead treated the Attorney General's conclusion regarding the illegality of benefits as sufficient to rescind both benefits and forbearance, without explanation.

That reasoning repeated the error we identified in one of our leading modern administrative law cases, *Motor Vehicle Manufacturers Association of the United States, Inc.* v. *State Farm Mutual Automobile Insurance Co.* . . .

State Farm teaches that when an agency rescinds a prior policy its reasoned analysis must consider the "alternative[s]" that are "within the ambit of the existing [policy]." Here forbearance was not simply "within the ambit of the existing [policy]," it was the centerpiece of the policy. . . .

That omission alone renders Acting Secretary Duke's decision arbitrary and capricious. But it is not the only defect. Duke also failed to address whether there was "legitimate reliance" on the DACA Memorandum. . . .

To the Government and lead dissent's point, DHS could respond that reliance on forbearance and benefits was unjustified in light of the express limitations in the DACA Memorandum. Or it might conclude that reliance interests in benefits that it views as unlawful are entitled to no or diminished weight. And, even if DHS ultimately concludes that the reliance interests rank as serious, they are but one factor to consider. DHS may determine, in the particular context before it, that other interests and policy concerns outweigh any reliance interests. Making that difficult decision was the agency's job, but the agency failed to do it. . . .

Justice Thomas, with whom Justice Alito and Justice Gorsuch join, [dissenting].

* * *

To lawfully implement such changes, DHS needed [in 2012] a grant of authority from Congress to either reclassify removable DACA recipients as lawfully present, or to exempt the entire class of aliens covered by DACA from statutory removal procedures. No party disputes that the immigration statutes lack an express delegation to accomplish either result. And, an examination of the highly reticulated immigration regime makes clear that DHS has no implicit discretion to create new classes of lawful presence or to grant relief from removal out of whole cloth. Accordingly, DACA is substantively unlawful.

This conclusion should begin and end our review. The decision to rescind an unlawful agency action is *per se* lawful. No additional policy justifications or considerations are necessary. And, the majority's contrary holding—that an agency is not only permitted, but required, to continue an ultra vires action—has no basis in law. . . .

The majority opts for a different path, all but ignoring DACA's substantive legal defect. On the majority's understanding of APA review, DHS was required to provide additional policy justifications in order to rescind an action that it had no authority to take. This rule "has no basis in our jurisprudence, and support for [it] is conspicuously absent from the Court's opinion." . . .

The majority's demanding review of DHS' decisionmaking process is especially perverse given that the 2012 memorandum flouted the APA's procedural requirements—the very requirements designed to prevent arbitrary decisionmaking. Even if DHS were authorized to create DACA, it could not do so without undertaking an administrative rulemaking. The fact that DHS did not engage in this process likely provides an independent basis for rescinding DACA. But at the very least, this procedural defect compounds the absurdity of the majority's position in these cases.

As described above, DACA fundamentally altered the immigration laws. It created a new category of aliens who, as a class, became exempt from statutory removal procedures, and it gave those aliens temporary lawful presence. Both changes contravened statutory limits. DACA is thus what is commonly called a substantive or legislative rule. . . .

Because DACA has the force and effect of law, DHS was required to observe the procedures set out in the APA if it wanted to promulgate a legislative rule. It is undisputed, however, that DHS did not do so. It provided no opportunity for interested parties to submit comments regarding the effect that the program's dramatic and very significant change in immigration law would have on various aspects of society. . . .

Given this state of affairs, it is unclear to me why DHS needed to provide any explanation whatsoever when it decided to rescind DACA. Nothing in the APA suggests that DHS was required to spill *any* ink justifying the rescission of an invalid legislative rule, let alone that it was required to provide policy justifications beyond acknowledging that the program was simply unlawful from the beginning. And, it is well established that we do not remand for an agency to correct its reasoning when it was required by law to take or abstain from an action. Here, remand would be futile, because no amount of policy explanation could cure the fact that DHS lacked statutory authority to enact DACA in the first place. . . .

At bottom, of course, none of this matters, because DHS *did* provide a sufficient explanation for its action. DHS' statement that DACA was ultra vires was more than sufficient to justify its rescission. By requiring more, the majority has distorted the APA review process beyond recognition, further burdening all future attempts to rescind unlawful programs. Plaintiffs frequently bring successful challenges to agency actions by arguing that the agency has impermissibly dressed up a legislative rule as a policy statement and must comply with the relevant procedures before functionally binding regulated parties. But going forward, when a rescinding agency inherits an invalid legislative rule that ignored virtually every rulemaking requirement of the APA, it will be obliged to overlook that reality. Instead of simply terminating the program because it did not go through the requisite process, the agency will be compelled to treat an invalid legislative rule as though it were legitimate. . . .

Neither State Farm nor any other decision cited by the majority addresses what an agency must do when it has inherited an unlawful program. . . .

[R]eliance interests are irrelevant when assessing whether to rescind an action that the agency lacked statutory authority to take. No amount of reliance could ever justify continuing a program that allows DHS to wield power that neither Congress nor the Constitution gave it. . . .

Justice Alito, [dissenting].

I join Justice Thomas's opinion. DACA presents a delicate political issue, but that is not our business. As Justice Thomas explains, DACA was unlawful from the start, and that alone is sufficient to justify its termination. But even if DACA were lawful, we would still have no basis for overturning its rescission. First, to the extent DACA represented a lawful exercise of prosecutorial discretion, its rescission represented an exercise of that same discretion, and it would therefore be unreviewable under the Administrative Procedure Act. 5 U. S. C. § 701(a)(2); see Heckler v. Chaney, 470 U. S. 821, 831–832 (1985) [excerpted infra Chapter 4.D—Ed.]. Second, to the extent we could review the rescission, it was not arbitrary and capricious for essentially the reasons explained by Justice Kavanaugh.

Justice Kavanaugh, [dissenting].

. . . . To begin with, all nine Members of the Court accept, as do the DACA plaintiffs themselves, that the Executive Branch possesses the legal authority to rescind DACA and to resume pre-DACA enforcement of the immigration laws enacted by Congress. Having previously adopted a policy of prosecutorial discretion and nonenforcement with respect to a particular class of offenses or individuals, the Executive Branch has the legal authority to rescind such a policy and resume enforcing the law enacted by Congress. . . .

The Nielsen Memorandum was issued nine months after the Duke Memorandum. Under the Administrative Procedure Act, the Nielsen Memorandum is itself a "rule" setting forth "an agency statement of general . . . applicability and future effect designed to implement . . . policy." 5 U. S. C. § 551(4). Because it is a rule, the Nielsen Memorandum constitutes "agency action." § 551(13). As the Secretary of Homeland Security, Secretary Nielsen had the authority to decide whether to stick with Secretary Duke's decision to rescind DACA, or to make a different decision. Like Secretary Duke, Secretary Nielsen chose to rescind DACA, and she provided additional explanation. Her memorandum was akin to common forms of agency action that follow earlier agency action on the same subject—for example, a supplemental or new agency statement of policy, or an agency order with respect to a motion for rehearing or reconsideration. Courts often consider an agency's additional explanations of policy or additional explanations made, for example, on agency rehearing or reconsideration, or on remand from a court, even if the agency's bottom-line decision itself does not change.

Yet the Court today jettisons the Nielsen Memorandum by classifying it as a *post hoc* justification for rescinding DACA. Under our precedents, however, the *post hoc* justification doctrine merely requires that courts assess agency action based on the official explanations of the agency decisionmakers, and not based on after-the-fact explanations advanced *by agency lawyers during litigation* (or by judges). . . .

Indeed, the ordinary judicial remedy for an agency's insufficient explanation is to remand for further explanation by the relevant agency personnel. It would make little sense for a court to exclude official explanations by agency personnel such as a Cabinet Secretary simply because the explanations are purportedly *post hoc*, and then to turn around and remand for further explanation by those same agency personnel. Yet that is the upshot of the Court's application of the *post hoc* justification doctrine today. The Court's refusal to look at the Nielsen Memorandum seems particularly mistaken, moreover, because the Nielsen Memorandum shows that the Department, back in 2018, considered the policy issues that the Court today says the Department did not consider. . . .

NOTES AND QUESTIONS

1. What should Secretary Nielsen have been done differently? There are several issues in the DACA case. One was whether to consider Secretary Nielsen's more elaborate explanation of the DACA rescission than the explanation made by Acting Secretary Duke. Why did the Court ignore it? What exactly does the Court mean that Secretary Nielsen should have engaged in new agency action? Wasn't her statement, as Justice Kavanaugh argues, precisely such a new agency action? If she

FOR DISCUSSION

Was Secretary Nielsen's memo a "rule" under the APA's definition?

had said "I therefore rescind DACA" instead of "I decline to disturb the prior rescission," would that really have made all the difference?

2.   *The legality of DACA.* The principal dissenters argue that the initial promulgation of DACA was unlawful because that program effectively rewrote the immigration laws and was promulgated in any event without notice-and-comment rulemaking. If either is true, should that be enough to rescind the program? If so, shouldn't the majority have addressed those arguments? Why did Justice Kavanaugh not join the principal dissent on this point? Was it ultimately unnecessary for the outcome? Would it be enough justification to rescind DACA if the *executive* branch *believed* (in good faith) that DACA was unconstitutional? Would that be enough justification if the Court held DACA was constitutional? Is the Executive bound by the Court's determination of what is constitutional? Compare Ilan Wurman, "Administrative Law and the DACA Decision," Newsweek, June 20, 2020 (arguing that it is not arbitrary and capricious to decline to exercise discretion based on a reasonable constitutional argument, even if the Court disagrees with that argument); with Daniel T. Deacon, "No, Agencies Are Not Allowed to be 'a Little Bit Wrong' About the Constitution," Yale J. on Reg. Notice & Comment Blog, June 22, 2020 (arguing that it's always arbitrary and capricious when the executive misunderstands the scope of its discretion, including when its view is based on an erroneous view of the Constitution).

3.   *Forbearance.* Is the majority's reading of the Fifth Circuit opinion fair? What exactly does the Fifth Circuit say about forbearance? Did the Fifth Circuit suggest that the wholesale forbearance of an entire category of cases was a lawful exercise of prosecutorial discretion, or only that individual forbearance decisions would be lawful exercises of such discretion? And if the latter, why would a new administration have to supply an explanation for its changed prosecutorial discretion priorities? (Such discretion is usually non-reviewable, see Section D of this Chapter.)

B.   Judicial Review of Agency Fact-Finding

Section 706 directs courts to set aside agency action that is "unsupported by substantial evidence" in matters decided under §§ 556–57, i.e. formal adjudications and rulemakings. This provision relates to factual findings. Although not limited to adjudications, this standard is most relevant in the context of findings of fact made by Administrative Law Judges or similar adjudicators, and hence arises most often in the context of adjudication. The next two cases apply this "substantial evidence" standard.

Universal Camera Corp. v. NLRB

340 U.S. 474 (1951)

MR. JUSTICE FRANKFURTER delivered the opinion of the Court.

[The underlying facts are not related in this Opinion, but they involve an employee of Universal Camera Corp. who testified against the interests of his company at a National Labor Relations Board hearing regarding union representation. The company fired him, claiming that the employee accused his manager of drunkenness during an argument; the employee claimed it was for retaliation. The hearing examiner—today, what would be an Administrative Law Judge—found in favor of the company, but the NLRB found otherwise and set aside the hearing examiner's findings. It ordered Universal Camera to hire back the employee with backpay. The Second Circuit upheld the NLRB's order.—Ed.]

The essential issue raised by this case and its companion is the effect of the Administrative Procedure Act and the legislation colloquially known as the Taft-Hartley Act on the duty of Courts of Appeals when called upon to review orders of the National Labor Relations Board.

The Court of Appeals for the Second Circuit granted enforcement of an order directing, in the main, that petitioner reinstate with back pay an employee found to have been discharged because he gave testimony under the Wagner Act, and cease and desist from discriminating against any employee who files charges or gives testimony under that Act. . . .

I

Want of certainty in judicial review of Labor Board decisions partly reflects the intractability of any formula to furnish definiteness of content for all the impalpable factors involved in judicial review. But in part doubts as to the nature of the reviewing power and uncertainties in its application derive from history, and to that extent an elucidation of this history may clear them away.

The Wagner Act provided: 'The findings of the Board as to the facts, if supported by evidence, shall be conclusive.' This Court read 'evidence' to mean 'substantial evidence,' and we said that '(s)ubstantial evidence is more than a mere scintilla. It means such relevant evidence as a reasonable mind might accept as adequate to support a conclusion.' Accordingly, it 'must do more than create a suspicion of the existence of the fact to be established. . . . [I]t must be enough to justify, if the trial were to a jury, a refusal to direct a verdict when the conclusion sought to be drawn from it is one of fact for the jury.'

The very smoothness of the 'substantial evidence' formula as the standard for reviewing the evidentiary validity of the Board's findings established its currency. But the inevitably variant applications of the standard to conflicting evidence soon brought contrariety of views and in due course bred criticism. Even though the whole record may have been canvassed in order to determine whether the evidentiary foundation of a determination by the Board was 'substantial,' the phrasing of this Court's process of review readily lent itself to the notion that it was enough that the evidence supporting the Board's result was 'substantial' when considered by itself. It is fair to say that by imperceptible steps regard for the fact-finding function of the Board led to the assumption that the requirements of the Wagner Act were met when the reviewing court could find in the record evidence which, when viewed in isolation, substantiated the Board's findings. This is not to say that every member of this Court was consciously guided by this view or that the Court ever explicitly avowed this practice as doctrine. What matters is that the belief justifiably arose that the Court had so construed the obligation to review.

Criticism of so contracted a reviewing power reinforced dissatisfaction felt in various quarters with the Board's administration of the Wagner Act in the years preceding the war. The scheme of the Act was attacked as an inherently unfair fusion of the functions of prosecutor and judge. Accusations of partisan bias were not wanting. The 'irresponsible admission and weighing of hearsay, opinion, and emotional speculation in place of factual evidence' was said to be a 'serious menace.' No doubt some, perhaps even much, of the criticism was baseless and some surely was reckless. What is here relevant, however, is the climate of opinion thereby generated and its effect on Congress. Protests against 'shocking injustices' and intimations of judicial 'abdication' with which some courts granted enforcement of the Board's order stimulated pressures for legislative relief from alleged administrative excesses.

The strength of these pressures was reflected in the passage in 1940 of the Walter-Logan Bill. It was vetoed by President Roosevelt, partly because it imposed unduly rigid limitations on the administrative process, and partly because of the investigation into the actual operation of the administrative process then being conducted by an experienced committee appointed by the Attorney General. . . .

The final report of the Attorney General's Committee was submitted in January, 1941. The majority concluded that '(d)issatisfaction with the existing standards as to the scope of judicial review derives largely from dissatisfaction with the fact-finding procedures now employed by the administrative bodies.' Departure from the 'substantial evidence' test, it thought, would either create unnecessary uncertainty or transfer to courts the responsibility for ascertaining and assaying matters the significance of which lies outside judicial competence. Accordingly, it recommended against Legislation embodying a general scheme of judicial review.

Three members of the Committee registered a dissent. Their view was that the 'present system or lack of system of judicial review' led to inconsistency and uncertainty. They reported that under a 'prevalent' interpretation of the 'substantial evidence' rule 'if what is called 'substantial evidence' is found anywhere in the record to support conclusions of fact, the courts are said to be obliged to sustain the decision without reference to how heavily the countervailing evidence may preponderate—unless indeed the stage of arbitrary decision is reached. Under this interpretation, the courts need to read only one side of the case and, if they find any evidence there, the administrative action is to be sustained and the record to the contrary is to be ignored.' Their view led them to recommend that Congress enact principles of review applicable to all agencies not excepted by unique characteristics. One of these principles was expressed by the formula that judicial review could extend to 'findings, inferences, or conclusions of fact unsupported, upon the whole record, by substantial evidence.' So far as the history of this movement for enlarged review reveals, the phrase 'upon the whole record' makes its first appearance in this recommendation of the minority of the Attorney General's Committee. This evidence of the close relationship between the phrase and the criticism out of which it arose is important, for the substance of this formula for judicial review found its way into the statute books when Congress with unquestioning—we might even say uncritical—unanimity enacted the Administrative Procedure Act.

One is tempted to say 'uncritical' because the legislative history of that Act hardly speaks with that clarity of purpose which Congress supposedly furnishes courts in order to enable them to enforce its true will. On the one hand, the sponsors of the legislation indicated that they were reaffirming the prevailing 'substantial evidence' test. But with equal clarity they expressed disapproval of the manner in which the courts were applying their own standard. The committee reports of both houses refer to the practice of agencies to rely upon 'suspicion, surmise, implications, or plainly incredible evidence,' and indicate that courts are to exact higher standards 'in the exercise of their independent judgment' and on consideration of 'the whole record.'

[In omitted paragraphs, the Court describes the enactment of the same standard in the Taft-Hartley Act.—Ed.]

It is fair to say that in all this Congress expressed a mood. And it expressed its mood not merely by oratory but by legislation. As legislation that mood must be respected, even though it can only serve as a standard for judgment and not as a body of rigid rules assuring sameness of applications. Enforcement of such broad standards implies subtlety of mind and solidity of judgment. But it is not for us to question that Congress may assume such qualities in the federal judiciary.

From the legislative story we have summarized, two concrete conclusions do emerge. One is the identity of aim of the Administrative Procedure Act and the Taft-Hartley Act regarding the proof with which the Labor Board must support a decision. The other is that now Congress has left no room for doubt as to the kind of scrutiny which a court of appeals must give the record before the Board to satisfy itself that the Board's order rests on adequate proof. . . .

Whether or not it was ever permissible for courts to determine the substantiality of evidence supporting a Labor Board decision merely on the basis of evidence which in and of itself justified it, without taking into account contradictory evidence or evidence from which conflicting inferences could be drawn, the new legislation definitively precludes such a theory of review and bars its practice. The substantiality of evidence must take into account whatever in the record fairly detracts from its weight. This is clearly the significance of the requirement in both statutes that courts consider the whole record. Committee reports and the adoption in the Administrative Procedure Act of the minority views of the Attorney General's Committee demonstrate that to enjoin such a duty on the reviewing court was one of the important purposes of the movement which eventuated in that enactment.

To be sure, the requirement for canvassing 'the whole record' in order to ascertain substantiality does not furnish a calculus of value by which a reviewing court can assess the evidence. Nor was it intended to negative the function of the Labor Board as one of those agencies presumably equipped or informed by experience to deal with a specialized field of knowledge, whose findings within that field carry the authority of an expertness which courts do not possess and therefore must respect. Nor does it mean that even as to matters not requiring expertise a court may displace the Board's choice between two fairly conflicting views, even though the court would justifiably have made a different choice had the matter been before it *de novo*. Congress has merely made it clear that a reviewing court is not barred from setting aside a Board decision when it cannot conscientiously find that the evidence supporting that decision is substantial, when viewed in the light that the record in its entirety furnishes, including the body of evidence opposed to the Board's view. . . .

We conclude, therefore, that the Administrative Procedure Act and the Taft-Hartley Act direct that courts must now assume more responsibility for the reasonableness and fairness of Labor Board decisions than some courts have shown in the past. Reviewing courts must be influenced by a feeling that they are not to abdicate the conventional judicial function. Congress has imposed on them responsibility for assuring that the Board keeps within reasonable grounds. . . .

II

. . . . The decision of the Court of Appeals is assailed . . . [for] holding that it was barred from taking into account the report of the examiner on questions of fact insofar as that report was rejected by the Board . . . .

III

. . . . We are aware that to give the examiner's findings less finality than a [special] master's and yet entitle them to consideration in striking the account, is to introduce another and an unruly factor into the judgmatical process of review. But we ought not to fashion an exclusionary rule merely to reduce the number of imponderables to be considered by reviewing courts. . . .

Surely an examiner's report is as much a part of the record as the complaint or the testimony. . . .

It is therefore difficult to escape the conclusion that the plain language of the statutes directs a reviewing court to determine the substantiality of evidence on the record including the examiner's report. The conclusion is confirmed by the indications in the legislative history that enhancement of the status and function of the trial examiner was one of the important purposes of the movement for administrative reform. . . .

We do not require that the examiner's findings be given more weight than in reason and in the light of judicial experience they deserve. The 'substantial evidence' standard is not modified in any way when the Board and its examiner disagree. We intend only to recognize that evidence supporting a conclusion may be less substantial when an impartial, experienced examiner who has observed the witnesses and lived with the case has drawn conclusions different from the Board's than when he has reached the same conclusion. The findings of the examiner are to be considered along with the consistency and inherent probability of testimony. The significance of his report, of course, depends largely on the importance of credibility in the particular case. To give it this significance does not seem to us materially more difficult than to heed the other factors which in sum determine whether evidence is 'substantial.' . . .

We therefore remand the cause to the Court of Appeals. On reconsideration of the record it should accord the findings of the trial examiner the relevance that they reasonably command in answering the comprehensive question whether the evidence supporting the Board's order is substantial. But the court need not limit its reexamination of the case to the effect of that report on its decision. We leave it free to grant or deny enforcement as it thinks the principles expressed in this opinion dictate.

Notes and Questions

1.   Relation to the jury standard. The substantial evidence standard was interpreted by the Court in *Universal Camera* and in prior cases to amount to the following: the evidence "must be enough to justify, if the trial were to a jury, a refusal to direct a verdict when the conclusion sought to be drawn from it is one of fact for the jury." Yet there is a slight difference between this standard and the one by which courts review a jury's fact-finding: when it comes to reviewing jury verdicts, all reasonable inferences must be drawn in favor of the verdict. When it comes to reviewing an agency decision, the question is whether a reasonable jury (or agency) could have concluded as the agency did in light of the evidence, but there does not appear to be a requirement that inferences be made in favor of the agency; in fact, "whole record" review seems to prohibit such inferences. Do you see the distinction? Do you think this distinction makes any difference?

2. *The importance of the initial determination.* In *Universal Camera*, the agency disagreed with the initial adjudicator. How much weight should be given by an appellate court to the findings of the initial adjudicator? The answer is rather intuitive: the more the initial adjudication involved testimonial facts and the credibility of witnesses, the more the court should (and the more the agency should have) deferred to that initial determination. But that does not mean the court or agency has to defer to the "secondary inferences" made by the initial adjudicator on the basis of the testimony. The agency can accept any "testimonial" or "primary" inferences, but does not have to accept conclusions or subsequent inferences that are not compelled by the primary, testimonial inferences. Put another way, the agency itself can still get deference if the inference it is making is a result of the agency's expertise and well-considered policy judgment. But the more the agency's inference hinges on the testimony itself, the more the initial adjudicator's credibility determinations will matter. See, e.g., Penasquitos Village, Inc. v. NLR, 565 F.2d 1074 (9th Cir. 1977).

When reviewing a jury verdict, courts make all reasonable inferences in favor of the verdict. When reviewing factual findings of agencies, courts ask whether a reasonable jury could have concluded as the agency had, but the court assesses the implications of the evidence for itself.

The standard of *Universal Camera* is easy enough to state, but not always easy to apply. Consider the Supreme Court's application of the rule in the following case.

Allentown Mack Sales and Services, Inc. v. NLRB

522 U.S. 359 (1998)

JUSTICE SCALIA delivered the opinion of the Court.

Under longstanding precedent of the National Labor Relations Board, an employer who believes that an incumbent union no longer enjoys the support of a majority of its employees has three options: to request a formal, Board-supervised election, to withdraw recognition from the union and refuse to bargain, or to conduct an internal poll of employee support for the union. The Board has held that the latter two are unfair labor practices unless the employer can show that it had a "good-faith reasonable doubt" about the union's majority support. We must decide whether the Board's standard for employer polling is rational and consistent with the National Labor Relations Act, and whether the Board's factual determinations in this case are supported by substantial evidence in the record.

I

Mack Trucks, Inc., had a factory branch in Allentown, Pennsylvania, whose service and parts employees were represented by Local Lodge 724 of the International Association of Machinists and Aerospace Workers, AFL-CIO (Local 724). Mack notified its Allentown managers in May 1990 that it intended to sell the branch, and several of those managers formed Allentown Mack Sales & Service, Inc., the petitioner here, which purchased the assets of the business on December 20, 1990, and began to operate it as an independent dealership. From December 21, 1990, to January 1, 1991, Allentown hired 32 of the original 45 Mack employees.

During the period before and immediately after the sale, a number of Mack employees made statements to the prospective owners of Allentown Mack Sales suggesting that the incumbent union had lost support among employees in the bargaining unit. In job interviews, eight employees made statements indicating, or at least arguably indicating, that they personally no longer supported the union. In addition, Ron Mohr, a member of the union's bargaining committee and shop steward for the Mack Trucks service department, told an Allentown manager that it was his feeling that the employees did not want a union, and that "with a new company, if a vote was taken, the Union would lose." And Kermit Bloch, who worked for Mack Trucks as a mechanic on the night shift, told a manager that the entire night shift (then five or six employees) did not want the union.

On January 2, 1991, Local 724 asked Allentown Mack Sales to recognize it as the employees' collective-bargaining representative, and to begin negotiations for a contract. The new employer rejected that request by letter dated January 25, claiming a "good faith doubt as to support of the Union among the employees." The letter also announced that Allentown had "arranged for an independent poll by secret ballot of its hourly employees to be conducted under guidelines prescribed by the National Labor Relations Board." The poll, supervised by a Roman Catholic priest, was conducted on February 8, 1991; the union lost 19 to 13. Shortly thereafter, the union filed an unfair-labor-practice charge with the Board.

The Administrative Law Judge (ALJ) concluded that Allentown was a "successor" employer to Mack Trucks, Inc., and therefore inherited Mack's bargaining obligation and a presumption of continuing majority support for the union. The ALJ held that Allentown's poll was conducted in compliance with the procedural standards enunciated by the Board . . . , but that it violated §§ 8(a)(1) and 8(a)(5) of the National Labor Relations Act (Act) because Allentown did not have an "objective reasonable doubt" about the majority status of the union. The Board adopted the ALJ's findings and agreed with his conclusion that Allentown "had not demonstrated that it harbored a reasonable doubt, based on objective considerations, as to the incumbent Union's continued majority status after the transition." The Board ordered Allentown to recognize and bargain with Local 724.

On review in the Court of Appeals for the District of Columbia Circuit, Allentown challenged both the facial rationality of the Board's test for employer polling and the Board's application of that standard to the facts of this case. The court enforced the Board's bargaining order, over a vigorous dissent. We granted certiorari.

* * *

III

The Board held Allentown guilty of an unfair labor practice in its conduct of the polling because it "ha[d] not demonstrated that it held a reasonable doubt, based on objective considerations, that the Union continued to enjoy the support of a majority of the bargaining unit employees." We must decide whether that conclusion is supported by substantial evidence on the record as a whole. Put differently, we must decide whether on this record it would have been possible for a reasonable jury to reach the Board's conclusion. . . .

The question presented for review, therefore, is whether, on the evidence presented to the Board, a reasonable jury could have found that Allentown lacked a genuine, reasonable uncertainty about whether Local 724 enjoyed the continuing support of a majority of unit employees. In our view, the answer is no. The Board's finding to the contrary rests on a refusal to credit probative circumstantial evidence, and on evidentiary demands that go beyond the substantive standard the Board purports to apply.

The Board adopted the ALJ's finding that 6 of Allentown's 32 employees had made "statements which could be used as objective considerations supporting a good-faith reasonable doubt as to continued majority status by the Union." (These included, for example, the statement of Rusty Hoffman that "he did not want to work in a union shop," and "would try to find another job if he had to work with the Union.") The Board seemingly also accepted (though this is not essential to our analysis) the ALJ's willingness to assume that the statement of a seventh employee (to the effect that he "did not feel comfortable with the Union and thought it was a waste of $35 a month") supported good-faith reasonable doubt of his support for the union—as in our view it unquestionably does. And it presumably accepted the ALJ's assessment that "7 of 32, or roughly 20 percent of the involved employees" was not alone sufficient to create "an objective reasonable doubt of union majority support." The Board did not specify how many express disavowals would have been enough to establish reasonable doubt, but the number must presumably be less than 16 (half of the bargaining unit), since that would establish reasonable *certainty*. Still, we would not say that 20% first-hand-confirmed opposition (even with no countering evidence of union support) is alone enough to *require* a conclusion of reasonable doubt. But there was much more.

For one thing, the ALJ and the Board totally disregarded the effect upon Allentown of the statement of an eighth employee, Dennis Marsh, who said that "he was not being represented for the $35 he was paying." The ALJ, whose findings were adopted by the Board, said that this statement "seems more an expression of a desire for better representation than one for no representation at all." It seems to us that it is, more accurately, simply an expression of dissatisfaction with the union's performance—which *could* reflect the speaker's desire that the union represent him more effectively, but *could also* reflect the speaker's desire to save his $35 and get rid of the union. The statement would assuredly engender an *uncertainty* whether the speaker supported the union, and so could not be entirely ignored.

But the most significant evidence excluded from consideration by the Board consisted of statements of two employees regarding not merely their own support of the union, but support among the work force in general. Kermit Bloch, who worked on the night shift, told an Allentown manager "the entire night shift did not want the Union." The ALJ refused to credit this, because "Bloch did not testify and thus could not explain how he formed his opinion about the views of his fellow employees." Unsubstantiated assertions that other employees do not support the union certainly do not establish *the fact of that disfavor* with the degree of reliability ordinarily demanded in legal proceedings. But under the Board's enunciated test for polling, it is not the fact of disfavor that is at issue (the poll itself is meant to establish that), but rather the existence of a reasonable uncertainty on the part of the employer regarding that fact. On that issue, absent some reason for the employer to know that Bloch had no basis for his information, or that Bloch was lying, reason demands that the statement be given considerable weight.

Another employee who gave information concerning overall support for the union was Ron Mohr, who told Allentown managers that "if a vote was taken, the Union would lose" and that "it was his feeling that the employees did not want a union." The ALJ again objected irrelevantly that "there is no evidence with respect to how he gained this knowledge." In addition, the Board held that Allentown "could not legitimately rely on [the statement] as a basis for doubting the Union's majority status" because Mohr was "referring to Mack's existing employee complement, not to the individuals who were later hired by [Allentown]." This basis for disregarding Mohr's statements is wholly irrational. Local 724 had never won an election, or even an informal poll, within the actual unit of 32 Allentown employees. Its claim to represent them rested entirely on the Board's presumption that the work force of a successor company has the same disposition regarding the union as did the work force of the predecessor company, if the majority of the new work force came from the old one. The Board cannot rationally adopt that presumption for purposes of imposing the duty to bargain, and adopt precisely the opposite presumption (*i.e.,* contend that there is no relationship between the sentiments of the two work forces) for purposes of determining what evidence tends to establish a reasonable doubt regarding union support. . .

It must be borne in mind that the issue here is not whether Mohr's statement clearly establishes a majority in opposition to the union, but whether it contributes to a reasonable uncertainty whether a majority in favor of the union existed. We think it surely does. Allentown would reasonably have given great credence to Mohr's assertion of lack of union support, since he was not hostile to the union, and was in a good position to assess antiunion sentiment. Mohr was a union shop steward for the service department, and a member of the union's bargaining committee; according to the ALJ, he "did not indicate personal dissatisfaction with the Union." It seems to us that Mohr's statement has undeniable and substantial probative value on the issue of "reasonable doubt."

Accepting the Board's apparent (and in our view inescapable) concession that Allentown received reliable information that 7 of the bargaining-unit employees did not support the union, the remaining 25 would have had to support the union by a margin of 17 to 8—a ratio of more than 2 to 1—if the union commanded majority support. The statements of Bloch and Mohr would cause anyone to doubt that degree of support, and neither the Board nor the ALJ discussed any evidence that Allentown should have weighed on the other side. . . . Giving fair weight to Allentown's circumstantial evidence, we think it quite impossible for a rational factfinder to avoid the conclusion that Allentown had reasonable, good-faith grounds to doubt—*to be uncertain about*—the union's retention of majority support.

[In an omitted section, the Court assesses the reasonableness of the Board's relevant policies under the arbitrary-and-capricious standard.—Ed.]

The same is true of the Board precedents holding that "an employee's statements of dissatisfaction with the quality of union representation may not be treated as opposition to union representation," and that "an employer may not rely on an employee's anti-union sentiments, expressed during a job interview in which the employer has indicated that there will be no union." It is of course true that such statements are not clear evidence of an employee's opinion about the union—and if the Board's substantive standard required clear proof of employee disaffection, it might be proper to ignore such statements altogether. But that is not the standard, and, depending on the circumstances, the statements can unquestionably be probative to some degree of the employer's good-faith reasonable doubt.

We conclude that . . . the Board's factual finding that Allentown Mack Sales lacked such a doubt is not supported by substantial evidence on the record as a whole. . . .

[An opinion concurring in part and dissenting in part—with respect to a part of the opinion not relevant to the above excerpts—by Chief Justice Rehnquist and Justices O'Connor, Kennedy, and Thomas is omitted.—Ed.]

Justice Breyer, with whom Justice Stevens, Justice Souter, and Justice Ginsburg join, concurring in part and dissenting in part.

. . . . To decide whether an agency's conclusion is supported by substantial evidence, a reviewing court must identify the conclusion and then examine and weigh the evidence. As this Court said in 1951, "[w]hether on the record as a whole there is substantial evidence to support agency findings is a question which Congress has placed in the keeping of the Courts of Appeals." *Universal Camera*, 340 U.S. at 491. The Court held that it would "intervene only in what ought to be the rare instance when the standard appears to have been *misapprehended or grossly misapplied*." *Ibid.* (emphasis added). Consequently, if the majority is to overturn a court of appeals' "substantial evidence" decision, it must identify the agency's conclusion, examine the evidence, and then determine whether the evidence is so *obviously* inadequate to support the conclusion that the reviewing court must have seriously misunderstood the nature of its legal duty.

The majority opinion begins by properly stating the Board's conclusion, namely, that the employer, Allentown Mack Sales & Service, Inc., did not demonstrate that it "held a reasonable doubt, *based on objective considerations,* that the Union continued to enjoy the support of a majority of the bargaining unit employees." The opinion, however, then omits the words I have italicized and transforms this conclusion, rephrasing it as: "Allentown lacked a genuine, reasonable uncertainty about whether Local 724 enjoyed the continuing support of a majority of unit employees."

Key words of a technical sort that the Board has used in hundreds of opinions written over several decades to express what the Administrative Law Judge (ALJ) here called "*objective* reasonable doubt" have suddenly disappeared, leaving in their place what looks like an ordinary jury standard that might reflect not an agency's specialized knowledge of the workplace, but a court's common understanding of human psychology. . . .

According to the ALJ, [Allentown Mack] sought to show that it had an "objective" good-faith doubt primarily by presenting the testimony of Allentown managers, who, in turn, reported statements made to them by 14 employees. The ALJ set aside the statements of 5 of those employees as insignificant for various reasons—for example because the employees were not among the rehired 32, because their statements were equivocal, or because they made the statements at a time too long before the transition. The majority does not take issue with the ALJ's reasoning with respect to these employees. The ALJ then found that statements made by six, and possibly seven, employees (22% of the 32) helped Allentown show an "objective" reasonable doubt. The majority does not quarrel with this conclusion. The majority does, however, take issue with the ALJ's decision not to count in Allentown's favor three further statements, made by employees Marsh, Bloch, and Mohr. The majority says that these statements *required* the ALJ and the Board to find for Allentown. I cannot agree.

Consider Marsh's statement. Marsh said, as the majority opinion notes, that " 'he was not being represented for the $35 he was paying.' " The majority says that the ALJ was wrong not to count this statement in the employer's favor. But the majority fails to mention that Marsh made this statement to an Allentown manager while the manager was interviewing Marsh to determine whether he would, or would not, be one of the 32 employees whom Allentown would reemploy. The ALJ, when evaluating all the employee statements, wrote that statements made to the Allentown managers during the job interviews were "somewhat tainted as it is likely that a job applicant will say whatever he believes the prospective employer wants to hear." In so stating, the ALJ was reiterating the Board's own normative general finding that employers should not "rely in asserting a good-faith doubt" upon "[s]tatements made by employees during the course of an interview with a prospective employer." The Board also has found that " '[e]mployee statements of dissatisfaction with a union are not deemed the equivalent of withdrawal of support for the union.' " Either of these general Board findings (presumably known to employers advised by the labor bar), applied by the ALJ in this particular case, provides more than adequate support for the ALJ's conclusion that the employer could not properly rely upon Marsh's statement as help in creating an "objective" employer doubt.

I do not see how, on the record before us, one could plausibly argue that these relevant general findings of the Board fall outside the Board's lawfully delegated authority. The Board in effect has said that an employee statement *made during a job interview with an employer who has expressed an interest in a nonunionized work force* will often tell us precisely *nothing* about that employee's true feelings. That Board conclusion represents an exercise of the kind of discretionary authority that Congress placed squarely within the Board's administrative and fact-finding powers and responsibilities. . . .

Consider next Bloch's statement, made during his job interview with Worth, that those on the night shift (five or six employees) "did not want the Union." . . .

The majority says that "reason demands" that Bloch's statement "be given considerable weight." But why? The Board, drawing upon both reason and experience, has said it will "view with suspicion and caution" one employee's statements "purporting to represent the views of other employees." . . . Indeed, the Board specifically has stated that this type of evidence does not qualify as "objective" within the meaning of the "objective reasonable doubt" standard. . . .

How is it unreasonable for the Board to provide this kind of guidance, about what kinds of evidence are more likely, and what kinds are less likely, to support an "objective reasonable doubt" (thereby helping an employer understand just when he may refuse to bargain with an established employee representative, in the absence of an employee-generated union decertification petition)? . . .

Finally, consider the Allentown manager's statement that Mohr told him that "if a vote was taken, the Union would lose." . . .

The lack of any specifics provides some support for the possibility that Mohr was overstating a conclusion, say, in a job-preserving effort to curry favor with Mack's new managers. More importantly, since the absence of detail or support brings Mohr's statement well within the Board's pre-existing cautionary evidentiary principle (about employee statements regarding the views of other employees), it diminishes the reasonableness of any employer reliance. . . .

The majority fails to mention the ALJ's third reason for discounting Mohr's statement, namely, that Mohr did not indicate "whether he was speaking about a large majority of the service employees being dissatisfied with the Union or a small majority." It fails to mention the ALJ's belief that the statement was "almost off-the-cuff." . . . The ALJ did not conclude that Mohr's statement lacked evidentiary significance. Rather, the ALJ concluded that the statement did not provide "*sufficient* basis, even when considered with other employee statements relied upon, to meet the Board's objective reasonable doubt standard." . . .

NOTES AND QUESTIONS

1. *How would you have ruled?* Do you agree, along with the majority, that the ALJ got this case wrong—that there was an objective basis for the company's subjective doubt as to whether the union continued to enjoy majority support? Even if you agree, do you think no reasonable agency could have concluded otherwise? Do deferential standards of review perhaps make more of a difference in the lower courts than at the Supreme Court?

 FOR DISCUSSION Do deference doctrines matter at the Supreme Court, or is there one set of standards for the lower courts, and the Supreme Court does something else?

2. Ex post *evidence.* What role do you think the actual result of the poll played in the Court's decision? The union did, after all, lose the vote. The determination of an objectively reasonable subjective doubt must be made *ex ante*—at the time the employer held the belief—but isn't the *ex post* result at least some evidence that the employer's doubt was reasonable? Should the *ex post* evidence be ignored?

3. *Factual findings in informal proceedings.* Thus far, the cases have involved formal adjudications under §§ 554, 556, and 557 of the APA. Section 706(2)(E) provides that in such cases, a court can set aside an agency decision if unsupported by substantial evidence. What about informal rulemakings and adjudications—does the substantial evidence standard apply to them? The following opinion addresses that question.

Ass'n of Data Processing Service Organizations, Inc. v. Board of Governors of the Federal Reserve System

745 F.2d 677 (D.C. Cir. 1984)

SCALIA, CIRCUIT JUDGE:

The Association of Data Processing Service Organizations, Inc. ("ADAP-SO"), a national trade association representing the data processing industry, and two of its members petition this court for review of two orders of the Board of Governors of the Federal Reserve System, pursuant to 12 U.S.C. § 1848 (1982).

In No. 82–1910, they seek review of the Board's July 9, 1982 order approving Citicorp's application to establish a subsidiary, Citishare, to engage in certain data processing and transmission services. ("Citicorp Order"). In No. 82–2108, they seek review of the Board's August 23, 1982 order, entered after notice and comment rulemaking, amending those portions of Regulation Y which dealt with the performance of data processing activities by bank holding companies. ("Regulation Y Order"). We consolidated the two appeals.

The Bank Holding Company Act of 1956 requires all bank holding companies to seek prior regulatory approval before engaging in nonbanking activities. The restrictions do not apply to:

> activities . . . which the Board after due notice and opportunity for hearing has determined (by order or regulation) to be so closely related to banking or managing or controlling banks as to be a proper incident thereto. . . . In determining whether a particular activity is a proper incident to banking or managing or controlling banks the Board shall consider whether its performance by an affiliate of a holding company can reasonably be expected to produce benefits to the public, such as greater convenience, increased competition, or gains in efficiency, that outweigh possible adverse effects, such as undue concentration of resources, decreased or unfair competition, conflicts of interests, or unsound banking practices.

12 U.S.C. § 1843(c)(8). Section 1848, the source of our review authority, provides that "[t]he findings of the Board as to the facts, if supported by substantial evidence, shall be conclusive." *Id.* at § 1848.

On February 23, 1979, Citicorp applied for authority to engage, through its subsidiary Citishare, in the processing and transmission of banking, financial, and economic related data through timesharing, electronic funds transfer, home banking and other techniques. It also sought permission to sell its excess computing capacity and some computer hardware. The Board published notice of Citicorp's application, which was protested by ADAPSO, and set it for formal hearing. Before the hearing was held, Citicorp amended its application to add certain activities and to request amendment of Regulation Y to permit the activities it had specified. The Board published an Amended Order for Hearing and invited public comments and participation. A formal hearing was held before an Administrative Law Judge in which the merits of both the application and the proposed rule were considered. In addition, more than sixty companies and individuals submitted written comments on the proposed rule. On March 29, 1982, the ALJ decided that the activities proposed by Citicorp were closely related to banking and would produce benefits to the public which would outweigh their costs. The ALJ also recommended amendments to Regulation Y that would permit those activities contained in the Citicorp application. On July 9, 1982, the Board adopted the ALJ's recommendation to approve the Citicorp application, with certain restrictions. On August 23, 1982, the Board adopted the ALJ's recommended amendments to Regulation Y, again with certain restrictions. ADAPSO, and two of its members, participants in the actions below, filed these petitions for review.

We are faced at the outset with a dispute regarding the proper standard of review. These consolidated appeals call for us to review both an on-the-record adjudication and an informal notice and comment rulemaking. Petitioners contend that the substantial evidence standard, which presumably authorizes more rigorous judicial review, should govern our review of both orders. The Board agrees, noting that § 1848 applies a substantial evidence standard to factual determinations. Intervenor Citicorp contends that while the substantial evidence standard should govern review of the Citicorp order, Regulation Y should be upset only if arbitrary or capricious. . . .

The courts of appeals, however, have applied the substantial evidence standard of § 1848 to Board adjudications such as the authorization in the first order here under review, while applying the arbitrary or capricious standard, despite § 1848, to Board rules, including specifically amendments of Regulation Y. In fact one appellate opinion has, like this one, addressed precisely the situation in which *both* an adjudicatory authorization *and* an amendment of Regulation Y were at issue in the same case—and applied the § 1848 substantial evidence standard to the former but the arbitrary or capricious standard to the latter. . . . That leaves the courts with the difficult task of explaining why the last sentence of § 1848, unlike all the rest of it, should be deemed to apply only to adjudication and not to rulemaking. . . .

We think that there is no basis for giving the last sentence of § 1848 anything less than the general application given to the rest of the section. . . . [T]he court of appeals decisions applying the arbitrary or capricious test to Board rulemaking, seem to us explicable on quite different grounds—namely, that in their application to the requirement of factual support the substantial evidence test and the arbitrary or capricious test are one and the same. The former is only a specific application of the latter, separately recited in the APA not to establish a more rigorous standard of factual support but to emphasize that in the case of formal proceedings the factual support must be found in the closed record as opposed to elsewhere. We shall elaborate upon this point because it is not uncommon for parties to expend great effort in appeals before us to establish which of the two standards is applicable where in fact their operation is precisely the same.

The "scope of review" provisions of the APA, 5 U.S.C. § 706(2), are cumulative. Thus, an agency action which is supported by the required substantial evidence may in another regard be "arbitrary, capricious, an abuse of discretion, or otherwise not in accordance with law"—for example, because it is an abrupt and unexplained departure from agency precedent. Paragraph (A) of subsection 706(2)—the "arbitrary or capricious" provision—is a catchall, picking up administrative misconduct not covered by the other more specific paragraphs. Thus, in those situations where paragraph (E) has no application (informal rulemaking, for example, which is not governed by §§ 556 and 557 to which paragraph (E) refers), paragraph (A) takes up the slack, so to speak, enabling the courts to strike down, as arbitrary, agency action that is devoid of needed factual support. When the arbitrary or capricious standard is performing that function of assuring factual support, there is no *substantive* difference between what it requires and what would be required by the substantial evidence test, since it is impossible to conceive of a "nonarbitrary" factual judgment supported only by evidence that is not substantial in the APA sense—*i.e.*, not " 'enough to justify, if the trial were to a jury, a refusal to direct a verdict when the conclusion sought to be drawn . . . is one of fact for the jury.' "

We have noted on several occasions that the distinction between the substantial evidence test and the arbitrary or capricious test [as applied to the required factual support] is "largely semantic," and have indeed described that view as "the emerging consensus of the Courts of Appeals." . . .

As noted earlier, this does not consign paragraph (E) of the APA's judicial review section to pointlessness. The distinctive function of paragraph (E)—what it achieves that paragraph (A) does not—is to require substantial evidence to be found *within the record of closed-record proceedings* to which it exclusively applies. The importance of that requirement should not be underestimated. It is true that, as the Supreme Court said in *Camp v. Pitts*, 411 U.S. 138, 142 (1973), even informal agency action (not governed by paragraph (E)) must be reviewed only on the basis of "the administrative record already in existence." But that is quite a different and less onerous requirement, meaning only that whether the administrator was arbitrary must be determined on the basis of what he had before him when he acted, and not on the basis of "some new record made initially in the reviewing court." That "administrative record" might well include crucial material that was neither shown to nor known by the private parties in the proceeding—as indeed appears to have been the situation in *Camp v. Pitts* itself. It is true that, in informal rulemaking, at least the most critical factual material that is used to support the agency's position on review must have been made public in the proceeding and exposed to refutation. That requirement, however, does not extend to all data; and it only applies in rulemaking and not in other informal agency action, since it derives not from the arbitrary or capricious test but from the command of 5 U.S.C. § 553(c) that "the agency . . . give interested persons an opportunity to participate in the rule making."

Consolidated cases such as those before us here—involving simultaneous review of a rule (whose factual basis is governed only by paragraph (A)'s catchall control against "arbitrary or capricious" action) and of a formal adjudication dealing with the same subject (whose factual basis is governed by paragraph (E)'s requirement of substantial evidence)—demonstrate why the foregoing interpretation of the two standards is the only interpretation that makes sense. If the standards were substantively different (and leaving aside for the moment consideration of any special effect of § 1848), the Citicorp order, authorizing one bank holding company's data processing services, would be subject to more rigorous judicial review of factual support than the Regulation Y order which, due to its general applicability, would affect the operations of every bank holding company in the nation. Or, to put the point another way: If the Board had never issued any Regulation Y, and simply determined in the context of a particular application that the provision of timesharing services is "closely related" to banking, that determination, which could be reconsidered and revised in the context of the next adjudication, would require more factual support than the same determination in a rulemaking, which would have immediate nationwide application and, until amended by further rulemaking, would have to be applied to all subsequent applications.

This seemingly upside-down application of varying standards is not an issue in the present case since, as we have observed, § 1848 makes it clear that only *one* standard—the substantial evidence test—applies to review of all Board actions. The relevance of the foregoing discussion here is to determine what that standard *means*. . . .

We hold, therefore, that the § 1848 "substantial evidence" requirement applicable to our review here demands a quantum of factual support no different from that demanded by the substantial evidence provision of the APA, which is in turn no different from that demanded by the arbitrary or capricious standard. . . .

NOTES AND QUESTIONS

1. Does the standard of review make a difference? In the fight over what standard of review to apply to the fact-findings of an agency during informal proceedings, the various parties advocated for different standards—either the "arbitrary and capricious" standard or the "substantial evidence" standard. Judge Scalia concluded that the standard was "substantial evidence," because informal agency action based on facts unsupported by substantial evidence would be "arbitrary and capricious." But why was there a fight at all? Is one standard more deferential than the other? The parties obviously thought it made a difference, yet Judge Scalia Is there any difference between the "substantial evidence" and "arbitrary and capricious" standards? Which one seems more deferential?

wrote that "the distinction between the substantial evidence test and the arbitrary or capricious test," at least as applied to the required factual support, is "largely semantic." Does one seem more rigorous to you than the other?

One scholar collected a variety of studies of agency affirmance rates under different standards of review—de novo, substantial evidence, arbitrary and capricious, and *Chevron* deference (more on that standard in the next section)—and showed that agency affirmance rates hover between 65 and 75 percent regardless of the standard used. David Zaring, *Reasonable Agencies*, 96 Va. L. Rev. 135, 170–86 (2010). Thus, there may be some difference in outcome, but the difference is likely not that large. Additionally, the affirmance rates vary greatly for some agencies; for example, social security determinations have a much lower affirmance rate overall. Paul R. Verkuil, *An Outcomes Analysis of Scope of Review Standards*, 44 Wm. & Mary L. Rev. 679, 704–9 (2002).

C.   Judicial Review of Legal Questions

In addition to making factual findings and policy choices, agencies also have to interpret their governing statutes. This is something they do every day. To administer the law, they have to know what the law requires of them. The APA provides that when courts review agency actions, the courts "shall decide all relevant questions of law, interpret constitutional and statutory provisions, and determine the meaning or applicability of the terms of an agency action." 5 U.S.C. § 706. What, however, is a court to do when a statute is very much ambiguous? When it leaves a gap? The modern doctrine, announced in *Chevron v. Natural Resources Defense Council* in 1984, maintains that courts defer to an agency's reasonable interpretation of a statute that it administers. Can you square that with the text of APA § 706, which requires courts to decide "all relevant questions of law" and to "interpret constitutional and statutory provisions"? Consider these questions as you read the materials in this section.

1.   From *Skidmore* to *Chevron* and *Auer*

Even before *Chevron* courts dealt with how much deference to give agency legal interpretations. The following is a leading case of an alternative approach to the modern-day judicial deference framework, and which still applies in important circumstances.

HISTORICAL PERSPECTIVE How much have deference doctrines changed over time? As you read the cases, ask yourself whether the modern deference regime is consistent with these older cases.

Skidmore v. Swift & Co.

323 U.S. 134 (1944)

MR. JUSTICE JACKSON delivered the opinion of the Court.

Seven employees of the Swift and Company packing plant at Fort Worth, Texas, brought an action under the Fair Labor Standards Act to recover overtime . . . .

It is not denied that the daytime employment of these persons was working time within the Act. Two were engaged in general fire hall duties and maintenance of fire-fighting equipment of the Swift plant. The others operated elevators or acted as relief men in fire duties. They worked from 7:00 a.m. to 3:30 p.m., with a half-hour lunch period, five days a week. They were paid weekly salaries.

Under their oral agreement of employment, however, petitioners undertook to stay in the fire hall on the Company premises, or within hailing distance, three and a half to four nights a week. This involved no task except to answer alarms, either because of fire or because the sprinkler was set off for some other reason. No fires occurred during the period in issue, the alarms were rare, and the time required for their answer rarely exceeded an hour. For each alarm answered the employees were paid in addition to their fixed compensation an agreed amount, fifty cents at first, and later sixty-four cents. The Company provided a brick fire hall equipped with steam heat and air-conditioned rooms. It provided sleeping quarters, a pool table, a domino table, and a radio. The men used their time in sleep or amusement as they saw fit, except that they were required to stay in or close by the fire hall and be ready to respond to alarms. It is stipulated that 'they agreed to remain in the fire hall and stay in it or within hailing distance, subject to call, in event of fire or other casualty, but were not required to perform any specific tasks during these periods of time, except in answering alarms.' The trial court found the evidentiary facts as stipulated; it made no findings of fact as such as to whether under the arrangement of the parties and the circumstances of this case, . . . the fire hall duty or any part thereof constituted working time. It said, however, as a 'conclusion of law' that 'the time plaintiffs spent in the fire hall subject to call to answer fire alarms does not constitute hours worked, for which overtime compensation is due them under the Fair Labor Standards Act, as interpreted by the Administrator and the Courts,' and in its opinion observed, 'of course we know pursuing such pleasurable occupations or performing such personal chores does not constitute work.' The Circuit Court of Appeals affirmed.

. . . [W]e hold that no principle of law found either in the statute or in Court decisions precludes waiting time from also being working time. We have not attempted to, and we cannot, lay down a legal formula to resolve cases so varied in their facts as are the many situations in which employment involves waiting time. Whether in a concrete case such time falls within or without the Act is a question of fact to be resolved by appropriate findings of the trial court. This involves scrutiny and construction of the agreements between the particular parties, appraisal of their practical construction of the working agreement by conduct, consideration of the nature of the service, and its relation to the waiting time, and all of the surrounding circumstances. Facts may show that the employee was engaged to wait, or they may show that he waited to be engaged. His compensation may cover both waiting and task, or only performance of the task itself. Living quarters may in some situations be furnished as a facility of the task and in another as a part of its compensation. The law does not impose an arrangement upon the parties. It imposes upon the courts the task of finding what the arrangement was.

We do not minimize the difficulty of such an inquiry where the arrangements of the parties have not contemplated the problem posed by the statute. But it does not differ in nature or in the standards to guide judgment from that which frequently confronts courts where they must find retrospectively the effect of contracts as to matters which the parties failed to anticipate or explicitly to provide for.

Congress did not utilize the services of an administrative agency to find facts and to determine in the first instance whether particular cases fall within or without the Act. Instead, it put this responsibility on the courts. But it did create the office of Administrator, impose upon him a variety of duties, endow him with powers to inform himself of conditions in industries and employments subject to the Act, and put on him the duties of bringing injunction actions to restrain violations. Pursuit of his duties has accumulated a considerable experience in the problems of ascertaining working time in employments involving periods of inactivity and a knowledge of the customs prevailing in reference to their solution. From these he is obliged to reach conclusions as to conduct without the law, so that he should seek injunctions to stop it, and that within the law, so that he has no call to interfere. He has set forth his views of the application of the Act under different circumstances in an interpretative bulletin and in informal rulings. They provide a practical guide to employers and employees as to how the office representing the public interest in its enforcement will seek to apply it. Wage and Hour Division, Interpretative Bulletin No. 13.

The Administrator thinks the problems presented by inactive duty require a flexible solution, rather than the all-in or all-out rules respectively urged by the parties in this case, and his Bulletin endeavors to suggest standards and examples to guide in particular situations. In some occupations, it says, periods of inactivity are not properly counted as working time even though the employee is subject to call. Examples are an operator of a small telephone exchange where the switchboard is in her home and she ordinarily gets several hours of uninterrupted sleep each night; or a pumper of a stripper well or watchman of a lumber camp during the off season, who may be on duty twenty-four hours a day but ordinarily 'has a normal night's sleep, has ample time in which to eat his meals, and has a certain amount of time for relaxation and entirely private pursuits.' Exclusion of all such hours the Administrator thinks may be justified. In general, the answer depends 'upon the degree to which the employee is free to engage in personal activities during periods of idleness when he is subject to call and the number of consecutive hours that the employee is subject to call without being required to perform active work.' 'Hours worked are not limited to the time spent in active labor but include time given by the employee to the employer. * * *'

The facts of this case do not fall within any of the specific examples given, but the conclusion of the Administrator, as expressed in the brief amicus curiae, is that the general tests which he has suggested point to the exclusion of sleeping and eating time of these employees from the work-week and the inclusion of all other on-call time: although the employees were required to remain on the premises during the entire time, the evidence shows that they were very rarely interrupted in their normal sleeping and eating time, and these are pursuits of a purely private nature which would presumably occupy the employees' time whether they were on duty or not and which apparently could be pursued adequately and comfortably in the required circumstances; the rest of the time is different because there is nothing in the record to suggest that, even though pleasurably spent, it was spent in the ways the men would have chosen had they been free to do so.

There is no statutory provision as to what, if any, deference courts should pay to the Administrator's conclusions. And, while we have given them notice, we have had no occasion to try to prescribe their influence. The rulings of this Administrator are not reached as a result of hearing adversary proceedings in which he finds facts from evidence and reaches conclusions of law from findings of fact. They are not, of course, conclusive, even in the cases with which they directly deal, much less in those to which they apply only by analogy. They do not constitute an interpretation of the Act or a standard for judging factual situations which binds a district court's processes, as an authoritative pronouncement of a higher court might do. But the Administrator's policies are made in pursuance of official duty, based upon more specialized experience and broader investigations and information than is likely to come to a judge in a particular case. They do determine the policy which will guide applications for enforcement by injunction on behalf of the Government. . . . The fact that the Administrator's policies and standards are not reached by trial in adversary form does not mean that they are not entitled to respect. This Court has long given considerable and in some cases decisive weight to Treasury Decisions and to interpretative regulations of the Treasury and of other bodies that were not of adversary origin.

We consider that the rulings, interpretations and opinions of the Administrator under this Act, while not controlling upon the courts by reason of their authority, do constitute a body of experience and informed judgment to which courts and litigants may properly resort for guidance. The weight of such a judgment in a particular case will depend upon the thoroughness evident in its consideration, the validity of its reasoning, its consistency with earlier and later pronouncements, and all those factors which give it power to persuade, if lacking power to control. . . .

. . . [I]n this case, although the District Court referred to the Administrator's Bulletin, its evaluation and inquiry were apparently restricted by its notion that waiting time may not be work, an understanding of the law which we hold to be erroneous. Accordingly, the judgment is reversed and the cause remanded for further proceedings consistent herewith.

Notes and Questions

1.   *How much deference is this?* *Skidmore* stands for the proposition that a reviewing court should give an agency's legal interpretation of its governing statute "respect," and while such interpretations are not "controlling," they "constitute a body of experience and informed judgment to which courts and litigants may properly resort for guidance." The weight given such judgments depends "upon the thoroughness evident in its consideration, the validity of its reasoning, its consistency with earlier and later pronouncements, and all those factors which give it power to persuade, if lacking power to control." The theory behind such "deference" or "weight" or "respect" is that by virtue of developing expertise in administering a particular statute, an agency may have important insights into the meaning of the statute. How much "deference" is this? Is the ultimate interpretive power with the courts? Is *Skidmore* deference a "thumb on the scales" in favor of the agency, or something more? Is an agency pronouncement under *Skidmore* entitled to more respect than a persuasive litigant's brief?

2.   *Cases prior to* Skidmore. Although *Skidmore* is by far the most famous of the early deference cases, the Supreme Court confronted the question of deference in other prominent cases. In NLRB v. Hearst Publications, 322 U.S. 111 (1944), the Court dealt with the National Labor Relations Board's interpretation of the term "employee" in the National Labor Relations Act. Hearst Publications argued that newsboys were not employees because at common law they would be considered independent contractors. The Court first held—as a pure matter of statutory construction—that the term "employee" in the Act does not necessarily incorporate the common-law distinction between employee and independent contractor. The Court then held, "Undoubtedly questions of statutory interpretation, especially when arising in the first instance in judicial proceedings, are for the courts to resolve, giving appropriate weight to the judgment of those whose special duty is to administer the questioned statute." Id. at 130–31. The Court went on to say, however, that "where the question is one of specific application of a *broad statutory term* in a proceeding in which the agency administering the statute must determine it initially, the reviewing court's function is limited." Id. at 131 (emphasis added).

Is the Court here distinguishing between two situations—those involving ordinary statutory interpretation, and those involving "broad statutory terms," perhaps like "reasonable," "practicable," and "in the public interest"? Is the word "employee" a broad statutory term? Is the word "work"? What about the word "family"? Note that these words include a set of mandated or required applications; "family," at a minimum, means "nuclear" family. These words also include a set of excluded applications; "family," no matter how one cuts it, does not include individuals with no genetic or marriage ties. But if the statute does not say anything else, what is the agency to do with in-laws? With first cousins? Assuming the statute provides no further guidance, within the space between those applications that are mandated and those that are prohibited, is it not a *policy* question whether to include first cousins or in-laws? And if it's a policy question and not truly an interpretive one, doesn't deference to agency judgments make sense? Is that what happened in *Hearst*? See Peter L. Strauss, *"Deference" Is Too Confusing—Let's Call Them "Chevron Space" and "Skidmore Weight,"* 112 Colum. L. Rev. 1143 (2012).

In Gray v. Powell, 314 U.S. 402 (1941), the Bituminous Coal Act of 1937 exempted from its requirements a "producer-consumer," i.e. those who produced and consumed their own coal. The question was whether a railroad company which had leased lands and mining equipment and contracted with an operator to mine the land's coal exclusively for the railroad's use counted as such a "producer-consumer." The agency concluded that the railroad was a consumer of coal, but not a producer. The Court observed that there were clear examples of separation and clear examples of unity between producers and consumers: "The separation of production and consumption is complete when a buyer obtains supplies from a seller totally free from buyer connection. Their identity is undoubted when the consumer extracts coal from its own land with its own employees." Id. at 413. "Between the two extremes," however, "are the innumerable variations that bring the arrangements closer to one pole or the other of the range between exemption and inclusion. To determine upon which side of the median line the particular instance falls calls for the expert experienced judgment of those familiar with the industry." Id. Is this another example of a court deciding for itself what is mandated by the statutory term and what is prohibited, leaving everything between the two for the agency to decide? Was the question of whether a certain factual arrangement made the railroad a consumer merely, or rather a producer-consumer, a factual question? Was it a policy question? A legal question? Does it matter?

How do you distinguish *Hearst, Gray,* and *Skidmore* from Packard Motor Car Co. v. NLRB, 330 U.S. 485 (1947)? In that case, the Court evaluated the

NLRB's conclusion that foremen were "employees" as opposed to "employers" under the National Labor Relations Act such that they could engage in collective bargaining. The Court had to interpret the same term—"employees"—as the Court did in *Hearst,* and yet the Court did not give any deference to the NLRB's interpretation. In fact, it did not even address the question of how much deference an agency receives on such matters. Is the distinction between employer and employee more amenable to judicial resolution than is the distinction between employee and independent contractor? Or was the Court just being inconsistent?

3. *Judicial inconsistency.* As the discussion of *Packard Motor Car Co.* might suggest, the Supreme Court's approach to deference seems to have varied considerably through 1983. Sometimes the Court deferred to an agency's construction of its statute, see, e.g., Bonanno Linen Service v. NLRB, 454 U.S. 404 (1982); INS v. Wang, 450 U.S. 139 (1981); Ford Motor Co. v. NLRB, 441 U.S. 488 (1979), and at other times the Court independently construed the statute, see, e.g., Dirks v. SEC, 463 U.S. 646 (1983); NLRB v. Bell Aerospace Co. Div. of Textron, Inc., 416 U.S. 267 (1974). That all changed with the issuance of the following landmark opinion.

Chevron USA, Inc. v. Natural Resources Defense Council, Inc.

467 U.S. 837 (1984)

JUSTICE STEVENS delivered the opinion of the Court.

In the Clean Air Act Amendments of 1977, Congress enacted certain requirements applicable to States that had not achieved the national air quality standards established by the Environmental Protection Agency (EPA) pursuant to earlier legislation. The amended Clean Air Act required these "nonattainment" States to establish a permit program regulating "new or modified major stationary sources" of air pollution. Generally, a permit may not be issued for a new or modified major stationary source unless several stringent conditions are met. The EPA regulation promulgated to implement this permit requirement allows a State to adopt a plantwide definition of the term "stationary source." Under this definition, an existing plant that contains several pollution-emitting devices may install or modify one piece of equipment without meeting the permit conditions if the alteration will not increase the total emissions from the plant. The question presented by these cases is whether EPA's decision to allow States to treat all of the pollution-emitting devices within the same industrial grouping as though they were encased within a single "bubble" is based on a reasonable construction of the statutory term "stationary source."

I

The EPA regulations containing the plantwide definition of the term stationary source were promulgated on October 14, 1981. . . . The Court of Appeals set aside the regulations. *Natural Resources Defense Council, Inc. v. Gorsuch*, 685 F.2d 718 (D.C. Cir. 1982).

The court observed that the relevant part of the amended Clean Air Act "does not explicitly define what Congress envisioned as a 'stationary source, to which the permit program . . . should apply," and further stated that the precise issue was not "squarely addressed in the legislative history." In light of its conclusion that the legislative history bearing on the question was "at best contradictory," it reasoned that "the purposes of the nonattainment program should guide our decision here." Based on two of its precedents concerning the applicability of the bubble concept to certain Clean Air Act programs, the court stated that the bubble concept was "mandatory" in programs designed merely to maintain existing air quality, but held that it was "inappropriate" in programs enacted to improve air quality. Since the purpose of the permit program—its "raison d'être," in the court's view—was to improve air quality, the court held that the bubble concept was inapplicable in these cases under its prior precedents. It therefore set aside the regulations embodying the bubble concept as contrary to law. We granted certiorari to review that judgment, and we now reverse.

The basic legal error of the Court of Appeals was to adopt a static judicial definition of the term "stationary source" when it had decided that Congress itself had not commanded that definition. . . .

II

When a court reviews an agency's construction of the statute which it administers, it is confronted with two questions. First, always, is the question whether Congress has directly spoken to the precise question at issue. If the intent of Congress is clear, that is the end of the matter; for the court, as well as the agency, must give effect to the unambiguously expressed intent of Congress.[9] If, however, the court determines Congress has not directly addressed the precise question at issue, the court does not simply impose its own construction on the statute, as would be necessary in the absence of an administrative interpretation. Rather, if the statute is silent or ambiguous with respect to the specific issue, the question for the court is whether the agency's answer is based on a permissible construction of the statute.[11]

"The power of an administrative agency to administer a congressionally created . . . program necessarily requires the formulation of policy and the making of rules to fill any gap left, implicitly or explicitly, by Congress." *Morton v. Ruiz*, 415 U.S. 199, 231 (1974). If Congress has explicitly left a gap for the agency to fill, there is an express delegation of authority to the agency to elucidate a specific provision of the statute by regulation. Such legislative regulations are given controlling weight unless they are arbitrary, capricious, or manifestly contrary to the statute. Sometimes the legislative delegation to an agency on a particular question is implicit rather than explicit. In such a case, a court may not substitute its own construction of a statutory provision for a reasonable interpretation made by the administrator of an agency.

We have long recognized that considerable weight should be accorded to an executive department's construction of a statutory scheme it is entrusted to administer, and the principle of deference to administrative interpretations

> has been consistently followed by this Court whenever decision as to the meaning or reach of a statute has involved reconciling conflicting policies, and a full understanding of the force of the statutory policy in the given situation has depended upon more than ordinary knowledge respecting the matters subjected to agency regulations.

> . . . If this choice represents a reasonable accommodation of conflicting policies that were committed to the agency's care by the statute, we should not disturb it unless it appears from the statute or its

---

[9]   The judiciary is the final authority on issues of statutory construction and must reject administrative constructions which are contrary to clear congressional intent. [Numerous citations omitted.—Ed.] If a court, employing traditional tools of statutory construction, ascertains that Congress had an intention on the precise question at issue, that intention is the law and must be given effect.

[11]   The court need not conclude that the agency construction was the only one it permissibly could have adopted to uphold the construction, or even the reading the court would have reached if the question initially had arisen in a judicial proceeding. [Citations omitted.—Ed.]

legislative history that the accommodation is not one that Congress would have sanctioned.

In light of these well-settled principles it is clear that the Court of Appeals misconceived the nature of its role in reviewing the regulations at issue. Once it determined, after its own examination of the legislation, that Congress did not actually have an intent regarding the applicability of the bubble concept to the permit program, the question before it was not whether in its view the concept is "inappropriate" in the general context of a program designed to improve air quality, but whether the Administrator's view that it is appropriate in the context of this particular program is a reasonable one. Based on the examination of the legislation and its history which follows, we agree with the Court of Appeals that Congress did not have a specific intention on the applicability of the bubble concept in these cases, and conclude that the EPA's use of that concept here is a reasonable policy choice for the agency to make.

III

In the 1950's and the 1960's Congress enacted a series of statutes designed to encourage and to assist the States in curtailing air pollution. . . . Section 109 of the 1970 Amendments directed the EPA to promulgate National Ambient Air Quality Standards (NAAQS's) and § 110 directed the States to develop plans (SIP's) to implement the standards within specified deadlines. In addition, § 111 provided that major new sources of pollution would be required to conform to technology-based performance standards; the EPA was directed to publish a list of categories of sources of pollution and to establish new source performance standards (NSPS) for each. Section 111(e) prohibited the operation of any new source in violation of a performance standard.

Section 111(a) defined the terms that are to be used in setting and enforcing standards of performance for new stationary sources. It provided: "For purposes of this section: . . . . (3) The term 'stationary source' means any building, structure, facility, or installation which emits or may emit any air pollutant."

In the 1970 Amendments that definition was not only applicable to the NSPS program required by § 111, but also was made applicable to a requirement of § 110 that each state implementation plan contain a procedure for reviewing the location of any proposed new source and preventing its construction if it would preclude the attainment or maintenance of national air quality standards. . . .

The 1970 legislation provided for the attainment of primary NAAQS's by 1975. In many areas of the country, particularly the most industrialized States, the statutory goals were not attained. In 1976, the 94th Congress was confronted with this fundamental problem . . . .

IV

The Clean Air Act Amendments of 1977 are a lengthy, detailed, technical, complex, and comprehensive response to a major social issue. A small portion of the statute . . . expressly deals with nonattainment areas. The focal point of this controversy is one phrase in that portion of the Amendments. . . .

Most significantly for our purposes, the statute provided that each [state implementation] plan shall "(6) require permits for the construction and operation of new or modified major stationary sources in accordance with section 173. . . ."

Before issuing a permit, § 173 requires . . . the state agency to determine that there will be sufficient emissions reductions in the region to offset the emissions from the new source and also to allow for reasonable further progress toward attainment . . . .

The 1977 Amendments contain no specific reference to the "bubble concept." Nor do they contain a specific definition of the term "stationary source," though they did not disturb the definition of "stationary source" contained in § 111(a)(3), applicable by the terms of the Act to the NSPS program. Section 302(j), however, defines the term "major stationary source" as follows:

(j) Except as otherwise expressly provided, the terms 'major stationary source' and 'major emitting facility' mean any stationary facility or source of air pollutants which directly emits, or has the potential to emit, one hundred tons per year or more of any air pollutant (including any major emitting facility or source of fugitive emissions of any such pollutant, as determined by rule by the Administrator).

V

The legislative history of the portion of the 1977 Amendments dealing with nonattainment areas does not contain any specific comment on the "bubble concept" or the question whether a plantwide definition of a stationary source is permissible under the permit program. It does, however, plainly disclose that in the permit program Congress sought to accommodate the conflict between the economic interest in permitting capital improvements to continue and the environmental interest in improving air quality. . . .

VI

. . . [P]rior to the 1977 Amendments, the EPA had adhered to a plantwide definition of the term "source" under a NSPS program. After adoption of the 1977 Amendments, proposals for a plantwide definition were considered in at least three formal proceedings. . . .

* * *

In August 1980 . . . the EPA adopted a regulation that, in essence, applied the basic reasoning of the Court of Appeals in these cases. The EPA took particular note of the two then-recent Court of Appeals decisions, which had created the bright-line rule that the "bubble concept" should be employed in a program designed to maintain air quality but not in one designed to enhance air quality. Relying heavily on those cases, EPA adopted a dual definition of "source" for nonattainment areas that required a permit whenever a change in either the entire plant, or one of its components, would result in a significant increase in emissions even if the increase was completely offset by reductions elsewhere in the plant. The EPA expressed the opinion that this interpretation was "more consistent with congressional intent" than the plantwide definition because it "would bring in more sources or modifications for review," but its primary legal analysis was predicated on the two Court of Appeals decisions.

In 1981 a new administration took office and initiated a "Government-wide reexamination of regulatory burdens and complexities." 46 Fed. Reg. 16281. In the context of that review, the EPA reevaluated the various arguments that had been advanced in connection with the proper definition of the term "source" and concluded that the term should be given the same definition in both nonattainment areas and PSD [preventing significant deterioration] areas.

In explaining its conclusion, the EPA first noted that the definitional issue was not squarely addressed in either the statute or its legislative history and therefore that the issue involved an agency "judgment as how to best carry out the Act." It then set forth several reasons for concluding that the plantwide definition was more appropriate. It pointed out that the dual definition "can act as a disincentive to new investment and modernization by discouraging modifications to existing facilities" and "can actually retard progress in air pollution control by discouraging replacement of older, dirtier processes or pieces of equipment with new, cleaner ones." Moreover, the new definition "would simplify EPA's rules by using the same definition of 'source' for PSD, nonattainment new source review and the construction moratorium. This reduces confusion and inconsistency." Finally, the agency explained that additional requirements that remained in place would accomplish the fundamental purposes of achieving attainment with NAAQS's as expeditiously as possible. These conclusions were expressed in a proposed rulemaking in August 1981 that was formally promulgated in October.

VII

In this Court [the NRDC et al.] expressly reject the basic rationale of the Court of Appeals' decision. That court viewed the statutory definition of the term "source" as sufficiently flexible to cover either a plantwide definition, a narrower definition covering each unit within a plant, or a dual definition that could apply to both the entire "bubble" and its components. It interpreted the policies of the statute, however, to mandate the plantwide definition in programs designed to maintain clean air and to forbid it in programs designed to improve air quality. [NRDC et al.] place a fundamentally different construction on the statute. They contend that the text of the Act requires the EPA to use a dual definition—if either a component of a plant, or the plant as a whole, emits over 100 tons of pollutant, it is a major stationary source. They thus contend that the EPA rules adopted in 1980, insofar as they apply to the maintenance of the quality of clean air, as well as the 1981 rules which apply to nonattainment areas, violate the statute.

The definition of the term "stationary source" in § 111(a)(3) refers to "any building, structure, facility, or installation" which emits air pollution. This definition is applicable only to the NSPS program by the express terms of the statute; the text of the statute does not make this definition applicable to the permit program. [The EPA] therefore maintain[s] that there is no statutory language even relevant to ascertaining the meaning of stationary source in the permit program aside from § 302(j), which defines the term "major stationary source." We disagree with [EPA] on this point.

The definition in § 302(j) tells us what the word "major" means—a source must emit at least 100 tons of pollution to qualify—but it sheds virtually no light on the meaning of the term "stationary source." It does equate a source with a facility—a "major emitting facility" and a "major stationary source" are synonymous under § 302(j). The ordinary meaning of the term "facility" is some collection of integrated elements which has been designed and constructed to achieve some purpose. Moreover, it is certainly no affront to common English usage to take a reference to a major facility or a major source to connote an entire plant as opposed to its constituent parts. Basically, however, the language of § 302(j) simply does not compel any given interpretation of the term "source."

[NRDC et al.] recognize that, and hence point to § 111(a)(3). Although the definition in that section is not literally applicable to the permit program, it sheds as much light on the meaning of the word "source" as anything in the statute. As [they] point out, use of the words "building, structure, facility, or installation," as the definition of source, could be read to impose the permit conditions on an individual building that is a part of a plant. . . . The language may reasonably be interpreted to impose the requirement on any discrete, but integrated, operation which pollutes. This gives meaning to all of the terms—a single building, not part of a larger operation, would be covered if it emits more than 100 tons of pollution, as would any facility, structure, or installation. Indeed, the language itself implies a "bubble concept" of sorts: each enumerated item would seem to be treated as if it were encased in a bubble. While respondents insist that each of these terms must be given a discrete meaning, they also argue that § 111(a)(3) defines "source" as that term is used in § 302(j). The latter section, however, equates a source with a facility, whereas the former defines "source" as a facility, among other items.

We are not persuaded that parsing of general terms in the text of the statute will reveal an actual intent of Congress. We know full well that this language is not dispositive; the terms are overlapping and the language is not precisely directed to the question of the applicability of a given term in the context of a larger operation. To the extent any congressional "intent" can be discerned from this language, it would appear that the listing of overlapping, illustrative terms was intended to enlarge, rather than to confine, the scope of the agency's power to regulate particular sources in order to effectuate the policies of the Act. . . .

Our review of the EPA's varying interpretations of the word "source"— both before and after the 1977 Amendments—convinces us that the agency primarily responsible for administering this important legislation has consistently interpreted it flexibly—not in a sterile textual vacuum, but in the context of implementing policy decisions in a technical and complex arena. The fact that the agency has from time to time changed its interpretation of the term "source" does not, as [NRDC et al.] argue, lead us to conclude that no deference should be accorded the agency's interpretation of the statute. An initial agency interpretation is not instantly carved in stone. On the contrary, the agency, to engage in informed rulemaking, must consider varying interpretations and the wisdom of its policy on a continuing basis. Moreover, the fact that the agency has adopted different definitions in different contexts adds force to the argument that the definition itself is flexible, particularly since Congress has never indicated any disapproval of a flexible reading of the statute.

Significantly, it was not the agency in 1980, but rather the Court of Appeals that read the statute inflexibly to command a plantwide definition for programs designed to maintain clean air and to forbid such a definition for programs designed to improve air quality. The distinction the court drew may well be a sensible one, but our labored review of the problem has surely disclosed that it is not a distinction that Congress ever articulated itself, or one that the EPA found in the statute before the courts began to review the legislative work product. . . .

In these cases, the Administrator's interpretation represents a reasonable accommodation of manifestly competing interests and is entitled to deference: the regulatory scheme is technical and complex, the agency considered the matter in a detailed and reasoned fashion, and the decision involves reconciling conflicting policies. Congress intended to accommodate both interests, but did not do so itself on the level of specificity presented by these cases. Perhaps that body consciously desired the Administrator to strike the balance at this level, thinking that those with great expertise and charged with responsibility for administering the provision would be in a better position to do so; perhaps it simply did not consider the question at this level; and perhaps Congress was unable to forge a coalition on either side of the question, and those on each side decided to take their chances with the scheme devised by the agency. For judicial purposes, it matters not which of these things occurred.

Judges are not experts in the field, and are not part of either political branch of the Government. Courts must, in some cases, reconcile competing political interests, but not on the basis of the judges' personal policy preferences. In contrast, an agency to which Congress has delegated policy-making responsibilities may, within the limits of that delegation, properly rely upon the incumbent administration's views of wise policy to inform its judgments. While agencies are not directly accountable to the people, the Chief Executive is, and it is entirely appropriate for this political branch of the Government to make such policy choices—resolving the competing interests which Congress itself either inadvertently did not resolve, or intentionally left to be resolved by the agency charged with the administration of the statute in light of everyday realities.

When a challenge to an agency construction of a statutory provision, fairly conceptualized, really centers on the wisdom of the agency's policy, . . . the challenge must fail. In such a case, federal judges—who have no constituency—have a duty to respect legitimate policy choices made by those who do. The responsibilities for assessing the wisdom of such policy choices and resolving the struggle between competing views of the public interest are not judicial ones . . . .

We hold that the EPA's definition of the term "source" is a permissible construction of the statute which seeks to accommodate progress in reducing air pollution with economic growth. . . .

NOTES AND QUESTIONS

1. Summary. *Chevron*'s two-step formulation is now canonical: "When a court reviews an agency's construction of the statute which it administers, it is confronted with two questions. First, always, is the question whether Congress has directly spoken to the precise question at issue. If the intent of Congress is clear, that is the end of the matter; for the court, as well as the agency, must give effect to the unambiguously expressed intent of Congress. If, however, the court determines Congress has not directly addressed the precise question at issue, the court does not simply impose its own construction on the statute, as would be necessary in the absence of an administrative interpretation. Rather, if the statute is silent or ambiguous with respect to the specific issue, the question for the court is whether the agency's

> **PRACTICE POINTER** If you are representing an agency, it is in your interest to make the standard of review as deferential as possible. If you are challenging an agency, you will want to convince the courts not to be excessively deferential to the agency.

answer is based on a permissible construction of the statute." In "step one" of the *Chevron* analysis, in other words, the court is to determine if the statute is clear about the question at hand—does it clearly preclude the agency's choice, or perhaps require it? If the statute is not clear on the matter—usually it is said if the statute is "ambiguous"—then the courts must defer to an agency's reasonable interpretation. In "step two," therefore—which takes place after a statute has been determined to be ambiguous—the court decides if the agency's interpretation is "reasonable."

2. *Is* **Chevron** *really two steps?* The first question that often arises is whether the *Chevron* analysis is really two steps. Isn't it just a single step? If at "step one" the court concludes that the statute is ambiguous on the question—that is, the statute does not clearly preclude the agency's choice—isn't the agency's interpretation therefore "reasonable"? In other words, doesn't the analysis boil down to this single question: is the agency's interpretation reasonable? If the statute clearly precludes the agency's interpretation, then it's quite clearly unreasonable. What else is there to do at "step two" of the analysis? See, e.g., Matthew C. Stephenson & Adrian Vermeule, Chevron *Has Only One Step*, 95 Va. L. Rev. 597 (2009); but see Kenneth A. Bamberger & Peter L. Strauss, Chevron's *Two Steps*, 95 Va. L. Rev. 611 (2009). We shall return to this question after reading more cases applying the *Chevron* framework.

3. **Chevron**'s *footnotes.* Two important footnotes were included in the case excerpt. In footnote 11, the Court makes exceptionally clear the import of the *Chevron* framework: even if the agency's interpretation is not the *best* interpretation—even if it is not the interpretation that the Court itself would have chosen as the best reading of the statute—the agency interpretation is upheld anyway (so long as it is reasonable). Can you square that with footnote 9, which said not only that the courts decide matters of statutory interpretation, but that they must use all the traditional tools of statutory interpretation? If a court arrives at a "best" reading of a statute using all the tools of statutory interpretation, does it nevertheless defer so long as that reading is not the only possible one? How plausible must the alternative reading be?

4. *Is* **Chevron** *deference constitutional?* The *Chevron* framework has been considered by some judges and scholars to be an abdication of the judicial duty to interpret law. Can you square the decision with the text of the APA, which provides that courts "shall decide all relevant questions of law, interpret constitutional and statutory provisions, and determine the meaning or applicability of

the terms of an agency action," 5 U.S.C. § 706? And what about the requirements of Article III? Justice Thomas wrote in a recent case that "[i]nterpreting federal statutes—including ambiguous ones administered by an agency—'calls for that exercise of independent judgment.' " Michigan v. EPA, 576 U.S. 743, 761 (2015) (Thomas, J., concurring) (citation omitted). According to Thomas, *Chevron* deference "wrests from Courts the ultimate interpretative authority," and that "[s]uch a transfer is in tension with Article III's Vesting Clause, which vests the judicial power exclusively in Article III courts, not administrative agencies." Id at 762. What do you think? We shall return to these issues later on, after reading some additional cases applying the *Chevron* framework.

5.   *Precedents for judicial deference?* One justification the Court offered in *Chevron* in favor of its deference framework was prior precedent. The Court wrote, "We have long recognized that considerable weight should be accorded to an executive department's construction of a statutory scheme it is entrusted to administer." Does that sound right to you? It's not at all clear that many (if any) cases had previously held that an agency interpretation stands even if it violates what the courts understand to be the *best* reading of the statute. Recall *Skidmore*, in which the Court gave the administrator's interpretation weight to the extent it was persuasive. Recall also one of our statutory interpretation lessons: it was a traditional tool of statutory interpretation to give some weight to executive interpretations contemporaneous with a law's enactment, as well as longstanding executive interpretations, because such interpretations were good evidence of what the law actually was. See generally Aditya Bamzai, *The Origins of Judicial Deference to Executive Interpretation,* 126 Yale L.J. 908 (2017). But in *Chevron*, the Court openly acknowledged that the EPA had been shifting its position on the bubble concept, and held, "An initial agency interpretation is not instantly carved in stone. On the contrary, the agency, to engage in informed rulemaking, must consider varying interpretations and the wisdom of its policy on a continuing basis." Is that consistent, or inconsistent, with the contemporaneous exposition and longstanding usage canons?

> **CROSS REFERENCE**
> Recall the contemporaneous and longstanding interpretation canons of construction. What is the relation of those canons to the principle announced in *Chevron*? Are these different principles?

6. *Mandamus justifications?* Justice Scalia once sought to root *Chevron* deference in old mandamus cases where the courts would refuse to compel the executive to interpret the law in a particular way. United States v. Mead, 533 U.S. 218, 242 (2001) (Scalia, J., dissenting). The mandamus precedents don't quite say what *Chevron* does, however. As the reader might recall from *Marbury v. Madison*, mandamus is a rare remedy used to compel executive action where the task at hand is "ministerial" and clearly required by law. If the executive officer had discretion, however, there could be no mandamus. Thus, courts sometimes refused to grant writs of mandamus

 Defined Term

MANDAMUS: A relatively rare judicial remedy whereby courts compel executive or judicial officers to undertake duties where the law does not leave the officer any discretion in the matter.

compelling the executive to adopt particular interpretations of statutes because legal interpretation requires a lot of discretion and judgment. But, in ordinary, non-mandamus lawsuits involving private rights, the courts would nevertheless interpret the statutes for themselves.

A classic example of this is the case of Decatur v. Paulding, 39 U.S. (14 Pet.) 497 (1840). There, the Court was confronted with two statutes, one which granted a pension to all widows of naval service members, and another which granted a pension specifically to the widow of Commodore Stephen Decatur. Mrs. Decatur sought to collect both pensions. The Court recognized that the interpretation of this law could leave room for discretion and even disagreement, and thus the Court would not compel the executive to adopt one interpretation over another through a writ of mandamus. But the Court also noted that had a non-mandamus action been brought, then "the Court certainly would not be bound to adopt the construction given by the head of a department" because in such cases it is the judges' "duty to interpret the act of Congress, in order to ascertain the rights of the parties in the cause before them." Id. at 515. In the very next year the Supreme Court again held that notwithstanding "the uniform construction" given to an act by the treasury department for two decades, "the judicial department has imposed upon it by the constitution, the solemn duty to interpret the laws, . . . however disagreeable that duty may be, in cases where its own judgment shall differ from that of other high functionaries." United States v. Dickson, 40 U.S. (15 Pet.) 141, 161–62 (1841).

7. *Interpretation or policy?* Perhaps defenses of the *Chevron* doctrine will have to be found elsewhere. The Court also said the following: "When a challenge to an agency construction of a statutory provision, fairly conceptualized, really centers on the wisdom of the agency's policy, . . . the challenge must fail." The Court here seems to suggest that some questions of interpretation are really questions of policy. This is a classic argument of the legal realists. As Cass Sunstein has written, the Court's rationales in *Chevron* amount to "a candid recognition that assessments of policy are sometimes indispensable to statutory interpretation." Cass R. Sunstein, *Beyond* Marbury: *The Executive's Power to Say What the Law Is,* 115 Yale L.J. 2580, 2587 (2006). This recognition is rooted in the arguments of the legal realists like Max Radin and Ernst Freund, who argued that "the inevitable ambiguities of language" make the interpretation of law "a controlling factor in the effect of legislative instruments," and thus make courts a "rival organ with the legislature in the development of the written law." Id. Supposing that the legal realists "were broadly right" to suggest that policymaking inheres in interpreting statutory ambiguity, Sunstein writes, "then there seems to be little reason to think that courts, rather than the executive, should be making the key judgments." Id. at 2592.

Do you agree? Is it impossible to separate interpretation from policymaking? Are all statutes so ambiguous or vague that one's choice of interpretation is inherently a legislative-type choice? Many scholars today argue that resolving "ambiguities" in statutes calls for policymaking. See, e.g., Kenneth A. Bamberger & Peter L. Strauss, Chevron's *Two Steps,* 95 Va. L. Rev. 611, 617 (2009); Henry P. Monaghan, Marbury *and the Administrative State,* 83 Colum. L. Rev. 1, 6–7, 26–28 (1983); Jonathan R. Siegel, *The Constitutional Case for* Chevron *Deference,* 71 Vand. L. Rev. 937, 963–65 (2018).

Maybe we can distinguish between interpretation and policymaking, but what's often at issue in these cases is in fact policymaking and not interpretation. If what's going on is really some kind of policymaking, then indeed it's hard to see why courts would be uniquely suited to the task. Thus, one could defend *Chevron* on the ground that agencies are more institutionally competent, as well as more politically accountable, than courts in making such policy decisions. As the Court in *Chevron* itself said, "Judges are not experts in the field, and are not part of either political branch of the Government."

What do you think? Is it possible that what the agencies are really doing when they are implementing broad statutory terms or filling gaps in statutes is *not* interpretation? When a statute requires an agency to act "reasonably" or "in the public interest," no one doubts the *meaning* of these terms; the disagreement is over whether particular *policies* are in fact reasonable or in the public interest. That is not an "interpretive" question, but rather a legislative question. In other words, when there's a broad statutory term, isn't the agency exercising a kind of legislative, or quasi-legislative, power? Go back to the questions in *Hearst* and *Gray*: were those interpretive questions, or more questions of policy?

8. *Implicit delegations.* Another rationale for deference is that statutory ambiguities are implicit delegations from Congress to agencies. As the Court wrote, "If Congress has explicitly left a gap for the agency to fill, there is an express delegation of authority to the agency to elucidate a specific provision of the statute by regulation. . . . Sometimes the legislative delegation to an agency on a particular question is implicit rather than explicit." Yet, if these are interpretive questions, can it really be said Congress intended to delegate power to agencies to resolve such questions? In fact, didn't Congress say the opposite in the APA? Does this rationale depend on such questions truly being policy questions, not interpretive ones?

The courts must defer not only to an agency's reasonable interpretation of a statute that it administers, but also to an agency's reasonable interpretation of its own regulations. The Court explained that doctrine in the following case.

Auer v. Robbins

519 U.S. 452 (1997)

Justice Scalia delivered the opinion of the Court.

The Fair Labor Standards Act of 1938 (FLSA) exempts "bona fide executive, administrative, or professional" employees from overtime pay requirements. This case presents the question whether the Secretary of Labor's "salary-basis" test for determining an employee's exempt status reflects a permissible reading of the statute as it applies to public-sector employees. We also consider whether the Secretary has reasonably interpreted the salary-basis test to deny an employee salaried status (and thus grant him overtime pay) when his compensation may "as a practical matter" be adjusted in ways inconsistent with the test.

I

Petitioners are sergeants and a lieutenant employed by the St. Louis Police Department. They brought suit in 1988 against respondents, members of the St. Louis Board of Police Commissioners, seeking payment of overtime pay that they claimed was owed under § 7(a)(1) of the FLSA, 29 U.S.C. § 207(a)(1). Respondents argued that petitioners were not entitled to such pay because they came within the exemption provided by § 213(a)(1) for "bona fide executive, administrative, or professional" employees.

Under regulations promulgated by the Secretary, one requirement for exempt status under § 213(a)(1) is that the employee earn a specified minimum amount on a "salary basis." 29 C.F.R. §§ 541.1(f), 541.2(e), 541.3(e) (1996). According to the regulations, "[a]n employee will be considered to be paid 'on a salary basis' . . . if under his employment agreement he regularly receives each pay period on a weekly, or less frequent basis, a predetermined amount constituting all or part of his compensation, which amount is not subject to reduction because of variations in the quality or quantity of the work performed." § 541.118(a). Petitioners contended that the salary-basis test was not met in their case because, under the terms of the St. Louis Metropolitan Police Department Manual, their compensation could be reduced for a variety of disciplinary infractions related to the "quality or quantity" of work performed. Petitioners also claimed that they did not meet the other requirement for exempt status under § 213(a)(1): that their duties be of an executive, administrative, or professional nature. . . .

II

The FLSA grants the Secretary broad authority to "defin[e] and delimi[t]" the scope of the exemption for executive, administrative, and professional employees. § 213(a)(1). Under the Secretary's chosen approach, exempt status requires that the employee be paid on a salary basis, which in turn requires that his compensation not be subject to reduction because of variations in the "quality or quantity of the work performed," 29 C.F.R. § 541.118(a) (1996). Because the regulation goes on to carve out an exception from this rule for "[p]enalties imposed . . . for infractions of safety rules of major significance," § 541.118(a)(5), it is clear that the rule embraces reductions in pay for disciplinary violations. The Secretary is of the view that employees whose pay is adjusted for disciplinary reasons do not deserve exempt status because as a general matter true "executive, administrative, or professional" employees are not "disciplined" by piecemeal deductions from their pay, but are terminated, demoted, or given restricted assignments. . . .

A

. . . . Respondents . . . contend . . . that the "no disciplinary deductions" element of the salary-basis test is invalid for public-sector employees because as applied to them it reflects an unreasonable interpretation of the statutory exemption. That is so, they say, because the ability to adjust public-sector employees' pay—even executive, administrative or professional employees' pay—as a means of enforcing compliance with work rules is a necessary component of effective government. In the public-sector context, they contend, fewer disciplinary alternatives to deductions in pay are available.

Because Congress has not "directly spoken to the precise question at issue," we must sustain the Secretary's approach so long as it is "based on a permissible construction of the statute." *Chevron U.S.A. Inc. v. Natural Resources Defense Council, Inc.,* 467 U.S. 837, 842–843 (1984). While respondents' objections would perhaps support a different application of the salary-basis test for public employees, we cannot conclude that they compel it. The Secretary's view that public employers are not *so* differently situated with regard to disciplining their employees as to require wholesale revision of his time-tested rule simply cannot be said to be unreasonable. . . .

III

A primary issue in the litigation unleashed by application of the salary-basis test to public-sector employees has been whether, under that test, an employee's pay is "subject to" disciplinary or other deductions whenever there exists a theoretical possibility of such deductions, or rather only when there is something more to suggest that the employee is actually vulnerable to having his pay reduced. Petitioners in effect argue for something close to the former view; they contend that because the police manual nominally subjects all department employees to a range of disciplinary sanctions that includes disciplinary deductions in pay, and because a single sergeant was actually subjected to a disciplinary deduction, they are "subject to" such deductions and hence nonexempt under the FLSA. . . .

The Secretary of Labor, in an *amicus* brief filed at the request of the Court, interprets the salary-basis test to deny exempt status when employees are covered by a policy that permits disciplinary or other deductions in pay "as a practical matter." That standard is met, the Secretary says, if there is either an actual practice of making such deductions or an employment policy that creates a "significant likelihood" of such deductions. The Secretary's approach rejects a wooden requirement of actual deductions, but in their absence it requires a clear and particularized policy—one which "effectively communicates" that deductions will be made in specified circumstances. . . .

Because the salary-basis test is a creature of the Secretary's own regulations, his interpretation of it is, under our jurisprudence, controlling unless " 'plainly erroneous or inconsistent with the regulation.' " *Robertson v. Methow Valley Citizens Council*, 490 U.S. 332, 359 (1989) (quoting *Bowles v. Seminole Rock & Sand Co.*, 325 U.S. 410, 414 (1945)). That deferential standard is easily met here. The critical phrase "subject to" comfortably bears the meaning the Secretary assigns.

The Secretary's approach is usefully illustrated by reference to this case. The policy on which petitioners rely is contained in a section of the police manual that lists a total of 58 possible rule violations and specifies the range of penalties associated with each. All department employees are nominally covered by the manual, and some of the specified penalties involve disciplinary deductions in pay. Under the Secretary's view, that is not enough to render petitioners' pay "subject to" disciplinary deductions within the meaning of the salary-basis test. This is so because the manual does not "effectively communicate" that pay deductions are an anticipated form of punishment for employees *in petitioners' category*, since it is perfectly possible to give full effect to every aspect of the manual without drawing any inference of that sort. If the statement of available penalties applied solely to petitioners, matters would be different; but since it applies both to petitioners and to employees who are unquestionably not paid on a salary basis, the expressed availability of disciplinary deductions may have reference only to the latter. No clear inference can be drawn as to the likelihood of a sanction's being applied to employees such as petitioners. Nor, under the Secretary's approach, is such a likelihood established by the one-time deduction in a sergeant's pay, under unusual circumstances.

Petitioners complain that the Secretary's interpretation comes to us in the form of a legal brief; but that does not, in the circumstances of this case, make it unworthy of deference. The Secretary's position is in no sense a "*post hoc* rationalizatio[n]" advanced by an agency seeking to defend past agency action against attack, *Bowen v. Georgetown Univ. Hospital*, 488 U.S. 204, 212 (1988). There is simply no reason to suspect that the interpretation does not reflect the agency's fair and considered judgment on the matter in question. . . .

NOTES AND QUESTIONS

1. **Seminole Rock.** *Auer* deference is the doctrine requiring courts to defer to reasonable interpretations of agency regulations. This is sometimes called *Seminole Rock* deference after Bowles v. Seminole Rock & Sand Co., 325 U.S. 410 (1945), cited in *Auer*. That case involved the interpretation of a World War II price control regulation setting the ceiling price for certain commodities as the highest price "charged" for those commodities in March of 1942. The question was whether such commodities also had to be *delivered* in March of 1942. The administrator said no, and the Court agreed, holding,

> Since this involves an interpretation of an administrative regulation a court must necessarily look to the administrative construction of the regulation if the meaning of the words used is in doubt. The intention of Congress or the principles of the Constitution in some situations may be relevant in the first instance in choosing between various constructions. But the ultimate criterion is the administrative interpretation, which becomes of controlling weight unless it is plainly erroneous or inconsistent with the regulation.

Id. at 413–14. In that case, however, the Court reviewed the statutory language for itself and concluded that it *compelled* the administrator's interpretation. Was the Court's statement about deference merely dicta?

2. Separation of powers questions. Scholars have argued that *Auer* deference raises distinct issues from *Chevron*. Under the latter doctrine, courts deal with an executive (agency) interpretation of a congressional statute; under the former, courts deal with an executive interpretation of an executive regulation. Does this raise more serious separation of powers concerns? Given how broadly Congress delegates power to agencies, does the *Auer* doctrine allow agencies to write their own laws, enforce those laws in front of their own adjudicators, and interpret those laws for themselves? Is that a problem? See John F. Manning, *Constitutional Structure and Judicial Deference to Agency Interpretations of Agency Rules,* 96 Colum. L. Rev. 612 (1996). The counter, of

FOR DISCUSSION

Do you agree with Professor Manning that *Auer* deference is more problematic than *Chevron* deference?

course, is that the agency, at least in theory, is not exercising legislative power at all; when it promulgates rules implementing a statutory standard it is exercising "executive" power. If it's all executive power, where is the violation of the separation of powers? If, as with *Chevron,* many of these questions are really policy questions, then isn't the agency more institutionally competent to fill the regulatory gaps?

3. Auer *still lives.* In 2019, many commentators thought that *Auer* deference was on its last legs given the widespread criticism of *Chevron* and the unique separation of powers issues involved with agency interpretations of agency regulations. In Kisor v. Wilkie, 139 S. Ct. 2400 (2019), however, the Supreme Court refused to overturn *Auer,* although it did limit the reach of the doctrine significantly. We shall encounter *Kisor* a bit later in the materials.

2. The *Chevron* Two-Step

The application of the *Chevron* doctrine raises many questions. This subsection examines three cases. The first, *Brand X,* deals with prior judicial interpretations of statutes and whether agencies may deviate from such prior interpretations under *Chevron.* It also raises the question of what exactly the courts do at "step two" of *Chevron,* and particularly its connection to "hard look" review. This question is then examined in more detail in the second case, *Encino Motorcars.* Finally, the third case, *FDA v. Brown & Williamson,* raises the issue of how courts are to engage in the first step of *Chevron:* do they use all the tools of statutory interpretation, or just some of them? How much ambiguity must exist to move from *Chevron*'s first step to its second step? What substantive interpretative canons can the courts deploy at the first step?

Nat'l Cable & Telecommunications Ass'n v. Brand X Internet Servs.

545 U.S. 967 (2005)

Justice Thomas delivered the opinion of the Court.

Title II of the Communications Act of 1934 subjects all providers of "telecommunications servic[e]" to mandatory common-carrier regulation, § 153(44). In the order under review, the Federal Communications Commission concluded that cable companies that sell broadband Internet service do not provide "telecommunications servic[e]" as the Communications Act defines that term, and hence are exempt from mandatory common-carrier regulation under Title II. We must decide whether that conclusion is a lawful construction of the Communications Act under *Chevron U.S.A. Inc. v. Natural Resources Defense Council, Inc.*, 467 U.S. 837 (1984), and the Administrative Procedure Act. We hold that it is.

I

The traditional means by which consumers in the United States access the network of interconnected computers that make up the Internet is through "dial-up" connections provided over local telephone facilities. Using these connections, consumers access the Internet by making calls with computer modems through the telephone wires owned by local phone companies. Internet service providers (ISPs), in turn, link those calls to the Internet network, not only by providing a physical connection, but also by offering consumers the ability to translate raw Internet data into information they may both view on their personal computers and transmit to other computers connected to the Internet. Technological limitations of local telephone wires, however, retard the speed at which data from the Internet may be transmitted through end users' dial-up connections. Dial-up connections are therefore known as "narrowband," or slower speed, connections.

"Broadband" Internet service, by contrast, transmits data at much higher speeds. There are two principal kinds of broadband Internet service: cable modem service and Digital Subscriber Line (DSL) service. Cable modem service transmits data between the Internet and users' computers via the network of television cable lines owned by cable companies. DSL service provides high-speed access using the local telephone wires owned by local telephone companies. Cable companies and telephone companies can either provide Internet access directly to consumers, thus acting as ISPs themselves, or can lease their transmission facilities to independent ISPs that then use the facilities to provide consumers with Internet access. Other ways of transmitting high-speed Internet data into homes, including terrestrial- and satellite-based wireless networks, are also emerging.

II

At issue in these cases is the proper regulatory classification under the Communications Act of broadband cable Internet service. The Act, as amended by the Telecommunications Act of 1996, defines two categories of regulated entities relevant to these cases: telecommunications carriers and information-service providers. The Act regulates telecommunications carriers, but not information-service providers, as common carriers. Telecommunications carriers, for example, must charge just and reasonable, nondiscriminatory rates to their customers, 47 U.S.C. §§ 201–209, design their systems so that other carriers can interconnect with their communications networks, § 251(a)(1), and contribute to the federal "universal service" fund, § 254(d). These provisions are mandatory, but the Commission must forbear from applying them if it determines that the public interest requires it. §§ 160(a), (b). Information-service providers, by contrast, are not subject to mandatory common-carrier regulation under Title II . . . .

These two statutory classifications originated in the late 1970's, as the Commission developed rules to regulate data-processing services offered over telephone wires. That regime . . . distinguished between "basic" service (like telephone service) and "enhanced" service (computer-processing service offered over telephone lines). The . . . rules defined both basic and enhanced services by reference to how the consumer perceives the service being offered.

In particular, the Commission defined "basic service" as "a pure transmission capability over a communications path that is virtually transparent in terms of its interaction with customer supplied information." By "pure" or "transparent" transmission, the Commission meant a communications path that enabled the consumer to transmit an ordinary-language message to another point, with no computer processing or storage of the information, other than the processing or storage needed to convert the message into electronic form and then back into ordinary language for purposes of transmitting it over the network—such as via a telephone or a facsimile. Basic service was subject to common-carrier regulation.

"[E]nhanced service," however, was service in which "computer processing applications [were] used to act on the content, code, protocol, and other aspects of the subscriber's information," such as voice and data storage services . . . . By contrast to basic service, the Commission decided not to subject providers of enhanced service, even enhanced service offered via transmission wires, to Title II common-carrier regulation. . . .

The definitions of the terms "telecommunications service" and "information service" established by the 1996 Act are similar to the . . . basic-and enhanced-service classifications. "Telecommunications service"—the analog to basic service—is "the offering of telecommunications for a fee directly to the public . . . regardless of the facilities used." 47 U.S.C. § 153(46). "Telecommunications" is "the transmission, between or among points specified by the user, of information of the user's choosing, without change in the form or content of the information as sent and received." § 153(43). "Telecommunications carrier[s]"—those subjected to mandatory Title II common-carrier regulation—are defined as "provider[s] of telecommunications services." § 153(44). And "information service"—the analog to enhanced service—is "the offering of a capability for generating, acquiring, storing, transforming, processing, retrieving, utilizing, or making available information via telecommunications. . . ." § 153(20).

In September 2000, the Commission initiated a rulemaking proceeding to, among other things, apply these classifications to cable companies that offer broadband Internet service directly to consumers. In March 2002, that rulemaking culminated in the *Declaratory Ruling* under review in these cases. In the *Declaratory Ruling,* the Commission concluded that broadband Internet service provided by cable companies is an "information service" but not a "telecommunications service" under the Act, and therefore not subject to mandatory Title II common-carrier regulation. . . . Because Internet access provides a capability for manipulating and storing information, the Commission concluded that it was an information service.

The integrated nature of Internet access and the high-speed wire used to provide Internet access led the Commission to conclude that cable companies providing Internet access are not telecommunications providers. This conclusion, the Commission reasoned, followed from the logic of the *Universal Service*

Report. The *Report* had concluded that, though Internet service "involves data transport elements" because "an Internet access provider must enable the movement of information between customers' own computers and distant computers with which those customers seek to interact," it also "offers end users information-service capabilities inextricably intertwined with data transport." . . . In other words, the Commission reasoned that consumers use their cable modems not to transmit information "transparently," such as by using a telephone, but instead to obtain Internet access.

The Commission applied this same reasoning to cable companies offering broadband Internet access. Its logic was that, like non-facilities-based ISPs, cable companies do not "offe[r] telecommunications service to the end user, but rather . . . merely us[e] telecommunications to provide end users with cable modem service." . . .

The Court of Appeals . . . vacated the ruling to the extent it concluded that cable modem service was not "telecommunications service" under the Communications Act. It held that the Commission could not permissibly construe the Communications Act to exempt cable companies providing Internet service from Title II regulation. Rather than analyzing the permissibility of that construction under the deferential framework of *Chevron*, however, the Court of Appeals grounded its holding in the *stare decisis* effect of *AT & T Corp. v. Portland*, 216 F.3d 871 (9th Cir. 2000). *Portland* held that cable modem service was a "telecommunications service," though the court in that case was not reviewing an administrative proceeding and the Commission was not a party to the case. Nevertheless, *Portland's* holding, the Court of Appeals reasoned, overrode the contrary interpretation reached by the Commission in the *Declaratory Ruling.* . . .

III

We first consider whether we should apply *Chevron's* framework to the Commission's interpretation of the term "telecommunications service." We conclude that we should. We also conclude that the Court of Appeals should have done the same, instead of following the contrary construction it adopted in *Portland*.

A

In *Chevron*, this Court held that ambiguities in statutes within an agency's jurisdiction to administer are delegations of authority to the agency to fill the statutory gap in reasonable fashion. Filling these gaps, the Court explained, involves difficult policy choices that agencies are better equipped to make than courts. If a statute is ambiguous, and if the implementing agency's construction is reasonable, *Chevron* requires a federal court to accept the agency's construction of the statute, even if the agency's reading differs from what the court believes is the best statutory interpretation. . . .

Some of the respondents dispute this conclusion, on the ground that the Commission's interpretation is inconsistent with its past practice. We reject this argument. Agency inconsistency is not a basis for declining to analyze the agency's interpretation under the *Chevron* framework. Unexplained inconsistency is, at most, a reason for holding an interpretation to be an arbitrary and capricious change from agency practice under the Administrative Procedure Act. See *Motor Vehicle Mfrs. Assn. of United States, Inc. v. State Farm Mut. Automobile Ins. Co.*, 463 U.S. 29, 46–57 (1983). For if the agency adequately explains the reasons for a reversal of policy, "change is not invalidating, since the whole point of *Chevron* is to leave the discretion provided by the ambiguities of a statute with the implementing agency." *Smiley v. Citibank (South Dakota), N. A.*, 517 U.S. 735, 742 (1996). "An initial agency interpretation is not instantly carved in stone. On the contrary, the agency . . . must consider varying interpretations and the wisdom of its policy on a continuing basis," *Chevron, supra*, at 863–864, for example, in response to changed factual circumstances, or a change in administrations, see *State Farm, supra*, at 59. That is no doubt why in *Chevron* itself, this Court deferred to an agency interpretation that was a recent reversal of agency policy. We therefore have no difficulty concluding that *Chevron* applies.

B

The Court of Appeals declined to apply *Chevron* because it thought the Commission's interpretation of the Communications Act foreclosed by the conflicting construction of the Act it had adopted in *Portland*. It based that holding on the assumption that *Portland*'s construction overrode the Commission's, regardless of whether *Portland* had held the statute to be unambiguous. That reasoning was incorrect.

A court's prior judicial construction of a statute trumps an agency construction otherwise entitled to *Chevron* deference only if the prior court decision holds that its construction follows from the unambiguous terms of the statute and thus leaves no room for agency discretion. This principle follows from *Chevron* itself. *Chevron* established a "presumption that Congress, when it left ambiguity in a statute meant for implementation by an agency, understood that the ambiguity would be resolved, first and foremost, by the agency, and desired the agency (rather than the courts) to possess whatever degree of discretion the ambiguity allows." *Smiley, supra,* at 740–741. Yet allowing a judicial precedent to foreclose an agency from interpreting an ambiguous statute, as the Court of Appeals assumed it could, would allow a court's interpretation to override an agency's. *Chevron*'s premise is that it is for agencies, not courts, to fill statutory gaps. The better rule is to hold judicial interpretations contained in precedents to the same demanding *Chevron* step one standard that applies if the court is reviewing the agency's construction on a blank slate: Only a judicial precedent holding that the statute unambiguously forecloses the agency's interpretation, and therefore contains no gap for the agency to fill, displaces a conflicting agency construction.

A contrary rule would produce anomalous results. It would mean that whether an agency's interpretation of an ambiguous statute is entitled to *Chevron* deference would turn on the order in which the interpretations issue: If the court's construction came first, its construction would prevail, whereas if the agency's came first, the agency's construction would command *Chevron* deference. . . .

The dissent answers that allowing an agency to override what a court believes to be the best interpretation of a statute makes "judicial decisions subject to reversal by executive officers." *Post,* at 2719 (opinion of SCALIA, J.). It does not. Since *Chevron* teaches that a court's opinion as to the best reading of an ambiguous statute an agency is charged with administering is not authoritative, the agency's decision to construe that statute differently from a court does not say that the court's holding was legally wrong. Instead, the agency may, consistent with the court's holding, choose a different construction, since the agency remains the authoritative interpreter (within the limits of reason) of such statutes. . . .

Against this background, the Court of Appeals erred in refusing to apply *Chevron* to the Commission's interpretation of the definition of "telecommunications service," 47 U.S.C. § 153(46). Its prior decision in *Portland* held only that the *best* reading of § 153(46) was that cable modem service was a "telecommunications service," not that it was the *only permissible* reading of the statute. . . .

IV

We next address whether the Commission's construction of the definition of "telecommunications service," 47 U.S.C. § 153(46), is a permissible reading of the Communications Act under the Chevron framework. Chevron established a familiar two-step procedure for evaluating whether an agency's interpretation of a statute is lawful. At the first step, we ask whether the statute's plain terms "directly addres[s] the precise question at issue." If the statute is ambiguous on the point, we defer at step two to the agency's interpretation so long as the construction is "a reasonable policy choice for the agency to make." The Commission's interpretation is permissible at both steps.

A

We first set forth our understanding of the interpretation of the Communications Act that the Commission embraced. The issue before the Commission was whether cable companies providing cable modem service are providing a "telecommunications service" in addition to an "information service."

The Commission first concluded that cable modem service is an "information service," a conclusion unchallenged here. The Act defines "information service" as "the offering of a capability for generating, acquiring, storing, transforming, processing, retrieving, utilizing, or making available information via telecommunications . . . ." § 153(20). Cable modem service is an information service, the Commission reasoned, because it provides consumers with a comprehensive capability for manipulating information using the Internet via high-speed telecommunications. That service enables users, for example, to browse the World Wide Web, to transfer files from file archives available on the Internet via the "File Transfer Protocol," and to access e-mail and Usenet newsgroups. Like other forms of Internet service, cable modem service also gives users access to the Domain Name System (DNS). DNS, among other things, matches the Web page addresses that end users type into their browsers (or "click" on) with the Internet Protocol (IP) addresses of the servers containing the Web pages the users wish to access. All of these features, the Commission concluded, were part of the information service that cable companies provide consumers.

At the same time, the Commission concluded that cable modem service was not "telecommunications service." "Telecommunications service" is "the offering of telecommunications for a fee directly to the public." 47 U.S.C. § 153(46). "Telecommunications," in turn, is defined as "the transmission, between or among points specified by the user, of information of the user's choosing, without change in the form or content of the information as sent and received." § 153(43). The Commission conceded that, like all information-service providers, cable companies use "telecommunications" to provide consumers with Internet service; cable companies provide such service via the high-speed wire that transmits signals to and from an end user's computer. For the Commission, however, the question whether cable broadband Internet providers "offer" telecommunications involved more than whether telecommunications was one necessary component of cable modem service. Instead, whether that service also includes a telecommunications "offering" "turn[ed] on the nature of the functions the *end user* is offered," for the statutory definition of "telecommunications service" does not "res[t] on the particular types of facilities used," see § 153(46) (definition of "telecommunications service" applies "regardless of the facilities used").

Seen from the consumer's point of view, the Commission concluded, cable modem service is not a telecommunications offering because the consumer uses the high-speed wire always in connection with the information-processing capabilities provided by Internet access, and because the transmission is a necessary component of Internet access: "As provided to the end user the telecommunications is part and parcel of cable modem service and is integral to its other capabilities." The wire is used, in other words, to access the World Wide Web, newsgroups, and so forth, rather than "transparently" to transmit and receive ordinary-language messages without computer processing or storage of the message. The integrated character of this offering led the Commission to conclude that cable modem service is not a "stand-alone," transparent offering of telecommunications.

B

This construction passes *Chevron*'s first step. Respondents argue that it does not, on the ground that cable companies providing Internet service necessarily "offe[r]" the underlying telecommunications used to transmit that service. The word "offering" as used in § 153(46), however, does not unambiguously require that result. Instead, "offering" can reasonably be read to mean a "stand-alone" offering of telecommunications, *i.e.*, an offered service that, from the user's perspective, transmits messages unadulterated by computer processing. That conclusion follows not only from the ordinary meaning of the word "offering," but also from the regulatory history of the Communications Act.

Cable companies in the broadband Internet service business "offe[r]" consumers an information service in the form of Internet access and they do so "via telecommunications," § 153(20), but it does not inexorably follow as a matter of ordinary language that they also "offe[r]" consumers the high-speed data transmission (telecommunications) that is an input used to provide this service, § 153(46). We have held that where a statute's plain terms admit of two or more reasonable ordinary usages, the Commission's choice of one of them is entitled to deference. . . . The term "offe[r]" as used in the definition of telecommunications service, § 153(46), is ambiguous in this way.

It is common usage to describe what a company "offers" to a consumer as what the consumer perceives to be the integrated finished product, even to the exclusion of discrete components that compose the product . . . . One might well say that a car dealership "offers" cars, but does not "offer" the integrated major inputs that make purchasing the car valuable, such as the engine or the chassis. . . .

The question, then, is whether the transmission component of cable modem service is sufficiently integrated with the finished service to make it reasonable to describe the two as a single, integrated offering. . . . What cable companies providing cable modem service and telephone companies providing telephone service "offer" is Internet service and telephone service respectively—the finished services, though they do so using (or "via") the discrete components composing the end product, including data transmission. Such functionally integrated components need not be described as distinct "offerings.". . .

Because the term "offer" can sometimes refer to a single, finished product and sometimes to the "individual components in a package being offered," . . . the statute fails unambiguously to classify the telecommunications component of cable modem service as a distinct offering. . . .

    * * *

C

We also conclude that the Commission's construction was "a reasonable policy choice for the [Commission] to make" at *Chevron*'s second step.

Respondents argue that the Commission's construction is unreasonable because it allows any communications provider to "evade" common-carrier regulation by the expedient of bundling information service with telecommunications. Respondents argue that under the Commission's construction a telephone company could, for example, offer an information service like voice mail together with telephone service, thereby avoiding common-carrier regulation of its telephone service.

We need not decide whether a construction that resulted in these consequences would be unreasonable because we do not believe that these results follow from the construction the Commission adopted. As we understand the *Declaratory Ruling,* the Commission did not say that any telecommunications service that is priced or bundled with an information service is automatically unregulated under Title II. The Commission said that a telecommunications input used to provide an information service that is not "separable from the data-processing capabilities of the service" and is instead "part and parcel of [the information service] and is integral to [the information service's] other capabilities" is not a telecommunications offering.

This construction does not leave all information-service offerings exempt from mandatory Title II regulation. "It is plain," for example, that a local telephone company "cannot escape Title II regulation of its residential local exchange service simply by packaging that service with voice mail." *Universal Service Report* 11530, ¶ 60. That is because a telephone company that packages voice mail with telephone service offers a transparent transmission path—telephone service—that transmits information independent of the information-storage capabilities provided by voice mail. For instance, when a person makes a telephone call, his ability to convey and receive information using the call is only trivially affected by the additional voice-mail capability. . . . By contrast, the high-speed transmission used to provide cable modem service is a functionally integrated component of that service because it transmits data only in connection with the further processing of information and is necessary to provide Internet service. . . .

* * *

The Commission is in a far better position to address these questions than we are. Nothing in the Communications Act or the Administrative Procedure Act makes unlawful the Commission's use of its expert policy judgment to resolve these difficult questions. The judgment of the Court of Appeals is reversed, and the cases are remanded for further proceedings consistent with this opinion.

[Concurring opinions by Justices Stevens and Breyer, and Part I of a dissent by Justice Scalia, joined by Justices Souter and Ginsburg, are omitted.—Ed.]

Justice Scalia, dissenting.

* * *

. . . . A court's interpretation is conclusive, the Court says, only if it holds that interpretation to be "the *only permissible* reading of the statute," and not if it merely holds it to be "the *best* reading." Does this mean that in future statutory-construction cases involving agency-administered statutes courts must specify (presumably in dictum) which of the two they are holding? And what of the many cases decided in the past, before this dictum's requirement was established? Apparently, silence on the point means that the court's decision is subject to agency reversal . . . . How much extra work will it entail for each court confronted with an agency-administered statute to determine whether it has reached, not only the right ("best") result, but "the only permissible" result? . . .

It is indeed a wonderful new world that the Court creates, one full of promise for administrative-law professors in need of tenure articles and, of course, for litigators. I would adhere to what has been the rule in the past: When a court interprets a statute without *Chevron* deference to agency views, its interpretation (whether or not asserted to rest upon an unambiguous text) is the law. . . .

Notes and Questions

1.   Summary. The Court's decision in *Brand X* seems to flow inevitably from the logic of *Chevron*. Even if a prior court has interpreted the statute in a certain way, the agency should be free to interpret the statute differently, so long as that interpretation is reasonable. The same rationales of institutional competence, political accountability, and implicit congressional delegation are present regardless of whether a court has interpreted the statute first. Is Justice Scalia—the lone dissenter on this point—wrong to worry about the difficulty of determining whether a court believed its prior interpretation was the only permissible reading? After all, isn't it the exact same inquiry a court would have to undertake even in the absence of a prior interpretation, viz. determining if the statute is ambiguous? On the other hand, would not Scalia's approach be more problematic, in that some agencies interpreting some statutes would get *Chevron* deference, but others wouldn't?

2. *The Net Neutrality saga.* In 2015, the FCC again did an about-face: it classified broadband Internet as a "telecommunications service" under the Communications Act of 1934 and subjected providers to "net neutrality" regulations. These regulations were highly controversial. Yet, under the Court's 2005 *Brand X* opinion, wasn't the FCC clearly free to adopt this change and impose common-carrier regulations? Note that the FCC, in 2018, repealed the 2015 regulations and reclassified broadband Internet once again as an "information service." What do you make of these constant changes in policy? Wouldn't it be better if the Supreme Court simply adopted what it thought was the "best" interpretation of the statute? Does the statute truly leave discretion for the agency to decide whether to subject Internet providers to regulation? If so, might that be a *nondelegation* problem?

 **POLITICAL INFLUENCE**
How much should administrative policies change with new presidential administrations? Does the *Net Neutrality* saga inform your views on the question?

---

3. *Step two and hard-look review.* What do you make of the Court's "step two" analysis? Once it concludes that, in this particular context, the word "offer" as applied to cable-supplied Internet services is ambiguous, doesn't it follow that the FCC's interpretation was reasonable? What was left to do at "step two"? The Court addressed an argument that the FCC's interpretation would let telecommunications providers get around their common-carrier obligations by bundling their service with an information service, no matter how insignificant. The Court rejected that argument. But in so doing, wasn't the Court simply affirming yet again that the agency's "interpretation" was reasonable? Or, perhaps, is it useful to think of *Chevron* as two steps even if it can be reconceptualized as one, in the sense that it forces the courts to declare whether the statute is clear on a question, and therefore whether the agency has choices and flexibility?

Consider some other examples that suggest that perhaps *Chevron* is really just one step. As Gary Lawson has written, "Courts generally affirm agencies at step two in cursory fashion, and often with no more than a single conclusory sentence." Gary Lawson, Federal Administrative Law 674–75 (7th ed. 2016). The D.C. Circuit in Adirondack Medical Center v. Sebelius, 740 F.3d 692 (2014), spent several pages on step one and then a single sentence at step two. Doesn't that suggest all the work was done in step one? Another example: In Utility Air Regulatory Group (UARG) v. EPA, 573 U.S. 302 (2014), the EPA sought to impose permitting requirements on stationary sources that emitted greenhouse gases because the Supreme Court had held in a prior case that greenhouse gases were included within the statutory definition of "pollutant" because it was an "airborne compound." In *UARG*, however, the Court held that the definitions of the various uses of the term pollutant in the statute were context-dependent. After all, if "any pollutant" really meant any airborne compound in every context, then major emitters of steam and oxygen—harmless airborne substances—would also have to be permitted. And, more to the point, if greenhouse gases were pollutants subject to the permitting requirements, then any source that emitted at least 250 tons of it would have to be permitted under the statute—raising the number of entities requiring permits from several hundred to tens of thousands. Indeed, the EPA recognized as much, which is why in its rule it proposed only to require permits of sources that emitted 100,000 tons of greenhouse gases, way above the statutory threshold of 250 tons. The Court held that the EPA's interpretation was "not permissible." Was this a step one decision, or a step two decision? It's not at all clear—and it's not clear that it matters.

So what was the Court doing in its robust step-two analysis in *Brand X*? Was it evaluating the agency's *policy* choice for reasonableness? Some scholars and judges have argued that *Chevron*'s second step, because it is redundant of step one, should really be reconceived as hard-look review under the arbitrary-and-capricious standard. If the statute, at step one, permits multiple options, the agency's policy choice still must meet the arbitrary-and-capricious standard. This will have nothing to do with statutory interpretation, but rather the agency's reasoning as a policy matter—whether it has considered the relevant factors. *See State Farm*, supra p. 285; *Overton Park*, supra p. 266. In *Kisor v.*

Wilkie, Justice Kavanaugh put it this way in a case involving *Auer* deference (judicial deference to an agency's interpretation of its own regulation, as opposed to a statute): "To be sure, some cases involve regulations that employ broad and open-ended terms like 'reasonable,' 'appropriate,' 'feasible,' or 'practicable.' Those kinds of terms afford agencies broad policy discretion, and courts allow an agency to reasonably exercise its discretion to choose among the options allowed by the text of the rule. But that is more *State Farm* than *Auer.*" 139 S. Ct. 2400, 2448–49 (2019) (Kavanaugh, J., concurring in the judgment). Do you think that's the best understanding of the Court's step-two analysis in *Brand X,* or was something else going on?

The next case, *Encino Motorcars,* raises the issue of the connection between *Chevron* and hard-look review in more depth. There is one complication of which the reader should be aware: the case was technically decided under *Chevron* "step zero," where the courts are supposed to ask whether the *Chevron* framework applies at all. That is, there are situations in which a court concludes that the agency is not entitled to the deference framework at all, so the courts will decide for themselves (or with less deference) what the best reading of the statute is. We shall get to "step zero" cases a bit later. That complication does not matter for our present purposes.

> **CROSS REFERENCE**
>
> At *Chevron* "step zero," courts ask whether they should even deploy the deference framework. We discuss step zero later in this chapter.

Encino Motorcars, LLC v. Navarro

136 S. Ct. 2117 (2016)

Justice Kennedy delivered the opinion of the Court.

This case addresses whether a federal statute requires payment of increased compensation to certain automobile dealership employees for overtime work. . . . Among its other provisions, the FLSA [Fair Labor Standards Act] requires employers to pay overtime compensation to covered employees who work more than 40 hours in a given week. The rate of overtime pay must be "not less than one and one-half times the regular rate" of the employee's pay. § 207(a).

Five current and former service advisors brought this suit alleging that the automobile dealership where they were employed was required by the FLSA to pay them overtime wages. The dealership contends that the position and duties of a service advisor bring these employees within § 213(b)(10)(A), which establishes an exemption from the FLSA overtime provisions for certain employees engaged in selling or servicing automobiles. The case turns on the interpretation of this exemption.

I

A

Automobile dealerships in many communities not only sell vehicles but also sell repair and maintenance services. Among the employees involved in providing repair and maintenance services are service advisors, partsmen, and mechanics. Service advisors interact with customers and sell them services for their vehicles. A service advisor's duties may include meeting customers; listening to their concerns about their cars; suggesting repair and maintenance services; selling new accessories or replacement parts; recording service orders; following up with customers as the services are performed (for instance, if new problems are discovered); and explaining the repair and maintenance work when customers return for their vehicles. . . .

[In omitted paragraphs, the Court detailed the agency's early regulations involving FLSA, which maintained that service advisors were not exempt from FLSA's overtime requirements, a position rejected by some courts.—Ed.]

Congress amended the statutory provision by enacting its present text, which now sets out the exemption in two subsections. The first subsection is at issue in this case. It exempts "any salesman, partsman, or mechanic primarily engaged in selling or servicing automobiles, trucks, or farm implements" at a covered dealership. 29 U.S.C. § 213(b)(10)(A). The second subsection exempts "any salesman primarily engaged in selling trailers, boats, or aircraft" at a covered dealership. § 213(b)(10)(B). . . .

In 1978, the Department issued an opinion letter departing from its previous position. Taking a position consistent with the cases decided by the courts, the opinion letter stated that service advisors could be exempt under § 213(b)(10)(A). . . .

Twenty-one years later, in 2008, the Department at last issued a notice of proposed rulemaking. The notice observed that every court that had considered the question had held service advisors to be exempt under § 213(b)(10)(A), and that the Department itself had treated service advisors as exempt since 1987. The Department proposed to revise its regulations to accord with existing practice by interpreting the exemption in § 213(b)(10)(A) to cover service advisors.

In 2011, however, the Department changed course yet again. It announced that it was "not proceeding with the proposed rule." Instead, the Department completed its 2008 notice-and-comment rulemaking by issuing a final rule that took the opposite position from the proposed rule. The new final rule followed the original 1970 regulation and interpreted the statutory term "salesman" to mean only an employee who sells automobiles, trucks, or farm implements.

The Department gave little explanation for its decision to abandon its decades-old practice of treating service advisors as exempt under § 213(b)(10)(A). . . .

B

Petitioner is a Mercedes-Benz automobile dealership in the Los Angeles area. Respondents are or were employed by petitioner as service advisors. They assert that petitioner required them to be at work from 7 a.m. to 6 p.m. at least five days per week, and to be available for work matters during breaks and while on vacation. Respondents were not paid a fixed salary or an hourly wage for their work; instead, they were paid commissions on the services they sold.

Respondents sued petitioner in the United States District Court for the Central District of California, alleging that petitioner violated the FLSA by failing to pay them overtime compensation when they worked more than 40 hours in a week. . . .

The Court of Appeals for the Ninth Circuit . . . construed the statute by deferring under *Chevron U.S.A. Inc. v. Natural Resources Defense Council, Inc.*, 467 U.S. 837 (1984), to the interpretation set forth by the Department in its 2011 regulation. . . .

II

A

The full text of the statutory subsection at issue states that the overtime provisions of the FLSA shall not apply to: "any salesman, partsman, or mechanic primarily engaged in selling or servicing automobiles, trucks, or farm implements, if he is employed by a nonmanufacturing establishment primarily engaged in the business of selling such vehicles or implements to ultimate purchasers." § 213(b)(10)(A).

The question presented is whether this exemption should be interpreted to include service advisors. To resolve that question, it is necessary to determine what deference, if any, the courts must give to the Department's 2011 interpretation.

In the usual course, when an agency is authorized by Congress to issue regulations and promulgates a regulation interpreting a statute it enforces, the interpretation receives deference if the statute is ambiguous and if the agency's interpretation is reasonable. This principle is implemented by the two-step analysis set forth in *Chevron*. At the first step, a court must determine whether Congress has "directly spoken to the precise question at issue." If so, "that is the end of the matter; for the court, as well as the agency, must give effect to the unambiguously expressed intent of Congress." If not, then at the second step the court must defer to the agency's interpretation if it is "reasonable."

A premise of *Chevron* is that when Congress grants an agency the authority to administer a statute by issuing regulations with the force of law, it presumes the agency will use that authority to resolve ambiguities in the statutory scheme. When Congress authorizes an agency to proceed through notice-and-comment rulemaking, that "relatively formal administrative procedure" is a "very good indicator" that Congress intended the regulation to carry the force of law, so *Chevron* should apply. But *Chevron* deference is not warranted where the regulation is "procedurally defective"—that is, where the agency errs by failing to follow the correct procedures in issuing the regulation. . . .

One of the basic procedural requirements of administrative rulemaking is that an agency must give adequate reasons for its decisions. The agency "must examine the relevant data and articulate a satisfactory explanation for its action including a rational connection between the facts found and the choice made." *Motor Vehicle Mfrs. Assn. of United States, Inc. v. State Farm Mut. Automobile Ins. Co.,* 463 U.S. 29, 43 (1983) (internal quotation marks omitted). That requirement is satisfied when the agency's explanation is clear enough that its "path may reasonably be discerned." *Bowman Transp., Inc. v. Arkansas-Best Freight System, Inc.,* 419 U.S. 281, 286 (1974). But where the agency has failed to provide even that minimal level of analysis, its action is arbitrary and capricious and so cannot carry the force of law. See 5 U.S.C. § 706(2)(A); *State Farm, supra,* at 42–43.

Agencies are free to change their existing policies as long as they provide a reasoned explanation for the change. See, *e.g., National Cable & Telecommunications Assn. v. Brand X Internet Services,* 545 U.S. 967, 981–982 (2005); *Chevron,* 467 U.S., at 863–864. When an agency changes its existing position, it "need not always provide a more detailed justification than what would suffice for a new policy created on a blank slate." *FCC v. Fox Television Stations, Inc.,* 556 U.S. 502, 515 (2009). But the agency must at least "display awareness that it is changing position" and "show that there are good reasons for the new policy." *Ibid.* In explaining its changed position, an agency must also be cognizant that longstanding policies may have "engendered serious reliance interests that must be taken into account." *Ibid.* "In such cases it is not that further justification is demanded by the mere fact of policy change; but that a reasoned explanation is needed for disregarding facts and circumstances that underlay or were engendered by the prior policy." *Fox Television Stations, supra,* at 515–516. It follows that an "[u]nexplained inconsistency" in agency policy is "a reason for holding an interpretation to be an arbitrary and capricious change from agency practice." *Brand X, supra,* at 981. An arbitrary and capricious regulation of this sort is itself unlawful and receives no *Chevron* deference.

B

Applying those principles here, the unavoidable conclusion is that the 2011 regulation was issued without the reasoned explanation that was required in light of the Department's change in position and the significant reliance interests involved. In promulgating the 2011 regulation, the Department offered barely any explanation. A summary discussion may suffice in other circumstances, but here—in particular because of decades of industry reliance on the Department's prior policy—the explanation fell short of the agency's duty to explain why it deemed it necessary to overrule its previous position.

The retail automobile and truck dealership industry had relied since 1978 on the Department's position that service advisors are exempt from the FLSA's overtime pay requirements. Dealerships and service advisors negotiated and structured their compensation plans against this background understanding. Requiring dealerships to adapt to the Department's new position could necessitate systemic, significant changes to the dealerships' compensation arrangements. . . . In light of this background, the Department needed a more reasoned explanation for its decision to depart from its existing enforcement policy. . . .

Whatever potential reasons the Department might have given, the agency in fact gave almost no reasons at all. In light of the serious reliance interests at stake, the Department's conclusory statements do not suffice to explain its decision. This lack of reasoned explication for a regulation that is inconsistent with the Department's longstanding earlier position results in a rule that cannot carry the force of law. It follows that this regulation does not receive *Chevron* deference in the interpretation of the relevant statute. . . .

Because the decision below relied on *Chevron* deference to this regulation, it is appropriate to remand for the Court of Appeals to interpret the statute in the first instance. . . .

[A concurring opinion by JUSTICES GINSBURG and SOTOMAYOR, and a dissenting opinion by JUSTICES THOMAS and ALITO, are omitted.—Ed.]

NOTES AND QUESTIONS

1. What does hard-look have to do with this? What, exactly, is the connection the Court draws between hard-look and *Chevron*? The Court seems to say that if the regulation is "arbitrary and capricious" because the agency did not sufficiently *explain* the policy change, the agency is not entitled to Chevron deference. But isn't that overdetermined? Why does it matter whether *Chevron* applies or not, if the policy change was independently arbitrary and capricious? Indeed, what does *Chevron* have to do with this at all? It could be that the statute is ambiguous, or leaves a gap, thereby leaving a range of options for the agency to pursue, much like in the *Fox Television* case. Thus, the agency's interpretation, or at least its choice among the possible options, is entitled to deference when it comes to interpreting the statute. But even if the agency has interpreted the statute reasonably, its action could still be unreasonable for *other* reasons—because it has failed to take into account reliance interests. Aren't these simply separate issues? Or, perhaps, is *Chevron* "step two"—the point at which courts recognize statutory ambiguity, but assess the agency's choice for "reasonableness"—the exact same thing as arbitrary-and-capricious review?

Putting aside the arbitrary-and-capricious analysis for the moment, even under *Chevron* itself do you think the statute is ambiguous? Justices Thomas and Alito, in dissent, thought not; the statute exempted "any salesman . . . primarily engaged in selling *or servicing* automobiles . . . ." Aren't car dealership service advisors clearly "salesmen" engaged in selling (which is what salesmen do) automobile servicing, such that they are exempt from the overtime requirements? Are courts too quick to find "ambiguity" at *Chevron*'s first step? The next case raises that, and other, "step one" questions.

FDA v. Brown & Williamson Tobacco Corp.

529 U.S. 120 (2000)

Justice O'Connor delivered the opinion of the Court.

This case involves one of the most troubling public health problems facing our Nation today: the thousands of premature deaths that occur each year because of tobacco use. In 1996, the Food and Drug Administration (FDA), after having expressly disavowed any such authority since its inception, asserted jurisdiction to regulate tobacco products. The FDA concluded that nicotine is a "drug" within the meaning of the Food, Drug, and Cosmetic Act (FDCA or Act), and that cigarettes and smokeless tobacco are "combination products" that deliver nicotine to the body. Pursuant to this authority, it promulgated regulations intended to reduce tobacco consumption among children and adolescents. The agency believed that, because most tobacco consumers begin their use before reaching the age of 18, curbing tobacco use by minors could substantially reduce the prevalence of addiction in future generations and thus the incidence of tobacco-related death and disease.

Regardless of how serious the problem an administrative agency seeks to address, however, it may not exercise its authority "in a manner that is inconsistent with the administrative structure that Congress enacted into law." And although agencies are generally entitled to deference in the interpretation of statutes that they administer, a reviewing "court, as well as the agency, must give effect to the unambiguously expressed intent of Congress." *Chevron U. S. A. Inc.* v. *Natural Resources Defense Council, Inc.*, 467 U. S. 837, 842–843 (1984). In this case, we believe that Congress has clearly precluded the FDA from asserting jurisdiction to regulate tobacco products. Such authority is inconsistent with the intent that Congress has expressed in the FDCA's overall regulatory scheme and in the tobacco-specific legislation that it has enacted subsequent to the FDCA. In light of this clear intent, the FDA's assertion of jurisdiction is impermissible.

I

The FDCA grants the FDA, as the designee of the Secretary of Health and Human Services (HHS), the authority to regulate, among other items, "drugs" and "devices." The Act defines "drug" to include "articles (other than food) intended to affect the structure or any function of the body." 21 U. S. C. § 321(g)(1)(C). It defines "device," in part, as "an instrument, apparatus, implement, machine, contrivance, . . . or other similar or related article, including any component, part, or accessory, which is . . . intended to affect the structure or any function of the body." § 321(h). The Act also grants the FDA the authority to regulate so-called "combination products," which "constitute a combination of a drug, device, or biological product." § 353(g)(1). The FDA has construed this provision as giving it the discretion to regulate combination products as drugs, as devices, or as both. . . .

On August 28, 1996, the FDA issued a final rule entitled "Regulations Restricting the Sale and Distribution of Cigarettes and Smokeless Tobacco to Protect Children and Adolescents." The FDA determined that nicotine is a "drug" and that cigarettes and smokeless tobacco are "drug delivery devices," and therefore it had jurisdiction under the FDCA to regulate tobacco products as customarily marketed—that is, without manufacturer claims of therapeutic benefit. First, the FDA found that tobacco products "affect the structure or any function of the body" because nicotine "has significant pharmacological effects." Specifically, nicotine "exerts psychoactive, or mood-altering, effects on the brain" that cause and sustain addiction, have both tranquilizing and stimulating effects, and control weight. Second, the FDA determined that these effects were "intended" under the FDCA because they "are so widely known and foreseeable that [they] may be deemed to have been intended by the manufacturers"; consumers use tobacco products "predominantly or nearly exclusively" to obtain these effects; and the statements, research, and actions of manufacturers revealed that they "have 'designed' cigarettes to provide pharmacologically active doses of nicotine to consumers." Finally, the agency concluded that cigarettes and smokeless tobacco are "combination products" because, in addition to containing nicotine, they include device components that deliver a controlled amount of nicotine to the body.

Having resolved the jurisdictional question, the FDA next explained the policy justifications for its regulations, detailing the deleterious health effects associated with tobacco use. . . . Based on these findings, the FDA promulgated regulations concerning tobacco products' promotion, labeling, and accessibility to children and adolescents. The access regulations prohibit the sale of cigarettes or smokeless tobacco to persons younger than 18; require retailers to verify through photo identification the age of all purchasers younger than 27; prohibit the sale of cigarettes in quantities smaller than 20; prohibit the distribution of free samples; and prohibit sales through self-service displays and vending machines except in adult-only locations. . . .

The FDA promulgated these regulations pursuant to its authority to regulate "restricted devices." See 21 U. S. C. § 360j(e). The FDA construed § 353(g) (1) as giving it the discretion to regulate "combination products" using the Act's drug authorities, device authorities, or both, depending on "how the public health goals of the act can be best accomplished." Given the greater flexibility in the FDCA for the regulation of devices, the FDA determined that "the device authorities provide the most appropriate basis for regulating cigarettes and smokeless tobacco." Under 21 U. S. C. § 360j(e), the agency may "require that a device be restricted to sale, distribution, or use . . . upon such other conditions as [the FDA] may prescribe in such regulation, if, because of its potentiality for harmful effect or the collateral measures necessary to its use, [the FDA] determines that there cannot otherwise be reasonable assurance of its safety and effectiveness." The FDA reasoned that its regulations fell within the authority granted by § 360j(e) because they related to the sale or distribution of tobacco products and were necessary for providing a reasonable assurance of safety.

* * *

II

The FDA's assertion of jurisdiction to regulate tobacco products is founded on its conclusions that nicotine is a "drug" and that cigarettes and smokeless tobacco are "drug delivery devices." . . .

A threshold issue is the appropriate framework for analyzing the FDA's assertion of authority to regulate tobacco products. Because this case involves an administrative agency's construction of a statute that it administers, our analysis is governed by *Chevron U. S. A. Inc.* v. *Natural Resources Defense Council, Inc.*, 467 U.S. 837 (1984). Under *Chevron*, a reviewing court must first ask "whether Congress has directly spoken to the precise question at issue." If Congress has done so, the inquiry is at an end; the court "must give effect to the unambiguously expressed intent of Congress." But if Congress has not specifically addressed the question, a reviewing court must respect the agency's construction of the statute so long as it is permissible. Such deference is justified because "[t]he responsibilities for assessing the wisdom of such policy choices and resolving the struggle between competing views of the public interest are not judicial ones," and because of the agency's greater familiarity with the ever-changing facts and circumstances surrounding the subjects regulated.

In determining whether Congress has specifically addressed the question at issue, a reviewing court should not confine itself to examining a particular statutory provision in isolation. The meaning—or ambiguity—of certain words or phrases may only become evident when placed in context. See *Brown* v. *Gardner*, 513 U. S. 115, 118 (1994) ("Ambiguity is a creature not of definitional possibilities but of statutory context"). It is a "fundamental canon of statutory construction that the words of a statute must be read in their context and with a view to their place in the overall statutory scheme." A court must therefore interpret the statute "as a symmetrical and coherent regulatory scheme," and "fit, if possible, all parts into an harmonious whole." Similarly, the meaning of one statute may be affected by other Acts, particularly where Congress has spoken subsequently and more specifically to the topic at hand. In addition, we must be guided to a degree by common sense as to the manner in which Congress is likely to delegate a policy decision of such economic and political magnitude to an administrative agency.

With these principles in mind, we find that Congress has directly spoken to the issue here and precluded the FDA's jurisdiction to regulate tobacco products.

A

Viewing the FDCA as a whole, it is evident that one of the Act's core objectives is to ensure that any product regulated by the FDA is "safe" and "effective" for its intended use. . . . This essential purpose pervades the FDCA. For instance, 21 U.S.C. § 393(b)(2) defines the FDA's "[m]ission" to include "protect[ing] the public health by ensuring that . . . drugs are safe and effective" and that "there is reasonable assurance of the safety and effectiveness of devices intended for human use." The FDCA requires pre-market approval of any new drug, with some limited exceptions, and states that the FDA "shall issue an order refusing to approve the application" of a new drug if it is not safe and effective for its intended purpose. §§ 355(d)(1)–(2), (4)–(5). . . . The Act also requires the FDA to classify all devices into one of three categories. Regardless of which category the FDA chooses, there must be a "reasonable assurance of the safety and effectiveness of the device." 21 U. S. C. §§ 360c(a) (1)(A)(i), (B), (C). Even the "restricted device" provision pursuant to which the FDA promulgated the regulations at issue here authorizes the agency to place conditions on the sale or distribution of a device specifically when "there cannot otherwise be reasonable assurance of its safety and effectiveness." 21 U.S.C. § 360j(e). Thus, the Act generally requires the FDA to prevent the marketing of any drug or device where the "potential for inflicting death or physical injury is not offset by the possibility of therapeutic benefit." *United States* v. *Rutherford*, 442 U. S. 544, 556 (1979).

In its rulemaking proceeding, the FDA quite exhaustively documented that "tobacco products are unsafe," "dangerous," and "cause great pain and suffering from illness." 61 Fed. Reg. 44412 (1996). It found that the consumption of tobacco products presents "extraordinary health risks," and that "tobacco use is the single leading cause of preventable death in the United States." . . .

These findings logically imply that, if tobacco products were "devices" under the FDCA, the FDA would be required to remove them from the market. Consider, first, the FDCA's provisions concerning the misbranding of drugs or devices. The Act prohibits "[t]he introduction or delivery for introduction into interstate commerce of any food, drug, device, or cosmetic that is adulterated or misbranded." 21 U. S. C. § 331(a). In light of the FDA's findings, two distinct FDCA provisions would render cigarettes and smokeless tobacco misbranded devices. First, § 352(j) deems a drug or device misbranded "[i]f it is dangerous to health when used in the dosage or manner, or with the frequency or duration prescribed, recommended, or suggested in the labeling thereof." The FDA's findings make clear that tobacco products are "dangerous to health" when used in the manner prescribed. Second, a drug or device is misbranded under the Act "[u]nless its labeling bears . . . adequate directions for use . . . in such manner and form, as are necessary for the protection of users," except where such directions are "not necessary for the protection of the public health." § 352(f)(1). Given the FDA's conclusions concerning the health consequences of tobacco use, there are no directions that could adequately protect consumers. . . . Contrary to the dissent's contention, the Act admits no remedial discretion once it is evident that the device is misbranded.

Second, the FDCA requires the FDA to place all devices that it regulates into one of three classifications. See § 360c(b)(1). . . . Given the FDA's findings regarding the health consequences of tobacco use, the agency would have to place cigarettes and smokeless tobacco in Class III because, even after the application of the Act's available controls, they would "presen[t] a potential unreasonable risk of illness or injury." 21 U. S. C. § 360c(a)(1)(C). As Class III devices, tobacco products would be subject to the FDCA's pre-market approval process. Under these provisions, the FDA would be prohibited from approving an application for premarket approval without "a showing of reasonable assurance that such device is safe under the conditions of use prescribed, recommended, or suggested in the proposed labeling thereof." 21 U.S.C. § 360e(d)(2)(A). In view of the FDA's conclusions regarding the health effects of tobacco use, the agency would have no basis for finding any such reasonable assurance of safety. Thus, once the FDA fulfilled its statutory obligation to classify tobacco products, it could not allow them to be marketed.

The FDCA's misbranding and device classification provisions therefore make evident that were the FDA to regulate cigarettes and smokeless tobacco, the Act would require the agency to ban them. . . .

Congress, however, has foreclosed the removal of tobacco products from the market. A provision of the United States Code currently in force states that "[t]he marketing of tobacco constitutes one of the greatest basic industries of the United States with ramifying activities which directly affect interstate and foreign commerce at every point, and stable conditions therein are necessary to the general welfare." 7 U.S.C. § 1311(a). More importantly, Congress has directly addressed the problem of tobacco and health through legislation on six occasions since 1965. . . . When Congress enacted these statutes, the adverse health consequences of tobacco use were well known, as were nicotine's pharmacological effects. . . . Nonetheless, Congress stopped well short of ordering a ban. Instead, it has generally regulated the labeling and advertisement of tobacco products, expressly providing that it is the policy of Congress that "commerce and the national economy may be . . . protected to the maximum extent consistent with" consumers "be[ing] adequately informed about any adverse health effects." 15 U. S. C. § 1331. . . . [T]he collective premise of these statutes is that cigarettes and smokeless tobacco will continue to be sold in the United States. A ban of tobacco products by the FDA would therefore plainly contradict congressional policy.

* * *

[T]he analogy made by the FDA and the dissent to highly toxic drugs used in the treatment of various cancers is unpersuasive. Although "dangerous" in some sense, these drugs are safe within the meaning of the Act because, for certain patients, the therapeutic benefits outweigh the risk of harm. Accordingly, such drugs cannot properly be described as "dangerous to health" under 21 U. S. C. § 352(j). The same is not true for tobacco products. As the FDA has documented in great detail, cigarettes and smokeless tobacco are an unsafe means to obtaining any pharmacological effect.

The dissent contends that our conclusion means that "the FDCA requires the FDA to ban outright 'dangerous' drugs or devices," and that this is a "perverse" reading of the statute. This misunderstands our holding. The FDA, consistent with the FDCA, may clearly regulate many "dangerous" products without banning them. Indeed, virtually every drug or device poses dangers under certain conditions. What the FDA may not do is conclude that a drug or device cannot be used safely for any therapeutic purpose and yet, at the same time, allow that product to remain on the market. Such regulation is incompatible with the FDCA's core objective of ensuring that every drug or device is safe and effective.

* * *

The inescapable conclusion is that there is no room for tobacco products within the FDCA's regulatory scheme. If they cannot be used safely for any therapeutic purpose, and yet they cannot be banned, they simply do not fit.

B

In determining whether Congress has spoken directly to the FDA's authority to regulate tobacco, we must also consider in greater detail the tobacco-specific legislation that Congress has enacted over the past 35 years. At the time a statute is enacted, it may have a range of plausible meanings. Over time, however, subsequent acts can shape or focus those meanings. The "classic judicial task of reconciling many laws enacted over time, and getting them to 'make sense' in combination, necessarily assumes that the implications of a statute may be altered by the implications of a later statute." *United States v. Fausto*, 484 U.S. at 453. This is particularly so where the scope of the earlier statute is broad but the subsequent statutes more specifically address the topic at hand. As we recognized recently in *United States v. Estate of Romani*, "a specific policy embodied in a later federal statute should control our construction of the [earlier] statute, even though it ha[s] not been expressly amended."

Congress has enacted six separate pieces of legislation since 1965 addressing the problem of tobacco use and human health. Those statutes, among other things, require that health warnings appear on all packaging and in all print and outdoor advertisements; prohibit the advertisement of tobacco products through "any medium of electronic communication" subject to regulation by the Federal Communications Commission (FCC); require the Secretary of HHS to report every three years to Congress on research findings concerning "the addictive property of tobacco"; and make States' receipt of certain federal block grants contingent on their making it unlawful "for any manufacturer, retailer, or distributor of tobacco products to sell or distribute any such product to any individual under the age of 18."

In adopting each statute, Congress has acted against the backdrop of the FDA's consistent and repeated statements that it lacked authority under the FDCA to regulate tobacco absent claims of therapeutic benefit by the manufacturer. In fact, on several occasions over this period, and after the health consequences of tobacco use and nicotine's pharmacological effects had become well known, Congress considered and rejected bills that would have granted the FDA such jurisdiction. Under these circumstances, it is evident that Congress' tobacco-specific statutes have effectively ratified the FDA's long-held position that it lacks jurisdiction under the FDCA to regulate tobacco products. Congress has created a distinct regulatory scheme to address the problem of tobacco and health, and that scheme, as presently constructed, precludes any role for the FDA.

[Omitted is a long discussion of the various statutes and legislative debates over tobacco legislation.—Ed.]

Although the dissent takes issue with our discussion of the FDA's change in position, our conclusion does not rely on the fact that the FDA's assertion of jurisdiction represents a sharp break with its prior interpretation of the FDCA. Certainly, an agency's initial interpretation of a statute that it is charged with administering is not "carved in stone." *Chevron*, 467 U.S. at 863. As we recognized in [*State Farm*], agencies "must be given ample latitude to 'adapt their rules and policies to the demands of changing circumstances.'" The consistency of the FDA's prior position is significant in this case for a different reason: It provides important context to Congress' enactment of its tobacco-specific legislation. When the FDA repeatedly informed Congress that the FDCA does not grant it the authority to regulate tobacco products, its statements were consistent with the agency's unwavering position since its inception, and with the position that its predecessor agency had first taken in 1914. Although not crucial, the consistency of the FDA's prior position bolsters the conclusion that when Congress created a distinct regulatory scheme addressing the subject of tobacco and health, it understood that the FDA is without jurisdiction to regulate tobacco products and ratified that position.

* * *

C

Finally, our inquiry into whether Congress has directly spoken to the precise question at issue is shaped, at least in some measure, by the nature of the question presented. Deference under *Chevron* to an agency's construction of a statute that it administers is premised on the theory that a statute's ambiguity constitutes an implicit delegation from Congress to the agency to fill in the statutory gaps. In extraordinary cases, however, there may be reason to hesitate before concluding that Congress has intended such an implicit delegation. . . .

This is hardly an ordinary case. Contrary to its representations to Congress since 1914, the FDA has now asserted jurisdiction to regulate an industry constituting a significant portion of the American economy. In fact, the FDA contends that, were it to determine that tobacco products provide no "reasonable assurance of safety," it would have the authority to ban cigarettes and smokeless tobacco entirely. Owing to its unique place in American history and society, tobacco has its own unique political history. Congress, for better or for worse, has created a distinct regulatory scheme for tobacco products, squarely rejected proposals to give the FDA jurisdiction over tobacco, and repeatedly acted to preclude any agency from exercising significant policymaking authority in the area. Given this history and the breadth of the authority that the FDA has asserted, we are obliged to defer not to the agency's expansive construction of the statute, but to Congress' consistent judgment to deny the FDA this power.

Our decision in *MCI Telecommunications Corp.* v. *American Telephone & Telegraph Co.*, 512 U.S. 218 (1994), is instructive. That case involved the proper construction of the term "modify" in § 203(b) of the Communications Act of 1934. The FCC contended that, because the Act gave it the discretion to "modify any requirement" imposed under the statute, it therefore possessed the authority to render voluntary the otherwise mandatory requirement that long distance carriers file their rates. We rejected the FCC's construction, finding "not the slightest doubt" that Congress had directly spoken to the question. In reasoning even more apt here, we concluded that "[i]t is highly unlikely that Congress would leave the determination of whether an industry will be entirely, or even substantially, rate-regulated to agency discretion—and even more unlikely that it would achieve that through such a subtle device as permission to 'modify' rate-filing requirements."

As in *MCI*, we are confident that Congress could not have intended to delegate a decision of such economic and political significance to an agency in so cryptic a fashion. . . . It is therefore clear, based on the FDCA's overall regulatory scheme and the subsequent tobacco legislation, that Congress has directly spoken to the question at issue and precluded the FDA from regulating tobacco products. . . .

Justice Breyer, with whom Justice Stevens, Justice Souter, and Justice Ginsburg join, dissenting.

The Food and Drug Administration (FDA) has the authority to regulate "articles (other than food) intended to affect the structure or any function of the body." Unlike the majority, I believe that tobacco products fit within this statutory language.

In its own interpretation, the majority nowhere denies the following two salient points. First, tobacco products (including cigarettes) fall within the scope of this statutory definition, read literally. Cigarettes achieve their mood stabilizing effects through the interaction of the chemical nicotine and the cells of the central nervous system. Both cigarette manufacturers and smokers alike know of, and desire, that chemically induced result. Hence, cigarettes are "intended to affect" the body's "structure" and "function," in the literal sense of these words.

Second, the statute's basic purpose—the protection of public health—supports the inclusion of cigarettes within its scope. . . .

I

* * *

As I have mentioned, the literal language of the third definition and the FDCA's general purpose both strongly support a pro-jurisdiction reading of the statute.

The statute's history offers further support. The FDA drafted the new language, and it testified before Congress that the third definition [of drugs and devices, which ended up in the statute—Ed.] would expand the FDCA's jurisdictional scope significantly. Indeed, "[t]he purpose" of the new definition was to "make possible the regulation of a great many products that have been found on the market that cannot be alleged to be treatments for diseased conditions." While the drafters focused specifically upon the need to give the FDA jurisdiction over "slenderizing" products such as "anti fat remedies," they were aware that, in doing so, they had created what was "admittedly an inclusive, a wide definition." And that broad language was included *deliberately,* so that jurisdiction could be had over "*all* substances and preparations, other than food, and *all* devices intended to affect the structure or any function of the body . . . ."

After studying the FDCA's history, experts have written that the statute "is a purposefully broad delegation of discretionary powers by Congress," and that, in a sense, the FDCA "must be regarded as a *constitution*" that "establish[es] general principles" and "permit[s] implementation within broad parameters" so that the FDA can "implement these objectives through the most effective and efficient controls that can be devised." . . .

Nor is it surprising that such a statutory delegation of power could lead after many years to an assertion of jurisdiction that the 1938 legislators might not have expected. Such a possibility is inherent in the very nature of a broad delegation. In 1938, it may well have seemed unlikely that the FDA would ever bring cigarette manufacturers within the FDCA's statutory language by proving that cigarettes produce chemical changes in the body and that the makers "intended" their product chemically to affect the body's "structure" or "function." Or, back then, it may have seemed unlikely that, even assuming such proof, the FDA actually would exercise its discretion to regulate so popular a product.

But it should not have seemed unlikely that, assuming the FDA decided to regulate and proved the particular jurisdictional prerequisites, the courts would rule such a jurisdictional assertion fully authorized. . . .

II

* * *

C

The majority nonetheless reaches the "inescapable conclusion" that the language and structure of the FDCA as a whole "simply do not fit" the kind of public health problem that tobacco creates. That is because, in the majority's view, the FDCA requires the FDA to ban outright "dangerous" drugs or devices (such as cigarettes); yet, the FDA concedes that an immediate and total cigarette-sale ban is inappropriate. . . .

First, the statute's language does not restrict the FDA's remedial powers in this way. . . . [T]he FDCA's "device" provisions explicitly grant the FDA wide remedial discretion. For example, where the FDA cannot "otherwise" obtain "reasonable assurance" of a device's "safety and effectiveness," the agency may restrict by regulation a product's "sale, distribution, or use" upon "*such . . . conditions as the Secretary may prescribe.*" § 360j(e)(1) (emphasis added). And the statutory section that most clearly addresses the FDA's power to ban (entitled "Banned devices") says that, where a device presents "an unreasonable and substantial risk of illness or injury," the Secretary "*may*"—not *must*—"*initiate* a proceeding . . . to make such device a banned device." § 360f(a) (emphasis added).

. . . . It is true, as the majority contends, that "the FDCA requires the FDA to place all devices" in "one of three classifications" and that Class III devices require "pre market approval." . . . [But] it is not entirely clear from the statute's text that a Class III categorization would require the FDA affirmatively to *withdraw* from the market dangerous devices, such as cigarettes, which are already widely distributed. . . .

Noting that the FDCA requires banning a "misbranded" drug, the majority also points to 21 U.S.C. § 352(j), which deems a drug or device "misbranded" if "it is dangerous to health when used" as "prescribed, recommended, or suggested in the labeling." . . . But this "misbranding" language is not determinative, for it permits the FDA to conclude that a drug or device is *not* "dangerous to health" and that it *does* have "adequate" directions *when regulated so as to render it as harmless as possible.* And surely the agency can determine that a substance is comparatively "safe" (*not* "dangerous") whenever it would be *less* dangerous to make the product available (subject to regulatory requirements) than suddenly to withdraw it from the market. . . .

In my view, where linguistically permissible, we should interpret the FDCA in light of Congress' overall desire to protect health. That purpose requires a flexible interpretation that both permits the FDA to take into account the realities of human behavior and allows it, in appropriate cases, to choose from its arsenal of statutory remedies. A statute so interpreted easily "fit[s]" this, and other, drug- and device-related health problems.

III

In the majority's view, laws enacted since 1965 require us to deny jurisdiction, whatever the FDCA might mean in their absence. But why? Do those laws contain language barring FDA jurisdiction? The majority must concede that they do not. Do they contain provisions that are inconsistent with the FDA's exercise of jurisdiction? With one exception, the majority points to no such provision. . . . [O]ne cannot automatically infer an anti-jurisdiction intent, as the majority does, for the later statutes are both (and similarly) consistent with quite a different congressional desire, namely, the intent to proceed without interfering with whatever authority the FDA otherwise may have possessed.

* * *

V

* * *

[O]ne might claim that courts, when interpreting statutes, should assume in close cases that a decision with "enormous social consequences," should be made by democratically elected Members of Congress rather than by unelected agency administrators. If there is such a background canon of interpretation, however, I do not believe it controls the outcome here.

Insofar as the decision to regulate tobacco reflects the policy of an administration, it is a decision for which that administration, and those politically elected officials who support it, must (and will) take responsibility. And the very importance of the decision taken here, as well as its attendant publicity, means that the public is likely to be aware of it and to hold those officials politically accountable. Presidents, just like Members of Congress, are elected by the public. Indeed, the President and Vice President are the *only* public officials whom the entire Nation elects. I do not believe that an administrative agency decision of this magnitude—one that is important, conspicuous, and controversial—can escape the kind of public scrutiny that is essential in any democracy. And such a review will take place whether it is the Congress or the Executive Branch that makes the relevant decision. . . .

STATUTORY INTERPRETATION LESSONS 13–16

Both the majority and the dissent used a variety of rules of statutory interpretation. What are they? Here are the prominent ones that we have not yet discussed in detail:

Lesson 13: The Whole Act Rule. You already encountered a similar lesson before (lesson 8) but it is worth repeating here using this new label. This rule maintains that the individual provisions of a statute (like the definitions of "drug" and "drug delivery device") must be read in light of the entire statute. The majority holds that cigarettes can't possibly be covered by the act because otherwise they'd be "misbranded," because they are not ever safe and effective for their intended use. And if they are misbranded, they would have to be withdrawn from the market, something Congress did not want and which the agency was not willing to do. Thus, the whole statutory scheme arguably falls apart, which militates against finding that tobacco and cigarettes fall within the statutory definition.

Lesson 14: The Whole Code Rule. This rule maintains that Congress legislates against the backdrop of other legislation in the statute books, and that as a general matter the courts will try to make all of Congress's statutory acts cohere. In *Brown & Williamson,* the Court observed that Congress had passed numerous other statutes with the intent that tobacco and cigarettes would stay on the market. In light of these other statutory provisions, the majority argued, regulating tobacco as a drug under the FDCA did not make sense because the FDA would have to withdraw tobacco from the market.

Lesson 15: Implied Repeals Are Disfavored. A corollary of the whole code rule—the reason courts try to make the various statutes cohere—is that implied repeals are generally disfavored in the law. The Supreme Court has held, "The cardinal rule is that repeals by implication are not favored. Where there are two acts upon the same subject, effect should be given to both if possible." Posadas v. Nat'l City Bank of New York, 296 U.S. 497, 503 (1936).

Lesson 16: The Elephants-in-Mouseholes Canon. Important to the majority's analysis was "the nature of the question presented." Here, the question was one of major political and economic significance. If Congress wanted the FDA to regulate tobacco, wouldn't it have said something—at least something more explicit? "[W]e are confident," the Court held, "that Congress could not have intended to delegate a decision of such economic and political significance to an agency in so cryptic a fashion." Justice Scalia colorfully described this canon of interpretation in a subsequent opinion that cited both to *Brown & Williamson* and to *MCI,* discussed in *Brown & Williamson*: Congress "does not alter the fundamental details of a regulatory scheme in vague terms or ancillary provisions—it does not, one might say, hide elephants in mouseholes." Whitman v. Am. Trucking Associations, 531 U.S. 457, 468 (2001). The upshot is simply that if the meaning of a statute is open to doubt, the courts should presume that Congress did not intend to make major changes to the law *sub silentio.*

Notes and Questions

   1.   Other tools? On what other rules of statutory interpretation did the two opinions in *Brown & Williamson* rely?

   2.   How clear is clear? There are two important questions that *Brown & Williamson* raises, both involving *Chevron*'s first step. The first is how much efforts should courts make at step one to begin with; should it use every tool of statutory interpretation in the arsenal? If a statute is ambiguous looking only at the text, is that sufficient for deference? What if looking at purpose, context, and legislative history makes clearer what Congress intended? Inversely, might resorting to a variety of tools sometimes make the statute *more* ambiguous? How much effort, in other words, should courts make before concluding a statute is ambiguous?

The second question is, how much "ambiguity" is necessary to make something ambiguous? Was the fact that the *Brown & Williamson* decision was a 5–4 split enough to suggest that the statute was ambiguous? If you're a judge and you are 90% confident that your reading of the statute is correct, is that ambiguous because there's a 10% chance there's an alternative reading? How plausible must a reading be to make a statute ambiguous? Then-Judge Kavanaugh raised this issue in a prominent law review article in 2016:

> But how do courts know when a statute is clear or ambiguous? In other words, how much clarity is sufficient to call a statute clear and end the case there without triggering the ambiguity-dependent canons?
>
> Unfortunately, there is often no good or predictable way for judges to determine whether statutory text contains "enough" ambiguity to cross the line beyond which courts may resort to the constitutional avoidance canon, legislative history, or *Chevron* deference. In my experience, judges will often go back and forth arguing over this point. One judge will say that the statute is clear, and that should be the end of it. The other judge will respond that the text is ambiguous, meaning that one or another canon of construction should be employed to decide the case. Neither judge can convince the other. That's because there is no right answer.
>
> It turns out that there are at least two separate problems facing those disagreeing judges.
>
> First, judges must decide how much clarity is needed to call a statute clear. If the statute is 60-40 in one direction, is that enough to call it clear? How about 80-20? Who knows?
>
> Second, let's imagine that we could agree on an 80-20 clarity threshold. In other words, suppose that judges may call a text "clear" only if it is 80-20 or more clear in one direction. Even if we say that 80-20 is the necessary level of clear, how do we then apply that 80-20 formula to particular statutory text? Again, who knows? Determining

the level of ambiguity in a given piece of statutory language is often not possible in any rational way. One judge's clarity is another judge's ambiguity. It is difficult for judges (or anyone else) to perform that kind of task in a neutral, impartial, and predictable fashion.

I tend to be a judge who finds clarity more readily than some of my colleagues but perhaps a little less readily than others. In practice, I probably apply something approaching a 65-35 rule. In other words, if the interpretation is at least 65-35 clear, then I will call it clear and reject reliance on ambiguity-dependent canons. I think a few of my colleagues apply more of a 90-10 rule, at least in certain cases. Only if the proffered interpretation is at least 90-10 clear will they call it clear. By contrast, I have other colleagues who appear to apply a 55-45 rule. If the statute is at least 55-45 clear, that's good enough to call it clear.

Who is right in that debate? Who knows? No case or canon of interpretation says that my 65-35 approach or my colleagues' 90-10 or 55-45 approach is the correct one (or even a better one). Of course, even if my colleagues and I could agree on 65-35, for example, as the appropriate trigger, we would still have to figure out whether the text in question surmounts that 65-35 threshold. And that itself is a difficult task for different judges to conduct neutrally, impartially, and predictably.

The simple and troubling truth is that no definitive guide exists for determining whether statutory language is clear or ambiguous.

Brett M. Kavanaugh, *Fixing Statutory Interpretation*, 129 Harv. L. Rev. 2118, 2136–38 (2016).

Is there a solution to now-Justice Kavanaugh's observations? Is the solution to abandon *Chevron* deference altogether, and simply let judges decide what they think is the best interpretation of the statute? Judges will of course disagree about what the best interpretation of a statute is in any particular case, but at least everyone is asking the same question: what does each judge think is the best reading of the statute?

3. Substantive canons. What other canons of interpretation should the courts consider at *Chevron*'s first step? Should it also consider *substantive* canons, like the rule of lenity or the rule of constitutional avoidance? In Solid Waste Agency of Northern Cook County v. United States Army Corps of Engineers, 531 U.S. 159 (2001), the Supreme Court dealt with an EPA interpretation of the Clean Water Act that was not clearly prohibited by the statutory language, but which would arguably stretch federal power to its outermost constitutional limits.

 Defined Term

RULE OF LENITY: The rule that provides that courts should interpret ambiguity in criminal statutes in favor of defendants.

"Where an administrative interpretation of a statute invokes the outer limits of Congress' power," the Court held, "we expect a clear indication that Congress intended that result." Id. at 172. Thus, the Court adopted a clear statement rule (like the elephants-in-mouseholes canon): an agency *could* adopt such a regulation if Congress has *explicitly* delegated it authority to do so; but the courts shouldn't uphold such regulations merely because the statute is "ambiguous" at *Chevron*'s first step.

In another case, the Court held that even though a regulation was a reasonable interpretation of the statute that would ordinarily be entitled to deference, the regulation raised serious First Amendment concerns and so the constitutional avoidance rule trumped the *Chevron* doctrine. Edward J. De-Bartolo Corp. v. Fla. Gulf Coast Bldg. & Const. Trades Council, 485 U.S. 568, 574–75 (1988). Thus, the agency had to choose the regulation that did not raise serious constitutional concerns.

4. ***"Major questions."*** Go back to the elephants-in-mouseholes canon. The idea behind this canon, again, is that Congress wouldn't delegate to an agency authority to decide questions of "major" political or economic significance without saying so explicitly or at least having an actual debate about it. Hence this canon is also sometimes called the "major question doctrine." Is this canon rooted in nondelegation concerns? The premise seems to be that Congress *could* delegate to an agency questions of major political and economic significance if it wanted, it would just have to say so clearly. But at least if Congress says so clearly, it will have made its own decision about delegating such major

CROSS REFERENCE What is the connection between the "major questions" analysis at *Chevron* step one, and the nondelegation doctrine? We will discuss the nondelegation doctrine in more detail in the next chapter.

questions. Thus, the canon does serve some nondelegation values. See Cass R. Sunstein, *Nondelegation Canons*, 67 U. Chi. L. Rev. 315 (2000). In a statement respecting the denial of certiorari in the case *Paul v. United States*, Justice Kavanaugh noted that the major questions doctrine had served to enforce nondelegation values, calling it "a closely related statutory interpretation doctrine." 140 S. Ct. 342 (2019).

The following case is the next case in which the Court confronted a potential "major question" in the context of *Chevron* deference: *Massachusetts v. EPA*, where the question was whether EPA had to decide whether carbon dioxide emissions contributed global climate change and, if it did conclude as much, whether it had to regulate such emissions from motor vehicles. How is *Chevron* deployed in this case? How is *Brown & Williamson*?

Massachusetts v. EPA

549 U.S. 497 (2007)

JUSTICE STEVENS delivered the opinion of the Court.

A well-documented rise in global temperatures has coincided with a significant increase in the concentration of carbon dioxide in the atmosphere. Respected scientists believe the two trends are related. For when carbon dioxide is released into the atmosphere, it acts like the ceiling of a greenhouse, trapping solar energy and retarding the escape of reflected heat. It is therefore a species—the most important species—of a "greenhouse gas."

Calling global warming "the most pressing environmental challenge of our time," a group of States, local governments, and private organizations alleged in a petition for certiorari that the Environmental Protection Agency (EPA) has abdicated its responsibility under the Clean Air Act to regulate the emissions of four greenhouse gases, including carbon dioxide. Specifically, petitioners asked us to answer two questions concerning the meaning of § 202(a)(1) of the Act: whether EPA has the statutory authority to regulate greenhouse gas emissions from new motor vehicles; and if so, whether its stated reasons for refusing to do so are consistent with the statute.

In response, EPA, supported by 10 intervening States and six trade associations, correctly argued that we may not address those two questions unless at least one petitioner has standing to invoke our jurisdiction under Article III of the Constitution. Notwithstanding the serious character of that jurisdictional argument and the absence of any conflicting decisions construing § 202(a)(1), the unusual importance of the underlying issue persuaded us to grant the writ.

I

Section 202(a)(1) of the Clean Air Act provides:

> "The [EPA] Administrator shall by regulation prescribe (and from time to time revise) in accordance with the provisions of this section, standards applicable to the emission of any air pollutant from any class or classes of new motor vehicles or new motor vehicle engines, which in his judgment cause, or contribute to, air pollution which may reasonably be anticipated to endanger public health or welfare . . . ."

The Act defines "air pollutant" to include "any air pollution agent or combination of such agents, including any physical, chemical, biological, radioactive . . . substance or matter which is emitted into or otherwise enters the ambient air." § 7602(g). "Welfare" is also defined broadly: among other things, it includes "effects on . . . weather . . . and climate." § 7602(h).

When Congress enacted these provisions, the study of climate change was in its infancy. In 1959, shortly after the U.S. Weather Bureau began monitoring atmospheric carbon dioxide levels, an observatory in Mauna Loa, Hawaii, recorded a mean level of 316 parts per million. This was well above the highest carbon dioxide concentration—no more than 300 parts per million—revealed in the 420,000-year-old ice-core record. By the time Congress drafted § 202(a)(1) in 1970, carbon dioxide levels had reached 325 parts per million.

In the late 1970's, the Federal Government began devoting serious attention to the possibility that carbon dioxide emissions associated with human activity could provoke climate change. In 1978, Congress enacted the National Climate Program Act, 92 Stat. 601, which required the President to establish a program to "assist the Nation and the world to understand and respond to natural and man-induced climate processes and their implications." President Carter, in turn, asked the National Research Council, the working arm of the National Academy of Sciences, to investigate the subject. The Council's response was unequivocal: "If carbon dioxide continues to increase, the study group finds no reason to doubt that climate changes will result and no reason to believe that these changes will be negligible. . . . A wait-and-see policy may mean waiting until it is too late."

Congress next addressed the issue in 1987, when it enacted the Global Climate Protection Act, 101 Stat. 1407. Finding that "manmade pollution—the release of carbon dioxide, chlorofluorocarbons, methane, and other trace gases into the atmosphere—may be producing a long-term and substantial increase in the average temperature on Earth," Congress directed EPA to propose to Congress a "coordinated national policy on global climate change," and ordered the Secretary of State to work "through the channels of multilateral diplomacy" and coordinate diplomatic efforts to combat global warming. Congress emphasized that "ongoing pollution and deforestation may be contributing now to an irreversible process" and that "[n]ecessary actions must be identified and implemented in time to protect the climate."

Meanwhile, the scientific understanding of climate change progressed. In 1990, the Intergovernmental Panel on Climate Change (IPCC), a multinational scientific body organized under the auspices of the United Nations, published its first comprehensive report on the topic. Drawing on expert opinions from across the globe, the IPCC concluded that "emissions resulting from human activities are substantially increasing the atmospheric concentrations of . . . greenhouse gases [which] will enhance the greenhouse effect, resulting on average in an additional warming of the Earth's surface."

Responding to the IPCC report, the United Nations convened the "Earth Summit" in 1992 in Rio de Janeiro. The first President Bush attended and signed the United Nations Framework Convention on Climate Change (UNFCCC), a nonbinding agreement among 154 nations to reduce atmospheric concentrations of carbon dioxide and other greenhouse gases for the purpose of "prevent[ing] dangerous anthropogenic [*i.e.*, human-induced] interference with the [Earth's] climate system." The Senate unanimously ratified the treaty.

Some five years later—after the IPCC issued a second comprehensive report in 1995 concluding that "[t]he balance of evidence suggests there is a discernible human influence on global climate"—the UNFCCC signatories met in Kyoto, Japan, and adopted a protocol that assigned mandatory targets for industrialized nations to reduce greenhouse gas emissions. Because those targets did not apply to developing and heavily polluting nations such as China and

India, the Senate unanimously passed a resolution expressing its sense that the United States should not enter into the Kyoto Protocol. See S. Res. 98, 105th Cong., 1st Sess. (July 25, 1997) (as passed). President Clinton did not submit the protocol to the Senate for ratification.

II

On October 20, 1999, a group of 19 private organizations filed a rulemaking petition asking EPA to regulate "greenhouse gas emissions from new motor vehicles under § 202 of the Clean Air Act." Petitioners maintained that 1998 was the "warmest year on record"; that carbon dioxide, methane, nitrous oxide, and hydrofluorocarbons are "heat trapping greenhouse gases"; that greenhouse gas emissions have significantly accelerated climate change; and that the IPCC's 1995 report warned that "carbon dioxide remains the most important contributor to [manmade] forcing of climate change." The petition further alleged that climate change will have serious adverse effects on human health and the environment. As to EPA's statutory authority, the petition observed that the Agency itself had already confirmed that it had the power to regulate carbon dioxide. In 1998, Jonathan Z. Cannon, then EPA's general counsel, prepared a legal opinion concluding that "$CO2$ emissions are within the scope of EPA's authority to regulate," even as he recognized that EPA had so far declined to exercise that authority. Cannon's successor, Gary S. Guzy, reiterated that opinion before a congressional committee just two weeks before the rulemaking petition was filed.

Fifteen months after the petition's submission, EPA requested public comment on "all the issues raised in [the] petition," adding a "particular" request for comments on "any scientific, technical, legal, economic or other aspect of these issues that may be relevant to EPA's consideration of this petition." EPA received more than 50,000 comments over the next five months.

Before the close of the comment period, the White House sought "assistance in identifying the areas in the science of climate change where there are the greatest certainties and uncertainties" from the National Research Council, asking for a response "as soon as possible." The result was a 2001 report titled Climate Change Science: An Analysis of Some Key Questions (NRC Report), which, drawing heavily on the 1995 IPCC report, concluded that "[g]reenhouse gases are accumulating in Earth's atmosphere as a result of human activities, causing surface air temperatures and subsurface ocean temperatures to rise. Temperatures are, in fact, rising."

On September 8, 2003, EPA entered an order denying the rulemaking petition. The Agency gave two reasons for its decision: (1) that contrary to the opinions of its former general counsels, the Clean Air Act does not authorize EPA to issue mandatory regulations to address global climate change; and (2) that even if the Agency had the authority to set greenhouse gas emission standards, it would be unwise to do so at this time.

In concluding that it lacked statutory authority over greenhouse gases, EPA observed that Congress "was well aware of the global climate change issue when it last comprehensively amended the [Clean Air Act] in 1990," yet it declined to adopt a proposed amendment establishing binding emissions limitations. Congress instead chose to authorize further investigation into climate change. EPA further reasoned that Congress' "specially tailored solutions to global atmospheric issues"—in particular, its 1990 enactment of a comprehensive scheme to regulate pollutants that depleted the ozone layer, see 42 U.S.C. §§ 7671–7671q—counseled against reading the general authorization of § 202(a)(1) to confer regulatory authority over greenhouse gases.

EPA stated that it was "urged on in this view" by this Court's decision in *FDA v. Brown & Williamson Tobacco Corp.*, 529 U.S. 120 (2000). In that case, relying on "tobacco['s] unique political history," we invalidated the Food and Drug Administration's reliance on its general authority to regulate drugs as a basis for asserting jurisdiction over an "industry constituting a significant portion of the American economy."

EPA reasoned that climate change had its own "political history": Congress designed the original Clean Air Act to address *local* air pollutants rather than a substance that "is fairly consistent in its concentration throughout the *world's* atmosphere"; declined in 1990 to enact proposed amendments to force EPA to set carbon dioxide emission standards for motor vehicles; and addressed global climate change in other legislation. Because of this political history, and because imposing emission limitations on greenhouse gases would have even greater economic and political repercussions than regulating tobacco, EPA was persuaded that it lacked the power to do so. In essence, EPA concluded that climate change was so important that unless Congress spoke with exacting specificity, it could not have meant the Agency to address it.

Having reached that conclusion, EPA believed it followed that green-house gases cannot be "air pollutants" within the meaning of the Act. . . . The Agency bolstered this conclusion by explaining that if carbon dioxide were an air pollutant, the only feasible method of reducing tailpipe emissions would be to improve fuel economy. But because Congress has already created detailed mandatory fuel economy standards subject to Department of Transportation (DOT) administration, the Agency concluded that EPA regulation would either conflict with those standards or be superfluous.

Even assuming that it had authority over greenhouse gases, EPA explained in detail why it would refuse to exercise that authority. The Agency began by recognizing that the concentration of greenhouse gases has dramatically increased as a result of human activities, and acknowledged the attendant increase in global surface air temperatures. EPA nevertheless gave controlling importance to the NRC Report's statement that a causal link between the two " 'cannot be unequivocally established.' " Given that residual uncertainty, EPA concluded that regulating greenhouse gas emissions would be unwise.

The Agency furthermore characterized any EPA regulation of motor-vehicle emissions as a "piecemeal approach" to climate change, and stated that such regulation would conflict with the President's "comprehensive approach" to the problem. That approach involves additional support for technological innovation, the creation of nonregulatory programs to encourage voluntary private-sector reductions in greenhouse gas emissions, and further research on climate change—not actual regulation. According to EPA, unilateral EPA regulation of motor-vehicle greenhouse gas emissions might also hamper the President's ability to persuade key developing countries to reduce greenhouse gas emissions.

* * *

IV

[In part IV of the Court's opinion, it finds that Massachusetts has Article III standing sufficient for judicial review. That part of the Court's opinion is addressed in Chapter 8.D, *infra*, on standing.—Ed.].

V

The scope of our review of the merits of the statutory issues is narrow. As we have repeated time and again, an agency has broad discretion to choose how best to marshal its limited resources and personnel to carry out its delegated responsibilities. See *Chevron U.S.A. Inc. v. Natural Resources Defense Council, Inc.*, 467 U.S. 837, 842–845 (1984). That discretion is at its height when the agency decides not to bring an enforcement action. Therefore, in *Heckler v. Chaney*, 470 U.S. 821 (1985), we held that an agency's refusal to initiate enforcement proceedings is not ordinarily subject to judicial review. Some debate remains, however, as to the rigor with which we review an agency's denial of a petition for rulemaking.

There are key differences between a denial of a petition for rulemaking and an agency's decision not to initiate an enforcement action. See *American Horse Protection Assn., Inc. v. Lyng*, 812 F.2d 1, 3–4 (D.C. Cir. 1987). In contrast to nonenforcement decisions, agency refusals to initiate rulemaking "are less frequent, more apt to involve legal as opposed to factual analysis, and subject to special formalities, including a public explanation." *Id.* at 4; see also 5 U.S.C. § 555(e). They moreover arise out of denials of petitions for rulemaking which (at least in the circumstances here) the affected party had an undoubted procedural right to file in the first instance. Refusals to promulgate rules are thus susceptible to judicial review, though such review is "extremely limited" and "highly deferential." *National Customs Brokers & Forwarders Assn. of America, Inc. v. United States*, 883 F.2d 93, 96 (D.C. Cir. 1989).

EPA concluded in its denial of the petition for rulemaking that it lacked authority under 42 U.S.C. § 7521(a)(1) to regulate new vehicle emissions because carbon dioxide is not an "air pollutant" as that term is defined in § 7602. In the alternative, it concluded that even if it possessed authority, it would decline to do so because regulation would conflict with other administration priorities. . . .

VI

On the merits, the first question is whether § 202(a)(1) of the Clean Air Act authorizes EPA to regulate greenhouse gas emissions from new motor vehicles in the event that it forms a "judgment" that such emissions contribute to climate change. We have little trouble concluding that it does. In relevant part, § 202(a)(1) provides that EPA "shall by regulation prescribe . . . standards applicable to the emission of any air pollutant from any class or classes of new motor vehicles or new motor vehicle engines, which in [the Administrator's] judgment cause, or contribute to, air pollution which may reasonably be anticipated to endanger public health or welfare." 42 U.S.C. § 7521(a)(1). Because

EPA believes that Congress did not intend it to regulate substances that contribute to climate change, the agency maintains that carbon dioxide is not an "air pollutant" within the meaning of the provision.

The statutory text forecloses EPA's reading. The Clean Air Act's sweeping definition of "air pollutant" includes "*any* air pollution agent or combination of such agents, including *any* physical, chemical . . . substance or matter which is emitted into or otherwise enters the ambient air . . . ." § 7602(g) (emphasis added). On its face, the definition embraces all airborne compounds of whatever stripe, and underscores that intent through the repeated use of the word "any." Carbon dioxide, methane, nitrous oxide, and hydrofluorocarbons are without a doubt "physical [and] chemical . . . substance [s] which [are] emitted into . . . the ambient air." The statute is unambiguous.

Rather than relying on statutory text, EPA invokes postenactment congressional actions and deliberations it views as tantamount to a congressional command to refrain from regulating greenhouse gas emissions. Even if such postenactment legislative history could shed light on the meaning of an otherwise-unambiguous statute, EPA never identifies any action remotely suggesting that Congress meant to curtail its power to treat greenhouse gases as air pollutants. That subsequent Congresses have eschewed enacting binding emissions limitations to combat global warming tells us nothing about what Congress meant when it amended § 202(a)(1) in 1970 and 1977. And unlike EPA, we have no difficulty reconciling Congress' various efforts to promote interagency collaboration and research to better understand climate change with the Agency's pre-existing mandate to regulate "any air pollutant" that may endanger the public welfare. Collaboration and research do not conflict with any thoughtful regulatory effort; they complement it.

EPA's reliance on *Brown & Williamson Tobacco Corp.*, 529 U.S. 120, is similarly misplaced. In holding that tobacco products are not "drugs" or "devices" subject to Food and Drug Administration (FDA) regulation pursuant to the Food, Drug and Cosmetic Act (FDCA), we found critical at least two considerations that have no counterpart in this case.

First, we thought it unlikely that Congress meant to ban tobacco products, which the FDCA would have required had such products been classified as "drugs" or "devices." Here, in contrast, EPA jurisdiction would lead to no such extreme measures. EPA would only *regulate* emissions, and even then, it would have to delay any action "to permit the development and application of the requisite technology, giving appropriate consideration to the cost of compliance," § 7521(a)(2). However much a ban on tobacco products clashed with the "common sense" intuition that Congress never meant to remove those products from circulation, there is nothing counterintuitive to the notion that EPA can curtail the emission of substances that are putting the global climate out of kilter.

Second, in *Brown & Williamson* we pointed to an unbroken series of congressional enactments that made sense only if adopted "against the backdrop of the FDA's consistent and repeated statements that it lacked authority under the FDCA to regulate tobacco." We can point to no such enactments here: EPA has not identified any congressional action that conflicts in any way with the regulation of greenhouse gases from new motor vehicles. Even if it had, Congress could not have acted against a regulatory "backdrop" of disclaimers of regulatory authority. Prior to the order that provoked this litigation, EPA had never disavowed the authority to regulate greenhouse gases, and in 1998 it in fact affirmed that it *had* such authority. See App. 54 (Cannon memorandum). There is no reason, much less a compelling reason, to accept EPA's invitation to read ambiguity into a clear statute.

EPA finally argues that it cannot regulate carbon dioxide emissions from motor vehicles because doing so would require it to tighten mileage standards, a job (according to EPA) that Congress has assigned to DOT. But that DOT sets mileage standards in no way licenses EPA to shirk its environmental responsibilities. EPA has been charged with protecting the public's "health" and "welfare," 42 U.S.C. § 7521(a)(1), a statutory obligation wholly independent of DOT's mandate to promote energy efficiency. The two obligations may overlap, but there is no reason to think the two agencies cannot both administer their obligations and yet avoid inconsistency.

While the Congresses that drafted § 202(a)(1) might not have appreciated the possibility that burning fossil fuels could lead to global warming, they did understand that without regulatory flexibility, changing circumstances and scientific developments would soon render the Clean Air Act obsolete. The broad language of § 202(a)(1) reflects an intentional effort to confer the flexibility necessary to forestall such obsolescence. Because greenhouse gases fit well within the Clean Air Act's capacious definition of "air pollutant," we hold that EPA has the statutory authority to regulate the emission of such gases from new motor vehicles.

VII

The alternative basis for EPA's decision—that even if it does have statutory authority to regulate greenhouse gases, it would be unwise to do so at this time—rests on reasoning divorced from the statutory text. While the statute does condition the exercise of EPA's authority on its formation of a "judgment," 42 U.S.C. § 7521(a)(1), that judgment must relate to whether an air pollutant "cause[s], or contribute[s] to, air pollution which may reasonably be anticipated to endanger public health or welfare." Put another way, the use of the word "judgment" is not a roving license to ignore the statutory text. It is but a direction to exercise discretion within defined statutory limits.

If EPA makes a finding of endangerment, the Clean Air Act requires the Agency to regulate emissions of the deleterious pollutant from new motor vehicles. *Ibid.* (stating that "[EPA] shall by regulation prescribe . . . standards applicable to the emission of any air pollutant from any class or classes of new motor vehicles"). EPA no doubt has significant latitude as to the manner, timing, content, and coordination of its regulations with those of other agencies. But once EPA has responded to a petition for rulemaking, its reasons for action or inaction must conform to the authorizing statute. Under the clear terms of the Clean Air Act, EPA can avoid taking further action only if it determines that greenhouse gases do not contribute to climate change or if it provides some reasonable explanation as to why it cannot or will not exercise its discretion to determine whether they do. To the extent that this constrains agency discretion to pursue other priorities of the Administrator or the President, this is the congressional design.

EPA has refused to comply with this clear statutory command. Instead, it has offered a laundry list of reasons not to regulate. For example, EPA said that a number of voluntary Executive Branch programs already provide an effective response to the threat of global warming, that regulating greenhouse gases might impair the President's ability to negotiate with "key developing nations" to reduce emissions, and that curtailing motor-vehicle emissions would reflect "an inefficient, piecemeal approach to address the climate change issue."

Although we have neither the expertise nor the authority to evaluate these policy judgments, it is evident they have nothing to do with whether greenhouse gas emissions contribute to climate change. Still less do they amount to a reasoned justification for declining to form a scientific judgment. In particular, while the President has broad authority in foreign affairs, that authority does not extend to the refusal to execute domestic laws. In the Global Climate Protection Act of 1987, Congress authorized the State Department—not EPA—to formulate United States foreign policy with reference to environmental matters relating to climate. EPA has made no showing that it issued the ruling in question here after consultation with the State Department. Congress did direct EPA to consult with other agencies in the formulation of its policies and rules, but the State Department is absent from that list. § 1103(b).

Nor can EPA avoid its statutory obligation by noting the uncertainty surrounding various features of climate change and concluding that it would therefore be better not to regulate at this time. If the scientific uncertainty is so profound that it precludes EPA from making a reasoned judgment as to whether greenhouse gases contribute to global warming, EPA must say so. That EPA would prefer not to regulate greenhouse gases because of some residual uncertainty . . . is irrelevant. The statutory question is whether sufficient information exists to make an endangerment finding.

In short, EPA has offered no reasoned explanation for its refusal to decide whether greenhouse gases cause or contribute to climate change. Its action was therefore "arbitrary, capricious, . . . or otherwise not in accordance with law." 42 U.S.C. § 7607(d)(9)(A). We need not and do not reach the question whether on remand EPA must make an endangerment finding, or whether policy concerns can inform EPA's actions in the event that it makes such a finding. Cf. *Chevron U.S.A. Inc. v. Natural Resources Defense Council, Inc.,* 467 U.S. 843–844. We hold only that EPA must ground its reasons for action or inaction in the statute.

[Chief Justice Roberts' dissent on standing is presented in Chapter 8.D.—Ed.]

Justice Scalia, with whom The Chief Justice, Justice Thomas, and Justice Alito join, dissenting.

I join The Chief Justice's opinion in full, and would hold that this Court has no jurisdiction to decide this case because petitioners lack standing. The Court having decided otherwise, it is appropriate for me to note my dissent on the merits.

I

A

The provision of law at the heart of this case is § 202(a)(1) of the Clean Air Act (CAA or Act), which provides that the Administrator of the Environmental Protection Agency (EPA) "shall by regulation prescribe . . . standards applicable to the emission of any air pollutant from any class or classes of new motor vehicles or new motor vehicle engines, which *in his judgment* cause, or contribute to, air pollution which may reasonably be anticipated to endanger public health or welfare." 42 U.S.C. § 7521(a)(1) (emphasis added). As the Court recognizes, the statute "condition[s] the exercise of EPA's authority on its formation of a 'judgment.' " There is no dispute that the Administrator has made no such judgment in this case. See *ante* ("We need not and do not reach the question whether on remand EPA must make an endangerment finding"); 68 Fed. Reg. 52929 (2003) ("[N]o Administrator has made a finding under any of the CAA's regulatory provisions that CO2 meets the applicable statutory criteria for regulation").

The question thus arises: Does anything *require* the Administrator to make a "judgment" whenever a petition for rulemaking is filed? Without citation of the statute or any other authority, the Court says yes. Why is that so? . . . Where does the CAA say that the EPA Administrator is required to come to a decision on this question whenever a rulemaking petition is filed? The Court points to no such provision because none exists.

Instead, the Court invents a multiple-choice question that the EPA Administrator must answer when a petition for rulemaking is filed. The Administrator must exercise his judgment in one of three ways: (a) by concluding that the pollutant *does* cause, or contribute to, air pollution that endangers public welfare (in which case EPA is required to regulate); (b) by concluding that the pollutant *does not* cause, or contribute to, air pollution that endangers public welfare (in which case EPA is *not* required to regulate); or (c) by "provid[ing] some reasonable explanation as to why it cannot or will not exercise its discretion to determine whether" greenhouse gases endanger public welfare (in which case EPA is *not* required to regulate).

I am willing to assume, for the sake of argument, that the Administrator's discretion in this regard is not entirely unbounded—that if he has no reasonable basis for deferring judgment he must grasp the nettle at once. The Court, however, with no basis in text or precedent, rejects all of EPA's stated "policy judgments" as not "amount[ing] to a reasoned justification," effectively narrowing the universe of potential reasonable bases to a single one: Judgment can be delayed *only* if the Administrator concludes that "the scientific uncertainty is [too] profound." The Administrator is precluded from concluding *for other reasons* "that it would . . . be better not to regulate at this time." Such other reasons—perfectly valid reasons—were set forth in the Agency's statement. . . .

When the Administrator *makes* a judgment whether to regulate greenhouse gases, that judgment must relate to whether they are air pollutants that "cause, or contribute to, air pollution which may reasonably be anticipated to endanger public health or welfare." 42 U.S.C. § 7521(a)(1). But the statute says *nothing at all* about the reasons for which the Administrator may *defer* making a judgment—the permissible reasons for deciding not to grapple with the issue at the present time. Thus, the various "policy" rationales that the Court criticizes are not "divorced from the statutory text," except in the sense that the statutory text is silent, as texts are often silent about permissible reasons for the exercise of agency discretion. The reasons EPA gave are surely considerations executive agencies *regularly* take into account (and *ought* to take into account) when deciding whether to consider entering a new field: the impact such entry would have on other Executive Branch programs and on foreign policy. There is no basis in law for the Court's imposed limitation.

EPA's interpretation of the discretion conferred by the statutory reference to "its judgment" is not only reasonable, it is the most natural reading of the text. The Court nowhere explains why this interpretation is incorrect, let alone why it is not entitled to deference under *Chevron U.S.A. Inc. v. Natural Resources Defense Council, Inc.*, 467 U.S. 837 (1984). As the Administrator acted within the law in declining to make a "judgment" for the policy reasons above set forth, I would uphold the decision to deny the rulemaking petition on that ground alone.

B

Even on the Court's own terms, however, the same conclusion follows. As mentioned above, the Court gives EPA the option of determining that the science is too uncertain to allow it to form a "judgment" as to whether greenhouse gases endanger public welfare. . . . But EPA *has* said precisely that—and at great length, based on information contained in a 2001 report by the National

Research Council (NRC) entitled Climate Change Science: An Analysis of Some Key Questions: "As the NRC noted in its report, . . . a [causal] linkage between the buildup of [GHGs] in the atmosphere and the observed climate changes during the 20th century cannot be unequivocally established. . . ."

I simply cannot conceive of what else the Court would like EPA to say.

II

A

Even before reaching its discussion of the word "judgment," the Court makes another significant error when it concludes that "§ 202(a)(1) of the Clean Air Act *authorizes* EPA to regulate greenhouse gas emissions from new motor vehicles in the event that it forms a 'judgment' that such emissions contribute to climate change." For such authorization, the Court relies on what it calls "the Clean Air Act's capacious definition of 'air pollutant.' "

"Air pollutant" is defined by the Act as "any air pollution agent or combination of such agents, including any physical, chemical, . . . substance or matter which is emitted into or otherwise enters the ambient air." 42 U.S.C. § 7602(g). The Court is correct that "[c]arbon dioxide, methane, nitrous oxide, and hydrofluorocarbons," fit within the second half of that definition: They are "physical, chemical, . . . substance[s] or matter which [are] emitted into or otherwise ente[r] the ambient air." But the Court mistakenly believes this to be the end of the analysis. In order to be an "air pollutant" under the Act's definition, the "substance or matter [being] emitted into . . . the ambient air" must also meet the *first* half of the definition—namely, it must be an "air pollution agent or combination of such agents." The Court simply pretends this half of the definition does not exist.

The Court's analysis faithfully follows the argument advanced by petitioners, which focuses on the word "including" in the statutory definition of "air pollutant." As that argument goes, anything that *follows* the word "including" must necessarily be a subset of whatever *precedes* it. Thus, if greenhouse gases qualify under the phrase following the word "including," they must qualify under the phrase preceding it. Since greenhouse gases come within the capacious phrase "any physical, chemical, . . . substance or matter which is emitted into or otherwise enters the ambient air," they must also be "air pollution agent[s] or combination[s] of such agents," and therefore meet the definition of "air pollutant[s]."

That is certainly one possible interpretation of the statutory definition. The word "including" can indeed indicate that what follows will be an "illustrative" sampling of the general category that precedes the word. Often, however, the examples standing alone are broader than the general category, and must be viewed as limited in light of that category. The Government provides a helpful (and unanswered) example: "The phrase 'any American automobile, including any truck or minivan,' would not naturally be construed to encompass a for-eign-manufactured [truck or] minivan." The general principle enunciated—that the speaker is talking about *American* automobiles—carries forward to the il-lustrative examples (trucks and minivans), and limits them accordingly, even though in isolation they are broader. Congress often uses the word "including" in this manner. In 28 U.S.C. § 1782(a), for example, it refers to "a proceeding in a foreign or international tribunal, including criminal investigations con-ducted before formal accusation." Certainly this provision would not encompass criminal investigations underway in a *domestic* tribunal.

In short, the word "including" does not require the Court's (or the peti-tioners') result. It is perfectly reasonable to view the definition of "air pollutant" in its entirety: An air pollutant *can* be "any physical, chemical, . . . substance or matter which is emitted into or otherwise enters the ambient air," but only if it retains the general characteristic of being an "air pollution agent or com-bination of such agents." This is precisely the conclusion EPA reached: "[A] substance does not meet the CAA definition of 'air pollutant' simply because it is a 'physical, chemical, . . . substance or matter which is emitted into or oth-erwise enters the ambient air.' It must also be an 'air pollution agent.' " 68 Fed. Reg. 52929, n. 3. See also *id.*, at 52928 ("The root of the definition indicates that for a substance to be an 'air pollutant,' it must be an 'agent' of 'air pollu-tion' "). Once again, in the face of textual ambiguity, the Court's application of *Chevron* deference to EPA s interpretation of the word "including" is nowhere to be found.[2] Evidently, the Court defers only to those reasonable interpreta-tions that it favors.

---

[2]   Not only is EPA's interpretation reasonable, it is far more plausible than the Court's alternative. As the Court correctly points out, "all airborne compounds of whatever stripe" would qualify as "physical, chemical, . . . substance[s] or matter which [are] emitted into or otherwise ente[r] the ambient air," 42 U.S.C. § 7602(g). It follows that *everything* airborne, from Frisbees to flatulence, qualifies as an "air pollutant." This reading of the statute defies common sense.

B

Using (as we ought to) EPA's interpretation of the definition of "air pollutant," we must next determine whether greenhouse gases are "agent[s]" of "air pollution." If so, the statute would authorize regulation; if not, EPA would lack authority.

Unlike "air pollutants," the term "air pollution" is not itself defined by the CAA; thus, once again we must accept EPA's interpretation of that ambiguous term, provided its interpretation is a "permissible construction of the statute." *Chevron,* 467 U.S. at 843. . . . EPA began with the commonsense observation that the "[p]roblems associated with atmospheric concentrations of CO2" bear little resemblance to what would naturally be termed "air pollution":

> ". . . . Since the inception of the Act, EPA has used these provisions to address air pollution problems that occur primarily at ground level or near the surface of the earth. For example, national ambient air quality standards (NAAQS) established under CAA section 109 address concentrations of substances in the ambient air and the related public health and welfare problems. This has meant setting NAAQS for concentrations of ozone, carbon monoxide, particulate matter and other substances in the air near the surface of the earth, not higher in the atmosphere . . . . CO2, by contrast, is fairly consistent in concentration throughout the world's atmosphere up to approximately the lower stratosphere." [68 Fed. Reg.] at 52926–52927.

In other words, regulating the buildup of CO2 and other greenhouse gases in the upper reaches of the atmosphere, which is alleged to be causing global climate change, is not akin to regulating the concentration of some substance that is *polluting* the *air.*

We need look no further than the dictionary for confirmation that this interpretation of "air pollution" is eminently reasonable. The definition of "pollute," of course, is "[t]o make or render impure or unclean." Webster's New International Dictionary 1910 (2d ed.1949). And the first three definitions of "air" are as follows: (1) "[t]he invisible, odorless, and tasteless mixture of gases which surrounds the earth"; (2) "[t]he body of the earth's atmosphere; esp., the part of it near the earth, as distinguished from the upper rarefied part"; (3) "[a] portion of air or of the air considered with respect to physical characteristics or as affecting the senses." *Id.* at 54. EPA's conception of "air pollution"—focusing on impurities in the "ambient air" "at ground level or near the surface of the earth"—is perfectly consistent with the natural meaning of that term. . . .

Once again, the Court utterly fails to explain why this interpretation is incorrect, let alone so unreasonable as to be unworthy of *Chevron* deference. . . .

The Court's alarm over global warming may or may not be justified, but it ought not distort the outcome of this litigation. This is a straightforward administrative-law case, in which Congress has passed a malleable statute giving broad discretion, not to us but to an executive agency. No matter how important the underlying policy issues at stake, this Court has no business substituting its own desired outcome for the reasoned judgment of the responsible agency.

Notes and Questions

1. ***Step one or step two?*** For the dissenting Justices, the case was effectively a step one question: the statute was at best ambiguous both as to whether the carbon dioxide was a "pollutant" within the meaning of the statute, and as to whether the Administrator had to make a judgment in the first place about the risks associated with known air pollutants. For the Justices in the majority, the case presented both a step one and a step two question. They held that carbon dioxide *was* a pollutant under the statute, and the Administrator *had* to make a judgment about that pollutant. Because the judgment the Administrator made in this case was based on an erroneous understanding of the statutory meaning of "pollutant," the Court remanded to the agency to make a judgment about the health impact of carbon dioxide emissions based on its impact on climate change. With which approach do you agree? Was the Court's arbitrary-and-capricious holding a step-two decision or a *State Farm* decision? Is there a difference between the two?

2. **Chevron *deference and consistency.*** Was the Court in *Massachusetts v. EPA* consistent with the Court in *Brown & Williamson*? Did the Court faithfully apply the "major questions" canon? On the other hand, in neither case did the majority of the Court defer to the agency. Is that a kind of consistency?

3. ***Step one or step zero?*** Was the Court's invocation of the major questions doctrine in *Brown & Williamson* and *Massachusetts v. EPA* part of its step one analysis? Or should the *Chevron* doctrine not apply at all to such major

questions? In *King v. Burwell*, 577 U.S. 988 (2015), the Supreme Court held that *Chevron* deference is inapplicable altogether when the question is one of major political and economic significance. Thus, the Court decided for itself, de novo, whether the Affordable Care Act permitted the federal government to provide personal health insurance subsidies in states with federal as opposed to state healthcare exchanges. On this account, the "major questions doctrine" is actually a "step zero" question: whether the *Chevron* doctrine should be deployed at all. The next section examines *Chevron* "step zero."

CROSS REFERENCE Although it has cropped up a few times, we have yet to address *Chevron* step zero fully. That is a preliminary step where courts ask whether to deploy the deference framework at all.

4. Follow-on case: UARG v. EPA.

In the aftermath of the Court's decision in *Massachusetts v. EPA*, the EPA decided during the administration of President Barack Obama to regulate greenhouse gasses as permitted by the Court's opinion. Recall that *Massachusetts* dealt with regulations of motor vehicle emissions. In another provision of the Clean Air Act, the EPA must regulate major stationary sources, like power plants, that emit pollution. The only problem was that the Act's definition of a "major emitting facility" subject to the relevant regulations was any stationary source that emitted at least, depending on the context, 100 or 250 tons of pollution a year. This is an astronomical amount of pollution for traditional pollutants like sulfur dioxide, and so the number of such sources regulated by the EPA is relatively small, but 100 or 250 tons are minuscule amounts for carbon dioxide emissions. If the EPA regulated any stationary source that emitted at least 100 or 250 tons of carbon dioxide, then EPA would get to regulate almost the entire economy. That didn't sound right or even feasible, and so the EPA promulgated a rule providing that it would regulate stationary sources that emitted at least 10,000 tons of carbon dioxide.

In *Utility Air Regulatory Group v. EPA*, the Court invalidated the regulation, holding that carbon dioxide simply could not fall within the meaning of "pollutant" in the relevant portion of the statute. 573 U.S. 302 (2014). The Court harkened back to *Brown & Williamson*: First, as a matter of statutory interpretation, carbon dioxide could not fall within the definition of air pollutant *in this part of the statute*, otherwise the entire statutory framework would fall apart. Second, the Court held that the EPA's interpretation was also unreasonable because it would bring about an enormous and transformative expansion in EPA's regulatory authority without clear congressional authorization. When an agency claims to discover in a long-extant statute an unheralded power to regulate "a significant portion of the American economy," *Brown & Williamson*, 529 U.S. at 159, we typically greet its announcement with a measure of skepticism. We expect Congress to speak clearly if it wishes to assign to an agency decisions of vast "economic and political significance."

573 U.S. at 324.

STATUTORY INTERPRETATION LESSON 17

The Court's analysis brings us to our next statutory interpretation lesson, which is related to lesson 8 on context and structure and lesson 13 on the whole act rule:

Lesson 17: Presumption of Consistent Usage, but This Presumption Yields to Context. There is no good name for this rule, and perhaps it is simply a variant of rules 8 and 13, as just noted. But here is how the Court put it in the *UARG* case:

> One ordinarily assumes " 'that identical words used in different parts of the same act are intended to have the same meaning.' " *Environmental Defense v. Duke Energy Corp.*, 549 U.S. 561, 574 (2007). . . . But we, and EPA, must do our best, bearing in mind the " 'fundamental canon of statutory construction that the words of a statute must be read in their context and with a view to their place in the overall statutory scheme.' " *FDA v. Brown & Williamson Tobacco Corp.*, 529 U.S. 120, 133 (2000). As we reiterated the same day we decided *Massachusetts,* the presumption of consistent usage " 'readily yields' " to context, and a statutory term—even one defined in the statute—"may take on distinct characters from association with distinct statutory objects calling for different implementation strategies." *Duke Energy, supra,* at 574.

Utility Air Regulatory Group v. EPA, 573 U.S. 302, 319–20 (2014).

3. *Chevron* Step Zero

In its canonical form, the *Chevron* doctrine has two steps: is the statute ambiguous, and if so, is the agency's interpretation reasonable? But preceding these questions is the question of whether the *Chevron* framework applies at all—and, if it doesn't, what kind of deference framework (if any) applies. These issues are sometimes labeled as "*Chevron* Step Zero." See generally Thomas W. Merrill & Kristin E. Hickman, Chevron's *Domain*, 89 Geo. L.J. 833 (2001); Cass R. Sunstein, Chevron *Step Zero*, 92 Va. L. Rev. 187 (2006). The following are some leading cases.

Christensen v. Harris County

529 U.S. 576 (2000)

JUSTICE THOMAS delivered the opinion of the Court.

Under the Fair Labor Standards Act of 1938 (FLSA), States and their political subdivisions may compensate their employees for overtime by granting them compensatory time or "comp time," which entitles them to take time off work with full pay. If the employees do not use their accumulated compensatory time, the employer is obligated to pay cash compensation under certain circumstances. §§ 207(*o*)(3)–(4). Fearing the fiscal consequences of having to pay for accrued compensatory time, Harris County adopted a policy requiring its employees to schedule time off in order to reduce the amount of accrued compensatory time. Employees of the Harris County Sheriff's Department sued, claiming that the FLSA prohibits such a policy. The Court of Appeals rejected their claim. Finding that nothing in the FLSA or its implementing regulations prohibits an employer from compelling the use of compensatory time, we affirm.

I

A

The FLSA generally provides that hourly employees who work in excess of 40 hours per week must be compensated for the excess hours at a rate not less than 1 ½ times their regular hourly wage. Although this requirement did not initially apply to public-sector employers, Congress amended the FLSA to subject States and their political subdivisions to its constraints . . . . States and their political subdivisions, however, did not feel the full force of this latter extension until our decision in *Garcia v. San Antonio Metropolitan Transit Authority*, 469 U.S. 528 (1985), which overruled our holding in *National League of Cities v. Usery*, 426 U.S. 833 (1976), that the FLSA could not constitutionally restrain traditional governmental functions.

In the months following *Garcia*, Congress acted to mitigate the effects of applying the FLSA to States and their political subdivisions, passing the Fair Labor Standards Amendments of 1985. Those amendments permit States and their political subdivisions to compensate employees for overtime by granting them compensatory time at a rate of 1 ½ hours for every hour worked. See 29 U.S.C. § 207(*o*)(1). To provide this form of compensation, the employer must arrive at an agreement or understanding with employees that compensatory time will be granted instead of cash compensation. § 207(*o*)(2); 29 CFR § 553.23 (1999).

The FLSA expressly regulates some aspects of accrual and preservation of compensatory time. For example, the FLSA provides that an employer must honor an employee's request to use compensatory time within a "reasonable period" of time following the request, so long as the use of the compensatory time would not "unduly disrupt" the employer's operations. § 207(*o*)(5); 29 CFR § 553.25 (1999). The FLSA also caps the number of compensatory time hours that an employee may accrue. After an employee reaches that maximum, the employer must pay cash compensation for additional overtime hours worked. § 207(*o*)(3)(A). In addition, the FLSA permits the employer at any time to cancel or "cash out" accrued compensatory time hours by paying the employee cash compensation for unused compensatory time. § 207(*o*)(3)(B); 29 CFR § 553.26(a) (1999). And the FLSA entitles the employee to cash payment for any accrued compensatory time remaining upon the termination of employment. § 207(*o*)(4).

B

Petitioners are 127 deputy sheriffs employed by respondents Harris County, Texas, and its sheriff, Tommy B. Thomas (collectively, Harris County). It is undisputed that each of the petitioners individually agreed to accept compensatory time, in lieu of cash, as compensation for overtime.

As petitioners accumulated compensatory time, Harris County became concerned that it lacked the resources to pay monetary compensation to employees who worked overtime after reaching the statutory cap on compensatory time accrual and to employees who left their jobs with sizable reserves of accrued time. As a result, the county began looking for a way to reduce accumulated compensatory time. It wrote to the United States Department of Labor's Wage and Hour Division, asking "whether the Sheriff may schedule non-exempt employees to use or take compensatory time." The Acting Administrator of the Division replied:

> "[I]t is our position that a public employer may schedule its nonexempt employees to use their accrued FLSA compensatory time as directed if the prior agreement specifically provides such a provision . . . .

> "Absent such an agreement, it is our position that neither the statute nor the regulations permit an employer to require an employee to use accrued compensatory time." Opinion Letter from Dept. of Labor, Wage and Hour Div. (Sept. 14, 1992).

After receiving the letter, Harris County implemented a policy under which the employees' supervisor sets a maximum number of compensatory hours that may be accumulated. When an employee's stock of hours approaches that maximum, the employee is advised of the maximum and is asked to take steps to reduce accumulated compensatory time. If the employee does not do so voluntarily, a supervisor may order the employee to use his compensatory time at specified times.

Petitioners sued, claiming that the county's policy violates the FLSA because § 207(*o*)(5)—which requires that an employer reasonably accommodate employee requests to use compensatory time—provides the exclusive means of utilizing accrued time in the absence of an agreement or understanding permitting some other method. . . .

II

Both parties, and the United States as *amicus curiae,* concede that nothing in the FLSA expressly prohibits a State or subdivision thereof from compelling employees to utilize accrued compensatory time. Petitioners and the United States, however, contend that the FLSA implicitly prohibits such a practice in the absence of an agreement or understanding authorizing compelled use. Title 29 U.S.C. § 207(*o*)(5) provides: "An employee . . . (A) who has accrued compensatory time off . . . , and (B) who has requested the use of such compensatory time, shall be permitted by the employee's employer to use such time within a reasonable period after making the request if the use of the compensatory time does not unduly disrupt the operations of the public agency."

Petitioners and the United States rely upon the canon *expressio unius est exclusio alterius,* contending that the express grant of control to employees to use compensatory time, subject to the limitation regarding undue disruptions of workplace operations, implies that all other methods of spending compensatory time are precluded.

We find this reading unpersuasive. . . . [V]iewed in the context of the overall statutory scheme, § 207(*o*)(5) is better read not as setting forth the exclusive method by which compensatory time can be used, but as setting up a safeguard to ensure that an employee will receive timely compensation for working overtime. Section 207(*o*)(5) guarantees that, at the very minimum, an employee will get to use his compensatory time (*i.e.,* take time off work with full pay) unless doing so would disrupt the employer's operations. . . .

At bottom, we think the better reading of § 207(*o*)(5) is that it imposes a restriction upon an employer's efforts to *prohibit* the use of compensatory time when employees request to do so; that provision says nothing about restricting an employer's efforts to *require* employees to use compensatory time. Because the statute is silent on this issue and because Harris County's policy is entirely compatible with § 207(*o*)(5), petitioners cannot, as they are required to do by 29 U.S.C. § 216(b), prove that Harris County has violated § 207. . . .

III

In an attempt to avoid the conclusion that the FLSA does not prohibit compelled use of compensatory time, petitioners and the United States contend that we should defer to the Department of Labor's opinion letter, which takes the position that an employer may compel the use of compensatory time only if the employee has agreed in advance to such a practice. Specifically, they argue that the agency opinion letter is entitled to deference under our decision in *Chevron U.S.A. Inc. v. Natural Resources Defense Council, Inc.,* 467 U.S. 837 (1984). In *Chevron,* we held that a court must give effect to an agency's regulation containing a reasonable interpretation of an ambiguous statute.

Here, however, we confront an interpretation contained in an opinion letter, not one arrived at after, for example, a formal adjudication or notice-and-comment rulemaking. Interpretations such as those in opinion letters—like interpretations contained in policy statements, agency manuals, and enforcement guidelines, all of which lack the force of law—do not warrant *Chevron*-style deference. Instead, interpretations contained in formats such as opinion letters are "entitled to respect" under our decision in *Skidmore v. Swift & Co.*, 323 U.S. 134, 140 (1944), but only to the extent that those interpretations have the "power to persuade," *ibid*. As explained above, we find unpersuasive the agency's interpretation of the statute at issue in this case.

Of course, the framework of deference set forth in *Chevron* does apply to an agency interpretation contained in a regulation. But in this case the Department of Labor's regulation does not address the issue of compelled compensatory time. . . .

Seeking to overcome the regulation's obvious meaning, the United States asserts that the agency's opinion letter interpreting the regulation should be given deference under our decision in *Auer v. Robbins*, 519 U.S. 452 (1997). In *Auer*, we held that an agency's interpretation of its own regulation is entitled to deference. See also *Bowles v. Seminole Rock & Sand Co.*, 325 U.S. 410 (1945). But *Auer* deference is warranted only when the language of the regulation is ambiguous. The regulation in this case, however, is not ambiguous—it is plainly permissive. . . .

As we have noted, no relevant statutory provision expressly or implicitly prohibits Harris County from pursuing its policy of forcing employees to utilize their compensatory time. In its opinion letter siding with the petitioners, the Department of Labor opined that "it is our position that neither the statute nor the regulations *permit* an employer to require an employee to use accrued compensatory time." Opinion Letter (emphasis added). But this view is exactly backwards. Unless the FLSA *prohibits* respondents from adopting its policy, petitioners cannot show that Harris County has violated the FLSA. And the FLSA contains no such prohibition.

Justice Scalia, concurring in part and concurring in the judgment.

I join the judgment of the Court and all of its opinion except Part III, which declines to give effect to the position of the Department of Labor in this case because its opinion letter is entitled only to so-called "*Skidmore* deference," see *Skidmore v. Swift & Co.*, 323 U.S. 134, 140 (1944). *Skidmore* deference to authoritative agency views is an anachronism, dating from an era in which we declined to give agency interpretations (including interpretive regulations, as opposed to "legislative rules") authoritative effect. . . .

That era came to an end with our watershed decision in *Chevron U.S.A. Inc. v. Natural Resources Defense Council, Inc.*, 467 U.S. 837, 844 (1984) . . . . While *Chevron* in fact involved an interpretive regulation, the rationale of the case was not limited to that context . . . . Quite appropriately, therefore, we have accorded *Chevron* deference not only to agency regulations, but to authoritative agency positions set forth in a variety of other formats. [Citing cases where deference was afforded to legal interpretations in agency adjudications, opinion letters, and other informal decisions.—Ed.]

In my view, therefore, the position that the county's action in this case was unlawful unless permitted by the terms of an agreement with the sheriff's department employees warrants *Chevron* deference if it represents the authoritative view of the Department of Labor. The fact that it appears in a single opinion letter signed by the Acting Administrator of the Wage and Hour Division might not alone persuade me that it occupies that status. But the Solicitor General of the United States, appearing as an *amicus* in this action, has filed a brief, cosigned by the Solicitor of Labor, which represents the position set forth in the opinion letter to be the position of the Secretary of Labor. That alone, even without existence of the opinion letter, would in my view entitle the position to *Chevron* deference. What we said in a case involving an agency's interpretation of its own regulations applies equally, in my view, to an agency's interpretation of its governing statute:

> "Petitioners complain that the Secretary's interpretation comes to us in the form of a legal brief; but that does not, in the circumstances of this case, make it unworthy of deference. The Secretary's position is in no sense a 'post hoc rationalizatio[n]' advanced by an agency seeking to defend past agency action against attack. There is simply no reason to suspect that the interpretation does not reflect the agency's fair and considered judgment on the matter in question." Auer v. Robbins, 519 U.S. 452, 462 (1997).

I nonetheless join the judgment of the Court because, for the reasons set forth in Part II of its opinion, the Secretary's position does not seem to me a reasonable interpretation of the statute.

Justice Souter, concurring.

I join the opinion of the Court on the assumption that it does not foreclose a reading of the Fair Labor Standards Act of 1938 that allows the Secretary of Labor to issue regulations limiting forced use.

Justice Stevens, with whom Justice Ginsburg and Justice Breyer join, dissenting.

Because the disagreement between the parties concerns the scope of an exception to a general rule, it is appropriate to begin with a correct identification of the relevant general rule. That rule gives all employees protected by the Fair Labor Standards Act of 1938 a statutory right to compensation for overtime work payable in cash, whether they work in the private sector of the economy or the public sector. In 1985, Congress enacted an exception to that general rule that permits States and their political subdivisions to use compensatory time instead of cash as compensation for overtime. The exception, however, is not applicable unless the public employer first arrives at an agreement with its employees to substitute that type of compensation for cash. § 207(*o*); 29 CFR § 553.23 (1999). As I read the statute, the employer has no right to impose compensatory overtime payment upon its employees except in accordance with the terms of the agreement authorizing its use. . . .

Justice Breyer, with whom Justice Ginsburg joins, dissenting.

Justice Scalia may well be right that the position of the Department of Labor, set forth in both brief and letter, is an "authoritative" agency view that warrants deference under *Chevron U.S.A. Inc. v. Natural Resources Defense Council, Inc.*, 467 U.S. 837 (1984). But I do not object to the majority's citing *Skidmore v. Swift & Co.*, 323 U.S. 134 (1944), instead. And I do disagree with Justice Scalia's statement that what he calls "*Skidmore* deference" is "an anachronism."

Skidmore made clear that courts may pay particular attention to the views of an expert agency where they represent "specialized experience," even if they do not constitute an exercise of delegated lawmaking authority. The Court held that the "rulings, interpretations and opinions of" an agency, "while not controlling upon the courts by reason of their authority, do constitute a body of experience and informed judgment to which courts and litigants may properly resort for guidance." As Justice Jackson wrote for the Court, those views may possess the "power to persuade," even where they lack the "power to control."

Chevron made no relevant change. It simply focused upon an additional, separate legal reason for deferring to certain agency determinations, namely, that Congress had delegated to the agency the legal authority to make those determinations. See *Chevron, supra,* at 843–844. And, to the extent there may be circumstances in which *Chevron*-type deference is inapplicable—*e.g.,* where one has doubt that Congress actually intended to delegate interpretive authority to the agency (an "ambiguity" that *Chevron* does not presumptively leave to agency resolution)—I believe that *Skidmore* nonetheless retains legal vitality. . . .

NOTES AND QUESTIONS

1. ***Three views of step zero.*** There seem to be three different views of what deference scheme should apply, and when. The majority opinion maintains that because the Department's legal interpretation did not have the "force of law"—i.e., it was not promulgated via notice-and-comment rulemaking—it was not entitled to *Chevron* deference, but it was entitled to *Skidmore* deference to the extent it had the power to persuade. Justice Scalia argued that any authoritative agency legal interpretation was entitled to *Chevron* deference, and that *Skidmore* deference was an anachronism. Justices Breyer and Ginsburg argue that the *Chevron* case simply focused on an *additional* reason to defer to an agency: when the agency is authorized to make rules, it can be assumed that Congresses intended the agency to use that rulemaking power to fill statutory gaps and resolve statutory ambiguities. But even where an agency does not use its rulemaking power, there may still be reason to give the agency plenty of deference under *Skidmore*. On their view, is there any difference between how much deference an agency is to receive under *Chevron* and *Skidmore*? Can you state what different levels of deference, if any, an agency would receive under the two tests?

2. ***The difference between "silence" and "ambiguity."*** Why is there a debate here about deference at all? According to the majority, there was simply no *law* on point. Put another way, there was no law prohibiting the forced use of compensatory time, and thus the FLSA was not ambiguous, nor did it a leave a "gap" to be filled. Are there differences between these types of statutory questions—whether there is a gap, an ambiguity, or simply no law to apply at all?

Do you agree with Justice Thomas's and Scalia's interpretation of the statute, viz. that there was no law prohibiting the forced use of compensatory time, or was Justice

FOR DISCUSSION

Do you see a difference between "silences," "ambiguities," and "gaps" in statutes?

Stevens right that there actually was some law on the question? Does the disagreement suggest an ambiguity after all?

In Barnhart v. Walton, 535 U.S. 212 (2002), also considered a "Step Zero" case, the Court had to interpret a provision of the Social Security Act that defined "disability" as an "inability to engage in any substantial gainful activity by reason of any medically determinable physical or mental impairment which can be expected to result in death or which has lasted or can be expected to last for a continuous period of not less than 12 months." The agency interpreted this to mean that the *inability to engage in substantial work* had to last for 12 months, even though linguistically the 12-month requirement modifies "physical or mental impairment," suggesting that the impairment is what must be expected to last for 12 months. The Supreme Court nonetheless held that "this linguistic point is insufficient[:] It shows that the particular statutory provision says nothing explicitly about the 'inability's' duration. But such silence, after all, normally creates ambiguity. It does not resolve it." Id. at 218.

Isn't that, well, crazy? If there is no law on a question, that doesn't make all the other laws on the statute books "ambiguous" as to that question. Suppose the only law in existence is a law prohibiting vehicles in the park. The law is ambiguous (or vague) on many questions—does it include tanks, bicycles, motorized wheelchairs?—but surely it is not "ambiguous" on the question of whether someone is entitled to overtime compensation or social security disability benefits, or is prohibited from shouting "fire" in a theater. The law in question simply doesn't speak to any of those issues. There's no ambiguity, and there's no gap; there's just no law. To be sure, maybe the Social Security Act authorizes the agency to *impose*, by regulation, a duration requirement on the inability to do work. But this would be a *new* legal requirement—a "legislative" rule that can be promulgated only after public participation—and not an "interpretation" of the statute, which says nothing at all about such a duration requirement.

3. *Revisiting interpretative and legislative rules.* The majority's position that ordinarily (although not always) notice-and-comment rulemaking is necessary to trigger *Chevron* deference suggests that for purposes of the *Chevron* analysis "legislative" rules with the "force of law" are considered "interpretations" of the relevant statutes. But aren't such "legislative" rules *not* "interpretative" rules for purposes of the APA notice-and-comment procedures, precisely because they are not interpreting any prior legal authority? So are these rules "with the force of law" interpreting something, or are they "legislative" in the sense that they make new policy? Or is the answer that to the extent a legislative rulemaking relies on an interpretation of the agency's statutory authority, that interpretation will get deference?

> **CROSS REFERENCE**
>
> What is the connection between step zero and the distinction between interpretative and legislative rules discussed in Chapter 2? "Force of law" seems to be a reference to legislative rules. Are those rules then interpreting some other legal authority? Is that a contradiction?

Although legislative formality is still a good indication that an agency's legal interpretation is entitled to deference, the analysis in *Christensen* has been refined by the following opinion.

United States v. Mead Corp.

533 U.S. 218 (2001)

JUSTICE SOUTER delivered the opinion of the Court.

The question is whether a tariff classification ruling by the United States Customs Service deserves judicial deference. The Federal Circuit rejected Customs's invocation of *Chevron U.S.A. Inc. v. Natural Resources Defense Council, Inc.,* 467 U.S. 837 (1984), in support of such a ruling, to which it gave no deference. We agree that a tariff classification has no claim to judicial deference under *Chevron,* there being no indication that Congress intended such a ruling to carry the force of law, but we hold that under *Skidmore v. Swift & Co.,* 323 U.S. 134 (1944), the ruling is eligible to claim respect according to its persuasiveness.

I

A

Imports are taxed under the Harmonized Tariff Schedule of the United States (HTSUS), 19 U.S.C. § 1202. Title 19 U.S.C. § 1500(b) provides that Customs "shall, under rules and regulations prescribed by the Secretary [of the Treasury,] . . . fix the final classification and rate of duty applicable to . . . merchandise" under the HTSUS. . . .

The Secretary provides for tariff rulings before the entry of goods by regulations authorizing "ruling letters" setting tariff classifications for particular imports. 19 CFR § 177.8 (2000). A ruling letter

> represents the official position of the Customs Service with respect to the particular transaction or issue described therein and is binding on all Customs Service personnel in accordance with the provisions of this section until modified or revoked. In the absence of a change of practice or other modification or revocation which affects the principle of the ruling set forth in the ruling letter, that principle may be cited as authority in the disposition of transactions involving the same circumstances. § 177.9(a).

After the transaction that gives it birth, a ruling letter is to "be applied only with respect to transactions involving articles identical to the sample submitted with the ruling request or to articles whose description is identical to the description set forth in the ruling letter." § 177.9(b)(2). As a general matter, such a letter is "subject to modification or revocation without notice to any person, except the person to whom the letter was addressed," § 177.9(c), and the regulations consequently provide that "no other person should rely on the ruling letter or assume that the principles of that ruling will be applied in connection with any transaction other than the one described in the letter," *ibid.* Since ruling letters respond to transactions of the moment, they are not subject to notice and comment before being issued, may be published but need only be made "available for public inspection," 19 U.S.C. § 1625(a), and, at the time this action arose, could be modified without notice and comment under most circumstances, 19 CFR § 177.10(c) (2000). A broader notice-and-comment requirement for modification of prior rulings was added by statute in 1993, and took effect after this case arose.

Any of the 46 port-of-entry Customs offices may issue ruling letters, and so may the Customs Headquarters Office, in providing "[a]dvice or guidance as to the interpretation or proper application of the Customs and related laws with respect to a specific Customs transaction [which] may be requested by Customs Service field offices . . . at any time, whether the transaction is prospective, current, or completed," 19 CFR § 177.11(a) (2000). Most ruling letters contain little or no reasoning, but simply describe goods and state the appropriate category and tariff. A few letters, like the Headquarters ruling at issue here, set out a rationale in some detail.

B

Respondent, the Mead Corporation, imports "day planners," three-ring binders with pages having room for notes of daily schedules and phone numbers and addresses, together with a calendar and suchlike. The tariff schedule on point falls under the HTSUS heading for "[r]egisters, account books, notebooks, order books, receipt books, letter pads, memorandum pads, diaries and similar articles," HTSUS subheading 4820.10, which comprises two subcategories. Items in the first, "[d]iaries, notebooks and address books, bound; memorandum pads, letter pads and similar articles," were subject to a tariff of 4.0% at the time in controversy. Objects in the second, covering "[o]ther" items, were free of duty.

Between 1989 and 1993, Customs repeatedly treated day planners under the "other" HTSUS subheading. In January 1993, however, Customs changed its position, and issued a Headquarters ruling letter classifying Mead's day planners as "Diaries . . . , bound" subject to tariff under subheading 4820.10.20. That letter was short on explanation, but after Mead's protest, Customs Headquarters issued a new letter, carefully reasoned but never published, reaching the same conclusion. This letter considered two definitions of "diary" from the Oxford English Dictionary, the first covering a daily journal of the past day's events, the second a book including " 'printed dates for daily memoranda and jottings; also . . . calendars . . . .' "

[After some lengthy lower-court proceedings, the Federal Circuit refused to give *Chevron* deference and set aside the agency's interpretation that "diaries" include day planners.—Ed.]

. . . . We hold that administrative implementation of a particular statutory provision qualifies for *Chevron* deference when it appears that Congress delegated authority to the agency generally to make rules carrying the force of law, and that the agency interpretation claiming deference was promulgated in the exercise of that authority. Delegation of such authority may be shown in a variety of ways, as by an agency's power to engage in adjudication or notice-and-comment rulemaking, or by some other indication of a comparable congressional intent. The Customs ruling at issue here fails to qualify, although the possibility that it deserves some deference under *Skidmore* leads us to vacate and remand.

II

A

When Congress has "explicitly left a gap for an agency to fill, there is an express delegation of authority to the agency to elucidate a specific provision of the statute by regulation," *Chevron*, 467 U.S. at 843–844, and any ensuing regulation is binding in the courts unless procedurally defective, arbitrary or capricious in substance, or manifestly contrary to the statute. But whether or not they enjoy any express delegation of authority on a particular question, agencies charged with applying a statute necessarily make all sorts of interpretive choices, and while not all of those choices bind judges to follow them, they certainly may influence courts facing questions the agencies have already answered. "[T]he well-reasoned views of the agencies implementing a statute 'constitute a body of experience and informed judgment to which courts and litigants may properly resort for guidance,' " and "[w]e have long recognized that considerable weight should be accorded to an executive department's construction of a statutory scheme it is entrusted to administer." The fair measure of deference to an agency administering its own statute has been understood to vary with circumstances, and courts have looked to the degree of the agency's care, its consistency, formality, and relative expertness, and to the persuasiveness of the agency's position, see *Skidmore, supra,* at 139–140. The approach has produced a spectrum of judicial responses, from great respect at one end, to near indifference at the other. Justice Jackson summed things up in *Skidmore v. Swift & Co.*:

> The weight [accorded to an administrative] judgment in a particular case will depend upon the thoroughness evident in its consideration, the validity of its reasoning, its consistency with earlier and later

pronouncements, and all those factors which give it power to persuade, if lacking power to control. 323 U.S. at 140.

Since 1984, we have identified a category of interpretive choices distinguished by an additional reason for judicial deference. This Court in *Chevron*
recognized that Congress not only engages in express delegation of specific
interpretive authority, but that "[s]ometimes the legislative delegation to an
agency on a particular question is implicit." 467 U.S. at 844. Congress, that
is, may not have expressly delegated authority or responsibility to implement
a particular provision or fill a particular gap. Yet it can still be apparent from
the agency's generally conferred authority and other statutory circumstances
that Congress would expect the agency to be able to speak with the force of
law when it addresses ambiguity in the statute or fills a space in the enacted
law, even one about which "Congress did not actually have an intent" as to a
particular result. When circumstances implying such an expectation exist, a
reviewing court has no business rejecting an agency's exercise of its generally
conferred authority to resolve a particular statutory ambiguity simply because
the agency's chosen resolution seems unwise, but is obliged to accept the agency's position if Congress has not previously spoken to the point at issue and the
agency's interpretation is reasonable, see *id.* at 842–845; cf. 5 U.S.C. § 706(2) (a
reviewing court shall set aside agency action, findings, and conclusions found
to be "arbitrary, capricious, an abuse of discretion, or otherwise not in accordance with law"). [Is the Court here, once again, equating *Chevron* Step Two
with arbitrary-and-capricious review?—Ed.]

We have recognized a very good indicator of delegation meriting *Chevron* treatment in express congressional authorizations to engage in the process
of rulemaking or adjudication that produces regulations or rulings for which
deference is claimed. It is fair to assume generally that Congress contemplates
administrative action with the effect of law when it provides for a relatively
formal administrative procedure tending to foster the fairness and deliberation
that should underlie a pronouncement of such force. Thus, the overwhelming
number of our cases applying *Chevron* deference have reviewed the fruits of
notice-and-comment rulemaking or formal adjudication. That said, and as significant as notice-and-comment is in pointing to *Chevron* authority, the want
of that procedure here does not decide the case, for we have sometimes found
reasons for *Chevron* deference even when no such administrative formality was
required and none was afforded. The fact that the tariff classification here was

not a product of such formal process does not alone, therefore, bar the application of *Chevron*.

There are, nonetheless, ample reasons to deny *Chevron* deference here. The authorization for classification rulings, and Customs's practice in making them, present a case far removed not only from notice-and-comment process, but from any other circumstances reasonably suggesting that Congress ever thought of classification rulings as deserving the deference claimed for them here.

B

No matter which angle we choose for viewing the Customs ruling letter in this case, it fails to qualify under *Chevron*. On the face of the statute, to begin with, the terms of the congressional delegation give no indication that Congress meant to delegate authority to Customs to issue classification rulings with the force of law. We are not, of course, here making any global statement about Customs's authority, for it is true that the general rulemaking power conferred on Customs authorizes some regulation with the force of law . . . . It is true as well that Congress had classification rulings in mind when it explicitly authorized, in a parenthetical, the issuance of "regulations establishing procedures for the issuance of binding rulings prior to the entry of the merchandise concerned," 19 U.S.C. § 1502(a). The reference to binding classifications does not, however, bespeak the legislative type of activity that would naturally bind more than the parties to the ruling, once the goods classified are admitted into this country. And though the statute's direction to disseminate "information" necessary to "secure" uniformity seems to assume that a ruling may be precedent in later transactions, precedential value alone does not add up to *Chevron* entitlement . . . . In any event, any precedential claim of a classification ruling is counterbalanced by the provision for independent review of Customs classifications by the CIT . . . .

It is difficult, in fact, to see in the agency practice itself any indication that Customs ever set out with a lawmaking pretense in mind when it undertook to make classifications like these. Customs does not generally engage in notice-and-comment practice when issuing them, and their treatment by the agency makes it clear that a letter's binding character as a ruling stops short of third parties; Customs has regarded a classification as conclusive only as between itself and the importer to whom it was issued . . . . Other importers are in fact warned against assuming any right of detrimental reliance.

Indeed, to claim that classifications have legal force is to ignore the reality that 46 different Customs offices issue 10,000 to 15,000 of them each year. Any suggestion that rulings intended to have the force of law are being churned out at a rate of 10,000 a year at an agency's 46 scattered offices is simply self-refuting. Although the circumstances are less startling here, with a Headquarters letter in issue, none of the relevant statutes recognizes this category of rulings as separate or different from others . . . .

In sum, classification rulings are best treated like "interpretations contained in policy statements, agency manuals, and enforcement guidelines." *Christensen*, 529 U.S. at 587. They are beyond the *Chevron* pale.

C

To agree with the Court of Appeals that Customs ruling letters do not fall within *Chevron* is not, however, to place them outside the pale of any deference whatever. *Chevron* did nothing to eliminate *Skidmore*'s holding that an agency's interpretation may merit some deference whatever its form, given the "specialized experience and broader investigations and information" available to the agency, and given the value of uniformity in its administrative and judicial understandings of what a national law requires.

There is room at least to raise a *Skidmore* claim here, where the regulatory scheme is highly detailed, and Customs can bring the benefit of specialized experience to bear on the subtle questions in this case . . . . Such a ruling may surely claim the merit of its writer's thoroughness, logic, and expertness, its fit with prior interpretations, and any other sources of weight.

D

. . . . If the primary objective is to simplify the judicial process of giving or withholding deference, then the diversity of statutes authorizing discretionary administrative action must be declared irrelevant or minimized. If, on the other hand, it is simply implausible that Congress intended such a broad range of statutory authority to produce only two varieties of administrative action, demanding either *Chevron* deference or none at all, then the breadth of the spectrum of possible agency action must be taken into account. Justice Scalia's first priority over the years has been to limit and simplify. The Court's choice has been to tailor deference to variety. This acceptance of the range of statutory variation has led the Court to recognize more than one variety of judicial deference, just as the Court has recognized a variety of indicators that Congress would expect *Chevron* deference. . . .

We think, in sum, that Justice Scalia's efforts to simplify ultimately run afoul of Congress's indications that different statutes present different reasons for considering respect for the exercise of administrative authority or deference to it. . . .

Justice Scalia, dissenting.

Today's opinion makes an avulsive change in judicial review of federal administrative action. Whereas previously a reasonable agency application of an ambiguous statutory provision had to be sustained so long as it represented the agency's authoritative interpretation, henceforth such an application can be set aside unless "it appears that Congress delegated authority to the agency generally to make rules carrying the force of law," as by giving an agency "power to engage in adjudication or notice-and-comment rulemaking, or . . . some other [procedure] indicati[ng] comparable congressional intent," and "the agency interpretation claiming deference was promulgated in the exercise of that authority." What was previously a general presumption of authority in agencies to resolve ambiguity in the statutes they have been authorized to enforce has been changed to a presumption of no such authority, which must be overcome by affirmative legislative intent to the contrary. And whereas previously, when agency authority to resolve ambiguity did not exist the court was free to give the statute what it considered the best interpretation, henceforth the court must supposedly give the agency view some indeterminate amount of so-called *Skidmore* deference. We will be sorting out the consequences of the *Mead* doctrine, which has today replaced the *Chevron* doctrine, for years to come. I would adhere to our established jurisprudence, defer to the reasonable interpretation the Customs Service has given to the statute it is charged with enforcing, and reverse the judgment of the Court of Appeals. . . .

The doctrine of *Chevron*—that all *authoritative* agency interpretations of statutes they are charged with administering deserve deference—was rooted in a legal presumption of congressional intent, important to the division of powers between the Second and Third Branches. When, *Chevron* said, Congress leaves an ambiguity in a statute that is to be administered by an executive agency, it is presumed that Congress meant to give the agency discretion, within the limits of reasonable interpretation, as to how the ambiguity is to be resolved.

By committing enforcement of the statute to an agency rather than the courts, Congress committed its initial and primary interpretation to that branch as well. . . .

The basis in principle for today's new doctrine can be described as follows: The background rule is that ambiguity in legislative instructions to agencies is to be resolved not by the agencies but by the judges. Specific congressional intent to depart from this rule must be found—and while there is no single touchstone for such intent it can generally be found when Congress has authorized the agency to act through (what the Court says is) relatively formal procedures such as informal rulemaking and formal (and informal?) adjudication, and when the agency in fact employs such procedures. . . . [T]he Court's principal criterion of congressional intent to supplant its background rule seems to me quite implausible. There is no necessary connection between the formality of procedure and the power of the entity administering the procedure to resolve authoritatively questions of law. The most formal of the procedures the Court refers to—formal adjudication—is modeled after the process used in trial courts, which of course are not generally accorded deference on questions of law. The purpose of such a procedure is to produce a closed record for determination and review of the facts—which implies nothing about the power of the agency subjected to the procedure to resolve authoritatively questions of law.

As for informal rulemaking: . . . Is it likely—or indeed even plausible— that Congress meant, when such an agency chooses rulemaking, to accord the administrators of that agency, *and their successors,* the flexibility of interpreting the ambiguous statute now one way, and later another; but, when such an agency chooses case-by-case administration, to eliminate all future agency discretion by having that same ambiguity resolved authoritatively (and forever) by the courts? Surely that makes no sense. . . .

Some decisions that are neither informal rulemaking nor formal adjudication are required to be made personally by a Cabinet Secretary, without any prescribed procedures. . . . Is it conceivable that decisions specifically committed to these high-level officers are meant to be accorded no deference, while decisions by an administrative law judge left in place without further discretionary agency review, see 5 U.S.C. § 557(b), are authoritative? This seems to me quite absurd, and not at all in accord with any plausible actual intent of Congress.

As for the practical effects of the new rule: The principal effect will be protracted confusion. As noted above, the one test for *Chevron* deference that the Court enunciates is wonderfully imprecise: whether "Congress delegated authority to the agency generally to make rules carrying the force of law, . . . as by . . . adjudication[,] notice-and-comment rulemaking, or . . . some other [procedure] indicati[ng] comparable congressional intent." But even this description does not do justice to the utter flabbiness of the Court's criterion, since, in order to maintain the fiction that the new test is really just the old one, applied consistently throughout our case law, the Court must make a virtually open-ended exception to its already imprecise guidance: In the present case, it tells us, the absence of notice-and-comment rulemaking . . . is not enough to decide the question of *Chevron* deference, "for we have sometimes found reasons for *Chevron* deference even when no such administrative formality was required and none was afforded." The opinion then goes on to consider a grab bag of other factors—including the factor that used to be the sole criterion for *Chevron* deference: whether the interpretation represented the *authoritative* position of the agency. It is hard to know what the lower courts are to make of today's guidance. . . .

And finally, the majority's approach compounds the confusion it creates by breathing new life into the anachronism of *Skidmore,* which sets forth a sliding scale of deference owed an agency's interpretation of a statute that is dependent "upon the thoroughness evident in [the agency's] consideration, the validity of its reasoning, its consistency with earlier and later pronouncements, and all those factors which give it power to persuade, if lacking power to control"; in this way, the appropriate measure of deference will be accorded the "body of experience and informed judgment" that such interpretations often embody. Justice Jackson's eloquence notwithstanding, the rule of *Skidmore* deference is an empty truism and a trifling statement of the obvious: A judge should take into account the well-considered views of expert observers.

It was possible to live with the indeterminacy of *Skidmore* deference in earlier times. But in an era when federal statutory law administered by federal agencies is pervasive, and when the ambiguities (intended or unintended) that those statutes contain are innumerable, totality-of-the-circumstances *Skidmore* deference is a recipe for uncertainty, unpredictability, and endless litigation. . . .

There is no doubt that the Customs Service's interpretation represents the authoritative view of the agency. Although the actual ruling letter was signed by only the Director of the Commercial Rulings Branch of Customs Head-quarters' Office of Regulations and Rulings, the Solicitor General of the United States has filed a brief, cosigned by the General Counsel of the Department of the Treasury, that represents the position set forth in the ruling letter to be the official position of the Customs Service. . . .

There is also no doubt that the Customs Service's interpretation is a reasonable one, whether or not judges would consider it the best. . . .

COURSE THEME

POLITICAL INFLUENCE
What happened in 1993 that might have made the agency change its views? Does that inform your view of the role of political influence?

Notes and Questions

1.   How much work does Skidmore do? Is Justice Scalia right that *Skidmore* is nothing but a truism? Don't courts consider litigation briefs to the extent they have the power to persuade? Or is there something more to *Skidmore* deference? Will a judge uphold an agency interpretation under *Skidmore* even if she does not believe the agency's interpretation is the best interpretation of the statute?

2.   Mead *has superseded* Christensen. In Barnhart v. Walton, 535 U.S. 212 (2002), discussed supra p. 437, the Court reaffirmed that any hard-and-fast rule imposed by *Christensen* was modified by *Mead*. There, the Court upheld an agency interpretation because of "the interstitial nature of the legal question, the related expertise of the Agency, the importance of the question to administration of the statute, the complexity of that administration, and the careful consideration the Agency has given the question over a long period of time." Id. at 222.

3.   Auer *step zero*. In Kisor v. Wilkie, 139 S. Ct. 2400 (2019), discussed in more depth starting infra p. 460, the Court dealt with calls to overturn *Auer* deference, judicial deference to an agency's reasonable interpretations of its own regulations. The Court refused to do so—but it did limit the applicability of *Auer* deference. The Court held that in applying *Auer*, "a court must make an independent inquiry into whether the character and context of the agency interpretation entitles it to controlling weight." The regulatory interpretation has to be "authoritative," it must "in some way implicate [the agency's] substantive expertise," and it must "reflect 'fair and considered judgment.'" *Kisor*, in other words, can be understood as a "step zero" case for *Auer* deference.

4. *Step zero and certain types of questions.* In the final "step zero" case excerpt, and in the notes, the Court dealt with the issue whether there are certain types of *questions* that an agency should never be able to decide for itself, no matter how authoritative and well-considered its interpretation. In the following case, the Court considered whether it should defer to an agency's interpretation of its own jurisdiction. Although the court said yes, in other cases (as explained in the notes) the Court seems to suggest that agencies should not get any deference when deciding questions of major political and economic significance—thus potentially transforming the "major questions doctrine" of *Brown & Williamson*, in which the doctrine was used at "step one" as a matter of statutory construction, into a "step zero" case.

City of Arlington, Tex. v. FCC

569 U.S. 290 (2013)

JUSTICE SCALIA delivered the opinion of the Court.

We consider whether an agency's interpretation of a statutory ambiguity that concerns the scope of its regulatory authority (that is, its jurisdiction) is entitled to deference under *Chevron U.S.A. Inc. v. Natural Resources Defense Council, Inc.*, 467 U.S. 837 (1984).

I

Wireless telecommunications networks require towers and antennas; proposed sites for those towers and antennas must be approved by local zoning authorities. In the Telecommunications Act of 1996, Congress "impose[d] specific limitations on the traditional authority of state and local governments to regulate the location, construction, and modification of such facilities," and incorporated those limitations into the Communications Act of 1934. Section 201(b) of that Act empowers the Federal Communications Commission to "prescribe such rules and regulations as may be necessary in the public interest to carry out [its] provisions." . . .

The Act imposes five substantive limitations, which are codified in 47 U.S.C. § 332(c)(7)(B); only one of them, § 332(c)(7)(B)(ii), is at issue here. That provision requires state or local governments to act on wireless siting applications "within a reasonable period of time after the request is duly filed." Two other features of § 332(c)(7) are relevant. First, subparagraph (A), known as the "saving clause," provides that nothing in the Act, *except* those limitations provided in § 332(c)(7)(B), "shall limit or affect the authority of a State or local government" over siting decisions. Second, § 332(c)(7)(B)(v) authorizes a person who believes a state or local government's wireless-siting decision to be inconsistent with any of the limitations in § 332(c)(7)(B) to "commence an action in any court of competent jurisdiction."

In theory, § 332(c)(7)(B)(ii) requires state and local zoning authorities to take prompt action on siting applications for wireless facilities. But in practice, wireless providers often faced long delays. In July 2008, CTIA—The Wireless Association, which represents wireless service providers, petitioned the FCC to clarify the meaning of § 332(c)(7)(B)(ii)'s requirement that zoning authorities act on siting requests "within a reasonable period of time." In November 2009, the Commission, relying on its broad statutory authority to implement the provisions of the Communications Act, issued a declaratory ruling responding to CTIA's petition. The Commission found that the "record evidence demonstrates that unreasonable delays in the personal wireless service facility siting process have obstructed the provision of wireless services" and that such delays "impede the promotion of advanced services and competition that Congress deemed critical in the Telecommunications Act of 1996." A "reasonable period of time" under § 332(c)(7)(B)(ii), the Commission determined, is presumptively (but rebuttably) 90 days to process a collocation application (that is, an application to place a new antenna on an existing tower) and 150 days to process all other applications.

Some state and local governments opposed adoption of the *Declaratory Ruling* on the ground that the Commission lacked "authority to interpret ambiguous provisions of Section 332(c)(7)." Specifically, they argued that the saving clause, § 332(c)(7)(A), and the judicial review provision, § 337(c)(7)(B)(v), together display a congressional intent to withhold from the Commission authority to interpret the limitations in § 332(c)(7)(B). Asserting that ground of objection, the cities of Arlington and San Antonio, Texas, petitioned for review of the *Declaratory Ruling* in the Court of Appeals for the Fifth Circuit.

Relying on Circuit precedent, the Court of Appeals held that the *Chevron* framework applied to the threshold question whether the FCC possessed statutory authority to adopt the 90- and 150-day timeframes. Applying *Chevron*, the Court of Appeals found "§ 332(c)(7)(A)'s effect on the FCC's authority to administer § 332(c)(7)(B)'s limitations ambiguous," and held that "the FCC's interpretation of its statutory authority" was a permissible construction of the statute. On the merits, the court upheld the presumptive 90- and 150-day deadlines as a "permissible construction of § 332(c)(7)(B)(ii) and . . . entitled to Chevron deference."

We granted certiorari, limited to the first question presented: "Whether . . . a court should apply *Chevron* to . . . an agency's determination of its own jurisdiction."

II

As this case turns on the scope of the doctrine enshrined in *Chevron*, we begin with a description of that case's now-canonical formulation. "When a court reviews an agency's construction of the statute which it administers, it is confronted with two questions." First, applying the ordinary tools of statutory construction, the court must determine "whether Congress has directly spoken to the precise question at issue. If the intent of Congress is clear, that is the end of the matter; for the court, as well as the agency, must give effect to the unambiguously expressed intent of Congress." But "if the statute is silent or ambiguous with respect to the specific issue, the question for the court is whether the agency's answer is based on a permissible construction of the statute." . . .

The question here is whether a court must defer under *Chevron* to an agency's interpretation of a statutory ambiguity that concerns the scope of the agency's statutory authority (that is, its jurisdiction). The argument against deference rests on the premise that there exist two distinct classes of agency interpretations: Some interpretations—the big, important ones, presumably—define the agency's "jurisdiction." Others—humdrum, run-of-the-mill stuff—are simply applications of jurisdiction the agency plainly has. That premise is false, because the distinction between "jurisdictional" and "nonjurisdictional" interpretations is a mirage. No matter how it is framed, the question a court faces when confronted with an agency's interpretation of a statute it administers is always, simply, *whether the agency has stayed within the bounds of its statutory authority.*

The misconception that there are, for *Chevron* purposes, separate "jurisdictional" questions on which no deference is due derives, perhaps, from a reflexive extension to agencies of the very real division between the jurisdictional and nonjurisdictional that is applicable to courts. In the judicial context, there *is* a meaningful line: Whether the court decided *correctly* is a question that has different consequences from the question whether it had the power to decide *at all*. Congress has the power (within limits) to tell the courts what classes of cases they may decide, but not to prescribe or superintend how they decide those cases. A court's power to decide a case is independent of whether its decision is correct, which is why even an erroneous judgment is entitled to res judicata effect. Put differently, a jurisdictionally proper but substantively incorrect judicial decision is not ultra vires.

That is not so for agencies charged with administering congressional statutes. Both their power to act and how they are to act is authoritatively prescribed by Congress, so that when they act improperly, no less than when they act beyond their jurisdiction, what they do is ultra vires. Because the question—whether framed as an incorrect application of agency authority or an assertion of authority not conferred—is always whether the agency has gone beyond what Congress has permitted it to do, there is no principled basis for carving out some arbitrary subset of such claims as "jurisdictional." . . .

This point is nicely illustrated by our decision in *National Cable & Telecommunications Assn., Inc. v. Gulf Power Co.*, 534 U.S. 327 (2002). That case considered whether the FCC's "jurisdiction" to regulate the rents utility-pole owners charge for "pole attachments" (defined as attachments by a cable television system or provider of telecommunications service) extended to attachments that provided both cable television and high-speed Internet access (attachments for so-called "commingled services"). We held, sensibly, that *Chevron* applied. Whether framed as going to the *scope* of the FCC's delegated authority or the FCC's *application* of its delegated authority, the underlying question was the same: Did the FCC exceed the bounds of its statutory authority to regulate rents for "pole attachments" when it sought to regulate rents for pole attachments providing commingled services?

The label is an empty distraction because every new application of a broad statutory term can be reframed as a questionable extension of the agency's jurisdiction. One of the briefs in support of petitioners explains, helpfully, that "[j]urisdictional questions concern the *who, what, where,* and *when* of regulatory power: which subject matters may an agency regulate and under what conditions." But an agency's *application* of its authority pursuant to statutory text answers the same questions. *Who* is an "outside salesman"? *What* is a "pole attachment"? *Where* do the "waters of the United States" end? *When* must a Medicare provider challenge a reimbursement determination in order to be entitled to an administrative appeal? These can all be reframed as questions about the scope of agencies' regulatory jurisdiction—and they are all questions to which the *Chevron* framework applies.

In sum, judges should not waste their time in the mental acrobatics needed to decide whether an agency's interpretation of a statutory provision is "jurisdictional" or "nonjurisdictional." Once those labels are sheared away, it becomes clear that the question in every case is, simply, whether the statutory text forecloses the agency's assertion of authority, or not. . . .

The U.S. Reports are shot through with applications of *Chevron* to agencies' constructions of the scope of their own jurisdiction. And we have applied *Chevron* where concerns about agency self-aggrandizement are at their apogee: in cases where an agency's expansive construction of the extent of its own power would have wrought a fundamental change in the regulatory scheme. In *FDA v. Brown & Williamson Tobacco Corp.*, 529 U.S. 120 (2000), the threshold question was the "appropriate framework for analyzing" the FDA's assertion of "jurisdiction to regulate tobacco products"—a question of vast "economic and political magnitude." "Because this case involves an administrative agency's construction of a statute that it administers," we held, *Chevron* applied. Similarly, in *MCI Telecommunications Corp. v. American Telephone & Telegraph Co.*, 512 U.S. 218 (1994), we applied the *Chevron* framework to the FCC's assertion that the statutory phrase "modify any requirement" gave it authority to eliminate rate-filing requirements, "the essential characteristic of a rate-regulated industry," for long-distance telephone carriers.

The false dichotomy between "jurisdictional" and "nonjurisdictional" agency interpretations may be no more than a bogeyman, but it is dangerous all the same. . . . The effect would be to transfer any number of interpretive decisions—archetypal *Chevron* questions, about how best to construe an ambiguous term in light of competing policy interests—from the agencies that administer the statutes to federal courts.[4] . . .

III

. . . . The dissent is correct that *United States v. Mead Corp.*, 533 U.S. 218 (2001), requires that, for *Chevron* deference to apply, the agency must have received congressional authority to determine the particular matter at issue in the particular manner adopted. No one disputes that. But *Mead* denied *Chevron* deference to action, by an agency with rulemaking authority, that was not rulemaking. What the dissent needs, and fails to produce, is a single case in which a general conferral of rulemaking or adjudicative authority has been held insufficient to support *Chevron* deference for an exercise of that authority within the agency's substantive field. There is no such case, and what the dissent proposes is a massive revision of our *Chevron* jurisprudence. . . .

[An opinion by Justice Breyer concurring in part and concurring in the judgment is omitted.—Ed.]

Chief Justice Roberts, with whom Justice Kennedy and Justice Alito join, dissenting.

My disagreement with the Court is fundamental. It is also easily expressed: A court should not defer to an agency until the court decides, on its own, that the agency is entitled to deference. Courts defer to an agency's interpretation of law when and because Congress has conferred on the agency interpretive authority over the question at issue. An agency cannot exercise interpretive authority until it has it; the question whether an agency enjoys that authority must be decided by a court, without deference to the agency.

I

One of the principal authors of the Constitution famously wrote that the "accumulation of all powers, legislative, executive, and judiciary, in the same hands, . . . may justly be pronounced the very definition of tyranny." The

---

[4]   The Chief Justice's discomfort with the growth of agency power is perhaps understandable. But the dissent overstates when it claims that agencies exercise "legislative power" and "judicial power." The former is vested exclusively in Congress, U.S. Const., Art. I, § 1, the latter in the "one supreme Court" and "such inferior Courts as the Congress may from time to time ordain and establish," Art. III, § 1. Agencies make rules ("Private cattle may be grazed on public lands *X, Y,* and *Z* subject to certain conditions") and conduct adjudications ("This rancher's grazing permit is revoked for violation of the conditions") and have done so since the beginning of the Republic. These activities take "legislative" and "judicial" forms, but they are exercises of—indeed, under our constitutional structure they *must be* exercises of—the "executive Power." Art. II, § 1, cl. 1.

Federalist No. 47, p. 324 (J. Cooke ed. 1961) (J. Madison). Although modern administrative agencies fit most comfortably within the Executive Branch, as a practical matter they exercise legislative power, by promulgating regulations with the force of law; executive power, by policing compliance with those regulations; and judicial power, by adjudicating enforcement actions and imposing sanctions on those found to have violated their rules. The accumulation of these powers in the same hands is not an occasional or isolated exception to the constitutional plan; it is a central feature of modern American government.

The administrative state "wields vast power and touches almost every aspect of daily life." The Framers could hardly have envisioned today's "vast and varied federal bureaucracy" and the authority administrative agencies now hold over our economic, social, and political activities. "[T]he administrative state with its reams of regulations would leave them rubbing their eyes." And the federal bureaucracy continues to grow; in the last 15 years, Congress has launched more than 50 new agencies. And more are on the way.

Although the Constitution empowers the President to keep federal officers accountable, administrative agencies enjoy in practice a significant degree of independence. As scholars have noted, "no President (or his executive office staff) could, and presumably none would wish to, supervise so broad a swath of regulatory activity." Kagan, Presidential Administration, 114 Harv. L. Rev. 2245, 2250 (2001); see also S. Breyer, Making Our Democracy Work 110 (2010) ("the president may not have the time or willingness to review [agency] decisions"). President Truman colorfully described his power over the administrative state by complaining, "I thought I was the president, but when it comes to these bureaucrats, I can't do a damn thing." See R. Nathan, The Administrative Presidency 2 (1986). President Kennedy once told a constituent, "I agree with you, but I don't know if the government will." See *id.* at 1. The collection of agencies housed outside the traditional executive departments, including the Federal Communications Commission, is routinely described as the "headless fourth branch of government," reflecting not only the scope of their authority but their practical independence.

As for judicial oversight, agencies enjoy broad power to construe statutory provisions over which they have been given interpretive authority. . . .

When it applies, *Chevron* is a powerful weapon in an agency's regulatory arsenal. Congressional delegations to agencies are often ambiguous—expressing "a mood rather than a message." Friendly, The Federal Administrative Agencies: The Need for Better Definition of Standards, 75 Harv. L. Rev. 1263, 1311 (1962). By design or default, Congress often fails to speak to "the precise question" before an agency. In the absence of such an answer, an agency's interpretation has the full force and effect of law, unless it "exceeds the bounds of the permissible."

It would be a bit much to describe the result as "the very definition of tyranny," but the danger posed by the growing power of the administrative state cannot be dismissed.

What the Court says in footnote 4 of its opinion is good, and true . . . . The Framers did divide governmental power in the manner the Court describes, for the purpose of safeguarding liberty. And yet . . . the citizen confronting thousands of pages of regulations—promulgated by an agency directed by Congress to regulate, say, "in the public interest"—can perhaps be excused for thinking that it is the agency really doing the legislating. And with hundreds of federal agencies poking into every nook and cranny of daily life, that citizen might also understandably question whether Presidential oversight—a critical part of the Constitutional plan—is always an effective safeguard against agency overreaching.

It is against this background that we consider whether the authority of administrative agencies should be augmented even further, to include not only broad power to give definitive answers to questions left to them by Congress, but also the same power to decide when Congress has given them that power.

Before proceeding to answer that question, however, it is necessary to sort through some confusion over what this litigation is about. The source of the confusion is a familiar culprit: the concept of "jurisdiction," which we have repeatedly described as a word with " 'many, too many, meanings.' " *Union Pacific R. Co. v. Locomotive Engineers*, 558 U.S. 67, 81 (2009).

The Court states that the question "is whether a court must defer under *Chevron* to an agency's interpretation of a statutory ambiguity that concerns the scope of the agency's statutory authority (that is, its jurisdiction)." That is fine—until the parenthetical. . . . The argument is instead that a court should not defer to an agency on whether Congress has granted the agency interpretive authority over the statutory ambiguity at issue.

You can call that "jurisdiction" if you'd like, as petitioners do in the question presented. But given that the term is ambiguous, more is required to understand its use in that question than simply "having read it." It is important to keep in mind that the term, in the present context, has the more precise meaning noted above, encompassing congressionally delegated authority to issue interpretations with the force and effect of law. And that has nothing do with whether the statutory provisions at issue are "big" or "small."

II

"It is emphatically the province and duty of the judicial department to say what the law is." *Marbury v. Madison*, 1 Cranch 137, 177 (1803). The rise of the modern administrative state has not changed that duty. Indeed, the Administrative Procedure Act, governing judicial review of most agency action, instructs reviewing courts to decide "all relevant questions of law." 5 U.S.C. § 706.

We do not ignore that command when we afford an agency's statutory interpretation *Chevron* deference; we respect it. We give binding deference to permissible agency interpretations of statutory ambiguities *because* Congress has delegated to the agency the authority to interpret those ambiguities "with the force of law." *United States v. Mead Corp.*, 533 U.S. 218, 229 (2001).

But before a court may grant such deference, it must on its own decide whether Congress—the branch vested with lawmaking authority under the Constitution—has in fact delegated to the agency lawmaking power over the ambiguity at issue. . . .

III

* * *

In *Mead*, we again made clear that the "category of interpretative choices" to which *Chevron* deference applies is defined by congressional intent. . . .

* * *

IV

Despite these precedents, the FCC argues that a court need only locate an agency and a grant of general rulemaking authority over a statute. *Chevron* deference then applies, it contends, to the agency's interpretation of any ambiguity in the Act, including ambiguity in a provision said to carve out specific provisions from the agency's general rulemaking authority. If Congress intends to exempt part of the statute from the agency's interpretive authority, the FCC says, Congress "can ordinarily be expected to state that intent explicitly."

If a congressional delegation of interpretive authority is to support *Chevron* deference, however, that delegation must extend to the specific statutory ambiguity at issue. The appropriate question is whether the delegation covers the "specific provision" and "particular question" before the court. A congressional grant of authority over some portion of a statute does not necessarily mean that Congress granted the agency interpretive authority over all its provisions. . . .

V

As the preceding analysis makes clear, I do not understand petitioners to ask the Court—nor do I think it necessary—to draw a "specious, but scary-sounding" line between "big, important" interpretations on the one hand and "humdrum, run-of-the-mill" ones on the other. Drawing such a line may well be difficult. Distinguishing between whether an agency's interpretation of an ambiguous term is reasonable and whether that term is for the agency to interpret is not nearly so difficult. . . .

* * *

In these cases, the FCC issued a declaratory ruling interpreting the term "reasonable period of time" in 47 U.S.C. § 332(c)(7) (B)(ii). The Fifth Circuit correctly recognized that it could not apply *Chevron* deference to the FCC's interpretation unless the agency "possessed statutory authority to administer § 332(c)(7)(B)(ii)," but it erred by granting *Chevron* deference to the FCC's view on that antecedent question. . . .

NOTES AND QUESTIONS

1. Summary. In *City of Arlington,* the majority held that *Chevron* deference applies to an agency's interpretation of its own jurisdiction, because there is no distinction (for *Chevron* purposes) between jurisdictional and nonjurisdictional questions. Justice Scalia is surely right that most of the time, there is no real distinction in this context because if an agency is misinterpreting its statute, then it is exercising power in excess of statutory authority. This can be understood as the agency exercising power beyond its jurisdiction, or simply that it's getting the statute wrong on the merits. There's no difference. Yet Chief Justice Roberts claimed that the term "jurisdictional" has a much narrower meaning in this context—it's simply the question of whether or not Congress has *conferred* authority on the agency to administer a part of the statute. The dispute in *City of Arlington* was whether the agency even had rulemaking authority to implement the "reasonable time" requirement as applied to local governments. Is that question distinct from the question of whether, assuming it has that authority, the agency has properly interpreted this particular substantive provision of the statute? Who's right?

2. ***Major questions revisited.*** In King v. Burwell, 576 U.S. 473 (2015), the Court confronted the question of whether, in the Affordable Care Act, the term "exchange established by a State" meant a health-care exchange established by a State *or by the federal government.* Chief Justice Roberts did not apply the *Chevron* framework. He cited *FDA v. Brown & Williamson* for the proposition that "[i]n extraordinary cases, . . . there may be reason to hesitate before concluding that Congress has intended such an implicit delegation" to the agency to interpret statutory ambiguities. The Court held: "The tax credits are among the Act's key reforms, involving billions of dollars in spending each year and affecting the price of health insurance for millions of people. Whether those credits are available on Federal Exchanges is thus a question of deep 'economic and political significance' that is central to this statutory scheme; had Congress wished to assign that question to an agency, it surely would have done so expressly." The Court therefore interpreted the statute for itself, affording not even *Skidmore* deference. Observe how the Court converted *Brown & Williamson* from a "step one" case to a "step zero" case.

CROSS REFERENCE Is the "major questions" doctrine a step one doctrine or a step zero doctrine? What is its connection to the nondelegation doctrine?

3. ***Some deference or no deference?*** The *Burwell* case raises another issue—what deference framework *does* apply if the court determines at "step zero" that *Chevron* deference is inappropriate? In *Mead*, the Court assumes that *Skidmore* deference would apply. In *Burwell*, the Court didn't apply any deference at all, and decided the case for itself *de novo*. Does this even matter? Is there a big difference between *Skidmore* deference and no particular deference at all?

4. Debating Deference

The debate over the validity of the deference frameworks continues to rage. The Supreme Court most fully engaged in that debate in a recent case involving *Auer* deference. As you read the next case, evaluate the arguments the majority makes against overturning *Auer*. Are they persuasive? What about the dissent's arguments in favor of overturning that deference doctrine?

Kisor v. Wilkie

139 S. Ct. 2400 (2019)

Justice Kagan announced the judgment of the Court and delivered the opinion of the Court with respect to Parts I, II-B, III-B, and IV, and an opinion with respect to Parts II-A and III-A, in which Justice Ginsburg, Justice Breyer, and Justice Sotomayor join.

This Court has often deferred to agencies' reasonable readings of genuinely ambiguous regulations. We call that practice *Auer* deference, or sometimes *Seminole Rock* deference, after two cases in which we employed it. See *Auer v. Robbins*, 519 U.S. 452 (1997); *Bowles v. Seminole Rock & Sand Co.*, 325 U.S. 410 (1945). The only question presented here is whether we should overrule those decisions, discarding the deference they give to agencies. We answer that question no. *Auer* deference retains an important role in construing agency regulations. But even as we uphold it, we reinforce its limits. *Auer* deference is sometimes appropriate and sometimes not. Whether to apply it depends on a range of considerations that we have noted now and again, but compile and further develop today. The deference doctrine we describe is potent in its place, but cabined in its scope. On remand, the Court of Appeals should decide whether it applies to the agency interpretation at issue.

I

We begin by summarizing how petitioner James Kisor's case made its way to this Court. Truth be told, nothing recounted in this Part has much bearing on the rest of our decision. The question whether to overrule *Auer* does not turn on any single application, whether right or wrong, of that decision's deference doctrine. But a recitation of the facts and proceedings below at least shows how the question presented arose.

Kisor is a Vietnam War veteran seeking disability benefits from the Department of Veterans Affairs (VA). He first applied in 1982, alleging that he had developed post-traumatic stress disorder (PTSD) as a result of his participation in a military action called Operation Harvest Moon. The report of the agency's evaluating psychiatrist noted Kisor's involvement in that battle, but found that he "d[id] not suffer from PTSD." The VA thus denied Kisor benefits. There matters stood until 2006, when Kisor moved to reopen his claim. Based on a new psychiatric report, the VA this time agreed that Kisor suffered from PTSD. But it granted him benefits only from the date of his motion to reopen, rather than (as he requested) from the date of his first application.

The Board of Veterans' Appeals—a part of the VA, represented in Kisor's case by a single administrative judge—affirmed that timing decision, based on its interpretation of an agency rule. Under the VA's regulation, the agency could grant Kisor retroactive benefits if it found there were "relevant official service department records" that it had not considered in its initial denial. The Board acknowledged that Kisor had come up with two new service records, both confirming his participation in Operation Harvest Moon. But according to the Board, those records were not "relevant" because they did not go to the reason for the denial—that Kisor did not have PTSD. The Court of Appeals for Veterans Claims, an independent Article I court that initially reviews the Board's decisions, affirmed for the same reason.

The Court of Appeals for the Federal Circuit also affirmed, but it did so based on deference to the Board's interpretation of the VA rule. Kisor had argued to the Federal Circuit that to count as "relevant," a service record need not (as the Board thought) "counter[ ] the basis of the prior denial"; instead, it could relate to some other criterion for obtaining disability benefits. The Federal Circuit found the regulation "ambiguous" as between the two readings. The rule, said the court, does not specifically address "whether 'relevant' records are those casting doubt on the agency's prior [rationale or] those relating to the veteran's claim more broadly." So how to choose between the two views? . . . [T]he court believed *Auer* deference appropriate: The agency's construction of its own regulation would govern unless "plainly erroneous or inconsistent with the VA's regulatory framework." Applying that standard, the court upheld the Board's reading—and so approved the denial of retroactive benefits.

We then granted certiorari to decide whether to overrule *Auer* and (its predecessor) *Seminole Rock*.

II

Before addressing that question directly, we spend some time describing what *Auer* deference is, and is not, for. . . . [O]ur account of why the doctrine emerged—and also how we have limited it—goes a long way toward explaining our view that it is worth preserving.

A

Begin with a familiar problem in administrative law: For various reasons, regulations may be genuinely ambiguous. They may not directly or clearly address every issue; when applied to some fact patterns, they may prove susceptible to more than one reasonable reading. Sometimes, this sort of ambiguity arises from careless drafting—the use of a dangling modifier, an awkward word, an opaque construction. But often, ambiguity reflects the well-known limits of expression or knowledge. The subject matter of a rule "may be so specialized and varying in nature as to be impossible"—or at any rate, impracticable—to capture in its every detail. *SEC v. Chenery Corp.*, 332 U.S. 194, 203 (1947). Or a "problem[ ] may arise" that the agency, when drafting the rule, "could not [have] reasonably foresee[n]." *Id.* at 202. Whichever the case, the result is to create real uncertainties about a regulation's meaning. . . .

[T]ake the facts of *Auer* itself. An agency must decide whether police captains are eligible for overtime under the Fair Labor Standards Act. According to the agency's regulations, employees cannot receive overtime if they are paid on a "salary basis." And in deciding whether an employee is salaried, one question is whether his pay is "subject to reduction" based on performance. A police department's manual informs its officers that their pay might be docked if they commit a disciplinary infraction. Does that fact alone make them "subject to" pay deductions? Or must the department have a practice of docking officer pay, so that the possibility of that happening is more than theoretical?

In each case, interpreting the regulation involves a choice between (or among) more than one reasonable reading. To apply the rule to some unanticipated or unresolved situation, the court must make a judgment call. How should it do so?

In answering that question, we have often thought that a court should defer to the agency's construction of its own regulation. For the last 20 or so years, we have referred to that doctrine as *Auer* deference, and applied it often.

But the name is something of a misnomer. Before the doctrine was called *Auer* deference, it was called *Seminole Rock* deference—for the 1945 decision in which we declared that when "the meaning of [a regulation] is in doubt," the agency's interpretation "becomes of controlling weight unless it is plainly erroneous or inconsistent with the regulation." And *Seminole Rock* itself was not built on sand. Deference to administrative agencies traces back to the late nineteenth century, and perhaps beyond.

We have explained *Auer* deference (as we now call it) as rooted in a presumption about congressional intent—a presumption that Congress would generally want the agency to play the primary role in resolving regulatory ambiguities. Congress, we have pointed out, routinely delegates to agencies the power to implement statutes by issuing rules. In doing so, Congress knows (how could it not?) that regulations will sometimes contain ambiguities. But Congress almost never explicitly assigns responsibility to deal with that problem, either to agencies or to courts. Hence the need to presume, one way or the other, what Congress would want. And as between those two choices, agencies have gotten the nod. We have adopted the presumption—though it is always rebuttable—that "the power authoritatively to interpret its own regulations is a component of the agency's delegated lawmaking powers." Or otherwise said, we have thought that when granting rulemaking power to agencies, Congress usually intends to give them, too, considerable latitude to interpret the ambiguous rules they issue.

In part, that is because the agency that promulgated a rule is in the "better position [to] reconstruct" its original meaning. Consider that if you don't know what some text (say, a memo or an e-mail) means, you would probably want to ask the person who wrote it. And for the same reasons, we have thought, Congress would too (though the person is here a collective actor). The agency that "wrote the regulation" will often have direct insight into what that rule was intended to mean. The drafters will know what it was supposed to include or exclude or how it was supposed to apply to some problem. To be sure, this justification has its limits. It does not work so well, for example, when the agency failed to anticipate an issue in crafting a rule (*e.g.*, if the agency never thought about whether and when chest X-rays would count as a "diagnosis"). Then, the agency will not be uncovering a specific intention; at most (though this is not nothing), it will be offering insight into the analogous issues the drafters considered and the purposes they designed the regulation to serve. And the defense works yet less well when lots of time has passed between the rule's issuance and its interpretation—especially if the interpretation differs from one that has come before. All that said, the point holds good for a significant category of "contemporaneous" readings. Want to know what a rule means? Ask its author.

In still greater measure, the presumption that Congress intended *Auer* deference stems from the awareness that resolving genuine regulatory ambiguities often "entail[s] the exercise of judgment grounded in policy concerns." Return to our TSA example. [Discussed above, but omitted from this excerpt.—Ed.] In most of their applications, terms like "liquids" and "gels" are clear enough. (Traveler checklist: Pretzels OK; water not.) But resolving the uncertain issues—the truffle pâtés or olive tapenades of the world—requires getting in the weeds of the rule's policy: Why does TSA ban liquids and gels in the first instance? What makes them dangerous? Can a potential hijacker use pâté jars in the same way as soda cans? Or take the less specialized-seeming ADA example. It is easy enough to know what "comparable lines of sight" means in a movie theater—but more complicated when, as in sports arenas, spectators sometimes stand up. How costly is it to insist that the stadium owner take that sporadic behavior into account, and is the viewing value received worth the added expense? That cost-benefit calculation, too, sounds more in policy than in law. . . .

And Congress, we have thought, knows just that: It is attuned to the comparative advantages of agencies over courts in making such policy judgments. Agencies (unlike courts) have "unique expertise," often of a scientific or technical nature, relevant to applying a regulation "to complex or changing circumstances." Agencies (unlike courts) can conduct factual investigations, can consult with affected parties, can consider how their experts have handled similar issues over the long course of administering a regulatory program. And agencies (again unlike courts) have political accountability, because they are subject to the supervision of the President, who in turn answers to the public. It is because of those features that Congress, when first enacting a statute, assigns rulemaking power to an agency and thus authorizes it to fill out the statutory scheme. And so too, when new issues demanding new policy calls come up within that scheme, Congress presumably wants the same agency, rather than any court, to take the laboring oar.

Finally, the presumption we use reflects the well-known benefits of uniformity in interpreting genuinely ambiguous rules. We have noted Congress's frequent "preference for resolving interpretive issues by uniform administrative decision, rather than piecemeal by litigation." That preference may be strongest when the interpretive issue arises in the context of a "complex and highly technical regulatory program." After all, judges are most likely to come to divergent conclusions when they are least likely to know what they are doing. . . . Consider *Auer* itself. There, four Circuits held that police captains were "subject to" pay deductions for disciplinary infractions if a police manual said they were, even if the department had never docked anyone. Two other Circuits held that captains were "subject to" pay deductions only if the department's actual practice made that punishment a realistic possibility. Had the agency issued an interpretation before all those rulings (rather than, as actually happened, in a brief in this Court), a deference rule would have averted most of that conflict and uncertainty. *Auer* deference thus serves to ensure consistency in federal regulatory law, for everyone who needs to know what it requires.

B

But all that said, *Auer* deference is not the answer to every question of interpreting an agency's rules. Far from it. As we explain in this section, the possibility of deference can arise only if a regulation is genuinely ambiguous. And when we use that term, we mean it—genuinely ambiguous, even after a court has resorted to all the standard tools of interpretation. Still more, not all reasonable agency constructions of those truly ambiguous rules are entitled to deference. As just explained, we presume that Congress intended for courts to defer to agencies when they interpret their own ambiguous rules. But when the reasons for that presumption do not apply, or countervailing reasons outweigh them, courts should not give deference to an agency's reading, except to the extent it has the "power to persuade." We have thus cautioned that *Auer* deference is just a "general rule"; it "does not apply in all cases." And although the limits of *Auer* deference are not susceptible to any rigid test, we have noted various circumstances in which such deference is "unwarranted." In particular, that will be so when a court concludes that an interpretation does not reflect an agency's authoritative, expertise-based, "fair[, or] considered judgment." [C]f. *United States v. Mead Corp.*, 533 U.S. 218, 229–231 (2001) (adopting a similar approach to *Chevron* deference).

We take the opportunity to restate, and somewhat expand on, those principles here to clear up some mixed messages we have sent. At times, this Court has applied *Auer* deference without significant analysis of the underlying regulation. At other times, the Court has given *Auer* deference without careful attention to the nature and context of the interpretation. And in a vacuum, our most classic formulation of the test—whether an agency's construction is "plainly erroneous or inconsistent with the regulation"—may suggest a caricature of the doctrine, in which deference is "reflexive." . . . So before we turn to Kisor's specific grievances, we think it worth reinforcing some of the limits inherent in the Auer doctrine.

First and foremost, a court should not afford *Auer* deference unless the regulation is genuinely ambiguous. If uncertainty does not exist, there is no plausible reason for deference. The regulation then just means what it means—and the court must give it effect, as the court would any law. Otherwise said, the core theory of *Auer* deference is that sometimes the law runs out, and policy-laden choice is what is left over. But if the law gives an answer—if there is only one reasonable construction of a regulation—then a court has no business deferring to any other reading, no matter how much the agency insists it would make more sense. Deference in that circumstance would "permit the agency, under the guise of interpreting a regulation, to create *de facto* a new regulation." See *Christensen*, 529 U.S. at 588. *Auer* does not, and indeed could not, go that far.

And before concluding that a rule is genuinely ambiguous, a court must exhaust all the "traditional tools" of construction. *Chevron U. S. A. Inc. v. Natural Resources Defense Council, Inc.*, 467 U.S. 837, 843, n. 9 (1984) (adopting the same approach for ambiguous statutes). For again, only when that legal toolkit is empty and the interpretive question still has no single right answer can a judge conclude that it is "more [one] of policy than of law." That means a court cannot wave the ambiguity flag just because it found the regulation impenetrable on first read. Agency regulations can sometimes make the eyes glaze over. But hard interpretive conundrums, even relating to complex rules, can often be solved. To make that effort, a court must "carefully consider[ ]" the text, structure, history, and purpose of a regulation, in all the ways it would if it had no agency to fall back on. Doing so will resolve many seeming ambiguities out of the box, without resort to *Auer* deference.

If genuine ambiguity remains, moreover, the agency's reading must still be "reasonable." In other words, it must come within the zone of ambiguity the court has identified after employing all its interpretive tools. . . . And let there be no mistake: That is a requirement an agency can fail.

Still, we are not done—for not every reasonable agency reading of a genuinely ambiguous rule should receive *Auer* deference. We have recognized in applying *Auer* that a court must make an independent inquiry into whether the character and context of the agency interpretation entitles it to controlling weight. As explained above, we give *Auer* deference because we presume, for a set of reasons relating to the comparative attributes of courts and agencies, that Congress would have wanted us to. But the administrative realm is vast and varied, and we have understood that such a presumption cannot always hold. Cf. *Mead*, 533 U.S. at 236 ("tailor[ing] deference to [the] variety" of administrative action). The inquiry on this dimension does not reduce to any exhaustive test. But we have laid out some especially important markers for identifying when *Auer* deference is and is not appropriate.

To begin with, the regulatory interpretation must be one actually made by the agency. In other words, it must be the agency's "authoritative" or "official position," rather than any more ad hoc statement not reflecting the agency's views. *Mead*, 533 U.S. at 257–259 (SCALIA, J., dissenting). That constraint follows from the logic of *Auer* deference—because Congress has delegated rulemaking power, and all that typically goes with it, to the agency alone. Of course, the requirement of "authoritative" action must recognize a reality of bureaucratic life: Not everything the agency does comes from, or is even in the name of, the Secretary or his chief advisers. So, for example, we have deferred to "official staff memoranda" that were "published in the Federal Register," even though never approved by the agency head. But there are limits. The interpretation must at the least emanate from those actors, using those vehicles, understood to make authoritative policy in the relevant context. If the interpretation does not do so, a court may not defer.

Next, the agency's interpretation must in some way implicate its substantive expertise. . . . Some interpretive issues may fall more naturally into a judge's bailiwick. Take one requiring the elucidation of a simple common-law property term, or one concerning the award of an attorney's fee. When the agency has no comparative expertise in resolving a regulatory ambiguity, Congress presumably would not grant it that authority.

Finally, an agency's reading of a rule must reflect "fair and considered judgment" to receive *Auer* deference. That means, we have stated, that a court should decline to defer to a merely "convenient litigating position" or "*post hoc* rationalizatio[n] advanced" to "defend past agency action against attack." And a court may not defer to a new interpretation, whether or not introduced in litigation, that creates "unfair surprise" to regulated parties. That disruption of expectations may occur when an agency substitutes one view of a rule for another. We have therefore only rarely given *Auer* deference to an agency construction "conflict[ing] with a prior" one. . . .

The upshot of all this goes something as follows. When it applies, *Auer* deference gives an agency significant leeway to say what its own rules mean. In so doing, the doctrine enables the agency to fill out the regulatory scheme Congress has placed under its supervision. But that phrase "when it applies" is important—because it often doesn't. As described above, this Court has cabined *Auer*'s scope in varied and critical ways—and in exactly that measure, has maintained a strong judicial role in interpreting rules. What emerges is a deference doctrine not quite so tame as some might hope, but not nearly so menacing as they might fear.

III

That brings us to the lone question presented here—whether we should abandon the longstanding doctrine just described. In contending that we should, Kisor raises statutory, policy, and constitutional claims (in that order). . . .

A

Kisor first attacks *Auer* as inconsistent with the judicial review provision of the Administrative Procedure Act (APA). See 5 U.S.C. § 706. As Kisor notes, Congress enacted the APA in 1946—the year after *Seminole Rock*—to serve as "the fundamental charter of the administrative state." Section 706 of the Act, governing judicial review of agency action, states (among other things) that reviewing courts shall "determine the meaning or applicability of the terms of an agency action" (including a regulation). According to Kisor, *Auer* violates that edict by thwarting "meaningful judicial review" of agency rules.

To begin with, that argument ignores the many ways, discussed above, that courts exercise independent review over the meaning of agency rules. As we have explained, a court must apply all traditional methods of interpretation to any rule, and must enforce the plain meaning those methods uncover. There can be no thought of deference unless, after performing that thoroughgoing review, the regulation remains genuinely susceptible to multiple reasonable meanings and the agency's interpretation lines up with one of them. And even if that is the case, courts must on their own determine whether the nature or context of the agency's construction reverses the usual presumption of deference. Most notably, a court must consider whether the interpretation is authoritative, expertise-based, considered, and fair to regulated parties. All of that figures as "meaningful judicial review."

And even when a court defers to a regulatory reading, it acts consistently with Section 706. That provision does not specify the standard of review a court should use in "determin[ing] the meaning" of an ambiguous rule. 5 U.S.C. § 706. One possibility, as Kisor says, is to review the issue *de novo*. But another is to review the agency's reading for reasonableness. To see the point, assume that a regulatory (say, an employment) statute expressly instructed courts to apply *Auer* deference when reviewing an agency's interpretations of its ambiguous rules. Nothing in that statute would conflict with Section 706. Instead, the employment law would simply make clear *how* a court is to "determine the meaning" of such a rule—by deferring to an agency's reasonable reading. Of course, that is not the world we know: Most substantive statutes do not say anything about *Auer* deference, one way or the other. But for all the reasons spelled out above, we have long presumed (subject always to rebuttal) that the Congress delegating regulatory authority to an agency intends as well to give that agency considerable latitude to construe its ambiguous rules. And that presumption operates just like the hypothesized statute above. Because of it, once again, courts do not violate Section 706 by applying *Auer*. To the contrary, they fulfill their duty to "determine the meaning" of a rule precisely by deferring to the agency's reasonable reading. . . .

Finally, Kisor goes big, asserting (though fleetingly) that *Auer* deference violates "separation-of-powers principles." In his view, those principles prohibit "vest[ing] in a single branch the law-making and law-interpreting functions." If that objection is to agencies' usurping the interpretive role of courts, this opinion has already met it head-on. Properly understood and applied, *Auer* does no such thing. In all the ways we have described, courts retain a firm grip on the interpretive function. If Kisor's objection is instead to the supposed commingling of functions (that is, the legislative and judicial) within an agency, this Court has answered it often before. That sort of mixing is endemic in agencies, and has been "since the beginning of the Republic." It does not violate the separation of powers, we have explained, because even when agency "activities take 'legislative' and 'judicial' forms," they continue to be "exercises of[ ] the 'executive Power' "—or otherwise said, ways of executing a statutory plan. . . .

IV

With that, we can finally return to Kisor's own case. You may remember that his retroactive benefits depend on the meaning of the term "relevant" records in a VA regulation. . . .

Applying the principles outlined in this opinion, we hold that a redo is necessary for two reasons. First, the Federal Circuit jumped the gun in declaring the regulation ambiguous. We have insisted that a court bring all its interpretive tools to bear before finding that to be so. . . .

And second, the Federal Circuit assumed too fast that *Auer* deference should apply in the event of genuine ambiguity. As we have explained, that is not always true. A court must assess whether the interpretation is of the sort that Congress would want to receive deference. . . .

[A concurring opinion by Chief Justice Roberts, in which he highlighted that the differences between the majority and Justice Gorsuch are not great, is omitted.—Ed.]

Justice Gorsuch, with whom Justice Thomas joins, with whom Justice Kavanaugh joins as to Parts I, II, III, IV, and V, and with whom Justice Alito joins as to Parts I, II, and III, concurring in the judgment.

It should have been easy for the Court to say goodbye to *Auer* v. *Robbins*. In disputes involving the relationship between the government and the people, *Auer* requires judges to accept an executive agency's interpretation of its own regulations even when that interpretation doesn't represent the best and fairest reading. This rule creates a "systematic judicial bias in favor of the federal government, the most powerful of parties, and against everyone else." Nor is *Auer*'s biased rule the product of some congressional mandate we are powerless to correct: This Court invented it, almost by accident and without any meaningful effort to reconcile it with the Administrative Procedure Act or the Constitution. A legion of academics, lower court judges, and Members of this Court—even *Auer*'s author—has called on us to abandon *Auer*. Yet today a bare majority flinches, and *Auer* lives on.

Still, today's decision is more a stay of execution than a pardon. The Court cannot muster even five votes to say that *Auer* is lawful or wise. Instead, a majority retains *Auer* only because of *stare decisis*. And yet, far from standing by that precedent, the majority proceeds to impose so many new and nebulous qualifications and limitations on *Auer* that THE CHIEF JUSTICE claims to see little practical difference between keeping it on life support in this way and overruling it entirely. So the doctrine emerges maimed and enfeebled—in truth, zombified.

Respectfully, we owe our colleagues on the lower courts more candid and useful guidance than this. And judges owe the people who come before them nothing less than a fair contest, where every party has an equal chance to persuade the court of its interpretation of the law's demands. One can hope that THE CHIEF JUSTICE is right, and that whether we formally overrule *Auer* or merely neuter it, the results in most cases will prove the same. But means, not just ends, matter, and retaining even this debilitated version of *Auer* threatens to force litigants and lower courts to jump through needless and perplexing new hoops and in the process deny the people the independent judicial decisions they deserve. . . .

Respectfully, I would stop this business of making up excuses for judges to abdicate their job of interpreting the law, and simply allow the court of appeals to afford Mr. Kisor its best independent judgment of the law's meaning. . . .

I. How We Got Here

. . . . Before the mid-20th century, few federal agencies engaged in extensive rulemaking, and those that did rarely sought deference for their regulatory interpretations. . . . Unsurprisingly, the government's early, longstanding, and consistent interpretation of a statute, regulation, or other legal instrument could count as powerful *evidence* of its original public meaning. But courts respected executive interpretations only because and to the extent "they embodied understandings made roughly contemporaneously with . . . enactment and stably maintained and practiced since that time," not "because they were executive as such." . . .

All this is borne out by the Court's later teachings in *Skidmore v. Swift & Co.* in 1944. . . . The Court first held, based on its own independent analysis, that "no principle of law found either in the statute or in Court decisions precludes waiting time from also being working time." Only then did the Court consider "what, if any, deference courts should pay" to the views of the Administrator of the Labor Department's Wage and Hour Division. . . .

* * *

II. The Administrative Procedure Act

When this Court speaks about the rules governing judicial review of federal agency action, we are not (or shouldn't be) writing on a blank slate or exercising some common-law-making power. We are supposed to be applying the Administrative Procedure Act. . . .

The first problem lies in § 706. That provision instructs reviewing courts to "decide all relevant questions of law" and "set aside agency action . . . found to be . . . not in accordance with law." Determining the meaning of a statute or regulation, of course, presents a classic legal question. But in case these directives were not clear enough, the APA further directs courts to "determine the meaning" of any relevant "agency action," including any rule issued by the agency. The APA thus requires a reviewing court to resolve for itself any dispute over the proper interpretation of an agency regulation. . . .

[The APA's] unqualified command requires the court to determine legal questions—including questions about a regulation's meaning—by its own lights, not by those of political appointees or bureaucrats who may even be self-interested litigants in the case at hand. Nor can there be any doubt that, when Congress wrote the APA, it knew perfectly well how to require judicial deference to an agency when it wished—in fact, Congress repeatedly specified deferential standards for judicial review *elsewhere* in the statute. But when it comes to the business of interpreting regulations, no such command exists; instead, Congress told courts to "determine" those matters for themselves. . . .

Nor does Justice Kagan's reading of § 706 offer any logical stopping point. If courts can "determine the meaning" of a regulation by deferring to any "reasonable" agency reading, then why not by deferring to *any* agency reading? . . .

* * *

III. The Constitution

Not only is *Auer* incompatible with the APA; it also sits uneasily with the Constitution. Article III, § 1 provides that the "judicial Power of the United States" is vested exclusively in this Court and the lower federal courts. A core component of that judicial power is " 'the duty of interpreting [the laws] and applying them in cases properly brought before the courts.' " As Chief Justice Marshall put it, "[i]t is emphatically the province and duty of the judicial department to say what the law is." And never, this Court has warned, should the "judicial power . . . be shared with [the] Executive Branch." Yet that seems to be exactly what *Auer* requires. . . .

Our Nation's founders . . . they designed a judiciary that would be able to interpret the laws "free from potential domination by other branches of government." To that end, they resisted proposals that would have subjected judicial decisions to review by political actors. And they rejected the British tradition of using the upper house of the legislature as a court of last resort, out of fear that a body with "even a partial agency in passing bad laws" would operate under the "same spirit" in "interpreting them." Instead, they gave federal judges life tenure, subject only to removal by impeachment; and they guaranteed that the other branches could not reduce judges' compensation so long as they remained in office.

The founders afforded these extraordinary powers and protections not for the comfort of judges, but so that an independent judiciary could better guard the people from the arbitrary use of governmental power. . . .

Auer represents no trivial threat to these foundational principles. . . . *Auer* tells the judge that he must interpret these binding laws to mean not what he thinks they mean, but what an executive agency says they mean. Unlike Article III judges, executive officials are not, nor are they supposed to be, "wholly impartial." They have their own interests, their own constituencies, and their own policy goals . . . .

IV. Policy Arguments

Lacking support elsewhere, Justice Kagan is forced to resort to policy arguments to defend *Auer*. . . .

If a court's goal in interpreting a regulation really were to determine what its author "intended," *Auer* would be an almost complete mismatch with the goal. Agency personnel change over time, and an agency's policy priorities may shift dramatically from one presidential administration to another. Yet *Auer* tells courts that they must defer to the agency's *current* view of what the regulation ought to mean, which may or may not correspond to the views of those who actually wrote it. . . .

Proceeding farther down this doubtful path, Justice Kagan asserts that resolving ambiguities in a regulation "sounds more in policy than in law" and is thus a task more suited to executive officials than judges. But this claim, too, contradicts a basic premise of our legal order: that we are governed not by the shifting whims of politicians and bureaucrats, but by written laws whose meaning is fixed and ascertainable—if not by all members of the public, then at least by lawyers who can advise them and judges who must apply the law to individual cases guided by the neutral principles found in our traditional tools of interpretation. The text of the regulation is treated *as* the law, and the agency's policy judgment has the force of law *only* insofar as it is embodied in the regulatory text. . . .

To be sure, during the period of *Auer*'s ascendancy some suggested that the meaning of written law is always "radically indeterminate" and that judges expounding it are "for the most part, guided by policy—not text." And in an environment like that it was perhaps thought a small step to conclude that, if legal disputes are going to be resolved on political grounds, then they ought to be resolved by real politicians in the executive branch rather than ersatz politicians on the bench. But the proposed cure proved worse than the disease. Arguments like these surrendered the judgment embodied in our Constitution and the APA that courts owe the people they serve their independent legal judgment about the law's meaning. Besides, we've long since come to realize that the real cure doesn't lie in turning judges into rubber stamps for politicians, but in redirecting the judge's interpretive task back to its roots, away from open-ended policy appeals and speculation about legislative intentions and toward the traditional tools of interpretation judges have employed for centuries to elucidate the law's original public meaning. . . .

Pursuing a more modest tack, Justice Kagan next suggests that *Auer* is justified by the respect due agencies' "technical" expertise. But no one doubts that courts should pay close attention to an expert agency's views on technical questions in its field. Just as a court "would want to know what John Henry Wigmore said about an issue of evidence law [or] what Arthur Corbin thought about a matter of contract law," so too should courts carefully consider what the Food and Drug Administration thinks about how its prescription drug safety regulations operate. The fact remains, however, that even agency experts "can be wrong; even Homer nodded." . . .

Justice Kagan's final policy argument is that *Auer* promotes "consistency" and "uniformity" . . . . But . . . [t]he judicial process is how we settle disputes about the meaning of written law, and our judicial system is more than capable of producing a single, uniform, and stable interpretation that will last until the regulation is amended or repealed.

* * *

Overruling *Auer* would have taken us directly back to *Skidmore*, liberating courts to decide cases based on their independent judgment and "follow [the] agency's [view] only to the extent it is persuasive." By contrast, the majority's attempt to remodel *Auer*'s rule into a multi-step, multi-factor inquiry guarantees more uncertainty and much litigation. . . .

But this cloud may have a silver lining: The majority leaves *Auer* so riddled with holes that, when all is said and done, courts may find that it does not constrain their independent judgment any more than *Skidmore*. . . . Alternatively, if *Auer* proves more resilient, this Court should reassert its responsibility to say what the law is and afford the people the neutral forum for their disputes that they expect and deserve.

Justice Kavanaugh, with whom Justice Alito joins, concurring in the judgment.

. . . . Importantly, the majority borrows from footnote 9 of this Court's opinion in *Chevron* to say that a reviewing court must "exhaust all the 'traditional tools' of construction" before concluding that an agency rule is ambiguous and deferring to an agency's reasonable interpretation. If a reviewing court employs all of the traditional tools of construction, the court will almost always reach a conclusion about the best interpretation of the regulation at issue. After doing so, the court then will have no need to adopt or defer to an agency's contrary interpretation. In other words, the footnote 9 principle, taken seriously, means that courts will have no reason or basis to put a thumb on the scale in favor of an agency when courts interpret agency regulations. Formally rejecting *Auer* would have been a more direct approach, but rigorously applying footnote 9 should lead in most cases to the same general destination. . . .

To be sure, some cases involve regulations that employ broad and open-ended terms like "reasonable," "appropriate," "feasible," or "practicable." Those kinds of terms afford agencies broad policy discretion, and courts allow an agency to reasonably exercise its discretion to choose among the options allowed by the text of the rule. But that is more *State Farm* than *Auer*. See *Motor Vehicle Mfrs. Assn. of United States, Inc. v. State Farm Mut. Automobile Ins. Co.*, 463 U.S. 29 (1983).

In short, after today's decision, a judge should engage in appropriately rigorous scrutiny of an agency's interpretation of a regulation, and can simultaneously be appropriately deferential to an agency's reasonable policy choices within the discretion allowed by a regulation.

NOTES AND QUESTIONS

1. Can Congress mandate deference? In portions of the opinions not excerpted, Justice Kagan claims that judicial deference to agency legal interpretations does not violate APA § 706 because Congress, if it wanted, could *tell* the courts to defer to reasonable agency interpretations. In other words, saying that courts should review questions of law does not answer the question of the *standard* or *scope* of that review. Justice Gorsuch doubted, although he did not directly address, the constitutionality of such a statute commanding courts to give deference. What's the answer?

Your casebook author suggests the following approach. It has to do with the distinction between private rights cases and public rights cases, discussed in Chapter 7. Here is a brief overview: Whether Congress can mandate deference depends entirely on the kind of case being adjudicated. If it is a public rights case, then Congress can require courts to defer to reasonable executive interpretations; if it is a private rights case, then Congress cannot constitutionally require courts to defer to interpretations that they do not believe are the best interpretations of the statute. Why the distinction?

> **CROSS REFERENCE** Chapter 7 discusses the distinction between private rights and public rights. Historically the executive branch could adjudicate matters of public right without any court involvement at all. If that's true, then wouldn't *Chevron* deference be perfectly constitutional as applied to public rights cases?

Public rights cases, as we shall see in Chapter 7, were historically the kinds of cases that needn't be resolved by Article III courts at all. The quintessential public rights cases are claims against the government, where a private citizen is seeking something *from* the government, like a land grant or welfare benefits. These cases could be entirely resolved in the executive branch with no court involvement at all. The theory was rooted in sovereign immunity: if the government did not have to consent to be sued, then it could consent on the condition that any adjudication be conducted in an executive branch tribunal. And if Congress did not have to authorize judicial review at all, then surely Congress could consent to judicial review on the condition that courts defer to reasonable agency interpretations.

In contrast, if we are dealing with *private rights* cases—as in where the government is trying to deprive a private citizen of liberty or property—those are the cases that *had* to be heard in traditional courts, and Congress therefore could not derogate from the judicial power to interpret law when deciding such cases.

2. **Kisor's *step one implications*.** An earlier note flagged that *Kisor* is a "step zero" case for *Auer* deference. But it also raises numerous other issues, for example, the scope of "step one." If all the tools of statutory construction are used at step one, how much occasion will the courts have to defer? Justice Kavanaugh says almost never. Do you agree? Does it depend on how much ambiguity or uncertainty is required before a judge will declare her view that the statute is sufficiently "ambiguous"? Should a judge decide the matter for herself if she is 51% confident that the regulation (or statute) meant *x* as opposed to *y*? If that's ambiguous, what if 60% of the evidence points in one direction? 65%? Do you see the point? Even using all the traditional tools of statutory construction at step one does not solve the threshold ambiguity question.

3. ***The hard-look connection*.** Justice Kavanaugh's concurrence raises the point that, even with a capacious step one in which judges deploy all the tools of statutory construction, there may still be broad delegations of authority and discretion to agencies, for example to make "reasonable" or "practicable" regulations. But, he says, that is more the stuff of *State Farm*. Under this view, is "step two" merely arbitrary-and-capricious review? In fact, are the courts at step two really dealing with *interpretation*, or pure policymaking?

In fact, isn't that what Justice Kagan's opinion seems to maintain? After all the tools of statutory construction are used, the statute still might not answer the question at hand. To be sure, she *describes* the agency's choice at this juncture as an "interpretation" of the statute. But is it really? If, after all the tools of statutory interpretation are deployed, the statute simply doesn't answer the question—if the law runs out, as Kagan says—then aren't we dealing with something very different from "interpretation"? If the law has run out, then what's being interpreted? Aren't we in a realm of pure policymaking? Aren't the agencies exercising a kind of *legislative*, or at least quasi-legislative, power?

Consider this possibility in light of the following law review excerpt, written by your casebook author, as well as the excerpt that follows, by Cass Sunstein.

Ilan Wurman, The Specification Power

168 U. Pa. L. Rev. 689 (2020)

The executive power to interpret law is at the center of modern debates over administrative law and the separation of powers. The doctrine announced in *Chevron, U.S.A., Inc. v. Natural Resources Defense Council* holds that courts must defer to an agency's reasonable interpretation of an ambiguous statute that it administers. The doctrine is justified on at least two grounds: when Congress enacts statutes with ambiguities, Congress is presumed to delegate implicitly to the agencies the authority to resolve those ambiguities; and agencies are more politically accountable, technically expert, and institutionally competent than courts to do so.

Chevron's "canonical" status in administrative law, however, may be fraying. Critics have noted the apparent inconsistency between Chevron deference and the Administrative Procedure Act ("APA"), which provides in § 706 that a reviewing court "shall decide all relevant questions of law, interpret constitutional and statutory provisions, and determine the meaning or applicability of the terms of an agency action." Deference to executive interpretations also appears inconsistent with the structural separation of powers: Article III assigns the judicial power to "say what the law is" to judges with life tenure and salary protections so they may exercise their legal judgment while insulated from the political accountability that seems to justify Chevron deference. Finally, recent scholarship has suggested that historically courts may have respected only those executive interpretations that were contemporaneous with the enactment of the law or were longstanding, and were thus good evidence of what the law actually was. For these reasons, even former Justice Kennedy has joined calls from his more formalist colleagues to reconsider "the premises that underlie Chevron."

Many scholars, however, maintain that deference is inevitable. Nicholas Bednar and Kristin Hickman recently argued, for example, that Chevron deference, or something much like it, "is a necessary consequence of and corollary to Congress's longstanding habit of relying on agencies to exercise substantial policymaking discretion to resolve statutory details." Unless Congress assumes "substantially more responsibility for making policy choices itself" or the courts "reinvigorate the nondelegation doctrine," they write, then "some variant of Chevron deference will be essential to guide and assist courts from intruding too deeply into a policy sphere for which they are ill-suited." A veritable legion of scholars has argued that deference is inevitable because the interpretation of broad statutory standards requires policymaking discretion, or the resolving of statutory "ambiguities" is for policymakers. And legal realists maintain that all interpretation inherently entails policymaking.

In short, when agencies implement statutory schemes, the doctrine treats their actions as "interpretations." This then raises the question of how much courts ought to defer to such interpretations of law, a question that remains unresolved by courts and scholars. The claim here is that this debate has stalled because, although the doctrine treats agency implementations of statutes as interpretation, something else is in fact usually going on. Agencies do interpret law as an incident to enforcing the law, but they also do something else: they exercise a kind of interstitial lawmaking, gap-filling, policymaking power where the statute is clear but does not specify a course of action, a power that I shall call the "specification power."

Although many deference proponents have intuited that agencies are doing something along these lines, they have been unable to escape the doctrinal vocabulary of interpretation and therefore have failed to provide an accurate descriptive or constitutional account of this power. A few scholars have recognized that the doctrine seems to conflate two different powers or activities, but none provides a complete constitutional account of why agencies may exercise this policymaking power, nor provides a satisfactory account of what distinguishes the "interpretation" that agencies do from their "policymaking." This Article supplements the work of these scholars, illustrating the distinction between interpretation and "specification" and providing arguments from the Constitution's text, structure, and history for why agencies may exercise this specification power.

American legal history is replete with examples of the exercise of both kinds of power. In the 1840 case of *Decatur v. Paulding*, the Court was confronted with two statutes, one which granted a pension to all widows of naval service members, and another which granted a pension specifically to the widow of Commodore Stephen Decatur. Mrs. Decatur sought to collect both pensions. The Court recognized that the interpretation of this law could leave room for discretion and even disagreement, and thus the Court would not compel the executive to adopt one interpretation over another through a writ of mandamus. But the Court also noted that had a non-mandamus action been brought, then "the Court certainly would not be bound to adopt the construction given by the head of a department" because in such cases it is the court's "duty to interpret the act of Congress, in order to ascertain the rights of the parties in the cause before them."

On the other hand, one of the earliest statutes provided that the military pensions which had been granted and paid by the states pursuant to the acts of the Confederation Congress to the wounded and disabled veterans of the Revolutionary War "shall be continued and paid by the United States, from the fourth day of March last, for the space of one year, under such regulations as the President of the United States may direct." President Washington's regulations stated that the sums owed were to be paid in "two equal payments," the first on March 5, 1790, and the second on June 5, 1790; and that each application for payment was to be accompanied by certain vouchers as evidence that the invalid served in a particular regiment or vessel at the time he was disabled.

This is a particularly clear example of an executive officer exercising a power not of interpretation, but of what we might call specification. The regulation concerning two equal payments to be made three months apart was certainly a reasonable interpretation of the statute, which required the payments to be made within one year. Yet the executive could have chosen any number of other options: daily installments for the entire year, three installments at varying intervals to be completed within the year, and so on. Each of these options, in and of itself, would have been a reasonable interpretation of the statute because the statute only required such payments to be made within a year.

The act of choosing among these various possible interpretations, however, was not an act of interpretation. Nothing in the statute demanded one regulation over another; all would have been reasonable interpretations because all would have been permitted by the statute. The choice among these options, then, was not an act of interpretation and that choice requires a different vocabulary. I suggest the term "specification": the executive officers specified this detail of implementation—this course of action—within the bounds of what the statute permitted but without more specific direction from the statute itself. Nothing in the statute bore on their choice, so long as it was within the range of options created by the best interpretation of the statute's limits.

Now consider another case: A statute provides that a "stationary source" is defined as "any building, structure, facility, or installation" which emits air pollution. The statute does not say, however, what to do when more than one of these definitions applies, for example when there is a facility that includes multiple structures and installations. A judge might do all the "interpretation" there is to do—ascertaining the meaning of all the relevant terms as well as the legal effect of those terms against the structure and backdrop of the entire statute and preexisting law more broadly—and the statute might simply not answer the question. The statute is not ambiguous, nor is it vague. It has simply left a "gap" or a "silence," a space within which the executive might specify the course of action in order to implement the statutory scheme. Here, again, the result of the executive's choice would, of course, be a reasonable interpretation of the statute; but the act of choosing among the multiple permissible options would not be an act of interpretation. These were the facts of *Chevron* itself, facts that call for an exercise of the specification power. This is the power to fill in the details where the statute is clear but does not specify the course of action.

Although agencies may not have final say over the interpretation of law, their exercise of the specification power is rooted in the text, structure, and history of both the "legislative power" and the "executive power." Chief Justice John Marshall recognized long ago that there was a category of power partly but not wholly legislative in its nature—we shall call it here "nonexclusive" legislative power—that Congress may exercise itself or delegate to the other branches. He described this power as the power to "fill up the details" of a general statutory provision. The specification power may also be deduced from the vesting of "the executive power" in the chief executive, whether one adopts the prevailing formalist account that the vesting clause is a residual grant of power or the view that it merely grants a power of law-execution.

* * *

Chief Justice Marshall proceeded to address the nondelegation argument. He wrote: "It will not be contended that Congress can delegate to the Courts, or to any other tribunals, powers which are strictly and exclusively legislative. But Congress may certainly delegate to others, powers which the legislature may rightfully exercise itself." The Judiciary Act and the Process Act "empower the Courts respectively to regulate their practice," and "[i]t certainly will not be contended, that this might not be done by Congress." Yet it also "will not be contended" that "mak[ing] rules, directing the returning of writs and processes, the filing of declarations and other pleadings, and other things of the same description . . . may not be conferred on the judicial department."

"The line has not been exactly drawn," Chief Justice Marshall continued, "which separates those important subjects, which must be entirely regulated by the legislature itself, from those of less interest, in which a general provision may be made, and power given to those who are to act under such general provisions to fill up the details." In other words, the power to make rules "fill[ing] up the details" of a general legislative provision is a kind of nonexclusive legislative power, a power partly but not wholly legislative in character and which Congress can exercise itself but which it can also confer on one of the other departments.

Chief Justice Marshall then assessed whether the power delegated by the proviso was an impermissible delegation, i.e., fell within the class of powers that was "exclusively legislative." He observed that it permitted the courts to specify where the executive officer might keep the goods of the debtor until the day of sale; to specify how notice is to be given before the execution of a judgment; and to specify whether the sale can be made on credit. Chief Justice Marshall thus recognized that a broad statutory provision might call for an exercise of what we have called the "specification" power to fill in interstitial legislative details, where there was no more interpretation to be done. Because it is quite impossible for Congress to anticipate every detail of implementation, there must exist this class of nonexclusive legislative power "to fill up the details" of a statutory scheme. . . .

Although the Process Act of 1792 explicitly delegated the power to the courts to "specify" particular details of that law, there may be other sources of constitutional power for the executive to specify at least certain kinds of details even in the absence of an explicit delegation to make regulations. The first possible source is the Take Care Clause; the second, more likely source is the Vesting Clause.

A specification power could inhere in the President's duty to take care that the laws be faithfully executed, assuming this textual provision is also a grant of power. If Congress left a detail to be specified, even if Congress did so unknowingly and even if Congress did not explicitly grant the executive the power to make regulations, how are executive officers to execute the laws faithfully without providing for that detail of implementation? This is what we ordinarily mean when we say a statute has a "gap." In Chevron itself, the agency was required to regulate "stationary sources." To execute this instruction, the agency had to decide what to consider as a stationary source when more than one of the statutory definitions applied. This gap had to be filled, in other words, for the law to be faithfully executed. . . .

Because the Take Care Clause may not even be a grant of power, the Vesting Clause is the more likely source of the specification power. . . .

Blackstone, whose work heavily influenced the Founders, described a prerogative power more along the lines presented here. "For, though the making of laws is entirely the work of a distinct part, the legislative branch, of the sovereign power," wrote Blackstone, "yet the manner, time, and circumstances of putting those laws in execution must frequently be left to the discretion of the executive magistrate." Therefore, the executive's edicts or proclamations on these points (its executive orders and regulations) "are binding upon the subject, where they do not either contradict the old laws, or tend to establish new ones; but only enforce the execution of such laws as are already in being, in such manner as the king shall judge necessary." If this power to specify the details necessary to enforce a law is a prerogative power, as Blackstone seems to describe, then it is vested in the executive department because such a power is not otherwise limited by the constitutional text.

* * *

Although a full exploration of the following implications must await another day, it is worth pointing out that two of administrative law's most persistent puzzles may also be resolved by distinguishing specification and interpretation.

First, under the APA, interpretative rules do not have to go through notice-and-comment rulemaking, in contrast to "legislative" rules. The test for distinguishing the two kinds of rules is that a rule is legislative if without that rule there would be an inadequate legislative basis for an enforcement action. This creates a puzzle. Under the theory of *Chevron,* most legislative rules are themselves interpretations of statutes. Indeed, the *Mead* doctrine says that deference to agency interpretation is warranted precisely where the agency has promulgated a legislative rule. . . .

The distinction between interpretation and specification may help resolve this puzzle. Insofar as a rule or agency statement is in fact merely an interpretation of a statute, then it would not have to go through notice-and-comment rulemaking because it is an "interpretative" rule under the APA. But the lack of public participation in the process of arriving at that interpretation ought to be acceptable because the courts would review such interpretations de novo, without deference. But insofar as the rule is not merely an interpretation, but actually a specification—the making of policy in the interstices of the acknowledged bounds of the statute—public participation through the notice-and-comment process is and ought to be required by the APA. Courts do not have much of a say here, but at least the public does.

This relates to a second puzzle: what is the relationship between "hard look" or arbitrary-and-capricious review of agency policymaking and Chevron's second step? If regulations are all interpretations of statutes, then courts should defer to reasonable choices made by an agency. But if that's the case, then there is no more room for hard-look review of the agency's policy choices—which by assumption are actually just constructions of the statute. Put another way, if hard look review requires agencies to base their decisions "on a consideration of the relevant factors," and the relevant factors are found in the statute, then Step Two and hard-look are identical. Several scholars and courts have therefore concluded that Chevron's second step is tantamount to hard-look review.

The distinction between interpretation and specification may resolve this puzzle as well. Insofar as an agency's act is truly an interpretive one, there is no need for hard-look review because the courts in any event review such interpretations de novo, and the analysis never proceeds past what is currently called Chevron Step One. But if the agency action was one of several possible policy choices, each of which would have been permissible under the statute, then the courts still could police such acts of specification to ensure their reasonableness if that is what Congress intended courts to do by granting courts the power of arbitrary-and-capricious review.

Cass R. Sunstein, Beyond *Marbury*: The Executive's Power to Say What the Law Is

115 Yale L.J. 2580 (2006)

My major goal in this Essay is to vindicate the law-interpreting authority of the executive branch. This authority, I suggest, is indispensable to the healthy operation of modern government; it can be defended on both democratic and technocratic grounds. Indeed, the executive's law-interpreting authority is a natural and proper outgrowth of both the legal realist attack on the autonomy of legal reasoning and the most important institutional development of the twentieth century: the shift from regulation through common law courts to regulation through administrative agencies. In the modern era, statutory interpretation must often be undertaken, at least in the first instance, by numerous institutions within the executive branch. For the resolution of ambiguities in statutory law, technical expertise and political accountability are highly relevant, and on these counts the executive has significant advantages over courts. Changed circumstances, involving new values and new understandings of fact, are relevant too, and they suggest further advantages on the part of the executive. . . .

What is most striking about the Court's analysis in *Chevron* is the suggestion that resolution of statutory ambiguities requires a judgment about resolving "competing interests." This is a candid recognition that assessments of policy are sometimes indispensable to statutory interpretation. Of course it is easy to find cases in which courts resolve ambiguities by using the standard legal sources—for example, by using dictionaries, consulting statutory structure, deploying canons of construction, or relying on legislative history if that technique is thought to be legitimate. Under the first step of *Chevron*, the executive will lose if the standard sources show that the agency is wrong. But sometimes those sources will leave gaps or reasonable disagreement; *Chevron* itself is such a case, and there are many others.

Suppose, for example, that the question involves the appropriate valuation of natural resources; the proper calculation of Medicare payments; or the proper extent of deregulation under the Telecommunications Act. If we emphasize the need to attend to "competing interests," four separate points support the executive's power to interpret the law. First, interpretation of statutes often calls for technical expertise, and here the executive has conspicuous advantages over the courts. The question in *Chevron* itself was highly technical, and it was difficult to answer that question without specialized knowledge. Second, interpretation of statutes often calls for political accountability, and the executive has conspicuous advantages on that count as well. When the executive is seeking to expand or limit the Endangered Species Act or deciding whether to apply the Clean Air Act to greenhouse gases, democratic forces undoubtedly play a significant role. Third, the executive administers laws that apply over extended periods and across heterogeneous contexts. Changes in both facts and values argue strongly in favor of considerable executive power in interpretation. Unlike the executive, courts are too decentralized—and their processes far too cumbersome—to do the relevant "updating," or to adapt statutes to diverse domains. Fourth, it is often important to permit the modern state to act promptly and decisively. Deference to executive interpretations promotes that goal far more effectively than a strong judicial role, for two different reasons. Deference to the executive reduces the likelihood that judicial disagreement will result in time-consuming remands to the agency for further proceedings. More subtly, such deference combats the risk that different lower courts will disagree about the appropriate interpretation of statutes—and thus counteracts the balkanization of federal law.

To be sure, it is possible to imagine some tension among these different considerations. Perhaps an issue calls for specialized competence, but perhaps the relevant agency has been buffeted about by political pressure imposed by an administration for which technical considerations are far from primary. Technical and political justifications for *Chevron* may not march hand-in-hand; they might well conflict with one another. But so long as the statute is genuinely ambiguous, and so long as the agency is not acting arbitrarily, it is entirely legitimate for the executive either to rely on its technical competence or to make its assessment on the basis of normative judgments that are not inconsistent with the governing statute.

Notice that so defended, *Chevron* stands for much more than the modest claim that courts may not invalidate executive action unless the standard legal sources require invalidation. Less modestly, *Chevron* means that courts must uphold reasonable agency interpretations even if they would reject those interpretations on their own. Courts must be prepared to say: "If we were interpreting the statute independently, we would read it to say X rather than Y; but because it is ambiguous, the executive is permitted to prefer Y." This argument applies most obviously to the national government, operated by the Chief Executive, who stands as the most visible official in the United States. But the same arguments can easily be invoked by other executive officers—above all, by governors and mayors—who are also entrusted with overseeing implementation of the law. For state and local officers, just as for federal officials, statutory ambiguities often cannot be resolved without judgments of policy. Those judgments should likewise be made by agencies with technical expertise or political accountability. . . .

The legal realists saw the interpretation of statutory ambiguities as necessarily involving judgments of policy and principle. They insisted that when courts understand statutes to mean one thing rather than another, they use judgments of their own, at least in genuinely hard cases. In a famous article, for example, Max Radin attacked the standard tools as largely unhelpful. . . . Radin said that, inevitably, a key question was, "Will the inclusion of this particular determinate in the statutory determinable lead to a desirable result? What is desirable will be what is just, what is proper, what satisfies the social emotions of the judge, what fits into the ideal scheme of society which he entertains."

Radin's argument was characteristic of the general period in which courts were being displaced by regulatory agencies. A specialist in administrative law, Ernst Freund saw at an early stage that for some statutes, "executive interpretation is an important factor." Freund noted, with evident concern, that "in view of the inevitable ambiguities of language, a power of interpretation is a controlling factor in the effect of legislative instruments, and makes the courts that exercise it a rival organ with the legislature in the development of the written law." After surveying the various sources of interpretation, Freund emphasized that policy, in the end, must be primary; therefore, "in cases of genuine ambiguity courts should use the power of interpretation consciously and deliberately to promote sound law and sound principles of legislation."

For his part, Karl Llewellyn contended that the standard sources of interpretation, above all the canons of construction, masked judgments that were really based on other grounds. He asked courts to "strive to make sense as a whole out of our law as a whole." In his view, the canons were plural and inconsistent, and thus unable to provide real help. Llewellyn argued that statutory meaning should be derived from "[t]he good sense of the situation and a simple construction of the available language to achieve that sense, by tenable means, out of the statutory language."

Radin, Freund, and Llewellyn overstated their arguments. Canons of construction, for example, can constrain judicial (or executive) interpretation, and it may well be better to rely on them than on a judge's individual, general sense of what is best. But suppose that the realists were broadly right to suggest that, in the face of genuine ambiguity, courts often make judgments of policy. Suppose that in hard cases, the search for "legislative intent" is often a fraud, and that when courts purport to rely on that intent, they often speak for their own preferred views. If Radin, Freund, and Llewellyn are indeed right, then there seems to be little reason to think that courts, rather than the executive, should be making the key judgments. The President himself should be in a better position to make the relevant judgments, simply because of his comparatively greater accountability. And if specialized knowledge is required, executive agencies have large advantages over generalist judges. In support of the realist position, consider strong evidence that, for hard statutory questions within the Supreme Court, policy arguments of one or another sort often play a central role, even in a period in which "textualism" has seemed on the ascendancy.

These points are easily linked with the post-New Deal transfer of effective lawmaking power from common law courts to federal bureaucracies. For much of the nation's history, the basic rules of regulation were elaborated by common law courts, using the principles of tort, contract, and property to set out the ground rules for social and economic relationships. In the early part of the twentieth century, some of those rules were taken to have constitutional status, so as to forbid legislative adjustments. But in a wholesale attack on the adequacy of the common law, the New Deal saw the rise and legitimation of a vast array of new agencies, including the National Labor Relations Board (NLRB), the Securities and Exchange Commission (SEC), the Social Security

Administration (SSA), the Federal Communications Commission (FCC), the Federal Deposit Insurance Corporation (FDIC), an expanded Federal Trade Commission (FTC), and an expanded Food and Drug Administration (FDA).

Many of the agencies were necessarily in the business of interpreting ambiguous statutory provisions; indeed, interpretation was the central part of their job. Agency-made common law dominated the early days of the administrative state. To take just one example, the NLRB was required to decide a number of fundamental questions about national labor policy. The statute did not speak plainly, and questions of policy were inevitably involved. While the federal courts also played a significant and sometimes aggressive role, the elaboration of the labor enactments of the New Deal was inevitably founded on the work of the NLRB. What can be said for the NLRB can also be said of the FDA, the FCC, the SEC, and the FTC, all of which, in the New Deal era, were also charged with implementing statutory law through the interpretation of largely open-ended statutory provisions.

There is an evident link between the realists' emphasis on the policy-driven nature of interpretation and the New Deal's enthusiasm for administrators, who were to be both expert and accountable. . . .

Chevron is best taken as a vindication of the realist claim that resolution of statutory ambiguities often calls for judgments of policy and principle. The allocation of law-interpreting power to the executive fits admirably well with the twentieth-century shift from common law courts to regulatory administration. . . .

D. Judicial Review of Agency Discretion and Inaction

The previous three sections covered judicial review of agency policymaking and reasoning, factual findings, and legal interpretations. This section now addresses judicial review of another kind of agency action. The next cases and notes deal with matters that are "committed to agency discretion by law" under the Administrative Procedure Act. According to APA § 701(a), the judicial review provisions of the APA apply except where an organic statute otherwise precludes judicial review, id. § 701(a)(1), or where the "agency action is committed to agency discretion by law," id. § 701(a)(2).

The Supreme Court has interpreted this to mean that there is no judicial review available in such cases, and that's indeed what the text of the APA seems to say. Thus, many casebooks include this material with the other "reviewability" cases, like those involving finality, ripeness, and exhaustion, which we tackle in the final chapter of this casebook. We include the "committed to agency discretion" material in this chapter, however, because it is important to understand that organic statutes commit lots of matters to agency discretion, including the policymaking discretion addressed earlier in this chapter, for which judicial review is available. Indeed, APA § 706(a)(2)(A), in the same pro-

INQUIRY What are the differences between an agency's policymaking discretion to which the arbitrary and capricious standard of review applies; discretionary acts that are reviewed for an abuse of discretion; and matters that are "committed to agency discretion by law," for which there is no judicial review at all?

vision as the arbitrary-and-capricious standard, requires agencies to set aside agency actions that are an "abuse of discretion." The question for us, then, is when is legal discretion judicially reviewable under, for example, the *State Farm* arbitrary-and-capricious standard or the abuse of discretion standard, and when is judicial review not available because the agency's discretion falls under matters "committed to agency discretion by law." Additionally, addressing this material now makes sense because we are trying to distinguish between *types* of agency action—reviewable discretionary decisions (such as agency policymaking and reasoning), factual findings, legal interpretations, and unreviewable discretionary decisions—whereas the reviewability doctrines of finality, ripeness, exhaustion, and standing can apply to preclude judicial review across the board, irrespective of the type of agency action at hand.

The first case deals with an agency's termination of an employee in the national security context, and the second case deals with agency *inaction,* or enforcement discretion. When an agency decides *not* to initiate a particular enforcement proceeding, or when it decides not to initiate a rulemaking, are those decisions judicially reviewable? Clearly some statutes give agencies discretion whether and when to deploy rulemaking, and every agency has enforcement discretion similar to prosecutorial discretion. On what basis can courts review such decisions? Are they "committed to agency discretion by law," are they more akin to policymaking discretion subject to arbitrary-and-capricious review, or are they to be reviewed under an abuse of discretion standard?

Webster v. Doe

486 U.S. 592 (1988)

Chief Justice Rehnquist delivered the opinion of the Court.

Section 102(c) of the National Security Act of 1947, 61 Stat. 498, as amended, provides that:

"[T]he Director of Central Intelligence may, in his discretion, terminate the employment of any officer or employee of the Agency whenever he shall deem such termination necessary or advisable in the interests of the United States. . . ." 50 U.S.C. § 403(c).

In this case we decide whether, and to what extent, the termination decisions of the Director under § 102(c) are judicially reviewable.

I

Respondent John Doe was first employed by the Central Intelligence Agency (CIA or Agency) in 1973 as a clerk-typist. He received periodic fitness reports that consistently rated him as an excellent or outstanding employee. By 1977, respondent had been promoted to a position as a covert electronics technician.

In January 1982, respondent voluntarily informed a CIA security officer that he was a homosexual. Almost immediately, the Agency placed respondent on paid administrative leave pending an investigation of his sexual orientation and conduct. On February 12 and again on February 17, respondent was extensively questioned by a polygraph officer concerning his homosexuality and possible security violations. Respondent denied having sexual relations with any foreign nationals and maintained that he had not disclosed classified information to any of his sexual partners. After these interviews, the officer told respondent that the polygraph tests indicated that he had truthfully answered all questions. The polygraph officer then prepared a five-page summary of his interviews with respondent, to which respondent was allowed to attach a two-page addendum.

On April 14, 1982, a CIA security agent informed respondent that the Agency's Office of Security had determined that respondent's homosexuality posed a threat to security, but declined to explain the nature of the danger. Respondent was then asked to resign. When he refused to do so, the Office of Security recommended to the CIA Director (petitioner's predecessor) that respondent be dismissed. After reviewing respondent's records and the evaluations of his subordinates, the Director "deemed it necessary and advisable in the interests of the United States to terminate [respondent's] employment with this Agency pursuant to section 102(c) of the National Security Act. . . ." Respondent was also advised that, while the CIA would give him a positive recommendation in any future job search, if he applied for a job requiring a security clearance the Agency would inform the prospective employer that it had concluded that respondent's homosexuality presented a security threat.

Respondent then filed an action against petitioner in the United States District Court for the District of Columbia. Respondent's amended complaint asserted a variety of statutory and constitutional claims against the Director. Respondent alleged that the Director's decision to terminate his employment violated the Administrative Procedure Act (APA), 5 U.S.C. § 706, because it was arbitrary and capricious, represented an abuse of discretion, and was reached without observing the procedures required by law and CIA regulations.[3] He also complained that the Director's termination of his employment deprived him of constitutionally protected rights to property, liberty, and privacy in violation of the First, Fourth, Fifth, and Ninth Amendments. Finally, he asserted that his dismissal transgressed the procedural due process and equal protection of the laws guaranteed by the Fifth Amendment. Respondent requested a declaratory judgment that the Director had violated the APA and the Constitution, and asked the District Court for an injunction ordering petitioner to reinstate him to the position he held with the CIA prior to his dismissal. As an alternative remedy, he suggested that he be returned to paid administrative leave and that petitioner be ordered to reevaluate respondent's employment termination and provide a statement of the reasons for any adverse final determination. Respondent sought no monetary damages in his amended complaint.

---

[3]   Title 5 U.S.C. § 706 provides in pertinent part:

    ". . . . The reviewing court shall . . . (2) hold unlawful and set aside agency action, findings, and conclusions found to be—

        "(A) arbitrary, capricious, an abuse of discretion, or otherwise not in accordance with law;

        "(B) contrary to constitutional right, power, privilege, or immunity;

        "(C) in excess of statutory jurisdiction, authority, or limitations, or short of statutory right;

        "(D) without observance of procedure required by law."

Petitioner moved to dismiss respondent's amended complaint on the ground that § 102(c) of the National Security Act (NSA) precludes judicial review of the Director's termination decisions under the provisions of the APA set forth in 5 U.S.C. §§ 701, 702, and 706. Section 702 provides judicial review to any "person suffering legal wrong because of agency action, or adversely affected or aggrieved by agency action within the meaning of a relevant statute." The section further instructs that "[a]n action in a court of the United States seeking relief other than money damages and stating a claim that an agency or an officer or employee thereof acted or failed to act in an official capacity or under color of legal authority shall not be dismissed nor relief therein be denied on the ground that it is against the United States or that the United States is an indispensable party." The scope of judicial review under § 702, however, is circumscribed by § 706, and its availability at all is predicated on satisfying the requirements of § 701, which provides:

> "(a) This chapter applies, according to the provisions thereof, except to the extent that—
>
> "(1) statutes preclude judicial review; or
>
> "(2) agency action is committed to agency discretion by law."

The District Court denied petitioner's motion to dismiss, and granted respondent's motion for partial summary judgment. The court determined that the APA provided judicial review of petitioner's termination decisions made under § 102(c) of the NSA, and found that respondent had been unlawfully discharged because the CIA had not followed the procedures described in its own regulations. . . .

A divided panel of the Court of Appeals for the District of Columbia Circuit vacated the District Court's judgment and remanded the case for further proceedings. The Court of Appeals first decided that judicial review under the APA of the Agency's decision to terminate respondent was not precluded by §§ 701(a)(1) or (a)(2). Turning to the merits, the Court of Appeals found that, while an agency must normally follow its own regulations, the CIA regulations cited by respondent do not limit the Director's discretion in making termination decisions. . . .

We granted certiorari to decide the question whether the Director's decision to discharge a CIA employee under § 102(c) of the NSA is judicially reviewable under the APA.

II

The APA's comprehensive provisions, set forth in 5 U.S.C. §§ 701–706, allow any person "adversely affected or aggrieved" by agency action to obtain judicial review thereof, so long as the decision challenged represents a "final agency action for which there is no other adequate remedy in a court." Typically, a litigant will contest an action (or failure to act) by an agency on the ground that the agency has neglected to follow the statutory directives of Congress. Section 701(a), however, limits application of the entire APA to situations in which judicial review is not precluded by statute, see § 701(a)(1), and the agency action is not committed to agency discretion by law, see § 701(a)(2).

In *Citizens to Preserve Overton Park, Inc. v. Volpe*, 401 U.S. 402 (1971), this Court explained the distinction between §§ 701(a)(1) and (a)(2). Subsection (a)(1) is concerned with whether Congress expressed an intent to prohibit judicial review; subsection (a)(2) applies "in those rare instances where 'statutes are drawn in such broad terms that in a given case there is no law to apply.' " 401 U.S. at 410 (citing S. Rep. No. 752, 79th Cong., 1st Sess., 26 (1945)).

We further explained what it means for an action to be "committed to agency discretion by law" in *Heckler v. Chaney*, 470 U.S. 821 (1985). *Heckler* required the Court to determine whether the Food and Drug Administration's decision not to undertake an enforcement proceeding against the use of certain drugs in administering the death penalty was subject to judicial review. We noted that, under § 701(a)(2), even when Congress has not affirmatively precluded judicial oversight, "review is not to be had if the statute is drawn so that a court would have no meaningful standard against which to judge the agency's exercise of discretion." 470 U.S. at 830. Since the statute conferring power on the Food and Drug Administration to prohibit the unlawful misbranding or misuse of drugs provided no substantive standards on which a court could base its review, we found that enforcement actions were committed to the complete discretion of the FDA to decide when and how they should be pursued.

Both *Overton Park* and *Heckler* emphasized that § 701(a)(2) requires careful examination of the statute on which the claim of agency illegality is based . . . . In the present case, respondent's claims against the CIA arise from the

Director's asserted violation of § 102(c) of the NSA. As an initial matter, it should be noted that § 102(c) allows termination of an Agency employee whenever the Director "shall *deem* such termination necessary or advisable in the interests of the United States" (emphasis added), not simply when the dismissal *is* necessary or advisable to those interests. This standard fairly exudes deference to the Director, and appears to us to foreclose the application of any meaningful judicial standard of review. Short of permitting cross-examination of the Director concerning his views of the Nation's security and whether the discharged employee was inimical to those interests, we see no basis on which a reviewing court could properly assess an Agency termination decision. The language of § 102(c) thus strongly suggests that its implementation was "committed to agency discretion by law."

So too does the overall structure of the NSA. Passed shortly after the close of the Second World War, the NSA created the CIA and gave its Director the responsibility "for protecting intelligence sources and methods from unauthorized disclosure." Section 102(c) is an integral part of that statute, because the Agency's efficacy, and the Nation's security, depend in large measure on the reliability and trustworthiness of the Agency's employees. . . .

This overriding need for ensuring integrity in the Agency led us to uphold the Director's use of § 102(d)(3) of the NSA to withhold the identities of protected intelligence sources . . . . Section 102(c), that portion of the NSA under consideration in the present case, is part and parcel of the entire Act, and likewise exhibits the Act's extraordinary deference to the Director in his decision to terminate individual employees.

We thus find that the language and structure of § 102(c) indicate that Congress meant to commit individual employee discharges to the Director's discretion, and that § 701(a)(2) accordingly precludes judicial review of these decisions under the APA. We reverse the Court of Appeals to the extent that it found such terminations reviewable by the courts.

III

In addition to his claim that the Director failed to abide by the statutory dictates of § 102(c), respondent also alleged a number of constitutional violations in his amended complaint. Respondent charged that petitioner's termination of his employment deprived him of property and liberty interests under the Due Process Clause of the Fifth Amendment, denied him equal protection of the laws, and unjustifiably burdened his right to privacy. Respondent asserts that he is entitled, under the APA, to judicial consideration of these claimed violations. . . .

Petitioner maintains that, no matter what the nature of respondent's constitutional claims, judicial review is precluded by the language and intent of § 102(c). In petitioner's view, all Agency employment termination decisions, even those based on policies normally repugnant to the Constitution, are given over to the absolute discretion of the Director, and are hence unreviewable under the APA. We do not think § 102(c) may be read to exclude review of constitutional claims. We emphasized in *Johnson v. Robison*, 415 U.S. 361 (1974), that where Congress intends to preclude judicial review of constitutional claims its intent to do so must be clear. In *Weinberger v. Salfi*, 422 U.S. 749 (1975), we reaffirmed that view. We require this heightened showing in part to avoid the "serious constitutional question" that would arise if a federal statute were construed to deny any judicial forum for a colorable constitutional claim.

Our review of § 102(c) convinces us that it cannot bear the preclusive weight petitioner would have it support. As detailed above, the section does commit employment termination decisions to the Director's discretion, and precludes challenges to these decisions based upon the statutory language of § 102(c). A discharged employee thus cannot complain that his termination was not "necessary or advisable in the interests of the United States," since that assessment is the Director's alone. Subsections (a)(1) and (a)(2) of § 701, however, remove from judicial review only those determinations specifically identified by Congress or "committed to agency discretion by law." Nothing in § 102(c) persuades us that Congress meant to preclude consideration of colorable constitutional claims arising out of the actions of the Director pursuant to that section; we believe that a constitutional claim based on an individual discharge may be reviewed by the District Court. We agree with the Court of Appeals that there must be further proceedings in the District Court on this issue.

Petitioner complains that judicial review even of constitutional claims will entail extensive "rummaging around" in the Agency's affairs to the detriment of national security. But petitioner acknowledges that Title VII claims attacking the hiring and promotion policies of the Agency are routinely entertained in federal court, and the inquiry and discovery associated with those proceedings would seem to involve some of the same sort of rummaging. Furthermore, the District Court has the latitude to control any discovery process which may be instituted so as to balance respondent's need for access to proof which would support a colorable constitutional claim against the extraordinary needs of the CIA for confidentiality and the protection of its methods, sources, and mission.

Petitioner also contends that even if respondent has raised a colorable constitutional claim arising out of his discharge, Congress in the interest of national security may deny the courts the authority to decide the claim and to order respondent's reinstatement if the claim is upheld. For the reasons previously stated, we do not think Congress meant to impose such restrictions when it enacted § 102(c) of the NSA. . . .

JUSTICE O'CONNOR, concurring in part and dissenting in part.

I agree that the Administrative Procedure Act (APA) does not authorize judicial review of the employment decisions referred to in § 102(c) of the National Security Act of 1947. Because § 102(c) does not provide a meaningful standard for judicial review, such decisions are clearly "committed to agency discretion by law" within the meaning of the provision of the APA set forth in 5 U.S.C. § 701(a)(2). I do not understand the Court to say that the exception in § 701(a)(2) is necessarily or fully defined by reference to statutes "drawn in such broad terms that in a given case there is no law to apply." Accordingly, I join Parts I and II of the Court's opinion.

I disagree, however, with the Court's conclusion that a constitutional claim challenging the validity of an employment decision covered by § 102(c) may nonetheless be brought in a federal district court. Whatever may be the exact scope of Congress' power to close the lower federal courts to constitutional claims in other contexts, I have no doubt about its authority to do so here. The functions performed by the Central Intelligence Agency and the Director of Central Intelligence lie at the core of "the very delicate, plenary and exclusive power of the President as the sole organ of the federal government in the field of international relations." *United States v. Curtiss-Wright Export Corp.*, 299 U.S. 304, 320 (1936). The authority of the Director of Central Intelligence to control access to sensitive national security information by discharging employees deemed to be untrustworthy flows primarily from this constitutional power of the President, and Congress may surely provide that the inferior federal courts are not used to infringe on the President's constitutional authority. Section 102(c) plainly indicates that Congress has done exactly that, and the Court points to nothing in the structure, purpose, or legislative history of the

National Security Act that would suggest a different conclusion. Accordingly, I respectfully dissent from the Court's decision to allow this lawsuit to go forward.

Justice Scalia, dissenting.

I agree with the Court's apparent holding in Part II of its opinion that the Director's decision to terminate a CIA employee is "committed to agency discretion by law" within the meaning of 5 U.S.C. § 701(a)(2). But because I do not see how a decision can, either practically or legally, be both unreviewable and yet reviewable for constitutional defect, I regard Part III of the opinion as essentially undoing Part II. I therefore respectfully dissent from the judgment of the Court.

I

Before proceeding to address Part III of the Court's opinion, which I think to be in error, I must discuss one significant element of the analysis in Part II. Though I subscribe to most of that analysis, I disagree with the Court's description of what is required to come within subsection (a)(2) of § 701, which provides that judicial review is unavailable "to the extent that . . . agency action is committed to agency discretion by law." The Court's discussion suggests that the Court of Appeals below was correct in holding that this provision is triggered only when there is "no law to apply." Our precedents amply show that "commit[ment] to agency discretion by law" includes, but is not limited to, situations in which there is "no law to apply."

The Court relies for its "no law to apply" formulation upon our discussion in *Heckler v. Chaney*, 470 U.S. 821 (1985)—which, however, did not apply that as the sole criterion of § 701(a)(2)'s applicability, but to the contrary discussed the subject action's "general unsuitability" for review, and adverted to "tradition, case law, and sound reasoning." 470 U.S. at 831. Moreover, the only supporting authority for the "no law to apply" test cited in *Chaney* was our observation in *Citizens to Preserve Overton Park, Inc. v. Volpe*, 401 U.S. 402 (1971), that "[t]he legislative history of the Administrative Procedure Act indicates that [§ 701(a)(2)] is applicable in those rare instances where 'statutes are drawn in such broad terms that in a given case there is no law to apply.' S. Rep. No. 752, 79th Cong., 1st Sess., 26 (1945)," *id.*, at 410. Perhaps *Overton Park* discussed only the "no law to apply" factor because that was the only basis for nonreviewability that was even arguably applicable. It surely could not have believed that factor to be exclusive, for that would contradict the very legislative history, both cited and quoted in the opinion, from which it had been derived, which read in full: "The basic exception of matters committed to agency discretion would apply even if not stated at the outset [of the judicial review Chapter]. If, *for example*, statutes are drawn in such broad terms that in a given case there is no law to apply, courts of course have no statutory question to review." S. Rep. No. 752, 79th Cong., 1st Sess., 26 (1945) (emphasis added).

The "no law to apply" test can account for the nonreviewability of certain issues, but falls far short of explaining the full scope of the areas from which the courts are excluded. For the fact is that there is no governmental decision that is not subject to a fair number of legal constraints precise enough to be susceptible of judicial application—beginning with the fundamental constraint that the decision must be taken in order to further a public purpose rather than a purely private interest; yet there are many governmental decisions that are not at all subject to judicial review. A United States Attorney's decision to prosecute, for example, will not be reviewed on the claim that it was prompted by personal animosity. Thus, "no law to apply" provides much less than the full answer to whether § 701(a)(2) applies.

The key to understanding the "committed to agency discretion *by law*" provision of § 701(a)(2) lies in contrasting it with the "*statutes* preclude judicial review" provision of § 701(a)(1). Why "statutes" for preclusion, but the much more general term "law" for commission to agency discretion? The answer is, as we implied in *Chaney*, that the latter was intended to refer to "the 'common law' of judicial review of agency action," 470 U.S. at 832—a body of jurisprudence that had marked out, with more or less precision, certain issues and certain areas that were beyond the range of judicial review. That jurisprudence included principles ranging from the "political question" doctrine, to sovereign immunity (including doctrines determining when a suit against an officer would be deemed to be a suit against the sovereign), to official immunity, to prudential limitations upon the courts' equitable powers, to what can be described no more precisely than a traditional respect for the functions of the other branches reflected in the statement in *Marbury v. Madison*, 1 Cranch 137, 170–171 (1803), that "[w]here the head of a department acts in a case, in which executive discretion is to be exercised; in which he is the mere organ of executive will; it is again repeated, that any application to a court to control, in any respect, his conduct, would be rejected without hesitation."

Only if all that "common law" were embraced within § 701(a)(2) could it have been true that, as was generally understood, "[t]he intended result of [§ 701(a)] is to restate the existing law as to the area of reviewable agency action." Attorney General's Manual on the Administrative Procedure Act 94 (1947). Because that is the meaning of the provision, we have continued to take into account for purposes of determining reviewability, post-APA as before, not only the text and structure of the statute under which the agency acts, but such factors as whether the decision involves "a sensitive and inherently discretionary judgment call," *Department of Navy v. Egan,* 484 U.S. 518, 527 (1988), whether it is the sort of decision that has traditionally been nonreviewable, *ICC v. Locomotive Engineers,* 482 U.S. 270, 282 (1987); *Chaney, supra,* 470 U.S. at 832[;] and whether review would have "disruptive practical consequences," see *Southern R. Co. v. Seaboard Allied Milling Corp.,* 442 U.S. 444, 457 (1979). This explains the seeming contradiction between § 701(a)(2)'s disallowance of review to the extent that action is "committed to agency discretion," and § 706's injunction that a court shall set aside agency action that constitutes "an abuse of discretion." Since, in the former provision, "committed to agency discretion by law" means "of the sort that is traditionally unreviewable," it operates to keep certain categories of agency action out of the courts; but when agency action is appropriately in the courts, abuse of discretion is of course grounds for reversal.

All this law, shaped over the course of centuries and still developing in its application to new contexts, cannot possibly be contained within the phrase "no law to apply." It is not surprising, then, that although the Court recites the test it does not really apply it. Like other opinions relying upon it, this one essentially announces the test, declares victory and moves on. It is not really true " 'that a court would have no meaningful standard against which to judge the agency's exercise of discretion.' " The standard set forth in § 102(c) of the National Security Act of 1947, "necessary or advisable in the interests of the United States," at least excludes dismissal out of personal vindictiveness, or because the Director wants to give the job to his cousin. Why, on the Court's theory, is respondent not entitled to assert the presence of such excesses, under the "abuse of discretion" standard of § 706?

If and when this Court does come to consider the reviewability of a dismissal such as the present one on the ground that it violated the agency's regulations—a question the Court avoids today—the difference between the "no law to apply" test and what I consider the correct test will be crucial.

Perhaps a dismissal in violation of the regulations can be reviewed, but not simply because the regulations provide a standard that makes review possible. Thus, I agree with the Court's holding in Part II of its opinion (though, as will soon appear, that holding seems to be undone by its holding in Part III), but on different reasoning.

II

Before taking the reader through the terrain of the Court's holding that respondent may assert constitutional claims in this suit, I would like to try to clear some of the underbrush, consisting primarily of the Court's ominous warning that "[a] 'serious constitutional question' . . . would arise if a federal statute were construed to deny any judicial forum for a colorable constitutional claim."

The first response to the Court's grave doubt about the constitutionality of denying all judicial review to a "colorable constitutional claim" is that the denial of all judicial review is not at issue here, but merely the denial of review in United States district courts. As to that, the law is, and has long been, clear. Article III, § 2, of the Constitution extends the judicial power to "all Cases . . . arising under this Constitution." But Article III, § 1, provides that the judicial power shall be vested "in one supreme Court, *and in such inferior Courts as the Congress may from time to time ordain and establish*" (emphasis added). We long ago held that the power not to create any lower federal courts at all includes the power to invest them with less than all of the judicial power. . . .

I turn, then, to the substance of the Court's warning that judicial review of all "colorable constitutional claims" arising out of the respondent's dismissal may well be constitutionally required. What could possibly be the basis for this fear? Surely not some general principle that *all* constitutional violations must be remediable in the courts. The very text of the Constitution refutes that principle, since it provides that "[e]ach House shall be the Judge of the Elections, Returns and Qualifications of its own Members," Art. I, § 5, and that "for any Speech or Debate in either House, [the Senators and Representatives] shall not be questioned in any other Place," Art. I, § 6. Claims concerning constitutional violations committed in these contexts—for example, the rather grave constitutional claim that an election has been stolen—cannot be addressed to the courts. Even apart from the strict text of the Constitution, we have found some constitutional claims to be beyond judicial review because they involve "political questions." The doctrine of sovereign immunity—not repealed by the

Constitution, but to the contrary at least partly reaffirmed as to the States by the Eleventh Amendment—is a monument to the principle that some constitutional claims can go unheard. No one would suggest that, if Congress had not passed the Tucker Act, 28 U.S.C. § 1491(a)(1), the courts would be able to order disbursements from the Treasury to pay for property taken under lawful authority (and subsequently destroyed) without just compensation. And finally, the doctrine of equitable discretion, which permits a court to refuse relief, even where no relief at law is available, when that would unduly impair the public interest, does not stand aside simply because the basis for the relief is a constitutional claim. In sum, it is simply untenable that there must be a judicial remedy for every constitutional violation. Members of Congress and the supervising officers of the Executive Branch take the same oath to uphold the Constitution that we do, and sometimes they are left to perform that oath unreviewed, as we always are. . . .

It seems to me clear that courts would not entertain, for example, an action for backpay by a dismissed Secretary of State claiming that the reason he lost his Government job was that the President did not like his religious views—surely a colorable violation of the First Amendment. I am confident we would hold that the President's choice of his Secretary of State is a "political question." . . . I think Congress can prescribe, at least within broad limits, that for certain jobs the dismissal decision will be unreviewable—that is, will be "committed to agency discretion by law."

Once it is acknowledged, as I think it must be, (1) that not all constitutional claims require a judicial remedy, and (2) that the identification of those that do not can, even if only within narrow limits, be determined by Congress, then it is clear that the "serious constitutional question" feared by the Court is an illusion. Indeed, it seems to me that if one is in a mood to worry about serious constitutional questions the one to worry about is not whether Congress can, by enacting § 102(c), give the President, through his Director of Central Intelligence, unreviewable discretion in firing the agents that he employs to gather military and foreign affairs intelligence, but rather whether Congress could constitutionally *permit* the courts to review all such decisions if it wanted to. [Here, Justice Scalia briefly discusses the President's foreign affairs and national security powers.—Ed.]

I think it entirely beyond doubt that if Congress intended, by the APA in 5 U.S.C. § 701(a)(2), to exclude judicial review of the President's decision (through the Director of Central Intelligence) to dismiss an officer of the Central Intelligence Agency, that disposition would be constitutionally permissible.

III

I turn, then, to whether that executive action is, within the meaning of § 701(a)(2), "committed to agency discretion by law." My discussion of this point can be brief, because the answer is compellingly obvious. . . . Given [the] statutory text, and given (as discussed above) that the area to which the text pertains is one of predominant executive authority and of traditional judicial abstention, it is difficult to conceive of a statutory scheme that more clearly reflects that "commit[ment] to agency discretion by law" to which § 701(a)(2) refers.

It is baffling to observe that the Court seems to agree with the foregoing assessment, . . . [but] reaches the conclusion that "a constitutional claim based on an individual discharge may be reviewed by the District Court." . . .

Even if we were to assume, however, contrary to all reason, that every constitutional claim is *ipso facto* more worthy, and every statutory claim less worthy, of judicial review, there would be no basis for writing that preference into a statute that makes no distinction between the two. . . . Neither of the two decisions cited by the Court to sustain its power to read in a limitation for constitutional claims remotely supports that proposition. In *Johnson v. Robison*, 415 U.S. 361 (1974), we considered a statute precluding judicial review of " 'the *decisions* of the Administrator on any question of law or fact *under* any law administered by the Veterans' Administration.' " We concluded that this statute did not bar judicial review of a challenge to the constitutionality of the statute itself, since that was a challenge not to a decision of the Administrator but to a decision of Congress. Our holding was based upon the text, and not upon some judicial power to read in a "constitutional claims" exception. And in *Weinberger v. Salfi*, 422 U.S. 749 (1975), we held that 42 U.S.C. § 405(h), a statute depriving district courts of federal-question jurisdiction over "any claim arising under" Title II of the Social Security Act, *did* embrace even constitutional challenges, since its language was "quite different" from that at issue in *Johnson* . . . . In *Salfi*, to be sure, another statutory provision was available that would enable judicial review of the constitutional claim, but as just observed, that distinction does not justify drawing a line that has no basis in the statute. . . .

The harm done by today's decision is that, contrary to what Congress knows is preferable, it brings a significant decision-making process of our intelligence services into a forum where it does not belong. Neither the Constitution, nor our laws, nor common sense gives an individual a right to come into court to litigate the reasons for his dismissal as an intelligence agent. . . . I would, in any event, not like to be the agent who has to explain to the intelligence services of other nations, with which we sometimes cooperate, that they need have no worry that the secret information they give us will be subjected to the notoriously broad discovery powers of our courts, because, although we have to litigate the dismissal of our spies, we have available a protection of somewhat uncertain scope known as executive privilege, which the President can invoke if he is willing to take the political damage that it often entails. . . .

Notes and Questions

1. **Summary.** In *Webster v. Doe*, the Court unanimously (although Justice Scalia's reasoning was different—more on that soon) held that judicial review under the statute was precluded by APA § 701(a)(2) because the question of whether any CIA employee should be terminated is committed to the agency's discretion by law. But six of the eight Justices held that judicial review was available for colorable *constitutional* claims. Do you agree with this approach? Is it sensible?

2. **Precluding federal judicial review.** In answering that question, Justice Scalia alluded to material that we will discuss in Chapter 7 on the Article III judicial power. In a nutshell, it certainly appears that the Constitution anticipates that Congress may foreclose judicial review of federal claims at least in lower federal courts because Congress does not have to create lower federal courts at all. Pursuant to the so-called "Madisonian Compromise" in the Constitutional Convention, the delegates left it up to the discretion of Congress whether to create lower federal courts, and the presumption was the state courts would be able to hear federal claims in the absence of lower federal courts. The state-court decisions could then be reviewed by the Supreme Court on appeal. But in the context of *Webster*, does that mean a *state* court could review Agent Doe's claim, but not a federal court, under Justice Scalia's approach? Justice Scalia anticipated this concern in an omitted part of his opinion, which is why he went on to explain that it is constitutional to foreclose *all* judicial review—including in state courts—of certain constitutional claims, for example under the "political question" doctrine. In any event, whether Congress can in fact foreclose review of constitutional questions is a hotly debated topic, and is the subject of a class on federal courts or jurisdiction. As of now, do you think you agree with the majority, or with Justice Scalia?

3.   *Reconciling §§ 701 and 706.* What is the connection between §§ 701 and 706? Surely § 701 cannot apply to *every* situation in which there is discretion committed to the agency. After all, § 706 permits review of such discretion under the abuse of discretion and arbitrary-and-capricious standards. Thus, § 706 tells us that discretion is usually reviewable, and so § 701 must be referring to a narrower class of discretionary questions.

4.   *What is the test for § 701(a)(2)?* Justice Scalia's dissent suggested that there was something of a debate about the precise scope of § 701(a)(2). The majority focused on the "no law to apply test" from *Overton Park.* Justice Scalia argued that the section codified the common law of reviewability, which included political questions, questions involving enforcement discretion, those involving foreign affairs and national security, etc. Even if there is law to apply, there may be reasons not to apply it.

Indeed, one component of the political question doctrine is the absence of any judicially manageable standards. Arguably the "no law to apply" test is a reference to this absence of a judicially manageable standard. If there is no law to apply—no judicially manageable standard—then that is one situation in which § 701(a)(2) indeed applies.

FOR DISCUSSION

If there is no law for the agency to apply, wouldn't that create a nondelegation problem? Or do the courts mean something different here?

Why the "no law to apply" test is likely a reference to judicially manageable standards makes sense when we consider that test in reference to the nondelegation doctrine. Recall that the doctrine holds that there must be an "intelligible principle" in the statute for the agency to administer. Is it true that there is really no law to apply in *Webster* and, if so, wouldn't that violate the nondelegation doctrine? The answer is that there *is* law to apply—only it's for the agency to apply it. Put another way, there is a principle—discharges must be in the national security interest of the United States—that is sufficiently intelligible for the agency to administer. The reason the decision falls within the scope of § 701(a)(2) is because there is no law for the *court* to apply—there is no judicially manageable standard.

5. Lincoln v. Virgil. The notes so far have spent significant space explaining Justice Scalia's opinion about § 701(a)(2) because his view may have ultimately prevailed. In Lincoln v. Virgil, 508 U.S. 182 (1993), the Supreme Court unanimously held that the termination of the Indian Health Service's Indian Children's Program was committed to agency discretion by law. The program was not specifically authorized by statute, and it had been funded through a general appropriations to the department. The Court held that an agency's discretion where to commit lump-sum appropriations, which give the agency the ability to adapt to changing circumstances, is committed to agency discretion by law. The Court cited *Webster* for the proposition that "§ 701(a)(2) precludes judicial review of a decision by the Direction of Central Intelligence to terminate an employee in the interests of national security, an area of executive action in which courts have long been hesitant to intrude." Did the Court reinterpret its holding in *Webster*?

6. *Revisiting the* Accardi *principle*. Recall that we have seen another case in which discretion was committed to the agency by law, but where the Court found judicial review available: United States ex rel. Accardi v. Shaugnessy, 347 U.S. 260 (1954), discussed supra p. 278. There, the petitioner was concededly deportable, and it was entirely up to the Attorney General's discretion whether to withhold removal. However, the Attorney General's decision was made contrary to the agency's own regulations respecting such decisions. In *Webster*, John Doe had also argued that the agency violated its own regulations, but the Court of Appeals had disagreed with that argument. Does the *Accardi* principle make sense where the matter is otherwise committed to agency discretion by law? Does the principle create a disincentive for the agency to create clarifying regulations that are binding on the agency, which then creates law to apply and thus opens up judicial review that otherwise would not exist?

 CROSS REFERENCE Recall that the *Accardi* principle holds that an agency can bind itself to its own regulations. Thus, an agency can bind itself even in matters that would otherwise be committed to agency discretion by law.

Heckler v. Chaney

470 U.S. 821 (1985)

Justice Rehnquist delivered the opinion of the Court.

This case presents the question of the extent to which a decision of an administrative agency to exercise its "discretion" not to undertake certain enforcement actions is subject to judicial review under the Administrative Procedure Act (APA). Respondents are several prison inmates convicted of capital offenses and sentenced to death by lethal injection of drugs. They petitioned the Food and Drug Administration (FDA), alleging that under the circumstances the use of these drugs for capital punishment violated the Federal Food, Drug, and Cosmetic Act (FDCA), and requesting that the FDA take various enforcement actions to prevent these violations. The FDA refused their request. We review here a decision of the Court of Appeals for the District of Columbia Circuit, which held the FDA's refusal to take enforcement actions both reviewable and an abuse of discretion, and remanded the case with directions that the agency be required "to fulfill its statutory function."

I

Respondents have been sentenced to death by lethal injection of drugs under the laws of the States of Oklahoma and Texas. Those States, and several others, have recently adopted this method for carrying out the capital sentence. Respondents first petitioned the FDA, claiming that the drugs used by the States for this purpose, although approved by the FDA for the medical purposes stated on their labels, were not approved for use in human executions. They alleged that the drugs had not been tested for the purpose for which they were to be used, and that, given that the drugs would likely be administered by untrained personnel, it was also likely that the drugs would not induce the quick and painless death intended. They urged that use of these drugs for human execution was the "unapproved use of an approved drug" and constituted a violation of the Act's prohibitions against "misbranding." They also suggested that the FDCA's requirements for approval of "new drugs" applied, since these drugs were now being used for a new purpose. Accordingly, respondents claimed that the FDA was required to approve the drugs as "safe and effective" for human execution before they could be distributed in interstate commerce. They therefore requested the FDA to take various investigatory and enforcement actions to prevent these perceived violations; they requested the FDA to affix warnings to the labels of all the drugs stating that they were unapproved and unsafe for human execution, to send statements to the drug manufacturers and prison administrators stating that the drugs should not be so used, and to adopt procedures for seizing the drugs from state prisons and to recommend the prosecution of all those in the chain of distribution who knowingly distribute or purchase the drugs with intent to use them for human execution.

The FDA Commissioner responded, refusing to take the requested actions. The Commissioner first detailed his disagreement with respondents' understanding of the scope of FDA jurisdiction over the unapproved use of approved drugs for human execution, concluding that FDA jurisdiction in the area was generally unclear but in any event should not be exercised to interfere with this particular aspect of state criminal justice systems. He went on to state:

> "Were FDA clearly to have jurisdiction in the area, moreover, we believe we would be authorized to decline to exercise it under our inherent discretion to decline to pursue certain enforcement matters. The unapproved use of approved drugs is an area in which the case law is far from uniform. Generally, enforcement proceedings in this area are initiated only when there is a serious danger to the public health or a blatant scheme to defraud. We cannot conclude that those dangers are present under State lethal injection laws, which are duly authorized statutory enactments in furtherance of proper State functions. . . ."

Respondents then filed the instant suit in the United States District Court for the District of Columbia, claiming the same violations of the FDCA and asking that the FDA be required to take the same enforcement actions requested in the prior petition. . . . The District Court granted summary judgment for [FDA]. It began with the proposition that "decisions of executive departments and agencies to *refrain* from instituting investigative and enforcement proceedings are essentially unreviewable by the courts." The court then cited case law stating that nothing in the FDCA indicated an intent to circumscribe the FDA's enforcement discretion or to make it reviewable.

A divided panel of the Court of Appeals for the District of Columbia Circuit reversed. The majority began by discussing the FDA's jurisdiction over the unapproved use of approved drugs for human execution, and concluded that the FDA did have jurisdiction over such a use. The court then addressed the Government's assertion of unreviewable discretion to refuse enforcement action. It first discussed this Court's opinions which have held that there is a general presumption that all agency decisions are reviewable under the APA . . . . Citing this Court's opinions in *Dunlop v. Bachowski*, 421 U.S. 560 (1975), and *Citizens to Preserve Overton Park v. Volpe*, 401 U.S. 402 (1971), for the view that these exceptions should be narrowly construed, the court held that the "committed to agency discretion by law" exception of § 701(a)(2) should be invoked only where the substantive statute left the courts with "no law to apply." . . .

The court found "law to apply" in the form of a FDA policy statement which indicated that the agency was "obligated" to investigate the unapproved use of an approved drug when such use became "widespread" or "endanger[ed] the public health." 37 Fed. Reg. 16504 (1972). . . .

The dissenting judge expressed the view that an agency's decision not to institute enforcement action generally is unreviewable, and that such exercises of "prosecutorial discretion" presumptively fall within the APA's exception for agency actions "committed to agency discretion by law." He noted that traditionally courts have been wary of second-guessing agency decisions not to enforce, given the agency's expertise and better understanding of its enforcement policies and available resources. . . .

We reverse.

II

. . . . For us, this case turns on the important question of the extent to which determinations by the FDA *not to exercise* its enforcement authority over the use of drugs in interstate commerce may be judicially reviewed. That decision in turn involves the construction of two separate but necessarily interrelated statutes, the APA and the FDCA.

The APA's comprehensive provisions for judicial review of "agency actions," are contained in 5 U.S.C. §§ 701–706. Any person "adversely affected or aggrieved" by agency action; see § 702, including a "failure to act," is entitled to "judicial review thereof," as long as the action is a "final agency action for which there is no other adequate remedy in a court," see § 704. The standards to be applied on review are governed by the provisions of § 706. But before any review at all may be had, a party must first clear the hurdle of § 701(a).

That section provides that the chapter on judicial review "applies, according to the provisions thereof, except to the extent that—(1) statutes preclude judicial review; or (2) agency action is committed to agency discretion by law." Petitioner urges that the decision of the FDA to refuse enforcement is an action "committed to agency discretion by law" under § 701(a)(2). . . .

On its face, the section does not obviously lend itself to any particular construction; indeed, one might wonder what difference exists between § (a)(1) and § (a)(2). The former section seems easy in application; it requires construction of the substantive statute involved to determine whether Congress intended to preclude judicial review of certain decisions. . . . But one could read the language "committed to agency discretion *by law*" in § (a)(2) to require a similar inquiry. In addition, commentators have pointed out that construction of § (a)(2) is further complicated by the tension between a literal reading of § (a)(2), which exempts from judicial review those decisions committed to agency "discretion," and the primary scope of review prescribed by § 706(2)(A)—whether the agency's action was "arbitrary, capricious, or an *abuse of discretion*." How is it, they ask, that an action committed to agency discretion can be unreviewable and yet courts still can review agency actions for abuse of that discretion? See 5 K. Davis, Administrative Law § 28:6 (1984). The APA's legislative history provides little help on this score. Mindful, however, of the common-sense principle of statutory construction that sections of a statute generally should be read "to give effect, if possible, to every clause," we think there is a proper construction of § (a)(2) which satisfies each of these concerns.

This Court first discussed § (a)(2) in *Citizens to Preserve Overton Park v. Volpe*, 401 U.S. 402 (1971). . . . [T]he Court stated: ". . . . The legislative history of the Administrative Procedure Act indicates that it is applicable in those rare instances where 'statutes are drawn in such broad terms that in a given case there is no law to apply.' S. Rep. No. 752, 79th Cong., 1st Sess., 26 (1945)."

The above quote answers several of the questions raised by the language of § 701(a), although it raises others. First, it clearly separates the exception provided by § (a)(1) from the § (a)(2) exception. The former applies when Congress has expressed an intent to preclude judicial review. The latter applies in different circumstances; even where Congress has not affirmatively precluded review, review is not to be had if the statute is drawn so that a court would have no meaningful standard against which to judge the agency's exercise of discretion. In such a case, the statute ("law") can be taken to have "committed" the decisionmaking to the agency's judgment absolutely. This construction avoids conflict with the "abuse of discretion" standard of review in § 706—if no judicially manageable standards are available for judging how and when an agency should exercise its discretion, then it is impossible to evaluate agency action for "abuse of discretion." . . .

We disagree, however, with [the Court of Appeal's] insistence that the "narrow construction" of § (a)(2) required application of a presumption of reviewability even to an agency's decision not to undertake certain enforcement actions. Here we think the Court of Appeals broke with tradition, case law, and sound reasoning.

Overton Park did not involve an agency's refusal to take requested enforcement action. It involved an affirmative act of approval under a statute that set clear guidelines for determining when such approval should be given. Refusals to take enforcement steps generally involve precisely the opposite situation, and in that situation we think the presumption is that judicial review is not available. This Court has recognized on several occasions over many years that an agency's decision not to prosecute or enforce, whether through civil or criminal process, is a decision generally committed to an agency's absolute discretion. This recognition of the existence of discretion is attributable in no small part to the general unsuitability for judicial review of agency decisions to refuse enforcement.

The reasons for this general unsuitability are many. First, an agency decision not to enforce often involves a complicated balancing of a number of factors which are peculiarly within its expertise. Thus, the agency must not only assess whether a violation has occurred, but whether agency resources are best spent on this violation or another, whether the agency is likely to succeed if it acts, whether the particular enforcement action requested best fits the agency's overall policies, and, indeed, whether the agency has enough resources to undertake the action at all. An agency generally cannot act against each technical violation of the statute it is charged with enforcing. The agency is far better equipped than the courts to deal with the many variables involved in the proper ordering of its priorities. . . .

In addition to these administrative concerns, we note that when an agency refuses to act it generally does not exercise its *coercive* power over an individual's liberty or property rights, and thus does not infringe upon areas that courts often are called upon to protect. Similarly, when an agency *does* act to enforce, that action itself provides a focus for judicial review, inasmuch as the agency must have exercised its power in some manner. The action at least can be reviewed to determine whether the agency exceeded its statutory powers. Finally, we recognize that an agency's refusal to institute proceedings shares to some extent the characteristics of the decision of a prosecutor in the Executive Branch not to indict—a decision which has long been regarded as the special province of the Executive Branch, inasmuch as it is the Executive who is charged by the Constitution to "take Care that the Laws be faithfully executed." U.S. Const., Art. II, § 3.

We of course only list the above concerns to facilitate understanding of our conclusion that an agency's decision not to take enforcement action should be presumed immune from judicial review under § 701(a)(2). For good reasons, such a decision has traditionally been "committed to agency discretion," and we believe that the Congress enacting the APA did not intend to alter that tradition. Cf. 5 Davis § 28:5 (APA did not significantly alter the "common law" of judicial review of agency action). In so stating, we emphasize that the decision is only presumptively unreviewable; the presumption may be rebutted where the substantive statute has provided guidelines for the agency to follow in exercising its enforcement powers. Thus, in establishing this presumption in the APA, Congress did not set agencies free to disregard legislative direction in the statutory scheme that the agency administers. Congress may limit an agency's exercise of enforcement power if it wishes, either by setting substantive priorities, or by otherwise circumscribing an agency's power to discriminate among issues or cases it will pursue. . . .

Dunlop v. Bachowski, 421 U.S. 560 (1975), relied upon heavily by respondents and the majority in the Court of Appeals, presents an example of statutory language which supplied sufficient standards to rebut the presumption of unreviewability. *Dunlop* involved a suit by a union employee, under the Labor-Management Reporting and Disclosure Act (LMRDA), asking the Secretary of Labor to investigate and file suit to set aside a union election. Section 482 provided that, upon filing of a complaint by a union member, "[t]he Secretary shall investigate such complaint and, if he finds probable cause to believe that a violation . . . has occurred . . . he shall . . . bring a civil action. . . ." After investigating the plaintiff's claims the Secretary of Labor declined to file suit, and the plaintiff sought judicial review under the APA. This Court held that review was available. It rejected the Secretary's argument that the statute precluded judicial review, and in a footnote it stated its agreement with the conclusion of the Court of Appeals that the decision was not "an unreviewable exercise of prosecutorial discretion." Our textual references to the "strong presumption" of reviewability in *Dunlop* were addressed only to the § (a)(1) exception; we were content to rely on the Court of Appeals' opinion to hold that the § (a)(2) exception did not apply. The Court of Appeals, in turn, had found the "principle of absolute prosecutorial discretion" inapplicable, because the language of the LMRDA indicated that the Secretary was required to file suit if certain "clearly defined" factors were present. The decision therefore was not " 'beyond the judicial capacity to supervise.' "

Dunlop is thus consistent with a general presumption of unreviewability of decisions not to enforce. The statute being administered quite clearly withdrew discretion from the agency and provided guidelines for exercise of its enforcement power. Our decision that review was available was not based on "pragmatic considerations," such as those cited by the Court of Appeals, that amount to an assessment of whether the interests at stake are important enough to justify intervention in the agencies' decisionmaking. The danger that agencies may not carry out their delegated powers with sufficient vigor does not necessarily lead to the conclusion that courts are the most appropriate body to police this aspect of their performance. That decision is in the first instance for Congress, and we therefore turn to the FDCA to determine whether in this case Congress has provided us with "law to apply." If it has indicated an intent to circumscribe agency enforcement discretion, and has provided meaningful standards for defining the limits of that discretion, there is "law to apply" under § 701(a)(2), and courts may require that the agency follow that law; if it has not, then an agency refusal to institute proceedings is a decision "committed to agency discretion by law" within the meaning of that section.

III

To enforce the various substantive prohibitions contained in the FDCA, the Act provides for injunctions, criminal sanctions, and seizure of any offending food, drug, or cosmetic article. The Act's general provision for enforcement, § 372, provides only that "[t]he Secretary is authorized to conduct examinations and investigations . . ." (emphasis added). Unlike the statute at issue in Dunlop, § 332 gives no indication of when an injunction should be sought, and § 334, providing for seizures, is framed in the permissive—the offending food, drug, or cosmetic "shall be liable to be proceeded against." . . . The Act's enforcement provisions thus commit complete discretion to the Secretary to decide how and when they should be exercised. [The Court then rejected reliance on the policy statement, noting that it dealt with prescribing physicians and conflicted with another regulation affirming the Secretary's discretion.—Ed.]

[Concurring opinions by Justices Brennan and Marshall are omitted.—Ed.]

Notes and Questions

1. ***Denial of rulemaking petitions.*** *Heckler v. Chaney* involved the refusal to take an enforcement action. What about refusal to promulgate a regulation? Recall the facts of *Massachusetts v. EPA*, supra p. 410. There, the Supreme Court held that carbon dioxide was an air pollutant within the meaning of the Clean Air Act and the EPA must therefore promulgate regulations of carbon dioxide if in EPA's judgment carbon dioxide contributed to climate change. When addressing the scope of review, the Court noted that "we have repeated time and again, an agency has broad discretion to choose how best to marshal its limited resources and personnel to carry out its delegated responsibilities," and that this "discretion is at its height when the agency decides not to bring an enforcement action." The Court cited *Chevron* and *Heckler* for these propositions. The Court, however, distinguished rulemaking petitions:

> In contrast to nonenforcement decisions, agency refusals to initiate rulemaking "are less frequent, more apt to involve legal as opposed to factual analysis, and subject to special formalities, including a public explanation." Refusals to promulgate rules are thus susceptible to judicial review, though such review is "extremely limited" and "highly deferential."

549 U.S. at 527–28.

 TEST YOUR KNOWLEDGE: To assess your understanding of the material in this chapter, **click here** to take a quiz.

CHAPTER FIVE

Legislative Power and Nondelegation

This is the first of three chapters that deal with administrative law and constitutional structure. What is the relationship of administrative agencies to the legislative power? When they promulgate "legislative" rules and regulations, are they exercising the "legislative power" that is vested in Congress? Can Congress delegate its legislative power? And if it can't, are agencies exercising legislative power anyway, in violation of the Constitution? This chapter deals with these questions. The next chapter addresses the relationship of agencies to "the executive power": Can the President appoint and remove administrative officials? Direct their activities? The final of the three chapters then addresses the relationship of agencies to "the judicial power" and to due process: When agencies engage in adjudications under their statutes, aren't they exercising the "judicial power," and aren't judges supposed to be exercising that power? Are there some kinds of cases that agencies can adjudicate, but others that must be heard in Article III courts? Finally, when they do adjudicate cases involving liberty and property, what kind of process must agencies afford the participants to the adjudication?

COURSE THEME

THE CONSTITUTIONAL PLACE OF AGENCIES
The next few chapters deal largely with this course theme: what is the relationship of agencies to the three named constitutional actors in the Constitution (Congress, President, courts)?

In addressing these questions, courts and scholars often distinguish between two competing methods of constitutional interpretation, formalism and functionalism. Although there is no single definition of formalism, in the constitutional context, and particularly in the separation of powers context, formalism stands at a minimum for the following two propositions: first, that the Constitution has clear rules for how legislative, executive, and judicial power are to be exercised; and second, that all exercises of governmental power can be categorized as either legislative, executive, or judicial.

Thus, in these separation of powers cases, for the formalist it is simply a matter of figuring out what kind of government power is at issue, and then to determine whether the exercise of that power matches the constitutional requirements for that kind of power. If we broaden our scope beyond constitutional law and to other legal fields, like contracts or civil procedure, formalism is usually taken to stand for the proposition that courts should prefer clear legal rules over balancing tests, even if the clear legal rules do not always conform to realities on the ground. Finally, it is worth observing that there is no necessary connection between formalism and "originalism," the idea that we should interpret the Constitution with its original meaning, but in constitutional law the two concepts tend to go together. After all, if the formalist believes in clear legal rules, those rules must come from somewhere—and the original meaning of the Constitution's text is, according to formalists, a clear and non-arbitrary source for these constitutional rules.

 FORMALISM: In separation of powers cases, formalism is the idea that the Constitution has clear rules for how legislative, executive, and judicial power are to be exercised, and that all exercises of governmental power can be categorized as either legislative, executive, or judicial.

Defined Term **ORIGINALISM:** The idea that we should interpret the Constitution with its original meaning—the meaning its words would have had to the Framers who wrote it and the public that ratified it.

Functionalism, on the other hand, is less concerned with getting "correct" constitutional answers in terms of the Constitution's formal rules for legislative, executive, and judicial power. This is so because, functionalists argue, it can be very challenging to determine the nature of the governmental power being exercised. Indeed, as you will see in some of the cases that follow, the exact same governmental act can be described as legislative, executive, or judicial depending on the branch that is exercising the power in question. Additionally, some functionalists argue, if formalism merely masks realities on the ground— for example, perhaps Congress really does delegate legislative power, even though the nondelegation doctrine (as we shall soon see) assumes that Congress is not so delegating—then formalism may lead to a constitutional imbalance of power that the doctrine would fail to recognize. Finally, many functionalists think that modern administrative government defies the Founders' expectations, but also that modern administrative government is inevitable. Therefore, if agencies are inevitably going to exercise combined legislative, executive, and judicial powers pursuant to broad delegations of power from Congress, constitutional law should be concerned with alternative (i.e., nonoriginalist)

> **Defined Term**
>
> **FUNCTIONALISM:** In separation of powers cases, functionalism is the idea that courts should take "functional," or practical, considerations into account when arriving at legal rules. Functionalists argue that government power is hard to characterize and courts should focus on ensuring a proper "balance" between the legislative and executive branches.

mechanisms for checking and balancing this administrative power. What ultimately matters to the functionalist, in summary, is *balance*: Is one branch intruding on the core functions of another? Are Congress and the Executive relatively evenly matched for exercising constitutional power? How do we make modern administrative government *workable*?

> **COURSE THEME**
>
> **FORMALISM VS. FUNCTIONALISM**
> A persistent question in the following cases is how should the Court approach separation of powers cases—through a formalist lens, or a functionalist one?

Consider these competing approaches to constitutional interpretation, and separation of powers cases in particular, as you read the material in this and the following two chapters.

A. Nondelegation: The Early Cases and History

The Constitution vests three kinds of powers in three different institutions. Article I, § 1 declares, "All legislative powers herein granted shall be vested in a Congress of the United States," and then Article I, § 8 enumerates the subjects to which this legislative power extends. Article II, § 1 declares, "The executive power shall be vested in a President of the United States," and then the rest of Article II seems to give the President additional powers—or perhaps these are limitations—such as the commander-in-chief and pardon powers, and the treaty and appointment powers, which are shared with the United States Senate. Article III, § 1, finally, declares, "The judicial power shall be vested in one supreme Court and in such inferior courts as Congress may from time to time ordain and establish." Article III, § 2 specifies that this judicial power "shall extend" to certain types of subjects and cases, including those "arising under" the Constitution and the laws of the United States.

There is no nondelegation clause in the Constitution. Article I does not say anywhere that "Congress may not delegate its legislative power" to other actors. Is a nondelegation principle nevertheless implied by the very structure of the Constitution? If the whole point of the Constitution was to distribute power in a certain way, then it would seem to undermine this objective if the national government could redistribute its own powers as it likes. Additionally, suppose Congress could or did delegate legislative power to the executive branch—the Executive would then be combining powers that *ought* to be separate. In Federalist No. 47, James Madison described "[t]he accumulation of all powers, legislative, executive, and judiciary, in the same hands, whether of one, a few, or many, and whether hereditary, self-appointed, or elective," as "the very definition of tyranny." Recall also the *expressio unius* canon: If the "executive" power is explicitly vested in the President, doesn't that imply that the executive branch is *excluded* from exercising the other powers—legislative and judicial—not mentioned?

CROSS REFERENCE The various tools of statutory interpretation that you have learned in the first half of this casebook can apply to constitutional interpretation as well.

Whatever one thinks of the lack of any express textual prohibition on the delegation of legislative power, early on both Congress and the Supreme Court concluded that Congress could not constitutionally delegate its legislative powers to other branches of the national government. In 1791, the House of Representatives debated a proposal to establish the post "by such route as the President of the United States shall, from time to time, cause to be established." 3 Annals of Cong. 229 (1791). The Constitution assigns Congress, however, the power to "establish post offices and post roads." Art. I, § 8, cl. 7. Madison argued against the proposal, stating that "there did not appear to be any necessity for alienating the powers of the House; and that if this should take place, it would be a violation of the Constitution." 3 Annals at 239. "However difficult it may be to determine with precision the exact boundaries of the Legislative and Executive powers," Madison said, such boundaries surely exist. Id. at 238. Other members of the House appear to have agreed, and the proposal was defeated. See, e.g., id. at 232–33. The House proceeded to establish the postal routes in great detail.

Do you agree with the House's conclusion? Doesn't the determination of what roads would serve most efficiently as postal routes seem like a question of administrative detail? Should Congress bother itself with such issues? On the other hand, in 1791, post roads were extremely important; whether one was established by a particular town could determine that town's prosperity. It was also the most crucial means of communication in that era. Gary Lawson, *Delegation and Original Meaning*, 88 Va. L. Rev. 327, 403 (2002) ("Postal routes were the eighteenth-century equivalent of water projects."); cf. David P. Currie, The Constitution in Congress: The Federalist Period, 1789–1801, at 149 (1997) (speculating that "the House's zest for detail" was attributable "to a taste for pork."). Perhaps Congress should be responsible for such important matters?

Notwithstanding this early conclusion by Congress—and the conclusion of the courts (as we shall see below) that Congress could not delegate its legislative power—Congress did enact statutes in the early Republic that granted quite broad policymaking discretion to the Executive. Consider the following examples, some of which we have already encountered in Chapter 1:

What role should historical practice play in constitutional interpretation today?

- In 1789, Congress enacted a statute requiring the new national government to assume the pension payments promised to invalid veterans of the revolutionary war under acts of the Confederation Congress, "under such regulations as the President of the United States may direct." Act of Sept. 29, 1789, ch. 24, 1 Stat. 95.

- In 1790, Congress enacted that no person could carry on trade with the Native American tribes without a license. The conditions on which a license was to be granted, and the rules the traders were to follow, "shall be governed . . . by such rules and regulations as the President shall prescribe." Act of July 22, 1790, ch. 33, 1 Stat. 137.

- In the same 1791 statute establishing the postal routes in great detail, the law also authorized the Postmaster General to extend the post roads and to establish the post offices. Specifically, the act authorized the Postmaster General to "enter into contracts, for a term not exceeding eight years, for extending the line of posts," and "to appoint . . . deputy postmasters, at all places where such shall be found necessary," and directing those postmasters to "keep an office." Act of Feb. 20, 1792, 1 Stat. 232, 233.

- The Judiciary Act of 1789 authorized the federal courts to "make and establish all necessary rules for the orderly conducting [of] business in the said courts, provided such rules are not repugnant to the laws of the United States." Act of Sept. 24, 1789, 1 Stat. 73. And the 1792 Process Act established that the practices prevailing in each respective state supreme court as of 1789, respecting "the forms of writs and executions" and the "modes of proceeding" in common law suits would govern in federal court proceedings in those states, subject "to such alterations and additions as the said courts respectively shall in their discretion deem expedient." Act of May 8, 1792, ch. 36, 1 Stat. 275.

- The Steamboat Act of 1852 granted discretion to the inspectors to license an engineer if "they are satisfied that his character, habits of life, knowledge, and experience in the duties of an engineer, are all such as to authorize the belief that the applicant is a suitable and safe person to be intrusted with the powers and duties of such a station"; to determine passenger limits on various kinds of vessels; and "to establish such rules and regulations to be obeyed by all such vessels in passing each other, as they shall from time to time deem necessary for safety." Act of Aug. 30, 1852, ch. 106, 10 Stat. 61.

Are those not delegations of "legislative power"? If not, what are they? Some of these examples, liked the 1792 Process Act, involved only *procedural* rules, i.e. those not affecting underlying substantive rights. Others permitted regulations of official conduct only. Recall that George Washington and Henry Knox's regulations respecting the invalid pensioners established only when the payments were to be made (within the year permitted by the statute) and what affidavits would be necessary as proof that one was entitled to the benefits. Neither Washington nor Knox had the authority to decide *who* should be paid, or *how much* to pay them. Those decisions had already been made by Congress.

On the other hand, Congress did delegate broad discretion to regulate private rights in the context of foreign affairs and relations with the native tribes. It also delegated such power over private rights and conduct to the steamboat inspectors, although more narrowly: they had the power only to make passenger limits and create the rules for passing ships. Can you come up with a coherent theory of what kind of power might be permissible to delegate, and what kind of power might be impermissible?

Defined Term

OFFICIAL CONDUCT and **PRIVATE CONDUCT:** Official conduct is the conduct of government officers and employees. Many regulations historically directed officers how to exercise their functions. Private conduct is the conduct of private citizens. Are regulations that affect private conduct on the same constitutional footing as those that affect official conduct?

The early cases came up with three possible approaches to the "nondelegation doctrine"—the doctrine that maintains Congress cannot delegate away its power. The first approach distinguished between making policy and finding facts on which certain policy outcomes were contingent. The second approach was to determine whether Congress had established a "primary" or "legislative" standard to guide the exercise of administrative discretion—the precursor to the modern "intelligible principle" test. The third approach was to distinguish between "important" matters and those of mere "administrative detail."

HISTORICAL PERSPECTIVE

There were three early approaches to identifying impermissible delegations of legislative power. The first asked whether the executive merely had to find "facts" upon which some congressional policy would be implemented. The second asked whether Congress has established a "primary" standard—the precursor to the modern intelligible principle test. The third asked whether Congress had resolved the "important subjects," leaving mere details to the executive.

Are the three approaches incompatible? Are they all interrelated?

In Cargo of the Brig Aurora v. United States, 11 U.S. 382 (1813), Congress had established an embargo against both France and England, who were then engaged in war with each other, and who were also violating the rights of American seamen by impressing them into service in their respective navies. After the Act establishing the embargo expired, Congress by another law authorized the President to determine if either of the belligerent powers had "ceased to violate the neutral commerce of the United States"; if one ceased to violate American rights but not the other, the previous embargo would be revived as to the nation that was still violating neutral commerce. The Court upheld this latter statute, noting that the President was not tasked with determining a *policy*, but merely the finding of a fact—whether France or England had stopped violating Americans' rights on the high seas—on which Congress's policy was contingent.

In Field v. Clark, 143 U.S. 649 (1892), Congress had enacted a statute establishing certain tariffs, but authorized the President to make a finding that the tariffs on like goods in foreign countries were "reciprocally unequal and unreasonable." The President did not have free rein to establish new rates upon such a finding; the statute itself directed what the alternative, higher tariffs would be. The Court upheld this statute, holding:

> What the president was required to do was simply in execution of the act of congress. It was not the making of law. He was the mere agent of the law-making department to ascertain and declare the event upon which its expressed will was to take effect. It was a part of the law itself, as it left the hands of congress, that the provisions, full and complete in themselves, permitting the free introduction of sugar, molasses, coffee, tea, and hides, from particular countries, should be suspended in a given contingency, and that in case of such suspension certain duties should be imposed.

"The legislature," the Court went on to say, "cannot delegate its power to make a law, but it can make a law to delegate a power to determine some fact or state of things upon which the law makes or intends to make its own action depend."

In other cases, however, it was far less clear that the President was merely finding facts. In Buttfield v. Stranahan, 192 U.S. 470 (1904), the Court confronted the Tea Inspection Act, the third section of which provided that the Secretary of the Treasury, upon the recommendation of a board charged with the inspection of tea, "shall fix and establish uniform standards of purity, quality, and fitness for consumption of all kinds of teas imported into the United States." The board's power here seems quite broader than merely the power to find facts; it actually had the power to establish the standards by which tea would be evaluated. The Court upheld the statute, however, partly by narrowing its scope: it concluded that by this particular act Congress intended to authorize the board to effectuate a prohibition in an earlier statute on tea "adulterated" with "exhausted" leaves. With the statute thus narrowed, the Court held that Congress, "in effect, was the fixing of a primary standard, and devolved upon the Secretary of the Treasury the mere executive duty to effectuate the legislative policy declared in the statute."

This case was a predecessor to the landmark case J.W. Hampton Jr. & Co. v. United States, 276 U.S. 394 (1928). There, Congress had enacted a tariff statute that went a step farther than the statute at issue in *Field v. Clark*: it allowed the President to *establish* tariff rates that would "equalize differences in costs of production" for particular products as compared to certain competing foreign countries. Arguably, this statute, too, authorized merely the findings of fact. But note how much discretion could go into that finding. What are "costs of production"? This could be a complicated calculation. Still, it does seem like the statute can be justified as merely authorizing the President to find facts.

The Court, however, did not rely on the distinction between policymaking and factual findings, and issued the following famous dictum: "If Congress shall lay down by legislative act an intelligible principle to which the person or body authorized to fix such rates is directed to conform, such legislative action is not a forbidden delegation of legislative power." Unlike the factual contingency test, the "intelligible principle" test is all about *discretion*: even if the executive gets to make some amount of policy, does Congress's statute give the executive sufficient "intelligible principles" to guide its exercise of this discretion?

The "intelligible principle" standard as stated in *J.W. Hampton* is the touchstone of the modern nondelegation doctrine. Before analyzing the modern cases that use this principle, however, it is worth pointing out the possibility of an alternative approach. In two cases, the Supreme Court distinguished between the power to legislate on the "important subjects," which belonged exclusively to Congress, and the power merely to fill up administrative details.

In United States v. Grimaud, 220 U.S. 506 (1911), the statute at issue authorized the President to designate forest reservations "to improve and protect the forest within the reservation, or for the purpose of securing favorable conditions of water flows, and to furnish a continuous supply of timber for the use and necessities of citizens of the United States." The statute authorized the Secretary of Agriculture to "make provisions for the protection against destruction by fire and depredations upon the public forests and forest reservations" and to "make such rules and regulations . . . to regulate their occupancy and use, and to preserve the forests thereon from destruction."

Under this provision, the Secretary prohibited grazing without a permit. An individual who was prosecuted for grazing without such a permit challenged the statute as an unconstitutional delegation of legislative power. The Court, however, concluded, that "[t]he determination of such questions . . . was a matter of administrative detail"; because "[e]ach reservation had its peculiar and special features," it was "impracticable for Congress to provide general regulations for these various and varying details of management." Here, the Court seemed to describe a distinction between matters of "administrative detail" where it was "impracticable" for Congress to legislate because of the "various and varying details" of the particular objects to be regulated, and matters that go beyond such details.

Prior to *Grimaud,* the Court decided Wayman v. Southard, 23 U.S. (10 Wheat.) 1 (1825)—the case dealing with the delegation of power in the 1792 Process Act to the courts to regulate their modes of proceeding—where Chief Justice John Marshall gave such a distinction more sustained analysis. Marshall observed, "It will not be contended that Congress can delegate to the Courts, or to any other tribunals, powers which are strictly and exclusively legislative." But, he wrote, "Congress may certainly delegate to others, powers which the legislature may rightfully exercise itself." He continued, "The line has not been exactly drawn which separates those important subjects, which must be entirely regulated by the legislature itself, from those of less interest, in which a general provision may be made, and power given to those who are to act under such general provisions to fill up the details."

NONEXCLUSIVE POWER

What does Chief Justice Marshall's dictum suggest about the nature of government power? Is all government power *either* legislative, executive, or judicial? Or can some government power be characterized as more than one, such that more than one branch can exercise that power?

In other words, Marshall seemed to be recognizing two types of legislative power. First, there is a "strictly and exclusively legislative" power that only Congress could exercise; this was the power to legislate on "important subjects," whatever those happened to be. Second, there is a category of power that "Congress may certainly delegate to others," but which it could also "rightfully exercise itself." This is the power to "fill up the details" pursuant to a "general provision" established by Congress. Can you think of examples of this second category of legislative power? Consider George Washington and Henry Knox's regulations respecting the payments to the invalid revolutionary war veterans. Those regulations established the timing of the payments (within the timeframe established by the statute), and also the affidavits that would be required as proof that one was entitled to the payments. Congress of course could have enacted such regulations itself. Thus, the creation of such regulations is at least partly a "legislative" power. But couldn't Congress legitimately leave such questions of administrative "detail" to the executive branch? Thus, the creation of those regulations was also partly an executive power.

Indeed, we might describe this second type of legislative power as "nonexclusive" legislative power to distinguish it from the category of power that is "strictly and exclusively" legislative. It is "nonexclusive" because either Congress or the executive (and even the courts) might be able to exercise it; and because the exercise of this power partakes of both legislative and executive (and maybe even judicial) characteristics.

But what, exactly, is an "important subject," and what exactly constitutes "strictly and exclusively" legislative power that Congress cannot delegate? No one knows for sure; Marshall did not even try to establish a definitive test. Yet there may be a number of factors we can look to—whether the question is one of fact or of policy; the breadth of the discretion; the *scope* of the delegated power (might Congress be able to delegate to an agency broad discretion to regulate a single industry, even if not the entire economy?); the nature of the power (maybe Congress can delegate more discretion to the Executive in foreign affairs, but less when it comes to defining crimes); and finally the extent to which the Executive is given power to affect private rights and conduct (as opposed to official conduct or procedural matters).

The analysis under the "important subjects" approach to nondelegation will not always be easy, but, as you read the following nondelegation cases, consider whether the test might make more sense than the modern "intelligible principle" standard. The next section explores how this test has been applied, first in two cases from 1935. These are the only two instances in which the Supreme Court has invalidated a congressional statute for unlawfully delegating legislative power. After 1935, however, the Supreme Court has not once struck down a congressional law for violating the nondelegation doctrine.

B. The Modern Doctrine

The Supreme Court has invalidated a law for violating the nondelegation doctrine only twice. The cases involved different parts of the same statute, the National Industrial Recovery Act, and both were decided in 1935. The first case also contains a short history and synthesis of the Court's prior nondelegation cases.

Panama Refining Co. v. Ryan

293 U.S. 388 (1935)

Mr. Chief Justice Hughes delivered the opinion of the Court.

On July 11, 1933, the President, by Executive Order No. 6199, prohibited 'the transportation in interstate and foreign commerce of petroleum and the products thereof produced or withdrawn from storage in excess of the amount permitted to be produced or withdrawn from storage by any State law or valid regulation or order prescribed thereunder, by any board, commission, officer, or other duly authorized agency of a State.' This action was based on section 9(c) of title 1 of the National Industrial Recovery Act of June 16, 1933, 15 U.S.C. § 709(c). That section provides: . . .

> 'The President is authorized to prohibit the transportation in interstate and foreign commerce of petroleum and the products thereof produced or withdrawn from storage in excess of the amount permitted to be produced or withdrawn from storage by any State law or valid regulation or order prescribed thereunder, by any board, commission, officer, or other duly authorized agency of a State. Any violation of any order of the President issued under the provisions of this subsection shall be punishable by fine of not to exceed $1,000, or imprisonment for not to exceed six months, or both.'

On July 14, 1933, the President, by Executive Order No. 6204, authorized the Secretary of the Interior to exercise all the powers vested in the President 'for the purpose of enforcing Section 9(c) of said act and said order' of July 11, 1933 . . . .

On July 15, 1933, the Secretary of the Interior issued regulations to carry out the President's orders of July 11 and 14, 1933. These regulations were amended by orders of July 25, 1933, and August 21, 1933, prior to the commencement of these suits. Regulation IV provided, in substance, that every producer of petroleum should file a monthly statement under oath, beginning August 15, 1933, with the Division of Investigations of the Department of the Interior giving information with respect to the residence and post office address of the producer, the location of his producing properties and wells, the allowable production as prescribed by state authority, the amount of daily production, all deliveries of petroleum, and declaring that no part of the petroleum or products produced and shipped had been produced or withdrawn from storage in excess of the amount permitted by state authority. Regulation V required every purchaser, shipper (other than a producer), and refiner of petroleum, including processors, similarly to file a monthly statement under oath, giving information as to residence and post office address, the place and date of receipt, the parties from whom and the amount of petroleum received and the amount held in storage, the disposition of the petroleum, particulars as to deliveries, and declaring, to the best of the affiant's information and belief, that none of the petroleum so handled had been produced or withdrawn from storage in excess of that allowed by state authority. Regulation VII provided that all persons embraced within the terms of section 9(c) of the act, and the executive orders and regulations issued thereunder, should keep 'available for inspection by the Division of Investigations of the Department of the Interior adequate books and records of all transactions involving the production and transportation of petroleum and the products thereof.' . . .

These suits were brought in October, 1933.

In No. 135, the Panama Refining Company, as owner of an oil refining plant in Texas, and its coplaintiff, a producer having oil and gas leases in Texas, sued to restrain the defendants, who were federal officials, from enforcing Regulations IV, V, and VII prescribed by the Secretary of the Interior under section 9(c) of the National Industrial Recovery Act. Plaintiffs attacked the validity of section 9(c) as an unconstitutional delegation to the President of legislative power and as transcending the authority of the Congress under the commerce clause. The regulations, and the attempts to enforce them by coming upon the properties of the plaintiffs, gauging their tanks, digging up pipe lines, and otherwise, were also assailed under the Fourth and Fifth Amendments of the Constitution. . . .

Section 9[c] is assailed upon the ground that it is an unconstitutional delegation of legislative power. The section purports to authorize the President to pass a prohibitory law. The subject to which this authority relates is defined. It is the transportation in interstate and foreign commerce of petroleum and petroleum products which are produced or withdrawn from storage in excess of the amount permitted by state authority. Assuming for the present purpose, without deciding, that the Congress has power to interdict the transportation of that excess in interstate and foreign commerce, the question whether that transportation shall be prohibited by law is obviously one of legislative policy. Accordingly, we look to the statute to see whether the Congress has declared a policy with respect to that subject; whether the Congress has set up a standard for the President's action; whether the Congress has required any finding by the President in the exercise of the authority to enact the prohibition.

Section 9(c) is brief and unambiguous. It does not attempt to control the production of petroleum and petroleum products within a state. It does not seek to lay down rules for the guidance of state Legislatures or state officers. It leaves to the states and to their constituted authorities the determination of what production shall be permitted. It does not qualify the President's authority by reference to the basis or extent of the state's limitation of production. Section 9(c) does not state whether or in what circumstances or under what conditions the President is to prohibit the transportation of the amount of petroleum or petroleum products produced in excess of the state's permission. It establishes no criterion to govern the President's course. It does not require any finding by the President as a condition of his action. The Congress in section 9(c) thus declares no policy as to the transportation of the excess production. So far as this section is concerned, it gives to the President an unlimited authority to determine the policy and to lay down the prohibition, or not to lay it down, as he may see fit. And disobedience to his order is made a crime punishable by fine and imprisonment.

We examine the context to ascertain if it furnishes a declaration of policy or a standard of action, which can be deemed to relate to the subject of section

9(c) and thus to imply what is not there expressed. . . . But the other provisions of section 9 afford no ground for implying a limitation of the broad grant of authority in section 9(c). . . .

We turn to the other provisions of title 1 of the act. The first section is a 'declaration of policy.' It declares that a national emergency exists which is 'productive of widespread unemployment and disorganization of industry, which burdens interstate and foreign commerce, affects the public welfare, and undermines the standards of living of the American people.' It is declared to be the policy of Congress 'to remove obstructions to the free flow of interstate and foreign commerce which tend to diminish the amount thereof;' 'to provide for the general welfare by promoting the organization of industry for the purpose of cooperative action among trade groups;' 'to induce and maintain united action of labor and management under adequate governmental sanctions and supervision;' 'to eliminate unfair competitive practices, to promote the fullest possible utilization of the present productive capacity of industries, to avoid undue restriction of production (except as may be temporarily required), to increase the consumption of industrial and agricultural products by increasing purchasing power, to reduce and relieve unemployment, to improve standards of labor, and otherwise to rehabilitate industry and to conserve natural resources.'

This general outline of policy contains nothing as to the circumstances or conditions in which transportation of petroleum or petroleum products should be prohibited—nothing as to the policy of prohibiting or not prohibiting the transportation of production exceeding what the states allow. The general policy declared is 'to remove obstructions to the free flow of interstate and foreign commerce.' As to production, the section lays down no policy of limitation. It favors the fullest possible utilization of the present productive capacity of industries. It speaks, parenthetically, of a possible temporary restriction of production, but of what, or in what circumstances, it gives no suggestion. The section also speaks in general terms of the conservation of natural resources, but it prescribes no policy for the achievement of that end. It is manifest that this broad outline is simply an introduction of the act, leaving the legislative policy as to particular subjects to be declared and defined, if at all, by the subsequent sections.

It is no answer to insist that deleterious consequences follow the transportation of 'hot oil'—oil exceeding state allowances. The Congress did not prohibit that transportation. The Congress did not undertake to say that the transportation of 'hot oil' was injurious. The Congress did not say that transportation of that oil was 'unfair competition.' The Congress did not declare in what circumstances that transportation should be forbidden, or require the President to make any determination as to any facts or circumstances. Among the numerous and diverse objectives broadly stated, the President was not required to choose. The President was not required to ascertain and proclaim the conditions prevailing in the industry which made the prohibition necessary. The Congress left the matter to the President without standard or rule, to be dealt with as he pleased. The effort by ingenious and diligent construction to supply a criterion still permits such a breadth of authorized action as essentially to commit to the President the functions of a Legislature rather than those of an executive or administrative officer executing a declared legislative policy. We find nothing in section 1 which limits or controls the authority conferred by section 9(c). . . .

The question whether such a delegation of legislative power is permitted by the Constitution is not answered by the argument that it should be assumed that the President has acted, and will act, for what he believes to be the public good. The point is not one of motives, but of constitutional authority, for which the best of motives is not a substitute. While the present controversy relates to a delegation to the President, the basic question has a much wider application. If the Congress can make a grant of legislative authority of the sort attempted by section 9(c), we find nothing in the Constitution which restricts the Congress to the selection of the President as grantee. . . . [And] there would appear to be no ground for denying a similar prerogative of delegation with respect to other subjects of legislation.

The Constitution provides that 'All legislative Powers herein granted shall be vested in a Congress of the United States, which shall consist of a Senate and House of Representatives.' Article 1, § 1. And the Congress is empowered 'To make all Laws which shall be necessary and proper for carrying into Execution' its general powers. Article 1, § 8, par. 18. The Congress manifestly is not permitted to abdicate or to transfer to others the essential legislative functions with which it is thus vested. Undoubtedly legislation must often be adapted to complex conditions involving a host of details with which the national Legislature cannot deal directly. The Constitution has never been regarded as denying to the Congress the necessary resources of flexibility and practicality, which will enable it to perform its function in laying down policies and establishing standards, while leaving to selected instrumentalities the making of subordinate rules within prescribed limits and the determination of facts to which the policy as declared by the Legislature is to apply. Without capacity to give authorizations of that sort we should have the anomaly of a legislative power which in many circumstances calling for its exertion would be but a futility. But the constant recognition of the necessity and validity of such provisions and the wide range of administrative authority which has been developed by means of them cannot be allowed to obscure the limitations of the authority to delegate, if our constitutional system is to be maintained.

The Court has had frequent occasion to refer to these limitations and to review the course of congressional action. At the very outset, amid the disturbances due to war in Europe, when the national safety was imperiled and our neutrality was disregarded, the Congress passed a series of acts, as a part of which the President was authorized, in stated circumstances, to lay and revoke embargoes, to give permits for the exportation of arms and military stores, to remit and discontinue the restraints and prohibitions imposed by acts suspending commercial intercourse with certain countries, and to permit or interdict the entrance into waters of the United States of armed vessels belonging to foreign nations. These early acts were not the subject of judicial decision, and, apart from that, they afford no adequate basis for a conclusion that the Congress assumed that it possessed an unqualified power of delegation. They were inspired by the vexations of American commerce through the hostile enterprises of the belligerent powers, they were directed to the effective execution of policies repeatedly declared by the Congress, and they confided to the President, for the purposes and under the conditions stated, an authority which was cognate to the conduct by him of the foreign relations of the government.

[A discussion of *The Brig Aurora, Field v. Clark, Wayman v. Southard,* and *Buttfield v. Stranahan* are omitted.—Ed.]

Another notable illustration is that of the authority given to the Secretary of War to determine whether bridges and other structures constitute unreasonable obstructions to navigation and to remove such obstructions. Act of March 3, 1899, 30 Stat. 1153, 1154. By that statute the Congress declared 'a general rule and imposed upon the Secretary of War the duty of ascertaining what particular cases came within the rule' as thus laid down. Upon this principle rests the authority of the Interstate Commerce Commission, in the execution of the declared policy of the Congress in enforcing reasonable rates, in preventing undue preferences and unjust discriminations, in requiring suitable facilities for transportation in interstate commerce, and in exercising other powers held to have been validly conferred. . . .

The provisions of the Radio Act of 1927, providing for assignments of frequencies or wave lengths to various stations, afford another instance. In granting licenses, the Radio Commission is required to act 'as public convenience, interest, or necessity requires.' In construing this provision, the Court found that the statute itself declared the policy as to 'equality of radio broadcasting service, both of transmission and of reception,' and that it conferred authority to make allocations and assignments in order to secure, according to stated criteria, an equitable adjustment in the distribution of facilities. The standard set up was not so indefinite 'as to confer an unlimited power.' Federal Radio Commission v. Nelson Brothers Co., 289 U.S. 266, 279, 285.

So also, from the beginning of the government, the Congress has conferred upon executive officers the power to make regulations—'not for the government of their departments, but for administering the laws which did govern.' United States v. Grimaud, 220 U.S. 506, 517. Such regulations become, indeed, binding rules of conduct, but they are valid only as subordinate rules and when found to be within the framework of the policy which the Legislature has sufficiently defined. . . .

The applicable considerations were reviewed in Hampton, Jr., & Co. v. United States, 276 U.S. 394, where the Court dealt with the so-called 'flexible tariff provision' of the Act of September 21, 1922, and with the authority which it conferred upon the President. The Court applied the same principle that permitted the Congress to exercise its ratemaking power in interstate commerce, and found that a similar provision was justified for the fixing of customs duties; that is, as the Court said: 'If Congress shall lay down by legislative act an intelligible principle to which the person or body authorized to fix such rates is directed to conform, such legislative action is not a forbidden delegation of legislative power. If it is thought wise to vary the customs duties according to changing conditions of production at home and abroad, it may authorize the Chief Executive to carry out this purpose, with the advisory assistance of a Tariff Commission appointed under congressional authority.' The Court sustained the provision upon the authority of Field v. Clark, supra, repeating with approval what was there said, that 'What the President was required to do was merely in execution of the act of Congress.'

Thus, in every case in which the question has been raised, the Court has recognized that there are limits of delegation which there is no constitutional authority to transcend. We think that section 9(c) goes beyond those limits. As to the transportation of oil production in excess of state permission, the Congress has declared no policy, has established no standard, has laid down no rule. There is no requirement, no definition of circumstances and conditions in which the transportation is to be allowed or prohibited.

If section 9(c) were held valid, it would be idle to pretend that anything would be left of limitations upon the power of the Congress to delegate its lawmaking function. The reasoning of the many decisions we have reviewed would be made vacuous and their distinctions nugatory. Instead of performing its lawmaking function, the Congress could at will and as to such subjects as it chooses transfer that function to the President or other officer or to an administrative body. The question is not of the intrinsic importance of the particular statute before us, but of the constitutional processes of legislation which are an essential part of our system of government. . . .

The executive order contains no finding, no statement of the grounds of the President's action in enacting the prohibition. . . . To hold that he is free to select as he chooses from the many and various objects generally described in the first section, and then to act without making any finding with respect to any object that he does select, and the circumstances properly related to that object, would be in effect to make the conditions inoperative and to invest him with an uncontrolled legislative power. . . .

Mr. Justice Cardozo, dissenting.

. . . . I am unable to assent to the conclusion that section 9(c) of the National Recovery Act, a section delegating to the President a very different power from any that is involved in the regulation of production or in the promulgation of a code, is to be nullified upon the ground that his discretion is too broad or for any other reason. My point of difference with the majority of the court is narrow. I concede that to uphold the delegation there is need to discover in the terms of the act a standard reasonably clear whereby discretion must be governed. I deny that such a standard is lacking in respect of the prohibitions permitted by this section when the act with all its reasonable implications is considered as a whole. What the standard is becomes the pivotal inquiry.

As to the nature of the act which the President is authorized to perform there is no need for implication. That at least is definite beyond the possibility of challenge. He may prohibit the transportation in interstate and foreign commerce of petroleum and the products thereof produced or withdrawn from storage in excess of the amount permitted by any state law or valid regulation or order prescribed thereunder. He is not left to roam at will among all the possible subjects of interstate transportation, picking and choosing as he pleases. I am far from asserting now that delegation would be valid if accompanied by all that latitude of choice. In the laying of his interdict he is to confine himself to a particular commodity, and to that commodity when produced or withdrawn from storage in contravention of the policy and statutes of the states. He has choice, though within limits, as to the occasion, but none whatever as to the means. The means have been prescribed by Congress. There has been no grant to the Executive of any roving commission to inquire into evils and then, upon discovering them, do anything he pleases. His act being thus defined, what else must he ascertain in order to regulate his discretion and bring the power into play? The answer is not given if we look to section 9(c) only, but it comes to us by implication from a view of other sections where the standards are defined. The prevailing opinion concedes that a standard will be as effective if imported into section 9(c) by reasonable implication as if put there in so many words. If we look to the whole structure of the statute, the test is plainly this, that the President is to forbid the transportation of the oil when he believes, in the light of the conditions of the industry as disclosed from time to time, that the prohibition will tend to effectuate the declared policies of the act—not merely his own conception of its policies, undirected by any extrinsic guide, but the policies announced by section in the forefront of the statute as an index to the meaning of everything that follows. . . .

A declared policy of Congress in the adoption of the act is 'to eliminate unfair competitive practices.' Beyond question an unfair competitive practice exists when 'hot oil' is transported in interstate commerce with the result that law-abiding dealers must compete with lawbreakers. Here is one of the standards set up in the act to guide the President's discretion. Another declared policy of Congress is 'to conserve natural resources.' Beyond question the disregard of statutory quotas is wasting the oil fields in Texas and other states and putting in jeopardy of exhaustion one of the treasures of the nation. All this is developed in the record and in the arguments of counsel for the government with a wealth of illustration. Here is a second standard.

Another declared policy of Congress is to 'promote the fullest possible utilization of the present productive capacity of industries,' and 'except as may be temporarily required' to 'avoid undue restriction of production.' Beyond question prevailing conditions in the oil industry have brought about the need for temporary restriction in order to promote in the long run the fullest productive capacity of business in all its many branches, for the effect of present practices is to diminish that capacity by demoralizing prices and thus increasing unemployment. The ascertainment of these facts at any time or place was a task too intricate and special to be performed by Congress itself through a general enactment in advance of the event. All that Congress could safely do was to declare the act to be done and the policies to be promoted, leaving to the delegate of its power the ascertainment of the shifting facts that would determine the relation between the doing of the act and the attainment of the stated ends. That is what it did. It said to the President, in substance: You are to consider whether the transportation of oil in excess of the statutory quotas is offensive to one or more of the policies enumerated in section 1, whether the effect of such conduct is to promote unfair competition or to waste the natural resources or to demoralize prices or to increase unemployment or to reduce the purchasing power of the workers of the nation. If these standards or some of them have been flouted with the result of a substantial obstruction to industrial recovery, you may then by a prohibitory order eradicate the mischief. . . .

To describe his conduct thus is to ignore the essence of his function. What he does is to inquire into the industrial facts as they exist from time to time. . . . He is to study the facts objectively, the violation of a standard impelling him to action or inaction according to its observed effect upon industrial recovery—the ultimate end, as appears by the very heading of the title, to which all the other ends are tributary and mediate. . . . When [Congress] clothed the President with power to impose such a restriction—to prohibit the flow of oil illegally produced—it laid upon him a mandate to inquire and determine whether the conditions in that particular industry were such at any given time as to make restriction helpful to the declared objectives of the act and to the ultimate attainment of industrial recovery. . . .

Under these decisions the separation of powers between the Executive and Congress is not a doctrinaire concept to be made use of with pedantic rigor. There must be sensible approximation, there must be elasticity of adjustment, in response to the practical necessities of government, which cannot foresee to-day the developments of tomorrow in their nearly infinite variety. . . . In the complex life of to-day, the business of government could not go on without the delegation, in greater or less degree, of the power to adapt the rule to the swiftly moving facts. . . .

There is no fear that the nation will drift from its ancient moorings as the result of the narrow delegation of power permitted by this section. What can be done under cover of that permission is closely and clearly circumscribed both as to subject-matter and occasion. The statute was framed in the shadow of a national disaster. A host of unforeseen contingencies would have to be faced from day to day, and faced with a fullness of understanding unattainable by any one except the man upon the scene. The President was chosen to meet the instant need. . . .

A.L.A. Schechter Poultry Corp. v. United States

295 U.S. 495 (1935)

Mr. Chief Justice Hughes delivered the opinion of the Court.

Petitioners in No. 854 were convicted in the District Court of the United States for the Eastern District of New York on eighteen counts of an indictment charging violations of what is known as the 'Live Poultry Code,' and on an additional count for conspiracy to commit such violations. By demurrer to the indictment and appropriate motions on the trial, the defendants contended (1) that the code had been adopted pursuant to an unconstitutional delegation by Congress of legislative power; (2) that it attempted to regulate intrastate transactions which lay outside the authority of Congress; and (3) that in certain provisions it was repugnant to the due process clause of the Fifth Amendment. . . .

A.L.A. Schechter Poultry Corporation and Schechter Live Poultry Market are corporations conducting wholesale poultry slaughterhouse markets in Brooklyn, New York City. Joseph Schechter operated the latter corporation and also guaranteed the credits of the former corporation, which was operated by Martin, Alex, and Aaron Schechter. Defendants ordinarily purchase their live poultry from commission men at the West Washington Market in New York City or at the railroad terminals serving the city, but occasionally they purchase from commission men in Philadelphia. They buy the poultry for slaughter and resale. After the poultry is trucked to their slaughterhouse markets in Brooklyn, it is there sold, usually within twenty-four hours, to retail poultry dealers and butchers who sell directly to consumers. . . .

The 'Live Poultry Code' was promulgated under section 3 of the National Industrial Recovery Act. That section, the pertinent provisions of which are set forth in the margin, authorizes the President to approve 'codes of fair competition.' Such a code may be approved for a trade or industry, upon application by one or more trade or industrial associations or groups, if the President finds (1) that such associations or groups 'impose no inequitable restrictions on admission to membership therein and are truly representative,' and (2) that such codes are not designed 'to promote monopolies or to eliminate or oppress small enterprises and will not operate to discriminate against them, and will tend to effectuate the policy' of title 1 of the act. Such codes 'shall not permit monopolies or monopolistic practices.' As a condition of his approval, the President may 'impose such conditions (including requirements for the making of reports and the keeping of accounts) for the protection of consumers, competitors, employees, and others, and in furtherance of the public interest, and may provide such exceptions to and exemptions from the provisions of such code as the President in his discretion deems necessary to effectuate the policy herein declared.' Where such a code has not been approved, the President may prescribe one, either on his own motion or on complaint. Violation of any provision of a code (so approved or prescribed) 'in any transaction in or affecting interstate or foreign commerce' is made a misdemeanor punishable by a fine of not more than $500 for each offense, and each day the violation continues is to be deemed a separate offense.

The 'Live Poultry Code' was approved by the President on April 13, 1934. Its divisions indicate its nature and scope. The code has eight articles entitled (1) 'purposes,' (2) 'definitions,' (3) 'hours,' (4) 'wages,' (5) 'general labor provisions,' (6) 'administration,' (7) 'trade practice provisions,' and (8) 'general.'

The declared purpose is 'To effect the policies of title I of the National Industrial Recovery Act.' The code is established as 'a code for fair competition for the live poultry industry of the metropolitan area in and about the City of New York.' . . .

The code fixes the number of hours for workdays. It provides that no employee, with certain exceptions, shall be permitted to work in excess of forty hours in any one week, and that no employees, save as stated, 'shall be paid in any pay period less than at the rate of fifty (50) cents per hour.' The article containing 'general labor provisions' prohibits the employment of any person under 16 years of age, and declares that employees shall have the right of 'collective bargaining' and freedom of choice with respect to labor organizations, in the terms of section 7(a) of the act. The minimum number of employees, who shall be employed by slaughterhouse operators, is fixed; the number being graduated according to the average volume of weekly sales. . . .

The seventh article, containing 'trade practice provisions,' prohibits various practices which are said to constitute 'unfair methods of competition.' . . .

The President approved the code by an executive order (No. 6675–A) . . . .

Of the eighteen counts of the indictment upon which the defendants were convicted, aside from the count for conspiracy, two counts charged violation of the minimum wage and maximum hour provisions of the code, and ten counts were for violation of the requirement (found in the 'trade practice provisions') of 'straight killing.' This requirement was really one of 'straight' selling. The term 'straight killing' was defined in the code as 'the practice of requiring persons purchasing poultry for resale to accept the run of any half coop, coop, or coops, as purchased by slaughterhouse operators, except for culls.' The charges in the ten counts, respectively, were that the defendants in selling to retail dealers and butchers had permitted 'selections of individual chickens taken from particular coops and half coops.' . . .

Two preliminary points are stressed by the government with respect to the appropriate approach to the important questions presented. We are told that the provision of the statute authorizing the adoption of codes must be viewed in the light of the grave national crisis with which Congress was confronted. Undoubtedly, the conditions to which power is addressed are always to be considered when the exercise of power is challenged. Extraordinary conditions may call for extraordinary remedies. But the argument necessarily stops short of an attempt to justify action which lies outside the sphere of constitutional authority. Extraordinary conditions do not create or enlarge constitutional power. The Constitution established a national government with powers deemed to be adequate, as they have proved to be both in war and peace, but these powers of the national government are limited by the constitutional grants. Those who act under these grants are not at liberty to transcend the imposed limits because they believe that more or different power is necessary. Such assertions of extra-constitutional authority were anticipated and precluded by the explicit terms of the Tenth Amendment—'The powers not delegated to the United States by the Constitution, nor prohibited by it to the States, are reserved to the States respectively, or to the people.'

The further point is urged that the national crisis demanded a broad and intensive co-operative effort by those engaged in trade and industry, and that this necessary co-operation was sought to be fostered by permitting them to initiate the adoption of codes. But the statutory plan is not simply one for voluntary effort. It does not seek merely to endow voluntary trade or industrial associations or groups with privileges or immunities. It involves the coercive exercise of the lawmaking power. The codes of fair competition which the statute attempts to authorize are codes of laws. If valid, they place all persons within their reach under the obligation of positive law, binding equally those who assent and those who do not assent. Violations of the provisions of the codes are punishable as crimes. . . .

We recently had occasion to review the pertinent decisions and the general principles which govern the determination of this [delegation] question. Panama Refining Company v. Ryan, 293 U.S. 388. . . .

Accordingly, we look to the statute to see whether Congress has overstepped these limitations—whether Congress in authorizing 'codes of fair competition' has itself established the standards of legal obligation, thus performing its essential legislative function, or, by the failure to enact such standards, has attempted to transfer that function to others.

The aspect in which the question is now presented is distinct from that which was before us in the case of the Panama Refining Company. There the subject of the statutory prohibition was defined. That subject was the transportation in interstate and foreign commerce of petroleum and petroleum products which are produced or withdrawn from storage in excess of the amount permitted by state authority. The question was with respect to the range of discretion given to the President in prohibiting that transportation. As to the 'codes of fair competition,' under section 3 of the act, the question is more fundamental.

It is whether there is any adequate definition of the subject to which the codes are to be addressed.

What is meant by 'fair competition' as the term is used in the act? Does it refer to a category established in the law, and is the authority to make codes limited accordingly? Or is it used as a convenient designation for whatever set of laws the formulators of a code for a particular trade or industry may propose and the President may approve (subject to certain restrictions), or the President may himself prescribe, as being wise and beneficent provisions for the government of the trade or industry in order to accomplish the broad purposes of rehabilitation, correction, and expansion which are stated in the first section of title 1?[9]

The act does not define 'fair competition.' 'Unfair competition,' as known to the common law, is a limited concept. Primarily, and strictly, it relates to the palming off of one's goods as those of a rival trader. In recent years, its scope has been extended. It has been held to apply to misappropriation as well as misrepresentation, to the selling of another's goods as one's own—to misappropriation of what equitably belongs to a competitor. Unfairness in competition has been predicated on acts which lie outside the ordinary course of business and are tainted by fraud or coercion or conduct otherwise prohibited by law. But it is evident that in its widest range, 'unfair competition,' as it has been understood in the law, does not reach the objectives of the codes which are authorized by the National Industrial Recovery Act. The codes may, indeed, cover conduct which existing law condemns, but they are not limited to conduct of that sort. The government does not contend that the act contemplates such a limitation. It would be opposed both to the declared purposes of the act and to its administrative construction.

The Federal Trade Commission Act introduced the expression 'unfair methods of competition,' which were declared to be unlawful. That was an

---

[9]   That section, under the heading 'Declaration of Policy,' is as follows: 'Section 1. A national emergency productive of widespread unemployment and disorganization of industry, which burdens interstate and foreign commerce, affects the public welfare, and undermines the standards of living of the American people, is hereby declared to exist. It is hereby declared to be the policy of Congress to remove obstructions to the free flow of interstate and foreign commerce which tend to diminish the amount thereof; and to provide for the general welfare by promoting the organization of industry for the purpose of co-operative action among trade groups, to induce and maintain united action of labor and management under adequate governmental sanctions and supervision, to eliminate unfair competitive practices, to promote the fullest possible utilization of the present productive capacity of industries, to avoid undue restriction of production (except as may be temporarily required), to increase the consumption of industrial and agricultural products by increasing purchasing power, to reduce and relieve unemployment, to improve standards of labor, and otherwise to rehabilitate industry and to conserve natural resources.'

expression new in the law. Debate apparently convinced the sponsors of the legislation that the words 'unfair competition,' in the light of their meaning at common law, were too narrow. We have said that the substituted phrase has a broader meaning, that it does not admit of precise definition; its scope being left to judicial determination as controversies arise. . . .

[T]he difference between the code plan of the Recovery Act and the scheme of the Federal Trade Commission Act lies not only in procedure but in subject-matter. We cannot regard the 'fair competition' of the codes as antithetical to the 'unfair methods of competition' of the Federal Trade Commission Act. The 'fair competition' of the codes has a much broader range and a new significance. The Recovery Act provides that it shall not be construed to impair the powers of the Federal Trade Commission, but, when a code is approved, its provisions are to be the 'standards of fair competition' for the trade or industry concerned, and any violation of such standards in any transaction in or affecting interstate or foreign commerce is to be deemed 'an unfair method of competition' within the meaning of the Federal Trade Commission Act.

For a statement of the authorized objectives and content of the 'codes of fair competition,' we are referred repeatedly to the 'Declaration of Policy' in section 1 of title 1 of the Recovery Act. . . . That declaration embraces a broad range of objectives. Among them we find the elimination of 'unfair competitive practices.' But, even if this clause were to be taken to relate to practices which fall under the ban of existing law, either common law or statute, it is still only one of the authorized aims described in section 1. It is there declared to be 'the policy of Congress'—'to remove obstructions to the free flow of interstate and foreign commerce which tend to diminish the amount thereof; and to provide for the general welfare by promoting the organization of industry for the purpose of cooperative action among trade groups, to induce and maintain united action of labor and management under adequate governmental sanctions and supervision, to eliminate unfair competitive practices, to promote the fullest possible utilization of the present productive capacity of industries, to avoid undue restriction of production (except as may be temporarily required), to increase the consumption of industrial and agricultural products by increasing purchasing power, to reduce and relieve unemployment, to improve standards of labor, and otherwise to rehabilitate industry and to conserve natural resources.'

Under section 3, whatever 'may tend to effectuate' these general purposes may be included in the 'codes of fair competition.' We think the conclusion is inescapable that the authority sought to be conferred by section 3 was not merely to deal with 'unfair competitive practices' which offend against existing law, and could be the subject of judicial condemnation without further legislation, or to create administrative machinery for the application of established principles of law to particular instances of violation. Rather, the purpose is clearly disclosed to authorize new and controlling prohibitions through codes of laws . . . .

The government urges that the codes will 'consist of rules of competition deemed fair for each industry by representative members of that industry—by the persons most vitally concerned and most familiar with its problems.' . . . But would it be seriously contended that Congress could delegate its legislative authority to trade or industrial associations or groups so as to empower them to enact the laws they deem to be wise and beneficent for the rehabilitation and expansion of their trade or industries? Could trade or industrial associations or groups be constituted legislative bodies for that purpose because such associations or groups are familiar with the problems of their enterprises? And could an effort of that sort be made valid by such a preface of generalities as to permissible aims as we find in section 1 of title 1? The answer is obvious. Such a delegation of legislative power is unknown to our law, and is utterly inconsistent with the constitutional prerogatives and duties of Congress. . . .

Congress cannot delegate legislative power to the President to exercise an unfettered discretion to make whatever laws he thinks may be needed or advisable for the rehabilitation and expansion of trade or industry.

Accordingly we turn to the Recovery Act to ascertain what limits have been set to the exercise of the President's discretion: . . . [T]he President is required to find that the code is not 'designed to promote monopolies or to eliminate or oppress small enterprises and will not operate to discriminate against them.' And to this is added a proviso that the code 'shall not permit monopolies or monopolistic practices.' But these restrictions leave virtually untouched the field of policy envisaged by section 1, and, in that wide field of legislative possibilities, the proponents of a code, refraining from monopolistic designs, may roam at will, and the President may approve or disapprove their proposals as he may see fit. . . .

As already noted, the President in approving a code may impose his own conditions, adding to or taking from what is proposed, as 'in his discretion' he thinks necessary 'to effectuate the policy' declared by the act. . . . And this authority relates to a host of different trades and industries, thus extending the President's discretion to all the varieties of laws which he may deem to be beneficial in dealing with the vast array of commercial and industrial activities throughout the country. . . .

Section 3 of the Recovery Act is without precedent. It supplies no standards for any trade, industry, or activity. It does not undertake to prescribe rules of conduct to be applied to particular states of fact determined by appropriate administrative procedure. Instead of prescribing rules of conduct, it authorizes the making of codes to prescribe them. For that legislative undertaking, section 3 sets up no standards, aside from the statement of the general aims of rehabilitation, correction, and expansion described in section 1. In view of the scope of that broad declaration and of the nature of the few restrictions that are imposed, the discretion of the President in approving or prescribing codes, and thus enacting laws for the government of trade and industry throughout the country, is virtually unfettered. We think that the code-making authority thus conferred is an unconstitutional delegation of legislative power. . . .

MR. JUSTICE CARDOZO, concurring.

The delegated power of legislation which has found expression in this code is not canalized within banks that keep it from overflowing. It is unconfined and vagrant, if I may borrow my own words in an earlier opinion. Panama Refining Co. v. Ryan, 293 U.S. 388, 440.

This court has held that delegation may be unlawful, though the act to be performed is definite and single, if the necessity, time, and occasion of performance have been left in the end to the discretion of the delegate. Panama Refining Co. v. Ryan, supra. I thought that ruling went too far. I pointed out in an opinion that there had been 'no grant to the Executive of any roving commission to inquire into evils and then, upon discovering them, do anything he pleases.' Choice, though within limits, had been given him 'as to the occasion, but none whatever as to the means.' Here, in the case before us, is an attempted delegation not confined to any single act nor to any class or group of acts identified or described by reference to a standard. Here in effect is a roving commission to inquire into evils and upon discovery correct them. . . .

If that conception shall prevail, anything that Congress may do within the limits of the commerce clause for the betterment of business may be done by the President upon the recommendation of a trade association by calling it

a code. This is delegation running riot. No such plenitude of power is susceptible of transfer. . . .

The code does not confine itself to the suppression of methods of competition that would be classified as unfair according to accepted business standards
or accepted norms of ethics. It sets up a comprehensive body of rules to promote
the welfare of the industry, if not the welfare of the nation, without reference
to standards, ethical or commercial, that could be known or predicted in advance of its adoption. One of the new rules, the source of ten counts in the
indictment, is aimed at an established practice, not unethical or oppressive, the
practice of selective buying. . . .

I am authorized to state that Mr. Justice Stone joins in this opinion.

Notes and Questions

1. Summary. In *Panama Refining,* the Supreme Court invalidated section 9(c) of the National Industrial Recovery Act (NIRA). That section allowed
the President by proclamation to prohibit the sale and shipping in interstate
commerce of "hot oil," i.e. oil produced in excess of production quotas in individual states. The statute did not give *any* guidance to the President on how he
was to exercise his discretion; the Court thought that the principles and objectives of section 1 of the act were too broad and competing. Justice Cardozo
dissented, arguing that the subject-matter was limited and defined; the President only had discretion with respect to one particular thing, namely whether
to prohibit interstate shipment of hot
oil. Given the well-defined and limited subject-matter, Justice Cardozo
seemed willing to finding an intelligible principle out of the overarching
objective of industrial recovery.
Schechter Poultry, on the other hand,
dealt with section 3 of the NIRA,
which allowed the President to approve and/or modify codes of
competition proposed by various industries for those industries. The

FOR DISCUSSION

What factors do you
think should play into
a nondelegation
analysis? Merely
whether Congress
has established suffi-
cient principles? Or does the breadth
of the conduct that it permits to be
regulated matter? What about the
nature of the regulation—should it
matter whether the regulation is of
official conduct or private conduct? Is
criminal or civil in nature? Relates to
foreign or domestic affairs?

breadth of the subject-matter was much greater; Justice Cardozo thought this created a "roving commission to inquire into evils and upon discovery correct them" as the President pleased. Was Justice Cardozo suggesting that the breadth of the *subject-matter* of the delegation should matter in addition to the breadth of the *discretion*? Do you think that should matter?

2. *Competing purposes.* Do the broad purposes of section 1 of the NIRA always coincide, or are they sometimes competing? When one policy effectuates one broad purpose of the act—say, removing obstructions to interstate commerce—but seems to undermine a different broad purpose of the act—for example, to improve standards of labor, and otherwise to rehabilitate industry and to conserve natural resources—can there be an intelligible principle?

After the famous "switch in time" in 1937, the Supreme Court regularly began upholding New Deal legislation. Never again would the Court invalidate a congressional law as a violation of the nondelegation doctrine. The broad delegations that have been upheld since 1935 are illustrated by the following handful of cases, some of which also raise quite interesting theoretical issues.

What role does political pressure and influence play on the Supreme Court?

Yakus v. United States

321 U.S. 414 (1944)

MR. CHIEF JUSTICE STONE delivered the opinion of the Court.

The questions for our decision are: (1) Whether the Emergency Price Control Act of January 30, 1942, as amended by the Inflation Control Act of October 2, 1942, involves an unconstitutional delegation to the Price Administrator of the legislative power of Congress to control prices . . . .

The Emergency Price Control Act provides for the establishment of the Office of Price Administration under the direction of a Price Administrator appointed by the President, and sets up a comprehensive scheme for the promulgation by the Administrator of regulations or orders fixing such maximum prices of commodities and rents as will effectuate the purposes of the Act and conform to the standards which it prescribes. The Act was adopted as a temporary wartime measure, and provides in § 1(b) for its termination on June 30, 1943, unless sooner terminated by Presidential proclamation or concurrent resolution of Congress. By the amendatory act of October 2, 1942, it was extended to June 30, 1944. . . .

The standards which are to guide the Administrator's exercise of his authority to fix prices, so far as now relevant, are prescribed by § 2(a) and by § 1 of the amendatory Act of October 2, 1942, and Executive Order 9250, promulgated under it. By § 2(a) the Administrator is authorized, after consultation with representative members of the industry so far as practicable, to promulgate regulations fixing prices of commodities which 'in his judgment will be generally fair and equitable and will effectuate the purposes of this Act' when, in his judgment, their prices 'have risen or threaten to rise to an extent or in a manner inconsistent with the purposes of this Act.'

[The section also directs the Administrator to give consideration to past prices in specific two-week windows, "and shall make adjustments for such relevant factors as he may determine and deem to be of general applicability."—Ed.]

By the Act of October 2, 1942, the President is directed to stabilize prices, wages and salaries 'so far as practicable' on the basis of the levels which existed on September 15, 1942 . . . .

Revised Maximum Price Regulation No. 169 was issued December 10, 1942, under authority of the Emergency Price Control Act as amended and Executive Order No. 9250. The Regulation established specific maximum prices for the sale at wholesale of specified cuts of beef and veal. . . .

Congress enacted the Emergency Price Control Act in pursuance of a defined policy and required that the prices fixed by the Administrator should further that policy and conform to standards prescribed by the Act. The boundaries of the field of the Administrator's permissible action are marked by the statute. It directs that the prices fixed shall effectuate the declared policy of the Act to stabilize commodity prices so as to prevent war-time inflation and its enumerated disruptive causes and effects. In addition the prices established must be fair and equitable, and in fixing them the Administrator is directed to give due consideration, so far as practicable, to prevailing prices during the designated base period, with prescribed administrative adjustments to compensate for enumerated disturbing factors affecting prices. In short the purposes of the Act specified in § 1 denote the objective to be sought by the Administrator in fixing prices—the prevention of inflation and its enumerated consequences. The standards set out in § 2 define the boundaries within which prices having that purpose must be fixed. It is enough to satisfy the statutory requirements that the Administrator finds that the prices fixed will tend to achieve that objective and will conform to those standards, and that the courts in an appropriate proceeding can see that substantial basis for those findings is not wanting.

The Act is thus an exercise by Congress of its legislative power. In it Congress has stated the legislative objective, has prescribed the method of achieving that objective—maximum price fixing—and has laid down standards to guide the administrative determination of both the occasions for the exercise of the price-fixing power, and the particular prices to be established. . . .

The Constitution as a continuously operative charter of government does not demand the impossible or the impracticable. It does not require that Congress find for itself every fact upon which it desires to base legislative action or that it make for itself detailed determinations which it has declared to be prerequisite to the application of the legislative policy to particular facts and circumstances impossible for Congress itself properly to investigate. The essentials of the legislative function are the determination of the legislative policy and its formulation and promulgation as a defined and binding rule of conduct—here the rule, with penal sanctions, that prices shall not be greater than those fixed by maximum price regulations which conform to standards and will tend to further the policy which Congress has established. . . .

Hence it is irrelevant that Congress might itself have prescribed the maximum prices or have provided a more rigid standard by which they are to be fixed; for example, that all prices should be frozen at the levels obtaining during a certain period or on a certain date. Congress is not confined to that method of executing its policy which involves the least possible delegation of discretion to administrative officers. It is free to avoid the rigidity of such a system, which might well result in serious hardship, and to choose instead the flexibility attainable by the use of less restrictive standards. Only if we could say that there is an absence of standards for the guidance of the Administrator's action, so that it would be impossible in a proper proceeding to ascertain whether the will of Congress has been obeyed, would we be justified in overriding its choice of means for effecting its declared purpose of preventing inflation. . . .

The directions that the prices fixed shall be fair and equitable, that in addition they shall tend to promote the purposes of the Act, and that in promulgating them consideration shall be given to prices prevailing in a stated base period, confer no greater reach for administrative determination than the power to fix just and reasonable rates; or the power to approve consolidations in the 'public interest'; or the power to regulate radio stations engaged in chain broadcasting 'as public interest, convenience or necessity requires' . . . ; or the power to prohibit 'unfair methods of competition' not defined or forbidden by the common law; or the direction that in allotting marketing quotas among states and producers due consideration be given to a variety of economic factors . . . ; or the similar direction that in adjusting tariffs to meet differences in costs of production the President 'take into consideration' 'in so far as he finds it practicable' a variety of economic matters, sustained in Hampton Jr. & Co. v. United States, supra; or the similar authority, in making classifications within an industry, to consider various named and unnamed 'relevant factors' and determine the respective weights attributable to each . . . .

Mr. Justice Roberts.

I dissent. I find it unnecessary to discuss certain of the questions treated in the opinion of the court. I am of opinion that the Act unconstitutionally delegates legislative power to the Administrator. As I read the opinion of the court it holds the Act valid on the ground that sufficiently precise standards are prescribed to confine the Administrator's regulations and orders within fixed limits, and that judicial review is provided effectively to prohibit his transgression of those limits. I believe that analysis demonstrates the contrary. . . .

The Act provides that any regulation or order must be 'generally fair and equitable' in the Administrator's judgment; but coupled with this injunction is another that the order and regulation must be such as, in the judgment of the Administrator, is necessary or proper to effectuate the purposes of the Act. . . .

Section 1(a) states seven purposes, which should be set forth separately as follows:

'to stabilize prices and to prevent speculative, unwarranted, and abnormal increases in prices and rents;'

In order to exercise his power [concerning] this purpose the Administrator will have to form a judgment as to what stabilization means, and what are speculative, unwarranted and abnormal increases in price. It hardly need be said that men may differ radically as to the connotation of these terms and that it would be very difficult to convict anyone of error of judgment in so classifying a given economic phenomenon.

'to eliminate and prevent profiteering, hoarding, manipulation, speculation, and other disruptive practices resulting from abnormal market conditions or scarcities caused by or contributing to the national emergency;'

To accomplish this purpose the Administrator must form a judgment as to what constitutes profiteering, hoarding, manipulation or speculation. As if the administrative discretion were not sufficiently broad there is added the phrase 'other disruptive practices', which seems to leave the Administrator at large in the formation of opinion as to whether any practice is disruptive.

'to assure that defense appropriations are not dissipated by excessive prices;'

It is not clear—to me at least—what is the limit of this purpose. I can conceive that an honest Administrator might, without laying himself open to the charge of exceeding his powers, make any kind of order or regulation based upon the view that otherwise defense appropriations by Congress might be dissipated by what he considers excessive prices. How his exercise of judgment in connection with this purpose could be thought excessive it is impossible for me to say.

'to protect persons with relatively fixed and limited incomes, consumers, wage earners, investors, and persons dependent on life insurance, annuities, and pensions, from undue impairment of their standard of living;'

The Administrator's judgment that any price policy will tend to affect the classes mentioned in this purpose from what he may decide to be 'undue impairment of their standard of living' would seem to be so sweeping that it would be impossible to convict him of an error of judgment in any conclusion he might reach.

'to prevent hardships to persons engaged in business, to schools, universities, and other institutions, and to the Federal, State, and local governments, which would result from abnormal increases in prices;'

Of course Congress might have included in the catalogue of beneficiaries churches, hospitals, labor unions, banks and trust companies and other praiseworthy organizations, without rendering the 'standard' any more vague.

'to assist in securing adequate production of commodities and facilities;'

Here is a purpose which seems, to some extent at least, to permit the easing of price restrictions; for it would appear that diminishment of price would hardly assist in promoting production. Thus the Administrator, and he alone, is to balance two competing policies and strike the happy mean between them. Who shall say his conclusion is so indubitably wrong as to be properly characterized as 'arbitrary or capricious'.

'to prevent a post emergency collapse of values;'

This purpose, or 'standard', seems to permit adoption by the Administrator of any conceivable policy. I have difficulty in envisaging any price policy in support of which some economic data or opinion could not be cited to show that it would tend to prevent post emergency collapse of values.

These seven purposes must, I submit, be considered as separate and independent. Any action taken by the Administrator which, in his judgment, promotes any one or more of them is within the granted power. If, in his judgment, any action by him is necessary or appropriate to the accomplishment of one or more of them, the Act gives sanction to his order or regulation.

Reflection will demonstrate that in fact the Act sets no limits upon the discretion or judgment of the Administrator. His commission is to take any action with respect to prices which he believes will preserve what he deems a sound economy during the emergency and prevent what he considers to be a disruption of such a sound economy in the post war period. His judgment, founded as it may be, on his studies and investigations, as well as other economic data, even though contrary to the great weight of current opinion or authority, is the final touchstone of the validity of his action. . . .

[A dissenting opinion by JUSTICES ROUTLEDGE and MURPHY, on unrelated issues, is omitted.—Ed.]

NOTES AND QUESTIONS

1. *The intelligible principle in* **Yakus.** *Yakus* is an interesting case because of the sheer breadth of the principle that the Court found to be "intelligible": the setting of prices for commodities that in the judgment of the Administrator would be "fair and equitable," and which would effectuate the purposes of the Act. And, as Justice Roberts explained in dissent, there were seven quite broad and often competing standards. If this delegation of authority is upheld, what delegation wouldn't be upheld? Justice Roberts wrote (in an omitted portion) that the Court effectively, even if not technically, overturned *Schechter Poultry.* Do you agree?

Justice Roberts, in dissent, claimed that it would be almost impossible to say that the Administrator had erred in fixing a particular price in light of the breadth of the standard and the purposes of the Act. If it's impossible to say that an agency made a mistake in light of the given principle, is that principle intelligible? Can you imagine at least some price which you would be willing to say violates Congress's policy choices in the statute? The majority seems to have agreed with Justice Roberts on the principle: "Only if we could say that there is an absence of standards for the guidance of the Administrator's action, so that it would be impossible in a proper proceeding to ascertain whether the will of Congress has been obeyed, would we be justified in overriding its choice of means for effecting its declared purpose of preventing inflation." Do you agree with Justice Roberts, or with the majority? Do you think it'd be possible to determine whether any particular price is consistent with the will of Congress?

2. *Other wage and price controls.* Perhaps *Yakus* could be justified as a wartime measure. But in 1970, Congress, in the Economic Stabilization Act, authorized the President "to issue such orders and regulations as he may deem appropriate to stabilize prices, rents, wages, and salaries at levels not less than those prevailing on May 25, 1970," but the President could make "such adjustments as may be necessary to prevent gross inequities." Pursuant to this authority, President Nixon imposed a 90-day freeze on wages and prices. An amendment the next year also required any price and wage freezes to be applicable to the entire economy, unless the President made specific findings that the wages and prices of one industry had been changing at a rate disproportionate to the rest of the economy. And the entire statute would expire after six months. Was this statute a violation of the nondelegation doctrine? Note that, just as in *Panama*

Refining, even if the subject-matter was limited—perhaps the President was authorized only to freeze wages and prices—the President was not given any guidance on when or why to impose such freezes. The statute authorized the President to make such regulations "as he may deem appropriate to stabilize prices, rents, wages, and salaries." A three-judge district court upheld the delegation. Amalgamated Meat Cutters & Butcher Workmen of N. Am., AFL-CIO v. Connally, 337 F. Supp. 737 (D.D.C. 1971).

3. ***Delegation and public choice theory.*** Can you understand why Congress might *want* to delegate its legislative power? In the 1970s, there was renewed interest in the nondelegation doctrine with the advent of "public choice theory," which basically posits that government actors act in their own self-interest just as do individuals in a private market. (See Chapter 1.B.4 for more detail.) Is delegating power in Congress's self-interest? John Hart Ely, in his famous *Democracy and Distrust,* thought it was:

> **CROSS REFERENCE**   Recall that Chapter 1 discussed the evolution of administrative law doctrine in response to "public choice theory," the idea the government actors are motivated by self-interest and profit-maximization just as private actors are in the free market. Does public choice theory help explain increasingly broad delegations of power?

The reasons things got switched around are not hard to discern. One is that it is simply easier, and it pays more visible political dividends, to play errand-boy-cum-ombudsman than to play one's part in a genuinely legislative process. How much more comfortable it must be simply to vote in favor of a bill calling for safe cars, clean air, or nondiscrimination, and to leave to others the chore of fleshing out what such a mandate might mean. . . . For the fact seems to be that on most hard issues our representatives quite shrewdly prefer not to have to stand up and be counted but rather to let some executive-branch bureaucrat, or perhaps some independent regulatory commission, "take the inevitable political heat." As Congressman Levitas put it, "When hard decisions have to be made, we pass the buck to the agencies with vaguely worded statutes." And as Congressman Flowers added, what comes later is a virtually no-loss situation: "[T]hen we stand back and say when our constituents are aggrieved or oppressed by various rules and regulations, 'Hey, it's not me. We didn't mean that. We passed this well-meaning legislation, and we intended for those people out there . . . to do exactly what we meant, and they did not do it.' "

John Hart Ely, Democracy and Distrust 131–32 (1980).

4. The Benzene Case. Ely was writing at the end of the 1970s, in which there was renewed interest in reinvigorating the nondelegation doctrine. In a single case in 1980, the Supreme Court kindled some hope that a nondelegation doctrine of some kind might be revived. In Industrial Union Dept., AFL-CIO v. American Petroleum Institute, 448 U.S. 607 (1980), known as "The Benzene Case," the Supreme Court narrowly construed a statute that otherwise might have posed a nondelegation problem. The Occupational Safety and Health Act of 1970 authorized the Secretary of Labor to promulgate occupational safety and health standards, which the statute defined as requiring "conditions, or the adoption or use of one or more practices, means, methods, operations, or processes, reasonably necessary or appropriate to provide safe or healthful employment and places of employment." § 3(8). The statute provided a further instruction for regulations involving toxic materials; for such materials, the Secretary had to "set the standard which most adequately assures, to the extent feasible, on the basis of the best available evidence, that no employee will suffer material impairment of health or functional capacity even if such employee has regular exposure to the hazard dealt with by such standard for the period of his working life." § 6(b)(5).

Pursuant to this statute, the Secretary promulgated a rule setting the exposure limit for the chemical benzene, a carcinogen, at one part per million parts of air (1 ppm). The best available data, however, showed that benzene created health risks at levels well above 10 ppm; the Court explained that the evidence of adverse effects at an exposure level of 1 ppm was "sketchy at best." Nevertheless, the Secretary had concluded that because "no safe exposure level can be determined," the exposure limit for benzene had to be set "at the lowest technologically feasible level that will not impair the viability of the industries regulated." The government argued that § 3(8), aside from a minimum requirement of rationality, imposed no limit on the agency's authority; the agency therefore looked only to § 6(b)(5), which seemed to allow it to set exposure limits to the lowest possible levels to ensure that "no employee will suffer material impairment of health or functional capacity."

The Supreme Court rejected the government's contention, and held "that § 3(8) requires the Secretary to find, as a threshold matter, that the toxic substance in question poses a *significant* health risk in the workplace" (emphasis added). The Court added, "If the Government was correct in arguing that neither § 3(8) nor § 6(b)(5) requires that the risk from a toxic substance be quantified sufficiently to enable the Secretary to characterize it as significant in an understandable way, the statute would make such a 'sweeping delegation of legislative power' that it might be unconstitutional under the Court's reasoning in" *Panama Refining* and *Schechter Poultry*. "A construction of the statute that avoids this kind of open-ended grant should certainly be favored." 448 U.S. at 646. Justice Rehnquist concurred in the judgment, but he would have held outright that the statute violated the nondelegation doctrine. The feasibility standard, he said, was a "mirage." Such a standard "renders meaningful judicial review impossible." The Court, Rehnquist wrote, "ought not to shy away from our judicial duty to invalidate unconstitutional delegations of legislative authority." Id. at 681, 686 (Rehnquist, J., concurring).

Note what the Court did in *The Benzene Case*. It did not invalidate the statute for violating the nondelegation doctrine, but *added*, as a matter of statutory "interpretation," a requirement that the agency make a finding that there was a significant health risk. The Court was deploying the canon of constitutional avoidance, by which it gives a statute an alternative plausible construction, even if not the best construction, to avoid serious constitutional doubts. Was the addition of a "significant health risk" finding a plausible alternative reading of the statute? Was the Court itself simply legislating here? Should it have struck down the statute instead? Whatever you think of the merits of deploying the canon of constitutional avoidance in this particular case, keep it in mind as a potential solution to nondelegation problems. The Supreme Court seems to have deployed this approach in its most recent nondelegation case.

 CROSS REFERENCE The canon of constitutional avoidance was one of our earlier statutory interpretation lessons. Do you see how it was deployed in *The Benzene Case*?

If there were any hopes that a nondelegation doctrine might be revived after *The Benzene Case,* those hopes were dashed in the following case, which the reader should analyze carefully: it raises some of the most fundamental questions about the role of agencies in our constitutional system.

Mistretta v. United States

488 U.S. 361 (1989)

JUSTICE BLACKMUN delivered the opinion of the Court.

In this litigation, we granted certiorari before judgment in the United States Court of Appeals for the Eighth Circuit in order to consider the constitutionality of the Sentencing Guidelines promulgated by the United States Sentencing Commission. . . .

I

For almost a century, the Federal Government employed in criminal cases a system of indeterminate sentencing. Statutes specified the penalties for crimes but nearly always gave the sentencing judge wide discretion to decide whether the offender should be incarcerated and for how long, whether he should be fined and how much, and whether some lesser restraint, such as probation, should be imposed instead of imprisonment or fine. This indeterminate-sentencing system was supplemented by the utilization of parole, by which an offender was returned to society under the "guidance and control" of a parole officer. . . .

As a result, the court and the officer were in positions to exercise, and usually did exercise, very broad discretion. . . .

Historically, federal sentencing—the function of determining the scope and extent of punishment—never has been thought to be assigned by the Constitution to the exclusive jurisdiction of any one of the three Branches of Government. Congress, of course, has the power to fix the sentence for a federal crime, and the scope of judicial discretion with respect to a sentence is subject to congressional control. Congress early abandoned fixed-sentence rigidity, however, and put in place a system of ranges within which the sentencer could choose the precise punishment. Congress delegated almost unfettered discretion to the sentencing judge to determine what the sentence should be within the customarily wide range so selected. This broad discretion was further enhanced by the power later granted the judge to suspend the sentence and by the resulting growth of an elaborate probation system. Also, with the advent of parole, Congress moved toward a "three-way sharing" of sentencing responsibility by granting corrections personnel in the Executive Branch the discretion to release a prisoner before the expiration of the sentence imposed by the judge. Thus, under the indeterminate-sentence system, Congress defined the maximum, the judge imposed a sentence within the statutory range (which he usually could replace with probation), and the Executive Branch's parole official eventually determined the actual duration of imprisonment. . . .

Fundamental and widespread dissatisfaction with the uncertainties and the disparities continued to be expressed. Congress had wrestled with the problem for more than a decade when, in 1984, it enacted the sweeping reforms that are at issue here. . . .

Before settling on a mandatory-guideline system, Congress considered other competing proposals for sentencing reform. It rejected strict determinate sentencing because it concluded that a guideline system would be successful in reducing sentence disparities while retaining the flexibility needed to adjust for unanticipated factors arising in a particular case. . . .

The Act, as adopted, revises the old sentencing process in several ways: . . . It makes the Sentencing Commission's guidelines binding on the courts, although it preserves for the judge the discretion to depart from the guideline applicable to a particular case if the judge finds an aggravating or mitigating factor present that the Commission did not adequately consider when formulating guidelines. §§ 3553(a) and (b). The Act also requires the court to state its reasons for the sentence imposed and to give "the specific reason" for imposing a sentence different from that described in the guideline. § 3553(c). . . .

The Commission is established "as an independent commission in the judicial branch of the United States." § 991(a). It has seven voting members (one of whom is the Chairman) appointed by the President "by and with the advice and consent of the Senate." "At least three of the members shall be Federal judges selected after considering a list of six judges recommended to the President by the Judicial Conference of the United States." No more than four members of the Commission shall be members of the same political party. The Attorney General, or his designee, is an ex officio non-voting member. The Chairman and other members of the Commission are subject to removal by the President "only for neglect of duty or malfeasance in office or for other good cause shown." Except for initial staggering of terms, a voting member serves for six years and may not serve more than two full terms. . . .

* * *

III

Petitioner argues that in delegating the power to promulgate sentencing guidelines for every federal criminal offense to an independent Sentencing Commission, Congress has granted the Commission excessive legislative discretion in violation of the constitutionally based nondelegation doctrine. We do not agree.

The nondelegation doctrine is rooted in the principle of separation of powers that underlies our tripartite system of Government. The Constitution provides that "[a]ll legislative Powers herein granted shall be vested in a Congress of the United States," U.S. Const., Art. I, § 1, and we long have insisted that "the integrity and maintenance of the system of government ordained by the Constitution" mandate that Congress generally cannot delegate its legislative power to another Branch. *Field v. Clark*, 143 U.S. 649, 692 (1892). We also have recognized, however, that the separation-of-powers principle, and the nondelegation doctrine in particular, do not prevent Congress from obtaining the assistance of its coordinate Branches. In a passage now enshrined in our jurisprudence, Chief Justice Taft, writing for the Court, explained our approach to such cooperative ventures: "In determining what [Congress] may do in seeking assistance from another branch, the extent and character of that assistance must be fixed according to common sense and the inherent necessities of the government co-ordination." *J.W. Hampton, Jr., & Co. v. United States*, 276 U.S. 394, 406 (1928). So long as Congress "shall lay down by legislative act an intelligible principle to which the person or body authorized to [exercise the delegated authority] is directed to conform, such legislative action is not a forbidden delegation of legislative power." *Id.* at 409.

Applying this "intelligible principle" test to congressional delegations, our jurisprudence has been driven by a practical understanding that in our increasingly complex society, replete with ever changing and more technical problems, Congress simply cannot do its job absent an ability to delegate power under broad general directives. See *Opp Cotton Mills, Inc. v. Administrator, Wage and Hour Div. of Dept. of Labor*, 312 U.S. 126, 145 (1941) ("In an increasingly complex society Congress obviously could not perform its functions if it were obliged to find all the facts subsidiary to the basic conclusions which support the defined legislative policy"). "The Constitution has never been regarded as denying to the Congress the necessary resources of flexibility and practicality, which will enable it to perform its function." *Panama Refining Co. v. Ryan*, 293

U.S. 388, 421 (1935). Accordingly, this Court has deemed it "constitutionally sufficient if Congress clearly delineates the general policy, the public agency which is to apply it, and the boundaries of this delegated authority." *American Power & Light Co. v. SEC,* 329 U.S. 90, 105 (1946).

Until 1935, this Court never struck down a challenged statute on delegation grounds. After invalidating in 1935 two statutes as excessive delegations, see *A.L.A. Schechter Poultry Corp. v. United States,* 295 U.S. 495, and Panama Refining Co. v. Ryan, supra, we have upheld, again without deviation, Congress' ability to delegate power under broad standards. See, *e.g., Lichter v. United States,* 334 U.S. 742, 785–786 (1948) (upholding delegation of authority to determine excessive profits); *American Power & Light Co. v. SEC,* 329 U.S. at 105 (upholding delegation of authority to Securities and Exchange Commission to prevent unfair or inequitable distribution of voting power among security holders); *Yakus v. United States,* 321 U.S. 414, 426 (1944) (upholding delegation to Price Administrator to fix commodity prices that would be fair and equitable, and would effectuate purposes of Emergency Price Control Act of 1942); *FPC v. Hope Natural Gas Co.,* 320 U.S. 591, 600 (1944) (upholding delegation to Federal Power Commission to determine just and reasonable rates); *National Broadcasting Co. v. United States,* 319 U.S. 190, 225–226 (1943) (upholding delegation to Federal Communications Commission to regulate broadcast licensing "as public interest, convenience, or necessity" require).

In light of our approval of these broad delegations, we harbor no doubt that Congress' delegation of authority to the Sentencing Commission is sufficiently specific and detailed to meet constitutional requirements. Congress charged the Commission with three goals: to "assure the meeting of the purposes of sentencing as set forth" in the Act; to "provide certainty and fairness in meeting the purposes of sentencing, avoiding unwarranted sentencing disparities among defendants with similar records . . . while maintaining sufficient flexibility to permit individualized sentences," where appropriate; and to "reflect, to the extent practicable, advancement in knowledge of human behavior as it relates to the criminal justice process." 28 U.S.C. § 991(b)(1). Congress further specified four "purposes" of sentencing that the Commission must pursue in carrying out its mandate: "to reflect the seriousness of the offense, to promote respect for the law, and to provide just punishment for the offense"; "to afford adequate deterrence to criminal conduct"; "to protect the public from further crimes of the defendant"; and "to provide the defendant with needed . . . correctional treatment." 18 U.S.C. § 3553(a)(2).

In addition, Congress prescribed the specific tool—the guidelines system—for the Commission to use in regulating sentencing. More particularly, Congress directed the Commission to develop a system of "sentencing ranges" applicable "for each category of offense involving each category of defendant." 28 U.S.C. § 994(b).[8] Congress instructed the Commission that these sentencing ranges must be consistent with pertinent provisions of Title 18 of the United States Code and could not include sentences in excess of the statutory maxima. Congress also required that for sentences of imprisonment, "the maximum of the range established for such a term shall not exceed the minimum of that range by more than the greater of 25 percent or 6 months, except that, if the minimum term of the range is 30 years or more, the maximum may be life imprisonment." § 994(b)(2). Moreover, Congress directed the Commission to use current average sentences "as a starting point" for its structuring of the sentencing ranges. § 994(m).

To guide the Commission in its formulation of offense categories, Congress directed it to consider seven factors: the grade of the offense; the aggravating and mitigating circumstances of the crime; the nature and degree of the harm caused by the crime; the community view of the gravity of the offense; the public concern generated by the crime; the deterrent effect that a particular sentence may have on others; and the current incidence of the offense. §§ 994(c)(1)–(7). Congress set forth 11 factors for the Commission to consider in establishing categories of defendants. These include the offender's age, education, vocational skills, mental and emotional condition, physical condition (including drug dependence), previous employment record, family ties and responsibilities, community ties, role in the offense, criminal history, and degree of dependence upon crime for a livelihood. § 994(d)(1)–(11). . . .

---

[8]   Congress mandated that the guidelines include:

"(A) a determination whether to impose a sentence [of] probation, a fine, or a term of imprisonment;

"(B) a determination as to the appropriate amount of a fine or the appropriate length of a term of probation or a term of imprisonment;

"(C) a determination whether a sentence to a term of imprisonment should include a requirement that the defendant be placed on a term of supervised release after imprisonment, and, if so, the appropriate length of such a term; and

"(D) a determination whether multiple sentences to terms of imprisonment should be ordered to run concurrently or consecutively." 28 U.S.C. § 994(a)(1).

In addition to these overarching constraints, Congress provided even more detailed guidance to the Commission about categories of offenses and offender characteristics. Congress directed that guidelines require a term of confinement at or near the statutory maximum for certain crimes of violence and for drug offenses, particularly when committed by recidivists. § 994(h). Congress further directed that the Commission assure a substantial term of imprisonment for an offense constituting a third felony conviction, for a career felon, for one convicted of a managerial role in a racketeering enterprise, for a crime of violence by an offender on release from a prior felony conviction, and for an offense involving a substantial quantity of narcotics. § 994(i). Congress also instructed "that the guidelines reflect . . . the general appropriateness of imposing a term of imprisonment" for a crime of violence that resulted in serious bodily injury. On the other hand, Congress directed that guidelines reflect the general inappropriateness of imposing a sentence of imprisonment "in cases in which the defendant is a first offender who has not been convicted of a crime of violence or an otherwise serious offense." § 994(j). Congress also enumerated various aggravating and mitigating circumstances, such as, respectively, multiple offenses or substantial assistance to the Government, to be reflected in the guidelines. §§ 994(*l*) and (n). In other words, although Congress granted the Commission substantial discretion in formulating guidelines, in actuality it legislated a full hierarchy of punishment—from near maximum imprisonment, to substantial imprisonment, to some imprisonment, to alternatives—and stipulated the most important offense and offender characteristics to place defendants within these categories.

We cannot dispute petitioner's contention that the Commission enjoys significant discretion in formulating guidelines. The Commission does have discretionary authority to determine the relative severity of federal crimes and to assess the relative weight of the offender characteristics that Congress listed for the Commission to consider. See §§ 994(c) and (d) (Commission instructed to consider enumerated factors as it deems them to be relevant). The Commission also has significant discretion to determine which crimes have been punished too leniently, and which too severely. § 994(m). Congress has called upon the Commission to exercise its judgment about which types of crimes and which types of criminals are to be considered similar for the purposes of sentencing. . . .

Developing proportionate penalties for hundreds of different crimes by a virtually limitless array of offenders is precisely the sort of intricate, labor-intensive task for which delegation to an expert body is especially appropriate. . . .

JUSTICE SCALIA, dissenting.

While the products of the Sentencing Commission's labors have been given the modest name "Guidelines," they have the force and effect of laws, prescribing the sentences criminal defendants are to receive. A judge who disregards them will be reversed. I dissent from today's decision because I can find no place within our constitutional system for an agency created by Congress to exercise no governmental power other than the making of laws.

I

There is no doubt that the Sentencing Commission has established significant, legally binding prescriptions governing application of governmental power against private individuals—indeed, application of the ultimate governmental power, short of capital punishment. Statutorily permissible sentences for particular crimes cover as broad a range as zero years to life, see, *e.g.*, 18 U.S.C. § 1201 (kidnapping), and within those ranges the Commission was given broad discretion to prescribe the "correct" sentence, 28 U.S.C. § 994(b)(2). Average prior sentences were to be a starting point for the Commission's inquiry, but it could and regularly did deviate from those averages as it thought appropriate. It chose, for example, to prescribe substantial increases over average prior sentences for white-collar crimes such as public corruption, antitrust violations, and tax evasion. Guidelines, at 2.31, 2.133, 2.140. For antitrust violations, before the Guidelines only 39% of those convicted served any imprisonment, and the average imprisonment was only 45 days, whereas the Guidelines prescribe base sentences (for defendants with no prior criminal conviction) ranging from 2-to-8 months to 10-to-16 months, depending upon the volume of commerce involved. See *id.* at 2.131, 5.2.

The Commission also determined when probation was permissible, imposing a strict system of controls because of its judgment that probation had been used for an "inappropriately high percentage of offenders guilty of certain economic crimes." *Id.* at 1.8. Moreover, the Commission had free rein in determining whether statutorily authorized fines should be imposed in addition to imprisonment, and if so, in what amounts. It ultimately decided that every nonindigent offender should pay a fine according to a schedule devised by the Commission. *Id.* at 5.18. Congress also gave the Commission discretion to determine whether 7 specified characteristics of offenses, and 11 specified characteristics of offenders, "have any relevance," and should be included among the factors varying the sentence. 28 U.S.C. §§ 994(c), (d). Of the latter, it included only three among the factors required to be considered, and declared the remainder not ordinarily relevant. Guidelines, at 5.29–5.31.

It should be apparent from the above that the decisions made by the Commission are far from technical, but are heavily laden (or ought to be) with value judgments and policy assessments. This fact is sharply reflected in the Commission's product, as described by the dissenting Commissioner:

> Under the guidelines, the judge could give the same sentence for abusive sexual contact that puts the child in fear as for unlawfully entering or remaining in the United States. Similarly, the guidelines permit equivalent sentences for the following pairs of offenses: drug trafficking and a violation of the Wild Free-Roaming Horses and Burros Act; arson with a destructive device and failure to surrender a cancelled naturalization certificate; operation of a common carrier under the influence of drugs that causes injury and alteration of one motor vehicle identification number; illegal trafficking in explosives and trespass; interference with a flight attendant and unlawful conduct relating to contraband cigarettes; aggravated assault and smuggling $11,000 worth of fish.

Petitioner's most fundamental and far-reaching challenge to the Commission is that Congress' commitment of such broad policy responsibility to any institution is an unconstitutional delegation of legislative power. It is difficult to imagine a principle more essential to democratic government than that upon which the doctrine of unconstitutional delegation is founded: Except in a few areas constitutionally committed to the Executive Branch, the basic policy decisions governing society are to be made by the Legislature. Our Members of Congress could not, even if they wished, vote all power to the President and adjourn *sine die*.

But while the doctrine of unconstitutional delegation is unquestionably a fundamental element of our constitutional system, it is not an element readily enforceable by the courts. Once it is conceded, as it must be, that no statute can be entirely precise, and that some judgments, even some judgments involving policy considerations, must be left to the officers executing the law and to the judges applying it, the debate over unconstitutional delegation becomes a debate not over a point of principle but over a question of degree. As Chief Justice Taft expressed the point for the Court in the landmark case of *J.W. Hampton, Jr., & Co. v. United States*, 276 U.S. 394, 406 (1928), the limits of delegation "must be fixed according to common sense and the inherent necessities of the governmental co-ordination." Since Congress is no less endowed with common sense than we are, and better equipped to inform itself of the "necessities" of government; and since the factors bearing upon those necessities are both multifarious and (in the nonpartisan sense) highly political . . . it is small wonder that we have almost never felt qualified to second-guess Congress regarding the permissible degree of policy judgment that can be left to those executing or applying the law. As the Court points out, we have invoked the doctrine of unconstitutional delegation to invalidate a law only twice in our history, over half a century ago. What legislated standard, one must wonder, can possibly be too vague to survive judicial scrutiny, when we have repeatedly upheld, in various contexts, a "public interest" standard? See, *e.g.*, *National Broadcasting Co. v. United States*, 319 U.S. 190, 216–217 (1943); *New York Central Securities Corp. v. United States*, 287 U.S. 12, 24–25 (1932).

In short, I fully agree with the Court's rejection of petitioner's contention that the doctrine of unconstitutional delegation of legislative authority has been violated because of the lack of intelligible, congressionally prescribed standards to guide the Commission.

II

Precisely because the scope of delegation is largely uncontrollable by the courts, we must be particularly rigorous in preserving the Constitution's structural restrictions that deter excessive delegation. The major one, it seems to me, is that the power to make law cannot be exercised by anyone other than Congress, except in conjunction with the lawful exercise of executive or judicial power.

The whole theory of *lawful* congressional "delegation" is not that Congress is sometimes too busy or too divided and can therefore assign its responsibility of making law to someone else; but rather that a certain degree of discretion, and thus of lawmaking, *inheres* in most executive or judicial action, and it is up to Congress, by the relative specificity or generality of its statutory commands, to determine—up to a point—how small or how large that degree shall be. Thus, the courts could be given the power to say precisely what constitutes a "restraint of trade," see *Standard Oil Co. of New Jersey v. United States*, 221 U.S. 1 (1911), or to adopt rules of procedure, see *Sibbach v. Wilson & Co.*, 312 U.S. 1, 22 (1941), or to prescribe by rule the manner in which their officers shall execute their judgments, *Wayman v. Southard*, 23 U.S. 1 (1825), because that "lawmaking" was ancillary to their exercise of judicial powers. And the Executive could be given the power to adopt policies and rules specifying in detail what radio and television licenses will be in the "public interest, convenience or necessity," because that was ancillary to the exercise of its executive powers in granting and policing licenses and making a "fair and equitable allocation" of the electromagnetic spectrum. See *Federal Radio Comm'n v. Nelson Brothers Bond & Mortgage Co.*, 289 U.S. 266, 285 (1933). Or to take examples closer to the case before us: Trial judges could be given the power to determine what factors justify a greater or lesser sentence within the statutorily prescribed limits because that was ancillary to their exercise of the judicial power of pronouncing sentence upon individual defendants. And the President, through the Parole Commission subject to his appointment and removal, could be given the power to issue Guidelines specifying when parole would be available, because that was ancillary to the President's exercise of the executive power to hold and release federal prisoners. . . .

The focus of controversy, in the long line of our so-called excessive delegation cases, has been whether the *degree* of generality contained in the authorization for exercise of executive or judicial powers in a particular field is so unacceptably high as to *amount* to a delegation of legislative powers. I say "so-called excessive delegation" because although that convenient terminology is often used, what is really at issue is whether there has been *any* delegation of legislative power, which occurs (rarely) when Congress authorizes the exercise of executive or judicial power without adequate standards. Strictly speaking, there is *no* acceptable delegation of legislative power. As John Locke put it almost 300 years ago, "[t]he power of the *legislative* being derived from the people by a positive voluntary grant and institution, can be no other, than what the positive grant conveyed, which being only to make *laws*, and not to make *legislators*, the *legislative* can have no power to transfer their authority of making laws, and place it in other hands." J. Locke, Second Treatise of Government 87 (R. Cox ed. 1982) (emphasis added). Or as we have less epigrammatically said: "That Congress cannot delegate legislative power to the President is a principle universally recognized as vital to the integrity and maintenance of the system of government ordained by the Constitution." *Field v. Clark, supra*, 143 U.S.

at 692. In the present case, however, a pure delegation of legislative power is precisely what we have before us. It is irrelevant whether the standards are adequate, because they are not standards related to the exercise of executive or judicial powers; they are, plainly and simply, standards for further legislation.

The lawmaking function of the Sentencing Commission is completely divorced from any responsibility for execution of the law or adjudication of private rights under the law. It is divorced from responsibility for execution of the law not only because the Commission is not said to be "located in the Executive Branch" (as I shall discuss presently, I doubt whether Congress can "locate" an entity within one Branch or another for constitutional purposes by merely saying so); but, more importantly, because the Commission neither exercises any executive power on its own, nor is subject to the control of the President who does. . . . And the Commission's lawmaking is completely divorced from the exercise of judicial powers since, not being a court, it has no judicial powers itself, nor is it subject to the control of any other body with judicial powers. The power to make law at issue here, in other words, is not ancillary but quite naked. The situation is no different in principle from what would exist if Congress gave the same power of writing sentencing laws to a congressional agency such as the General Accounting Office, or to members of its staff.

The delegation of lawmaking authority to the Commission is, in short, unsupported by any legitimating theory to explain why it is not a delegation of legislative power. To disregard structural legitimacy is wrong in itself—but since structure has purpose, the disregard also has adverse practical consequences. In this case, as suggested earlier, the consequence is to facilitate and encourage judicially uncontrollable delegation. Until our decision last Term in *Morrison v. Olson*, 487 U.S. 654 (1988), it could have been said that Congress could delegate lawmaking authority only at the expense of increasing the power of either the President or the courts. . . .

By reason of today's decision, I anticipate that Congress will find delegation of its lawmaking powers much more attractive in the future. If rulemaking can be entirely unrelated to the exercise of judicial or executive powers, I foresee all manner of "expert" bodies, insulated from the political process, to which Congress will delegate various portions of its lawmaking responsibility. How tempting to create an expert Medical Commission (mostly M.D.'s, with perhaps a few Ph.D.'s in moral philosophy) to dispose of such thorny, "no-win" political issues as the withholding of life-support systems in federally funded hospitals, or the use of fetal tissue for research. This is an undemocratic precedent that we set—not because of the scope of the delegated power, but because its recipient is not one of the three Branches of Government. The only governmental power the Commission possesses is the power to make law; and it is not the Congress.

* * *

Today's decision follows the regrettable tendency of our recent separation-of-powers jurisprudence to treat the Constitution as though it were no more than a generalized prescription that the functions of the Branches should not be commingled too much—how much is too much to be determined, case-by-case, by this Court. The Constitution is not that. Rather, as its name suggests, it is a prescribed structure, a framework, for the conduct of government. In designing that structure, the Framers *themselves* considered how much commingling was, in the generality of things, acceptable, and set forth their conclusions in the document. . . .

I think the Court errs, in other words, not so much because it mistakes the degree of commingling, but because it fails to recognize that this case is not about commingling, but about the creation of a new Branch altogether, a sort of junior-varsity Congress. It may well be that in some circumstances such a Branch would be desirable; perhaps the agency before us here will prove to be so. But there are many desirable dispositions that do not accord with the constitutional structure we live under. And in the long run the improvisation of a constitutional structure on the basis of currently perceived utility will be disastrous.

Notes and Questions

1. **Summary.** In *Mistretta*, the Supreme Court upheld a delegation of power to the U.S. Sentencing Commission to create mandatory sentencing guidelines for a variety of criminal offenses. The Court held that Congress's statute contained an intelligible principle. Justice Scalia did not disagree on this point; he agreed that the statute contained such a principle. His point was different. Scalia argued that most delegations of power have been upheld because the exercise of that delegated discretionary and policymaking power could be considered to be executive or judicial power when exercised by another branch of the government. Here, however, the Sentencing Commission did not exercise any *executive* or *judicial* powers. It merely prescribed the rules for sentencing. Do you understand why Justice Scalia thought this should make a difference? Do you agree that it should?

EXPERTISE VS. ACCOUNTABILITY
The Court in *Mistretta* argued societal complexity justifies modern delegations of legislative power. Do you agree?

---

2. Societal complexity. Citing earlier cases, the Court in Mistretta issued the following famous dictum: "[I]n our increasingly complex society, replete with ever changing and more technical problems, Congress simply cannot do its job absent an ability to delegate power under broad general directives." Do you agree with the Court? Is society too complex for Congress to decide on criminal sentencing? If complexity and expertise justify the delegation here, can you think of another solution that would have allowed Congress to take advantage of the Commission's expertise? Could the Commission have simply proposed its guidelines to Congress, which would then have to approve them? Or is there a reason Congress should not have to vote on the guidelines after they are proposed, or perhaps a reason why it might be impracticable for it to do so?

 **HISTORICAL PERSPECTIVE** Where else have we seen the argument that societal complexity demands administrative governance? Did Woodrow Wilson make a similar argument in 1887? What do you make of the fact that even 130 years ago some thought society was too complex for Congress to legislate in much detail?

Whitman v. American Trucking Ass'ns

531 U.S. 457 (2001)

JUSTICE SCALIA delivered the opinion of the Court.

These cases present the following question[ ]: (1) Whether § 109(b)(1) of the Clean Air Act (CAA) delegates legislative power to the Administrator of the Environmental Protection Agency (EPA). . . .

I

Section 109(a) of the CAA, 42 U.S.C. § 7409(a), requires the Administrator of the EPA to promulgate NAAQS [National Ambient Air Quality Standards] for each air pollutant for which "air quality criteria" have been issued under § 108. Once a NAAQS has been promulgated, the Administrator must review the standard (and the criteria on which it is based) "at five-year intervals" and make "such revisions . . . as may be appropriate." These cases arose when, on July 18, 1997, the Administrator revised the NAAQS for particulate matter and ozone. American Trucking Associations, Inc., and its co-respondents in No. 99–1257—which include, in addition to other private companies, the States of Michigan, Ohio, and West Virginia—challenged the new standards in the Court of Appeals for the District of Columbia Circuit . . . .

The District of Columbia Circuit . . . agreed . . . that § 109(b)(1) delegated legislative power to the Administrator in contravention of the United States Constitution, Art. I, § 1, because it found that the EPA had interpreted the statute to provide no "intelligible principle" to guide the agency's exercise of authority. *American Trucking Assns., Inc. v. EPA*, 175 F.3d 1027, 1034 (D.C. Cir. 1999). The court thought, however, that the EPA could perhaps avoid the unconstitutional delegation by adopting a restrictive construction of § 109(b)(1), so instead of declaring the section unconstitutional the court remanded the NAAQS to the agency. . . .

II

. . . . Section 109(b)(1) instructs the EPA to set primary ambient air quality standards "the attainment and maintenance of which . . . are requisite to protect the public health" with "an adequate margin of safety." 42 U.S.C. § 7409(b)(1). Were it not for the hundreds of pages of briefing respondents have submitted on the issue, one would have thought it fairly clear that this text does not permit the EPA to consider costs in setting the standards. The language, as one scholar has noted, "is absolute." The EPA, "based on" the information about health effects contained in the technical "criteria" documents compiled under § 108(a)(2), is to identify the maximum airborne concentration of a pollutant that the public health can tolerate, decrease the concentration to provide an "adequate" margin of safety, and set the standard at that level. . . .

* * *

III

Section 109(b)(1) of the CAA instructs the EPA to set "ambient air quality standards the attainment and maintenance of which in the judgment of the Administrator, based on [the] criteria [documents of § 108] and allowing an adequate margin of safety, are requisite to protect the public health." 42 U.S.C. § 7409(b)(1). The Court of Appeals held that this section as interpreted by the Administrator did not provide an "intelligible principle" to guide the EPA's exercise of authority in setting NAAQS. "[The] EPA," it said, "lack[ed] any determinate criteria for drawing lines. It has failed to state intelligibly how much is too much." 175 F.3d, at 1034. The court hence found that the EPA's interpretation (but not the statute itself) violated the nondelegation doctrine. *Id.* at 1038. We disagree.

In a delegation challenge, the constitutional question is whether the statute has delegated legislative power to the agency. Article I, § 1, of the Constitution vests "[a]ll legislative Powers herein granted . . . in a Congress of the United States." This text permits no delegation of those powers, and so we repeatedly have said that when Congress confers decisionmaking authority upon agencies *Congress* must "lay down by legislative act an intelligible principle to which the person or body authorized to [act] is directed to conform." *J.W. Hampton, Jr., & Co. v. United States*, 276 U.S. 394, 409 (1928). We have never suggested that an agency can cure an unlawful delegation of legislative power by adopting in its discretion a limiting construction of the statute. . . . The idea that an agency can cure an unconstitutionally standardless delegation of power by declining to exercise some of that power seems to us internally contradictory. The very choice of which portion of the power to exercise—that is to say, the prescription of the standard that Congress had omitted—would *itself* be an exercise of the forbidden legislative authority. Whether the statute delegates legislative power is a question for the courts, and an agency's voluntary self-denial has no bearing upon the answer.

We agree with the Solicitor General that the text of § 109(b)(1) of the CAA at a minimum requires that "[f]or a discrete set of pollutants and based on published air quality criteria that reflect the latest scientific knowledge, [the] EPA must establish uniform national standards at a level that is requisite to protect public health from the adverse effects of the pollutant in the ambient air." Requisite, in turn, "mean[s] sufficient, but not more than necessary." These limits on the EPA's discretion are strikingly similar to the ones we approved in *Touby v. United States*, 500 U.S. 160 (1991), which permitted the Attorney General to designate a drug as a controlled substance for purposes of criminal drug enforcement if doing so was " 'necessary to avoid an imminent hazard to the public safety.' " They also resemble the Occupational Safety and Health Act of 1970 provision requiring the agency to " 'set the standard which most adequately assures, to the extent feasible, on the basis of the best available evidence, that no employee will suffer any impairment of health' "—which the Court upheld in *Industrial Union Dept., AFL-CIO v. American Petroleum Institute*, 448 U.S. 607, 646 (1980) . . . .

The scope of discretion § 109(b)(1) allows is in fact well within the outer limits of our nondelegation precedents. In the history of the Court we have found the requisite "intelligible principle" lacking in only two statutes, one of which provided literally no guidance for the exercise of discretion, and the other of which conferred authority to regulate the entire economy on the basis of no more precise a standard than stimulating the economy by assuring "fair competition." See *Panama Refining Co. v. Ryan*, 293 U.S. 388 (1935); *A.L.A. Schechter Poultry Corp. v. United States*, 295 U.S. 495 (1935). We have, on the other hand, upheld the validity of § 11(b)(2) of the Public Utility Holding Company Act of 1935, which gave the Securities and Exchange Commission authority to modify the structure of holding company systems so as to ensure that they are not "unduly or unnecessarily complicate[d]" and do not "unfairly or inequitably distribute voting power among security holders." *American Power & Light Co. v. SEC*, 329 U.S. 90, 104 (1946). We have approved the wartime conferral of agency power to fix the prices of commodities at a level that " 'will be generally fair and equitable and will effectuate the [in some respects conflicting] purposes of th[e] Act." *Yakus v. United States*, 321 U.S. 414, 420, 423–426 (1944). And we have found an "intelligible principle" in various statutes authorizing regulation in the "public interest." See, *e.g.*, *National Broadcasting Co. v. United States*, 319 U.S. 190, 225–226 (1943) (Federal Communications Commission's power to regulate airwaves); *New York Central Securities Corp. v. United States*, 287 U.S. 12, 24–25 (1932) (Interstate Commerce Commission's power to approve railroad consolidations). In short, we have "almost never felt qualified to second-guess Congress regarding the permissible degree of policy judgment that can be left to those executing or applying the law." *Mistretta v. United States*, 488 U.S. 361, 416 (1989) (SCALIA, J., dissenting); see *id.* at 373 (majority opinion).

It is true enough that the degree of agency discretion that is acceptable varies according to the scope of the power congressionally conferred. See *Loving v. United States,* 517 U.S. at 772–773; *United States v. Mazurie,* 419 U.S. 544, 556–557 (1975). While Congress need not provide any direction to the EPA regarding the manner in which it is to define "country elevators," which are to be exempt from new-stationary-source regulations governing grain elevators, see 42 U.S.C. § 7411(i), it must provide substantial guidance on setting air standards that affect the entire national economy. But even in sweeping regulatory schemes we have never demanded, as the Court of Appeals did here, that statutes provide a "determinate criterion" for saying "how much [of the regulated harm] is too much." 175 F.3d, at 1034. In *Touby,* for example, we did not require the statute to decree how "imminent" was too imminent, or how "necessary" was necessary enough, or even—most relevant here—how "hazardous" was too hazardous. . . . "[A] certain degree of discretion, and thus of lawmaking, inheres in most executive or judicial action." *Mistretta v. United States, supra,* at 417 (SCALIA, J., dissenting) (emphasis deleted). Section 109(b)(1) of the CAA, which to repeat we interpret as requiring the EPA to set air quality standards at the level that is "requisite"—that is, not lower or higher than is necessary—to protect the public health with an adequate margin of safety, fits comfortably within the scope of discretion permitted by our precedent. . . .

JUSTICE THOMAS, concurring.

I agree with the majority that § 109's directive to the agency is no less an "intelligible principle" than a host of other directives that we have approved. I also agree that the Court of Appeals' remand to the agency to make its own corrective interpretation does not accord with our understanding of the delegation issue. I write separately, however, to express my concern that there may nevertheless be a genuine constitutional problem with § 109, a problem which the parties did not address.

The parties to these cases who briefed the constitutional issue wrangled over constitutional doctrine with barely a nod to the text of the Constitution. Although this Court since 1928 has treated the "intelligible principle" requirement as the only constitutional limit on congressional grants of power to administrative agencies, the Constitution does not speak of "intelligible principles." Rather, it speaks in much simpler terms: *"All* legislative Powers herein granted shall be vested in a Congress." U.S. Const., Art. 1, § 1 (emphasis added). I am not convinced that the intelligible principle doctrine serves to prevent all cessions of legislative power. I believe that there are cases in which the principle is intelligible and yet the significance of the delegated decision is simply too great for the decision to be called anything other than "legislative."

As it is, none of the parties to these cases has examined the text of the Constitution or asked us to reconsider our precedents on cessions of legislative power. On a future day, however, I would be willing to address the question whether our delegation jurisprudence has strayed too far from our Founders' understanding of separation of powers.

JUSTICE STEVENS, with whom JUSTICE SOUTER joins, concurring in part and concurring in the judgment.

Section 109(b)(1) delegates to the Administrator of the Environmental Protection Agency (EPA) the authority to promulgate national ambient air quality standards (NAAQS). In Part III of its opinion, the Court convincingly explains why the Court of Appeals erred when it concluded that § 109 effected "an unconstitutional delegation of legislative power." I wholeheartedly endorse the Court's result and endorse its explanation of its reasons, albeit with the following caveat.

The Court has two choices. We could choose to articulate our ultimate disposition of this issue by frankly acknowledging that the power delegated to the EPA is "legislative" but nevertheless conclude that the delegation is constitutional because adequately limited by the terms of the authorizing statute. Alternatively, we could pretend, as the Court does, that the authority delegated to the EPA is somehow not "legislative power." Despite the fact that there is language in our opinions that supports the Court's articulation of our holding, I am persuaded that it would be both wiser and more faithful to what we have actually done in delegation cases to admit that agency rulemaking authority is "legislative power."

The proper characterization of governmental power should generally depend on the nature of the power, not on the identity of the person exercising it. See Black's Law Dictionary 899 (6th ed. 1990) (defining "legislation" as, *inter alia*, "[f]ormulation of rule[s] for the future"); 1 K. Davis & R. Pierce, Administrative Law Treatise § 2.3, p. 37 (3d ed. 1994) ("If legislative power means the power to make rules of conduct that bind everyone based on resolution of major policy issues, scores of agencies exercise legislative power routinely by promulgating what are candidly called 'legislative rules' "). If the NAAQS that the EPA promulgated had been prescribed by Congress, everyone would agree that those rules would be the product of an exercise of "legislative power." The same characterization is appropriate when an agency exercises rulemaking authority pursuant to a permissible delegation from Congress.

My view is not only more faithful to normal English usage, but is also fully consistent with the text of the Constitution. In Article I, the Framers vested "All legislative Powers" in the Congress, Art. I, § 1, just as in Article II they vested the "executive Power" in the President, Art. II, § 1. Those provisions do not purport to limit the authority of either recipient of power to delegate authority to others. Surely the authority granted to members of the Cabinet and federal law enforcement agents is properly characterized as "Executive" even though not exercised by the President.

It seems clear that an executive agency's exercise of rulemaking authority pursuant to a valid delegation from Congress is "legislative." As long as the delegation provides a sufficiently intelligible principle, there is nothing inherently unconstitutional about it. . . .

[A concurrence by JUSTICE BREYER, on a separate issue, is omitted.—Ed.]

NOTES AND QUESTIONS

1. Summary. In *Whitman,* the D.C. Circuit had held that the agency's interpretation of its statutory authority violated the nondelegation doctrine because the regulation did not specify or clarify how much of a given pollution was too much for purposes of the Act. The Supreme Court rejected this reasoning, noting that it is the *statute itself* that either violates or does not violate the nondelegation doctrine. After all, an agency's regulation isn't a delegation of power from Congress; it is made *pursuant to* a delegation from Congress.

2. Isn't this all legislative power? Justice Stevens, in concurrence, argued intriguingly that the Court ought to acknowledge openly that Congress had delegated legislative power to the EPA. Justice Stevens, however, thought there was no constitutional problem with such a delegation. After all, the Constitution doesn't say Congress can't delegate its power; indeed, the executive power is vested in the President, but many executive branch officers like FBI agents and prosecutors exercise "executive power," presumably delegated from the President. Do you find Stevens' point about executive power persuasive? Does it depend on your view of the President's authority to direct, control, and possibly remove officers that she disagrees with? If the President can do those things, isn't the executive power still ultimately vested in the President, even if lower-level officers exercise a part of that executive power?

NONEXCLUSIVE POWER

Justice Stevens argues that the EPA was in fact exercising legislative power, but that delegations of such power were constitutional. Do you agree? Might it make more sense to think of the EPA's power as "nonexclusive"—that is, both Congress and the executive could have exercised that power?

Whether or not you find Justice Stevens' point about the ability of the executive to delegate power, isn't he right that Congress routinely delegates legislative power in fact, even if the Supreme Court's doctrine refuses to recognize it as "legislative"? Recall what Justice Scalia wrote for the Court in *City of Arlington v. FCC*: "Agencies make rules . . . and conduct adjudications . . . and have done so since the beginning of the Republic. These activities take 'legislative' and 'judicial' forms, but they are exercises of—indeed, under our constitutional structure they *must be* exercises of—the 'executive Power.' " City of Arlington v. FCC, 569 U.S. 290, 304 n.4 (2013). Perhaps they must be exercises of executive power to be constitutional, but are they *actually* exercises of executive power, or would it be better to recognize rulemakings as exercises of legislative power? Your present casebook author once flirted with this idea, although he now disclaims it. See Ilan Wurman, *Constitutional Administration*, 69 Stan. L. Rev. 359 (2017).

   3.   *What is "legislative power"?* What exactly is "legislative power"? Justice Stevens quoted Black's Law Dictionary for the proposition that it is the "[f]ormulation of rule[s] for the future." What do you think of this definition? Might it be overbroad? Weren't George Washington's regulations respecting the invalid veterans of the revolutionary war the "formulation of rules for the future"? Surely Congress could have made those regulations for itself, but did it have to? Recall that Justice Thomas, in the *Amtrak* case, see supra p. 57, argued that legislative power was the making of only specific kinds of rules: those that affected private rights or private conduct. Is that a better test? Wouldn't the regulations of the steamboat inspectors under the 1852 Steamboat Act setting

passenger limits and creating the rules for passing ships affect private rights and conduct? Did Congress unlawfully delegate power to the steamboat inspectors? Keep these questions in mind as you read the final nondelegation case. We shall revisit theories of what constitutes "legislative power" in the notes to that case.

Gundy v. United States

139 S. Ct. 2116 (2019)

Justice Kagan announced the judgment of the Court and delivered an opinion, in which Justice Ginsburg, Justice Breyer, and Justice Soto-mayor join.

The nondelegation doctrine bars Congress from transferring its legislative power to another branch of Government. This case requires us to decide whether 34 U. S. C. § 20913(d), enacted as part of the Sex Offender Registration and Notification Act (SORNA), violates that doctrine. We hold it does not. Under § 20913(d), the Attorney General must apply SORNA's registration requirements as soon as feasible to offenders convicted before the statute's enactment. That delegation easily passes constitutional muster.

I

Congress has sought, for the past quarter century, to combat sex crimes and crimes against children through sex-offender registration schemes. In 1994, Congress first conditioned certain federal funds on States' adoption of registration laws meeting prescribed minimum standards. Two years later, Congress strengthened those standards, most notably by insisting that States inform local communities of registrants' addresses. By that time, every State and the District of Columbia had enacted a sex-offender registration law. But the state statutes varied along many dimensions, and Congress came to realize that their "loopholes and deficiencies" had allowed over 100,000 sex offenders (about 20% of the total) to escape registration. In 2006, to address those failings, Congress enacted SORNA.

SORNA makes "more uniform and effective" the prior "patchwork" of sex-offender registration systems. *Reynolds v. United States*, 565 U.S. 432, 435 (2012). The Act's express "purpose" is "to protect the public from sex offenders and offenders against children" by "establish[ing] a comprehensive national system for [their] registration." § 20901. To that end, SORNA covers more sex offenders, and imposes more onerous registration requirements, than most States had before. The Act also backs up those requirements with new criminal penalties. Any person required to register under SORNA who knowingly fails to do so (and who travels in interstate commerce) may be imprisoned for up to ten years.

The basic registration scheme works as follows. A "sex offender" is defined as "an individual who was convicted of" specified criminal offenses: all offenses "involving a sexual act or sexual contact" and additional offenses "against a minor." Such an individual must register—provide his name, address, and certain other information—in every State where he resides, works, or studies. And he must keep the registration current, and periodically report in person to a law enforcement office, for a period of between fifteen years and life (depending on the severity of his crime and his history of recidivism).

Section 20913—the disputed provision here—elaborates the "[i]nitial registration" requirements for sex offenders. Subsection (b) sets out the general rule: An offender must register "before completing a sentence of imprisonment with respect to the offense giving rise to the registration requirement" (or, if the offender is not sentenced to prison, "not later than [three] business days after being sentenced"). Two provisions down, subsection (d) addresses (in its title's words) the "[i]nitial registration of sex offenders unable to comply with subsection (b)." The provision states:

> "The Attorney General shall have the authority to specify the applicability of the requirements of this subchapter to sex offenders convicted before the enactment of this chapter . . . and to prescribe rules for the registration of any such sex offenders and for other categories of sex offenders who are unable to comply with subsection (b)."

Subsection (d), in other words, focuses on individuals convicted of a sex offense before SORNA's enactment—a group we will call pre-Act offenders. Many of these individuals were unregistered at the time of SORNA's enactment, either because pre-existing law did not cover them or because they had successfully evaded that law (so were "lost" to the system). And of those potential new registrants, many or most could not comply with subsection (b)'s registration rule because they had already completed their prison sentences. For the entire group of pre-Act offenders, once again, the Attorney General "shall have the authority" to "specify the applicability" of SORNA's registration requirements and "to prescribe rules for [their] registration."

Under that delegated authority, the Attorney General issued an interim rule in February 2007, specifying that SORNA's registration requirements apply in full to "sex offenders convicted of the offense for which registration is required prior to the enactment of that Act." 72 Fed. Reg. 8897. The final rule, issued in December 2010, reiterated that SORNA applies to all pre-Act offenders. 75 Fed. Reg. 81850. That rule has remained the same to this day.

Petitioner Herman Gundy is a pre-Act offender. The year before SOR-NA's enactment, he pleaded guilty under Maryland law for sexually assaulting a minor. After his release from prison in 2012, Gundy came to live in New York. But he never registered there as a sex offender. A few years later, he was convicted for failing to register, in violation of § 2250. He argued below (among other things) that Congress unconstitutionally delegated legislative power when it authorized the Attorney General to "specify the applicability" of SORNA's registration requirements to pre-Act offenders. § 20913(d). The District Court and Court of Appeals for the Second Circuit rejected that claim, as had every other court (including eleven Courts of Appeals) to consider the issue. We nonetheless granted certiorari. Today, we join the consensus and affirm.

II

Article I of the Constitution provides that "[a]ll legislative Powers herein granted shall be vested in a Congress of the United States." § 1. Accompanying that assignment of power to Congress is a bar on its further delegation. Congress, this Court explained early on, may not transfer to another branch "powers which are strictly and exclusively legislative." *Wayman* v. *Southard*, 10 Wheat. 1, 42–43 (1825). But the Constitution does not "deny[ ] to the Congress the necessary resources of flexibility and practicality [that enable it] to perform its function[s]." *Yakus* v. *United States*, 321 U.S. 414, 425 (1944). Congress may "obtain[ ] the assistance of its coordinate Branches"—and in particular, may confer substantial discretion on executive agencies to implement and enforce the laws. *Mistretta* v. *United States*, 488 U.S. 361, 372 (1989). "[I]n our increasingly complex society, replete with ever changing and more technical problems," this Court has understood that "Congress simply cannot do its job absent an ability to delegate power under broad general directives." *Ibid.* So we have held, time and again, that a statutory delegation is constitutional as long as Congress "lay[s] down by legislative act an intelligible principle to which the person or body authorized to [exercise the delegated authority] is directed to conform." *Ibid.* (quoting *J. W. Hampton, Jr., & Co.* v. *United States*, 276 U.S. 394, 409 (1928)).

Given that standard, a nondelegation inquiry always begins (and often almost ends) with statutory interpretation. The constitutional question is whether Congress has supplied an intelligible principle to guide the delegee's use of discretion. So the answer requires construing the challenged statute to figure out what task it delegates and what instructions it provides. Only after a court has determined a challenged statute's meaning can it decide whether the law sufficiently guides executive discretion to accord with Article I. And indeed, once a court interprets the statute, it may find that the constitutional question all but answers itself.

That is the case here, because § 20913(d) does not give the Attorney General anything like the "unguided" and "unchecked" authority that Gundy says. The provision, in Gundy's view, "grants the Attorney General plenary power to determine SORNA's applicability to pre-Act offenders—to require them to register, or not, as she sees fit, and to change her policy for any reason and at any time." If that were so, we would face a nondelegation question. But it is not. This Court has already interpreted § 20913(d) to say something different—to require the Attorney General to apply SORNA to all pre-Act offenders as soon as feasible. See *Reynolds*, 565 U. S. at 442–443. And revisiting that issue yet more fully today, we reach the same conclusion. The text, considered alongside its context, purpose, and history, makes clear that the Attorney General's discretion extends only to considering and addressing feasibility issues. Given that statutory meaning, Gundy's constitutional claim must fail. Section 20913(d)'s delegation falls well within permissible bounds.

* * *

B

Recall again the delegation provision at issue. Congress gave the Attorney General authority to "specify the applicability" of SORNA's requirements to pre-Act offenders. § 20913(d). And in the second half of the same sentence, Congress gave him authority to "prescribe rules for the registration of any such sex offenders . . . who are unable to comply with" subsection (b)'s initial registration requirement. What does the delegation in § 20913(d) allow the Attorney General to do?

The different answers on offer here reflect competing views of statutory interpretation. As noted above, Gundy urges us to read § 20913(d) to empower the Attorney General to do whatever he wants as to pre-Act offenders: He may make them all register immediately or he may exempt them from registration forever (or he may do anything in between). Gundy bases that argument on the first half of § 20913(d), isolated from everything else—from the second half of the same section, from surrounding provisions in SORNA, and from any conception of the statute's history and purpose. . . .

This Court has long refused to construe words "in a vacuum," as Gundy attempts. *Davis* v. *Michigan Dept. of Treasury*, 489 U.S. 803, 809 (1989). "It is a fundamental canon of statutory construction that the words of a statute must be read in their context and with a view to their place in the overall statutory scheme." *National Assn. of Home Builders* v. *Defenders of Wildlife*, 551 U.S. 644, 666 (2007). And beyond context and structure, the Court often looks to "history [and] purpose" to divine the meaning of language. *Maracich* v. *Spears*, 570 U.S. 48, 76 (2013). . . .

So begin at the beginning, with the "[d]eclaration of purpose" that is SOR-NA's first sentence. There, Congress announced . . . that "to protect the public," it was "establish[ing] a comprehensive national system for the registration" of "sex offenders and offenders against children." § 20901. The term "comprehensive" has a clear meaning—something that is all-encompassing or sweeping. That description could not fit the system SORNA created if the Attorney General could decline, for any reason or no reason at all, to apply SORNA to all pre-Act offenders. After all, for many years after SORNA's enactment, the great majority of sex offenders in the country would be pre-Act offenders. If Gundy were right, all of those offenders could be exempt from SORNA's registration requirements. So the mismatch between SORNA's statement of purpose and Gundy's view of § 20913(d) is as stark as stark comes. Responding to that patent disparity, Gundy urges us to ignore SORNA's statement of purpose because it is "located in the Act's preface" rather than "tied" specifically to § 20913(d). But the placement of such a statement within a statute makes no difference. See A. Scalia & B. Garner, Reading Law: The Interpretation of Legal Texts 220 (2012). Wherever it resides, it is "an appropriate guide" to the "meaning of the [statute's] operative provisions." *Id.*, at 218. And here it makes clear that SORNA was supposed to apply to all pre-Act offenders—which precludes Gundy's construction of § 20913(d).

The Act's definition of "sex offender" . . . makes the same point. Under that definition, a "sex offender" is "an individual who was convicted of a sex offense." § 0911(1). Note the tense: "was," not "is." This Court has often "looked to Congress' choice of verb tense to ascertain a statute's temporal reach," including when interpreting other SORNA provisions. Here, Congress's use of the past tense to define the term "sex offender" shows that SORNA was not merely forward-looking. The word "is" would have taken care of all future offenders. The word "was" served to bring in the hundreds of thousands of persons previously found guilty of a sex offense, and thought to pose a current threat to the public. The tense of the "sex offender" definition thus confirms that the delegation allows only temporary exclusions, as necessary to address feasibility issues. Contra Gundy, it does not sweep so wide as to make a laughingstock of the statute's core definition.

The Act's legislative history backs up everything said above by showing that the need to register pre-Act offenders was front and center in Congress's thinking. . . . Recall that Congress designed SORNA to address "loopholes and deficiencies" in existing registration laws. And no problem attracted greater attention than the large number of sex offenders who had slipped the system. . . .

With that context and background established, we may return to § 20913(d). As we have noted, Gundy makes his stand there (and there only), insisting that the lonesome phrase "specify the applicability" ends this case. But in so doing, Gundy ignores even the rest of the section that phrase is in. Both the title and the remaining text of that section pinpoint one of the "practical problems" discussed above: . . . The phrase instead means "specify *how* to apply SORNA" to pre-Act offenders if transitional difficulties require some delay. . . . Under the law, he had to order their registration as soon as feasible.

And no Attorney General has used (or, apparently, thought to use) § 20913(d) in any more expansive way. To the contrary. Within a year of SORNA's enactment (217 days, to be precise), the Attorney General determined that SORNA would apply immediately to pre-Act offenders. That rule has remained in force ever since . . . .

C

Now that we have determined what § 20913(d) means, we can consider whether it violates the Constitution. The question becomes: Did Congress make an impermissible delegation when it instructed the Attorney General to apply

SORNA's registration requirements to pre-Act offenders as soon as feasible? Under this Court's long-established law, that question is easy. Its answer is no.

As noted earlier, this Court has held that a delegation is constitutional so long as Congress has set out an "intelligible principle" to guide the delegee's exercise of authority. . . . Those standards, the Court has made clear, are not demanding. "[W]e have 'almost never felt qualified to second-guess Congress regarding the permissible degree of policy judgment that can be left to those executing or applying the law.'" *Whitman*, 531 U.S. at 474–475. Only twice in this country's history (and that in a single year) have we found a delegation excessive—in each case because "Congress had failed to articulate *any* policy or standard" to confine discretion. By contrast, we have over and over upheld even very broad delegations. Here is a sample: We have approved delegations to various agencies to regulate in the "public interest." We have sustained authorizations for agencies to set "fair and equitable" prices and "just and reasonable" rates. We more recently affirmed a delegation to an agency to issue whatever air quality standards are "requisite to protect the public health." And so forth.

In that context, the delegation in SORNA easily passes muster . . . .

Indeed, if SORNA's delegation is unconstitutional, then most of Government is unconstitutional—dependent as Congress is on the need to give discretion to executive officials to implement its programs. . . . Among the judgments often left to executive officials are ones involving feasibility. In fact, standards of that kind are ubiquitous in the U. S. Code. . . .

We therefore affirm the judgment of the Court of Appeals.

JUSTICE ALITO, concurring in the judgment.

The Constitution confers on Congress certain "legislative [p]owers," Art. I, § 1, and does not permit Congress to delegate them to another branch of the Government. Nevertheless, since 1935, the Court has uniformly rejected nondelegation arguments and has upheld provisions that authorized agencies to adopt important rules pursuant to extraordinarily capacious standards. See *ibid.*

If a majority of this Court were willing to reconsider the approach we have taken for the past 84 years, I would support that effort. But because a majority is not willing to do that, it would be freakish to single out the provision at issue here for special treatment.

Because I cannot say that the statute lacks a discernable standard that is adequate under the approach this Court has taken for many years, I vote to affirm.

Justice Gorsuch, with whom The Chief Justice and Justice Thomas join, dissenting.

[Justice Gorsuch puts all of his citations in footnotes. The citations which are retained in the following excerpt are moved in-line to the text.—Ed.]

The Constitution promises that only the people's elected representatives may adopt new federal laws restricting liberty. Yet the statute before us scrambles that design. It purports to endow the nation's chief prosecutor with the power to write his own criminal code governing the lives of a half-million citizens. Yes, those affected are some of the least popular among us. But if a single executive branch official can write laws restricting the liberty of this group of persons, what does that mean for the next? . . .

I

For individuals convicted of sex offenses *after* Congress adopted the Sex Offender Registration and Notification Act (SORNA) in 2006, the statute offers detailed instructions. It requires them "to provide state governments with (and to update) information, such as names and current addresses, for inclusion on state and federal sex offender registries." The law divides offenders into three tiers based on the seriousness of their crimes: Some must register for 15 years, others for 25 years, and still others for life. The statute proceeds to set registration deadlines: Offenders sentenced to prison must register before they're released, while others must register within three business days after sentencing. The statute explains when and how offenders must update their registrations. And the statute specifies particular penalties for failing to comply with its commands. On and on the statute goes for more than 20 pages of the U. S. Code.

But what about those convicted of sex offenses *before* the Act's adoption? At the time of SORNA's enactment, the nation's population of sex offenders exceeded 500,000, and Congress concluded that something had to be done about these "pre-Act" offenders too. But it seems Congress couldn't agree what that should be. The treatment of pre-Act offenders proved a "controversial issue with major policy significance and practical ramifications for states." Logan, The Adam Walsh Act and the Failed Promise of Administrative Federalism, 78 Geo. Wash. L. Rev. 993, 999–1000 (2010). Among other things, applying

SORNA immediately to this group threatened to impose unpopular and costly burdens on States and localities by forcing them to adopt or overhaul their own sex offender registration schemes. So Congress simply passed the problem to the Attorney General. For all half-million pre-Act offenders, the law says only this, in 34 U. S. C. § 20913(d):

> "The Attorney General shall have the authority to specify the applicability of the requirements of this subchapter to sex offenders convicted before the enactment of this chapter . . . and to prescribe rules for the registration of any such sex offender."

Yes, that's it. The breadth of the authority Congress granted to the Attorney General in these few words can only be described as vast. As the Department of Justice itself has acknowledged, SORNA "does not require the Attorney General" to impose registration requirements on pre-Act offenders "within a certain time frame or by a date certain; it does not require him to act at all." If the Attorney General does choose to act, he can require all pre-Act offenders to register, or he can "require some but not all to register." For those he requires to register, the Attorney General may impose "some but not all of [SORNA's] registration requirements," as he pleases. And he is free to change his mind on any of these matters "at any given time or over the course of different [political] administrations." Congress thus gave the Attorney General free rein to write the rules for virtually the entire existing sex offender population in this country—a situation that promised to persist for years or decades until pre-Act offenders passed away or fulfilled the terms of their registration obligations and post-Act offenders came to predominate.

Unsurprisingly, different Attorneys General have exercised their discretion in different ways. See, *e.g.,* 72 Fed. Reg. 8894 (2007); 73 Fed. Reg. 38030 (2008); 76 Fed. Reg. 1639 (2011). For six months after SORNA's enactment, Attorney General Gonzales left past offenders alone. Then the pendulum swung the other direction when the Department of Justice issued an interim rule requiring pre-Act offenders to follow all the same rules as post-Act offenders. 28 CFR § 72.3 (2007); 72 Fed. Reg. 8894. A year later, Attorney General Mukasey issued more new guidelines, this time directing the States to register some but not all past offenders. See 73 Fed. Reg. 38030. Three years after that, Attorney General Holder required the States to register only those pre-Act offenders convicted of a new felony after SORNA's enactment. See 76 Fed. Reg. 1639. Various Attorneys General have also taken different positions on whether pre-Act offenders might be entitled to credit for time spent in the community before SORNA was enacted. Compare 73 Fed. Reg. 38036 (no credit given) with 75 Fed. Reg. 81851 (full credit given).

These unbounded policy choices have profound consequences for the people they affect. Take our case. Before SORNA's enactment, Herman Gundy pleaded guilty in 2005 to a sexual offense. After his release from prison five years later, he was arrested again, this time for failing to register as a sex offender according to the rules the Attorney General had then prescribed for pre-Act offenders. As a result, Mr. Gundy faced an additional 10-year prison term—10 years more than if the Attorney General had, in his discretion, chosen to write the rules differently.

II

A

Our founding document begins by declaring that "We the People . . . ordain and establish this Constitution." At the time, that was a radical claim, an assertion that sovereignty belongs not to a person or institution or class but to the whole of the people. From that premise, the Constitution proceeded to vest the authority to exercise different aspects of the people's sovereign power in distinct entities. In Article I, the Constitution entrusted all of the federal government's legislative power to Congress. In Article II, it assigned the executive power to the President. And in Article III, it gave independent judges the task of applying the laws to cases and controversies.

To the framers, each of these vested powers had a distinct content. When it came to the legislative power, the framers understood it to mean the power to adopt generally applicable rules of conduct governing future actions by private persons—the power to "prescrib[e] the rules by which the duties and rights of every citizen are to be regulated," The Federalist No. 78, p. 465 (C. Rossiter ed. 1961) (A. Hamilton), or the power to "prescribe general rules for the government of society." *Fletcher* v. *Peck*, 6 Cranch 87, 136 (1810); see also J. Locke, The Second Treatise of Civil Government and a Letter Concerning Toleration § 22, p. 13 (1947) (Locke, Second Treatise); 1 W. Blackstone, Commentaries on the Laws of England 44 (1765).

The framers understood, too, that it would frustrate "the system of government ordained by the Constitution" if Congress could merely announce vague aspirations and then assign others the responsibility of adopting legislation to realize its goals. *Marshall Field & Co. v. Clark*, 143 U.S. 649, 692 (1892). Through the Constitution, after all, the people had vested the power to prescribe rules limiting their liberties in Congress alone. No one, not even Congress, had the right to alter that arrangement. As Chief Justice Marshall explained, Congress may not "delegate . . . powers which are strictly and exclusively legislative." *Wayman v. Southard*, 10 Wheat. 1, 42–43 (1825). Or as John Locke, one of the thinkers who most influenced the framers' understanding of the separation of powers, described it:

> "The legislative cannot transfer the power of making laws to any other hands; for it being but a delegated power from the people, they who have it cannot pass it over to others. The people alone can appoint the form of the commonwealth, which is by constituting the legislative, and appointing in whose hands that shall be. And when the people have said we will submit to rules, and be governed by laws made by such men, and in such forms, nobody else can say other men shall make laws for them; nor can the people be bound by any laws but such as are enacted by those whom they have chosen and authorised to make laws for them." Locke, Second Treatise § 141, at 71.

Why did the framers insist on this particular arrangement? They believed the new federal government's most dangerous power was the power to enact laws restricting the people's liberty. The Federalist No. 48, at 309–312 (J. Madison). An "excess of law-making" was, in their words, one of "the diseases to which our governments are most liable." *Id.*, No. 62, at 378. See also *id.*, No. 73, at 441–442 (Hamilton); Locke, Second Treatise § 143.

To address that tendency, the framers went to great lengths to make lawmaking difficult. In Article I, by far the longest part of the Constitution, the framers insisted that any proposed law must win the approval of two Houses of Congress—elected at different times, by different constituencies, and for different terms in office—and either secure the President's approval or obtain enough support to override his veto. Some occasionally complain about Article I's detailed and arduous processes for new legislation, but to the framers these were bulwarks of liberty.

Nor was the point only to limit the government's capacity to restrict the people's freedoms. Article I's detailed processes for new laws were also designed to promote deliberation. . . .

If Congress could pass off its legislative power to the executive branch, the "[v]esting [c]lauses, and indeed the entire structure of the Constitution," would "make no sense." Lawson, Delegation and Original Meaning, 88 Va. L. Rev. 327, 340 (2002). Without the involvement of representatives from across the country or the demands of bicameralism and presentment, legislation would risk becoming nothing more than the will of the current President. And if laws could be simply declared by a single person, they would not be few in number, the product of widespread social consensus, likely to protect minority interests, or apt to provide stability and fair notice. Accountability would suffer too. Legislators might seek to take credit for addressing a pressing social problem by sending it to the executive for resolution, while at the same time blaming the executive for the problems that attend whatever measures he chooses to pursue. In turn, the executive might point to Congress as the source of the problem. These opportunities for finger-pointing might prove temptingly advantageous for the politicians involved . . . .

B

Accepting, then, that we have an obligation to decide whether Congress has unconstitutionally divested itself of its legislative responsibilities, the question follows: What's the test? Madison acknowledged that "no skill in the science of government has yet been able to discriminate and define, with sufficient certainty, its three great provinces—the legislative, executive, and judiciary." The Federalist No. 37, at 228 (Madison). Chief Justice Marshall agreed that policing the separation of powers "is a subject of delicate and difficult inquiry." *Wayman*, 10 Wheat. at 46. Still, the framers took this responsibility seriously and offered us important guiding principles.

First, we know that as long as Congress makes the policy decisions when regulating private conduct, it may authorize another branch to "fill up the details." In *Wayman* v. *Southard,* this Court upheld a statute that instructed the federal courts to borrow state-court procedural rules but allowed them to make certain "alterations and additions." Writing for the Court, Chief Justice Marshall distinguished between those "important subjects, which must be entirely regulated by the legislature itself," and "those of less interest, in which a general provision may be made, and power given to those who are to act . . . to fill up the details." *Id.* at 31, 43. The Court upheld the statute before it because Congress had announced the controlling general policy when it ordered federal courts to follow state procedures, and the residual authority to make "alterations and additions" did no more than permit courts to fill up the details. . . .

Second, once Congress prescribes the rule governing private conduct, it may make the application of that rule depend on executive fact-finding. Here, too, the power extended to the executive may prove highly consequential. During the Napoleonic Wars, for example, Britain and France each tried to block the United States from trading with the other. Congress responded with a statute instructing that, if the President found that either Great Britain or France stopped interfering with American trade, a trade embargo would be imposed against the other country. In *Cargo of Brig Aurora* v. *United States,* this Court explained that it could "see no sufficient reason, why the legislature should not exercise its discretion [to impose an embargo] either expressly or *conditionally,* as their judgment should direct." 7 Cranch 382, 388 (1813) (emphasis added). Half a century later, Congress likewise made the construction of the Brooklyn Bridge depend on a finding by the Secretary of War that the bridge wouldn't interfere with navigation of the East River. The Court held that Congress "did not abdicate any of its authority" but "simply declared that, upon a certain fact being established, the bridge should be deemed a lawful structure, and employed the secretary of war as an agent to ascertain that fact." *Miller* v. *Mayor of New York,* 109 U.S. 385, 393 (1883).

Third, Congress may assign the executive and judicial branches certain non-legislative responsibilities. While the Constitution vests all federal legislative power in Congress alone, Congress's legislative authority sometimes overlaps with authority the Constitution separately vests in another branch. So, for example, when a congressional statute confers wide discretion to the executive, no separation-of-powers problem may arise if "the discretion is to be exercised over matters already within the scope of executive power." Though the case was decided on different grounds, the foreign-affairs-related statute in *Cargo of the Brig Aurora* may be an example of this kind of permissible lawmaking, given that many foreign affairs powers are constitutionally vested in the president under Article II. *Wayman* itself might be explained by the same principle as applied to the judiciary: Even in the absence of any statute, courts have the power under Article III "to regulate their practice."

C

Before the 1930s, federal statutes granting authority to the executive were comparatively modest and usually easily upheld. But then the federal government began to grow explosively. And with the proliferation of new executive programs came new questions about the scope of congressional delegations. Twice the Court responded by striking down statutes for violating the separation of powers. . . .

After *Schechter Poultry* and *Panama Refining* . . . the Court hasn't held another statute to violate the separation of powers in the same way. . . . [M]aybe the most likely explanation of all lies in the story of the evolving "intelligible principle" doctrine.

This Court first used that phrase in 1928 in *J. W. Hampton, Jr., & Co.* v. *United States,* . . . No one at the time thought the phrase meant to effect some revolution in this Court's understanding of the Constitution. While the exact line between policy and details, lawmaking and fact-finding, and legislative and non-legislative functions had sometimes invited reasonable debate, everyone agreed these were the relevant inquiries. And when Chief Justice Taft wrote of an "intelligible principle," it seems plain enough that he sought only to explain the operation of these traditional tests; he gave no hint of a wish to overrule or revise them. . . .

There's a good argument, as well, that the statute in *J. W. Hampton* passed muster under the traditional tests. To boost American competitiveness in international trade, the legislation directed the President to " 'investigat[e]' " the relative costs of production for American companies and their foreign counterparts and impose tariffs or duties that would " 'equalize' " those costs. It also offered guidance on how to determine costs of production, listing several relevant factors and establishing a process for interested parties to submit evidence. The President's fact-finding responsibility may have required intricate calculations, but it could be argued that Congress had made all the relevant policy decisions, and the Court's reference to an "intelligible principle" was just another way to describe the traditional rule that Congress may leave the executive the responsibility to find facts and fill up details.

Still, it's undeniable that the "intelligible principle" remark eventually began to take on a life of its own. . . . For two decades, no one thought to invoke the "intelligible principle" comment as a basis to uphold a statute that would have failed more traditional separation-of-powers tests. . . .

Still, the scope of the problem can be overstated. At least some of the results the Court has reached under the banner of the abused "intelligible principle" doctrine may be consistent with more traditional teachings. . . .

While it's been some time since the Court last held that a statute improperly delegated the legislative power to another branch—thanks in no small measure to the intelligible principle misadventure—the Court has hardly abandoned the business of policing improper legislative delegations. When one legal doctrine becomes unavailable to do its intended work, the hydraulic pressures of our constitutional system sometimes shift the responsibility to different doctrines. And that's exactly what's happened here. We still regularly rein in Congress's efforts to delegate legislative power; we just call what we're doing by different names.

Consider, for example, the "major questions" doctrine. Under our precedents, an agency can fill in statutory gaps where "statutory circumstances" indicate that Congress meant to grant it such powers. *United States* v. *Mead Corp.*, 533 U.S. 218, 229 (2001). But we don't follow that rule when the "statutory gap" concerns "a question of deep 'economic and political significance' that is central to the statutory scheme." *King* v. *Burwell*, 576 U. S. ___, ___ (2015) (slip op., at 8). So we've rejected agency demands that we defer to their attempts to rewrite rules for billions of dollars in healthcare tax credits, *ibid.*, to assume control over millions of small greenhouse gas sources, *Utility Air Regulatory Group* v. *EPA*, 573 U.S. 302, 324 (2014), and to ban cigarettes. *FDA* v. *Brown & Williamson Tobacco Corp.*, 529 U.S. 120, 159–160 (2000). Although it is nominally a canon of statutory construction, we apply the major questions doctrine in service of the constitutional rule that Congress may not divest itself of its legislative power by transferring that power to an executive agency.

Consider, too, this Court's cases addressing vagueness. "A vague law," this Court has observed, "impermissibly delegates basic policy matters to policemen, judges, and juries for resolution on an *ad hoc* and subjective basis." *Grayned* v. *City of Rockford*, 408 U.S. 104, 108–109 (1972). And we have explained that our doctrine prohibiting vague laws is an outgrowth and "corollary of the separation of powers." . . .

To leave this aspect of the constitutional structure alone undefended would serve only to accelerate the flight of power from the legislative to the executive branch, turning the latter into a vortex of authority that was constitutionally reserved for the people's representatives in order to protect their liberties.

III

A

Returning to SORNA with this understanding of our charge in hand, problems quickly emerge. Start with this one: It's hard to see how SORNA leaves the Attorney General with only details to fill up. . . . As the government itself admitted in *Reynolds,* SORNA leaves the Attorney General free to impose on 500,000 pre-Act offenders all of the statute's requirements, some of them, or none of them. The Attorney General may choose which pre-Act offenders to subject to the Act. And he is free to change his mind at any point or over the course of different political administrations. In the end, there isn't a single policy decision concerning pre-Act offenders on which Congress even tried to speak, and not a single other case where we have upheld executive authority over matters like these on the ground they constitute mere "details." This much appears to have been deliberate, too. Because members of Congress could not reach consensus on the treatment of pre-Act offenders, it seems this was one of those situations where they found it expedient to hand off the job to the executive and direct there the blame for any later problems that might emerge. . . .

If allowing the President to draft a "cod[e] of fair competition" for slaughterhouses was "delegation running riot," then it's hard to see how giving the nation's chief prosecutor the power to write a criminal code rife with his own policy choices might be permissible. And if Congress may not give the President the discretion to ban or allow the interstate transportation of petroleum, then it's hard to see how Congress may give the Attorney General the discretion to apply or not apply any or all of SORNA's requirements to pre-Act offenders, and then change his mind at any time. If the separation of powers means anything, it must mean that Congress cannot give the executive branch a blank check to write a code of conduct governing private conduct for a half-million people.

The statute here also sounds all the alarms the founders left for us. Because Congress could not achieve the consensus necessary to resolve the hard problems associated with SORNA's application to pre-Act offenders, it passed the potato to the Attorney General. And freed from the need to assemble a broad supermajority for his views, the Attorney General did not hesitate to apply the statute retroactively to a politically unpopular minority. . . .

Nor would enforcing the Constitution's demands spell doom for what some call the "administrative state." The separation of powers does not prohibit any particular policy outcome, let alone dictate any conclusion about the proper size and scope of government. Instead, it is a procedural guarantee that requires Congress to assemble a social consensus before choosing our nation's course on policy questions like those implicated by SORNA. . . .

B

What do the government and the plurality have to say about the constitutional concerns SORNA poses? Most everyone, the plurality included, concedes that if SORNA allows the Attorney General as much authority as we have outlined, it would present "a nondelegation question." So the only remaining available tactic is to try to make this big case "small-bore" by recasting the statute in a way that might satisfy any plausible separation-of-powers test. So, yes, just a few years ago in *Reynolds* the government represented to this Court that SORNA granted the Attorney General nearly boundless discretion with respect to pre-Act offenders. But *now*, faced with a constitutional challenge, the government speaks out of the other side of its mouth and invites us to reimagine SORNA as compelling the Attorney General to register pre-Act offenders "to the maximum extent feasible." And, as thus reinvented, the government insists, the statute supplies a clear statement of legislative policy, with only details for the Attorney General to clean up.

But even this new dream of a statute wouldn't be free from doubt. A statute directing an agency to regulate private conduct to the extent "feasible" can have many possible meanings: It might refer to "technological" feasibility, "economic" feasibility, "administrative" feasibility, or even "political" feasibility. Such an "evasive standard" could threaten the separation of powers if effectively allowed the agency to make the "important policy choices" that belong to Congress while frustrating "meaningful judicial review." And that seems exactly the case here, where the Attorney General is left free to make all the important policy decisions and it is difficult to see what standard a court might later use to judge whether he exceeded the bounds of the authority given to him.

But don't worry over that; return to the real world. The bigger problem is that the feasibility standard is a figment of the government's (very recent) imagination. The only provision addressing pre-Act offenders, § 20913(d), says *nothing* about feasibility. And the omission can hardly be excused as some oversight: No one doubts that Congress knows exactly how to write a feasibility standard into law when it wishes. Unsurprisingly, too, the existence of some imaginary statutory feasibility standard seemed to have escaped notice at the Department of Justice during the Attorney General's many rulemakings; in those proceedings, as we have seen, the Attorney General has repeatedly admitted that the statute affords him the authority to "balance" the burdens on sex offenders with "public safety interests" as and how he sees fit. 75 Fed. Reg. 81851–81852.

Unable to muster a feasibility standard from the only statutory provision addressing pre-Act offenders, the plurality invites us to hunt in other and more unlikely corners. It points first to SORNA's "[d]eclaration of purpose," which announces that Congress, "[i]n order to protect the public from sex offenders and offenders against children . . . establishes a comprehensive national system for the registration of those offenders." But nowhere is feasibility mentioned here either. . . .

Besides, even if we were to pretend that § 20901 amounted to a directive *telling* the Attorney General to establish a "comprehensive national system" for pre-Act offenders, the plurality reads too much into the word "comprehensive." Comprehensive coverage does not mean coverage to the maximum extent feasible. . . . [A] criminal justice system may be called "comprehensive" even though many crimes go unpursued. And SORNA itself contains all sorts of coverage exceptions for *post-Act* offenders yet claims to comprehensively address them. In the same way, . . . [t]he statute still "comprehensively" addresses [pre-Act offenders] by indicating they must abide whatever rules an Attorney General may choose. . . .

Finding it impossible to conscript the statute's declaration of purpose into doing the work it needs done, the government and plurality next ask us to turn to SORNA's definition of " 'sex offender.' " . . . To say that pre-Act sex offenders fall within the definition of "sex offenders" is merely a truism: Yes, of course, these people have already been convicted of sex offenses under state law. But whether these individuals are *also* subject to federal registration requirements is a different question entirely. . . .

The only real surprise is that the Court fails to make good on the consequences the government invited, resolving nothing and deferring everything. In a future case with a full panel, I remain hopeful that the Court may yet recognize that, while Congress can enlist considerable assistance from the executive branch in filling up details and finding facts, it may never hand off to the nation's chief prosecutor the power to write his own criminal code. That "is delegation running riot." *Schechter Poultry*, 295 U. S., at 553 (Cardozo, J., concurring).

Notes and Questions

1. Nondelegation as a canon of avoidance. In *Gundy*, the plurality interpreted SORNA to *require* the Attorney General to apply its provisions to pre-Act offenders as soon as feasible. With this interpretation of the Act, the plurality easily upheld the statute as containing an intelligible principle. Do you agree with the plurality's interpretation? Even if you don't think it's the best interpretation, is it a plausible one? Could the plurality be deploying the nondelegation doctrine as a canon of constitutional avoidance? Recall the *Benzene* case. There, the Court added a "significant health risk" component to the statute that otherwise seemed to give broad authority to the agency to regulate any amount of carcinogens, however trivial; the Court noted that otherwise there might have been a nondelegation problem. Is *Gundy* a revival of the *Benzene* approach? In fact, can we interpret the "major questions" doctrine along these lines? Was the Court in *Brown & Williamson* interpreting the statute to deny the FDA a choice whether to regulate tobacco in order to avoid a nondelegation problem? See generally John F. Manning, *The Nondelegation Doctrine as a Canon of Avoidance*, 2000 Sup. Ct. Rev. 223; Cass R. Sunstein, *Nondelegation Canons*, 67 U. Chi. L. Rev. 315 (2000); Ilan Wurman, *As-Applied Nondelegation*, 96 Tex. L. Rev. 975 (2018).

 CROSS REFERENCE Do you see similarities between *Gundy* and *The Benzene Case*? Do they both deploy the canon of constitutional avoidance?

2. The definition of "legislative power." Recall our earlier question about what exactly constitutes the legislative power that Congress can't delegate. Justice Gorsuch, in dissent in *Gundy*, surveys the historical cases and concludes that Congress could delegate to the executive the power to find facts upon which certain policies would be contingent, and also the power to "fill up the details" as long as "Congress makes the policy decisions when regulating private conduct." Here, the dissent seems to adopt Justice Thomas's view from the *Amtrak* case that any regulation of private rights or private conduct is legislative power that Congress cannot delegate. But this seems not to square with the history—consider the Steamboat Act of 1852—and also seems impractical. Would we expect Congress to enact a statute specifying exactly what passenger and weight limits apply to particular aircraft models?

 **HISTORICAL PERSPECTIVE** Did the 1852 steamboat legislation authorize the regulation of private conduct? Does that suggest Justice Gorsuch was wrong in *Gundy*? Does the narrowness of the delegation matter?

Additionally, isn't there a level-of-generality problem with the Thomas/Gorsuch approach? Consider *Grimaud*: There, the statute did not specifically mention grazing permits. It granted the Secretary authority to "make provisions for the protection against destruction by fire and depredations upon the public forests and forest reservations" and to "make such rules and regulations . . . to regulate their occupancy and use, and to preserve the forests thereon from destruction." The regulations respecting grazing clearly affected private conduct—was it enough that Congress merely authorized the making of regulations respecting "occupancy and use" even if not grazing specifically? If so, isn't that just the intelligible principle doctrine?

Recall that earlier we introduced Chief Justice Marshall's distinction between "exclusively legislative power" over the "important subjects," and what we might describe as "nonexclusive" legislative power to "fill up the details." Might that be the better general test? Might some regulations affecting private rights be relatively unimportant, and in fact might some regulations that are entirely procedural be extremely important? Recall that there may be a number of factors we can look to—whether the question is one of fact or of policy; the breadth of the discretion; the scope of the subject-matter over which the executive is given authority; the nature of the power; and finally the extent to which the executive is given power to affect private rights and conduct.

C. Debating Delegation

In this section, we consider four excerpts on the merits of delegating power to agencies. The first excerpt argues that delegation to agencies reduces political accountability and likely leads to worse policy outcomes. The next two excerpts respond to these arguments and argue in favor of delegating to agencies. The fourth and final excerpt argues that delegating authority undermines "republicanism." Note that none of these excerpts deals with the question of whether a nondelegation doctrine is or is not constitutionally mandated. The questions here relate to political philosophy, public choice theory, and policy. How do you come down on these questions?

David Schoenbrod, Power Without Responsibility

Yale University Press, 1993, pp. 9–11, 99, 119–21

Delegation can shield our elected lawmakers from blame for harming the public not only when a regulatory program, such as the navel orange marketing order, serves no legitimate public purpose, but also when a regulatory program should serve an important public purpose. Then the consequences of delegation for the public can be even greater because lawmakers can use delegation to escape blame both for failing to achieve that purpose and for imposing unnecessary costs. . . .

Even though all statutory laws require some interpretation, statutes that state laws differ in a critical way from statutes that delegate. In making laws, Congress has to allocate both rights and duties in the very course of stating what conduct it prohibits, and so must make manifest the benefits and costs of regulation. When Congress delegates, it tends to do only half its job—to distribute rights without imposing the commensurate duties. So it promises clean air without restricting polluters and higher incomes for farmers without increasing the price of groceries. In striking poses popular to each and every constituency, Congress ducks the key conflicts. Those conflicts, however, will inevitably surface when the agency tries to translate the popular abstractions of the statutory goals—such as "clean" air or "orderly" agricultural markets—into rules of conduct.

Congress and the president delegate for much the same reason that they continue to run budget deficits. With deficit spending, they can claim credit for the benefits of their expenditures yet escape blame for the costs. The public must pay ultimately of course, but through taxes levied at some future time by some other officials. The point is not that deficits always have bad economic consequences, but that they have the political consequence of allowing officials to duck responsibility for costs.

Likewise, delegation allows legislators to claim credit for the benefits which a regulatory statute promises yet escape the blame for the burdens it will impose, because they do not issue the laws needed to achieve those benefits. The public inevitably must suffer regulatory burdens to realize regulatory benefits, but the laws will come from an agency that legislators can then criticize for imposing excessive burdens on their constituents. Just as deficit spending allows legislators to appear to deliver money to some people without taking it from others, delegation allows them to appear to deliver regulatory benefits without imposing regulatory costs. It provides "a handy set of mirrors—so useful in Washington—by which a politician can appear to kiss both sides of the apple."

Politicians understand that delegation helps them to avoid blame. For example, in 1988 legislators used delegation to try to give themselves a 50-percent pay raise without losing votes in the next election. They enacted a statute that delegated to a commission the power to set pay for themselves and other top officials whose pay they linked to their own. Under the statute, if the commission grants a pay increase, another statute passed before (but not after) the increase goes into effect could cancel it. When the commission recommended the 50-percent increase, some legislators introduced bills to cancel it. But that action was part of a plan in which the congressional leadership would prevent a vote on the bills until it was too late to stop the increase. Legislators could then tell their constituents that they would have voted against the increase if given a chance. Thus they could get the pay raise and also credit for opposing it. However, the size of the increase, in an atmosphere of antipathy to Congress, provoked such a storm of protest and publicity that the public came to see through the charade. Embarrassed, the House leadership conducted a secret ballot among members to determine whether to hold a roll-call vote on the pay increase. Fifty-seven percent of the members who responded opposed a roll call, although 95 percent of the House members surveyed by the Public Citizen group claimed that they had supported it. After public opposition to the pay increase rose to an extraordinary 88 percent, Congress passed a bill to cancel it. . . .

In those statutes, Congress and the president generally did not resolve the key conflicts between business and environmental groups but instead promised to satisfy each side and instructed the Environmental Protection Agency (EPA) to make the laws accordingly. Subsequently, when EPA attempted to issue a law that industry did not like legislators—sometimes even those who took the strongest environmental positions on the floor of Congress—would tell EPA to back off. . . .

The Constitution gives the people control over the laws that govern them by requiring that statutes be affirmed personally by legislators and a president whom the people have elected. Through delegation, these elected officials grant the power to make laws to unelected officials in the agencies. In theory, the elected lawmakers give the agency general instructions, oversee implementation of the directions, provide more specific instructions, and so on until the agency does what the elected officials want. In the words of Robert Dahl, proponents of such a government maintain that it grafts "the expertness of [Platonic] guardianship to the popular sovereignty of the demos," but he warns that it may instead graft "the symbols of democracy to the de facto guardianship of the policy elites." When the elected lawmakers delegate, the people lose control over the laws that govern them. . . .

In the ideal picture of delegation, agency officials are experts who make technical decisions, and legislators are generalists who make broad policy decisions. The picture is incorrect, even in theory. Congress usually cannot delegate the technical issues in lawmaking without also delegating the broad issues of policy. Lawmaking after all is not just a matter of making expert judgments: laws inevitably reflect moral judgments about how to balance and attain competing goals. According to Robert Dahl:

> No intellectually defensible claim can be made that policy elites . . . possess superior moral knowledge or more specifically superior knowledge of what constitutes the public good. Indeed, we have some reason for thinking that specialization, which is the very ground for the influence of policy elites, may itself impair their capacity for moral judgment. Likewise, precisely because the knowledge of the policy elites is specialized, their expert knowledge ordinarily provides

too narrow a base for the instrumental judgments that an intelligent policy would require.

Perhaps for this reason as well as because of the politics of the appointment process, most agency heads are not scientists, engineers, economists, or other kinds of technical experts. From EPA's inception in 1970, seven of its eight administrators and six of its eight assistant administrators for air pollution were lawyers. One observer has noted that "the New Deal concept of the 'expert agency' breaks down in the modern context of health and environmental regulation. An agency addressing complex scientific, economic, and technological issues must draw upon so many different kinds of expertise that no individual employee can know very much about all of the issues involved in a typical rulemaking." Meanwhile, generalist legislators often vote on laws—such as those setting the emission limits for new cars—the merits of which depend upon the resolution of hotly contested technical disputes.

Although both agency heads and legislators often lack the expertise to evaluate technical arguments by themselves, they can get help from agency staff, government institutes (for example, the Center for Disease Control), and private sources (for example, medical associations, private think tanks, and university scientists). In addition, legislators request advice from committee staffs and the congressional Office of Technology Assessment. By paying attention to the source, amount, and tenor of competing advice, agency heads and legislators can make judgments involving technical issues without fully understanding them.

In my experience, however, legislators choose politically convenient answers to technical questions. For example, in setting the emission limits on new cars in 1970, 1977, and 1990, Congress apparently was driven as much by politics as by technical information. Congress is free to decide in this way because the legitimacy and legality of its laws flows from political representation. In contrast, the legitimacy and legality of agency laws depends upon a reasoned explanation. Nonetheless, as the Clean Air Act experience illustrates, agencies also often find politically convenient answers to technical questions. The charade of rationalizing these answers makes agency lawmaking more complicated but not necessarily more reasonable.

Some political leaders fear that separation of powers, of which the Article I lawmaking process is a part, is unworkable, because it leads to gridlock when the president and majorities in the House and the Senate do not all come from the same party. *Gridlock* is a value-laden word for a decision not to make a law; such a gridlock is no problem to those, such as the Framers, who believed that laws should not be made unless they have the broad support that usually is sufficient to get them through the Article I process. Solutions proposed by those who see gridlock as a problem vary from amending the Constitution to change the method of electing legislators to reduce the chance of divided government, to dispensing with separation of powers altogether by adopting a parliamentary form of government.

Whether these proposals have any merit or not, delegation is no cure for divided government. Delegation might seem to be a cure because the statutes let an agency make law without the permission of the House, Senate, or president. But, as we know, the president, the legislators, and their staffs influence the agency. So, with delegation the stalemate often continues, but in a new context. Yet, because delegation has ostensibly given the agency the job of making the law, our elected lawmakers can shift to the agency much of the blame for failing to resolve the dispute. Delegation thus shortcircuits the nation's only authoritative method of resolving disputes about what the law should be and so puts protection of the public into an administrative limbo. The EPA s delays in producing the rules required by the Clean Air Act are typical of what happens under many other statutes.

The supposed ability of agencies to protect the public quickly is more apparent than real for other reasons. The Administrative Procedure Act theoretically allows agencies to make law in two months, and even less in an emergency. It is tempting to compare such potential speed with the years that can pass while bills languish in Congress. Yet, in fact, Congress can react quickly when it senses public support for quick action, while agencies ordinarily need years to make law. . . .

Jerry L. Mashaw, Greed, Chaos, and Governance

Yale University Press, 1997, pp. 136, 139–41, 146–48, 152–54

I will argue that by thinking through the ways in which interest group pluralism may structure different forms of political contests, elections, and accountability systems, one can construct a public choice argument for broad delegations of authority to administrators that looks at least as good on both welfare and accountability grounds as do the critics' calls for specificity in statutory drafting. . . .

The dynamics of accountability apparently involve voters willing to vote upon the basis of their representative's record in the legislature. Assuming that our current representatives in the legislature vote for laws that contain vague delegations of authority, we are presumably holding them accountable for that at the polls. How is it that we are not being represented? . . .

Even if we were to imagine that statutory precision would be informative, it is hard to envisage how rational voter calculation is appreciably improved. When one votes for Congressperson X, presumably one votes on the basis of a prediction about what X will do in the next time period in the legislature. How much better off are voters likely to be in making that prediction—that is, in determining how well Congressperson X is likely to represent them over a range of presently unspecified issues—by knowing that he or she voted yes or no on the specific language in certain specific bills in some preceding legislature?

After all, the voter will also know that X could not have controlled all or even a substantial portion of the language of those bills. Votes must have been cast "all things considered." Therefore, when making a general appraisal of X's likely behavior in the future, it is surely much more important that voters know the general ideological tendencies that inform those votes (prolabor, probusiness, prodisarmament, prodefense) than that X votes for or against the particular language of particular bill. I know of no one who argues that statutory vagueness prevents the electorate from becoming informed on the general proclivities of their representatives. . . .

[S]ome scholars have claimed that vague delegations are precisely a device for avoiding responsibility in the face of difficult political decisions and perhaps intractable interest group conflict. . . . Vague delegations are a means to reduce accountability. . . .

To summarize, Schoenbrod's argument is that broad delegations provide legislators with the opportunity to provide information selectively, to legislate without reaching consensus, and to disguise inconsistent positions. I have no quarrel with Schoenbrod that legislators do all of these things in the context of broad delegations of authority to administrators. My argument is that not all of these things are unqualifiedly bad, and that those things that do reduce accountability are equally available to legislators in the context of enacting highly specific legislation.

As previously suggested, I do not believe that failure to reach consensus on detail should disable legislators from legislating because I see no reason to believe that it has negative consequences either for public welfare or for political accountability. A decision to go forward notwithstanding continuing ambiguity or disagreement about the details of implementation is a decision that the polity is better off legislating generally than maintaining the status quo. Citizens may disagree, but they can also hold legislators accountable for their choice. If citizens want more specific statutes, or fear that legislating without serious agreement on implementing details is dangerous, they can, after all, throw the bums out.

To be sure, it may be argued that this requires a significant level of sophistication on the part of voters. But that is precisely the problem with the suggestion that broad delegations of authority in legislation enhance the ability of representatives either to dissemble or to be inconsistent, by comparison with more specific legislative action. The sad truth is that legislators can as easily convey information selectively or take up inconsistent positions in specific statutes as in more general ones.

The Clean Air Act that Schoenbrod uses as an example for his view as easily supports mine. There are indeed some critical gaps in this statute and its many amendments that leave substantial policy discretion to administrators. On the other hand, the statute goes on for hundreds of pages, many of them containing hypertechnical provisions that few citizens could possibly understand. Moreover, to the extent that the Clean Air Act and its amendments do things that dramatically depart from citizens' expectation, I would suggest that they are largely in the detailed provisions, not in the broad aspirational sections. Voters do not read bills and would have little chance of understanding most of them if they did. Hence, legislators can selectively convey information about legislation whether they legislate specifically or generally.

Nor does specificity help voters police for inconsistency in legislators' ideological positions. Indeed, it would seem to me much easier for a voter to detect the inconsistency in a legislator's statement that he or she intended "to protect the public health through strict air quality regulation while avoiding any serious economic dislocation" than by attempting to figure out that the specific provisions of a bill were indeed trading off these values and in precisely what ways.

The long and short of the matter seems to be this: No one has been able to demonstrate any systematic relationship between improving accountability, or enhancing the public welfare, or respecting the rule of law, and the specificity of legislation. Plausible abstract hypotheses can be connected with selective examples to demonstrate that both generality and specificity can impair one or all of the public values I have been discussing. If that is the case, then surely the Supreme Court has been wise to leave the choice of statutory generality to the legislature itself. . . .

Strangely enough, it may make sense to imagine the delegation of political authority to administrators as a device for improving the responsiveness of government to the desires of the general electorate. This argument can be made even if we accept many of the insights of the political and economic literature that premises its predictions of congressional and voter behavior on a direct linkage between benefits transferred to constituents and the election or reelection of representatives. All we need do is not forget there are also presidential elections . . . .

The president has no particular constituency to which he or she has special responsibility to deliver benefits. Presidents are hardly cut off from pork-barrel politics. Yet issues of national scope and the candidates' positions on those issues are the essence of presidential politics. Citizens vote for a president based almost wholly on a perception of the difference that one or another candidate might make to general governmental policies.

If this description of voting in national elections is reasonably plausible, then the utilization of vague delegations to administrative agencies takes on significance as a device for facilitating responsiveness to voter preferences expressed in presidential elections. The high transactions costs of legislating specifically suggests that legislative activity directed to the modification of administration mandates will be infrequent. Agencies will thus persist with their statutory empowering provisions relatively intact over substantial periods of time.

Voter preferences on the direction and intensity of governmental activities, however, are not likely to be so stable. Indeed, one can reasonably expect that a president will be able to affect policy in a four-year term only because being elected president entails acquiring the power to exercise, direct, or influence policy discretion. The group of executive officers we commonly call "the administration" matters only because of the relative malleability of the directives that administrators have in their charge. If congressional statutes were truly specific with respect to the actions that administrators were to take, presidential politics would be a mere beauty contest. For, in the absence of a parliamentary system, or a system of strict party loyalty, specific statutes would mean that presidents and administrations could respond to voter preferences only if they were able to convince the legislature to make specific changes in the existing set of specific statutes. Arguments for specific statutory provisions constraining administrative discretion may therefore reflect a desire merely for conservative, not responsive, governance.

Of course, the vision of a president or an administration having to negotiate with the Congress for changes in policy is not one that is without its own attractiveness. Surely, we desire some limits on the degree to which a president can view a national election as a referendum approving all the president's (or the president's colleagues') pet projects, whether disclosed or undisclosed during the campaign. Those who abhor the policies of any administration, for example, might surely be attracted to a system that would have required that particular president to act almost exclusively through proposals for legislative change. Yet it seems likely that the flexibility that is currently built into the processes of administrative governance by relatively broad delegations of statutory authority permits a more appropriate degree of administrative, or administration, responsiveness to the voter's will than would a strict nondelegation doctrine. For if we were to be serious about restricting the discretion of administrators, we would have to go much beyond what most nondelegation theorists seem to presume would represent clear congressional choices. . . .

Peter H. Schuck, Delegation and Democracy

20 Cardozo L. Rev. 775 (1999)

I think that Professor Schoenbrod has the problem wrong. The real problem with delegation is not a lack of political "responsibility," a concept that he deploys frequently but never defines. I understand responsibility to be the accountability of elected officials (and the indirect accountability of their appointed agents) to the electorate for significant policy choices. If anything, our political system produces too much of this kind of responsibility. Our system creates incentives for legislators (especially those with relatively short terms of office, like members of Congress) to think so obsessively about their immediate electoral prospects that they are unduly timorous, lacking the leeway that a more Burkean conception of representation requires. Hence, they may neglect longer term social problems whose solutions require immediate sacrifices for delayed gains, problems that demand as much of the legislators' attention, prudence, and political courage as they can muster.

Whether we have struck the best balance between accountability and stewardship that can be achieved in light of the realistic constraints on democratic governance is a vital question to which no one really knows the answer. But, I feel quite certain that non-accountability in Professor Schoenbrod's sense is, relatively speaking, a non-problem. The greater dilemma, I think, is that growing social complexity has made it far more difficult for legislators (not to mention voters) to accurately predict the consequences of their choices so that they can reason their way to a conclusion as to the best policy choice. If I am right about this, we may need more delegation to agencies, not less. . . .

More to the point, responsibility is only one value among others. Let me suggest some additional constitutional and quasi-constitutional goals that any democratic, just, and effective lawmaking system should seek to both reify and advance. Lawmaking should encourage active, meaningful participation by individual citizens and groups affected by the law. It should facilitate and reflect mature deliberation among members of the public and among the lawmakers themselves. Lawmaking should exhibit instrumental competence, in the sense that it implements a satisfactory level of legislative purposes. Lawmaking, as Mashaw notes, should promote justice in individual cases, not merely at wholesale. It should also achieve responsiveness to public preferences, in Professor Schoenbrod's sense of giving the voters what they (think they) want. Finally, of course, lawmaking in both its procedural and substantive aspects should exemplify and secure the rule of law.

The political responsibility that Professor Schoenbrod wants to achieve through more specific statutes must coexist with these goals and will sometimes conflict with them. Even if the nondelegation doctrine would in fact promote political responsibility, which I very much doubt, it would also frustrate some or all of these other values. Mashaw explains, for example, how more specific statutes can undercut both justice in the individual case and responsiveness to diverse local conditions.

Professor Schoenbrod seems innocent of, or at least unimpressed by, these poignant and inescapable normative and empirical tradeoffs. He assumes that the legislature is the site where the virtues of responsible lawmaking are best achieved; it is there, he suggests, that the public's values should be expressed and the hard policy choices made. He fails to see, however, that the particular attributes of the legislature's delegation—its breadth, type, and level—are themselves fundamental policy choices. Moreover, these issues are hardly peripheral to legislative choice. Along with the closely related issue of the scope of the agency's regulatory authority, they are almost always—and quite explicitly—at the heart of the political debates in Congress over the shape and content of particular pieces of legislation. The optimal specificity and other delegation-related features of the legislation are among the questions on which almost all of the parties to these legislative struggles—congressional committees, legislative staffs, the White House, regulated firms, "public interest" groups, state and local governments, and others—tend to stake out clear positions, for they know the resolution of these questions may well determine the nature and effectiveness of the regulatory scheme being established. The issue of statutory specificity is not resolved sub silentio or by default, as Professor Schoenbrod suggests. Rather, it is a focal point of the political maneuvering in the legislature.

Legislation is only part of the process of responsible lawmaking, and it is becoming a less important part. In some important respects, this is for the better. Today, the administrative agency is often the site where public participation in lawmaking is most accessible, most meaningful, and most effective.

The administrative agency is often the most accessible site for public participation because the costs of participating in the rulemaking and more informal agency processes, where many of the most important policy choices are in fact made, are likely to be lower than the costs of lobbying or otherwise seeking to influence Congress. Moreover, the institutional culture of the administrative agency, despite its often daunting opacity, is probably more familiar to the average citizen, who deals with bureaucracies constantly and probably works in one, than the exotic, intricate, unruly (and "un-ruley"), insider's culture of Congress.

The agency is often a more meaningful site for public participation than Congress, because the policy stakes for individuals and interest groups are most immediate, transparent, and well-defined at the agency level. One can scarcely exaggerate the importance of this consideration to the legitimacy of democratic politics and to the substantive content of public policy. After all, it is only at the agency level that the generalities of legislation are broken down and concretized into discrete, specific issues with which affected parties can hope to deal. It is there that the agency commits itself to a particular course of action; because only there does it propose the specific rate it will set, the particular emission level it will prescribe, the precise restrictions on private activity it will impose, the exact regulatory definitions it will employ, the kinds of enforcement techniques it will use, the types of information it will collect, and the details relating to the administrative state's myriad other impacts on citizens and groups. In short, it is only at the agency level that the citizen can know precisely what the statute means to her; how, when, and to what extent it will affect her interests; whether she supports, opposes, or wants changes in what the agency is proposing; whether it is worth her while to participate actively in seeking to influence this particular exercise of governmental power, and if so, how best to go about it; and where other citizens or groups stand on these questions. . . .

Finally, the agency is often the site in which public participation is most effective. This is not only because the details of the regulatory impacts are hammered out there. It is also because the agency is where the public can best educate the government about the true nature of the problem that Congress has tried to address. Only the interested parties, reacting to specific agency proposals for rules or other actions, possess (or have the incentives to acquire) the information necessary to identify, explicate, quantify, and evaluate the real-world consequences of these and alternative proposals. Even when Congress can identify the first-order effects of the laws that it enacts, these direct impacts seldom exhaust the laws' policy consequences. Indeed, first-order effects of policies usually are less significant than the aggregate of more remote effects that ripple through a complex, interrelated, opaque society. When policies fail, it is usually not because the congressional purpose was misunderstood. More commonly, they fail because Congress did not fully appreciate how the details of policy implementation would confound its purpose. Often, however, this knowledge can only be gained through active public participation in the policymaking process at the agency level where these implementation issues are most clearly focused and the stakes in their correct resolution are highest. . . .

If the rule of law is a central goal . . . , then our desideratum should not be statutes of a certain specificity with that level of specificity enforced by courts as a matter of constitutional law. Instead, we should seek to assure that bureaucratic power is checked and effectively bent to the legislative purpose, that the agency, in Professor Schoenbrod's words, is not "free to do as it pleases." Now, no one would suggest that this essential goal of constraining and guiding bureaucratic power is easily accomplished. If it were, Congress could take longer recesses and most administrative lawyers would be out of a job. Developing agency cost theory and other approaches have painstakingly detailed the tensions between this goal and other important goals such as technical rationality, policy flexibility, procedural simplicity, speed of decision, justice in the individual case, individual dignity, and the like.

Federal agencies, however, are hardly at liberty. They are surrounded by watchdogs with sharp, penetrating teeth. Indeed, what most clearly distinguishes the American administrative state from that of other countries is the pervasive public philosophy of mistrust of government bureaucracies and the subordination of bureaucracy to numerous, diverse, external, power-checking institutions and processes. These institutions, moreover, are remarkably powerful; they routinely shape policy and delve into the intricate details of administration. . . . I do not claim that this control is complete, nor should it be if the advantages of technocratic administration are to be realized. Agencies enjoy some leeway and sometimes abuse it. The controls, however, are extensive.

Some of these external constraints on bureaucratic policymaking are: (1) Congress; (2) the Executive Office of the President; (3) judicial review; (4) interest group monitors; (5) media; and (6) informal agency norms. It is important, moreover, to remember that these and other constraints on bureaucracy's freedom to "do as it pleases" all operate simultaneously. . . .

Joseph Postell, Bureaucracy in America

University of Missouri Press, 2016, pp. 42–49

In comparing Madison's definition of republicanism to contemporary administrative power, two questions emerge. The first question is what kind of connection must be present between citizens and officials in order to legitimize the exercise of coercive power. Madison's admission that officials in a republican form of government may be appointed "either directly or indirectly" might be interpreted to permit policymaking by officials who are only indirectly chosen by the people such as administrators are today. Second, since Madison's definition of representation demands that officials resist popular opinion if necessary, administrators who are far removed from practical politics might be seen as a reflection, rather than a contradiction, of Madison's understanding of republicanism. These two questions, raised recently by scholars, merit further attention.

The first question asserts that Madison's conception of republicanism can accommodate policymaking by unelected officials. After all, if republicanism merely requires *some* connection, however indirect or remote, between the people and federal office-holders, federal administrators today would satisfy the requirements of republican government. The manner of their selection, it may be urged, is no more remote than that of a U.S. senator (prior to the 17th Amendment) or a federal judge. The filling of an office by a civil service examination certainly does not provide an "immediate" connection, but it might be said to be an "indirect" appointment by the people. And presidential appointments (or appointments by heads of departments) are certainly "indirectly" based on popular elections.

In response to this argument, we must note that one of the critical elements of Madison's conception of republicanism is its practical ability to control the exercise of government power. Madison argued that representation must be structured in a way that controls and guides the use of delegated power in the interest of the people. This aspect of Madison's definition of republicanism *precludes* lawmaking by unelected—or even indirectly elected—officials.

As just noted, Madison's definition of republicanism in *Federalist 39* repeatedly draws a distinction between direct (sometimes referred to as "immediate") and indirect elections. This is a phrase that both Madison and Hamilton used carefully and systematically throughout *The Federalist*. For instance, Hamilton in *Federalist 84* proclaims that the U.S. Constitution is "professedly founded upon the power of the people, and executed by their *immediate representatives and servants*." Hamilton made the same argument almost verbatim more than sixty essays earlier: "The fabric of American Empire ought to rest on the solid basis of THE CONSENT OF THE PEOPLE. The streams of national power ought to flow *immediately* from that pure original fountain of all legitimate authority." While the choice of whether to follow the immediate influence of the people belongs to the representative, the relationship between the government and the people must be immediate.

Combining these statements with the principles of republican government set forth by Madison in *Federalist 39*, we may conclude that officials may be *appointed* either directly or indirectly by the people, but this does not mean that the connection between the people and their representatives can be anything less than "immediate." The manner in which officials are *chosen* is understood differently than the relationship between officials and the people once those

officials are in office. For the theory of representation to be effectual in practice the connection between the people and their representatives must always
be immediate, in the basic sense that the public, the sovereign authority, must
be able to remove delinquent public officials from office. This means that the
principle of election is a necessary condition for the preservation of representative government. Election can be applied indirectly, meaning that an elected
official could fill another office through appointment; this would still satisfy the
republican principle. What is impermissible, however, is to fill offices without
the direct or indirect appointment of the people, such as by lottery or heredity.
The manner of choosing an official can be indirect or remote but still representative. The crucial cord that cannot be severed is the principle of election. . . .

For Madison the manner in which the office is filled is critical to understanding the connection between the people and the occupant of the office. In
Federalist 52, for instance, Madison stated clearly and emphatically: "As it is
essential to liberty that the government in general, should have a common interest with the people; so it is particularly essential that the branch of it under
consideration, should have an immediate dependence on, & an intimate sympathy with the people. Frequent elections are *unquestionably the only policy* by
which this dependence and sympathy can be effectually secured." . . .

In this view, representation must preserve the immediate connection between the people and their representatives in the legislature, thereby ensuring
that the interest of representatives coincides with their duty to serve the people. It demands that the representatives of the people are so situated that their
interest will lie in discerning and pursuing the best interests of the people. The
most obvious way to situate the representatives of the people to secure this end
is to render their reelection contingent upon winning the favor of the people.
Ensuring that the power of government is in the hands of the people's representatives ensures the security of the people because they are able to exercise
control over their representatives. They are able to exercise control over their
representatives because they are in charge of perpetuating their representatives'
tenure in office. This explains why the Framers refused to grant legitimacy to
the idea that the elected representatives in the legislature could delegate the
lawmaking power to indirectly chosen officers in the executive branch.

In summary, the Federalists argued that representation was fundamental
to republicanism. In their view political officials must be incentivized to exercise
their powers in a manner conducive to the public good. Representation secures

this practical end by making the representative's interest—reelection—one and the same with the representative's duty, namely pursuing the public good. In order to achieve this practical end, an immediate connection between the people and their representatives is required. . . . [W]ith regard to the making of binding laws, immediate election is the only method that promotes a common interest and sympathy between rulers and the people.

The second question asserts not that election is irrelevant to legitimizing administrative power, but that it is actually detrimental to good policymaking, and that Madison would draw the same conclusion. This argument fixes on the nature of representation as articulated by Madison and Hamilton in *The Federalist*. According to this argument, Madison and Hamilton emphasized the need for representatives to resist popular opinion in certain situations, for the good of the country, and federal administrators have the same ability, thus vindicating some of the original purposes of representation. This argument suggests that administrative policymaking is actually more consistent with the idea of republican government than any other potential alternative. . . .

A closer examination of the way in which representation refines public opinion suggests that there are critical differences between the way representation filters public opinion and the way in which the administrative process does this. . . .

First, it is critical to note *how* the Senate is designed to correct the errors of the public in these "critical moments." The purpose of the Senate is not to *thwart* the will of the public, but to *enlighten* it. Madison maintains that "in all free governments" the "cool and deliberate sense of the community" will "prevail over the views of its rulers." The purpose of the Senate is simply to provide the cooling effect necessary to allow reason to regain its control over the public mind, not to operate independently of the people. The connection between the Senate and the people is not severed in this process.

Second, Madison's explanation of the means by which the Senate accomplishes this cooling effect illustrates another difference between the Senate and an independent bureaucracy. Superficial analysis of this passage leads one to the conclusion that the Senate cools the public will simply by resisting it. On the contrary, Madison says that the Senate must be a "temperate and respectable body of citizens" in order to check the public passions. But the Senate can only be respectable because of its connection to the people. As Madison remarks elsewhere, representatives will "have been distinguished by the preference of their fellow citizens." Therefore, "we are to presume, that in general, they will be somewhat distinguished also, by those qualities which entitle them to it. . . ." Representatives may need to resist public opinion, but in Madison's view they can only do so if they are connected to the people through election.

Therefore, the purpose of the Senate is not simply to ignore the public will when it is in error; Madison maintains consistently that the public will is to prevail in republican governments. The purpose of the Senate is to enlighten or cool the public will so that it can rule according to reason rather than passion. In order for a governmental institution to do this, it has to be "respectable." As Madison remarks elsewhere, a "numerous legislature" is "best adapted to deliberation and wisdom, and best calculated to conciliate the confidence of the people and to secure their privileges and interests." The legislature in general, and the Senate in particular, will be respectable and possess "the confidence of the people" by virtue of their connection to the people. The Senate fulfills this requirement in a way that an administrator cannot, because of the core differences in the design of the two institutions.

A second aspect of the Senate that allowed it to resist public opinion, at the time of the Founding, was the method of electing Senators. Under the original Constitution senators were to be elected indirectly by the state legislatures. This would seem to suggest that senators and bureaucrats are both equally legitimate lawmakers from a constitutional perspective. After all, if a legislative body can be severed from direct connection to the people, why is it illegitimate for administrative agencies, with a similarly indirect connection to the people, to make law?

Madison would have rejected this claim for several reasons, some of which have already been indicated. First, many administrative officers are not even indirectly selected by the people. They are chosen impersonally by a civil service examination. Second, as earlier mentioned, Madison explicitly granted that frequent elections for legislators are critical to ensuring that the government have a common interest and immediate sympathy with the people. Most decisively, however, is the fact that Senators alone do not make policy. Bureaucrats do. Senators are *part* of the policymaking process, but it is impossible for senators to make policy on their own according to the Constitution. The only way for senators to take part in a policymaking process is in concert with other, directly elected officials. Because of bicameralism and the requirement to present legislation to the President for signing, no indirectly elected member of the United States government may make law without the concurrence of a directly elected official. . . .

[W]hile Madison recommended that the representatives use their own, often superior judgment regarding whether to *follow* the will of the people, he did not recommend eliminating the immediate *connection* between the people and their representatives.

D. Delegation and the Separation of Powers

This chapter concludes with a discussion of some of the separation of powers implications of the nondelegation doctrine. Starting in the 1930s, as Congress delegated increasingly broad power to agencies, Congress tried to retain control over agency action on the back end by providing for the possibility of a "legislative veto" of administrative action. By these legislative veto provisions, Congress, or one house, or even one committee of one house, could negate an administrative action. The Supreme Court analyzed this practice—and put an end to it— in the following famous case.

 Does the Supreme Court in *Chadha* take a formalist or functionalist approach to the legislative veto question? What about the dissent? With which approach do you agree?

INS v. Chadha

462 U.S. 919 (1983)

Chief Justice Burger delivered the opinion of the Court.

. . . . [This case] presents a challenge to the constitutionality of the provision in § 244(c)(2) of the Immigration and Nationality Act, 8 U.S.C. § 1254(c)(2), authorizing one House of Congress, by resolution, to invalidate the decision of the Executive Branch, pursuant to authority delegated by Congress to the Attorney General of the United States, to allow a particular deportable alien to remain in the United States.

I

Chadha is an East Indian who was born in Kenya and holds a British passport. He was lawfully admitted to the United States in 1966 on a nonimmigrant student visa. His visa expired on June 30, 1972. On October 11, 1973, the District Director of the Immigration and Naturalization Service ordered Chadha to show cause why he should not be deported for having "remained in the United States for a longer time than permitted." Pursuant to § 242(b) of the Immigration and Nationality Act (Act), 8 U.S.C. § 1252(b), a deportation hearing was held before an immigration judge on January 11, 1974. Chadha conceded that he was deportable for overstaying his visa and the hearing was adjourned to enable him to file an application for suspension of deportation under § 244(a)(1) of the Act, 8 U.S.C. § 1254(a)(1). Section 244(a)(1) provides:

> "(a) As hereinafter prescribed in this section, the Attorney General may, in his discretion, suspend deportation and adjust the status to that of an alien lawfully admitted for permanent residence, in the case of an alien who . . . has been physically present in the United States for a continuous period of not less than seven years immediately preceding the date of such application, and proves that during all of such period he was and is a person of good moral character; and is a person whose deportation would, in the opinion of the Attorney General, result in extreme hardship to the alien or to his spouse, parent, or child, who is a citizen of the United States or an alien lawfully admitted for permanent residence."

After Chadha submitted his application for suspension of deportation, the deportation hearing was resumed on February 7, 1974. On the basis of evidence adduced at the hearing, affidavits submitted with the application, and the results of a character investigation conducted by the INS, the immigration judge, on June 25, 1974, ordered that Chadha's deportation be suspended. The immigration judge found that Chadha met the requirements of § 244(a)(1): he had resided continuously in the United States for over seven years, was of good moral character, and would suffer "extreme hardship" if deported.

Pursuant to § 244(c)(1) of the Act, 8 U.S.C. § 1254(c)(1), the immigration judge suspended Chadha's deportation and a report of the suspension was transmitted to Congress. Section 244(c)(1) provides:

> "Upon application by any alien who is found by the Attorney General to meet the requirements of subsection (a) of this section the Attorney General may in his discretion suspend deportation of such alien. If the deportation of any alien is suspended under the provisions of this subsection, a complete and detailed statement of the

facts and pertinent provisions of law in the case shall be reported to the Congress with the reasons for such suspension. Such reports shall be submitted on the first day of each calendar month in which Congress is in session."

Once the Attorney General's recommendation for suspension of Chadha's deportation was conveyed to Congress, Congress had the power under § 244(c)(2) of the Act, 8 U.S.C. § 1254(c)(2), to veto the Attorney General's determination that Chadha should not be deported. Section 244(c)(2) provides:

"(2) In the case of an alien specified in paragraph (1) of subsection (a) of this subsection—

if during the session of the Congress at which a case is reported, or prior to the close of the session of the Congress next following the session at which a case is reported, either the Senate or the House of Representatives passes a resolution stating in substance that it does not favor the suspension of such deportation, the Attorney General shall thereupon deport such alien or authorize the alien's voluntary departure at his own expense under the order of deportation in the manner provided by law. If, within the time above specified, neither the Senate nor the House of Representatives shall pass such a resolution, the Attorney General shall cancel deportation proceedings."

The June 25, 1974 order of the immigration judge suspending Chadha's deportation remained outstanding as a valid order for a year and a half. For reasons not disclosed by the record, Congress did not exercise the veto authority reserved to it under § 244(c)(2) until the first session of the 94th Congress. This was the final session in which Congress, pursuant to § 244(c)(2), could act to veto the Attorney General's determination that Chadha should not be deported. The session ended on December 19, 1975. Absent Congressional action, Chadha's deportation proceedings would have been cancelled after this date and his status adjusted to that of a permanent resident alien.

On December 12, 1975, Representative Eilberg, Chairman of the Judiciary Subcommittee on Immigration, Citizenship, and International Law, introduced a resolution opposing "the granting of permanent residence in the United States to [six] aliens," including Chadha. The resolution was referred to the House Committee on the Judiciary. On December 16, 1975, the resolution was discharged from further consideration by the House Committee on the

Judiciary and submitted to the House of Representatives for a vote. The resolution had not been printed and was not made available to other Members of the House prior to or at the time it was voted on. So far as the record before us shows, the House consideration of the resolution was based on Representative Eilberg's statement from the floor that "[i]t was the feeling of the committee, after reviewing 340 cases, that the aliens contained in the resolution [Chadha and five others] did not meet these statutory requirements, particularly as it relates to hardship; and it is the opinion of the committee that their deportation should not be suspended."

The resolution was passed without debate or recorded vote. Since the House action was pursuant to § 244(c)(2), the resolution was not treated as an Article I legislative act; it was not submitted to the Senate or presented to the President for his action.

After the House veto of the Attorney General's decision to allow Chadha to remain in the United States, the immigration judge reopened the deportation proceedings to implement the House order deporting Chadha. Chadha moved to terminate the proceedings on the ground that § 244(c)(2) is unconstitutional. The immigration judge held that he had no authority to rule on the constitutional validity of § 244(c)(2). On November 8, 1976, Chadha was ordered deported pursuant to the House action. . . .

Pursuant to § 106(a) of the Act, Chadha filed a petition for review of the deportation order in the United States Court of Appeals for the Ninth Circuit. The Immigration and Naturalization Service agreed with Chadha's position before the Court of Appeals and joined him in arguing that § 244(c)(2) is unconstitutional. In light of the importance of the question, the Court of Appeals invited both the Senate and the House of Representatives to file briefs *amici curiae*.

After full briefing and oral argument, the Court of Appeals held that the House was without constitutional authority to order Chadha's deportation; accordingly it directed the Attorney General "to cease and desist from taking any steps to deport this alien based upon the resolution enacted by the House of Representatives." *Chadha v. INS*, 634 F.2d 408, 436 (9th Cir. 1980). The essence of its holding was that § 244(c)(2) violates the constitutional doctrine of separation of powers.

We granted certiorari . . . and we now affirm.

* * *

III

We turn now to the question whether action of one House of Congress under § 244(c)(2) violates strictures of the Constitution. . . .

[T]he fact that a given law or procedure is efficient, convenient, and useful in facilitating functions of government, standing alone, will not save it if it is contrary to the Constitution. Convenience and efficiency are not the primary objectives—or the hallmarks—of democratic government and our inquiry is sharpened rather than blunted by the fact that Congressional veto provisions are appearing with increasing frequency in statutes which delegate authority to executive and independent agencies:

> "Since 1932, when the first veto provision was enacted into law, 295 congressional veto-type procedures have been inserted in 196 different statutes as follows: from 1932 to 1939, five statutes were affected; from 1940–49, nineteen statutes; between 1950–59, thirty-four statutes; and from 1960–69, forty-nine. From the year 1970 through 1975, at least one hundred sixty-three such provisions were included in eighty-nine laws."

Abourezk, The Congressional Veto: A Contemporary Response to Executive Encroachment on Legislative Prerogatives, 52 Ind. L. Rev. 323, 324 (1977).

Justice WHITE undertakes to make a case for the proposition that the one-House veto is a useful "political invention," and we need not challenge that assertion. We can even concede this utilitarian argument although the long range political wisdom of this "invention" is arguable. . . . But policy arguments supporting even useful "political inventions" are subject to the demands of the Constitution which defines powers and, with respect to this subject, sets out just how those powers are to be exercised.

Explicit and unambiguous provisions of the Constitution prescribe and define the respective functions of the Congress and of the Executive in the legislative process. Since the precise terms of those familiar provisions are critical to the resolution of this case, we set them out verbatim. Art. I provides:

"All legislative Powers herein granted shall be vested in a Congress of the United States, which shall consist of a Senate *and* a House of Representatives." Art. I, § 1. (Emphasis added).

"Every Bill which shall have passed the House of Representatives *and* the Senate, *shall*, before it becomes a Law, be presented to the President of the United States; . . ." Art. I, § 7, cl. 2. (Emphasis added).

"*Every* Order, Resolution, or Vote to which the Concurrence of the Senate and House of Representatives may be necessary (except on a question of Adjournment) *shall be* presented to the President of the United States; and before the Same shall take Effect, *shall be* approved by him, or being disapproved by him, *shall be* repassed by two thirds of the Senate and House of Representatives, according to the Rules and Limitations prescribed in the Case of a Bill." Art. I, § 7, cl. 3. (Emphasis added).

These provisions of Art. I are integral parts of the constitutional design for the separation of powers. . . .

The records of the Constitutional Convention reveal that the requirement that all legislation be presented to the President before becoming law was uniformly accepted by the Framers. Presentment to the President and the Presidential veto were considered so imperative that the draftsmen took special pains to assure that these requirements could not be circumvented. During the final debate on Art. I, § 7, cl. 2, James Madison expressed concern that it might easily be evaded by the simple expedient of calling a proposed law a "resolution" or "vote" rather than a "bill." 2 M. Farrand, The Records of the Federal Convention of 1787 301–302. As a consequence, Art. I, § 7, cl. 3 was added. *Id.*, at 304–305.

The decision to provide the President with a limited and qualified power to nullify proposed legislation by veto was based on the profound conviction of the Framers that the powers conferred on Congress were the powers to be most carefully circumscribed. It is beyond doubt that lawmaking was a power to be shared by both Houses and the President. In The Federalist No. 73, Hamilton focused on the President's role in making laws: "If even no propensity had ever discovered itself in the legislative body to invade the rights of the Executive, the rules of just reasoning and theoretic propriety would of themselves teach us that the one ought not to be left to the mercy of the other, but ought to possess a constitutional and effectual power of self-defense."

The President's role in the lawmaking process also reflects the Framers' careful efforts to check whatever propensity a particular Congress might have to enact oppressive, improvident, or ill-considered measures. . . . The Court also has observed that the Presentment Clauses serve the important purpose of assuring that a "national" perspective is grafted on the legislative process . . . .

The bicameral requirement of Art. I, §§ 1, 7 was of scarcely less concern to the Framers than was the Presidential veto and indeed the two concepts are interdependent. By providing that no law could take effect without the concurrence of the prescribed majority of the Members of both Houses, the Framers reemphasized their belief, already remarked upon in connection with the Presentment Clauses, that legislation should not be enacted unless it has been carefully and fully considered by the Nation's elected officials. . . .

These observations are consistent with what many of the Framers expressed, none more cogently than Hamilton in pointing up the need to divide and disperse power in order to protect liberty: "In republican government, the legislative authority necessarily predominates. The remedy for this inconveniency is to divide the legislature into different branches; and to render them, by different modes of election and different principles of action, as little connected with each other as the nature of their common functions and their common dependence on the society will admit." The Federalist No. 51. . . .

However familiar, it is useful to recall that apart from their fear that special interests could be favored at the expense of public needs, the Framers were also concerned, although not of one mind, over the apprehensions of the smaller states. . . .

We see therefore that the Framers were acutely conscious that the bicameral requirement and the Presentment Clauses would serve essential constitutional functions. The President's participation in the legislative process was to protect the Executive Branch from Congress and to protect the whole people from improvident laws. The division of the Congress into two distinctive bodies assures that the legislative power would be exercised only after opportunity for full study and debate in separate settings. The President's unilateral veto power, in turn, was limited by the power of two thirds of both Houses of Congress to overrule a veto thereby precluding final arbitrary action of one person. It emerges clearly that the prescription for legislative action in Art. I, §§ 1, 7 represents the Framers' decision that the legislative power of the Federal government be exercised in accord with a single, finely wrought and exhaustively considered, procedure.

IV

The Constitution sought to divide the delegated powers of the new federal government into three defined categories, legislative, executive and judicial, to assure, as nearly as possible, that each Branch of government would confine itself to its assigned responsibility. The hydraulic pressure inherent within each of the separate Branches to exceed the outer limits of its power, even to accomplish desirable objectives, must be resisted.

Although not "hermetically" sealed from one another, the powers delegated to the three Branches are functionally identifiable. When any Branch acts, it is presumptively exercising the power the Constitution has delegated to it. When the Executive acts, it presumptively acts in an executive or administrative capacity as defined in Art. II. And when, as here, one House of Congress purports to act, it is presumptively acting within its assigned sphere.

Beginning with this presumption, we must nevertheless establish that the challenged action under § 244(c)(2) is of the kind to which the procedural requirements of Art. I, § 7 apply. Not every action taken by either House is subject to the bicameralism and presentment requirements of Art. I. Whether actions taken by either House are, in law and fact, an exercise of legislative power depends not on their form but upon "whether they contain matter which is properly to be regarded as legislative in its character and effect."

Examination of the action taken here by one House pursuant to § 244(c)(2) reveals that it was essentially legislative in purpose and effect. In purporting to exercise power defined in Art. I, § 8, cl. 4 to "establish an uniform Rule of Naturalization," the House took action that had the purpose and effect of altering the legal rights, duties and relations of persons, including the Attorney General, Executive Branch officials and Chadha, all outside the legislative branch. Section 244(c)(2) purports to authorize one House of Congress to require the Attorney General to deport an individual alien whose deportation otherwise would be cancelled under § 244. The one-House veto operated in this case to overrule the Attorney General and mandate Chadha's deportation; absent the House action, Chadha would remain in the United States. Congress has *acted* and its action has altered Chadha's status.

The legislative character of the one-House veto in this case is confirmed by the character of the Congressional action it supplants. Neither the House of Representatives nor the Senate contends that, absent the veto provision in § 244(c)(2), either of them, or both of them acting together, could effectively require the Attorney General to deport an alien once the Attorney General, in the exercise of legislatively delegated authority,[16] had determined the alien should remain in the United States. Without the challenged provision in § 244(c)(2), this could have been achieved, if at all, only by legislation requiring deportation. Similarly, a veto by one House of Congress under § 244(c)(2) cannot be justified as an attempt at amending the standards set out in § 244(a)(1), or as a repeal of § 244 as applied to Chadha. Amendment and repeal of statutes, no less than enactment, must conform with Art. I.

The nature of the decision implemented by the one-House veto in this case further manifests its legislative character. After long experience with the clumsy, time consuming private bill procedure, Congress made a deliberate choice to delegate to the Executive Branch, and specifically to the Attorney General, the authority to allow deportable aliens to remain in this country in certain specified circumstances. It is not disputed that this choice to delegate authority is precisely the kind of decision that can be implemented only in accordance with the procedures set out in Art. I. Disagreement with the Attorney General's decision on Chadha's deportation—that is, Congress' decision to deport Chadha—no less than Congress' original choice to delegate to the Attorney General the authority to make that decision, involves determinations of policy

---

[16]   Congress protests that affirming the Court of Appeals in this case will sanction "lawmaking by the Attorney General. . . . Why is the Attorney General exempt from submitting his proposed changes in the law to the full bicameral process?" Brief of the United States House of Representatives 40. To be sure, some administrative agency action—rule making, for example—may resemble "lawmaking." See 5 U.S.C. § 551(4), which defines an agency's "rule" as "the whole or part of an agency statement of general or particular applicability and future effect designed to implement, interpret, or prescribe *law* or policy. . . ." This Court has referred to agency activity as being "quasi-legislative" in character. *Humphrey's Executor v. United States*, 295 U.S. 602, 628 (1935). Clearly, however, "[i]n the framework of our Constitution, the President's power to see that the laws are faithfully executed refutes the idea that he is to be a lawmaker." *Youngstown Sheet & Tube Co. v. Sawyer*, 343 U.S. 579, 587 (1952). When the Attorney General performs his duties pursuant to § 244, he does not exercise "legislative" power. The bicameral process is not necessary as a check on the Executive's administration of the laws because his administrative activity cannot reach beyond the limits of the statute that created it—a statute duly enacted pursuant to Art. I, §§ 1, 7. . . . It is clear, therefore, that the Attorney General acts in his presumptively Art. II capacity when he administers the Immigration and Nationality Act. Executive action under legislatively delegated authority that might resemble "legislative" action in some respects is not subject to the approval of both Houses of Congress and the President for the reason that the Constitution does not so require. That kind of Executive action is always subject to check by the terms of the legislation that authorized it; and if that authority is exceeded it is open to judicial review as well as the power of Congress to modify or revoke the authority entirely. A one-House veto is clearly legislative in both character and effect and is not so checked; the need for the check provided by Art. I, §§ 1, 7 is therefore clear. Congress' authority to delegate portions of its power to administrative agencies provides no support for the argument that Congress can constitutionally control administration of the laws by way of a Congressional veto.

that Congress can implement in only one way; bicameral passage followed by presentment to the President. Congress must abide by its delegation of authority until that delegation is legislatively altered or revoked.

Finally, we see that when the Framers intended to authorize either House of Congress to act alone and outside of its prescribed bicameral legislative role, they narrowly and precisely defined the procedure for such action. There are but four provisions in the Constitution, explicit and unambiguous, by which one House may act alone with the unreviewable force of law, not subject to the President's veto: (a) The House of Representatives alone was given the power to initiate impeachments. Art. I, § 2, cl. 6; (b) The Senate alone was given the power to conduct trials following impeachment on charges initiated by the House and to convict following trial. Art. I, § 3, cl. 5; (c) The Senate alone was given final unreviewable power to approve or to disapprove presidential appointments. Art. II, § 2, cl. 2; (d) The Senate alone was given unreviewable power to ratify treaties negotiated by the President. Art. II, § 2, cl. 2.

Clearly, when the Draftsmen sought to confer special powers on one House, independent of the other House, or of the President, they did so in explicit, unambiguous terms. . . .

The choices we discern as having been made in the Constitutional Convention impose burdens on governmental processes that often seem clumsy, inefficient, even unworkable, but those hard choices were consciously made by men who had lived under a form of government that permitted arbitrary governmental acts to go unchecked. There is no support in the Constitution or decisions of this Court for the proposition that the cumbersomeness and delays often encountered in complying with explicit Constitutional standards may be avoided, either by the Congress or by the President. With all the obvious flaws of delay, untidiness, and potential for abuse, we have not yet found a better way to preserve freedom than by making the exercise of power subject to the carefully crafted restraints spelled out in the Constitution.

JUSTICE POWELL, concurring in the judgment.

The Court's decision, based on the Presentment Clauses, Art. I, § 7, cls. 2 and 3, apparently will invalidate every use of the legislative veto. The breadth of this holding gives one pause. Congress has included the veto in literally hundreds of statutes, dating back to the 1930s. Congress clearly views this procedure as essential to controlling the delegation of power to administrative agencies. One reasonably may disagree with Congress' assessment of the veto's utility, but the respect due its judgment as a coordinate branch of Government cautions that our holding should be no more extensive than necessary to decide this case. In my view, the case may be decided on a narrower ground. When Congress finds that a particular person does not satisfy the statutory criteria for permanent residence in this country it has assumed a judicial function in violation of the principle of separation of powers. Accordingly, I concur only in the judgment.

I

The Framers perceived that "[t]he accumulation of all powers legislative, executive and judiciary in the same hands, whether of one, a few or many, and whether hereditary, self appointed, or elective, may justly be pronounced the very definition of tyranny." The Federalist No. 47 (J. Madison). Theirs was not a baseless fear. Under British rule, the colonies suffered the abuses of unchecked executive power that were attributed, at least popularly, to an hereditary monarchy. During the Confederation, the States reacted by removing power from the executive and placing it in the hands of elected legislators. But many legislators proved to be little better than the Crown. . . .

One abuse that was prevalent during the Confederation was the exercise of judicial power by the state legislatures. The Framers were well acquainted with the danger of subjecting the determination of the rights of one person to the "tyranny of shifting majorities." . . .

It was to prevent the recurrence of such abuses that the Framers vested the executive, legislative, and judicial powers in separate branches. Their concern that a legislature should not be able unilaterally to impose a substantial deprivation on one person was expressed not only in this general allocation of power, but also in more specific provisions, such as the Bill of Attainder Clause, Art. I, § 9, cl. 3. As the Court recognized in *United States v. Brown*, 381 U.S. 437, 442 (1965), "the Bill of Attainder Clause was intended not as a narrow, technical . . . prohibition, but rather as an implementation of the separation of powers, a general safeguard against legislative exercise of the judicial function, or more simply—trial by legislature." This Clause, and the separation of powers doctrine generally, reflect the Framers' concern that trial by a legislature lacks the safeguards necessary to prevent the abuse of power.

The Constitution does not establish three branches with precisely defined boundaries. Rather, as Justice Jackson wrote, "[w]hile the Constitution diffuses power the better to secure liberty, it also contemplates that practice will integrate the dispersed powers into a workable government. It enjoins upon its branches separateness but interdependence, autonomy but reciprocity." *Youngstown Sheet & Tube Co. v. Sawyer*, 343 U.S. 579, 635 (1952) (concurring opinion). The Court thus has been mindful that the boundaries between each branch should be fixed "according to common sense and the inherent necessities of the governmental co-ordination." *J.W. Hampton, Jr. & Co. v. United States*, 276 U.S. 394, 406 (1928). But where one branch has impaired or sought to assume a power central to another branch, the Court has not hesitated to enforce the doctrine. . . .

II

Before considering whether Congress impermissibly assumed a judicial function, it is helpful to recount briefly Congress' actions. Jagdish Rai Chadha, a citizen of Kenya, stayed in this country after his student visa expired. Although he was scheduled to be deported, he requested the Immigration and Naturalization Service to suspend his deportation because he met the statutory criteria for permanent residence in this country. After a hearing, the Service granted Chadha's request and sent—as required by the reservation of the veto right—a report of its action to Congress.

In addition to the report on Chadha, Congress had before it the names of 339 other persons whose deportations also had been suspended by the Service. The House Committee on the Judiciary decided that six of these persons, including Chadha, should not be allowed to remain in this country. . . . Without further explanation and without a recorded vote, the House rejected the Service's determination that these six people met the statutory criteria.

On its face, the House's action appears clearly adjudicatory. The House did not enact a general rule; rather it made its own determination that six specific persons did not comply with certain statutory criteria. It thus undertook the type of decision that traditionally has been left to other branches. . . .

The impropriety of the House's assumption of this function is confirmed by the fact that its action raises the very danger the Framers sought to avoid—the exercise of unchecked power. In deciding whether Chadha deserves to be deported, Congress is not subject to any internal constraints that prevent it from arbitrarily depriving him of the right to remain in this country. Unlike the judiciary or an administrative agency, Congress is not bound by established substantive rules. Nor is it subject to the procedural safeguards, such as the right to counsel and a hearing before an impartial tribunal, that are present when a court or an agency adjudicates individual rights. The only effective constraint on Congress' power is political, but Congress is most accountable politically when it prescribes rules of general applicability. When it decides rights of specific persons, those rights are subject to "the tyranny of a shifting majority."

Chief Justice Marshall observed: "It is the peculiar province of the legislature to prescribe general rules for the government of society; the application of those rules would seem to be the duty of other departments." *Fletcher v. Peck*, 6 Cranch 87, 136 (1810). In my view, when Congress undertook to apply its rules to Chadha, it exceeded the scope of its constitutionally prescribed authority. I would not reach the broader question whether legislative vetoes are invalid under the Presentment Clauses.

Justice White, dissenting.

Today the Court not only invalidates § 244(c)(2) of the Immigration and Nationality Act, but also sounds the death knell for nearly 200 other statutory provisions in which Congress has reserved a "legislative veto." For this reason, the Court's decision is of surpassing importance. And it is for this reason that the Court would have been well-advised to decide the case, if possible, on the narrower grounds of separation of powers, leaving for full consideration the constitutionality of other congressional review statutes operating on such varied matters as war powers and agency rulemaking, some of which concern the independent regulatory agencies.

The prominence of the legislative veto mechanism in our contemporary political system and its importance to Congress can hardly be overstated. It has become a central means by which Congress secures the accountability of executive and independent agencies. Without the legislative veto, Congress is faced with a Hobson's choice: either to refrain from delegating the necessary authority, leaving itself with a hopeless task of writing laws with the requisite specificity to cover endless special circumstances across the entire policy landscape, or in the alternative, to abdicate its law-making function to the executive branch and independent agencies. To choose the former leaves major national problems unresolved; to opt for the latter risks unaccountable policymaking by those not elected to fill that role. Accordingly, over the past five decades, the legislative veto has been placed in nearly 200 statutes. The device is known in every field of governmental concern: reorganization, budgets, foreign affairs, war powers, and regulation of trade, safety, energy, the environment and the economy.

I

The legislative veto developed initially in response to the problems of reorganizing the sprawling government structure created in response to the Depression. The Reorganization Acts established the chief model for the legislative veto. When President Hoover requested authority to reorganize the government in 1929, he coupled his request that the "Congress be willing to delegate its authority over the problem (subject to defined principles) to the Executive" with a proposal for legislative review. He proposed that the Executive "should act upon approval of a joint committee of Congress or with the reservation of power of revision by Congress within some limited period adequate for its consideration." Congress followed President Hoover's suggestion and authorized reorganization subject to legislative review. Although the reorganization authority reenacted in 1933 did not contain a legislative veto provision, the provision returned during the Roosevelt Administration and has since been renewed numerous times. Over the years, the provision was used extensively. Presidents submitted 115 reorganization plans to Congress of which 23 were disapproved by Congress pursuant to legislative veto provisions.

Shortly after adoption of the Reorganization Act of 1939, Congress and the President applied the legislative veto procedure to resolve the delegation problem for national security and foreign affairs. World War II occasioned the need to transfer greater authority to the President in these areas. The legislative veto offered the means by which Congress could confer additional authority while preserving its own constitutional role. During World War II, Congress enacted over thirty statutes conferring powers on the Executive with legislative veto provisions. President Roosevelt accepted the veto as the necessary price for obtaining exceptional authority.

Over the quarter century following World War II, Presidents continued to accept legislative vetoes by one or both Houses as constitutional, while regularly denouncing provisions by which Congressional committees reviewed Executive activity. The legislative veto balanced delegations of statutory authority in new areas of governmental involvement: the space program, international agreements on nuclear energy, tariff arrangements, and adjustment of federal pay rates.

During the 1970's the legislative veto was important in resolving a series of major constitutional disputes between the President and Congress over claims of the President to broad impoundment, war, and national emergency powers. The key provision of the War Powers Resolution, 50 U.S.C. § 1544(c), authorizes the termination by concurrent resolution of the use of armed forces in hostilities. A similar measure resolved the problem posed by Presidential claims of inherent power to impound appropriations. In conference, a compromise was achieved under which permanent impoundments, termed "rescissions," would require approval through enactment of legislation. In contrast, temporary impoundments, or "deferrals," would become effective unless disapproved by one House. This compromise provided the President with flexibility, while preserving ultimate Congressional control over the budget. Although the War Powers Resolution was enacted over President Nixon's veto, the Impoundment Control Act was enacted with the President's approval. These statutes were followed by others . . . .

Even this brief review suffices to demonstrate that the legislative veto is more than "efficient, convenient, and useful." It is an important if not indispensable political invention that allows the President and Congress to resolve major constitutional and policy differences, assures the accountability of independent regulatory agencies, and preserves Congress' control over lawmaking. Perhaps there are other means of accommodation and accountability, but the increasing reliance of Congress upon the legislative veto suggests that the alternatives to which Congress must now turn are not entirely satisfactory.

The history of the legislative veto also makes clear that it has not been a sword with which Congress has struck out to aggrandize itself at the expense of the other branches—the concerns of Madison and Hamilton. Rather, the veto has been a means of defense, a reservation of ultimate authority necessary if Congress is to fulfill its designated role under Article I as the nation's lawmaker. While the President has often objected to particular legislative vetoes, generally those left in the hands of congressional committees, the Executive has more often agreed to legislative review as the price for a broad delegation of authority. To be sure, the President may have preferred unrestricted power, but that could be precisely why Congress thought it essential to retain a check on the exercise of delegated authority.

II

For all these reasons, the apparent sweep of the Court's decision today is regretable. The Court's Article I analysis appears to invalidate all legislative vetoes irrespective of form or subject. Because the legislative veto is commonly found as a check upon rulemaking by administrative agencies and upon broad-based policy decisions of the Executive Branch, it is particularly unfortunate that the Court reaches its decision in a case involving the exercise of a veto over deportation decisions regarding particular individuals. Courts should always be wary of striking statutes as unconstitutional; to strike an entire class of statutes based on consideration of a somewhat atypical and more-readily indictable exemplar of the class is irresponsible. . . .

The reality of the situation is that the constitutional question posed today is one of immense difficulty over which the executive and legislative branches—as well as scholars and judges—have understandably disagreed. That disagreement stems from the silence of the Constitution on the precise question: The Constitution does not directly authorize or prohibit the legislative veto. Thus, our task should be to determine whether the legislative veto is consistent with the purposes of Art. I and the principles of Separation of Powers which are reflected in that Article and throughout the Constitution. We should not find the lack of a specific constitutional authorization for the legislative veto surprising, and I would not infer disapproval of the mechanism from its absence. From the summer of 1787 to the present the government of the United States has become an endeavor far beyond the contemplation of the Framers. Only within the last half century has the complexity and size of the Federal Government's responsibilities grown so greatly that the Congress must rely on the legislative veto as the most effective if not the only means to insure their role as the nation's lawmakers. But the wisdom of the Framers was to anticipate that the nation would grow and new problems of governance would require different solutions. Accordingly, our Federal Government was intentionally chartered with the flexibility to respond to contemporary needs without losing sight of fundamental democratic principles. . . .

In my view, neither Article I of the Constitution nor the doctrine of separation of powers is violated by this mechanism by which our elected representatives preserve their voice in the governance of the nation.

III

The Court holds that the disapproval of a suspension of deportation by the resolution of one House of Congress is an exercise of legislative power without compliance with the prerequisites for lawmaking set forth in Art. I . . . .

I do not dispute the Court's truismatic exposition of these clauses. . . .

It does not, however, answer the constitutional question before us. The power to exercise a legislative veto is not the power to write new law without bicameral approval or presidential consideration. The veto must be authorized by statute and may only negative what an Executive department or independent agency has proposed. On its face, the legislative veto no more allows one House of Congress to make law than does the presidential veto confer such power upon the President. . . .

The terms of the Presentment Clauses suggest only that bills and their equivalent are subject to the requirements of bicameral passage and presentment to the President. . . .

There is no record that the Convention contemplated, let alone intended, that these Article I requirements would someday be invoked to restrain the scope of Congressional authority pursuant to duly-enacted law.

When the Convention did turn its attention to the scope of Congress' lawmaking power, the Framers were expansive. The Necessary and Proper Clause, Art. I, § 8, cl. 18, vests Congress with the power "to make all laws which shall be necessary and proper for carrying into Execution the foregoing Powers [the enumerated powers of § 8], and all other Powers vested by this Constitution in the government of the United States, or in any Department or Officer thereof." It is long-settled that Congress may "exercise its best judgment in the selection of measures, to carry into execution the constitutional powers of the government," and "avail itself of experience, to exercise its reason, and to accommodate its legislation to circumstances." *McCulloch v. Maryland*, 4 Wheat. 316, 415–416, 420 (1819).

The Court heeded this counsel in approving the modern administrative state. The Court's holding today that all legislative-type action must be enacted through the lawmaking process ignores that legislative authority is routinely delegated to the Executive branch, to the independent regulatory agencies, and to private individuals and groups. . . .

This Court's decisions sanctioning such delegations make clear that Article I does not require all action with the effect of legislation to be passed as a law.

Theoretically, agencies and officials were asked only to "fill up the details," and the rule was that "Congress cannot delegate any part of its legislative power except under a limitation of a prescribed standard." Chief Justice Taft elaborated the standard in *J.W. Hampton & Co. v. United States*, 276 U.S. 394, 409 (1928): "If Congress shall lay down by legislative act an intelligible principle to which the person or body authorized to fix such rates is directed to conform, such legislative action is not a forbidden delegation of legislative power." In practice, however, restrictions on the scope of the power that could be delegated diminished and all but disappeared. In only two instances did the Court find an unconstitutional delegation. In other cases, the "intelligible principle" through which agencies have attained enormous control over the economic affairs of the country was held to include such formulations as "just and reasonable," "public interest," "public convenience, interest, or necessity," and "unfair methods of competition."

The wisdom and the constitutionality of these broad delegations are matters that still have not been put to rest. But for present purposes, these cases establish that by virtue of congressional delegation, legislative power can be exercised by independent agencies and Executive departments without the passage of new legislation. For some time, the sheer amount of law—the substantive rules that regulate private conduct and direct the operation of government—made by the agencies has far outnumbered the lawmaking engaged in by Congress through the traditional process. There is no question but that agency rulemaking is lawmaking in any functional or realistic sense of the term. The Administrative Procedure Act, 5 U.S.C. § 551(4), provides that a "rule" is an agency statement "designed to implement, interpret, or prescribe law or policy." When agencies are authorized to prescribe law through substantive rulemaking, the administrator's regulation is not only due deference, but is accorded "legislative effect." These regulations bind courts and officers of the federal government, may preempt state law, and grant rights to and impose obligations on the public. In sum, they have the force of law.

If Congress may delegate lawmaking power to independent and executive agencies, it is most difficult to understand Article I as forbidding Congress from also reserving a check on legislative power for itself. Absent the veto, the agencies receiving delegations of legislative or quasi-legislative power may issue regulations having the force of law without bicameral approval and without the President's signature. It is thus not apparent why the reservation of a veto over the exercise of that legislative power must be subject to a more exacting test. In both cases, it is enough that the initial statutory authorizations comply with the Article I requirements. . . .

The Court's opinion in the present case comes closest to facing the reality of administrative lawmaking in considering the contention that the Attorney General's action in suspending deportation under § 244 is itself a legislative act. The Court posits that the Attorney General is acting in an Article II enforcement capacity under § 244. . . .

[E]ven if the Court correctly characterizes the Attorney General's authority under § 244 as an Article II Executive power, the Court concedes that certain administrative agency action, such as rulemaking, "may resemble lawmaking" and recognizes that "[t]his Court has referred to agency activity as being 'quasi-legislative' in character. Such rules and adjudications by the agencies meet the Court's own definition of legislative action for they "alter [ ] the legal rights, duties, and relations of persons . . . outside the legislative branch," and involve "determinations of policy." Under the Court's analysis, the Executive Branch and the independent agencies may make rules with the effect of law while Congress, in whom the Framers confided the legislative power, may not exercise a veto which precludes such rules from having operative force. If the effective functioning of a complex modern government requires the delegation of vast authority which, by virtue of its breadth, is legislative or "quasi-legislative" in character, I cannot accept that Article I—which is, after all, the source of the non-delegation doctrine—should forbid Congress from qualifying that grant with a legislative veto. . . .

[A dissent by Justices Rehnquist and White on severability is omitted.—Ed.]

Notes and Questions

1. The power at issue in Chadha. What kind of power was Congress purporting to exercise? The Court says legislative power. Do you agree? If Congress was exercising legislative power by seeking to stop the suspension of a deportation, why was the President's suspension in the first place not also an exercise of legislative power? Does the nature of the power depend on the branch exercising that power? Is there an argument that Congress's action was unconstitutional on any account of the power it was seeking to exercise?

2. *The delegation trade-off.* Justice White, in dissent, argued that the legislative veto was the price the executive had to pay in exchange for broad delegations of power from Congress to the executive. Do you agree with Justice White that the ex-

HISTORICAL PERSPECTIVE The majority in *Chadha* cites *The Federalist Papers* for the proposition that the Framers feared legislative aggrandizement. Is that still of concern today? Or should we be more fearful of executive aggrandizement?

ecutive branch sometimes exercises legislative power in fact, even if the doctrine claims that the executive branch merely exercises executive power? Would it be better to recognize the reality that Congress in fact delegates legislative power? Or is rulemaking "nonexclusive" legislative power? Is Justice White's functionalist approach more attractive than the majority's formalist one?

3. *The REINS Act.* A bill, The Regulations from the Executive in Need of Scrutiny Act, or the REINS Act, has been previously introduced in Congress. This Act would require that all "major" regulations, defined as those having more than $100 million in economic effect, would first have to be enacted by Congress and the President in order to take effect. If Congress and the President did not enact such regulations, those regulations would not take effect. Do you see how this proposal is different than the legislative veto the Court struck down in *Chadha*? Nevertheless, is this proposal constitutional?

Bowsher v. Synar

478 U.S. 714 (1986)

CHIEF JUSTICE BURGER delivered the opinion of the Court.

The question presented by these appeals is whether the assignment by Congress to the Comptroller General of the United States of certain functions under the Balanced Budget and Emergency Deficit Control Act of 1985 violates the doctrine of separation of powers.

I

A

On December 12, 1985, the President signed into law the Balanced Budget and Emergency Deficit Control Act of 1985, popularly known as the "Gramm-Rudman-Hollings Act." The purpose of the Act is to eliminate the federal budget deficit. To that end, the Act sets a "maximum deficit amount" for federal spending for each of fiscal years 1986 through 1991. The size of that maximum deficit amount progressively reduces to zero in fiscal year 1991. If in any fiscal year the federal budget deficit exceeds the maximum deficit amount by more than a specified sum, the Act requires across-the-board cuts in federal spending to reach the targeted deficit level, with half of the cuts made to defense programs and the other half made to nondefense programs. The Act exempts certain priority programs from these cuts.

These "automatic" reductions are accomplished through a rather complicated procedure, spelled out in § 251, the so-called "reporting provisions" of the Act. Each year, the Directors of the Office of Management and Budget (OMB) and the Congressional Budget Office (CBO) independently estimate the amount of the federal budget deficit for the upcoming fiscal year. If that deficit exceeds the maximum targeted deficit amount for that fiscal year by more than a specified amount, the Directors of OMB and CBO independently calculate, on a program-by-program basis, the budget reductions necessary to ensure that the deficit does not exceed the maximum deficit amount. The Act then requires the Directors to report jointly their deficit estimates and budget reduction calculations to the Comptroller General.

The Comptroller General, after reviewing the Directors' reports, then reports his conclusions to the President. § 251(b). The President in turn must issue a "sequestration" order mandating the spending reductions specified by the Comptroller General. § 252. There follows a period during which Congress may by legislation reduce spending to obviate, in whole or in part, the need for the sequestration order. If such reductions are not enacted, the sequestration order becomes effective and the spending reductions included in that order are made.

Anticipating constitutional challenge to these procedures, the Act also contains a "fallback" deficit reduction process to take effect "[i]n the event that any of the reporting procedures described in section 251 are invalidated." § 274(f). Under these provisions, the report prepared by the Directors of OMB and the

CBO is submitted directly to a specially created Temporary Joint Committee on Deficit Reduction, which must report in five days to both Houses a joint resolution setting forth the content of the Directors' report. Congress then must vote on the resolution under special rules, which render amendments out of order. If the resolution is passed and signed by the President, it then serves as the basis for a Presidential sequestration order.

B

Within hours of the President's signing of the Act, Congressman Synar, who had voted against the Act, filed a complaint seeking declaratory relief that the Act was unconstitutional. Eleven other Members later joined Congressman Synar's suit. A virtually identical lawsuit was also filed by the National Treasury Employees Union. The Union alleged that its members had been injured as a result of the Act's automatic spending reduction provisions, which have suspended certain cost-of-living benefit increases to the Union's members.

A three-judge District Court . . . invalidated the reporting provisions. *Synar v. United States*, 626 F. Supp. 1374 (D.C. Cir. 1986) (Scalia, Johnson and Gasch, JJ.). The District Court concluded that the Union had standing to challenge the Act since the members of the Union had suffered actual injury by suspension of certain benefit increases. The District Court also concluded that Congressman Synar and his fellow Members had standing under the so-called "congressional standing" doctrine. . . .

[T]he District Court . . . held that the role of the Comptroller General in the deficit reduction process violated the constitutionally imposed separation of powers. The court first explained that the Comptroller General exercises executive functions under the Act. However, the Comptroller General, while appointed by the President with the advice and consent of the Senate, is removable not by the President but only by a joint resolution of Congress or by impeachment. . . .

* * *

III

We noted recently that "[t]he Constitution sought to divide the delegated powers of the new Federal Government into three defined categories, Legislative, Executive, and Judicial." *INS v. Chadha*, 462 U.S. 919, 951 (1983). The declared purpose of separating and dividing the powers of government, of course, was to "diffus[e] power the better to secure liberty." *Youngstown Sheet & Tube Co. v. Sawyer*, 343 U.S. 579, 635 (1952) (Jackson, J., concurring).

[In omitted paragraphs, the Court goes through various removal-power precedents, which we encounter in Chapter 6.—Ed.]

In light of these precedents, we conclude that Congress cannot reserve for itself the power of removal of an officer charged with the execution of the laws except by impeachment. To permit the execution of the laws to be vested in an officer answerable only to Congress would, in practical terms, reserve in Congress control over the execution of the laws. . . .

Our decision in *INS v. Chadha* supports this conclusion. In *Chadha*, we struck down a one-House "legislative veto" provision by which each House of Congress retained the power to reverse a decision Congress had expressly authorized the Attorney General to make . . . .

To permit an officer controlled by Congress to execute the laws would be, in essence, to permit a congressional veto. Congress could simply remove, or threaten to remove, an officer for executing the laws in any fashion found to be unsatisfactory to Congress. This kind of congressional control over the execution of the laws, *Chadha* makes clear, is constitutionally impermissible.

The dangers of congressional usurpation of Executive Branch functions have long been recognized. "[T]he debates of the Constitutional Convention, and the Federalist Papers, are replete with expressions of fear that the Legislative Branch of the National Government will aggrandize itself at the expense of the other two branches." *Buckley v. Valeo*, 424 U.S. 1, 129 (1976). . . .

* * *

V

The primary responsibility of the Comptroller General under the instant Act is the preparation of a "report." This report must contain detailed estimates of projected federal revenues and expenditures. The report must also specify the reductions, if any, necessary to reduce the deficit to the target for the appropriate fiscal year. The reductions must be set forth on a program-by-program basis.

In preparing the report, the Comptroller General is to have "due regard" for the estimates and reductions set forth in a joint report submitted to him by the Director of CBO and the Director of OMB, the President's fiscal and budgetary adviser. However, the Act plainly contemplates that the Comptroller General will exercise his independent judgment and evaluation with respect to those estimates. . . .

Appellants suggest that the duties assigned to the Comptroller General in the Act are essentially ministerial and mechanical so that their performance does not constitute "execution of the law" in a meaningful sense. On the contrary, we view these functions as plainly entailing execution of the law in constitutional terms. Interpreting a law enacted by Congress to implement the legislative mandate is the very essence of "execution" of the law. Under § 251, the Comptroller General must exercise judgment concerning facts that affect the application of the Act. He must also interpret the provisions of the Act to determine precisely what budgetary calculations are required. Decisions of that kind are typically made by officers charged with executing a statute.

The executive nature of the Comptroller General's functions under the Act is revealed in § 252(a)(3) which gives the Comptroller General the ultimate authority to determine the budget cuts to be made. Indeed, the Comptroller General commands the President himself to carry out, without the slightest variation . . . the directive of the Comptroller General as to the budget reductions . . . .

Congress of course initially determined the content of the Balanced Budget and Emergency Deficit Control Act; and undoubtedly the content of the Act determines the nature of the executive duty. However, as *Chadha* makes clear, once Congress makes its choice in enacting legislation, its participation ends. Congress can thereafter control the execution of its enactment only indirectly—by passing new legislation. By placing the responsibility for execution of the Balanced Budget and Emergency Deficit Control Act in the hands of an officer who is subject to removal only by itself, Congress in effect has retained control over the execution of the Act and has intruded into the executive function. The Constitution does not permit such intrusion. . . .

Justice Stevens, with whom Justice Marshall joins, concurring in the judgment.

. . . . I agree with the Court that the "Gramm-Rudman-Hollings" Act contains a constitutional infirmity so severe that the flawed provision may not stand. I disagree with the Court, however, on the reasons why the Constitution prohibits the Comptroller General from exercising the powers assigned to him by § 251(b) and § 251(c)(2) of the Act. It is not the dormant, carefully circumscribed congressional removal power that represents the primary constitutional evil. Nor do I agree with the conclusion of both the majority and the dissent that the analysis depends on a labeling of the functions assigned to the Comptroller General as "executive powers." Rather, I am convinced that the Comptroller General must be characterized as an agent of Congress because of his longstanding statutory responsibilities; that the powers assigned to him under the Gramm-Rudman-Hollings Act require him to make policy that will bind the Nation; and that, when Congress, or a component or an agent of Congress, seeks to make policy that will bind the Nation, it must follow the procedures mandated by Article I of the Constitution—through passage by both Houses and presentment to the President. In short, Congress may not exercise its fundamental power to formulate national policy by delegating that power to one of its two Houses, to a legislative committee, or to an individual agent of the Congress such as the Speaker of the House of Representatives, the Sergeant at Arms of the Senate, or the Director of the Congressional Budget Office. *INS v. Chadha*, 462 U.S. 919 (1983). That principle, I believe, is applicable to the Comptroller General. . . .

       * * *

III

Everyone agrees that the powers assigned to the Comptroller General by § 251(b) and § 251(c)(2) of the Gramm-Rudman-Hollings Act are extremely important. They require him to exercise sophisticated economic judgment concerning anticipated trends in the Nation's economy, projected levels of unemployment, interest rates, and the special problems that may be confronted by the many components of a vast federal bureaucracy. His duties are anything but ministerial—he is not merely a clerk wearing a "green eye-shade" as he undertakes these tasks. Rather, he is vested with the kind of responsibilities that Congress has elected to discharge itself under the fallback provision that will become effective if and when § 251(b) and § 251(c)(2) are held invalid. Unless we make the naive assumption that the economic destiny of the Nation could be safely entrusted to a mindless bank of computers, the powers that this Act vests in the Comptroller General must be recognized as having transcendent importance.

The Court concludes that the Gramm-Rudman-Hollings Act impermissibly assigns the Comptroller General "executive powers." Justice White's dissent agrees that "the powers exercised by the Comptroller under the Act may be characterized as 'executive' in that they involve the interpretation and carrying out of the Act's mandate." This conclusion is not only far from obvious but also rests on the unstated and unsound premise that there is a definite line that distinguishes executive power from legislative power. . . .

"The men who met in Philadelphia in the summer of 1787 were practical statesmen, experienced in politics, who viewed the principle of separation of powers as a vital check against tyranny. But they likewise saw that a hermetic sealing off of the three branches of Government from one another would preclude the establishment of a Nation capable of governing itself effectively." *Buckley v. Valeo*, 424 U.S. 1, 121 (1976). . . .

One reason that the exercise of legislative, executive, and judicial powers cannot be categorically distributed among three mutually exclusive branches of Government is that governmental power cannot always be readily characterized with only one of those three labels. On the contrary, as our cases demonstrate, a particular function, like a chameleon, will often take on the aspect of the office to which it is assigned. For this reason, "[w]hen any Branch acts, it is presumptively exercising the power the Constitution has delegated to it." *INS v. Chadha*, 462 U.S. at 951.

The *Chadha* case itself illustrates this basic point. The governmental decision that was being made was whether a resident alien who had overstayed his student visa should be deported. From the point of view of the Administrative Law Judge who conducted a hearing on the issue—or as JUSTICE POWELL saw the issue in his concurrence—the decision took on a judicial coloring. From the point of view of the Attorney General of the United States to whom Congress had delegated the authority to suspend deportation of certain aliens, the decision appeared to have an executive character. But, as the Court held, when the House of Representatives finally decided that Chadha must be deported, its action "was essentially legislative in purpose and effect."

The powers delegated to the Comptroller General by § 251 of the Act before us today have a similar chameleon-like quality. The District Court persuasively explained why they may be appropriately characterized as executive powers. But, when that delegation is held invalid, the "fallback provision" provides that the report that would otherwise be issued by the Comptroller General shall be issued by Congress itself. In the event that the resolution is enacted, the congressional report will have the same legal consequences as if it had been issued by the Comptroller General. In that event, moreover, surely no one would suggest that Congress had acted in any capacity other than "legislative." . . .

Under the District Court's analysis, and the analysis adopted by the majority today, it would therefore appear that the function at issue is "executive" if performed by the Comptroller General but "legislative" if performed by the Congress. In my view, however, the function may appropriately be labeled "legislative" even if performed by the Comptroller General or by an executive agency.

Despite the statement in Article I of the Constitution that "All legislative Powers herein granted shall be vested in a Congress of the United States," it is far from novel to acknowledge that independent agencies do indeed exercise legislative powers. . . .

Thus, I do not agree that the Comptroller General's responsibilities under the Gramm-Rudman-Hollings Act must be termed "executive powers," or even that our inquiry is much advanced by using that term. For, whatever the label given the functions to be performed by the Comptroller General under § 251—or by the Congress under § 274—the District Court had no difficulty in concluding that Congress could delegate the performance of those functions to another branch of the Government. If the delegation to a stranger is permissible, why may not Congress delegate the same responsibilities to one of its own agents? That is the central question before us today.

IV

. . . . The Gramm-Rudman-Hollings Act assigns to the Comptroller General the duty to make policy decisions that have the force of law. The Comptroller General's report is, in the current statute, the engine that gives life to the ambitious budget reduction process. . . . It is, in short, the Comptroller General's report that will have a profound, dramatic, and immediate impact on the Government and on the Nation at large.

Article I of the Constitution specifies the procedures that Congress must follow when it makes policy that binds the Nation: its legislation must be approved by both of its Houses and presented to the President. . . .

If Congress were free to delegate its policymaking authority to one of its components, or to one of its agents, it would be able to evade "the carefully crafted restraints spelled out in the Constitution." That danger—congressional action that evades constitutional restraints—is not present when Congress delegates lawmaking power to the executive or to an independent agency. . . .

In short, even though it is well settled that Congress may delegate legislative power to independent agencies or to the Executive, and thereby divest itself of a portion of its lawmaking power, when it elects to exercise such power itself, it may not authorize a lesser representative of the Legislative Branch to act on its behalf. It is for this reason that I believe § 251(b) and § 251(c)(2) of the Act are unconstitutional. . . .

Justice White, dissenting.

The Court, acting in the name of separation of powers, takes upon itself to strike down the Gramm-Rudman-Hollings Act, one of the most novel and far-reaching legislative responses to a national crisis since the New Deal. . . . Like the Court, I will not purport to speak to the wisdom of the policies incorporated in the legislation the Court invalidates; that is a matter for the Congress and the Executive, *both* of which expressed their assent to the statute barely half a year ago. I will, however, address the wisdom of the Court's willingness to interpose its distressingly formalistic view of separation of powers as a bar to the attainment of governmental objectives through the means chosen by the Congress and the President in the legislative process established by the Constitution. . . . As I will explain, the Court's decision rests on a feature of the legislative scheme that is of minimal practical significance and that presents no substantial threat to the basic scheme of separation of powers. In attaching dispositive significance to what should be regarded as a triviality, the Court neglects what has in the past been recognized as a fundamental principle governing consideration of disputes over separation of powers:

> "The actual art of governing under our Constitution does not and cannot conform to judicial definitions of the power of any of its branches based on isolated clauses or even single Articles torn from context. While the Constitution diffuses power the better to secure liberty, it also contemplates that practice will integrate the dispersed powers into a workable government."

Youngstown Sheet & Tube Co. v. Sawyer, 343 U.S. 579, 635 (1952) (Jackson, J., concurring).

I

* * *

It is evident . . . that the powers exercised by the Comptroller General under the Gramm-Rudman-Hollings Act are not such that vesting them in an officer not subject to removal at will by the President would in itself improperly interfere with Presidential powers. Determining the level of spending by the Federal Government is not by nature a function central either to the exercise of the President's enumerated powers or to his general duty to ensure execution of the laws; rather, appropriating funds is a peculiarly legislative function, and one expressly committed to Congress by Art. I, § 9, which provides that "No Money shall be drawn from the Treasury, but in Consequence of Appropriations made by Law." In enacting Gramm-Rudman-Hollings, Congress has chosen to exercise this legislative power to establish the level of federal spending by providing a detailed set of criteria for reducing expenditures below the level of appropriations in the event that certain conditions are met. Delegating the execution of this legislation—that is, the power to apply the Act's criteria and make the required calculations—to an officer independent of the President's will does not deprive the President of any power that he would otherwise have or that is essential to the performance of the duties of his office. . . .

In Gramm-Rudman-Hollings . . . Congress . . . created a precise and articulated set of criteria designed to minimize the degree of policy choice exercised by the officer executing the statute and to ensure that the relative spending priorities established by Congress in the appropriations it passes into law remain unaltered. Given that the exercise of policy choice by the officer executing the statute would be inimical to Congress' goal in enacting "automatic" budget-cutting measures, it is eminently reasonable and proper for Congress to vest the budget-cutting authority in an officer who is to the greatest degree possible nonpartisan and independent of the President and his political agenda and who therefore may be relied upon not to allow his calculations to be colored by political considerations. Such a delegation deprives the President of no authority that is rightfully his.

II

* * *

More importantly, the substantial role played by the President in the process of removal through joint resolution reduces to utter insignificance the possibility that the threat of removal will induce subservience to the Congress. As I have pointed out above, a joint resolution must be presented to the President and is ineffective if it is vetoed by him, unless the veto is overridden by the constitutionally prescribed two-thirds majority of both Houses of Congress. The requirement of Presidential approval obviates the possibility that the Comptroller will perceive himself as so completely at the mercy of Congress that he will function as its tool. . . .

The practical result of the removal provision is not to render the Comptroller unduly dependent upon or subservient to Congress, but to render him one of the most independent officers in the entire federal establishment. . . .

Realistic consideration of the nature of the Comptroller General's relation to Congress thus reveals that the threat to separation of powers conjured up by the majority is wholly chimerical. . . .

[A separate dissent by JUSTICE BLACKMUN is omitted.—Ed.]

NOTES AND QUESTIONS

1. *The power at issue in* Bowsher. Was the Comptroller exercising legislative power, or executive power? Can the argument be made that on either account of the power, it was unconstitutional for the Comptroller to exercise it?

2. *Stevens's concurrence.* Justice Stevens in his concurrence takes up Justice White's notion in *Chadha*, which Stevens would repeat later in *Whitman v. American Trucking*, that Congress in fact routinely delegates legislative power. He joined the majority, however, because he argued that while it was constitutional for Congress to delegate its legislative powers to the executive branch, it was *not* constitutional for Congress to delegate its legislative powers to a subcomponent of itself. Why would that be the case? If it's acceptable to delegate legislative power to the executive, why not to one House of Congress, or one committee? Recall that under the majority's approach, and as Justice Scalia reminds us in *City of Arlington v. FCC*, the whole theory of nondelegation is that when the executive exercises delegated power, it is not exercising legislative power but rather executive power. Under that approach, it would make sense for the executive to exercise such power.

NONEXCLUSIVE POWER
Justice Stevens makes arguments in *Bowsher* that he would later repeat in *Whitman*, discussed earlier in this chapter. Do you agree with Justice Stevens' characterization of government power?

Justice Stevens also suggests that there is no definite test for distinguishing between legislative and executive power, and that governmental power is in fact "chameleon like," taking on the characteristic of the branch exercising that power. Do you agree? Are the budget cuts executive when the President does them, but legislative when Congress does? Would a better approach be to recognize categories of *exclusive* powers and *nonexclusive* powers? Recall that Chief Justice Marshall, in *Wayman v. Southard*, argued that there was a category of "exclusively legislative" power that Congress could not delegate. Recall also George Washington's regulations respecting the payments to be made to the invalid veterans of the Revolutionary War. Surely Congress could have made those regulations by legislation if it had wanted; but did Congress *have* to make them? Could those regulations be characterized as either legislative or executive—or perhaps *partly* legislative and *partly* executive—because either branch could create them? Wouldn't identifying exclusive powers that only the particular branch can exercise, and nonexclusive powers that more than one branch can exercise, clarify the nature of governmental power?

TEST YOUR KNOWLEDGE: To assess your understanding of the material in this chapter, **click here** to take a quiz.

CHAPTER SIX

The President and the Administration

The previous chapter dealt with the relationship of agencies to Congress and their activities to legislative power. This chapter deals with the relationship of agencies to the President and their activities to the executive power. Recall from the introductory chapter that the Constitution clearly contemplates the existence of executive departments and officers; it was widely understood that the President would need assistants to help execute the laws. The predominant question running through these cases and materials is whether the President can control these assistants by the powers to appoint, direct, and remove them, or whether Congress can insulate administrative officers from presidential control and influence. The chapter begins with the appointment power, proceeds to the removal power, and concludes with some thoughts on the President's ability to influence administration.

COURSE THEME

POLITICAL INFLUENCE
We previously discussed what role politics should play in administration. In this chapter, we explore whether the Constitution itself has something to say on the matter.

A. Appointments

Article II of the Constitution provides the mechanism for appointing officers of the United States. Article II, Section 2, Paragraph 2 provides:

> [The President] . . . shall nominate, and by and with the Advice and Consent of the Senate, shall appoint Ambassadors, other public Ministers and Consuls, Judges of the supreme Court, and all other Officers of the United States, whose Appointments are not herein

otherwise provided for, and which shall be established by Law: but the Congress may by Law vest the Appointment of such inferior Officers, as they think proper, in the President alone, in the Courts of Law, or in the Heads of Departments.

From this text it becomes clear that there are two kinds of officers contemplated by the Constitution: principal officers and inferior officers. Principal officers *must* be appointed by the President by and with the advice and consent of the Senate. In contrast, Congress can choose to vest the appointment of inferior officers in the President alone, the heads of departments, or the courts of law. If Congress does not choose to vest the appointment of an inferior officer according to this exception, then the default mode of appointment is the same as for principal officers—by the President by and with advice and consent of the Senate.

> **Defined Term**
>
> **PRINCIPAL OFFICER:** An officer, like a cabinet secretary, who must be appointed by and with the advice and consent of the Senate.

For purposes of administrative law, then, there are two issues. First, who qualifies as an "officer of the United States," such that they must be appointed pursuant to the mechanisms provided in Article II, Section 2, Paragraph 2? Some individuals who work for the executive branch are considered mere *employees*, and they can be appointed or employed by whatever means Congress provides. For example, many civil servants are classified as employees. The second issue is, once we know we are dealing with an officer, is that officer a principal officer or an inferior officer?

> **Defined Term**
>
> **INFERIOR OFFICER:** A subordinate officer whose appointment Congress, if it chooses, can place in the hands of a principal officer, the President, or the courts, without the advice and consent of the Senate.

1.   Who Is an Officer?

Lucia v. SEC

138 S. Ct. 2044 (2018)

JUSTICE KAGAN delivered the opinion of the Court.

The Appointments Clause of the Constitution lays out the permissible methods of appointing "Officers of the United States," a class of government officials distinct from mere employees. Art. II, § 2, cl. 2. This case requires us to decide whether administrative law judges (ALJs) of the Securities and Exchange Commission (SEC or Commission) qualify as such "Officers." In keeping with *Freytag v. Commissioner,* 501 U.S. 868 (1991), we hold that they do.

I

The SEC has statutory authority to enforce the nation's securities laws. One way it can do so is by instituting an administrative proceeding against an alleged wrongdoer. By law, the Commission may itself preside over such a proceeding. See 17 C.F.R. § 201.110 (2017). But the Commission also may, and typically does, delegate that task to an ALJ. See *ibid.;* 15 U.S.C. § 78d–1(a). The SEC currently has five ALJs. Other staff members, rather than the Commission proper, selected them all.

An ALJ assigned to hear an SEC enforcement action has extensive powers—the "authority to do all things necessary and appropriate to discharge his or her duties" and ensure a "fair and orderly" adversarial proceeding. §§ 201.111, 200.14(a). Those powers "include, but are not limited to," supervising discovery; issuing, revoking, or modifying subpoenas; deciding motions; ruling on the admissibility of evidence; administering oaths; hearing and examining witnesses; generally "[r]egulating the course of" the proceeding and the "conduct of the parties and their counsel"; and imposing sanctions for "[c]ontemptuous conduct" or violations of procedural requirements. §§ 201.111, 201.180; see §§ 200.14(a), 201.230. As that list suggests, an SEC ALJ exercises authority "comparable to" that of a federal district judge conducting a bench trial.

After a hearing ends, the ALJ issues an "initial decision." § 201.360(a)(1). That decision must set out "findings and conclusions" about all "material issues of fact [and] law"; it also must include the "appropriate order, sanction, relief, or denial thereof." § 201.360(b). The Commission can then review the ALJ's decision, either upon request or *sua sponte*. See § 201.360(d)(1). But if it opts against review, the Commission "issue[s] an order that the [ALJ's] decision has become final." § 201.360(d)(2). At that point, the initial decision is "deemed the action of the Commission." § 78d–1(c).

This case began when the SEC instituted an administrative proceeding against petitioner Raymond Lucia and his investment company. Lucia market-ed a retirement savings strategy called "Buckets of Money." In the SEC's view, Lucia used misleading slideshow presentations to deceive prospective clients. The SEC charged Lucia under the Investment Advisers Act, § 80b–1 *et seq.*, and assigned ALJ Cameron Elliot to adjudicate the case. After nine days of testimony and argument, Judge Elliot issued an initial decision concluding that Lucia had violated the Act and imposing sanctions, including civil penalties of $300,000 and a lifetime bar from the investment industry. In his decision, Judge Elliot made factual findings about only one of the four ways the SEC thought Lucia's slideshow misled investors. The Commission thus remanded for factfinding on the other three claims, explaining that an ALJ's "personal experience with the witnesses" places him "in the best position to make find-ings of fact" and "resolve any conflicts in the evidence." Judge Elliot then made additional findings of deception and issued a revised initial decision, with the same sanctions.

On appeal to the SEC, Lucia argued that the administrative proceeding was invalid because Judge Elliot had not been constitutionally appointed. Ac-cording to Lucia, the Commission's ALJs are "Officers of the United States" and thus subject to the Appointments Clause. Under that Clause, Lucia noted, only the President, "Courts of Law," or "Heads of Departments" can appoint "Officers." See Art. II, § 2, cl. 2. And none of those actors had made Judge Elliot an ALJ. To be sure, the Commission itself counts as a "Head[ ] of De-partment[ ]." [S]ee *Free Enterprise Fund v. Public Company Accounting Oversight Bd.*, 561 U.S. 477, 511–513 (2010). But the Commission had left the task of appointing ALJs, including Judge Elliot, to SEC staff members. As a result, Lucia contended, Judge Elliot lacked constitutional authority to do his job.

The Commission rejected Lucia's argument. It held that the SEC's ALJs are not "Officers of the United States." Instead, they are "mere employees"—officials with lesser responsibilities who fall outside the Appointments Clause's ambit. The Commission reasoned that its ALJs do not "exercise significant authority independent of [its own] supervision." Because that is so (said the SEC), they need no special, high-level appointment. . . .

II

The sole question here is whether the Commission's ALJs are "Officers of the United States" or simply employees of the Federal Government. The Appointments Clause prescribes the exclusive means of appointing "Officers." Only the President, a court of law, or a head of department can do so. See Art. II, § 2, cl. 2. And as all parties agree, none of those actors appointed Judge Elliot before he heard Lucia's case; instead, SEC staff members gave him an ALJ slot. So if the Commission's ALJs are constitutional officers, Lucia raises a valid Appointments Clause claim. The only way to defeat his position is to show that those ALJs are not officers at all, but instead non-officer employees—part of the broad swath of "lesser functionaries" in the Government's workforce. *Buckley v. Valeo*, 424 U.S. 1, 126, n. 162 (1976). For if that is true, the Appointments Clause cares not a whit about who named them. See *United States v. Germaine*, 99 U.S. 508, 510 (1879).

Two decisions set out this Court's basic framework for distinguishing between officers and employees. *Germaine* held that "civil surgeons" (doctors hired to perform various physical exams) were mere employees because their duties were "occasional or temporary" rather than "continuing and permanent." *Id.* at 511–512. Stressing "ideas of tenure [and] duration," the Court there made clear that an individual must occupy a "continuing" position established by law to qualify as an officer. *Id.* at 511. *Buckley* then set out another requirement, central to this case. It determined that members of a federal commission were officers only after finding that they "exercis[ed] significant authority pursuant to the laws of the United States." 424 U.S. at 126. The inquiry thus focused on the extent of power an individual wields in carrying out his assigned functions. . . .

[I]n *Freytag v. Commissioner*, 501 U.S. 868 (1991), we applied the unadorned "significant authority" test to adjudicative officials who are near-carbon copies of the Commission's ALJs. As we now explain, our analysis there . . . necessarily decides this case.

The officials at issue in *Freytag* were the "special trial judges" (STJs) of the United States Tax Court. The authority of those judges depended on the significance of the tax dispute before them. In "comparatively narrow and minor matters," they could both hear and definitively resolve a case for the Tax Court. In more major matters, they could preside over the hearing, but could not issue the final decision; instead, they were to "prepare proposed findings and an opinion" for a regular Tax Court judge to consider. The proceeding challenged in *Freytag* was a major one, involving $1.5 billion in alleged tax deficiencies. After conducting a 14-week trial, the STJ drafted a proposed decision in favor of the Government. A regular judge then adopted the STJ's work as the opinion of the Tax Court. The losing parties argued on appeal that the STJ was not constitutionally appointed.

This Court held that the Tax Court's STJs are officers, not mere employees. Citing *Germaine,* the Court first found that STJs hold a continuing office established by law. See 501 U.S. at 881. They serve on an ongoing, rather than a "temporary [or] episodic [,] basis"; and their "duties, salary, and means of appointment" are all specified in the Tax Code. The Court then considered, as *Buckley* demands, the "significance" of the "authority" STJs wield. In addressing that issue, the Government had argued that STJs are employees, rather than officers, in all cases (like the one at issue) in which they could not "enter a final decision." But the Court thought the Government's focus on finality "ignore[d] the significance of the duties and discretion that [STJs] possess." Describing the responsibilities involved in presiding over adversarial hearings, the Court said: STJs "take testimony, conduct trials, rule on the admissibility of evidence, and have the power to enforce compliance with discovery orders." *Id.* at 881–882. And the Court observed that "[i]n the course of carrying out these important functions, the [STJs] exercise significant discretion." *Id.* at 882. That fact meant they were officers, even when their decisions were not final.

Freytag says everything necessary to decide this case. To begin, the Commission's ALJs, like the Tax Court's STJs, hold a continuing office established by law. Indeed, everyone here—Lucia, the Government, and the *amicus*—agrees on that point. Far from serving temporarily or episodically, SEC ALJs "receive[ ] a career appointment." 5 C.F.R. § 930.204(a) (2018). And that appointment is to a position created by statute, down to its "duties, salary, and means of appointment." *Freytag,* 501 U.S. at 878; see 5 U.S.C. §§ 556–557, 5372, 3105.

Still more, the Commission's ALJs exercise the same "significant discretion" when carrying out the same "important functions" as STJs do. Both sets of officials have all the authority needed to ensure fair and orderly adversarial hearings—indeed, nearly all the tools of federal trial judges. Consider in order the four specific (if overlapping) powers *Freytag* mentioned. First, the Commission's ALJs (like the Tax Court's STJs) "take testimony." More precisely, they "[r]eceiv[e] evidence" and "[e]xamine witnesses" at hearings, and may also take pre-hearing depositions. Second, the ALJs (like STJs) "conduct trials." As detailed earlier, they administer oaths, rule on motions, and generally "regulat[e] the course of" a hearing, as well as the conduct of parties and counsel. Third, the ALJs (like STJs) "rule on the admissibility of evidence." They thus critically shape the administrative record (as they also do when issuing document subpoenas). And fourth, the ALJs (like STJs) "have the power to enforce compliance with discovery orders." In particular, they may punish all "[c]ontemptuous conduct," including violations of those orders, by means as severe as excluding the offender from the hearing. So point for point—straight from *Freytag*'s list—the Commission's ALJs have equivalent duties and powers as STJs in conducting adversarial inquiries.

And at the close of those proceedings, ALJs issue decisions much like that in *Freytag*—except with potentially more independent effect. As the *Freytag* Court recounted, STJs "prepare proposed findings and an opinion" adjudicating charges and assessing tax liabilities. Similarly, the Commission's ALJs issue decisions containing factual findings, legal conclusions, and appropriate remedies. And what happens next reveals that the ALJ can play the more autonomous role. In a major case like *Freytag*, a regular Tax Court judge must always review an STJ's opinion. And that opinion counts for nothing unless the regular judge adopts it as his own. By contrast, the SEC can decide against reviewing an ALJ decision at all. And when the SEC declines review (and issues an order saying so), the ALJ's decision itself "becomes final" and is "deemed the action of the Commission." That last-word capacity makes this an *a fortiori* case: If the Tax Court's STJs are officers, as *Freytag* held, then the Commission's ALJs must be too. . . .

The only issue left is remedial. For all the reasons we have given, and all those *Freytag* gave before, the Commission's ALJs are "Officers of the United States," subject to the Appointments Clause. And as noted earlier, Judge Elliot heard and decided Lucia's case without the kind of appointment the Clause requires. . . . This Court has . . . held that the "appropriate" remedy for an adjudication tainted with an appointments violation is a new "hearing before a properly appointed" official. And we add today one thing more. That official cannot be Judge Elliot, even if he has by now received (or receives sometime in the future) a constitutional appointment. Judge Elliot has already both heard Lucia's case and issued an initial decision on the merits. He cannot be expected to consider the matter as though he had not adjudicated it before. To cure the constitutional error, another ALJ (or the Commission itself) must hold the new hearing to which Lucia is entitled. . . .

Justice Thomas, with whom Justice Gorsuch joins, concurring.

I agree with the Court that this case is indistinguishable from *Freytag v. Commissioner*, 501 U.S. 868 (1991). . . . Moving forward, however, this Court will not be able to decide every Appointments Clause case by comparing it to *Freytag*. And, as the Court acknowledges, our precedents in this area do not provide much guidance. While precedents like *Freytag* discuss what is *sufficient* to make someone an officer of the United States, our precedents have never clearly defined what is *necessary*. I would resolve that question based on the original public meaning of "Officers of the United States." To the Founders, this term encompassed all federal civil officials " 'with responsibility for an ongoing statutory duty.' " Mascott, Who Are "Officers of the United States"? 70 Stan. L. Rev. 443, 564 (2018) (Mascott).

The Appointments Clause provides the exclusive process for appointing "Officers of the United States." While principal officers must be nominated by the President and confirmed by the Senate, Congress can authorize the appointment of "inferior Officers" by "the President alone," "the Courts of Law," or "the Heads of Departments." Art. II, § 2, cl. 2.

This alternative process for appointing inferior officers strikes a balance between efficiency and accountability. Given the sheer number of inferior officers, it would be too burdensome to require each of them to run the gauntlet of Senate confirmation. But, by specifying only a limited number of actors who can appoint inferior officers without Senate confirmation, the Appointments Clause maintains clear lines of accountability—encouraging good appointments and giving the public someone to blame for bad ones.

The Founders likely understood the term "Officers of the United States" to encompass all federal civil officials who perform an ongoing, statutory duty—no matter how important or significant the duty. See Mascott 454. "Officers of the United States" was probably not a term of art that the Constitution used to signify some special type of official. Based on how the Founders used it and similar terms, the phrase "of the United States" was merely a synonym for "federal," and the word "Office[r]" carried its ordinary meaning. The ordinary meaning of "officer" was anyone who performed a continuous public duty. See *id.* at 484–507; *e.g., United States v. Maurice,* 26 F.Cas. 1211, 1214 (No. 15,747) (C.C.D. Va. 1823) (defining officer as someone in " 'a public charge or employment' " who performed a "continuing" duty); 8 Annals of Cong. 2304–2305 (1799) (statement of Rep. Harper) (explaining that the word officer "is derived from the Latin word *officium*" and "includes all persons holding posts which require the performance of some public duty"). For federal officers, that duty is "established by Law"—that is, by statute. Art. II, § 2, cl. 2. The Founders considered individuals to be officers even if they performed only ministerial statutory duties—including recordkeepers, clerks, and tidewaiters (individuals who watched goods land at a customhouse). See Mascott 484–507. Early congressional practice reflected this understanding. With exceptions not relevant here, Congress required all federal officials with ongoing statutory duties to be appointed in compliance with the Appointments Clause. See *id.* at 507–545.

Applying the original meaning here, the administrative law judges of the Securities and Exchange Commission easily qualify as "Officers of the United States." These judges exercise many of the agency's statutory duties, including issuing initial decisions in adversarial proceedings. As explained, the importance or significance of these statutory duties is irrelevant. All that matters is that the judges are continuously responsible for performing them.

In short, the administrative law judges of the Securities Exchange Commission are "Officers of the United States" under the original meaning of the Appointments Clause. They have " 'responsibility for an ongoing statutory duty,' " which is sufficient to resolve this case. Because the Court reaches the same conclusion by correctly applying *Freytag*, I join its opinion.

[An opinion concurring in part and dissenting in part by Justice Breyer, joined partly by Justices Ginsburg and Sotomayor, as well as a dissenting opinion by Justice Sotomayor, joined by Justice Ginsburg, are omitted.—Ed.]

Notes and Questions

1. **Buckley v. Valeo.** The *Lucia* case is the Supreme Court's most recent and perhaps most lucid explanation of the distinction between officers and employees. Justice Kagan was not, however, writing on a clean slate. In addition to Freytag v. Commissioner, 501 U.S. 868 (1991), in which the Court had found the special tax judges were officers even though their decisions were reviewable and not final, the Court also had available the earlier precedent of Buckley v. Valeo, 424 U.S. 1 (1976). In that case, the Supreme Court dealt with the creation of the Federal Election Commission. Among the many issues in that case was an appointments clause issue. The Commission included two presidential appointments subject to approval by House as well as Senate, and four commissioners were appointed by the president pro tem of the Senate and the Speaker of House. If the commissioners were merely employees then this appointment scheme would be constitutional. If they were officers, it would be unconstitutional. After observing the rulemaking, policymaking, and enforcement functions of the Commission, the Court concluded that the commissioners exercised "significant authority" under the statute and therefore were officers. The Court also held, however, that the commissioners could continue to undertake their informational work, by which they investigated matters for potential legislation and reported their findings to Congress, even absent the constitutional appointment.

2. **Who is a "head of department"?** After *Lucia* was decided, the SEC commissioners ratified the appointments of the ALJs. Is that still unconstitutional? The excepting clause for inferior officers still requires such officers to be appointed by the President, the courts of law, or a head of department. Do the SEC commissioners jointly constitute a "head of department"? In Free Enterprise Fund v. Public Company Accounting and Oversight Board, 561 U.S. 477 (2010), the Supreme Court said yes. Of course, with this holding, *Buckley v. Valeo* would have been much easier to decide: a head of department is usually (if not always) a principal officer.

 CROSS REFERENCE We will encounter *Free Enterprise Fund* again later in this chapter in the context of the removal power.

3. **The original meaning of "officers."** Justices Thomas and Gorsuch, in concurrence, argued that the original meaning of "officers of the United States"

included all personnel who existed by virtue of a statute and who exercised on-going duties pursuant to statute. On this view, almost every civil servant—and perhaps each and every one—would be considered an "officer" of the United States and would have to be appointed by the President or a head of department. Is this plausible? Arguably, this would give a lot more political control to political appointees over the civil service. Is that a good thing? Is it even practical for the heads of department to appoint every single government employee? Might they just rubber-stamp a slate of employees given to them by other staff or the Civil Service? Would that be a practical

 CROSS REFERENCE Recall that we previously defined "originalism." What role should original meaning play in constitutional interpretation today?

accommodation of the competing interests? Take a look at Section 9 of the Steamboat Act of 1852, reproduced in Appendix C. Does a similar scheme for appointing various officers sound feasible today?

2.   Principal or Inferior?

Recall once more that *Lucia* dealt with the question of who was an employee and who was an officer. The question of whether an officer is an inferior or principal officer arose in the next two cases. As you read them, ask yourself, what kind of interpretive methodology does the court employ in each case? What methodology is better?

Morrison v. Olson

487 U.S. 654 (1988)

CHIEF JUSTICE REHNQUIST delivered the opinion of the Court.

This case presents us with a challenge to the independent counsel provisions of the Ethics in Government Act of 1978. We hold today that these provisions of the Act do not violate the Appointments Clause of the Constitution, Art. II, § 2, cl. 2, . . . nor do they impermissibly interfere with the President's authority under Article II in violation of the constitutional principle of separation of powers.

I

Briefly stated, Title VI of the Ethics in Government Act allows for the appointment of an "independent counsel" to investigate and, if appropriate, prosecute certain high-ranking Government officials for violations of federal criminal laws. The Act requires the Attorney General, upon receipt of information that he determines is "sufficient to constitute grounds to investigate whether any person [covered by the Act] may have violated any Federal criminal law," to conduct a preliminary investigation of the matter. When the Attorney General has completed this investigation, or 90 days has elapsed, he is required to report to a special court (the Special Division) created by the Act "for the purpose of appointing independent counsels." 28 U.S.C. § 49. If the Attorney General determines that "there are no reasonable grounds to believe that further investigation is warranted," then he must notify the Special Division of this result. In such a case, "the division of the court shall have no power to appoint an independent counsel." § 592(b)(1). If, however, the Attorney General has determined that there are "reasonable grounds to believe that further investigation or prosecution is warranted," then he "shall apply to the division of the court for the appointment of an independent counsel." The Attorney General's application to the court "shall contain sufficient information to assist the [court] in selecting an independent counsel and in defining that independent counsel's prosecutorial jurisdiction." § 592(d). Upon receiving this application, the Special Division "shall appoint an appropriate independent counsel and shall define that independent counsel's prosecutorial jurisdiction." § 593(b).

With respect to all matters within the independent counsel's jurisdiction, the Act grants the counsel "full power and independent authority to exercise all investigative and prosecutorial functions and powers of the Department of Justice, the Attorney General, and any other officer or employee of the Department of Justice." § 594(a). The functions of the independent counsel include conducting grand jury proceedings and other investigations, participating in civil and criminal court proceedings and litigation, and appealing any decision in any case in which the counsel participates in an official capacity. §§ 594(a)(1)–(3). Under § 594(a)(9), the counsel's powers include "initiating and conducting prosecutions in any court of competent jurisdiction, framing and signing indictments, filing informations, and handling all aspects of any case, in the name of the United States." The counsel may appoint employees, § 594(c), may request and obtain assistance from the Department of Justice, § 594(d), and may accept referral of matters from the Attorney General if the matter falls within the counsel's jurisdiction as defined by the Special Division, § 594(e). The Act also states that an independent counsel "shall, except where not possible, comply with the written or other established policies of the Department of Justice respecting enforcement of the criminal laws." § 594(f). In addition, whenever a matter has been referred to an independent counsel under the Act, the Attorney General and the Justice Department are required to suspend all investigations and proceedings regarding the matter. § 597(a). An independent counsel has "full authority to dismiss matters within [his or her] prosecutorial jurisdiction without conducting an investigation or at any subsequent time before prosecution, if to do so would be consistent" with Department of Justice policy. § 594(g).

Two statutory provisions govern the length of an independent counsel's tenure in office. The first defines the procedure for removing an independent counsel. Section 596(a)(1) provides: "An independent counsel appointed under this chapter may be removed from office, other than by impeachment and conviction, only by the personal action of the Attorney General and only for good cause, physical disability, mental incapacity, or any other condition that substantially impairs the performance of such independent counsel's duties."

If an independent counsel is removed pursuant to this section, the Attorney General is required to submit a report to both the Special Division and the Judiciary Committees of the Senate and the House "specifying the facts found and the ultimate grounds for such removal." § 596(a)(2). Under the current version of the Act, an independent counsel can obtain judicial review of the Attorney General's action by filing a civil action in the United States District Court for the District of Columbia. Members of the Special Division "may not hear or determine any such civil action or any appeal of a decision in any such civil action." The reviewing court is authorized to grant reinstatement or "other appropriate relief." § 596(a)(3).

The other provision governing the tenure of the independent counsel defines the procedures for "terminating" the counsel's office. Under § 596(b)(1), the office of an independent counsel terminates when he or she notifies the Attorney General that he or she has completed or substantially completed any investigations or prosecutions undertaken pursuant to the Act. In addition, the Special Division, acting either on its own or on the suggestion of the Attorney General, may terminate the office of an independent counsel at any time if it finds that "the investigation of all matters within the prosecutorial jurisdiction of such independent counsel . . . have been completed or so substantially completed that it would be appropriate for the Department of Justice to complete such investigations and prosecutions." § 596(b)(2). . . .

The Attorney General . . . requested appointment of an independent counsel to investigate whether Olson's March 10, 1983, testimony "regarding the completeness of [OLC's] response to the Judiciary Committee's request for OLC documents, and regarding his knowledge of EPA's willingness to turn over certain disputed documents to Congress, violated 18 U.S.C. § 1505, § 1001, or any other provision of federal criminal law." The Attorney General also requested that the independent counsel have authority to investigate "any other matter related to that allegation." . . .

[I]n May and June 1987, appellant caused a grand jury to issue and serve subpoenas *ad testificandu* and *duces tecum* on appellees. All three appellees moved to quash the subpoenas, claiming, among other things, that the independent counsel provisions of the Act were unconstitutional and that appellant accordingly had no authority to proceed. . . .

* * *

III

. . . . The parties do not dispute that "[t]he Constitution for purposes of appointment . . . divides all its officers into two classes." *United States v. Germaine*, 99 U.S. 508, 509 (1879). As we stated in *Buckley v. Valeo*, 424 U.S. 1 (1976): "[P]rincipal officers are selected by the President with the advice and consent of the Senate. Inferior officers Congress may allow to be appointed by the President alone, by the heads of departments, or by the Judiciary." The initial question is, accordingly, whether appellant is an "inferior" or a "principal" officer. If she is the latter, as the Court of Appeals concluded, then the Act is in violation of the Appointments Clause.

The line between "inferior" and "principal" officers is one that is far from clear, and the Framers provided little guidance into where it should be drawn. See, *e.g.*, 2 J. Story, Commentaries on the Constitution § 1536, pp. 397–398 (3d ed. 1858) ("In the practical course of the government there does not seem to have been any exact line drawn, who are and who are not to be deemed *inferior* officers, in the sense of the constitution, whose appointment does not necessarily require the concurrence of the senate"). We need not attempt here to decide exactly where the line falls between the two types of officers, because in our view appellant clearly falls on the "inferior officer" side of that line. Several factors lead to this conclusion.

First, appellant is subject to removal by a higher Executive Branch official. Although appellant may not be "subordinate" to the Attorney General (and the President) insofar as she possesses a degree of independent discretion to exercise the powers delegated to her under the Act, the fact that she can be removed by the Attorney General indicates that she is to some degree "inferior" in rank and authority. Second, appellant is empowered by the Act to perform only certain, limited duties. An independent counsel's role is restricted primarily to investigation and, if appropriate, prosecution for certain federal crimes. Admittedly, the Act delegates to appellant "full power and independent authority to exercise all investigative and prosecutorial functions and powers of the Department of Justice," § 594(a), but this grant of authority does not include any authority to formulate policy for the Government or the Executive Branch, nor does it give appellant any administrative duties outside of those necessary to operate her office. The Act specifically provides that in policy matters appellant is to comply to the extent possible with the policies of the Department. § 594(f).

Third, appellant's office is limited in jurisdiction. Not only is the Act itself restricted in applicability to certain federal officials suspected of certain serious federal crimes, but an independent counsel can only act within the scope of the jurisdiction that has been granted by the Special Division pursuant to a request by the Attorney General. Finally, appellant's office is limited in tenure. There is concededly no time limit on the appointment of a particular counsel. Nonetheless, the office of independent counsel is "temporary" in the sense that an independent counsel is appointed essentially to accomplish a single task, and when that task is over the office is terminated, either by the counsel herself or by action of the Special Division. Unlike other prosecutors, appellant has no ongoing responsibilities that extend beyond the accomplishment of the mission that she was appointed for and authorized by the Special Division to undertake. In our view, these factors relating to the "ideas of tenure, duration . . . and duties" of the independent counsel, *Germaine, supra,* at 511, are sufficient to establish that appellant is an "inferior" officer in the constitutional sense. . . .

This does not, however, end our inquiry under the Appointments Clause. Appellees argue that even if appellant is an "inferior" officer, the Clause does not empower Congress to place the power to appoint such an officer outside the Executive Branch. They contend that the Clause does not contemplate congressional authorization of "interbranch appointments," in which an officer of one branch is appointed by officers of another branch. The relevant language of the Appointments Clause is worth repeating. It reads: ". . . but the Congress may by Law vest the Appointment of such inferior Officers, as they think proper, in the President alone, in the courts of Law, or in the Heads of Departments." On its face, the language of this "excepting clause" admits of no limitation on interbranch appointments. Indeed, the inclusion of "as they think proper" seems clearly to give Congress significant discretion to determine whether it is "proper" to vest the appointment of, for example, executive officials in the "courts of Law." . . .

We also note that the history of the Clause provides no support for appellees' position. . . . [T]here was little or no debate on the question whether the Clause empowers Congress to provide for interbranch appointments, and there is nothing to suggest that the Framers intended to prevent Congress from having that power.

We do not mean to say that Congress' power to provide for interbranch appointments of "inferior officers" is unlimited. In addition to separation-of-powers concerns, which would arise if such provisions for appointment had the potential to impair the constitutional functions assigned to one of the branches, . . . Congress' decision to vest the appointment power in the courts would be improper if there was some "incongruity" between the functions normally performed by the courts and the performance of their duty to appoint. In this case, however, we do not think it impermissible for Congress to vest the power to appoint independent counsel in a specially created federal court. We thus disagree with the Court of Appeals' conclusion that there is an inherent incongruity about a court having the power to appoint prosecutorial officers. We have recognized that courts may appoint private attorneys to act as prosecutor for judicial contempt judgments. . . . [And] we indicated that judicial appointment of federal marshals, who are "executive officer[s]," would not be inappropriate. Lower courts have also upheld interim judicial appointments of United States Attorneys, and Congress itself has vested the power to make these interim appointments in the district courts. Congress, of course, was concerned when it created the office of independent counsel with the conflicts of interest that could arise in situations when the Executive Branch is called upon to investigate its own high-ranking officers. If it were to remove the appointing authority from the Executive Branch, the most logical place to put it was in the Judicial Branch. . . .

Justice Scalia, dissenting.

* * *

. . . . Because appellant . . . was not appointed by the President with the advice and consent of the Senate, but rather by the Special Division of the United States Court of Appeals, her appointment is constitutional only if (1) she is an "inferior" officer within the meaning of the [Appointments] Clause, and (2) Congress may vest her appointment in a court of law.

As to the first of these inquiries, the Court does not attempt to "decide exactly" what establishes the line between principal and "inferior" officers, but is confident that, whatever the line may be, appellant "clearly falls on the 'inferior officer' side" of it. The Court gives three reasons: *First*, she "is subject to removal by a higher Executive Branch official," namely, the Attorney General. *Second*, she is "empowered by the Act to perform only certain, limited duties." *Third*, her office is "limited in jurisdiction" and "limited in tenure."

The first of these lends no support to the view that appellant is an inferior officer. Appellant is removable only for "good cause" or physical or mental incapacity. By contrast, most (if not all) *principal* officers in the Executive Branch may be removed by the President *at will*. I fail to see how the fact that appellant is more difficult to remove than most principal officers helps to establish that she is an inferior officer. . . . If she were removable at will by the Attorney General, then she would be subordinate to him and thus properly designated as inferior; but the Court essentially admits that she is not subordinate. If it were common usage to refer to someone as "inferior" who is subject to removal for cause by another, then one would say that the President is "inferior" to Congress.

The second reason offered by the Court—that appellant performs only certain, limited duties—may be relevant to whether she is an inferior officer, but it mischaracterizes the extent of her powers. As the Court states: "Admittedly, the Act delegates to appellant [the] '*full power and independent authority to exercise all investigative and prosecutorial functions and powers of the Department of Justice.*'" . . .

The final set of reasons given by the Court for why the independent counsel clearly is an inferior officer emphasizes the limited nature of her jurisdiction and tenure. Taking the latter first, I find nothing unusually limited about the independent counsel's tenure. To the contrary, unlike most high-ranking Executive Branch officials, she continues to serve until she (or the Special Division) decides that her work is substantially completed. This particular independent prosecutor has already served more than two years, which is at least as long as many Cabinet officials. As to the scope of her jurisdiction, there can be no doubt that is small (though far from unimportant). But within it she exercises more than the full power of the Attorney General. The Ambassador to Luxembourg is not anything less than a principal officer, simply because Luxembourg is small. And the federal judge who sits in a small district is not for that reason "inferior in rank and authority." If the mere fragmentation of executive responsibilities into small compartments suffices to render the heads of each of those compartments inferior officers, then Congress could deprive the President of the right to appoint his chief law enforcement officer by dividing up the Attorney General's responsibilities among a number of "lesser" functionaries.

More fundamentally, however, it is not clear from the Court's opinion why the factors it discusses—even if applied correctly to the facts of this case—are determinative of the question of inferior officer status. The apparent source of these factors is a statement in *United States v. Germaine*, 99 U.S. 508, 511 (1879), that "the term [officer] embraces the ideas of tenure, duration, emolument, and duties." Besides the fact that this was dictum, it was dictum in a case where the distinguishing characteristics of inferior officers versus superior officers were in no way relevant, but rather only the distinguishing characteristics of an "officer of the United States" (to which the criminal statute at issue applied) as opposed to a mere *employee*. Rather than erect a theory of who is an inferior officer on the foundation of such an irrelevancy, I think it preferable to look to the text of the Constitution and the division of power that it establishes. These demonstrate, I think, that the independent counsel is not an inferior officer because she is not *subordinate* to any officer in the Executive Branch (indeed, not even to the President). Dictionaries in use at the time of the Constitutional Convention gave the word "inferiour" two meanings which it still bears today: (1) "[l]ower in place, . . . station, . . . rank of life, . . . value or excellency," and (2) "[s]ubordinate." S. Johnson, Dictionary of the English Language (6th ed. 1785). In a document dealing with the structure (the constitution) of a government, one would naturally expect the word to bear the latter meaning—indeed, in such a context it would be unpardonably careless to use the word *unless* a relationship of subordination was intended. If what was meant was merely "lower in station or rank," one would use instead a term such as "lesser officers." At the only other point in the Constitution at which the word "inferior" appears, it plainly connotes a relationship of subordination. Article III vests the judicial power of the United States in "one supreme Court, and in such *inferior* Courts as the Congress may from time to time ordain and establish." U.S. Const., Art. III, § 1 (emphasis added). In Federalist No. 81, Hamilton pauses to describe the "inferior" courts authorized by Article III as inferior in the sense that they are "subordinate" to the Supreme Court. . . .

Because appellant is not subordinate to another officer, she is not an "inferior" officer and her appointment other than by the President with the advice and consent of the Senate is unconstitutional. . . .

Edmond v. United States

520 U.S. 651 (1997)

JUSTICE SCALIA delivered the opinion of the Court.

We must determine in this case whether Congress has authorized the Secretary of Transportation to appoint civilian members of the Coast Guard Court of Criminal Appeals, and if so, whether this authorization is constitutional under the Appointments Clause of Article II.

I

The Coast Guard Court of Criminal Appeals . . . is an intermediate court within the military justice system. It is one of four military Courts of Criminal Appeals; others exist for the Army, the Air Force, and the Navy-Marine Corps. The Coast Guard Court of Criminal Appeals hears appeals from the decisions of courts-martial, and its decisions are subject to review by the United States Court of Appeals for the Armed Forces (formerly known as the United States Court of Military Appeals).

Appellate military judges who are assigned to a Court of Criminal Appeals must be members of the bar, but may be commissioned officers or civilians. Art. 66(a), Uniform Code of Military Justice (UCMJ), 10 U.S.C. § 866(a). During the times relevant to this case, the Coast Guard Court of Criminal Appeals has had two civilian members, Chief Judge Joseph H. Baum and Associate Judge Alfred F. Bridgman, Jr. These judges were originally assigned to serve on the court by the General Counsel of the Department of Transportation, who is, ex officio, the Judge Advocate General of the Coast Guard, Art. 1(1), UCMJ, 10 U.S.C. § 801(1). Subsequent events, however, called into question the validity of these assignments. . . .

In *Weiss v. United States*, 510 U.S. 163 (1994), we . . . held that military trial and appellate judges are officers of the United States and must be appointed pursuant to the Appointments Clause. . . .

In anticipation of our decision in *Weiss*, Chief Judge Baum sent a memorandum to the Chief Counsel of the Coast Guard requesting that the Secretary, in his capacity as a department head, reappoint the judges so the court would be constitutionally valid beyond any doubt. On January 15, 1993, the Secretary of Transportation issued a memorandum "adopting" the General Counsel's assignments to the Coast Guard Court of Military Review "as judicial appointments of my own." The memorandum then listed the names of "[t]hose judges presently assigned and appointed by me," including Chief Judge Baum and Judge Bridgman. . . .

II

Petitioners argue that the Secretary's civilian appointments to the Coast Guard Court of Criminal Appeals are invalid . . . [because] judges of military Courts of Criminal Appeals are principal, not inferior, officers within the meaning of the Appointments Clause, and must therefore be appointed by the President with the advice and consent of the Senate. . . .

* * *

[T]he Appointments Clause of Article II is more than a matter of "etiquette or protocol"; it is among the significant structural safeguards of the constitutional scheme. By vesting the President with the exclusive power to select the principal (noninferior) officers of the United States, the Appointments Clause prevents congressional encroachment upon the Executive and Judicial Branches. This disposition was also designed to assure a higher quality of appointments: The Framers anticipated that the President would be less vulnerable to interest-group pressure and personal favoritism than would a collective body. "The sole and undivided responsibility of one man will naturally beget a livelier sense of duty, and a more exact regard to reputation." The Federalist No. 76 (A. Hamilton); accord, 3 J. Story, Commentaries on the Constitution of the United States 374–375 (1833). The President's power to select principal officers of the United States was not left unguarded, however, as Article II further requires the "Advice and Consent of the Senate." This serves both to curb Executive abuses of the appointment power, and "to promote a judicious choice of [persons] for filling the offices of the union," The Federalist No. 76. By requiring the joint participation of the President and the Senate, the Appointments Clause was designed to ensure public accountability for both the making of a bad appointment and the rejection of a good one. . . .

The prescribed manner of appointment for principal officers is also the default manner of appointment for inferior officers. "[B]ut," the Appointments Clause continues, "the Congress may by Law vest the Appointment of such inferior Officers, as they think proper, in the President alone, in the Courts of Law, or in the Heads of Departments." . . . [The statute], which confers appointment power upon the Secretary of Transportation, can constitutionally be applied to the appointment of Court of Criminal Appeals judges only if those judges are "inferior Officers."

Our cases have not set forth an exclusive criterion for distinguishing between principal and inferior officers for Appointments Clause purposes. Among the offices that we have found to be inferior are that of a district court clerk, *Ex parte Hennen*, 38 U.S. (13 Pet.) 225, 229 (1839), an election supervisor, *Ex parte Siebold*, 100 U.S. 371, 397–398 (1880), a vice consul charged temporarily with the duties of the consul, *United States v. Eaton*, 169 U.S. 331, 343 (1898), and a "United States commissioner" in district court proceedings, *Go-Bart Importing Co. v. United States*, 282 U.S. 344, 352–354 (1931). Most recently, in *Morrison v. Olson*, 487 U.S. 654 (1988), we held that the independent counsel created by provisions of the Ethics in Government Act of 1978, was an inferior officer. In reaching that conclusion, we relied on several factors: that the independent counsel was subject to removal by a higher officer (the Attorney General), that she performed only limited duties, that her jurisdiction was narrow, and that her tenure was limited.

Petitioners are quite correct that the last two of these conclusions do not hold with regard to the office of military judge at issue here. It is not "limited in tenure," as that phrase was used in *Morrison* to describe "appoint[ment] essentially to accomplish a single task [at the end of which] the office is terminated." Nor are military judges "limited in jurisdiction," as used in *Morrison* to refer to the fact that an independent counsel may investigate and prosecute only those individuals, and for only those crimes, that are within the scope of jurisdiction granted by the special three judge appointing panel. However, *Morrison* did not purport to set forth a definitive test for whether an office is "inferior" under the Appointments Clause. To the contrary, it explicitly stated: "We need not attempt here to decide exactly where the line falls between the two types of officers, because in our view [the independent counsel] clearly falls on the 'inferior officer' side of that line." . . .

Generally speaking, the term "inferior officer" connotes a relationship with some higher ranking officer or officers below the President: Whether one is an "inferior" officer depends on whether he has a superior. It is not enough that other officers may be identified who formally maintain a higher rank, or possess responsibilities of a greater magnitude. If that were the intention, the Constitution might have used the phrase "lesser officer." Rather, in the context of a Clause designed to preserve political accountability relative to important Government assignments, we think it evident that "inferior officers" are officers whose work is directed and supervised at some level by others who were appointed by Presidential nomination with the advice and consent of the Senate. . . .

Supervision of the work of Court of Criminal Appeals judges is divided between the Judge Advocate General (who in the Coast Guard is subordinate to the Secretary of Transportation) and the Court of Appeals for the Armed Forces. The Judge Advocate General exercises administrative oversight over the Court of Criminal Appeals. He is charged with the responsibility to "prescribe uniform rules of procedure" for the court, and must "meet periodically [with other Judge Advocates General] to formulate policies and procedure in regard to review of court-martial cases." Art. 66(f), UCMJ, 10 U.S.C. § 866(f). It is conceded by the parties that the Judge Advocate General may also remove a Court of Criminal Appeals judge from his judicial assignment without cause. The power to remove officers, we have recognized, is a powerful tool for control.

The Judge Advocate General's control over Court of Criminal Appeals judges is, to be sure, not complete. He may not attempt to influence (by threat of removal or otherwise) the outcome of individual proceedings, Art. 37, UCMJ, 10 U.S.C. § 837, and has no power to reverse decisions of the court. This latter power does reside, however, in another Executive Branch entity, the Court of

Appeals for the Armed Forces. That court reviews every decision of the Courts of Criminal Appeals in which: (a) the sentence extends to death; (b) the Judge Advocate General orders such review; or (c) the court itself grants review upon petition of the accused. Id., Art. 67(a), § 867(a). The scope of review is narrower than that exercised by the Court of Criminal Appeals: so long as there is some competent evidence in the record to establish each element of the offense beyond a reasonable doubt, the Court of Appeals for the Armed Forces will not reevaluate the facts. This limitation upon review does not in our opinion render the judges of the Court of Criminal Appeals principal officers. What is significant is that the judges of the Court of Criminal Appeals have no power to render a final decision on behalf of the United States unless permitted to do so by other Executive officers. . . .

We conclude . . . that [these] appointment[s] [are] in conformity with the Appointments Clause of the Constitution, since [these] judges are "inferior Officers" within the meaning of that provision, by reason of the supervision over their work exercised by the General Counsel of the Department of Transportation in his capacity as Judge Advocate General and the Court of Appeals for the Armed Forces. The judicial appointments at issue in this case are therefore valid.

[An opinion by Justice Souter, concurring in part and concurring in the judgment, is omitted.—Ed.]

Notes and Questions

1. Comparing the two cases. In *Morrison v. Olson*, the eight-justice majority did not purport "to decide exactly where the line falls between the two types of officers," and instead relied on "[s]everal factors" to determine that the independent counsel was an inferior officer. These factors included the ability of the Attorney General to remove the counsel, even though the Attorney General could only do so "for cause"; and the counsel's limited duties, jurisdiction, and tenure.

COMPARATIVE PERSPECTIVE After *Morrison* and *Edmond*, are there two competing tests—one functionalist, one formalist—for determining whether an officer is principal or inferior?

In *Edmond*, Justice Scalia—who was the lone dissenter in *Morrison*—wrote for the majority that what makes an officer inferior is whether she is subordinate to another officer. An officer is usually subordinate if she is removable at-will by a another officer or if her work is reviewable and revisable by another officer (or both). Is the Court deploying different methodologies in these two cases? Is one functionalist and the other formalist? Note that *Edmond* barely even paid lip service to *Morrison*. Are there now two competing approaches for determining who is an inferior officer?

2. *Functionalism versus formalism.* One concern that the Court had in *Morrison* was, who will police the police? Who will prosecute the prosecutors? Who will ensure, that is, that high government officials responsible for the execution of the laws themselves do not commit violations of the law? The Court seems to have thought an "independent" prosecutor was necessary. This is the essence of functionalism: what matters is not the formal constitutional requirements, but rather making government work effectively. What was the dissent's response? What powers does Congress have to oversee and investigate potentially illegal executive branch activities? Are those powers sufficient?

FORMALISM VS. FUNCTIONALISM
Are there functionalist reasons for the decision in *Morrison*? Do you agree with them?

B. Removals

Unlike with appointments, the Constitution says nothing about the power to remove officers, except for impeachment. How do we interpret the Constitution on this point, given the Constitution's silence? Does the President have the power to remove officers as part of "the executive power"? Because the President has the duty to take care that the laws be faithfully executed? Should the Senate have a role in removals, just as it does in appointments? Or maybe Congress's power to establish offices includes a power to condition how the officers who are to fill those offices are to be removed. In addressing this question, the Supreme Court has vacillated between formalist and functionalist methods of constitutional interpretation, as the following cases show.

1. "The Executive Power": 1789–1935

The very first Congress debated the question who has the power to remove at least a principal executive officer. When establishing the first department of the national government—a department of foreign affairs—Congress provided for a principal officer "to be removable by the President." 1 Annals of Cong. 455 (1789) (Joseph Gales ed., 1834); 11 Doc. Hist. of First Fed. Cong., 1789–1791, at 842 (Bickford et al. eds., 1992). A wide-ranging debate ensued on the constitutional and policy merits of having the Secretary removable by the President. The First Congress voted to leave the power of removal in the President, but some members who supported this position believed that the Constitution vested the removal power in the President, and others believed that Congress in its discretion could choose to vest the removal power in the President. 1 Annals at 580. It is therefore not entirely clear how to interpret this debate. See generally Edward S. Corwin, *Tenure of Office and the Removal Power Under the Constitution*, 27 Colum. L. Rev. 353, 362–63 (1927); David P. Currie, The Constitution in Congress: The Federalist Period, 1789–1801, at 40–41 (1997). Moreover, was the determination applicable only to principal officers, or also to inferior officers?

Very few *inferior* executive officers were removed by Presidents in the first few decades of the Presidency. See Leonard D. White, The Federalists: A Study in Administrative History 257 (1956). The era of the Jacksonian "spoils system," however, ushered in widespread removals of both principal and inferior officers, who were replaced by party lackeys and presidential favorites. Jackson also fired two secretaries of treasury when they refused to withdraw federal money from the Bank of the United States; some Whigs in Congress, including the famous Daniel Webster and Henry Clay, argued that such removals were unconstitutional, but their argument lost the day. David P. Currie, The Constitution in Congress: Democrats and Whigs, 1829–1861, at 67, 70 (2005). Then in the height of Reconstruction, the radical Republicans in Congress feared that President Andrew Johnson would stymie Reconstruction efforts by removing the executive officers that had served under Lincoln. They enacted over a presidential veto the Tenure of Office Act, which purported to require the President to obtain Senate consent before removing a principal officer. Andrew Johnson nevertheless proceeded to remove from office Lincoln's Secretary of War, Edwin Stanton, for which (among other things) Johnson was impeached by the House of Representatives. The Senate, however, was one vote shy of the two-thirds majority necessary for conviction. Ever since the 1860s, some version of the Tenure of Office Act and similar acts had stayed on the statute books, until the following case, which discusses in great detail this history of the removal power in the United States.

Myers v. United States

272 U.S. 52 (1926)

Mr. Chief Justice Taft delivered the opinion of the Court.

This case presents the question whether under the Constitution the President has the exclusive power of removing executive officers of the United States whom he has appointed by and with the advice and consent of the Senate.

Myers, appellant's intestate, was on July 21, 1917, appointed by the President, by and with the advice and consent of the Senate, to be a postmaster of the first class at Portland, Or., for a term of four years. On January 20, 1920, Myers' resignation was demanded. He refused the demand. On February 2, 1920, he was removed from office by order of the Postmaster General, acting by direction of the President. February 10th, Myers sent a petition to the President and another to the Senate committee on post offices, asking to be heard, if any charges were filed. He protested to the department against his removal, and continued to do so until the end of his term. He pursued no other occupation and drew compensation for no other service during the interval. On April 21, 1921, he brought this suit in the Court of Claims for his salary from the date of his removal, which, as claimed by supplemental petition filed after July 21, 1921, the end of his term, amounted to $8,838.71. In August, 1920, the President made a recess appointment of one Jones, who took office September 19, 1920. . . .

By the sixth section of the Act of Congress of July 12, 1876, 19 Stat. 80, 81, under which Myers was appointed with the advice and consent of the Senate as a first-class postmaster, it is provided that: 'Postmasters of the first, second, and third classes shall be appointed and may be removed by the President by and with the advice and consent of the Senate, and shall hold their offices for four years unless sooner removed or suspended according to law.'

The Senate did not consent to the President's removal of Myers during his term. If this statute in its requirement that his term should be four years unless sooner removed by the President by and with the consent of the Senate is valid, the appellant, Myers' administratrix, is entitled to recover his unpaid salary for his full term and the judgment of the Court of Claims must be reversed. The government maintains that the requirement is invalid, for the reason that under article 2 of the Constitution the President's power of removal of executive officers appointed by him with the advice and consent of the Senate is full and complete without consent of the Senate. If this view is sound, the removal of Myers by the President without the Senate's consent was legal, and the judgment of the Court of Claims against the appellant was correct, and must be affirmed, though for a different reason from the given by that court. We are therefore confronted by the constitutional question and cannot avoid it.

The relevant parts of article 2 of the Constitution are as follows:

'Section 1. The executive Power shall be vested in a President of the United States of America. * * *

'Section 2. The President shall be Commander in Chief of the Army and Navy of the United States, and of the Militia of the several States, when called into the actual Service of the United States; he may require the Opinion, in writing, of the principal Officer in each of the executive Departments, upon any subject relating to the Duties of their respective Officers, and he shall have Power to grant Reprieves and Pardons for Offenses against the United States, except in Cases of Impeachment.

'He shall have Power, by and with the Advice and Consent of the Senate, to make Treaties, provided two thirds of the Senators present concur; and he shall nominate, and by and with the Advice and Consent of the Senate, shall appoint Ambassadors, other public Ministers and Consuls, Judges of the Supreme Court, and all other Officers of the United States, whose Appointments are not herein otherwise provided for, and which shall be established by Law; but the Congress may by Law vest the Appointment of such inferior Officers, as they think proper, in the President alone, in the Courts of Law, or in the Heads of Departments.

'The President shall have Power to fill up all Vacancies that may happen during the Recess of the Senate, by granting Commissions which shall expire at the End of their next Session.

'Section 3. He shall from time to time give to the Congress information of the State of the Union, and recommend to their consideration such measures as he shall judge necessary and expedient; he may, on extraordinary occasions, convene both Houses, or either of them, and in case of disagreement between them, with respect to the time of adjournment, he may adjourn them to such time as he shall think proper; he shall receive Ambassadors and other public Ministers; he shall take Care that the Laws be faithfully executed, and shall Commission all the Officers of the United States.

'Section 4. The President, Vice President and all civil Officers of the United States, shall be removed from Office on Impeachment for, and Conviction of, Treason, Bribery, or other high Crimes and Misdemeanors.'

. . . . The question where the power of removal of executive officers appointed by the President by and with the advice and consent of the Senate was vested, was presented early in the first session of the First Congress. There is no express provision respecting removals in the Constitution, except as section 4 of article 2, above quoted, provides for removal from office by impeachment. The subject was not discussed in the Constitutional Convention. . . .

In the House of Representatives of the First Congress, on Tuesday, May 18, 1789, Mr. Madison moved in the committee of the whole that there should be established three executive departments, one of Foreign Affairs, another of the Treasury, and a third of War, at the head of each of which there should be a Secretary, to be appointed by the President by and with the advice and consent of the Senate, and to be removable by the President. The committee agreed to the establishment of a Department of Foreign Affairs, but a discussion ensued as to making the Secretary removable by the President. 'The question was now taken and carried, by a considerable majority, in favor of declaring the power of removal to be in the President.'

On June 16, 1789, the House resolved itself into a committee of the whole on a bill proposed by Mr. Madison for establishing an executive department to be denominated the Department of Foreign Affairs, in which the first clause, after stating the title of the officer and describing his duties, had these words 'to be removable from office by the President of the United States.' After a very full discussion the question was put; Shall the words 'to be removable by the President' be struck out? It was determined in the negative—yeas 20, nays 34.

[The Court then describes a motion on June 22 by Representative Benson to amend the act to provide that a chief clerk, 'whenever the said principal officer shall be removed from office by the President of the United States, or in any other case of vacancy,' should during such vacancy, have the charge and custody of all records, books, and papers appertaining to the department. Mr. Benson explained his motion as follows:—Ed.]

'Mr. Benson stated that his objection to the clause 'to be removable by the President' arose from an idea that the power of removal by the President hereafter might appear to be exercised by virtue of a legislative grant only, and consequently be subjected to legislative instability, when he was well satisfied in his own mind that it was fixed by a fair legislative construction of the Constitution.' 1 Annals of Congress, 579.

'Mr. Benson declared, if he succeeded in this amendment, he would move to strike out the words in the first clause, 'to be removable by the President,' which appeared somewhat like a grant. Now, the mode he took would evade that point and establish a legislative construction of the Constitution. He also hoped his amendment would succeed in reconciling both sides of the House to the decision, and quieting the minds of gentlemen.' 1 Annals of Congress, 578.

Mr. Madison admitted the objection made by [Benson] to the words in the bill. He said:

'They certainly may be construed to imply a legislative grant of the power. He wished everything like ambiguity expunged, and the sense of the House explicitly declared, and therefore seconded the motion. Gentlemen have all along proceeded on the idea that the Constitution vests the power in the President, and what arguments were brought forward respecting the convenience or inconvenience of such disposition of the power were intended only to throw light upon what was meant by the compilers of the Constitution. Now, as the words proposed by the gentleman from New York expressed to his mind the meaning of the Constitution, he should be in favor of them, and would agree to strike out those agreed to in the committee.' 1 Annals of Congress, 578, 579.

[The first amendment, inserting the passive-voice language "whenever the principal officer shall be removed from office by the President of the United States," passed by a vote of 30 to 18. The second motion to strike out the original language, "to be removable by the President," passed by a vote of 31 to 18, although by different majorities, as the dissent points out.—Ed.]

It is very clear from this history that the exact question which the House voted upon was whether it should recognize and declare the power of the President under the Constitution to remove the Secretary of Foreign Affairs without the advice and consent of the Senate. That was what the vote was taken for. Some effort has been made to question whether the decision carries the result claimed for it, but there is not the slightest doubt, after an examination of the record, that the vote was, and was intended to be, a legislative declaration that the power to remove officers appointed by the President and the Senate vested in the President alone, and until the Johnson impeachment trial in 1868 its meaning was not doubted, even by those who questioned its soundness. . . .

It is convenient in the course of our discussion of this case to review the reasons advanced by Mr. Madison and his associates for their conclusion, supplementing them, so far as may be, by additional considerations which lead this court to concur therein.

First. Mr. Madison insisted that article 2 by vesting the executive power in the President was intended to grant to him the power of appointment and removal of executive officers except as thereafter expressly provided in that article. He pointed out that one of the chief purposes of the convention was to separate the legislative from the executive functions. . . .

[T]he Constitution was so framed as to vest in the Congress all legislative powers therein granted, to vest in the President the executive power, and to vest in one Supreme Court and such inferior courts as Congress might establish the judicial power. From this division on principle, the reasonable construction of the Constitution must be that the branches should be kept separate in all cases in which they were not expressly blended, and the Constitution should be expounded to blend them no more than it affirmatively requires. . . .

The debates in the Constitutional Convention indicated an intention to create a strong executive, and after a controversial discussion the executive power of the government was vested in one person and many of his important functions were specified so as to avoid the humiliating weakness of the Congress during the Revolution and under the Articles of Confederation. . . .

The vesting of the executive power in the President was essentially a grant of the power to execute the laws. But the President alone and unaided could not execute the laws. He must execute them by the assistance of subordinates. This view has since been repeatedly affirmed by this court. As he is charged specifically to take care that they be faithfully executed, the reasonable implication, even in the absence of express words, was that as part of his executive power he should select those who were to act for him under his direction in the execution of the laws. The further implication must be, in the absence of any express limitation respecting removals, that as his selection of administrative officers is essential to the execution of the laws by him, so must be his power of removing those for whom he cannot continue to be responsible. Fisher Ames, 1 Annals of Congress, 474. It was urged that the natural meaning of the term 'executive power' granted the President included the appointment and removal of executive subordinates. If such appointments and removals were not an exercise of the executive power, what were they? They certainly were not the exercise of legislative or judicial power in government as usually understood. . . .

The requirement of the second section of article 2 that the Senate should advise and consent to the presidential appointments, was to be strictly construed. The words of section 2, following the general grant of executive power under section 1, were either an enumeration and emphasis of specific functions of the executive, not all inclusive, or were limitations upon the general grant of the executive power, and as such, being limitations, should not be enlarged beyond the words used. Madison, 1 Annals, 462, 463, 464. The executive power was given in general terms strengthened by specific terms where emphasis was regarded as appropriate, and was limited by direct expressions where limitation was needed, and the fact that no express limit was placed on the power of removal by the executive was convincing indication that none was intended. . . .

Second. The view of Mr. Madison and his associates was that not only did the grant of executive power to the President in the first section of article 2 carry with it the power of removal, but the express recognition of the power of appointment in the second section enforced this view on the well-approved principle of constitutional and statutory construction that the power of removal of executive officers was incident to the power of appointment. . . . The reason for the principle is that those in charge of and responsible for administering functions of government, who select their executive subordinates, need in meeting their responsibility to have the power to remove those whom they appoint.

Under section 2 of article 2, however, the power of appointment by the executive is restricted in its exercise by the provision that the Senate, a part of the legislative branch of the government, may check the action of the executive by rejecting the officers he selects. Does this make the Senate part of the removing power? And this, after the whole discussion in the House is read attentively, is the real point which was considered and decided in the negative by the vote already given. . . .

It was pointed out in this great debate that the power of removal, though equally essential to the executive power is different in its nature from that of appointment. A veto by the Senate—a part of the legislative branch of the government—upon removals is a much greater limitation upon the executive branch, and a much more serious blending of the legislative with the executive, than a rejection of a proposed appointment. It is not to be implied. The rejection of a nominee of the President for a particular office does not greatly embarrass him in the conscientious discharge of his high duties in the selection of those who are to aid him, because the President usually has an ample field from which to select for office, according to his preference, competent and capable men. The Senate has full power to reject newly proposed appointees whenever the President shall remove the incumbents. Such a check enables the Senate to prevent the filling of offices with bad or incompetent men, or with those against whom there is tenable objection.

The power to prevent the removal of an officer who has served under the President is different from the authority to consent to or reject his appointment. When a nomination is made, it may be presumed that the Senate is, or may become, as well advised as to the fitness of the nominee as the President, but in the nature of things the defects in ability or intelligence or loyalty in the administration of the laws of one who has served as an officer under the President are facts as to which the President, or his trusted subordinates, must be better informed than the Senate, and the power to remove him may therefore be regarded as confined for very sound and practical reasons, to the governmental authority which has administrative control. The power of removal is incident to the power of appointment, not to the power of advising and consenting to appointment, and when the grant of the executive power is enforced by the express mandate to take care that the laws be faithfully executed, it emphasizes the necessity for including within the executive power as conferred the exclusive power of removal. . . .

Another argument urged against the constitutional power of the President alone to remove executive officers appointed by him with the consent of the Senate is that, in the absence of an express power of removal granted to the President, power to make provision for removal of all such officers is vested in the Congress by section 8 of article 1 [the Necessary and Proper Clause.—Ed.]. Mr. Madison . . . answered it as follows:

> '[Mr. Sherman] seems to think (if I understand him rightly) that the power of displacing from office is subject to legislative discretion, because, it having a right to create, it may limit or modify as it thinks proper. I shall not say but at first view this doctrine may seem to have some plausibility. But when I consider that the Constitution clearly intended to maintain a marked distinction between the legislative, executive and judicial powers of government, and when I consider that, if the Legislature has a power such as is contended for, they may subject and transfer at discretion powers from one department of our government to another, they may, on that principle, exclude the President altogether from exercising any authority in the removal of officers, they may give to the Senate alone, or the President and Senate combined, they may vest it in the whole Congress, or they may reserve it to be exercised by this house. When I consider the consequences of this doctrine, and compare them with the true principles of the Constitution, I own that I cannot subscribe to it.' 1 Annals of Congress, 495, 496.

. . . . [The] point is that by the specific constitutional provision for appointment of executive officers with its necessary incident of removal, the power of appointment and removal is clearly provided for by the Constitution, and the legislative power of Congress in respect to both is excluded save by the specific exception as to inferior offices in the clause that follows. This is 'but the Congress may by law vest the appointment of such inferior officers, as they think proper, in the President alone, in the Courts of Law, or in the Heads of Departments.' These words, it has been held by this court, give to Congress the power to limit and regulate removal of such inferior officers by heads of departments when it exercises its constitutional power to lodge the power of appointment with them. United States v. Perkins, 116 U. S. 483, 485. Here then is an express provision introduced in words of exception for the exercise by Congress of legislative power in the matter of appointments and removals in the case of inferior executive officers. The phrase, 'But Congress may by law vest,' is equivalent to 'excepting that Congress may by law vest.' By the plainest implication it excludes congressional dealing with appointments or removals of executive officers not falling within the exception and leaves unaffected the executive power of the President to appoint and remove them.

A reference of the whole power of removal to general legislation by Congress is quite out of keeping with the plan of government devised by the framers of the Constitution. It could never have been intended to leave to Congress unlimited discretion to vary fundamentally the operation of the great independent executive branch of government and thus most seriously to weaken it. . . .

It is reasonable to suppose also that had it been intended to give to Congress power to regulate or control removals in the manner suggested, it would have been included among the specifically enumerated legislative powers in article 1, or in the specified limitations on the executive power in article 2. The difference between the grant of legislative power under article 1 to Congress which is limited to powers therein enumerated, and the more general grant of the executive power to the President under article 2 is significant. The fact that the executive power is given in general terms strengthened by specific terms where emphasis is appropriate, and limited by direct expressions where limitation is needed, and that no express limit is placed on the power of removal by the executive is a convincing indication that none was intended.

It is argued that the denial of the legislative power to regulate removals in some way involves the denial of power to prescribe qualifications for office, or reasonable classification for promotion, and yet that has been often exercised. We see no conflict between the latter power and that of appointment and removal, provided of course that the qualifications do not so limit selection and so trench upon executive choice as to be in effect legislative designation. . . .

To Congress under its legislative power is given the establishment of offices, the determination of their functions and jurisdiction, the prescribing of reasonable and relevant qualifications and rules of eligibility of appointees, and the fixing of the term for which they are to be appointed and their compensation—all except as otherwise provided by the Constitution. . . .

Mr. Madison and his associates pointed out with great force the unreasonable character of the view that the convention intended, without express provision, to give to Congress or the Senate, in case of political or other differences, the means of thwarting the executive in the exercise of his great powers and in the bearing of his great responsibility by fastening upon him, as subordinate executive officers, men who by their inefficient service under him, by their lack of loyalty to the service, or by their different views of policy might make his taking care that the laws be faithfully executed most difficult or impossible. . . .

Made responsible under the Constitution for the effective enforcement of the law, the President needs as an indispensable aid to meet it the disciplinary influence upon those who act under him of a reserve power of removal. But it is contended that executive officers appointed by the President with the consent of the Senate are bound by the statutory law, and are not his servants to do his will, and that his obligation to care for the faithful execution of the laws does not authorize him to treat them as such. The degree of guidance in the discharge of their duties that the President may exercise over executive officers varies with the character of their service as prescribed in the law under which they act. The highest and most important duties which his subordinates perform are those in which they act for him. In such cases they are exercising not their own but his discretion. This field is a very large one. It is sometimes described as political. Each head of a department is and must be the President's alter ego in the matters of that department where the President is required by law to exercise authority. . . .

The duties of the heads of departments and bureaus in which the discretion of the President is exercised and which we have described are the most important in the whole field of executive action of the government. There is nothing in the Constitution which permits a distinction between the removal of the head of a department or a bureau, when he discharges a political duty of the President or exercises his discretion, and the removal of executive officers engaged in the discharge of their other normal duties. The imperative reasons requiring an unrestricted power to remove the most important of his subordinates in their most important duties must therefore control the interpretation of the Constitution as to all appointed by him.

But this is not to say that there are not strong reasons why the President should have a like power to remove his appointees charged with other duties than those above described. The ordinary duties of officers prescribed by statute come under the general administrative control of the President by virtue of the general grant to him of the executive power, and he may properly supervise and guide their construction of the statutes under which they act in order to secure that unitary and uniform execution of the laws which article 2 of the Constitution evidently contemplated in vesting general executive power in the President alone. Laws are often passed with specific provision for adoption of regulations by a department or bureau head to make the law workable and effective. The ability and judgment manifested by the official thus empowered, as well as his energy and stimulation of his subordinates, are subjects which the President must consider and supervise in his administrative control. Finding such officers to be negligent and inefficient, the President should have the power to remove them. Of course there may be duties so peculiarly and specifically committed to the discretion of a particular officer as to raise a question whether the President may overrule or revise the officer's interpretation of his statutory duty in a particular instance. Then there may be duties of a quasi judicial character imposed on executive officers and members of executive tribunals whose decisions after hearing affect interests of individuals, the discharge of which the President cannot in a particular case properly influence or control. But even in such a case he may consider the decision after its rendition as a reason for removing the officer, on the ground that the discretion regularly entrusted to that officer by statute has not been on the whole intelligently or wisely exercised. Otherwise he does not discharge his own constitutional duty of seeing that the laws be faithfully executed.

We have devoted much space to this discussion and decision of the question of the presidential power of removal in the First Congress, not because a congressional conclusion on a constitutional issue is conclusive, but first because of our agreement with the reasons upon which it was avowedly based, second because this was the decision of the First Congress on a question of primary importance in the organization of the government made within two years after the Constitutional Convention and within a much shorter time after its ratification, and third because that Congress numbered among its leaders those who had been members of the convention. It must necessarily constitute a precedent upon which many future laws supplying the machinery of the new government would be based and, if erroneous, would be likely to evoke dissent and departure in future Congresses. It would come at once before the executive branch of the government for compliance and might well be brought before the judicial branch for a test of its validity. As we shall see, it was soon accepted as a final decision of the question by all branches of the government.

It was, of course, to be expected that the decision would be received by lawyers and jurists with something of the same division of opinion as that manifested in Congress, and doubts were often expressed as to its correctness. But the acquiescence which was promptly accorded it after a few years was universally recognized. . . .

[In omitted paragraphs, the Court discussed Chief Justice Marshall's opinion in *Marbury v. Madison*, in which the Court compelled President Jefferson and Secretary of State Madison to deliver a signed commission to William Marbury, who had been appointed as Justice of the Peace for the District of Columbia. In dictum, Marshall suggested that the result might be different if Marbury were removable at will, but noted that the statute does not allow the President to remove Marbury until Marbury's five-year term was up. The Court dismissed this as dictum, expressly disavowed in a subsequent case, and which Marshall himself seems to have disavowed a few years later.—Ed.]

Congress in a number of acts followed and enforced the legislative decision of 1789 for 74 years. . . . [Chief Justice Taft proceeds to discuss several congressional acts assuming or specifying that various executive officers were removable at pleasure by the President, and cites several cases and commentaries for the proposition that the whole country had acquiesced in the legislative construction of the Constitution in the decision of 1789.—Ed.]

We come now to consider an argument, advanced and strongly pressed on behalf of the complainant, that this case concerns only the removal of a postmaster, that a postmaster is an inferior officer, and that such an office was not included within the legislative decision of 1789, which related only to superior officers to be appointed by the President by and with the advice and consent of the Senate. This, it is said, is the distinction which Chief Justice Marshall had in mind in Marbury v. Madison in the language already discussed in respect to the President's power of removal of a District of Columbia justice of the peace appointed and confirmed for a term of years. We find nothing in Marbury v. Madison to indicate any such distinction. It cannot be certainly affirmed whether the conclusion there stated was based on a dissent from the legislative decision of 1789, or on the fact that the office was created under the special power of Congress exclusively to legislate for the District of Columbia, or on the fact that the office was a judicial one, or on the circumstance that it was an inferior office. In view of the doubt as to what was really the basis of the remarks relied on and their obiter dictum character, they can certainly not be used to give weight to the argument that the 1789 decision only related to superior officers.

The very heated discussions during General Jackson's administration, except as to the removal of Secretary Duane, related to the distribution of offices, which were most of them inferior offices, and it was the operation of the legislative decision of 1789 upon the power of removal of incumbents of such offices that led the General to refuse to comply with the request of the Senate that he give his reasons for the removals therefrom. It was to such inferior officers that Chancellor Kent's letter to Mr. Webster already quoted was chiefly directed, and the language cited from his commentaries on the decision of 1789 was used with reference to the removal of United States marshals. It was such inferior offices that Mr. Justice Story conceded to be covered by the legislative decision in his treatise on the Constitution, already cited, when he suggested a method by which the abuse of patronage in such offices might be avoided. It was with reference to removals from such inferior offices that the already cited opinions of the Attorneys General, in which the legislative decision of 1789 was referred to as controlling authority, were delivered. That of Attorney General Legare (4 Op. A. G. 1) affected the removal of a surgeon in the Navy. The opinion of Attorney General Clifford (4 Op A. G. 603, 612) involved an officer of the same rank. The opinion of Attorney General Cushing (6 Op. A. G. 4) covered the office of military storekeeper. Finally, Parsons' Case, where it was the point in judgment, conclusively establishes for this court that the legislative decision of 1789 applied to a United States attorney, an inferior officer.

It is further pressed on us that, even though the legislative decision of 1789 included inferior officers, yet under the legislative power given Congress with respect to such officers it might directly legislate as to the method of their removal without changing their method of appointment by the President with the consent of the Senate. We do not think the language of the Constitution justifies such a contention.

Section 2 of article 2, after providing that the President shall nominate and with the consent of the Senate appoint ambassadors, other public ministers, consuls, judges of the Supreme Court and all other officers of the United States whose appointments are not herein otherwise provided for, and which shall be established by law, contains the proviso: 'But the Congress may by law vest the appointment of such inferior officers, as they think proper, in the President alone, in the courts of law or in the heads of departments.'

In United States v. Perkins, 116 U. S. 483, a cadet engineer, a graduate of the Naval Academy, brought suit to recover his salary for the period after his removal by the Secretary of the Navy. It was decided that his right was established by Revised Statutes, § 1229, providing that no officer in the military or naval service should in time of peace be dismissed from service, except in pursuance of a sentence of court-martial. The section was claimed to be an infringement upon the constitutional prerogative of the executive. The Court of Claims refused to yield to this argument and said:

> 'Whether or not Congress can restrict the power of removal incident to the power of appointment of those officers who are appointed by the President by and with the advice and consent of the Senate under the authority of the Constitution (article 2, section 2), does not arise in this case and need not be considered. We have no doubt that, when Congress by law vests the appointment of inferior officers in the heads of departments it may limit and restrict the power of removal as it deems best for the public interest. The constitutional authority in Congress to thus vest the appointment implies authority to limit, restrict, and regulate the removal by such laws as Congress may enact in relation to the officers so appointed. The head of a department has no constitutional prerogative of appointment to offices independently of the legislation of Congress, and by such legislation he must be governed, not only in making appointments, but in all that is incident thereto.'

This language of the Court of Claims was approved by this court and the judgment was affirmed.

The power to remove inferior executive officers, like that to remove superior executive officers, is an incident of the power to appoint them, and is in its nature an executive power. The authority of Congress given by the excepting clause to vest the appointment of such inferior officers in the heads of departments carries with it authority incidentally to invest the heads of departments with power to remove. It has been the practice of Congress to do so and this court has recognized that power. The court also has recognized in the Perkins Case that Congress, in committing the appointment of such inferior officers to the heads of departments, may prescribe incidental regulations controlling and restricting the latter in the exercise of the power of removal. But the court never has held, nor reasonably could hold, although it is argued to the contrary on behalf of the appellant, that the excepting clause enables Congress to draw to itself, or to either branch of it, the power to remove or the right to participate in the exercise of that power. To do this would be to go beyond the words and implications of that clause, and to infringe the constitutional principle of the separation of governmental powers.

Assuming, then, the power of Congress to regulate removals as incidental to the exercise of its constitutional power to vest appointments of inferior officers in the heads of departments, certainly so long as Congress does not exercise that power, the power of removal must remain where the Constitution places it, with the President, as part of the executive power, in accordance with the legislative decision of 1789 which we have been considering.

Whether the action of Congress in removing the necessity for the advice and consent of the Senate and putting the power of appointment in the President alone would make his power of removal in such case any more subject to Congressional legislation than before is a question this court did not decide in the Perkins Case. Under the reasoning upon which the legislative decision of 1789 was put, it might be difficult to avoid a negative answer, but it is not before us and we do not decide it.

The Perkins Case is limited to the vesting by Congress of the appointment of an inferior officer in the head of a department. The condition upon which the power of Congress to provide for the removal of inferior officers rests is that it shall vest the appointment in some one other than the President with the consent of the Senate. Congress may not obtain the power and provide for the removal of such officer except on that condition. If it does not choose to intrust the appointment of such inferior officers to less authority than the President with the consent of the Senate, it has no power of providing for their removal. . . .

Summing up, then, the facts as to acquiescence by all branches of the government in the legislative decision of 1789 as to executive officers, whether superior or inferior, we find that from 1789 until 1863, a period of 74 years, there was no act of Congress, no executive act, and no decision of this court at variance with the declaration of the First Congress; but there was, as we have seen, clear affirmative recognition of it by each branch of the government.

Our conclusion on the merits, sustained by the arguments before stated, is that article 2 grants to the President the executive power of the government—i.e., the general administrative control of those executing the laws, including the power of appointment and removal of executive officers—a conclusion confirmed by his obligation to take care that the laws be faithfully executed; that article 2 excludes the exercise of legislative power by Congress to provide for appointments and removals, except only as granted therein to Congress in the matter of inferior offices; that Congress is only given power to provide for appointments and removals of inferior officers after it has vested, and on condition that it does vest, their appointment in other authority than the President with the Senate's consent; that the provisions of the second section of article 2, which blend action by the legislative branch, or by part of it, in the work of the executive, are limitations to be strictly construed, and not to be extended by implication; that the President's power of removal is further established as an incident to his specifically enumerated function of appointment by and with the advice of the Senate, but that such incident does not by implication extend to removals the Senate's power of checking appointments; and, finally, that to hold otherwise would make it impossible for the President, in case of political or other difference with the Senate or Congress, to take care that the laws be faithfully executed.

We come now to a period in the history of the government when both houses of Congress attempted to reverse this constitutional construction, and to subject the power of removing executive officers appointed by the President and confirmed by the Senate to the control of the Senate, indeed finally to the assumed power in Congress to place the removal of such officers anywhere in the government.

This reversal grew out of the serious political difference between the two houses of Congress and President Johnson. There was a two-thirds majority of the Republican party, in control of each house of Congress, which resented what it feared would be Mr. Johnson's obstructive course in the enforcement of the reconstruction measures in respect to the states whose people had lately been at war against the national government. . . .

[T]he chief legislation in support of the reconstruction policy of Congress was the Tenure of Office Act of March 2, 1867, 14 Stat. 430, c. 154, providing that all officers appointed by and with the consent of the Senate should hold their offices until their successors should have in like manner been appointed and qualified; that certain heads of departments, including the Secretary of War, should hold their offices during the term of the President by whom appointed and one month thereafter, subject to removal by consent of the Senate. The

Tenure of Office Act was vetoed, but it was passed over the veto. The House of Representatives preferred articles of impeachment against President Johnson for refusal to comply with, and for conspiracy to defeat, the legislation above referred to, but he was acquitted for lack of a two-thirds vote for conviction in the Senate. . . .

The extreme provisions of all this legislation were a full justification for the considerations, so strongly advanced by Mr. Madison and his associates in the First Congress, for insisting that the power of removal of executive officers by the President alone was essential in the division of powers between the executive and the legislative bodies. It exhibited in a clear degree the paralysis to which a partisan Senate and Congress could subject to executive arm, and destroy the principle of executive responsibility, and separation of the powers sought for by the framers of our government, if the President had no power of removal save by consent of the Senate. It was an attempt to redistribute the powers and minimize those of the President.

After President Johnson's term ended, the injury and invalidity of the Tenure of Office Act in its radical innovation were immediately recognized by the executive and objected to. General Grant, succeeding Mr. Johnson in the presidency, earnestly recommended in his first message the total repeal of the act . . . .

The attitude of the Presidents on this subject has been unchanged and uniform to the present day whenever an issue has clearly been raised. . . .

In spite of the foregoing presidential declarations, it is contended that, since the passage of the Tenure of Office Act, there has been general acquiescence by the executive in the power of Congress to forbid the President alone to remove executive officers, an acquiescence which has changed any formerly accepted constitutional construction to the contrary. Instances are cited of the signed approval by President Grant and other Presidents of legislation in derogation of such construction. We think these are all to be explained, not by acquiescence therein, but by reason of the otherwise valuable effect of the legislation approved. Such is doubtless the explanation of the executive approval of the act of 1876, which we are considering, for it was an appropriation act on which the section here in question was imposed as a rider. . . .

When instances which actually involve the question are rare or have not in fact occurred, the weight of the mere presence of acts on the statute book for a considerable time as showing general acquiescence in the legislative assertion of a questioned power is minimized. . . .

Other acts of Congress are referred to which contain provisions said to be inconsistent with the 1789 decision. Since the provision for an Interstate Commerce Commission in 1887, many administrative boards have been created whose members are appointed by the President, by and with the advice and consent of the Senate, and in the statutes creating them have been provisions for the removal of the members for specified causes. Such provisions are claimed to be inconsistent with the independent power of removal by the President. This, however, is shown to be unfounded by the case of Shurtleff v. United States, 189 U. S. 311 (1903). That concerned an act creating a board of general appraisers, 26 Stat. 131, 136, c. 407, § 12, and provided for their removal for inefficiency, neglect of duty, or malfeasance in office. The President removed an appraiser without notice or hearing. It was forcibly contended that the affirmative language of the statute implied the negative of the power to remove except for cause and after a hearing. This would have been the usual rule of construction, but the court declined to apply it. Assuming for the purpose of that case only, but without deciding, that Congress might limit the President's power to remove, the court held that, in the absence of constitutional or statutory provision otherwise, the President could by virtue of his general power of appointment remove an officer, though appointed by and with the advice and consent of the Senate, and notwithstanding specific provisions for his removal for cause, on the ground that the power of removal inhered in the power to appoint. This is an indication that many of the statutes cited are to be reconciled to the unrestricted power of the President to remove, if he chooses to exercise his power. . . .

An argument [from inconvenience] has been made against our conclusion in favor of the executive power of removal by the President, without the consent of the Senate, that it will open the door to a reintroduction of the spoils system. The evil of the spoils system aimed at in the Civil Service Law and its amendments is in respect to inferior offices. . . . The independent power of removal by the President alone under present conditions works no practical interference with the merit system. Political appointments of inferior officers are still maintained in one important class, that of the first, second, and third class postmasters, collectors of internal revenue, marshals, collectors of customs, and other officers of that kind distributed through the country. They are appointed by the President with the consent of the Senate. It is the intervention of the Senate in their appointment, and not in their removal, which prevents their classification into the merit system. If such appointments were vested in the heads of departments to which they belong, they could be entirely removed from politics, and that is what a number of Presidents have recommended. . . .

What, then, are the elements that enter into our decision of this case? We have, first, a construction of the Constitution made by a Congress which was to provide by legislation for the organization of the government in accord with the Constitution which had just then been adopted, and in which there were, as Representatives and Senators, a considerable number of those who had been members of the convention that framed the Constitution and presented it for ratification. . . . This construction was followed by the legislative department and the executive department continuously for 73 years, and this, although the matter in the heat of political differences between the executive and the Senate in President Jackson's time, was the subject of bitter controversy, as we have seen. This court has repeatedly laid down the principle that a contemporaneous legislative exposition of the Constitution, when the founders of our government and framers of our Constitution were actively participating in public affairs, acquiesced in for a long term of years, fixes the construction to be given its provisions. . . .

When on the merits we find our conclusion strongly favoring the view which prevailed in the First Congress, we have no hesitation in holding that conclusion to be correct; and it therefore follows that the Tenure of Office Act of 1867, in so far as it attempted to prevent the President from removing executive officers who had been appointed by him by and with the advice and consent of the Senate, was invalid, and that subsequent legislation of the same effect was equally so. . . .

The separate [dissenting] opinion of Mr. Justice McReynolds.

* * *

V.   For the United States it is asserted: Except certain judges, the President may remove all officers whether executive or judicial appointed by him with the Senate's consent, and therein he cannot be limited or restricted by Congress. The argument runs thus: The Constitution gives the President all executive power of the national government, except as this is checked or controlled by some other definite provision; power to remove is executive and unconfined; accordingly, the President may remove at will. Further, the President is required to take care that the laws be faithfully executed; he cannot do this unless he may remove at will all officers whom he appoints; therefore he has such authority.

The argument assumes far too much. Generally, the actual ouster of an officer is executive action; but to prescribe the conditions under which this may be done is legislative. . . .

The Legislature may create post offices and prescribe qualifications, duties, compensation, and term. And it may protect the incumbent in the enjoyment of his term unless in some way restrained therefrom. The real question, therefore, comes to this: Does any constitutional provision definitely limit the otherwise plenary power of Congress over postmasters, when they are appointed by the President with the consent of the Senate? The question is not the much-mooted one whether the Senate is part of the appointing power under the Constitution and therefore must participate in removals.

Here the restriction is imposed by statute alone and thereby made a condition of the tenure. I suppose that beyond doubt Congress could authorize the Postmaster General to appoint all postmasters and restrain him in respect of removals.

Concerning the insistence that power to remove is a necessary incident of the President's duty to enforce the laws, it is enough now to say: The general duty to enforce all laws cannot justify infraction of some of them. Moreover, Congress, in the exercise of its unquestioned power, may deprive the President of the right either to appoint or to remove any inferior officer, by vesting the authority to appoint in another. Yet in that event his duty touching enforcement of the laws would remain. He must utilize the force which Congress gives. He cannot, without permission, appoint the humblest clerk or expend a dollar of the public funds. . . .

Nor is the situation the one which arises when the statute creates an office without a specified term, authorizes appointment and says nothing of removal. In the latter event, under long-continued practice and supposed early legislative construction, it is now accepted doctrine that the President may remove at pleasure. This is entirely consistent with implied legislative assent; power to remove is commonly incident to the right to appoint when not forbidden by law. But there has never been any such usage where the statute prescribed restrictions. From its first session down to the last one Congress has consistently asserted its power to prescribe conditions concerning the removal of inferior officers. The executive has habitually observed them, and this court has affirmed the power of Congress therein.

* * *

XIV. If the framers of the Constitution had intended 'the executive power,' in article 2, § 1, to include all power of an executive nature, they would not have added the carefully defined grants of section 2. They were scholarly men, and it exceeds belief 'that the known advocates in the convention for a jealous grant and cautious definition of federal powers should have silently permitted the introduction of words and phrases in a sense rendering fruitless the restrictions and definitions elaborated by them.' Why say, the President shall be commander-in-chief; may require opinions in writing of the principal officers in each of the executive departments; shall have power to grant reprieves and pardons; shall give information to Congress concerning the state of the union; shall receive ambassadors; shall take care that the laws be faithfully executed—if all of these things and more had already been vested in him by the general words? . . .

* * *

XVIII. In any rational search for answer to the questions arising upon this record, it is important not to forget—

That this is a government of limited powers, definitely enumerated and granted by a written Constitution.

That the Constitution must be interpreted by attributing to its words the meaning which they bore at the time of its adoption, and in view of commonly-accepted canons of construction, its history, early and long-continued practices under it, and relevant opinions of this court. . . .

That the Constitution contains no words which specifically grant to the President power to remove duly appointed officers. And it is definitely settled that he cannot remove those whom he has not appointed—certainly they can be removed only as Congress may permit. . . .

That many Presidents have approved statutes limiting the power of the executive to remove, and that from the beginning such limitations have been respected in practice.

That this court, as early as 1803, in an opinion [in Marbury v. Madison] never overruled and rendered in a case where it was necessary to decide the question, positively declared that the President had no power to remove at will an inferior officer appointed with consent of the Senate to serve for a definite term fixed by an act of Congress. . . .

Considering all these things, it is impossible for me to accept the view that the President may dismiss, as caprice may suggest, any inferior officer whom he has appointed with consent of the Senate, notwithstanding a positive inhibition by Congress. In the last analysis, that view has no substantial support, unless it be the polemic opinions expressed by Mr. Madison (and eight others) during the debate of 1789, when he was discussing questions relating to a 'superior officer' to be appointed for an indefinite term. Notwithstanding his justly exalted reputation as one of the creators and early expounder of the Constitution, sentiments expressed under such circumstances ought not now to outweigh the conclusion which Congress affirmed by deliberate action while he was leader in the House and has consistently maintained down to the present year, the opinion of this court solemnly announced through the great Chief Justice more than a century ago, and the canons of construction approved over and over again.

Mr. Justice Brandeis, dissenting.

In 1833 Mr. Justice Story, after discussing in sections 1537–1543 his Commentaries on the Constitution the much debated question concerning the President's power of removal, said in section 1544:

> 'If there has been any aberration from the true constitutional exposition of the power of removal (which the reader must decide for himself), it will be difficult, and perhaps impracticable, after forty years' experience, to recall the practice to the correct theory. But, at all events, it will be a consolation to those who love the Union, and honor a devotion to the patriotic discharge of duty, that in regard to 'inferior officers' (which appellation probably includes ninety-nine out of a hundred of the lucrative offices in the government), the remedy for any permanent abuse is still within the power of Congress, by the simple expedient of requiring the consent of the Senate to removals in such cases.'

Postmasters are inferior officer. Congress might have vested their appointment in the head of the department. The Act of July 12, 1876, re-enacted earlier legislation, provided that: 'Postmasters of the first, second, and third classes shall be appointed and may be removed by the President by and with the advice and consent of the Senate, and shall hold their offices for four years unless sooner removed or suspended according to law.'

That statute has been in force unmodified for half a century. Throughout the period, it has governed a large majority of all civil officers to which appointments are made by and with the advice and consent of the Senate. May the President, having acted under the statute in so far as it creates the office and authorizes the appointment, ignore, while the Senate is in session, the provision which prescribes the condition under which a removal may take place?

It is this narrow question, and this only, which we are required to decide. We need not consider what power the President, being Commander-in-Chief, has over officers in the Army and the Navy. We need not determine whether the President, acting alone, may remove high political officers. We need not even determine whether, acting alone, he may remove inferior civil officers when the Senate is not in session. It was in session when the President purported to remove Myers, and for a long time thereafter. All questions of statutory construction have been eliminated by the language of the act. It is settled that, in the absence of a provision expressly providing for the consent of the Senate to a removal, the clause fixing the tenure will be construed as a limitation, not as a grant, and that, under such legislation, the President, acting alone, has the power of removal. Parsons v. United States, 167 U. S. 324. But, in defining the tenure, this statute used words of grant. Congress clearly intended to preclude a removal without the consent of the Senate.

Other questions have been eliminated by the facts found, by earlier decisions of this court, and by the nature of the claim made. . . . It is settled that if Congress had, under clause 2 of section 2, art. 2, vested the appointment in the Postmaster General, it could have limited his power of removal by requiring consent of the Senate. United States v. Perkins, 116 U. S. 483. It is not questioned here that the President, acting alone, has the constitutional power to suspend an officer in the executive branch of the government. But Myers was not suspended. . . . The sole question is whether, in respect to inferior offices, Congress may impose upon the Senate both responsibilities, as it may deny to it participation in the exercise of either function.

In Marbury v. Madison, 1 Cranch, 137, 167, it was assumed, as the basis of decision, that the President, acting alone, is powerless to remove an inferior civil officer appointed for a fixed term with the consent of the Senate; and that case was long regarded as so deciding. In no case, has this court determined that the President's power of removal is beyond control, limitation, or regulation by Congress. . . . This is true of the power as it affects officers in the Army or the Navy and the high political officers like heads of departments, as well as of the power in respect to inferior statutory offices in the executive branch. Continuously, for the last 58 years, laws comprehensive in character, enacted from time to time with the approval of the President, have made removal from the great majority of the inferior presidential offices dependent upon the consent of the Senate. Throughout that period these laws have been continuously applied. We are requested to disregard the authority of Marbury v. Madison and to overturn this long-established constitutional practice.

The contention that Congress is powerless to make consent of the Senate a condition of removal by the President from an executive office rests mainly upon the clause in section 1 of article 2 which declares that 'the executive Power shall be vested in a President.' The argument is that appointment and removal of officials are executive prerogatives; that the grant to the President of 'the executive power' confers upon him, as inherent in the office, the power to exercise these two functions without restriction by Congress, except in so far as the power to restrict his exercise of then is expressly conferred upon Congress by the Constitution; that in respect to appointment certain restrictions of the executive power are so provided for; but that in respect to removal there is no express grant to Congress of any power to limit the President's prerogative.

The simple answer to the argument is this: The ability to remove a subordinate executive officer, being an essential of effective government, will, in the absence of express constitutional provision to the contrary, be deemed to have been vested in some person or body. But it is not a power inherent in a chief executive. The President's power of removal from statutory civil inferior offices, like the power of appointment to them, comes immediately from Congress. It is true that the exercise of the power of removal is said to be an executive act, and that when the Senate grants or withholds consent to a removal by the President, it participates in an executive act. But the Constitution has confessedly granted to Congress the legislative power to create offices, and to prescribe the tenure thereof; and it has not in terms denied to Congress the power to control removals. To prescribe the tenure involves prescribing the conditions under which incumbency shall cease. For the possibility of removal is a condition or qualification of the tenure. When Congress provides that the incumbent shall hold the office for four years unless sooner removed with the consent of the Senate, it prescribes the term of the tenure.

It is also argued that the clauses in article 2, § 3, of the Constitution, which declare that the President 'shall take Care that the Laws be faithfully executed, and shall Commission all the Officers of the United States' imply a grant to the President of the alleged uncontrollable power of removal. . . . There is no express grant to the President of incidental powers resembling those conferred upon Congress by clause 18 of article 1, § 8 [the Necessary and Proper Clause.—Ed.]. A power implied on the ground that it is inherent in the executive, must, according to established principles of constitutional construction, be limited to 'the least possible power adequate to the end proposed.' The end to which the President's efforts are to be directed is not the most efficient civil service conceivable, but the faithful execution of the laws consistent with the provisions therefor made by Congress. A power essential to protection against pressing dangers incident to disloyalty in the civil service may well be deemed inherent in the executive office. But that need, and also insubordination and neglect of duty, are adequately provided against by implying in the President the constitutional power of suspension. . . . But power to remove an inferior administrative officer appointed for a fixed term cannot conceivably be deemed an essential of government.

To imply a grant to the President of the uncontrollable power of removal from statutory inferior executive offices involves an unnecessary and indefensible limitation upon the constitutional power of Congress to fix the tenure of the inferior statutory offices. . . .

Over removal from inferior civil offices, Congress has, from the foundation of our government, exercised continuously some measure of control by legislation. . . . Thus, the Act of September 2, 1789, c. 12, 1 Stat. 65, 67, establishing the Treasury Department, provided by section 8, that if any person appointed to any office by that act should be convicted of offending against any of its provisions, he shall 'upon conviction be removed from office.' . . . The Act of January 31, 1823, 3 Stat. 723, directed that officers receiving public money and failing to account quarterly shall be dismissed by the President unless they shall account for such default to his satisfaction. . . . The Act of July 17, 1854,

10 Stat. 305, 306, which authorized the President to appoint registers and receivers, provided that 'on satisfactory proof that either of said officers, or any other officer, has charged or received fees or other rewards not authorized by law, he shall be forthwith removed from office.'

In the later period, which began after the spoils system had prevailed for a generation, the control of Congress over inferior offices was exerted to prevent removals. The removal clause here in question was first introduced by the Currency Act of February 25, 1863, 12 Stat. 665, which was approved by President Lincoln. That statute provided for the appointment of the Comptroller, and that he 'shall hold his office for the term of five years unless sooner removed by the President, by and with the advice and consent of the Senate.' In 1867 this provision was inserted in the Tenure of Office Act of March 2, 1867, 14 Stat. 430, 431, which applied, in substance, to all presidential offices. It was passed over President Johnson's veto. . . .

It is significant that President Johnson, who vetoed in 1867 the Tenure of Office Act, which required the Senate's consent to the removal of high political officers, approved other acts containing the removal clause which related only to inferior officers. Thus, he had approved the Act of July 13, 1866, 14 Stat. 90, 92, which provided that 'no officer in the military or naval service shall in time of peace, be dismissed from service except upon and in pursuance of the sentence of a court-martial to that effect, or in commutation thereof.' And in 1868 he approved the Wyoming Act, which required such consent to the removal of inferior officers who had been appointed for fixed terms. . . .

The practice of Congress to control the exercise of the executive power of removal from inferior offices is evidenced by many statutes which restrict it in many ways besides the removal clause here in question. Each of these restrictive statutes became law with the approval of the President. Every President who has held office since 1861, except President Garfield, approved one or more of such statutes. Some of these statutes, prescribing a fixed term, provide that removal shall be made only for one of several specified causes. Some provide a fixed term, subject generally to removal for cause. Some provide for removal only after hearing. Some provide a fixed term, subject to removal for reasons to be communicated by the President to the Senate. . . .

The assertion that the mere grant by the Constitution of executive power confers upon the President as a prerogative the unrestricted power of appointment and of removal from executive offices, except so far as otherwise expressly provided by the Constitution, is clearly inconsistent also with those statutes which restrict the exercise by the President of the power of nomination. There is not a word in the Constitution which in terms authorizes Congress to limit the President's freedom of choice in making nominations for executive offices. It is to appointment as distinguished from nomination that the Constitution imposes in terms the requirement of Senatorial consent. But a multitude of laws have been enacted which limit the President's power to make nominations, and which through the restrictions imposed, may prevent the selection of the person deemed by him best fitted. Such restriction upon the power to nominate has been exercised by Congress continuously since the foundation of the government. Every President has approved one or more of such acts. Every President has consistently observed them. This is true of those offices to which he makes appointments without the advice and consent of the Senate as well as of those for which its consent is required.

Thus Congress has, from time to time, restricted the President's selection by the requirement of citizenship. It has limited the power of nomination by providing that the office may be held only by a resident of the United States; of a state; of a particular state; of a particular district; of a particular territory; of the District of Columbia; of a particular foreign country. It has limited the power of nomination further by prescribing specific professional attainments, or occupational experience. . . .

The practical disadvantage to the public service of denying to the President the uncontrollable power of removal from inferior civil offices would seem to have been exaggerated. Upon the service, the immediate effect would ordinarily be substantially the same, whether the President, acting alone, has or has not the power of removal. For he can, at any time, exercise his constitutional right to suspend an officer and designate some other person to act temporarily in his stead; and he cannot while the Senate is in session, appoint a successor without its consent. On the other hand, to the individual in the public service, and to the maintenance of its morale, the existence of a power in Congress to impose upon the Senate the duty to share in the responsibility for a removal is of paramount importance. The Senate's consideration of a proposed removal may be necessary to protect reputation and emoluments of office from arbitrary executive action. Equivalent protection is afforded to other inferior officers whom Congress has placed in the classified civil service and which it authorizes the heads of departments to appoint and to remove without the consent of the Senate. . . .

The fact that the removal clause had been inserted in the currency bill of 1863 (12 Stat. 665) shows that it did not originate in the contest of Congress with President Johnson, as has been sometimes stated. Thirty years before that, it had been recommended by Mr. Justice Story as a remedial measure, after the wholesale removals of the first Jackson administration. The Post Office Department was then the chief field for plunder. Vacancies had been created in order that the spoils of office might be distributed among political supporters. . . .

The long delay in adopting legislation to curb removals was not because Congress accepted the doctrine that the Constitution had vested in the President uncontrollable power over removal. It was because the spoils system held sway.

The historical data submitted present a legislative practice, established by concurrent affirmative action of Congress and the President, to make consent of the Senate a condition of removal from statutory inferior, civil, executive offices to which the appointment is made for a fixed term by the President with such consent. They show that the practice has existed, without interruption, continuously for the last 58 years; that throughout this period, it has governed a great majority of all such offices; that the legislation applying the removal clause specifically to the office of postmaster was enacted more than half a century ago; and that recently the practice has, with the President's approval, been extended to several newly created offices. . . . A persistent legislative practice which involves a delimitation of the respective powers of Congress and the President, and which has been so established and maintained, should be deemed tantamount to judicial construction, in the absence of any decision by any court to the contrary. . . .

The action taken by Congress in 1789 after the great debate . . . did not involve a decision that the President had uncontrollable power. It did not involve a decision of the question whether Congress could confer upon the Senate the right, and impose upon it the duty, to participate in removals. It involved merely the decision that the Senate does not, in the absence of legislative grant thereof, have the right to share in the removal of an officer appointed with its consent, and that the President has, in the absence of restrictive legislation, the constitutional power of removal without such consent. Moreover, as Chief

Justice Marshall recognized, the debate and the decision related to a high political office, not to inferior ones.

Nor does the debate show that the majority of those then in Congress thought that the President had the uncontrollable power of removal. The Senators divided equally in their votes [Vice President John Adams had to break the tie in the Senate.—Ed.]. As to their individual views we lack knowledge; for the debate was secret. In the House only 24 of the 54 members voting took part in the debate. Of the 24, only 6 appear to have held the opinion that the President possessed the uncontrollable power of removal. The clause which involved a denial of the claim that the Senate had the constitutional right to participate in removals was adopted, so far as appears, by aid of the votes of others who believed it expedient for Congress to confer the power of removal upon the President alone. This is indicated both by Madison's appeal for support and by the action taken on Benson's motions. . . .

The separation of the powers of government did not make each branch completely autonomous. It left each in some measure, dependent upon the others, as it left to each power to exercise, in some respects, functions in their nature executive, legislative and judicial. Obviously the President cannot secure full execution of the laws, if Congress denies to him adequate means of doing so. Full execution may be defeated because Congress declines to create offices indispensable for that purpose; or because Congress, having created the office, declines to make the indispensable appropriation; or because Congress, having both created the office and made the appropriation, prevents, by restrictions which it imposes, the appointment of officials who in quality and character are indispensable to the efficient execution of the law. If, in any such way, adequate means are denied to the President, the fault will lie with Congress. The President performs his full constitutional duty, if, with the means and instruments provided by Congress and within the limitations prescribed by it, he uses his best endeavors to secure the faithful execution of the laws enacted. . . .

Checks and balances were established in order that this should be 'a government of laws and not of men.' As White said in the House in 1789, an uncontrollable power of removal in the Chief Executive 'is a doctrine not to be learned in American governments.' Such power had been denied in colonial charters, and even under proprietary grants and royal commissions. It had been denied in the thirteen states before the framing of the federal Constitution. The doctrine of the separation of powers was adopted by the convention of 1787 not to promote efficiency but to preclude the exercise of arbitrary power. . . . Nothing in support of the claim of uncontrollable power can be inferred from the silence of the convention of 1787 on the subject of removal. For the outstanding fact remains that every specific proposal to confer such uncontrollable power upon the President was rejected. In America, as in England, the conviction prevailed then that the people must look to representative assemblies for the protection of their liberties. And protection of the individual, even if he be an official, from the arbitrary or capricious exercise of power was then believed to be an essential of free government.

MR. JUSTICE HOLMES, dissenting.

My Brothers McREYNOLDS and BRANDEIS have discussed the question before us with exhaustive research and I say a few words merely to emphasize my agreement with their conclusion.

The arguments drawn from the executive power of the President, and from his duty to appoint officers of the United States (when Congress does not vest the appointment elsewhere), to take care that the laws be faithfully executed, and to commission all officers of the United States, seem to me spiders' webs inadequate to control the dominant facts.

We have to deal with an office that owes its existence to Congress and that Congress may abolish to-morrow. Its duration and the pay attached to it while it lasts depend on Congress alone. Congress alone confers on the President the power to appoint to it and at any time may transfer the power to other hands. With such power over its own creation, I have no more trouble in believing that Congress has power to prescribe a term of life for it free from any interference than I have in accepting the undoubted power of Congress to decree its end. I have equally little trouble in accepting its power to prolong the tenure of an incumbent until Congress or the Senate shall have assented to his removal. The duty of the President to see that the laws be executed is a duty that does not go beyond the laws or require him to achieve more than Congress sees fit to leave within his power.

Notes and Questions

1. Summary. In *Myers*, the Supreme Court held that a first-class postmaster who had been appointed by and with the advice and consent of the Senate could be removed by the President alone, without the Senate's involvement, and that a statute purporting to require the President to seek Senate consent for a removal was unconstitutional. It is not entirely clear how far the Court's decision goes. What did Chief Justice Taft say about inferior officers generally? If Congress had chosen to vest the appointment of the first-class postmaster (an inferior officer) in the Postmaster General rather than leaving in place the default appointment process of advice and consent, could Congress restrict the power of the President to remove him? Taft wrote that the Court's ruling applied only to those officers appointed by and with advice and consent of the Senate, but doesn't its logic apply to all principal and inferior officers, no matter how appointed?

Finally, does the Court's opinion disallow for-cause removal provisions, which leave the removal power with the President but require that certain conditions be met, or does it only disallow Congress and the Senate from retaining a role in the removal of officers?

2. The Decision of 1789. There is a lot to unpack in the competing opinions in *Myers*. Start with the so-called "Decision of 1789." As Taft's opinion for the Court explains, when establishing the first executive department—the Department of Foreign Affairs—the draft statute provided that the principal officer of the department would be removable by the President. A debate on the propriety of presidential removal ensued, and there were four positions that various representatives took: (1) the power to remove the principal officer was constitutionally vested in the President; (2) the power to remove was incident to the power to appoint, and therefore the officer could not be removed by the President without the advice and consent of the Senate; (3) Congress had the power under the Necessary and Proper Clause to establish offices, and therefore Congress in its discretion could confer the removal power (or not) on the President;

 CROSS REFERENCE Although *INS v. Chadha* was not decided for another 60 years, is there a "legislative veto" problem if Congress or the Senate were to veto the President's decision to remove an officer?

and (4) impeachment was the only available mechanism for removing civil officers. The impeachment argument was quickly dropped; as Madison and others argued, impeachment was a mechanism by which *Congress* could remove officers, but that did not imply that the *President* could not remove officers by other means.

Over the five days or so of debate, much of which was constitutional in its tenor, the representatives in the House took a series of votes. First, the representatives voted to retain the provision that the principal officer was to be removable by the President. Then Representative Benson put forward two amendments. The first would provide that when "whenever the said principal officer shall be removed from office by the President of the United States," the chief clerk shall have responsibility for the department's papers. The second amendment would strike the original language, which had provided simply that there would be a principal officer "removable by the President of the United States." Benson sought the change so that it would not appear as though Congress were conferring the removal power on the President, and that the statute would instead reflect the House's judgment that the removal power belonged to the President as a matter of constitutional right. 1 Annals of Cong. 505 (1789) (Joseph Gales ed., 1834); 11 Doc. Hist. of First Fed. Cong., 1789–1791, at 931–32 (Bickford et al. eds., 1992).

HISTORICAL PERSPECTIVE What information about constitutional meaning can we discern from this debate in 1789? And should that matter for constitutional interpretation today?

Both amendments were agreed to. Taft argued that "[i]t is very clear from this history . . . that the vote was, and was intended to be, a legislative declaration that the power to remove officers appointed by the President and the Senate vested in the President alone." Brandeis argued, however, that the two majorities supporting the respective amendments were different. In a footnote omitted above, he wrote that the first vote "succeeded only as a result of coalition between those who accepted Madison's views and those who considered removal subject to congressional control but deemed it advisable to vest the power in the President." A different majority agreed to the second amendment, and that majority "exhibits a combination of diverse views—those who held to Madison's construction, those who initially had sought to strike out the clause on the ground that the Senate should share in removals, and those who deemed it unwise to make any legislative declaration of the Constitution." Thus, Brandeis argued, "the votes on Benson's amendments reveal that the success of this endeavor was due to the strategy of dividing the opposition and not to unanimity of constitutional conceptions." 272 U.S. at 285 n.75. If Brandeis is correct, was the "decision of 1789" really a decision at all? Was it in fact a legislative construction of the Constitution entitled to continued respect? For elaborations on this argument, see Edward S. Corwin, *Tenure of Office and the Removal Power Under the Constitution*, 27 Colum. L. Rev. 353, 362–63 (1927); David P. Currie, The Constitution in Congress: The Federalist Period, 1789–1801, at 40–41 (1997).

On the other hand, consider Madison's statement toward the end of the debate: "Gentlemen have all along proceeded on the idea that the Constitution vests the power in the President; and what arguments were brought forward respecting the convenience or inconvenience of such a disposition of power, were intended only to throw light upon what was meant by the compilers of the Constitution." 1 Annals 579. And Madison later explained in a letter to Thomas Jefferson that the House's decision about the removal power was "most consonant to the text of the Constitution, to the policy of mixing the Legislative and Executive Departments as little as possible, and to the requisite responsibility and harmony in the Executive Department." Letter from James Madison to Thomas Jefferson (June 30, 1789), in Correspondence, First Session: June-August 1789, 16 Documentary History of the First Federal Congress, 1789–1791, at 890, 893 (Charlene Bangs Bickford et al. eds., 2004). Alexander Hamilton and Chief Justice Marshall also appeared to believe that Congress's decision reflected its constitutional interpretation that the removal power was constitutionally vested in the President. See 15 Alexander Hamilton, The Papers of Alexander Hamilton 33, 40 (Harold C. Syrett ed., 1969); 5 John Marshall, The Life of George Washington 200 (1807).

IN QUIRY Who had the better interpretation of the 1789 debate—Chief Justice Taft or Justice Brandeis? Was that "decision" really a decision at all?

3. *Legislative construction.* Even if the debate suggests a consensus in the First Congress that the removal power was constitutionally vested in the President, what kind of precedential force should such a decision have? Is it precedential only because it's good evidence of what the Constitution actually requires? Recall two of our canons of statutory interpretation: longstanding and contemporaneous executive interpretations of statutes are good evidence of what the law is. Here, similarly, a longstanding and contemporaneous exposition of the Constitution by members of Congress is good evidence of what the Constitution requires. Madison explained in the course of the debates that the House's interpretation would become the "permanent exposition of the Constitution" on this point. 1 Annals 495. Alternatively, perhaps the Constitution does not compel a single answer on this question; might Congress's choice "liquidate" the meaning of the Constitution within the range of possible alternatives, and settle on the answer that way? See William Baude, *Constitutional Liquidation*, 71 Stan. L. Rev. 1 (2019). Or does the force of the First Congress's decision depend on the force of the reasoning of the various representatives?

COMPARATIVE PERSPECTIVE Just as a longstanding and contemporaneous executive interpretation of a congressional statute can be good evidence of what the statute means, so too can a longstanding and contemporaneous congressional law be evidence of what the Constitution means.

4. *"The executive power."* Neither Taft nor Brandeis went into much detail about the actual arguments made by the participants in the debate of 1789. The winning argument of James Madison and Fisher Ames are worth repeating because they relate to the modern debate over the meaning of "the executive power" vested in the President. Madison argued that vesting clause of Article II vested all of "the executive power" in the President, subject to a limitation elsewhere in the text—the limitation on the President's power to appoint. This part of "the executive power" is shared with the Senate and with Congress as a whole (pursuant to its power to establish offices). Therefore, if the removal power was part of the executive power, and nothing in the Constitution otherwise limited that power, it belonged to the President. Madison argued:

> The Constitution affirms, that the Executive power shall be vested in the President. Are there exceptions to this proposition? Yes, there are. The Constitution says, that in appointing to office, the Senate shall be associated with the President, unless in the case of inferior

officers, when the law shall otherwise direct. Have we a right to extend this exception? I believe not.

1 Annals 463; see also id. at 496 (Madison) ("[T]he Executive power shall be vested in a President of the United States. The association of the Senate with the President in exercising that particular function, is an exception to this general rule; and exceptions to general rules, I conceive, are ever to be taken strictly.").

Was removal part of "the executive power"? "The Constitution places all Executive power in the hands of the President," argued Fisher Ames, "and could he personally execute all the laws, there would be no occasion for establishing auxiliaries; but the circumscribed powers of human nature in one man, demand the aid of others." 1 Annals 474. Because the President cannot possibly handle all the minutiae of administration, he "must therefore have assistants." Id. But "in order that he may be responsible to his country, he must have a choice in selecting his assistants, a control over them, with power to remove them when he finds the qualifications which induced their appointment cease to exist." Id. The executive power thus includes a "choice in selecting . . . assistants, a control over them, with power to remove them." Id.

For his part, Madison conceived "that if any power whatsoever is in its nature Executive, it is the power of appointing, overseeing, and controlling those who execute the laws." Id. at 463. "[I]f any thing in its nature is executive," he later added, "it must be that power which is employed in superintending and seeing that the laws are faithfully executed." Id. at 500. He also argued that the Take Care Clause supported this inference. Id. at 496 ("[T]here is another part of the Constitution, which inclines, in my judgment, to favor the construction I put upon it; the President is required to take care that the laws be faithfully executed. If the duty to see the laws faithfully executed be required at the hands of the Executive Magistrate, it would seem that it was generally intended he should have that species of power which is necessary to accomplish that end.").

These arguments from Madison and Ames are often thought to support the proposition that the vesting clause of Article II is a residual grant of all executive-type powers, including royal prerogatives historically exercised by the British monarch. See, e.g., Saikrishna B. Prakash & Michael D. Ramsey, *The Executive Power over Foreign Affairs*, 111 Yale L.J. 231 (2001) (arguing that many presidential foreign affairs powers can only be explained if the vesting clause is a residual grant of executive powers). However, other scholars have argued that "the executive power" was not a residual grant of executive powers, but was a grant of a single power only: the power to carry law into execution. See Julian Davis Mortenson, *The Executive Power Clause*, 168 U. Pa. L. Rev. 1269 (2020); Julian Davis Mortenson, *Article II Vests Executive Power, Not the Royal Prerogative*, 119 Colum. L. Rev. 1169 (2019). Your author happens to agree with Professor Mortenson—the executive power was only the power to carry law into execution. But can Madison still be right about the removal power even under this reading of Article II's vesting clause? See Ilan Wurman, *In Search of Prerogative*, 70 Duke L.J. 93 (2020).

   5. The Take Care Clause. Is it possible that the Vesting Clause of Article II is not a grant of power at all, and that it merely identifies who is to exercise the subsequently granted powers? This was Justice Jackson's view in his *Youngstown* concurrence: "I cannot accept the view that [the executive power] clause is a grant in bulk of all conceivable executive power but regard it as an allocation to the presidential office of the generic powers thereafter stated." Youngstown Sheet & Tube Co. v. Sawyer, 343 U.S. 579, 641 (1952) (Jackson, J., concurring). If the vesting clause is not a grant of power, then the President's power to execute law must derive from the Take Care Clause. But this is framed as a duty: the president "shall take care that the laws be faithfully executed." If the President's power is only that which can be derived from this clause, then are the implications for the removal power different? Can the President "take care" if the Senate retains a role in removal?

PRACTICE POINTER It is good practice to see how different parts of a statute—or the Constitution—work together. Why have the Take Care Clause if the Vesting Clause is a grant of power? Does that imply the Vesting Clause is not a grant of power? Or, perhaps, is the Take Care Clause a limit on how the executive power is to be exercised?

   6. Inferior officers. The decision of 1789 arguably only had to do with principal officers. Justice Story, for example, thought it did not apply to inferior officers. Joseph Story, Commentaries on the Constitution of the United States § 1544 (1833). Chief Justice Taft argued, on the other hand, that there is in fact a provision in Article II for inferior officers—Congress may vest their appointment in the President, the heads of departments, or the courts of law. Thus, it was held in the *Perkins* case, United States v. Perkins, 116 U. S. 483 (1886), that by vesting the appointment of an inferior officer in the head of department, Congress could also put conditions on the ability of that head of department to remove the inferior officer. Conditioning the grounds on which a principal officer may remove an inferior officer dates back from the earliest days of the Republic; for example, in 1796 a statute authored the Surveyor General to hire "skilful surveyors" and only authorized the Surveyor General to remove them for negligence or misconduct. Leonard D. White, The Federalists: A Study in Administrative History 384 (1956).

But the *Perkins* case, and this prior historical practice, says nothing about the President's power to remove such officers. Perhaps the principal officers can be limited by law in how they exercise their authority over inferior officers, but can the President be so controlled? And what if the appointment of the inferior officer is vested not in a head of department, but in the President alone? Can the President's power be restricted in this circumstance? If so, would that violate the executive power clause under Chief Justice Taft's reading? Indeed, in *Myers*, Chief Justice Taft doubted whether such an extension of *Perkins* would be constitutional. Do inferior officers also assist the president in exercising the executive power?

7. *The civil service.* What are the implications of the *Myers* opinion for the civil service? To the extent civil servants are inferior officers, they can be protected from removal by the principals who appoint them. But can they be protected from removal by the President? If civil servants are classified as "employees" as opposed to inferior officers, can they be protected from removal?

8. *Congress's power to establish offices.* Justices McReynolds, Brandeis, and Holmes all argued that Congress's power to establish offices in the first place allowed Congress to create those offices with conditions on how the officers are to be removed. Indeed, Congress had routinely created conditions as

HISTORICAL PERSPECTIVE In 1789, there was no "civil service" like there is today, but many inferior officers did serve for several years across multiple administrations. Andrew Jackson introduced the "spoils system" where political supporters would fill government positions with a new administration. Starting in the 1880s or so, Congress and the President began classifying more and more officers as "civil servants" who would be protected from removal.

to whom could be appointed to particular offices. What do you make of these arguments? From a historical perspective, it was widely understood at the time of the Founding that "the executive power" was the power to execute law *and* to appoint officers *not otherwise provided for by law.* The idea seems to have been that the appointment power—unlike the power to remove officers—was at least partly a legislative function. See Ilan Wurman, *In Search of Prerogative,* 70 Duke L.J. 93 (2020). Both Madison and Wilson, for example, defined the executive power in the Constitutional Convention as including the power "to appoint to offices *in cases not otherwise provided for.*" 1 The Records of the Federal Convention of 1787, at 66–67 (Max Farrand ed. 1911) (cleaned up) (Madison); id. at 70 (Wilson) ("Extive. powers are designed for the execution of Laws, and appointing Officers not otherwise to be appointed."). Might that answer Brandeis's objection? If Congress has part of the appointment power and can set qualifications for nominees, does that mean it must also have the power to condition removals?

9. *The power to suspend officers.* More than once in his opinion Justice Brandeis argued that the President does not have a unitary power to remove officers, but that the President could *suspend* those officers until the Senate could act. Why does Brandeis think the President has the power to suspend officers? Where does the Constitution say that? If it is part of "the executive power," why is it unreasonable to conclude that this executive power includes the power of removal itself? Is there a way to interpret the Constitution to imply that the President has a power of suspension but not removal? Was Justice Brandeis's argument here a functionalist one? Is Brandeis's view plausible if one thinks the Vesting Clause is not a grant of power, and the President's only power to remove is that which can be implied from the duty to "take care"?

10. *Statutory removal provisions.* Justice Brandeis also described a series of statutes by which Congress directed that the President remove officers on certain conditions, such as after conviction. Does this stand for the proposition that the President's removal power can be restricted? It seems to suggest that Congress might be able to *require* certain removals by statute, but that does not limit the *President*'s ability to remove in other circumstances. Still, where does Congress get the power to require certain removals? Does it derive from Congress's necessary and proper power? Might Congress have a necessary and proper power to direct certain removals, but not to prevent removals? Does one help the President carry law into execution, and the other derogate from that power?

Alternatively, is it possible that Congress was simply referring to its impeachment power? For example, in the statute establishing the Treasury department, the act provided that if any officer "shall offend against any of the prohibitions of this act, he shall be deemed guilty of a high misdemeanor . . . and shall upon conviction be removed from office, and forever thereafter incapable of holding any office under the United States." 1 Stat. 65, 67. Here, the "conviction" could refer to conviction by the Senate after an impeachment; and the punishment parallels the Constitution's disqualification clause, which provides that "Judgment in Cases of Impeachment shall not extend further than to removal from Office, and disqualification to hold and enjoy any Office of honor, Trust or Profit under the United States." U.S. Const. art. I, § 3, cl. 7. On the other hand, the statute also required paying a monetary penalty, and also mentions a "public prosecutor." Thus, what Congress had in mind here was a bit ambiguous. Would it have been unconstitutional if it were referring to something other than impeachment?

11. **Marbury v. Madison.** Consider, finally, Chief Justice Marshall's opinion in *Marbury v. Madison.* Recall that Marshall held that President Jefferson and Secretary of State Madison had to deliver a signed commission to William Marbury, who had been appointed a Justice of the Peace for the District of Columbia by President John Adams. Why would Jefferson have to deliver the commission, if Jefferson could simply have removed Marbury at will? Marshall's opinion thus at a minimum assumes that Marbury was not removable and was entitled to his office for its full five-year term. Chief Justice Taft, in *Myers,* treats all this as dicta, whereas the dissenting Justices found this all quite decisive in their favor. What do you think? Might a distinction be that justices of the peace for territories are really local officials who do not have any part in exercising "the executive power of the United States"? Or was Marshall wrong about this point? Or on the contrary, was he right and Chief Justice Taft wrong?

2. The Functionalist Approach: 1935–2010

The Court's opinion in *Myers* reflects a formalist and "originalist" approach to interpreting the Constitution. In the next two cases—one decided within a decade of *Myers,* the other in more recent times—the Supreme Court arguably changed tacks and adopted more functionalist approaches to analyzing the President's removal power. The next case, upholding for-cause removal provisions for independent agencies, is often considered to be a cornerstone of the modern administrative state.

COURSE THEME

FORMALISM VS. FUNCTIONALISM

Did the Supreme Court take a functionalist approach
in the next two cases?

Humphrey's Executor v. United States

295 U.S. 602 (1935)

MR. JUSTICE SUTHERLAND delivered the opinion of the Court.

Plaintiff brought suit in the Court of Claims against the United States to recover a sum of money alleged to be due the deceased for salary as a Federal Trade Commissioner from October 8, 1933, when the President undertook to remove him from office, to the time of his death on February 14, 1934. . . . The material facts which give rise to the questions are as follows:

William E. Humphrey, the decedent, on December 10, 1931, was nominated by President Hoover to succeed himself as a member of the Federal Trade Commission, and was confirmed by the United States Senate. He was duly commissioned for a term of seven years, expiring September 25, 1938; and, after taking the required oath of office, entered upon his duties. On July 25, 1933, President Roosevelt addressed a letter to the commissioner asking for his resignation, on the ground 'that the aims and purposes of the Administration with respect to the work of the Commission can be carried out most effectively with personnel of my own selection,' but disclaiming any reflection upon the commissioner personally or upon his services. The commissioner replied, asking time to consult his friends. After some further correspondence upon the subject, the President on August 31, 1933, wrote the commissioner expressing the hope that the resignation would be forthcoming, and saying: 'You will, I know, realize that I do not feel that your mind and my mind go along together on either the policies or the administering of the Federal Trade Commission, and, frankly, I think it is best for the people of this country that I should have a full confidence.'

The commissioner declined to resign; and on October 7, 1933, the President wrote him: 'Effective as of this date you are hereby removed from the office of Commissioner of the Federal Trade Commission.'

Humphrey never acquiesced in this action, but continued thereafter to insist that he was still a member of the commission, entitled to perform its duties and receive the compensation provided by law at the rate of $10,000 per annum. Upon these and other facts set forth in the certificate, which we deem it unnecessary to recite, the following questions are certified:

'1. Do the provisions of section 1 of the Federal Trade Commission Act, stating that 'any commissioner may be removed by the President for inefficiency, neglect of duty, or malfeasance in office', restrict or limit the power of the President to remove a commissioner except upon one or more of the causes named?

'If the foregoing question is answered in the affirmative, then—

'2. If the power of the President to remove a commissioner is restricted or limited as shown by the foregoing interrogatory and the answer made thereto, is such a restriction or limitation valid under the Constitution of the United States?'

The Federal Trade Commission Act creates a commission of five members to be appointed by the President by and with the advice and consent of the Senate, and section 1 provides: 'Not more than three of the commissioners shall be members of the same political party. . . . [T]heir successors shall be appointed for terms of seven years . . . . Any commissioner may be removed by the President for inefficiency, neglect of duty, or malfeasance in office.'

[In omitted paragraphs, the Court describes the Commission's role in implementing the statutory prohibition on "unfair methods of competition in commerce."—Ed.]

First. The question first to be considered is whether, by the provisions of section 1 of the Federal Trade Commission Act already quoted, the President's power is limited to removal for the specific causes enumerated therein. The negative contention of the government is based principally upon the decision of this court in Shurtleff v. United States, 189 U.S. 311. That case involved the power of the President to remove a general appraiser of merchandise appointed under the Act of June 10, 1890, 26 Stat. 131. Section 12 of the act provided for the appointment by the President, by and with the advice and consent of the Senate, of nine general appraisers of merchandise, who 'may be removed from office at any time by the President for inefficiency, neglect of duty, or malfeasance in office.' The President removed Shurtleff without assigning any cause therefor.

The Court of Claims dismissed plaintiff's petition to recover salary, upholding the President's power to remove for causes other than those stated. In this court Shurtleff relied upon the maxim expressio unius est exclusio alterius; but this court held that, while the rule expressed in the maxim was a very proper one and founded upon justifiable reasoning in many instances, it 'should not be accorded controlling weight when to do so would involve the alteration of the universal practice of the government for over a century, and the consequent curtailment of the powers of the Executive in such an unusual manner.' What the court meant by this expression appears from a reading of the opinion. That opinion, after saying that no term of office was fixed by the act and that, with the exception of judicial officers provided for by the Constitution, no civil officer had ever held office by life tenure since the foundation of the government, points out that to construe the statute as contended for by Shurtleff would give the appraiser the right to hold office during his life or until found guilty of some act specified in the statute, the result of which would be a complete revolution in respect of the general tenure of office, effected by implication with regard to that particular office only.

'We think it quite inadmissible,' the court said, 'to attribute an intention on the part of Congress to make such an extraordinary change in the usual rule governing the tenure of office, and one which is to be applied to this particular office only, without stating such intention in plain and explicit language, instead of leaving it to be implied from doubtful inferences. . . . '

These circumstances, which led the court to reject the maxim as inapplicable, are exceptional. In the face of the unbroken precedent against life tenure, except in the case of the judiciary, the conclusion that Congress intended that, from among all other civil officers, appraisers alone should be selected to hold office for life was so extreme as to forbid, in the opinion of the court, any ruling which would produce that result if it reasonably could be avoided. The situation here presented is plainly and wholly different. The statute fixes a term of office, in accordance with many precedents. . . .

[T]he fixing of a definite term subject to removal for cause, unless there be some countervailing provision or circumstance indicating the contrary, which here we are unable to find, is enough to establish the legislative intent that the term is not to be curtailed in the absence of such cause. But if the intention of Congress that no removal should be made during the specified term except for one or more of the enumerated causes were not clear upon the face of the statute, as we think it is, it would be made clear by a consideration of the character of the commission and the legislative history which accompanied and preceded the passage of the act.

The commission is to be nonpartisan; and it must, from the very nature of its duties, act with entire impartiality. It is charged with the enforcement of no policy except the policy of the law. Its duties are neither political nor executive, but predominantly quasi judicial and quasi legislative. Like the Interstate Commerce Commission, its members are called upon to exercise the trained judgment of a body of experts 'appointed by law and informed by experience.'

The legislative reports in both houses of Congress clearly reflect the view that a fixed term was necessary to the effective and fair administration of the law. In the report to the Senate the Senate Committee on Interstate Commerce . . . declares that one advantage which the commission possessed . . . lay in the fact of its independence, and that it was essential that the commission should not be open to the suspicion of partisan direction. . . .

The debates in both houses demonstrate that the prevailing view was that the Commission was not to be 'subject to anybody in the government but . . . only to the people of the United States'; free from 'political domination or control' or the 'probability or possibility of such a thing'; to be 'separate and apart from any existing department of the government—not subject to the orders of the President.' . . .

Thus, the language of the act, the legislative reports, and the general purposes of the legislation as reflected by the debates, all combine to demonstrate the congressional intent to create a body of experts who shall gain experience by length of service; a body which shall be independent of executive authority, except in its selection, and free to exercise its judgment without the leave or hindrance of any other official or any department of the government. To the accomplishment of these purposes, it is clear that Congress was of opinion that length and certainty of tenure would vitally contribute. And to hold that, nevertheless, the members of the commission continue in office at the mere will of the President, might be to thwart, in large measure, the very ends which Congress sought to realize by definitely fixing the term of office.

We conclude that the intent of the act is to limit the executive power of removal to the causes enumerated, the existence of none of which is claimed here; and we pass to the second question.

Second. To support its contention that the removal provision of section 1, as we have just construed it, is an unconstitutional interference with the executive power of the President, the government's chief reliance is Myers v. United States, 272 U.S. 52. That case has been so recently decided, and the prevailing and dissenting opinions so fully review the general subject of the power of executive removal, that further discussion would add little of value to the wealth of material there collected. These opinions examine at length the historical, legislative, and judicial data bearing upon the question, beginning with what is called 'the decision of 1789' in the first Congress and coming down almost to the day when the opinions were delivered. They occupy 243 pages of the volume in which they are printed. Nevertheless, the narrow point actually decided was only that the President had power to remove a postmaster of the first class, without the advice and consent of the Senate as required by act of Congress. In the course of the opinion of the court, expressions occur which tend to sustain the government's contention, but these are beyond the point involved and, therefore, do not come within the rule of stare decisis. In so far as they are out of harmony with the views here set forth, these expressions are disapproved. . . .

The office of a postmaster is so essentially unlike the office now involved that the decision in the Myers Case cannot be accepted as controlling our decision here. A postmaster is an executive officer restricted to the performance of executive functions. He is charged with no duty at all related to either the legislative or judicial power. The actual decision in the Myers Case finds support in the theory that such an officer is merely one of the units in the executive department and, hence, inherently subject to the exclusive and illimitable power of removal by the Chief Executive, whose subordinate and aid he is. Putting aside dicta, which may be followed if sufficiently persuasive but which are not controlling, the necessary reach of the decision goes far enough to include all purely executive officers. It goes no farther; much less does it include an officer who occupies no place in the executive department and who exercises no part of the executive power vested by the Constitution in the President.

The Federal Trade Commission is an administrative body created by Congress to carry into effect legislative policies embodied in the statute in accordance with the legislative standard therein prescribed, and to perform other specified duties as a legislative or as a judicial aid. Such a body cannot in any proper sense be characterized as an arm or an eye of the executive. Its duties are performed without executive leave and, in the contemplation of the statute, must be free from executive control. In administering the provisions of the statute in respect of 'unfair methods of competition,' that is to say, in filling in and administering the details embodied by that general standard, the commission acts in part quasi legislatively and in part quasi judicially. In making investigations and reports thereon for the information of Congress under section 6, in aid of the legislative power, it acts as a legislative agency. Under section 7, which authorizes the commission to act as a master in chancery under rules prescribed by the court, it acts as an agency of the judiciary. To the extent that it exercises any executive function, as distinguished from executive power in the constitutional sense, it does so in the discharge and effectuation of its quasi legislative or quasi judicial powers, or as an agency of the legislative or judicial departments of the government. . . .

We think it plain under the Constitution that illimitable power of removal is not possessed by the President in respect of officers of the character of those just named. The authority of Congress, in creating quasi legislative or quasi judicial agencies, to require them to act in discharge of their duties independently of executive control cannot well be doubted; and that authority includes, as an appropriate incident, power to fix the period during which they shall continue, and to forbid their removal except for cause in the meantime. For it is quite evident that one who holds his office only during the pleasure of another cannot be depended upon to maintain an attitude of independence against the latter's will. . . .

The power of removal here claimed for the President . . . threatens the independence of a commission, which is not only wholly disconnected from the executive department, but which, as already fully appears, was created by Congress as a means of carrying into operation legislative and judicial powers, and as an agency of the legislative and judicial departments.

In the light of the question now under consideration, we have re-examined the precedents referred to in the Myers Case, and find nothing in them to justify a conclusion contrary to that which we have reached. The so-called 'decision of 1789' had relation to a bill proposed by Mr. Madison to establish an executive Department of Foreign Affairs. The bill provided that the principal officer was 'to be removable from office by the President of the United

States.' This clause was changed to read 'whenever the principal officer shall be removed from office by the President of the United States,' certain things should follow, thereby, in connection with the debates, recognizing and confirming, as the court thought in the Myers Case, the sole power of the President in the matter. We shall not discuss the subject further, since it is so fully covered by the opinions in the Myers Case, except to say that the office under consideration by Congress was not only purely executive, but the officer one who was responsible to the President, and to him alone, in a very definite sense. A reading of the debates shows that the President's illimitable power of removal was not considered in respect of other than executive officers. And it is pertinent to observe that when, at a later time, the tenure of office for the Comptroller of the Treasury was under consideration, Mr. Madison quite evidently thought that, since the duties of that office were not purely of an executive nature but partook of the judiciary quality as well, a different rule in respect of executive removal might well apply. 1 Annals of Congress 611–612. . . .

The result of what we now have said is this: Whether the power of the President to remove an officer shall prevail over the authority of Congress to condition the power by fixing a definite term and precluding a removal except for cause will depend upon the character of the office; the Myers decision, affirming the power of the President alone to make the removal, is confined to purely executive officers; and as to officers of the kind here under consideration, we hold that no removal can be made during the prescribed term for which the officer is appointed, except for one or more of the causes named in the applicable statute. . . .

NOTES AND QUESTIONS

1. Summary. *Humphrey's Executor* stands for the proposition that Congress can restrict the President's ability to remove even principal officers, although Congress cannot necessarily impose any restriction—for example, it might still not be able to require Senate consent to removals. And Congress cannot impose the restrictions on just any officer. The case stands for the proposition that Congress may impose at least for-cause removal provisions applicable to principal officers who are not exercising "purely executive" power. The theory here is that some principal officers—those heading independent commissions—are exercising "quasi-legislative" or "quasi-judicial" power. This means, presumably, that at least some category of principal officers are exercising purely executive power—perhaps those involved in defense and foreign affairs, and maybe those involved in criminal prosecutions—and that others are involved in activities that aren't "purely" executive. Do you see a distinction between executive power when it comes to foreign affairs and defense—or when it comes to postmasters—and executive power in the context of administering the federal trade commission laws?

2. ***Quasi-legislative power, or nonexclusive legislative power?*** What exactly is the "quasi-legislative" power the Court describes? The Court says: "In administering the provisions of the statute in respect of 'unfair methods of competition,' that is to say, in filling in and administering the details embodied by that general standard, the commission acts in part quasi legislatively and in part quasi judicially." But how is that different than "executive power"? Is that different from implementing or administering the law by making regulations? Were George Washington's regulations respecting the invalid veterans of the revolutionary war "quasi-legislative"? Maybe they were quasi-legislative, but weren't they ultimately exercises of *executive* power? At least, were those regulations sufficiently administrative and executive in nature, even if Congress could have made them itself? Isn't what the Court describes in *Humphrey's Executor* really nonexclusive legislative power, i.e., the kind of power that either Congress or the Executive could exercise?

COURSE THEME

NONEXCLUSIVE POWER
What is the difference between the "quasi" powers identified in *Humphrey's Executor* and the "nonexclusive powers" that we have discussed throughout these materials? Is the answer that nonexclusive power must at least be exercised by one of the three named constitutional actors?

---

3. ***Can originalism justify*** **Humphrey's Executor?** Is it possible to defend for-cause removal restrictions on originalist grounds? Does it depend on one's view of the executive power clause (Article II's vesting clause)? If the executive power clause is not a grant of substantive power, then the only power the President has with respect to law execution is whatever power can be implied for the *duty* to take care that the laws be faithfully executed. So long as an officer is exercising discretion within the bounds permitted by statute, then that

would seem to be "faithful" execution even if the President would prefer the officer to exercise the discretion in a different way. Put another way, subordinate officers do not have to follow the President's general policy preferences to faithfully execute their legal obligations. On the other hand, if the executive power clause is a grant of substantive power—at least the power to execute law—then is *Humphrey's Executor* harder to justify? Isn't the core of the power to execute law the choice how to proceed when the law leaves discretion?

4. **Wiener v. United States.** In Wiener v. United States, 357 U.S. 349 (1958), Wiener was a member of the War Claims Commission, which Congress had created to adjudicate claims involving compensation to "internees, prisoners of war, and religious organizations who suffered personal injury or property damage at the hands of the enemy in connection with World War II." Wiener was appointed by President Truman and then removed by President Eisenhower. The Court invalidated the removal and reiterated that nothing in *Myers* applied to "quasi-judicial" bodies like the War Claims Commission. On why the War Claims Commission could adjudicate such disputes at all, see the discussion of "public rights" in the next chapter.

Morrison v. Olson

487 U.S. 654 (1988)

CHIEF JUSTICE REHNQUIST delivered the opinion of the Court.

[The facts of the case are excerpted above in the appointments clause section, supra pp. 653–656. Recall that at issue is the constitutionality of the "independent counsel," who by statute could exercise all the prosecutorial authority of the Department of Justice in the matters assigned to her by the special court, and was removable only for-cause by the Attorney General. In the part of the opinion excerpted previously, the Court concluded that the independent counsel was an "inferior" officer and thus could be appointed by the special court. Justice Scalia dissented, arguing that she was a principal officer because subordinate to no one. The following excerpts deal with whether the removal provision is separately unconstitutional.—Ed.]

 CROSS REFERENCE We read another part of *Morrison v. Olson* earlier in this chapter in the appointments section.

* * *

V

We now turn to consider whether the Act is invalid under the constitutional principle of separation of powers. Two related issues must be addressed: The first is whether the provision of the Act restricting the Attorney General's power to remove the independent counsel to only those instances in which he can show "good cause," taken by itself, impermissibly interferes with the President's exercise of his constitutionally appointed functions. The second is whether, taken as a whole, the Act violates the separation of powers by reducing the President's ability to control the prosecutorial powers wielded by the independent counsel.

A

Two Terms ago we had occasion to consider whether it was consistent with the separation of powers for Congress to pass a statute that authorized a Government official who is removable only by Congress to participate in what we found to be "executive powers." *Bowsher v. Synar*, 478 U.S. 714, 730 (1986). We held in *Bowsher* that "Congress cannot reserve for itself the power of removal of an officer charged with the execution of the laws except by impeachment." A primary antecedent for this ruling was our 1926 decision in *Myers v. United States*, 272 U.S. 52 (1926). *Myers* had considered the propriety of a federal statute by which certain postmasters of the United States could be removed by the President only "by and with the advice and consent of the Senate." There too, Congress' attempt to involve itself in the removal of an executive official was found to be sufficient grounds to render the statute invalid. . . .

Unlike both *Bowsher* and *Myers,* this case does not involve an attempt by Congress itself to gain a role in the removal of executive officials other than its established powers of impeachment and conviction. The Act instead puts the removal power squarely in the hands of the Executive Branch; an independent counsel may be removed from office, "only by the personal action of the Attorney General, and only for good cause." § 596(a)(1). There is no requirement of congressional approval of the Attorney General's removal decision, though the decision is subject to judicial review. § 596(a)(3). In our view, the removal provisions of the Act make this case more analogous to *Humphrey's Executor v. United States*, 295 U.S. 602 (1935), and *Wiener v. United States*, 357 U.S. 349(1958), than to *Myers* or *Bowsher.* . . .

Appellees contend that *Humphrey's Executor* and *Wiener* are distinguishable from this case because they did not involve officials who performed a "core executive function." They argue that our decision in *Humphrey's Executor* rests on a distinction between "purely executive" officials and officials who exercise "quasi-legislative" and "quasi-judicial" powers. In their view, when a "purely executive" official is involved, the governing precedent is *Myers*, not *Humphrey's Executor*. And, under *Myers*, the President must have absolute discretion to discharge "purely" executive officials at will.

We undoubtedly did rely on the terms "quasi-legislative" and "quasi-judicial" to distinguish the officials involved in *Humphrey's Executor* and *Wiener* from those in *Myers*, but our present considered view is that the determination of whether the Constitution allows Congress to impose a "good cause"-type restriction on the President's power to remove an official cannot be made to turn on whether or not that official is classified as "purely executive." The analysis contained in our removal cases is designed not to define rigid categories of those officials who may or may not be removed at will by the President, but to ensure that Congress does not interfere with the President's exercise of the "executive power" and his constitutionally appointed duty to "take care that the laws be faithfully executed" under Article II. *Myers* was undoubtedly correct in its holding, and in its broader suggestion that there are some "purely executive" officials who must be removable by the President at will if he is to be able to accomplish his constitutional role. . . .

At the other end of the spectrum from *Myers*, the characterization of the agencies in *Humphrey's Executor* and *Wiener* as "quasi-legislative" or "quasi-judicial" in large part reflected our judgment that it was not essential to the President's proper execution of his Article II powers that these agencies be headed up by individuals who were removable at will. We do not mean to suggest that an analysis of the functions served by the officials at issue is irrelevant. But the real question is whether the removal restrictions are of such a nature that they impede the President's ability to perform his constitutional duty, and the functions of the officials in question must be analyzed in that light.

Considering for the moment the "good cause" removal provision in isolation from the other parts of the Act at issue in this case, we cannot say that the imposition of a "good cause" standard for removal by itself unduly trammels on executive authority. There is no real dispute that the functions performed by the independent counsel are "executive" in the sense that they are law enforcement functions that typically have been undertaken by officials within the Executive Branch. As we noted above, however, the independent counsel is an inferior officer under the Appointments Clause, with limited jurisdiction and tenure and lacking policymaking or significant administrative authority. Although the counsel exercises no small amount of discretion and judgment in deciding how to carry out his or her duties under the Act, we simply do not see how the President's need to control the exercise of that discretion is so central to the functioning of the Executive Branch as to require as a matter of constitutional law that the counsel be terminable at will by the President.

Nor do we think that the "good cause" removal provision at issue here impermissibly burdens the President's power to control or supervise the independent counsel, as an executive official, in the execution of his or her duties under the Act. This is not a case in which the power to remove an executive official has been completely stripped from the President, thus providing no means for the President to ensure the "faithful execution" of the laws. Rather, because the independent counsel may be terminated for "good cause," the Executive, through the Attorney General, retains ample authority to assure that the counsel is competently performing his or her statutory responsibilities in a manner that comports with the provisions of the Act. . . . We do not think that this limitation as it presently stands sufficiently deprives the President of control over the independent counsel to interfere impermissibly with his constitutional obligation to ensure the faithful execution of the laws.

B

The final question to be addressed is whether the Act, taken as a whole, violates the principle of separation of powers by unduly interfering with the role of the Executive Branch. . . .

We observe first that this case does not involve an attempt by Congress to increase its own powers at the expense of the Executive Branch. . . .

Finally, we do not think that the Act "impermissibly undermine[s]" the powers of the Executive Branch, or "disrupts the proper balance between the coordinate branches [by] prevent[ing] the Executive Branch from accomplishing its constitutionally assigned functions." It is undeniable that the Act reduces the amount of control or supervision that the Attorney General and, through him, the President exercises over the investigation and prosecution of a certain class of alleged criminal activity. . . . Nonetheless, the Act does give the

Attorney General several means of supervising or controlling the prosecutorial powers that may be wielded by an independent counsel. Most importantly, the Attorney General retains the power to remove the counsel for "good cause," a power that we have already concluded provides the Executive with substantial ability to ensure that the laws are "faithfully executed" by an independent counsel. . . . In addition, the jurisdiction of the independent counsel is defined with reference to the facts submitted by the Attorney General . . . . Notwithstanding the fact that the counsel is to some degree "independent" and free from executive supervision to a greater extent than other federal prosecutors, in our view these features of the Act give the Executive Branch sufficient control over the independent counsel to ensure that the President is able to perform his constitutionally assigned duties. . . .

Justice Scalia, dissenting.

. . . . The Framers of the Federal Constitution . . . viewed the principle of separation of powers as the absolutely central guarantee of a just Government. . . . Without a secure structure of separated powers, our Bill of Rights would be worthless, as are the bills of rights of many nations of the world that have adopted, or even improved upon, the mere words of ours.

The principle of separation of powers is expressed in our Constitution in the first section of each of the first three Articles. Article I, § 1, provides that "[a]ll legislative Powers herein granted shall be vested in a Congress of the United States, which shall consist of a Senate and House of Representatives." Article III, § 1, provides that "[t]he judicial Power of the United States, shall be vested in one supreme Court, and in such inferior Courts as the Congress may from time to time ordain and establish." And the provision at issue here, Art. II, § 1, cl. 1, provides that "[t]he executive Power shall be vested in a President of the United States of America." . . .

[T]he Founders conspicuously and very consciously declined to sap the Executive's strength in the same way they had weakened the Legislature: by dividing the executive power. Proposals to have multiple executives, or a council of advisers with separate authority were rejected. Thus, while "[a]ll legislative Powers herein granted shall be vested in a Congress of the United States, which shall consist of a Senate *and* House of Representatives," U.S. Const., Art. I, § 1(emphasis added), "[t]he executive Power shall be vested in *a President of the United States*," Art. II, § 1, cl. 1 (emphasis added).

That is what this suit is about. Power. The allocation of power among Congress, the President, and the courts in such fashion as to preserve the equilibrium the Constitution sought to establish—so that "a gradual concentration of the several powers in the same department," Federalist No. 51, p. 321 (J. Madison), can effectively be resisted. Frequently an issue of this sort will come before the Court clad, so to speak, in sheep's clothing: the potential of the asserted principle to effect important change in the equilibrium of power is not immediately evident, and must be discerned by a careful and perceptive analysis. But this wolf comes as a wolf.

I

The present case began when the Legislative and Executive Branches became "embroiled in a dispute concerning the scope of the congressional investigatory power," which—as is often the case with such interbranch conflicts—became quite acrimonious. . . .

[T]he Judiciary Committee remained disturbed by the possibility that the Department had persuaded the President to assert executive privilege despite reservations by the EPA; that the Department had "deliberately and unnecessarily precipitated a constitutional confrontation with Congress"; that the Department had not properly reviewed and selected the documents as to which executive privilege was asserted; that the Department had directed the United States Attorney not to present the contempt certification involving the EPA Administrator to a grand jury for prosecution; that the Department had made the decision to sue the House of Representatives; and that the Department had not adequately advised and represented the President, the EPA, and the EPA Administrator. Accordingly, staff counsel of the House Judiciary Committee were commissioned . . . to investigate the Justice Department's role in the controversy. That investigation lasted 2 ½ years, and produced a 3,000-page report issued by the Committee over the vigorous dissent of all but one of its minority-party members. That report, which among other charges questioned the truthfulness of certain statements made by Assistant Attorney General Olson during testimony in front of the Committee during the early stages of its investigation, was sent to the Attorney General along with a formal request that he appoint an independent counsel to investigate Mr. Olson and others.

As a general matter, the Act before us here requires the Attorney General to apply for the appointment of an independent counsel within 90 days after receiving a request to do so, unless he determines within that period that "there are no reasonable grounds to believe that further investigation or prosecution is warranted." 28 U.S.C. § 592(b)(1). As a practical matter, it would be surprising if the Attorney General had any choice (assuming this statute is constitutional) but to seek appointment of an independent counsel to pursue the charges against the principal object of the congressional request, Mr. Olson. Merely the political consequences (to him and the President) of seeming to break the law by refusing to do so would have been substantial. How could it not be, the public would ask, that a 3,000-page indictment drawn by our representatives over 2 ½ years does not even establish "reasonable grounds to believe" that further investigation or prosecution is warranted with respect to at least the principal alleged culprit? But the Act establishes more than just practical compulsion. Although the Court's opinion asserts that the Attorney General had "no duty to comply with the [congressional] request," that is not entirely accurate. He *had* a duty to comply unless he could conclude that there were "*no reasonable grounds to believe*," not that prosecution was warranted, but merely that "*further investigation*" was warranted . . . . The Court also makes much of the fact that "the courts are specifically prevented from reviewing the Attorney General's decision not to seek appointment, § 592(f)." Yes, but *Congress* is not prevented from reviewing it. The context of this statute is acrid with the smell of threatened impeachment. . . .

Thus, by the application of this statute in the present case, Congress has effectively compelled a criminal investigation of a high-level appointee of the President in connection with his actions arising out of a bitter power dispute between the President and the Legislative Branch. Mr. Olson may or may not be guilty of a crime; we do not know. But we do know that the investigation of him has been commenced, not necessarily because the President or his authorized subordinates believe it is in the interest of the United States, in the sense that it warrants the diversion of resources from other efforts, and is worth the cost in money and in possible damage to other governmental interests; and not even, leaving aside those normally considered factors, because the President or his authorized subordinates necessarily believe that an investigation is likely to unearth a violation worth prosecuting; but only because the Attorney General cannot affirm, as Congress demands, that there are *no reasonable grounds to believe* that further investigation is warranted. The decisions regarding the scope of that further investigation, its duration, and, finally, whether or not prosecution should ensue, are likewise beyond the control of the President and his subordinates.

II

If to describe this case is not to decide it, the concept of a government of separate and coordinate powers no longer has meaning. The Court devotes most of its attention to such relatively technical details as the Appointments Clause and the removal power, addressing briefly and only at the end of its opinion the separation of powers. As my prologue suggests, I think that has it backwards. . . . [W]hile I will subsequently discuss why our appointments and removal jurisprudence does not support today's holding, I begin with a consideration of the fountainhead of that jurisprudence, the separation and equilibration of powers. . . .

To repeat, Article II, § 1, cl. 1, of the Constitution provides: "The executive Power shall be vested in a President of the United States."

As I described at the outset of this opinion, this does not mean *some of* the executive power, but *all of* the executive power. It seems to me, therefore, that the decision of the Court of Appeals invalidating the present statute must be upheld on fundamental separation-of-powers principles if the following two questions are answered affirmatively: (1) Is the conduct of a criminal prosecution (and of an investigation to decide whether to prosecute) the exercise of purely executive power? (2) Does the statute deprive the President of the United States of exclusive control over the exercise of that power? Surprising to say, the Court appears to concede an affirmative answer to both questions, but seeks to avoid the inevitable conclusion that since the statute vests some purely executive power in a person who is not the President of the United States it is void.

The Court concedes that "[t]here is no real dispute that the functions performed by the independent counsel are 'executive'," though it qualifies that concession by adding "in the sense that they are law enforcement functions that typically have been undertaken by officials within the Executive Branch." The qualifier adds nothing but atmosphere. In what *other* sense can one identify "the executive Power" that is supposed to be vested in the President (unless it includes everything the Executive Branch is given to do) *except* by reference to what has always and everywhere—if conducted by government at all—been conducted never by the legislature, never by the courts, and always by the executive. There is no possible doubt that the independent counsel's functions fit this description. She is vested with the "full power and independent authority to exercise all *investigative and prosecutorial* functions and powers of the Department of Justice [and] the Attorney General." 28 U.S.C. § 594(a). Governmental investigation and prosecution of crimes is a quintessentially executive function.

As for the second question, whether the statute before us deprives the President of exclusive control over that quintessentially executive activity: The Court does not, and could not possibly, assert that it does not. That is indeed the whole object of the statute. Instead, the Court points out that the President, through his Attorney General, has at least *some* control. That concession is alone enough to invalidate the statute, but I cannot refrain from pointing out that the Court greatly exaggerates the extent of that "some" Presidential control. "Most importan[t]" among these controls, the Court asserts, is the Attorney General's "power to remove the counsel for 'good cause.'" This is somewhat like referring to shackles as an effective means of locomotion. As we recognized in *Humphrey's Executor v. United States*, 295 U.S. 602 (1935)— indeed, what *Humphrey's Executor* was all about—limiting removal power to "good cause" is an impediment to, not an effective grant of, Presidential control. . . . What we in *Humphrey's Executor* found to be a means of eliminating Presidential control, the Court today considers the "most importan[t]" means of assuring Presidential control. . . .

Moving on to the presumably "less important" controls that the President retains, the Court notes that no independent counsel may be appointed without a specific request from the Attorney General. As I have discussed above, the condition that renders such a request mandatory (inability to find "no reasonable grounds to believe" that further investigation is warranted) is so insubstantial that the Attorney General's discretion is severely confined. And once the referral is made, it is for the Special Division to determine the scope and duration of the investigation. And in any event, the limited power over referral is irrelevant to the question whether, *once appointed,* the independent counsel exercises executive power free from the President's control. . . .

It effects a revolution in our constitutional jurisprudence for the Court, once it has determined that (1) purely executive functions are at issue here, and (2) those functions have been given to a person whose actions are not fully within the supervision and control of the President, nonetheless to proceed further to sit in judgment of whether "the President's need to control the exercise of [the independent counsel's] discretion is *so central* to the functioning of the Executive

Branch" as to require complete control, whether the conferral of his powers upon someone else "*sufficiently* deprives the President of control over the independent counsel to interfere impermissibly with [his] constitutional obligation to ensure the faithful execution of the laws," and whether "the Act give[s] the Executive Branch *sufficient* control over the independent counsel to ensure that the President is able to perform his constitutionally assigned duties." It is not for us to determine, and we have never presumed to determine, how much of the purely executive powers of government must be within the full control of the President. The Constitution prescribes that they *all* are. . . .

Is it conceivable that if Congress passed a statute depriving itself of less than full and entire control over some insignificant area of legislation, we would inquire whether the matter was "*so central* to the functioning of the Legislative Branch" as really to require complete control, or whether the statute gives Congress "*sufficient* control over the surrogate legislator to ensure that Congress is able to perform its constitutionally assigned duties"? Of course we would have none of that. . . . Or to bring the point closer to home, consider a statute giving to non-Article III judges just a tiny bit of purely judicial power in a relatively insignificant field, with substantial control, though not total control, in the courts—perhaps "clear error" review, which would be a fair judicial equivalent of the Attorney General's "for cause" removal power here. Is there any doubt that we would not pause to inquire whether the matter was "*so central* to the functioning of the Judicial Branch" as really to require complete control, or whether we retained "*sufficient* control over the matters to be decided that we are able to perform our constitutionally assigned duties"? We would say that our "constitutionally assigned duties" include *complete* control over all exercises of the judicial power—or, as the plurality opinion said in *Northern Pipeline Construction Co. v. Marathon Pipe Line Co.*, 458 U.S. 50, 58–59 (1982): "The inexorable command of [Article III] is clear and definite: The judicial power of the United States must be exercised by courts having the attributes prescribed in Art. III." We should say here that the President's constitutionally assigned duties include *complete* control over investigation and prosecution of violations of the law, and that the inexorable command of Article II is clear and definite: the executive power must be vested in the President of the United States.

Is it unthinkable that the President should have such exclusive power, even when alleged crimes by him or his close associates are at issue? No more so than that Congress should have the exclusive power of legislation, even when what is at issue is its own exemption from the burdens of certain laws. See Civil Rights Act of 1964, Title VII, 42 U.S.C. § 2000e *et seq.* (prohibiting "employers," not defined to include the United States, from discriminating on the basis of race, color, religion, sex, or national origin). No more so than that this Court should have the exclusive power to pronounce the final decision on justiciable cases and controversies, even those pertaining to the constitutionality of a statute reducing the salaries of the Justices. See *United States v. Will,* 449 U.S. 200, 211–217 (1980). A system of separate and coordinate powers necessarily involves an acceptance of exclusive power that can theoretically be abused. . . . The checks against any branch's abuse of its exclusive powers are twofold: First, retaliation by one of the other branch's use of *its* exclusive powers: Congress, for example, can impeach the executive who willfully fails to enforce the laws; the executive can decline to prosecute under unconstitutional statutes; and the courts can dismiss malicious prosecutions. Second, and ultimately, there is the political check that the people will replace those in the political branches . . . who are guilty of abuse. Political pressures produced special prosecutors—for Teapot Dome and for Watergate, for example—long before this statute created the independent counsel.

The Court has, nonetheless, replaced the clear constitutional prescription that the executive power belongs to the President with a "balancing test." What are the standards to determine how the balance is to be struck, that is, how much removal of Presidential power is too much? Many countries of the world get along with an executive that is much weaker than ours—in fact, entirely dependent upon the continued support of the legislature. Once we depart from the text of the Constitution, just where short of that do we stop? The most amazing feature of the Court's opinion is that it does not even purport to give an answer. It simply *announces,* with no analysis, that the ability to control the decision whether to investigate and prosecute the President's closest advisers, and indeed the President himself, is not "so central to the functioning of the Executive Branch" as to be constitutionally required to be within the President's control. Apparently that is so because we say it is so. Having abandoned as the basis for our decision-making the text of Article II that "the executive Power" must be vested in the President, the Court does not even attempt to craft a *substitute* criterion . . . . Evidently, the governing standard is to be what might be called the unfettered wisdom of a majority of this Court, revealed to an obedient people on a case-by-case basis. This is not only not the government of laws that the Constitution established; it is not a government of laws at all. . . .

Besides weakening the Presidency by reducing the zeal of his staff, it must also be obvious that the institution of the independent counsel enfeebles him more directly in his constant confrontations with Congress, by eroding his public support. Nothing is so politically effective as the ability to charge that one's opponent and his associates are not merely wrongheaded, naive, ineffective, but, in all probability, "crooks." And nothing so effectively gives an appearance of validity to such charges as a Justice Department investigation and, even better, prosecution. The present statute provides ample means for that sort of attack, assuring that massive and lengthy investigations will occur, not merely when the Justice Department in the application of its usual standards believes they are called for, but whenever it cannot be said that there are "no reasonable grounds to believe" they are called for. The statute's highly visible procedures assure, moreover, that unlike most investigations these will be widely known and prominently displayed. Thus, in the 10 years since the institution of the independent counsel was established by law, there have been nine highly publicized investigations, a source of constant political damage to two administrations. . . .

In sum, this statute does deprive the President of substantial control over the prosecutory functions performed by the independent counsel, and it does substantially affect the balance of powers. That the Court could possibly conclude otherwise demonstrates both the wisdom of our former constitutional system, in which the degree of reduced control and political impairment were irrelevant, since *all* purely executive power had to be in the President; and the folly of the new system of standardless judicial allocation of powers we adopt today.

   * * *

IV

I will not discuss at any length why the restrictions upon the removal of the independent counsel also violate our established precedent dealing with that specific subject. . . . I cannot avoid commenting, however, about the essence of what the Court has done to our removal jurisprudence today.

There is, of course, no provision in the Constitution stating who may remove executive officers, except the provisions for removal by impeachment. Before the present decision it was established, however, (1) that the President's power to remove principal officers who exercise purely executive powers could not be restricted, see *Myers v. United States*, 272 U.S. 52, 127 (1926), and (2) that his power to remove inferior officers who exercise purely executive powers, and whose appointment Congress had removed from the usual procedure of Presidential appointment with Senate consent, could be restricted, at least where the appointment had been made by an officer of the Executive Branch, see *ibid.*; *United States v. Perkins*, 116 U.S. 483, 485 (1886).

The Court could have resolved the removal power issue in this case by simply relying upon its erroneous conclusion that the independent counsel was an inferior officer, and then extending our holding that the removal of inferior officers appointed by the Executive can be restricted, to a new holding that even the removal of inferior officers appointed by the courts can be restricted. That would in my view be a considerable and unjustified extension, giving the Executive full discretion in *neither* the selection *nor* the removal of a purely executive officer. The course the Court has chosen, however, is even worse.

Since our 1935 decision in *Humphrey's Executor v. United States*, 295 U.S. 602—which was considered by many at the time the product of an activist, anti-New Deal Court bent on reducing the power of President Franklin Roosevelt—it has been established that the line of permissible restriction upon removal of principal officers lies at the point at which the powers exercised by those officers are no longer purely executive. Thus, removal restrictions have been generally regarded as lawful for so-called "independent regulatory agencies," . . . which engage substantially in what has been called the "quasi-legislative activity" of rulemaking, and for members of Article I courts, such as the Court of Military Appeals, who engage in the "quasi-judicial" function of adjudication. It has often been observed, correctly in my view, that the line between "purely executive" functions and "quasi-legislative" or "quasi-judicial" functions is not a clear one or even a rational one. But at least it permitted the identification of certain officers, and certain agencies, whose functions were entirely within the control of the President. Congress had to be aware of that restriction in its legislation.

Today, however, *Humphrey's Executor* is swept into the dustbin of repudiated constitutional principles. "[O]ur present considered view," the Court says, "is that the determination of whether the Constitution allows Congress to impose a 'good cause'-type restriction on the President's power to remove an official cannot be made to turn on whether or not that official is classified as 'purely executive.'" What *Humphrey's Executor* (and presumably *Myers*) really means, we are now told, is not that there are any "rigid categories of those officials who may or may not be removed at will by the President," but simply that Congress cannot "interfere with the President's exercise of the 'executive power' and his constitutionally appointed duty to 'take care that the laws be faithfully executed.'"

One can hardly grieve for the shoddy treatment given today to *Humphrey's Executor*, which, after all, accorded the same indignity (with much less justification) to Chief Justice Taft's opinion 10 years earlier in *Myers v. United States*, 272 U.S. 52 (1926)—gutting, in six quick pages devoid of textual or historical precedent for the novel principle it set forth, a carefully researched and reasoned 70-page opinion. It is in fact comforting to witness the reality that he who lives by the *ipse dixit* dies by the *ipse dixit*. But one must grieve for the Constitution. *Humphrey's Executor* at least had the decency formally to observe the constitutional principle that the President had to be the repository of *all* executive power, which, as *Myers* carefully explained, necessarily means that he must be able to discharge those who do not perform executive functions according to his liking. . . . By contrast, "our present considered view" is simply that *any* executive officer's removal can be restricted, so long as the President remains "able to accomplish his constitutional role." There are now no lines. If the removal of a prosecutor, the virtual embodiment of the power to "take care that the laws be faithfully executed," can be restricted, what officer's removal cannot? This is an open invitation for Congress to experiment. What about a special Assistant Secretary of State, with responsibility for one very narrow area of foreign policy, who would not only have to be confirmed by the Senate but could also be removed only pursuant to certain carefully designed restrictions? . . . As far as I can discern from the Court's opinion, it is now open season upon the President's removal power for all executive officers, with not even the superficially principled restriction of *Humphrey's Executor* as cover. The Court essentially says to the President: "Trust us. We will make sure that you are able to accomplish your constitutional role." I think the Constitution gives the President—and the people—more protection than that.

* * *

By its shortsighted action today, I fear the Court has permanently encumbered the Republic with an institution that will do it great harm.

Worse than what it has done, however, is the manner in which it has done it. A government of laws means a government of rules. Today's decision on the basic issue of fragmentation of executive power is ungoverned by rule, and hence ungoverned by law. It extends into the very heart of our most significant constitutional function the "totality of the circumstances" mode of analysis that this Court has in recent years become fond of. Taking all things into account, we conclude that the power taken away from the President here is not really *too* much. The next time executive power is assigned to someone other than the President we may conclude, taking all things into account, that it *is* too much. That opinion, like this one, will not be confined by any rule. . . .

The ad hoc approach to constitutional adjudication has real attraction, even apart from its work-saving potential. It is guaranteed to produce a result, in every case, that will make a majority of the Court happy with the law. The law is, by definition, precisely what the majority thinks, taking all things into account, it *ought* to be. I prefer to rely upon the judgment of the wise men who constructed our system, and of the people who approved it, and of two centuries of history that have shown it to be sound. Like it or not, that judgment says, quite plainly, that "[t]he executive Power shall be vested in a President of the United States."

NOTES AND QUESTIONS

***1. Functionalism in* Morrison.** *Humphrey's Executor* supplied a kind of functionalist test: the Court purported functionally to distinguish between categories of "purely" executive power and power that is quasi-legislative or quasi-judicial in nature. In *Morrison v. Olson*, the Court seems to have taken the argument a step further: Congress can restrict the President's ability to control and remove even officers exercising purely executive functions, so long as those restrictions do not "impermissibly interfere"—that is, do not interfere too much—with the President's ability to exercise her constitutional functions. Is Justice Scalia right that there are now no lines? Or might this case be limited to the context of investigating wrongdoing at the highest levels of government? Isn't Congress concerned here with who will police the police, and who will prosecute the prosecutors? Without the ability to

FORMALISM VS. FUNCTIONALISM
Are there functionalist justifications for the decision in *Morrison*?

restrict the President's authority to direct and remove the independent counsel, would Congress's powers be too limited to ferret out and remedy high-level government misconduct?

2. *Is prosecution purely executive power?* It could be that *Morrison* is merely an application of *Humphrey's Executor*, at least if criminal prosecution were not historically considered a purely executive power. There have been numerous arguments along these lines in the scholarly literature, though your casebook author has found such arguments unpersuasive. For a sampling of the debate, compare Lawrence Lessig & Cass R. Sunstein, *The President and the Administration*, 94 Colum. L. Rev. 1, 7–9, 16–19, 22 (1994) (arguing that the President did not have directory authority over prosecutors); Harold J. Krent, *Executive Control over Criminal Law Enforcement: Some Lessons from History*, 38 Am. U. L. Rev. 275 (1989) (similar); and Peter M. Shane, *Prosecutors at the Periphery*, 94 Chi-Kent L. Rev. 241, 251–62 (2019) (arguing that prosecution was considered more of a judicial power); with Steven G. Calabresi & Saikrishna B. Prakash, *The President's Power to Execute the Laws*, 104 Yale L.J. 541, 659 (1994) (arguing that the President did have directory authority over prosecutors); Ilan Wurman, *In Search of Prerogative*, 70 Duke L.J. 93 (2020) (same).

3.　The Return of Formalism?

Humphrey's Executor and *Morrison v. Olson* took functionalist approaches to the removal power question. In the following two cases, the Supreme Court seems to have returned to a formalist mode of constitutional interpretation. How do the next two cases describe *Humphrey's Executor* and *Morrison v. Olson*? Are those cases still good law? Is the Court likely to limit them to their specific facts in future cases?

Free Enterprise Fund v. PCAOB

561 U.S. 477 (2010)

Chief Justice Roberts delivered the opinion of the Court.

Our Constitution divided the "powers of the new Federal Government into three defined categories, Legislative, Executive, and Judicial." *INS v. Chadha*, 462 U.S. 919, 951 (1983). Article II vests "[t]he executive Power . . . in a

President of the United States of America," who must "take Care that the Laws be faithfully executed." Art. II, § 1, cl. 1; *id.*, § 3. In light of "[t]he impossibility that one man should be able to perform all the great business of the State," the Constitution provides for executive officers to "assist the supreme Magistrate in discharging the duties of his trust." 30 Writings of George Washington 334 (J. Fitzpatrick ed.1939).

Since 1789, the Constitution has been understood to empower the President to keep these officers accountable—by removing them from office, if necessary. See generally *Myers v. United States*, 272 U.S. 52 (1926). This Court has determined, however, that this authority is not without limit. In *Humphrey's Executor v. United States*, 295 U.S. 602 (1935), we held that Congress can, under certain circumstances, create independent agencies run by principal officers appointed by the President, whom the President may not remove at will but only for good cause. Likewise, in *United States v. Perkins*, 116 U.S. 483 (1886), and *Morrison v. Olson*, 487 U.S. 654 (1988), the Court sustained similar restrictions on the power of principal executive officers—themselves responsible to the President—to remove their own inferiors. The parties do not ask us to reexamine any of these precedents, and we do not do so.

We are asked, however, to consider a new situation not yet encountered by the Court. The question is whether these separate layers of protection may be combined. May the President be restricted in his ability to remove a principal officer, who is in turn restricted in his ability to remove an inferior officer, even though that inferior officer determines the policy and enforces the laws of the United States?

We hold that such multilevel protection from removal is contrary to Article II's vesting of the executive power in the President. The President cannot "take Care that the Laws be faithfully executed" if he cannot oversee the faithfulness of the officers who execute them. Here the President cannot remove an officer who enjoys more than one level of good-cause protection, even if the President determines that the officer is neglecting his duties or discharging them improperly. That judgment is instead committed to another officer, who may or may not agree with the President's determination, and whom the President cannot remove simply because that officer disagrees with him. This contravenes the President's "constitutional obligation to ensure the faithful execution of the laws." *Id.* at 693.

I

A

After a series of celebrated accounting debacles, Congress enacted the Sarbanes-Oxley Act of 2002, 116 Stat. 745. Among other measures, the Act introduced tighter regulation of the accounting industry under a new Public Company Accounting Oversight Board. The Board is composed of five members, appointed to staggered 5-year terms by the Securities and Exchange Commission. It was modeled on private self-regulatory organizations in the securities industry—such as the New York Stock Exchange—that investigate and discipline their own members subject to Commission oversight. Congress created the Board as a private "nonprofit corporation," and Board members and employees are not considered Government "officer[s] or employee[s]" for statutory purposes. The Board can thus recruit its members and employees from the private sector by paying salaries far above the standard Government pay scale.

Unlike the self-regulatory organizations, however, the Board is a Government-created, Government-appointed entity, with expansive powers to govern an entire industry. Every accounting firm—both foreign and domestic—that participates in auditing public companies under the securities laws must register with the Board, pay it an annual fee, and comply with its rules and oversight. The Board is charged with enforcing the Sarbanes-Oxley Act, the securities laws, the Commission's rules, its own rules, and professional accounting standards. To this end, the Board may regulate every detail of an accounting firm's practice, including hiring and professional development, promotion, supervision of audit work, the acceptance of new business and the continuation of old, internal inspection procedures, professional ethics rules, and "such other requirements as the Board may prescribe." § 7213(a)(2)(B).

The Board promulgates auditing and ethics standards, performs routine inspections of all accounting firms, demands documents and testimony, and initiates formal investigations and disciplinary proceedings. The willful violation of any Board rule is treated as a willful violation of the Securities Exchange Act of 1934—a federal crime punishable by up to 20 years' imprisonment or $25 million in fines ($5 million for a natural person). And the Board itself can issue severe sanctions in its disciplinary proceedings, up to and including the permanent revocation of a firm's registration, a permanent ban on a person's associating with any registered firm, and money penalties of $15 million

($750,000 for a natural person). Despite the provisions specifying that Board members are not Government officials for statutory purposes, the parties agree that the Board is "part of the Government" for constitutional purposes, and that its members are " 'Officers of the United States' " who "exercis[e] significant authority pursuant to the laws of the United States."

The Act places the Board under the SEC's oversight, particularly with respect to the issuance of rules or the imposition of sanctions (both of which are subject to Commission approval and alteration). But the individual members of the Board—like the officers and directors of the self-regulatory organizations—are substantially insulated from the Commission's control. The Commission cannot remove Board members at will, but only "for good cause shown," "in accordance with" certain procedures. § 7211(e)(6).

Those procedures require a Commission finding, "on the record" and "after notice and opportunity for a hearing," that the Board member

¶ "(A) has willfully violated any provision of th[e] Act, the rules of the Board, or the securities laws;

¶ "(B) has willfully abused the authority of that member; or

¶ "(C) without reasonable justification or excuse, has failed to enforce compliance with any such provision or rule, or any professional standard by any registered public accounting firm or any associated person thereof." § 7217(d)(3).

Removal of a Board member requires a formal Commission order and is subject to judicial review. Similar procedures govern the Commission's removal of officers and directors of the private self-regulatory organizations. The parties agree that the Commissioners cannot themselves be removed by the President except under the *Humphrey's Executor* standard of "inefficiency, neglect of duty, or malfeasance in office," and we decide the case with that understanding.

* * *

III

We hold that the dual for-cause limitations on the removal of Board members contravene the Constitution's separation of powers.

A

The Constitution provides that "[t]he executive Power shall be vested in a President of the United States of America." Art. II, § 1, cl. 1. As Madison stated on the floor of the First Congress, "if any power whatsoever is in its nature Executive, it is the power of appointing, overseeing, and controlling those who execute the laws." 1 Annals of Cong. 463 (1789).

The removal of executive officers was discussed extensively in Congress when the first executive departments were created. The view that "prevailed, as most consonant to the text of the Constitution" and "to the requisite responsibility and harmony in the Executive Department," was that the executive power included a power to oversee executive officers through removal; because that traditional executive power was not "expressly taken away, it remained with the President." Letter from James Madison to Thomas Jefferson (June 30, 1789), 16 Documentary History of the First Federal Congress 893 (2004). "This Decision of 1789 provides contemporaneous and weighty evidence of the Constitution's meaning since many of the Members of the First Congress had taken part in framing that instrument." *Bowsher v. Synar,* 478 U.S. 714, 723–724 (1986). . . .

The landmark case of *Myers v. United States* reaffirmed the principle that Article II confers on the President "the general administrative control of those executing the laws." 272 U.S. at 164. It is *his* responsibility to take care that the laws be faithfully executed. The buck stops with the President, in Harry Truman's famous phrase. As we explained in *Myers,* the President therefore must have some "power of removing those for whom he can not continue to be responsible." *Id.* at 117.

Nearly a decade later in *Humphrey's Executor,* this Court held that *Myers* did not prevent Congress from conferring good-cause tenure on the principal officers of certain independent agencies. That case concerned the members of the Federal Trade Commission, who held 7-year terms and could not be removed by the President except for "inefficiency, neglect of duty, or malfeasance in office." The Court distinguished *Myers* on the ground that *Myers* concerned "an officer [who] is merely one of the units in the executive department and, hence, inherently subject to the exclusive and illimitable power of removal by the Chief Executive, whose subordinate and aid he is." 295 U.S. at 627. By contrast, the Court characterized the FTC as "quasi-legislative and quasi-judicial" rather than "purely executive," and held that Congress could require it "to act . . . independently of executive control." *Id.* at 627–629. Because "one who holds his office only during the pleasure of another, cannot be depended upon to maintain an attitude of independence against the latter's will," the Court held that Congress had power to "fix the period during which [the Commissioners] shall continue in office, and to forbid their removal except for cause in the meantime." *Id.* at 629.

Humphrey's Executor did not address the removal of inferior officers, whose appointment Congress may vest in heads of departments. If Congress does so, it is ordinarily the department head, rather than the President, who enjoys the power of removal. This Court has upheld for-cause limitations on that power as well.

In *Perkins*, a naval cadet-engineer was honorably discharged from the Navy because his services were no longer required. He brought a claim for his salary under statutes barring his peacetime discharge except by a court-martial or by the Secretary of the Navy "for misconduct." This Court adopted verbatim the reasoning of the Court of Claims, which had held that when Congress "vests the appointment of inferior officers in the heads of Departments[,] it may limit and restrict the power of removal as it deems best for the public interest." . . .

We again considered the status of inferior officers in *Morrison*. That case concerned the Ethics in Government Act, which provided for an independent counsel to investigate allegations of crime by high executive officers. The counsel was appointed by a special court, wielded the full powers of a prosecutor, and was removable by the Attorney General only "for good cause." We recognized that the independent counsel was undoubtedly an executive officer, rather than "quasi-legislative" or "quasi-judicial," but we stated as "our present considered view" that Congress had power to impose good-cause restrictions on her removal. 487 U.S. at 689–691. The Court noted that the statute "g[a]ve the Attorney General," an officer directly responsible to the President and "through [whom]" the President could act, "several means of supervising or controlling" the independent counsel—"[m]ost importantly . . . the power to remove the counsel for good cause." *Id.* at 695–696. Under those circumstances, the Court sustained the statute. *Morrison* did not, however, address the consequences of more than one level of good-cause tenure . . . .

B

As explained, we have previously upheld limited restrictions on the President's removal power. In those cases, however, only one level of protected tenure separated the President from an officer exercising executive power. It was the President—or a subordinate he could remove at will—who decided whether the officer's conduct merited removal under the good-cause standard.

The Act before us does something quite different. It not only protects Board members from removal except for good cause, but withdraws from the President any decision on whether that good cause exists. That decision is vested instead in other tenured officers—the Commissioners—none of whom is subject to the President's direct control. The result is a Board that is not accountable to the President, and a President who is not responsible for the Board.

The added layer of tenure protection makes a difference. Without a layer of insulation between the Commission and the Board, the Commission could remove a Board member at any time, and therefore would be fully responsible for what the Board does. The President could then hold the Commission to account for its supervision of the Board, to the same extent that he may hold the Commission to account for everything else it does.

A second level of tenure protection changes the nature of the President's review. Now the Commission cannot remove a Board member at will. The President therefore cannot hold the Commission fully accountable for the Board's conduct, to the same extent that he may hold the Commission accountable for everything else that it does. The Commissioners are not responsible for the Board's actions. They are only responsible for their own determination of whether the Act's rigorous good-cause standard is met. And even if the President disagrees with their determination, he is powerless to intervene—unless that determination is so unreasonable as to constitute "inefficiency, neglect of duty, or malfeasance in office." *Humphrey's Executor*, 295 U.S. at 620.

This novel structure does not merely add to the Board's independence, but transforms it. Neither the President, nor anyone directly responsible to him, nor even an officer whose conduct he may review only for good cause, has full control over the Board. The President is stripped of the power our precedents have preserved, and his ability to execute the laws—by holding his subordinates accountable for their conduct—is impaired. . . .

Indeed, if allowed to stand, this dispersion of responsibility could be multiplied. If Congress can shelter the bureaucracy behind two layers of good-cause tenure, why not a third? At oral argument, the Government was unwilling to concede that even *five* layers between the President and the Board would be too many. The officers of such an agency—safely encased within a Matryoshka doll of tenure protections—would be immune from Presidential oversight, even as they exercised power in the people's name. . . .

The diffusion of power carries with it a diffusion of accountability. The people do not vote for the "Officers of the United States." Art. II, § 2, cl. 2. They instead look to the President to guide the "assistants or deputies . . . subject to his superintendence." The Federalist No. 72. Without a clear and effective chain of command, the public cannot "determine on whom the blame or the punishment of a pernicious measure, or series of pernicious measures ought really to fall." *Id.* That is why the Framers sought to ensure that "those who are employed in the execution of the law will be in their proper situation, and the chain of dependence be preserved; the lowest officers, the middle grade, and the highest, will depend, as they ought, on the President, and the President on the community." 1 Annals of Cong. at 499 (J. Madison).

By granting the Board executive power without the Executive's oversight, this Act subverts the President's ability to ensure that the laws are faithfully executed—as well as the public's ability to pass judgment on his efforts. The Act's restrictions are incompatible with the Constitution's separation of powers.

C

Respondents and the dissent resist this conclusion, portraying the Board as "the kind of practical accommodation between the Legislature and the Executive that should be permitted in a 'workable government.'" According to the dissent, Congress may impose multiple levels of for-cause tenure between the President and his subordinates when it "rests agency independence upon the need for technical expertise." The Board's mission is said to demand both "technical competence" and "apolitical expertise," and its powers may only be exercised by "technical experts." In this respect the statute creating the Board is, we are told, simply one example of the "vast numbers of statutes governing vast numbers of subjects, concerned with vast numbers of different problems, [that] provide for, or foresee, their execution or administration through the work of administrators organized within many different kinds of administrative structures, exercising different kinds of administrative authority, to achieve their legislatively mandated objectives."

No one doubts Congress's power to create a vast and varied federal bureaucracy. But where, in all this, is the role for oversight by an elected President? The Constitution requires that a President chosen by the entire Nation oversee the execution of the laws. And the "fact that a given law or procedure is efficient, convenient, and useful in facilitating functions of government, standing alone, will not save it if it is contrary to the Constitution," for "[c]onvenience and efficiency are not the primary objectives—or the hallmarks—of democratic government." *Bowsher*, 478 U.S. at 736 (quoting *Chadha*, 462 U.S. at 944).

One can have a government that functions without being ruled by functionaries, and a government that benefits from expertise without being ruled by experts. Our Constitution was adopted to enable the people to govern themselves, through their elected leaders. The growth of the Executive Branch, which now wields vast power and touches almost every aspect of daily life, heightens the concern that it may slip from the Executive's control, and thus from that of the people. This concern is largely absent from the dissent's paean to the administrative state. . . .

* * *

[M]any civil servants within independent agencies would not qualify as "Officers of the United States," . . . We do not decide the status of other Government employees, nor do we decide whether "lesser functionaries subordinate to officers of the United States" must be subject to the same sort of control as those who exercise "significant authority pursuant to the laws."

Nor do the employees referenced by the dissent enjoy the same significant and unusual protections from Presidential oversight as members of the Board. Senior or policymaking positions in government may be excepted from the competitive service to ensure Presidential control, and members of the Senior Executive Service may be reassigned or reviewed by agency heads (and entire agencies may be excluded from that Service by the President). While the full extent of that authority is not before us, any such authority is of course wholly absent with respect to the Board. Nothing in our opinion, therefore, should be read to cast doubt on the use of what is colloquially known as the civil service system within independent agencies. . . .

* * *

The Constitution that makes the President accountable to the people for executing the laws also gives him the power to do so. That power includes, as a general matter, the authority to remove those who assist him in carrying out his duties. . . .

While we have sustained in certain cases limits on the President's removal power, the Act before us imposes a new type of restriction—two levels of protection from removal for those who nonetheless exercise significant executive power. Congress cannot limit the President's authority in this way. . . .

JUSTICE BREYER, with whom JUSTICE STEVENS, JUSTICE GINSBURG, and JUSTICE SOTOMAYOR, join, dissenting.

The Court holds unconstitutional a statute providing that the Securities and Exchange Commission (SEC or Commission) can remove members of the Public Company Accounting Oversight Board from office only for cause. . . . But in my view the statute does not significantly interfere with the President's "executive Power." Art. II, § 1. It violates no separation-of-powers principle. And the Court's contrary holding threatens to disrupt severely the fair and efficient administration of the laws. I consequently dissent.

I

A

The legal question before us arises at the intersection of two general constitutional principles. On the one hand, Congress has broad power to enact statutes "necessary and proper" to the exercise of its specifically enumerated constitutional authority. Art. I, § 8, cl. 18. As Chief Justice Marshall wrote for the Court nearly 200 years ago, the Necessary and Proper Clause reflects the Framers' efforts to create a Constitution that would "endure for ages to come." *McCulloch v. Maryland*, 17 U.S. 316, 4 Wheat. 316, 415 (1819). It embodies their recognition that it would be "unwise" to prescribe "the means by which government should, in all future time, execute its powers." Such "immutable rules" would deprive the Government of the needed flexibility to respond to future "exigencies which, if foreseen at all, must have been seen dimly." Thus the Necessary and Proper Clause affords Congress broad authority to "create" governmental "offices" and to structure those offices "as it chooses." *Buckley v. Valeo*, 424 U.S. 1, 138 (1976). . . .

On the other hand, the opening sections of Articles I, II, and III of the Constitution separately and respectively vest "[a]ll legislative Powers" in Congress, the "executive Power" in the President, and the "judicial Power" in the Supreme Court (and such "inferior Courts as Congress may from time to time ordain and establish"). In doing so, these provisions imply a structural separation-of-powers principle. And that principle, along with the instruction in Article II, § 3, that the President "shall take Care that the Laws be faithfully executed," limits Congress' power to structure the Federal Government. Indeed, this Court has held that the separation-of-powers principle guarantees the President the authority to dismiss certain Executive Branch officials at will. *Myers v. United States*, 272 U.S. 52 (1926).

But neither of these two principles is absolute in its application to removal cases. The Necessary and Proper Clause does not grant Congress power to free all Executive Branch officials from dismissal at the will of the President. Nor does the separation-of-powers principle grant the President an absolute authority to remove *any and all* Executive Branch officials at will. Rather, depending on, say, the nature of the office, its function, or its subject matter, Congress sometimes may, consistent with the Constitution, limit the President's authority to remove an officer from his post. See *Humphrey's Executor v. United States*, 295 U.S. 602 (1935); *Morrison v. Olson*, 487 U.S. 654 (1988). And we must here decide whether the circumstances surrounding the statute at issue justify such a limitation. . . .

In short, the question presented lies at the intersection of two sets of conflicting, broadly framed constitutional principles. And no text, no history, perhaps no precedent provides any clear answer.

B

When previously deciding this kind of nontextual question, the Court has emphasized the importance of examining how a particular provision, taken in context, is likely to function. . . . The Court has thereby written into law Justice Jackson's wise perception that "the Constitution . . . contemplates that practice will integrate the dispersed powers into *a workable government*." *Youngstown Sheet & Tube Co. v. Sawyer*, 343 U.S. 579, 635 (1952) (opinion concurring in judgment) (emphasis added).

It is not surprising that the Court in these circumstances has looked to function and context, and not to bright-line rules. . . .

[A] functional approach permits Congress and the President the flexibility needed to adapt statutory law to changing circumstances. . . . Indeed, the Federal Government at the time of the founding consisted of about 2,000 employees and served a population of about 4 million. Today, however, the Federal Government employs about *4.4 million workers* who serve a Nation of more than 310 million people living in a society characterized by rapid technological, economic, and social change.

Federal statutes now require or permit Government officials to provide, regulate, or otherwise administer, not only foreign affairs and defense, but also a wide variety of such subjects as taxes, welfare, social security, medicine, pharmaceutical drugs, education, highways, railroads, electricity, natural gas, nuclear power, financial instruments, banking, medical care, public health and safety, the environment, fair employment practices, consumer protection, and much else besides. Those statutes create a host of different organizational structures. Sometimes they delegate administrative authority to the President directly; sometimes they place authority in a long-established Cabinet department; sometimes they delegate authority to an independent commission or board; sometimes they place authority directly in the hands of a single senior administrator; sometimes they place it in a subcabinet bureau, office, division, or other agency; sometimes they vest it in multimember or multiagency task groups; sometimes they vest it in commissions or advisory committees made up of members of more than one branch; sometimes they divide it among groups of departments, commissions, bureaus, divisions, and administrators; and sometimes they permit state or local governments to participate as well. Statutes similarly grant administrators a wide variety of powers—for example, the power to make rules, develop informal practices, investigate, adjudicate, impose sanctions, grant licenses, and provide goods, services, advice, and so forth.

The upshot is that today vast numbers of statutes governing vast numbers of subjects, concerned with vast numbers of different problems, provide for, or foresee, their execution or administration through the work of administrators organized within many different kinds of administrative structures, exercising different kinds of administrative authority, to achieve their legislatively mandated objectives. And, given the nature of the Government's work, it is not surprising that administrative units come in many different shapes and sizes.

The functional approach required by our precedents recognizes this administrative complexity and, more importantly, recognizes the various ways

Presidential power operates within this context—and the various ways in which a removal provision might affect that power. . . .

These practical reasons not only support our precedents' determination that cases such as this should examine the specific functions and context at issue; they also indicate that judges should hesitate before second-guessing a "for cause" decision made by the other branches. Compared to Congress and the President, the Judiciary possesses an inferior understanding of the realities of administration, and the manner in which power, including and most especially political power, operates in context. . . .

II

A

To what extent then is the Act's "for cause" provision likely, as a practical matter, to limit the President's exercise of executive authority? . . .

[W]e should . . . conclude that the "for cause" restriction before us will not restrict Presidential power significantly. . . .

[T]he Court fails to show why *two* layers of "for cause" protection—layer 1 insulating the Commissioners from the President, and layer 2 insulating the Board from the Commissioners—impose any more serious limitation upon the *President's* powers than *one* layer. Consider the four scenarios that might arise:

1.   The President and the Commission both want to keep a Board member in office. Neither layer is relevant.

2.   The President and the Commission both want to dismiss a Board member. Layer 2 stops them both from doing so without cause. The President's ability to remove the Commission (layer 1) is irrelevant, for he and the Commission are in agreement.

3.   The President wants to dismiss a Board member, but the Commission wants to keep the member. Layer 1 allows the Commission to make that determination notwithstanding the President's contrary view. Layer 2 is irrelevant because the Commission does not seek to remove the Board member.

4.   The President wants to keep a Board member, but the Commission wants to dismiss the Board member. Here, layer 2 *helps the President*, for it

hinders the Commission's ability to dismiss a Board member whom the President wants to keep in place.

Thus, the majority's decision to eliminate only *layer 2* accomplishes virtually nothing. . . .

In order to avoid this elementary logic, the Court creates two alternative scenarios. In the first, the Commission and the President *both* want to remove a Board member, but have varying judgments as to whether they have good "cause" to do so—*i.e.*, the President and the Commission both conclude that a Board member should be removed, but disagree as to whether that conclusion (which they have both reached) is *reasonable*. In the second, the President wants to remove a Board member and the Commission disagrees; but, notwithstanding its freedom to make reasonable decisions independent of the President (afforded by layer 1), the Commission (while apparently telling the President that it agrees with him and would like to remove the Board member) uses layer 2 as an "excuse" to pursue its actual aims—an excuse which, given layer 1, it does not need.

Both of these circumstances seem unusual. I do not know if they have ever occurred. But I do not deny their logical possibility. I simply doubt their importance. And the fact that, with respect to the President's power, the double layer of for-cause removal sometimes might help, sometimes might hurt, leads me to conclude that its overall effect is at most indeterminate. . . .

* * *

B

At the same time, Congress and the President had good reason for enacting the challenged "for cause" provision. First and foremost, the Board adjudicates cases. This Court has long recognized the appropriateness of using "for cause" provisions to protect the personal independence of those who even only sometimes engage in adjudicatory functions. . . .

Moreover, in addition to their adjudicative functions, the Accounting Board members supervise, and are themselves, technical professional experts. This Court has recognized that the "difficulties involved in the preparation of" sound auditing reports require the application of "scientific accounting principles." And this Court has recognized the constitutional legitimacy of a justification that rests agency independence upon the need for technical expertise. . . .

Here, the justification for insulating the "technical experts" on the Board from fear of losing their jobs due to political influence is particularly strong. Congress deliberately sought to provide that kind of protection. It did so for good reason. And historically, this regulatory subject matter—financial regulation—has been thought to exhibit a particular need for independence. . . .

[I]n a world in which we count on the Federal Government to regulate matters as complex as, say, nuclear-power production, the Court's assertion that we should simply learn to get by "without being" regulated "by experts" is, at best, unrealistic—at worst, dangerously so.

* * *

. . . I . . . see no way to avoid sweeping hundreds, perhaps thousands of high-level Government officials within the scope of the Court's holding, putting their job security and their administrative actions and decisions constitutionally at risk. To make even a conservative estimate, one would have to begin by listing federal departments, offices, bureaus, and other agencies whose heads are by statute removable only "for cause." I have found 48 such agencies . . . . Then it would be necessary to identify the senior officials in those agencies (just below the top) who themselves are removable only "for cause." I have identified 573 such high-ranking officials . . . .

My research reflects that the Federal Government relies on 1,584 ALJs to adjudicate administrative matters in over 25 agencies. These ALJs adjudicate Social Security benefits, employment disputes, and other matters highly important to individuals. Does every losing party before an ALJ now have grounds to appeal on the basis that the decision entered against him is unconstitutional?

And what about the military? Commissioned military officers "are 'inferior officers.'" There are over 210,000 active-duty commissioned officers currently serving in the Armed Forces. Numerous statutory provisions provide that such officers may not be removed from office except for cause (at least in peacetime). And such officers can generally be so removed only by *other* commissioned officers, who themselves enjoy the same career protections. . . .

Thus, notwithstanding the majority's assertions to the contrary, the potential consequences of today's holding are worrying. . . .

[In an omitted part of the opinion, the dissenters argue that the Court should have actually sought to determine whether the SEC commissioners are in fact removable only for-cause; everyone assumes they are, but the Securities and Exchange Act does not mention removal.—Ed.]

NOTES AND QUESTIONS

1. Dual for-cause removal and ALJs. Recall in *Lucia v. SEC*, the Supreme Court held that SEC ALJs are inferior officers. Those ALJs are protected by for-cause removal provisions; and the SEC commissioners, as we just saw, may also be protected by for-cause removal provisions. Is this removal framework for the ALJs unconstitutional? Should it make a difference that ALJs engage *only* in adjudicatory functions? Will the answer depend on whether the Supreme Court adopts a formalist or functionalist approach?

FOR DISCUSSION

Is the removal scheme for the SEC ALJs in *Lucia* unconstitutional under *Free Enterprise Fund*? Can you make an argument that adjudicative officers should be treated differently? Would that be a functionalist argument, or a formalist one?

Seila Law v. Consumer Financial Protection Bureau

140 S. Ct. 2183 (2020)

CHIEF JUSTICE ROBERTS delivered the opinion of the Court with respect to [the relevant parts of the opinion].

In the wake of the 2008 financial crisis, Congress established the Consumer Financial Protection Bureau (CFPB), an independent regulatory agency tasked with ensuring that consumer debt products are safe and transparent. In organizing the CFPB, Congress deviated from the structure of nearly every other independent administrative agency in our history. Instead of placing the agency under the leadership of a board with multiple members, Congress provided that the CFPB would be led by a single Director, who serves for a longer term than the President and cannot be removed by the President except for inefficiency, neglect, or malfeasance. The CFPB Director has no boss, peers, or voters to report to. Yet the Director wields vast rulemaking, enforcement, and adjudicatory authority over a significant portion of the U.S. economy. The question before us is whether this arrangement violates the Constitution's separation of powers.

Under our Constitution, the "executive Power"—all of it—is "vested in a President," who must "take Care that the Laws be faithfully executed." Art. II, § 1, cl. 1; *id.* § 3. Because no single person could fulfill that responsibility alone, the Framers expected that the President would rely on subordinate officers for assistance. Ten years ago, in *Free Enterprise Fund* v. *Public Company Accounting Oversight Bd.*, 561 U.S. 477 (2010), we reiterated that, "as a general matter," the Constitution gives the President "the authority to remove those who assist him in carrying out his duties," *id.* at 513–514. "Without such power, the President could not be held fully accountable for discharging his own responsibilities; the buck would stop somewhere else." *Id.* at 514.

The President's power to remove—and thus supervise—those who wield executive power on his behalf follows from the text of Article II, was settled by the First Congress, and was confirmed in the landmark decision *Myers* v. *United States*, 272 U.S. 52 (1926). Our precedents have recognized only two exceptions to the President's unrestricted removal power. In *Humphrey's Executor v. United States*, 295 U.S. 602 (1935), we held that Congress could create expert agencies led by a *group* of principal officers removable by the President only for good cause. And in *United States* v. *Perkins*, 116 U.S. 483 (1886), and *Morrison* v. *Olson*, 487 U.S. 654 (1988), we held that Congress could provide tenure protections to certain *inferior* officers with narrowly defined duties.

We are now asked to extend these precedents to a new configuration: an independent agency that wields significant executive power and is run by a single individual who cannot be removed by the President unless certain statutory criteria are met. We decline to take that step. While we need not and do not revisit our prior decisions allowing certain limitations on the President's removal power, there are compelling reasons not to extend those precedents to the novel context of an independent agency led by a single Director. Such an agency lacks a foundation in historical practice and clashes with constitutional structure by concentrating power in a unilateral actor insulated from Presidential control.

We therefore hold that the structure of the CFPB violates the separation of powers. . . .

I

A

. . . . In 2010, Congress . . . created the Consumer Financial Protection Bureau (CFPB) as an independent financial regulator within the Federal Reserve System. . . . Congress transferred the administration of 18 existing federal statutes to the CFPB, including the Fair Credit Reporting Act, the Fair Debt Collection Practices Act, and the Truth in Lending Act. In addition, Congress enacted a new prohibition on "any unfair, deceptive, or abusive act or practice" by certain participants in the consumer-finance sector. Congress authorized the CFPB to implement that broad standard (and the 18 pre-existing statutes placed under the agency's purview) through binding regulations.

Congress also vested the CFPB with potent enforcement powers. The agency has the authority to conduct investigations, issue subpoenas and civil investigative demands, initiate administrative adjudications, and prosecute civil actions in federal court. To remedy violations of federal consumer financial law, the CFPB may seek restitution, disgorgement, and injunctive relief, as well as civil penalties of up to $1,000,000 (inflation adjusted) for each day that a violation occurs. . . .

The CFPB's rulemaking and enforcement powers are coupled with extensive adjudicatory authority. The agency may conduct administrative proceedings to "ensure or enforce compliance with" the statutes and regulations it administers. When the CFPB acts as an adjudicator, it has "jurisdiction to grant any appropriate legal or equitable relief." The "hearing officer" who presides over the proceedings may issue subpoenas, order depositions, and resolve any motions filed by the parties. At the close of the proceedings, the hearing officer issues a "recommended decision," and the CFPB Director considers that recommendation and "issue[s] a final decision and order." . . .

Rather than create a traditional independent agency headed by a multimember board or commission, Congress elected to place the CFPB under the leadership of a single Director. The CFPB Director is appointed by the President with the advice and consent of the Senate. The Director serves for a term of five years, during which the President may remove the Director from office only for "inefficiency, neglect of duty, or malfeasance in office."

Unlike most other agencies, the CFPB does not rely on the annual appropriations process for funding. Instead, the CFPB receives funding directly from the Federal Reserve, which is itself funded outside the appropriations process through bank assessments. . . .

III

We hold that the CFPB's leadership by a single individual removable only for inefficiency, neglect, or malfeasance violates the separation of powers.

A

Article II provides that "[t]he executive Power shall be vested in a President," who must "take Care that the Laws be faithfully executed." Art. II, § 1, cl. 1; *id.* § 3. The entire "executive Power" belongs to the President alone. But because it would be "impossib[le]" for "one man" to "perform all the great business of the State," the Constitution assumes that lesser executive officers will "assist the supreme Magistrate in discharging the duties of his trust." 30 Writings of George Washington 334 (J. Fitzpatrick ed. 1939).

These lesser officers must remain accountable to the President, whose authority they wield. As Madison explained, "[I]f any power whatsoever is in its nature Executive, it is the power of appointing, overseeing, and controlling those who execute the laws." 1 Annals of Cong. 463 (1789). That power, in turn, generally includes the ability to remove executive officials, for it is "only the authority that can remove" such officials that they "must fear and, in the performance of [their] functions, obey." *Bowsher,* 478 U.S. at 726.

The President's removal power has long been confirmed by history and precedent. It "was discussed extensively in Congress when the first executive departments were created" in 1789. *Free Enterprise Fund,* 561 U.S. at 492. "The view that 'prevailed, as most consonant to the text of the Constitution' and 'to the requisite responsibility and harmony in the Executive Department,' was that the executive power included a power to oversee executive officers through removal." *Ibid.* (quoting Letter from James Madison to Thomas Jefferson (June 30, 1789), 16 Documentary History of the First Federal Congress 893 (2004)). The First Congress's recognition of the President's removal power in 1789 "provides contemporaneous and weighty evidence of the Constitution's meaning," *Bowsher,* 478 U.S. at 723, and has long been the "settled and well understood construction of the Constitution," *Ex parte Hennen,* 13 Pet. 230, 259 (1839).

The Court recognized the President's prerogative to remove executive officials in *Myers* v. *United States*, 272 U.S. 52. Chief Justice Taft, writing for the Court, conducted an exhaustive examination of the First Congress's determination in 1789, the views of the Framers and their contemporaries, historical practice, and our precedents up until that point. He concluded that Article II "grants to the President" the "general administrative control of those executing the laws, including the power of appointment *and removal* of executive officers." *Id.* at 163–164 (emphasis added). Just as the President's "selection of administrative officers is essential to the execution of the laws by him, so must be his power of removing those for whom he cannot continue to be responsible." *Id.* at 117. "[T]o hold otherwise," the Court reasoned, "would make it impossible for the President . . . to take care that the laws be faithfully executed." *Id.* at 164.

We recently reiterated the President's general removal power in *Free Enterprise Fund*. "Since 1789," we recapped, "the Constitution has been understood to empower the President to keep these officers accountable—by removing them from office, if necessary." 561 U.S. at 483. Although we had previously sustained congressional limits on that power in certain circumstances, we declined to extend those limits to "a new situation not yet encountered by the Court"—an official insulated by *two* layers of for-cause removal protection. In the face of that novel impediment to the President's oversight of the Executive Branch, we adhered to the general rule that the President possesses "the authority to remove those who assist him in carrying out his duties."

Free Enterprise Fund left in place two exceptions to the President's unrestricted removal power. First, in *Humphrey's Executor*, decided less than a decade after *Myers*, the Court upheld a statute that protected the Commissioners of the FTC from removal except for "inefficiency, neglect of duty, or malfeasance in office." In reaching that conclusion, the Court stressed that Congress's ability to impose such removal restrictions "will depend upon the character of the office." 295 U.S. at 631.

Because the Court limited its holding "to officers of the kind here under consideration," the contours of the *Humphrey's Executor* exception depend upon the characteristics of the agency before the Court. Rightly or wrongly, the Court viewed the FTC (as it existed in 1935) as exercising "no part of the executive power." *Id.* at 628. Instead, it was "an administrative body" that performed "specified duties as a legislative or as a judicial aid." It acted "as a legislative agency" in "making investigations and reports" to Congress and "as an agency of the judiciary" in making recommendations to courts as a master in chancery. "To the extent that [the FTC] exercise[d] any executive *function*[,] as distinguished from executive *power* in the constitutional sense," it did so only in the discharge of its "quasi-legislative or quasi-judicial powers."

The Court identified several organizational features that helped explain its characterization of the FTC as non-executive. Composed of five members— no more than three from the same political party—the Board was designed to be "non-partisan" and to "act with entire impartiality." The FTC's duties were "neither political nor executive," but instead called for "the trained judgment of a body of experts" "informed by experience." And the Commissioners' staggered, seven-year terms enabled the agency to accumulate technical expertise and avoid a "complete change" in leadership "at any one time."

In short, *Humphrey's Executor* permitted Congress to give for-cause removal protections to a multimember body of experts, balanced along partisan lines, that performed legislative and judicial functions and was said not to exercise any executive power. Consistent with that understanding, the Court later applied "[t]he philosophy of *Humphrey's Executor*" to uphold for-cause removal protections for the members of the War Claims Commission—a three-member "adjudicatory body" tasked with resolving claims for compensation arising from World War II. *Wiener v. United States*, 357 U.S. 349, 356 (1958).

While recognizing an exception for multimember bodies with "quasi-judicial" or "quasi-legislative" functions, *Humphrey's Executor* reaffirmed the core holding of *Myers* that the President has "unrestrictable power . . . to remove purely executive officers." . . .

We have recognized a second exception for inferior officers in two cases, *United States* v. *Perkins* and *Morrison* v. *Olson*. In *Perkins*, we upheld tenure protections for a naval cadet-engineer. And, in *Morrison*, we upheld a provision granting good-cause tenure protection to an independent counsel appointed to investigate and prosecute particular alleged crimes by high-ranking Government officials. Backing away from the reliance in *Humphrey's Executor* on the concepts of "quasi-legislative" and "quasi-judicial" power, we viewed the ultimate question as whether a removal restriction is of "such a nature that [it] impede[s] the President's ability to perform his constitutional duty." 487 U.S. at 691. Although the independent counsel was a single person and performed "law enforcement functions that typically have been undertaken by officials within the Executive Branch," we concluded that the removal protections did not unduly interfere with the functioning of the Executive Branch because "the independent counsel [was] an inferior officer under the Appointments Clause, with limited jurisdiction and tenure and lacking policymaking or significant administrative authority."

These two exceptions—one for multimember expert agencies that do not wield substantial executive power, and one for inferior officers with limited duties and no policymaking or administrative authority—"represent what up to now have been the outermost constitutional limits of permissible congressional restrictions on the President's removal power."

B

Neither *Humphrey's Executor* nor *Morrison* resolves whether the CFPB Director's insulation from removal is constitutional. Start with *Humphrey's Executor*. Unlike the New Deal-era FTC upheld there, the CFPB is led by a single Director who cannot be described as a "body of experts" and cannot be considered "non-partisan" in the same sense as a group of officials drawn from both sides of the aisle. Moreover, while the staggered terms of the FTC Commissioners prevented complete turnovers in agency leadership and guaranteed that there would always be some Commissioners who had accrued significant expertise, the CFPB's single-Director structure and five-year term guarantee abrupt shifts in agency leadership and with it the loss of accumulated expertise.

In addition, the CFPB Director is hardly a mere legislative or judicial aid. Instead of making reports and recommendations to Congress, as the 1935 FTC did, the Director possesses the authority to promulgate binding rules fleshing out 19 federal statutes, including a broad prohibition on unfair and deceptive practices in a major segment of the U.S. economy. And instead of submitting recommended dispositions to an Article III court, the Director may unilaterally issue final decisions awarding legal and equitable relief in administrative adjudications. Finally, the Director's enforcement authority includes the power to seek daunting monetary penalties against private parties on behalf of the United States in federal court—a quintessentially executive power not considered in *Humphrey's Executor*.

The logic of *Morrison* also does not apply. Everyone agrees the CFPB Director is not an inferior officer, and her duties are far from limited. Unlike the independent counsel, who lacked policymaking or administrative authority, the

Director has the sole responsibility to administer 19 separate consumer-protection statutes that cover everything from credit cards and car payments to mortgages and student loans. It is true that the independent counsel in *Morrison* was empowered to initiate criminal investigations and prosecutions, and in that respect wielded core executive power. But that power, while significant, was trained inward to high-ranking Governmental actors identified by others, and was confined to a specified matter in which the Department of Justice had a potential conflict of interest. By contrast, the CFPB Director has the authority to bring the coercive power of the state to bear on millions of private citizens and businesses, imposing even billion-dollar penalties through administrative adjudications and civil actions.

In light of these differences, the constitutionality of the CFPB Director's insulation from removal cannot be settled by *Humphrey's Executor* or *Morrison* alone.

C

The question instead is whether to extend those precedents to the "new situation" before us, namely an independent agency led by a single Director and vested with significant executive power. We decline to do so. Such an agency has no basis in history and no place in our constitutional structure.

1

"Perhaps the most telling indication of [a] severe constitutional problem" with an executive entity "is [a] lack of historical precedent" to support it. An agency with a structure like that of the CFPB is almost wholly unprecedented. After years of litigating the agency's constitutionality, the Courts of Appeals, parties, and *amici* have identified "only a handful of isolated" incidents in which Congress has provided good-cause tenure to principal officers who wield power alone rather than as members of a board or commission. "[T]hese few scattered examples"—four to be exact—shed little light. *NLRB* v. *Noel Canning*, 573 U.S. 513, 538 (2014).

First, the CFPB's defenders point to the Comptroller of the Currency, who enjoyed removal protection for *one year* during the Civil War. That example has rightly been dismissed as an aberration. It was "adopted without discussion" during the heat of the Civil War and abandoned before it could be "tested by executive or judicial inquiry." *Myers*, 272 U.S. at 165. (At the time, the

Comptroller may also have been an inferior officer, given that he labored "under the general direction of the Secretary of the Treasury." Ch. 58, 12 Stat. 665.)

Second, the supporters of the CFPB point to the Office of the Special Counsel (OSC), which has been headed by a single officer since 1978. But this first enduring single-leader office, created nearly 200 years after the Constitution was ratified, drew a contemporaneous constitutional objection from the Office of Legal Counsel under President Carter and a subsequent veto on constitutional grounds by President Reagan. In any event, the OSC exercises only limited jurisdiction to enforce certain rules governing Federal Government employers and employees. It does not bind private parties at all or wield regulatory authority comparable to the CFPB.

Third, the CFPB's defenders note that the Social Security Administration (SSA) has been run by a single Administrator since 1994. That example, too, is comparatively recent and controversial. President Clinton questioned the constitutionality of the SSA's new single-Director structure upon signing it into law. In addition, unlike the CFPB, the SSA lacks the authority to bring enforcement actions against private parties. Its role is largely limited to adjudicating claims for Social Security benefits.

The only remaining example is the Federal Housing Finance Agency (FHFA), created in 2008 to assume responsibility for Fannie Mae and Freddie Mac. That agency is essentially a companion of the CFPB, established in response to the same financial crisis. It regulates primarily Government-sponsored enterprises, not purely private actors. And its single-Director structure is a source of ongoing controversy. Indeed, it was recently held unconstitutional by the Fifth Circuit, sitting en banc. See *Collins* v. *Mnuchin*, 938 F. 3d 553, 587–588 (2019).

With the exception of the one-year blip for the Comptroller of the Currency, these isolated examples are modern and contested. And they do not involve regulatory or enforcement authority remotely comparable to that exercised by the CFPB. The CFPB's single-Director structure is an innovation with no foothold in history or tradition.

2

In addition to being a historical anomaly, the CFPB's single-Director configuration is incompatible with our constitutional structure. Aside from the sole exception of the Presidency, that structure scrupulously avoids concentrating power in the hands of any single individual. "The Framers recognized that, in the long term, structural protections against abuse of power were critical to preserving liberty." *Bowsher,* 478 U.S. at 730. Their solution to governmental power and its perils was simple: divide it. To prevent the "gradual concentration" of power in the same hands, they enabled "[a]mbition . . . to counteract ambition" at every turn. The Federalist No. 51, p. 349 (J. Cooke ed. 1961) (J. Madison). At the highest level, they "split the atom of sovereignty" itself into one Federal Government and the States. They then divided the "powers of the new Federal Government into three defined categories, Legislative, Executive, and Judicial." *Chadha,* 462 U.S. at 951. They did not stop there. Most prominently, the Framers bifurcated the federal legislative power into two Chambers: the House of Representatives and the Senate, each composed of multiple Members and Senators. Art. I, §§ 2, 3. The Executive Branch is a stark departure from all this division. . . .

The Framers deemed an energetic executive essential to "the protection of the community against foreign attacks," "the steady administration of the laws," "the protection of property," and "the security of liberty." [The Federalist] No. 70, at 471. Accordingly, they chose not to bog the Executive down with the "habitual feebleness and dilatoriness" that comes with a "diversity of views and opinions." *Id.,* at 476. Instead, they gave the Executive the "[d]ecision, activity, secrecy, and dispatch" that "characterise the proceedings of one man." *Id.,* at 472.

To justify and check *that* authority—unique in our constitutional structure—the Framers made the President the most democratic and politically accountable official in Government. Only the President (along with the Vice President) is elected by the entire Nation. . . .

The resulting constitutional strategy is straightforward: divide power everywhere except for the Presidency, and render the President directly accountable to the people through regular elections. . . .

The CFPB's single-Director structure contravenes this carefully calibrated system by vesting significant governmental power in the hands of a single individual accountable to no one. The Director is neither elected by the people nor meaningfully controlled (through the threat of removal) by someone who is. The Director does not even depend on Congress for annual appropriations.

Yet the Director may *unilaterally*, without meaningful supervision, issue final regulations, oversee adjudications, set enforcement priorities, initiate prosecutions, and determine what penalties to impose on private parties. With no colleagues to persuade, and no boss or electorate looking over her shoulder, the Director may dictate and enforce policy for a vital segment of the economy affecting millions of Americans.

The CFPB Director's insulation from removal by an accountable President is enough to render the agency's structure unconstitutional. But several other features of the CFPB combine to make the Director's removal protection even more problematic. In addition to lacking the most direct method of presidential control—removal at will—the agency's unique structure also forecloses certain indirect methods of Presidential control.

Because the CFPB is headed by a single Director with a five-year term, some Presidents may not have any opportunity to shape its leadership and thereby influence its activities. A President elected in 2020 would likely not appoint a CFPB Director until 2023, and a President elected in 2028 may *never* appoint one. That means an unlucky President might get elected on a consumer-protection platform and enter office only to find herself saddled with a holdover Director from a competing political party who is dead set *against* that agenda. To make matters worse, the agency's single-Director structure means the President will not have the opportunity to appoint any other leaders—such as a chair or fellow members of a Commission or Board—who can serve as a check on the Director's authority and help bring the agency in line with the President's preferred policies.

The CFPB's receipt of funds outside the appropriations process further aggravates the agency's threat to Presidential control. The President normally has the opportunity to recommend or veto spending bills that affect the operation of administrative agencies. See Art. I, § 7, cl. 2; Art. II, § 3. And, for the past century, the President has annually submitted a proposed budget to Congress for approval. Presidents frequently use these budgetary tools "to influence the policies of independent agencies." But no similar opportunity exists for the President to influence the CFPB Director. Instead, the Director receives over $500 million per year to fund the agency's chosen priorities. And the Director receives that money from the Federal Reserve, which is itself funded outside of the annual appropriations process. This financial freedom makes it even more likely that the agency will "slip from the Executive's control, and thus from that of the people." *Free Enterprise Fund*, 561 U.S. at 499. . . .

The dissent, for its part, largely reprises points that the Court has already considered and rejected: It notes the lack of an express removal provision, invokes Congress's general power to create and define executive offices, highlights isolated statements from individual Framers, downplays the decision of 1789, minimizes *Myers*, brainstorms methods of Presidential control short of removal, touts the need for creative congressional responses to technological and economic change, and celebrates a pragmatic, flexible approach to American governance.

If these arguments sound familiar, it's because they are. They were raised by the dissent in *Free Enterprise Fund*. . . .

As we explained in *Free Enterprise Fund*, "One can have a government that functions without being ruled by functionaries, and a government that benefits from expertise without being ruled by experts." While "[n]o one doubts Congress's power to create a vast and varied federal bureaucracy," the expansion of that bureaucracy into new territories the Framers could scarcely have imagined only sharpens our duty to ensure that the Executive Branch is overseen by a President accountable to the people. . . .

Justice Thomas, with whom Justice Gorsuch joins, [concurring].

The decision in *Humphrey's Executor* poses a direct threat to our constitutional structure and, as a result, the liberty of the American people. The Court concludes that it is not strictly necessary for us to overrule that decision. But with today's decision, the Court has repudiated almost every aspect of *Humphrey's Executor*. In a future case, I would repudiate what is left of this erroneous precedent. . . .

Despite the defined structural limitations of the Constitution and the clear vesting of executive power in the President, Congress has increasingly shifted executive power to a *de facto* fourth branch of Government—independent agencies. These agencies wield considerable executive power without Presidential oversight. They are led by officers who are insulated from the President by removal restrictions, "reduc[ing] the Chief Magistrate to [the role of] cajoler-in-chief." . . .

Humphrey's Executor laid the foundation for a fundamental departure from our constitutional structure with nothing more than handwaving and obfuscating phrases such as "quasi-legislative" and "quasi-judicial." . . .

Humphrey's Executor relies on one key premise: the notion that there is a category of "quasi-legislative" and "quasi-judicial" power that is not exercised by Congress or the Judiciary, but that is also not part of "the executive power vested by the Constitution in the President." Working from that premise, the Court distinguished the "illimitable" power of removal recognized in *Myers*, and upheld the FTC Act's removal restriction, while simultaneously acknowledging that the Constitution vests the President with the entirety of the executive power.

The problem is that the Court's premise was entirely wrong. The Constitution does not permit the creation of officers exercising "quasi-legislative" and "quasi-judicial powers" in "quasi-legislative" and "quasi-judicial agencies." No such powers or agencies exist. Congress lacks the authority to delegate its legislative power, *Whitman* v. *American Trucking Assns., Inc.*, 531 U.S. 457, 472 (2001), and it cannot authorize the use of judicial power by officers acting outside of the bounds of Article III, *Stern* v. *Marshall*, 564 U.S. 462, 484 (2011). Nor can Congress create agencies that straddle multiple branches of Government. The Constitution sets out three branches of Government and provides each with a different form of power—legislative, executive, and judicial. . . . "[I]t is hard to dispute that the powers of the FTC at the time of *Humphrey's Executor* would at the present time be considered 'executive,' at least to some degree." *Morrison*, at 690, n. 28; [see also footnote seven of Justice Kagan's dissent, below.—Ed.].

[T]oday's decision builds upon *Morrison* and *Free Enterprise Fund*, further eroding the foundation of *Humphrey's Executor*. . . .

Justice Kagan, with whom Justice Ginsburg, Justice Breyer, and Justice Sotomayor join, [dissenting].

Throughout the Nation's history, this Court has left most decisions about how to structure the Executive Branch to Congress and the President, acting through legislation they both agree to. In particular, the Court has commonly allowed those two branches to create zones of administrative independence by limiting the President's power to remove agency heads. The Federal Reserve Board. The Federal Trade Commission (FTC). The National Labor Relations Board. Statute after statute establishing such entities instructs the President that he may not discharge their directors except for cause—most often phrased as inefficiency, neglect of duty, or malfeasance in office. Those statutes, whose language the Court has repeatedly approved, provide the model for the removal restriction before us today. If precedent were any guide, that provision would have survived its encounter with this Court—and so would the intended independence of the Consumer Financial Protection Bureau (CFPB).

Our Constitution and history demand that result. The text of the Constitution allows these common for-cause removal limits. Nothing in it speaks of removal. And it grants Congress authority to organize all the institutions of American governance, provided only that those arrangements allow the President to perform his own constitutionally assigned duties. Still more, the Framers' choice to give the political branches wide discretion over administrative offices has played out through American history in ways that have settled the constitutional meaning. From the first, Congress debated and enacted measures to create spheres of administration—especially of financial affairs—detached from direct presidential control. As the years passed, and governance became ever more complicated, Congress continued to adopt and adapt such measures— confident it had latitude to do so under a Constitution meant to "endure for ages to come." *McCulloch* v. *Maryland,* 4 Wheat. 316, 415 (1819) (approving the Second Bank of the United States). Not every innovation in governance— not every experiment in administrative independence—has proved successful. And debates about the prudence of limiting the President's control over regulatory agencies, including through his removal power, have never abated. But the Constitution—both as originally drafted and as practiced—mostly leaves disagreements about administrative structure to Congress and the President, who have the knowledge and experience needed to address them. Within broad bounds, it keeps the courts—who do not—out of the picture.

The Court today fails to respect its proper role. It recognizes that this Court has approved limits on the President's removal power over heads of agencies much like the CFPB. Agencies possessing similar powers, agencies charged with similar missions, agencies created for similar reasons. The majority's explanation is that the heads of those agencies fall within an "exception"—one for multimember bodies and another for inferior officers—to a "general rule" of unrestricted presidential removal power. And the majority says the CFPB Director does not. That account, though, is wrong in every respect. The majority's general rule does not exist. Its exceptions, likewise, are made up for the occasion—gerrymandered so the CFPB falls outside them. And the distinction doing most of the majority's work—between multimember bodies and single directors—does not respond to the constitutional values at stake. If a removal provision violates the separation of powers, it is because the measure so deprives the President of control over an official as to impede his own constitutional functions. But with or without a for-cause removal provision, the President has at least as much control over an individual as over a commission—and possibly more. That means the constitutional concern is, if anything, ameliorated when the agency has a single head. . . .

In second-guessing the political branches, the majority second-guesses as well the wisdom of the Framers and the judgment of history. It writes in rules to the Constitution that the drafters knew well enough not to put there. It repudiates the lessons of American experience, from the 18th century to the present day. And it commits the Nation to a static version of governance, incapable of responding to new conditions and challenges. Congress and the President established the CFPB to address financial practices that had brought on a devastating recession, and could do so again. Today's decision wipes out a feature of that agency its creators thought fundamental to its mission—a measure of independence from political pressure. I respectfully dissent.

I

The text of the Constitution, the history of the country, the precedents of this Court, and the need for sound and adaptable governance—all stand against the majority's opinion. They point not to the majority's "general rule" of "unrestricted removal power" with two grudgingly applied "exceptions." Rather, they bestow discretion on the legislature to structure administrative institutions as the times demand, so long as the President retains the ability to carry out his constitutional duties. And most relevant here, they give Congress wide leeway to limit the President's removal power in the interest of enhancing independence from politics in regulatory bodies like the CFPB.

A

What does the Constitution say about the separation of powers—and particularly about the President's removal authority? (Spoiler alert: about the latter, nothing at all.) The majority offers the civics class version of separation of powers—call it the Schoolhouse Rock definition of the phrase. The Constitution's first three articles, the majority recounts, "split the atom of sovereignty" among Congress, the President, and the courts. And by that mechanism, the Framers provided a "simple" fix "to governmental power and its perils." There is nothing wrong with that as a beginning (except the adjective "simple"). It is of course true that the Framers lodged three different kinds of power in three different entities. And that they did so for a crucial purpose—because, as James Madison wrote, "there can be no liberty where the legislative and executive powers are united in the same person[ ] or body" or where "the power of judging [is] not separated from the legislative and executive powers." The Federalist No. 47, p. 325 (J. Cooke ed. 1961) (quoting Baron de Montesquieu).

The problem lies in treating the beginning as an ending too—in failing to recognize that the separation of powers is, by design, neither rigid nor complete. Blackstone, whose work influenced the Framers on this subject as on others, observed that "every branch" of government "supports and is supported, regulates and is regulated, by the rest." 1 W. Blackstone, Commentaries on the Laws of England 151 (1765). So as James Madison stated, the creation of distinct branches "did not mean that these departments ought to have no partial agency in, or no controul over the acts of each other." The Federalist No. 47, at 325. To the contrary, Madison explained, the drafters of the Constitution—like those of then-existing state constitutions—opted against keeping the branches of government "absolutely separate and distinct." Or as Justice Story reiterated a half-century later: "[W]hen we speak of a separation of the three great departments of government," it is "not meant to affirm, that they must be kept wholly and entirely separate." 2 J. Story, Commentaries on the Constitution of the United States § 524, p. 8 (1833). Instead, the branches have—as they must for the whole arrangement to work—"common link[s] of connexion [and] dependence."

One way the Constitution reflects that vision is by giving Congress broad authority to establish and organize the Executive Branch. Article II presumes the existence of "Officer[s]" in "executive Departments." § 2, cl. 1. But it does not, as you might think from reading the majority opinion, give the President authority to decide what kinds of officers—in what departments, with what responsibilities—the Executive Branch requires. Instead, Article I's Necessary and Proper Clause puts those decisions in the legislature's hands. Congress has the power"[t]o make all Laws which shall be necessary and proper for carrying into Execution" not just its own enumerated powers but also "all other Powers vested by this Constitution in the Government of the United States, or in any

Department or Officer thereof." § 8, cl. 18. Similarly, the Appointments Clause reflects Congress's central role in structuring the Executive Branch. Yes, the President can appoint principal officers, but only as the legislature "shall . . . establish[ ] by Law" (and of course subject to the Senate's advice and consent). Art. II, § 2, cl. 2. And Congress has plenary power to decide not only what inferior officers will exist but also who (the President or a head of department) will appoint them. So as Madison told the first Congress, the legislature gets to "create[ ] the office, define[ ] the powers, [and] limit[ ] its duration." 1 Annals of Cong. 582 (1789). The President, as to the construction of his own branch of government, can only try to work his will through the legislative process.[3]

The majority relies for its contrary vision on Article II's Vesting Clause, but the provision can't carry all that weight. Or as Chief Justice Rehnquist wrote of a similar claim in *Morrison* v. *Olson,* 487 U.S. 654 (1988), "extrapolat[ing]" an unrestricted removal power from such "general constitutional language"— which says only that "[t]he executive Power shall be vested in a President"—is "more than the text will bear." Dean John Manning has well explained why, even were it not obvious from the Clause's "open-ended language." Separation of Powers as Ordinary Interpretation, 124 Harv. L. Rev. 1939, 1971 (2011). The Necessary and Proper Clause, he writes, makes it impossible to "establish a constitutional violation simply by showing that Congress has constrained the way '[t]he executive Power' is implemented"; that is exactly what the Clause gives Congress the power to do. Only "a *specific* historical understanding" can bar Congress from enacting a given constraint.

And nothing of that sort broadly prevents Congress from limiting the President's removal power. I'll turn soon to the Decision of 1789 and other evidence of Post-Convention thought. For now, note two points about practice before the Constitution's drafting. First, in that era, Parliament often restricted the King's power to remove royal officers—and the President, needless to say, wasn't supposed to be a king. See Birk, Interrogating the Historical Basis for a Unitary Executive, 73 Stan. L. Rev. (forthcoming 2021). Second, many States at the time allowed limits on gubernatorial removal power even though their

---

[3]   Article II's Opinions Clause also demonstrates the possibility of limits on the President's control over the Executive Branch. Under that Clause, the President "may require the Opinion, in writing, of the principal Officer in each of the executive Departments, upon any Subject relating to the Duties of their respective Offices." § 2, cl. 1. For those in the majority's camp, that Clause presents a puzzle: If the President must always have the direct supervisory control they posit, including by threat of removal, why would he ever need a constitutional warrant to demand agency heads' opinions? The Clause becomes at least redundant—though really, inexplicable—under the majority's idea of executive power.

constitutions had similar vesting clauses. See Shane, The Originalist Myth of the Unitary Executive, 19 U. Pa. J. Const. L. 323, 334–344 (2016). Historical understandings thus belie the majority's "general rule."

Nor can the Take Care Clause come to the majority's rescue. . . . To begin with, the provision—"he shall take Care that the Laws be faithfully executed"—speaks of duty, not power. Art. II, § 3. New scholarship suggests the language came from English and colonial oaths taken by, and placing fiduciary obligations on, all manner and rank of executive officers. See Kent, Leib, & Shugerman, Faithful Execution and Article II, 132 Harv. L. Rev. 2111, 2121–2178 (2019). To be sure, the imposition of a duty may imply a grant of power sufficient to carry it out. But again, the majority's view of that power ill comports with founding-era practice, in which removal limits were common. See, *e.g.*, Corwin, Tenure of Office and the Removal Power Under the Constitution, 27 Colum. L. Rev. 353, 385 (1927) (noting that New York's Constitution of 1777 had nearly the same clause, though the State's executive had "very little voice" in removals). And yet more important, the text of the Take Care Clause requires only enough authority to make sure "the laws [are] faithfully executed"—meaning with fidelity to the law itself, not to every presidential policy preference. As this Court has held, a President can ensure " 'faithful execution' of the laws"—thereby satisfying his "take care" obligation—with a removal provision like the one here. . . .

B

History no better serves the majority's cause. As Madison wrote, "a regular course of practice" can "liquidate & settle the meaning of" disputed or indeterminate constitutional provisions. Letter to Spencer Roane (Sept. 2, 1819), in 8 Writings of James Madison 450 (G. Hunt ed. 1908); see *NLRB* v. *Noel Canning*, 573 U. S. 513, 525 (2014). The majority lays claim to that kind of record, asserting that its muscular view of "[t]he President's removal power has long been confirmed by history." But that is not so. The early history—including the fabled Decision of 1789—shows mostly debate and division about removal authority. And when a "settle[ment of] meaning" at last occurred, it was not on the majority's terms. Instead, it supports wide latitude for Congress to create spheres of administrative independence.

1

Begin with evidence from the Constitution's ratification. And note that this moment is indeed the beginning: Delegates to the Constitutional Convention never discussed whether or to what extent the President would have power to remove executive officials. As a result, the Framers advocating ratification had no single view of the matter. In Federalist No. 77, Hamilton presumed that under the new Constitution "[t]he consent of [the Senate] would be necessary to displace as well as to appoint" officers of the United States. He thought that scheme would promote "steady administration": "Where a man in any station had given satisfactory evidence of his fitness for it, a new president would be restrained" from substituting "a person more agreeable to him." By contrast, Madison thought the Constitution allowed Congress to decide how any executive official could be removed. He explained in Federalist No. 39: "The tenure of the ministerial offices generally will be a subject of legal regulation, conformably to the reason of the case, and the example of the State Constitutions." Neither view, of course, at all supports the majority's story.[4]

The second chapter is the Decision of 1789, when Congress addressed the removal power while considering the bill creating the Department of Foreign Affairs. Speaking through Chief Justice Taft—a judicial presidentialist if ever there was one—this Court in *Myers* v. *United States*, 272 U.S. 52 (1926), read that debate as expressing Congress's judgment that the Constitution gave the President illimitable power to remove executive officials. . . .

The best view is that the First Congress was "deeply divided" on the President's removal power, and "never squarely addressed" the central issue here. The congressional debates revealed three main positions. See Corwin, 27 Colum. L. Rev., at 361. Some shared Hamilton's Federalist No. 77 view: The Constitution required Senate consent for removal. At the opposite extreme, others claimed that the Constitution gave absolute removal power to the President. And a third faction maintained that the Constitution placed Congress in the driver's seat: The legislature could regulate, if it so chose, the President's authority to remove. In the end, Congress passed a bill saying nothing about removal, leaving the President free to fire the Secretary of Foreign Affairs at will. But the only one of the three views definitively rejected was Hamilton's theory of

---

[4]   The majority dismisses Federalist Nos. 77 and 39 as "reflect[ing] initial impressions later abandoned." But even Hamilton's and Madison's later impressions are less helpful to the majority than it suggests. . . . [S]uch changing minds and inconstant opinions don't usually prove the existence of constitutional rules.

necessary Senate consent. As even strong proponents of executive power have shown, Congress never "endorse[d] the view that [it] lacked authority to modify" the President's removal authority when it wished to. . . .

At the same time, the First Congress gave officials handling financial affairs—as compared to diplomatic and military ones—some independence from the President. The title and first section of the statutes creating the Departments of Foreign Affairs and War designated them "executive departments." The law creating the Treasury Department conspicuously avoided doing so. See Act of Sept. 2, 1789, ch. 12, 1 Stat. 65. That difference in nomenclature signaled others of substance. Congress left the organization of the Departments of Foreign Affairs and War skeletal, enabling the President to decide how he wanted to staff them. By contrast, Congress listed each of the offices within the Treasury Department, along with their functions. Of the three initial Secretaries, only the Treasury's had an obligation to report to Congress when requested. And perhaps most notable, Congress soon deemed the Comptroller of the Treasury's settlements of public accounts "final and conclusive." Act of Mar. 3, 1795, ch. 48, § 4, 1 Stat. 441–442. That decision, preventing presidential overrides, marked the Comptroller as exercising independent judgment.[5] True enough, no statute shielded the Comptroller from discharge. But even James Madison, who at this point opposed most removal limits, told Congress that "there may be strong reasons why an officer of this kind should not hold his office at the pleasure" of the Secretary or President. 1 Annals of Cong. 612. . . .

Contrary to the majority's view, then, the founding era closed without any agreement that Congress lacked the power to curb the President's removal authority. And as it kept that question open, Congress took the first steps— which would launch a tradition—of distinguishing financial regulators from diplomatic and military officers. The latter mainly helped the President carry out his own constitutional duties in foreign relations and war. The former chiefly carried out statutory duties, fulfilling functions Congress had assigned to their offices. In addressing the new Nation's finances, Congress had begun

---

[5]   As President Jefferson explained: "[W]ith the settlement of the accounts at the Treasury I have no right to interfere in the least," because the Comptroller of the Treasury "is the sole & supreme judge for all claims of money against the US. and would no more receive a direction from me" than would "one of the judges of the supreme court." Letter from T. Jefferson to B. Latrobe (June 2, 1808), in Thomas Jefferson and the National Capital 429, 431 (S. Padover ed. 1946). A couple of decades later, Attorney General William Wirt reached the same conclusion, stating that "the President has no right to interpose in the settling of accounts" because Congress had "separated" the Comptroller from the President's authority. 1 Op. Atty. Gen. 636, 637 (1824); 1 Op. Atty. Gen. 678, 680 (1824). And indeed, Wirt believed that Congress could restrict the President's authority to remove such officials, at least so long as it "express[ed] that intention clearly." 1 Op. Atty. Gen. 212, 213 (1818).

to use its powers under the Necessary and Proper Clause to design effective administrative institutions. And that included taking steps to insulate certain officers from political influence.

2

As the decades and centuries passed, those efforts picked up steam. Confronting new economic, technological, and social conditions, Congress—and often the President—saw new needs for pockets of independence within the federal bureaucracy. And that was especially so, again, when it came to financial regulation. . . .

Take first Congress's decision in 1816 to create the Second Bank of the United States—"the first truly independent agency in the republic's history." Lessig & Sunstein, The President and the Administration, 94 Colum. L. Rev. 1, 30 (1994). Of the twenty-five directors who led the Bank, the President could appoint and remove only five. See Act of Apr. 10, 1816, § 8, 3 Stat. 269. Yet the Bank had a greater impact on the Nation than any but a few institutions, regulating the Nation's money supply in ways anticipating what the Federal Reserve does today. Of course, the Bank was controversial—in large part because of its freedom from presidential control. Andrew Jackson chafed at the Bank's independence and eventually fired his Treasury Secretary for keeping public moneys there (a dismissal that itself provoked a political storm). No matter. Innovations in governance always have opponents; administrative independence predictably (though by no means invariably) provokes presidential ire. The point is that by the early 19th century, Congress established a body wielding enormous financial power mostly outside the President's dominion.

The Civil War brought yet further encroachments on presidential control over financial regulators. In response to wartime economic pressures, President Lincoln (not known for his modest view of executive power) asked Congress to establish an office called the Comptroller of the Currency. The statute he signed made the Comptroller removable only with the Senate's consent . . . . A year later, Congress amended the statute to permit removal by the President alone, but only upon "reasons to be communicated by him to the Senate." . . .

And then, nearly a century and a half ago, the floodgates opened. In 1887, the growing power of the railroads over the American economy led Congress to create the Interstate Commerce Commission. Under that legislation, the President could remove the five Commissioners only "for inefficiency, neglect of duty, or malfeasance in office"—the same standard Congress applied to the CFPB Director. More—many more—for-cause removal provisions followed. In 1913, Congress gave the Governors of the Federal Reserve Board for-cause protection to ensure the agency would resist political pressure and promote economic stability. The next year, Congress provided similar protection to the FTC . . . . The Federal Deposit Insurance Corporation (FDIC), the Securities and Exchange Commission (SEC), the Commodity Futures Trading Commission. . . . By one count, across all subject matter areas, 48 agencies have heads (and below them hundreds more inferior officials) removable only for cause. So year by year by year, the broad sweep of history has spoken to the constitutional question before us: Independent agencies are everywhere.

C

What is more, the Court's precedents before today have accepted the role of independent agencies in our governmental system. To be sure, the line of our decisions has not run altogether straight. But we have repeatedly upheld provisions that prevent the President from firing regulatory officials except for such matters as neglect or malfeasance. . . .

According to *Humphrey's*, the Commissioners' primary work was to "carry into effect legislative policies"—"filling in and administering the details embodied by [a statute's] general standard." 295 U. S., at 627–628. In addition, the Court noted, the Commissioners recommended dispositions in court cases, much as a special master does. Given those "quasi-legislative" and "quasi-judicial"—as opposed to "purely executive"—functions, Congress could limit the President's removal authority. Id., at 628.[7] . . .

The majority's description of *Morrison* is not true to the decision. . . . [T]he decision, with care, set out the governing rule—again, that removal restrictions are permissible so long as they do not impede the President's performance of his own constitutionally assigned duties. Second, as all that suggests, *Morrison* is not limited to inferior officers. In the eight pages addressing the removal issue, the Court constantly spoke of "officers" and "officials" in general. . . .

---

[7]　The majority is quite right that today we view *all* the activities of administrative agencies as exercises of "the 'executive Power.' " *Arlington* v. *FCC*, 569 U. S. 290, 305, n. 4 (2013) (quoting Art. II, § 1, cl.1); see *ante*, at 14, n. 2. But we well understand, just as the *Humphrey's* Court did, that those activities may "take 'legislative' and 'judicial' forms." *Arlington*, 569 U. S., at 305, n. 4. The classic examples are agency rule-makings and adjudications, endemic in agencies like the FTC and CFPB. In any event, the Court would soon make clear that Congress can also constrain the President's removal authority over officials performing even the most "executive" of functions. See *infra*, at 19–20.

D

The deferential approach this Court has taken gives Congress the flexibility it needs to craft administrative agencies. Diverse problems of government demand diverse solutions. They call for varied measures and mixtures of democratic accountability and technical expertise, energy and efficiency. Sometimes, the arguments push toward tight presidential control of agencies. The President's engagement, some people say, can disrupt bureaucratic stagnation, counter industry capture, and make agencies more responsive to public interests. See, well, Kagan, Presidential Administration, 114 Harv. L. Rev. 2245, 2331–2346 (2001) [discussed later in this chapter.—Ed.]. At other times, the arguments favor greater independence from presidential involvement. Insulation from political pressure helps ensure impartial adjudications. It places technical issues in the hands of those most capable of addressing them. It promotes continuity, and prevents short-term electoral interests from distorting policy. (Consider, for example, how the Federal Reserve's independence stops a President trying to win a second term from manipulating interest rates.) Of course, the right balance between presidential control and independence is often uncertain, contested, and value-laden. No mathematical formula governs institutional design; trade-offs are endemic to the enterprise. But that is precisely why the issue is one for the political branches to debate—and then debate again as times change. And it's why courts should stay (mostly) out of the way. . . .

A given agency's independence (or lack of it) depends on a wealth of features, relating not just to removal standards, but also to appointments practices, procedural rules, internal organization, oversight regimes, historical traditions, cultural norms, and (inevitably) personal relationships. It is hard to pinpoint how those factors work individually, much less in concert, to influence the distance between an agency and a President. In that light, even the judicial opinions' perennial focus on removal standards is a bit of a puzzle. Removal is only the most obvious, not necessarily the most potent, means of control. . . . [I]n spurning a "pragmatic, flexible approach to American governance" in favor of a dogmatic, inflexible one, the majority makes a serious error. . . .

II

. . . . [T]he CFPB's powers are nothing unusual in the universe of independent agencies. The CFPB, as the majority notes, can issue regulations, conduct its own adjudications, and bring civil enforcement actions in court—all backed by the threat of penalties. But then again, so too can (among others) the FTC and SEC, two agencies whose regulatory missions parallel the CFPB's. . . .

The analysis is as simple as simple can be. The CFPB Director exercises the same powers, and receives the same removal protections, as the heads of other, constitutionally permissible independent agencies. How could it be that this opinion is a dissent? . . .

Still more important, novelty is not the test of constitutionality when it comes to structuring agencies. See *Mistretta* v. *United States*, 488 U.S. 361, 385 (1989) ("[M]ere anomaly or innovation" does not violate the separation of powers). Congress regulates in that sphere under the Necessary and Proper Clause, not (as the majority seems to think) a Rinse and Repeat Clause. The Framers understood that new times would often require new measures, and exigencies often demand innovation. In line with that belief, the history of the administrative sphere—its rules, its practices, its institutions—is replete with experiment and change. Indeed, each of the agencies the majority says now fits within its "exceptions" was once new; there is, as the saying goes, "a first time for everything." So even if the CFPB differs from its forebears in having a single director, that departure is not itself "telling" of a "constitutional problem." In deciding what *this* moment demanded, Congress had no obligation to make a carbon copy of a design from a bygone era.

And Congress's choice to put a single director, rather than a multimember commission, at the CFPB's head violates no principle of separation of powers. The purported constitutional problem here is that an official has "slip[ped] from the Executive's control" and "supervision"—that he has become unaccountable to the President. So to make sense on the majority's own terms, the distinction between singular and plural agency heads must rest on a theory about why the former more easily "slip" from the President's grasp. But the majority has nothing to offer. In fact, the opposite is more likely to be true: To the extent that such matters are measurable, individuals are easier than groups to supervise. . . .

Because it has no answer on that score, the majority slides to a different question: Assuming presidential control of any independent agency is vanishingly slim, is a single-head or a multi-head agency more capable of exercising power, and so of endangering liberty? . . .

[T]he premise of the majority's argument—that the CFPB head is a mini-dictator, not subject to meaningful presidential control—is wrong. As this

Court has seen in the past, independent agencies are not fully independent. A for-cause removal provision, as noted earlier, leaves "ample" control over agency heads in the hands of the President. . . .

III

"While the Constitution diffuses power the better to secure liberty, it also contemplates that practice will integrate the dispersed powers into a workable government." *Youngstown Sheet & Tube Co.* v. *Sawyer*, 343 U.S. 579, 635 (1952) (Jackson, J., concurring). The Framers took pains to craft a document that would allow the structures of governance to change, as times and needs change. The Constitution says only a few words about administration. As Chief Justice Marshall wrote: Rather than prescribing "immutable rules," it enables Congress to choose "the means by which government should, in all future time, execute its powers." *McCulloch*, 4 Wheat. at 415. It authorizes Congress to meet new exigencies with new devices. So Article II does not generally prohibit independent agencies. Nor do any supposed structural principles. Nor do any odors wafting from the document. Save for when those agencies impede the President's performance of his own constitutional duties, the matter is left up to Congress. Our history has stayed true to the Framers' vision. Congress has accepted their invitation to experiment with administrative forms—nowhere more so than in the field of financial regulation. . . .

[T]here was no need to send Congress back to the drawing board. The Constitution does not distinguish between single-director and multimember independent agencies. It instructs Congress, not this Court, to decide on agency design. Because this Court ignores that sensible—indeed, that obvious—division of tasks, I respectfully dissent.

NOTES AND QUESTIONS

1. What's left of **Humphrey's Executor?** Take another look at footnote 7 of Justice Kagan's dissent. Do all nine justices agree that the reasoning of the Court in *Humphrey's Executor* is not sustainable? Do all agree that there is no such thing as "quasi-legislative" or "quasi-judicial" power that is not ultimately also executive power? If nothing is left of *Humphrey's* reasoning, should *Humphrey's* have been overruled? Or, should the Court have analyzed the other possible justification for that decision, i.e., if Article II's vesting clause is not a substantive grant of power and the President only has whatever power can be derived from the Take Care Clause?

2.   *The Opinions Clause.* In another footnote, Justice Kagan suggests that on the majority's reading, the Opinions Clause would be redundant. Indeed, why would the Constitution specify that the President can demand the opinions in writing of the principal executive officers? If the President could fire them at-will, doesn't that imply the power to ask them to do things? Is redundancy a bad thing in constitutions, anyway? Could the Opinions Clause confirm that the President is to be unitary and confirm the Convention's rejection of a privy council? And could it actually be a limitation on the President's power by denying the President the ability to seek the opinions of officers in the other branches? See 2 The Records of the Federal Convention of 1787, at 342, 367 (Max Farrand ed., 1966) (1911) (showing that the reference to "executive" departments in the Opinions Clause may have been in response to proposals that would have given the President power to demand opinions from the Chief Justice and officers of the House and Senate).

FOR DISCUSSION We noted earlier that it is useful to look at how various parts of a statute, or the Constitution, work together. Here, why have an Opinions Clause if the Vesting Clause is a grant of executive power? Wouldn't the ability to direct officers flow from that grant of power? Is the Opinions Clause superfluous?

3.   *Madison and Hamilton in The Federalist.* Justice Kagan also cites to statements from Madison and Hamilton in The Federalist. In Federalist No. 77, Hamilton wrote that the "[t]he consent of [the Senate] would be necessary to displace as well as to appoint" officers of the United States. And in Federalist No. 39 Madison wrote: "The tenure of the ministerial offices generally will be a subject of legal regulation, conformably to the reason of the case, and the example of the State Constitutions."

Do these statements prove that Madison and Hamilton, at least initially, thought Senate consent was necessary to removal or that Congress could limit the President's removal authority? Hamilton's paragraph is rather ambiguous. He starts by noting that "one of the advantages to be expected the co-operation of the Senate, in the business of *appointments*," is "that it would contribute to the stability of the administration." Hamilton's entire discussion seems to be about "appointments," not removals. Thus, he speaks of "displacing" an officer after a *new President* is elected:

> The consent of that body would be necessary to displace as well as to appoint. *A change of the Chief Magistrate*, therefore, would not occasion so violent or so general a revolution in the officers of the government as might be expected, if he were the sole disposer of offices. Where a man in any station had given satisfactory evidence of his fitness for it, a new President would be restrained from attempting a change *in favor of a person* more agreeable to him, by the apprehension that a discountenance of the Senate might frustrate the attempt, and bring some degree of discredit upon himself.

Does this paragraph seem more logically to be referring to the advice and consent of the Senate to a *new* appointment? The President would not need the advice and consent to *remove* an officer, but to *displace* the officer (i.e., replace the officer with a new one), the President certainly would need the advice and consent of the Senate. See Joseph Story, Commentaries on the Constitution of the United States §§ 1532–33 (1833) (making similar argument); see also Seth Barrett Tillman, *The Puzzle of Hamilton's Federalist No. 77*, 33 Harv. J.L. Pub. Pol'y 149 (2010) (similar); but see Jeremy D. Bailey, *The Traditional View of Hamilton's Federalist No. 77 and an Unexpected Challenge: A Response to Seth Barrett Tillman*, 33 Harv. J.L. Pub. Pol'y 169 (2010) (arguing that Hamilton did mean that removals would require senatorial consent).

 What do we do with historical evidence when the evidence is contradictory, or there are competing interpretations of the evidence, as with Hamilton in Federalist No. 77?

As for Madison's statement, it is true that Congress regulates the "tenure" of "offices" by establishing the length of the term, i.e., the length of time before a new individual has to be nominated and appointed to the position. Does that necessarily imply anything about removal?

4.   *Evidence from British practice and state constitutions.* How much does evidence of practices under the British or state constitutions matter for interpreting the federal Constitution? Did the Framers reject or embrace many elements of state constitutions? For an interpretation of the evidence from British and state practices at odds with the dissent's interpretation in *Seila Law*, see Ilan Wurman, *In Search of Prerogative*, 70 Duke L.J. 93 (2020); Ilan Wurman, *The Removal Power: A Critical Guide*, 2020 Cato Sup. Ct. Rev. 157. For an alternative interpretation of the evidence involving financial institutions, see Wurman, The Removal Power, at 178–81.

C. Presidential Control of Agencies and Officers

The answer to whether the President can control administrative agencies, and direct them in exercising their statutory duties, will depend on one's view of the removal power cases discussed previously. If one is of the view that the President must be able to supervise and therefore remove officers as a constitutional matter, then the President can direct the activities of these officers. If one is of the view that Congress can put a check on the President's ability to remove, then presumably the President also cannot interfere with how these officers exercise their administrative duties. (Although of course the President would still be able to remove such officers "for cause"—typically for inefficiency, neglect of duty, or malfeasance in office.)

Within the "formalist" camp—those who believe the President is in charge of administration—there are two competing views. Some scholars believe the President can execute the law him or herself, even if Congress assigns the particularly statutory duty to a particular officer. See Saikrishna Prakash, *The Essential Meaning of Executive Power*, 2003 U. Ill. L. Rev. 701, 716. The more conventional view (among the formalists) is that the President executes the law by overseeing the officers to whom Congress has assigned specific statutory duties; if the President is displeased, the President can remove the officer. This was the view of Attorney General William Wirt in an influential 1823 opinion, in which he wrote that "the constitutional charge to the President to take care that the laws be faithfully executed" does not require the President "to perform the duty, but to see that the officer assigned by law performs his duty *faithfully*," and the President "has power to remove him—to appoint a successor; and through the medium of such successor, and by his instrumentality, to remove the deputy, and to see that his place be honestly supplied." 1 U.S. Opp. Att'y Gen. 624, 626 (1823).

At least until very recent years, the modern, non-formalist view has been that Congress has plenary control over who gets to administer the law and how to structure administrative agencies, and therefore Presidential involvement is rulemaking and directing administrative agencies was broadly discouraged. This started to change in the 1980s as President Reagan began to reassert presidential control over administration generally. And in the 1990s, President Clinton specifically directed agencies within the executive branch—not independent agencies—to engage in rulemakings that advanced the political priorities of his administration. President Clinton's practice was supported by then-professor, now-Justice Elena Kagan in the following prominent Article.

COURSE THEME

**FORMALISM VS. FUNCTIONALISM
POLITICAL INFLUENCE**

Are there functionalist reasons why we might want administrative officers to be insulated from presidential control? Are there functionalist reasons we might, on the contrary, desire presidential influence?

Elena Kagan, Presidential Administration

114 Harv. L. Rev. 2245, 2246–52, 2322–28 (2001)

The history of the American administrative state is the history of competition among different entities for control of its policies. All three branches of government—the President, Congress, and Judiciary—have participated in this competition; so too have the external constituencies and internal staff of the agencies. Because of the stakes of the contest and the strength of the claims and weapons possessed by the contestants, no single entity has emerged finally triumphant, or is ever likely to do so. But at different times, one or another has come to the fore and asserted at least a comparative primacy in setting the direction and influencing the outcome of administrative process. In this time, that institution is the Presidency. We live today in an era of presidential administration.

This assertion may seem jarring to those who have immersed themselves in the recent work of constitutional law scholars on the relationship between the Presidency and the administration. In this work, scholars have debated the constitutional basis for a fully "unitary executive"—otherwise put, a system in which all of what now counts as administrative activity is controllable by the President. Because Congress has deprived (or, in the view of the "unitarians," unconstitutionally purported to deprive) the President of such plenary authority in one obvious respect—by creating the so-called independent agencies, whose heads the President may not remove at will—the common ground of this debate is that the current system of administration is not strongly unitary. And because this much is common ground, the participants in the debate largely have failed to register, much less to comment on, the recent trend toward presidential control over administration generally.

For administrative law scholars, the claim of presidential administration may seem puzzling for a different reason. These scholars—concerned as they are with the actual practices of administrative control, as carried out in executive branch as well as independent agencies—may well have viewed the claim as arguable, though perhaps premature, if made ten or fifteen years ago, when President Reagan or Bush was in office. In the first month of his tenure, Reagan issued an executive order creating a mechanism by which the Office of Management and Budget (OMB), an entity within the Executive Office of the President (EOP), would review all major regulations of executive branch agencies. As Reagan's and then Bush's terms proceeded, and the antiregulatory effects of this system of review became increasingly evident, administrative law scholars took part in a sharp debate about its propriety. With the advent of the Clinton Administration, however, this debate receded. Although President Clinton issued his own executive order providing for OMB review of regulations, the terms of this order struck most observers as moderating the aggressive approach to oversight of administration taken in the Reagan and Bush Presidencies. Perhaps as important, the Clinton OMB chose to implement the order in a way generally sympathetic to regulatory efforts. Because objections to OMB review in the Reagan and Bush era arose in large part from its deregulatory tendencies, this reversal of substantive direction contributed to the waning of interest in, and even recognition of, the involvement of the President and his EOP staff in administration.

In fact, as this Article will show, presidential control of administration, in critical respects, expanded dramatically during the Clinton years, making the regulatory activity of the executive branch agencies more and more an extension of the President's own policy and political agenda. Faced for most of his time in office with a hostile Congress but eager to show progress on domestic issues, Clinton and his White House staff turned to the bureaucracy to achieve, to the extent it could, the full panoply of his domestic policy goals. Whether the subject was health care, welfare reform, tobacco, or guns, a self-conscious and central object of the White House was to devise, direct, and/or finally announce administrative actions—regulations, guidance, enforcement strategies, and reports—to showcase and advance presidential policies. In executing this strategy, the White House in large measure set the administrative agenda for key agencies, heavily influencing what they would (or would not) spend time on and what they would (or would not) generate as regulatory product.

The resulting policy orientation diverged substantially from that of the Reagan and Bush years, disproving the assumption some scholars have made, primarily on the basis of that earlier experience, that presidential supervision of administration inherently cuts in a deregulatory direction. Where once presidential supervision had worked to dilute or delay regulatory initiatives, it served in the Clinton years as part of a distinctly activist and pro-regulatory governing agenda. Where once presidential supervision had tended to favor politically conservative positions, it generally operated during the Clinton Presidency as a mechanism to achieve progressive goals. Or expressed in the terms most sympathetic to all these Presidents (and therefore most contestable), if Reagan and Bush showed that presidential supervision could thwart regulators intent on regulating no matter what the cost, Clinton showed that presidential supervision could jolt into action bureaucrats suffering from bureaucratic inertia in the face of unmet needs and challenges.

The methods of presidential supervision used in the Clinton years also differed substantially from what had come before, enabling the President to use more numerous and direct means of controlling administrative activity. The Clinton OMB continued to manage a regulatory review process, but with certain variations from the Reagan and Bush model: although the process provoked fewer confrontations with agencies, it in fact articulated a broader understanding of the President's appropriate authority to direct administrative actions. More important, the Clinton White House sandwiched regulatory review between two other methods for guiding and asserting ownership over administrative activity, used episodically by prior Presidents but elevated by Clinton to something near a governing philosophy. At the front end of the regulatory process, Clinton regularly issued formal directives to the heads of executive agencies to set the terms of administrative action and prevent deviation from his proposed course. And at the back end of the process (which could not but affect prior stages as well), Clinton personally appropriated significant regulatory action through communicative strategies that presented regulations and other agency work product, to both the public and other governmental actors, as his own, in a way new to the annals of administrative process.

By the close of the Clinton Presidency, a distinctive form of administration and administrative control—call it "presidential administration"—had emerged, at the least augmenting, and in significant respects subordinating, other modes of bureaucratic governance. Triggered mainly by the re-emergence of divided government and built on the foundation of President Reagan's regulatory review process, President Clinton's articulation and use of directive authority over regulatory agencies, as well as his assertion of personal ownership over regulatory product, pervaded crucial areas of administration. Of course, presidential control did not show itself in all, or even all important, regulation; no President (or his executive office staff) could, and presumably none would wish to, supervise so broad a swath of regulatory activity. And of course, presidential control co-existed and competed with other forms of influence and control over administration, exerted by other actors within and outside the government. At times, indeed, presidential administration surely seemed to Clinton and his staff, as it surely also had to their pioneering predecessors, more an aspiration than an achievement. Still, these officials put in place a set of mechanisms and practices, likely to survive into the future, that greatly enhanced presidential supervision of agency action, thus changing the very nature of administration (and, perhaps too, of the Presidency).

A key aspect of this system of administrative control raises serious legal questions. Accepted constitutional doctrine holds that Congress possesses broad, although not unlimited, power to structure the relationship between the President and the administration, even to the extent of creating independent agencies, whose heads have substantial protection from presidential removal. The conventional view further posits, although no court has ever decided the matter, that by virtue of this power, Congress can insulate discretionary decisions of even removable (that is, executive branch) officials from presidential dictation—and, indeed, that Congress has done so whenever (as is usual) it has delegated power not to the President, but to a specified agency official. Clinton's use of what I call directive authority—his commands to executive branch officials to take specified actions within their statutorily delegated discretion— ill-comports with this view. The unitarians would defend the practice simply by insisting, against the weight of precedent, that the Constitution provides the

President with plenary authority over administration, so that Congress can no more interfere with the President's directive authority than with his removal power. I too defend the practice, but not on this basis. I accept Congress's broad power to insulate administrative activity from the President, but argue here that Congress has left more power in presidential hands than generally is recognized. More particularly, I argue that a statutory delegation to an executive agency official—although not to an independent agency head—usually should be read as allowing the President to assert directive authority, as Clinton did, over the exercise of the delegated discretion.

This rule of statutory construction is based in part (though only in part) on policy considerations relating to the desirability of presidential control over administration. Those considerations also should govern the questions how Congress and the President should act within the legal framework I posit: whether and when Congress should override the interpretive rule, and whether and when the President should exercise the power conferred under this rule in the absence of such congressional action. Policy arguments for presidential control over administration are surprisingly undeveloped in the legal literature, in large part because most of the unitarians, the strongest proponents of presidential power in public law scholarship, believe that all important questions surrounding this subject are settled by resort to originalist inquiry. My analysis focuses on the values of accountability and effectiveness—the principal values that all models of administration must attempt to further. I aver that in comparison with other forms of control, the new presidentialization of administration renders the bureaucratic sphere more transparent and responsive to the public, while also better promoting important kinds of regulatory competence and dynamism. I make these claims against the backdrop of notable features of contemporary American government, including the emergent relationship between the President and public, the rise of divided government, and the increased ossification of federal bureaucracies. I also consider objections to a system of presidential administration and note appropriate limitations on it.

* * *

But what if Congress had delegated specifically to the Secretary of Commerce the authority to seize property in certain circumstances? [Here, Professor Kagan is referring, of course, to the famous *Youngstown* Steel Seizure Case.— Ed.] Could President Truman then have issued the order that he did? Could he effectively have substituted his decision as to the propriety of the seizure for that of the Secretary? This is essentially the question posed by Clinton's use of directive authority—by his assumption, expressed in formal terms, that when Congress designates an agency official as a decisionmaker, the President himself may step into that official's shoes.

Because no Supreme Court cases specifically address this question, analysis of it under current law must begin with the body of cases relating to the President's removal power. Just nine years after the Court in *Myers v. United States* appeared to recognize a plenary power on the part of the President to remove administrative officeholders, the Court approved in *Humphrey's Executor v. United States* a statute providing that the President could dismiss a member of the Federal Trade Commission (FTC) only for "inefficiency, neglect of duty, or malfeasance in office." The Court distinguished *Myers* on the basis that the FTC Commissioner exercised "quasi-legislative" and "quasi-judicial" duties, as opposed to performing purely "executive function[s]." Later cases downplayed the importance of this distinction, focusing instead on the question whether the removal provision at issue only limited the President (thus creating a more "independent" entity) or also gave Congress a hand in determining the official's tenure (thus effecting a legislative "aggrandizement" of executive power). If the former, but only if the former, the removal provision was permissible, provided it did not "unduly interfer[e]" with the President's constitutionally assigned functions.

These cases strongly suggest that Congress may limit the President's capacity to direct administrative officials in the exercise of their substantive discretion. If Congress can create a zone of independent administration by preventing the President from removing officials at will, then it can advance the same end by barring the President from imposing his policy choices on them. This is true regardless whether Congress in fact has chosen to insulate the official from the President's at-will removal authority. If Congress has done so, the limit on the President's directive power seems but a necessary corollary: a for-cause removal provision would buy little substantive independence if the President, though unable to fire an official, could command or, if necessary, supplant his every decision. And even if Congress has not done so, it should be able, as an alternate means of ensuring a measure of independence, to limit the President's directive authority, thus forcing him to bear the burden of removing an official (and substituting a more compliant person) when he wishes to dictate an agency's decision. Indeed, a dictum from *Myers* suggests that even when Congress cannot at all limit the President's power to remove an official, Congress may be able to confine the President's capacity to direct that official as to the exercise of his delegated discretion. Said the Court: "Of course there may be duties so peculiarly and specifically committed to the discretion of a particular officer as to raise a question whether the President may overrule or revise the officer's interpretation of his statutory duty in a particular instance."

The conventional view in administrative law, in apparent accord with these cases, holds that the President lacks the power to direct an agency official to take designated actions within the sphere of that official's delegated discretion. The President may have the power to remove an official at will, because Congress either has not taken or (more rarely) could not take that power away. In addition, and critically, the President may have what Peter Strauss and Cass Sunstein have called "procedural" supervisory authority over administrative officers, enabling the President to demand information from and engage in consultation with them. Congress usually has done nothing to suggest that it wishes to interfere with this authority as to executive branch agencies; and even if Congress has indicated this intent as to the independents, Article II of the Constitution, most notably its Opinions Clause, may bar Congress from such interference. This procedural oversight power, most administrative law experts agree, supports OMB review of at least executive agency (and perhaps independent agency) actions, so long as ultimate decisionmaking power resides in the hands of agency officials; the review system then operates as a channel through which the President can obtain information from and offer advice to the relevant administrators. So too this oversight power sustains Clinton's directives to agency officials demanding reports on various issues, even if these directives, like the demands of OMB review, suggested a preferred policy position. But there the line is drawn. The President has no authority to act as the decisionmaker, either by resolving disputes in the OMB process or by issuing substantive directives. This is because Congress, under the removal precedents, can insulate administrative policymaking from the President, and Congress has exercised this power by delegating the relevant discretion to a specified agency official, rather than to the President.

The work of the scholars and lawyers known as unitarians provides a basis for contesting this view by attacking the removal decisions on which it rests. The unitarians argue that, contrary to these decisions, Article II of the Constitution establishes a President with plenary control over all heads of agencies involved in executing, implementing, or administering federal law. Most unitarians make this claim on the basis of the original meaning of the constitutional text. A few rely on the identification of broad constitutional values and the translation of those founding values into the contemporary context. In either event, the unitarians insist that the Court has allowed Congress too much power to insulate the agencies from the President. Although focusing on the question of removal, the unitarian position equally would bar legislative inroads into the President's directive authority.

I do not espouse the unitarian position in this Article, instead taking the Supreme Court's removal cases, and all that follows from them, as a given. I adopt this stance for two reasons. First, although I am highly sympathetic to the view that the President should have broad control over administrative activity, I believe, for reasons I can only sketch here, that the unitarians have failed to establish their claim for plenary control as a matter of constitutional mandate. The original meaning of Article II is insufficiently precise and, in this area of staggering change, also insufficiently relevant to support the unitarian position. And the constitutional values sometimes offered in defense of this claim are too diffuse, too diverse, and for these reasons, too easily manipulable to justify removing from the democratic process all decisions about the relationship between the President and administration—especially given that this result would reverse decades' worth of established law and invalidate the defining features of numerous and entrenched institutions of government. Second and equally important, the cases sustaining restrictions on the President's removal authority, whether or not justified, are almost certain to remain the law (at least in broad terms, if not in specifics); as a result, any serious attempt to engage the actual practice of presidential-agency relations must incorporate these holdings and their broader implications as part of its framework.

But my acceptance of congressional authority in this area does not require the conclusion, assumed on the conventional view, that the President lacks all power to direct administrative officials as to the exercise of their delegated discretion. That Congress could bar the President from directing discretionary action does not mean that Congress has done so; whether it has is a matter of statutory construction. If Congress, in a particular statute, has stated its intent with respect to presidential involvement, then that is the end of the matter. But if Congress, as it usually does, simply has assigned discretionary authority to an agency official, without in any way commenting on the President's role in the delegation, then an interpretive question arises. One way to read a statute of this kind is to assume that the delegation runs to the agency official specified and to that official alone. But a second way to read such a statute is to assume that the delegation runs to the agency official specified, rather than to any other agency official, but still subject to the ultimate control of the President. The lawfulness of a President's use of directive power depends on the choice between these two readings.

The availability of presidential directive authority thus usually will turn on the selection of an interpretive principle—really, a presumption—with which to approach a statutory delegation to an administrative official. The principle that advocates of the conventional view implicitly have adopted reads a standard delegation as excluding the President, in the absence of evidence to the contrary. The contrary principle would read a standard delegation as including the President, unless Congress indicates otherwise. Either principle would give clear guidance to courts and, equally important, provide Congress with a clear default rule against which to legislate. The choice between them appropriately rests on other considerations: in the first instance, on a judgment about legislative intentions; and to the extent these are in doubt, on a judgment about institutional competencies.

When the delegation in question runs to the members of an independent agency, the choice between these two interpretive principles seems fairly obvious. In establishing such an agency, Congress has acted self-consciously, by means of limiting the President's appointment and removal power, to insulate agency decisionmaking from the President's influence. In then delegating power to that agency (rather than to a counterpart in the executive branch), Congress must be thought to intend the exercise of that power to be independent. In such a case, the agency's heads are not subordinate to the President in other respects; making the heads subordinate in this single way would subvert the very structure and premises of the agency.

When the delegation runs to an executive branch official, however, Congress's intent (to the extent it exists) may well cut in the opposite direction. Congress knows, after all, that executive officials stand in all other respects in a subordinate position to the President, given that the President nominates them without restriction, can remove them at will, and can subject them to potentially far-ranging procedural oversight. All these powers establish a general norm of deference among executive officials to presidential opinions, such that when Congress delegates to an executive official, it in some necessary and obvious sense also delegates to the President. . . .

Notes and Questions

1.   *Summary.* Professor Kagan's view is that just because Congress can insulate administrative officials from presidential supervision, doesn't mean that Congress has in fact done so. Whether it has or hasn't is a matter of statutory interpretation. For Professor Kagan, the default rule should be that if Congress has created an independent agency, then Congress intends their officials to be insulated from presidential control; if Congress has created an agency or office as part of the executive branch itself, then the default rule is that the President can control and direct those officers. Do you agree with this interpretive presumption? If Congress assigns duties to subordinate officials, does Congress intend the President to have a say in how that subordinate executes the statutory duties?

2.   *The values of presidential administration.* Although left out of the excerpt, Professor Kagan also argued that presidential administration advances important values of democratic accountability, administrative effectiveness, and dynamism. Do you agree? What are the benefits and costs of presidential administration? All else being equal, is it better to have the President, who is elected, supervise and direct all administrative officers? What are the countervailing values? Go back to the course themes; think about administrative expertise and also consistency. How do those values cut?

COURSE THEME

EXPERTISE VS. ACCOUNTABILITY
What do you make of the expertise-accountability tradeoff that now-Justice Kagan discusses in her Harvard Law Review article?

---

3.   *Executive Order 12,291.* Although presidents had exercised varying degrees of control over administrative agencies prior to 1981, President Ronald Reagan systematized White House review of agency regulations in Executive Order 12,291, issued in 1981. The order required agencies, "to the extent permitted by law," to create a Regulatory Impact Analysis for any proposed "major rule," which was defined as a rule with an "annual effect on the economy of $100 million or more." These analyses had to present the costs and benefits of the proposed rules. The order required each agency to submit the proposed rules and the analyses to the White House Office of Management and Budget (OMB), which was given a period of time to review the rules and analyses, and required agencies to incorporate the OMB's views. The bottom line is that all major rules were to be reviewed by the President's staff, who would have an opportunity to comment on the proposed rules, and the agencies would have to take those comments into consideration "to the extent permitted by law." As Professor Kagan wrote, many thought that when President Clinton assumed office in 1993, he would revoke this executive order. Instead, he maintained the bulk of it in the following executive order, which still provides the fundamental framework for White House review of regulations.

Executive Order 12,866

The American people deserve a regulatory system that works for them, not against them: a regulatory system that protects and improves their health, safety, environment, and well-being and improves the performance of the economy without imposing unacceptable or unreasonable costs on society; regulatory policies that recognize that the private sector and private markets are the best engine for economic growth; regulatory approaches that respect the role of State, local, and tribal governments; and regulations that are effective, consistent, sensible, and understandable. We do not have such a regulatory system today.

With this Executive order, the Federal Government begins a program to reform and make more efficient the regulatory process. The objectives of this Executive order are to enhance planning and coordination with respect to both new and existing regulations; to reaffirm the primacy of Federal agencies in the regulatory decision-making process; to restore the integrity and legitimacy of regulatory review and oversight; and to make the process more accessible and open to the public. In pursuing these objectives, the regulatory process shall be conducted so as to meet applicable statutory requirements and with due regard to the discretion that has been entrusted to the Federal agencies.

Accordingly, by the authority vested in me as President by the Constitution and the laws of the United States of America, it is hereby ordered as follows:

Section 1. *Statement of Regulatory Philosophy and Principles.*

(a) *The Regulatory Philosophy.* Federal agencies should promulgate only such regulations as are required by law, are necessary to interpret the law, or are made necessary by compelling public need, such as material failures of private markets to protect or improve the health and safety of the public, the environment, or the well-being of the American people. In deciding whether and how to regulate, agencies should assess all costs and benefits of available regulatory alternatives, including the alternative of not regulating. Costs and benefits shall be understood to include both quantifiable measures (to the fullest extent that these can be usefully estimated) and qualitative measures of costs and benefits that are difficult to quantify, but nevertheless essential to consider. Further, in choosing among alternative regulatory approaches, agencies should select those approaches that maximize net benefits (including potential economic, environmental, public health and safety, and other advantages; distributive impacts; and equity), unless a statute requires another regulatory approach.

(b) *The Principles of Regulation.* To ensure that the agencies' regulatory programs are consistent with the philosophy set forth above, agencies should adhere to the following principles, to the extent permitted by law and where applicable:

(1)   Each agency shall identify the problem that it intends to address (including, where applicable, the failures of private markets or public institutions that warrant new agency action) as well as assess the significance of that problem.

(2)   Each agency shall examine whether existing regulations (or other law) have created, or contributed to, the problem that a new regulation is intended to correct and whether those regulations (or other law) should be modified to achieve the intended goal of regulation more effectively.

(3)   Each agency shall identify and assess available alternatives to direct regulation, including providing economic incentives to encourage the desired behavior, such as user fees or marketable permits, or providing information upon which choices can be made by the public.

(4)   In setting regulatory priorities, each agency shall consider, to the extent reasonable, the degree and nature of the risks posed by various substances or activities within its jurisdiction.

(5)   When an agency determines that a regulation is the best available method of achieving the regulatory objective, it shall design its regulations in the most cost-effective manner to achieve the regulatory objective. . . .

(6)   Each agency shall assess both the costs and the benefits of the intended regulation and, recognizing that some costs and benefits are difficult to quantify, propose or adopt a regulation only upon a reasoned determination that the benefits of the intended regulation justify its costs.

(7)   Each agency shall base its decisions on the best reasonably obtainable scientific, technical, economic, and other information concerning the need for, and consequences of, the intended regulation. . . .

(10)   Each agency shall avoid regulations that are inconsistent, incompatible, or duplicative with its other regulations or those of other Federal agencies.

(11)   Each agency shall tailor its regulations to impose the least burden on society, including individuals, businesses of differing sizes, and other entities (including small communities and governmental entities), consistent with obtaining the regulatory objectives, taking into account, among other things, and to the extent practicable, the costs of cumulative regulations.

(12)   Each agency shall draft its regulations to be simple and easy to understand, with the goal of minimizing the potential for uncertainty and litigation arising from such uncertainty.

Sec. 2. *Organization.*

An efficient regulatory planning and review process is vital to ensure that the Federal Government's regulatory system best serves the American people.

(a)   *The Agencies.* Because Federal agencies are the repositories of significant substantive expertise and experience, they are responsible for developing regulations and assuring that the regulations are consistent with applicable law, the President's priorities, and the principles set forth in this Executive order.

(b) *The Office of Management and Budget.* Coordinated review of agency rulemaking is necessary to ensure that regulations are consistent with applicable law, the President's priorities, and the principles set forth in this Executive order, and that decisions made by one agency do not conflict with the policies or actions taken or planned by another agency. The Office of Management and Budget (OMB) shall carry out that review function. Within OMB, the Office of Information and Regulatory Affairs (OIRA) is the repository of expertise concerning regulatory issues, including methodologies and procedures that affect more than one agency, this Executive order, and the President's regulatory policies. To the extent permitted by law, OMB shall provide guidance to agencies and assist the President, the Vice President, and other regulatory policy advisors to the President in regulatory planning and shall be the entity that reviews individual regulations, as provided by this Executive order. . . .

Sec. 3. *Definitions.*

For purposes of this Executive order: . . .

(b) "Agency," unless otherwise indicated, means any authority of the United States that is an "agency" under 44 U.S.C. 3502(1), other than those considered to be independent regulatory agencies, as defined in 44 U.S.C. 3502(10).

(c) "Director" means the Director of OMB.

(d) "Regulation" or "rule" means an agency statement of general applicability and future effect, which the agency intends to have the force and effect of law, that is designed to implement, interpret, or prescribe law or policy or to describe the procedure or practice requirements of an agency. It does not, however, include:

(1) Regulations or rules issued in accordance with the formal rulemaking provisions of 5 U.S.C. 556, 557;

(2) Regulations or rules that pertain to a military or foreign affairs function of the United States . . . .

(3) Regulations or rules that are limited to agency organization, management, or personnel matters; or

(4) Any other category of regulations exempted by the Administrator of OIRA.

(e) "Regulatory action" means any substantive action by an agency (normally published in the Federal Register) that promulgates or is expected to lead to the promulgation of a final rule or regulation, including notices of inquiry, advance notices of proposed rulemaking, and notices of proposed rulemaking.

(f) "Significant regulatory action" means any regulatory action that is likely to result in a rule that may:

(1) Have an annual effect on the economy of $100 million or more or adversely affect in a material way the economy, a sector of the economy, productivity, competition, jobs, the environment, public health or safety, or State, local, or tribal governments or communities; . . .

(4) Raise novel legal or policy issues arising out of legal mandates, the President's priorities, or the principles set forth in this Executive order.

Sec. 4. *Planning Mechanism.*

In order to have an effective regulatory program, to provide for coordination of regulations, to maximize consultation and the resolution of potential conflicts at an early stage, to involve the public and its State, local, and tribal officials in regulatory planning, and to ensure that new or revised regulations promote the President's priorities and the principles set forth in this Executive order, these procedures shall be followed, to the extent permitted by law: . . .

(b) *Unified Regulatory Agenda.* For purposes of this subsection, the term "agency" or "agencies" shall also include those considered to be independent regulatory agencies, as defined in 44 U.S.C. 3502(10). Each agency shall prepare an agenda of all regulations under development or review, at a time and in a manner specified by the Administrator of OIRA. The description of each regulatory action shall contain, at a minimum, a regulation identifier number, a brief summary of the action, the legal authority for the action, any legal deadline for the action, and the name and telephone number of a knowledgeable agency official. Agencies may incorporate the information required under 5 U.S.C. 602 and 41 U.S.C. 402 into these agendas.

(c) *The Regulatory Plan.* For purposes of this subsection, the term "agency" or "agencies" shall also include those considered to be independent regulatory agencies, as defined in 44 U.S.C. 3502(10).

(1) As part of the Unified Regulatory Agenda, beginning in 1994, each agency shall prepare a Regulatory Plan (Plan) of the most important significant regulatory actions that the agency reasonably expects to issue in proposed or final form in that fiscal year or thereafter. . . .

(7) The Plans developed by the issuing agency shall be published annually in the October publication of the Unified Regulatory Agenda. This publication shall be made available to the Congress; State, local, and tribal governments; and the public. . . .

Sec. 6. *Centralized Review of Regulations.*

The guidelines set forth below shall apply to all regulatory actions, for both new and existing regulations, by agencies other than those agencies specifically exempted by the Administrator of OIRA:

(a) *Agency Responsibilities.*

(1) Each agency shall (consistent with its own rules, regulations, or procedures) provide the public with meaningful participation in the regulatory process. . . .In addition, each agency should afford the public a meaningful opportunity to comment on any proposed regulation, which in most cases should include a comment period of not less than 60 days. . . .

(3) In addition to adhering to its own rules and procedures and to the requirements of the Administrative Procedure Act, the Regulatory Flexibility Act, the Paperwork Reduction Act, and other applicable law, each agency shall develop its regulatory actions in a timely fashion and adhere to the following procedures with respect to a regulatory action:

(A) Each agency shall provide OIRA, at such times and in the manner specified by the Administrator of OIRA, with a list of its planned regulatory actions, indicating those which the agency believes are significant regulatory actions within the meaning of this Executive order. . . .

(B)   For each matter identified as, or determined by the Administrator of OIRA to be, a significant regulatory action, the issuing agency shall provide to OIRA:

(i)   The text of the draft regulatory action, together with a reasonably detailed description of the need for the regulatory action and an explanation of how the regulatory action will meet that need; and

(ii)   An assessment of the potential costs and benefits of the regulatory action, including an explanation of the manner in which the regulatory action is consistent with a statutory mandate and, to the extent permitted by law, promotes the President's priorities . . . .

(b) *OIRA Responsibilities.* The Administrator of OIRA shall provide meaningful guidance and oversight so that each agency's regulatory actions are consistent with applicable law, the President's priorities, and the principles set forth in this Executive order and do not conflict with the policies or actions of another agency. OIRA shall, to the extent permitted by law, adhere to the following guidelines:

(1) OIRA may review only actions identified by the agency or by OIRA as significant regulatory actions under subsection (a)(3)(A) of this section.

(2) OIRA shall waive review or notify the agency in writing of the results of its review within the following time periods:

(A)   For any notices of inquiry, advance notices of proposed rulemaking, or other preliminary regulatory actions prior to a Notice of Proposed Rulemaking, within 10 working days after the date of submission of the draft action to OIRA;

(B)   For all other regulatory actions, within 90 calendar days after the date of submission . . . .

(3) For each regulatory action that the Administrator of OIRA returns to an agency for further consideration of some or all of its provisions, the Administrator of OIRA shall provide the issuing agency a written explanation for such return, setting forth the pertinent

provision of this Executive order on which OIRA is relying. If the agency head disagrees with some or all of the bases for the return, the agency head shall so inform the Administrator of OIRA in writing. . . .

Sec. 7. *Resolution of Conflicts.*

To the extent permitted by law, disagreements or conflicts between or among agency heads or between OMB and any agency that cannot be resolved by the Administrator of OIRA shall be resolved by the President, or by the Vice President acting at the request of the President, with the relevant agency head (and, as appropriate, other interested government officials). . . .

At the end of this review process, the President, or the Vice President acting at the request of the President, shall notify the affected agency and the Administrator of OIRA of the President's decision with respect to the matter.

Sec. 8. *Publication.*

Except to the extent required by law, an agency shall not publish in the Federal Register or otherwise issue to the public any regulatory action that is subject to review under section 6 of this Executive order until (1) the Administrator of OIRA notifies the agency that OIRA has waived its review of the action or has completed its review without any requests for further consideration, or (2) the applicable time period in section 6(b)(2) expires without OIRA having notified the agency that it is returning the regulatory action for further consideration under section 6(b)(3), whichever occurs first. . . .

Sec. 9. *Agency Authority.*

Nothing in this order shall be construed as displacing the agencies' authority or responsibilities, as authorized by law.

Sec. 10. *Judicial Review.*

Nothing in this Executive order shall affect any otherwise available judicial review of agency action. This Executive order is intended only to improve the internal management of the Federal Government and does not create any right or benefit, substantive or procedural, enforceable at law or equity by a party against the United States, its agencies or instrumentalities, its officers or employees, or any other person.

Notes and Questions

1. *Elaborating on opportunity to comment.* Recall that the APA does not actually establish a minimum time period for the notice-and-comment period for informal rulemaking. E.O. 12,866 does establish a presumptive minimum.

2. *To the extent permitted by law.* Nothing in the Executive Order changes existing laws. The order, of course, would otherwise be an unconstitutional act of lawmaking. The order merely required agencies to exercise their discretion in a certain way. Thus, if a particular organic statute does not, say, permit the analysis of costs, then the agency cannot engage in a cost-benefit analysis.

3. *OIRA.* President Reagan's order centralized review in the Office of Management and Budget (OMB); President Clinton's centralized review in the Office of Information and Regulatory Affairs (OIRA), a subunit of the OMB, which still conducts regulatory review under this executive order to this day.

4. *Subsequent amendments to E.O. 12,866.* All subsequent presidents have kept E.O. 12,866 more or less intact. In 2007, President George W. Bush amended E.O. 12,866 with E.O. 13,422, which included major guidance documents within OIRA's purview. President Obama repealed that order. President Obama supplemented 12,866 with E.O. 13,563 in 2011, which principally announced President Obama's regulatory philosophy. In 2017, President Trump promulgated E.O. 13,771, which directed agencies to eliminate two regulations for each additional new regulation promulgated—of course, "to the extent permitted by law." And E.O. 13,777, also promulgated in 2017, created "regulatory reform officers" whose task is to identify regulations for repeal or modification. President Biden has, in the early days of his administration, repealed both of these Trump Administration executive orders.

D. Debating Presidential Control

In her article, then-Professor Kagan argued that although Congress can structure the executive branch as it sees fit, there is value in presuming that Congress intended the President to have the power to direct the activities of at least non-independent agencies. She argued that such an approach enhances accountability and dynamism. Recall also that Jerry Mashaw argued that delegation enhances accountability because that way presidential elections have real policy consequences. See pp. 599–603 supra.

This section takes a deeper dive into the policy benefits and normative values of presidential control on the one hand, and agency independence on the other. It starts with a full-throated defense of a "unitary executive" in *The Federalist*. But, do the values of a unitary executive still have resonance in a world of broad delegations to the executive? Recall the discussion in *INS v. Chadha*. Today, do we have to fear "legislative aggrandizement," as the Framers feared, or on the contrary executive aggrandizement? Thus, following the excerpts from *The Federalist*, we shall explore a relatively recent functionalist argument by Martin Flaherty for more agency independence because of the aggrandizement of executive power. Our final excerpt argues that the place of agencies in government is subordinate to all three constitutionally named branches, that each shares important controls, and that there should be a balance among the three branches for control. In that excerpt, Peter Strauss argues that we should not sharply distinguish between independent agencies and other executive-branch agencies.

COURSE THEME

EXPERTISE VS. ACCOUNTABILITY
What does Hamilton's argument tell us about the ongoing debate between expertise and accountability today?

Alexander Hamilton, The Federalist No. 70

The New York Packet, March 18, 1788

There is an idea, which is not without its advocates, that a vigorous Executive is inconsistent with the genius of republican government. The enlightened well-wishers to this species of government must at least hope that the supposition is destitute of foundation; since they can never admit its truth, without at the same time admitting the condemnation of their own principles. Energy in the Executive is a leading character in the definition of good government. It is essential to the protection of the community against foreign attacks; it is not less essential to the steady administration of the laws; to the protection of property against those irregular and high-handed combinations which sometimes interrupt the ordinary course of justice; to the security of liberty against the enterprises and assaults of ambition, of faction, and of anarchy. Every man the least conversant in Roman story, knows how often that republic was obliged to take refuge in the absolute power of a single man, under the formidable title of Dictator, as well against the intrigues of ambitious individuals who aspired to the tyranny, and the seditions of whole classes of the community whose conduct threatened the existence of all government, as against the invasions of external enemies who menaced the conquest and destruction of Rome.

There can be no need, however, to multiply arguments or examples on this head. A feeble Executive implies a feeble execution of the government. A feeble execution is but another phrase for a bad execution; and a government ill executed, whatever it may be in theory, must be, in practice, a bad government.

Taking it for granted, therefore, that all men of sense will agree in the necessity of an energetic Executive, it will only remain to inquire, what are the ingredients which constitute this energy? How far can they be combined with those other ingredients which constitute safety in the republican sense? And how far does this combination characterize the plan which has been reported by the convention?

The ingredients which constitute energy in the Executive are, first, unity; secondly, duration; thirdly, an adequate provision for its support; fourthly, competent powers.

The ingredients which constitute safety in the republican sense are, first, a due dependence on the people, secondly, a due responsibility.

Those politicians and statesmen who have been the most celebrated for the soundness of their principles and for the justice of their views, have declared in favor of a single Executive and a numerous legislature. They have with great propriety, considered energy as the most necessary qualification of the former, and have regarded this as most applicable to power in a single hand, while they have, with equal propriety, considered the latter as best adapted to deliberation and wisdom, and best calculated to conciliate the confidence of the people and to secure their privileges and interests.

That unity is conducive to energy will not be disputed. Decision, activity, secrecy, and despatch will generally characterize the proceedings of one man in a much more eminent degree than the proceedings of any greater number; and in proportion as the number is increased, these qualities will be diminished.

This unity may be destroyed in two ways: either by vesting the power in two or more magistrates of equal dignity and authority; or by vesting it ostensibly in one man, subject, in whole or in part, to the control and co-operation of others, in the capacity of counsellors to him. Of the first, the two Consuls of Rome may serve as an example; of the last, we shall find examples in the constitutions of several of the States. New York and New Jersey, if I recollect right, are the only States which have intrusted the executive authority wholly to single men. Both these methods of destroying the unity of the Executive have their partisans; but the votaries of an executive council are the most numerous. They are both liable, if not to equal, to similar objections, and may in most lights be examined in conjunction.

The experience of other nations will afford little instruction on this head. As far, however, as it teaches any thing, it teaches us not to be enamoured of plurality in the Executive. We have seen that the Achaeans, on an experiment of two Praetors, were induced to abolish one. The Roman history records many instances of mischiefs to the republic from the dissensions between the Consuls, and between the military Tribunes, who were at times substituted for the Consuls. But it gives us no specimens of any peculiar advantages derived to the state from the circumstance of the plurality of those magistrates. That the dissensions between them were not more frequent or more fatal, is a matter of astonishment, until we advert to the singular position in which the republic was almost continually placed, and to the prudent policy pointed out by the circumstances of the state, and pursued by the Consuls, of making a division of the government between them. . . .

But quitting the dim light of historical research, attaching ourselves purely to the dictates of reason and good sense, we shall discover much greater cause to reject than to approve the idea of plurality in the Executive, under any modification whatever.

Wherever two or more persons are engaged in any common enterprise or pursuit, there is always danger of difference of opinion. If it be a public trust or office, in which they are clothed with equal dignity and authority, there is peculiar danger of personal emulation and even animosity. From either, and especially from all these causes, the most bitter dissensions are apt to spring. Whenever these happen, they lessen the respectability, weaken the authority, and distract the plans and operation of those whom they divide. If they should unfortunately assail the supreme executive magistracy of a country, consisting of a plurality of persons, they might impede or frustrate the most important measures of the government, in the most critical emergencies of the state. And what is still worse, they might split the community into the most violent and irreconcilable factions, adhering differently to the different individuals who composed the magistracy. . . .

But one of the weightiest objections to a plurality in the Executive . . . is, that it tends to conceal faults and destroy responsibility. Responsibility is of two kinds to censure and to punishment. The first is the more important of the two, especially in an elective office. Man, in public trust, will much oftener act in such a manner as to render him unworthy of being any longer trusted, than in such a manner as to make him obnoxious to legal punishment. But the multiplication of the Executive adds to the difficulty of detection in either case. It often becomes impossible, amidst mutual accusations, to determine on whom the blame or the punishment of a pernicious measure, or series of pernicious measures, ought really to fall. It is shifted from one to another with so much dexterity, and under such plausible appearances, that the public opinion is left in suspense about the real author. The circumstances which may have led to any national miscarriage or misfortune are sometimes so complicated that, where there are a number of actors who may have had different degrees and kinds of agency, though we may clearly see upon the whole that there has been mismanagement, yet it may be impracticable to pronounce to whose account the evil which may have been incurred is truly chargeable. . . .

It is evident from these considerations, that the plurality of the Executive tends to deprive the people of the two greatest securities they can have for the faithful exercise of any delegated power, first, the restraints of public opinion, which lose their efficacy, as well on account of the division of the censure attendant on bad measures among a number, as on account of the uncertainty on whom it ought to fall; and, secondly, the opportunity of discovering with facility and clearness the misconduct of the persons they trust, in order either to their removal from office or to their actual punishment in cases which admit of it. . . .

Martin S. Flaherty, The Most Dangerous Branch

105 Yale L.J. 1725 (1996)

As a general matter, developments in American government over the past two centuries undercut the modern formalist case . . . . [T]wo centuries of change have profoundly reshaped the context in which each of the principal

Founding values so far considered are to be implemented today if they are to be implemented at all. . . .

By far the greatest changes concern the goal of balance, the Founding's most important separation of powers value. As Forrest McDonald recently observed, "[i]t is a commonplace among students of the presidency that the two-plus centuries of American experience under the Constitution have been characterized by a general if irregular drift of authority and responsibility toward the executive branch." This is not to say that Congress cannot, on occasion, still seize the initiative when, as now, it benefits from an effective leadership and a rudderless Chief Executive. But from a larger perspective the overall drift has been inexorable and shows few signs of any long-term shift. It often surprises students to discover Madison's statement, previously noted, that "[t]he legislative department is . . . drawing all power into its impetuous vortex." Were Madison to consider the same problem in light of subsequent developments, he would have little choice but to conclude that if there were any one branch against which "the people ought to indulge all their jealousy and exhaust all their precautions," it would be the executive. . . .

[T]he most clearcut shift toward presidential power has yet to be mentioned. This is, of course, the grand-scale emergence of executive and independent agencies, the "fourth branch of government" also known as the "administrative state." As the nation's problems grew, Progressives and New Dealers believed that so too should the federal response. Congress therefore "not only passed more laws, requiring more execution; it also passed more laws requiring broad-scale policy making before execution." Once more the net beneficiary would be the President, the nominal head of the agencies that would both execute and make policy. But unlike many of the transfers considered so far, this one crossed bright doctrinal lines. Previously, a formalist-minded Supreme Court had held that, while Congress could enact laws that required execution, it could not franchise away its legislative power by passing laws that required broad-scale policymaking. Twice the Court invoked this "nondelegation doctrine" to strike down congressional giveaways. These were, however, the last times the Court tried to keep the floodgates shut.

Here, then, was a threat to separation of powers that functionalists and even formalists could (or should) agree on, though for different reasons. For formalists, the rise of the administrative state could not count as a simple expansion of laws to be executed. . . . As the Court elsewhere indicated, its new stance acknowledged that the administrative state typically wielded "quasi" executive, legislative, and judicial power that could not be easily shoved into any of the three traditional categories. The Federal Trade Commission, for example, was not only "to carry into effect" certain policies, but was "to perform other specified duties as a legislative or as a judicial aid." Broad delegation of authority to what, on the formalist view, is the executive was not therefore necessarily troubling, least of all because it crossed borders that had formally been policed, so long as Congress did not delegate in such a way that threatened such foundational values as balance.

Yet this is just what Congress continued to do. With the New Deal, and the attendant death of the nondelegation doctrine, the giveaway of what had been seen as legislative authority (or something close) became massive. Between 1934 and 1936 alone, Congress established the Securities and Exchange Commission, the National Labor Relations Board, the Bituminous Coal Commission, and the United States Maritime Commission, to name a few. This trend, moreover, has generally accelerated during the five decades since F.D.R.'s death. At least as important as the scope of modern delegation, however, is to whom the power has been delegated. If there has been any net beneficiary of Congress's abdication of authority, it has been the President. In formal terms, Presidents ultimately exercise the appointments and removal powers over the heads of both executive and independent agencies (a distinction that is becoming increasingly difficult to maintain). Informally, Presidents influence agencies through ex parte and secret contacts and through executive agencies established to coordinate agency activities. This is not to say that Congress lacks methods of influencing agency conduct. It is to say, however, that a substantial measure of power that under the nondelegation doctrine would by definition have resided in Congress has since fallen to the President.

Any approach that ignores changes bearing upon ongoing constitutional commitments overlooks them not so much at its own peril, but at the peril of the commitments it purports to further. Where the commitment is balance, even the most glancing survey indicates that the executive branch long ago supplanted its legislative counterpart as the most powerful—and therefore most dangerous—in the sense that the Founders meant. This shift toward presidential government suggests that at a minimum we need an approach that would permit Congress to maintain some control over the authority the Court now permits it to delegate away to the administrative state. More broadly, this shift implies that invoking separation of powers to invalidate congressional attempts to keep pace with the presidency is not only wrong headed but, more important still, fundamentally unfaithful to our founding values. . . .

Two hundred years of practice have also affected the Founding commitment to accountability, properly recaptured. On this view, accountability should no longer be the province of one branch of government but instead should rest with both houses of the legislature, the executive, and, less directly, even the judiciary. In this way, separation of powers tamed accountability by ensuring that government, or any part of it, could threaten liberty in the name of last year's election results. It also refined accountability by ensuring that government action could not proceed legitimately only if it rested on sustained, widespread, and deliberative support as reflected in the agreement of several components of the government, in turn reflecting several soundings of popular will through staggered congressional and presidential elections.

If any branch at first seemed the most likely to claim electoral mandates for tyrannical or precipitous actions, it was the legislature. By contrast, the Founders generally conceived of the presidency not first and foremost as a representative post, but as a relatively apolitical award for men who had demonstrated extraordinary virtue and character through selfless public service. No longer. As unitarians are quick to point out, at present no elected official plausibly claims to be more representative or accountable than the President. He, or one day she, can do this on the strength of elections that, far from filtered affairs envisioned by the electoral college process, long ago evolved into tournaments that are in part plebiscite, in larger part popularity contests. . . .

In this light, accountability appears as nearly the opposite of the trump card that proponents, and even many opponents, of the unitary executive take it to be. As with balance, the changes in government practice since the Founding cut against, not for, executive power. In each case the trick is to avoid confusing original applications of a constitutional norm with the norm itself, properly reconstructed. Contrary to the usual assumption, here was not the rudimentary accountability that modern unitarians extol. Instead, the Founders reconceptualized the idea to render it more safe and more reflective of considered popular choice. Initially, Congress put the greatest pressure on this more sophisticated commitment by virtue of its superior representativeness. As unitarians are the first to argue, this is exactly the area in which the President now advances a comparable, if not more compelling, claim. Any response faithful to the Founding, therefore, should greet this development not as a cause for celebration but concern. . . .

From this perspective—the Founding emphasis on purpose and process— the Court's historically novel forays into separation of powers have been bad enough. From the perspective of changed circumstances—outlined earlier— the outcome of those sallies has been even worse. Now should it be clear how much worse. Too often the Court has managed to get matters exactly wrong, going out of its way to exacerbate the very evils that separation of powers was designed to curb. Most often these missteps have come about when the Court has invalidated mechanisms that the political branches had developed as responses to presidential government, including the legislative veto as well as limits on executive removal and appointment authority. . . .

The analysis is much the same when applied to removal authority, only stronger. Congress early on considered placing statutory limitations on the executive's presumed authority to dismiss government officials, at first balking, but then reversing itself with the Tenure of Office Act of 1820. Only in this century have limitations on presidential removal authority, mainly restricting the exercise of that authority "for cause," become a staple of the Court's separation of powers jurisprudence. These have included restrictions upon the discharge of "executive" officials in *Myers,* of officials in "independent agencies" in *Humphrey's Executor,* of Congress's own officials who ostensibly executed the law in *Bowsher,* and, coming full circle, of "executive" officials in *Morrison.* Each of these variations raises its own particular considerations, especially *Bowsher.* Nonetheless, they all share the common thread of remaining faithful to the Founding conception as applied to contemporary practice.

The removal issue, in fact, exposes formalist analysis at its least grounded. Unlike the legislative veto, arguably no specific text serves as a candidate to determine matters. Absent a "Removals Clause," or something reasonably close, opponents of legislative involvement must retreat to an originalist baseline that assumes that the removal of government officials is categorically an executive task. In this way, unitarians can claim that the removal authority is inherently executive, bootstrap the power to the all-purpose Executive Vesting Clause, or both. Yet such an originalist baseline is precisely what the original understanding does not support. While some of the Founders may have believed that removal was necessarily an executive act, many, including the proexecutive Hamilton, did not—too many to assume sufficient agreement on the matter.

Rather, the Constitution's silence left the issue, as it did so many others, to the political processes that it explicitly set forth.

By contrast, limitations on executive removal authority comport with those values that did initially command widespread support—or at least they comport with modern values. Start again by considering balance. As the *Humphrey's* Court recognized, preventing Congress from imposing neutral restrictions on the dismissal of "independent" agency officials would accord the President a powerful weapon for controlling administrative policymaking, even as Congress was ceding even more policymaking control to such officials. As Brandeis earlier recognized—and as the Court came to appreciate in *Morrison*—similar threat to balance may arise from unrestricted presidential control over "purely executive" officials as well. In the abstract, policymaking by officials subject to congressional approval may well present a closer case. In the real world of presidential dominance, however, such arrangements should not necessarily trigger constitutional concern. They may even function to maintain interbranch balance, especially when Congress limits its own removal authority to neutral, "for cause" reasons.

As with the legislative veto, a proper reconstruction of accountability turns this value against its usual champions. When the goal is diffusing accountability rather than concentrating it, and when the presidency lays the most plausible claim to the concentrated version, congressional involvement in the critical area of removal should meet with approval instead of invalidation. Moreover, the case is even more compelling than that of the legislative veto. Here, Congress would have no other way of checking officials who, to follow the example, promulgated massive environmental legislation at the President's behest, in a manner consistent with a general statutory delegation but not reflective of an electorate that has yet to back the President's approach fully by returning a compliant House and Senate. Admittedly, the value of joint accountability provides less support for arrangements in which, as in *Bowsher*, Congress itself wields removal authority absent presidential involvement. In this situation, even a "for cause" limitation on removals would not expand the input of the elected branches. That said, the restriction to neutral criteria would at least lessen concern about the concentration of unlimited authority.

As a final matter, efficiency concerns again may not support the device in question, but they do not undermine it either. Once more, it is not clear that removal limitations will always work to produce less government rather than more. Insulated officials may just as easily resist presidential attempts to reduce governmental activity as expand it, a discovery made by President Reagan much to his chagrin. But even if they did produce stasis, removal limitations would not rise to the level of constitutional concern. As with the legislative veto, post-New Deal experience suggests that the mechanism has not exactly impeded the government's ability to act with sufficient energy. Short of that, the extent to which it hampers the President's efficient "chain of command" is simply the price of balance and joint accountability. . . .

Peter L. Strauss, The Place of Agencies in Government

84 Colum. L. Rev. 573, 575–80 (1984)

At the root of these problems lies a difficulty in understanding the relationships between the agencies that actually do the work of law-administration, whose existence is barely hinted at in the Constitution, and the three constitutionally named repositories of all governmental power—Congress, President, and Supreme Court. When, for example, a federal agency adopts a legislative "rule" following the procedures of the Administrative Procedure Act, how is this act to be understood constitutionally? In a colloquial sense, the agency is acting legislatively—that is, creating general statements of positive law whose application to an indefinite class awaits future acts and proceedings. Validly adopted legislative rules are identical to statutes in their impact on all relevant legal actors—those subject to their constraints, those responsible for their administration, and judges or others who may have occasion to consider them in the course of their activities. Does it follow that in the constitutional sense what the agency is doing should be regarded as an exercise of the "legislative Powers . . . granted" by article I, "all" of which are vested in Congress? Or, given statutory authorization, is it to be regarded as an exercise of the executive authority vested in the President by article II, the judicial power placed in the Supreme Court (and statutorily created inferior courts) by article III, or authority merely statutory in provenance? The Constitution names and ascribes functions only to the Congress, President and Supreme Court, sitting in uneasy relation at the apex of the governmental structure; it leaves undiscussed what might be the necessary and permissible relationships of each of these three constitutional bodies to the agency making the rule. Is it significant for any of these purposes whether the rulemaking authority has been assigned to a cabinet department or to an independent regulatory commission? Indeed, does it make sense to look to the Constitution, written so many years ago, for contemporary guidance or limits on the sorts of arrangements Congress can make?

Three differing approaches have been used in the effort to understand issues such as these. The first, "separation of powers," supposes that what government does can be characterized in terms of the kind of act performed—legislating, enforcing, and determining the particular application of law—and that for the safety of the citizenry from tyrannous government these three functions must be kept in distinct places. Congress legislates, and it only legislates; the President sees to the faithful execution of those laws and, in the domestic context at least, that is all he does; the courts decide specific cases of law-application, and that is their sole function. These three powers of government are kept radically separate, because if the same body exercised all three of them, or even two, it might no longer be possible to keep it within the constraints of law.

"Separation of functions" suggests a somewhat different idea, grounded more in considerations of individual fairness in particular proceedings than in the need for structural protection against tyrannical government generally. It admits that for agencies (as distinct from the constitutionally named heads of government) the same body often does exercise all three of the characteristic governmental powers, albeit in a web of other controls—judicial review and legislative and executive oversight. As these controls are thought to give reasonable assurance against systemic lawlessness, the separation-of-functions inquiry asks to what extent constitutional due process for the particular individual(s) who may be involved with an agency in a given proceeding requires special measures to assure the objectivity or impartiality of that proceeding. The powers are not kept separate, at least in general, but certain procedural protections—for example, the requirement of an on-the-record hearing before an "impartial" trier—may be afforded.

"Checks and balances" is the third idea, one that to a degree bridges the gap between these two domains. Like separation of powers, it seeks to protect the citizens from the emergence of tyrannical government by establishing multiple heads of authority in government, which are then pitted one against another in a continuous struggle; the intent of that struggle is to deny to any one (or two) of them the capacity ever to consolidate all governmental authority in itself, while permitting the whole effectively to carry forward the work of government. Unlike separation of powers, however, the checks-and-balances idea does not suppose a radical division of government into three parts, with particular functions neatly parceled out among them. Rather, the focus is on relationships and interconnections, on maintaining the conditions in which the intended struggle at the apex may continue. From this perspective, as from the perspective of separation of functions, it is not important how powers below the apex are treated; the important question is whether the relationship of each of the three named actors of the Constitution to the exercise of those powers is such as to promise a continuation of their effective independence and interdependence.

In the pages following I argue that, for any consideration of the structure given law-administration below the very apex of the governmental structure, the rigid separation-of-powers compartmentalization of governmental functions should be abandoned in favor of analysis in terms of separation of functions and checks and balances. Almost fifty years of experience has accustomed lawyers and judges to accepting the independent regulatory commissions, in the metaphor, as a "headless 'fourth branch'" of government. Although the resulting theoretical confusion has certainly been noticed, we accept the idea of potent actors in government joining judicial, legislative and executive functions, yet falling outside the constitutionally described schemata of three named branches embracing among them the entire allocated authority of government. What would be the consequences of so viewing all government regulators? I believe such a shift in view would carry with it significant analytical advantages by directing our focus away from the truly insignificant structural and procedural differences between the "independent regulatory commissions" and other agencies to the relationships existing between each such agency and the three named branches. Each such agency is to some extent "independent" of each of the named branches and to some extent in relationship with each. The continued achievement of the intended balance and interaction among the three named actors at the top of government, with each continuing to have effective responsibility for its unique core function, depends on the existence of relationships between each of these actors and each agency within which that function can find voice. A shorthand way of putting the argument is that we should stop pretending that all our government (as distinct from its highest levels) can be allocated into three neat parts. The theory of separation-of-powers breaks down when attempting to locate administrative and regulatory agencies within one of the three branches; its vitality, rather, lies in the formulation and specification of the controls that Congress, the Supreme Court and the President may exercise over administration and regulation.

Bits and pieces of history contribute to our assumptions about the place of agencies in government—most notably, that there is a something called an "independent regulatory commission" that is somehow different in what it does from a cabinet department, and that need have no relation with the President though it is strongly associated with Congress and the courts. These bits and pieces have led us astray. The Department of Agriculture and the Securities and Exchange Commission both adopt rules, execute laws, and adjudicate cases, all pursuant to statutory authority. Why is that not the forbidden conjoining of powers? The question has been more obscured than answered, perhaps, by describing what the agencies do as "quasi-adjudication" or "quasi-legislation," as if the operations performed were in fact not the same three characteristic operations of government our eighteenth-century political theorists insisted must be kept separate for public protection. If the constitutional scheme were to require locating these agencies in one or another part of government, as more formalistic separation-of-powers opinions have sometimes hinted, which part would they be in? And how could they then be authorized to perform the functions associated with another part?

From the perspective suggested here, the important fact is that an agency is neither Congress nor President nor Court, but an inferior part of government. Each agency is subject to control relationships with some or all of the three constitutionally named branches, and those relationships give an assurance—functionally similar to that provided by the separation-of-powers notion for the constitutionally named bodies—that they will not pass out of control. Powerful and potentially arbitrary as they may be, the Secretary of Agriculture and the Chairman of the SEC for this reason do not present the threat that led the framers to insist on a splitting of the authority of government at its very top. What we have, then, are three named repositories of authorizing power and control, and an infinity of institutions to which parts of the authority of each may be lent. The three must share the reins of control; means must be found of assuring that no one of them becomes dominant. But it is not terribly important to number or allocate the horses that pull the carriage of government. . . .

 TEST YOUR KNOWLEDGE: To assess your understanding of the material in this chapter, **click here** to take a quiz.

CHAPTER SEVEN

Agency Adjudications, Article III, and Due Process

This final chapter on administrative agencies and the Constitution addresses their relationship to the judicial power and due process. When agencies adjudicate cases, are they not deciding cases "arising under . . . the laws of the United States," Art. III, § 2, and thus exercising the judicial power of the United States? And if so, aren't such adjudications supposed to take place in Article III federal courts whose judges are protected by lifetime tenure and salary protections? Finally, when an agency adjudication might deprive someone of a benefit or privilege, does the due process clause apply? If so, what amount of process is required? This chapter addresses Article III first, and then the due process clause. As we shall see, the two parts of the Constitution are related, at least historically, and this ordering will make some logical sense as we proceed with the following materials.

A. Article III Limits

1. Judicial Power and Executive Branch Adjudications

Not every adjudication requires an Article III court to hear or resolve. Some cases are sufficiently judicial in nature that they are amenable to resolution by a court, but are not "exclusively" judicial such that a court *must* hear them. The distinction between those cases that a court must hear, and those for which a court is not necessary, was historically described as the distinction between "private rights" cases and "public rights" cases.

COURSE THEME

NONEXCLUSIVE POWER

As you read these materials, can you distinguish those cases that must be heard by a judicial court and those that can be heard either by a court or by an agency? Could the latter types of cases be considered "nonexclusive" judicial power—Congress can, but doesn't have to, assign them to the courts?

One quintessential example of a private rights case is a criminal case or civil suit between a private individual and the government, where the government is seeking to deprive that individual of life, liberty, or property. (Hence, the due process clause would also apply.) Another classic example of a private rights case is a tort or contract suit between two private individuals. The government or public has nothing to do with such cases,

Defined Term

PRIVATE RIGHTS: Private rights are generally those rights you have in the state of nature, that do not depend on government for their existence: primarily your rights to life, liberty, and real and personal property.

except of course that the government can establish the law governing these private relations (the stuff of a first-year law school curriculum). Traditionally, private rights cases such as these had to be heard in real courts. Indeed, Article III, section 2, paragraph 3 of the Constitution, and the Sixth Amendment, require jury trials for criminal cases, and the Seventh Amendment also preserves the jury trial right for suits at common law with an amount-in-controversy of at least twenty dollars, suggesting that real courts probably had to hear such cases. Historically, "due process of law" probably also required judicial trials, with real juries and proper judges, for these kinds of cases.

Defined Term

PUBLIC RIGHTS: In contrast to private rights, public rights are typically rights that the government might choose to grant some of its citizens, like a land grant, a patent, or welfare benefits. Once the government actually makes the grant, however, the granted land or money usually becomes the private property of the recipient.

On the other hand, the classic example of a "public rights" case is a claim against the government of the United States. The due process clause would not apply because the government is not seeking to deprive anyone of life, liberty, or property; it is the private person seeking to get something from the government. Such cases could include not only tort claims against the government, but also claims for an entitlement. Recall one of our earliest statutes, the statute assuming the payments to the invalid veterans of the revolutionary war. If the War Department had denied a claim for a pension (suppose the department concluded that the individual was not actually an invalid, or was not actually a veteran), there was no remedy in court. The individual could petition Congress for a private bill, but that was about it.

Indeed, in the 1792 version of the Invalid Pensions Act, Congress allowed circuit courts to decide on pension claims, but their decisions had to be forwarded to the Secretary of War for final decision. Several justices of the Supreme Court, while riding circuit, had declared this Act to be unconstitutional because it either assigned non-judicial duties to the courts, or because it made judicial decisions reviewable by an executive-branch official. Congress remedied the statute by providing that the *judges* of the circuit courts, but not the circuit courts themselves, could hear such claims, thereby effectively assigning the judges, but not the courts themselves, non-judicial duties. There is nothing in the Constitution preventing judges from also exercising some executive duties; there is an "Incompatibility Clause," but this prohibits members of *Congress* from simultaneously holding executive offices. U.S. Const. art. I, § 6, para. 2. There was also no question that the Secretary of War (or Congress) could have had final say in such matters, and the statute did give the Secretary of War final say. David P. Currie, The Constitution in Congress: The Federalist Period, 1789–1801 at 55 & n. 305 (1997); id. at 155.

Why? Why was a court not needed? The traditional view was rooted in the government's sovereign immunity—the government's immunity from suit without its consent. If the government doesn't have to consent to be sued, then there's quite literally nothing that one can do if the government denies a claim to an entitlement. And if the government can choose not to consent to be sued, then it can consent to be sued on certain conditions—for example, by adjudicating the case in the executive branch itself. Simply put, because the government never had to agree to give a privilege such as a pension in the first place, and because the government never had to consent to be sued if such a privilege were wrongfully withheld, the government could permit the adjudication of such public rights

Defined Term

SOVEREIGN IMMUNITY: The government's traditional immunity from suits for money damages. The government can waive this immunity.

cases in an executive tribunal or agency. See William Baude, *Adjudication Outside Article III*, 133 Harv. L. Rev. 1511, 1542–44, 1567 (2020).

Perhaps it is a mistake to define public rights as those to which sovereign immunity applies. It could be that sovereign immunity is merely consistent with the private-rights, public-rights distinction. As Caleb Nelson has argued, sovereign immunity only applied where private rights were not at stake. Caleb Nelson, *Adjudication in the Political Branches*, 107 Colum. L. Rev. 559, 582–85 (2007). Private rights are those rights we could have exercised in the state of nature, where we have the right to life, the right to move about freely and pursue an occupation, the right to acquire and possess property. We don't enjoy such rights by the grace of government. In contrast, "public rights" or "privileges" only exist because government exists and has chosen to confer such rights on individuals. In other words, we all have a "private right" to work and acquire property for ourselves, but if we have a "right" to a welfare check, it is only because society has chosen to give us that right. It is therefore not a private right, but a "public" right or a public "privilege." Id. at 567–68.

Whether the distinction is rooted in sovereign immunity, natural rights, or both, the Supreme Court recognized the distinction between private and public rights cases in *Murray's Lessee v. Hoboken Land & Improvement Company*, where the Court observed that

> there are matters, involving public rights, which may be presented in such form that the judicial power is capable of acting on them, and which are susceptible of judicial determination, but which congress may or may not bring within the cognizance of the courts of the United States, as it may deem proper.

59 U.S. (18 How.) 272, 284 (1856). Thus public rights cases *could* be decided by courts, but Congress did not have to assign such cases to the court system. It could assign such cases to the executive branch, or could even decide such claims by congressional committee. For the first several years of the Republic, Congress directly decided many claims against the government by private bill, and it eventually assigned the resolution of such claims to a *non*-Article III court of claims. David P. Currie, The Constitution in Congress, Democrats and Whigs, 1829–1861, at 199–202 (2005) (discussing evolution of the court of claims and congressional resolution of petitions).

Importantly, there do appear to be prominent examples in which non-Article III courts hear private-rights claims. Perhaps the most prominent are the state courts, the territorial courts, and the courts of the District of Columbia, most of whose judges do *not* enjoy lifetime tenure or salary protections. These courts do routinely hear private rights cases. The idea appears to have been that these

Defined Term

ARTICLE III COURT: A court whose judges enjoy lifetime tenure and salary protections, as provided in Article III of the Constitution.

courts are exercising the authority of another sovereign altogether. State courts can hear federal claims, and that's constitutional even though many state-court judges do not have the same protections as do Article III judges because state courts are also exercising the sovereignty and judicial power of the states. And in the District of Columbia and the territories, the courts not only adjudicate federal claims, but also the traditional stuff of state courts—from local crimes to small tort and contract disputes that usually could not have been heard in a federal court of an established state. Thus, these courts exercise judicial power, but not the

Defined Term

NON-ARTICLE III COURT: A court whose judges do not enjoy lifetime tenure or salary protections, and who usually serve for a term of years.

"judicial power of the United States." They exercise the judicial power of the state, of the territory, or of the District of Columbia, and can hear claims based under federal law or under another state's law under basic conflict-of-laws principles that require courts to decide what substantive law governs a dispute between parties. See generally Baude, *Adjudication Outside Article III*, supra, at 1523–40. Importantly, the framers of the Constitution expected state courts to hear federal cases pursuant to the so-called "Madisonian Compromise" in the Convention: to resolve the difference between the New Jersey Plan (no lower federal courts) and the Virginia Plan (which proposed the establishment of a national court system), the framers compromised by establishing one supreme court, and leaving it up to Congress whether or

Defined Term

MADISONIAN COMPROMISE: The term for the decision of the Constitutional Convention to mandate the establishment only of one supreme court, leaving to Congress whether to establish lower federal courts.

not to establish lower federal courts. Id. at 1524.

The other exception is purely historical: Military courts in the executive branch most assuredly have tried private rights cases. These courts can even order the execution of American citizens. Outside of the military context, only a federal court could have heard such claims. The use of military courts for military discipline and punishment is simply a historical exception permitting the executive branch, in those cases, to exercise what otherwise looks like pure, exclusive judicial power—the power to apply existing law to facts and adjudicate deprivations of life, liberty, or property—that ordinarily would have to be exercised by a federal court. Whether we call the exercise of this power by military tribunals (and the President) "executive power" or "judicial power" might matter at least some of the time. If military justice is merely an exercise of executive power, then appeals of such military decisions to the federal courts cannot go straight to the Supreme Court, but must first be filed in a lower federal court. See Marbury v. Madison, 5 U.S. (1 Cranch) 137 (1803) (holding that Congress cannot expand the original jurisdiction of the Supreme Court). If at least some military justice decisions are "judicial," then the Supreme Court can hear such cases directly via its appellate jurisdiction. See Ortiz v. United States, 138 S. Ct. 2165 (2018) (holding that decisions of the Court of Appeals for the Armed Forces, whose judges do not enjoy lifetime tenure and salary protections, are nevertheless "judicial" such that the Supreme Court could hear a direct appeal).

With all of this context in hand, the question for administrative law is whether and when can the executive branch adjudicate cases over, for example, social security benefits, or order an employer to pay backpay to an employee, and so on. As we have seen, administrative agencies adjudicate cases all the time. Why can they do so? Are these all "public rights" cases? Many certainly are. But it also seems that administrative agencies often adjudicate cases that traditionally would have been considered to be private rights cases. Is that constitutional? The next section addresses a watershed case confronting such issues.

2. Birth of the Modern Era

Crowell v. Benson

285 U.S. 22 (1932)

MR. CHIEF JUSTICE HUGHES delivered the opinion of the Court.

This suit was brought in the District Court to enjoin the enforcement of an award made by petitioner Crowell, as Deputy Commissioner of the United States Employees' Compensation Commission, in favor of the petitioner Knudsen and against the respondent Benson. The award was made under the Longshoremen's and Harbor Workers' Compensation Act (Act of March 4, 1927, 44 Stat. 1424), and rested upon the finding of the deputy commissioner that Knudsen was injured while in the employ of Benson and performing service upon the navigable waters of the United States. The complainant alleged that the award was contrary to law for the reason that Knudsen was not at the time of his injury an employee of the complainant and his claim was not 'within the jurisdiction' of the Deputy Commissioner. An amended complaint charged that the act was unconstitutional upon the grounds that it violated the due process clause of the Fifth Amendment, the provision of the Seventh Amendment as to trial by jury, that of the Fourth Amendment as to unreasonable search and seizure, and the provisions of article 3 with respect to the judicial power of the United States. The District Judge denied motions to dismiss and granted a hearing de novo upon the facts and the law, expressing the opinion that the act would be invalid if not construed to permit such a hearing. The case was transferred to the admiralty docket, answers were filed presenting the issue as to the fact of employment, and, the evidence of both parties having been heard, the District Court decided that Knudsen was not in the employ of the petitioner and restrained the enforcement of the award. The decree was affirmed by the Circuit Court of Appeals and this Court granted writs of certiorari.

The question of the validity of the act may be considered in relation to (1) its provisions defining substantive rights and (2) its procedural requirements.

First. The act has two limitations that are fundamental. It deals exclusively with compensation in respect of disability or death resulting 'from an injury occurring upon the navigable waters of the United States' if recovery 'through workmen's compensation proceedings may not validly be provided by State law,' and it applies only when the relation of master and servant exists. Section 3. 'Injury,' within the statute, 'means accidental injury or death arising out of and in the course of employment,' and the term 'employer' means one 'any of whose employees are employed in maritime employment, in whole or in part,' upon such navigable waters. . . .

The propriety of providing by federal statute for compensation of employees in such cases had been expressly recognized by this Court, and within its sphere the statute was designed to accomplish the same general purpose as the Workmen's Compensation Laws of the states. In defining substantive rights, the act provides for recovery in the absence of fault, classifies disabilities resulting from injuries, fixes the range of compensation in case of disability or death, and designates the classes of beneficiaries. In view of federal power to alter and revise the maritime law, there appears to be no room for objection on constitutional grounds to the creation of these rights . . . .

Second. The objections to the procedural requirements of the act relate to the extent of the administrative authority which it confers. The administration of the act—'except as otherwise specifically provided'—was given to the United States Employees' Compensation Commission, which was authorized to establish compensation districts, appoint deputy commissioners, and make regulations. Claimants must give written notice to the deputy commissioner and to the employer of the injury or death within thirty days thereafter; the deputy commissioner may excuse failure to give such notice for satisfactory reasons. If the employer contests the right to compensation, he is to file notice to that effect. A claim for compensation must be filed with the deputy commissioner within a prescribed period, and it is provided that the deputy commissioner shall have full authority to hear and determine all questions in respect to the claim. Sections 13, 19(a).

Within ten days after the claim is filed, the deputy commissioner, in accordance with regulations prescribed by the Commission, must notify the employer and any other person who is considered by the deputy commissioner to be an interested party. The deputy commissioner is required to make, or cause to be made, such investigations as he deems to be necessary, and upon application of any interested party must order a hearing, upon notice, at which the claimant and the employer may present evidence. Employees claiming compensation must submit to medical examination. In conducting investigations and hearings, the deputy commissioner is not bound by common law or statutory rules of evidence, or by technical or formal rules or procedure, except as the act provides, but he is to proceed in such manner 'as to best ascertain the rights of the parties.' Section 23(a). He may issue subpoenas, administer oaths, compel the attendance and testimony of witnesses, the production of documents or other evidence or the taking of depositions, and may do all things conformable to law which may be necessary to enable him effectively to discharge his duties. . . .

A compensation order becomes effective when filed, and, unless proceedings are instituted to suspend it or set it aside it becomes final at the expiration of thirty days. . . .

The act further provides that, if a compensation order is 'not in accordance with law,' it 'may be suspended or set aside, in whole or in part, through injunction proceedings, mandatory or otherwise, brought by any party in interest' against the deputy commissioner making the order and instituted in the federal District Court for the judicial district in which the injury occurred. . . . Beneficiaries of awards or the deputy commissioner may apply for enforcement to the federal District Court, and, if the court determines that the order 'was made and served in accordance with law,' obedience may be compelled by writ of injunction or other proper process. Section 21(c).

As the claims which are subject to the provisions of the act are governed by the maritime law as established by the Congress and are within the admiralty jurisdiction, the objection raised by the respondent's pleading as to the right to a trial by jury under the Seventh Amendment [right to a jury] is unavailing [because there were no jury trials in admiralty—Ed.] . . . . The other objections as to procedure invoke the due process clause and the provision as to the judicial power of the United States.

1.   The contention under the due process clause of the Fifth Amendment relates to the determination of questions of fact. Rulings of the deputy commissioner upon questions of law are without finality. So far as the latter are concerned, full opportunity is afforded for their determination by the federal courts through proceedings to suspend or to set aside a compensation order . . . [or] in a proceeding by a beneficiary to compel obedience to a compensation order is dependent upon a determination by the court that the order was lawfully made and served. Moreover, the statute contains no express limitation attempting to preclude the court, in proceedings to set aside an order as not in accordance with law, from making its own examination and determination of

facts whenever that is deemed to be necessary to enforce a constitutional right properly asserted. . . .

Apart from cases involving constitutional rights to be appropriately enforced by proceedings in court, there can be no doubt that the act contemplates that as to questions of fact, arising with respect to injuries to employees within the purview of the act, the findings of the deputy commissioner, supported by evidence and within the scope of his authority, shall be final. To hold otherwise would be to defeat the obvious purpose of the legislation to furnish a prompt, continuous, expert, and inexpensive method for dealing with a class of questions of fact which are peculiarly suited to examination and determination by an administrative agency specially assigned to that task. The object is to secure within the prescribed limits of the employer's liability an immediate investigation and a sound practical judgment, and the efficacy of the plan depends upon the finality of the determinations of fact with respect to the circumstances, nature, extent, and consequences of the employee's injuries and the amount of compensation that should be awarded . . . . The use of the administrative method for these purposes, assuming due notice, proper opportunity to be heard, and that findings are based upon evidence, falls easily within the principle of the decisions sustaining similar procedure against objections under the due process clauses of the Fifth and Fourteenth Amendments. . . .

2. The contention based upon the judicial power of the United States, as extended 'to all Cases of admiralty and maritime Jurisdiction' (Const. art. 3), presents a distinct question. In *Murray's Lessee v. Hoboken Land & Improvement Company,* 18 How. 272, 284, this Court, speaking through Mr. Justice Curtis, said: 'To avoid misconstruction upon so grave a subject, we think it proper to state that we do not consider congress can either withdraw from judicial cognizance any matter which, from its nature, is the subject of a suit at the common law, or in equity, or admiralty; nor, on the other hand, can it bring under the judicial power a matter which, from its nature, is not a subject for judicial determination.'

The question in the instant case, in this aspect, can be deemed to relate only to determinations of fact. . . . The Congress did not attempt to define questions of law, and the generality of the description leaves no doubt of the intention to reserve to the Federal court full authority to pass upon all matters which this Court had held to fall within that category. . . .

As to determinations of fact, the distinction is at once apparent between cases of private right and those which arise between the government and persons subject to its authority in connection with the performance of the constitutional functions of the executive or legislative departments. The Court referred to this distinction in *Murray's Lessee v. Hoboken Land & Improvement Company, supra*, pointing out that 'there are matters, involving public rights, which may be presented in such form that the judicial power is capable of acting on them, and which are susceptible of judicial determination, but which congress may or may not bring within the cognizance of the courts of the United States, as it may deem proper.' Thus the Congress, in exercising the powers confided to it, may establish 'legislative' courts (as distinguished from 'constitutional courts in which the judicial power conferred by the Constitution can be deposited') which are to form part of the government of territories or of the District of Columbia, or to serve as special tribunals 'to examine and determine various matters, arising between the government and others, which from their nature do not require judicial determination and yet are susceptible of it.' But 'the mode of determining matters of this class is completely within congressional control. Congress may reserve to itself the power to decide, may delegate that power to executive officers, or may commit it to judicial tribunals.' *Ex parte Bakelite Corporation*, 279 U. S. 438, 451. Familiar illustrations of administrative agencies created for the determination of such matters are found in connection with the exercise of the congressional power as to interstate and foreign commerce, taxation, immigration, the public lands, public health, the facilities of the post office, pensions, and payments to veterans.

The present case does not fall within the categories just described, but is one of private right, that is, of the liability of one individual to another under the law as defined. But, in cases of that sort, there is no requirement that, in order to maintain the essential attributes of the judicial power, all determinations of fact in constitutional courts shall be made by judges. On the common-law side of the federal courts, the aid of juries is not only deemed appropriate but is required by the Constitution itself. In cases of equity and admiralty, it is historic practice to call to the assistance of the courts, without the consent of the parties, masters, and commissioners or assessors, to pass upon certain classes of questions, as, for example, to take and state an account or to find the amount of damages. While the reports of masters and commissioners in such cases are essentially of an advisory nature, it has not been the practice to disturb their findings when they are properly based upon evidence, in the absence of errors of law, and the parties have no right to demand that the court shall redetermine the facts thus found. . . .

Findings of fact by the deputy commissioner . . . are closely analogous to the findings of the amount of damages that are made according to familiar practice by commissioners or assessors, and the reservation of full authority to the court to deal with matters of law provides for the appropriate exercise of the judicial function in this class of cases. For the purposes stated, we are unable to find any constitutional obstacle to the action of the Congress in availing itself of a method shown by experience to be essential in order to apply its standards to the thousands of cases involved, thus relieving the courts of a most serious burden while preserving their complete authority to insure the proper application of the law.

3.   What has been said thus far relates to the determination of claims of employees within the purview of the act. A different question is presented where the determinations of fact are fundamental or 'jurisdictional,' in the sense that their existence is a condition precedent to the operation of the statutory scheme. These fundamental requirements are that the injury occurs upon the navigable waters of the United States, and that the relation of master and servant exists. These conditions are indispensable to the application of the statute, not only because the Congress has so provided explicitly (section 3), but also because the power of the Congress to enact the legislation turns upon the existence of these conditions.

In amending and revising the maritime law, the Congress cannot reach beyond the constitutional limits which are inherent in the admiralty and maritime jurisdiction. Unless the injuries to which the act relates occur upon the navigable waters of the United States, they fall outside that jurisdiction. Not only is navigability itself a question of fact, as waters that are navigable in fact are navigable in law, but, where navigability is not in dispute, the locality of the injury, that is, whether it has occurred upon the navigable waters of the United States, determines the existence of the congressional power to create the liability prescribed by the statute. . . . If the person injured was not an employee of the person sought to be held, or if the injury did not occur upon the navigable waters of the United States, there is no ground for an assertion that the person against whom the proceeding was directed could constitutionally be subjected, in the absence of fault upon his part, to the liability which the statute creates.

In relation to these basic facts, the question is not the ordinary one as to the propriety of provision for administrative determinations. Nor have we simply the question of due process in relation to notice and hearing. It is rather a question of the appropriate maintenance of the federal judicial power in requiring the observance of constitutional restrictions. It is the question whether the Congress may substitute for constitutional courts, in which the judicial power of the United States is vested, an administrative agency—in this instance a single deputy commissioner—for the final determination of the existence of the facts upon which the enforcement of the constitutional rights of the citizen depend. The recognition of the utility and convenience of administrative agencies for the investigation and finding of facts within their proper province, and the support of their authorized action, does not require the conclusion that there is no limitation of their use, and that the Congress could completely oust the courts of all determinations of fact by vesting the authority to make them with finality in its own instrumentalities or in the executive department. That would be to sap the judicial power as it exists under the federal Constitution, and to establish a government of a bureaucratic character alien to our system, wherever fundamental rights depend, as not infrequently they do depend, upon the facts, and finality as to facts becomes in effect finality in law.

. . . . [W]here administrative bodies have been appropriately created to meet the exigencies of certain classes of cases and their action is of a judicial character, the question of the conclusiveness of their administrative findings of fact generally arises where the facts are clearly not jurisdictional and the scope of review as to such facts has been determined by the applicable legislation. None of the decisions of this sort touch the question which is presented where the facts involved are jurisdictional or where the question concerns the proper exercise of the judicial power of the United States in enforcing constitutional limitations. . . .

In cases brought to enforce constitutional rights, the judicial power of the United States necessarily extends to the independent determination of all questions, both of fact and law, necessary to the performance of that supreme function. . . .

The Congress has not expressly provided that the determinations by the deputy commissioner of the fundamental or jurisdictional facts as to the locality of the injury and the existence of the relation of master and servant shall be final. . . . [T]here is no violation of the purpose of the Congress in sustaining the determinations of fact of the deputy commissioner where he acts within his authority in passing upon compensation claims while denying finality to his conclusions as to the jurisdictional facts upon which the valid application of the statute depends.

Assuming that the federal court may determine for itself the existence of these fundamental or jurisdictional facts, we come to the question, Upon what record is the determination to be made? . . . By providing for injunction proceedings, the Congress evidently contemplated a suit as in equity, and in such a suit the complainant would have full opportunity to plead and prove either that the injury did not occur upon the navigable waters of the United States or that the relation of master and servant did not exist, and hence that the case lay outside the purview of the statute. As the question is one of the constitutional authority of the deputy commissioner as an administrative agency, the court is under no obligation to give weight to his proceedings pending the determination of that question. . . . We think that the essential independence of the exercise of the judicial power of the United States, in the enforcement of constitutional rights requires that the federal court should determine such an issue upon its own record and the facts elicited before it. . . .

We are of the opinion that the District Court did not err in permitting a trial de novo on the issue of employment. . . .

Mr. Justice Brandeis, [joined by Justices Stone and Roberts,] dissenting.

. . . . The safeguards with which Congress has surrounded the proceedings before the deputy commissioner would be without meaning if those proceedings were to serve merely as an inquiry preliminary to a contest in the courts. Specific provisions of the Longshoremen's Act make clear that it was the aim of Congress to expedite the relief afforded. With a view to obviating the delays incident to judicial proceedings the act substitutes an administrative tribunal for the court; and, besides providing for notice and opportunity to be heard, endows the proceedings before the deputy commissioner with the customary incidents of a judicial hearing. . . . Procedure of this character, instead of expediting relief, would entail useless expense and delay if the proceedings before the deputy commissioner were to be repeated in court and the case tried from the beginning, at the option of either party. . . .

Nothing in the statute warrants the construction that the right to a trial de novo which Congress has concededly denied as to most issues of fact determined by the deputy commissioner has been granted in respect to the issue of the existence of the employer-employee relation. The language which is held sufficient to foreclose the right to such a trial on some issues forecloses it as to all. Whether the peculiar relation which the fact of employment is asserted to bear to the scheme of the statute and to the constitutional authority under which it was passed might conceivably have induced Congress to provide a special method of review upon that question, it is not necessary to inquire. For Congress expressly declared its intention to put, for purposes of review, all the issues of fact on the same basis, by conferring upon the deputy commissioner 'full power to hear and determine all questions in respect of such claim,' subject only to the power of the court to set aside his order 'if not in accordance with law.'

The suggestion that 'such claim' may be construed to mean only a claim within the purview of the act seems to me without substance. . . . It is not reasonable to suppose that Congress intended to set up a fact-finding tribunal of first instance, shorn of power to find a portion of the facts required for any decision of the case; or that, in enacting legislation designed to withdraw from litigation the great bulk of maritime accidents, it contemplated a procedure whereby the same facts must be twice litigated before a longshoreman could be assured the benefits of compensation. . . .

It is suggested that this exception is required as to issues of fact involving claims of constitutional right. For reasons which I shall later discuss, I cannot believe that the issue of employment is one of constitutional right. But even assuming it to be so, the conclusion does not follow that trial of the issue must therefore be upon a record made in the District Court. That the function of collecting evidence may be committed to an administrative tribunal is settled by a host of cases, and supported by persuasive analogies, none of which justify a distinction between issues of constitutional right and any others. Resort to administrative remedies may be made a condition precedent to a judicial hearing. This is so even though a party is asserting deprivation of rights secured by the Federal Constitution. . . .

Even in respect to the question, discussed by the Court, of the finality to be accorded administrative findings of fact in a civil case involving pecuniary liability, I see no reason for making special exception as to issues of constitutional right, unless it be that, under certain circumstances, there may arise difficulty in reaching conclusions of law without consideration of the evidence [and] the findings of fact. . . .

I see no basis for a contention that the denial of the right to a trial de novo upon the issue of employment is in any manner subversive of the independence of the federal judicial power. Nothing in the Constitution, or in any prior decision of this Court to which attention has been called, lends support to the doctrine that a judicial finding of any fact involved in any civil proceeding to enforce a pecuniary liability may not be made upon evidence introduced before a properly constituted administrative tribunal, or that a determination so made may not be deemed an independent judicial determination. . . .

The 'judicial power' of article 3 of the Constitution is the power of the federal government, and not of any inferior tribunal. There is in that article nothing which requires any controversy to be determined as of first instance in the federal District Courts. The jurisdiction of those courts is subject to the control of Congress. Matters which may be placed within their jurisdiction may instead be committed to the state courts. If there be any controversy to which the judicial power extends that may not be subjected to the conclusive determination of administrative bodies or federal legislative courts, it is not because of any prohibition against the diminution of the jurisdiction of the federal District Courts as such, but because, under certain circumstances, the constitutional requirement of due process is a requirement of judicial process. . . .

Notes and Questions

1. **Overview.** *Crowell v. Benson* is not a public-rights case. It does not arise between an individual and the government where the individual is seeking a privilege like a public land grant or a welfare benefit. It is about the liability of one private individual (the employer) to another (the employee). It is exactly the kind of case that would be decided by a judge and jury in state common-law courts, or by federal courts sitting in admiralty or diversity. The difference here is that the substantive law is a federal statute but, as the Court held, the source of substantive law doesn't determine whether the matter is one of private rights. Common law, state law, and federal law each can define the liability of one private individual to another.

Why did the Court hold this administrative tribunal was constitutional? What kind of facts did the Court hold could be decided by the administrative tribunal, and what kind of facts did the Court hold are still decided by—or *must* be decided by—the federal courts themselves? Why can *any* facts be found by an administrative agency and not a court? Is fact-finding upon which the application of law depends not part of the "judicial power"?

2. *The agency as "adjunct" and the evolution of deferential review.* The Court in *Crowell* emphasized that in that case the federal courts maintained the "essential attributes" of judicial power, and the agency was merely serving as an adjunct like a jury or a special master, because the courts decided (1) questions of law, (2) questions of jurisdictional fact, and (3) questions of constitutional rights and limits. But are these still true? Today, do courts review questions of law de novo? (What does the *Chevron* doctrine say?) And it may not surprise you, in light of Justice Brandeis's dissent, that courts now defer even to findings of jurisdictional facts. After all, it

 CROSS REFERENCE In an earlier chapter, we saw how under *Chevron v. NRDC* courts are supposed to defer to reasonable agency interpretations of their organic statutes. Is *Crowell* outdated in this regard?

would be terribly inefficient to let the tribunal decide only certain factual questions but not others. Moreover, can we really distinguish questions of jurisdictional fact from those of nonjurisdictional fact? Is there "jurisdiction" if there hasn't been an injury? Is that question any different from asking if there is an employer-employee relationship and therefore "jurisdiction"?

In short, today agencies get deference on questions of law as well as questions of fact, which are as a general matter, you will recall, reviewed under the substantial evidence standard. Does that change your view of *Crowell*? Do courts that substantially defer on both factual and legal questions maintain the "essential attributes" of judicial power?

Further: was the agency in *Crowell* truly an "adjunct" if it could conclusively determine *any* matter? Putting aside the jury comparison—it is not at all clear that the jury is an "adjunct" to the court, and it could be that the jury exercises its own power—special masters certainly do not get any "deference" from the courts. Of course, they get "deference" to the extent they're experts. But their work, legally speaking, is reviewed de novo. Magistrate judges are also "adjuncts" to district court judges, and they cannot determine anything conclusively—they must issue "proposed findings and recommendations" which are reviewed de novo by district court judges. 28 U.S.C. § 636(b)(I)(A), (C) (2018). (To the extent magistrate judges do conclusively adjudicate certain cases like petty offenses, they may be unconstitutional.) Do you think the analogy to adjuncts holds?

3. *The relevance of the Madisonian Compromise.* Brandeis argued that it is inefficient to allow only some facts but not all to be conclusively found by the tribunal. More still, he said the judicial power does not require the courts to find any facts at all. His argument was that Congress need not create district courts at all, and so state courts hear cases; and state courts, of course, are not federal courts. But recall that state courts can hear cases because of the Madisonian compromise. They are *already* exercising some judicial power of their own—that of the states—and they can have concurrent federal jurisdiction with the federal courts. But isn't that very different from saying that the *executive branch* can therefore exercise the federal judicial power? Consider the motives of the antifederalists who feared the federal judicial power: They did not want a farmer dragged into a federal court in a faraway state capital and, eventually, in a faraway national capital. Such federal courts might also favor the eastern commercial interests. Do these arguments for allowing *state* courts to hear federal cases apply to the *executive branch itself* hearing cases? Would that not have greatly alarmed the antifederalists?

4. *Is the Seventh Amendment relevant?* The Seventh Amendment provides, "In Suits at common law, where the value in controversy shall exceed twenty dollars, the right of trial by jury shall be preserved." In Granfinanciera v. Nordberg, 492 U.S. 33 (1989), the Court held the Seventh Amendment applied to a claim of fraudulent conveyance under the bankruptcy code, and so

> **Defined Term**
>
> **LAW VERSUS EQUITY:** Equitable rights did not require a jury. The difference between suits in law and suits in equity is that in the former, defendants could usually just pay money after a judgment. In equity, courts could require defendants to do things—to take certain actions, like specific performance, beyond simply paying money.

the bankruptcy court (an Article I legislative court, whose judges do not enjoy lifetime tenure and salary protections) had to empanel a jury to hear such a claim. (The Court reserved the question whether such a claim had to be heard in an Article III court.) The Court held that the Seventh Amendment applies to cases where "legal rights were to be ascertained and determined," as opposed to "equitable rights alone," and therefore the Amendment "also applies to actions brought to enforce *statutory* rights that are analogous to common-law causes of action ordinarily decided in English law courts in the 18th century."

Why weren't the parties in *Crowell* entitled to a jury trial? Weren't the legal rights of the parties to be ascertained and determined? The point passed quickly in the excerpt, but the answer is that juries were not required in admiralty cases. Suppose, however, that this case was not an admiralty case. Suppose, instead, that this was simply a matter of the National Labor Relations Board determining whether an employer owes backpay to an employee—a classic private rights case. Wouldn't the parties be entitled to a jury? But administrative agencies don't empanel juries. Does *Crowell* apply only to fact-finding in cases in which no jury is necessary? Is that a small or large subset of cases?

5.   *Subsequent expansion of "public rights."* Following *Crowell*, in a number of cases, the Supreme Court approved the use of administrative agencies to determine conclusively (or at least with minimal judicial review) private-rights cases involving administrative statutes. Unlike in *Crowell*, where the Court recognized that the issue at hand was a matter of private right, the Court in these subsequent cases redesignated them as "public rights" cases because they involved rights created by "statute." The two most prominent cases are *Atlas Roofing v. Occupational Safety and Health Administration*, and *National Labor Relations Board v. Jones & Laughlin Steel Corp.* As you read about these two cases in the following paragraphs, ask yourself whether you agree that these are really public rights cases. Does the fact that a statute creates the right make a difference? (Did it make a difference in *Crowell*?) And, what about the right to a jury trial?

(a)   Atlas Roofing. In the Occupational Safety and Heath Act of 1970, Congress created a statutory duty to maintain safe and healthy working conditions and permitted the Occupational Safety and Health Administration (OSHA) to institute actions not only for an abatement of health and safety risks, but also for civil fines. The factual findings of the agency, and the "fact" of violation, were conclusive upon federal courts.

In Atlas Roofing v. OSHA, 430 U.S. 442 (1977), the Supreme Court upheld these administrative proceedings for civil fines and penalties brought by the United States against an individual for violations of newly created statutory obligations. The Court first held that the case involved a "public right"—it was a case in which the government was suing "in its sovereign capacity to enforce public rights created by statutes." Is this convincing? Although the full extent of public rights is disputed, ordinarily when we think of public rights the right at issue belongs to the public as a whole, for example the public lands or the right to use an invention, or to the government itself if it is a claim against the government. Recall that the justification for doing away with Article III adjudications in these cases is the government's sovereign immunity. If the government need not consent to be sued, then this greater power to deny consent includes a lesser power to consent to an executive-branch adjudication. There does not appear to have been a "public right" in this sense at issue in *Atlas Roofing*, but rather rights and obligations of particular private parties—employer and employee—created by statute.

The Court further held that the case was not like an action "at common law," but rather was like one in equity, because Congress determined that the existing common-law remedies against negligent employers were insufficient to protect the safety of workers; thus there was no right to a jury trial. Is this argument convincing? Recall what the Court said in *Granfinanciera v. Nordberg*: the Seventh Amendment applies to cases where "legal rights were to be ascertained and determined," as opposed to equitable rights alone, and therefore the Amendment "also applies to actions brought to enforce *statutory* rights that are analogous to common-law causes of action ordinarily decided in English law courts in the 18th century." Are you convinced that when the government sues an individual for civil penalties for violating statutory obligations toward other private parties, it's merely an equitable suit, rather than one in which "legal rights [are] to be ascertained and determined"?

(b) **Jones & Laughlin.** In NLRB v. Jones & Laughlin Steel Corp., 301 U.S. 1 (1937), cited and discussed in *Atlas Roofing*, the Court similarly held that NLRB adjudications could determine whether there had been an unfair labor practice and could also order backpay to wronged employees where appropriate—all without a jury or Article III adjudication—because the case involved "public rights." Do you agree? Wasn't that actually a private-rights case, like *Crowell*?

3.   A (Partial) Return to Formalism?

Whatever their merits, the holdings in *Crowell*, *Atlas Roofing*, and *Jones & Laughlin* remain a core justification for much administrative adjudication today.

So long as the case involves a *statutory* obligation enacted by Congress which the federal government is given the right to enforce through an administrative agency, the administrative agency is permitted to adjudicate violations of such obligation and not only seek equitable remedies like abatement, but also monetary penalties; indeed, administrative agencies, like the NLRB, can even require one party to pay another.

Starting with the following case in 1982, however, the Supreme Court started limiting the kinds of claims that could be heard by non-Article III tribunals, including agencies. In particular, the Court has limited the ability of agencies to hear cases that actually exist at common-law or are based in state law (as opposed to congressional statute). Ask yourself, again, whether that should really matter. What does the source of the underlying substantive law have to do with whether a case is about private or public rights?

Note that in the following case, the Court confronts the jurisdiction of bankruptcy courts. Such courts are not administrative agencies, but they're not Article III courts either. Their judges don't enjoy lifetime tenure or salary protections, but they can empanel juries—something agencies can't do. Do the constitutional rules that apply to legislative courts apply also to agencies, and vice versa? If the rules are different, is there any constitutional basis for the difference? If bankruptcy courts aren't exercising judicial power (if they were, their judges would need Article III salary and tenure protections), then don't they have to be exercising executive power? Or, perhaps, are they adjuncts to actual Article III courts?

Northern Pipeline Construction Co. v. Marathon Pipe Line Co.

458 U.S. 50 (1982)

Justice Brennan announced the judgment of the Court and delivered an opinion in which Justice Marshall, Justice Blackmun, and Justice Stevens joined.

The question presented is whether the assignment by Congress to bankruptcy judges of the jurisdiction granted . . . by § 241(a) of the Bankruptcy Act of 1978 violates Art. III of the Constitution.

I

A

In 1978, after almost 10 years of study and investigation, Congress enacted a comprehensive revision of the bankruptcy laws. The Bankruptcy Act of 1978 (Act) made significant changes in both the substantive and procedural law of bankruptcy. It is the changes in the latter that are at issue in this case.

Before the Act, federal district courts served as bankruptcy courts and employed a "referee" system. Bankruptcy proceedings were generally conducted before referees, except in those instances in which the district court elected to withdraw a case from a referee. The referee's final order was appealable to the district court. The bankruptcy courts were vested with "summary jurisdiction"—that is, with jurisdiction over controversies involving property in the actual or constructive possession of the court. And, with consent, the bankruptcy court also had jurisdiction over some "plenary" matters—such as disputes involving property in the possession of a third person.

The Act eliminates the referee system and establishes "in each judicial district, as an adjunct to the district court for such district, a bankruptcy court which shall be a court of record known as the United States Bankruptcy Court for the district." 28 U.S.C. § 151(a). The judges of these courts are appointed to office for 14-year terms by the President, with the advice and consent of the Senate. They are subject to removal by the "judicial council of the circuit" on account of "incompetency, misconduct, neglect of duty or physical or mental disability." § 153(b). In addition, the salaries of the bankruptcy judges are set by statute and are subject to adjustment under the Federal Salary Act.

The jurisdiction of the bankruptcy courts created by the Act is much broader than that exercised under the former referee system. Eliminating the distinction between "summary" and "plenary" jurisdiction, the Act grants the new courts jurisdiction over all "civil proceedings arising under title 11 [the Bankruptcy title] or arising in or *related to* cases under title 11." 28 U.S.C. § 1471(b) (emphasis added). This jurisdictional grant empowers bankruptcy courts to entertain a wide variety of cases involving claims that may affect the property of the estate once a petition has been filed under Title 11. Included within the bankruptcy courts' jurisdiction are suits to recover accounts, controversies involving exempt property, actions to avoid transfers and payments as preferences or fraudulent conveyances, and causes of action owned by the debtor at the time of the petition for bankruptcy. The bankruptcy courts can hear claims based on state law as well as those based on federal law.

The judges of the bankruptcy courts are vested with all of the "powers of a court of equity, law, and admiralty," except that they "may not enjoin another court or punish a criminal contempt not committed in the presence of the judge of the court or warranting a punishment of imprisonment." 28 U.S.C. § 1481. In addition to this broad grant of power, Congress has allowed bankruptcy judges the power to hold jury trials, § 1480; to issue declaratory judgments, § 2201; to issue writs of habeas corpus under certain circumstances, § 2256; to issue all writs necessary in aid of the bankruptcy court's expanded jurisdiction, § 451; and to issue any order, process or judgment that is necessary or appropriate to carry out the provisions of Title 11, 11 U.S.C. § 105(a).

The Act also establishes a special procedure for appeals from orders of bankruptcy courts. The circuit council is empowered to direct the chief judge of the circuit to designate panels of three bankruptcy judges to hear appeals. These panels have jurisdiction of all appeals from final judgments, orders, and decrees of bankruptcy courts, and, with leave of the panel, of interlocutory appeals. If no such appeals panel is designated, the district court is empowered to exercise appellate jurisdiction. The court of appeals is given jurisdiction over appeals from the appellate panels or from the district court. If the parties agree, a direct appeal to the court of appeals may be taken from a final judgment of a bankruptcy court. . . .

B

This case arises out of proceedings initiated in the United States Bankruptcy Court for the District of Minnesota after appellant Northern Pipeline Construction Co. (Northern) filed a petition for reorganization in January 1980. In March 1980 Northern, pursuant to the Act, filed in that court a suit against appellee Marathon Pipe Line Co. (Marathon). Appellant sought damages for alleged breaches of contract and warranty, as well as for alleged misrepresentation, coercion, and duress. Marathon sought dismissal of the suit, on the ground that the Act unconstitutionally conferred Art. III judicial power upon judges who lacked life tenure and protection against salary diminution. The United States intervened to defend the validity of the statute.

The Bankruptcy Judge denied the motion to dismiss. But on appeal the District Court entered an order granting the motion, on the ground that "the delegation of authority in 28 U.S.C. § 1471 to the Bankruptcy Judges to try cases which are otherwise relegated under the Constitution to Article III judges" was unconstitutional. . . .

II

A

Basic to the constitutional structure established by the Framers was their recognition that "[t]he accumulation of all powers, legislative, executive, and judiciary, in the same hands, whether of one, a few, or many, and whether hereditary, self-appointed, or elective, may justly be pronounced the very definition of tyranny." The Federalist No. 47 (J. Madison). To ensure against such tyranny, the Framers provided that the Federal Government would consist of three distinct Branches, each to exercise one of the governmental powers recognized by the Framers as inherently distinct. "The Framers regarded the checks and balances that they had built into the tripartite Federal Government as a self-executing safeguard against the encroachment or aggrandizement of one branch at the expense of the other." *Buckley v. Valeo,* 424 U.S. 1, 122 (1976).

The Federal Judiciary was therefore designed by the Framers to stand independent of the Executive and Legislature—to maintain the checks and balances of the constitutional structure, and also to guarantee that the process of adjudication itself remained impartial. Hamilton explained the importance of an independent Judiciary:

> "Periodical appointments, however regulated, or by whomsoever made, would, in some way or other, be fatal to [the courts'] necessary independence. If the power of making them was committed either to the Executive or legislature, there would be danger of an improper complaisance to the branch which possessed it; if to both, there would be an unwillingness to hazard the displeasure of either; if to the people, or to persons chosen by them for the special purpose, there would be too great a disposition to consult popularity, to justify a reliance that nothing would be consulted but the Constitution and the laws." The Federalist No. 78.

The Court has only recently reaffirmed the significance of this feature of the Framers' design: "A Judiciary free from control by the Executive and Legislature is essential if there is a right to have claims decided by judges who are free from potential domination by other branches of government." *United States v. Will*, 449 U.S. 200, 217–218 (1980).

As an inseparable element of the constitutional system of checks and balances, and as a guarantee of judicial impartiality, Art. III both defines the power and protects the independence of the Judicial Branch. It provides that "The judicial Power of the United States, shall be vested in one supreme Court, and in such inferior Courts as the Congress may from time to time ordain and establish." Art. III, § 1. The inexorable command of this provision is clear and definite. The judicial power of the United States must be exercised by courts having the attributes prescribed in Art. III. Those attributes are also clearly set forth:

> "The Judges, both of the supreme and inferior Courts, shall hold their Offices during good Behaviour, and shall, at stated Times, receive for their Services, a Compensation, which shall not be diminished during their Continuance in Office." Art. III, § 1.

The "good Behaviour" Clause guarantees that Art. III judges shall enjoy life tenure, subject only to removal by impeachment. The Compensation Clause guarantees Art. III judges a fixed and irreducible compensation for their services. Both of these provisions were incorporated into the Constitution to ensure the independence of the Judiciary from the control of the Executive and Legislative Branches of government. . . .

In sum, our Constitution unambiguously enunciates a fundamental principle—that the "judicial Power of the United States" must be reposed in an independent Judiciary. It commands that the independence of the Judiciary be jealously guarded, and it provides clear institutional protections for that independence.

B

It is undisputed that the bankruptcy judges whose offices were created by the Bankruptcy Act of 1978 do not enjoy the protections constitutionally afforded to Art. III judges. The bankruptcy judges do not serve for life subject to their continued "good Behaviour." Rather, they are appointed for 14-year terms, and can be removed by the judicial council of the circuit in which they serve on grounds of "incompetency, misconduct, neglect of duty, or physical or mental disability." Second, the salaries of the bankruptcy judges are not immune from diminution by Congress. In short, there is no doubt that the bankruptcy judges created by the Act are not Art. III judges. . . .

[W]e turn to the question presented for decision: whether the Bankruptcy Act of 1978 violates the command of Art. III that the judicial power of the United States must be vested in courts whose judges enjoy the protections and safeguards specified in that Article.

Appellants suggest two grounds for upholding the Act's conferral of broad adjudicative powers upon judges unprotected by Art. III. First, it is urged that "pursuant to its enumerated Article I powers, Congress may establish legislative courts that have jurisdiction to decide cases to which the Article III judicial power of the United States extends." Referring to our precedents upholding the validity of "legislative courts," appellants suggest that "the plenary grants of power in Article I permit Congress to establish non-Article III tribunals in 'specialized areas having particularized needs and warranting distinctive treatment,' " such as the area of bankruptcy law. Second, appellants contend that even if the Constitution does require that this bankruptcy-related action be adjudicated in an Art. III court, the Act in fact satisfies that requirement. "Bankruptcy jurisdiction was vested in the district court" of the judicial district in which the bankruptcy court is located, "and the exercise of that jurisdiction by the adjunct bankruptcy court was made subject to appeal as of right to an Article III court." Analogizing the role of the bankruptcy court to that of a special master, appellants urge us to conclude that this "adjunct" system established by Congress satisfies the requirements of Art. III. We consider these arguments in turn.

III

Congress did not constitute the bankruptcy courts as legislative courts. Appellants contend, however, that the bankruptcy courts could have been so constituted, and that as a result the "adjunct" system in fact chosen by Congress does not impermissibly encroach upon the judicial power. In advancing this argument, appellants rely upon cases in which we have identified certain matters that "congress may or may not bring within the cognizance of [Art. III courts], as it may deem proper." *Murray's Lessee v. Hoboken Land & Improvement Co.*, 18 How. 272, 284 (1856). But when properly understood, these precedents represent no broad departure from the constitutional command that the judicial power of the United States must be vested in Art. III courts.

Rather, they reduce to three narrow situations not subject to that command, each recognizing a circumstance in which the grant of power to the Legislative and Executive Branches was historically and constitutionally so exceptional that the congressional assertion of a power to create legislative courts was consistent with, rather than threatening to, the constitutional mandate of separation of powers. These precedents simply acknowledge that the literal command of Art. III, assigning the judicial power of the United States to courts insulated from Legislative or Executive interference, must be interpreted in light of the historical context in which the Constitution was written, and of the structural imperatives of the Constitution as a whole.

Appellants first rely upon a series of cases in which this Court has upheld the creation by Congress of non-Art. III "territorial courts." This exception from the general prescription of Art. III dates from the earliest days of the Republic, when it was perceived that the Framers intended that as to certain geographical areas, in which no State operated as sovereign, Congress was to exercise the general powers of government. For example, in *American Ins. Co. v. Canter*, 1 Pet. 511 (1828), the Court observed that Art. IV bestowed upon Congress alone a complete power of government over territories not within the States that constituted the United States. The Court then acknowledged Congress' authority to create courts for those territories that were not in conformity with Art. III. Such courts were

> "created in virtue of the general right of sovereignty which exists in the government, or in virtue of that clause which enables Congress to make all needful rules and regulations, respecting the territory belonging to the United States. . . . In legislating for them, Congress exercises the combined powers of the general, and of a state government." 1 Pet., at 546.

The Court followed the same reasoning when it reviewed Congress' creation of non-Art. III courts in the District of Columbia. It noted that there was in the District

> "no division of powers between the general and state governments. Congress has the entire control over the district for every purpose of government; and it is reasonable to suppose, that in organizing a judicial department here, all judicial power necessary for the purposes

of government would be vested in the courts of justice." *Kendall v. United States*, 12 Pet. 524, 619 (1838).

Appellants next advert to a second class of cases—those in which this Court has sustained the exercise by Congress and the Executive of the power to establish and administer courts-martial. The situation in these cases strongly resembles the situation with respect to territorial courts: It too involves a constitutional grant of power that has been historically understood as giving the political Branches of Government extraordinary control over the precise subject matter at issue. . . . The Fifth Amendment, which requires a presentment or indictment of a grand jury before a person may be held to answer for a capital or otherwise infamous crime, contains an express exception for "cases arising in the land or naval forces." And Art. II, § 2, cl. 1, provides that "The President shall be Commander in Chief of the Army and Navy of the United States, and of the Militia of the several States, when called into the actual Service of the United States." Noting these constitutional directives, the Court in *Dynes v. Hoover*, 20 How. 65 (1857), explained:

> "These provisions show that Congress has the power to provide for the trial and punishment of military and naval offences in the manner then and now practiced by civilized nations; and that the power to do so is given without any connection between it and the 3d article of the Constitution defining the judicial power of the United States; indeed, that the two powers are entirely independent of each other." *Id.* at 79.

Finally, appellants rely on a third group of cases, in which this Court has upheld the constitutionality of legislative courts and administrative agencies created by Congress to adjudicate cases involving "public rights." The "public rights" doctrine was first set forth in *Murray's Lessee v. Hoboken Land & Improvement Co.*, 18 How. 272 (1856):

> "[W]e do not consider congress can either withdraw from judicial cognizance any matter which, from its nature, is the subject of a suit at the common law, or in equity, or admiralty; nor, on the other hand, can it bring under the judicial power a matter which, from its nature, is not a subject for judicial determination. At the same time there are matters, *involving public rights*, which may be presented in such form that the judicial power is capable of acting on them, and

which are susceptible of judicial determination, but which congress may or may not bring within the cognizance of the courts of the United States, as it may deem proper." *Id.* at 284 (emphasis added).

This doctrine may be explained in part by reference to the traditional principle of sovereign immunity, which recognizes that the Government may attach conditions to its consent to be sued. But the public-rights doctrine also draws upon the principle of separation of powers, and a historical understanding that certain prerogatives were reserved to the political Branches of Government. The doctrine extends only to matters arising "between the Government and persons subject to its authority [as opposed to between two private persons— Ed.] in connection with the performance of the constitutional functions of the executive or legislative departments," *Crowell v. Benson,* 285 U.S. 22, 50 (1932), and only to matters that historically could have been determined exclusively by those departments. The understanding of these cases is that the Framers expected that Congress would be free to commit such matters completely to nonjudicial executive determination, and that as a result there can be no constitutional objection to Congress' employing the less drastic expedient of committing their determination to a legislative court or an administrative agency. *Crowell v. Benson, supra,* 285 U.S. at 50.

The public-rights doctrine is grounded in a historically recognized distinction between matters that could be conclusively determined by the Executive and Legislative Branches and matters that are "inherently . . . judicial." For example, the Court in *Murray's Lessee* looked to the law of England and the States at the time the Constitution was adopted, in order to determine whether the issue presented was customarily cognizable in the courts. Concluding that the matter had not traditionally been one for judicial determination, the Court perceived no bar to Congress' establishment of summary procedures, outside of Art. III courts, to collect a debt due to the Government from one of its customs agents. On the same premise, the Court in *Ex parte Bakelite Corp.* . . . held that the Court of Customs Appeals had been properly constituted by Congress as a legislative court . . . .

The distinction between public rights and private rights has not been definitively explained in our precedents. Nor is it necessary to do so in the present cases, for it suffices to observe that a matter of public rights must at a minimum arise "between the government and others." *Ex parte Bakelite Corp.,* [279 U.S. 438, 451 (1929)]. In contrast, "the liability of one individual to another under the law as defined," *Crowell v. Benson, supra,* at 51, is a matter of private rights. Our precedents clearly establish that *only* controversies in the former category may be removed from Art. III courts and delegated to legislative courts or administrative agencies for their determination. See *Atlas Roofing Co. v. Occupational Safety and Health Review Comm'n,* 430 U.S. 442, 450, n. 7 (1977); *Crowell v. Benson, supra,* 285 U.S. at 50–51. Private-rights disputes, on the other hand, lie at the core of the historically recognized judicial power.

In sum, this Court has identified three situations in which Art. III does not bar the creation of legislative courts. In each of these situations, the Court has recognized certain exceptional powers bestowed upon Congress by the Constitution or by historical consensus. Only in the face of such an exceptional grant of power has the Court declined to hold the authority of Congress subject to the general prescriptions of Art. III.

We discern no such exceptional grant of power applicable in the cases before us. The courts created by the Bankruptcy Act of 1978 do not lie exclusively outside the States of the Federal Union, like those in the District of Columbia and the Territories. Nor do the bankruptcy courts bear any resemblance to courts-martial . . . . Finally, the substantive legal rights at issue in the present action cannot be deemed "public rights." Appellants argue that a discharge in bankruptcy is indeed a "public right," similar to such congressionally created benefits as "radio station licenses, pilot licenses, or certificates for common carriers" granted by administrative agencies. But the restructuring of debtor-creditor relations, which is at the core of the federal bankruptcy power, must be distinguished from the adjudication of state-created private rights, such as the right to recover contract damages that is at issue in this case. The former may well be a "public right," but the latter obviously is not. Appellant Northern's right to recover contract damages to augment its estate is "one of private right, that is, of the liability of one individual to another under the law as defined." *Crowell v. Benson,* 285 U.S. at 51. . . .

IV

Appellants advance a second argument for upholding the constitutionality of the Act: that "viewed within the entire judicial framework set up by Congress," the bankruptcy court is merely an "adjunct" to the district court, and that the delegation of certain adjudicative functions to the bankruptcy court is accordingly consistent with the principle that the judicial power of the United

States must be vested in Art. III courts. As support for their argument, appellants rely principally upon *Crowell v. Benson,* 285 U.S. 22, 52 (1932), and *United States v. Raddatz,* 447 U.S. 667 (1980), cases in which we approved the use of administrative agencies and magistrates as adjuncts to Art. III courts. . . .

It is, of course, true that while the power to adjudicate "private rights" must be vested in an Art. III court, see Part III, *supra,* "this Court has accepted factfinding by an administrative agency, . . . as an adjunct to the Art. III court, analogizing the agency to a jury or a special master and permitting it in admiralty cases to perform the function of the special master. . . ." *Atlas Roofing Co. v. Occupational Safety and Health Review Comm'n,* 430 U.S. at 450, n. 7.

The use of administrative agencies as adjuncts was first upheld in *Crowell v. Benson, supra.* . . .

Crowell involved the adjudication of congressionally created rights. But this Court has sustained the use of adjunct factfinders even in the adjudication of constitutional rights—so long as those adjuncts were subject to sufficient control by an Art. III district court. In *United States v. Raddatz, supra,* the Court upheld the 1978 Federal Magistrates Act, which permitted district court judges to refer certain pretrial motions, including suppression motions based on alleged violations of constitutional rights, to a magistrate for initial determination. The Court observed that the magistrate's proposed findings and recommendations were subject to *de novo* review by the district court, which was free to rehear the evidence or to call for additional evidence. . . .

Together these cases establish two principles that aid us in determining the extent to which Congress may constitutionally vest traditionally judicial functions in non-Art. III officers. First, it is clear that when Congress creates a substantive federal right, it possesses substantial discretion to prescribe the manner in which that right may be adjudicated—including the assignment to an adjunct of some functions historically performed by judges. Thus *Crowell* recognized that Art. III does not require "all determinations of fact [to] be made by judges"; with respect to congressionally created rights, some factual determinations may be made by a specialized factfinding tribunal designed by Congress, without constitutional bar. Second, the functions of the adjunct must be limited in such a way that "the essential attributes" of judicial power are retained in the Art. III court. Thus in upholding the adjunct scheme challenged in *Crowell,* the Court emphasized that "the reservation of full authority to the court to deal with matters of law provides for the appropriate exercise of the judicial function in this class of cases." . . .

These two principles assist us in evaluating the "adjunct" scheme presented in these cases. Appellants assume that Congress' power to create "adjuncts" to consider all cases related to those arising under Title 11 is as great as it was in the circumstances of *Crowell*. But while *Crowell* certainly endorsed the proposition that Congress possesses broad discretion to assign factfinding functions to an adjunct created to aid in the adjudication of congressionally created statutory rights, *Crowell* does not support the further proposition necessary to appellants' argument—that Congress possesses the same degree of discretion in assigning traditionally judicial power to adjuncts engaged in the adjudication of rights not created by Congress. . . .

[W]hen Congress creates a statutory right, it clearly has the discretion, in defining that right, to create presumptions, or assign burdens of proof, or prescribe remedies; it may also provide that persons seeking to vindicate that right must do so before particularized tribunals created to perform the specialized adjudicative tasks related to that right. Such provisions do, in a sense, affect the exercise of judicial power, but they are also incidental to Congress' power to define the right that it has created. No comparable justification exists, however, when the right being adjudicated is not of congressional creation. . . .

[T]he cases before us, which center upon appellant Northern's claim for damages for breach of contract and misrepresentation, involve a right created by *state* law, a right independent of and antecedent to the reorganization petition that conferred jurisdiction upon the Bankruptcy Court. Accordingly, Congress' authority to control the manner in which that right is adjudicated, through assignment of historically judicial functions to a non-Art. III "adjunct," plainly must be deemed at a minimum. . . .

Unlike the administrative scheme that we reviewed in *Crowell*, the Act vests all "essential attributes" of the judicial power of the United States in the "adjunct" bankruptcy court. First, the agency in *Crowell* made only specialized, narrowly confined factual determinations regarding a particularized area of law. In contrast, the subject-matter jurisdiction of the bankruptcy courts encompasses not only traditional matters of bankruptcy, but also "all civil proceedings arising under title 11 or arising in or *related to* cases under title 11." 28 U.S.C. § 1471(c) (emphasis added). Second, while the agency in *Crowell* engaged in statutorily channeled factfinding functions, the bankruptcy courts exercise "*all of the jurisdiction*" conferred by the Act on the district courts, § 1471(c) (emphasis added). Third, the agency in *Crowell* possessed only a limited power to issue compensation orders pursuant to specialized procedures, and its orders could be enforced only by order of the district court. By contrast, the bankruptcy courts exercise all ordinary powers of district courts, including the power to preside over jury trials, the power to issue declaratory judgments, the power to issue writs of habeas corpus, and the power to issue any order, process, or judgment appropriate for the enforcement of the provisions of Title 11. Fourth, while orders issued by the agency in *Crowell* were to be set aside if "not supported by the evidence," the judgments of the bankruptcy courts are apparently subject to review only under the more deferential "clearly erroneous" standard. Finally, the agency in *Crowell* was required by law to seek enforcement of its compensation orders in the district court. In contrast, the bankruptcy courts issue final judgments, which are binding and enforceable even in the absence of an appeal. . . .

We conclude that 28 U.S.C. § 1471, as added by § 241(a) of the Bankruptcy Act of 1978, has impermissibly removed most, if not all, of "the essential attributes of the judicial power" from the Art. III district court, and has vested those attributes in a non-Art. III adjunct. Such a grant of jurisdiction cannot be sustained as an exercise of Congress' power to create adjuncts to Art. III courts. . . .

JUSTICE REHNQUIST, with whom JUSTICE O'CONNOR joins, concurring in the judgment.

. . . . From the record before us, the lawsuit in which Marathon was named defendant seeks damages for breach of contract, misrepresentation, and other counts which are the stuff of the traditional actions at common law tried by the courts at Westminster in 1789. There is apparently no federal rule of decision provided for any of the issues in the lawsuit; the claims of Northern arise entirely under state law. No method of adjudication is hinted, other than the traditional common-law mode of judge and jury. The lawsuit is before the Bankruptcy Court only because the plaintiff has previously filed a petition for reorganization in that court.

The cases dealing with the authority of Congress to create courts other than by use of its power under Art. III do not admit of easy synthesis. . . .

DOCTRINE AND PRACTICE SERIES: ADMINISTRATIVE LAW

None of the cases has gone so far as to sanction the type of adjudication to which Marathon will be subjected against its will under the provisions of the 1978 Act. To whatever extent different powers granted under that Act might be sustained under the "public rights" doctrine of *Murray's Lessee v. Hoboken Land & Improvement Co.*, 18 How. 272 (1856), and succeeding cases, I am satisfied that the adjudication of Northern's lawsuit cannot be so sustained. . . .

CHIEF JUSTICE BURGER, dissenting.

I join JUSTICE WHITE's dissenting opinion, but I write separately to emphasize that, notwithstanding the plurality opinion, the Court does *not* hold today that Congress' broad grant of jurisdiction to the new bankruptcy courts is generally inconsistent with Art. III of the Constitution. Rather, the Court's holding is limited to the proposition stated by JUSTICE REHNQUIST in his concurrence in the judgment—that a "traditional" state common-law action, not made subject to a federal rule of decision, and related only peripherally to an adjudication of bankruptcy under federal law, must, absent the consent of the litigants, be heard by an "Art. III court" if it is to be heard by any court or agency of the United States. . . .

The problems arising from today's judgment can be resolved simply by providing that ancillary common-law actions, such as the one involved in these cases, be routed to the United States district court of which the bankruptcy court is an adjunct.

JUSTICE WHITE, with whom THE CHIEF JUSTICE and JUSTICE POWELL join, dissenting.

. . . . [The] question is what limits Art. III places on Congress' ability to create adjudicative institutions designed to carry out federal policy established pursuant to the substantive authority given Congress elsewhere in the Constitution. Whether fortunate or unfortunate, at this point in the history of constitutional law that question can no longer be answered by looking only to the constitutional text. This Court's cases construing that text must also be considered. In its attempt to pigeonhole these cases, the plurality does violence to their meaning and creates an artificial structure that itself lacks coherence. . . .

* * *

The distinction between public and private rights as the principle delineating the proper domains of legislative and constitutional courts respectively received its death blow, I had believed, in *Crowell v. Benson*, 285 U.S. 22 (1932). In that case, the Court approved an administrative scheme for the determination, in the first instance, of maritime employee compensation claims. Although acknowledging the framework set out in *Murray's Lessee* and *Ex parte Bakelite Corp.*, the Court specifically distinguished the case before it: "The present case does not fall within the categories just described but is one of private right, that is, of the liability of one individual to another under the law as defined." 285 U.S. at 51. Nevertheless, the Court approved of the use of an Art. I adjudication mechanism on the new theory that "there is no requirement that, in order to maintain the essential attributes of the judicial power, all determinations of fact in constitutional courts shall be made by judges." *Ibid.* Article I courts could deal not only with public rights, but also, to an extent, with private rights. . . .

The complicated and contradictory history of the issue before us leads me to conclude that . . . [t]here is no difference in principle between the work that Congress may assign to an Art. I court and that which the Constitution assigns to Art. III courts. Unless we want to overrule a large number of our precedents upholding a variety of Art. I courts—not to speak of those Art. I courts that go by the contemporary name of "administrative agencies"—this conclusion is inevitable. It is too late to go back that far; too late to return to the simplicity of the principle pronounced in Art. III and defended so vigorously and persuasively by Hamilton in The Federalist Nos. 78–82.

To say that the Court has failed to articulate a principle by which we can test the constitutionality of a putative Art. I court, or that there is no such abstract principle, is not to say that this Court must always defer to the legislative decision to create Art. I, rather than Art. III, courts. Article III is not to be read out of the Constitution; rather, it should be read as expressing one value that must be balanced against competing constitutional values and legislative responsibilities. This Court retains the final word on how that balance is to be struck. . . .

I do not suggest that the Court should simply look to the strength of the legislative interest and ask itself if that interest is more compelling than the values furthered by Art. III. The inquiry should, rather, focus equally on those Art. III values and ask whether and to what extent the legislative scheme accommodates them or, conversely, substantially undermines them. The burden on Art. III values should then be measured against the values Congress hopes to serve through the use of Art. I courts. . . .

To be more concrete: *Crowell, supra,* suggests that the presence of appellate review by an Art. III court will go a long way toward insuring a proper separation of powers. Appellate review of the decisions of legislative courts, like appellate review of state-court decisions, provides a firm check on the ability of the political institutions of government to ignore or transgress constitutional limits on their own authority. Obviously, therefore, a scheme of Art. I courts that provides for appellate review by Art. III courts should be substantially less controversial than a legislative attempt entirely to avoid judicial review in a constitutional court. . . .

I believe that the new bankruptcy courts established by the Bankruptcy Act of 1978, satisfy this standard.

First, ample provision is made for appellate review by Art. III courts. . . .

Second, no one seriously argues that the Bankruptcy Act of 1978 represents an attempt by the political branches of government to aggrandize themselves at the expense of the third branch or an attempt to undermine the authority of constitutional courts in general. Indeed, the congressional perception of a lack of judicial interest in bankruptcy matters was one of the factors that led to the establishment of the bankruptcy courts . . . .

Finally, I have no doubt that the ends that Congress sought to accomplish by creating a system of non-Art. III bankruptcy courts were at least as compelling as the ends . . . that have traditionally justified the creation of legislative courts. The stresses placed upon the old bankruptcy system by the tremendous increase in bankruptcy cases were well documented and were clearly a matter to which Congress could respond. . . .

The real question is not whether Congress was justified in establishing a specialized bankruptcy court, but rather whether it was justified in failing to create a specialized, Art. III bankruptcy court. My own view is that the very fact of extreme specialization may be enough, and certainly has been enough in the past, to justify the creation of a legislative court. Congress may legitimately consider the effect on the federal judiciary of the addition of several hundred specialized judges: We are, on the whole, a body of generalists. The addition of several hundred specialists may substantially change, whether for good or bad, the character of the federal bench. Moreover, Congress may have desired to maintain some flexibility in its possible future responses to the general problem of bankruptcy. There is no question that the existence of several hundred bankruptcy judges with life tenure would have severely limited Congress' future options. Furthermore, the number of bankruptcies may fluctuate, producing a substantially reduced need for bankruptcy judges. Congress may have thought that, in that event, a bankruptcy specialist should not as a general matter serve as a judge in the countless nonspecialized cases that come before the federal district courts. It would then face the prospect of large numbers of idle federal judges. . . .

Notes and Questions

1.   Summary. The principal holding of *Northern Pipeline* is that state-law or common-law claims must as a general matter be heard by Article III courts (or state courts). As put in the oft-quoted phrase of Justice Rehnquist's concurrence, if the claim is "the stuff of the traditional actions at common law tried by the courts at Westminster in 1789," then it must be heard by a traditional court exercising "judicial power." As articulated in *Northern Pipeline*, then, administrative agencies (or other non-Article III tribunals) can hear private-rights cases only if (1) the substantive law is supplied by congressional statute, as opposed to state law or common law; and (2) the essential attributes of the judicial power are maintained in the courts—in other words, the agency, in theory, is really merely an "adjunct" to the court in a narrow and specialized area of law.

2.   Why those two factors? Does either of the Court's two factors pass the smell test? First, a private rights case is a private rights case because it is between two private individuals, or the government is seeking to deprive one individual of a private right (such as a vested liberty or property interest). The law that actually determines one's rights and obligations shouldn't matter. Indeed, *Crowell* involved a congressional statute, but the Court there agreed it was a private rights case. Plus, doesn't the judicial power extend explicitly to cases "arising under . . . the laws of the United States," and aren't congressional laws explicitly contemplated by this provision? Moreover, why should it matter that the congressional statute involves a narrow and specialized area of law? Can Congress mostly eliminate the role of the federal courts simply by creating hundreds of thousands of agencies all responsible for discrete areas of law?

Second, are administrative agencies really "adjuncts"? The decisions of magistrate judges, who truly are adjuncts, are reviewed de novo, at least those parts of their reports and recommendations that are specifically objected to. In *Crowell*, on the other hand, the district courts deferred to the agency on many important factual questions—after all, what would be the point of the agency adjudication otherwise? And as explained in the notes following *Crowell*, today courts defer to agencies on questions of law and essentially all questions of fact, too—are courts maintaining the "essential attributes" of the judicial power under such circumstances?

Are administrative agencies like magistrate judges? Or are they different in important ways?

3. *Functionalism.* The majority's argument may be characterized as formalist, while Justice White's dissent is decidedly functionalist: he would balance the interests of Congress in creating specialized tribunals with the interests underlying Article III. Do you think White's test would be better? In fact, do you trust Article III judges to get the balance right? What do you make of White's argument that Congress could not have made bankruptcy courts into Article III courts because adding hundreds of specialized judges would change the "character of the federal bench"? Isn't White worried about the diluting the prestige that comes with being a federal judge? Is that concern legitimate? White argued that "[t]here is no difference in principle between the work that Congress may assign to an Art. I court [a non-Article III tribunal] and that which the Constitution assigns to Art. III courts." Can that possibly be right?

FORMALISM VS. FUNCTIONALISM
How would you characterize the majority and minority opinions: Is one formalist, the other functionalist?

Just a few years after *Northern Pipeline*, the Supreme Court tacked back to a functionalist approach in the following case.

Commodity Futures Trading Comm'n v. Schor

478 U.S. 833 (1986)

JUSTICE O'CONNOR delivered the opinion of the Court.

The question presented is whether the Commodity Exchange Act (CEA or Act) empowers the Commodity Futures Trading Commission (CFTC or Commission) to entertain state law counterclaims in reparation proceedings and, if so, whether that grant of authority violates Article III of the Constitution.

I

The CEA broadly prohibits fraudulent and manipulative conduct in connection with commodity futures transactions. In 1974, Congress "overhaul[ed]" the Act in order to institute a more "comprehensive regulatory structure to oversee the volatile and esoteric futures trading complex." Congress also determined that the broad regulatory powers of the CEA were most appropriately vested in an agency which would be relatively immune from the "political winds that sweep Washington." It therefore created an independent agency, the CFTC, and entrusted to it sweeping authority to implement the CEA.

Among the duties assigned to the CFTC was the administration of a reparations procedure through which disgruntled customers of professional commodity brokers could seek redress for the brokers' violations of the Act or CFTC regulations. Thus, § 14 of the CEA provides that any person injured by such violations may apply to the Commission for an order directing the offender to pay reparations to the complainant and may enforce that order in federal district court. Congress intended this administrative procedure to be an "inexpensive and expeditious" alternative to existing fora available to aggrieved customers, namely, the courts and arbitration.

In conformance with the congressional goal of promoting efficient dispute resolution, the CFTC promulgated a regulation in 1976 which allows it to adjudicate counterclaims "aris[ing] out of the transaction or occurrence or series of transactions or occurrences set forth in the complaint." 17 CFR § 12.23(b)(2) (1983). This permissive counterclaim rule leaves the respondent in a reparations proceeding free to seek relief against the reparations complainant in other fora.

The instant dispute arose in February 1980, when respondents Schor and Mortgage Services of America, Inc., invoked the CFTC's reparations jurisdiction by filing complaints against petitioner ContiCommodity Services, Inc. (Conti), a commodity futures broker, and Richard L. Sandor, a Conti employee. Schor had an account with Conti which contained a debit balance because Schor's net futures trading losses and expenses, such as commissions, exceeded the funds deposited in the account. Schor alleged that this debit balance was the result of Conti's numerous violations of the CEA.

Before receiving notice that Schor had commenced the reparations proceeding, Conti had filed a diversity action in Federal District Court to recover the debit balance. Schor counterclaimed in this action, reiterating his charges that the debit balance was due to Conti's violations of the CEA. Schor also moved on two separate occasions to dismiss or stay the District Court action, arguing that the continuation of the federal action would be a waste of judicial resources and an undue burden on the litigants in view of the fact that "[t]he reparations proceedings . . . will fully . . . resolve and adjudicate all the rights of the parties to this action with respect to the transactions which are the subject matter of this action."

Although the District Court declined to stay or dismiss the suit, Conti voluntarily dismissed the federal court action and presented its debit balance claim by way of a counterclaim in the CFTC reparations proceeding. Conti denied violating the CEA and instead insisted that the debit balance resulted from Schor's trading, and was therefore a simple debt owed by Schor.

After discovery, briefing, and a hearing, the Administrative Law Judge (ALJ) in Schor's reparations proceeding ruled in Conti's favor on both Schor's claims and Conti's counterclaims. After this ruling, Schor for the first time challenged the CFTC's statutory authority to adjudicate Conti's counterclaim. The ALJ rejected Schor's challenge, stating himself "bound by agency regulations and published agency policies." The Commission declined to review the decision and allowed it to become final, at which point Schor filed a petition for review with the Court of Appeals for the District of Columbia Circuit. Prior to oral argument, the Court of Appeals, *sua sponte*, raised the question whether CFTC could constitutionally adjudicate Conti's counterclaims in light of *Northern Pipeline Construction Co. v. Marathon Pipe Line Co.*, 458 U.S. 50 (1982), in which this Court held that "Congress may not vest in a non-Article III court the power to adjudicate, render final judgment, and issue binding orders in a traditional contract action arising under state law, without consent of the litigants, and subject only to ordinary appellate review." *Thomas v. Union Carbide Agricultural Products Co.*, 473 U.S. 568, 584 (1985) (*Thomas*).

After briefing and argument, the Court of Appeals upheld the CFTC's decision on Schor's claim in most respects, but ordered the dismissal of Conti's counterclaims on the ground that "the CFTC lacks authority (subject matter competence) to adjudicate" common law counterclaims. In support of this latter ruling, the Court of Appeals reasoned that the CFTC's exercise of jurisdiction over Conti's common law counterclaim gave rise to "[s]erious constitutional problems" under *Northern Pipeline*. . . .

This Court granted the CFTC's petition for certiorari, vacated the Court of Appeals' judgment, and remanded the case for further consideration in light of *Thomas, supra*. We had there ruled that the arbitration scheme established under the Federal Insecticide, Fungicide, and Rodenticide Act (FIFRA), does not contravene Article III and, more generally, held that "Congress, acting for a valid legislative purpose pursuant to its constitutional powers under Article I, may create a seemingly 'private' right that is so closely integrated into a public regulatory scheme as to be a matter appropriate for agency resolution with limited involvement by the Article III judiciary." 473 U.S. at 593.

On remand, the Court of Appeals reinstated its prior judgment. It reaffirmed its earlier view that *Northern Pipeline* drew into serious question the Commission's authority to decide debit-balance counterclaims in reparations proceedings; concluded that nothing in *Thomas* altered that view; and again held that, in light of the constitutional problems posed by the CFTC's adjudication of common law counterclaims, the CEA should be construed to authorize the CFTC to adjudicate only counterclaims arising from violations of the Act or CFTC regulations.

We again granted certiorari, and now reverse.

* * *

III

Article III, § 1, directs that the "judicial Power of the United States shall be vested in one supreme Court and in such inferior Courts as the Congress may from time to time ordain and establish," and provides that these federal courts shall be staffed by judges who hold office during good behavior, and whose compensation shall not be diminished during tenure in office. Schor claims that these provisions prohibit Congress from authorizing the initial adjudication of common law counterclaims by the CFTC, an administrative agency whose adjudicatory officers do not enjoy the tenure and salary protections embodied in Article III.

Although our precedents in this area do not admit of easy synthesis, they do establish that the resolution of claims such as Schor's cannot turn on conclusory reference to the language of Article III. Rather, the constitutionality of a given congressional delegation of adjudicative functions to a non-Article III body must be assessed by reference to the purposes underlying the requirements of Article III. This inquiry, in turn, is guided by the principle that "practical attention to substance rather than doctrinaire reliance on formal categories should inform application of Article III." *Thomas, supra,* at 587. See also *Crowell v. Benson,* 285 U.S. at 53.

A

Article III, § 1, serves both to protect "the role of the independent judiciary within the constitutional scheme of tripartite government," *Thomas, supra,* at 583, and to safeguard litigants' "right to have claims decided before judges who are free from potential domination by other branches of government." *United States v. Will,* 449 U.S. 200, 218 (1980). Although our cases have provided us with little occasion to discuss the nature or significance of this latter safeguard, our prior discussions of Article III, § 1's guarantee of an independent and impartial adjudication by the federal judiciary of matters within the judicial power of the United States intimated that this guarantee serves to protect primarily personal, rather than structural, interests.

. . . . [A]s a personal right, Article III's guarantee of an impartial and independent federal adjudication is subject to waiver, just as are other personal constitutional rights that dictate the procedures by which civil and criminal matters must be tried. Indeed, the relevance of concepts of waiver to Article III challenges is demonstrated by our decision in *Northern Pipeline,* in which the absence of consent to an initial adjudication before a non-Article III tribunal was relied on as a significant factor in determining that Article III forbade such adjudication. See, *e.g.,* 458 U.S. at 80, n. 31.

In the instant cases, Schor indisputably waived any right he may have possessed to the full trial of Conti's counterclaim before an Article III court. Schor expressly demanded that Conti proceed on its counterclaim in the reparations proceeding rather than before the District Court, and was content to have the entire dispute settled in the forum he had selected until the ALJ ruled against him on all counts; it was only after the ALJ rendered a decision to which he objected that Schor raised any challenge to the CFTC's consideration of Conti's counterclaim. . . .

B

As noted above, our precedents establish that Article III, § 1, not only preserves to litigants their interest in an impartial and independent federal adjudication of claims within the judicial power of the United States, but also serves as "an inseparable element of the constitutional system of checks and balances." *Northern Pipeline, supra,* 458 U.S. at 58. Article III, § 1 safeguards the role of the Judicial Branch in our tripartite system by barring congressional attempts "to transfer jurisdiction [to non-Article III tribunals] for the purpose of emasculating" constitutional courts, *National Insurance Co. v. Tidewater Co.,* 337 U.S. 582, 644 (1949) (Vinson, C.J., dissenting), and thereby preventing "the encroachment or aggrandizement of one branch at the expense of the other." *Buckley v. Valeo,* 424 U.S. 1, 122 (1976). To the extent that this structural principle is implicated in a given case, the parties cannot by consent cure the constitutional difficulty for the same reason that the parties by consent cannot confer on federal courts subject-matter jurisdiction beyond the limitations imposed by Article III, § 2. When these Article III limitations are at issue, notions of consent and waiver cannot be dispositive because the limitations serve institutional interests that the parties cannot be expected to protect.

In determining the extent to which a given congressional decision to authorize the adjudication of Article III business in a non-Article III tribunal impermissibly threatens the institutional integrity of the Judicial Branch, the Court has declined to adopt formalistic and unbending rules. Although such rules might lend a greater degree of coherence to this area of the law, they might also unduly constrict Congress' ability to take needed and innovative action pursuant to its Article I powers. Thus, in reviewing Article III challenges, we have weighed a number of factors, none of which has been deemed determinative, with an eye to the practical effect that the congressional action will have on the constitutionally assigned role of the federal judiciary. Among the factors upon which we have focused are the extent to which the "essential attributes of judicial power" are reserved to Article III courts, and, conversely, the extent to which the non-Article III forum exercises the range of jurisdiction and powers normally vested only in Article III courts, the origins and importance of the right to be adjudicated, and the concerns that drove Congress to depart from the requirements of Article III.

An examination of the relative allocation of powers between the CFTC and Article III courts in light of the considerations given prominence in our precedents demonstrates that the congressional scheme does not impermissibly intrude on the province of the judiciary. The CFTC's adjudicatory powers depart from the traditional agency model in just one respect: the CFTC's jurisdiction over common law counterclaims. While wholesale importation of concepts of pendent or ancillary jurisdiction into the agency context may create greater constitutional difficulties, we decline to endorse an absolute prohibition on such jurisdiction out of fear of where some hypothetical "slippery slope" may deposit us. . . .

In the instant cases, we are . . . persuaded that there is little practical reason to find that this single deviation from the agency model is fatal to the congressional scheme. Aside from its authorization of counterclaim jurisdiction, the CEA leaves far more of the "essential attributes of judicial power" to Article III courts than did that portion of the Bankruptcy Act found unconstitutional in *Northern Pipeline*. The CEA scheme in fact hews closely to the agency model approved by the Court in *Crowell v. Benson*, 285 U.S. 22 (1932).

The CFTC, like the agency in *Crowell*, deals only with a "particularized area of law," whereas the jurisdiction of the bankruptcy courts found unconstitutional in *Northern Pipeline* extended to broadly "all civil proceedings arising under title 11 or arising in or *related to* cases under title 11." CFTC orders, like those of the agency in *Crowell*, but unlike those of the bankruptcy courts under the 1978 Act, are enforceable only by order of the district court. CFTC orders are also reviewed under the same "weight of the evidence" standard sustained in *Crowell*, rather than the more deferential standard found lacking in *Northern Pipeline*. The legal rulings of the CFTC, like the legal determinations of the agency in *Crowell*, are subject to *de novo* review. Finally, the CFTC, unlike the bankruptcy courts under the 1978 Act, does not exercise "all ordinary powers of district courts," and thus may not, for instance, preside over jury trials or issue writs of habeas corpus.

Of course, the nature of the claim has significance in our Article III analysis quite apart from the method prescribed for its adjudication. The counterclaim asserted in this litigation is a "private" right for which state law provides the rule of decision. It is therefore a claim of the kind assumed to be at the "core" of matters normally reserved to Article III courts. Yet this conclusion does not end our inquiry; just as this Court has rejected any attempt to make determinative for Article III purposes the distinction between public rights and private rights, there is no reason inherent in separation of powers principles to accord the state law character of a claim talismanic power in Article III inquiries. . . .

The risk that Congress may improperly have encroached on the federal judiciary is obviously magnified when Congress "withdraw[s] from judicial cognizance any matter which, from its nature, is the subject of a suit at the common law, or in equity, or admiralty" and which therefore has traditionally been tried in Article III courts, and allocates the decision of those matters to a non-Article III forum of its own creation. *Murray's Lessee v. Hoboken Land & Improvement Co.*, 18 How. 272, 284 (1856). Accordingly, where private, common law rights are at stake, our examination of the congressional attempt to control the manner in which those rights are adjudicated has been searching. In this litigation, however, '[l]ooking beyond form to the substance of what" Congress has done, we are persuaded that the congressional authorization of limited CFTC jurisdiction over a narrow class of common law claims as an incident to the CFTC's primary, and unchallenged, adjudicative function does not create a substantial threat to the separation of powers. . . .

The CFTC adjudication of common law counterclaims is incidental to, and completely dependent upon, adjudication of reparations claims created by federal law, and in actual fact is limited to claims arising out of the same transaction or occurrence as the reparations claim.

In such circumstances, the magnitude of any intrusion on the Judicial Branch can only be termed *de minimis*. Conversely, were we to hold that the Legislative Branch may not permit such limited cognizance of common law counterclaims at the election of the parties, it is clear that we would "defeat the obvious purpose of the legislation to furnish a prompt, continuous, expert and inexpensive method for dealing with a class of questions of fact which are peculiarly suited to examination and determination by an administrative agency specially assigned to that task." *Crowell v. Benson, supra,* 285 U.S. at 46. We do not think Article III compels this degree of prophylaxis. . . .

[T]his case raises no question of the aggrandizement of congressional power at the expense of a coordinate branch. Instead, the separation of powers question presented in this litigation is whether Congress impermissibly undermined, without appreciable expansion of its own power, the role of the Judicial Branch. . . .

[W]e have also been faithful to our Article III precedents, which counsel that bright-line rules cannot effectively be employed to yield broad principles applicable in all Article III inquiries. Rather, due regard must be given in each case to the unique aspects of the congressional plan at issue and its practical consequences in light of the larger concerns that underlie Article III. We conclude that the limited jurisdiction that the CFTC asserts over state law claims as a necessary incident to the adjudication of federal claims willingly submitted by the parties for initial agency adjudication does not contravene separation of powers principles or Article III. . . .

JUSTICE BRENNAN, with whom JUSTICE MARSHALL joins, dissenting.

Article III, § 1, of the Constitution provides that "[t]he judicial Power of the United States, shall be vested in one supreme Court, and in such inferior Courts as the Congress may from time to time ordain and establish." It further specifies that the federal judicial power must be exercised by judges who "shall hold their Offices during good Behaviour, and [who] shall, at stated Times, receive for their Services a Compensation, which shall not be diminished during their Continuance in Office."

On its face, Article III, § 1, seems to prohibit the vesting of *any* judicial functions in either the Legislative or the Executive Branch. The Court has, however, recognized three narrow exceptions to the otherwise absolute mandate of Article III: territorial courts; courts-martial; and courts that adjudicate certain disputes concerning public rights . . . .

Article III's prophylactic protections were intended to prevent just this sort of abdication to claims of legislative convenience. The Court requires that the legislative interest in convenience and efficiency be weighed against the competing interest in judicial independence. In doing so, the Court pits an interest the benefits of which are immediate, concrete, and easily understood against one, the benefits of which are almost entirely prophylactic, and thus often seem remote and not worth the cost in any single case. . . .

Perhaps the resolution of reparations claims such as respondents' may be accomplished more conveniently under the Court's decision than under my approach, but the Framers foreswore this sort of convenience in order to preserve freedom. . . .

The decision today may authorize the administrative adjudication only of state-law claims that stem from the same transaction or set of facts that allow the customer of a professional commodity broker to initiate reparations proceedings before the CFTC, but the *reasoning* of this decision strongly suggests that, given "legislative necessity" and party consent, any federal agency may decide state-law issues that are ancillary to federal issues within the agency's jurisdiction. . . .

The Court's reliance on Schor's "consent" to a non-Article III tribunal is also misplaced. . . .

In my view, the structural and individual interests served by Article III are inseparable. . . . I do not believe that a litigant may ever waive his right to an Article III tribunal where one is constitutionally required. . . .

NOTES AND QUESTIONS

1. Summary. In *Schor*, the Court once again focused on whether the federal courts maintained the "essential attributes" of the judicial power. The CFTC, like the agency in *Crowell*, dealt only with a "particularized area of law," whereas in *Northern Pipeline* the bankruptcy court's jurisdiction extended to "all civil proceedings arising under title 11 or arising in or related to cases under title 11." The CFTC orders, like those in *Crowell*, were enforceable only by order of the district court. The CFTC orders were reviewed under the less deferential standard in *Crowell*. The Court also noted that questions of law were reviewed de novo by the courts, but note that this will sometimes be incorrect under *Chevron*. Finally, the CFTC had less power than the bankruptcy court—it couldn't empanel juries or issue writs of habeas corpus.

Recall, however, that in addition to requiring that the courts maintain the essential attributes of judicial power, the Court in *Northern Pipeline* also held that the nature of the claim mattered. A claim deriving from federal statute, if the courts maintained the essential attributes of judicial power, could be heard by an agency. But the Court in *Northern Pipeline* seemed to say that this did not apply to any common-law or state-law claim. In *Schor*, the Court makes an exception: a common-law or state-law claim can be heard by an agency if adjudication of the claim "is incidental to, and completely dependent upon, adjudication of reparations claims created by federal law, and in actual fact is limited to claims arising out of the same transaction or occurrence as the reparations claim."

The identity of the relevant facts raises an interesting point: This is, ultimately, a private-rights case. It is about the liability of one private party to another, as was the case in *Crowell*. Isn't Justice O'Connor right that it shouldn't matter whether the substantive law is state law or federal law? It's a private rights claim either way. But isn't that a reason why this case should be heard in a federal court, and not in an administrative agency?

2. ***Is the Seventh Amendment relevant?*** (Revisited.) If Schor had not consented to the administrative adjudication, there is no doubt that, under *Granfinanciera*, he would have been entitled to a jury trial. And thus at least Conti's common law claim would have had to be heard by a jury. Is it fair to say, then, that the "rule" of *Schor* is that state-law or common-law claims can be heard as part of an otherwise valid administrative adjudication if those claims "aris[e] out of the same transaction or occurrence" as the federal statutory claim *and* the individual consents to the administrative adjudication of those claims?

3. ***Formalism and* Stern v. Marshall.** The Court in *Schor* took a decidedly functionalist approach to the use of administrative adjudications and explicitly rejected the formalism. In recent years, however, the Court has pivoted yet again to formalism. In Stern v. Marshall, 564 U.S. 462 (2011), the Supreme Court held that a bankruptcy court could not constitutionally adjudicate a defamation suit brought by a third party against the estate. The Court held, along the lines of *Northern Pipeline*, that this was a suit "under state common law between two private parties." Of course, so was the suit at issue in *Schor*. Thus, to distinguish *Schor*, the Court in *Stern* explained that *Schor* was a unique exception because there the common-law counterclaim and the administrative claim had involved a "single dispute" in a "narrow class of common law claims" in a "particularized area of law" governed by a "specific and limited federal regulatory scheme" in which the agency has "obvious expertise," and whose orders could only be enforceable by a district court. The Court held that for similar reasons *Crowell v. Benson* was distinguishable.

FORMALISM VS. FUNCTIONALISM
Having now seen formalism and functionalism play out in cases involving legislative, executive, and judicial power, which approach to constitutional interpretation do you prefer? Why?

Justice Scalia was not persuaded by the surfeit of factors that went into the Court's analysis. He would have held simply that an Article III judge is required in all federal adjudications, except where there is a "firmly established historical practice to the contrary," for example respecting territorial courts, military courts, and true "public rights" cases—the same point Justices Brennan and Marshall made in *Schor*. Justice Scalia also would have excepted administrative adjudications, which, "for better or worse," are governed by the Court's "landmark decision in *Crowell v. Benson.*"

The four dissenting Justices found it difficult to distinguish the kind of claim involved with those in *Crowell v. Benson*. The dissent therefore thought the Court's opinion cast doubt on the validity of numerous administrative adjudications that resolved disputes between private parties, like those undertaken by the National Labor Relations Board, the CFTC, and many other agencies. Weren't they right?

4. *A solution?* Is one solution to the potential Article III problem with allowing agencies to hear private rights cases simply to make the agencies true "adjuncts" of the district courts? Is it impracticable to treat agency decisions in private rights cases like reports from magistrate judges? Such reports are reviewable de novo, but only those parts that are specifically objected to. Wouldn't such a system create efficiency but also satisfy Article III? See Ilan Wurman, *Constitutional Administration*, 69 Stan. L. Rev. 359, 423–24 (2017).

PRACTICE POINTER It is worth remembering that administrative law is not all about courts or the executive, it is also about Congress, which can always amend the relevant statutes. What kind of statutory reforms might you recommend to Congress in light of the materials covered in this and other chapters?

4. Synthesis

The Court noted in both *Schor* and *Northern Pipeline* that its cases in this area do not admit of "easy synthesis." Yet some synthesis can be had. There are some "easy" cases that, it would seem, must be heard by Article III courts, and also some "easy" cases that can most certainly be heard in the executive branch.

Criminal cases. One "easy" set of cases are criminal cases involving loss of life and liberty (in the sense of imprisonment). These must be tried by Article III courts. Federal criminal cases clearly "arise under the laws of the United States." They fall within the core of the "judicial power," because they involve the core private rights to life and liberty. Article III, § 3 further says that the trials of all crimes shall be by jury, implying both the need for a jury and an Article III tribunal. (Remember, administrative agencies don't have juries.) Finally, the Fifth Amendment's due process clause likely also requires at least that much, if by "due process of law" is meant that no one can be deprived of life or liberty without the protection afforded by a jury or a judge with life tenure and salary protections. No case has allowed an administrative agency to deprive someone of life or liberty in this sense.

State-law or common-law claims. After *Stern v. Marshall*, it is probably a correct statement of law that state-law or common-law claims must ordinarily be heard by an Article III court. The most obvious exception to this rule is *Schor*, where the state-law claims arose out of the same occurrence and the jury trial right had been waived.

Public rights cases. In contrast to cases existing at state or common law or criminal cases, those involving truly public rights can be adjudicated by administrative agencies. Although the scope of the public rights doctrine is disputed, these cases include *at least* the adjudication of claims against the government itself, like a claim for veterans' benefits or public welfare. As explained, the traditional argument in favor of executive-branch adjudication in these cases is that they involve rights that only exist by the grace of government, and because of the government's sovereign immunity—the government doesn't have to consent to be sued at all, let alone to be sued in an Article III court.

Non-criminal federal statutory rights. Now we come to the most difficult and contested category of cases. The cases (including *Atlas Roofing* and *Jones & Laughlin* and *Crowell v. Benson*) seem to allow administrative adjudication of certain disputes between private parties without the requirement of a jury or Article III court, so long as they involve new "statutory" rights and obligations. What distinguishes such disputes from other private disputes?

First, don't such disputes "arise under the laws of the United States," such that they must be heard by an Article III court that can exercise the "judicial power" of the United States? Indeed, keep in mind that normally cases arising under federal statutes, like the Sherman Act or 42 U.S.C. § 1983, *are* heard by Article III courts. What distinguishes "administrative statutes" like the Occupational Safety and Health Act or the National Labor Relations Act from these other "non-administrative" federal statutes? Don't both kinds of statutes arise under the laws of the United States? Isn't the only difference whom Congress chooses to task with enforcement (i.e., the U.S. Attorney offices or some administrative agency)?

Second, don't such disputes equally deprive persons of liberty or property by forcing them to pay monetary damages or enjoining them from doing certain things? The due process clause does not distinguish between deprivations of property resulting from common law claims, federal statutes, or "administrative" federal statutes. It says simply that no person shall be deprived of life, liberty, or property without due process of law. Why would the full import of the due process clause apply only to common-law claims or federal statutes like the Sherman Act or 42 U.S.C. § 1983, but not cases arising under "administrative" statutes, if the resulting deprivation is the same?

Whatever the constitutional infirmities, this is the current state of the doctrine: if a federal statute creates an administrative, regulatory regime enforceable by an agency, then an agency may hear a claim even between two private parties so long as there is some amount of review in the federal courts, even if deferential, such that the federal courts retain the "essential attributes" of judicial power as articulated in *Crowell* and *Northern Pipeline*.

B. Due Process

In addition to Article III, the due process clause may impose limits on how adjudications are conducted. The due process clause of the Fifth Amendment provides, "No person shall . . . be deprived of life, liberty, or property without due process of law." There are two due process questions that must be addressed in the context of administrative law: Does the due process clause even apply? And if it does, what process is due?

1.   When Does Due Process Apply?

Not every agency action is subject to the due process clause. Are you enti-tled to a personal adjudication before an agency makes a regulation? Or are you only entitled to a hearing in an adjudication? That is the subject of the following pair of famous cases.

 CROSS REFERENCE We introduced the *Londoner/Bi-Metallic* distinction in Chapter 2, when discussing the distinction be-tween rulemakings and adjudications.

Londoner v. Denver

210 U.S. 373 (1908)

MR. JUSTICE MOODY delivered the opinion of the court:

The plaintiffs in error began this proceeding in a state court of Colora-do to relieve lands owned by them from an assessment of a tax for the cost of paving a street upon which the lands abutted. The relief sought was granted by the trial court, but its action was reversed by the supreme court of the state, which ordered judgment for the defendants. . . .

The tax complained of was assessed under the provisions of the charter of the city of Denver, which confers upon the city the power to make local im-provements and to assess the cost upon property specially benefited. . . .

It appears from the charter that, in the execution of the power to make lo-cal improvements and assess the cost upon the property specially benefited, the main steps to be taken by the city authorities . . . [include] [t]he assessment of the cost upon the landowners after due notice and opportunity for hearing. . . .

The fifth assignment [of error], though general, vague, and obscure, fair-ly raises, we think, the question whether the assessment was made without notice and opportunity for hearing to those affected by it, thereby denying to them due process of law. The trial court found as a fact that no opportunity for hearing was afforded, and the supreme court did not disturb this finding. . . .

The facts out of which the question on this assignment arises may be com-pressed into small compass. The first step in the assessment proceedings was by the certificate of the board of public works of the cost of the improvement and a preliminary apportionment of it. The last step was the enactment of the assessment ordinance. From beginning to end of the proceedings the landowners, although allowed to formulate and file complaints and objections, were not afforded an opportunity to be heard upon them. Upon these facts, was there a denial by the state of the due process of law guaranteed by the 14th Amendment to the Constitution of the United States? . . .

[W]here the legislature of a state, instead of fixing the tax itself, commits to some subordinate body the duty of determining whether, in what amount, and upon whom it shall be levied, and of making its assessment and apportionment, due process of law requires that, at some stage of the proceedings, before the tax becomes irrevocably fixed, the taxpayer shall have an opportunity to be heard, of which he must have notice, either personal, by publication, or by a law fixing the time and place of the hearing. . . .

If it is enough that, under such circumstances, an opportunity is given to submit in writing all objections to and complaints of the tax to the board, then there was a hearing afforded in the case at bar. But we think that something more than that, even in proceedings for taxation, is required by due process of law. Many requirements essential in strictly judicial proceedings may be dispensed with in proceedings of this nature. But even here a hearing, in its very essence, demands that he who is entitled to it shall have the right to support his allegations by argument, however brief: and, if need be, by proof, however informal.

It is apparent that such a hearing was denied to the plaintiffs in error. The denial was by the city council, which, while acting as a board of equalization, represents the state. The assessment was therefore void, and the plaintiffs in error were entitled to a decree discharging their lands from a lien on account of it. . . .

The Chief Justice and Mr. Justice Holmes dissent [without written opinion—Ed.].

Bi-Metallic Investment Co. v. State Bd. of Equalization

<u>239 U.S. 441 (1915)</u>

MR. JUSTICE HOLMES delivered the opinion of the court:

This is a suit to enjoin the State Board of Equalization and the Colorado Tax Commission from putting in force and the defendant Pitcher, as assessor of Denver, from obeying, an order of the boards, increasing the valuation of all taxable property in Denver 40 per cent. . . . The plaintiff is the owner of real estate in Denver, and brings the case here on the ground that it was given no opportunity to be heard, and that therefore its property will be taken without due process of law, contrary to the 14th Amendment of the Constitution of the United States. . . . The question, then, is whether all individuals have a constitutional right to be heard before a matter can be decided in which all are equally concerned . . . .

Where a rule of conduct applies to more than a few people, it is impracticable that everyone should have a direct voice in its adoption. The Constitution does not require all public acts to be done in town meeting or an assembly of the whole. General statutes within the state power are passed that affect the person or property of individuals, sometimes to the point of ruin, without giving them a chance to be heard. Their rights are protected in the only way that they can be in a complex society, by their power, immediate or remote, over those who make the rule.

If the result in this case had been reached, as it might have been by the state's doubling the rate of taxation, no one would suggest that the 14th Amendment was violated unless every person affected had been allowed an opportunity to raise his voice against it before the body intrusted by the state Constitution with the power. In considering this case in this court we must assume that the proper state machinery has been used, and the question is whether, if the state Constitution had declared that Denver had been undervalued as compared with the rest of the state, and had decreed that for the current year the valuation should be 40 per cent higher, the objection now urged could prevail.

It appears to us that to put the question is to answer it. There must be a limit to individual argument in such matters if government is to go on. In Londoner v. Denver, 210 U.S. 373, a local board had to determine 'whether, in what amount, and upon whom' a tax for paving a street should be levied for special benefits. A relatively small number of persons was concerned, who were exceptionally affected, in each case upon individual grounds, and it was held that they had a right to a hearing. But that decision is far from reaching a general determination dealing only with the principle upon which all the assessments in a county had been laid.

Judgment affirmed.

NOTES AND QUESTIONS

1.   What do these cases stand for? *Londoner* and *Bi-Metallic* are a pair of cases often discussed when courts make determinations of whether the due process clause applies to a particular agency action. *Bi-Metallic* stands for the rather commonsense proposition that a general legislative-type rule—in that case, the tax rate on all taxable property in the city of Denver shall increase by 40 percent—does not trigger the due process clause. After all, it is up to the *legislature,* or in the context of local government, perhaps the board of equalization, to determine as a legislative matter what the prospective tax rates shall be. The only "process" that is required is the standard legislative process established in the federal, state, or city constitution.

In *Londoner,* in contrast, the general legislative provision allowed the city to make improvements and to assess the cost on the property owners abutting the improvement; the question seems to have been, at least in part, whether the assessment was correctly applied in that particular case. (*Londoner* raised many other issues, too, most of which were entirely frivolous.) Understood thus, *Londoner* can perhaps stand for the proposition that in *applying* a general law to a particular person or set of facts, some amount of "process" is due to the individuals against whom the law is being applied. That is a standard account of the meaning of "due process of law." In this sense, presumably someone could have even challenged the 40 percent increase in *Bi-Metallic* as applied to their own property if, for example, they claimed their property wasn't in fact in the city of Denver, or perhaps if it was otherwise exempt.

Londoner and *Bi-Metallic* can easily be misinterpreted. In *Bi-Metallic,* Justice Holmes distinguished *Londoner* on the ground that, there, "[a] relatively small number of persons was concerned, who were exceptionally affected, in each case upon individual grounds." Yet that surely cannot be the determining factor in whether the due process clause applies. If 100 people are all indicted in a criminal conspiracy, the sheer size of the conspiracy does not negate the relevance of the due process clause. Each would still be entitled to a trial. And on the other side of the coin, sometimes legislatively enacted laws affect a very small number of people. A state legislature might enact a statute prohibiting certain structures on, say, large beachfront properties, even if only 10 residents have such properties. These residents could of course petition the legislature itself or otherwise make themselves heard in the legislative and political process, but they would not be entitled to an adjudication or to "due process of law" before the legislature enacted such a law. They would, however, be entitled to "due process of law" in an adjudication if they believed the law was being improperly *applied* to them.

The due process clause, in summary, applies when a law is applied to particular individuals and as a result those individuals might be deprived of life, liberty, or property. (In the administrative context, obviously, life is not at stake; but liberty and property rights often are.) Translating this to administrative law, general and prospective regulations do not trigger the due process clause, just as generally enacted laws do not trigger the clause, unless the agency or the legislature is actually seeking to deprive someone of their liberty or property directly by regulation or statute. As a general matter, the due process clause applies when the prospective law or rule is then applied to individuals, for example those who have violated the law or rule, and the result might be a deprivation of liberty or property. For additional discussion of these matters, consider revisiting the note on retroactivity on pp. 237–239, supra.

2. *Due process and "public rights."* The due process clause only comes into play if an individual is to be deprived of "life, liberty, or property." To determine whether the clause applies, then, the agency also has to know what counts as "liberty" or "property." Historically, "public rights" or "privileges" such as land grants or welfare benefits did not count as property for purposes of the due process clause. As explained in the preceding section on Article III, historically court adjudications were not even required for such matters because of sovereign immunity. If the government does not have to give welfare benefits in the first place—and, if it chooses to afford such benefits, it does not have to agree to be sued in the event that someone feels those benefits are wrongfully withheld—then clearly the due process clause cannot apply. The government can consent to be sued, of course, but it can do so on conditions—for example, on the condition that there be an executive-branch-only adjudication, or perhaps an executive adjudication with limited judicial review. The greater power to refuse consent, in other words, includes the lesser power to consent on conditions.

 CROSS REFERENCE The sections in this chapter on judicial power introduced the distinction between private and public rights. Does that distinction matter for purposes of the Due Process Clause? To which kind of rights does the clause refer?

In short, just as a federal court adjudication was not constitutionally necessary to hear these "public rights" cases, the due process clause did not apply to them, either. The clause only applied to traditional, private rights, such as property earned or obtained in a free market. That all changed with the next, landmark case.

Goldberg v. Kelly

397 U.S. 254 (1970)

Mr. Justice Brennan delivered the opinion of the Court.

The question for decision is whether a State that terminates public assistance payments to a particular recipient without affording him the opportunity for an evidentiary hearing prior to termination denies the recipient procedural due process in violation of the Due Process Clause of the Fourteenth Amendment.

This action was brought in the District Court for the Southern District of New York by residents of New York City receiving financial aid under the federally assisted program of Aid to Families with Dependent Children (AFDC) or under New York State's general Home Relief program. Their complaint alleged that the New York State and New York City officials administering these programs terminated, or were about to terminate, such aid without prior notice and hearing, thereby denying them due process of law. At the time the suits were filed there was no requirement of prior notice or hearing of any kind before termination of financial aid. However, the State and city adopted procedures for notice and hearing after the suits were brought, and the plaintiffs, appellees here, then challenged the constitutional adequacy of those procedures.

The State Commissioner of Social Services amended the State Department of Social Services' Official Regulations to require that local social services officials proposing to discontinue or suspend a recipient's financial aid do so according to a procedure that conforms to either subdivision (a) or subdivision (b) of § 351.26 of the regulations as amended. The City of New York elected to promulgate a local procedure according to subdivision (b). That subdivision, so far as here pertinent, provides that the local procedure must include the giving of notice to the recipient of the reasons for a proposed discontinuance or suspension at least seven days prior to its effective date, with notice also that upon request the recipient may have the proposal reviewed by a local welfare official holding a position superior to that of the supervisor who approved the proposed discontinuance or suspension, and, further, that the recipient may submit, for purposes of the review, a written statement to demonstrate why his grant should not be discontinued or suspended. The decision by the reviewing official whether to discontinue or suspend aid must be made expeditiously, with written notice of the decision to the recipient. . . .

Pursuant to subdivision (b), the New York City Department of Social Services promulgated Procedure No. 68–18. A caseworker who has doubts about the recipient's continued eligibility must first discuss them with the recipient. If the caseworker concludes that the recipient is no longer eligible, he recommends termination of aid to a unit supervisor. If the latter concurs, he sends the recipient a letter stating the reasons for proposing to terminate aid and notifying him that within seven days he may request that a higher official review the record, and may support the request with a written statement prepared personally or with the aid of an attorney or other person. If the reviewing official affirms the determination of ineligibility, aid is stopped immediately and the recipient is informed by letter of the reasons for the action. Appellees' challenge to this procedure emphasizes the absence of any provisions for the personal appearance of the recipient before the reviewing official, for oral presentation of evidence, and for confrontation and cross-examination of adverse witnesses. However, the letter does inform the recipient that he may request a post-termination 'fair hearing.' This is a proceeding before an independent state hearing officer at which the recipient may appear personally, offer oral evidence, confront and cross-examine the witnesses against him, and have a record made of the hearing. If the recipient prevails at the 'fair hearing' he is paid all funds erroneously withheld. A recipient whose aid is not restored by a 'fair hearing' decision may have judicial review. . . .

I

The constitutional issue to be decided, therefore, is the narrow one whether the Due Process Clause requires that the recipient be afforded an evidentiary hearing before the termination of benefits. The District Court held that only a pre-termination evidentiary hearing would satisfy the constitutional command, and rejected the argument of the state and city officials that the combination of the post-termination 'fair hearing' with the informal pre-termination review disposed of all due process claims. The court said: 'While post-termination review is relevant, there is one overpowering fact which controls here. By hypothesis, a welfare recipient is destitute, without funds or assets. . . . Suffice it to say that to cut off a welfare recipient in the face of . . . 'brutal need' without a prior hearing of some sort is unconscionable, unless overwhelming considerations justify it.' The court rejected the argument that the need to protect the public's tax revenues supplied the requisite 'overwhelming consideration.' . . . We affirm.

Appellant does not contend that procedural due process is not applicable to the termination of welfare benefits. Such benefits are a matter of statutory entitlement for persons qualified to receive them.[8] Their termination involves state action that adjudicates important rights. The constitutional challenge cannot be answered by an argument that public assistance benefits are "a 'privilege' and not a 'right.'" Shapiro v. Thompson, 394 U.S. 618, 627 n. 6 (1969). Relevant constitutional restraints apply as much to the withdrawal of public assistance benefits as to disqualification for unemployment compensation, Sherbert v. Verner, 374 U.S. 398 (1963); or to denial of a tax exemption, Speiser v. Randall, 357 U.S. 513 (1958); or to discharge from public employment, Slochower v. Board of Higher Education, 350 U.S. 551 (1956). The extent to which procedural due

---

[8]   It may be realistic today to regard welfare entitlements as more like 'property' than a 'gratuity.' Much of the existing wealth in this country takes the form of rights that do not fall within traditional common-law concepts of property. It has been aptly noted that

'(s)ociety today is built around entitlement. The automobile dealer has his franchise, the doctor and lawyer their professional licenses, the worker his union membership, contract, and pension rights, the executive his contract and stock options; all are devices to aid security and independence. Many of the most important of these entitlements now flow from government: subsidies to farmers and businessmen, routes for airlines and channels for television stations; long term contracts for defense, space, and education; social security pensions for individuals. Such sources of security, whether private or public, are no longer regarded as luxuries or gratuities; to the recipients they are essentials, fully deserved, and in no sense a form of charity. It is only the poor whose entitlements, although recognized by public policy, have not been effectively enforced.'

Reich, Individual Rights and Social Welfare: The Emerging Legal Issues, 74 Yale L.J. 1245, 1255 (1965). See also Reich, The New Property, 73 Yale L.J. 733 (1964).

process must be afforded the recipient is influenced by the extent to which he may be 'condemned to suffer grievous loss,' Joint Anti-Fascist Refugee Committee v. McGrath, 341 U.S. 123, 168 (1951) (Frankfurter, J., concurring), and depends upon whether the recipient's interest in avoiding that loss outweighs the governmental interest in summary adjudication. Accordingly, as we said in Cafeteria & Restaurant Workers Union, etc. v. McElroy, 367 U.S. 886, 895 (1961), 'consideration of what procedures due process may require under any given set of circumstances must begin with a determination of the precise nature of the government function involved as well as of the private interest that has been affected by governmental action.'

It is true, of course, that some governmental benefits may be administratively terminated without affording the recipient a pre-termination evidentiary hearing. But we agree with the District Court that when welfare is discontinued, only a pre-termination evidentiary hearing provides the recipient with procedural due process. For qualified recipients, welfare provides the means to obtain essential food, clothing, housing, and medical care. Thus the crucial factor in this context—a factor not present in the case of the blacklisted government contractor, the discharged government employee, the taxpayer denied a tax exemption, or virtually anyone else whose governmental entitlements are ended—is that termination of aid pending resolution of a controversy over eligibility may deprive an eligible recipient of the very means by which to live while he waits. Since he lacks independent resources, his situation becomes immediately desperate. His need to concentrate upon finding the means for daily subsistence, in turn, adversely affects his ability to seek redress from the welfare bureaucracy.

Moreover, important governmental interests are promoted by affording recipients a pre-termination evidentiary hearing. From its founding the Nation's basic commitment has been to foster the dignity and well-being of all persons within its borders. We have come to recognize that forces not within the control of the poor contribute to their poverty. This perception, against the background of our traditions, has significantly influenced the development of the contemporary public assistance system. Welfare, by meeting the basic demands of subsistence, can help bring within the reach of the poor the same opportunities that are available to others to participate meaningfully in the life of the community. At the same time, welfare guards against the societal malaise that may flow from a widespread sense of unjustified frustration and insecurity. Public assistance, then, is not mere charity, but a means to 'promote the general Welfare, and secure the Blessings of Liberty to ourselves and our Posterity.' The same governmental interests that counsel the provision of welfare, counsel as well its uninterrupted provision to those eligible to receive it; pre-termination evidentiary hearings are indispensable to that end.

Appellant does not challenge the force of these considerations but argues that they are outweighed by countervailing governmental interests in conserving fiscal and administrative resources. These interests, the argument goes, justify the delay of any evidentiary hearing until after discontinuance of the grants. Summary adjudication protects the public fisc by stopping payments promptly upon discovery of reason to believe that a recipient is no longer eligible. Since most terminations are accepted without challenge, summary adjudication also conserves both the fisc and administrative time and energy by reducing the number of evidentiary hearings actually held.

We agree with the District Court, however, that these governmental interests are not overriding in the welfare context. The requirement of a prior hearing doubtless involves some greater expense, and the benefits paid to ineligible recipients pending decision at the hearing probably cannot be recouped, since these recipients are likely to be judgment-proof. But the State is not without weapons to minimize these increased costs. Much of the drain on fiscal and administrative resources can be reduced by developing procedures for prompt pre-termination hearings and by skillful use of personnel and facilities. Indeed, the very provision for a post-termination evidentiary hearing in New York's Home Relief program is itself cogent evidence that the State recognizes the primacy of the public interest in correct eligibility determinations and therefore in the provision of procedural safeguards. Thus, the interest of the eligible recipient in uninterrupted receipt of public assistance, coupled with the State's interest that his payments not be erroneously terminated, clearly outweighs the State's competing concern to prevent any increase in its fiscal and administrative burdens. . . .

II

We also agree with the District Court, however, that the pre-termination hearing need not take the form of a judicial or quasi-judicial trial. We bear in mind that the statutory 'fair hearing' will provide the recipient with a full administrative review. Accordingly, the pre-termination hearing has one function only: to produce an initial determination of the validity of the welfare department's grounds for discontinuance of payments in order to protect a recipient against an erroneous termination of his benefits. Thus, a complete record and a comprehensive opinion, which would serve primarily to facilitate judicial review and to guide future decisions, need not be provided at the pre-termination stage. We recognize, too, that both welfare authorities and recipients have an interest in relatively speedy resolution of questions of eligibility, that they are used to dealing with one another informally, and that some welfare departments have very burdensome caseloads. These considerations justify the limitation of the pre-termination hearing to minimum procedural safeguards, adapted to the particular characteristics of welfare recipients, and to the limited nature of the controversies to be resolved. We wish to add that we, no less than the dissenters, recognize the importance of not imposing upon the States or the Federal Government in this developing field of law any procedural requirements beyond those demanded by rudimentary due process.

'The fundamental requisite of due process of law is the opportunity to be heard.' Grannis v. Ordean, 234 U.S. 385, 394 (1914). The hearing must be 'at a meaningful time and in a meaningful manner.' Armstrong v. Manzo, 380 U.S. 545, 552 (1965). In the present context these principles require that a recipient have timely and adequate notice detailing the reasons for a proposed termination, and an effective opportunity to defend by confronting any adverse witnesses and by presenting his own arguments and evidence orally. These rights are important in cases such as those before us, where recipients have challenged proposed terminations as resting on incorrect or misleading factual premises or on misapplication of rules or policies to the facts of particular cases.

We are not prepared to say that the seven-day notice currently provided by New York City is constitutionally insufficient per se, although there may be cases where fairness would require that a longer time be given. Nor do we see any constitutional deficiency in the content or form of the notice. New York employs both a letter and a personal conference with a caseworker to inform a recipient of the precise questions raised about his continued eligibility. Evidently the recipient is told the legal and factual bases for the Department's doubts. This combination is probably the most effective method of communicating with recipients.

The city's procedures presently do not permit recipients to appear personally with or without counsel before the official who finally determines continued eligibility. Thus a recipient is not permitted to present evidence to that official orally, or to confront or cross-examine adverse witnesses. These omissions are fatal to the constitutional adequacy of the procedures.

The opportunity to be heard must be tailored to the capacities and circumstances of those who are to be heard. It is not enough that a welfare recipient may present his position to the decision maker in writing or second-hand through his caseworker. Written submissions are an unrealistic option for most recipients, who lack the educational attainment necessary to write effectively and who cannot obtain professional assistance. Moreover, written submissions do not afford the flexibility of oral presentations; they do not permit the recipient to mold his argument to the issues the decision maker appears to regard as important. Particularly where credibility and veracity are at issue, as they must be in many termination proceedings, written submissions are a wholly unsatisfactory basis for decision. The second-hand presentation to the decisionmaker by the caseworker has its own deficiencies; since the caseworker usually gathers the facts upon which the charge of ineligibility rests, the presentation of the recipient's side of the controversy cannot safely be left to him. Therefore a recipient must be allowed to state his position orally. Informal procedures will suffice; in this context due process does not require a particular order of proof or mode of offering evidence.

In almost every setting where important decisions turn on questions of fact, due process requires an opportunity to confront and cross-examine adverse witnesses. . . .

'The right to be heard would be, in many cases, of little avail if it did not comprehend the right to be heard by counsel.' Powell v. Alabama, 287 U.S. 45, 68–69 (1932). We do not say that counsel must be provided at the pre-termination hearing, but only that the recipient must be allowed to retain an attorney if he so desires. . . . We do not anticipate that this assistance will unduly prolong or otherwise encumber the hearing. . . .

Finally, the decisionmaker's conclusion as to a recipient's eligibility must rest solely on the legal rules and evidence adduced at the hearing. To demonstrate compliance with this elementary requirement, the decision maker should state the reasons for his determination and indicate the evidence he relied on, though his statement need not amount to a full opinion or even formal findings of fact and conclusions of law. And, of course, an impartial decision maker is essential. We agree with the District Court that prior involvement in some aspects of a case will not necessarily bar a welfare official from acting as a decision maker. He should not, however, have participated in making the determination under review.

MR. JUSTICE BLACK, dissenting.

In the last half century the United States, along with many, perhaps most, other nations of the world, has moved far toward becoming a welfare state, that is, a nation that for one reason or another taxes its most affluent people to help support, feed, clothe, and shelter its less fortunate citizens. The result is that today more than nine million men, women, and children in the United States receive some kind of state or federally financed public assistance in the form of allowances or gratuities, generally paid them periodically, usually by the week, month, or quarter. Since these gratuities are paid on the basis of need, the list of recipients is not static, and some people go off the lists and others are added from time to time. These ever-changing lists put a constant administrative burden on government and it certainly could not have reasonably anticipated that this burden would include the additional procedural expense imposed by the Court today. . . .

[W]hen federal judges use [their] judicial power for legislative purposes, I think they wander out of their field of vested powers and transgress into the area constitutionally assigned to the Congress and the people. That is precisely what I believe the Court is doing in this case. Hence my dissent.

The more than a million names on the relief rolls in New York, and the more than nine million names on the rolls of all the 50 States, were not put there at random. The names are there because state welfare officials believed that those people were eligible for assistance. Probably in the officials' haste to make out the lists many names were put there erroneously in order to alleviate immediate suffering, and undoubtedly some people are drawing relief who are not entitled under the law to do so. Doubtless some draw relief checks from time to time who know they are not eligible, either because they are not actually in need or for some other reason. Many of those who thus draw undeserved gratuities are without sufficient property to enable the government to collect back from them any money they wrongfully receive. But the Court today holds that it would violate the Due Process Clause of the Fourteenth Amendment to stop paying those people weekly or monthly allowances unless the government first affords them a full 'evidentiary hearing' even though welfare officials are persuaded that the recipients are not rightfully entitled to receive a penny under the law. In other words, although some recipients might be on the lists for payment wholly because of deliberate fraud on their part, the Court holds that the government is helpless and must continue, until after an evidentiary hearing, to pay money that it does not owe, never has owed, and never could owe. I do not believe there is any provision in our Constitution that should thus paralyze the government's efforts to protect itself against making payments to people who are not entitled to them. . . .

The Court, however, relies upon the Fourteenth Amendment and in effect says that failure of the government to pay a promised charitable instalment to an individual deprives that individual of his own property, in violation of the Due Process Clause of the Fourteenth Amendment. It somewhat strains credulity to say that the government's promise of charity to an individual is property belonging to that individual when the government denies that the individual is honestly entitled to receive such a payment.

I would have little, if any, objection to the majority's decision in this case if it were written as the report of the House Committee on Education and Labor, but as an opinion ostensibly resting on the language of the Constitution I find it woefully deficient. Once the verbiage is pared away it is obvious that this Court today adopts the views of the District Court 'that to cut off a welfare recipient in the face of . . . 'brutal need' without a prior hearing of some sort is unconscionable,' and therefore, says the Court, unconstitutional. The majority reaches this result by a process of weighing 'the recipient's interest in avoiding' the termination of welfare benefits against 'the governmental interest in summary adjudication.' Today's balancing act requires a 'pre-termination evidentiary hearing,' yet there is nothing that indicates what tomorrow's balance will be. Although the majority attempts to bolster its decision with limited quotations from prior cases, it is obvious that today's result doesn't depend on the language of the Constitution itself or the principles of other decisions, but solely on the collective judgment of the majority as to what would be a fair and humane procedure in this case.

This decision is thus only another variant of the view often expressed by some members of this Court that the Due Process Clause forbids any conduct that a majority of the Court believes 'unfair,' 'indecent,' or 'shocking to their consciences.' Neither these words nor any like them appear anywhere in the

Due Process Clause. If they did, they would leave the majority of Justices free to hold any conduct unconstitutional that they should conclude on their own to be unfair or shocking to them. Had the drafters of the Due Process Clause meant to leave judges such ambulatory power to declare laws unconstitutional, the chief value of a written constitution, as the Founders saw it, would have been lost. In fact, if that view of due process is correct, the Due Process Clause could easily swallow up all other parts of the Constitution. And truly the Constitution would always be 'what the judges say it is' at a given moment, not what the Founders wrote into the document. A written constitution, designed to guarantee protection against governmental abuses, including those of judges, must have written standards that mean something definite and have an explicit content. I regret very much to be compelled to say that the Court today makes a drastic and dangerous departure from a Constitution written to control and limit the government and the judges and moves toward a constitution designed to be no more and no less than what the judges of a particular social and economic philosophy declare on the one hand to be fair or on the other hand to be shocking and unconscionable. . . .

The Court apparently feels that this decision will benefit the poor and needy. In my judgment the eventual result will be just the opposite. While today's decision requires only an administrative, evidentiary hearing, the inevitable logic of the approach taken will lead to constitutionally imposed, time-consuming delays of a full adversary process of administrative and judicial review. In the next case the welfare recipients are bound to argue that cutting off benefits before judicial review of the agency's decision is also a denial of due process. Since, by hypothesis, termination of aid at that point may still 'deprive an eligible recipient of the very means by which to live while he waits,' I would be surprised if the weighing process did not compel the conclusion that termination without full judicial review would be unconscionable. After all, at each step, as the majority seems to feel, the issue is only one of weighing the government's pocketbook against the actual survival of the recipient, and surely that balance must always tip in favor of the individual. Similarly today's decision requires only the opportunity to have the benefit of counsel at the administrative hearing, but it is difficult to believe that the same reasoning process would not require the appointment of counsel, for otherwise the right to counsel is a meaningless one since these people are too poor to hire their own advocates. Cf. Gideon v. Wainwright, 372 U.S. 335, 344 (1963). Thus the end result of today's decision may well be that the government, once it decides to give welfare benefits, cannot reverse that decision until the recipient has had the benefits of full administrative and judicial review, including, of course, the opportunity to present his case to this Court. Since this process will usually entail a delay of several years, the inevitable result of such a constitutionally imposed burden will be that the government will not put a claimant on the rolls initially until it has made an exhaustive investigation to determine his eligibility. While this Court will perhaps have insured that no needy person will be taken off the rolls without a full 'due process' proceeding, it will also have insured that many will never get on the rolls, or at least that they will remain destitute during the lengthy proceedings followed to determine initial eligibility.

For the foregoing reasons I dissent from the Court's holding. The operation of a welfare state is a new experiment for our Nation. For this reason, among others, I feel that new experiments in carrying out a welfare program should not be frozen into our constitutional structure. They should be left, as are other legislative determinations, to the Congress and the legislatures that the people elect to make our laws.

Notes and Questions

1. Unconstitutional conditions. Recall that earlier we said that public rights like welfare benefits would not have required any court adjudication at all, and for a similar reason the due process clause would not have applied. The Court rejects the distinction between public and private rights by citing a variety of cases: Sherbert v. Verner, 374 U.S. 398 (1963); Speiser v. Randall, 357 U.S. 513 (1958); and Slochower v. Board of Higher Education, 350 U.S. 551 (1956). These cases, however, were all "unconstitutional conditions" cases. The question in those cases is whether the govern-

COMPARATIVE PERSPECTIVE

The unconstitutional conditions doctrine features in many areas of law. Not just here, in administrative law, but also in First Amendment law and elsewhere.

ment can *condition* someone's receipt of a public benefit or privilege on that person forgoing a constitutional right. For example, can the government deny welfare benefits where the applicant had refused employment that would have required her to work on the Sabbath, contrary to her religious principles?

Sherbert, 374 U.S. 398. Can it condition a tax benefit on forgoing First Amendment rights by requiring the applicant to attest loyalty to the United States? *Speiser*, 350 U.S. 551. Can it   require that a government employee not exercise her First Amendment rights, as a condition of employment? Pickering v. Board of Education, 391 U.S. 563 (1968). Thus, the unconstitutional conditions cases all involve "public rights," because those are the only rights that the government has the power to condition in this way. Those cases do not say anything about whether due process applies to public as well as private rights. The government is not conditioning the receipt of benefits on forgoing due process rights; the very question is whether there is a due process right at all.

2. *What's the test?* What exactly is the test for when the due process clause applies to a statutory entitlement? Is it the degree of the loss that will be experienced? What factors does the Court inquire into to make this determination? Are those the same factors it considers for determining how much process is due?

The following cases and the notes explore additional liberty and property interests protected by the due process clause. Note that, in the latter of these two cases, the Court moves away from *Goldberg v. Kelly*'s "grievous loss" test for determining whether there is a protected liberty or property interest. This reflects a limiting of the "due process revolution" ushered by *Goldberg v. Kelly* and similar cases. Do you agree with these new limitations? Following the next two cases, we will debate the merits of the "due process revolution" that *Goldberg* ushered.

Wisconsin v. Constantineau

400 U.S. 433 (1971)

MR. JUSTICE DOUGLAS delivered the opinion of the Court.

Appellee is an adult resident of Hartford, Wis. She brought suit in a federal district court in Wisconsin to have a Wisconsin statute declared unconstitutional. . . .

The Act provides that designated persons may in writing forbid the sale or gift of intoxicating liquors to one who 'by excessive drinking' produces described conditions or exhibits specified traits, such as exposing himself or family 'to want' or becoming 'dangerous to the peace' of the community.

The chief of police of Hartford, without notice or hearing to appellee, caused to be posted a notice in all retail liquor outlets in Hartford that sales or gifts of liquors to appellee were forbidden for one year. . . .

We have no doubt as to the power of a State to deal with the evils described in the Act. The police power of the States over intoxicating liquors was extremely broad even prior to the Twenty-first Amendment. The only issue present here is whether the label or characterization given a person by 'posting,' though a mark of serious illness to some, is to others such a stigma or badge of disgrace that procedural due process requires notice and an opportunity to be heard. We agree with the District Court that the private interest is such that those requirements of procedural due process must be met. . . .

Generalizations are hazardous as some state and federal administrative procedures are summary by reason of necessity or history. Yet certainly where the State attaches 'a badge of infamy' to the citizen, due process comes into play. Wieman v. Updegraff, 344 U.S. 183, 191. '(T)he right to be heard before being condemned to suffer grievous loss of any kind, even though it may not involve the stigma and hardships of a criminal conviction, is a principle basic to our society.' Joint Anti-Fascist Refugee Committee v. McGrath, 341 U.S. 123, 168 (Frankfurter, J., concurring).

Where a person's good name, reputation, honor, or integrity is at stake because of what the government is doing to him, notice and an opportunity to be heard are essential. 'Posting' under the Wisconsin Act may to some be merely the mark of illness, to others it is a stigma, an official branding of a person. The label is a degrading one. Under the Wisconsin Act, a resident of Hartford is given no process at all. This appellee was not afforded a chance to defend herself. She may have been the victim of an official's caprice. Only when the whole proceedings leading to the pinning of an unsavory label on a person are aired can oppressive results be prevented. . . .

[Dissenting opinions by Chief Justice Burger and Justice Black, both joined by Justice Blackmun, on an unrelated federal jurisdiction question, are omitted.—Ed.].

Notes and Questions

1. *What is the liberty interest?* What, exactly, is the liberty interest at stake in *Constantineau*? It seems to depend on the stigma and reputational harm to be suffered by the person against whom the statute was applied. But what if there was no stigma at all? Wouldn't the statute still violate due process? The statute effectively allows the police chief to declare that stores cannot sell liquor to a particular person—and therefore that this person cannot buy liquor. Is that itself not a deprivation of liberty? The government may of course make such a declaration as a punishment for doing some act, just like it imposes any number of punishments for violations of any number of laws. Ordinarily, however, it is only a court judgment that can impose such punishments. Is there any reason why the substantive rule and the punishment at issue in *Constantineau* should be treated any differently?

Board of Regents of State Colleges v. Roth

408 U.S. 564 (1972)

Mr. Justice Stewart delivered the opinion of the Court.

In 1968 the respondent, David Roth, was hired for his first teaching job as assistant professor of political science at Wisconsin State University-Oshkosh. He was hired for a fixed term of one academic year. The notice of his faculty appointment specified that his employment would begin on September 1, 1968, and would end on June 30, 1969. The respondent completed that term. But he was informed that he would not be rehired for the next academic year.

The respondent had no tenure rights to continued employment. Under Wisconsin statutory law a state university teacher can acquire tenure as a 'permanent' employee only after four years of year-to-year employment. Having acquired tenure, a teacher is entitled to continued employment 'during efficiency and good behavior.' A relatively new teacher without tenure, however, is under Wisconsin law entitled to nothing beyond his one-year appointment. There are no statutory or administrative standards defining eligibility for re-employment. State law thus clearly leaves the decision whether to rehire a nontenured teacher for another year to the unfettered discretion of university officials.

The procedural protection afforded a Wisconsin State University teacher before he is separated from the University corresponds to his job security. As a matter of statutory law, a tenured teacher cannot be 'discharged except for cause upon written charges' and pursuant to certain procedures. A nontenured teacher, similarly, is protected to some extent during his one-year term. Rules promulgated by the Board of Regents provide that a nontenured teacher 'dismissed' before the end of the year may have some opportunity for review of the 'dismissal.' But the Rules provide no real protection for a nontenured teacher who simply is not re-employed for the next year. He must be informed by February 1 'concerning retention or non-retention for the ensuing year.' But 'no reason for non-retention need be given. No review or appeal is provided in such case.'

In conformance with these Rules, the President of Wisconsin State University-Oshkosh informed the respondent before February 1, 1969, that he would not be rehired for the 1969–1970 academic year. He gave the respondent no reason for the decision and no opportunity to challenge it at any sort of hearing.

The respondent then brought this action in Federal District Court alleging that the decision not to rehire him for the next year infringed his Fourteenth Amendment rights. He attacked the decision both in substance and procedure. First, he alleged that the true reason for the decision was to punish him for certain statements critical of the University administration, and that it therefore violated his right to freedom of speech. Second, he alleged that the failure of University officials to give him notice of any reason for nonretention and an opportunity for a hearing violated his right to procedural due process of law. . . .

The only question presented to us at this stage in the case is whether the respondent had a constitutional right to a statement of reasons and a hearing on the University's decision not to rehire him for another year. We hold that he did not.

I

The requirements of procedural due process apply only to the deprivation of interests encompassed by the Fourteenth Amendment's protection of liberty and property. When protected interests are implicated, the right to some kind of prior hearing is paramount. But the range of interests protected by procedural due process is not infinite.

The District Court decided that procedural due process guarantees apply in this case by assessing and balancing the weights of the particular interests involved. It concluded that the respondent's interest in re-employment at Wisconsin State University-Oshkosh outweighed the University's interest in denying him re-employment summarily. Undeniably, the respondent's re-employment prospects were of major concern to him—concern that we surely cannot say was insignificant. And a weighing process has long been a part of any determination of the form of hearing required in particular situations by procedural due process. But, to determine whether due process requirements apply in the first place, we must look not to the 'weight' but to the nature of the interest at stake. We must look to see if the interest is within the Fourteenth Amendment's protection of liberty and property.

'Liberty' and 'property' are broad and majestic terms. . . . For that reason, the Court has fully and finally rejected the wooden distinction between 'rights' and 'privileges' that once seemed to govern the applicability of procedural due process rights. The Court has also made clear that the property interests protected by procedural due process extend well beyond actual ownership of real estate, chattels, or money. By the same token, the Court has required due process protection for deprivations of liberty beyond the sort of formal constraints imposed by the criminal process.

Yet, while the Court has eschewed rigid or formalistic limitations on the protection of procedural due process, it has at the same time observed certain boundaries. For the words 'liberty' and 'property' in the Due Process Clause of the Fourteenth Amendment must be given some meaning.

II

'While this court has not attempted to define with exactness the liberty . . . guaranteed (by the Fourteenth Amendment), the term has received much consideration and some of the included things have been definitely stated. Without doubt, it denotes not merely freedom from bodily restraint but also the right of the individual to contract, to engage in any of the common occupations of life, to acquire useful knowledge, to marry, establish a home and bring up children, to worship God according to the dictates of his own conscience, and generally to enjoy those privileges long recognized . . . as essential to the orderly pursuit of happiness by free men.' Meyer v. Nebraska, 262 U.S. 390, 399. . . .

There might be cases in which a State refused to re-employ a person under such circumstances that interests in liberty would be implicated. But this is not such a case.

The State, in declining to rehire the respondent, did not make any charge against him that might seriously damage his standing and associations in his community. It did not base the nonrenewal of his contract on a charge, for example, that he had been guilty of dishonesty, or immorality. Had it done so, this would be a different case. For '(w)here a person's good name, reputation, honor, or integrity is at stake because of what the government is doing to him, notice and an opportunity to be heard are essential.' Wisconsin v. Constantineau, 400 U.S. 433, 437. In such a case, due process would accord an opportunity to refute the charge before University officials. In the present case, however, there is no suggestion whatever that the respondent's 'good name, reputation, honor, or integrity' is at stake.

Similarly, there is no suggestion that the State, in declining to re-employ the respondent, imposed on him a stigma or other disability that foreclosed his freedom to take advantage of other employment opportunities. The State, for example, did not invoke any regulations to bar the respondent from all other public employment in state universities. Had it done so, this, again, would be a different case. . . .

To be sure, the respondent has alleged that the nonrenewal of his contract was based on his exercise of his right to freedom of speech. But this allegation is not now before us. The District Court stayed proceedings on this issue, and the respondent has yet to prove that the decision not to rehire him was, in fact, based on his free speech activities.

Hence, on the record before us, all that clearly appears is that the respondent was not rehired for one year at one university. It stretches the concept too far to suggest that a person is deprived of 'liberty' when he simply is not rehired in one job but remains as free as before to seek another.

III

The Fourteenth Amendment's procedural protection of property is a safeguard of the security of interests that a person has already acquired in specific benefits. These interests—property interests—may take many forms.

Thus, the Court has held that a person receiving welfare benefits under statutory and administrative standards defining eligibility for them has an interest in continued receipt of those benefits that is safeguarded by procedural due process. Goldberg v. Kelly, 397 U.S. 254. Similarly, in the area of public employment, the Court has held that a public college professor dismissed from an office held under tenure provisions, Slochower v. Board of Education, 350 U.S. 551, and college professors and staff members dismissed during the terms of their contracts, Wieman v. Updegraff, 344 U.S. 183, have interests in continued employment that are safeguarded by due process. Only last year, the Court held that this principle 'proscribing summary dismissal from public employment without hearing or inquiry required by due process' also applied to a teacher recently hired without tenure or a formal contract, but nonetheless with a clearly implied promise of continued employment. Connell v. Higginbotham, 403 U.S. 207, 208.

Certain attributes of 'property' interests protected by procedural due process emerge from these decisions. To have a property interest in a benefit, a person clearly must have more than an abstract need or desire for it. He must have more than a unilateral expectation of it. He must, instead, have a legitimate claim of entitlement to it. It is a purpose of the ancient institution of property to protect those claims upon which people rely in their daily lives, reliance that must not be arbitrarily undermined. It is a purpose of the constitutional right to a hearing to provide an opportunity for a person to vindicate those claims.

Property interests, of course, are not created by the Constitution. Rather they are created and their dimensions are defined by existing rules or understandings that stem from an independent source such as state law—rules or understandings that secure certain benefits and that support claims of entitlement to those benefits. Thus, the welfare recipients in Goldberg v. Kelly, supra, had a claim of entitlement to welfare payments that was grounded in the statute defining eligibility for them. The recipients had not yet shown that they were, in fact, within the statutory terms of eligibility. But we held that they had a right to a hearing at which they might attempt to do so.

Just as the welfare recipients' 'property' interest in welfare payments was created and defined by statutory terms, so the respondent's 'property' interest in employment at Wisconsin State University-Oshkosh was created and defined by the terms of his appointment. Those terms secured his interest in employment up to June 30, 1969. But the important fact in this case is that they specifically provided that the respondent's employment was to terminate on June 30. They did not provide for contract renewal absent 'sufficient cause.' Indeed, they made no provision for renewal whatsoever.

Thus, the terms of the respondent's appointment secured absolutely no interest in re-employment for the next year. They supported absolutely no possible claim of entitlement to re-employment. Nor, significantly, was there any state statute or University rule or policy that secured his interest in re-employment or that created any legitimate claim to it. In these circumstances, the respondent surely had an abstract concern in being rehired, but he did not have a property interest sufficient to require the University authorities to give him a hearing when they declined to renew his contract of employment. . . .

[A dissenting opinion by Justice Douglas is omitted.—Ed.]

Justice Marshall, dissenting.

Respondent was hired as an assistant professor of political science at Wisconsin State University-Oshkosh for the 1968–1969 academic year. During the course of that year he was told that he would not be rehired for the next academic term, but he was never told why. . . .

I would go further than the Court does in defining the terms 'liberty' and 'property.' . . .

In my view, every citizen who applies for a government job is entitled to it unless the government can establish some reason for denying the employment. This is the 'property' right that I believe is protected by the Fourteenth Amendment and that cannot be denied 'without due process of law.' And it is also liberty—liberty to work—which is the 'very essence of the personal freedom and opportunity' secured by the Fourteenth Amendment. . . .

[W]hen an application for public employment is denied or the contract of a government employee is not renewed, the government must say why, for it is only when the reasons underlying government action are known that citizens feel secure and protected against arbitrary government action.

Employment is one of the greatest, if not the greatest, benefits that governments offer in modern-day life. When something as valuable as the opportunity to work is at stake, the government may not reward some citizens and not others without demonstrating that its actions are fair and equitable. And it is procedural due process that is our fundamental guarantee of fairness, our protection against arbitrary, capricious, and unreasonable government action. . . .

Notes and Questions

1. Summary. The Court in *Roth* changed the test for determining what is a protected liberty or property interest. The test is no longer the extent to which someone can be expected to suffer a "grievous loss," the apparent test in *Goldberg v. Kelly*. The *weight* of the loss is not a factor, but rather the *nature* of the liberty or property interest is what matters. What kind of liberty and property interests does the Court list as creating due process claims?

■ *Problem 7.1*

In Perry v. Sindermann, 408 U.S. 593 (1972), a companion case to *Roth*, Sindermann was a nontenured college professor in the Texas college system with a year-to-year contract, which was not renewed for an additional year allegedly because of testimony Sindermann gave in front of the Texas state legislature. Sindermann had worked in the state college system for 10 years. A Faculty Guide provided that the college had "no tenure system," but that faculty members should "feel" as though they have "permanent tenure as long as [their] teaching services are satisfactory and as long as [they] display[ ] a cooperative attitude" toward co-workers and superiors. Additionally, Sindermann claimed that guidelines promulgated by the Coordinating Board of the Texas College and University System had provided that anyone employed as a teacher in the state college and university system for at least seven years "has some form of job tenure." The district court granted summary judgment on the ground that the school had not adopted the tenure system. Sindermann appealed. How would you have ruled on appeal?

---

2. "Stigma plus." In Paul v. Davis, 424 U.S. 693 (1976), police chiefs distributed fliers of "active shoplifters" to a variety of stores, and included the name of Davis, who had had shoplifting charges filed against him, which had yet to be resolved. Davis cited *Constantineau* and argued that he was entitled to procedural due process because his inclusion on the list could lead to reputational harm, diminished employment prospects, and being refused at stores. The Court rejected the claim, distinguishing *Constantineau* on the ground that there liberty had actually been lost. Here, in contrast, Davis hadn't lost any liberty. To be sure, he may have a defamation claim—but that is something to be pursued after the fact in court, and has nothing to do with procedural due process. "While we have in a number of our prior cases pointed out the frequently drastic effect of the 'stigma' which may result from defamation by the government in a variety of contexts," the Court held, "this line of cases does not establish the proposition that reputation alone, apart from some more tangible interests such as employment, is either 'liberty' or 'property' by itself sufficient to invoke the procedural protection of the Due Process Clause." 424 U.S. at 701.

After *Paul v. Davis*, the courts began to conclude that stigma alone was not enough to state a procedural due process claim, and that limited liberty or property interests like nontenured employment were insufficient to state a claim, but that depriving someone of such a minimal liberty or property interest in combination with stigma could still amount to a due process claim. The key language comes from *Roth*. Recall there the Court held that Roth did not state a claim because he did not have a genuine entitlement to continued employment. But, the Court had added, there was "no suggestion that the State, in declining to reemploy the respondent, imposed on him a sigma or other disability that foreclosed his freedom to take advantage of other employment opportunities." *Roth*, 408 U.S. at 573. This has come to be known as the "stigma plus" test: even if a plaintiff might not otherwise have a genuine entitlement to the continued receipt of a particular privilege, if the plaintiff is denied that privilege in combination with a stigma, that might state a due process claim.

3. Due process and prison litigation. In the early 1970s, when assessing whether prison inmates had liberty or property interests—say, in visitation rights, or credit for good behavior—the Supreme Court still focused on the "grievous loss" test and the severity of the harm suffered by the inmates. See, e.g., Wolff v. McDonnell, 418 U.S. 539 (1974). In the late 1970s, perhaps following the lead of *Roth*, the Court shifted focus and the inquiry was whether official state or prison policies created mandatory duties on prison officers, or otherwise cabined the discretion of prison officers in mandatory language. See, e.g., Kentucky Dep't of Corrections v. Thompson, 490 U.S. 454 (1989). If the official policy left discretion on the part of the officers, the prisoners had no liberty or property interest. What kind of incentives did this new test create?

In Sandin v. Conner, 515 U.S. 472 (1995), the Court changed course yet again. The Court observed that the mandatory/discretionary dichotomy incentivized prisons to have no official policy and to make all decisions purely discretionary (surely not to the benefit of the inmates or the officers), and required significant judicial resources to determine whether various policies were mandatory or discretionary. The Court went back to something like the grievous loss test: the question became whether official action "imposes atypical and significant hardship on the inmate in relation to the ordinary incidents of prison life." For example, if an inmate was convicted to a year's sentence, and the prison decided to put that inmate in solitary confinement for a year, that could trigger due process requirements. Indeed, wouldn't such a decision deprive the inmate of "liberty" in the traditional sense of the term?

2.   Debating the Due Process Revolution

In the cases discussed in the previous section, the Court expanded and then somewhat, but not totally, contracted the scope of protected due process rights. What do you think of the initial expansion, and the subsequent semi-contraction? Whatever you think of the Court's reasoning as a matter of constitutional text, history, or precedent in *Goldberg v. Kelly*, might it be good to require the government to provide due process before depriving someone of a statutory entitlement? Could the argument be made that *if* the government is going to create a class of dependent individuals—individuals who have grown to depend on the government itself, as opposed to family, charity, or some other institution—that the government ought to ensure that the individuals that depend on it are not arbitrarily deprived of the very thing they depend on to live? What do you make of footnote 8 of the Court's opinion in *Goldberg*, citing the scholarship of

 **COMPARATIVE PERSPECTIVE** What role do social and political developments play in constitutional law? What role should they play?

Charles Reich on the prevalence of "new property" in the modern age? Here is a more extended excerpt from one of his law review articles cited by the Court; do you agree with him?

In the sampling of issues already given there were many instances of welfare decisions capable of having a major impact on the lives of individuals. Many of these decisions are made in a manner that is lacking in basic safeguards. In the case of a decision removing a family from public housing, or a decision denying aid to families with dependent children, generally the matter is finally determined at some level within the appropriate agency, after investigation by the agency, and with comparatively informal procedures, if any, available to the persons affected. In the welfare area procedures often exist on paper, but are not pursued in practice. This contrasts sharply with what happens in agencies dealing with business regulation, where lawyers have made paper procedures a practical reality.

In the past thirty years a large body of experience and law has grown up with respect to the procedures of government agencies which undertake regulation of economic affairs, or dispensation of benefits such as airline routes or television licenses. In a general way, the standards which have developed are as follows. (1) The rules which are to furnish the standard of decision should be clearly formulated in advance of any action; (2) the rules should be available to the public; (3) every action should begin with actual notice of the proposed action and a full statement of the basis for it; (4) the relevant facts should be determined in a proceeding at which the person or company affected can know the evidence and have an opportunity to rebut it; factual findings should not be based on hearsay or secret evidence known only to the agency; (5) the person or company should have the right to be represented by counsel; (6) there should be a distinct separation between those officials who investigate and initiate action and those who find the facts and make the decision; the latter officials should be subject to different authority than the former and free of any of the atmosphere in which the action was begun; (7) the decision, once made, should be accompanied by findings and reasons; (8) there should be opportunity for review of the decision within the agency, and, ultimately, in the courts.

These procedures, however cumbersome they may seem, have come to represent a fundamental standard of fairness in administrative process. They may be exaggerated and misused until they produce inordinate delay and expense, but they represent effective checks on the characteristic evils of proceedings in any large public or private organization: closed doors, Kafka-like uncertainty, difficulty in locating responsibility, and rigid adherence to a particular point of view. They are fundamental safeguards for those who must deal with government.

In a society where a significant portion of the population is dependent on social welfare, decisions about eligibility for benefits are among the most important that a government can make. By one set of values the granting of a license to broadcast over a television channel, or to build a hydroelectric project on a river, might seem of more far-reaching significance. But in a society that considers the individual as its basic unit a decision affecting the life of a person or a family should not be taken by means that would be unfair for a television station or power company. Indeed, full adjudicatory procedures are far more appropriate in welfare cases than in most of the areas of administrative procedure. In the licensing of television or hydroelectric dams, policy-making and planning are so mixed with fact-finding as to severely limit the possibility of reaching "objective" decisions. Welfare cases rest on comparatively objective statutory criteria, are less subject to ad hoc policy-making, and demand high standards of fairness and equitable treatment for large numbers of individuals. At a minimum, there should be notice to beneficiaries of regulations and proposed adverse action, and fact finding should be carried on in a scrupulous fashion. There is much to be said for a genuine separation of the functions of investigator and judge, so that welfare workers are not put in the psychologically impossible position of having to evaluate their own actions, or those of their colleagues. And a clear statement of reasons, plus some form of review, would give a beneficiary one more opportunity to argue his side of the case. Procedures can develop gradually and pragmatically, but as welfare grows in importance in our society, it will be necessary to give increasing attention to the procedures by which welfare rights are granted or refused. Here the experience of lawyers can be of great assistance; whatever the outcome of particular decisions, adequate procedure gives a sense of fairness that is vital to community acceptance of a welfare program.

Charles A. Reich, *Individual Rights and Social Welfare: The Emerging Legal Issues*, 74 Yale L.J. 1245, 1252–53 (1965).

Compare Reich's argument to those of Stephen F. Williams before he became a judge on the D.C. Circuit, responding to the other of Reich's articles cited by the Court in *Goldberg*. Williams argued:

> The branch of Reich's argument that sees traditional private property as functioning to protect the individual from the state is surely correct. It performs the function in a variety of ways. An owner of real property has a fairly broad right to determine what happens within its physical boundaries. Income-producing property cushions its owner against destitution and thus affords a degree of independence. Private property makes it possible for individual citizens to meet the expenses of publicizing antigovernment positions (as through newspaper advertisements). Finally, private property means that the resources needed for the distribution of dissident positions (paper, printing machines, labor, etc.) can be obtained from nongovernment sources.

> Property plays an even greater role as a bulwark against government if one takes it to encompass what Madison called the "broad" concept of property. . . . This broader property, essentially individuals' ownership of their own skills, is an important-probably essential-source of independence of government. If individuals can sell their labor to persons other than the government (and obtain secure property rights in the wealth transferred to them in exchange for their labor), they can derive a security comparable to that of owners of income-producing property.

> As a shield of the individual against the government, property in both its broad and narrow senses can operate as an external check on government's expansive tendencies. Accordingly, judicial protection of traditional property interests from procedural incursion might play some role—necessarily rather a slight one, I suspect—in assuring the persistence of external checks. In a society with substantial power centers outside the government, judicial enforcement of procedural due process might shore up the external power centers against encroachment by the nonjudicial branches of government.

Reich's extension of this analysis, however, weakens it to the breaking point. In arguing that procedural due process can play a comparable role in a society that (according to his premises) has incorporated all power centers into the government, he seems to rely on a romantically grandiose idea of judicial effectiveness. . . . It seems unrealistic to picture the judiciary single-handedly assuring meaningful independence for a citizenry that had accepted substantive dependence upon the legislative and executive branches.

As we have not adopted a society as statist as that envisioned by Reich, one might argue that in the present environment due process protection for government benefits can reinforce individual independence of the state. But anyone advocating that view must somehow meet the linguistic dilemma that Reich confronted—On what basis are such interests sufficiently "like" liberty or property to enjoy the protection of a clause that protects only life, liberty, and property? Whatever theory he invokes to resolve that dilemma, the theory must sacrifice the special claims of traditional liberty and property. The latter are grounded in the idea of individuals' ownership of their selves, their talents, and the resulting wealth; it is thus inherent in traditional liberty and property that they should serve as counterweights to government. Over the long pull, relinquishing those special claims may have a far more detrimental impact on individual independence from the state than denying due process protection for conditioned government benefits.

Stephen F. Williams, *Liberty and Property: The Problem of Government Benefits*, 12 J. Legal Stud. 3, 11–13 (1983).

Professor Richard Pierce has also advocated a distinction between rights and privileges. The rights-privileges distinction the Court rejected in *Goldberg*, Pierce has written,

is the fundamental distinction between the private and public spheres. The "old" property that the Court discounted is private property. It is created by individuals in the private sphere, with the government existing simply to recognize and to protect the fruits of individual labor and capital. In sharp contrast, the "new" property consists of entitlements to government largesse. It exists and is created entirely in the public sphere through governmental redistribution of private wealth. Thus, by eliminating the distinction between "rights" and "privileges," the Court rejected both the distinction between public and private political spheres and the individualistic liberal political philosophy such a distinction represents. In essence, the Court rejected the social and political philosophies that motivated the Framers of the Constitution.

Richard J. Pierce Jr., *The Due Process Counterrevolution of the 1990s?*, 96 Colum. L. Rev. 1973, 1980 (1996). With which view do you agree?

Even if you agree that entitlements should fall within the scope of due process protections, does it follow that an adversarial, judicial-like process is the best way to protect such rights? A few years after *Goldberg* was decided, Judge Henry J. Friendly delivered a lecture entitled "Some Kind of Hearing," in which he questioned the Supreme Court's insistence on the need for an adversarial process to satisfy the requirements of due process. Here are some snippets—do you agree with Judge Friendly?

 **HISTORICAL PERSPECTIVE** Circuit Judge Henry Friendly, who did not sit on the Supreme Court, was one of the most prominent and cited judges of the twentieth century.

> To be sure, counsel can often perform useful functions even in welfare cases or other instances of mass justice; they may bring out facts ignored by or unknown to the authorities, or help to work out satisfactory compromises. But this is only one side of the coin. Under our adversary system the role of counsel is not to make sure the truth is ascertained but to advance his client's cause by any ethical means. Within the limits of professional propriety, causing delay and sowing confusion not only are his right but may be his duty. The appearance of counsel for the citizen is likely to lead the government to provide one—or at least to cause the government's representative to act like one. The result may be to turn what might have been a short conference leading to an amicable result into a protracted controversy. . . . It is thus fortunate that subsequent cases have not taken this portion of *Goldberg* as an absolute governing other types of hearings. . . .

These problems concerning counsel and confrontation inevitably bring up the question whether we would not do better to abandon the adversary system in certain areas of mass justice, notably in the many ramifications of the welfare system, in favor of one in which an examiner—or administrative law judge if you will—with no connection with the agency would have the responsibility for developing all the pertinent facts and making a just decision. Under such a model the "judge" would assume a much more active role with respect to the course of the hearing; for example, he would examine the parties, might call his own experts if needed, request that certain types of evidence be presented, and, if necessary, aid the parties in acquiring that evidence.

Many parts of the mass justice area would be particularly suitable for such an experiment since the guidelines are sufficiently definite to avoid the danger that an outside reviewing panel might endeavor to remake agency policy. Although questions of fact and policy may inevitably become intertwined, for the most part the tribunals would simply be determining the facts and then applying pertinent statutes and agency rules or regulations. The hearing boards presumably would have access to government officials and program administrators for pertinent information concerning agency policies. While such an experiment would be a sharp break with our tradition of adversary process, that tradition . . . was not formulated for a situation in which many thousands of hearings must be provided each month. . . .

If we are to experiment with the investigatory model anywhere, this is the ideal place to do it. Strongly embedded traditions, specific constitutional limitations, and resistance of the bar will prevent its use not only in criminal but also, to a lesser extent, in ordinary civil litigation. There is no constitutional mandate requiring use of the adversary process in administrative hearings unless the Court chooses to construct one out of the vague contours of the due process clause. But that clause does not forbid reasonable experimentation. . . .

Henry J. Friendly, *"Some Kind of Hearing"*, 123 U. Pa. L. Rev. 1267, 1287–91 (1975).

In another article, Jerry Mashaw argued that welfare determinations are not like ordinary judicial proceedings, and judicial-like processes may be inappropriate. Do you agree or disagree? He argued:

> Perhaps the most general consideration which supports a management strategy for assuring accuracy, fairness, and timeliness in social welfare adjudications is the positive focus inherent in the administration of programs involving benefits and compensation. The purposes of claims adjudication in social welfare systems are somewhat different from the purposes served by most judicial adjudications. The adjudication of claims in social welfare programs is an outgrowth of a positive legislative program to insure or protect qualified claimants against certain economic hazards. The claims adjudicator's role, whether at the initial consideration of a completed claim file or after an oral hearing, is essentially the same—to provide benefits to eligible individuals and to deny the claims of ineligible individuals.

> This is a quite different posture from that which is customary for a court in judicial proceedings. A court generally has no responsibility for "administering" the substance of legislative programs relevant to the lawsuit before it; and in most cases, the adversaries may compromise their dispute and withdraw it from judicial jurisdiction without judicial approval. This compromise may be quite different from the judgment the court would have rendered, but this difference in result does not mean that the judicial process has failed. Adversaries may use the judicial forum as a vehicle for facilitating their bargaining, and to the extent that compromise resolves their differences, judicial involvement is successful. One of the purposes of judicial decisionmaking—the resolution of conflicts which might otherwise disturb the public peace—is served regardless of the substance of the outcome and the absence of judicial judgment. Additional purposes of judicial decisionmaking, such as developing decisional rules which promote efficient resource allocation, may be served as well (or better) by the parties' bargain as by a judicial decision.

> The same opportunity for "successful" compromise solutions between adversaries is not available in social welfare claims processing. Law in this area is not a loose framework within which private ordering is dominant. A regime of strict law applies, and within that

regime adjudicative success can be tested only by whether the allowed claims are consistent with the statutory and regulatory scheme. Although a partially satisfied claimant may decline to appeal, thus in effect compromising his claim, there is no way to satisfy a claimant, even partially, without rendering an initial decision on the validity of his claim.

The notion that claims adjudicators are engaged, not in providing a forum for the resolution of conflicts, but rather in the systematic and affirmative implementation of certain prescribed legislative policies is reflected in the nonadversary and informal procedures of most social welfare claims processes. No one acts specifically as the representative of the government in these proceedings. Nor is the claimant, who is usually unrepresented and often uninformed of his rights, an adversary in any realistic sense. In this context, the theoretical model of the passive adjudicator ruling on the basis of facts and arguments presented by opposing parties is wholly inappropriate. Hence, agency policy and practice recognize that claims adjudicators must assist in the development of facts, as well as sit in judgment on evidence presented to them. . . .

There also appear to be special problems with the development and dissemination of precedent in social welfare claims systems. Cost is clearly a major factor. Adjudicators in large programs such as Aid to Families with Dependent Children or Social Security Disability Insurance process thousands of hearings per month. This workload cannot be managed at an acceptable cost if each adjudicator is expected to write a full narrative description of his cases and his reasons for decision. . . .

Other disadvantages may also attend a fully adversary-type of proceeding. It is unlikely, for example, that adversary proceedings would accelerate the process of decision. Adversariness almost necessarily has a strong association with formal procedure and with a punctilious regard for procedural rights. Formality and punctiliousness take time—time that can have harsh consequences for the social welfare claimant who is awaiting a decision.

This is not to say that present nonadversary hearing procedures are faultless or that adversary procedure would produce no gains. It is only to suggest that before imposing formal adversary procedures for the adjudication of social welfare claims there should be no doubt that the benefits in accuracy and fairness which might thereby be achieved would outweigh the attendant administrative costs to the public and delay to claimants. But there is little evidence to substantiate the proposition that increased formality or adversariness would improve social welfare adjudications. No controlled experiments have been conducted; the data on the effects of representation in claims adjudications is highly ambiguous, and there is some evidence from the AFDC program that the implementation of formal procedures may be resisted in systems which are already under stress and therefore are suspected of making a large number of errors. . . .

Jerry L. Mashaw, *The Management Side of Due Process*, 59 Cornell L. Rev. 772 (1974).

3.   What Process Is Due?

Justice Black warned in his dissent in *Goldberg v. Kelly* that the result of the Court's holding will be that many individuals don't get on the welfare rolls at all—or that a state would roll back welfare programs altogether because the adjudicatory requirements are too costly. Perhaps in response to these concerns, the Court, in the following case, also walked back the holding of *Goldberg v. Kelly* as to what procedures are typically sufficient before an agency terminates a welfare recipient's benefits.

Mathews v. Eldridge

424 U.S. 319 (1976)

MR. JUSTICE POWELL delivered the opinion of the Court.

The issue in this case is whether the Due Process Clause of the Fifth Amendment requires that prior to the termination of Social Security disability benefit payments the recipient be afforded an opportunity for an evidentiary hearing.

I

Cash benefits are provided to workers during periods in which they are completely disabled under the disability insurance benefits program created by the 1956 amendments to Title II of the Social Security Act. Respondent Eldridge was first awarded benefits in June 1968. In March 1972, he received a questionnaire from the state agency charged with monitoring his medical condition. Eldridge completed the questionnaire, indicating that his condition had not improved and identifying the medical sources, including physicians, from whom he had received treatment recently. The state agency then obtained reports from his physician and a psychiatric consultant. After considering these reports and other information in his file the agency informed Eldridge by letter that it had made a tentative determination that his disability had ceased in May 1972. The letter included a statement of reasons for the proposed termination of benefits, and advised Eldridge that he might request reasonable time in which to obtain and submit additional information pertaining to his condition.

In his written response, Eldridge disputed one characterization of his medical condition and indicated that the agency already had enough evidence to establish his disability. The state agency then made its final determination that he had ceased to be disabled in May 1972. This determination was accepted by the Social Security Administration (SSA), which notified Eldridge in July that his benefits would terminate after that month. The notification also advised him of his right to seek reconsideration by the state agency of this initial determination within six months.

Instead of requesting reconsideration Eldridge commenced this action challenging the constitutional validity of the administrative procedures established by the Secretary of Health, Education, and Welfare for assessing whether there exists a continuing disability. He sought an immediate reinstatement of benefits pending a hearing on the issue of his disability. The Secretary moved to dismiss on the grounds that Eldridge's benefits had been terminated in accordance with valid administrative regulations and procedures and that he had failed to exhaust available remedies. In support of his contention that due process requires a pretermination hearing, Eldridge relied exclusively upon this Court's decision in *Goldberg v. Kelly*, 397 U.S. 254 (1970), which established a right to an "evidentiary hearing" prior to termination of welfare benefits. The Secretary contended that Goldberg was not controlling since eligibility for disability benefits, unlike eligibility for welfare benefits, is not based on financial need and since issues of credibility and veracity do not play a significant role in the disability entitlement decision, which turns primarily on medical evidence.

The District Court concluded that the administrative procedures pursuant to which the Secretary had terminated Eldridge's benefits abridged his right to procedural due process. The court viewed the interest of the disability recipient in uninterrupted benefits as indistinguishable from that of the welfare recipient in Goldberg. It further noted that decisions subsequent to Goldberg demonstrated that the due process requirement of pretermination hearings is not limited to situations involving the deprivation of vital necessities. Reasoning that disability determinations may involve subjective judgments based on conflicting medical and nonmedical evidence, the District Court held that prior to termination of benefits Eldridge had to be afforded an evidentiary hearing of the type required for welfare beneficiaries under Title IV of the Social Security Act. Relying entirely upon the District Court's opinion, the Court of Appeals for the Fourth Circuit affirmed the injunction barring termination of Eldridge's benefits prior to an evidentiary hearing. We reverse.

* * *

III

A

Procedural due process imposes constraints on governmental decisions which deprive individuals of "liberty" or "property" interests within the meaning of the Due Process Clause of the Fifth or Fourteenth Amendment. The Secretary does not contend that procedural due process is inapplicable to terminations of Social Security disability benefits. He recognizes, as has been implicit in our prior decisions, that the interest of an individual in continued receipt of these benefits is a statutorily created "property" interest protected by the Fifth Amendment. Rather, the Secretary contends that the existing administrative procedures, detailed below, provide all the process that is constitutionally due before a recipient can be deprived of that interest.

This Court consistently has held that some form of hearing is required before an individual is finally deprived of a property interest. The "right to be heard before being condemned to suffer grievous loss of any kind, even though it may not involve the stigma and hardships of a criminal conviction, is a principle basic to our society." *Joint Anti-Fascist Comm. v. McGrath*, 341 U.S. 123,

168 (1951) (Frankfurter, J., concurring). The fundamental requirement of due process is the opportunity to be heard "at a meaningful time and in a meaningful manner." *Armstrong v. Manzo,* 380 U.S. 545, 552 (1965). Eldridge agrees that the review procedures available to a claimant before the initial determination of ineligibility becomes final would be adequate if disability benefits were not terminated until after the evidentiary hearing stage of the administrative process. The dispute centers upon what process is due prior to the initial termination of benefits, pending review.

In recent years this Court increasingly has had occasion to consider the extent to which due process requires an evidentiary hearing prior to the deprivation of some type of property interest even if such a hearing is provided thereafter. In only one case, *Goldberg v. Kelly,* 397 U.S. at 266–271, has the Court held that a hearing closely approximating a judicial trial is necessary. In other cases requiring some type of pretermination hearing as a matter of constitutional right the Court has spoken sparingly about the requisite procedures. . . . *Bell v. Burson,* 91 S. Ct. at 1590, held, in the context of the revocation of a state-granted driver's license, that due process required only that the prerevocation hearing involve a probable-cause determination as to the fault of the licensee, noting that the hearing "need not take the form of a full adjudication of the question of liability." More recently, in *Arnett v. Kennedy,* we sustained the validity of procedures by which a federal employee could be dismissed for cause. They included notice of the action sought, a copy of the charge, reasonable time for filing a written response, and an opportunity for an oral appearance. Following dismissal, an evidentiary hearing was provided. 416 U.S. at 142–146. . . .

"(D)ue process is flexible and calls for such procedural protections as the particular situation demands." *Morrissey v. Brewer,* 408 U.S. 471, 481 (1972). Accordingly, resolution of the issue whether the administrative procedures provided here are constitutionally sufficient requires analysis of the governmental and private interests that are affected. More precisely, our prior decisions indicate that identification of the specific dictates of due process generally requires consideration of three distinct factors: First, the private interest that will be affected by the official action; second, the risk of an erroneous deprivation of such interest through the procedures used, and the probable value, if any, of additional or substitute procedural safeguards; and finally, the Government's interest, including the function involved and the fiscal and administrative burdens that the additional or substitute procedural requirement would entail. *See, e.g., Goldberg v. Kelly,* 397 U.S. at 263–271.

We turn first to a description of the procedures for the termination of Social Security disability benefits and thereafter consider the factors bearing upon the constitutional adequacy of these procedures.

B

. . . . The principal reasons for benefits terminations are that the worker is no longer disabled or has returned to work. As Eldridge's benefits were terminated because he was determined to be no longer disabled, we consider only the sufficiency of the procedures involved in such cases.

The continuing-eligibility investigation is made by a state agency acting through a "team" consisting of a physician and a nonmedical person trained in disability evaluation. The agency periodically communicates with the disabled worker, usually by mail in which case he is sent a detailed questionnaire or by telephone, and requests information concerning his present condition, including current medical restrictions and sources of treatment, and any additional information that he considers relevant to his continued entitlement to benefits.

Information regarding the recipient's current condition is also obtained from his sources of medical treatment. If there is a conflict between the information provided by the beneficiary and that obtained from medical sources such as his physician, or between two sources of treatment, the agency may arrange for an examination by an independent consulting physician. Whenever the agency's tentative assessment of the beneficiary's condition differs from his own assessment, the beneficiary is informed that benefits may be terminated, provided a summary of the evidence upon which the proposed determination to terminate is based, and afforded an opportunity to review the medical reports and other evidence in his case file. He also may respond in writing and submit additional evidence.

The state agency then makes its final determination, which is reviewed by an examiner in the SSA Bureau of Disability Insurance. If, as is usually the case, the SSA accepts the agency determination it notifies the recipient in writing, informing him of the reasons for the decision, and of his right to seek de novo reconsideration by the state agency. Upon acceptance by the SSA, benefits are terminated effective two months after the month in which medical recovery is found to have occurred.

If the recipient seeks reconsideration by the state agency and the determination is adverse, the SSA reviews the reconsideration determination and notifies the recipient of the decision. He then has a right to an evidentiary hearing before an SSA administrative law judge. The hearing is nonadversary, and the SSA is not represented by counsel. As at all prior and subsequent stages of the administrative process, however, the claimant may be represented by counsel or other spokesmen. If this hearing results in an adverse decision, the claimant is entitled to request discretionary review by the SSA Appeals Council, and finally may obtain judicial review.

Should it be determined at any point after termination of benefits, that the claimant's disability extended beyond the date of cessation initially established, the worker is entitled to retroactive payments. If, on the other hand, a beneficiary receives any payments to which he is later determined not to be entitled, the statute authorizes the Secretary to attempt to recoup these funds in specified circumstances.

C

Despite the elaborate character of the administrative procedures provided by the Secretary, the courts below held them to be constitutionally inadequate, concluding that due process requires an evidentiary hearing prior to termination. In light of the private and governmental interests at stake here and the nature of the existing procedures, we think this was error.

Since a recipient whose benefits are terminated is awarded full retroactive relief if he ultimately prevails, his sole interest is in the uninterrupted receipt of this source of income pending final administrative decision on his claim. . . .

Only in *Goldberg* has the Court held that due process requires an evidentiary hearing prior to a temporary deprivation. It was emphasized there that welfare assistance is given to persons on the very margin of subsistence . . . .

Eligibility for disability benefits, in contrast, is not based upon financial need. Indeed, it is wholly unrelated to the worker's income or support from many other sources, such as earnings of other family members, workmen's compensation awards, tort claims awards, savings, private insurance, public or private pensions, veterans' benefits, food stamps, public assistance, or the "many other important programs, both public and private, which contain provisions for disability payments affecting a substantial portion of the work force . . . ."

As *Goldberg* illustrates, the degree of potential deprivation that may be created by a particular decision is a factor to be considered in assessing the validity of any administrative decisionmaking process. The potential deprivation here is generally likely to be less than in Goldberg, although the degree of difference can be overstated. . . .

In view of the torpidity of this administrative review process, and the typically modest resources of the family unit of the physically disabled worker the hardship imposed upon the erroneously terminated disability recipient may be significant. Still, the disabled worker's need is likely to be less than that of a welfare recipient. In addition to the possibility of access to private resources, other forms of government assistance will become available where the termination of disability benefits places a worker or his family below the subsistence level. In view of these potential sources of temporary income, there is less reason here than in *Goldberg* to depart from the ordinary principle, established by our decisions, that something less than an evidentiary hearing is sufficient prior to adverse administrative action.

D

An additional factor to be considered here is the fairness and reliability of the existing pretermination procedures, and the probable value, if any, of additional procedural safeguards. Central to the evaluation of any administrative process is the nature of the relevant inquiry. In order to remain eligible for benefits the disabled worker must demonstrate by means of "medically acceptable clinical and laboratory diagnostic techniques," that he is unable "to engage in any substantial gainful activity by reason of any medically determinable physical or mental impairment . . . ." In short, a medical assessment of the worker's physical or mental condition is required. This is a more sharply focused and easily documented decision than the typical determination of welfare entitlement. In the latter case, a wide variety of information may be deemed relevant, and issues of witness credibility and veracity often are critical to the decisionmaking process. *Goldberg* noted that in such circumstances "written submissions are a wholly unsatisfactory basis for decision." 397 U.S. at 269.

By contrast, the decision whether to discontinue disability benefits will turn, in most cases, upon "routine, standard, and unbiased medical reports by physician specialists," *Richardson v. Perales,* 402 U.S. at 404, concerning a subject whom they have personally examined. . . . To be sure, credibility and veracity may be a factor in the ultimate disability assessment in some cases. But procedural due process rules are shaped by the risk of error inherent in the truthfinding process as applied to the generality of cases, not the rare exceptions. The potential value of an evidentiary hearing, or even oral presentation to the decisionmaker, is substantially less in this context than in Goldberg.

The decision in Goldberg also was based on the Court's conclusion that written submissions were an inadequate substitute for oral presentation because they did not provide an effective means for the recipient to communicate his case to the decisionmaker. . . .

The detailed questionnaire which the state agency periodically sends the recipient identifies with particularity the information relevant to the entitlement decision, and the recipient is invited to obtain assistance from the local SSA office in completing the questionnaire. More important, the information critical to the entitlement decision usually is derived from medical sources, such as the treating physician. Such sources are likely to be able to communicate more effectively through written documents than are welfare recipients or the lay witnesses supporting their cause. . . .

E

In striking the appropriate due process balance the final factor to be assessed is the public interest. This includes the administrative burden and other societal costs that would be associated with requiring, as a matter of constitutional right, an evidentiary hearing upon demand in all cases prior to the termination of disability benefits. The most visible burden would be the incremental cost resulting from the increased number of hearings and the expense of providing benefits to ineligible recipients pending decision. No one can predict the extent of the increase, but the fact that full benefits would continue until after such hearings would assure the exhaustion in most cases of this attractive option. Nor would the theoretical right of the Secretary to recover undeserved benefits result, as a practical matter, in any substantial offset to the added outlay of public funds. The parties submit widely varying estimates of the probable additional financial cost. We only need say that experience with the constitutionalizing of government procedures suggests that the ultimate additional cost in terms of money and administrative burden would not be insubstantial.

Financial cost alone is not a controlling weight in determining whether due process requires a particular procedural safeguard prior to some administrative decision. But the Government's interest, and hence that of the public, in conserving scarce fiscal and administrative resources is a factor that must be weighed. At some point the benefit of an additional safeguard to the individual affected by the administrative action and to society in terms of increased assurance that the action is just, may be outweighed by the cost. Significantly, the cost of protecting those whom the preliminary administrative process has identified as likely to be found undeserving may in the end come out of the pockets of the deserving since resources available for any particular program of social welfare are not unlimited.

But more is implicated in cases of this type than ad hoc weighing of fiscal and administrative burdens against the interests of a particular category of claimants. The ultimate balance involves a determination as to when, under our constitutional system, judicial-type procedures must be imposed upon administrative action to assure fairness. We reiterate the wise admonishment of Mr. Justice Frankfurter that differences in the origin and function of administrative agencies "preclude wholesale transplantation of the rules of procedure, trial and review which have evolved from the history and experience of courts." *FCC v. Pottsville Broadcasting Co.*, 309 U.S. 134, 143 (1940). The judicial model of an evidentiary hearing is neither a required, nor even the most effective, method of decisionmaking in all circumstances. . . .

We conclude that an evidentiary hearing is not required prior to the termination of disability benefits and that the present administrative procedures fully comport with due process.

[A short dissenting opinion by Justices Brennan and Marshall is omitted.—Ed.].

Notes and Questions

1. Summary. Mathews v. Eldridge establishes a three-part test for determining how much process is due in these procedural due process cases. The court must consider the private interest at stake, the interest of the government, and the probative value of any additional procedures along with the risk of an erroneous deprivation with the existing procedures. Applying this test, the Court in *Mathews* held that a trial-like hearing was not necessary before a social security disability recipient is deprived of benefits. Do you agree with how the Court distinguished *Goldberg v. Kelly*? When addressing the government's interest, the Court noted, "We only need say that experience with the constitutionalizing of government procedures suggests that the ultimate additional cost in terms of money and administrative burden would not be insubstantial." Was the Court regretting its decision in *Goldberg*? Had Justice Black been right?

2. ***The bitter with the sweet model.*** In a further attempt to limit the reach of *Goldberg*, the Court in Arnett v. Kennedy, 416 U.S. 134 (1974), rejected the procedural due process claim of a federal employee who had been discharged under the for-cause provisions governing the termination of federal employees in the competitive civil service. Justice Rehnquist wrote for a three-Justice plurality that the procedures established in the statute governing the termination were conditions on the right to employment that the statute created in the first

FOR DISCUSSION

What do you think: If Congress or a state legislature establishes a public entitlement, should the recipient be subject to all the various procedural conditions that come with it?

Or, if the state decides to create a class of citizens who are dependent on public rights for their welfare, should it not be left to the legislatures to determine what process is sufficient?

place, and therefore those were the only procedures that had to be followed. If the statute creates a right, in other words, it creates it subject to all the limitations in the statute. Civil servants "must take the bitter with the sweet." The Court rejected this approach in the following case, decided just over a decade later. Was the Court right to reject it?

Cleveland Bd. of Education v. Loudermill

470 U.S. 532 (1985)

Justice White delivered the opinion of the Court.

In these cases we consider what pretermination process must be accorded a public employee who can be discharged only for cause.

I

In 1979 the Cleveland Board of Education hired respondent James Loudermill as a security guard. On his job application, Loudermill stated that he had never been convicted of a felony. Eleven months later, as part of a routine examination of his employment records, the Board discovered that in fact Loudermill had been convicted of grand larceny in 1968. By letter dated November 3, 1980, the Board's Business Manager informed Loudermill that he had been dismissed because of his dishonesty in filling out the employment application. Loudermill was not afforded an opportunity to respond to the charge of dishonesty or to challenge his dismissal. On November 13, the Board adopted a resolution officially approving the discharge.

Under Ohio law, Loudermill was a "classified civil servant." Ohio Rev. Code Ann. § 124.11 (1984). Such employees can be terminated only for cause, and may obtain administrative review if discharged. § 124.34. Pursuant to this provision, Loudermill filed an appeal with the Cleveland Civil Service Commission on November 12. The Commission appointed a referee, who held a hearing on January 29, 1981. Loudermill argued that he had thought that his 1968 larceny conviction was for a misdemeanor rather than a felony. The referee recommended reinstatement. On July 20, 1981, the full Commission heard argument and orally announced that it would uphold the dismissal. Proposed findings of fact and conclusions of law followed on August 10, and Loudermill's attorneys were advised of the result by mail on August 21.

Although the Commission's decision was subject to judicial review in the state courts, Loudermill instead brought the present suit in the Federal District Court for the Northern District of Ohio. The complaint alleged that § 124.34 was unconstitutional on its face because it did not provide the employee an opportunity to respond to the charges against him prior to removal. As a result, discharged employees were deprived of liberty and property without due process. The complaint also alleged that the provision was unconstitutional as applied because discharged employees were not given sufficiently prompt postremoval hearings.

Before a responsive pleading was filed, the District Court dismissed for failure to state a claim on which relief could be granted. It held that because the very statute that created the property right in continued employment also specified the procedures for discharge, and because those procedures were followed, Loudermill was, by definition, afforded all the process due. The post-termination hearing also adequately protected Loudermill's liberty interests. Finally, the District Court concluded that, in light of the Commission's crowded docket, the delay in processing Loudermill's administrative appeal was constitutionally acceptable. . . .

[The Court proceeds to describe the facts of the other case on review.—Ed.]

II

Respondents' federal constitutional claim depends on their having had a property right in continued employment. *Board of Regents v. Roth*, 408 U.S. 564, 576–578 (1972). If they did, the State could not deprive them of this property without due process.

Property interests are not created by the Constitution, "they are created and their dimensions are defined by existing rules or understandings that stem from an independent source such as state law. . . ." *Board of Regents v. Roth*, 408 U.S. at 577. The Ohio statute plainly creates such an interest. Respondents were "classified civil service employees," Ohio Rev. Code Ann. § 124.11(1984), entitled to retain their positions "during good behavior and efficient service," who could not be dismissed "except . . . for . . . misfeasance, malfeasance, or nonfeasance in office," § 124.34. The statute plainly supports the conclusion, reached by both lower courts, that respondents possessed property rights in continued employment. Indeed, this question does not seem to have been disputed below.

The . . . Board argues, however, that the property right is defined by, and conditioned on, the legislature's choice of procedures for its deprivation. The Board stresses that in addition to specifying the grounds for termination, the statute sets out procedures by which termination may take place. The procedures were adhered to in these cases. . . .

This argument, which was accepted by the District Court, has its genesis in the plurality opinion in *Arnett v. Kennedy*, 416 U.S. 134 (1974). *Arnett* involved a challenge by a former federal employee to the procedures by which he was dismissed. The plurality reasoned that where the legislation conferring the substantive right also sets out the procedural mechanism for enforcing that right, the two cannot be separated:

> "The employee's statutorily defined right is not a guarantee against removal without cause in the abstract, but such a guarantee

as enforced by the procedures which Congress has designated for the determination of cause.

"[W]here the grant of a substantive right is inextricably intertwined with the limitations on the procedures which are to be employed in determining that right, a litigant in the position of appellee must take the bitter with the sweet."

Id. at 152–154.

This view garnered three votes in *Arnett*, but was specifically rejected by the other six Justices. Since then, this theory has at times seemed to gather some additional support. More recently, however, the Court has clearly rejected it. . . .

[T]he "bitter with the sweet" approach misconceives the constitutional guarantee. . . . The point is straightforward: the Due Process Clause provides that certain substantive rights—life, liberty, and property—cannot be deprived except pursuant to constitutionally adequate procedures. The categories of substance and procedure are distinct. Were the rule otherwise, the Clause would be reduced to a mere tautology. "Property" cannot be defined by the procedures provided for its deprivation any more than can life or liberty. The right to due process "is conferred, not by legislative grace, but by constitutional guarantee. While the legislature may elect not to confer a property interest in [public] employment, it may not constitutionally authorize the deprivation of such an interest, once conferred, without appropriate procedural safeguards." *Arnett v. Kennedy*, 416 U.S. at 167 (POWELL, J., concurring in part and concurring in result in part); see *id.* at 185 (WHITE, J., concurring in part and dissenting in part).

In short, once it is determined that the Due Process Clause applies, "the question remains what process is due." *Morrissey v. Brewer*, 408 U.S. 471, 481 (1972). The answer to that question is not to be found in the Ohio statute.

III

An essential principle of due process is that a deprivation of life, liberty, or property "be preceded by notice and opportunity for hearing appropriate to the nature of the case." *Mullane v. Central Hanover Bank & Trust Co.*, 339 U.S. 306, 313 (1950). We have described "the root requirement" of the Due Process Clause as being "that an individual be given an opportunity for a hearing before he is deprived of any significant property interest." *Boddie v. Connecticut*, 401 U.S. 371, 379 (1971) (emphasis in original). This principle requires "some kind of a hearing" prior to the discharge of an employee who has a constitutionally protected property interest in his employment. *Board of Regents v. Roth*, 408 U.S. at 569–570; *Perry v. Sindermann*, 408 U.S. 593, 599 (1972). . . .

The need for some form of pretermination hearing, recognized in these cases, is evident from a balancing of the competing interests at stake. These are the private interests in retaining employment, the governmental interest in the expeditious removal of unsatisfactory employees and the avoidance of administrative burdens, and the risk of an erroneous termination. See *Mathews v. Eldridge*, 424 U.S. 319, 335 (1976).

First, the significance of the private interest in retaining employment cannot be gainsaid. We have frequently recognized the severity of depriving a person of the means of livelihood. While a fired worker may find employment elsewhere, doing so will take some time and is likely to be burdened by the questionable circumstances under which he left his previous job.

Second, some opportunity for the employee to present his side of the case is recurringly of obvious value in reaching an accurate decision. Dismissals for cause will often involve factual disputes. Even where the facts are clear, the appropriateness or necessity of the discharge may not be; in such cases, the only meaningful opportunity to invoke the discretion of the decisionmaker is likely to be before the termination takes effect.

The cases before us illustrate these considerations. Both respondents had plausible arguments to make that might have prevented their discharge. . . . As for Loudermill, given the Commission's ruling we cannot say that the discharge was mistaken. Nonetheless, in light of the referee's recommendation, neither can we say that a fully informed decisionmaker might not have exercised its discretion and decided not to dismiss him, notwithstanding its authority to do so. In any event, the termination involved arguable issues, and the right to a hearing does not depend on a demonstration of certain success.

The governmental interest in immediate termination does not outweigh these interests. As we shall explain, affording the employee an opportunity to respond prior to termination would impose neither a significant administrative burden nor intolerable delays. Furthermore, the employer shares the employee's interest in avoiding disruption and erroneous decisions; and until the matter is settled, the employer would continue to receive the benefit of the employee's labors. It is preferable to keep a qualified employee on than to train a new one.

A governmental employer also has an interest in keeping citizens usefully employed rather than taking the possibly erroneous and counterproductive step of forcing its employees onto the welfare rolls. Finally, in those situations where the employer perceives a significant hazard in keeping the employee on the job, it can avoid the problem by suspending with pay.

IV

The foregoing considerations indicate that the pretermination "hearing," though necessary, need not be elaborate. We have pointed out that "[t]he formality and procedural requisites for the hearing can vary, depending upon the importance of the interests involved and the nature of the subsequent proceedings." In general, "something less" than a full evidentiary hearing is sufficient prior to adverse administrative action. Under state law, respondents were later entitled to a full administrative hearing and judicial review. The only question is what steps were required before the termination took effect.

In only one case, *Goldberg v. Kelly*, 397 U.S. 254 (1970), has the Court required a full adversarial evidentiary hearing prior to adverse governmental action. However, as the *Goldberg* Court itself pointed out, that case presented significantly different considerations than are present in the context of public employment. Here, the pretermination hearing need not definitively resolve the propriety of the discharge. It should be an initial check against mistaken decisions—essentially, a determination of whether there are reasonable grounds to believe that the charges against the employee are true and support the proposed action.

The essential requirements of due process . . . are notice and an opportunity to respond. The opportunity to present reasons, either in person or in writing, why proposed action should not be taken is a fundamental due process requirement. See Friendly, "Some Kind of Hearing," 123 U. Pa. L. Rev. 1267, 1281 (1975). The tenured public employee is entitled to oral or written notice of the charges against him, an explanation of the employer's evidence, and an opportunity to present his side of the story. To require more than this prior to termination would intrude to an unwarranted extent on the government's interest in quickly removing an unsatisfactory employee.

Our holding rests in part on the provisions in Ohio law for a full post-termination hearing. . . .

We conclude that all the process that is due is provided by a pretermination opportunity to respond, coupled with post-termination administrative procedures as provided by the Ohio statute. Because respondents allege in their complaints that they had no chance to respond, the District Court erred in dismissing for failure to state a claim. . . .

Justice Marshall, concurring in part and concurring in the judgment.

I agree wholeheartedly with the Court's express rejection of the theory of due process, urged upon us by the petitioner Boards of Education, that a public employee who may be discharged only for cause may be discharged by whatever procedures the legislature chooses. . . .

I write separately, however, to reaffirm my belief that public employees who may be discharged only for cause are entitled, under the Due Process Clause of the Fourteenth Amendment, to more than respondents sought in this case. I continue to believe that *before the decision is made to terminate an employee's wages,* the employee is entitled to an opportunity to test the strength of the evidence "by confronting and cross-examining adverse witnesses and by presenting witnesses on his own behalf, whenever there are substantial disputes in testimonial evidence," *Arnett v. Kennedy,* 416 U.S. 134, 214 (1974) (Marshall, J., dissenting). . . .

To my mind, the disruption caused by a loss of wages may be so devastating to an employee that, whenever there are substantial disputes about the evidence, additional pre-deprivation procedures are necessary to minimize the risk of an erroneous termination. . . .

[An opinion by Justice Brennan concurring in part and dissenting in part is omitted.—Ed.]

Justice Rehnquist, dissenting.

In *Arnett v. Kennedy,* 416 U.S. 134 (1974), six Members of this Court agreed that a public employee could be dismissed for misconduct without a full hearing prior to termination. A plurality of Justices agreed that the employee was entitled to exactly what Congress gave him, and no more. The Chief Justice, Justice Stewart, and I said:

> "Here appellee did have a statutory expectancy that he not be removed other than for 'such cause as will promote the efficiency

of [the] service.' But the very section of the statute which granted him that right, a right which had previously existed only by virtue of administrative regulation, expressly provided also for the procedure by which 'cause' was to be determined, and expressly omitted the procedural guarantees which appellee insists are mandated by the Constitution. Only by bifurcating the very sentence of the Act of Congress which conferred upon appellee the right not to be removed save for cause could it be said that he had an expectancy of that substantive right without the procedural limitations which Congress attached to it. . . . Congress was obviously intent on according a measure of statutory job security to governmental employees which they had not previously enjoyed, but was likewise intent on excluding more elaborate procedural requirements which it felt would make the operation of the new scheme unnecessarily burdensome in practice. Where the focus of legislation was thus strongly on the procedural mechanism for enforcing the substantive right which was simultaneously conferred, we decline to conclude that the substantive right may be viewed wholly apart from the procedure provided for its enforcement. The employee's statutorily defined right is not a guarantee against removal without cause in the abstract, but such a guarantee as enforced by the procedures which Congress has designated for the determination of cause."

Id. at 151–152.

In these cases, the relevant Ohio statute provides in its first paragraph that

"[t]he tenure of every officer or employee in the classified service of the state and the counties, civil service townships, cities, city health districts, general health districts, and city school districts thereof, holding a position under this chapter of the Revised Code, shall be during good behavior and efficient service and no such officer or employee shall be reduced in pay or position, suspended, or removed, except . . . for incompetency, inefficiency, dishonesty, drunkenness, immoral conduct, insubordination, discourteous treatment of the public, neglect of duty, violation of such sections or the rules of the director of administrative services or the commission, or any other failure of good behavior, or any other acts of misfeasance, malfeasance, or nonfeasance in office."

Ohio Rev. Code Ann. § 124.34 (1984).

The very next paragraph of this section of the Ohio Revised Code provides that in the event of suspension of more than three days or removal the appointing authority shall furnish the employee with the stated reasons for his removal. The next paragraph provides that within 10 days following the receipt of such a statement, the employee may appeal in writing to the State Personnel Board of Review or the Commission, such appeal shall be heard within 30 days from the time of its filing, and the Board may affirm, disaffirm, or modify the judgment of the appointing authority.

Thus in one legislative breath Ohio has conferred upon civil service employees such as respondents in these cases a limited form of tenure during good behavior, and prescribed the procedures by which that tenure may be terminated. . . . We stated in *Board of Regents v. Roth*, 408 U.S. 564, 577 (1972):

> "Property interests, of course, are not created by the Constitution. Rather, they are created and their dimensions are defined by existing rules or understandings that stem from an independent source such as state law—rules or understandings that secure certain benefits and that support claims of entitlement to those benefits."

We ought to recognize the totality of the State's definition of the property right in question, and not merely seize upon one of several paragraphs in a unitary statute to proclaim that in that paragraph the State has inexorably conferred upon a civil service employee something which it is powerless under the United States Constitution to qualify in the next paragraph of the statute. This practice ignores our duty under *Roth* to rely on state law as the source of property interests for purposes of applying the Due Process Clause of the Fourteenth Amendment. While it does not impose a federal definition of property, the Court departs from the full breadth of the holding in *Roth* by its selective choice from among the sentences the Ohio Legislature chooses to use in establishing and qualifying a right.

Having concluded by this somewhat tortured reasoning that Ohio has created a property right in the respondents in these cases, the Court naturally proceeds to inquire what process is "due" before the respondents may be divested of that right. This customary "balancing" inquiry conducted by the Court in these cases reaches a result that is quite unobjectionable, but it seems to me that it is devoid of any principles which will either instruct or endure. The balance is simply an ad hoc weighing which depends to a great extent upon how the Court subjectively views the underlying interests at stake. The results in previous cases and in these cases have been quite unpredictable. To paraphrase Justice Black, today's balancing act requires a "pretermination opportunity to respond" but there is nothing that indicates what tomorrow's will be. *Goldberg v. Kelly*, 397 U.S. 254, 276 (1970) (Black, J., dissenting). The results from today's balance certainly do not jibe with the result in *Goldberg* or *Mathews v. Eldridge*, 424 U.S. 319 (1976). The lack of any principled standards in this area means that these procedural due process cases will recur time and again. Every different set of facts will present a new issue on what process was due and when. One way to avoid this subjective and varying interpretation of the Due Process Clause in cases such as these is to hold that one who avails himself of government entitlements accepts the grant of tenure along with its inherent limitations. . . .

Notes and Questions

1.   Summary. In *Loudermill*, the Court rejected the bitter with the sweet model articulated by Justice Rehnquist in *Arnett v. Kennedy*. The Court argued that the categories of protected interests are distinct from procedures. That proposition is obviously true under the traditional understanding of liberty and property rights. Such traditional liberty and property—one's life, freedom of locomotion, and the property one has acquired on one's own—all existed independently of government and of whatever procedures the government had to use to deprive one of such rights. But is the proposition true of statutory entitlements? If the government does not have to give out entitlements at all, can it not decide on what conditions it will give them out, including the conditions for terminating the benefit? Put another way, is the "right" to a statutory entitlement independent of the other conditions in the statute establishing that right?

■   *Problem 7.2*

In Gilbert v. Homar, 520 U.S. 924 (1997), Homar was a police officer at East Stroudsburg University, a branch of the state university system in Pennsylvania. On August 26, 1992, Homar was at a friend's home when the police conducted a drug raid, arresting Homar along with his friend. The state police filed drug charges against Homar, and notified the state university system, which promptly suspended Homar without pay pending an investigation of the charges. The state police had also forwarded its police report, which included a confession, to the university. Ultimately, the criminal charges were dropped on September 1, but the suspension continued. On September 18, university officials met with Homar to get his side of the story, and on September 23, the university notified Homar that he was being demoted. Homar filed suit, arguing that suspending him without pay violated his due process rights. How would you rule?

---

2. Hamdi v. Rumsfeld. In perhaps one of the most interesting procedural due process cases, the Supreme Court applied the *Mathews v. Eldridge* test to determine the constitutionality of a military detention of an American citizen who was captured in Afghanistan fighting for the Taliban in the aftermath of the attacks on the World Trade Center on September 11, 2001. Hamdi v. Rumsfeld, 542 U.S. 507 (2004). The majority concluded that the citizen-detainee "must receive notice of the factual basis for his classification, and a fair opportunity to rebut the Government's factual assertions before a neutral decisionmaker." However, "exigencies of the circumstances may demand that, aside from these core elements, enemy-combatant proceedings may be tailored to alleviate their uncommon potential to burden the Executive at a time of ongoing military conflict." The majority suggested, for example, that hearsay may be appropriate, as well as a presumption in favor of the government's evidence. What do you think of the Court's balancing of the *Mathews v. Eldridge* factors? Does applying those factors even make sense in Hamdi's context? Would they apply to the imprisonment of an ordinary American citizen on American soil?

 TEST YOUR KNOWLEDGE: To assess your understanding of the material in this chapter, **click here** to take a quiz.

CHAPTER EIGHT

Reviewability

The previous chapter dealt with the *scope* of judicial review. The scope—the standard of review—depends on the nature of the agency action at hand. But to get judicial review at all, one has to be able to get into court in the first place. To do so, one has to clear a variety of hurdles that are bundled under the description "reviewability." Some of these hurdles are not unique to administrative law, like the requirements of a cause of action and Article III standing. Others are more unique to administrative law, such as the requirement of finality and administrative exhaustion. To get judicial review, all the boxes need to be checked: the agency action must be "final," administrative remedies must be "exhausted," the case must be "ripe" for adjudication, and the plaintiff must have both Article III standing and a cause of action.

CAUSE OF ACTION: When one's legal rights have been invaded such that one is legally entitled to bring a lawsuit for relief, one has a cause of action.

We begin from the beginning. To sue, one needs to have a *legal right* that has been violated. The first two sections of this chapter deal with causes of action, i.e., whether someone has a legal right that has been infringed and therefore a right to sue for a vindication of that legal right. We then turn to constitutional standing, and finally to timing of judicial review. As noted in the introductory chapter, the organization of these materials is a bit different than in the typical casebook. The student may have heard elsewhere of the concept of "statutory standing" as a prudential limitation related to constitutional

STANDING: Closely related to a cause of action, standing is a complicated term which will be more fully defined later in this chapter. It has to do with the prerequisites for getting into federal court: there must be an actual injury, traceable to a defendant, that the court can redress.

standing. This is a mistake. Statutory standing is really about causes of action, and so it is addressed in this chapter before constitutional standing. The "preclusion" material—has the statute precluded judicial review?—is also about causes of action. As for the timing doctrines, finality and exhaustion are still treated together, but ripeness is now part of a unique section on equitable remedies and preenforcement review of administrative action.

> **Defined Term**
>
> **PRECLUSION:** When Congress statutorily precludes judicial review of administrative actions. Sometimes preclusion might be unconstitutional.

A. Non-APA Causes of Action

When an agency or administrative officer does something unlawful, and you are harmed thereby, how do you challenge the agency's or officer's action? The answer to that question has changed dramatically over the last two centuries, but to understand the modern landscape one must also understand the history.

1. Common Law, Officers, and Sovereign Immunity

Historically, a plaintiff could only sue if she had a *legal right* that was infringed; or, put another way, if she had a *cause of action*. This is a very important point: not everyone who is "harmed" by the actions of another has a cause of action to sue. Recall that infamous case from your first-year torts class, Palsgraf v. Long Island Railroad Co., 162 N.E. 99 (N.Y. Ct. App. 1928). Palsgraf was very much harmed by the negligence of the railroad company: a railroad employee negligently assisted another passenger with boarding a train, leading to that passenger dropping a package that exploded, leading to a large scale hitting Ms. Palsgraf elsewhere on the train platform. There were so many intervening factors that led to this freak accident such that, according to then-Judge Benjamin Cardozo, Ms. Palsgraf did not have any legal right against the railroad. There was no cause of action. Thus in tort, we learn that the "cause of action" for negligence in general has four elements: (1) a duty, (2) a breach of that duty by negligence, (3) causation, and (4) damages. Only if a plaintiff can show all four elements is there a cause of action. Ms. Palsgraf was not a reasonably foreseeable plaintiff and so there was not "duty" to her on the part of the railroad.

Similarly, not everyone that is harmed by government action has a cause of action. As we shall see later in this section, government often takes actions that benefit one economic competitor over another. Historically, there was no cause of action for the competitor to sue. Competitive harm was simply not a harm cognizable in the courts. Likewise, someone might also be emotionally harmed by government action with which he or she disagrees. That hardly means that that person's legal rights have been invaded. There is no general, freestanding right to be free of all types of harm. Only certain types of harm are legally cognizable, for example, trespass, conversion of property, intentional infliction of emotional distress, and so on.

Although not every government action could be challenged in tort, tort causes of action were the traditional way one could challenge unlawful agency action. If an administrative officer entered property unlawfully, and perhaps unlawfully seized property, then the owner would bring a suit *against the officer* for trespass or conversion. The officer would then raise some administrative regulation or congressional statute as a defense, i.e., the officer would claim legal authorization for his or her actions. Then the plaintiff would challenge the legality of that authorization. And if the plaintiff prevailed—if the plaintiff proved that the officer's actions were not authorized, or that the regulation or statute pursuant to which the officer acted was unlawful or unconstitutional— then the officer would have to pay damages.

It may seem odd to require the officer to pay, but this is exactly how things used to be done. The famous case Little v. Barreme, 6 U.S. (2 Cranch) 170 (1804), involved a congressional statute that authorized the seizure of American ships travelling *to* French ports. The Secretary of the Navy, however, instructed commanders to seize any vessels travelling to *or from* a French port. The *Flying Fish* had been travelling from France when it was seized by one Captain Little pursuant to these orders. The owner of the vessel brought a suit against Captain Little for damages. Chief Justice Marshall held that Captain Little was indeed liable:

> I confess the first bias of my mind was very strong in favor of the opinion that though the instructions of the executive could not give a right, they might yet excuse from damages. . . . I was strongly inclined to think that where, in consequence of orders from the legitimate authority, a vessel is seized with pure intention, the claim of the injured party for damages would be against that government from which the orders proceeded, and would be a proper subject for negotiation. But I have been convinced that I was mistaken, and I have receded from this first opinion. I acquiesce in that of my

brethren, which is that the instructions cannot change the nature of the transaction or legalize an act which without those instructions would have been a plain trespass. . . .

Captain Little, then, must be answerable in damages to the owner of this neutral vessel . . . .

6 U.S. at 179. Put another way, the administrative officer was liable for damages at law because the "legal authorization" for his actions were in fact unlawful. Nothing prevented the government from *indemnifying* Captain Little if it chose to do so, and paying for the judgment. The point was only that nothing *immunized* Captain Little from ordinary actions at law for unlawful behavior, even if he acted pursuant to what he believed to be a lawful order.

Chief Justice Marshall observed that he initially had believed that "the claim of the injured party for damages would be against that government from which the orders proceeded," but that his colleagues on the Supreme Court changed his mind about that. Why? Why would the action not be against the government? You learned the answer in the previous chapter: sovereign immunity. Because the government did not have to consent to be sued, there was no action available against the government for damages. That is why the *officers* were sued in their individual capacities. The government could indemnify them, but sovereign immunity did not immunize the government's officers if their actions were not taken pursuant to a lawful order. This may seem like a legal fiction—why have sovereign immunity, if you can just sue the officers themselves?—but it was the way things worked. (Indeed, in England, the government historically did not indemnify officers, and public officers were expected to be substantially wealthy so that they could pay any damages for wrongdoing.)

> **CROSS REFERENCE** We have introduced the concept of sovereign immunity elsewhere, both in the Article III and due process materials. Does sovereign immunity help explain why historically a harmed individual could sue an administrative officer personally?

Over time, and for a variety of (perhaps obvious) reasons, Congress waived sovereign immunity in a variety of statutes. Most prominently, the Tucker Act, enacted in 1887, waived sovereign immunity for claims for money damages not sounding in tort, i.e., those claims based on contract disputes with the government or takings of private property for public use. 28 U.S.C. § 1491(a)(1)

("The United States Court of Federal Claims shall have jurisdiction to render judgment upon any claim against the United States founded either upon the Constitution, or any Act of Congress or any regulation of an executive department, or upon any express or implied contract with the United States, or for liquidated or unliquidated damages in cases not sounding in tort.").

Many decades later, in 1946, Congress waived sovereign immunity for many, but not all, tort claims, in the Federal Tort Claims Act (FTCA). The Act provides that "[t]he head of each Federal agency," pursuant to general regulation promulgated by the Attorney General, may determine and settle

> any claim for money damages against the United States for injury or loss of property or personal injury or death caused by the negligent or wrongful act or omission of any employee of the agency while acting within the scope of his office or employment, under circumstances where the United States, if a private person, would be liable to the claimant in accordance with the law of the place where the act or omission occurred.

28 U.S.C. § 2672. An action in court may be instituted for damages after a claim has been presented to the agency and denied. Id. § 2675; id. § 1346(b) (1) (district court jurisdiction). The FTCA does exempt some claims, however. For example, the Act does not authorize tort suits stemming from the miscarriage of mail by postal carriers, damages as a result of national quarantines, claims arising out of wartime military activities, and certain other categories of claims. Id. § 2680.

Between the Tucker Act and the FTCA, that still leaves a lot of administrative action where the government has not waived sovereign immunity. Basically, the Tucker Act and FTCA waive sovereign immunity *where a private party would have been liable*—that is, for what would be traditionally private-rights claims if they were between two private individuals. Thus, there is a traditional cause of action (tort, contract, takings) and a waiver of sovereign immunity for those actions. But what about where the government wrongfully deprives a veteran of veterans' benefits to which she is entitled? Up until the modern day, there was still no cause of action, nor a waiver of sovereign immunity.

In 1976, Congress amended the APA to waive sovereign immunity for *equitable relief*—that is, non-monetary relief—where there otherwise was a cause of action (we will discuss equity in more detail shortly). See 5 U.S.C. § 702 ("An action in a court of the United States seeking relief other than money damages and stating a claim that an agency or an officer or employee thereof acted or failed to act in an official capacity or under color of legal authority shall not be dismissed nor relief therein be denied on the ground that it is against the United States or that the United States is an indispensable party."). But that provision does not in and of itself *create* a cause of action—there still must be some preexisting legal right to sue. And it does not waive sovereign immunity for monetary damages.

Thus, a cause of action for the veteran, and a waiver of sovereign immunity, still has to be found elsewhere. The most obvious candidate is the specific organic statute governing that particular area of law. As we shall see in Part B of this chapter, however, the Administrative Procedure Act itself has since been interpreted as creating a general cause of action. But put that aside for the moment.

It is worth making one final observation. If the government has waived sovereign immunity, can you still sue an officer? And can you sue an officer for unlawful actions even where sovereign immunity has not been waived? The answer is generally yes, but with the ever-increasing waivers of sovereign immunity there has been a concomitant increase in *official immunity*. That is, the Supreme Court has developed a number of doctrines—contrary to *Little v. Barreme*—that immunize administrative officers. The most prominent example today is the doctrine of "qualified immunity,"

 **HISTORICAL PERSPECTIVE** As Congress increasingly waived sovereign immunity, courts correspondingly increased the immunity that individual officers would receive.

whereby police officers (federal and state) who would historically have been liable in tort for trespass, conversion of property, unlawful imprisonment, and the like, are now immune even for their unlawful actions, so long as the unlawfulness of the actions was not "clearly established" by existing court precedent or other law.

Do you think it's constitutional for Congress to immunize federal officers in this way? What if Congress does not create an adequate alternative remedy, for instance by waiving sovereign immunity and authorizing suit against itself? Is the answer to that question to be found in interpretations of the Necessary and Proper Clause? See McCulloch v. Maryland, 17 U.S. (4 Wheat.) 316, 411 (1819) (observing that "a great substantive and independent power . . . cannot be implied as incidental to other powers" pursuant to the Necessary and Proper Clause). If the government has violated a "right," must there generally be a "remedy"? See Marbury v. Madison, 5 U.S. (1 Cranch) 137, 163 (1803) ("The very essence of civil liberty certainly consists in the right of every individual to claim the protection of the laws whenever he receives an injury. . . . The Government of the United States has been emphatically termed a government of laws, and not of men. It will certainly cease to deserve this high appellation if the laws furnish no remedy for the violation of a vested legal right.").

2. Injunctions

The previous section described how someone could historically challenge administrative action where the government had caused harm to known legal interests at law, such as when government officials committed torts under color of legal authority. Another way that administrative action was challenged was in *enforcement proceedings*. Often the government did not actually cause harm, or threaten to cause harm, until the government criminally prosecuted someone for violating a statute, or went to court to seek an enforcement of some administrative order. Recall, for example, that the Interstate Commerce Commission could only enforce its orders in a court, and the United States Employees' Compensation Commission awards, at issue in *Crowell v. Benson*, could only be enforced in the district court. In these situations, the invalidity of the government action could be raised as a defense to the proceedings.

Was there any way to challenge the government's action *before* the government brought an enforcement proceeding, or *before* it undertook actions that might cause some harm? This was the realm of equity jurisdiction. Courts could *enjoin* the government from taking some threatened action under certain circumstances. The most important

 CROSS REFERENCE The material in this section will be revisited in a subsequent section on "preenforcement review." The cases here are precursors to the modern ones discussed in that section.

criterion to trigger equity jurisdiction, which is still a factor in an analysis of injunctions today, is whether the remedy at law was adequate. If the after-the-fact legal remedy for damages was "inadequate," for whatever reason, then the interested party might have been able to get an injunction beforehand.

Importantly, equity jurisdiction did not create new legal rights. If the veteran could not sue for wrongfully withheld veterans' benefits at law, then she couldn't sue for an injunction in equity either to set aside the administrative regulation pursuant to which the administrative officer was acting, or otherwise compel the agency to act (with a narrow exception for ministerial duties, to which we come shortly). Equity was rather a form of *relief.* The interested party had to have some known legal right that was threatened—for example, a trespass, conversion of property, or an imprisonment—and then she could get relief before the harm occurred if the remedy at law was inadequate. In other words, equity closely tracked the actions at law, and there was no freestanding right to sue agencies in equity.

An injunction of this type was issued in the classic case of Ex Parte Young, 209 U.S. 123 (1908). The case involved a state agency, but its principles apply just the same to federal agencies. The Minnesota railroad commission had established certain rates, and the existing statutes provided that violations were punishable by thousands of dollars for each occurrence. The

Defined Term

INJUNCTION: A court order enjoining—mandating—that a person do a certain thing or take a certain action.

state legislature subsequently passed a statute changing the railroad rates and making violations thereof a felony, with punishment up to five years in prison. The directors and officers of several railroad companies sued in equity for an injunction; they argued that the penalties provided by the statutes were "so drastic that no owner or operator of a railway property could invoke the jurisdiction of any court to test the validity thereof, except at the risk of confiscation of its property, and the imprisonment for long terms in jails and penitentiaries of its officers, agents, and employees." 209 U.S. at 131.

The federal circuit court issued a preliminary injunction enjoining Young from enforcing the various orders. Young, however, proceeded to get an order against the railroads from a state court. The federal court then imprisoned Young for contempt of court. Young then sought a writ of habeas corpus; it was upon review of this writ that the Supreme Court decided the issues in the case.

The Court's decision is famous for concluding that sovereign immunity is not violated where the suit is against an officer for an injunction enjoining enforcement of an unconstitutional statute. This should come as no surprise to readers of *Little v. Barreme* and this casebook. If a plaintiff could sue an officer in tort even though the officer was acting pursuant to some ostensible legal authorization, then surely the officer could be enjoined in equity, too (assuming the remedy at law was inadequate). The only difference in *Ex Parte Young* was that the railroads did not have any common-law right that was invaded; they were simply going to be "harmed" by the application of an onerous statute that they believed to be unconstitutional. The Court explained that, if an officer could be enjoined from interfering with common law rights, then the officer could also be enjoined before causing irreparable harm by applying an unconstitutional statute:

> The difference between an actual and direct interference with tangible property and the enjoining of state officers from enforcing an unconstitutional act, is not of a radical nature, and does not extend, in truth, the jurisdiction of the courts over the subject-matter.
>
> In the case of the interference with property, the person enjoined is assuming to act in his capacity as an official of the state, and justification for his interference is claimed by reason of his position as a state official. Such official cannot so justify when acting under an unconstitutional enactment of the legislature. So, where the state official, instead of directly interfering with tangible property, is about to commence suits which have for their object the enforcement of an act which violates the Federal Constitution, to the great and irreparable injury of the complainants, he is seeking the same justification from the authority of the state as in other cases. The sovereignty of the state is, in reality, no more involved in one case than in the other. The state cannot, in either case, impart to the official immunity from responsibility to the supreme authority of the United States.

Ex Parte Young, 209 U.S. at 167 (paragraph breaks added). Put another way, if acting under color of legal authority does not immunize an administrative officer from an action for damages if that purported legal authority was actually unlawful or unconstitutional, then nothing in theory prevented an injunction of that behavior beforehand, assuming, again, that the legal remedy was inadequate.

On the inadequacy of the legal remedy, the Court observed:

> We do not say the company could not interpose this defense in an action to recover penalties or upon the trial of an indictment, but the facility of proving it in either case falls so far below that which would obtain in a court of equity that comparison is scarcely possible.

> To await proceedings against the company in a state court, grounded upon a disobedience of the act, and then, if necessary, obtain a review in this court by writ of error to the highest state court, would place the company in peril of large loss and its agents in great risk of fines and imprisonment if it should be finally determined that the act was valid. This risk the company ought not to be required to take. . . .

> All the objections to a remedy at law as being plainly inadequate are obviated by a suit in equity, making all who are directly interested parties to the suit, and enjoining the enforcement of the act until the decision of the court upon the legal question.

Ex Parte Young, 209 U.S. at 165. Do you agree that the legal remedy was inadequate? Would you be willing to risk years in prison in order to challenge the validity of the statute and orders? Professor John Harrison argues that the facts represented a classic case for an "anti-suit injunction":

> A core function of equity, and a classic use of the remedy of injunction, especially in systems that separated law and equity, was to interfere with proceedings at law by enjoining parties from bringing legal actions, from raising certain claims or defenses in them, or from executing judgments obtained at law. In one standard configuration a potential defendant at law would sue in equity in order to present a defense that was not recognized at law, or would be inadequately protected by being raised as a defense in a legal proceeding. . . .

> Crucial to understanding *Young* is that injunctions to restrain proceedings at law were sometimes granted to enforce defenses that could be raised at law but the assertion of which would nevertheless not afford the equity plaintiff full protection. If the bill in equity could explain why the legal defense, even though technically available, would not do full justice, then the defense at law would constitute

a legal remedy that was inadequate, and equity could act. [Joseph] Story devoted several sections of his treatise on equity jurisprudence to describing situations in which a legal defense was inadequate and an injunction against bringing the lawsuit was appropriate. . . .

To apply the familiar principle that equity will act only when the remedy at law is inadequate, the court must identify the legal remedy. [Justice] Peckham discussed the question in detail, giving several grounds on which it would be unreasonable to demand that the railroads violate the rates, wait to be sued by Minnesota, and present their federal arguments as defenses.

John Harrison, *Ex Parte* Young, 60 Stan. L. Rev. 989, 997–98, 1002 (2008). To be sure, it may be that *Ex Parte Young* and its predecessors actually expanded the availability of injunctions from the historical baseline. Is the implication of *Ex Parte Young* that injunctive relief will always be available if the punishment for lack of compliance is criminal? The general rule, however, was that a court would not restrain state officials from instituting criminal proceedings. Davis & Farnum Mfg. Co. v. City of Los Angeles, 189 U.S. 207, 217 (1903) ("a court of equity has no general power to enjoin or stay criminal proceedings unless they are instituted by a party to a suit already pending before it"). Still, injunctions to prevent the invasion of property interests were sometimes allowed. As the Supreme Court noted in *Davis & Farnum,* "in a few cases, an injunction has been allowed to issue to restrain an invasion of rights of property by the enforcement of an unconstitutional law, where such enforcement would result in irreparable damages to the plaintiff." 189 U.S. at 218.

Whether or not *Ex Parte Young* represented an expansion of the availability of injunctions to situations in which the regulated parties risked severe penalties if they challenged the regulation at law, it was nevertheless consistent with the principles of equity jurisprudence: injunctions were only available where (1) there would have been a corresponding action at law, or the defendant-turned-plaintiff had a known legal right, and (2) the remedy at law was inadequate. As we shall see, this doctrine still plays an important role in determining whether federal courts will engage in preenforcement review of regulatory actions, which we discuss in the final section of this chapter. The Court does not always recognize that such cases are about equity jurisprudence. For example, the cases about "ripeness," usually discussed with materials on "finality" and "exhaustion," are really about these old rules regarding injunctions.

3. Mandamus and Declaratory Judgments

Before leaving the subject of equitable remedies, it is important to identify a few other legal mechanisms to challenge agency action that were not based in actions at law. In addition to tort suits against the officer (or against the sovereign), to defenses to criminal proceedings or enforcement actions, and to suits in equity where the legal remedy was inadequate, there was (and is) the writ of

Defined Term

MANDAMUS: A type of injunction that compels an officer to take affirmative actions where the law leaves that officer no discretion.

mandamus, which does not prohibit a government officer from taking some unlawful action but rather *compels* the officer to take *affirmative* action that she has a duty to undertake.

This was the writ at issue in Marbury v. Madison, 5 U.S. (1 Cranch) 137 (1803). Secretary of State James Madison refused to deliver to William Marbury his commission, signed by the previous President, John Adams, to become a Justice of the Peace for the District of Columbia. Marbury sued Madison, and Chief Justice Marshall explained that a writ of mandamus was warranted because the law clearly required the delivering of the commission and so it was a "ministerial duty," rather than a mere discretionary action of the executive. Here is some of the famous language from the case:

> This is not a proceeding which may be varied, if the judgment of the executive shall suggest one more eligible; but is a precise course accurately marked out by law, and is to be strictly pursued. It is the duty of the secretary of state to conform to the law, and in this he is an officer of the United States, bound to obey the laws. He acts, in this respect, as has been very properly stated at the bar, under the authority of law, and not by the instructions of the President. It is a ministerial act which the law enjoins on a particular officer for a particular purpose. . . .
>
> By the constitution of the United States, the President is invested with certain important political powers, in the exercise of which he is to use his own discretion, and is accountable only to his country in his political character, and to his own conscience. To aid him in the performance of these duties, he is authorized to appoint certain officers, who act by his authority and in conformity with his orders.

In such cases, their acts are his acts; and whatever opinion may be entertained of the manner in which executive discretion may be used, still there exists, and can exist, no power to control that discretion. The subjects are political. They respect the nation, not individual rights, and being entrusted to the executive, the decision of the executive is conclusive. . . .

But when the legislature proceeds to impose on that officer other duties; when he is directed peremptorily to perform certain acts; when the rights of individuals are dependent on the performance of those acts; he is so far the officer of the law; is amenable to the laws for his conduct; and cannot at his discretion sport away the vested rights of others.

The conclusion from this reasoning is, that where the heads of departments are the political or confidential agents of the executive, merely to execute the will of the President, or rather to act in cases in which the executive possesses a constitutional or legal discretion, nothing can be more perfectly clear than that their acts are only politically examinable. But where a specific duty is assigned by law, and individual rights depend upon the performance of that duty, it seems equally clear that the individual who considers himself injured, has a right to resort to the laws of his country for a remedy.

5 U.S. at 158, 164–66. Although the "political question" doctrine has evolved—as we know from the materials on judicial review of agency action, not all discretionary acts are unexaminable—it remains the case that to compel an agency action by writ of mandamus, there must be a "specific duty . . . assigned by law." The only other way to compel agency action is if the specific statute provides for review of an agency's failure to act (think back to *Massachusetts v. EPA*).

The final important mechanism for review of administrative action is the declaratory judgment, which is a concept closely connected to injunctions. Recall that to get an injunction, the regulated party had to have a known legal right and the remedy at law had to be inadequate. The injunction remained a rather rare remedy until modern times. In an effort to expand the availability of preenforcement review, Congress enacted the Declaratory Judgment Act of 1934, now codified at 28 U.S.C. § 2201. It provides:

In a case of actual controversy within its jurisdiction [excepting certain cases, such as tax matters], any court of the United States, upon the filing of an appropriate pleading, may declare the rights and other legal relations of any interested party seeking such declaration, whether or not further relief is or could be sought.

The declaratory judgment effectively creates a new cause of action for a plaintiff who might otherwise have had to wait to bring a legal action in tort or under some other known cause of action to sue beforehand and obtain a declaration of her legal rights and interests. The declaratory judgment does not result in an injunction, however, which must be sued for separately if, for example, the declaratory judgment is ignored. But see Samuel L Bray, *The Myth of the Mild Declaratory Judgment*, 63 Duke L.J. 1091, 1109–13 (2014) (arguing that almost all declaratory judgments are obeyed because of the incentives that motivated a plaintiff to seek the declaratory judgment in the first place). Even more importantly, the Declaratory Judgment Act does not *expand* the universe of known legal rights. It merely creates a mechanism by which the known, existing legal rights can be ascertained and declared.

Defined Term

DECLARATORY JUDGMENT: Closely related to an injunction, a declaratory judgment is a declaration of one's legal rights. Theoretically, however, a declaratory judgment does not actually command any person to do any particular thing.

4.   Special Statutory Causes of Action

As explained previously, not everyone who suffers a harm has a cause of action to sue. Not everyone who is harmed has suffered a *legal* harm. People are harmed all the time for all sorts of reasons; people are given offense; that doesn't mean they can take their grievances to court. There used to be a saying, perhaps apocryphal: don't turn a schoolyard dispute into a federal lawsuit. And that's because most schoolyard disputes *can't* be the stuff of a federal lawsuit. Again, not every harm is a legal harm.

For purposes of administrative law, the most important kind of harm that was traditionally not cognizable in court was the economic harm that a competitor might suffer as a result of a government action. The classic case of this type was Alabama Power Co. v. Ickes, 302 U.S. 464 (1938). Alabama Power sued the Federal Emergency Administrator of Public Works to prevent him from giving loans and grants to municipalities for the purpose of constructing electricity-distribution systems. Such systems would compete directly with Alabama Power. The Supreme Court held there was no cause of action. "[T]he mere fact that petitioner will sustain financial loss by reason of the lawful competition which will result from the use by the municipalities of the proposed loans and grants" does not create a "legal injury as enables [Alabama Power] to maintain the present suits." The question, the Court noted, is: "Can any one who will suffer injurious consequences from the lawful use of money about to be unlawfully loaned maintain a suit to enjoin the loan?" The answer is no because "the lender owes the sufferer no enforceable duty to refrain from making the unauthorized loan." 302 U.S. at 478–80. Just as the Long Island Railroad Company had no enforceable duty to an unforeseeable plaintiff, the lender had no enforceable duty toward a firm who might be harmed by the lender giving money to a competitor.

The problem with this state of affairs was that often economic competitors were the only entities with sufficient incentive to sue to prevent unlawful government action of this type. Thus, Congress began to create new causes of action by statute to permit such competitors to sue. The "leading" example, see Caleb Nelson, *"Standing" and Remedial Rights in Administrative Law*, 105 Va. L. Rev. 703, 721 (2019), was Section 402(b)(2) of the Communications Act of 1934, which is now codified in 47 U.S.C. § 402(b)(6): "Appeals may be taken from decisions and orders of the [FCC] to the United States Court of Appeals for the District of Columbia . . . [b]y and . . . person who is aggrieved or whose interests are adversely affected by any order of the Commission granting or denying any application."

The language that any "aggrieved" party, or a party "whose interests are adversely affected" by an order of the commission, was included to create a cause of action allowing economic competitors to sue. If the FCC unlawfully granted a license, who better to sue than a competitor of the licensee? The Supreme Court explained as much in FCC v. Sanders Bros. Radio Station, 309 U.S. 470 (1940), in allowing a competitor to sue for an allegedly unlawful granting of a license. Congress, the Court explained, "may have been of opinion that one likely to be financially injured by the issue of a license would be the only person having a sufficient interest to bring to the attention of the appellate court errors of law in the action of the Commission in granting the license." 309 U.S. at 477.

Caleb Nelson has explained that Congress had broad power to create these new causes of action, and that lawyers started to refer to these causes of action as creating "statutory review" of agency action. This distinguished such causes of action from "nonstatutory review," i.e., the causes of action that derive from non-written law, like torts, contracts, and equity jurisprudence. Nelson, *Remedial Rights*, supra, at 725. Nelson explains that "[b]y the time Congress enacted the APA, a number of federal regulatory statutes contained provisions allowing certain decisions by specific federal agencies to be reviewed in court at the behest of people who were "aggrieved" (or, occasionally, "adversely affected"), but who might not otherwise have been eligible for judicial relief." Id. at 729. One survey of such statutes in 1949 explained that although an administrative stat-

>
> **Defined Term**
>
> **NONSTATUTORY REVIEW:** Another term for causes of action that do not depend on statutes for their existence, such as suits in tort or contract.

ute "may be silent about the area of review, or it may limit it to those against whom the order runs, . . . the most common provision is that 'persons aggrieved,' or 'parties in interest,' or 'persons adversely affected' may seek review of orders

> **Defined Term**
>
> **STATUTORY REVIEW:** Causes of action created by statute, particularly where there is no corresponding cause of action at common law.

promulgated under the authority of the statute." *Note, Statutory Standing to Review Administrative Action*, 98 U. Pa. L. Rev. 70, 71; see also id. at n. 13a (collecting such statutes).

In summary, by the time of the APA's enactment, the only way to challenge an agency's action was in a common law suit, as a defense to enforcement proceedings, in an equitable action (or declaratory judgment action) that more or less mirrored the common law action, or where an organic statute specifically created a cause of action to sue.

B. The APA Cause of Action

We now come to some of the most difficult of the reviewability materials. Our question is: did the APA change the law respecting whether someone could sue an agency? Recall from the previous section that an agency action could only be reviewed by a court if it was reviewed as part of some known action at law or in equity. Thus, a criminal defendant could raise invalidity of the agency action as a defense. A property owner could sue an officer under the known causes of action in tort such as trespass or conversion, and later could sue the government directly under the FTCA or the Tucker Act. Regulated businesses could sometimes bring declaratory judgment actions or anti-suit injunctions for preenforcement review. And some special statutes gave "aggrieved" or "adversely affected" competitors the right to sue for economic harm.

That still left a large amount of agency action unreviewable, especially in the public rights context. Recall again that sovereign immunity insulated government action from judicial review in public rights cases. The government waived some of its sovereign immunity in the Tucker Act and the FTCA for those actions that would be private rights cases if they were between two private parties (breach of contract, takings of private property, torts, etc.). But there was no general statute waiving sovereign immunity in "core" public rights cases: those involving discretionary government benefits. Could a veteran sue if she believed the federal government wrongly denied her veterans' benefits? What about a Medicare or Social Security recipient? There was no general waiver of sovereign immunity, and no general authorization for suit, in these cases; the relevant causes of action and waivers of sovereign immunity had to be found in the specific organic statutes.

 CROSS REFERENCE We have encountered the concepts of sovereign immunity and public rights several times before.

That is where the Administrative Procedure Act comes in—sort of. Historically, the APA did *not* expand the realm of judicial review. It was not intended to create new causes of action. Section 702 of the APA provides: "A person suffering legal wrong because of agency action, or adversely affected or aggrieved by agency action within the meaning of a relevant statute, is entitled to judicial review thereof." The rest of that section then waives sovereign immunity in such cases. (The sovereign immunity waiver was added, as previously explained, in 1976.) Does this create a cause of action for anyone who is "aggrieved" by any agency action? Can a veteran "aggrieved" by a wrongful benefits decision sue?

The answer historically was no. This provision did not expand causes of action. It simply codified the existing law respecting causes of action. Anyone who suffered a "legal wrong"—a breach of contract, a tort, a taking of private property—could already sue, either the officer or (after sovereign immunity was waived) the government itself. Section 702 also provides, however, that a person who is "adversely affected or aggrieved by agency action within the meaning of the relevant statute" is also entitled to review. There are two possible ways to interpret this to the modern ear: (1) a person is aggrieved "within the meaning of the relevant statute" *if* the specific statute has already granted that person a cause of action, as in those special statutory review provisions for economic competitors; *or* (2) the APA is now a freestanding cause of action for anyone aggrieved by any statute, whether or not the specific statute says anything about judicial review or causes of action at all.

The scholarly consensus is that the "original" answer was the first of the two. Caleb Nelson, *"Standing" and Remedial Rights in Administrative Law*, 105 Va. L. Rev. 703, 727 (2019) ("Scholars largely agree that rather than expanding judicial review, . . . Section [702] was simply meant to codify existing doctrines and to accommodate the variety of forms of review that were already in use."). If the special statute expanded judicial review by creating a cause of action for, say, economic competitors, then APA § 702 now said that those actions are brought within the APA, including its scope of review provisions in § 706. But the APA did not by itself create new causes of action. This was confirmed by § 703 about the "form" of action; that section provides,

> The form of proceeding for judicial review is the special statutory review proceeding relevant to the subject matter in a court specified by statute or, in the absence or inadequacy thereof, any applicable form of legal action, including actions for declaratory judgments or writs of prohibitory or mandatory injunction or habeas corpus, in a court of competent jurisdiction.

Section 703 thus confirmed that the only "forms" or "causes" of action known to the APA were (1) the traditional "form[s] of legal action" including not just torts, but also declaratory judgments, injunctions, mandamus, and habeas corpus; and (2) any *new* causes of action provided by *specific statutes*. This understanding was also confirmed by a leading case from the D.C. Circuit in 1955. In Kansas City Power & Light Co. v. McKay, 225 F.2d 924 (1955), the question was "whether utility companies which claim they are in competition with a federally-supported power program can obtain the aid of the courts in challenging the validity of that program." 225 F.2d at 926. Clearly, at law, these competitors had no legally cognizable interest. There was no breach of a contract to which they were a party, no tort, no taking. The only way they could bring suit was under a special statutory review provision creating a cause of action for "aggrieved" economic competitors. But there was no such statute. So what about APA § 702? The court explained,

> Section [702] is for the benefit of 'any person suffering legal wrong', that is, one whose legal rights have been violated. As we have seen, these plaintiffs cannot effectively make such a claim. Nor are we confronted with any relevant statute within the meaning of which the plaintiffs are 'adversely affected or aggrieved.'

Id. at 932. Section 702, simply put, seems to have codified existing law and created no new causes of action.

1. Presumption of Review

Very quickly after the APA's enactment, however, language in a variety of Supreme Court cases seemed to suggest that the APA did provide a general right of review, *unless* the organic statute otherwise precluded review. See, e.g., Shaughnessy v. Pedreiro, 349 U.S. 48, 51 (1955) (the purpose of the APA's review provisions "was to remove obstacles to judicial review of agency action under subsequently enacted statutes"); Rusk v. Cort, 369 U.S. 367, 379–80 (1962) ("[T]he Court will not hold that the broadly remedial provisions of the Administrative Procedure Act are unavailable to review administrative decisions under the 1952 Act in the absence of clear and convincing evidence that Congress so intended.").

The leading case is Abbott Laboratories v. Gardner, 387 U.S. 136 (1967), where the Court held that there is a "presumption of judicial review" under the APA. (This case is also the leading case on ripeness, i.e. "when" judicial review may be had assuming that review is available, and the opinion is excerpted in detail later in this chapter.) The Court's cases, the Court observed, "show[ ] that judicial review of a final agency action by an aggrieved person will not be cut off unless there is persuasive reason to believe that such was the purpose of Congress." 387 U.S. at 140. Or as the Court explained it more recently, the APA "creates a 'presumption favoring judicial review of administrative action,' but as with most presumptions, this one 'may be overcome by inferences of intent drawn from the statutory scheme as a whole.'" Sackett v. EPA, 566 U.S. 120, 128 (2012) (quoting Block v. Community Nutrition Institute, 467 U.S. 340, 349 (1984)).

Abbott Laboratories itself, however, was not actually a groundbreaking case. The question was whether a party regulated by the FDA could challenge an FDA regulation before there was any enforcement proceeding. The question thus really turned on equitable remedies—whether, as in *Ex Parte Young,* a party could sue for an injunction before a regulation or statute was enforced against it. There was no question, however, that Abbott Laboratories, as the regulated party, had known legal rights at stake. If the FDA brought an enforcement proceeding, Abbott would have been able to raise the invalidity of the regulation as a defense. Although in this respect *Abbott Labs.* was not a groundbreaking case (it was groundbreaking, as we shall see later in this chapter, by expanding the availability of the preenforcement injunction as a remedy), it is often cited for this general "presumption of judicial review."

2.   The Zone of Interests Test

What was groundbreaking was the next case, *Data Processing,* decided in 1970. There, the Supreme Court established the "zone of interests" test. As you shall see as you read, the Supreme Court seems to be—and it has since been understood to be—expanding the availability of causes of action. *Data Processing* seems to hold that § 702 authorizes a cause of action for anyone aggrieved by any statute, whether or not that statute has its own special review provisions and creates its own cause of action. The Court seems to hold that so long as one "arguably" comes within the "zone of interests" that Congress intended the particular statute to protect, that person has a cause of action or "standing" to sue. Because the Court uses the word "standing," the zone of interests test is often taken to be a prudential element of standing analysis—not required by Article III, but imposed as a prudential matter by the courts. Thus, *Data Processing* is usually included within a dedicated chapter on standing, right after the constitutional standing material that we will address shortly. But, as you shall see when you read this, *Data Processing* is really about causes of action.

IN QUIRY What work does the "zone of interests" test do? Is it about standing? Causes of action? Something else?

Association of Data Processing Service Organizations, Inc. v. Camp

397 U.S. 150 (1970)

MR. JUSTICE DOUGLAS delivered the opinion of the Court.

Petitioners sell data processing services to businesses generally. In this suit they seek to challenge a ruling by respondent Comptroller of the Currency that, as an incident to their banking services, national banks, including respondent American National Bank & Trust Company, may make data processing services available to other banks and to bank customers. The District Court dismissed the complaint for lack of standing of petitioners to bring the suit. The Court of Appeals affirmed. The case is here on a petition for writ of certiorari which we granted.

Generalizations about standing to sue are largely worthless as such. One generalization is, however, necessary and that is that the question of standing in the federal courts is to be considered in the framework of Article III which restricts judicial power to 'cases' and 'controversies.' As we recently stated in Flast v. Cohen, 392 U.S. 83, 101, '(I)n terms of Article III limitations on federal court jurisdiction, the question of standing is related only to whether the dispute sought to be adjudicated will be presented in an adversary context and in a form historically viewed as capable of judicial resolution.' Flast was a taxpayer's suit. The present is a competitor's suit. And while the two have the same Article III starting point, they do not necessarily track one another.

The first question is whether the plaintiff alleges that the challenged action has caused him injury in fact, economic or otherwise. There can be no doubt but that petitioners have satisfied this test. The petitioners not only allege that competition by national banks in the business of providing data processing services might entail some future loss of profits for the petitioners, they also allege that respondent American National Bank & Trust Company was performing or preparing to perform such services for two customers for whom petitioner Data Systems, Inc., had previously agreed or negotiated to perform such services. The petitioners' suit was brought not only against the American National Bank & Trust Company, but also against the Comptroller of the Currency. The Comptroller was alleged to have caused petitioners injury in fact by his 1966 ruling which stated: 'Incidental to its banking services, a national bank may make available its data processing equipment or perform data processing services on such equipment for other banks and bank customers.'

The Court of Appeals viewed the matter differently, stating:

'(A) plaintiff may challenge alleged illegal competition when as complainant it pursues (1) a legal interest by reason of public charter or contract, . . . (2) a legal interest by reason of statutory protection, . . . or (3) a 'public interest' in which Congress has recognized the need for review of administrative action and plaintiff is significantly involved to have standing to represent the public. . . .'

Those tests were based on prior decisions of this Court, such as Tennessee Electric Power Co. v. TVA, 306 U.S. 118 [(1939)], where private power companies sought to enjoin TVA from operating, claiming that the statutory plan under which it was created was unconstitutional. The Court denied the competitors' standing, holding that they did not have that status 'unless the right invaded is a legal right,—one of property, one arising out of contract, one protected against tortious invasion, or one founded on a statute which confers a privilege.' Id. at 137–138.

The 'legal interest' test goes to the merits. The question of standing is different. It concerns, apart from the 'case' or 'controversy' test, the question whether the interest sought to be protected by the complainant is arguably within the zone of interests to be protected or regulated by the statute or constitutional guarantee in question. Thus the Administrative Procedure Act grants standing to a person 'aggrieved by agency action within the meaning of a relevant statute.' 5 U.S.C. § 702. That interest, at times, may reflect 'aesthetic, conservational, and recreational' as well as economic values. A person or a family may have a spiritual stake in First Amendment values sufficient to give standing to raise issues concerning the Establishment Clause and the Free Exercise Clause. We mention these noneconomic values to emphasize that standing may stem from them as well as from the economic injury in which petitioners rely here. . . .

Apart from Article III jurisdictional questions, problems of standing, as resolved by this Court for its own governance, have involved a 'rule of self-restraint.' Barrows v. Jackson, 346 U.S. 249, 255 [(1953)]. Congress can, of course, resolve the question one way or another, save as the requirements of Article III dictate otherwise.

Where statutes are concerned, the trend is toward enlargement of the class of people who may protest administrative action. The whole drive for enlarging the category of aggrieved 'persons' is symptomatic of that trend. In a closely analogous case we held that an existing entrepreneur had standing to challenge the legality of the entrance of a newcomer into the business, because the established business was allegedly protected by a valid city ordinance that protected it from unlawful competition. Chicago v. Atchison, T. & S.F.R. Co., 357 U.S. 77, 83–84 [(1958)]. In that tradition was Hardin v. Kentucky Utilities Co., 390 U.S. 1 [(1968)], which involved a section of the TVA Act designed primarily to protect, through area limitations, private utilities against TVA competition. We held that no explicit statutory provision was necessary to confer standing, since the private utility bringing suit was within the class of persons that the statutory provision was designed to protect.

It is argued that the Chicago case and the Hardin case are relevant here because of § 4 of the Bank Service Corporation Act of 1962, which provides: 'No bank service corporation may engage in any activity other than the performance of bank services for banks.'

The Court of Appeals for the First Circuit [has] held . . . that by reason of § 4 a data processing company has standing to contest the legality of a national bank performing data processing services for other banks and bank customers:

> "Section 4 had a broader purpose than regulating only the service corporations. It was also a response to the fears expressed by a few senators, that without such a prohibition, the bill would have enabled 'banks to engage in a nonbanking activity,' S. Rep. No. 2105 (87th Cong., 2d Sess. 7–12) (Supplemental views of Senators Proxmire, Douglas, and Neuberger), and thus constitute 'a serious exception to the accepted public policy which strictly limits banks to banking.' (Supplemental views of Senators Muskie and Clark). We think Congress has provided the sufficient statutory aid to standing even though the competition may not be the precise kind Congress legislated against."

We do not put the issue in those words, for they implicate the merits. We do think, however, that § 4 arguably brings a competitor within the zone of interests protected by it.

That leaves the remaining question, whether judicial review of the Comptroller's action has been precluded. We do not think it has been. . . .

The Administrative Procedure Act provides that the provisions of the Act authorizing judicial review apply 'except to the extent that—(1) statutes preclude judicial review; or (2) agency action is committed to agency discretion by law.' 5 U.S.C. § 701(a). . . .

There is no presumption against judicial review and in favor of administrative absolutism unless that purpose is fairly discernible in the statutory scheme.

We find no evidence that Congress in either the Bank Service Corporation Act or the National Bank Act sought to preclude judicial review of administrative rulings by the Comptroller as to the legitimate scope of activities available to national banks under those statutes. . . . It is clear that petitioners, as competitors of national banks which are engaging in data processing services, are within that class of 'aggrieved' persons who, under § 702, are entitled to judicial review of 'agency action.' . . .

We hold that petitioners have standing to sue and that the case should be remanded for a hearing on the merits.

Mr. Justice Brennan, with whom Mr. Justice White joins, concurring and dissenting.

I concur in the result in both cases but dissent from the Court's treatment of the question of standing to challenge agency action.

The Court's approach to standing, set out in Data Processing, has two steps: (1) since 'the framework of Article III . . . restricts judicial power to 'cases' and 'controversies,' the first step is to determine 'whether the plaintiff alleges that the challenged action has caused him injury in fact'; (2) if injury in fact is alleged, the relevant statute or constitutional provision is then examined to determine 'whether the interest sought to be protected by the complainant is arguably within the zone of interests to be protected or regulated by the statute or constitutional guarantee in question.'

My view is that the inquiry in the Court's first step is the only one that need be made to determine standing. I had thought we discarded the notion of any additional requirement when we discussed standing solely in terms of its constitutional content in Flast v. Cohen, 392 U.S. 83 (1968). By requiring a second, nonconstitutional step, the Court comes very close to perpetuating the discredited requirement that conditioned standing on a showing by the plaintiff that the challenged governmental action invaded one of his legally protected interests. . . .

Before the plaintiff is allowed to argue the merits, it is true that a canvass of relevant statutory materials must be made in cases challenging agency action. But the canvass is made, not to determine standing, but to determine an aspect of reviewability, that is, whether Congress meant to deny or to allow judicial review of the agency action at the instance of the plaintiff. [2] The Court in the present cases examines the statutory materials for just this purpose but only after making the same examination during the second step of its standing inquiry. Thus in Data Processing the Court determines that the petitioners have standing because they alleged injury in fact and because '§ 4 (of the Bank Service Corporation Act of 1962) arguably brings a competitor within the zone of interests protected by it.' . . .

I submit that in making such examination of statutory materials an element in the determination of standing, the Court not only performs a useless and unnecessary exercise but also encourages badly reasoned decisions, which may well deny justice in this complex field. When agency action is challenged, standing, reviewability, and the merits pose discrete, and often complicated, issues which can best be resolved by recognizing and treating them as such. . . .

The objectives of the Article III standing requirement are simple: the avoidance of any use of a 'federal court as a forum (for the airing of) generalized grievances about the conduct of government,' . . .

In light of Flast, standing exists when the plaintiff alleges, as the plaintiffs in each of these cases alleged, that the challenged action has caused him injury in fact, economic or otherwise. . . .

When the legality of administrative action is at issue, standing alone will not entitle the plaintiff to a decision on the merits. Pertinent statutory language, legislative history, and public policy considerations must be examined to determine whether Congress precluded all judicial review, and, if not, whether

---

[2]   Reviewability has often been treated as if it involved a single issue: whether agency action is conclusive and beyond judicial challenge by anyone. In reality, however, reviewability is equally concerned with a second issue: whether the particular plaintiff then requesting review may have it. Both questions directly concern the extent to which persons harmed by agency action may challenge its legality.

Congress nevertheless foreclosed review to the class to which the plaintiff belongs. Under the Administrative Procedure Act (APA), 'statutes (may) preclude judicial review' or 'agency action (may be) committed to agency discretion by law.' 5 U.S.C. § 701(a). In either case, the plaintiff is out of court, not because he has no standing to enter, but because Congress has stripped the judiciary of authority to review agency action. Review may be totally foreclosed . . . or, if permitted, it may nonetheless be denied to the plaintiff's class. . . .

The APA provides that '(a) person suffering legal wrong because of agency action, or adversely affected or aggrieved by agency action within the meaning of a relevant statute, is entitled to judicial review thereof.' 5 U.S.C. § 702. Congressional intent that a particular plaintiff have review may be found either in express statutory language granting it to the plaintiff's class, or, in the absence of such express language, in statutory indicia from which a right to review may be inferred. Where, as in the instant cases, there is no express grant of review, reviewability has ordinarily been inferred from evidence that Congress intended the plaintiff's class to be a beneficiary of the statute under which the plaintiff raises his claim. . . .

If it is determined that a plaintiff who alleged injury in fact is entitled to judicial review, inquiry proceeds to the merits—to whether the specific legal interest claimed by the plaintiff is protected by the statute and to whether the protested agency action invaded that interest. It is true, of course, that matters relevant to the merits will already have been touched tangentially in the determination of standing and, in some cases, in the determination of reviewability. The aspect of the merits touched in establishing standing is the identification of injury in fact, the existence of which the plaintiff must prove. The merits are also touched in establishing reviewability in cases where the plaintiff's right to review must be inferred from evidence that his class is a statutory beneficiary. The same statutory indicia that afford the plaintiff a right to review also bear on the merits, because they provide evidence that the statute protects his class, and thus that he is entitled to relief if he can show that the challenged agency action violated the statute. Evidence that the plaintiff's class is a statutory beneficiary, however, need not be as strong for the purpose of obtaining review as for the purpose of establishing the plaintiff's claim on the merits. . . .

To reiterate, in my view alleged injury in fact, reviewability, and the merits pose questions that are largely distinct from one another, each governed by its own considerations. To fail to isolate and treat each inquiry independently of the other two, so far as possible, is to risk obscuring what is at issue in a given case, and thus to risk uninformed, poorly reasoned decisions that may result in injustice. Too often these various questions have been merged into one confused inquiry, lumped under the general rubric of 'standing.' The books are full of opinions that dismiss a plaintiff for lack of 'standing' when dismissal, if proper at all, actually rested either upon the plaintiff's failure to prove on the merits the existence of the legally protected interest that he claimed, or on his failure to prove that the challenged agency action was reviewable at his instance.

The risk of ambiguity and injustice can be minimized by cleanly severing, so far as possible, the inquiries into reviewability and the merits from the determination of standing. Today's decisions, however, will only compound present confusion and breed even more litigation over standing. In the first place, the Court's formulation of its non-constitutional element of standing is obscure. What precisely must a plaintiff do to establish that 'the interest sought to be protected . . . is arguably within the zone of interests to be protected or regulated by the statute'? . . .

Finally, . . . [t]he Constitution requires for standing only that the plaintiff allege that actual harm resulted to him from the agency action. Investigation to determine whether the constitutional requirement has been met has nothing in common with the inquiry into statutory language, legislative history, and public policy that must be made to ascertain whether Congress has precluded or limited judicial review. More fundamentally, an approach that treats separately the distinct issues of standing, reviewability, and the merits, and decides each on the basis of its own criteria, assures that these often complex questions will be squarely faced, thus contributing to better reasoned decisions and to greater confidence that justice has in fact been done. . . .

NOTES AND QUESTIONS

1. *A dramatic shift in the law.* The *Data Processing* case was, according to Professor Gary Lawson, "an earth-shattering kaboom." Gary Lawson, Federal Administrative Law 1051 (7th ed. 2016). Isn't he right? In *Data Processing,* the Court confronted a lawsuit filed by an economic competitor, and the statute, as in the D.C. Circuit's 1955 case *Kansas City Power & Light Co. v. McKay* (discussed above), did not provide a special cause of action for economic

competitors. In the D.C. Circuit case, the court dismissed the suit because APA § 702 merely codified the existing legal rules about causes of action. But in *Data Processing*, the Supreme Court seemed to hold that § 702 authorizes a lawsuit where the complainant is "arguably within the zone of interests to be protected or regulated by the statute or constitutional guarantee in question."

This was a dramatic expansion of judicial review. Now a potential litigant does not need a special statute authorizing a cause of action to proceed against the agency; a lawsuit is now available under *any* statute—except to the extent the statute actually *precludes* judicial review. Recall that the APA, in numerous places, specifies that it does not apply where the statute precludes review. Section 701(a)(1) provides: "This chapter applies, according to the provisions thereof, except to the extent that . . . statutes preclude judicial review." And § 704 provides, "Agency action *made reviewable by statute* and final agency action for which there is no other adequate remedy in a court are subject to judicial review" (emphasis added).

Hence in *Data Processing*, once the Court concluded that the plaintiffs were within the "zone of interests" protected by the banking statute and could sue even though the statute had no special review provision, the Court *also* had to ask the secondary question of whether anything in the statute precluded that review. Note how this gets things backward. Before *Data Processing*, there would be no cause of action in these circumstances, and no right to sue, unless the statute specifically *provided* authorization to sue. This is probably what Justice Brennan was getting at in his dissent, and in his second footnote: the question of reviewability had always been whether the statute authorizes this kind of suit for this kind of plaintiff.

After *Data Processing*, however, the general presumption is reversed: now the APA permits review, and so we have to look at the specific statutes to see if anything *precludes* that review. Congress no longer has to affirmatively act to authorize review; it has to affirmatively act to preclude it. The question of statutory "preclusion" of judicial review—on the assumption, post-*Data Processing*, the judicial review is otherwise generally available—has created an entirely new line of cases. We address those cases in the next subsection.

2. *Have we misinterpreted* Data Processing? Note the Court here doesn't say the complainant has to be within the zone of interests; rather, the complainant only has to be "arguably" within the zone of interests. Could subsequent cases and commentators who have interpreted the *Data Processing* case as expanding causes of action be misinterpreting the Court's opinion? Professor Caleb Nelson, in a recent and important article, argues yes. He writes that a better reading of the opinion is that the Court was indeed engaging in a threshold "standing" analysis. To have "standing" to sue at all, a party at least had to "arguably" be within the zone of interests protected by the statute. But that did not mean that party actually *had* a legally protected interest. That was a question that might only be answerable at the merits stage. See Caleb Nelson, *"Standing" and Remedial Rights in Administrative Law,* 105 Va. L. Rev. 703 (2019).

3. ***Prudential standing or causes of action?*** It is important to repeat that the student will often encounter the zone-of-interests test in an analysis of "statutory standing," which is thought to be a prudential limit to the jurisdictions of the courts, above and beyond the jurisdictional limits actually imposed by Article III of the Constitution. (We get to Article III standing in the next part of this chapter.) Importantly, however, the Supreme Court has at least once recognized that these cases are really about causes of action. In Lexmark Int'l, Inc. v. Static Control Components, Inc., 572 U.S. 118 (2014), the Court explained that "[t]he zone-of-interests test is" a "concept that we have previously classified as an aspect of 'prudential standing' but . . . upon closer inspection, we have found that label inapt." 527 U.S. at 127 n.3. It also explained that "[w]e have on occasion referred to this inquiry as 'statutory standing' and treated it as effectively jurisdictional," but this label, "too, is misleading, since 'the absence of a valid . . . cause of action does not implicate . . . the court's statutory or constitutional power to adjudicate the case.' " Id. at 128 n.4. In short, "a statutory *cause of action* extends only to plaintiffs whose interests 'fall within the zone of interests protected by the law invoked.' " Id. at 129 (emphasis added). If a plaintiff is within the zone of interests that Congress intended the statute to protect, then that plaintiff has a "cause of action" to sue.

4. ***Applying the test.*** Justice Brennan was also concerned about the vagueness of the zone-of-interests test. How specific must the interest be? Indeed, what does it mean to "arguably" be within the zone of interests? The Court was silent for many years on these questions. Although it did decide some zone-of-interests cases in the late 1980s and early 1990s, the following case is one of the more recent leading cases on the question. Note that the courts below and the Supreme Court all used the term "prudential standing" several times. The excerpt occasionally includes an editor's note to remind the reader that what the courts are really talking about is a cause of action.

National Credit Union Admin. v. First Nat. Bank & Trust Co.

522 U.S. 479 (1998)

Justice Thomas delivered the opinion of the Court, except as to footnote 6. [Footnote 6 included a discussion of legislative history, which Justice Scalia refused to join.—Ed.]

Section 109 of the Federal Credit Union Act (FCUA) provides that "[f]ederal credit union membership shall be limited to groups having a common bond of occupation or association, or to groups within a well-defined neighborhood, community, or rural district." Since 1982, the National Credit Union Administration (NCUA), the agency charged with administering the FCUA, has interpreted § 109 to permit federal credit unions to be composed of multiple unrelated employer groups, each having its own common bond of occupation. In this action, respondents, five banks and the American Bankers Association, have challenged this interpretation on the ground that § 109 unambiguously requires that the *same* common bond of occupation unite every member of an occupationally defined federal credit union. We granted certiorari to answer ... [whether] respondents have standing [that is, a cause of action—Ed.] under the Administrative Procedure Act to seek federal-court review of the NCUA's interpretation[.] ... We answer ... in the affirmative and ... therefore affirm.

I

A

In 1934, during the Great Depression, Congress enacted the FCUA, which authorizes the chartering of credit unions at the national level and provides that federal credit unions may, as a general matter, offer banking services only to their members. Section 109 of the FCUA, which has remained virtually unaltered since the FCUA's enactment, expressly restricts membership in federal credit unions. In relevant part, it provides[ ] "... *that Federal credit union membership shall be limited to groups having a common bond of occupation or association, or to groups within a well-defined neighborhood, community, or rural district.*" 12 U.S.C. § 1759 (emphasis added).

Until 1982, the NCUA and its predecessors consistently interpreted § 109 to require that the *same* common bond of occupation unite every member of an occupationally defined federal credit union. In 1982, however, the NCUA reversed its longstanding policy in order to permit credit unions to be composed of multiple unrelated employer groups. It thus interpreted § 109's common bond requirement to apply only to each employer group in a multiple-group credit union, rather than to every member of that credit union. Under the NCUA's new interpretation, all of the employer groups in a multiple-group credit union had to be located "within a well-defined area," but the NCUA later revised this requirement to provide that each employer group could be located within "an area surrounding the [credit union's] home or a branch office that can be reasonably served by the [credit union] as determined by NCUA." Since 1982, therefore, the NCUA has permitted federal credit unions to be composed of wholly unrelated employer groups, each having its own distinct common bond.

B

After the NCUA revised its interpretation of § 109, petitioner AT&T Family Federal Credit Union (ATTF) expanded its operations considerably by adding unrelated employer groups to its membership. As a result, ATTF now has approximately 110,000 members nationwide, only 35% of whom are employees of AT&T and its affiliates. The remaining members are employees of such diverse companies as the Lee Apparel Company, the Coca-Cola Bottling Company, the Ciba-Geigy Corporation, the Duke Power Company, and the American Tobacco Company.

In 1990, after the NCUA approved a series of amendments to ATTF's charter that added several such unrelated employer groups to ATTF's membership, respondents brought this action. Invoking the judicial review provisions of the Administrative Procedure Act (APA), 5 U.S.C. § 702, respondents claimed that the NCUA's approval of the charter amendments was contrary to law because the members of the new groups did not share a common bond of occupation with ATTF's existing members, as respondents alleged § 109 required. ATTF and petitioner Credit Union National Association were permitted to intervene in the action as defendants.

The District Court dismissed the complaint. It held that respondents lacked prudential standing [that is, a cause of action—Ed.] to challenge the NCUA's chartering decision because their interests were not within the "zone of interests" to be protected by § 109, as required by this Court's cases inter-preting the APA. The District Court rejected as irrelevant respondents' claims that the NCUA's interpretation had caused them competitive injury, stating that the legislative history of the FCUA demonstrated that it was passed "to establish a place for credit unions within the country's financial market, and specifically not to protect the competitive interest of banks." The District Court also determined that respondents were not "suitable challengers" to the NCUA's interpretation, as that term had been used in prior prudential standing cases from the Court of Appeals for the District of Columbia Circuit.

The Court of Appeals for the District of Columbia Circuit reversed. The Court of Appeals agreed that "Congress did not, in 1934, intend to shield banks from competition from credit unions," and hence respondents could not be said to be "intended beneficiaries" of § 109. Relying on two of our pru-dential standing cases involving the financial services industry, the Court of Appeals nonetheless concluded that respondents' interests were sufficiently congruent with the interests of § 109's intended beneficiaries that respondents were "suitable challengers" to the NCUA's chartering decision; therefore, their suit could proceed. . . .

Because of the importance of the issues presented, we granted certiorari.

II

Respondents claim a right to judicial review of the NCUA's chartering decision under § 10(a) of the APA, which provides: "A person suffering legal wrong because of agency action, or adversely affected or aggrieved by agency action within the meaning of a relevant statute, is entitled to judicial review thereof." 5 U.S.C. § 702.

We have interpreted § 10(a) of the APA to impose a prudential stand-ing requirement in addition to the requirement, imposed by Article III of the Constitution, that a plaintiff have suffered a sufficient injury in fact. See, *e.g.*, *Association of Data Processing Service Organizations, Inc. v. Camp*, 397 U.S. 150, 152 (1970) *(Data Processing)*.[4] For a plaintiff to have prudential standing [that is, a cause of action—Ed.] under the APA, "the interest sought to be protected

---

[4]   In this action, it is not disputed that respondents have suffered an injury in fact because the NCUA's inter-pretation allows persons who might otherwise be their customers to be members, and therefore customers, of ATTF.

by the complainant [must be] arguably within the zone of interests to be protected or regulated by the statute . . . in question." *Id.* at 153.

Based on four of our prior cases finding that competitors of financial institutions have standing to challenge agency action relaxing statutory restrictions on the activities of those institutions, we hold that respondents interest in limiting the markets that federal credit unions can serve is arguably within the zone of interests to be protected by § 109. Therefore, respondents have prudential standing [a cause of action—Ed.] under the APA to challenge the NCUA's interpretation.

A

Although our prior cases have not stated a clear rule for determining when a plaintiff's interest is "arguably within the zone of interests" to be protected by a statute, they nonetheless establish that we should not inquire whether there has been a congressional intent to benefit the would-be plaintiff. In *Data Processing*, . . . [i]n determining that the plaintiffs' interest met this requirement, we noted that although the relevant federal statutes—the National Bank Act and the Bank Service Corporation Act—did not "in terms protect a specified group[,] . . . their general policy is apparent; and those whose interests are directly affected by a broad or narrow interpretation of the Acts are easily identifiable." *Data Processing*, 397 U.S. at 157. "[A]s competitors of national banks which are engaging in data processing services," the plaintiffs were within that class of "aggrieved persons" entitled to judicial review of the Comptroller's interpretation. *Ibid.*

Less than a year later, we applied the "zone of interests" test in *Arnold Tours, Inc. v. Camp*, 400 U.S. 45 (1970). There, certain travel agencies challenged a ruling by the Comptroller, similar to the one contested in *Data Processing*, that permitted national banks to operate travel agencies. In holding that the plaintiffs had prudential standing under the APA, we noted that it was incorrect to view our decision in *Data Processing* as resting on the peculiar legislative history of § 4 of the Bank Service Corporation Act, which had been passed in part at the behest of the data processing industry. See 400 U.S. at 46. We stated explicitly that "we did not rely on any legislative history showing that Congress desired to protect data processors alone from competition." *Ibid.* We further explained:

"In *Data Processing* . . . [w]e held that § 4 arguably brings a competitor within the zone of interests protected by it. Nothing in the opinion limited § 4 to protecting only competitors in the data-processing field. When national banks begin to provide travel services for their customers, they compete with travel agents no less than they compete with data processors when they provide data-processing services to their customers." *Ibid.*

A year later, we decided *Investment Company Institute v. Camp*, 401 U.S. 617 (1971). In that case, an investment company trade association and several individual investment companies alleged that the Comptroller had violated, *inter alia*, § 21 of the Glass-Steagall Act, by permitting national banks to establish and operate what in essence were early versions of mutual funds. We held that the plaintiffs, who alleged that they would be injured by the competition resulting from the Comptroller's action, had standing under the APA and stated that the case was controlled by *Data Processing*. See 401 U.S. at 621. Significantly, we found unpersuasive Justice Harlan's argument in dissent that the suit should be dismissed because "neither the language of the pertinent provisions of the Glass-Steagall Act nor the legislative history evince[d] any congressional concern for the interests of petitioners and others like them in freedom from competition." *Id.* at 640.

Our fourth case in this vein was *Clarke v. Securities Industry Assn.*, 479 U.S. 388 (1987). There, a securities dealers trade association sued the Comptroller, this time for authorizing two national banks to offer discount brokerage services both at their branch offices and at other locations inside and outside their home States. The plaintiff contended that the Comptroller's action violated the McFadden Act, which permits national banks to carry on the business of banking only at authorized branches, and to open new branches only in their home States and only to the extent that state-chartered banks in that State can do so under state law.

We again held that the plaintiff had standing under the APA. Summarizing our prior holdings, we stated that although the "zone of interests" test "denies a right of review if the plaintiff's interests are . . . marginally related to or inconsistent with the purposes implicit in the statute," *id.* at 399, "there need be no indication of congressional purpose to benefit the would-be plaintiff," *id.* at 399–400. We then determined that by limiting the ability of national banks to do business outside their home States, "Congress ha[d] shown a concern to keep national banks from gaining a monopoly control over credit and money." 479 U.S. at 403. The interest of the securities dealers in preventing national banks from expanding into the securities markets directly implicated this concern . . . .

B

Our prior cases, therefore, have consistently held that for a plaintiff's interests to be arguably within the "zone of interests" to be protected by a statute, there does not have to be an "indication of congressional purpose to benefit the would-be plaintiff." The proper inquiry is simply "whether the interest sought to be protected by the complainant is *arguably* within the zone of interests to be protected . . . by the statute." *Data Processing,* 397 U.S. at 153 (emphasis added). Hence in applying the "zone of interests" test, we do not ask whether, in enacting the statutory provision at issue, Congress specifically intended to benefit the plaintiff. Instead, we first discern the interests "arguably . . . to be protected" by the statutory provision at issue; we then inquire whether the plaintiff's interests affected by the agency action in question are among them. . . .

By its express terms, § 109 limits membership in every federal credit union to members of definable "groups." Because federal credit unions may, as a general matter, offer banking services only to members, § 109 also restricts the markets that every federal credit union can serve. Although these markets need not be small, they unquestionably are limited. The link between § 109's regulation of federal credit union membership and its limitation on the markets that federal credit unions can serve is unmistakable. Thus, even if it cannot be said that Congress had the specific purpose of benefiting commercial banks, one of the interests "arguably . . . to be protected" by § 109 is an interest in limiting the markets that federal credit unions can serve. This interest is precisely the interest of respondents affected by the NCUA's interpretation of § 109. As competitors of federal credit unions, respondents certainly have an interest in limiting the markets that federal credit unions can serve, and the NCUA's interpretation has affected that interest by allowing federal credit unions to increase their customer base.[7]

---

[7]   Contrary to the dissent's contentions, our formulation does not "eviscerat[e]" or "abolis[h]" the zone of interests requirement. Nor can it be read to imply that, in order to have standing under the APA, a plaintiff must merely have an interest in enforcing the statute in question. The test we have articulated—discerning the interests "arguably . . . to be protected" by the statutory provision at issue and inquiring whether the plaintiff's interests affected by the agency action in question are among them—differs only as a matter of semantics from the formulation that the dissent has accused us of "eviscerating" or "abolishing" (. . . that the plaintiff must establish that "the injury he complains of . . . falls within the zone of interests sought to be protected by the statutory provision whose violation forms the legal basis for his complaint").

Section 109 cannot be distinguished from the statutory provisions at issue in *Clarke, ICI, Arnold Tours,* and *Data Processing.* Although in *Clarke . . .* Congress did not intend specifically to protect securities dealers, one of the interests "arguably . . . to be protected" by the statute was an interest in restricting national bank market power. The plaintiff securities dealers, as competitors of national banks, had that interest, and that interest had been affected by the interpretation of the McFadden Act they sought to challenge, because that interpretation had allowed national banks to expand their activities and serve new customers.

Similarly, in *ICI,* even though in enacting the Glass-Steagall Act, Congress did not intend specifically to benefit investment companies and may have sought only to protect national banks and their depositors, one of the interests "arguably . . . to be protected" by the statute was an interest in restricting the ability of national banks to enter the securities business. The investment company plaintiffs, as competitors of national banks, had that interest, and that interest had been affected by the Comptroller's interpretation allowing national banks to establish mutual funds.

So too, in *Arnold Tours* and *Data Processing,* although in enacting the National Bank Act and the Bank Service Corporation Act, Congress did not intend specifically to benefit travel agents and data processors and may have been concerned only with the safety and soundness of national banks, one of the interests "arguably . . . to be protected" by the statutes was an interest in preventing national banks from entering other businesses' product markets. As competitors of national banks, travel agents and data processors had that interest, and that interest had been affected by the Comptroller's interpretations opening their markets to national banks.

C

. . . . We therefore cannot accept petitioners' argument that respondents do not have standing because there is no evidence that the Congress that enacted § 109 was concerned with the competitive interests of commercial banks. To accept that argument, we would have to reformulate the "zone of interests"

Our only disagreement with the dissent lies in the application of the "zone of interests" test. Because of the unmistakable link between § 109's express restriction on credit union membership and the limitation on the markets that federal credit unions can serve, there is objectively "some indication in the statute" that respondents' interest is "arguably within the zone of interests to be protected" by § 109. Hence respondents are more than merely incidental beneficiaries of § 109's effects on competition.

test to require that Congress have specifically intended to benefit a particular class of plaintiffs before a plaintiff from that class could have standing under the APA to sue. We have refused to do this in our prior cases, and we refuse to do so today.

Petitioners also mistakenly rely on our decision in *Air Courier Conference v. Postal Workers*, 498 U.S. 517 (1991). In *Air Courier*, we held that the interest of Postal Service employees in maximizing employment opportunities was not within the "zone of interests" to be protected by the postal monopoly statutes, and hence those employees did not have standing under the APA to challenge a Postal Service regulation suspending its monopoly over certain international operations. We stated that the purposes of the statute were solely to increase the revenues of the Post Office and to ensure that postal services were provided in a manner consistent with the public interest. Only those interests, therefore, and not the interests of Postal Service employees in their employment, were "arguably within the zone of interests to be protected" by the statute. We further noted that although the statute in question regulated competition, the interests of the plaintiff employees had nothing to do with competition. . . .

Respondents' interest in limiting the markets that credit unions can serve is "arguably within the zone of interests to be protected" by § 109. Under our precedents, it is irrelevant that in enacting the FCUA, Congress did not specifically intend to protect commercial banks. . . .

JUSTICE O'CONNOR, with whom JUSTICE STEVENS, JUSTICE SOUTER, and JUSTICE BREYER join, dissenting.

In determining that respondents have standing under the zone-of-interests test to challenge the National Credit Union Administration's (NCUA's) interpretation of the "common bond" provision of the Federal Credit Union Act (FCUA), the Court applies the test in a manner that is contrary to our decisions and, more importantly, that all but eviscerates the zone-of-interests requirement. In my view, under a proper conception of the inquiry, "the interest sought to be protected by" respondents in this action is not "arguably within the zone of interests to be protected" by the common bond provision. *Association of Data Processing Service Organizations, Inc. v. Camp*, 397 U.S. 150 (1970). Accordingly, I respectfully dissent.

I

Respondents brought this suit under § 10(a) of the Administrative Procedure Act (APA), 5 U.S.C. § 702. To establish their standing to sue here, respondents must demonstrate that they are "adversely affected or aggrieved by agency action within the meaning of a relevant statute." . . .

First, respondents must show that they are "adversely affected or aggrieved," *i.e.*, have suffered injury in fact. In addition, respondents must establish that the injury they assert is "within the meaning of a relevant statute," *i.e.*, satisfies the zone-of-interests test. Specifically, "the plaintiff must establish that the injury he complains of (*his* aggrievement, or the adverse effect *upon him*), falls within the 'zone of interests' sought to be protected by the statutory provision whose violation forms the legal basis for his complaint." [*Lujan v. National Wildlife Federation*, 497 U.S. 871, 873 (1990).

The "injury respondents complain of," . . . is a loss of respondents' customer base to a competing entity, or more generally, an injury to respondents' commercial interest as a competitor. The relevant question under the zone-of-interests test, then, is whether injury to respondents' commercial interest as a competitor "falls within the zone of interests sought to be protected by the [common bond] provision." . . .

The Court adopts a quite different approach to the zone-of-interests test today, eschewing any assessment of whether the common bond provision was intended to protect respondents' commercial interest. . . . [T]he Court reasons that one interest sought to be protected by the common bond provision "is an interest in limiting the markets that federal credit unions can serve." . . .

Under the Court's approach, every litigant who establishes injury in fact under Article III will automatically satisfy the zone-of-interests requirement, rendering the zone-of-interests test ineffectual. . . .

[T]he Court's conclusion that respondents "have" an interest in "limiting the [customer] markets that federal credit unions can serve" means little more than that respondents "have" an interest in enforcing the statute. The common bond requirement limits a credit union's membership, and hence its customer base, to certain groups, and in the Court's view, it is enough to establish standing that respondents "have" an interest in limiting the customers a credit union can serve. The Court's additional observation that respondents' interest has been "affected" by the NCUA's interpretation adds little to the analysis; agency interpretation of a statutory restriction will of course affect a party who has an interest in the restriction. Indeed, a party presumably will bring suit to vindicate an interest only if the interest has been affected by the challenged action. The crux of the Court's zone-of-interests inquiry, then, is simply that the plaintiff must "have" an interest in enforcing the pertinent statute.

A party, however, will invariably have an interest in enforcing a statute when he can establish injury in fact caused by an alleged violation of that statute. An example we used in *National Wildlife Federation* illustrates the point. There, we hypothesized a situation involving "the failure of an agency to comply with a statutory provision requiring 'on the record' hearings." 497 U.S. at 883. That circumstance "would assuredly have an adverse effect upon the company that has the contract to record and transcribe the agency's proceedings," and so the company would establish injury in fact. *Ibid.* But the company would not satisfy the zone-of-interests test, because "the provision was obviously enacted to protect the interests of the parties to the proceedings and not those of the reporters." *Ibid.* Under the Court's approach today, however, the reporting company would have standing under the zone-of-interests test: Because the company is injured by the failure to comply with the requirement of on-the-record hearings, the company would certainly "have" an interest in enforcing the statute.

Our decision in *Air Courier*, likewise, cannot be squared with the Court's analysis in this action. *Air Courier* involved a challenge by postal employees to a decision of the Postal Service suspending its statutory monopoly over certain international mailing services. The postal employees alleged a violation of the Private Express Statutes (PES)—the provisions that codify the Service's postal monopoly—citing as their injury in fact that competition from private mailing companies adversely affected their employment opportunities. 498 U.S. at 524. We concluded that the postal employees did not have standing under the zone-of-interests test, because "the PES were not designed to protect postal employment or further postal job opportunities." *Id.* at 528. As with the example from *National Wildlife Federation*, though, the postal employees would have established standing under the Court's analysis in this action: The employees surely "had" an interest in enforcing the statutory monopoly, given that suspension of the monopoly caused injury to their employment opportunities.

In short, requiring simply that a litigant "have" an interest in enforcing the relevant statute amounts to hardly any test at all. That is why our decisions have required instead that a party "establish that the *injury he complains* of . . . falls within the 'zone of interests' sought to be protected by the statutory provision" in question. *National Wildlife Federation, supra,* at 883. In *Air Courier,* for instance, after noting that the asserted injury in fact was "an adverse effect on employment opportunities of postal workers," we characterized "[t]he question before us" as "whether the adverse effect on the employment opportunities of postal workers . . . is within the zone of interests encompassed by the PES." 498 U.S., at 524; see also *National Wildlife Federation, supra,* at 885–886 (noting that asserted injury is to the plaintiffs' interests in "recreational use and aesthetic enjoyment," and finding those particular interests "are among the *sorts* of interests [the] statutes were specifically designed to protect"). . . .

The same approach should lead the Court to ask in this action whether respondents' injury to their commercial interest as competitors falls within the zone of interests protected by the common bond provision. Respondents recognize that such an inquiry is mandated by our decisions. They argue that "the competitive interests of banks *were* among Congress's concerns when it enacted the Federal Credit Union Act," and that the common bond provision was motivated by "[c]ongressional concerns that chartering credit unions could inflict an unwanted competitive injury on the commercial banking industry." Brief for Respondents 24–25. The Court instead asks simply whether respondents have an interest in enforcing the common bond provision, an approach tantamount to abolishing the zone-of-interests requirement altogether.

II

Contrary to the Court's suggestion, its application of the zone-of-interests test in this action is not in concert with the approach we followed in a series of cases in which the plaintiffs, like respondents here, alleged that agency interpretation of a statute caused competitive injury to their commercial interests. . . .

[O]ur decisions in *Arnold Tours* and *Data Processing* turned on the conclusion that economic injury to competitors fell within the zone of interests protected by the relevant statute. . . .

We found [in *ICI*] that the investment companies had standing, but did not rest that determination simply on the notion that the companies had an interest in enforcing the prohibition against banks entering the investment business. Instead, we observed that, as in *Data Processing,* "Congress had arguably legislated against . . . competition" . . . .

We held [in *Clarke*] that the plaintiffs had standing under the zone-of-interests test, but again, not simply on the ground that they had an interest in enforcing the branching limits. Instead, we found that, as in *ICI*, Congress had "arguably legislated against . . . competition" . . . .

It is true, as the Court emphasizes repeatedly, that we did not require in this line of decisions that the statute at issue was designed to benefit the particular party bringing suit. . . .

In each of the competitor standing cases, though, we found that Congress had enacted an "anti-competition limitation," or, alternatively, that Congress had "legislated against . . . competition," and accordingly, that the plaintiff-competitor's "commercial interest was sought to be protected by the anti-competition limitation" at issue. We determined, in other words, that "the injury [the plaintiff] complain[ed] of . . . [fell] within the zone of interests sought to be protected by the [relevant] statutory provision." *National Wildlife Federation*, 497 U.S. at 883. The Court fails to undertake that analysis here.

III

Applying the proper zone-of-interests inquiry to this action, I would find that competitive injury to respondents' commercial interests does not arguably fall within the zone of interests sought to be protected by the common bond provision. The terms of the statute do not suggest a concern with protecting the business interests of competitors. The common bond provision limits "[f]ederal credit union membership . . . to groups having a common bond of occupation or association, or to groups within a well-defined neighborhood, community, or rural district." 12 U.S.C. § 1759. And the provision is framed as an exception to the preceding clause, which confers membership on "incorporators and such other persons and incorporated and unincorporated organizations . . . as may be elected . . . and as such shall each, subscribe to at least one share of its stock and pay the initial installment thereon and a uniform entrance fee." *Ibid.* The language suggests that the common bond requirement is an internal organizational principle concerned primarily with defining membership in a way that secures a financially sound organization. There is no indication in the text of the provision or in the surrounding language that the membership limitation was even arguably designed to protect the commercial interests of competitors.

Nor is there any nontextual indication to that effect. Significantly, the operation of the common bond provision is much different from the statutes at issue in *Clarke, ICI,* and *Data Processing.* Those statutes evinced a congressional intent to legislate against competition because they imposed direct restrictions on banks generally, specifically barring their entry into certain markets. In *Data Processing* and *ICI,* "the question was what activities banks could engage in at all," and in *Clarke,* "the question [was] what activities banks [could] engage in without regard to the limitations imposed by state branching law."

The operation of the common bond provision does not likewise denote a congressional desire to legislate against competition. First, the common bond requirement does not purport to restrict credit unions from becoming large, nationwide organizations, as might be expected if the provision embodied a congressional concern with the competitive consequences of credit union growth.

More tellingly, although the common bond provision applies to all credit unions, the restriction operates against credit unions individually: The common bond requirement speaks only to whether a *particular* credit union's membership can include a given group of customers, not to whether credit unions *in general* can serve that group. . . .

In *Data Processing, ICI,* and *Clarke,* by contrast, the statutes operated against national banks generally, prohibiting all banks from competing in a particular market: Banks in general were barred from providing a specific type of service (*Data Processing* and *ICI*), or from providing services at a particular location (*Clarke*) Thus, whereas in *Data Processing* customers could not obtain data processing services from *any* national bank, and in *Clarke* customers outside of the permissible branching area likewise could not obtain financial services from *any* national bank, in this action customers who lack an adequate bond with the members of a particular credit union can still receive financial services from a *different* credit union. Unlike the statutes in *Data Processing, ICI,* and *Clarke,* then, the common bond provision does not erect a competitive boundary excluding credit unions from any identifiable market. . . .

That the common bond requirement would later come to be viewed by competitors as a useful tool for curbing a credit union's membership should not affect the zone-of-interests inquiry. The pertinent question under the zone-of-interests test is whether Congress *intended* to protect certain interests through a particular provision, not whether, irrespective of congressional intent, a provision may have the *effect* of protecting those interests. . . .

In this light, I read our decisions as establishing that there must at least be *some* indication in the statute, beyond the mere fact that its enforcement has the effect of incidentally benefiting the plaintiff, from which one can draw an inference that the plaintiff's injury arguably falls within the zone of interests sought to be protected by that statute. . . .

NOTES AND QUESTIONS

1. "Arguably." The Supreme Court decided that the NCUA was "arguably" within the zone of interests protected by the statute. Ask yourself again (see the second note following the *Data Processing* case): if the plaintiff is only "arguably" within the zone of interests, isn't it possible to prove at trial that the plaintiff is not *actually* within the zone of interests? And if the plaintiff is not actually within the zone of interests, there is no cause of action, and no basis to sue? Would it be better to understand *Data Processing* as indeed being about "standing"—the plaintiff at least has to show at the initial stages of litigation that her claim is "arguably" within the zone of interests, and therefore she "arguably" has a cause of action, before she can bring a lawsuit—but that the court might ultimately conclude that there isn't a cause of action and dismiss the case later?

2. Is this a higher- or lower-order dispute? All of the Justices in this case agreed that the zone-of-interests test does not require a finding that a particular type or class of plaintiff was intended by Congress to be protected by the statute. Rather, the question is what interests Congress intended the statute to protect, and whether the plaintiff happens to share any of those interests. In light of that agreement, what exactly is the dissent's disagreement with the majority? The dissent argues that the majority's description of the zone-of-interests test is wrong, that it would simply require "that a litigant 'have' an interest in enforcing the relevant statute," which "amounts to hardly any test at all." Is that really what the majority said? Or was the dispute really a lower-order dispute about the *application* of the test?

The true disagreement seems to be about what the majority believed the statute was intended to protect. Here is the key passage from the majority:

By its express terms, § 109 limits membership in every federal credit union to members of definable "groups." Because federal credit unions may, as a general matter, offer banking services only to members, § 109 also restricts the markets that every federal credit union can serve. Although these markets need not be small, they unquestionably are limited. The link between § 109's regulation of federal credit union membership and its limitation on the markets that federal credit unions can serve is unmistakable. Thus, even if it cannot be said that Congress had the specific purpose of benefiting commercial banks, one of the interests "arguably . . . to be protected" by § 109 is an interest in limiting the markets that federal credit unions can serve. This interest is precisely the interest of respondents affected by the NCUA's interpretation of § 109.

The dissent, in contrast, argued that the statute was not intended to protect the interests of competitors or to limit the size of the federal credit union market. The dissent argued that each *individual* credit union was limited in size by the common bond provision, but nothing prevented thousands of credit unions across the country from completely crowding out other banking institutions such as the plaintiffs in this case. Which view do you find more persuasive? Does your answer change when you recall that the test is only whether the plaintiff's interest must "arguably" be within the zone of interests?

3. *Legislative history.* In footnote 6 of the Court's opinion, omitted from the excerpt, four Justices in the majority (Justice Scalia did not join that footnote) discussed the legislative history to argue that Congress believed that the common bond provision would promote the "safety and soundness" of credit unions "and allow access to credit to persons otherwise unable to borrow." The plurality went on to say, "Because, by its very nature, a cooperative institution must serve a limited market, the legislative history of § 109 demonstrates that one of the interests 'arguably . . . to be protected' by § 109 is an interest in limiting the markets that federal credit unions can serve." The dissent also discussed the legislative history (in an omitted portion), observing that the common bond requirement was "meant to ensure that each credit union remains a cooperative

 CROSS REFERENCE Recall our earlier discussions over using legislative history in statutory interpretation. Does legislative history help at all in interpreting the statute in *National Credit Union*?

institution that is economically stable and responsive to its members' needs," that it was "a principle of internal governance designed to secure the viability of individual credit unions in the interests of the membership," and therefore "was in no way designed to impose a restriction on all credit unions in the interests of institutions that might one day become competitors."

Is the legislative history at all helpful here? Both sides agree that Congress intended to protect the soundness of the institutions by limiting the size of individual credit unions. But the plurality and dissent extrapolate different conclusions. The dissent says that has nothing to do with protection competitors; the plurality says Congress's purpose also represented "an interest in limiting the markets that the federal credit unions can serve." With which do you agree? Should legislative history be used at all in a zone-of-interests analysis?

4. **Expansive approach to zone of interests.** Because the plaintiff's interest must only be "arguably" within the zone-of-interests test, it may not surprise you that the Supreme Court has expansively interpreted statutes to find plaintiffs within the zone of interests. In that regard, the majority's decision in *National Credit Union* is more representative of the modern cases. A more recent example is Match-E-Be-Nash-She-Wish Band of Pottawatomi Indians v. Patchak, 567 U.S. 209 (2012). That case involved a provision of the Indian Reorganization Act that authorized the Secretary of the Interior to acquire property "for the purpose of providing land for Indians." The Secretary acquired land in trust for the Matche-E-Be-Nash-She-Wish Band to open a casino. An individual, not a member of the tribe, who lived near that land, challenged the Secretary's decision, arguing (probably correctly) that the Band did not qualify under the statute, enacted in 1934 for the benefit of then-existing tribes, because the Band was not recognized until 1999. The Court held that the "economic, environmental, or aesthetic" interests of neighbors "at least arguably" fell within the land-use interests Congress intended the statute to protect.

3. Statutory Preclusion of Review

Before *Data Processing*, the question of whether someone had a cause of action to sue was identical to the question of whether the statute allowed a particular type of person to sue a particular kind of agency action. The default presumption was no review (outside some other cause of action), but a statute could specially confer new causes of action and thus permit judicial review. After *Data Processing*, the APA creates a general cause of action to any aggrieved party, but only to the extent judicial review is not "preclude[d]" by statute. APA § 701(a)(1). Thus, now the student of administrative law must ask, even if the plaintiff arguably falls within the zone of interests, and even if there otherwise would be constitutional standing (which we discuss later in this chapter), does the organic statute otherwise *preclude* review? That was the question addressed in the following three leading cases. Can you reconcile them?

Johnson v. Robison

415 U.S. 361 (1974)

Mr. Justice Brennan delivered the opinion of the Court.

A draftee accorded Class I-O conscientious objector status and completing performance of required alternative civilian service does not qualify under 38 U.S.C. § 1652(a)(1) as a 'veteran who . . . served on active duty' (defined in 38 U.S.C. § 101(21) as 'full-time duty in the Armed Forces'), and is therefore not an 'eligible veteran' entitled under 38 U.S.C. § 1661(a) to veterans' educational benefits provided by the Veterans' Readjustment Benefits Act of 1966. Appellants, the Veterans' Administration and the Administrator of Veterans' Affairs, for that reason, denied the application for educational assistance of appellee Robison, a conscientious objector who filed his application after he satisfactorily completed two years of alternative civilian service at the Peter Bent Brigham Hospital, Boston. Robison thereafter commenced this class action in the United States District Court for the District of Massachusetts, seeking a declaratory judgment that 38 U.S.C. §§ 101(21), 1652(a)(1), and 1661(a), read together, violated the First Amendment's guarantee of religious freedom and the Fifth Amendment's guarantee of equal protection of the laws. Appellants moved to dismiss the action on the ground, among others, that the District Court lacked jurisdiction because of 38 U.S.C. § 211(a) which prohibits judicial review of decisions of the Administrator.[5] The District Court denied the motion . . . . We hold, in agreement with the District Court, that § 211(a) is

---

[5]   Title 38 U.S.C. § 211(a) provides: '(a) On and after October 17, 1940, . . . the decisions of the Administrator on any question of law or fact under any law administered by the Veterans' Administration providing benefits for veterans and their dependents or survivors shall be final and conclusive and no other official or any court of the United States shall have power or jurisdiction to review any such decision by an action in the nature of mandamus or otherwise.'

inapplicable to this action and therefore that appellants' motion to dismiss for lack of jurisdiction of the subject matter was properly denied. . . .

We consider first appellants' contention that § 211(a) bars federal courts from deciding the constitutionality of veterans' benefits legislation. Such a construction would, of course, raise serious questions concerning the constitutionality of § 211(a), and in such case 'it is a cardinal principle that this Court will first ascertain whether a construction of the statute is fairly possible by which the (constitutional) question(s) may be avoided.' United States v. Thirty-seven Photographs, 402 U.S. 363, 369 (1971).

Plainly, no explicit provision of § 211(a) bars judicial consideration of appellee's constitutional claims. That section provides that 'the decisions of the Administrator on any question of law or fact under any law administered by the Veterans' Administration providing benefits for veterans . . . shall be final and conclusive and no . . . court of the United States shall have power or jurisdiction to review any such decision . . . .' The prohibitions would appear to be aimed at review only of those decisions of law or fact that arise in the administration by the Veterans' Administration of a statute providing benefits for veterans. A decision of law or fact 'under' a statute is made by the Administrator in the interpretation or application of a particular provision of the statute to a particular set of facts, Appellee's constitutional challenge is not to any such decision of the Administrator, but rather to a decision of Congress to create a statutory class entitled to benefits that does not include I-O conscientious objectors who performed alternative civilian service. . . .

This construction is also supported by the administrative practice of the Veterans' Administration. . . . The Board of Veterans' Appeals expressly disclaimed authority to decide constitutional questions . . . .

Nor does the legislative history accompanying the 1970 amendment of § 211(a) demonstrate a congressional intention to bar judicial review even of constitutional questions. . . . [T]he Administrator, in a letter written in 1952 in connection with a revision of the clause under consideration by the Subcommittee of the House Committee on Veterans' Affairs, comprehensively explained the policies necessitating the no-review clause and identified two primary purposes: (1) to insure that veterans' benefits claims will not burden the courts and the Veterans' Administration with expensive and time-consuming litigation, and (2) to insure that the technical and complex determinations and applications of Veterans' Administration policy connected with veterans' benefits decisions will be adequately and uniformly made. . . .

Congress was concerned that the judicial interpretation of § 211(a) would involve the courts in day-to-day determination and interpretation of Veterans' Administration policy. . . .

Nothing whatever in the legislative history of the 1970 amendment, or predecessor no-review clauses, suggests any congressional intent to preclude judicial cognizance of constitutional challenges to veterans' benefits legislation. Such challenges obviously do not contravene the purposes of the no-review clause, for they cannot be expected to burden the courts by their volume, nor do they involve technical considerations of Veterans' Administration policy. We therefore conclude, in agreement with the District Court, that a construction of § 211(a) that does not extend the prohibitions of that section to actions challenging the constitutionality of laws providing benefits for veterans is not only 'fairly possible' but is the most reasonable construction, for neither the text nor the scant legislative history of § 211(a) provides the 'clear and convincing' evidence of congressional intent required by this Court before a statute will be construed to restrict access to judicial review. See Abbott Laboratories v. Gardner, 387 U.S. 136, 141 (1967). . . .

[A dissent by Justice Douglas on the merits is omitted.—Ed.]

Notes and Questions

1. ***What's the cause of action?*** *Robison* involved a matter of quintessential public rights, namely public benefits. Historically, then, there was no cause of action in tort or contract, Robison's arguments were not made as a defense to a criminal proceedings, and the case would not fit within any known equitable suits. Thus, for Robison to be able to sue, Congress would have had to provide him with a cause of action. This it did not do, and in fact Congress attempted to preclude judicial review. Under the modern understanding of the APA, however, judicial review is presumed, and so the Court held that Congress's preclusion of review applied only to those matters specifically precluded (non-constitutional claims). Can you square that with the next case?

2.   *Constitutional avoidance.* Although the Court concludes that the best reading of the statute is that it does not preclude review of constitutional claims, it begins with the idea that with-holding review of constitutional questions would raise serious constitutional concerns. Why? Do you recall the discussion in *Webster v. Doe,* discussed in Chapter 4 on the question of what it means to be "committed to agency discretion by law"? Think back also to our discussions of sovereign immunity. Again, *Robison* involves a pure public rights case. Historically, sovereign immunity meant that there would have been no right to sue at all. If that's true, how can it raise constitutional concerns to foreclose judicial review of constitutional questions?

CROSS REFERENCE   We have encountered the doctrine of constitutional avoidance several times in this course. Did the Court deploy that canon in *Robison*? Should it have?

Block v. Community Nutrition Institute

467 U.S. 340 (1984)

Justice O'Connor delivered the opinion of the Court.

This case presents the question whether ultimate consumers of dairy products may obtain judicial review of milk market orders issued by the Secretary of Agriculture (Secretary) under the authority of the Agricultural Marketing Agreement Act of 1937 (Act). We conclude that consumers may not obtain judicial review of such orders.

I

A

In the early 1900's, dairy farmers engaged in intense competition in the production of fluid milk products. To bring this destabilizing competition under control, the 1937 Act authorizes the Secretary to issue milk market orders setting the minimum prices that handlers (those who process dairy products) must pay to producers (dairy farmers) for their milk products. 7 U.S.C. § 608c. The "essential purpose [of this milk market order scheme is] to raise producer prices," S. Rep. No. 1011, 74th Cong., 1st Sess., 3 (1935), and thereby to ensure that the benefits and burdens of the milk market are fairly and proportionately shared by all dairy farmers.

Under the scheme established by Congress, the Secretary must conduct an appropriate rulemaking proceeding before issuing a milk market order. The public must be notified of these proceedings and provided an opportunity for public hearing and comment. . . . Moreover, before any market order may become effective, it must be approved by the handlers of at least 50% of the volume of milk covered by the proposed order and at least two-thirds of the affected dairy producers in the region. If the handlers withhold their consent, the Secretary may nevertheless impose the order. But the Secretary's power to do so is conditioned upon at least two-thirds of the producers consenting to its promulgation and upon his making an administrative determination that the order is "the only practical means of advancing the interests of the producers."

The Secretary currently has some 45 milk market orders in effect. Each order covers a different region of the country, and collectively they cover most, though not all, of the United States. The orders divide dairy products into separately priced classes based on the uses to which raw milk is put. Raw milk that is processed and bottled for fluid consumption is termed "Class I" milk. Raw milk that is used to produce milk products such as butter, cheese, or dry milk powder is termed "Class II" milk.

For a variety of economic reasons, fluid milk products would command a higher price than surplus milk products in a perfectly functioning market. Accordingly, the Secretary's milk market orders require handlers to pay a higher order price for Class I products than for Class II products. To discourage destabilizing competition among producers for the more desirable fluid milk sales, the orders also require handlers to submit their payments for either class of milk to a regional pool. Administrators of these regional pools are then charged with distributing to dairy farmers a weighted average price for each milk product they have produced, irrespective of its use.

In particular, the Secretary has regulated the price of "reconstituted milk"—that is, milk manufactured by mixing milk powder with water—since 1964. The Secretary's orders assume that handlers will use reconstituted milk to manufacture surplus milk products. Handlers are therefore required to pay only the lower Class II minimum price. However, handlers are required to make a "compensatory payment" on any portion of the reconstituted milk that their records show has not been used to manufacture surplus milk products. 7 CFR §§ 1012.44(a)(5)(i), 1012.60(e) (1984). The compensatory payment is equal to the difference between the Class I and Class II milk product prices. Handlers make these payments to the regional pool, from which moneys are then distributed to producers of fresh fluid milk in the region where the reconstituted milk was manufactured and sold. § 1012.71(a)(1).

B

In December 1980, respondents brought suit in District Court, contending that the compensatory payment requirement makes reconstituted milk uneconomical for handlers to process. Respondents, as plaintiffs in the District Court, included three individual consumers of fluid dairy products, a handler regulated by the market orders, and a nonprofit organization. The District Court concluded that the consumers and the nonprofit organization did not have standing to challenge the market orders. In addition, it found that Congress had intended by the Act to preclude such persons from obtaining judicial review. The District Court dismissed the milk handler's complaint because he had failed to exhaust his administrative remedies.

The Court of Appeals affirmed in part and reversed in part, and remanded the case for a decision on the merits. The Court of Appeals agreed that the milk handler and the nonprofit organization had been properly dismissed by the District Court. But the court concluded that the individual consumers had standing: they had suffered an injury-in-fact, their injuries were redressable, and they were within the zone of interests arguably protected by the Act. The Court also concluded that the statutory structure and purposes of the Act did not reveal "the type of clear and convincing evidence of congressional intent needed to overcome the presumption in favor of judicial review." . . .

We now reverse the judgment of the Court of Appeals in this case.

II

Respondents filed this suit under the Administrative Procedure Act (APA). The APA confers a general cause of action upon persons "adversely affected or aggrieved by agency action within the meaning of a relevant statute," 5 U.S.C. § 702, but withdraws that cause of action to the extent the relevant statute "preclude[s] judicial review," 5 U.S.C. § 701(a)(1). Whether and to what extent a particular statute precludes judicial review is determined not only from its express language, but also from the structure of the statutory scheme, its objectives, its legislative history, and the nature of the administrative action involved. Therefore, we must examine this statutory scheme "to determine whether Congress precluded all judicial review, and, if not, whether Congress nevertheless foreclosed review to the class to which the [respondents] belon[g]." Barlow v. Collins, 397 U.S. 159, 173 (1970) (opinion of Brennan, J.,); see also Data Processing Service v. Camp, 397 U.S. 150, 156 (1970).

It is clear that Congress did not intend to strip the judiciary of all authority to review the Secretary's milk market orders. The Act's predecessor, the Agricultural Adjustment Act of 1933, contained no provision relating to administrative or judicial review. In 1935, however, Congress added a mechanism by which dairy handlers could obtain review of the Secretary's market orders. That mechanism was retained in the 1937 legislation and remains in the Act as § 608c(15) today. Section 608c(15) requires handlers first to exhaust the administrative remedies made available by the Secretary. 7 U.S.C. § 608c(15)(A). After these formal administrative remedies have been exhausted, handlers may obtain judicial review of the Secretary's ruling in the federal district court in any district "in which [they are] inhabitant[s], or ha[ve their] principal place[s] of business." 7 U.S.C. § 608c(15)(B). These provisions for handler-initiated review make evident Congress' desire that some persons be able to obtain judicial review of the Secretary's market orders.

The remainder of the statutory scheme, however, makes equally clear Congress' intention to limit the classes entitled to participate in the development of market orders. The Act contemplates a cooperative venture among the Secretary, handlers, and producers the principal purposes of which are to raise the price of agricultural products and to establish an orderly system for marketing them. Handlers and producers—but not consumers—are entitled to participate in the adoption and retention of market orders. 7 U.S.C. §§ 608c(8), (9), (16)(B). The Act provides for agreements among the Secretary, producers, and handlers, 7 U.S.C. § 608(2), for hearings among them, §§ 608(5), 608c(3), and for votes by producers and handlers, §§ 608c(8)(A), (9)(B), (12), 608c(19). Nowhere in the Act, however, is there an express provision for participation by consumers in any proceeding. In a complex scheme of this type, the omission of such a provision is sufficient reason to believe that Congress intended to foreclose consumer participation in the regulatory process.

To be sure, the general purpose sections of the Act allude to general consumer interests. See 7 U.S.C. §§ 602(2), (4). But the preclusion issue does not only turn on whether the interests of a particular class like consumers are implicated. Rather, the preclusion issue turns ultimately on whether Congress intended for that class to be relied upon to challenge agency disregard of the law. See Barlow v. Collins, supra, at 167. The structure of this Act indicates that Congress intended only producers and handlers, and not consumers, to ensure that the statutory objectives would be realized.

Respondents would have us believe that, while Congress unequivocally directed handlers first to complain to the Secretary that the prices set by milk market orders are too high, it was nevertheless the legislative judgment that the same challenge, if advanced by consumers, does not require initial administrative scrutiny. There is no basis for attributing to Congress the intent to draw such a distinction. The regulation of agricultural products is a complex, technical undertaking. Congress channelled disputes concerning marketing orders to the Secretary in the first instance because it believed that only he has the expertise necessary to illuminate and resolve questions about them. Had Congress intended to allow consumers to attack provisions of marketing orders, it surely would have required them to pursue the administrative remedies provided in § 608c(15)(A) as well. The restriction of the administrative remedy to handlers strongly suggests that Congress intended a similar restriction of judicial review of market orders.

Allowing consumers to sue the Secretary would severely disrupt this complex and delicate administrative scheme. It would provide handlers with a convenient device for evading the statutory requirement that they first exhaust their administrative remedies. A handler may also be a consumer and, as such, could sue in that capacity. Alternatively, a handler would need only to find a consumer who is willing to join in or initiate an action in the district court. The consumer or consumer-handler could then raise precisely the same exceptions that the handler must raise administratively. Consumers or consumer-handlers could seek injunctions against the operation of market orders that "impede, hinder, or delay" enforcement actions, even though such injunctions are expressly prohibited in proceedings properly instituted under 7 U.S.C. § 608c(15). Suits of this type would effectively nullify Congress' intent to establish an "equitable and expeditious procedure for testing the validity of orders, without hampering the Government's power to enforce compliance with their terms." S. Rep.

No. 1011, 74th Cong., 1st Sess., 14 (1935). For these reasons, we think it clear that Congress intended that judicial review of market orders issued under the Act ordinarily be confined to suits brought by handlers in accordance with 7 U.S.C. § 608c(15).

III

The Court of Appeals viewed the preclusion issue from a somewhat different perspective. First, it recited the presumption in favor of judicial review of administrative action that this Court usually employs. It then noted that the Act has been interpreted to authorize producer challenges to the administration of market order settlement funds, and that no legislative history or statutory language directly and specifically supported the preclusion of consumer suits. In these circumstances, the Court of Appeals reasoned that the Act could not fairly be interpreted to overcome the presumption favoring judicial review and to leave consumers without a judicial remedy. We disagree with the Court of Appeals' analysis.

The presumption favoring judicial review of administrative action is just that—a presumption. This presumption, like all presumptions used in interpreting statutes, may be overcome by specific language or specific legislative history that is a reliable indicator of congressional intent. The congressional intent necessary to overcome the presumption may also be inferred from contemporaneous judicial construction barring review and the congressional acquiescence in it, or from the collective import of legislative and judicial history behind a particular statute. More important for purposes of this case, the presumption favoring judicial review of administrative action may be overcome by inferences of intent drawn from the statutory scheme as a whole. In particular, at least when a statute provides a detailed mechanism for judicial consideration of particular issues at the behest of particular persons, judicial review of those issues at the behest of other persons may be found to be impliedly precluded. . . .

In this case, the Court of Appeals . . . recited this Court's oft-quoted statement that "only upon a showing of 'clear and convincing evidence' of a contrary legislative intent should the courts restrict access to judicial review." Abbott Laboratories v. Gardner, 387 U.S. 136, 141 (1967). According to the Court of Appeals, the "clear and convincing evidence" standard required it to find unambiguous proof, in the traditional evidentiary sense, of a congressional intent to preclude judicial review at the consumers' behest. Since direct statutory language or legislative history on this issue could not be found, the Court of Appeals found the presumption favoring judicial review to be controlling.

This Court has, however, never applied the "clear and convincing evidence" standard in the strict evidentiary sense the Court of Appeals thought necessary in this case. Rather, the Court has found the standard met, and the presumption favoring judicial review overcome, whenever the congressional intent to preclude judicial review is "fairly discernible in the statutory scheme." Data Processing Service v. Camp, 397 U.S. at 157. In the context of preclusion analysis, the "clear and convincing evidence" standard is not a rigid evidentiary test but a useful reminder to courts that, where substantial doubt about the congressional intent exists, the general presumption favoring judicial review of administrative action is controlling. That presumption does not control in cases such as this one, however, since the congressional intent to preclude judicial review is "fairly discernible" in the detail of the legislative scheme. Congress simply did not intend for consumers to be relied upon to challenge agency disregard of the law.

It is true, as the Court of Appeals also noted, that this Court determined, in Stark v. Wickard, 321 U.S. 288 (1944), that dairy producers could challenge certain administrative actions even though the Act did not expressly provide them a right to judicial review. The producers challenged certain deductions the Secretary had made from the "producer settlement fund" established in connection with the milk market order in effect at the time. "[T]he challenged deduction[s] reduce[d] pro tanto the amount actually received by the producers for their milk." Id. at 302. These deductions injured what the producers alleged were "definite personal rights" that were "not possessed by the people generally," id. at 304, 309, and gave the producers standing to object to the administration of the settlement fund. See id., at 306. Though the producers' standing could not by itself ensure judicial review of the Secretary's action at their behest, the statutory scheme as a whole, the Court concluded, implicitly authorized producers' suits concerning settlement fund administration. "[H]andlers [could not] question the use of the fund, because handlers had no financial interest in the fund or its use." Id. at 308. Thus, there was "no forum" in which this aspect of the Secretary's actions could or would be challenged. Judicial review of the producers' complaint was therefore necessary to ensure achievement of the Act's most fundamental objectives—to wit, the protection of the producers of milk and milk products.

By contrast, preclusion of consumer suits will not threaten realization of the fundamental objectives of the statute. Handlers have interests similar to those of consumers. Handlers, like consumers, are interested in obtaining reliable supplies of milk at the cheapest possible prices. Handlers can therefore be expected to challenge unlawful agency action and to ensure that the statute's objectives will not be frustrated. Indeed, as noted above, consumer suits might themselves frustrate achievement of the statutory purposes. The Act contemplates a cooperative venture among the Secretary, producers, and handlers; consumer participation is not provided for or desired under the complex scheme enacted by Congress. Consumer suits would undermine the congressional preference for administrative remedies and provide a mechanism for disrupting administration of the congressional scheme. Thus, preclusion of consumer suits is perfectly consistent with the Court's contrary conclusion concerning producer challenges . . . .

The structure of this Act implies that Congress intended to preclude consumer challenges to the Secretary's market orders.

NOTES AND QUESTIONS

1. Summary. In *Block*, the Court held that the statute precluded consumers from suing the Secretary of Agriculture over marketing orders after examining the structure of the Act as a whole. The Act provided for an elaborate process between producers, handlers, and the agency, including the requirement that administrative remedies be exhausted before a handler could bring suit. Allowing consumers to sue would undermine this whole structure; indeed, handlers are often consumers, too, and could arguably sue as consumers and thereby forgo the carefully reticulated structure that Congress designed. Thus, *Block* is often taken for the proposition that, notwithstanding the presumption of judicial review, preclusion of review can be implied and need not be explicit in Congress's statute.

2. Stark v. Wickard. In *Stark*, discussed in *Block*, the Court had held that producers could sue the Secretary even though "the Act did not expressly provide them a right to judicial review." How does the Court distinguish *Stark*? Do you find it convincing?

3. Causes of action—again. Would this case be easier to analyze under the framework of causes of action? How would such an analysis go? The handlers clearly had a cause of action: the statute explicitly gave them a right to sue under certain circumstances. Did consumers have a cause of action? Did the producers? Is this a simpler approach?

4. Should consumers be able to sue? In what way were the consumers aggrieved? Because they had to pay higher prices for milk? If they could sue on that basis, can anyone sue to stop any government action that will have the effect of raising prices of services or commodities? Although the Supreme Court did not address standing in this case, as you shall learn later in this chapter Article III standing stands for the proposition that "generalized grievances" against government action is not sufficient to bring a lawsuit. Don't most regulations affect prices in some way? Is that kind of harm to consumers from government regulations too generalized?

 Is *Block* consistent with the following case?

Bowen v. Michigan Academy of Family Physicians

476 U.S. 667 (1980)

Justice Stevens delivered the opinion of the Court.

The question presented in this case is whether Congress, in either § 1395ff or § 1395ii of Title 42 of the United States Code, barred judicial review of regulations promulgated under Part B of the Medicare program.

Respondents, who include an association of family physicians and several individual doctors, filed suit to challenge the validity of 42 CFR § 405.504(b) (1985), which authorizes the payment of benefits in different amounts for similar physicians' services. The District Court held that the regulation contravened several provisions of the statute governing the Medicare program:

> "There is no basis to justify the segregation of allopathic family physicians from all other types of physicians. Such segregation is not rationally related to any legitimate purpose of the Medicare statute. To lump MDs who are family physicians, but who have chosen not

to become board certified family physicians for whatever motive, with chiropractors, dentists, and podiatrists for the purpose of determining Medicare reimbursement defies all reason."

. . . . The Court of Appeals agreed with the District Court that the Secretary's regulation was "obvious[ly] inconsisten[t] with the plain language of the Medicare statute" and held that "this regulation is irrational and is invalid." . . .

The Secretary of Health and Human Services has not sought review of the decision on the merits invalidating the regulation. Instead, he renews the contention, rejected by both the District Court and the Court of Appeals, that Congress has forbidden judicial review of all questions affecting the amount of benefits payable under Part B of the Medicare program. . . . We now affirm.

I

We begin with the strong presumption that Congress intends judicial review of administrative action. From the beginning "our cases [have established] that judicial review of a final agency action by an aggrieved person will not be cut off unless there is persuasive reason to believe that such was the purpose of Congress." *Abbott Laboratories v. Gardner*, 387 U.S. 136, 140 (1967) (citing cases). In *Marbury v. Madison*, 1 Cranch 137, 163 (1803), a case itself involving review of executive action, Chief Justice Marshall insisted that "[t]he very essence of civil liberty certainly consists in the right of every individual to claim the protection of the laws." Later, in the lesser known but nonetheless important case of *United States v. Nourse*, 9 Pet. 8, 28–29 (1835), the Chief Justice noted the traditional observance of this right and laid the foundation for the modern of judicial review:

> "It would excite some surprise if, in a government of laws and of principle, furnished with a department whose appropriate duty it is to decide questions of right, not only between individuals, but between the government and individuals; a ministerial officer might, at his discretion, issue this powerful process . . . leaving to the debtor no remedy, no appeal to the laws of his country, if he should believe the claim to be unjust. But this anomaly does not exist; this imputation cannot be cast on the legislature of the United States."

Committees of both Houses of Congress have endorsed this view. In undertaking the comprehensive rethinking of the place of administrative agencies in a regime of separate and divided powers that culminated in the passage of the Administrative Procedure Act (APA) . . . .

The Committee on the Judiciary of the House of Representatives agreed [with the Senate Judiciary Committee] that Congress ordinarily intends that there be judicial review, and emphasized the clarity with which a contrary intent must be expressed . . . .

Subject to constitutional constraints, Congress can, of course, make exceptions to the historic practice whereby courts review agency action. The presumption of judicial review is, after all, a presumption, and "like all presumptions used in interpreting statutes, may be overcome by," *inter alia*, "specific language or specific legislative history that is a reliable indicator of congressional intent," or a specific congressional intent to preclude judicial review that is " 'fairly discernible' in the detail of the legislative scheme." *Block v. Community Nutrition Institute*, 467 U.S. 340, 349 (1984).

In this case, the Government asserts that two statutory provisions remove the Secretary's regulation from review under the grant of general federal-question jurisdiction found in 28 U.S.C. § 1331. First, the Government contends that 42 U.S.C. § 1395ff(b), which authorizes "Appeal by individuals," impliedly forecloses administrative or judicial review of any action taken under Part B of the Medicare program by failing to authorize such review while simultaneously authorizing administrative and judicial review of [Part A]. § 1395ff(b)(1)(C). Second, the Government asserts that 42 U.S.C. § 1395ii, which makes applicable 42 U.S.C. § 405(h), of the Social Security Act to the Medicare program, expressly precludes all administrative or judicial review not otherwise provided in that statute. We find neither argument persuasive.

II

Section 1395ff on its face is an explicit authorization of judicial review, not a bar. As a general matter, " '[t]he mere fact that some acts are made reviewable should not suffice to support an implication of exclusion as to others. The right to review is too important to be excluded on such slender and indeterminate evidence of legislative intent.' " *Abbott Laboratories v. Gardner*, 387 U.S. at 141 (quoting L. Jaffe, Judicial Control of Administrative Action 357 (1965)). See *Barlow v. Collins*, 397 U.S. 159, 166 (1970); *Stark v. Wickard*, 321 U.S. 288, 309 (1944).

In the Medicare program, however, the situation is somewhat more complex. Under Part B of that program, which is at issue here, the Secretary contracts with private health insurance carriers to provide benefits for which individuals voluntarily remit premiums. This optional coverage, which is federally subsidized, supplements the mandatory institutional health benefits (such as coverage for hospital expenses) provided by Part A. Subject to an amount-in-controversy requirement, individuals aggrieved by delayed or insufficient payment with respect to benefits payable under Part B are afforded an "opportunity for a fair hearing by the *carrier*," 42 U.S.C. § 1395u(b)(3)(C) (emphasis added); in comparison, and subject to a like amount-in-controversy requirement, a similarly aggrieved individual under Part A is entitled "to a hearing thereon by the *Secretary* . . . and to judicial review," 42 U.S.C. §§ 1395ff(b)(1)(C), (b)(2). "In the context of the statute's precisely drawn provisions," we held in *United States v. Erika, Inc.*, 456 U.S. 201, 208 (1982), that the failure "to authorize further review for determinations of the amount of Part B awards . . . provides persuasive evidence that Congress deliberately intended to foreclose further review of such claims." . . .

Respondents' federal-court challenge to the validity of the Secretary's regulation is not foreclosed by § 1395ff as we construed that provision in *Erika*. The reticulated statutory scheme, which carefully details the forum and limits of review of "any determination . . . of . . . the amount of benefits under part A," 42 U.S.C. § 1395ff(b)(1)(C), and of the "amount of . . . payment" of benefits under Part B, 42 U.S.C. § 1395u(b)(3)(C), simply does not speak to challenges mounted against the *method* by which such amounts are to be *determined* rather than the determinations themselves. As the Secretary has made clear, "the legality, constitutional or otherwise, of any provision of the Act or regulations relevant to the Medicare Program" is not considered in a "fair hearing" held by a carrier to resolve a grievance related to a determination of the amount of a Part B award. As a result, an attack on the validity of a regulation is not the kind of administrative action that we described in *Erika* as an "amount determination" which decides "the amount of the Medicare payment to be made on a particular claim" and with respect to which the Act impliedly denies judicial review. . . .

We conclude, therefore, that those matters which Congress did *not* leave to be determined in a "fair hearing" conducted by the carrier—including challenges to the validity of the Secretary's instructions and regulations—are not impliedly insulated from judicial review by 42 U.S.C. § 1395ff.

[Discussion of the second statutory argument made by the government is omitted.—Ed.]

C. Constitutional Standing

Even if a plaintiff has a cause of action, that does not mean the plaintiff can necessarily sue. There is another hurdle that has to be cleared: the plaintiff must have *constitutional standing* to bring the case within the Article III judicial power. To bring her case within the federal judicial power, the plaintiff must show that she has an injury that is caused by the defendant, and that the injury is redressable by the courts.

Historically, one might have thought about constitutional standing before causes of action. That's because many individuals might suffer sufficient injury to satisfy standing but that did not mean they'd have a cause of action. Third parties are often harmed by actions taken by two other parties, including, recall, when the federal government subsidizes or licenses a competitor. That did not mean the third party could sue (see the economic competition cases). Thus, as a general matter, it used to be the case that one could regularly find cases in which there was sufficient injury for standing, but no cause of action.

> **Defined Term**
>
> **STANDING:** We are now in a better position to define standing. A plaintiff must have an injury before bringing a lawsuit. An injury caused by the defendant would be sufficient to confer standing. But, that did not mean there was a cause of action, which was also necessary to bring a lawsuit and obtain relief.

Today things are generally (although not always) reversed. After *Data Processing*, almost everyone has a cause of action, or "statutory standing." Of course, not quite everyone does. Some plaintiffs will still be beyond the zone of interests. But even *if* a plaintiff is within the zone of interests—perhaps the statute includes a citizen-suit provision allowing anyone to bring a lawsuit—and thus has a cause of action (or "statutory standing"), the plaintiff may not have an injury within the meaning of Article III of the Constitution.

The following decision is the leading case on constitutional standing today, and might be the most cited public-law case in history, on par and possibly ahead of *Chevron* and *Marbury*. It includes just such a citizen-suit provision. In the following case, six Justices joined the entirety of the Court's opinion with the exception of Part III-B on redressability, which two Justices thought the Court did not need to reach because the case was resolved by the ruling on the injury requirement. Three Justices dissented on the reasoning, although one of these three concurred in the judgment on the merits.

Lujan v. Defenders of Wildlife

504 U.S. 555 (1992)

Justice Scalia delivered the opinion of the Court with respect to Parts I, II, III-A, and IV, and an opinion with respect to Part III-B, in which The Chief Justice, Justice White, and Justice Thomas join.

This case involves a challenge to a rule promulgated by the Secretary of the Interior interpreting § 7 of the Endangered Species Act of 1973 (ESA), 16 U.S.C. § 1536, in such fashion as to render it applicable only to actions within the United States or on the high seas. The preliminary issue, and the only one we reach, is whether respondents here, plaintiffs below, have standing to seek judicial review of the rule.

I

The ESA seeks to protect species of animals against threats to their continuing existence caused by man. The ESA instructs the Secretary of the Interior to promulgate by regulation a list of those species which are either endangered or threatened under enumerated criteria, and to define the critical habitat of these species. 16 U.S.C. §§ 1533, 1536. Section 7(a)(2) of the Act then provides, in pertinent part:

> "Each Federal agency shall, in consultation with and with the assistance of the Secretary [of the Interior], insure that any action authorized, funded, or carried out by such agency . . . is not likely to jeopardize the continued existence of any endangered species or threatened species or result in the destruction or adverse modification of habitat of such species which is determined by the Secretary, after consultation as appropriate with affected States, to be critical." 16 U.S.C. § 1536(a)(2).

In 1978, the Fish and Wildlife Service (FWS) and the National Marine Fisheries Service (NMFS), on behalf of the Secretary of the Interior and the Secretary of Commerce respectively, promulgated a joint regulation stating that the obligations imposed by § 7(a)(2) extend to actions taken in foreign nations. 43 Fed. Reg. 874 (1978). The next year, however, the Interior Department began to reexamine its position. A revised joint regulation, reinterpreting § 7(a)(2) to require consultation only for actions taken in the United States or on the high seas, was proposed in 1983, and promulgated in 1986[.] 50 CFR 402.01 (1991).

Shortly thereafter, respondents, organizations dedicated to wildlife conservation and other environmental causes, filed this action against the Secretary of the Interior, seeking a declaratory judgment that the new regulation is in error as to the geographic scope of § 7(a)(2) and an injunction requiring the Secretary to promulgate a new regulation restoring the initial interpretation. [The District Court on remand from the Eighth Circuit, with the Eighth Circuit subsequently affirming, found standing.—Ed.]

II

While the Constitution of the United States divides all power conferred upon the Federal Government into "legislative Powers," Art. I, § 1, "[t]he executive Power," Art. II, § 1, and "[t]he judicial Power," Art. III, § 1, it does not attempt to define those terms. To be sure, it limits the jurisdiction of federal courts to "Cases" and "Controversies," but an executive inquiry can bear the name "case" (the Hoffa case) and a legislative dispute can bear the name "controversy" (the Smoot-Hawley controversy). Obviously, then, the Constitution's central mechanism of separation of powers depends largely upon common understanding of what activities are appropriate to legislatures, to executives, and to courts. In The Federalist No. 48, Madison expressed the view that "[i]t is not infrequently a question of real nicety in legislative bodies whether the operation of a particular measure will, or will not, extend beyond the legislative sphere," whereas "the executive power [is] restrained within a narrower compass and . . . more simple in its nature," and "the judiciary [is] described by landmarks still less uncertain." The Federalist No. 48. One of those landmarks, setting apart the "Cases" and "Controversies" that are of the justiciable sort referred to in Article III—"serv[ing] to identify those disputes which are appropriately resolved through the judicial process," *Whitmore v. Arkansas,* 495 U.S. 149, 155 (1990)—is the doctrine of standing. Though some of its elements express merely prudential considerations that are part of judicial self-government, the core component of standing is an essential and unchanging part of the case-or-controversy requirement of Article III. See, *e.g., Allen v. Wright*, 468 U.S. 737, 751 (1984).

Over the years, our cases have established that the irreducible constitutional minimum of standing contains three elements. First, the plaintiff must have suffered an "injury in fact"—an invasion of a legally protected interest which is (a) concrete and particularized, see *id.* at 756; and (b) "actual or imminent, not 'conjectural' or 'hypothetical,'" *Whitmore, supra*, 495 U.S. at 155 (quoting *Los Angeles v. Lyons*, 461 U.S. 95, 102 (1983)). Second, there must be a causal connection between the injury and the conduct complained of—the injury has to be "fairly . . . trace[able] to the challenged action of the defendant, and not . . . th[e] result [of] the independent action of some third party not before the court." *Simon v. Eastern Ky. Welfare Rights Organization*, 426 U.S. 26, 41–42 (1976). Third, it must be "likely," as opposed to merely "speculative," that the injury will be "redressed by a favorable decision." *Id.* at 38, 43.

The party invoking federal jurisdiction bears the burden of establishing these elements. Since they are not mere pleading requirements but rather an indispensable part of the plaintiff's case, each element must be supported in the same way as any other matter on which the plaintiff bears the burden of proof, *i.e.*, with the manner and degree of evidence required at the successive stages of the litigation. See *Lujan v. National Wildlife Federation*, 497 U.S. 871, 883–889 (1990). At the pleading stage, general factual allegations of injury resulting from the defendant's conduct may suffice, for on a motion to dismiss we "presum[e] that general allegations embrace those specific facts that are necessary to support the claim." [*Id.*] at 889. In response to a summary judgment motion, however, the plaintiff can no longer rest on such "mere allegations," but must "set forth" by affidavit or other evidence "specific facts," Fed. Rule Civ. Proc. 56(e), which for purposes of the summary judgment motion will be taken to be true. And at the final stage, those facts (if controverted) must be "supported adequately by the evidence adduced at trial."

When the suit is one challenging the legality of government action or inaction, the nature and extent of facts that must be averred (at the summary judgment stage) or proved (at the trial stage) in order to establish standing depends considerably upon whether the plaintiff is himself an object of the action (or forgone action) at issue. If he is, there is ordinarily little question that the action or inaction has caused him injury, and that a judgment preventing or requiring the action will redress it. When, however, as in this case, a plaintiff's asserted injury arises from the government's allegedly unlawful regulation (or lack of regulation) of *someone else,* much more is needed. In that circumstance, causation and redressability ordinarily hinge on the response of the regulated (or regulable) third party to the government action or inaction—and perhaps on the response of others as well. The existence of one or more of the essential elements of standing "depends on the unfettered choices made by independent actors not before the courts and whose exercise of broad and legitimate discretion the courts cannot presume either to control or to predict," *ASARCO Inc. v. Kadish,* 490 U.S. 605, 615 (1989) (opinion of KENNEDY, J.), and it becomes the burden of the plaintiff to adduce facts showing that those choices have been or will be made in such manner as to produce causation and permit redressability of injury. Thus, when the plaintiff is not himself the object of the government action or inaction he challenges, standing is not precluded, but it is ordinarily "substantially more difficult" to establish. *Allen, supra,* 468 U.S. at 758.

III

We think the Court of Appeals failed to apply the foregoing principles in denying the Secretary's motion for summary judgment. Respondents had not made the requisite demonstration of (at least) injury and redressability.

A

Respondents' claim to injury is that the lack of consultation with respect to certain funded activities abroad "increas[es] the rate of extinction of endangered and threatened species." Of course, the desire to use or observe an animal species, even for purely esthetic purposes, is undeniably a cognizable interest for purpose of standing. See, *e.g., Sierra Club v. Morton,* 405 U.S. [727, 734 (1972)]. "But the 'injury in fact' test requires more than an injury to a cognizable interest. It requires that the party seeking review be himself among the injured." *Id.* at 734–735. To survive the Secretary's summary judgment motion, respondents had to submit affidavits or other evidence showing, through specific facts, not only that listed species were in fact being threatened by funded activities abroad, but also that one or more of respondents' members would thereby be "directly" affected apart from their " 'special interest' in th[e] subject." *Id.* at 735, 739.

With respect to this aspect of the case, the Court of Appeals focused on the affidavits of two [of] Defenders' members—Joyce Kelly and Amy Skilbred. Ms. Kelly stated that she traveled to Egypt in 1986 and "observed the traditional habitat of the endangered nile crocodile there and intend[s] to do so again, and hope[s] to observe the crocodile directly," and that she "will suffer harm in fact as the result of [the] American . . . role . . . in overseeing the rehabilitation of the Aswan High Dam on the Nile . . . and [in] develop[ing] . . . Egypt's . . . Master Water Plan." Ms. Skilbred averred that she traveled to Sri Lanka in 1981 and "observed th[e] habitat" of "endangered species such as the Asian elephant and the leopard" at what is now the site of the Mahaweli project funded by the Agency for International Development (AID), although she "was unable to see any of the endangered species"; "this development project," she continued, "will seriously reduce endangered, threatened, and endemic species habitat including areas that I visited . . . [, which] may severely shorten the future of these species"; that threat, she concluded, harmed her because she "intend[s] to return to Sri Lanka in the future and hope[s] to be more fortunate in spotting at least the endangered elephant and leopard." When Ms. Skilbred was asked at a subsequent deposition if and when she had any plans to return to Sri Lanka, she reiterated that "I intend to go back to Sri Lanka," but confessed that she had no current plans: "I don't know [when]. There is a civil war going on right now. I don't know. Not next year, I will say. In the future."

We shall assume for the sake of argument that these affidavits contain facts showing that certain agency-funded projects threaten listed species—though that is questionable. They plainly contain no facts, however, showing how damage to the species will produce "imminent" injury to Mses. Kelly and Skilbred. That the women "had visited" the areas of the projects before the projects commenced proves nothing. As we have said in a related context, " 'Past exposure to illegal conduct does not in itself show a present case or controversy regarding injunctive relief . . . if unaccompanied by any continuing, present adverse effects.' " *Lyons,* 461 U.S. at 102. And the affiants' profession of an "inten[t]" to return to the places they had visited before—where they will presumably, this time, be deprived of the opportunity to observe animals of the endangered species—is simply not enough. Such "some day" intentions—without any description of concrete plans, or indeed even any specification of *when* the some day will be—do not support a finding of the "actual or imminent" injury that our cases require.

Besides relying upon the Kelly and Skilbred affidavits, respondents propose a series of novel standing theories. The first, inelegantly styled "ecosystem nexus," proposes that any person who uses *any part* of a "contiguous ecosystem" adversely affected by a funded activity has standing even if the activity is located a great distance away. This approach, as the Court of Appeals correctly observed, is inconsistent with our opinion in *National Wildlife Federation*, which held that a plaintiff claiming injury from environmental damage must use the area affected by the challenged activity and not an area roughly "in the vicinity" of it. 497 U.S. at 887–889; see also *Sierra Club*, 405 U.S. at 735. It makes no difference that the general-purpose section of the ESA states that the Act was intended in part "to provide a means whereby the ecosystems upon which endangered species and threatened species depend may be conserved," 16 U.S.C. § 1531(b). To say that the Act protects ecosystems is not to say that the Act creates (if it were possible) rights of action in persons who have not been injured in fact, that is, persons who use portions of an ecosystem not perceptibly affected by the unlawful action in question.

Respondents' other theories are called, alas, the "animal nexus" approach, whereby anyone who has an interest in studying or seeing the endangered animals anywhere on the globe has standing; and the "vocational nexus" approach, under which anyone with a professional interest in such animals can sue. Under these theories, anyone who goes to see Asian elephants in the Bronx Zoo, and anyone who is a keeper of Asian elephants in the Bronx Zoo, has standing to sue because the Director of the Agency for International Development (AID) did not consult with the Secretary regarding the AID-funded project in Sri Lanka. This is beyond all reason. . . . It is clear that the person who observes or works with a particular animal threatened by a federal decision is facing perceptible harm, since the very subject of his interest will no longer exist. It is even plausible—though it goes to the outermost limit of plausibility—to think that a person who observes or works with animals of a particular species in the very area of the world where that species is threatened by a federal decision is facing such harm, since some animals that might have been the subject of his interest will no longer exist. It goes beyond the limit, however, and into pure speculation and fantasy, to say that anyone who observes or works with an endangered species, anywhere in the world, is appreciably harmed by a single project affecting some portion of that species with which he has no more specific connection.

B

Besides failing to show injury, respondents failed to demonstrate redressability. Instead of attacking the separate decisions to fund particular projects allegedly causing them harm, respondents chose to challenge a more general-ized level of Government action (rules regarding consultation), the invalidation of which would affect all overseas projects. This programmatic approach has obvious practical advantages, but also obvious difficulties insofar as proof of causation or redressability is concerned. . . .

The most obvious problem in the present case is redressability. Since the agencies funding the projects were not parties to the case, the District Court could accord relief only against the Secretary: He could be ordered to revise his regulation to require consultation for foreign projects. But this would not rem-edy respondents' alleged injury unless the funding agencies were bound by the Secretary's regulation, which is very much an open question. Whereas in other contexts the ESA is quite explicit as to the Secretary's controlling authority, see, *e.g.*, 16 U.S.C. § 1533(a)(1) ("The Secretary shall" promulgate regulations determining endangered species); § 1535(d)(1) ("The Secretary is authorized to provide financial assistance to any State"), with respect to consultation the initiative, and hence arguably the initial responsibility for determining statuto-ry necessity, lies with the agencies, see § 1536(a)(2) (*"Each Federal agency shall, in consultation with and with the assistance of the Secretary, insure that any"* funded action is not likely to jeopardize endangered or threatened species) (em-phasis added). When the Secretary promulgated the regulation at issue here, he thought it was binding on the agencies. The Solicitor General, however, has repudiated that position here, and the agencies themselves apparently deny the Secretary's authority. (During the period when the Secretary took the view that § 7(a)(2) did apply abroad, AID and FWS engaged in a running controversy over whether consultation was required with respect to the Mahaweli project, AID insisting that consultation applied only to domestic actions.)

Respondents assert that this legal uncertainty did not affect redressability (and hence standing) because the District Court itself could resolve the issue of the Secretary's authority as a necessary part of its standing inquiry. Assuming that it is appropriate to resolve an issue of law such as this in connection with a threshold standing inquiry, resolution by the District Court would not have remedied respondents' alleged injury anyway, because it would not have been binding upon the agencies. They were not parties to the suit, and there is no reason they should be obliged to honor an incidental legal determination the suit produced. The Court of Appeals tried to finesse this problem by simply proclaiming that "[w]e are satisfied that an injunction requiring the Secretary

to publish [respondents' desired] regulatio[n] . . . would result in consultation."
We do not know what would justify that confidence, particularly when the
Justice Department (presumably after consultation with the agencies) has tak-
en the position that the regulation is not binding. The short of the matter is
that redress of the only injury in fact respondents complain of requires action
(termination of funding until consultation) by the individual funding agencies;
and any relief the District Court could have provided in this suit against the
Secretary was not likely to produce that action.

A further impediment to redressability is the fact that the agencies generally supply only a fraction of the funding for a foreign project. AID, for
example, has provided less than 10% of the funding for the Mahaweli project.
Respondents have produced nothing to indicate that the projects they have
named will either be suspended, or do less harm to listed species, if that fraction is eliminated. . . . There is no standing.

IV

The Court of Appeals found that respondents had standing for an additional reason: because they had suffered a "procedural injury." The so-called
"citizen-suit" provision of the ESA provides, in pertinent part, that "any person
may commence a civil suit on his own behalf (A) to enjoin any person, including the United States and any other governmental instrumentality or agency
. . . who is alleged to be in violation of any provision of this chapter." 16 U.S.C.
§ 1540(g). The court held that, because § 7(a)(2) requires interagency consultation, the citizen-suit provision creates a "procedural righ[t]" to consultation
in all "persons"—so that *anyone* can file suit in federal court to challenge the
Secretary's (or presumably any other official's) failure to follow the assertedly
correct consultative procedure, notwithstanding his or her inability to allege
any discrete injury flowing from that failure. To understand the remarkable
nature of this holding one must be clear about what it does *not* rest upon: This
is not a case where plaintiffs are seeking to enforce a procedural requirement
the disregard of which could impair a separate concrete interest of theirs (*e.g.*,
the procedural requirement for a hearing prior to denial of their license application, or the procedural requirement for an environmental impact statement
before a federal facility is constructed next door to them). Nor is it simply a
case where concrete injury has been suffered by many persons, as in mass fraud
or mass tort situations. Nor, finally, is it the unusual case in which Congress
has created a concrete private interest in the outcome of a suit against a private

party for the government's benefit, by providing a cash bounty for the victorious plaintiff. Rather, the court held that the injury-in-fact requirement had been satisfied by congressional conferral upon *all* persons of an abstract, self-contained, noninstrumental "right" to have the Executive observe the procedures required by law. We reject this view.

We have consistently held that a plaintiff raising only a generally available grievance about government—claiming only harm to his and every citizen's interest in proper application of the Constitution and laws, and seeking relief that no more directly and tangibly benefits him than it does the public at large—does not state an Article III case or controversy. For example, in *Fairchild v. Hughes*, 258 U.S. 126, 129–130 (1922), we dismissed a suit challenging the propriety of the process by which the Nineteenth Amendment was ratified. Justice Brandeis wrote for the Court:

> "[This is] not a case within the meaning of . . . Article III. . . . Plaintiff has [asserted] only the right, possessed by every citizen, to require that the Government be administered according to law and that the public moneys be not wasted. Obviously this general right does not entitle a private citizen to institute in the federal courts a suit. . . ."

In *Massachusetts v. Mellon*, 262 U.S. 447 (1923), we dismissed for lack of Article III standing a taxpayer suit challenging the propriety of certain federal expenditures. We said:

> "The party who invokes the power [of judicial review] must be able to show not only that the statute is invalid but that he has sustained or is immediately in danger of sustaining some direct injury as the result of its enforcement, and not merely that he suffers in some indefinite way in common with people generally. . . . Here the parties plaintiff have no such case. . . . [T]heir complaint . . . is merely that officials of the executive department of the government are executing and will execute an act of Congress asserted to be unconstitutional; and this we are asked to prevent. To do so would be not to decide a judicial controversy, but to assume a position of authority over the governmental acts of another and co-equal department, an authority which plainly we do not possess."

In *Ex parte Lévitt*, 302 U.S. 633 (1937), we dismissed a suit contending that Justice Black's appointment to this Court violated the Ineligibility Clause,

Art. I, § 6, cl. 2. "It is an established principle," we said, "that to entitle a private individual to invoke the judicial power to determine the validity of executive or legislative action he must show that he has sustained or is immediately in danger of sustaining a direct injury as the result of that action and it is not sufficient that he has merely a general interest common to all members of the public." 302 U.S. at 634.

More recent cases are to the same effect. In *United States v. Richardson*, 418 U.S. 166 (1974), we dismissed for lack of standing a taxpayer suit challenging the Government's failure to disclose the expenditures of the Central Intelligence Agency, in alleged violation of the constitutional requirement, Art. I, § 9, cl. 7, that "a regular Statement and Account of the Receipts and Expenditures of all public Money shall be published from time to time." We held that such a suit rested upon an impermissible "generalized grievance," and was inconsistent with "the framework of Article III" because "the impact on [plaintiff] is plainly undifferentiated and 'common to all members of the public.' " And in *Schlesinger v. Reservists Comm. to Stop the War*, 418 U.S. 208 (1974), we dismissed for the same reasons a citizen-taxpayer suit contending that it was a violation of the Incompatibility Clause, Art. I, § 6, cl. 2, for Members of Congress to hold commissions in the military Reserves. . . .

To be sure, our generalized-grievance cases have typically involved Government violation of procedures assertedly ordained by the Constitution rather than the Congress. But there is absolutely no basis for making the Article III inquiry turn on the source of the asserted right. Whether the courts were to act on their own, or at the invitation of Congress, in ignoring the concrete injury requirement described in our cases, they would be discarding a principle fundamental the separate and distinct constitutional role of the Third Branch—one of the essential elements that identifies those "Cases" and "Controversies" that are the business of the courts rather than of the political branches. "The province of the court," as Chief Justice Marshall said in *Marbury v. Madison*, 5 U.S. (1 Cranch) 137, 170 (1803), "is, solely, to decide on the rights of individuals." Vindicating the *public* interest (including the public interest in Government observance of the Constitution and laws) is the function of Congress and the Chief Executive. The question presented here is whether the public interest in proper administration of the laws (specifically, in agencies' observance of a particular, statutorily prescribed procedure) can be converted into an individual right by a statute that denominates it as such, and that permits all citizens (or, for that matter, a subclass of citizens who suffer no distinctive concrete harm) to sue. If the concrete injury requirement has the separation-of-powers significance we have always said, the answer must be obvious: To permit Congress to convert the undifferentiated public interest in executive officers' compliance with the law into an "individual right" vindicable in the courts is to permit Congress to transfer from the President to the courts the Chief Executive's most important constitutional duty, to "take Care that the Laws be faithfully executed," Art. II, § 3. It would enable the courts, with the permission of Congress, "to assume a position of authority over the governmental acts of another and co-equal department," *Massachusetts v. Mellon*, 262 U.S. at 489, and to become " 'virtually continuing monitors of the wisdom and soundness of Executive action.' " *Allen, supra,* 468 U.S. at 760. We have always rejected that vision of our role:

> "When Congress passes an Act empowering administrative agencies to carry on governmental activities, the power of those agencies is circumscribed by the authority granted. This permits the courts to participate in law enforcement entrusted to administrative bodies only to the extent necessary to protect justiciable individual rights against administrative action fairly beyond the granted powers. . . . This is very far from assuming that the courts are charged more than administrators or legislators with the protection of the rights of the people. Congress and the Executive supervise the acts of administrative agents. . . . But under Article III, Congress established courts to adjudicate cases and controversies as to claims of infringement of individual rights whether by unlawful action of private persons or by the exertion of unauthorized administrative power." *Stark v. Wickard,* 321 U.S. 288, 309–310 (1944).

"Individual rights," within the meaning of this passage, do not mean public rights that have been legislatively pronounced to belong to each individual who forms part of the public.

Nothing in this contradicts the principle that "[t]he . . . injury required by Art. III may exist solely by virtue of 'statutes creating legal rights, the invasion of which creates standing.' " [*Warth v. Seldin*, 422 U.S. 490, 500 (1975)]. . . . [Prior cases involved] Congress' elevating to the status of legally cognizable injuries concrete, *de facto* injuries that were previously inadequate in law (namely, injury to an individual's personal interest in living in a racially integrated community, and injury to a company's interest in marketing its product free from competition). As we said in *Sierra Club*, "[Statutory] broadening [of] the categories of injury that may be alleged in support of standing is a different matter from abandoning the requirement that the party seeking review must himself have suffered an injury." 405 U.S. at 738. Whether or not the principle set forth in *Warth* can be extended beyond that distinction, it is clear that in suits against the Government, at least, the concrete injury requirement must remain. . . .

We hold that respondents lack standing to bring this action . . . .

JUSTICE KENNEDY, with whom JUSTICE SOUTER joins, concurring in part and concurring in the judgment.

Although I agree with the essential parts of the Court's analysis, I write separately to make several observations.

I agree with the Court's conclusion in Part III-A that, on the record before us, respondents have failed to demonstrate that they themselves are "among the injured." . . .

While it may seem trivial to require that Mses. Kelly and Skilbred acquire airline tickets to the project sites or announce a date certain upon which they will return, this is not a case where it is reasonable to assume that the affiants will be using the sites on a regular basis, nor do the affiants claim to have visited the sites since the projects commenced. . . .

In light of the conclusion that respondents have not demonstrated a concrete injury here sufficient to support standing under our precedents, I would not reach the issue of redressability that is discussed by the plurality in Part III-B.

I also join Part IV of the Court's opinion with the following observations. As Government programs and policies become more complex and far-reaching, we must be sensitive to the articulation of new rights of action that do not have clear analogs in our common-law tradition. Modern litigation has progressed far from the paradigm of Marbury suing Madison to get his commission, *Marbury v. Madison*, 5 U.S. (1 Cranch) 137 (1803), or Ogden seeking an injunction to halt Gibbons' steamboat operations, *Gibbons v. Ogden*, 22 U.S. (9 Wheat.) 1 (1824). In my view, Congress has the power to define injuries and articulate chains of causation that will give rise to a case or controversy where none existed before, and I do not read the Court's opinion to suggest a contrary view. In exercising this power, however, Congress must at the very least identify the injury it seeks to vindicate and relate the injury to the class of persons entitled to bring suit. The citizen-suit provision of the Endangered Species Act does not meet these minimal requirements, because while the statute purports to confer a right on "any person . . . to enjoin . . . the United States and any other governmental instrumentality or agency . . . who is alleged to be in violation of any provision of this chapter," it does not of its own force establish that there is an injury in "any person" by virtue of any "violation." 16 U.S.C. § 1540(g)(1)(A).

The Court's holding that there is an outer limit to the power of Congress to confer rights of action is a direct and necessary consequence of the case and controversy limitations found in Article III. I agree that it would exceed those limitations if, at the behest of Congress and in the absence of any showing of concrete injury, we were to entertain citizen suits to vindicate the public's non-concrete interest in the proper administration of the laws. While it does not matter how many persons have been injured by the challenged action, the party bringing suit must show that the action injures him in a concrete and personal way. This requirement is not just an empty formality. It preserves the vitality of the adversarial process by assuring both that the parties before the court have an actual, as opposed to professed, stake in the outcome, and that "the legal questions presented . . . will be resolved, not in the rarified atmosphere of a debating society, but in a concrete factual context conducive to a realistic appreciation of the consequences of judicial action." *Valley Forge Christian College v. Americans United for Separation of Church and State, Inc.*, 454 U.S. 464, 472 (1982). In addition, the requirement of concrete injury confines the Judicial Branch to its proper, limited role in the constitutional framework of Government.

An independent judiciary is held to account through its open proceedings and its reasoned judgments. In this process it is essential for the public to know what persons or groups are invoking the judicial power, the reasons that they have brought suit, and whether their claims are vindicated or denied. The concrete injury requirement helps assure that there can be an answer to these questions; and, as the Court's opinion is careful to show, that is part of the constitutional design.

With these observations, I concur in Parts I, II, III-A, and IV of the Court's opinion and in the judgment of the Court.

Justice Stevens, concurring in the judgment.

Because I am not persuaded that Congress intended the consultation requirement in § 7(a)(2) of the Endangered Species Act of 1973 (ESA), 16 U.S.C.

§ 1536(a)(2), to apply to activities in foreign countries, I concur in the judgment of reversal. I do not, however, agree with the Court's conclusion that respondents lack standing because the threatened injury to their interest in protecting the environment and studying endangered species is not "imminent." Nor do I agree with the plurality's additional conclusion that respondents' injury is not "redressable" in this litigation.

I

In my opinion a person who has visited the critical habitat of an endangered species has a professional interest in preserving the species and its habitat, and intends to revisit them in the future has standing to challenge agency action that threatens their destruction. Congress has found that a wide variety of endangered species of fish, wildlife, and plants are of "aesthetic, ecological, educational, historical, recreational, and scientific value to the Nation and its people." 16 U.S.C. § 1531(a)(3). Given that finding, we have no license to demean the importance of the interest that particular individuals may have in observing any species or its habitat, whether those individuals are motivated by esthetic enjoyment, an interest in professional research, or an economic interest in preservation of the species. Indeed, this Court has often held that injuries to such interests are sufficient to confer standing, and the Court reiterates that holding today.

The Court nevertheless concludes that respondents have not suffered "injury in fact" because they have not shown that the harm to the endangered species will produce "imminent" injury to them. I disagree. An injury to an individual's interest in studying or enjoying a species and its natural habitat occurs when someone (whether it be the Government or a private party) takes action that harms that species and habitat. In my judgment, therefore, the "imminence" of such an injury should be measured by the timing and likelihood of the threatened environmental harm, rather than—as the Court seems to suggest—by the time that might elapse between the present and the time when the individuals would visit the area if no such injury should occur.

To understand why this approach is correct and consistent with our precedent, it is necessary to consider the purpose of the standing doctrine. Concerned about "the proper—and properly limited—role of the courts in a democratic society," we have long held that "Art. III judicial power exists only to redress or otherwise to protect against injury to the complaining party." *Warth v. Seldin,*

422 U.S. 490, 498–499 (1975). The plaintiff must have a "personal stake in the outcome" sufficient to "assure that concrete adverseness which sharpens the presentation of issues upon which the court so largely depends for illumination of difficult . . . questions." *Baker v. Carr,* 369 U.S. 186, 204 (1962). For that reason, "[a]bstract injury is not enough. . . ."

Consequently, we have denied standing to plaintiffs whose likelihood of suffering any concrete adverse effect from the challenged action was speculative. In this case, however, the likelihood that respondents will be injured by the destruction of the endangered species is not speculative. If respondents are genuinely interested in the preservation of the endangered species and intend to study or observe these animals in the future, their injury will occur as soon as the animals are destroyed. Thus the only potential source of "speculation" in this case is whether respondents' intent to study or observe the animals is genuine. In my view, Joyce Kelly and Amy Skilbred have introduced sufficient evidence to negate petitioner's contention that their claims of injury are "speculative" or "conjectural." As JUSTICE BLACKMUN explains, a reasonable finder of fact could conclude, from their past visits, their professional backgrounds, and their affidavits and deposition testimony, that Ms. Kelly and Ms. Skilbred will return to the project sites and, consequently, will be injured by the destruction of the endangered species and critical habitat.

The plurality also concludes that respondents' injuries are not redressable in this litigation for two reasons. First, . . . even if respondents succeed and a new regulation is promulgated, there is no guarantee that federal agencies that are not parties to this case will actually consult with the Secretary. Furthermore, the plurality continues, respondents have not demonstrated that federal agencies can influence the behavior of the foreign governments where the affected projects are located. Thus, even if the agencies consult with the Secretary and terminate funding for foreign projects, the foreign governments might nonetheless pursue the projects and jeopardize the endangered species. Neither of these reasons is persuasive.

We must presume that if this Court holds that § 7(a)(2) requires consultation, all affected agencies would abide by that interpretation and engage in the requisite consultations. Certainly the Executive Branch cannot be heard to argue that an authoritative construction of the governing statute by this Court may simply be ignored by any agency head. Moreover, if Congress has required consultation between agencies, we must presume that such consultation will have a serious purpose that is likely to produce tangible results. As JUSTICE BLACKMUN explains, it is not mere speculation to think that foreign governments, when faced with the threatened withdrawal of United States assistance, will modify their projects to mitigate the harm to endangered species.

II

Although I believe that respondents have standing, I nevertheless concur in the judgment of reversal because I am persuaded that the Government is correct in its submission that § 7(a)(2) does not apply to activities in foreign countries. As with all questions of statutory construction, the question whether a statute applies extraterritorially is one of congressional intent. . . .

Nothing in this text indicates that the section applies in foreign countries. Indeed, the only geographic reference in the section is in the "critical habitat" clause, which mentions "affected States." . . .

The lack of an express indication that the consultation requirement applies extraterritorially is particularly significant because other sections of the ESA expressly deal with the problem of protecting endangered species abroad. . . .

In short, a reading of the entire statute persuades me that Congress did not intend the consultation requirement in § 7(a)(2) to apply to activities in foreign countries. Accordingly, notwithstanding my disagreement with the Court's disposition of the standing question, I concur in its judgment.

JUSTICE BLACKMUN, with whom JUSTICE O'CONNOR joins, dissenting.

I part company with the Court in this case in two respects. First, I believe that respondents have raised genuine issues of fact—sufficient to survive summary judgment—both as to injury and as to redressability. Second, I question the Court's breadth of language in rejecting standing for "procedural" injuries. I fear the Court seeks to impose fresh limitations on the constitutional authority of Congress to allow citizen suits in the federal courts for injuries deemed "procedural" in nature. I dissent.

I

Article III of the Constitution confines the federal courts to adjudication of actual "Cases" and "Controversies." To ensure the presence of a "case" or "controversy," this Court has held that Article III requires, as an irreducible minimum, that a plaintiff allege (1) an injury that is (2) "fairly traceable to the defendant's allegedly unlawful conduct" and that is (3) "likely to be redressed by the requested relief." *Allen v. Wright*, 468 U.S. 737, 751 (1984).

A

To survive petitioner's motion for summary judgment on standing, respondents need not prove that they are actually or imminently harmed. They need show only a "genuine issue" of material fact as to standing. Fed. Rule Civ. Proc. 56(c). This is not a heavy burden. A "genuine issue" exists so long as "the evidence is such that a reasonable jury could return a verdict for the nonmoving party [respondents]." . . .

I think a reasonable finder of fact could conclude from the information in the affidavits and deposition testimony that either Kelly or Skilbred will soon return to the project sites, thereby satisfying the "actual or imminent" injury standard. The Court dismisses Kelly's and Skilbred's general statements that they intended to revisit the project sites as "simply not enough." But those statements did not stand alone. A reasonable finder of fact could conclude, based not only upon their statements of intent to return, but upon their past visits to the project sites, as well as their professional backgrounds, that it was likely that Kelly and Skilbred would make a return trip to the project areas. . . .

No substantial barriers prevent Kelly or Skilbred from simply purchasing plane tickets to return to the Aswan and Mahaweli projects. This case differs from other cases in which the imminence of harm turned largely on the affirmative actions of third parties beyond a plaintiff's control. . . .

I fear the Court's demand for detailed descriptions of future conduct will do little to weed out those who are genuinely harmed from those who are not. More likely, it will resurrect a code-pleading formalism in federal court summary judgment practice, as federal courts, newly doubting their jurisdiction, will demand more and more particularized showings of future harm. . . .

The Court also concludes that injury is lacking, because respondents' allegations of "ecosystem nexus" failed to demonstrate sufficient proximity to the site of the environmental harm. To support that conclusion, the Court mischaracterizes our decision in *Lujan v. National Wildlife Federation*, 497 U.S. 871 (1990), as establishing a general rule that "a plaintiff claiming injury from environmental damage must use the area affected by the challenged activity." In *National Wildlife Federation*, the Court required specific geographical proximity because of the particular type of harm alleged in that case: harm to the plaintiff's visual enjoyment of nature from mining activities. 497 U.S. at 888. One cannot suffer from the sight of a ruined landscape without being close enough to see the sites actually being mined. Many environmental injuries, however, cause harm distant from the area immediately affected by the challenged action. Environmental destruction may affect animals traveling over vast geographical ranges, or rivers running long geographical courses. It cannot seriously be contended that a litigant's failure to use the precise or exact site where animals are slaughtered or where toxic waste is dumped into a river means he or she cannot show injury.

The Court also rejects respondents' claim of vocational or professional injury. The Court says that it is "beyond all reason" that a zoo "keeper" of Asian elephants would have standing to contest his Government's participation in the eradication of all the Asian elephants in another part of the world. I am unable to see how the distant location of the destruction *necessarily* (for purposes of ruling at summary judgment) mitigates the harm to the elephant keeper. If there is no more access to a future supply of the animal that sustains a keeper's livelihood, surely there is harm.

I have difficulty imagining this Court applying its rigid principles of geographic formalism anywhere outside the context of environmental claims. As I understand it, environmental plaintiffs are under no special constitutional standing disabilities. Like other plaintiffs, they need show only that the action they challenge has injured them, without necessarily showing they happened to be physically near the location of the alleged wrong. . . .

B

A plurality of the Court suggests that respondents have not demonstrated redressability: a likelihood that a court ruling in their favor would remedy their injury. The plurality identifies two obstacles. The first is that the "action agencies" (*e.g.*, AID) cannot be required to undertake consultation with petitioner Secretary, because they are not directly bound as parties to the suit and are otherwise not indirectly bound by being subject to petitioner Secretary's regulation. Petitioner, however, officially and publicly has taken the position that his regulations regarding consultation under § 7 of the Act are binding on action agencies. . . .

Emphasizing that none of the action agencies are parties to this suit (and having rejected the possibility of their being indirectly bound by petitioner's regulation), the plurality concludes that "there is no reason they should be obliged to honor an incidental legal determination the suit produced." I am not as willing as the plurality is to assume that agencies at least will not try to follow the law. . . .

The second redressability obstacle relied on by the plurality is that "the [action] agencies generally supply only a fraction of the funding for a foreign project." What this Court might "generally" take to be true does not eliminate the existence of a genuine issue of fact to withstand summary judgment. Even if the action agencies supply only a fraction of the funding for a particular foreign project, it remains at least a question for the finder of fact whether threatened withdrawal of that fraction would affect foreign government conduct sufficiently to avoid harm to listed species.

The plurality states that "AID, for example, has provided less than 10% of the funding for the Mahaweli project." The plurality neglects to mention that this "fraction" amounts to $170 million, not so paltry a sum for a country of only 16 million people with a gross national product of less than $6 billion in 1986 when respondents filed the complaint in this action. Federal Research Division, Library of Congress, Sri Lanka: A Country Study (Area Handbook Series) xvi-xvii (1990). . . .

I do not share the plurality's astonishing confidence that, on the record here, a factfinder could only conclude that AID was powerless to ensure the protection of listed species at the Mahaweli project. . . .

II

The Court concludes that any "procedural injury" suffered by respondents is insufficient to confer standing. It rejects the view that the "injury-in-fact requirement [is] satisfied by congressional conferral upon *all* persons of an abstract, self-contained, noninstrumental 'right' to have the Executive observe the procedures required by law." . . .

The Court expresses concern that allowing judicial enforcement of "agencies' observance of a particular, statutorily prescribed procedure" would "transfer from the President to the courts the Chief Executive's most important constitutional duty, to 'take Care that the Laws be faithfully executed,' Art. II, § 3." In fact, the principal effect of foreclosing judicial enforcement of such procedures is to transfer power into the hands of the Executive at the expense—not of the courts—but of Congress, from which that power originates and emanates.

Under the Court's anachronistically formal view of the separation of powers, Congress legislates pure, substantive mandates and has no business structuring the procedural manner in which the Executive implements these mandates. To be sure, in the ordinary course, Congress does legislate in black-and-white terms of affirmative commands or negative prohibitions on the conduct of officers of the Executive Branch. In complex regulatory areas, however, Congress often legislates, as it were, in procedural shades of gray. That is, it sets forth substantive policy goals and provides for their attainment by requiring Executive Branch officials to follow certain procedures, for example, in the form of reporting, consultation, and certification requirements. . . .

Just as Congress does not violate separation of powers by structuring the procedural manner in which the Executive shall carry out the laws, surely the federal courts do not violate separation of powers when, at the very instruction and command of Congress, they enforce these procedures.

To prevent Congress from conferring standing for "procedural injuries" is another way of saying that Congress may not delegate to the courts authority deemed "executive" in nature. Here Congress seeks not to delegate "executive" power but only to strengthen the procedures it has legislatively mandated. . . .

I dissent.

NOTES AND QUESTIONS

1. Summary. Article III standing has three requirements: (1) there must be an injury-in-fact, or an imminent injury, that is concrete and not hypothetical; (2) the injury must be caused by, or "fairly traceable" to, the defendant's conduct; and (3) it must be "likely" that the court will be able to redress the injury. In *Defenders of Wildlife*, the Justices addressed only the first and the third prongs. Note that there is substantial overlap between the causation requirement and redressability. If the defendant's action isn't the cause of the injury, then surely there is nothing for the court to redress. The interaction between these two factors is discussed in the next case.

2. *The standard of review.* The majority and dissent disagree over the standard of review. The majority decides for itself whether the plaintiffs have alleged sufficient injury. The majority agrees that the analysis depends on "the manner and degree of evidence required at the successive stages of the litigation," and that at summary judgment "the plaintiff can no longer rest on such 'mere allegations,' but must 'set forth' by affidavit or other evidence 'specific facts,' Fed. Rule Civ. Proc. 56(e), which for purposes of the summary judgment motion will be taken to be true." The dissent, in contrast, argues that the Court should simply ask whether there is a genuine issue of material fact as to their injury, i.e., whether a reasonably jury could find that there is sufficient injury. The dissent's notion seems to be that a court can proceed to the merits, and if a trial shows no injury, dismiss the action at that time. With which approach do you agree? Would you apply that approach not just to injury, but also redressability? That is, redressability must be "likely." Is it up for the Court to decide whether it can in fact likely redress the injury on the facts averred, or is the question whether "a reasonable jury" could conclude that it's likely? Doesn't it actually have to *be* likely, if the court is to entertain the action in the first place?

3. *What's the point of standing?* What is the reason standing requires concrete injuries, and precludes citizens from suing for a generalized grievance? A majority of six Justices argued that allowing suits for generalized grievances would put the courts in a position of supervision over the general administration of the laws, contrary not just to Article III but also to Article II. Do you agree? Do you find Justice Blackmun's response on this point persuasive? Justice Blackmun seemed to suggest that the majority was holding that Congress couldn't structure the procedures by which the Executive administers the law. But of course, as you all know, Congress does that routinely. The Administrative Procedure Act is precisely such a statute. And Congress could always legislate as specifically as it wants, cabining executive discretion. Was the majority really casting doubt on these general principles, or did it have some other point?

4. *Citizen-suit provisions as causes of action.* What do you make of the Court's discussion of Congress's ability to create, or not to create, citizen suits? You already know enough to answer: it has to do with causes of action. Although the Court does not speak in terms of causes of action (it speaks rather confusingly about "procedural injury"), isn't it accurate to say that the citizen-suit provision in the Endangered Species Act creates a *cause of action* for anyone to sue? But, as previously explained, not everyone can actually deploy a cause of action. To sue, one still must have Article III standing. Although the Supreme Court today does not seem to understand citizen-suit provisions as causes of action (everything is rather muddled after *Data Processing*), elsewhere the Supreme Court has connected these citizen-suit provisions to "statutory standing," which effectively is about causes of action. In *Bennett v. Spear*, addressed elsewhere in this chapter in the context of finality, the Supreme Court explained that citizen-suit provisions negate the "zone of interests" test—in other words, such provisions effectively say

> **Defined Term**
>
> **STANDING (REVISITED):** We can now further refine our understanding of standing. Sometimes Congress creates a cause of action—"statutory standing," if you will—but the plaintiff will not have a sufficient injury for constitutional standing, and thus the lawsuit would still be precluded.

that everyone is within the zone protected by the statute. 520 U.S. 154, 164–65 (1997). The best way to think about citizen-suit provisions, then, is that they provide a cause of action such that the zone-of-interests test is met. That does not mean, however, that the constitutional standing requirements have been met.

Massachusetts v. EPA

549 U.S. 497 (2007)

JUSTICE STEVENS delivered the opinion of the Court.

[The facts of Massachusetts v. EPA are recounted starting on p. 410, supra. In a nutshell, the EPA was presented with a petition by Massachusetts, among others, requesting that the EPA regulate carbon dioxide under the Clean Air Act so as to help combat global warming. In the following excerpts, the majority and dissent debate the issue of standing.—Ed.]

* * *

IV

Article III of the Constitution limits federal-court jurisdiction to "Cases" and "Controversies." Those two words confine "the business of federal courts to questions presented in an adversary context and in a form historically viewed as capable of resolution through the judicial process." *Flast v. Cohen*, 392 U.S.

83, 95 (1968). It is therefore familiar learning that no justiciable "controversy" exists when parties seek adjudication of a political question, *Luther v. Borden,* 7 How. 1 (1849), when they ask for an advisory opinion, *Hayburn's Case,* 2 Dall. 409 (1792), or when the question sought to be adjudicated has been mooted by subsequent developments, *California v. San Pablo & Tulare R. Co.,* 149 U.S. 308 (1893). This case suffers from none of these defects.

The parties' dispute turns on the proper construction of a congressional statute, a question eminently suitable to resolution in federal court. Congress has moreover authorized this type of challenge to EPA action. See 42 U.S.C. § 7607(b)(1). That authorization is of critical importance to the standing inquiry: "Congress has the power to define injuries and articulate chains of causation that will give rise to a case or controversy where none existed before." *Lujan,* 504 U.S. at 580 (Kennedy, J., concurring in part and concurring in judgment). "In exercising this power, however, Congress must at the very least identify the injury it seeks to vindicate and relate the injury to the class of persons entitled to bring suit." *Ibid.* We will not, therefore, "entertain citizen suits to vindicate the public's nonconcrete interest in the proper administration of the laws." *Id.* at 581.

EPA maintains that because greenhouse gas emissions inflict widespread harm, the doctrine of standing presents an insuperable jurisdictional obstacle. We do not agree. At bottom, "the gist of the question of standing" is whether petitioners have "such a personal stake in the outcome of the controversy as to assure that concrete adverseness which sharpens the presentation of issues upon which the court so largely depends for illumination." *Baker v. Carr,* 369 U.S. 186, 204 (1962). . . .

To ensure the proper adversarial presentation, *Lujan* holds that a litigant must demonstrate that it has suffered a concrete and particularized injury that is either actual or imminent, that the injury is fairly traceable to the defendant, and that it is likely that a favorable decision will redress that injury. However, a litigant to whom Congress has "accorded a procedural right to protect his concrete interests"—here, the right to challenge agency action unlawfully withheld, § 7607(b)(1)—"can assert that right without meeting all the normal standards for redressability and immediacy." When a litigant is vested with a procedural right, that litigant has standing if there is some possibility that the requested relief will prompt the injury-causing party to reconsider the decision that allegedly harmed the litigant.

Only one of the petitioners needs to have standing to permit us to consider the petition for review. We stress here, as did Judge Tatel below, the special position and interest of Massachusetts. It is of considerable relevance that the party seeking review here is a sovereign State and not, as it was in *Lujan*, a private individual.

Well before the creation of the modern administrative state, we recognized that States are not normal litigants for the purposes of invoking federal jurisdiction. As Justice Holmes explained in *Georgia v. Tennessee Copper Co.*, 206 U.S. 230, 237 (1907), a case in which Georgia sought to protect its citizens from air pollution originating outside its borders: ". . . . [T]he State has an interest independent of and behind the titles of its citizens, in all the earth and air within its domain. It has the last word as to whether its mountains shall be stripped of their forests and its inhabitants shall breathe pure air."

Just as Georgia's independent interest "in all the earth and air within its domain" supported federal jurisdiction a century ago, so too does Massachusetts' well-founded desire to preserve its sovereign territory today. That Massachusetts does in fact own a great deal of the "territory alleged to be affected" only reinforces the conclusion that its stake in the outcome of this case is sufficiently concrete to warrant the exercise of federal judicial power.

When a State enters the Union, it surrenders certain sovereign prerogatives. Massachusetts cannot invade Rhode Island to force reductions in greenhouse gas emissions, it cannot negotiate an emissions treaty with China or India, and in some circumstances the exercise of its police powers to reduce in-state motor-vehicle emissions might well be pre-empted.

These sovereign prerogatives are now lodged in the Federal Government, and Congress has ordered EPA to protect Massachusetts (among others) by prescribing standards applicable to the "emission of any air pollutant from any class or classes of new motor vehicle engines, which in [the Administrator's] judgment cause, or contribute to, air pollution which may reasonably be anticipated to endanger public health or welfare." 42 U.S.C. § 7521(a)(1). Congress has moreover recognized a concomitant procedural right to challenge the rejection of its rulemaking petition as arbitrary and capricious. § 7607(b)(1). Given that procedural right and Massachusetts' stake in protecting its quasi-sovereign interests, the Commonwealth is entitled to special solicitude in our standing analysis.

With that in mind, it is clear that petitioners' submissions as they pertain to Massachusetts have satisfied the most demanding standards of the adversarial process. EPA's steadfast refusal to regulate greenhouse gas emissions presents a risk of harm to Massachusetts that is both "actual" and "imminent." *Lujan*, 504 U.S. at 560. There is, moreover, a "substantial likelihood that the judicial relief requested" will prompt EPA to take steps to reduce that risk.

The Injury

The harms associated with climate change are serious and well recognized. Indeed, the NRC Report itself—which EPA regards as an "objective and independent assessment of the relevant science"—identifies a number of environmental changes that have already inflicted significant harms, including "the global retreat of mountain glaciers, reduction in snow-cover extent, the earlier spring melting of ice on rivers and lakes, [and] the accelerated rate of rise of sea levels during the 20th century relative to the past few thousand years."

Petitioners allege that this only hints at the environmental damage yet to come. According to the climate scientist Michael MacCracken, "qualified scientific experts involved in climate change research" have reached a "strong consensus" that global warming threatens (among other things) a precipitate rise in sea levels by the end of the century, MacCracken Decl. ¶ 5, "severe and irreversible changes to natural ecosystems," ¶ 5(d), a "significant reduction in water storage in winter snowpack in mountainous regions with direct and important economic consequences," *ibid.*, and an increase in the spread of disease, ¶ 28. He also observes that rising ocean temperatures may contribute to the ferocity of hurricanes. ¶¶ 23–25.

That these climate-change risks are "widely shared" does not minimize Massachusetts' interest in the outcome of this litigation. See *Federal Election Comm'n v. Akins*, 524 U.S. 11, 24 (1998) ("[W]here a harm is concrete, though widely shared, the Court has found 'injury in fact' "). According to petitioners' unchallenged affidavits, global sea levels rose somewhere between 10 and 20 centimeters over the 20th century as a result of global warming. These rising seas have already begun to swallow Massachusetts' coastal land. Because the Commonwealth "owns a substantial portion of the state's coastal property," it has alleged a particularized injury in its capacity as a landowner. The severity of that injury will only increase over the course of the next century: If sea levels continue to rise as predicted, one Massachusetts official believes that a significant fraction of coastal property will be "either permanently lost through inundation or temporarily lost through periodic storm surge and flooding events." Remediation costs alone, petitioners allege, could run well into the hundreds of millions of dollars.

Causation

EPA does not dispute the existence of a causal connection between man-made greenhouse gas emissions and global warming. At a minimum, therefore, EPA's refusal to regulate such emissions "contributes" to Massachusetts' injuries.

EPA nevertheless maintains that its decision not to regulate greenhouse gas emissions from new motor vehicles contributes so insignificantly to petitioners' injuries that the Agency cannot be haled into federal court to answer for them. For the same reason, EPA does not believe that any realistic possibility exists that the relief petitioners seek would mitigate global climate change and remedy their injuries. That is especially so because predicted increases in greenhouse gas emissions from developing nations, particularly China and India, are likely to offset any marginal domestic decrease.

But EPA overstates its case. Its argument rests on the erroneous assumption that a small incremental step, because it is incremental, can never be attacked in a federal judicial forum. Yet accepting that premise would doom most challenges to regulatory action. Agencies, like legislatures, do not generally resolve massive problems in one fell regulatory swoop. They instead whittle away at them over time, refining their preferred approach as circumstances change and as they develop a more nuanced understanding of how best to proceed. That a first step might be tentative does not by itself support the notion that federal courts lack jurisdiction to determine whether that step conforms to law.

And reducing domestic automobile emissions is hardly a tentative step. Even leaving aside the other greenhouse gases, the United States transportation sector emits an enormous quantity of carbon dioxide into the atmosphere—according to the MacCracken affidavit, more than 1.7 billion metric tons in 1999 alone. That accounts for more than 6% of worldwide carbon dioxide emissions. To put this in perspective: Considering just emissions from the transportation sector, which represent less than one-third of this country's total carbon dioxide emissions, the United States would still rank as the third-largest emitter of carbon dioxide in the world, outpaced only by the European Union and China. Judged by any standard, U.S. motor-vehicle emissions make a meaningful contribution to greenhouse gas concentrations and hence, according to petitioners, to global warming.

The Remedy

While it may be true that regulating motor-vehicle emissions will not by itself *reverse* global warming, it by no means follows that we lack jurisdiction to decide whether EPA has a duty to take steps to *slow* or *reduce* it. Because of the enormity of the potential consequences associated with manmade climate change, the fact that the effectiveness of a remedy might be delayed during the (relatively short) time it takes for a new motor-vehicle fleet to replace an older one is essentially irrelevant. Nor is it dispositive that developing countries such as China and India are poised to increase greenhouse gas emissions substantially over the next century: A reduction in domestic emissions would slow the pace of global emissions increases, no matter what happens elsewhere. . . .

In sum—at least according to petitioners' uncontested affidavits—the rise in sea levels associated with global warming has already harmed and will continue to harm Massachusetts. The risk of catastrophic harm, though remote, is nevertheless real. That risk would be reduced to some extent if petitioners received the relief they seek. We therefore hold that petitioners have standing to challenge EPA's denial of their rulemaking petition. . . .

Chief Justice Roberts, with whom Justice Scalia, Justice Thomas, and Justice Alito join, dissenting.

Global warming may be a "crisis," even "the most pressing environmental problem of our time." Indeed, it may ultimately affect nearly everyone on the planet in some potentially adverse way, and it may be that governments have done too little to address it. It is not a problem, however, that has escaped the attention of policymakers in the Executive and Legislative Branches of our Government, who continue to consider regulatory, legislative, and treaty-based means of addressing global climate change.

Apparently dissatisfied with the pace of progress on this issue in the elected branches, petitioners have come to the courts claiming broad-ranging injury, and attempting to tie that injury to the Government's alleged failure to comply with a rather narrow statutory provision. I would reject these challenges as nonjusticiable. Such a conclusion involves no judgment on whether global warming exists, what causes it, or the extent of the problem. Nor does it render petitioners without recourse. This Court's standing jurisprudence simply recognizes that redress of grievances of the sort at issue here "is the function of Congress and the Chief Executive," not the federal courts. *Lujan v. Defenders of Wildlife*, 504 U.S. 555, 576 (1992). I would vacate the judgment below and remand for dismissal of the petitions for review.

I

Article III, § 2, of the Constitution limits the federal judicial power to the adjudication of "Cases" and "Controversies." . . .

Our modern framework for addressing standing is familiar: "A plaintiff must allege personal injury fairly traceable to the defendant's allegedly unlawful conduct and likely to be redressed by the requested relief." Applying that standard here, petitioners bear the burden of alleging an injury that is fairly traceable to the Environmental Protection Agency's failure to promulgate new motor vehicle greenhouse gas emission standards, and that is likely to be redressed by the prospective issuance of such standards.

Before determining whether petitioners can meet this familiar test, however, the Court changes the rules. It asserts that "States are not normal litigants for the purposes of invoking federal jurisdiction," and that given "Massachusetts' stake in protecting its quasi-sovereign interests, the Commonwealth is entitled to *special solicitude* in our standing analysis."

Relaxing Article III standing requirements because asserted injuries are pressed by a State, however, has no basis in our jurisprudence, and support for any such "special solicitude" is conspicuously absent from the Court's opinion. . . .

Nor does the case law cited by the Court provide any support for the notion that Article III somehow implicitly treats public and private litigants differently. The Court has to go back a full century in an attempt to justify its novel standing rule, but even there it comes up short. The Court's analysis hinges on *Georgia v. Tennessee Copper Co.*, 206 U.S. 230 (1907)—a case that did indeed draw a distinction between a State and private litigants, but solely with respect to available remedies. The case had nothing to do with Article III standing. . . .

There was certainly no suggestion that the State could show standing where the private parties could not . . . . Nothing about a State's ability to sue in that capacity dilutes the bedrock requirement of showing injury, causation, and redressability to satisfy Article III. . . .

Just as an association suing on behalf of its members must show not only that it represents the members but that at least one satisfies Article III requirements, so too a State asserting quasi-sovereign interests as *parens patriae* must still show that its citizens satisfy Article III. Focusing on Massachusetts's interests as quasi-sovereign makes the required showing here harder, not easier. The Court, in effect, takes what has always been regarded as a *necessary* condition for *parens patriae* standing—a quasi-sovereign interest—and converts it into a *sufficient* showing for purposes of Article III. . . .

On top of everything else, the Court overlooks the fact that our cases cast significant doubt on a State's standing to assert a quasi-sovereign interest—as opposed to a direct injury—against the Federal Government. As a general rule, we have held that while a State might assert a quasi-sovereign right as *parens patriae* "for the protection of its citizens, it is no part of its duty or power to enforce their rights in respect of their relations with the Federal Government. In that field it is the United States, and not the State, which represents them." *Massachusetts v. Mellon,* 262 U.S. 447, 485–486 (1923).

All of this presumably explains why petitioners never cited *Tennessee Copper* in their briefs before this Court or the D.C. Circuit. It presumably explains why not one of the legion of *amici* supporting petitioners ever cited the case. And it presumably explains why not one of the three judges writing below ever cited the case either. . . .

II

It is not at all clear how the Court's "special solicitude" for Massachusetts plays out in the standing analysis, except as an implicit concession that petitioners cannot establish standing on traditional terms. But the status of Massachusetts as a State cannot compensate for petitioners' failure to demonstrate injury in fact, causation, and redressability.

When the Court actually applies the three-part test, it focuses . . . on the Commonwealth's asserted loss of coastal land as the injury in fact. If petitioners rely on loss of land as the Article III injury, however, they must ground the rest of the standing analysis in that specific injury. That alleged injury must be "concrete and particularized," "distinct and palpable." Central to this concept of "particularized" injury is the requirement that a plaintiff be affected in a "personal and individual way," *Defenders of Wildlife*, 504 U.S. at 560, n. 1, and seek relief that "directly and tangibly benefits him" in a manner distinct from its impact on "the public at large," *id.* at 573–574. . . .

The very concept of global warming seems inconsistent with this particularization requirement. Global warming is a phenomenon "harmful to humanity at large," and the redress petitioners seek is focused no more on them than on the public generally—it is literally to change the atmosphere around the world.

If petitioners' particularized injury is loss of coastal land, it is also that injury that must be "actual or imminent, not conjectural or hypothetical," "real and immediate," and "certainly impending."

As to "actual" injury, the Court observes that "global sea levels rose somewhere between 10 and 20 centimeters over the 20th century as a result of global warming" and that "[t]hese rising seas have already begun to swallow Massachusetts' coastal land." But none of petitioners' declarations supports that connection. One declaration states that "a rise in sea level due to climate change is occurring on the coast of Massachusetts, in the metropolitan Boston area," but there is no elaboration. And the declarant goes on to identify a "significan[t]" *non*-global-warming cause of Boston's rising sea level: land subsidence. Thus, aside from a single conclusory statement, there is nothing in petitioners' 43 standing declarations and accompanying exhibits to support an inference of actual loss of Massachusetts coastal land from 20th-century global sea level increases. It is pure conjecture.

The Court's attempts to identify "imminent" or "certainly impending" loss of Massachusetts coastal land fares no better. One of petitioners' declarants predicts global warming will cause sea level to rise by 20 to 70 centimeters *by the year 2100*. Another uses a computer modeling program to map the Commonwealth's coastal land and its current elevation, and calculates that the high-end estimate of sea level rise would result in the loss of significant state-owned coastal land. But the computer modeling program has a conceded average error of about 30 centimeters and a maximum observed error of 70 centimeters. As an initial matter, if it is possible that the model underrepresents the elevation of coastal land to an extent equal to or in excess of the projected sea level rise, it is difficult to put much stock in the predicted loss of land. But even placing that problem to the side, accepting a century-long time horizon and a series of compounded estimates renders requirements of imminence and immediacy utterly toothless. . . .

III

Petitioners' reliance on Massachusetts's loss of coastal land as their injury in fact for standing purposes creates insurmountable problems for them with respect to causation and redressability. To establish standing, petitioners must show a causal connection between that specific injury and the lack of new motor vehicle greenhouse gas emission standards, and that the promulgation of such standards would likely redress that injury. As is often the case, the questions of causation and redressability overlap. And importantly, when a party is challenging the Government's allegedly unlawful regulation, or lack of regulation, of a third party, satisfying the causation and redressability requirements becomes "substantially more difficult." *Defenders of Wildlife*, 504 U.S. at 562.

Petitioners view the relationship between their injuries and EPA's failure to promulgate new motor vehicle greenhouse gas emission standards as simple and direct: Domestic motor vehicles emit carbon dioxide and other greenhouse gases. Worldwide emissions of greenhouse gases contribute to global warming and therefore also to petitioners' alleged injuries. Without the new vehicle standards, greenhouse gas emissions—and therefore global warming and its attendant harms—have been higher than they otherwise would have been; once EPA changes course, the trend will be reversed.

The Court ignores the complexities of global warming, and does so by now disregarding the "particularized" injury it relied on in step one, and using the dire nature of global warming itself as a bootstrap for finding causation and redressability. First, it is important to recognize the extent of the emissions at issue here. Because local greenhouse gas emissions disperse throughout the atmosphere and remain there for anywhere from 50 to 200 years, it is global emissions data that are relevant. According to one of petitioners' declarations, domestic motor vehicles contribute about 6 percent of global carbon dioxide emissions and 4 percent of global greenhouse gas emissions. The amount of global emissions at issue here is smaller still; § 202(a)(1) of the Clean Air Act covers only *new* motor vehicles and *new* motor vehicle engines, so petitioners' desired emission standards might reduce only a fraction of 4 percent of global emissions.

This gets us only to the relevant greenhouse gas emissions; linking them to global warming and ultimately to petitioners' alleged injuries next requires consideration of further complexities. As EPA explained in its denial of petitioners' request for rulemaking,

"predicting future climate change necessarily involves a complex web of economic and physical factors including: our ability to predict future global anthropogenic emissions of [greenhouse gases] and aerosols; the fate of these emissions once they enter the atmosphere (e.g., what percentage are absorbed by vegetation or are taken up by the oceans); the impact of those emissions that remain in the atmosphere on the radiative properties of the atmosphere; changes in critically important climate feedbacks (e.g., changes in cloud cover and ocean circulation); changes in temperature characteristics (e.g., average temperatures, shifts in daytime and evening temperatures); changes in other climatic parameters (e.g., shifts in precipitation, storms); and ultimately the impact of such changes on human health and welfare (e.g., increases or decreases in agricultural productivity, human health impacts)."

Petitioners are never able to trace their alleged injuries back through this complex web to the fractional amount of global emissions that might have been limited with EPA standards. In light of the bit-part domestic new motor vehicle greenhouse gas emissions have played in what petitioners describe as a 150-year global phenomenon, and the myriad additional factors bearing on petitioners' alleged injury—the loss of Massachusetts coastal land—the connection is far too speculative to establish causation.

IV

Redressability is even more problematic. To the tenuous link between petitioners' alleged injury and the indeterminate fractional domestic emissions at issue here, add the fact that petitioners cannot meaningfully predict what will come of the 80 percent of global greenhouse gas emissions that originate outside the United States. As the Court acknowledges, "developing countries such as China and India are poised to increase greenhouse gas emissions substantially over the next century," so the domestic emissions at issue here may become an increasingly marginal portion of global emissions, and any decreases produced by petitioners' desired standards are likely to be overwhelmed many times over by emissions increases elsewhere in the world.

Petitioners offer declarations attempting to address this uncertainty, contending that "[i]f the U.S. takes steps to reduce motor vehicle emissions, other countries are very likely to take similar actions regarding their own motor vehicles using technology developed in response to the U.S. program." . . . The Court previously has explained that when the existence of an element of standing "depends on the unfettered choices made by independent actors not before the courts and whose exercise of broad and legitimate discretion the courts cannot presume either to control or to predict," a party must present facts supporting an assertion that the actor will proceed in such a manner. *Defenders of Wildlife,* 504 U.S. at 562. The declarations' conclusory (not to say fanciful) statements do not even come close.

No matter, the Court reasons, because *any* decrease in domestic emissions will "slow the pace of global emissions increases, no matter what happens elsewhere." Every little bit helps, so Massachusetts can sue over any little bit.

The Court's sleight of hand is in failing to link up the different elements of the three-part standing test. What must be *likely* to be redressed is the particular injury in fact. The injury the Court looks to is the asserted loss of land. The Court contends that regulating domestic motor vehicle emissions will reduce carbon dioxide in the atmosphere, *and therefore* redress Massachusetts's injury. But even if regulation *does* reduce emissions—to some indeterminate degree, given events elsewhere in the world—the Court never explains why that makes it *likely* that the injury in fact—the loss of land—will be redressed. Schoolchildren know that a kingdom might be lost "all for the want of a horseshoe nail," but "likely" redressability is a different matter. The realities make it pure conjecture to suppose that EPA regulation of new automobile emissions will *likely* prevent the loss of Massachusetts coastal land.

V

Petitioners' difficulty in demonstrating causation and redressability is not surprising given the evident mismatch between the source of their alleged injury—catastrophic global warming—and the narrow subject matter of the Clean Air Act provision at issue in this suit. The mismatch suggests that petitioners' true goal for this litigation may be more symbolic than anything else.

The constitutional role of the courts, however, is to decide concrete cases—not to serve as a convenient forum for policy debates.

When dealing with legal doctrine phrased in terms of what is "fairly" traceable or "likely" to be redressed, it is perhaps not surprising that the matter is subject to some debate. But in considering how loosely or rigorously to define those adverbs, it is vital to keep in mind the purpose of the inquiry. The limitation of the judicial power to cases and controversies "is crucial in maintaining the tripartite allocation of power set forth in the Constitution." *DaimlerChrysler*, 547 U.S. at 341. In my view, the Court today—addressing Article III's "core component of standing," *Defenders of Wildlife, supra*, at 560—fails to take this limitation seriously. . . .

To be fair, it is not the first time the Court has done so. Today's decision recalls the previous high-water mark of diluted standing requirements, *United States v. Students Challenging Regulatory Agency Procedures (SCRAP)*, 412 U.S. 669 (1973). . . . In SCRAP, the Court based an environmental group's standing to challenge a railroad freight rate surcharge on the group's allegation that increases in railroad rates would cause an increase in the use of nonrecyclable goods, resulting in the increased need for natural resources to produce such goods. According to the group, some of these resources might be taken from the Washington area, resulting in increased refuse that might find its way into area parks, harming the group's members.

Over time, *SCRAP* became emblematic not of the looseness of Article III standing requirements, but of how utterly manipulable they are if not taken seriously as a matter of judicial self-restraint. *SCRAP* made standing seem a lawyer's game, rather than a fundamental limitation ensuring that courts function as courts and not intrude on the politically accountable branches. Today's decision is *SCRAP* for a new generation.

Perhaps the Court recognizes as much. How else to explain its need to devise a new doctrine of state standing to support its result? The good news is that the Court's "special solicitude" for Massachusetts limits the future applicability of the diluted standing requirements applied in this case. The bad news is that the Court's self-professed relaxation of those Article III requirements has caused us to transgress "the proper—and properly limited—role of the courts in a democratic society."

I respectfully dissent.

NOTES AND QUESTIONS

1. *The Supreme Court's recent cases.* The Supreme Court has decided standing decisions since *Massachusetts v. EPA.* How would you address the following facts?

■ *Problem 8.1*

The Foreign Intelligence Surveillance Act (FISA) establishes a secret surveillance program. The Act allows the government to surveille individuals who are not "U.S. persons," reasonably believed to be located outside the United States, even if one side of the communications is a U.S. person within the United States. The plaintiffs—a group of attorneys, human rights activists, and media organizations—filed suit, arguing that their communications were likely to be caught up in the secret surveillance because they represented individuals, such as Guantanamo Bay detainees, whose communications were likely to be surveilled. Is there standing? See Clapper v. Amnesty International, 568 U.S. 398 (2013).

D. Timing (I): Finality and Exhaustion

Even if there is a cause of action, and even if one has standing to sue, other legal doctrines affect the timing of such lawsuits. In this section, we explore the two prominent timing doctrines in administrative law: finality and exhaustion. First, courts will not review an agency action until it is the "final" action of the agency. If there are no actual legal consequences because the agency has not finally made up its mind about something, or hasn't made a final decision, then the courts can't review the intermediate decisions, actions, and thoughts of the agency. Second, sometimes the courts or Congress require that a potential litigant exhaust administrative remedies before filing suit in court. This means that if there are internal procedures for appeal within the agency, the potential litigant first has to try to use those procedures. Put

FINALITY: The requirement that an agency action be "final" before a lawsuit can be brought.

another way, an agency action can be "final" but the complainant nevertheless has to work her way through the administrative appeals process first.

1. Finality

APA § 704 provides, "Agency action made reviewable by statute and final agency action for which there is no other adequate remedy in a court are subject to judicial review." This is known as the "finality" requirement, upon which the Supreme Court elaborated in the following two cases.

Defined Term

EXHAUSTION: The requirement that an aggrieved person exhaust all administrative remedies before bringing a lawsuit in court.

Bennett v. Spear

520 U.S. 154 (1997)

JUSTICE SCALIA delivered the opinion of the Court.

This is a challenge to a biological opinion issued by the Fish and Wildlife Service in accordance with the Endangered Species Act of 1973 (ESA), concerning the operation of the Klamath Irrigation Project by the Bureau of Reclamation, and the project's impact on two varieties of endangered fish. The question for decision is whether the petitioners, who have competing economic and other interests in Klamath Project water, have standing to seek judicial review of the biological opinion under the citizen-suit provision of the ESA, § 1540(g)(1), and the Administrative Procedure Act (APA).

I

The ESA requires the Secretary of the Interior to promulgate regulations listing those species of animals that are "threatened" or "endangered" under specified criteria, and to designate their "critical habitat." 16 U.S.C. § 1533. The ESA further requires each federal agency to "insure that any action authorized, funded, or carried out by such agency . . . is not likely to jeopardize the continued existence of any endangered species or threatened species or result in the destruction or adverse modification of habitat of such species which is determined by the Secretary . . . to be critical." § 1536(a)(2). If an agency determines that action it proposes to take may adversely affect a listed species, it must engage in formal consultation with the Fish and Wildlife Service, as delegate of the Secretary, after which the Service must provide the agency with a written statement (the Biological Opinion) explaining how the proposed action will affect the species or its habitat, 16 U.S.C. § 1536(b)(3)(A). If the Service concludes that the proposed action will "jeopardize the continued existence of any [listed] species or threatened species or result in the destruction or adverse modification of [critical habitat]," § 1536(a)(2), the Biological Opinion must outline any "reasonable and prudent alternatives" that the Service believes will avoid that consequence, § 1536(b)(3)(A). Additionally, if the Biological Opinion concludes that the agency action will not result in jeopardy or adverse habitat modification, or if it offers reasonable and prudent alternatives to avoid that consequence, the Service must provide the agency with a written statement (known as the Incidental Take Statement) specifying the "impact of such incidental taking on the species," any "reasonable and prudent measures that the [Service] considers necessary or appropriate to minimize such impact," and setting forth "the terms and conditions . . . that must be complied with by the Federal agency . . . to implement [those measures]." § 1536(b)(4).

The Klamath Project, one of the oldest federal reclamation schemes, is a series of lakes, rivers, dams, and irrigation canals in northern California and southern Oregon. The project was undertaken by the Secretary of the Interior pursuant to the Reclamation Act of 1902, and the Act of Feb. 9, 1905, and is administered by the Bureau of Reclamation, which is under the Secretary's jurisdiction. In 1992, the Bureau notified the Service that operation of the project might affect the Lost River Sucker (*Deltistes luxatus*) and Shortnose Sucker (*Chasmistes brevirostris*), species of fish that were listed as endangered in 1988. After formal consultation with the Bureau in accordance with 50 CFR § 402.14 (1995), the Service issued a Biological Opinion which concluded that the " 'long-term operation of the Klamath Project was likely to jeopardize the continued existence of the Lost River and shortnose suckers.' " The Biological Opinion identified "reasonable and prudent alternatives" the Service believed would avoid jeopardy, which included the maintenance of minimum water levels on Clear Lake and Gerber reservoirs. The Bureau later notified the Service that it intended to operate the project in compliance with the Biological Opinion.

Petitioners, two Oregon irrigation districts that receive Klamath Project water and the operators of two ranches within those districts, filed the present action against the director and regional director of the Service and the Secretary of the Interior. Neither the Bureau nor any of its officials is named as defendant.

The complaint asserts that the Bureau "has been following essentially the same procedures for storing and releasing water from Clear Lake and Gerber reservoirs throughout the twentieth century"; that "[t]here is no scientifically or commercially available evidence indicating that the populations of endangered suckers in Clear Lake and Gerber reservoirs have declined, are declining, or will decline as a result" of the Bureau's operation of the Klamath Project; that "[t]here is no commercially or scientifically available evidence indicating that the restrictions on lake levels imposed in the Biological Opinion will have any beneficial effect on the . . . populations of suckers in Clear Lake and Gerber reservoirs"; and that the Bureau nonetheless "will abide by the restrictions imposed by the Biological Opinion."

Petitioners' complaint included three claims for relief that are relevant here. The first and second claims allege that the Service's jeopardy determination with respect to Clear Lake and Gerber reservoirs, and the ensuing imposition of minimum water levels, violated § 7 of the ESA, 16 U.S.C. § 1536. The third claim is that the imposition of minimum water elevations constituted an implicit determination of critical habitat for the suckers, which violated § 4 of the ESA, 16 U.S.C. § 1533(b)(2), because it failed to take into consideration the designation's economic impact. Each of the claims also states that the relevant action violated the APA's prohibition of agency action that is "arbitrary, capricious, an abuse of discretion, or otherwise not in accordance with law." 5 U.S.C. § 706(2)(A).

The complaint asserts that petitioners' use of the reservoirs and related waterways for "recreational, aesthetic and commercial purposes, as well as for their primary sources of irrigation water," will be "irreparably damaged" by the actions complained of, and that the restrictions on water delivery "recommended" by the Biological Opinion "adversely affect plaintiffs by substantially reducing the quantity of available irrigation water." In essence, petitioners claim a competing interest in the water the Biological Opinion declares necessary for the preservation of the suckers.

The District Court dismissed the complaint for lack of jurisdiction. . . .

[The Court first addressed the "zone of interests" tests for prudential standing, and the requirements of Article III standing, doctrines that are addressed in subsequent subsections of this chapter. It then held that judicial review was not available under the Endangered Species Act with respect to the Biological Opinion, and so turned to the question of judicial review under the APA—Ed.]

    * * *

IV

. . . . The Government contends that petitioners may not obtain judicial review under the APA on the theory that the Biological Opinion does not constitute "final agency action," 5 U.S.C. § 704, because it does not conclusively determine the manner in which Klamath Project water will be allocated:

> "Whatever the practical likelihood that the [Bureau] would adopt the reasonable and prudent alternatives (including the higher lake levels) identified by the Service, the Bureau was not legally obligated to do so. Even if the Bureau decided to adopt the higher lake levels, moreover, nothing in the biological opinion would constrain the [Bureau's] discretion as to how the available water should be allocated among potential users." Brief for Respondents 33.

This confuses the question whether the Secretary's action is final with the separate question whether petitioners' harm is "fairly traceable" to the Secretary's action . . . . As a general matter, two conditions must be satisfied for agency action to be "final": First, the action must mark the "consummation" of the agency's decisionmaking process, *Chicago & Southern Air Lines, Inc. v. Waterman S.S. Corp.*, 333 U.S. 103, 113 (1948)—it must not be of a merely tentative or interlocutory nature. And second, the action must be one by which "rights or obligations have been determined," or from which "legal consequences will flow," *Port of Boston Marine Terminal Assn. v. Rederiaktiebolaget Transatlantic*, 400 U.S. 62, 71 (1970). It is uncontested that the first requirement is met here; and the second is met because, as we have discussed above, the Biological Opinion and accompanying Incidental Take Statement alter the legal regime to which the [Bureau] is subject, authorizing it to take the endangered species if (but only if) it complies with the prescribed conditions.

In this crucial respect the present case is different from the cases upon which the Government relies, *Franklin v. Massachusetts*, 505 U.S. 788 (1992), and *Dalton v. Specter*, 511 U.S. 462 (1994). In the former case, the agency action in question was the Secretary of Commerce's presentation to the President of a report tabulating the results of the decennial census; our holding that this did not constitute "final agency action" was premised on the observation that the report carried "no direct consequences" and served "more like a tentative recommendation than a final and binding determination." 505 U.S. at 798. And in the latter case, the agency action in question was submission to the President of base closure recommendations by the Secretary of Defense and the Defense Base Closure and Realignment Commission; our holding that this was not "final agency action" followed from the fact that the recommendations were in no way binding on the President, who had absolute discretion to accept or reject them. 511 U.S. at 469–471. Unlike the reports in *Franklin* and *Dalton*, which were purely advisory and in no way affected the legal rights of the relevant actors, the Biological Opinion at issue here has direct and appreciable legal consequences. . . .

[P]etitioners' . . . claims are reviewable under the APA. . . .

Sackett v. EPA

566 U.S. 120 (2012)

JUSTICE SCALIA delivered the opinion of the Court.

We consider whether Michael and Chantell Sackett may bring a civil action under the Administrative Procedure Act to challenge the issuance by the Environmental Protection Agency (EPA) of an administrative compliance order under § 309 of the Clean Water Act, 33 U.S.C. § 1319. The order asserts that the Sacketts' property is subject to the Act, and that they have violated its provisions by placing fill material on the property; and on this basis it directs them immediately to restore the property pursuant to an EPA work plan.

I

The Clean Water Act prohibits, among other things, "the discharge of any pollutant by any person," § 1311, without a permit, into the "navigable waters," § 1344—which the Act defines as "the waters of the United States," § 1362(7). If the EPA determines that any person is in violation of this restriction, the Act directs the agency either to issue a compliance order or to initiate a civil enforcement action. § 1319(a)(3). When the EPA prevails in a civil action, the Act provides for "a civil penalty not to exceed [$37,500] per day for each violation." § 1319(d). And according to the Government, when the EPA prevails against any person who has been issued a compliance order but has failed to comply, that amount is increased to $75,000—up to $37,500 for the statutory violation and up to an additional $37,500 for violating the compliance order.

The particulars of this case flow from a dispute about the scope of "the navigable waters" subject to this enforcement regime. Today we consider only whether the dispute may be brought to court by challenging the compliance order—we do not resolve the dispute on the merits. The reader will be curious, however, to know what all the fuss is about. In *United States v. Riverside Bayview Homes, Inc.*, 474 U.S. 121 (1985), we upheld a regulation that construed "the navigable waters" to include "freshwater wetlands," themselves not actually navigable, that were adjacent to navigable-in-fact waters. Later, in *Solid Waste Agency of Northern Cook Cty. v. Army Corps of Engineers*, 531 U.S. 159 (2001), we held that an abandoned sand and gravel pit, which "seasonally ponded" but which was not adjacent to open water, was not part of the navigable waters. Then most recently, in *Rapanos v. United States*, 547 U.S. 715 (2006), we considered whether a wetland not adjacent to navigable-in-fact waters fell within the scope of the Act. Our answer was no, but no one rationale commanded a majority of the Court. In his separate opinion, THE CHIEF JUSTICE expressed the concern that interested parties would lack guidance "on precisely how to read Congress' limits on the reach of the Clean Water Act" and would be left "to feel their way on a case-by-case basis."

The Sacketts are interested parties feeling their way. They own a 2/3-acre residential lot in Bonner County, Idaho. Their property lies just north of Priest Lake, but is separated from the lake by several lots containing permanent structures. In preparation for constructing a house, the Sacketts filled in part of their lot with dirt and rock. Some months later, they received from the EPA a compliance order. The order contained a number of "Findings and Conclusions," including [that Sacketts' property contained wetlands that were adjacent to Priest Lake, which is a navigable water under the statute, and therefore that the Sacketts had unlawfully discharged pollutants into the waters of the United States without a permit.—Ed.]

On the basis of these findings and conclusions, the order directs the Sacketts, among other things, "immediately [to] undertake activities to restore the Site in accordance with [an EPA-created] Restoration Work Plan" and to "provide and/or obtain access to the Site . . . [and] access to all records and documentation related to the conditions at the Site . . . to EPA employees and/ or their designated representatives."

The Sacketts, who do not believe that their property is subject to the Act, asked the EPA for a hearing, but that request was denied. They then brought this action in the United States District Court for the District of Idaho, seeking declaratory and injunctive relief. Their complaint contended that the EPA's issuance of the compliance order was "arbitrary [and] capricious" under the Administrative Procedure Act (APA), 5 U.S.C. § 706(2)(A), and that it deprived them of "life, liberty, or property, without due process of law," in violation of the Fifth Amendment. The District Court dismissed the claims for want of subject-matter jurisdiction, and the United States Court of Appeals for the Ninth Circuit affirmed. It concluded that the Act "preclude[s] pre-enforcement judicial review of compliance orders," and that such preclusion does not violate the Fifth Amendment's due process guarantee. We granted certiorari.

II

The Sacketts brought suit under Chapter 7 of the APA, which provides for judicial review of "final agency action for which there is no other adequate remedy in a court." 5 U.S.C. § 704. We consider first whether the compliance order is final agency action. There is no doubt it is agency action, which the APA defines as including even a "failure to act." §§ 551(13), 701(b)(2). But is it *final*? It has all of the hallmarks of APA finality that our opinions establish. Through the order, the EPA " 'determined' " " 'rights or obligations.' " *Bennett v. Spear,* 520 U.S. 154, 178 (1997). By reason of the order, the Sacketts have the legal obligation to "restore" their property according to an agency-approved Restoration Work Plan, and must give the EPA access to their property and to "records and documentation related to the conditions at the Site." Also, " 'legal consequences . . . flow' " from issuance of the order. *Bennett, supra,* at 178. For one, according to the Government's current litigating position, the order exposes the Sacketts to double penalties in a future enforcement proceeding. It also severely limits the Sacketts' ability to obtain a permit for their fill from the Army Corps of Engineers, see 33 U.S.C. § 1344. The Corps' regulations provide that, once the EPA has issued a compliance order with respect to certain property, the Corps will not process a permit application for that property unless doing so "is clearly appropriate." 33 CFR § 326.3(e)(1)(iv) (2011).

The issuance of the compliance order also marks the " 'consummation' " of the agency's decisionmaking process. *Bennett, supra,* at 178. As the Sacketts learned when they unsuccessfully sought a hearing, the "Findings and Conclusions" that the compliance order contained were not subject to further agency review. The Government resists this conclusion, pointing to a portion of the order that invited the Sacketts to "engage in informal discussion of the terms and requirements" of the order with the EPA and to inform the agency of "any allegations [t]herein which [they] believe[d] to be inaccurate." But that confers no entitlement to further agency review. The mere possibility that an agency might reconsider in light of "informal discussion" and invited contentions of inaccuracy does not suffice to make an otherwise final agency action nonfinal.

The APA's judicial review provision also requires that the person seeking APA review of final agency action have "no other adequate remedy in a court," 5 U.S.C. § 704. In Clean Water Act enforcement cases, judicial review ordinarily comes by way of a civil action brought by the EPA under 33 U.S.C. § 1319. But the Sacketts cannot initiate that process, and each day they wait for the agency to drop the hammer, they accrue, by the Government's telling, an additional $75,000 in potential liability. The other possible route to judicial review—applying to the Corps of Engineers for a permit and then filing suit under the APA if a permit is denied—will not serve either. The remedy for denial of action that might be sought from one agency does not ordinarily provide an "adequate remedy" for action already taken by another agency. The Government, to its credit, does not seriously contend that other available remedies alone foreclose review under § 704. . . .

We conclude that the compliance order in this case is final agency action for which there is no adequate remedy other than APA review . . . .

[A short concurrence by Justice Ginsburg is omitted.—Ed.].

Justice Alito, concurring.

The position taken in this case by the Federal Government—a position that the Court now squarely rejects—would have put the property rights of ordinary Americans entirely at the mercy of Environmental Protection Agency (EPA) employees.

The reach of the Clean Water Act is notoriously unclear. Any piece of land that is wet at least part of the year is in danger of being classified by EPA employees as wetlands covered by the Act, and according to the Federal Government, if property owners begin to construct a home on a lot that the agency thinks possesses the requisite wetness, the property owners are at the agency's mercy. The EPA may issue a compliance order demanding that the owners cease construction, engage in expensive remedial measures, and abandon any use of the property. If the owners do not do the EPA's bidding, they may be fined up to $75,000 per day ($37,500 for violating the Act and another $37,500 for violating the compliance order). And if the owners want their day in court to show that their lot does not include covered wetlands, well, as a practical matter, that is just too bad. Until the EPA sues them, they are blocked from access to the courts, and the EPA may wait as long as it wants before deciding to sue. By that time, the potential fines may easily have reached the millions. In a nation that values due process, not to mention private property, such treatment is unthinkable.

The Court's decision provides a modest measure of relief. At least, property owners like petitioners will have the right to challenge the EPA's jurisdictional determination under the Administrative Procedure Act. . . .

NOTES AND QUESTIONS

1. **Franklin *and* Dalton.** Franklin v. Massachusetts, 505 U.S. 788 (1992), and Dalton v. Specter, 511 U.S. 462 (1994), both cited in *Bennett,* are also leading cases on finality. Unlike in *Bennett* and *Sackett,* the Court in Franklin and Dalton held there was no final agency action. The consequence of that determination, however, was that there was no judicial review available at all. As you may recall from the "what is an agency" discussion from Chapter 1, *Franklin* involved the decennial census and the question of whether the President was an "agency" within

 CROSS REFERENCE We saw *Franklin v. Massachusetts* earlier in the casebook, in the first chapter, on the question whether the President is an "agency" within the meaning of the APA.

the meaning of the APA. The Secretary of Commerce, through the Census Bureau, issued a report allocating overseas defense and military employees to states based on their "home of record," as opposed to the alternative options of legal residence or last duty station. As a result, Massachusetts would lose seats in the House of Representatives. The Supreme Court held, however, that no review was available. The Court held first that the agency action was not final because the President still had discretion to make corrections to the Bureau's report, and could even have directed the Bureau to change the way it assigned overseas personnel. The action was not final until the President submitted the relevant data and information to Congress. The "final agency action" would therefore be the President's. But, the Court held, the President was not an agency within the meaning of the APA, and so there was no review to be had at all—at least not under the APA.

Similarly, *Dalton* involved a decision by the Defense Base Closure and Realignment Commission to recommend to the President the closing of the Philadelphia Naval Shipyard. The statute left it up to the President to approve or disapprove of *all* of the Commission's recommendation as a slate; the President could not pick and choose. Before the President made the decision, Arlen Specter, a powerful U.S. Senator from Pennsylvania, and others sued the Commission under the APA. The Supreme Court held that the Commission's decision was not final agency action—indeed, the base might not close at all if the President rejected the Commission's report. But if the President did approve of the report, there would be no opportunity for APA review because, again, the President was not an agency.

How do you feel about the unavailability of judicial review in these cases? Just because there is no APA review, does that mean there is no review at all for an appropriate plaintiff under other causes of action? If there is in fact no review, is that nevertheless acceptable because these questions are ultimately better determined by the political branches of government? Or, should the President be subject to APA review? Would that even be constitutional?

2.   Exhaustion

Even if an agency's action is final, there is yet another reviewability hurdle that must be overcome: a potential litigant must generally first exhaust any available administrative remedies. Put another way, the initial decision of the agency—for example, an ALJ decision, or a cease-and-desist order—can be final agency action. But the agency might have an internal appeals process, for example to the commission as a whole. No one is *required* to appeal the agency's initial decision. One could always just submit to that decision. But the exhaustion requirement says a potential litigant has to exhaust this administrative process before proceeding in federal court.

The exhaustion requirement has two sources: statute and judicial common law. Let us start with statutory exhaustion.

Sometimes a statute specifically requires that a litigant exhaust the administrative process, including any appeals within the agency, before that litigant can bring a case in federal court. For example, the Prison Litigation Reform Act (PLRA) of 1996 provides that "[n]o action shall be brought with respect to prison conditions . . . by a prisoner . . . until such administrative remedies as are available are exhausted." 42 U.S.C. § 1997e(a). This decision effectively overturned a judge-made exception to exhaustion in McCarthy v. Madigan, 503 U.S. 140 (1992), presented later in this section.

Note that the courts might still develop a significant body of case law *interpreting* these statutory exhaustion requirements. Thus in Ross v. Blake, 136 S. Ct. 1850 (2016), the Supreme Court remanded a case for development of a prisoner's claim that administrative remedies were not actually "available" to him under the PLRA. The Court explained that "an administrative procedure is unavailable when (despite what regulations or guidance materials may promise) it operates as a simple dead end—with officers unable or consistently unwilling to provide any relief to aggrieved inmates," and that "an administrative scheme might be so opaque that it becomes, practically speaking, incapable of use."

What about cases under the Administrative Procedure Act—that is, where the organic statute does not provide any specific mechanism for judicial review, and therefore judicial review is to be had under the APA? Section 704 of the APA supplies the answer:

> Except as otherwise expressly required by statute, agency action otherwise final is final for the purposes of this section whether or not there has been presented or determined an application for a declaratory order, for any form of reconsideration, or, unless the agency otherwise requires by rule and provides that the action meanwhile is inoperative, for an appeal to superior agency authority.

Section 704 therefore provides that final agency actions may be reviewed whether or not administrative appeals (to "superior agency authority") have been exhausted, *unless* "otherwise expressly required by statute" or "the agency otherwise requires by rule." Thus, in Darby v. Cisneros, 509 U.S. 137 (1993), the Supreme Court held that "[w]hile federal courts may be free to apply, where appropriate, other prudential doctrines of judicial administration to limit the scope and timing of judicial review," § 704 of the APA, "by its very terms, has limited the availability of the doctrine of exhaustion of administrative remedies to that which the statute or rule clearly mandates." 509 U.S. at 146. Put another way, if judicial review is taking place under the provisions of the APA, as opposed to under unique judicial review provisions of the organic statute, judges cannot require exhaustion unless the organic statute or agency rule provides for exhaustion. Note that for an agency rule to require exhaustion under § 704, the agency must provide that the initial action is "inoperative" during the appeal to the superior agency authority.

In short, if (1) Congress has required exhaustion in a particular statute, or (2) an agency rule specifically requires exhaustion (for cases decided under the APA), then litigants must follow the procedures established in the statutes or regulations before filing suit, but the courts are not otherwise free to add to these exhaustion requirements. That still leaves a third situation: administrative statutes with their own judicial review provisions, or actions brought or defenses raised under non-APA causes of action, where the statute at hand does not specify any exhaustion requirement. Can the federal courts nevertheless require exhaustion of administrative proceedings in such cases?

This is the realm of common-law exhaustion requirements. The general rule is that, even in the absence of a specific statutory requirement to exhaust, litigants must exhaust available administrative remedies. This judge-made exhaustion requirement, however, is subject to numerous judge-made exceptions. Put another way, if (1) there is no statute that *requires* exhaustion, and (2) the case is not brought under the APA, then it is entirely up to the

 PRACTICE POINTER It is important to distinguish between common-law exhaustion requirements and statutory exhaustion requirements.

courts as a matter of judicial discretion whether or not to require exhaustion. This section presents three cases that deal with this common law of administrative exhaustion.

McKart v. United States

395 U.S. 185 (1969)

Mr. Justice Marshall, delivered the opinion of the Court.

Petitioner was indicted for willfully and knowingly failing to report for and submit to induction into the Armed Forces of the United States. At trial, petitioner's only defense was that he should have been exempt from military service because he was the 'sole surviving son' of a family whose father had been killed in action while serving in the Armed Forces of the United States. The District Court held that he could not raise that defense because he had failed to exhaust the administrative remedies provided by the Selective Service System. Accordingly, petitioner was convicted and sentenced to three years' imprisonment. The Court of Appeals affirmed, with one judge dissenting. We granted certiorari.

I

The facts are not in dispute. Petitioner registered with his local Selective Service board shortly after his 18th birthday and thereafter completed his classification questionnaire. On that form he indicated that he was 'the sole surviving son of a family of which one or more sons or daughters were killed in action . . . while serving in the Armed Forces of the United States . . . .' On February 25, 1963, petitioner's local board placed him in Class I-A, available for military service; he made no attempt to appeal that classification.

On March 23, 1964, he was ordered to report for a pre-induction physical, but failed to do so. He was declared a delinquent and ordered to report for induction on May 11, 1964. He failed to report, but instead wrote a letter to his local board indicating that his moral beliefs prevented him from cooperating with the Selective Service System. The local board replied by sending petitioner the form for claiming conscientious objector status. The board also referred to petitioner's indication in his original questionnaire that he was a sole surviving son and requested further information on that subject.

On May 20, 1964, petitioner returned the blank form, stating that he did not wish to be a conscientious objector. In response to the board's request for information about his claim to be a sole surviving son, petitioner indicated that his father had been killed in World War II. The local board, after consulting the

State Director, again wrote petitioner requesting more information about his father. Petitioner supplied some of the information. The local board forwarded this information to the State Director, who requested the local board to reopen petitioner's classification. The board canceled his induction order and reclassified him IV-A, the appropriate classification for a registrant exempted as a sole surviving son. Petitioner remained in that classification until February 14, 1966.

Early in 1966, the local board learned of the death of petitioner's mother. After checking with the State Director, the board returned petitioner to Class I-A. The board rested this decision on the theory that a IV-A classification became improper when petitioner's 'family unit' ceased to exist on the death of his mother. Petitioner was ordered to report for a pre-induction physical. He failed to report and was declared a delinquent and ordered to report for induction. He again failed to report and, after further investigation, his criminal prosecution followed.

II

We think it clear that petitioner was exempt from military service as a sole surviving son. The sole surviving son exemption originated in the Selective Service Act of 1948, § 6(*o*). As originally enacted, that section provided exemption for the sole surviving son only '(w)here one or more sons or daughters of a family were killed in action . . . while serving in the armed forces of the United States.' In 1964, the section was amended to extend the exemption to sole surviving sons whose fathers were killed in action. The section now reads in relevant part as follows:

'(W)here the father or one or more sons or daughters of a family were killed in action or died in line of duty while serving in the Armed Forces . . . the sole surviving son of such family shall not be inducted for service . . . .' 50 U.S.C. App. § 456(*o*).

There is no question that petitioner was entitled to an exemption before the death of his mother. The issue is whether her death, and the end of the immediate 'family unit,' ended that exemption. . . .

The section says nothing about the continuing existence of a family unit, even though other provisions of the Selective Service laws make similar conditions explicit in other contexts. . . .

The local board erred in classifying petitioner I-A and ordering him to report for induction. . . .

III

The Government maintains, however, that petitioner cannot raise the invalidity of his I-A classification and subsequent induction order as a defense to a criminal prosecution for refusal to report for induction. According to the Government, petitioner's failure to appeal his reclassification after the death of his mother constitutes a failure to exhaust available administrative remedies and therefore should bar all judicial review. For the reasons set out below, we cannot agree.

The doctrine of exhaustion of administrative remedies is well established in the jurisprudence of administrative law. The doctrine provides 'that no one is entitled to judicial relief for a supposed or threatened injury until the prescribed administrative remedy has been exhausted.' Myers v. Bethlehem Shipbuilding Corp., 303 U.S. 41, 50–51 (1938). The doctrine is applied in a number of different situations and is, like most judicial doctrines, subject to numerous exceptions. Application of the doctrine to specific cases requires an understanding of its purposes and of the particular administrative scheme involved.

Perhaps the most common application of the exhaustion doctrine is in cases where the relevant statute provides that certain administrative procedures shall be exclusive. The reasons for making such procedures exclusive, and for the judicial application of the exhaustion doctrine in cases where the statutory requirement of exclusivity is not so explicit, are not difficult to understand. A primary purpose is, of course, the avoidance of premature interruption of the administrative process. The agency, like a trial court, is created for the purpose of applying a statute in the first instance. Accordingly, it is normally desirable to let the agency develop the necessary factual background upon which decisions should be based. And since agency decisions are frequently of a discretionary nature or frequently require expertise, the agency should be given the first chance to exercise that discretion or to apply that expertise. And of course it is generally more efficient for the administrative process to go forward without interruption than it is to permit the parties to seek aid from the courts at various intermediate stages. The very same reasons lie behind judicial rules sharply limiting interlocutory appeals.

Closely related to the above reasons is a notion peculiar to administrative law. The administrative agency is created as a separate entity and invested with certain powers and duties. The courts ordinarily should not interfere with an agency until it has completed its action, or else has clearly exceeded its jurisdiction. As Professor Jaffe puts it, '(t)he exhaustion doctrine is, therefore, an expression of executive and administrative autonomy.' This reason is particularly pertinent where the function of the agency and the particular decision sought to be reviewed involve exercise of discretionary powers granted the agency by Congress, or require application of special expertise.

Some of these reasons apply equally to cases like the present one, where the administrative process is at an end and a party seeks judicial review of a decision that was not appealed through the administrative process. Particularly, judicial review may be hindered by the failure of the litigant to allow the agency to make a factual record, or to exercise its discretion or apply its expertise. In addition, other justifications for requiring exhaustion in cases of this sort have nothing to do with the dangers of interruption of the administrative process. Certain very practical notions of judicial efficiency come into play as well. A complaining party may be successful in vindicating his rights in the administrative process. If he is required to pursue his administrative remedies, the courts may never have to intervene. And notions of administrative autonomy require that the agency be given a chance to discover and correct its own errors. Finally, it is possible that frequent and deliberate flouting of administrative processes could weaken the effectiveness of an agency by encouraging people to ignore its procedures.

In Selective Service cases, the exhaustion doctrine must be tailored to fit the peculiarities of the administrative system Congress has created. At the heart of the Selective Service System are the local boards, which are charged in the first instance with registering and classifying those subject to the Selective Service laws. Upon being classified by the local board, the registrant has a right of appeal to a state appeal board, and, in some instances, to the President. No registrant is required to appeal. A registrant cannot be ordered to report for induction while his classification is being considered by the local board or by an appeal board.

At some stage during this process, normally shortly before he is expected to be ordered to report for induction, the registrant is required to complete a pre-induction physical examination. If he passes this examination, he ordinarily will be ordered to report for induction. The next, and last, step is to report to the induction center and submit to induction. At this point, the administrative process is at an end.

If the registrant fails to report for induction, he is, like petitioner in the present case, subject to criminal prosecution. Although the Universal Military Training and Service Act, as it stood at the time of petitioner's trial, provided that the decisions of the local boards were 'final,' it was long ago established that a registrant charged with failure to report can raise the defense that there was 'no basis in fact' for his classification. It is also established that there can be no judicial review at all, with some exceptions, until the registrant has refused to submit to induction and is prosecuted, or else has submitted to induction and seeks release by habeas corpus.

This case raises a different question. We are not here faced with a premature resort to the courts—all administrative remedies are now closed to petitioner. We are asked instead to hold that petitioner's failure to utilize a particular administrative process—an appeal—bars him from defending a criminal prosecution on grounds which could have been raised on that appeal. We cannot agree that application of the exhaustion doctrine would be proper in the circumstances of the present case.

First of all, it is well to remember that use of the exhaustion doctrine in criminal cases can be exceedingly harsh. The defendant is often stripped of his only defense; he must go to jail without having any judicial review of an assertedly invalid order. The deprivation of judicial review occurs not when the affected person is affirmatively asking for assistance from the courts but when the Government is attempting to impose criminal sanctions on him. Such a result should not be tolerated unless the interests underlying the exhaustion rule clearly outweigh the severe burden imposed upon the registrant if he is denied judicial review. The statute as it stood when petitioner was reclassified said nothing which would require registrants to raise all their claims before the appeal boards. We must ask, then, whether there is in this case a governmental interest compelling enough to outweigh the severe burden placed on petitioner. Even if there is no such compelling interest when petitioner's case is viewed in isolation, we must also ask whether allowing all similarly situated registrants to bypass administrative appeal procedures would seriously impair the Selective Service System's ability to perform its functions.

The question of whether petitioner is entitled to exemption as a sole surviving son is, as we have seen, solely one of statutory interpretation. The resolution of that issue does not require any particular expertise on the part of the appeal board; the proper interpretation is certainly not a matter of discretion. In this sense, the issue is different from many Selective Service classification questions which do involve expertise or the exercise of discretion, both by the local boards and the appeal boards. Petitioner's failure to take his claim through all available administrative appeals only deprived the Selective Service System of the opportunity of having its appellate boards resolve a question of statutory interpretation. Since judicial review would not be significantly aided by an additional administrative decision of this sort, we cannot see any compelling reason why petitioner's failure to appeal should bar his only defense to a criminal prosecution. There is simply no overwhelming need for the court to have the agency finally resolve this question in the first instance, at least not where the administrative process is at an end and the registrant is faced with criminal prosecution.

We are thus left with the Government's argument that failure to require exhaustion in the present case will induce registrants to bypass available administrative remedies. The Government fears an increase in litigation and a consequent danger of thwarting the primary function of the Selective Service System, the rapid mobilization of manpower. This argument is based upon the proposition that the Selective Service System will, through its own processes, correct most errors and thus avoid much litigation. The exhaustion doctrine is assertedly necessary to compel resort to these processes. The Government also speculates that many more registrants will risk criminal prosecution if their claims need not carry into court the stigma of denial not only by their local boards, but also by at least one appeal board.

We do not, however, take such a dire view of the likely consequences of today's decision. At the outset, we doubt whether many registrants will be foolhardy enough to deny the Selective Service System the opportunity to correct its own errors by taking their chances with a criminal prosecution and a possibility of five years in jail. The very presence of the criminal sanction is sufficient to ensure that the great majority of registrants will exhaust all administrative remedies before deciding whether or not to continue the challenge to their classifications. And, today's holding does not apply to every registrant who fails to take advantage of the administrative remedies provided by the Selective Service

System. For, as we have said, many classifications require exercise of discretion or application of expertise; in these cases, it may be proper to require a registrant to carry his case through the administrative process before he comes into court. Moreover, we are not convinced that many in this rather small class of registrants will bypass the Selective Service System with the thought that their ultimate chances of success in the courts are enhanced thereby. In short, we simply do not think that the exhaustion doctrine contributes significantly to the fairly low number of registrants who decide to subject themselves to criminal prosecution for failure to submit to induction. Accordingly, in the present case, where there appears no significant interest to be served in having the System decide the issue before it reaches the courts, we do not believe that petitioner's failure to appeal his classification should foreclose all judicial review. . . .

MR. JUSTICE DOUGLAS, concurring.

The principle of Oestereich v. Selective Service System Local Board No. 11, 393 U.S. 233, should dispose of this case. There a registrant was plainly entitled to a statutory exemption from service because he was a divinity student. Yet he was denied the exemption because, having burned his draft card, he was classified as a 'delinquent' by Selective Service. He challenged that action in a civil suit for pre-induction review; and we granted relief. . . .

If Oestereich could raise his claim to statutory exemption in a civil suit at a pre-induction stage, it follows a fortiori that petitioner can do so in a criminal prosecution for failure to obey the Act's mandate. . . .

MR. JUSTICE WHITE, concurring in the result.

The Court's opinion, as I understand it, does not dispense with the necessity of presenting an issue under the draft laws to the registrant's local board for consideration in the first instance. Petitioner did exactly this, and by its decision, the Court provides no avenue for totally bypassing the Selective Service System and using the courts as an alternative to the local draft boards. . . .

It is petitioner's failure to exhaust appellate remedies available within the Selective Service System which presents the obstacle to the challenge of his classification in the courts. And while this facet of the exhaustion doctrine, like its other facets, admits of exceptions when special circumstances warrant, I cannot agree with the Court's conclusion that petitioner's failure to exhaust appellate remedies within the System can be disregarded on the broader ground that only a question of law is involved. Questions of law have not, in the past, been thought to be immune from exhaustion requirements. Indeed, this Court has often emphasized that the expertise of the responsible agency is entitled to great deference in matters of statutory construction, thus refuting any contention that questions of law are somehow beyond the expertise of the agency and do not give rise to the considerations which underlie the exhaustion doctrine.

Although I would stop far short of the broad strokes used by the Court in this respect, I do agree that petitioner's failure to exhaust appellate remedies does not bar review of his classification on the facts of this case. Undoubtedly, Congress could require such exhaustion as a prerequisite to judicial review, but Congress has not chosen to do so. In the absence of any such requirement, I do not think review of petitioner's classification is an impermissible encroachment upon the bailiwick of the Selective Service System. We are not faced with a situation in which consideration of the issue involved has stopped at the first level of the administrative machinery. Rather, petitioner's case and the scope of the § 6(*o*) exemption for sole surviving sons have received the attention of both the State and the National Directors of the Selective Service System. Petitioner has not exhausted the channels for formal appellate review within the System, but the informal review given petitioner's case and the ratification by the State and National Directors of the position taken by petitioner's local board are sufficient justification to permit the courts to entertain petitioner's defense that his classification is improper under § 6(*o*).

Notes and Questions

1. ***Relevant factors for analysis.*** *McKart* remains a leading case on non-statutory administrative exhaustion. What was the basis of the Court's decision not to require exhaustion of remedies? The Court discussed a variety of factors. As a general matter, exhaustion is necessary where (1) administrative expertise is relevant; (2) where administrators decisions are particularly discretionary; (3) where further factual development is necessary (do you see the overlap with ripeness?); and/or (4) if Congress indicates in the statute that the administrative process is to be exclusive. The Court held that exhaustion was less necessary in *McKart* in part because it involved a matter of pure statutory interpretation. But what do you make of Justice White's argument that administrative expertise and discretion is often necessary to resolve statutory questions, especially in light of the subsequent development of *Chevron* deference?

2. ***Exceptions are still exceptions, not the rule.*** It is important to remember that the exception to exhaustion in *McKart* was just that—an exception. The general rule remains that litigants must typically exhaust. The next case, also in the context of the Selective Service and decided just two years after *McKart,* is thus more representative of the exhaustion requirement.

McGee v. United States

402 U.S. 479 (1971)

MR. JUSTICE MARSHALL delivered the opinion of the Court.

Petitioner was convicted of failing to submit to induction and other violations of the draft laws. His principal defense involves the contention that he had been incorrectly classified by his local Selective Service board. The Court of Appeals ruled that this defense was barred because petitioner had failed to pursue and exhaust his administrative remedies. . . .

I

In February 1966, while attending the University of Rochester, petitioner applied to his local Selective Service board for conscientious objector status. In support of his claim to that exemption he submitted the special form for conscientious objectors (SSS Form 150), setting forth his views concerning participation in war. The board continued petitioner's existing classification—student deferment—and advised him that the conscientious objector claim would be passed upon when student status no longer applied.

In April 1967 petitioner wrote to President Johnson, enclosing the charred remnants of his draft cards and declaring his conviction that he must 'sever every link with violence and war.' The letter included a statement that petitioner had 'already been accepted for graduate study in a program where I would probably qualify for the theological deferment.' A copy of the letter was forwarded to the local board; the board continued petitioner's student deferment. Petitioner graduated in June 1967, and thereafter the board sent him a current information questionnaire (SSS Form 127), which asked inter alia for specific information concerning his future educational plans and generally for any information he thought should be called to the board's attention. Petitioner returned the questionnaire unanswered and announced in a cover letter that henceforth he would adhere to a policy of non-cooperation with the Selective Service System.

In September 1967 the board reviewed petitioner's file, rejected the pending conscientious objector claim, and reclassified petitioner I-A. In response to his reclassification petitioner sought neither a personal appearance before the local board nor review by the appeal board. Indeed, pursuant to his policy of noncooperation, he returned to the board, unopened, the communication notifying him of the reclassification and of his right to appear before the local board, to confer with the Government appeal agent, and to appeal. Petitioner did not appear for a physical examination ordered to take place in October 1967. He did respond to an order to appear for induction in January 1968, and he took a physical examination at that time. However, he refused to submit to induction.

Petitioner was prosecuted, under § 12(a) of the Military Selective Service Act of 1967, 50 U.S.C. App. § 462(a) and applicable Selective Service regulations, for failing to submit to induction (count I), failing to report for a pre-induction physical examination (count II), failing to keep possession of a valid classification notice (count III), and failing to submit requested information relevant to his draft status (count IV). Petitioner was convicted on all four counts and sentenced to two years' imprisonment on each count, the sentences to run concurrently. Petitioner's principal defense to liability for refusing induction was that the local board had erred in classifying him I-A. The Court of Appeals, with one judge dissenting, held that the defense of incorrect classification was barred because petitioner had failed to exhaust the administrative remedies available for correction of such an error. The conviction was affirmed by the Court of Appeals.

II

Two Terms ago, in McKart v. United States, 395 U.S. 185 (1969), the Court surveyed the place of the exhaustion doctrine in Selective Service cases, and the policies that underpin the doctrine. . . . McKart stands for the proposition that the doctrine is not to be applied inflexibly in all situations, but that decision also plainly contemplates situations where a litigant's claims will lose vitality because the litigant has failed to contest his rights in an administrative forum. The result in a criminal context is no doubt a substantial detriment to the defendant whose claims are barred. Still this unhappy result may be justified in particular circumstances by considerations relating to the integrity of the Selective Service classification process and the limited role of the courts in deciding the proper classification of draft registrants.

A

After McKart the task for the courts, in deciding the applicability of the exhaustion doctrine to the circumstances of a particular case, is to ask 'whether allowing all similarly situated registrants to bypass (the administrative avenue in question) would seriously impair the Selective Service System's ability to perform its functions.' 395 U.S. at 197. McKart specified the salient interests that may be jeopardized by a registrant's failure to pursue administrative remedies. Certain failures to exhaust may deny the administrative system important opportunities 'to make a factual record' for purposes of classification, or 'to exercise its discretion or apply its expertise' in the course of decisionmaking. Id. at 194. There may be a danger that relaxation of exhaustion requirements, in certain circumstances, would induce 'frequent and deliberate flouting of administrative processes,' thereby undermining the scheme of decisionmaking that Congress has created. Id. at 195. And of course, a strict exhaustion requirement tends to ensure that the agency have additional opportunities 'to discover and correct its own errors,' and thus may help to obviate all occasion for judicial review.

To be weighed against the interests in exhaustion is the harsh impact of the doctrine when it is invoked to bar any judicial review of a registrant's claims. Surely an insubstantial procedural default by a registrant should not shield an invalid order from judicial correction, simply because the interest in time-saving self-correction by the agency is involved. That single interest is conceivably slighted by any failure to exhaust, however innocuous the bypass in other respects, and McKart recognizes that the exhaustion requirement is not to be applied 'blindly in every case.' Id. at 201. McKart also acknowledges that the fear of 'frequent and deliberate flouting' can easily be overblown, since in the normal case a registrant would be 'foolhardy' indeed to withhold a valid claim from administrative scrutiny. Id. at 200. Thus the contention that the rigors of the exhaustion doctrine should be relaxed is not to be met by mechanical recitation of the broad interests usually served by the doctrine but rather should be assessed in light of a discrete analysis of the particular default in question, to see whether there is 'a governmental interest compelling enough' to justify the forfeiting of judicial review. Id. at 197. . . .

[H]ere it is apparent that McGee's failure to exhaust did jeopardize the interest in full administrative fact gathering and utilization of agency expertise, rather than the contrary. Unlike the dispute about statutory interpretation involved in McKart, McGee's claims to exempt status—as a ministerial student or a conscientious objector—depended on the application of expertise by administrative bodies in resolving underlying issues of fact. Factfinding for purposes of Selective Service classification is committed primarily to the administrative process, with very limited judicial review to ascertain whether there is a 'basis in fact' for the administrative determination. . . .

Petitioner argues that denial of exemption as a ministerial student was erroneous, but he had never requested that classification nor had he submitted information that would have been pertinent to such a claim. . . .

Such a default directly jeopardizes the functional autonomy of the administrative bodies on which Congress has conferred the primary responsibility to decide questions of fact relating to the proper classification of Selective Service registrants. Here the bypass was deliberate and without excuse, and this is not a case where entitlement to an exemption would be automatically made out, given a minimal showing by the registrant or minimal investigatory effort by the local board. . . .

Petitioner contends that denial of conscientious objector status was erroneous but after the claim was rejected he did not invoke the administrative processes available to correct the error. He did not seek a personal appearance before the local board, nor did he take an administrative appeal to contest the denial before the appeal board, which classifies de novo. . . .

Conscientious objector claims turn on the resolution of factual questions relating to the nature of a registrant's beliefs concerning war, the basis of the objection in conscience and religion, and the registrant's sincerity. See 50 U.S.C. App. § 456(j). Petitioner declined to contest the denial of his conscientious objector claim before the local board by securing a personal appearance, and the Selective Service System was thereby deprived of one opportunity to supplement the record of relevant facts. The opportunity would have been restored had petitioner sought review by the appeal board. While the local board apparently was satisfied that classification should be made on the basis of the record it confronted, the appeal board, which classifies de novo, might have determined that the record should be supplemented by the local board. In the circumstances of this case, petitioner's failure to take an administrative appeal not only deprived the appeal board of the opportunity to 'apply its expertise' in factfinding to the record that was available; it also removed an opportunity to supplement a record containing petitioner's own submissions but not containing the results of any specific inquiry into sincerity. . . .

And it is not fanciful to think that 'frequent and deliberate flouting of administrative processes' might occur if McGee and others similarly situated were allowed to press their claims in court despite a dual failure to exhaust.

Mr. Justice Douglas, dissenting.

This is a case where so far every judge has agreed that McGee is a conscientious objector. He expressed his belief 'in a personal Supreme Being to whom obligation is superior when duties of human relations are considered'; he said that 'taking part in any form of military operation indicates an approval/consent situation repugnant . . . to love and service of God and fellowman.' . . .

Petitioner was a Roman Catholic studying at the Union Theological Seminary in New York City, preparing for the ministry. His sincerity and dedication to his moral cause are not questioned.

The critical issue in the case is whether the Selective Service Board in 1966 did 'consider' and reject the claim of the registrant that he was a conscientious objector. . . .

It is, with all due respect, I think, a clear miscarriage of justice to allow a man to be sent off to prison where there are at best only dubious grounds for saying that the board discharged its statutory duty of considering and passing upon the conscientious objector claim. . . .

The man was a theological student studying for the priesthood, and to send him off to prison on this record is either to sanction a form of administrative trickery or to allow the Selective Service board to act quite irresponsibly. . . .

Notes and Questions

1. *The basis of decision.* What was the most important factor for the Court in *McGee*, in terms of distinguishing the case from *McKart*? Was it the need for factual development of McGee's actual conscientious beliefs? Is that a question that the agency is better suited to address in the first instance? What role did McGee's flouting of the Selective Service process play?

FOR DISCUSSION — Can you distinguish *McKart* and *McGee*?

McCarthy v. Madigan

503 U.S. 140 (1992)

Justice Blackmun delivered the opinion of the Court.

The issue in this case is whether a federal prisoner must resort to the internal grievance procedure promulgated by the Federal Bureau of Prisons before he may initiate a suit, pursuant to the authority of *Bivens v. Six Unknown Fed. Narcotics Agents*, 403 U.S. 388 (1971), solely for money damages. . . .

I

While he was a prisoner in the federal penitentiary at Leavenworth, petitioner John J. McCarthy filed a *pro se* complaint in the United States District Court for the District of Kansas against four prison employees: the hospital administrator, the chief psychologist, another psychologist, and a physician. McCarthy alleged that respondents had violated his constitutional rights under the Eighth Amendment by their deliberate indifference to his needs and medical condition resulting from a back operation and a history of psychiatric problems. On the first page of his complaint, he wrote: "This Complaint seeks Money Damages Only."

The District Court dismissed the complaint on the ground that petitioner had failed to exhaust prison administrative remedies. Under 28 CFR pt. 542 (1991), setting forth the general "Administrative Remedy Procedure for Inmates" at federal correctional institutions, a prisoner may "seek formal review of a complaint which relates to any aspect of his imprisonment." § 542.10. When an inmate files a complaint or appeal, the responsible officials are directed to acknowledge the filing with a "signed receipt" which is returned to the inmate, to "[c]onduct an investigation," and to "[r]espond to and sign all complaints or appeals." §§ 542.11(a)(2) to (4). The general grievance regulations do not provide for any kind of hearing or for the granting of any particular type of relief.

To promote efficient dispute resolution, the procedure includes rapid filing and response timetables. An inmate first seeks informal resolution of his claim by consulting prison personnel. § 542.13(a). If this informal effort fails, the prisoner "may file a formal written complaint on the appropriate form, within fifteen (15) calendar days of the date on which the basis of the complaint occurred." § 542.13(b). Should the warden fail to respond to the inmate's satisfaction within 15 days, the inmate has 20 days to appeal to the Bureau's Regional Director, who has 30 days to respond. If the inmate still remains unsatisfied, he has 30 days to make a final appeal to the Bureau's general counsel, who has another 30 days to respond. §§ 542.14 and 542.15. If the inmate can demonstrate a "valid reason for delay," he "shall be allowed" an extension of any of these time periods for filing. § 542.13(b).

Petitioner McCarthy filed with the District Court a motion for reconsideration under Federal Rule of Civil Procedure 60(b), arguing that he was not required to exhaust his administrative remedies, because he sought only money damages which, he claimed, the Bureau could not provide. The court denied the motion.

The Court of Appeals, in affirming, observed that because *Bivens* actions are a creation of the judiciary, the courts may impose reasonable conditions upon their filing. The exhaustion rule, the court reasoned, "is not keyed to the type of relief sought, but to the need for preliminary fact-finding" to determine "whether there is a possible *Bivens* cause of action." Accordingly, " '[a]lthough the administrative apparatus could not award money damages . . . , administrative consideration of the possibility of corrective action and a record would have aided a court in measuring liability and determining the *extent* of the damages.' " Exhaustion of the general grievance procedure was required notwithstanding the fact that McCarthy's request was solely for money damages.

II

The doctrine of exhaustion of administrative remedies is one among related doctrines—including abstention, finality, and ripeness—that govern the timing of federal-court decisionmaking. Of "paramount importance" to any exhaustion inquiry is congressional intent. *Patsy v. Board of Regents of Florida*, 457 U.S. 496, 501 (1982). Where Congress specifically mandates, exhaustion is required. *Coit Independence Joint Venture v. FSLIC*, 489 U.S. 561, 579 (1989); *Patsy*, 457 U.S. at 502, n. 4. But where Congress has not clearly required exhaustion, sound judicial discretion governs. *McGee v. United States*, 402 U.S. 479, 483, n. 6 (1971). Nevertheless, even in this field of judicial discretion, appropriate deference to Congress' power to prescribe the basic procedural scheme under which a claim may be heard in a federal court requires fashioning of exhaustion principles in a manner consistent with congressional intent and any applicable statutory scheme.

A

This Court long has acknowledged the general rule that parties exhaust prescribed administrative remedies before seeking relief from the federal courts. See, *e.g.*, *Myers v. Bethlehem Shipbuilding Corp.*, 303 U.S. 41, 50–51, and n. 9 (1938) (discussing cases as far back as 1898). Exhaustion is required because it serves the twin purposes of protecting administrative agency authority and promoting judicial efficiency.

As to the first of these purposes, the exhaustion doctrine recognizes the notion, grounded in deference to Congress' delegation of authority to coordinate branches of Government, that agencies, not the courts, ought to have primary responsibility for the programs that Congress has charged them to administer. Exhaustion concerns apply with particular force when the action under review involves exercise of the agency's discretionary power or when the agency proceedings in question allow the agency to apply its special expertise. *McKart v. United States*, 395 U.S. 185, 194 (1969). The exhaustion doctrine also acknowledges the commonsense notion of dispute resolution that an agency ought to have an opportunity to correct its own mistakes with respect to the programs it administers before it is haled into federal court. Correlatively, exhaustion principles apply with special force when "frequent and deliberate flouting of administrative processes" could weaken an agency's effectiveness by encouraging disregard of its procedures. *McKart v. United States*, 395 U.S. at 195.

As to the second of the purposes, exhaustion promotes judicial efficiency in at least two ways. When an agency has the opportunity to correct its own errors, a judicial controversy may well be mooted, or at least piecemeal appeals may be avoided. And even where a controversy survives administrative review, exhaustion of the administrative procedure may produce a useful record for subsequent judicial consideration, especially in a complex or technical factual context.

B

Notwithstanding these substantial institutional interests, federal courts are vested with a "virtually unflagging obligation" to exercise the jurisdiction given them. *Colorado River Water Conservation Dist. v. United States*, 424 U.S. 800, 817–818 (1976). "We have no more right to decline the exercise of jurisdiction which is given, than to usurp that which is not given." *Cohens v. Virginia*, 6 Wheat. 264, 404 (1821). Accordingly, this Court has declined to require exhaustion in some circumstances even where administrative and judicial interests would counsel otherwise. In determining whether exhaustion is required, federal courts must balance the interest of the individual in retaining prompt access to a federal judicial forum against countervailing institutional interests favoring exhaustion. . . .

C

This Court's precedents have recognized at least three broad sets of circumstances in which the interests of the individual weigh heavily against requiring administrative exhaustion. First, requiring resort to the administrative remedy may occasion undue prejudice to subsequent assertion of a court action. Such prejudice may result, for example, from an unreasonable or indefinite timeframe for administrative action. See *Gibson v. Berryhill*, 411 U.S. 564, 575, n. 14 (1973) (administrative remedy deemed inadequate "[m]ost often . . . because of delay by the agency"). See also *Walker v. Southern R. Co.*, 385 U.S. 196, 198 (1966) (possible delay of 10 years in administrative proceedings makes exhaustion unnecessary); *Smith v. Illinois Bell Telephone Co.*, 270 U.S. 587, 591–592 (1926) (claimant "is not required indefinitely to await a decision of the rate-making tribunal before applying to a federal court for equitable relief"). Even where the administrative decisionmaking schedule is otherwise reasonable and definite, a particular plaintiff may suffer irreparable harm if unable to secure immediate judicial consideration of his claim. *Bowen v. City of New York*, 476 U.S. [467, 483 (1986)] (disability-benefit claimants "would be irreparably injured were the exhaustion requirement now enforced against them"); *Aircraft & Diesel Equipment Corp. v. Hirsch*, 331 U.S. 752, 773 (1947) ("impending irreparable injury flowing from delay incident to following the prescribed procedure" may contribute to finding that exhaustion is not required). By the same token, exhaustion principles apply with less force when an individual's failure to exhaust may preclude a defense to criminal liability. *McKart v. United States*, 395 U.S. at 197.

Second, an administrative remedy may be inadequate "because of some doubt as to whether the agency was empowered to grant effective relief." *Gibson v. Berryhill*, 411 U.S. at 575, n. 14. For example, an agency, as a preliminary matter, may be unable to consider whether to grant relief because it lacks institutional competence to resolve the particular type of issue presented, such as the constitutionality of a statute. See, *e.g., Moore v. East Cleveland*, 431 U.S. [494, 497, n. 5 (1977)]; *Mathews v. Diaz*, 426 U.S. 67, 76 (1976). In a similar vein, exhaustion has not been required where the challenge is to the adequacy of the agency procedure itself, such that " 'the question of the adequacy of the administrative remedy . . . [is] for all practical purposes identical with the merits of [the plaintiff's] lawsuit.' " *Barry v. Barchi*, 443 U.S. 55, 63, n. 10 (1979) (quoting *Gibson v. Berryhill*, 411 U.S. at 575). Alternatively, an agency may be competent to adjudicate the issue presented, but still lack authority to grant the type of relief requested. *McNeese v. Board of Ed. for Community Unit School Dist. 187*, 373 U.S. 668, 675 (1963) (students seeking to integrate public school need not file complaint with school superintendent because the "Superintendent himself apparently has no power to order corrective action" except to request the Attorney General to bring suit); *Montana National Bank of Billings v. Yellowstone County*, 276 U.S. 499, 505 (1928) (taxpayer seeking refund not required to exhaust where "any such application [would have been] utterly futile since the county board of equalization was powerless to grant any appropriate relief" in face of prior controlling court decision).

Third, an administrative remedy may be inadequate where the administrative body is shown to be biased or has otherwise predetermined the issue before it. *Gibson v. Berryhill*, 411 U.S. at 575, n. 14; *Houghton v. Shafer*, 392 U.S. 639, 640 (1968) (in view of Attorney General's submission that the challenged rules of the prison were "validly and correctly applied to petitioner," requiring administrative review through a process culminating with the Attorney General "would be to demand a futile act"); [other citations omitted—Ed.].

III

In light of these general principles, we conclude that petitioner McCarthy need not have exhausted his constitutional claim for money damages. As a preliminary matter, we find that Congress has not meaningfully addressed the appropriateness of requiring exhaustion in this context. Although respondents' interests are significant, we are left with a firm conviction that, given the type of claim McCarthy raises and the particular characteristics of the Bureau's general grievance procedure, McCarthy's individual interests outweigh countervailing institutional interests favoring exhaustion.

Turning first to congressional intent, we note that the general grievance procedure was neither enacted nor mandated by Congress. Respondents, however, urge that Congress, in effect, has acted to require exhaustion by delegating power to the Attorney General and the Bureau of Prisons to control and manage the federal prison system. We think respondents confuse what Congress could be claimed to allow by implication with what Congress affirmatively has requested or required. By delegating authority, in the most general of terms, to the Bureau to administer the federal prison system, Congress cannot be said to have spoken to the particular issue whether prisoners in the custody of the Bureau should have direct access to the federal courts. . . .

Because Congress has not *required* exhaustion of a federal prisoner's *Bivens* claim, we turn to an evaluation of the individual and institutional interests at stake in this case. The general grievance procedure heavily burdens the individual interests of the petitioning inmate in two ways. First, the procedure imposes short, successive filing deadlines that create a high risk of forfeiture of a claim for failure to comply. Second, the administrative "remedy" does not authorize an award of monetary damages—the only relief requested by McCarthy in this action. The combination of these features means that the prisoner seeking only money damages has everything to lose and nothing to gain from being required to exhaust his claim under the internal grievance procedure. . . .

We do not find the interests of the Bureau of Prisons to weigh heavily in favor of exhaustion in view of the remedial scheme and particular claim presented here. To be sure, the Bureau has a substantial interest in encouraging internal resolution of grievances and in preventing the undermining of its authority by unnecessary resort by prisoners to the federal courts. But other institutional concerns relevant to exhaustion analysis appear to weigh in hardly at all. The Bureau's alleged failure to render medical care implicates only tangentially its authority to carry out the control and management of the federal prisons. Furthermore, the Bureau does not bring to bear any special expertise on the type of issue presented for resolution here.

The interests of judicial economy do not stand to be advanced substantially by the general grievance procedure. No formal factfindings are made. The paperwork generated by the grievance process might assist a court somewhat in ascertaining the facts underlying a prisoner's claim more quickly than if it has only a prisoner's complaint to review. But the grievance procedure does not create a formal factual record of the type that can be relied on conclusively by a court for disposition of a prisoner's claim on the pleadings or at summary judgment without the aid of affidavits. . . .

The judgment of the Court of Appeals is reversed.

CHIEF JUSTICE REHNQUIST, with whom JUSTICE SCALIA and JUSTICE THOMAS join, concurring in the judgment.

I agree with the Court's holding that a federal prisoner need not exhaust the procedures promulgated by the Federal Bureau of Prisons. My view, however, is based entirely on the fact that the grievance procedure at issue does not provide for any award of monetary damages. As a result, in cases such as this one where prisoners seek monetary relief, the Bureau's administrative remedy furnishes no effective remedy at all, and it is therefore improper to impose an exhaustion requirement.

Because I would base the decision on this ground, I do not join the Court's extensive discussion of the general principles of exhaustion . . . . In particular, I disagree with the Court's reliance on the grievance procedure's filing deadlines as a basis for excusing exhaustion. As the majority observes, we have previously refused to require exhaustion of administrative remedies where the administrative process subjects plaintiffs to unreasonable delay or to an indefinite timeframe for decision. This principle rests on our belief that when a plaintiff might have to wait seemingly forever for an agency decision, agency procedures are "inadequate" and therefore need not be exhausted.

But the Court makes strange use of this principle in holding that filing deadlines imposed by agency procedures may provide a basis for finding that those procedures need not be exhausted. Whereas before we have held that procedures without "reasonable time limit[s]" may be inadequate because they make a plaintiff wait too long, today the majority concludes that strict filing deadlines might also contribute to a finding of inadequacy because they make a plaintiff move too quickly. But surely the second proposition does not follow from the first. In fact, short filing deadlines will almost always promote quick decisionmaking by an agency, the very result that we have advocated repeatedly in the cases cited above. So long as there is an escape clause, as there is here, and the time limit is within a zone of reasonableness, as I believe it is here, the length of the period should not be a factor in deciding the adequacy of the remedy.

NOTES AND QUESTIONS

1. **_The three common exceptions to exhaustion._** _McCarthy_ is another case involving the common-law exhaustion requirement. Recall that Congress overrode the Court's decision in _McCarthy_ by enacting the Prison Litigation Reform Act, which specifically required exhaustion. But until the PLRA was enacted, no specific statute required exhaustion of such claims. And McCarthy's claim was brought under _Bivens_—that is, directly under the Fourth Amendment. It was not brought under the APA and so APA § 704 did not apply. This meant that the Court was free to require exhaustion, but it also could choose not to require it.

The Court chose not to require exhaustion. In so doing, it identified three common exceptions to exhaustion: where proceeding through the agency may cause undue delay; where the agency may not have the power to decide the question at hand; and where the agency is biased. Do you see why these are exceptions? Do you agree that they should be? How would you balance these against the reasons the courts created an exhaustion requirement in the first place? Would it just be easier if courts got out of the exhaustion business altogether, leaving it entirely up to Congress (or the agency, by rule) to determine whether and to what extent exhaustion is necessary?

 CROSS REFERENCE Recall that the analysis of statutory exhaustion is distinct from that of common-law exhaustion.

2. **_Issue exhaustion/waiver._** If a potential litigant is required to exhaust administrative remedies, does that mean the litigant must also have raised the particular arguments she plans to make in federal court with the agency? The answer is typically yes. In general, a similar doctrine within the federal court system is simply called "waiver": if you plan to raise an issue on appeal, you generally must raise it at the trial court, too. But there are exceptions to waiver doctrine, especially if the argument is purely legal and there was some explanation for why it was not raised, although the exact rules for waivers and exceptions to waiver vary from circuit to circuit. In administrative law, the related doctrine is called "issue exhaustion": if you're supposed to exhaust remedies so the agency can deploy its specialized expertise, that means you typically have to raise the particular arguments with the agency, too. There are some exceptions to this doctrine, too, although their scope is unclear. For example, in Sims v. Apfel, 530 U.S. 103 (2000), a plurality of the Supreme Court held that a social security disability claimant did not have to exhaust the particular argument before the agency first because the agency proceeding was more inquisitorial than adversarial.

    3.   ***Exhaustion in the rulemaking context.*** It is not entirely clear the extent to which exhaustion requirements apply in the rulemaking context, and whether they should apply in the rulemaking context at all; but some exhaustion requirement is occasionally required. This will be particularly true if the statute requires a party to raise an objection to the rulemaking as a precondition to judicial review. See, e.g., 42 U.S.C. § 7607(d)(7)(B) ("Only an objection to a rule . . . raised with reasonably specificity during the period for public comment . . . may be raised during judicial review."). The D.C. Circuit has sometimes made more general and conclusive statements in the rulemaking context to the effect that "[i]t is a hard and fast rule of administrative law, rooted in simple fairness, that issues not raised before an agency are waived and will not be considered by a court on review." Nuclear Energy Inst., Inc. v. EPA, 373 F.3d 1251, 1297 (D.C. Cir. 2004). But can that possibly be true? After all, no one is *required* to participate in the public comment process. Does that mean an injured party can never sue to invalidate a rule? What do you think?

    4.   ***Primary jurisdiction.*** There is another doctrine related to exhaustion, that sounds in the same values. Sometimes there is no doubt that both the federal court and the agency have jurisdiction over a particular case or controversy. But there may be an issue in the case that is more amenable to resolution by the agency because of the agency's expertise. In other words, the agency might have "primary jurisdiction" over a particular matter, even though the federal court certainly has jurisdiction over the suit. In such cases, the "primary jurisdiction" is an abstention doctrine: the court will abstain from hearing the case until the issue over which the agency has primary jurisdiction is resolved by the agency. The Supreme Court has explained the difference between exhaustion and primary jurisdiction as follows:

> The doctrine of primary jurisdiction, like the rule requiring exhaustion of administrative remedies, is concerned with promoting proper relationships between the courts and administrative agencies charged with particular regulatory duties. 'Exhaustion' applies where a claim is cognizable in the first instance by an administrative agency alone; judicial interference is withheld until the administrative process has run its course. 'Primary jurisdiction,' on the other hand, applies where a claim is originally cognizable in the courts, and comes into play whenever enforcement of the claim requires the resolution of issues which, under a regulatory scheme, have been placed within the special competence of an administrative body; in such a case the judicial process is suspended pending referral of such issues to the administrative body for its views.

United States v. W. Pac. R. Co., 352 U.S. 59, 63–64 (1956). This abstention doctrine is similar to other abstention doctrines where the federal court has jurisdiction but will hold the federal proceedings in abeyance, for example, until an issue of state-law is resolved by the state courts. See R.R. Comm'n of Tex. v. Pullman Co., 312 U.S. 496, 497 (1941) (*"Pullman* abstention").

E. Timing (II): Preenforcement Injunctions

Another set of important cases respecting the "timing" of review has to do with whether a federal court can enjoin administrative action before it occurs. These cases are therefore of course related to "timing," but really they're about the power of federal courts to grant equitable relief as in *Ex Parte Young* and similar cases. Some of the following cases are sometimes described as "preenforcement review" cases. Some predominantly discuss statutory preclusion of review. Some discuss administrative exhaustion. Others even have to do with finality. And the cases involving "ripeness"—whether a regulation is "ripe" for judicial review in the absence of an enforcement proceeding—are usually included with the materials on finality and exhaustion, but are really about the power of courts to grant equitable relief. Such cases are all discussed in this final section on reviewability.

1.   Injunctions Since *Ex Parte Young*

Recall the principle of *Ex Parte Young*, discussed earlier in this chapter. If an individual (1) had a known action at law or otherwise a known legal right, and (2) the remedy at law was inadequate, then that individual could sue for an injunction: she could sue in equity to enjoin the administrative officer from engaging in unlawful behavior. *Ex Parte Young* involved a state statute, but just a few years before *Ex Parte Young*, the Supreme Court applied those same principles of equity to a case involving a federal administrative officer. In American School of Magnetic Healing v. McAnnulty, 187 U.S. 94 (1902), the federal postmaster, pursuant to a determination by the Postmaster General after administrative proceedings, stopped delivering mail to the American School of Magnetic Healing on the grounds that they were engaged in a fraud. The central tenet of the school was "the physical and practical proposition that the mind of the human race is largely responsible for its ills, and is a perceptible factor in the treating, curing, benefiting, and remedying thereof," and that "through proper exercise of the faculty of the brain and mind," individuals could "largely control and remedy the ills that humanity is heir to."

> **CROSS REFERENCE**   We discussed *Ex Parte Young* earlier in this chapter, when exploring early remedies against administrative actions.

The Court concluded that injunctive relief was available:

> Conceding, for the purpose of this case, that Congress has full and absolute jurisdiction over the mails, and that it may provide who may and who may not use them, and that its action is not subject to review by the courts, and also conceding the conclusive character of the determination by the Postmaster General of any material and relevant questions of fact arising in the administration of the statutes of Congress relating to his department, the question still remains as to the power of the court to grant relief where the Postmaster General has assumed and exercised jurisdiction in a case not covered by the statutes, and where he has ordered the detention of mail matter, when the statutes have not granted him power so to order. Has Congress intrusted the administration of these statutes wholly to the discretion of the Postmaster General, and to such an extent that his determination is conclusive upon all questions arising under those statutes, even though the evidence which is adduced before him is

wholly uncontradicted, and shows, beyond any room for dispute or doubt, that the case, in any view, is beyond the statutes, and not covered or provided for by them?

That the conduct of the post office is a part of the administrative department of the government is entirely true, but that does not necessarily and always oust the courts of jurisdiction to grant relief to a party aggrieved by any action by the head, or one of the subordinate officials, of that Department, which is unauthorized by the statute under which he assumes to act. The acts of all its officers must be justified by some law, and in case an official violates the law to the injury of an individual the courts generally have jurisdiction to grant relief. . . .

In our view of these statutes the complainants had the legal right, under the general acts of Congress relating to the mails, to have their letters delivered at the post office as directed. They had violated no law which Congress had passed, and their letters contained checks, drafts, money orders, and money itself, all of which were their property as soon as they were deposited in the various post offices for transmission by mail. They allege, and it is not difficult to see that the allegation is true, that, if such action be persisted in, these complainants will be entirely cut off from all mail facilities, and their business will necessarily be greatly injured, if not wholly destroyed, such business being, so far as the laws of Congress are concerned, legitimate and lawful. In other words, irreparable injury will be done to these complainants by the mistaken act of the Postmaster General in directing the defendant to retain and refuse to deliver letters addressed to them. The Postmaster General's order, being the result of a mistaken view of the law, could not operate as a defense to this action on the part of the defendant [the local postmaster], though it might justify his obedience thereto until some action of the court. In such a case as the one before us there is no adequate remedy at law, the injunction to prohibit the further withholding of the mail from complainants being the only remedy at all adequate to the full relief to which the complainants are entitled.

187 U.S. at 107–08, 110. All the themes from *Ex Parte Young* are present. The school had a *legal right* to the receipt of mail, which right was established

in the federal statutes establishing the post office. The money shipped to it by customers was the school's *property*. The first prong of the equitable relief analysis was therefore satisfied. And, secondly, the remedy at law was inadequate. If an injunction did not issue, and the postmaster continued to withhold the school's mail, then the school "will be entirely cut off from all mail facilities, and [its] business will necessarily be greatly injured, if not wholly destroyed." Note also that the Court explained that the Postmaster General's order to the local postmaster did not immunize the local postmaster from liability, just as in *Little v. Barreme*.

McAnnulty was not an anomaly. By "the early part of the twentieth century," Professor Caleb Nelson has written, "the most common path for plaintiffs who wanted courts to control the behavior of federal officials was to bring a suit in equity for an injunction." Caleb Nelson, *"Standing" and Administrative Rights in Administrative Law*, 105 Va. L. Rev. 703, 713 (2019); see also John F. Duffy, *Administrative Common Law in Judicial Review*, 77 Tex. L. Rev. 113, 121–30 (1998). In fact, recall from your constitutional law classes one more famous case along these lines, Youngstown Sheet & Tube Co. v. Sawyer, 343 U.S. 579 (1952) ("The Steel Seizure Case."). That case involved a labor strike at steel mills while the Korean War was ongoing. To prevent a steel shortage, President Truman issued an executive order pursuant to which the Secretary of Commerce, Charles Sawyer, proceeded to seize the still mills and have the government operate them. The owners of the steel mills sought an injunction to have Sawyer return to them possession of the mills. The Supreme Court affirmed the District Court's ordering the requested injunctive relief against this high-ranking administrative officer, who was directly following the President's own orders.

COMPARATIVE PERSPECTIVE

How much should these early cases factor into modern judicial decision-making?

2. Expansion: Modern Ripeness Doctrine

As of 1967, injunctions were regularly used to enjoin administrative action, but these injunctions were still the exception and not the rule. One still had to show that the remedy at law was still inadequate. Thus, as a general matter, courts refused to authorize preenforcement review of federal statutes—and regulations—where the penalties for violation were not particularly steep. The mere cost of complying with the administrative order was not deemed sufficient irreparable injury to justify injunctive relief. And where employees could recover their salary after-the-fact if discharged, the Court held that a pre-violation constitutional challenge to a federal statute was premature. United Public Workers of America (CIO) v. Mitchell, 330 U.S. 75 (1947).

In 1967, however, the Court relaxed the availability of preenforcement injunctions with the following case, *Abbott Laboratories*, which permitted judicial review of a regulation before the agency brought an enforcement proceeding. The Court seems to hold that a regulation that immediately imposes obligations on regulated parties may be challenged without first complying with the regulation or waiting for an enforcement action. *Abbott Laboratories* is the leading modern case on "ripeness." Ripeness is the notion that a judicial decision will be

Defined Term

RIPENESS: Closely related to other reviewability doctrines, ripeness is the notion that some lawsuits are premature, such that judicial review would be inappropriate.

premature, usually because relevant facts have not been sufficiently developed, and therefore judicial review of the regulation would be inappropriate. But these cases really have to do with equitable relief. Ask yourself: Do the regulated parties in the following case have an adequate remedy at law? Is the remedy inadequate merely because a regulated party might have to expend some amount of resources conforming to a regulation, even if the penalty for a violation is not severe? What might explain the expansion of preenforcement review? Might it have something to do with the growing skepticism of agencies along with the rise of public choice theory in the 1960s?

Abbott Laboratories v. Gardner

387 U.S. 136 (1967)

MR. JUSTICE HARLAN delivered the opinion of the Court.

In 1962 Congress amended the Federal Food, Drug, and Cosmetic Act to require manufacturers of prescription drugs to print the 'established name' of the drug 'prominently and in type at least half as large as that used thereon for any proprietary name or designation for such drug,' on labels and other printed material, 21 U.S.C. § 352(e)(1)(B). The 'established name' is one designated by the Secretary of Health, Education, and Welfare pursuant to § 502(e)(2) of the Act, 21 U.S.C. § 352(e)(2); the 'proprietary name' is usually a trade name under which a particular drug is marketed. The underlying purpose of the 1962 amendment was to bring to the attention of doctors and patients the fact that many of the drugs sold under familiar trade names are actually identical to drugs sold under their 'established' or less familiar trade names at significantly lower prices. The Commissioner of Food and Drugs, exercising authority delegated to him by the Secretary, published proposed regulations designed to implement the statute. After inviting and considering comments submitted by interested parties the Commissioner promulgated the following regulation for the 'efficient enforcement' of the Act, 21 U.S.C. § 371(a):

> 'If the label or labeling of a prescription drug bears a proprietary name or designation for the drug or any ingredient thereof, the established name, if such there be, corresponding to such proprietary name or designation, shall accompany each appearance of such proprietary name or designation.' 21 CFR § 1.104(g)(1).

A similar rule was made applicable to advertisements for prescription drugs, 21 CFR § 1.105(b)(1).

The present action was brought by a group of 37 individual drug manufacturers and by the Pharmaceutical Manufacturers Association, of which all the petitioner companies are members, and which includes manufacturers of more than 90% of the Nation's supply of prescription drugs. They challenged the regulations on the ground that the Commissioner exceeded his authority under the statute by promulgating an order requiring labels, advertisements, and other printed matter relating to prescription drugs to designate the established name of the particular drug involved every time its trade name is used anywhere in such material. . . .

The Court of Appeals for the Third Circuit . . . held first that under the statutory scheme provided by the Federal Food, Drug, and Cosmetic Act pre-enforcement review of these regulations was unauthorized and therefore beyond the jurisdiction of the District Court. Second, the Court of Appeals held that no 'actual case or controversy' existed and, for that reason, that no relief under the Administrative Procedure Act, or under the Declaratory Judgment Act, was in any event available. Because of the general importance of the question, and the apparent conflict with the decision of the Court of Appeals for the Second Circuit in Toilet Goods Assn. v. Gardner, 360 F.2d 677, which we also review today, 387 U.S. 158, we granted certiorari.

[The Court first finds that the statute does not preclude review.—Ed.]

II

. . . . The injunctive and declaratory judgment remedies are discretionary, and courts traditionally have been reluctant to apply them to administrative determinations unless these arise in the context of a controversy 'ripe' for judicial resolution. Without undertaking to survey the intricacies of the ripeness doctrine it is fair to say that its basic rationale is to prevent the courts, through avoidance of premature adjudication, from entangling themselves in abstract disagreements over administrative policies, and also to protect the agencies from judicial interference until an administrative decision has been formalized and its effects felt in a concrete way by the challenging parties. The problem is best seen in a twofold aspect, requiring us to evaluate both the fitness of the issues for judicial decision and the hardship to the parties of withholding court consideration.

As to the former factor, we believe the issues presented are appropriate for judicial resolution at this time. First, all parties agree that the issue tendered is a purely legal one: whether the statute was properly construed by the Commissioner to require the established name of the drug to be used every time the proprietary name is employed. Both sides moved for summary judgment in the District Court, and no claim is made here that further administrative proceedings are contemplated. It is suggested that the justification for this rule might vary with different circumstances, and that the expertise of the Commissioner is relevant to passing upon the validity of the regulation. This of course is true, but the suggestion overlooks the fact that both sides have approached this case as one purely of congressional intent, and that the Government made no effort to justify the regulation in factual terms.

Second, the regulations in issue we find to be 'final agency action' within the meaning of s 10 of the Administrative Procedure Act, 5 U.S.C. § 704, as construed in judicial decisions. An 'agency action' includes any 'rule,' defined by the Act as 'an agency statement of general or particular applicability and future effect designed to implement, interpret, or prescribe law or policy,' 5 U.S.C. §§ 551(4), 551(13). . . . Thus in Columbia Broadcasting System v. United

States, 316 U.S. 407, . . . this Court held reviewable a regulation of the Federal Communications Commission setting forth certain proscribed contractual arrangements between chain broadcasters and local stations. The FCC did not have direct authority to regulate these contracts, and its rule asserted only that it would not license stations which maintained such contracts with the networks. Although no license had in fact been denied or revoked, and the FCC regulation could properly be characterized as a statement only of its intentions, the Court held that 'Such regulations have the force of law before their sanctions are invoked as well as after. . . .'

. . . . The regulation challenged here, promulgated in a formal manner after announcement in the Federal Register and consideration of comments by interested parties is quite clearly definitive. There is no hint that this regulation is informal, or only the ruling of a subordinate official, or tentative. It was made effective upon publication, and the Assistant General Counsel for Food and Drugs stated in the District Court that compliance was expected.

The Government argues, however, that the present case can be distinguished from [prior] cases . . . on the ground that in those instances the agency involved could implement its policy directly, while here the Attorney General must authorize criminal and seizure actions for violations of the statute. In the context of this case, we do not find this argument persuasive. These regulations are not meant to advise the Attorney General, but purport to be directly authorized by the statute. Thus, if within the Commissioner's authority, they have the status of law and violations of them carry heavy criminal and civil sanctions. . . .

This is also a case in which the impact of the regulations upon the petitioners is sufficiently direct and immediate as to render the issue appropriate for judicial review at this stage. These regulations purport to give an authoritative interpretation of a statutory provision that has a direct effect on the day-to-day business of all prescription drug companies; its promulgation puts petitioners in a dilemma that it was the very purpose of the Declaratory Judgment Act to ameliorate. As the District Court found on the basis of uncontested allegations, 'Either they must comply with the every time requirement and incur the costs of changing over their promotional material and labeling or they must follow their present course and risk prosecution.' The regulations are clear-cut, and were made effective immediately upon publication; as noted earlier the agency's counsel represented to the District Court that immediate compliance with their terms was expected. . . .

It is relevant at this juncture to recognize that petitioners deal in a sensitive industry, in which public confidence in their drug products is especially important. To require them to challenge these regulations only as a defense to an action brought by the Government might harm them severely and unnecessarily. Where the legal issue presented is fit for judicial resolution, and where a regulation requires an immediate and significant change in the plaintiffs' conduct of their affairs with serious penalties attached to noncompliance, access to the courts under the Administrative Procedure Act and the Declaratory Judgment Act must be permitted, absent a statutory bar or some other unusual circumstance, neither of which appears here.

The Government does not dispute the very real dilemma in which petitioners are placed by the regulation, but contends that 'mere financial expense' is not a justification for pre-enforcement judicial review. It is of course true that cases in this Court dealing with the standing of particular parties to bring an action have held that a possible financial loss is not by itself a sufficient interest to sustain a judicial challenge to governmental action. But there is no question in the present case that petitioners have sufficient standing as plaintiffs: the regulation is directed at them in particular; it requires them to make significant changes in their everyday business practices; if they fail to observe the Commissioner's rule they are quite clearly exposed to the imposition of strong sanctions. . . .

Finally, the Government urges that to permit resort to the courts in this type of case may delay or impede effective enforcement of the Act. We fully recognize the important public interest served by assuring prompt and unimpeded administration of the Pure Food, Drug, and Cosmetic Act, but we do not find the Government's argument convincing. First, in this particular case, a pre-enforcement challenge by nearly all prescription drug manufacturers is calculated to speed enforcement. If the Government prevails, a large part of the industry is bound by the decree; if the Government loses, it can more quickly revise its regulation. . . .

[I]t is important to note that the institution of this type of action does not by itself stay the effectiveness of the challenged regulation. There is nothing in the record to indicate that petitioners have sought to stay enforcement of the 'every time' regulation pending judicial review. See 5 U.S.C. § 705. If the agency believes that a suit of this type will significantly impede enforcement or will harm the public interest, it need not postpone enforcement of the regulation and may oppose any motion for a judicial stay on the part of those challenging the regulation. It is scarcely to be doubted that a court would refuse to postpone the effective date of an agency action if the Government could show, as it made no effort to do here, that delay would be detrimental to the public health or safety. . . .

Mr. Justice Fortas, with whom The Chief Justice and Mr. Justice Clark join, . . . dissenting . . . .

[The first part of Justice Fortas's opinion on reviewability is omitted.—Ed.]

II

I come then to the questions whether the review otherwise available under the statute is 'adequate,' whether the controversies are 'ripe' or appropriate for review in terms of the evaluation of the competing private and public interests. I discuss these together because the questions of adequacy and ripeness or appropriateness for review are interrelated. I again note that no constitutional issues are raised, and, indeed, no issues as to the authority of the agency to issue regulations of the general sort involved. The only issue is whether that authority was properly exercised.

There is, of course, no abstract or mechanical method for determining the adequacy of review provisions. Where personal status or liberties are involved, the courts may well insist upon a considerable ease of challenging administrative orders or regulations. But in situations where a regulatory scheme designed to protect the public is involved, this Court has held that postponement of the opportunity to obtain judicial relief in the interest of avoiding disruption of the regulatory plan is entirely justifiable. . . .

The regulation . . . relates to a 1962 amendment to the Act requiring manufacturers of prescription drugs to print on the labels or other printed material, the 'established name' of the drug 'prominently and in type at least half as large as that used thereon for any proprietary name or designation for such drug.' § 502(e)(1). Obviously, this requires some elucidation, either case-by-case or by general regulation or pronouncement, because the statute does not say that this must be done 'every time,' or only once on each label or in each pamphlet, or once per panel, etc., or that it must be done differently on labels than on circulars, or doctors' literature than on directions to the patients, etc.

This is exactly the traditional purpose and function of an administrative agency. The Commissioner, acting by delegation from the Secretary, took steps to provide for the specification. He invited and considered comments and then issued a regulation requiring that the 'established name' appear every time the proprietary name is used. A manufacturer—or other person who violates this regulation—has mislabeled his product. The product may be seized; or injunction may be sought; or the mislabeler may be criminally prosecuted. In any of these actions he may challenge the regulation and obtain a judicial determination.

The Court, however, moved by petitioners' claims as to the expense and inconvenience of compliance and the risks of deferring challenge by noncompliance, decrees that the manufacturers may have their suit for injunction at this time and reverses the Third Circuit. The Court says that this confronts the manufacturer with a 'real dilemma.' But the fact of the matter is that the dilemma is no more than citizens face in connection with countless statutes and with the rules of the SEC, FTC, FCC, ICC, and other regulatory agencies. This has not heretofore been regarded as a basis for injunctive relief unless Congress has so provided. . . .

With all respect, we should refuse to accept the invitation to abandon the traditional insistence of the courts upon specific, concrete facts, and instead entertain this massive onslaught in which it will be utterly impossible to make the kind of discrete judgments which are within judicial competence. With all respect we should not permit the administration of a law of the Congress to be disrupted by this non-adjudicable mass assault.

NOTES AND QUESTIONS

1.   The test for ripeness. *Abbott Labs.* and its companion case, *Toilet Goods* (which we discuss presently), has come to stand for the proposition that there is a two-part test for ripeness: "The problem is best seen in a twofold aspect, requiring us to evaluate both the fitness of the issues for judicial decision and the hardship to the parties of withholding court consideration." *Abbott Labs.,* 387 U.S. at 149; see also Toilet Goods Ass'n, Inc. v. Gardner, 387 U.S. 158, 162 (1967) ("In determining whether a challenge to an administrative regulation is ripe for review a twofold inquiry must be made: first to determine whether the issues tendered are appropriate for judicial resolution, and second to assess the hardship to the parties if judicial relief is denied at that stage."); Nat'l Park Hosp. Ass'n v. Dep't of Interior, 538 U.S. 803, 808 (2003) ("Determining whether administrative action is ripe for judicial review requires us to evaluate (1) the fitness of the issues for judicial decision and (2) the hardship to the parties of withholding court consideration.").

As to the first factor, the issue will generally not be fit for judicial decision if further factual development is necessary; purely legal issues, in contrast, are generally fit for judicial resolution. See, e.g., Thomas v. Union Carbide Agr. Prod. Co., 473 U.S. 568, 581 (1985).

Hardship typically depends on the actual adverse legal consequences, and the likelihood of suffering those consequences. In *National Park Hospitality*, the Court found no hardship because at issue was a mere policy statement without the force of law, and it simply stated the agency's view that certain legal requirement did *not* apply to the plaintiffs. 538 U.S. 803, 810–11.

2.   *Is this case really about reviewability?* This case is often treated as a "reviewability" case, and the leading case on "ripeness." But isn't it just a case about the availability of equitable *remedies*? Note how the Court responded to the government's argument that relief was available in an enforcement proceeding: "[T]here is no question in the present case that petitioners have sufficient standing as plaintiffs: the regulation is directed at them in particular; it requires them to make significant changes in their everyday business practices; if they fail to observe the Commissioner's rule they are quite clearly exposed to the imposition of strong sanctions."

Is that enough, however, to conclude that the legal remedy was sufficiently "inadequate" as to justify equitable relief? Although the Court does observe that in some situations there may be strong sanctions, that need not be the case; often the FDA simply sought an injunction, or simply seized the goods. And what do you think of Justice Fortas's response to the argument that Abbott Laboratories would have to expend significant cost in complying with the regulation? Isn't that the "dilemma" faced by all citizens when confronting new regulations by all sorts of government entities? Does that now mean that equitable relief is always available? Can this case be seen as consistent with the prior cases on equitable relief because, as the Court noted, violations of the regulations "carry heavy criminal and civil sanctions"?

3. *The relation of ripeness to other reviewability doctrines.* You'll notice
that in *Abbott Labs.*, a case about ripeness, the Court spent a lot of time addressing finality, and also a bit of time on standing. This is not surprising: these
reviewability doctrines have significant overlap. The Court held that the basic
rationale of ripeness doctrine "is to prevent the courts, through avoidance of
premature adjudication, from entangling themselves in abstract disagreements
over administrative policies, and also to protect the agencies from judicial interference until an administrative decision has been formalized and its effects
felt in a concrete way by the challenging parties." This seems quite similar to
the injury requirement for constitutional standing. And surely if the agency
action is not final, judicial review also will not be ripe—suggesting that finality
may be a subset of ripeness, even in the absence of the explicit statutory requirement for finality in APA § 704. And the factors in the ripeness analysis
about factual development and administrative expertise are similar to the factors in an administrative exhaustion case.

It is no surprise that these doctrines overlap and cause confusion. Famously, in Ticor Title Insurance Co. v. FTC, 814 F.2d 731 (D.C. Cir. 1987), the
three-judge panel all agreed that the case was reviewable, but disagreed on the
rationale: one judge thought the case
was not ripe, another that the agency
action was not final, and the third
that the litigant had not exhausted
administrative remedies.

Toilet Goods was a
companion case to
Abbott Labs. What
distinguishes these
cases?

Toilet Goods Ass'n, Inc. v. Gardner

387 U.S. 158 (1967)

MR. JUSTICE HARLAN delivered the opinion of the Court.

Petitioners in this case are the Toilet Goods Association, an organization
of cosmetics manufacturers accounting for some 90% of annual American sales
in this field, and 39 individual cosmetics manufacturers and distributors. They
brought this action in the United States District Court for the Southern District
of New York seeking declaratory and injunctive relief against the Secretary of
Health, Education, and Welfare and the Commissioner of Food and Drugs, on
the ground that certain regulations promulgated by the Commissioner exceeded

his statutory authority under the Color Additive Amendments to the Federal Food, Drug and Cosmetic Act. The District Court held that the Act did not prohibit this type of preenforcement suit . . . .

Each side below sought review here from the portions of the Court of Appeals' decision adverse to it, the Government as petitioner in Gardner v. Toilet Goods Assn., 387 U.S. 167, and the Toilet Goods Association and other plaintiffs in the present case. . . .

In our decisions reversing the judgment in Abbott Laboratories, 387 U.S. 136, and affirming the judgment in Gardner v. Toilet Goods Assn., 387 U.S. 167, both decided today, we hold that nothing in the Food, Drug, and Cosmetic Act bars a pre-enforcement suit under the Administrative Procedure Act and the Declaratory Judgment Act. We nevertheless agree with the Court of Appeals that judicial review of this particular regulation in this particular context is inappropriate at this stage because, applying the standards set forth in Abbott Laboratories v. Gardner, the controversy is not presently ripe for adjudication.

The regulation in issue here was promulgated under the Color Additive Amendments of 1960, a statute that revised and somewhat broadened the authority of the Commissioner to control the ingredients added to foods, drugs, and cosmetics that impart color to them. The Commissioner of Food and Drugs, exercising power delegated by the Secretary, under statutory authority 'to promulgate regulations for the efficient enforcement' of the Act, issued the following regulation after due public notice, and consideration of comments submitted by interested parties:

> '(a) When it appears to the Commissioner that a person has:

> '(4) Refused to permit duly authorized employees of the Food and Drug Administration free access to all manufacturing facilities, processes, and formulae involved in the manufacture of color additives and intermediates from which such color additives are derived; 'he may immediately suspend certification service to such person and may continue such suspension until adequate corrective action has been taken.'

28 Fed. Reg. 6445–6446; 21 CFR § 8.28.

The petitioners maintain that this regulation is an impermissible exercise of authority, that the FDA has long sought congressional authorization for free access to facilities, processes, and formulae, but that Congress has always denied the agency this power except for prescription drugs. Framed in this way, we agree with petitioners that a 'legal' issue is raised, but nevertheless we are not persuaded that the present suit is properly maintainable.

In determining whether a challenge to an administrative regulation is ripe for review a twofold inquiry must be made: first to determine whether the issues tendered are appropriate for judicial resolution, and second to assess the hardship to the parties if judicial relief is denied at that stage.

As to the first of these factors, we agree with the Court of Appeals that the legal issue as presently framed is not appropriate for judicial resolution. This is not because the regulation is not the agency's considered and formalized determination . . . . Also, we recognize the force of petitioners' contention that the issue as they have framed it presents a purely legal question: whether the regulation is totally beyond the agency's power under the statute, the type of legal issue that courts have occasionally dealt with without requiring a specific attempt at enforcement, or exhaustion of administrative remedies.

These points which support the appropriateness of judicial resolution are, however, outweighed by other considerations. The regulation serves notice only that the Commissioner may under certain circumstances order inspection of certain facilities and data, and that further certification of additives may be refused to those who decline to permit a duly authorized inspection until they have complied in that regard. At this juncture we have no idea whether or when such an inspection will be ordered and what reasons the Commissioner will give to justify his order. The statutory authority asserted for the regulation is the power to promulgate regulations 'for the efficient enforcement' of the Act. Whether the regulation is justified thus depends not only, as petitioners appear to suggest, on whether Congress refused to include a specific section of the Act authorizing such inspections, although this factor is to be sure a highly relevant one, but also on whether the statutory scheme as a whole justified promulgation of the regulation. This will depend not merely on an inquiry into statutory purpose, but concurrently on an understanding of what types of enforcement problems are encountered by the FDA, the need for various sorts of supervision in order to effectuate the goals of the Act, and the safeguards devised to protect legitimate trade secrets. We believe that judicial appraisal of these factors is likely to stand on a much surer footing in the context of a specific application of this regulation than could be the case in the framework of the generalized challenge made here.

We are also led to this result by considerations of the effect on the petitioners of the regulation, for the test of ripeness, as we have noted, depends not only on how adequately a court can deal with the legal issue presented, but also on the degree and nature of the regulation's present effect on those seeking relief. The regulation challenged here is not analogous to those . . . where the impact of the administrative action could be said to be felt immediately by those subject to it in conducting their day-to-day affairs.

This is not a situation in which primary conduct is affected—when contracts must be negotiated, ingredients tested or substituted, or special records compiled. This regulation merely states that the Commissioner may authorize inspectors to examine certain processes or formulae; no advance action is required of cosmetics manufacturers, who since the enactment of the 1938 Act have been under a statutory duty to permit reasonable inspection of a 'factory, warehouse, establishment, or vehicle and all pertinent equipment, finished and unfinished materials; containers, and labeling therein.' § 704(a). Moreover, no irremediable adverse consequences flow from requiring a later challenge to this regulation by a manufacturer who refuses to allow this type of inspection. Unlike the other regulations challenged in this action, in which seizure of goods, heavy fines, adverse publicity for distributing 'adulterated' goods, and possible criminal liability might penalize failure to comply, a refusal to admit an inspector here would at most lead only to a suspension of certification services to the particular party, a determination that can then be promptly challenged through an administrative procedure, which in turn is reviewable by a court. Such review will provide an adequate forum for testing the regulation in a concrete situation. . . .

NOTES AND QUESTIONS

1.   Summary. In *Toilet Goods,* the companion case to *Abbott Labs.,* the Supreme Court held that a regulation promulgated via notice-and-comment rulemaking was nevertheless not ripe for judicial decision. Thus, not all regulations with the force of law are ripe for review, even after *Abbott Labs.*

The careful reader should already be able to spot the difference between the regulation in *Abbott Labs.*, which immediately required every participant in the industry to take a certain action, and the regulation at issue in *Toilet Goods*, which did not require any immediate action by anyone. Moreover, the Court noted that "no irremediable adverse consequences flow from requiring a later challenge to this regulation by a manufacturer who refuses to allow this type of inspection." Is this just a classic restatement of when equitable relief is unavailable?

FOR DISCUSSION

Can you distinguish *Abbott Laboratories* and T*oilet Goods*? Would you have ruled the same way as the Court in both cases?

Reno v. Catholic Social Services

509 U.S. 43 (1993)

JUSTICE SOUTER delivered the opinion of the Court.

This petition joins two separate suits, each challenging a different regulation issued by the Immigration and Naturalization Service (INS) in administering the alien legalization program created by Title II of the Immigration Reform and Control Act of 1986. In each instance, a District Court struck down the regulation challenged and issued a remedial order directing the INS to accept legalization applications beyond the statutory deadline; the Court of Appeals consolidated the INS's appeals from these orders, and affirmed the District Courts' judgments. We are now asked to consider whether the District Courts had jurisdiction to hear the challenges . . . .

I

On November 6, 1986, the President signed the Immigration Reform and Control Act of 1986, Title II of which established a scheme under which certain aliens unlawfully present in the United States could apply, first, for the status of a temporary resident and then, after a 1-year wait, for permission to reside permanently. An applicant for temporary resident status must have resided continuously in the United States in an unlawful status since at least January 1, 1982, 8 U.S.C. § 1255a(a)(2)(A); must have been physically present in the United States continuously since November 6, 1986, the date the Reform Act was enacted, § 1255a(a)(3)(A); and must have been otherwise admissible as an immigrant, § 1255a(a)(4). The applicant must also have applied during the 12-month period beginning on May 5, 1987. § 1255a(a)(1).

The two separate suits joined before us challenge regulations addressing, respectively, the first two of these four requirements. The first, *Reno v. Catholic Social Services, Inc. (CSS), et al.*, focuses on an INS interpretation of 8 U.S.C. § 1255a(a)(3), the Reform Act's requirement that applicants for temporary residence prove "continuous physical presence" in the United States since November 6, 1986. To mitigate this requirement, the Reform Act provides that "brief, casual, and innocent absences from the United States" will not break the required continuity. § 1255a(a)(3)(B). In a telex sent to its regional offices on November 14, 1986, however, the INS treated the exception narrowly, stating that it would consider an absence "brief, casual, and innocent" only if the alien had obtained INS permission, known as "advance parole," before leaving the United States; aliens who left without it would be "ineligible for legalization." The INS later softened this limitation somewhat by regulations issued on May 1, 1987, forgiving a failure to get advance parole for absences between November 6, 1986, and May 1, 1987. But the later regulation confirmed that any absences without advance parole on or after May 1, 1987, would not be considered "brief, casual, and innocent" and would therefore be taken to have broken the required continuity.

The *CSS* plaintiffs challenged the advance parole regulation as an impermissible construction of the Reform Act. After certifying the case as a class action, the District Court eventually defined a class comprising "persons prima facie eligible for legalization under [8 U.S.C. § 1255a] who departed and reentered the United States without INS authorization (i.e. 'advance parole') after the enactment of the [Reform Act] following what they assert to have been a brief, casual and innocent absence from the United States." On April 22, 1988, 12 days before the end of the legalization program's 12-month application period, the District Court granted partial summary judgment invalidating the regulation and declaring that "brief, casual, and innocent" absences did not require prior INS approval. . . .

The second of the two lawsuits, styled *INS v. League of United Latin American Citizens (LULAC) et al.*, goes to the INS's interpretation of 8

U.S.C. § 1255a(a)(2)(A), the Reform Act's "continuous unlawful residence" requirement. . . .

      * * *

As we said in *Abbott Laboratories,* . . . the presumption of available judicial review is subject to an implicit limitation: "injunctive and declaratory judgment remedies," what the respondents seek here, "are discretionary, and courts traditionally have been reluctant to apply them to administrative determinations unless these arise in the context of a controversy 'ripe' for judicial resolution," 387 U.S. at 148, that is to say, unless the effects of the administrative action challenged have been "felt in a concrete way by the challenging parties," *id.* at 148–149. In some cases, the promulgation of a regulation will itself affect parties concretely enough to satisfy this requirement, as it did in *Abbott Laboratories* itself. There, for example, as well as in *Gardner v. Toilet Goods Assn., Inc.,* 387 U.S. 167 (1967), the promulgation of the challenged regulations presented plaintiffs with the immediate dilemma to choose between complying with newly imposed, disadvantageous restrictions and risking serious penalties for violation. But that will not be so in every case. In *Toilet Goods Assn., Inc. v. Gardner,* 387 U.S. 158 (1967), for example, we held that a challenge to another regulation, the impact of which could not "be said to be felt immediately by those subject to it in conducting their day-to-day affairs," would not be ripe before the regulation's application to the plaintiffs in some more acute fashion, since "no irremediabl[y] adverse consequences flow[ed] from requiring a later challenge."

The regulations challenged here fall on the latter side of the line. They impose no penalties for violating any newly imposed restriction, but limit access to a benefit created by the Reform Act but not automatically bestowed on eligible aliens. Rather, the Act requires each alien desiring the benefit to take further affirmative steps, and to satisfy criteria beyond those addressed by the disputed regulations. It delegates to the INS the task of determining on a case-by-case basis whether each applicant has met all of the Act's conditions, not merely those interpreted by the regulations in question. In these circumstances, the promulgation of the challenged regulations did not itself give each *CSS* and *LULAC* class member a ripe claim; a class member's claim would ripen only once he took the affirmative steps that he could take before the INS blocked his path by applying the regulation to him.

Ordinarily, of course, that barrier would appear when the INS formally denied the alien's application on the ground that the regulation rendered him ineligible for legalization. A plaintiff who sought to rely on the denial of his application to satisfy the ripeness requirement, however, would then still find himself at least temporarily barred by the Reform Act's exclusive review provisions, since he would be seeking "judicial review of a determination respecting an application." 8 U.S.C. § 1255a(f)(1). The ripeness doctrine and the Reform Act's jurisdictional provisions would thus dovetail neatly, and not necessarily by mere coincidence. Congress may well have assumed that, in the ordinary case, the courts would not hear a challenge to regulations specifying limits to eligibility before those regulations were actually applied to an individual, whose challenge to the denial of an individual application would proceed within the Reform Act's limited scheme. The *CSS* and *LULAC* plaintiffs do not argue that this limited scheme would afford them inadequate review of a determination based on the regulations they challenge, presumably because they would be able to obtain such review on appeal from a deportation order, if they become subject to such an order . . . .

JUSTICE O'CONNOR, concurring in the judgment.

I agree that the District Courts in these two cases . . . erred in extending the application period for legalization beyond May 4, 1988, the end of the 12-month interval specified by the Immigration Reform and Control Act of 1986. I would not, however, reach this result on ripeness grounds. . . .

Our prior cases concerning anticipatory challenges to agency rules do not specify when an anticipatory suit may be brought against a benefit-conferring rule, such as the INS regulations here. An anticipatory suit by a would-be beneficiary, who has not yet applied for the benefit that the rule denies him, poses different ripeness problems than a pre-enforcement suit against a duty-creating rule, see *Abbott Laboratories v. Gardner*, 387 U.S. 136, 148–156 (1967) (permitting pre-enforcement suit). Even if he succeeds in his anticipatory action, the would-be beneficiary will not receive the benefit until he actually applies for it; and the agency might then deny him the benefit on grounds other than his ineligibility under the rule. By contrast, a successful suit against the duty-creating rule will relieve the plaintiff immediately of a burden that he otherwise would bear.

Yet I would not go so far as to state that a suit challenging a benefit-conferring rule is necessarily unripe simply because the plaintiff has not yet applied for the benefit. "Where the inevitability of the operation of a statute against certain individuals is patent, it is irrelevant to the existence of a justiciable controversy that there will be a time delay before the disputed provisions will come into effect." *Regional Rail Reorganization Act Cases*, 419 U.S. 102, 143 (1974). If it is "inevitable" that the challenged rule will "operat[e]" to the plaintiff's disadvantage—if the court can make a firm prediction that the plaintiff will apply for the benefit, and that the agency will deny the application by virtue of the rule—then there may well be a justiciable controversy that the court may find prudent to resolve.

I do not mean to suggest that a simple anticipatory challenge to the INS regulations would be ripe under the approach I propose. . . . My intent is rather to criticize the Court's reasoning—its reliance on a categorical rule that would-be beneficiaries cannot challenge benefit-conferring regulations until they apply for benefits.

Certainly the line of cases beginning with *Abbott Laboratories* does not support this categorical approach. That decision itself discusses with approval an earlier case that involved an anticipatory challenge to a benefit-conferring rule[:]

> "[I]n *United States v. Storer Broadcasting Co.*, 351 U.S. 192 [(1956)], the Court held to be a final agency action . . . an FCC regulation announcing a Commission policy that it would not issue a television license to an applicant already owning five such licenses, even though no specific application was before the Commission."

387 U.S. at 151 (emphasis added).

More recently, in *EPA v. National Crushed Stone Assn.*, 449 U.S. 64 (1980), the Court held that a facial challenge to the variance provision of an EPA pollution-control regulation was ripe even "prior to application of the regulation to a particular [company's] request for a variance." And in *Pacific Gas & Elec. Co. v. State Energy Resources Conservation and Development Comm'n*, 461 U.S. 190 (1983), the Court permitted utilities to challenge a state law imposing a moratorium on the certification of nuclear power plants, even though the utilities had not yet applied for a certificate. To be sure, all of these decisions involved licenses, certificates, or variances, which exempt the bearer from otherwise-applicable duties; but the same is true of the instant cases. The benefit conferred by the Reform Act—an adjustment in status to lawful temporary resident alien—readily can be conceptualized as a "license" or "certificate" to remain in the United States, or a "variance" from the immigration laws. . . .

At the very least, where the challenge to the benefit-conferring rule is purely legal, and where the plaintiff will suffer hardship if he cannot raise his challenge until later, a justiciable, anticipatory challenge to the rule may well be ripe in the prudential sense. Thus I cannot agree with the Court that ripeness will never obtain until the plaintiff actually applies for the benefit. . . .

JUSTICE STEVENS, with whom JUSTICE WHITE and JUSTICE BLACKMUN join, dissenting.

After Congress authorized a major amnesty program in 1986, the Government promulgated two regulations severely restricting access to that program. If valid, each regulation would have rendered ineligible for amnesty the members of the respective classes of respondents in this case. . . .

This Court . . . finds a basis for prolonging the litigation on a theory that was not argued in either the District Courts or the Court of Appeals, and was barely mentioned in this Court: that respondents' challenges are not, for the most part, "ripe" for adjudication. I agree with JUSTICE O'CONNOR that the Court's rationale is seriously flawed. Unlike JUSTICE O'CONNOR, however, I have no doubt that respondents' claims were ripe as soon as the concededly invalid regulations were promulgated.

Our test for ripeness is two pronged, "requiring us to evaluate both the fitness of the issues for judicial decision and the hardship to the parties of withholding court consideration." *Abbott Laboratories v. Gardner*, 387 U.S. 136, 149 (1967). Whether an issue is fit for judicial review, in turn, often depends on "the degree and nature of [a] regulation's present effect on those seeking relief," *Toilet Goods Assn., Inc. v. Gardner*, 387 U.S. 158, 164 (1967), or, put differently, on whether there has been some "concrete action applying the regulation to the claimant's situation in a fashion that harms or threatens to harm him," *Lujan v. National Wildlife Federation*, 497 U.S. 871, 891 (1990). As JUSTICE O'CONNOR notes, we have returned to this two-part test for ripeness time and again, and there is no question but that the *Abbott Laboratories* formulation should govern this case.

As to the first *Abbott Laboratories* factor, I think it clear that the challenged regulations have an impact on respondents sufficiently "direct and immediate," that they are fit for judicial review. My opinion rests, in part, on the unusual character of the amnesty program in question. . . .

A major purpose of this ambitious effort was to eliminate the fear in which these immigrants lived . . . . Indeed, in recognition of this fear of governmental authority, Congress established a special procedure through which "qualified designated entities," or "QDE's," would serve as a channel of communication between undocumented aliens and the INS, providing reasonable assurance that "emergence from the shadows" would result in amnesty and not deportation.

Under these circumstances, official advice that specified aliens were ineligible for amnesty was certain to convince those aliens to retain their "shadow" status rather than come forward. At the moment that decision was made—at the moment respondents conformed their behavior to the invalid regulations—those regulations concretely and directly affected respondents, consigning them to the shadow world from which the Reform Act was designed to deliver them, and threatening to deprive them of the statutory entitlement that would otherwise be theirs. . . .

The second *Abbott Laboratories* factor, which focuses on the cost to the parties of withholding judicial review, also weighs heavily in favor of ripeness in this case. Every day during which the invalid regulations were effective meant another day spent in the shadows for respondents, with the attendant costs of that way of life. Even more important, with each passing day, the clock on the application period continued to run, increasing the risk that review, when it came, would be meaningless because the application period had already expired. . . .

Under *Abbott Laboratories*, then, I think it plain that respondents' claims were ripe for adjudication at the time they were filed. The Court's contrary holding, which seems to rest on the premise that respondents cannot challenge a condition of legalization until they have satisfied all other conditions, is at odds not only with our ripeness case law, but also with our more general understanding of the way in which government regulation affects the regulated. In *Northeastern Fla. Chapter, Associated Gen. Contractors of America v. Jacksonville*, 508 U.S. 656 (1993), for instance, we held that a class of contractors could challenge an ordinance making it more difficult for them to compete for public business without making any showing that class members were actually in a position to receive such business, absent the challenged regulation. . . .

Notes and Questions

1. ***What is the holding of* CSS?** Why, exactly, did the majority conclude that the case was not ripe? Was it because the plaintiffs were applying for a benefit and the regulation did not have any immediate coercive effect on any individuals? Do you think that's a distinction that should matter for a ripeness analysis? Or did the Court conclude the case was not ripe because the plaintiffs might have had their legalization applications denied for reasons unrelated to the regulation being challenged? If the Court *knows* that the plaintiffs' applications will be denied *at least* because of the challenged regulation, shouldn't that be enough? Why or why not? If we thought about this case in terms of equitable remedies, do you think the remedy at law was adequate or inadequate?

3.   Other Examples of Inadequate Remedies at Law

The following cases are not usually discussed together, and they involve questions of statutory preclusion, administrative exhaustion, and finality. We have seen some of them before—*Mathews v. Eldridge, Free Enterprise Fund v. PCAOB*, and *Sackett v. EPA*. What they all have in common, however, is the issue of the availability of preenforcement review and injunctions. As you read these cases, ask yourself whether they can all cohere on the understanding that the remedy at law was inadequate.

 We saw *Mathews v. Eldridge* in Chapter 7. It is a seminal procedural due process case.

Mathews v. Eldridge

<u>424 U.S. 319 (1976)</u>

MR. JUSTICE POWELL delivered the opinion of the Court.

[The facts of this case were presented above on p. 891, in the due process chapter. The facts are repeated here for the reader's convenience.—Ed.]

The issue in this case is whether the Due Process Clause of the Fifth Amendment requires that prior to the termination of Social Security disability benefit payments the recipient be afforded an opportunity for an evidentiary hearing.

I

Cash benefits are provided to workers during periods in which they are completely disabled under the disability insurance benefits program created by the 1956 amendments to Title II of the Social Security Act. Respondent Eldridge was first awarded benefits in June 1968. In March 1972, he received a questionnaire from the state agency charged with monitoring his medical condition. Eldridge completed the questionnaire, indicating that his condition had not improved and identifying the medical sources, including physicians, from whom he had received treatment recently. The state agency then obtained reports from his physician and a psychiatric consultant. After considering these reports and other information in his file the agency informed Eldridge by letter that it had made a tentative determination that his disability had ceased in May 1972. The letter included a statement of reasons for the proposed termination of benefits, and advised Eldridge that he might request reasonable time in which to obtain and submit additional information pertaining to his condition.

In his written response, Eldridge disputed one characterization of his medical condition and indicated that the agency already had enough evidence to establish his disability. The state agency then made its final determination that he had ceased to be disabled in May 1972. This determination was accepted by the Social Security Administration (SSA), which notified Eldridge in July that his benefits would terminate after that month. The notification also advised him of his right to seek reconsideration by the state agency of this initial determination within six months.

Instead of requesting reconsideration Eldridge commenced this action challenging the constitutional validity of the administrative procedures established by the Secretary of Health, Education, and Welfare for assessing whether there exists a continuing disability. He sought an immediate reinstatement of benefits pending a hearing on the issue of his disability. The Secretary moved to dismiss on the grounds that Eldridge's benefits had been terminated in accordance with valid administrative regulations and procedures and that he had failed to exhaust available remedies. In support of his contention that due process requires a pretermination hearing, Eldridge relied exclusively upon this Court's decision in *Goldberg v. Kelly*, 397 U.S. 254 (1970), which established a right to an "evidentiary hearing" prior to termination of welfare benefits. The Secretary contended that Goldberg was not controlling since eligibility for disability benefits, unlike eligibility for welfare benefits, is not based on financial need and since issues of credibility and veracity do not play a significant role in the disability entitlement decision, which turns primarily on medical evidence.

The District Court concluded that the administrative procedures pursuant to which the Secretary had terminated Eldridge's benefits abridged his right to procedural due process. The court viewed the interest of the disability recipient in uninterrupted benefits as indistinguishable from that of the welfare recipient in Goldberg. It further noted that decisions subsequent to Goldberg demonstrated that the due process requirement of pretermination hearings is not limited to situations involving the deprivation of vital necessities. Reasoning that disability determinations may involve subjective judgments based on conflicting medical and nonmedical evidence, the District Court held that prior to termination of benefits Eldridge had to be afforded an evidentiary hearing of the type required for welfare beneficiaries under Title IV of the Social Security Act. Relying entirely upon the District Court's opinion, the Court of Appeals for the Fourth Circuit affirmed the injunction barring termination of Eldridge's benefits prior to an evidentiary hearing. We reverse.

II

At the outset we are confronted by a question as to whether the District Court had jurisdiction over this suit. The Secretary contends that our decision last Term in Weinberger v. Salfi, 422 U.S. 749 (1975), bars the District Court from considering Eldridge's action. *Salfi* was an action challenging the Social Security Act's duration-of-relationship eligibility requirements for surviving wives and stepchildren of deceased wage earners. We there held that 42 U.S.C.

§ 405(h) precludes federal-question jurisdiction in an action challenging denial of claimed benefits. The only avenue for judicial review is 42 U.S.C. § 405(g), which requires exhaustion of the administrative remedies provided under the Act as a jurisdictional prerequisite.

Section 405(g) in part provides:

"Any individual, after any final decision of the Secretary made after a hearing to which he was a party, irrespective of the amount in controversy, may obtain a review of such decision by a civil action commenced within sixty days after the mailing to him of notice of such decision or within such further time as the Secretary may allow."

On its face § 405(g) thus bars judicial review of any denial of a claim of disability benefits until after a "final decision" by the Secretary after a "hearing." It is uncontested that Eldridge could have obtained full administrative review of the termination of his benefits, yet failed even to seek reconsideration of the initial determination. Since the Secretary has not "waived" the finality requirement as he had in *Salfi*, he concludes that Eldridge cannot properly invoke § 405(g) as a basis for jurisdiction. We disagree.

Salfi identified several conditions which must be satisfied in order to obtain judicial review under § 405(g). Of these, the requirement that there be a final decision by the Secretary after a hearing was regarded as "central to the requisite grant of subject-matter jurisdiction . . . ." Implicit in *Salfi* however, is the principle that this condition consists of two elements, only one of which is purely "jurisdictional" in the sense that it cannot be "waived" by the Secretary in a particular case. The waivable element is the requirement that the administrative remedies prescribed by the Secretary be exhausted. The nonwaivable element is the requirement that a claim for benefits shall have been presented to the Secretary. Absent such a claim there can be no "decision" of any type. And some decision by the Secretary is clearly required by the statute. . . .

Eldridge has fulfilled this crucial prerequisite. Through his answers to the state agency questionnaire, and his letter in response to the tentative determination that his disability had ceased, he specifically presented the claim that his benefits should not be terminated because he was still disabled. This claim was denied by the state agency and its decision was accepted by the SSA.

The fact that Eldridge failed to raise with the Secretary his constitutional claim to a pretermination hearing is not controlling. As construed in *Salfi*, § 405(g) requires only that there be a "final decision" by the Secretary with respect to the claim of entitlement to benefits. . . . It is unrealistic to expect that the Secretary would consider substantial changes in the current administrative review system at the behest of a single aid recipient raising a constitutional challenge in an adjudicatory context. The Secretary would not be required even to consider such a challenge.

As the nonwaivable jurisdictional element was satisfied, we next consider the waivable element. The question is whether the denial of Eldridge's claim to continued benefits was a sufficiently "final" decision with respect to his constitutional claim to satisfy the statutory exhaustion requirement. Eldridge concedes that he did not exhaust the full set of internal-review procedures provided by the Secretary. . . . But cases may arise where a claimant's interest in having a particular issue resolved promptly is so great that deference to the agency's judgment is inappropriate. This is such a case.

Eldridge's constitutional challenge is entirely collateral to his substantive claim of entitlement. Moreover, there is a crucial distinction between the nature of the constitutional claim asserted here and that raised in *Salfi*. A claim to a predeprivation hearing as a matter of constitutional right rests on the proposition that full relief cannot be obtained at a postdeprivation hearing. In light of the Court's prior decisions, see, e.g., Goldberg v. Kelly, 397 U.S. 254 (1970), Eldridge has raised at least a colorable claim that because of his physical condition and dependency upon the disability benefits, an erroneous termination would damage him in a way not recompensable through retroactive payments. Thus . . . denying Eldridge's substantive claim . . . at the post-termination stage would not answer his constitutional challenge.

We conclude that the denial of Eldridge's request for benefits constitutes a final decision for purposes of 405(g) jurisdiction over his constitutional claim. We now proceed to the merits of that claim. [The reader will recall that the Court held that a pretermination hearing was not required, applying a now-famous three-part balancing test.—Ed.]

NOTES AND QUESTIONS

1.   Why was preenforcement review available? What was the basis of the Court's decision? Was *Mathews* a finality case? An exhaustion case? A statutory preclusion case? A bit of all three? The statute appeared to require exhaustion and, as the student will recall from the materials on exhaustion, usually that means such administrative remedies must indeed be exhausted. But in *Mathews* the Court does not find that dispositive. The Court notes that the constitutional question—whether the amount of process given meets the requirements of the due process clause—is entirely collateral to the merits of Eldridge's claim for benefits. Moreover, the Court held, "[a] claim to a predeprivation hearing as a matter of constitutional right rests on the proposition that full relief cannot be obtained at a postdeprivation hearing."

Is *Mathews* thus just an equitable relief case? How does it compare to the following case, where the Supreme Court held that preenforcement review was not available?

Thunder Basin Coal Co. v. Reich

510 U.S. 200 (1994)

JUSTICE BLACKMUN delivered the opinion of the Court.

In this case, we address the question whether the statutory-review scheme in the Federal Mine Safety and Health Amendments Act of 1977 prevents a district court from exercising subject-matter jurisdiction over a pre-enforcement challenge to the Act. We hold that it does.

I

Congress adopted the Mine Act "to protect the health and safety of the Nation's coal or other miners." 30 U.S.C. § 801(g). The Act requires the Secretary of Labor or his representative to conduct periodic, unannounced health and safety inspections of the Nation's mines. Section § 813(f) provides:

> "[A] representative of the operator and a representative authorized by
> his miners shall be given an opportunity to accompany the Secretary
> or his authorized representative during the physical inspection of any

coal or other mine . . . for the purpose of aiding such inspection and to participate in pre- or post-inspection conferences held at the mine."

Regulations promulgated under this section define a miners' representative as "[a]ny person or organization which represents two or more miners at a coal or other mine for the purposes of the Act." 30 CFR § 40.1(b)(1) (1993).

In addition to exercising these "walk-around" inspection rights under § 813(f), persons designated as representatives of the miners may obtain certain health and safety information and promote health and safety enforcement. Once the mine employees designate one or more persons as their representatives, the employer must post at the mine information regarding these designees. 30 CFR § 40.4.

The Secretary has broad authority to compel immediate compliance with Mine Act provisions through the use of mandatory civil penalties, discretionary daily civil penalties, and other sanctions.[4] Challenges to enforcement are reviewed by the Federal Mine Safety and Health Review Commission, 30 U.S.C. §§ 815 and 823, which is independent of the Department of Labor, and by the appropriate United States court of appeals, § 816.

II

Petitioner Thunder Basin Coal Company operates a surface coal mine in Wyoming with approximately 500 nonunion employees. In 1990, petitioner's employees selected two employees of the United Mine Workers of America (UMWA), who were not employees of the mine, to serve as their miners' representatives pursuant to § 813(f). Petitioner did not post the information regarding the miners' representatives as required by 30 CFR § 40.4, but complained to the Mine Safety and Health Administration (MSHA) that the designation compromised its rights under the National Labor Relations Act (NLRA). The MSHA district manager responded with a letter instructing petitioner to post the miners' representative designations.

Rather than post the designations and before receiving the MSHA letter, petitioner filed suit in the United States District Court for the District of

---

[4]   The Secretary must issue a citation and recommend assessment of a civil penalty of up to $50,000 against any mine operator believed to have violated the Act. If an operator fails to abate the violation within the time allotted, the Secretary may assess additional daily civil penalties of up to $5,000 per day pending abatement. The Secretary's representative also may issue a "withdrawal order," directing all individuals to withdraw from the affected mine area, or pursue criminal penalties.

Wyoming for pre-enforcement injunctive relief. Petitioner contended that the designation of nonemployee UMWA "representatives" violated the principles of collective-bargaining representation under the NLRA as well as the company's NLRA rights to exclude union organizers from its property. Petitioner argued then, as it does here, that deprivation of these rights would harm the company irreparably by "giv[ing] the union organizing advantages in terms of access, personal contact and knowledge that would not be available under the labor laws, as well as enhanced credibility flowing from the appearance of government imprimatur."

Petitioner additionally alleged that requiring it to challenge the MSHA's interpretation of 30 U.S.C. § 813(f) and 30 CFR pt. 40 through the statutory-review process would violate the Due Process Clause of the Fifth Amendment, since the company would be forced to choose between violating the Act and incurring possible escalating daily penalties,[6] or, on the other hand, complying with the designations and suffering irreparable harm. The District Court enjoined respondents from enforcing 30 CFR pt. 40, finding that petitioner had raised serious questions going to the merits and that it might face irreparable harm.

The Court of Appeals for the Tenth Circuit reversed, holding that the Mine Act's comprehensive enforcement and administrative-review scheme precluded district court jurisdiction over petitioner's claims. The court stated:

"[T]he gravamen of Thunder Basin's case is a dispute over an anticipated citation and penalty. . . . Operators may not avoid the Mine Act's administrative review process simply by filing in a district court before actually receiving an anticipated citation, order, or assessment of penalty."

To hold otherwise, the court reasoned, "would permit preemptive strikes that could seriously hamper effective enforcement of the Act, disrupting the review scheme Congress intended." The court also concluded that the Mine Act's review procedures adequately protected petitioner's due process rights.

---

[6]   Petitioner relied for this proposition on a similar case in which a mine operator refused to post the designation of a UMWA employee, a citation was issued, and the MSHA ordered abatement within 24 hours and threatened to impose daily civil penalties. See *Kerr-McGee Coal Corp. v. Secretary,* 15 F.M.S.H.R.C. 352 (1993), appeal pending, No. 93–1250 (CADC). Kerr-McGee complied but contested the citation. An administrative law judge rejected the operator's claim, and the Commission affirmed, holding that § 813(f) did not violate the NLRA. 15 F.M.S.H.R.C., at 362–363. The Commission eventually fined Kerr-McGee a total of $300 for its non-compliance.

We granted certiorari on the jurisdictional question . . . .

III

In cases involving delayed judicial review[8] of final agency actions, we shall find that Congress has allocated initial review to an administrative body where such intent is "fairly discernible in the statutory scheme." *Block v. Community Nutrition Institute,* 467 U.S. 340, 351 (1984), quoting *Association of Data Processing Service Organizations, Inc. v. Camp,* 397 U.S. 150, 157 (1970). Whether a statute is intended to preclude initial judicial review is determined from the statute's language, structure, and purpose, its legislative history, *Block,* 467 U.S. at 345, and whether the claims can be afforded meaningful review.

A

Applying this analysis to the review scheme before us, we conclude that the Mine Act precludes district court jurisdiction over the pre-enforcement challenge made here. The Act establishes a detailed structure for reviewing violations of "any mandatory health or safety standard, rule, order, or regulation promulgated" under the Act. § 814(a). A mine operator has 30 days to challenge before the Commission any citation issued under the Act, after which time an uncontested order becomes "final" and "not subject to review by any court or agency." §§ 815(a) and (d). Timely challenges are heard before an administrative law judge (ALJ), § 823(d)(1), with possible Commission review.[9] Only the Commission has authority actually to impose civil penalties proposed by the Secretary, § 820(i), and the Commission reviews all proposed civil penalties *de novo* according to six criteria. The Commission may grant temporary relief pending review of most orders, § 815(b)(2), and must expedite review where necessary, § 815(d).

Mine operators may challenge adverse Commission decisions in the appropriate court of appeals, § 816(a)(1), whose jurisdiction "shall be exclusive and its judgment and decree shall be final" except for possible Supreme Court review. The court of appeals must uphold findings of the Commission that are

---

[8]   Because court of appeals review is available, this case does not implicate " 'the strong presumption that Congress did not mean to prohibit all judicial review.' " *Bowen v. Michigan Academy of Family Physicians,* 476 U.S. 667, 672 (1986).

[9]   30 U.S.C. § 823(d)(2). The Commission exercises discretionary review over any case involving, among others, a "substantial question of law, policy or discretion," and may review on its own initiative any decision "contrary to law or Commission policy" or in which "a novel question of policy has been presented." Any ALJ decision not granted review by the Commission within 40 days becomes a "final decision of the Commission." § 823(d)(1).

substantially supported by the record, but may grant temporary relief pending final determination of most proceedings, § 816(a)(2).

Although the statute establishes that the Commission and the courts of appeals have exclusive jurisdiction over challenges to agency enforcement proceedings, the Act is facially silent with respect to pre-enforcement claims. The structure of the Mine Act, however, demonstrates that Congress intended to preclude challenges such as the present one. The Act's comprehensive review process does not distinguish between preenforcement and postenforcement challenges, but applies to all violations of the Act and its regulations. Contrary to petitioner's suggestion, actions before the Commission are initiated not by the Secretary but by a mine operator who claims to be aggrieved. See § 815(a). The Act expressly authorizes district court jurisdiction in only two provisions, §§ 818(a) and 820(j), which respectively empower the *Secretary* to enjoin habitual violations of health and safety standards and to coerce payment of civil penalties. Mine operators enjoy no corresponding right but are to complain to the Commission and then to the court of appeals.

B

The legislative history of the Mine Act confirms this interpretation. At the time of the Act's passage, at least 1 worker was killed and 66 miners were disabled every working day in the Nation's mines. Frequent and tragic mining disasters testified to the ineffectiveness of then-existing enforcement measures. Under existing legislation, civil penalties were not always mandatory and were too low to compel compliance, and enforcement was hobbled by a cumbersome review process.

Congress expressed particular concern that under the previous Coal Act mine operators could contest civil-penalty assessments *de novo* in federal district court once the administrative review process was complete, thereby "seriously hamper[ing] the collection of civil penalties." Concluding that "rapid abatement of violations is essential for the protection of miners," Congress accordingly made improved penalties and enforcement measures a primary goal of the Act.

The 1977 Mine Act thus strengthened and streamlined health and safety enforcement requirements. The Act authorized the Secretary to compel payment of penalties and to enjoin habitual health and safety violators in federal district court. Assessment of civil penalties was made mandatory for all mines, and Congress expressly eliminated the power of a mine operator to challenge a final penalty assessment *de novo* in district court. Cf. [*Whitney Nat. Bank in Jefferson Parish v. Bank of New Orleans & Trust Co.*, 379 U.S. 411, 420 (1965)] (that "Congress rejected a proposal for a *de novo* review in the district courts of Board decisions" supports a finding of district court preclusion). We consider the legislative history and these amendments to be persuasive evidence that Congress intended to direct ordinary challenges under the Mine Act to a single review process.

Abbott Laboratories v. Gardner, 387 U.S. 136 (1967), is not to the contrary. In that case, this Court held that statutory review of certain provisions of the Federal Food, Drug, and Cosmetic Act did not preclude district court jurisdiction over a pre-enforcement challenge to regulations promulgated under separate provisions of that Act. In so holding, the Court found that the presence of a statutory saving clause and the statute's legislative history demonstrated "rather conclusively that the specific review provisions were designed to give an additional remedy and not to cut down more traditional channels of review." It concluded that Congress' primary concern in adopting the administrative-review procedures was to supplement review of specific agency determinations over which traditional forms of review might be inadequate. Contrary to petitioner's contentions, no comparable statutory language or legislative intent is present here. Indeed, as discussed above, the Mine Act's text and legislative history suggest precisely the opposite. The prospect that federal jurisdiction might thwart effective enforcement of the statute also was less immediate in *Abbott Laboratories*, since the *Abbott* petitioners did not attempt to stay enforcement of the challenged regulation pending judicial review, as petitioner did here.

C

We turn to the question whether petitioner's claims are of the type Congress intended to be reviewed within this statutory structure. This Court previously has upheld district court jurisdiction over claims considered "wholly 'collateral' " to a statute's review provisions and outside the agency's expertise, *Heckler v. Ringer*, 466 U.S. 602, 618 (1984), discussing *Mathews v. Eldridge*, 424 U.S. 319 (1976), particularly where a finding of preclusion could foreclose all meaningful judicial review. See *Traynor v. Turnage*, 485 U.S. 535, 544–545 (1988) (statutory prohibition of all judicial review of Veterans Administration benefits determinations did not preclude jurisdiction over an otherwise unreviewable collateral statutory claim); *Bowen v. Michigan Academy of Family Physicians*, 476 U.S. 667, 678–680 (1986); Johnson v. Robison, 415 U.S. 361,

373–374 (1974); *Oestereich v. Selective Ser. System Local Bd. No. 11*, 393 U.S. 233, 237–238 (1968); *Leedom v. Kyne*, 358 U.S. 184, 190 (1958) (upholding injunction of agency action where petitioners had "no other means, within their control . . . to protect and enforce that right"). In *Mathews v. Eldridge*, for example, it was held that 42 U.S.C. § 405(g), which requires exhaustion of administrative remedies before the denial of Social Security disability benefits may be challenged in district court, was not intended to bar federal jurisdiction over a due process challenge that was "entirely collateral" to the denial of benefits, and where the petitioner had made a colorable showing that full postdeprivation relief could not be obtained.

McNary v. Haitian Refugee Center, Inc., 498 U.S. 479 (1991), similarly held that an alien could bring a due process challenge to Immigration and Naturalization Service amnesty determination procedures, despite an Immigration and Nationality Act provision expressly limiting judicial review of individual amnesty determinations to deportation or exclusion proceedings. This Court held that the statutory language did not evidence an intent to preclude broad "pattern and practice" challenges to the program, and acknowledged that "if not allowed to pursue their claims in the District Court, respondents would not as a practical matter be able to obtain meaningful judicial review."

An analogous situation is not presented here. Petitioner pressed two primary claims below: that the UMWA designation under § 813(f) violates the principles of collective bargaining under the NLRA and petitioner's right "to exclude nonemployee union organizers from [its] property," *Lechmere, Inc. v. NLRB*, 502 U.S. 527, 532 (1992), and that adjudication of petitioner's claims through the statutory-review provisions will violate due process by depriving petitioner of meaningful review. Petitioner's statutory claims at root require interpretation of the parties' rights and duties under § 813(f) and 30 CFR pt. 40, and as such arise under the Mine Act and fall squarely within the Commission's expertise. The Commission, which was established as an independent-review body to "develop a uniform and comprehensive interpretation" of the Mine Act, has extensive experience interpreting the walk-around rights and recently addressed the precise NLRA claims presented here. Although the Commission has no particular expertise in construing statutes other than the Mine Act, we conclude that exclusive review before the Commission is appropriate since "agency expertise [could] be brought to bear on" the statutory questions presented here. *Whitney Nat. Bank*, 379 U.S. at 420.

As for petitioner's constitutional claim, we agree that "[a]djudication of the constitutionality of congressional enactments has generally been thought beyond the jurisdiction of administrative agencies." Johnson v. Robison, 415 U.S. at 368. This rule is not mandatory, however, and is perhaps of less consequence where, as here, the reviewing body is not the agency itself but an independent commission established exclusively to adjudicate Mine Act disputes. The Commission has addressed constitutional questions in previous enforcement proceedings. Even if this were not the case, however, petitioner's statutory and constitutional claims here can be meaningfully addressed in the Court of Appeals.

We conclude that the Mine Act's comprehensive enforcement structure, combined with the legislative history's clear concern with channeling and streamlining the enforcement process, establishes a "fairly discernible" intent to preclude district court review in the present case. See *Block v. Community Nutrition Institute*, 467 U.S. at 351. Petitioner's claims are "pre-enforcement" only because the company sued before a citation was issued, and its claims turn on a question of statutory interpretation that can be meaningfully reviewed under the Mine Act. Had petitioner persisted in its refusal to post the designation, the Secretary would have been required to issue a citation and commence enforcement proceedings. Nothing in the language and structure of the Act or its legislative history suggests that Congress intended to allow mine operators to evade the statutory-review process by enjoining the Secretary from commencing enforcement proceedings, as petitioner sought to do here. To uphold the District Court's jurisdiction in these circumstances would be inimical to the structure and the purposes of the Mine Act.

IV

Petitioner finally contends, in the alternative, that due process requires district court review because the absence of pre-enforcement declaratory relief before the Commission will subject petitioner to serious and irreparable harm. We need not consider this claim, however, because neither compliance with, nor continued violation of, the statute will subject petitioner to a serious prehearing deprivation.

The record before us contains no evidence that petitioner will be subject to serious harm if it complies with 30 U.S.C. § 813(f) and 30 CFR pt. 40 by posting the designations, and the potential for abuse of the miners' representative position appears limited. As the district manager of the MSHA stated to petitioner, designation as a miners' representative does not convey "an uncontrolled access right to the mine property to engage in any activity that the miners' representative wants." Statutory inspections of petitioner's mine need occur only twice annually and are conducted with representatives of the Secretary and the operator. Because the miners' representative cannot receive advance notice of an inspection, the ability of the nonemployee UMWA designees to exercise these limited walk-around rights is speculative. Although it is possible that a miners' representative could abuse his privileges, we agree with the Court of Appeals that petitioner has failed to demonstrate that such abuse, entirely hypothetical on the record before us, cannot be remedied on an individual basis under the Mine Act.

Nor will petitioner face any serious prehearing deprivation if it refuses to post the designations while challenging the Secretary's interpretation. Although the Act's civil penalties unquestionably may become onerous if petitioner chooses not to comply, the Secretary's penalty assessments become final and payable only after full review by both the Commission and the appropriate court of appeals. A mine operator may request that the Commission expedite its proceedings, and temporary relief of certain orders is available from the Commission and the court of appeals. Thus, this case does not present the situation confronted in *Ex parte Young*, 209 U.S. 123, 148 (1908), in which the practical effect of coercive penalties for noncompliance was to foreclose all access to the courts. Nor does this approach a situation in which compliance is sufficiently onerous and coercive penalties sufficiently potent that a constitutionally intolerable choice might be presented.

V

We conclude that the Mine Act's administrative structure was intended to preclude district court jurisdiction over petitioner's claims and that those claims can be meaningfully reviewed through that structure consistent with due process.[23] The judgment of the Court of Appeals is affirmed.

JUSTICE SCALIA, with whom JUSTICE THOMAS joins, concurring in part and concurring in the judgment.

---

[23] Because we have resolved this dispute on statutory preclusion grounds, we do not reach the parties' arguments concerning final agency action, a cause of action, ripeness, and exhaustion.

I join all except Parts III-B, IV, and V of the Court's opinion. The first of these consists of a discussion of the legislative history . . . . I find that discussion unnecessary to the decision. It serves to maintain the illusion that legislative history is an important factor in this Court's deciding of cases . . . .

As to Part V: The only additional analysis introduced in that brief section is the proposition that "the parties' arguments concerning final agency action, a cause of action, ripeness, and exhaustion" need not be reached "[b]ecause we have resolved this dispute on statutory preclusion grounds." That is true enough as to the claims disposed of in Part III, but quite obviously not true as to the constitutional claim disposed of in Part IV, which is rejected not on preclusion grounds but on the merits. The alleged impediments to entertaining that claim must be considered. It suffices here to say that I do not consider them valid.

And finally, as to Part IV: The Court holds that the preclusion of review is constitutional "because neither compliance with, nor continued violation of, the statute will subject petitioner to a serious prehearing deprivation." . . . It seems to me, however, that compliance with the inspection regulations *will* cause petitioner more than *de minimis* harm . . . . Compliance will compel the company to allow union officials to enter its premises (and in a position of apparent authority, at that), notwithstanding its common-law right to exclude them. And compliance will provide at least some confidential business information to officers of the union. (The UMWA's contention, on which the Court relies, that it is "speculative" whether a nonemployee miners' representative will be able to accompany the walk-arounds means only that such a representative may not *always* be able to do so. He will surely *often* be able to do so, since the statute *requires* that he "be given an opportunity to accompany" the inspector.)

In my view, however, the preclusion of pre-enforcement judicial review is constitutional *whether or not* compliance produces irreparable harm—at least if a summary penalty does not cause irreparable harm (*e.g.,* if it is a recoverable summary fine) or if judicial review *is* provided before a penalty for *non*-compliance can be imposed. . . . Were it otherwise, the availability of pre-enforcement challenges would have to be the rule rather than the exception, since complying with a regulation later held invalid almost *always* produces the irreparable harm of nonrecoverable compliance costs. Petitioner's claim is that the imposition of a choice between (1) complying with what the Government says to be the law, and (2) risking potential penalties (without a prior opportunity to challenge the law in district court) denies due process. This is similar to the constitutional challenge brought in the line of cases beginning with *Ex parte Young*, 209 U.S. 123 (1908), but with one crucial difference. As the Court notes, petitioner, unlike the plaintiff in *Young*, had the option of complying *and then* bringing a judicial challenge. The constitutional defect in *Young* was that the dilemma of either obeying the law and thereby forgoing any possibility of judicial review, or risking "enormous" and "severe" penalties, effectively cut off all access to the courts. That constitutional problem does not exist here, nor does any other of which I am aware. I would decide the second constitutional challenge (Part IV) on the simple grounds that the company can obtain judicial review if it complies with the agency's request, and can obtain presanction judicial review if it does not.

NOTES AND QUESTIONS

1. How to analyze preenforcement review. What kind of case is *Thunder Basin*? An exhaustion case? A statutory preclusion case? The Court decides it largely on the basis of the statutory preclusion cases, assessing whether Congress's creation of an administrative review scheme with federal appellate review precludes preenforcement judicial review in the district court. The Mine Act did not expressly preclude district-court review pursuant to the general federal-question jurisdiction statute, so the Court had to assess whether the Mine Act implicitly precluded that review. The Court thus examined Congress's intent, looking at the text, structure, and purpose of the Act (as well as the legislative history).

What is the relationship between preenforcement review cases, statutory preclusion cases, and exhaustion cases? Should these preenforcement cases be reconceptualized to fit into one of those other boxes?

The Court considered the availability of meaningful review later in the process; the importance of agency expertise; the need for prompt enforcement; and whether the question at hand was collateral to the challenge on the merits, among other factors. Some of these factors also play a role in exhaustion analysis. The Court concluded that Congress intended to channel review of these types of claims through the administrative process.

How does this case relate to *Ex Parte Young* and all those prior cases about equitable relief? The Court distinguishes *Young* on the ground that there "the practical effect of coercive penalties for noncompliance was to foreclose all access to the courts," and "compliance [was] sufficiently onerous and coercive penalties sufficiently potent that a constitutionally intolerable choice might be presented." The Court seems to be saying here that equitable relief would still be available *even if Congress had precluded review,* so long as the harm from awaiting review through the administrative scheme would be irreparable. The Court seems to be suggesting that precluding preenforcement review where there would be irreparable harm would be *unconstitutional.* Do you agree? Is that because some ability to access the courts is required by the principle of "equal protection of the laws" (reverse-incorporated against the federal government through the Fifth Amendment)? Or does "due process of law" itself require a sufficient opportunity to challenge government action without risking the incurring of intolerable losses simply from engaging in such a challenge?

Now consider the converse: Imagine that the Court had concluded that federal-court jurisdiction, pursuant to the general federal-question jurisdiction statute, was not precluded by the statute at issue in *Thunder Basin.* Would that be enough to make a preenforcement injunction available? Even if the statute did not preclude review, was Thunder Basin's remedy at law—before the agency in an enforcement action, or perhaps in an action against the miners' representative in an action for trespass—inadequate?

The Supreme Court did not analyze the case in precisely these terms. But, properly understood, there are—or ought to be—two prerequisites for obtaining preenforcement, federal district-court review: (1) the statute cannot preclude review, expressly or impliedly, and (2) the remedy at law must also be inadequate. In other words, even if federal district court review is otherwise available, the legal remedy—pursuing one's action through the administrative process as a defense to an enforcement proceeding, or suing the purported mining representatives for trespass—must also be inadequate. And on the other hand, if the statute does preclude review, the question becomes whether that preclusion is constitutional. If the remedy at law is adequate, there is no issue. But what if Congress precludes review *and* the remedy at law is "inadequate"? Would that be constitutional?

One might think of these cases through the following graphic:

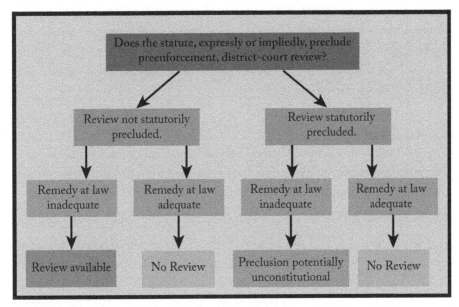

How would you apply this analysis where the challenge is to the constitutionality of the statute the agency is tasked with enforcing? In the first case that follows, the Supreme Court held that preenforcement review was available; in the second, it held such preenforcement review was not available. Can you reconcile them?

 CROSS REFERENCE We encountered *Free Enterprise Fund* in Chapter 6. It is an important removal power case.

Free Enterprise Fund v. PCAOB

561 U.S. 477 (2010)

CHIEF JUSTICE ROBERTS delivered the opinion of the Court.

[The facts of *Free Enterprise Fund* are recounted supra p. 730. In a nutshell, Congress created a Public Company Accounting Oversight Board under the Securities and Exchange Commission. The board members on the PCAOB were removable only for-cause by the SEC, whose own commissioners were removable only for-cause by the President. Recall that the Supreme Court invalidated this dual for-cause removal scheme. In the part of the case excerpted below, the Supreme Court addressed whether the federal courts had jurisdiction to address this constitutional question *before* an enforcement proceeding was brought against Free Enterprise Fund, or whether it had to wait until the conclusion of the proceeding after the agency had decided upon the constitutional question for itself.—Ed.]

II

We first consider whether the District Court had jurisdiction. We agree with both courts below that the statutes providing for judicial review of Commission action did not prevent the District Court from considering petitioners' claims.

The Sarbanes-Oxley Act empowers the Commission to review any Board rule or sanction. See 15 U.S.C. §§ 7217(b)(2)–(4), (c)(2). Once the Commission has acted, aggrieved parties may challenge "a final order of the Commission" or "a rule of the Commission" in a court of appeals under § 78y, and "[n]o objection . . . may be considered by the court unless it was urged before the Commission or there was reasonable ground for failure to do so." §§ 78y(a)(1), (b)(1), (c)(1).

The Government reads § 78y as an exclusive route to review. But the text does not expressly limit the jurisdiction that other statutes confer on district courts. See, *e.g.*, 28 U.S.C. §§ 1331, 2201. Nor does it do so implicitly. Provisions for agency review do not restrict judicial review unless the "statutory scheme" displays a "fairly discernible" intent to limit jurisdiction, and the claims at issue "are of the type Congress intended to be reviewed within th[e] statutory structure." *Thunder Basin Coal Co. v. Reich*, 510 U.S. 200, 207 (1994) (internal quotation marks omitted). Generally, when Congress creates procedures "designed to permit agency expertise to be brought to bear on particular problems," those procedures "are to be exclusive." *Whitney Nat. Bank in Jefferson Parish v. Bank of New Orleans & Trust Co.*, 379 U.S. 411, 420 (1965). But we presume that Congress does not intend to limit jurisdiction if "a finding of preclusion could foreclose all meaningful judicial review"; if the suit is "wholly collateral to a statute's review provisions"; and if the claims are "outside the agency's expertise." *Thunder Basin*, *supra*, at 212–213). These considerations point against any limitation on review here.

We do not see how petitioners could meaningfully pursue their constitutional claims under the Government's theory. Section 78y provides only for judicial review of *Commission* action, and not every Board action is encapsulated in a final Commission order or rule.

The Government suggests that petitioners could first have sought Commission review of the Board's "auditing standards, registration requirements, or other rules." But petitioners object to the Board's existence, not to any of its auditing standards. Petitioners' general challenge to the Board is "collateral" to any Commission orders or rules from which review might be sought. Cf. *McNary v. Haitian Refugee Center, Inc.*, 498 U.S. 479, 491–492 (1991). Requiring petitioners to select and challenge a Board rule at random is an odd procedure for Congress to choose, especially because only *new* rules, and not existing ones, are subject to challenge. See 15 U.S.C. §§ 78s(b)(2), 78y(a)(1), 7217(b)(4).

Alternatively, the Government advises petitioners to raise their claims by appealing a Board sanction. But the investigation of Beckstead and Watts produced no sanction, and an uncomplimentary inspection report is not subject to judicial review, see § 7214(h)(2). So the Government proposes that Beckstead and Watts *incur* a sanction (such as a sizable fine) by ignoring Board requests for documents and testimony. If the Commission then affirms, the firm will win access to a court of appeals—and severe punishment should its challenge fail. We normally do not require plaintiffs to "bet the farm . . . by taking the violative action" before "testing the validity of the law," *MedImmune, Inc. v. Genentech, Inc.*, 549 U.S. 118, 129 (2007); accord, *Ex parte Young*, 209 U.S. 123 (1908), and we do not consider this a "meaningful" avenue of relief, *Thunder Basin*, 510 U.S. at 212.

Petitioners' constitutional claims are also outside the Commission's competence and expertise. In *Thunder Basin*, the petitioner's primary claims were statutory . . . . No similar expertise is required here . . . .

We therefore conclude that § 78y did not strip the District Court of jurisdiction over these claims, which are properly presented for our review.

NOTES AND QUESTIONS

1. Summary. Once again, the Court's analysis is mostly about statutory preclusion of review. There is no *express* preclusion of district-court review of constitutional claims in the first instance, so the Court must determine if such preclusion is implied, i.e., that it is "fairly discernable" from the statute's text, structure, and purpose. The Court examines the availability of meaningful review; whether the claim is collateral to the issues the agency is tasked with reviewing; and the importance of agency expertise.

In *Free Enterprise Fund*, it seems clear that the SEC's expertise is irrelevant to the question of whether a dual for-cause removal provision is constitutional, a question which is also wholly collateral to the securities issues the Commission is tasked with enforcing.

How does the Court address the "meaningful review" prong of the analysis? The Court suggests that the agency can make the constitutional claim unreviewable because not all types of agency action is reviewable under the statute. Additionally, incurring a sanction for the purpose of review would be costly—and here the Court cites to *Ex Parte Young*. Is this a classic case of an anti-suit injunction? The Court did not analyze the severity of the sanctions, however. Is the Court saying that if the statute precludes preenforcement review, that would be unconstitutional?

In sum, once again the Supreme Court addresses a variety of factors as part of a statutory preclusion analysis. But that is only part of the question. Even if the statute does not preclude an injunction, the remedy at law must be inadequate. Would it have been?

2.   *Similar challenges to the SEC and FTC.* Notwithstanding the Court's decision in *Free Enterprise Fund*, several courts of appeal have rejected preenforcement constitutional challenges against the Securities and Exchange Commission. For example, in Bebo v. SEC, 799 F.3d 765 (7th Cir. 2015), the Court rejected a preenforcement challenge to the SEC's dual for-cause removal protections for its ALJs. In Axon Enterp. Inc. v. FTC, No. CV–20–00014, a federal district court in Arizona held a similar challenge to the Federal Trade Commission's dual for-cause removal protections for its ALJs had to go through the administrative process first.

Elgin v. Department of Treasury

567 U.S. 1 (2012)

Justice Thomas delivered the opinion of the Court.

Under the Civil Service Reform Act of 1978 (CSRA), certain federal employees may obtain administrative and judicial review of specified adverse employment actions. The question before us is whether the CSRA provides the exclusive avenue to judicial review when a qualifying employee challenges an adverse employment action by arguing that a federal statute is unconstitutional. We hold that it does.

I

The CSRA "established a comprehensive system for reviewing personnel action taken against federal employees." *United States v. Fausto,* 484 U.S. 439, 455 (1988). As relevant here, Subchapter II of Chapter 75 governs review of major adverse actions taken against employees "for such cause as will promote the efficiency of the service." 5 U.S.C. §§ 7503(a), 7513(a). Employees entitled to review are those in the "competitive service" and "excepted service" who meet certain requirements regarding probationary periods and years of service. § 7511(a)(1). The reviewable agency actions are removal, suspension for more than 14 days, reduction in grade or pay, or furlough for 30 days or less. § 7512.

When an employing agency proposes a covered action against a covered employee, the CSRA gives the employee the right to notice, representation by counsel, an opportunity to respond, and a written, reasoned decision from the agency. § 7513(b). If the agency takes final adverse action against the employee, the CSRA gives the employee the right to a hearing and to be represented by an attorney or other representative before the Merit Systems Protection Board (MSPB). §§ 7513(d), 7701(a)(1)–(2). The MSPB is authorized to order relief to prevailing employees, including reinstatement, backpay, and attorney's fees. §§ 1204(a)(2), 7701(g).

An employee who is dissatisfied with the MSPB's decision is entitled to judicial review in the United States Court of Appeals for the Federal Circuit. That court "shall review the record and hold unlawful and set aside any agency action, findings, or conclusions" that are "arbitrary, capricious, an abuse of discretion, or otherwise not in accordance with law," "obtained without procedures required by law, rule, or regulation having been followed," or "unsupported by substantial evidence." § 7703(a)(1), (c). The Federal Circuit has "exclusive jurisdiction" over appeals from a final decision of the MSPB. 28 U.S.C. § 1295(a)(9); see also 5 U.S.C. § 7703(b)(1) (judicial review of an MSPB decision "shall be" in the Federal Circuit).

II

Petitioners are former federal competitive service employees who failed to comply with the Military Selective Service Act. That Act requires male citizens and permanent-resident aliens of the United States between the ages of 18 and 26 to register for the Selective Service. Another federal statute, 5 U.S.C. § 3328 (hereinafter Section 3328), bars from employment by an Executive agency anyone who has knowingly and willfully failed to register. Pursuant to Section 3328, petitioners were discharged (or allegedly constructively discharged) by respondents, their employing agencies.

Among petitioners, only Michael Elgin appealed his removal to the MSPB. Elgin argued that Section 3328 is an unconstitutional bill of attainder and unconstitutionally discriminates on the basis of sex when combined with the registration requirement of the Military Selective Service Act. The MSPB referred Elgin's appeal to an administrative law judge (ALJ) for an initial decision. The ALJ dismissed the appeal for lack of jurisdiction, concluding that an employee is not entitled to MSPB review of agency action that is based on an absolute statutory bar to employment. The ALJ also held that Elgin's constitutional claims could not "confer jurisdiction" on the MSPB because it "lacks authority to determine the constitutionality of a statute."

Elgin neither petitioned for review by the full MSPB nor appealed to the Federal Circuit. Instead, he joined the other petitioners in filing suit in the United States District Court for the District of Massachusetts, raising the same constitutional challenges to Section 3328 and the Military Selective Service Act. Petitioners sought equitable relief in the form of a declaratory judgment that the challenged statutes are unconstitutional, an injunction prohibiting enforcement of Section 3328, reinstatement to their former positions, backpay, benefits, and attorney's fees.

The District Court rejected respondents' argument that it lacked jurisdiction and denied petitioners' constitutional claims on the merits. The District Court held that the CSRA did not preclude it from hearing petitioners' claims, because the MSPB had no authority to determine the constitutionality of a federal statute. Hence, the District Court concluded that it retained jurisdiction under the general grant of federal-question jurisdiction in 28 U.S.C. § 1331.

The United States Court of Appeals for the First Circuit vacated the judgment and remanded with instructions to dismiss for lack of jurisdiction. The Court of Appeals held that challenges to a removal are not exempted from the CSRA review scheme simply because the employee argues that the statute authorizing the removal is unconstitutional. According to the Court of Appeals, the CSRA provides a forum—the Federal Circuit—that may adjudicate the constitutionality of a federal statute, and petitioners "were obliged to use it."

We granted certiorari to decide whether the CSRA precludes district court jurisdiction over petitioners' claims even though they are constitutional claims for equitable relief. We conclude that it does, and we therefore affirm.

III

We begin with the appropriate standard for determining whether a statutory scheme of administrative and judicial review provides the exclusive means of review for constitutional claims. Petitioners argue that even if they may obtain judicial review of their constitutional claims before the Federal Circuit, they are not precluded from pursuing their claims in federal district court. According to petitioners, the general grant of federal-question jurisdiction in 28 U.S.C. § 1331, which gives district courts authority over constitutional claims, remains undisturbed unless Congress explicitly directs otherwise. In support of this argument, petitioners rely on *Webster v. Doe*, 486 U.S. 592, 603 (1988), which held that "where Congress intends to preclude judicial review of constitutional claims[,] its intent to do so must be clear." The *Webster* Court noted that this "heightened showing" was required "to avoid the 'serious constitutional question' that would arise if a federal statute were construed to deny any judicial forum for a colorable constitutional claim." *Ibid.* (quoting *Bowen v. Michigan Academy of Family Physicians*, 476 U.S. 667, 681, n. 12 (1986)). Petitioners contend that the CSRA does not meet this standard because it does not expressly bar suits in district court.

Petitioners' argument overlooks a necessary predicate to the application of *Webster*'s heightened standard: a statute that purports to "deny any judicial forum for a colorable constitutional claim." 486 U.S. at 603. *Webster*'s standard does not apply where Congress simply channels judicial review of a constitutional claim to a particular court. We held as much in *Thunder Basin Coal Co. v. Reich*, 510 U.S. 200 (1994). In that case, we considered whether a statutory scheme of administrative review followed by judicial review in a federal appellate court precluded district court jurisdiction over a plaintiff's statutory and constitutional claims. We noted that the plaintiff's claims could be "meaningfully addressed in the Court of Appeals" and that the case therefore did "not present the 'serious constitutional question' that would arise if an agency statute were construed to preclude all judicial review of a constitutional claim." Accordingly, we . . . asked only whether Congress' intent to preclude district court jurisdiction was " 'fairly discernible in the statutory scheme.' "

Like the statute in *Thunder Basin*, the CSRA does not foreclose all judicial review of petitioners' constitutional claims, but merely directs that judicial review shall occur in the Federal Circuit. Moreover, as we explain below, the Federal Circuit is fully capable of providing meaningful review of petitioners' claims. Accordingly, the appropriate inquiry is whether it is "fairly discernible" from the CSRA that Congress intended covered employees appealing covered agency actions to proceed exclusively through the statutory review scheme, even in cases in which the employees raise constitutional challenges to federal statutes.

IV

To determine whether it is "fairly discernible" that Congress precluded district court jurisdiction over petitioners' claims, we examine the CSRA's text, structure, and purpose.

A

This is not the first time we have addressed the impact of the CSRA's text and structure on the availability of judicial review of a federal employee's challenge to an employment decision. In *Fausto*, we considered whether a so-called "nonpreference excepted service employe[e]" could challenge his suspension in the United States Claims Court, even though the CSRA did not then afford him a right to review in the MSPB or the Federal Circuit. Citing "[t]he comprehensive nature of the CSRA, the attention that it gives throughout to the rights of nonpreference excepted service employees, and the fact that it does not include them in provisions for administrative and judicial review contained in Chapter 75," the Court concluded that "the absence of provision for these employees to obtain judicial review" was a "considered congressional judgment."

The Court thus found it "fairly discernible" that Congress intended to preclude all judicial review of Fausto's statutory claims.

Just as the CSRA's "elaborate" framework demonstrates Congress' intent to entirely foreclose judicial review to employees to whom the CSRA *denies* statutory review, it similarly indicates that extrastatutory review is not available to those employees to whom the CSRA *grants* administrative and judicial review. Indeed, in *Fausto* we expressly assumed that "competitive service employees, who *are* given review rights by Chapter 75, cannot expand these rights by resort to" judicial review outside of the CSRA scheme. As *Fausto* explained, the CSRA "prescribes in great detail the protections and remedies applicable to" adverse personnel actions against federal employees. For example, Subchapter II of Chapter 75, the portion of the CSRA relevant to petitioners, specifically enumerates the major adverse actions and employee classifications to which the CSRA's procedural protections and review provisions apply. 5 U.S.C. §§ 7511, 7512. The subchapter then sets out the procedures due an employee prior to final agency action. § 7513. And, Chapter 77 of the CSRA exhaustively details the system of review before the MSPB and the Federal Circuit. §§ 7701, 7703. Given the painstaking detail with which the CSRA sets out the method for covered employees to obtain review of adverse employment actions, it is fairly discernible that Congress intended to deny such employees an additional avenue of review in district court.

Petitioners do not dispute that they are employees who suffered adverse actions covered by the foregoing provisions of the CSRA. Nor do they contest that the CSRA's text and structure support implied preclusion of district court jurisdiction, at least as a general matter. Petitioners even acknowledge that the MSPB routinely adjudicates some constitutional claims, such as claims that an agency took adverse employment action in violation of an employee's First or Fourth Amendment rights, and that these claims must be brought within the CSRA scheme. Nevertheless, petitioners seek to carve out an exception to CSRA exclusivity for facial or as-applied constitutional challenges to federal statutes.

The text and structure of the CSRA, however, provide no support for such an exception. The availability of administrative and judicial review under the CSRA generally turns on the type of civil service employee and adverse employment action at issue. Nothing in the CSRA's text suggests that its exclusive review scheme is inapplicable simply because a covered employee challenges a covered action on the ground that the statute authorizing that action is unconstitutional. . . .

In only one situation does the CSRA expressly exempt a covered employee's appeal of a covered action from Federal Circuit review based on the type of claim at issue. When a covered employee "alleges that a basis for the action was discrimination" prohibited by enumerated federal employment laws, the CSRA allows the employee to obtain judicial review of an unfavorable MSPB decision by filing a civil action as provided by the applicable employment law. [This] demonstrates that Congress knew how to provide alternative forums for judicial review based on the nature of an employee's claim. That Congress declined to include an exemption from Federal Circuit review for challenges to a statute's constitutionality indicates that Congress intended no such exception.

B

The purpose of the CSRA also supports our conclusion that the statutory review scheme is exclusive, even for employees who bring constitutional challenges to federal statutes. . . .

The CSRA's objective of creating an integrated scheme of review would be seriously undermined if, as petitioners would have it, a covered employee could challenge a covered employment action first in a district court, and then again in one of the courts of appeals, simply by alleging that the statutory authorization for such action is unconstitutional. Such suits would reintroduce the very potential for inconsistent decisionmaking and duplicative judicial review that the CSRA was designed to avoid. . . .

Finally, we note that a jurisdictional rule based on the nature of an employee's constitutional claim would deprive the aggrieved employee, the MSPB, and the district court of clear guidance about the proper forum for the employee's claims at the outset of the case. For example, petitioners contend that facial and as-applied constitutional challenges to statutes may be brought in district court, while other constitutional challenges must be heard by the MSPB. But . . . that line is hazy at best and incoherent at worst. . . . Accordingly, we conclude that the better interpretation of the CSRA is that its exclusivity does not turn on the constitutional nature of an employee's claim, but rather on the type of the employee and the challenged employment action.

V

Petitioners raise three additional factors in arguing that their claims are not the type that Congress intended to be reviewed within the CSRA scheme. Specifically, petitioners invoke our "presum[ption] that Congress does not intend to limit [district court] jurisdiction if 'a finding of preclusion could foreclose all meaningful judicial review'; if the suit is 'wholly collateral to a statute's review provisions'; and if the claims are 'outside the agency's expertise.'" *Free Enterprise Fund v. Public Company Accounting Oversight Bd.*, 130 S.Ct. 3138, 3150 (2010) (quoting *Thunder Basin*, 510 U.S. at 212–213). Contrary to petitioners' suggestion, none of those characteristics are present here.

A

First, petitioners argue that the CSRA review scheme provides no meaningful review of their claims because the MSPB lacks authority to declare a federal statute unconstitutional. Petitioners are correct that the MSPB has repeatedly refused to pass upon the constitutionality of legislation. This Court has also stated that "adjudication of the constitutionality of congressional enactments has generally been thought beyond the jurisdiction of administrative agencies." *Thunder Basin*, 510 U.S. at 215.

We need not, and do not, decide whether the MSPB's view of its power is correct, or whether the oft-stated principle that agencies cannot declare a statute unconstitutional is truly a matter of jurisdiction. In *Thunder Basin*, we held that Congress' intent to preclude district court jurisdiction was fairly discernible in the statutory scheme "[e]ven if" the administrative body could not decide the constitutionality of a federal law. That issue, we reasoned, could be "meaningfully addressed in the Court of Appeals" . . . .

B

Petitioners next contend that the CSRA does not preclude district court jurisdiction over their claims because they are "wholly collateral" to the CSRA scheme. According to petitioners, their bill-of-attainder and sex discrimination claims "have nothing to do with the types of day-to-day personnel actions adjudicated by the MSPB," and petitioners "are not seeking the CSRA's 'protections and remedies.'" We disagree.

As evidenced by their district court complaint, petitioners' constitutional claims are the vehicle by which they seek to reverse the removal decisions, to return to federal employment, and to receive the compensation they would have earned but for the adverse employment action. A challenge to removal is precisely the type of personnel action regularly adjudicated by the MSPB and the Federal Circuit within the CSRA scheme. Likewise, reinstatement, backpay, and attorney's fees are precisely the kinds of relief that the CSRA empowers the MSPB and the Federal Circuit to provide. Far from a suit wholly collateral to the CSRA scheme, the case before us is a challenge to CSRA-covered employment action brought by CSRA-covered employees requesting relief that the CSRA routinely affords.

C

Relatedly, petitioners argue that their constitutional claims are not the sort that Congress intended to channel through the MSPB because they are outside the MSPB's expertise. But petitioners overlook the many threshold questions that may accompany a constitutional claim and to which the MSPB can apply its expertise. Of particular relevance here, preliminary questions unique to the employment context may obviate the need to address the constitutional challenge. For example, petitioner Henry Tucker asserts that his resignation amounted to a constructive discharge. That issue falls squarely within the MSPB's expertise, and its resolution against Tucker would avoid the need to reach his constitutional claims. In addition, the challenged statute may be one that the MSPB regularly construes, and its statutory interpretation could alleviate constitutional concerns. . . .

For the foregoing reasons, we conclude that it is fairly discernible that the CSRA review scheme was intended to preclude district court jurisdiction over petitioners' claims. . . .

Justice Alito, with whom Justice Ginsburg and Justice Kagan join, dissenting.

. . . . The problem with the majority's reasoning is that petitioners' constitutional claims are a far cry from the type of claim that Congress intended to channel through the Board. The Board's mission is to adjudicate fact-specific employment disputes within the existing statutory framework. By contrast, petitioners argue that one key provision of that framework is facially unconstitutional. Not only does the Board lack authority to adjudicate facial constitutional challenges, but such challenges are wholly collateral to the type of claims that the Board is authorized to hear.

The majority attempts to defend its holding by noting that, although the Board cannot consider petitioners' claims, petitioners may appeal from the Board to the Federal Circuit, which *does* have authority to address facial constitutional claims. But that does not cure the oddity of requiring such claims to be filed initially before the Board, which can do nothing but pass them along unaddressed, leaving the Federal Circuit to act as a court of first review, but with little capacity for factfinding.

Because I doubt that Congress intended to channel petitioners' constitutional claims into an administrative tribunal that is powerless to decide them, I respectfully dissent.

I

As a general matter, federal district courts have "original jurisdiction of all civil actions arising under the Constitution, laws, or treaties of the United States." 28 U.S.C. § 1331. . . . In light of § 1331, the question is not whether Congress has specifically conferred jurisdiction, but whether it has taken it away. . . . When dealing with an express preclusion clause . . . we determine the scope of preclusion simply by interpreting the words Congress has chosen.

We have also recognized that preclusion can be implied. When Congress creates an administrative process to handle certain types of claims, it impliedly removes those claims from the ordinary jurisdiction of the federal courts. Under these circumstances, the test is whether "the 'statutory scheme' displays a 'fairly discernible' intent to limit jurisdiction and the claims at issue 'are of the type Congress intended to be reviewed within th[e] statutory structure.'" *Free Enterprise Fund v. Public Company Accounting Oversight Bd.*, 130 S.Ct. 3138, 3150 (2010) (quoting *Thunder Basin Coal Co. v. Reich*, 510 U.S. 200, 207 (1994)). . . .

We have emphasized two important factors for determining whether Congress intended an agency to have exclusive original jurisdiction over a claim. The first is whether the claim falls within the agency's area of expertise . . . .

Second, even if a claim would not benefit from agency expertise, we nonetheless consider whether the claim is legally or factually related to the type of dispute the agency is authorized to hear. If so, the claim may be channeled through the administrative process to guard against claim-splitting, which could involve redundant analysis of overlapping issues of law and fact. But for claims that fall outside the agency's expertise and are "wholly collateral" to the type of dispute the agency is authorized to hear, the interest in requiring unified administrative review is considerably reduced. . . .

II

. . . . The parties agree that petitioners are covered employees who may file an appeal to the Board protesting their removal from federal employment. The parties also agree, however, that the Board lacks authority to adjudicate claims like those asserted by petitioners, which attack the validity of a federal statute as a facial matter. . . . Thus, the Board's own self-described role in the administrative process is simply to apply the relevant statutes as written, without addressing any facial challenges to the validity of those statutes.

III

There is no basis for the majority's conclusion that petitioners must file their constitutional challenges before the Board instead of a federal district court. Congress has not expressly curtailed the jurisdiction of the federal courts to consider facial constitutional claims relating to federal employment, and no such limitation can be fairly discerned from the CSRA. Not only are petitioners' claims "wholly collateral to [the CSRA's] review provisions and outside the agency's expertise," but the Board itself admits that it is completely powerless to consider the merits of petitioners' arguments. In short, neither efficiency nor agency expertise can explain why Congress would want the Board to have exclusive jurisdiction over claims like these. To the contrary, imposing a scheme of exclusive administrative review in this context breeds inefficiency and creates a procedural framework that is needlessly vexing. . . .

Administrative agencies typically do not adjudicate facial constitutional challenges to the laws that they administer. Such challenges not only lie outside the realm of special agency expertise, but they are also wholly collateral to other types of claims that the agency is empowered to consider. . . .

The wholly collateral nature of petitioners' claims makes them readily distinguishable from claims that this Court has held to be impliedly excluded from the original jurisdiction of the federal courts. In *Fausto*, for example, we held that the CSRA precluded a statutory Back Pay Act claim involving a dispute over whether an employee had engaged in unauthorized use of a Government vehicle. The plaintiff in that case did not challenge the constitutional validity of the applicable legal framework, but argued instead that the framework had been improperly applied to him. . . .

Finally, the majority's reliance on *Thunder Basin* is entirely misplaced. In that case, we found that a statutory scheme impliedly precluded a pre-enforcement challenge brought by a mining company seeking to enjoin an order issued by the Mine Safety and Health Administration. 510 U.S. at 205. Importantly, the plaintiff company was seeking review of purely statutory claims that were reviewable in the first instance by the administrative commission that Congress had established. . . .

By requiring facial constitutional claims to be filed before the Board, the majority's holding sets up an odd sequence of procedural hoops for petitioners to jump through. As the Government concedes, the Board is powerless to adjudicate facial constitutional claims, and so these claims cannot be addressed on the merits until they reach the Federal Circuit on appeal. As a result, the Federal Circuit will be forced to address the claims in the first instance, without the benefit of any relevant factfinding at the administrative level. This is a strange result . . . .

The Government admits that the absence of first-tier factfinding might very well result in "the initial record" being "insufficient to permit meaningful consideration of a constitutional claim," but suggests that the court could always "remand the case to the [Board] for further factual development." The majority accepts this solution, but it is hard to see how it will work in practice. Without any authority to decide merits issues, the Board may find it difficult to adjudicate disputes about the relevancy of evidence sought in discovery. Nor will the Board find it easy to figure out which facts it must find before sending the case back to the Federal Circuit.

Even if these problems can be overcome, that will not resolve the needless complexity of the majority's approach. According to the majority, petitioners should file their claims with the Board, which must then kick the claims up to the Federal Circuit, which must then remand the claims back to the Board, which must then develop the record and send the case back to the Federal Circuit, which can only then consider the constitutional issues.

To be sure, this might be sufficient to afford "meaningful review" of petitioners' claims, but that is not the only consideration. The question is whether it is "fairly discernible" that Congress intended to impose these pinball procedural requirements instead of permitting petitioners' claims to be decided in a regular lawsuit in federal district court. And why would it? As already noted, the benefits of preventing claim-splitting are considerably reduced with respect to facial constitutional claims that are wholly collateral to an administrative proceeding. Because collateral constitutional claims have no overlap with the issues of law and fact that will pertain to the administrative proceeding, allowing the constitutional claims to be adjudicated separately before a district court does not invite wasteful or duplicative review. It simply allows the district court to develop the factual record and then provide a first-tier legal analysis, thereby enhancing both the quality and efficiency of appellate review. . . .

IV

The presumptive power of the federal courts to hear constitutional challenges is well established. In this case, however, the majority relies on a very weak set of inferences to strip the courts of their original jurisdiction over petitioners' claims. Because I believe Congress would have been very surprised to learn that it implied this result when it passed the CSRA, I respectfully dissent.

Notes and Questions

1. Can you distinguish PCAOB and Elgin? Both *Free Enterprise Fund* and *Elgin* involved a constitutional claim. Can you distinguish the cases? One of the most obvious distinctions is that the constitutional claim in *Elgin* was not actually "collateral." Resolving the constitutional claim would have resolved the merits question, i.e., whether Elgin had been rightly or wrongly discharged. In contrast, in *Free Enterprise Fund* the structure of the PCAOB was entirely collateral to the separate questions of whether its regulations were lawful, or whether the companies subject to enforcement actions acted unlawfully.

What do you make of the Court's analysis of the availability of meaningful review, in light of the fact that the agency did not believe it had authority to address the constitutional claim? Is review really meaningful in the first instance at the federal circuit? Is the Court simply saying that the legal remedy is adequate?

Indeed, isn't the legal remedy adequate? Elgin had already been discharged and could recover whatever salary was owed in an action at law, through the administrative proceedings and federal-circuit review. There was no risk of incurring severe penalties. Is that the true distinction between *Elgin* and *Free Enterprise Fund*?

The final case in this chapter was excerpted above in the section on finality. Re-read the excerpt below. Is the preenforcement injunction framework better for making sense of it?

> **CROSS REFERENCE**
> This is our second time encountering *Sackett v. EPA*. We first discussed the case earlier in this chapter in the section on finality. Is *Sackett* really a finality case?

Sackett v. EPA

566 U.S. 120 (2012)

JUSTICE SCALIA delivered the opinion of the Court.

We consider whether Michael and Chantell Sackett may bring a civil action under the Administrative Procedure Act to challenge the issuance by the Environmental Protection Agency (EPA) of an administrative compliance order under § 309 of the Clean Water Act, 33 U.S.C. § 1319. The order asserts that the Sacketts' property is subject to the Act, and that they have violated its provisions by placing fill material on the property; and on this basis it directs them immediately to restore the property pursuant to an EPA work plan.

I

The Clean Water Act prohibits, among other things, "the discharge of any pollutant by any person," § 1311, without a permit, into the "navigable waters," § 1344—which the Act defines as "the waters of the United States," § 1362(7). If the EPA determines that any person is in violation of this restriction, the Act directs the agency either to issue a compliance order or to initiate a civil enforcement action. § 1319(a)(3). When the EPA prevails in a civil action, the Act provides for "a civil penalty not to exceed [$37,500] per day for each violation." § 1319(d). And according to the Government, when the EPA prevails against any person who has been issued a compliance order but has failed to comply, that amount is increased to $75,000—up to $37,500 for the statutory violation and up to an additional $37,500 for violating the compliance order.

The particulars of this case flow from a dispute about the scope of "the navigable waters" subject to this enforcement regime. Today we consider only whether the dispute may be brought to court by challenging the compliance order—we do not resolve the dispute on the merits. . . .

The Sacketts . . . own a 2/3-acre residential lot in Bonner County, Idaho. Their property lies just north of Priest Lake, but is separated from the lake by several lots containing permanent structures. In preparation for constructing a house, the Sacketts filled in part of their lot with dirt and rock. Some months later, they received from the EPA a compliance order. The order contained a number of "Findings and Conclusions," including [that Sacketts' property contained wetlands that were adjacent to Priest Lake, which is a navigable water under the statute, and therefore that the Sacketts had unlawfully discharged pollutants into the waters of the United States without a permit.—Ed.]

On the basis of these findings and conclusions, the order directs the Sacketts, among other things, "immediately [to] undertake activities to restore the Site in accordance with [an EPA-created] Restoration Work Plan" and to "provide and/or obtain access to the Site . . . [and] access to all records and documentation related to the conditions at the Site . . . to EPA employees and/ or their designated representatives."

The Sacketts, who do not believe that their property is subject to the Act, asked the EPA for a hearing, but that request was denied. They then brought this action in the United States District Court for the District of Idaho, seeking declaratory and injunctive relief. Their complaint contended that the EPA's issuance of the compliance order was "arbitrary [and] capricious" under the Administrative Procedure Act (APA), 5 U.S.C. § 706(2)(A), and that it deprived them of "life, liberty, or property, without due process of law," in violation of the Fifth Amendment. The District Court dismissed the claims for want of subject-matter jurisdiction, and the United States Court of Appeals for the Ninth Circuit affirmed. It concluded that the Act "preclude[s] pre-enforcement judicial review of compliance orders," and that such preclusion does not violate the Fifth Amendment's due process guarantee. We granted certiorari.

II

The Sacketts brought suit under Chapter 7 of the APA, which provides for judicial review of "final agency action for which there is no other adequate remedy in a court." 5 U.S.C. § 704. We consider first whether the compliance order is final agency action. There is no doubt it is agency action, which the APA defines as including even a "failure to act." §§ 551(13), 701(b)(2). But is it *final*? It has all of the hallmarks of APA finality that our opinions establish. Through the order, the EPA " 'determined' " " 'rights or obligations.' " *Bennett v. Spear,* 520 U.S. 154, 178 (1997). By reason of the order, the Sacketts have the legal obligation to "restore" their property according to an agency-approved Restoration Work Plan, and must give the EPA access to their property and to "records and documentation related to the conditions at the Site." Also, " 'legal consequences . . . flow' " from issuance of the order. *Bennett, supra,* at 178. For one, according to the Government's current litigating position, the order exposes the Sacketts to double penalties in a future enforcement proceeding. It also severely limits the Sacketts' ability to obtain a permit for their fill from the Army Corps of Engineers, see 33 U.S.C. § 1344. The Corps' regulations provide that, once the EPA has issued a compliance order with respect to certain property, the Corps will not process a permit application for that property unless doing so "is clearly appropriate." 33 CFR § 326.3(e)(1)(iv) (2011).

The issuance of the compliance order also marks the " 'consummation' " of the agency's decisionmaking process. *Bennett, supra,* at 178. As the Sacketts learned when they unsuccessfully sought a hearing, the "Findings and Conclusions" that the compliance order contained were not subject to further agency review. . . .

The APA's judicial review provision also requires that the person seeking APA review of final agency action have "no other adequate remedy in a court," 5 U.S.C. § 704. In Clean Water Act enforcement cases, judicial review ordinarily comes by way of a civil action brought by the EPA under 33 U.S.C. § 1319. But the Sacketts cannot initiate that process, and each day they wait for the agency to drop the hammer, they accrue, by the Government's telling, an additional $75,000 in potential liability. . . .

We conclude that the compliance order in this case is final agency action for which there is no adequate remedy other than APA review . . . .

4.   Debating "Universal" Injunctions

What exactly happens when a federal court issues an injunction against an administrative officer or regulation? Does the entire regulation fall by the wayside, or is the court's order binding only on the particular plaintiffs who brought the lawsuit? What exactly does it mean in § 706 of the APA that a reviewing court may "set aside agency action" that's arbitrary or capricious or otherwise contrary to law? Is the whole regulation invalidated, or is it merely held to have no legal effect in the case before it? Does a single district judge, in a particularly favorable forum, have the ability to enjoin the administration of an entire part of the executive branch? These are questions that are hotly contested today. The following excerpts provide a window into the debate.

Samuel L. Bray, Multiple Chancellors: Reforming the National Injunction

131 Harv. L. Rev. 417 (2017)

Federal district judges have taken to an odd practice: they are issuing injunctions that apply across the nation, controlling the defendant's behavior with respect to nonparties. A prominent example is the preliminary injunction in *Texas v. United States,* which shut down the implementation of the Obama Administration's most important immigration program. Another is the preliminary injunction in *Washington v. Trump,* which halted the implementation of President Trump's first executive order restricting entry by individuals from seven countries. How did this practice of issuing national injunctions begin? Is it defensible?

This Article offers a new analysis of the scope of injunctions to restrain the enforcement of a federal statute, regulation, or order. Without much controversy, federal courts have increasingly been acting as if they have the authority to issue "national injunctions." That is, in non-class actions, federal courts are issuing injunctions that are universal in scope—injunctions that prohibit the enforcement of a federal statute, regulation, or order *not only against the plaintiff, but also against anyone.* There is a small but growing literature critical of the national injunction. The criticisms expressed in this literature are essentially correct, including that the national injunction encourages forum shopping and that it arrests the development of the law in the federal system. But there is a strange disconnect between the diagnosis and the cure. The solutions proposed in this literature rely heavily on existing principles and appeals to judicial self-restraint. If these solutions would work, they would already have worked. . . .

[T]he national injunction is a recent development in the history of equity, traceable to the second half of the twentieth century. The older English and American practice was that an injunction would restrain the defendant's conduct vis-à-vis the plaintiff, not vis-à-vis the world. Thus, judicial behavior about the scope of injunctions has changed. But more has changed than judicial behavior.

If the English Chancellor had given national injunctions, they would not have been particularly problematic. There would have been no forum shopping and no risk of conflicting injunctions issued to the same defendant. The reason is a structural feature of English equity: there was one Chancellor. By contrast, in the federal courts of the United States, every judge is a "Chancellor" in the sense of having power to issue equitable relief. The current problems from the national injunction are thus a result of two transformations. One involved judicial institutions (the number of Chancellors). That transformation was a necessary precondition for the second, which involved judicial behavior (the scope of relief granted). The multiple-chancellor model of the federal courts requires better behavior from judges about the scope of equitable relief, behavior we can no longer count on.

. . . [T]his Article proposes a single clear rule for the scope of injunctions against federal defendants. A federal court should give a plaintiff-protective injunction, enjoining the defendant's conduct only with respect to the plaintiff. No matter how important the question and no matter how important the value of uniformity, a federal court should not award a national injunction. This rule, if adopted by the courts or by Congress, would alleviate the forum-shopping problem. It would restore the percolation of legal questions through different courts of appeals, allowing each circuit to reach its own conclusion pending resolution by the Supreme Court. And it would nearly eliminate the risk of directly conflicting injunctions.

This rule is rooted in the authority of the federal courts. Article III gives the federal courts the "judicial Power," which is a power to decide cases for parties, not questions for everyone. A further source of this rule is equitable principles. The federal courts are obligated to trace their equitable doctrines and remedies to the historic tradition of equity. In equity, however, injunctions did not control the defendant's behavior against nonparties. It is true that traditional equity lacked the sharply defined rule that is advanced here: because there was one Chancellor, Chancery never needed to develop rules to constrain the scope of injunctive relief. But translating traditional equity into the present, with sensitivity to the changed institutional setting, requires this rule.

The central objection to the proposal here is that it will lead to disuniformity in the law. That disuniformity will be of two kinds. First, if an injunction protects only the plaintiff, the federal government may continue to apply the invalidated statute, regulation, or order to other people. Second, once the disuniformity within a circuit is ended, usually but not always by a holding from the court of appeals, the federal government may continue enforcement in other circuits.

Is the bitter worth the sweet? Our system already tolerates a substantial amount of legal disuniformity. Without a decision by the Supreme Court, state courts and lower federal courts can reach different conclusions on the same question. The national government is not subject to offensive issue preclusion in later suits with different parties. When federal agencies lose in one circuit, they often continue litigating the question in other circuits.

If this seems like madness, it has a method. If the circuits all agree, their precedents resolve the question; if they disagree, the Supreme Court gains from the clash of opposing views. We sacrifice immediate resolution for what we hope will be better decisionmaking. The national injunction requires the opposite sacrifice, giving up deliberate decisionmaking for accelerated resolution. Cases still go to the Supreme Court, but without the benefit of decisions from multiple courts of appeals. If the national injunction issued by the district court is a preliminary one, the Supreme Court might even decide a major constitutional question on a motion for a stay. In that procedural posture, the Court would be reviewing lower court decisions reached in haste, and without the benefit of a record. Indeed, that very nearly occurred with the Take Care Clause claim in *Texas v. United States*, and with important questions about executive power and religious freedom in challenges to the immigration orders of President Trump. By returning to the older practice with respect to the scope of injunctions—the practice that obtained for more than a century and a half in the federal courts, and that is still followed in many cases—we choose patience and get better decisions. Measure twice, cut once.

The proposal made here differs sharply from the solutions proposed by most commentators. The limiting principles they have suggested include the physical boundaries of the court's jurisdiction, whether a broad injunction is necessary to provide "complete relief," whether "the court believes the underlying right to be highly significant," whether the challenge is to "a generally applicable policy or practice maintained by a defendant," and whether "the challenged provision can coherently be applied just to people other than the plaintiffs." These approaches and proposals are all indeterminate. Some are question-begging, such as allowing national injunctions only against generally applicable policies. Some are even perverse, such as allowing national injunctions only in the most significant cases—a principle that would allow national injunctions only when the forum-shopping temptation is irresistible. They also tend to exhort judges to apply the existing principles in a restrained way. But if the rise of the national injunction was not due to willful judging—if it was latent in the structure of the federal courts and then manifested with changes in ideology—then we must look elsewhere for the answer. Exhortation is not a solution to structural problems and ideological forces.

For the rule proposed here, the historical account of the origins of the national injunction is not mere background. The equitable doctrines and remedies of the federal courts must have a basis in traditional equity. The national injunction lacks the requisite basis. Moreover, this account exposes a complexity that scholars and courts need to consider when asking what is part of traditional equity. It is not enough to look at the past to see if some contemporary phenomenon can be spotted there, as if it were a beast in the wild. One must also consider the institutional setting—*the one-chancellor setting*—in which traditional equitable doctrines were fashioned. In that setting, certain powers and limits were developed. Other powers and limits were not developed, because there was no occasion for them. But we live in a multiple-chancellor world. Given the gap between equity's past and present, sometimes a translation has to be made. Sometimes equity's principles have to change in order to stay the same. . . .

I

. . . . In English equity before the Founding of the United States, there were no injunctions against the Crown. No doubt part of the explanation was the identification of the Chancellor with the King, an identification that was important in the early development and self-understanding of the Court of

Chancery. Without injunctions against the Crown, it would be easy to see why there were no broad injunctions against the enforcement of statutes. There were sometimes suits to restrain the actions of particular officers against particular plaintiffs. And the Attorney General could be a defendant in Chancery in certain kinds of cases "in which the interests of the Crown" were not "immediately concerned." Still, there was nothing remotely like a national injunction.

Equity would sometimes resolve a number of claims at once. To get into equity, a plaintiff needed to show that his case fit under one of the heads of equitable jurisdiction. One of these, "multiplicity of suits," could be invoked when the equity plaintiff wanted to avoid repeated instances of litigation with the same opposing party (for example, repeated trespass).

In addition, to avoid a multiplicity of suits, equity would give a "bill of peace." With this device, the Chancellor would consolidate a number of suits that would not be sequential between two parties. These might be suits involving some kind of common claim the plaintiff could have against multiple defendants (for example, a lord suing all of his tenants, or a vicar suing all of his parishioners). Or these might be suits involving some kind of common claim that multiple plaintiffs could have against a single defendant (for example, the tenants suing the lord, or the parishioners suing the vicar).

A bill of peace with multiple plaintiffs who represented the whole set of possible plaintiffs—some tenants representing all of the tenants, or some parishioners representing all of the parishioners—is probably the closest analogy in traditional equity to the national injunction. The analogy is not close. A bill of peace was not used to resolve a question of legal interpretation for the entire realm. It was not enough that many people were interested in or affected by the outcome. It was instead a kind of proto-class action. The group was small and cohesive; in present terms, we might say its interest was common. One could think of the Chancellor as hearing the plaintiffs' claim, which was identical to the claims of others within a preexisting social group, and then rounding up the scope of the decision (from most tenants to all tenants, for example). The Chancellor would then control the defendant's conduct with respect to this rounded-up group of plaintiffs and nonplaintiffs. The Chancellor would not control the defendant's conduct against the world, or against other potential plaintiffs who might bring other kinds of claims.

These principles were carried over into American equity. A suit had to fall under one of the recognized heads of equity jurisprudence. Courts would "take care to make no decree [that would] affect" the rights of nonparties. As for the bill of peace, one application and extension came in suits by taxpayers against tax collectors. Beginning in the mid-nineteenth century, some state courts were willing to enjoin the collection of an illegal tax, not only with respect to the plaintiffs but with respect to any taxpayer; other state courts disagreed, and would give relief only as to the plaintiffs. Yet when courts did give broader relief it was in cases involving municipal or county taxes. The theory was still that the bill of peace, or the injunction in the nature of a bill of peace, was resolving the common claims of a cohesive group, what might be called a micropolity.

There is evidence that late in the nineteenth century courts extended this reasoning from suits to enjoin tax collection to other challenges, allowing a successful plaintiff to obtain an injunction protecting all similarly situated persons. Again what was challenged were not federal or state laws but municipal ordinances. . . .

[I]n the nineteenth century, the idea of suing to restrain the enforcement of a federal statute everywhere in the nation seems not to have found any acceptance, and it may never even have been raised. . . .

Beginning in 1906, Congress gave the federal courts power to review the orders of the Interstate Commerce Commission (ICC). . . . When shippers challenged these ratemaking orders from the ICC in federal court, and succeeded, the injunction would be limited in scope to the parties. . . .

In *Panama Refining Co. v. Ryan*, the plaintiffs challenged a statutory provision allowing the President to restrict interstate shipment of oil, as well as regulations promulgated by the Department of the Interior under the statutory provision. The provision was part of the National Industrial Recovery Act, a central piece of New Deal legislation. It was exactly the kind of case that today would feature a request for a national injunction. But the plaintiffs did not seek one. Instead they sought an injunction against three federal officers—all then residing in Texas—to keep them from enforcing the law against the plaintiffs. In particular, they sought an injunction that would keep "the defendants from further coming upon the refining plant of the plaintiff, Panama Refining Company, or interfering with it in any manner" in its refining, purchasing, and disposing of oil; restrain the defendants "from coming upon the property of the plaintiff, A. F. Anding"; prohibit them "from further demanding of either of the plaintiffs reports called for" in regulations promulgated under the Act; and restrain them "from instituting any criminal proceedings against these plaintiffs because of the violation" of the regulations. . . .

Indeed, the litigation resulting in *Panama Refining Co. v. Ryan* was only part of a larger wave of challenges to New Deal legislation. As then-Attorney General Robert Jackson described it, after the Supreme Court held various New Deal acts unconstitutional, " 'hell broke loose' in the lower courts." The precise form that hell took was the grant of "injunctions restraining officers of the Federal Government from carrying out acts of Congress." How many injunctions were there? Against the enforcement of just one statutory provision, the processing tax in the Agricultural Adjustment Act, there were 1600 injunctions. . . .

Almost two decades later, in *Youngstown Sheet & Tube Co. v. Sawyer,* the district court issued a preliminary injunction that did not restrain the seizure of all steel mills. In its initial form, the preliminary injunction protected all the plaintiffs save one. . . .

II

. . . . Why did it take a century and a half after the establishment of the federal courts before the national injunction arrived? The question is difficult, and the answer here is tentative. With enough judicial restraint or certain ideological views about courts and law, the vulnerabilities of the multiple-chancellor structure would not have been exposed. Yet two ideological shifts—in the sense of changes in thinking about law—made it easier for federal judges to grant national injunctions.

First, judges once thought of injunctions against enforcement not as challenges to the validity of a statute (something offensive) as much as *antisuit injunctions* (something defensive). A plaintiff seeking an injunction against public officials would be trying to forestall an enforcement action in which the parties would be reversed. (That is, the plaintiff seeking an injunction would otherwise have been the defendant in the hypothetical future enforcement action.) The court would decide the validity of a law being applied, but only when there was, and only to the extent that there was, a threatened enforcement action. . . .

No one has yet charted exactly when the shift occurred, this shift in thinking of an injunction against enforcement of a federal law primarily in antisuit terms to thinking of it primarily as a challenge to the law itself. It is possible that the adoption in 1934 of the federal Declaratory Judgment Act encouraged this change in thinking. . . .

Second, there has been a change for some judges in their self-conception of what they are doing vis-à-vis an unconstitutional statute. The traditional conception is that a judge does not so much strike down an unconstitutional law as refuse to apply it. A judge has a duty to follow the law. Where there is a conflict among legal authorities, that duty compels the judge to follow the higher law. When a statute is "repugnant" to the Constitution, that is, when a statute is inconsistent with the Constitution, a judge simply does not apply it. This view is represented by *Marbury v. Madison*.

A different view is common today, and it can be found in the metaphorical language of courts and commentators. We speak of a statute, regulation, or order being "struck down," words that are physical and violent. Such language has accompanied a shift in the idea of what courts do with an unconstitutional statute. Instead of seeing courts as preventing or remedying a specific wrong to a person and only incidentally determining the constitutionality of a law, now many see courts as determining the constitutionality of a law and only incidentally preventing or remedying a specific wrong to a person. . . .

If a court strikes down a statute, regulation, or order, why should it give it respect by allowing its continued enforcement? Wouldn't enforcement, anywhere, offend the court's determination that it was invalid, struck down, *obliterated*? If a law is unconstitutional in all its applications, why should the court permit it to be applied to anyone? Again, reasons can be given for stopping short— ones grounded in equitable remedies, judicial competence, humility, separation of powers, federalism, and so on. But the logic of the national injunction is certainly strengthened by the newer view of what judges do when one law is inconsistent with a higher one, as well as by the metaphorical language used to express that view. . . .

Another change that might have led to national injunctions was an increase in general rulemaking by federal agencies. A number of statutes enacted in the 1960s and 1970s authorized general rulemaking, such as the National Traffic and Motor Vehicle Safety Act, the Clean Air Act, and the Clean Water Act.

At roughly the same time, Judge Wright and Judge Friendly offered revisionist statutory interpretations that gave several federal agencies legislative rulemaking powers. Meanwhile, as federal rulemaking expanded, the Supreme Court revised its ripeness doctrines, making it easier to bring pre-enforcement challenges to agency action. And Congress joined in, encouraging pre-enforcement review of agency actions. The total effect was to markedly increase the number of pre-enforcement challenges.

Even so, it is not obvious that more rulemaking and more pre-enforcement challenges have any logical implication for the scope of injunctions. It does seem that agencies now act more often in a legislative mode, making general rules, rather than taking relatively specific actions such as setting rates for a railroad operating between Shreveport and Dallas. But before the shift to national injunctions, there were many statutes enacted by Congress. Those statutes could be challenged before enforcement, with the litigant seeking an antisuit injunction or what might be called an antisuit declaratory judgment. As already discussed, there were many such challenges to New Deal legislation. But there were no national injunctions. Thus there is no logical or practical inconsistency between (a) plaintiff-protective injunctions and (b) a large quantity of pre-enforcement challenges to generally applicable legal norms.

Yet another change that might have influenced the development of the national injunction was the desegregation cases of the 1950s and 1960s. . . . After the *Brown* era, judges became more willing to give commands to federal and state officers. After the *Brown* era, those officers became more willing to follow the judges' commands.

Moreover, the desegregation decrees gave federal judges experience with broader injunctions. As Southern officials engaged in massive resistance to *Brown*, the personal cost of being a plaintiff was high. One solution was class actions; these may have encouraged judges to think of desegregation injunctions in systemic terms. Another solution was an injunction—in an individual suit— that went beyond the plaintiff and desegregated the entire school district. . . .

Yet there are also reasons to doubt that desegregation decrees led directly to national injunctions. The geographic scope of the injunctions, when they went beyond the plaintiffs, was usually the school district, not anything like the entire nation. An injunction against a school or a school district has a much firmer basis in traditional equity: it is easier to analogize such an injunction to the bill of peace . . . .

Finally, there is the impact of the 1966 amendments to Rule 23 of the Federal Rules of Civil Procedure. Among the changes was the addition of the Rule 23(b)(2) class action—a class action for injunctive and declaratory relief that was especially meant for civil rights cases. There is something logically odd about Rule 23(b)(2) leading to broader injunctions in non-class actions. One would have thought the implication was the reverse: because there was express authorization for class actions that could secure injunctive relief for a class of plaintiffs, there was *less* need for broad injunctions in non-class actions. . . .

In short, the rise of the national injunction seems to have been gradual and unplanned. . . .

III

. . . . National injunctions have increasingly thwarted the policies of the Federal Executive. When George W. Bush was President, national injunctions against the Administration's regulatory initiatives were issued by district court judges in California. For example, the Sierra Club and other plaintiffs challenged Bush Administration Forest Service regulations in *Earth Island Institute v. Pengilly*. The district court held several of the regulations invalid, enjoining their operation. After separate briefing directly on the scope of the court's order, the court insisted on giving a national injunction. "The appropriate remedy," the court concluded, "is to prevent such injury from occurring again by the operation of the invalidated regulations, be it in the Eastern District of California, another district within the Ninth Circuit, or anywhere else in the nation." The Ninth Circuit upheld the district court's national injunction, and it went even further, concluding that once the district court had found the regulations invalid, a national injunction was actually "compelled by the text of the Administrative Procedure Act," because the Act requires a court to "hold unlawful and *set aside* agency action" found to be invalid.

Near the end of the Obama Administration, national injunctions stymied many of the President's policies. Most prominent was the injunction in *Texas v. United States*, a case brought by Texas and a number of other states to challenge an immigration program, "Deferred Action for Parents of Americans and Lawful Permanent Residents," which gave lawful presence to millions of aliens for various federal-law purposes. The district court concluded that the program was likely a violation of the Administrative Procedure Act. The district court also concluded that a preliminary injunction should be issued halting the implementation of the program. But what would be the scope of that remedy? The court enjoined implementation for everyone, not just with respect to the twenty-six states that were plaintiffs. That preliminary injunction was affirmed by the Fifth Circuit, and by an evenly divided U.S. Supreme Court.

Texas v. United States was not a unique challenge to the policies of the Obama Administration. In 2016, a district court judge issued a national preliminary injunction against a major Department of Labor regulation, the "persuader rule." Another issued a national preliminary injunction regarding a "Dear Colleague" letter from the Department of Education about the statutory term "sex" and public school restrooms. Another issued a preliminary injunction against enforcement of a regulation requiring federal contractors to report labor violations. Another issued a national preliminary injunction against the enforcement of a Department of Labor regulation that would have made about four million workers eligible for overtime pay. Still another issued a national preliminary injunction against a rule interpreting an antidiscrimination provision in the Affordable Care Act (ACA). These national injunctions were all issued against a Democratic administration by federal district court judges in Texas.

At the start of the Trump Administration, the President's executive order restricting entry to the United States from seven countries was blocked by a federal district judge in the State of Washington, who issued a national preliminary injunction. Other district judges also issued national preliminary injunctions against the original or later versions of the order. Another district court issued a national preliminary injunction against an executive order on "sanctuary cities." In another challenge to the Administration's policies on "sanctuary cities," a district court issued a national preliminary injunction against grant conditions imposed by the Attorney General. In another case, involving representation in immigration proceedings, a district court blocked the enforcement of a cease-and-desist order with a national preliminary injunction. All these national injunctions came in the first eight months of the Trump Administration.

It is no accident which courts have given the major national injunctions in the last three administrations. In the George W. Bush Administration, it was federal courts in California. In the Obama Administration, it was federal courts in Texas. Now, in the Trump Administration, the national preliminary injunctions have come from federal courts in several less conservative circuits (the Fourth, Seventh, and Ninth). The forum selection happens not only for the district court, but also for the appellate court. The pattern is as obvious as it is disconcerting. Given the sweeping power of the individual judge to issue a national injunction, and the plaintiff's ability to select a forum, it is unsurprising that there would be rampant forum shopping.

The opportunity for forum shopping is extended by the asymmetric effect of decisions upholding and invalidating a statute, regulation, or order. If a plaintiff brings an individual action seeking a national injunction, and the district judge *upholds* the challenged law, that decision has no effect on other potential plaintiffs. But if one district judge *invalidates* it and issues a national injunction, the injunction controls the defendant's actions with respect to everyone. Shop 'til the statute drops. . . .

National injunctions interfere with good decisionmaking by the federal judiciary. . . .

The district court's injunction may halt federal enforcement everywhere. There may be no opportunity, then, for more circuits to express their views, because parties in other circuits might no longer bring their own challenges to the statute, regulation, or order. The Supreme Court is thus more likely to hear a case without the benefit of disagreement from the courts of appeals. It is denied what Judge Leventhal famously described as the "value in percolation among the circuits, with room for a healthful difference that may balance the final result." . . .

The forum shopping and decisionmaking effects of the national injunction can obscure a less common but also potentially serious problem, namely, conflicting injunctions. The most colorful example involves the battle for the control of the Erie Railroad in the late nineteenth century. There were repeated instances of conflicting injunctions, as multiple judges wielding equitable powers would give diverging commands to litigants, one judge mandating the sale of stock and another judge prohibiting it.

Nor are all the examples historical. At the very end of the Obama Administration, two lawsuits were filed by immigrants not legally in the United States challenging the scope of the district court injunction in *Texas v. United States*. . . . The plaintiffs also sought injunctions requiring the federal government to ignore the Texas injunction in their own cases. In the New York case, the judge even signaled his willingness to accept the plaintiff's argument . . . .

There are a number of doctrines and patterns of judicial decisionmaking that are premised on the absence of national injunctions. The availability of national injunctions allows a plaintiff suing a federal defendant to make an end run around these doctrines and patterns. . . .

Rule 23(b)(2) makes a class-wide injunctive remedy available if certain conditions are met; the implication is that the remedy is available *only* if those conditions are met. Nevertheless, the need for and value of this class action provision is greatly diminished if plaintiffs can get the same relief in an individual suit that they can in a class action. . . .

[T]here are limitations on the power of a federal district court to establish precedent. A federal district judge's decision does not bind other district courts. Indeed, it is not even an authoritative precedent for other judges in the same district court. Nor can a federal district court decision assure "clearly established law" for purposes of qualified immunity. Given these limitations on a federal district judge's authority to recognize and determine the law for anyone but the parties, it would be strange if a district judge could do so by means of a national injunction. . . .

IV

. . . . To be sure, the cases do have apparent constraints on the granting of national injunctions. The one most commonly raised by courts and commentators is the principle of "complete relief," which is that "injunctive relief should be no more burdensome to the defendant than necessary to provide complete relief to the plaintiffs." This principle suggests that when a national injunction is needed for complete relief a court *should* award one, and when it is not needed for complete relief a court *should not* award one. It is thus two sided, by turns a shield for defendants and a sword for plaintiffs, depending on the case. The complete-relief principle is intuitively appealing, and it suits the most basic aim of the law of remedies: to put the plaintiff in her rightful position.

Nevertheless, despite its acceptance by courts and commentators, the complete-relief principle is problematic. . . .

What counts as complete relief will often be indeterminate, as even supporters of this principle acknowledge. To get past this indeterminacy, a frequent move in judicial opinions is to look to the "extent of the violation." That inquiry ... drains the complete-relief principle of any limiting power. The question of whether to issue a national injunction arises precisely because the extent of the violation—the unconstitutional statute or the unlawful regulation or executive order—is national. The extent of the violation is national and so (courts reason) to give complete relief the injunction should also be national. In this way, the complete-relief principle can be taken by courts as a constraint on national injunctions or an impetus to give them, which is to say that it is no constraint at all. . . .

V

. . . . Given that national injunctions are problematic, and that the existing doctrine is inadequate, what can be done? Let's begin with a simple rule: injunctions should not protect nonparties. . . .

How would this work in practice? When a plaintiff sues to restrain the enforcement of a federal statute, regulation, or order, and wins, the national government will be unable to enforce the challenged law as to the plaintiff. Depending on the number of plaintiffs and their identity, the result might be broad but still partial nonenforcement.

For example, in *Texas v. United States* there were twenty-six state plaintiffs. The states sued in their own capacity, alleging that they would suffer injuries such as financial costs from issuing drivers' licenses on the basis of the federal grant of lawful presence. A more sound injunction would have prohibited the federal government from enforcing its statutes and regulations so as to require the states to grant drivers' licenses on the basis of the federally granted lawful presence. Beyond their alleged injuries, the states had no basis for securing a remedy from the court. All other states—and even private parties within the geographic borders of the twenty-six plaintiff states—had no claim to an injunction against the Obama Administration's immigration policy.

Or consider the case of President Trump's initial executive order restricting entry to the United States by individuals from seven nations. For an individual litigant seeking entry to the United States, a successful challenge should bring an injunction forbidding the officers of the United States from denying him or her that entry. A federal court should not award that litigant a national injunction controlling the government's conduct toward those who are not parties before the court.

In *Washington v. Trump*, the plaintiffs who obtained the preliminary injunction were the states of Washington and Minnesota. Although the states alleged various kinds of injury, in denying a stay the Ninth Circuit relied on the states' strongest claim of irreparable injury, namely, their claim on behalf of students and faculty affiliated with their state universities who would be injured by denial of entry to and departure from the United States. That basis for the preliminary injunction points the way to its proper scope. The injunction should have restrained the federal government from enforcing the executive order against students and faculty affiliated with the state universities of Washington and Minnesota. . . .

The [first] basis for the rule advanced here is . . . Article III of the Constitution of the United States[, which] confers the "judicial Power." This is a power to decide a case for a particular claimant. . . .

In decision after decision, the Supreme Court has understood Article III as giving shape and definition to the remedial authority of the federal courts. Many of these cases have involved equitable remedies, with the Court insisting that the plaintiff show standing that is specifically correlated with the requested injunction. . . .

A second basis is the Judiciary Act of 1789, which has been interpreted as requiring the federal courts to trace their equitable doctrines to traditional equity. . . .

[One] objection is that the successful plaintiff will be treated differently from others. . . . [This] question should be about the right moment to achieve uniformity—at what point should the uncertainty be liquidated, by what legal actor, and in what posture? With the question posed that way, it is impossible to think the best legal actor is a single district judge selected through forum shopping. . . . The better way to resolve the question is either through the unanimous alignment of lower courts or through disagreement among the lower courts followed by a series of decisions by the Supreme Court. In other words, the way to resolve legal questions for nonparties is through precedent, not through injunctions.

Precedent should be the ordinary way one case ripples out to others. What that means, in practical terms, is that a single plaintiff can win an injunction that protects her from the enforcement of a statute, regulation, or order. When the government appeals, if the appellate court affirms, its decision is a precedent within the circuit. There is no need for dozens of other suits in the circuit; the law of the circuit can be settled promptly, and can then be applied to every new plaintiff. . . .

If there is disagreement among the circuits, the likelihood is high that the Supreme Court will take the case and resolve the circuit split. In the meantime, each circuit's precedents apply only in that circuit.

Such disagreement is not merely tolerable; it is good. The possibility that the federal government would apply a rule in some circuits but not others was blessed in *United States v. Mendoza*, the decision holding that nonmutual offensive issue preclusion does not apply against the United States. . . .

Admittedly, there may be cases in which an injunction protecting only the plaintiff proves too narrow. But in such cases there is an obvious answer: a class action. . . .

Conclusion

. . . . It is possible, in a sense, to solve the problem of the national injunction. But the national injunction is intimately connected to another, deeper problem, namely, the speed at which legal questions are answered. Imagine that legal questions were resolved quickly, comprehensively, and with immediate finality. That system would be criticized as rash, perhaps even as an illegitimate exercise of authority. Imagine, by contrast, that legal questions were resolved slowly, piecemeal, and with a resolution that was only eventually final. That system would also be open to criticism. For one person it might offer justice, but for others it might offer only justice delayed or outright denied.

This choice is a deep problem that will never be solved. Each legal system can pick its poison, tending toward the vices of immediate, final resolution or the vices of slow, provisional resolution. In this regard, there is a sharp contrast between the English Chancery and the federal courts. A medieval Chancellor spoke on behalf of God and King; an early modern Chancellor spoke on behalf of conscience and King. These claims of epistemic certainty and political authority fit hand-in-glove with the existence of a single Chancellor. But the authority of federal judges is different. Power in the American political system is pervasively divided—through federalism, through the separation of powers, and through the sprawling system of federal courts. A legal question is resolved through patience and the consideration of many minds. Which system is better, if starting from scratch, is a difficult question. The question of which system obtains in the United States is easy to answer: a fragmented, many-minds system. In a system like ours, there is no room for the national injunction.

Notes and Questions

1. Is geography relevant? What is the relevance of geography? Is it fair to say that Professor Bray supports injunctions that are "national" in scope, as applied to the parties to the case? After all, if the defendant's action is enjoined, surely it is enjoined anywhere it might occur. Thus, in principle, there is no need to limit the *geographic* scope of the injunction—only the scope of the parties to whom it applies. For an argument that courts should also limit the geographic scope of injunctions only to those areas necessary to afford a plaintiff "complete relief," see Zayn Siddique, *Nationwide Injunctions*, 117 Colum. L. Rev. 2095 (2017).

2. Debating the history. In another Harvard Law Review article, Professor Mila Sohoni argues that there is a "lost" history of what she calls "universal" injunctions. Mila Sohoni, *The Lost History of the "Universal" Injunction*, 133 Harv. L. Rev. 920 (2020). She argues that courts effectively bound nonparties in many kinds of cases. For example, actions in rem to determine ownership of a piece of property necessarily bound the whole world as to that determination. Public nuisance decisions redounded to the benefit of others around the nuisance. What do you make of these analogies? Is invalidating a federal regulation the same thing as abating a nuisance? Or declaring that a piece of property belongs to a particular person, which must necessarily bind the whole world?

FOR DISCUSSION We earlier asked what role history should play when there is conflicting evidence or conflicting interpretations of the evidence. Is the evidence here conflicting, or do you agree with one or the other of the participants in this historical debate?

Professor Sohoni also points to cases in which courts appear to issue injunctions restraining government officials that are not named parties, and even private parties who might bring lawsuits to enforce government orders. In these cases, however, the injunction only protected the particular plaintiffs suing. Can such cases be explained on the ground that courts of equity have the power to craft a remedy that will give "complete relief" to the plaintiff? See Michael T. Morley, *Disaggregating the History of Nationwide Injunctions: A Response to Professor Sohoni*, 72 Ala. L. Rev. 239 (2020).

3. *Is the APA relevant?* Professor Bray once mentions the APA in the above excerpt, in the context of a Ninth Circuit decision holding that a nationwide injunction was compelled by the language of APA § 706 that an agency may "set aside" agency action held to be unlawful. What do you make of that conclusion? Can a court "set aside" an agency regulation in a particular case by simply refusing to enforce it? Why does "setting aside" require the invalidation of the regulation as to all people, even those not parties to the suit?

In a recent post, Professor John Harrison argues that the APA does not authorize nationwide injunctions; rather, the remedy depends on the form of action, which is governed by APA § 703. This section provides that "[t]he form of proceeding for judicial review is the special statutory review proceeding relevant to the subject matter in a court specified by statute or, in the absence or inadequacy thereof, any applicable form of legal action, including actions for declaratory judgments or writs of prohibitory or mandatory injunction or habeas corpus," and that "agency action is subject to judicial review in civil or criminal proceedings for judicial enforcement." In some of these actions—such as habeas corpus or as a defense to an enforcement proceeding—"setting aside" the agency action results in no affirmative remedy at all. Setting aside means simply that the regulation is not enforced against the private party and thus she suffers no sanctions. And, if setting aside simply meaning ignoring the law in such cases, then it can't compel a nationwide injunction in other cases. If a nationwide injunction is justified, it can only be justified on the basis of existing equitable principles.

What do you make of this argument? Harrison explains it in more detail:

> The view that section 706 directs that courts give a remedy that sets aside agency action appears to be quite common. That view is wrong. Section 706 operates at a point in the court's decision process before the remedy is considered. When that provision tells courts to set agency action aside, it instructs them not to decide the case according to that action. The court is to put the agency action off to the side, in a manner of speaking. The remedial consequences of not

deciding the case according to the agency action depend on the form of proceeding for judicial review being used in the case. In an enforcement proceeding, setting the agency action aside means treating it as legally ineffective, so that it does not impose any obligations on the defendant. In a proceeding in which the court acts like an appellate tribunal with respect to the agency, setting the action aside may entail rendering it wholly ineffective. . . .

One mode of judicial review contemplated by section 703, enforcement proceedings, does not produce any affirmative remedy at all. If a private defendant argues successfully that a regulation should have been promulgated with notice and comment but was not, the defendant prevails but the court gives no affirmative remedy. If section 706 directs courts to give a remedy of setting aside, it cannot operate in enforcement proceedings. But section 706 deals with the scope of judicial review generally, and must operate in all the proceedings referred to by section 703.

Some of the other modes of judicial review contemplated by section 703 do involve an affirmative remedy, but not one that sets agency action aside the way an appellate court sets a judgment aside. A successful petitioner in habeas obtains an order of release from custody, but nothing else. A private plaintiff who obtains an injunction against the institution of enforcement proceedings, and thereby anticipates the defense that would be available were the regulation enforced, obtains the injunction but no more. In neither of those modes of judicial review does the court give an affirmative remedy making the agency action inoperative. If section 706 directs courts to give such orders, it cannot apply in habeas or anti-enforcement proceedings.

If by "set aside" section 706 means, put to the side in deciding the case and so do not follow the agency action, section 706 provides a principle that can be applied in all the modes of judicial review contemplated by section 703. In an enforcement proceeding, not deciding according to the agency action means deciding in favor of the defendant. In habeas and anti-enforcement proceedings, it means giving affirmative relief that follows from the principle that the agency action is not legally binding, which follows from not deciding according to it.

In appellate-type proceedings, deciding not according to the agency action means overturning the action, if the court is authorized to do so by the applicable special review statute. . . .

Section 706 does not instruct or authorize reviewing courts to give a remedy that operates on the effectiveness of the agency action under review. Any instruction or authorization along those lines must come from the form of proceeding applicable pursuant to section 703. . . .

John Harrison, *"Section 706 of the Administrative Procedure Act Does Not Call for Universal Injunctions or Other Universal Remedies," Notice & Comment Blog,* Yale Journal on Regulation (Apr. 12, 2020).

Professor Mila Sohoni disagrees with Professor Harrison. See Mila Sohoni, *The Power to Vacate a Rule,* 88 Geo. Wash. L. Rev. 1121 (2020). She argues that the APA does authorize nationwide (or universal) injunctions. She notes that the APA was intended to codify existing equitable principles, and then cites to several of the equitable cases she cites in the Harvard Law Review article on universal injunctions. Does the meaning of the APA thus depend on one's interpretation of the historical cases?

In any event, in DHS v. Regents, the 2020 DACA case excerpted in the section on arbitrary and capricious review, the Supreme Court, in a footnote, said the following: "Our affirmance of [one court's] order vacating the rescission [of DACA] makes it unnecessary to examine the propriety of the nationwide scope of the injunctions issued by the [other courts]." Does the Supreme Court therefore agree with Professor Sohoni? Does the question deserve more treatment than it received in this footnote?

Amanda Frost, In Defense of Nationwide Injunctions

93 N.Y.U. L Rev. 1065 (2018)

Over the past few years, courts have issued nationwide injunctions barring the executive from enforcing federal laws and policies against *anyone*, not just the plaintiffs in the case before them. Nationwide injunctions halted President Obama's initiative granting deferred action to undocumented parents of U.S. citizens and lawful permanent residents, his Department of Education's interpretive guidance on the treatment of transgender students in public schools, and enforcement of a federal regulation requiring that federal contractors report labor violations. A few years later, district courts enjoined nationwide President Trump's ban on entry into the United States by refugees and nationals of six predominantly Muslim countries, and his administration's policy of withholding federal funds from so-called "sanctuary cities" that refused to assist federal officials in enforcing immigration laws. Most recently, a district court issued a nationwide injunction that barred the federal government from rescinding the deferred action status granted to 690,000 undocumented immigrants brought to the United States as children.

The whiplash-inducing effect of the change in presidential administrations has highlighted the power of a single district court judge to halt executive programs in their tracks. Legal scholars have criticized the practice, Congress is considering legislation to prohibit it, and commentators are calling for the Supreme Court to address it. A consensus is rapidly forming that courts should *never* issue nationwide injunctions, period. Indeed, at least one scholar has argued that federal courts lack the constitutional authority to do so under any circumstances.

This Article is a defense of nationwide injunctions, albeit a qualified one. Nationwide injunctions come with significant costs and should never be the default remedy in cases challenging federal executive action. As their critics point out, nationwide injunctions encourage forum shopping, politicize the courts, create the risk of conflicting injunctions, and potentially give enormous power to a single district court judge. But in some cases, nationwide injunctions are also the only means to provide plaintiffs with complete relief and avoid harm to thousands of individuals similarly situated to the plaintiffs. And sometimes anything short of a nationwide injunction would be impossible to administer. When a district court is asked to pass on the validity of certain types of federal policies with nationwide effects—such as those affecting the air or water, or the nation's immigration system—it would be extremely difficult to enjoin application of the policy to some plaintiffs but not others.

Nothing in the Constitution's text or structure bars federal courts from issuing a remedy that extends beyond the parties; to the contrary, such injunctions enable federal courts to play their essential role as a check on the political branches. Without nationwide injunctions, the federal courts would be powerless to protect thousands or millions of people from potentially illegal or unconstitutional government policies—policies that can be applied with minimal notice or process, and to many who lack the ability to bring their individual cases before the courts. The need for such injunctions is particularly great in an era when major policy choices are increasingly made through unilateral executive action affecting millions.

As a theoretical matter, the debate over nationwide injunctions reveals deep divisions among scholars over the role of the federal courts, and particularly the lower federal courts, in our system of government. Do the federal courts exist primarily to resolve disputes between parties, or to declare the meaning of law for everyone? Is precedent alone a sufficient tool with which to correct the government's legal and constitutional errors, or may courts use injunctions to accomplish the same goals? May courts adjust their traditional equitable powers to counter expanding executive power—particularly when the executive can act strategically to avoid both judgments in individual cases and decisions by the Supreme Court? As these questions suggest, one's view of the propriety of nationwide injunctions may turn on one's deep-seated beliefs about the role of the judiciary and the scope of judicial power vis-à-vis the political branches. . . .

I

. . . . This Article uses the term "nationwide injunction" to refer to an injunction at any stage of the litigation that bars the defendant from taking action against individuals who are not parties to the lawsuit in a case that is not brought as a class action. That term is somewhat misleading, however, because no one denies that district courts have the power to enjoin a defendant's conduct anywhere in the nation (indeed, the world) as it relates to *the plaintiff*; rather, the dispute is about *who* can be included in the scope of the injunction, not *where* the injunction applies or is enforced. For that reason, some scholars refer to injunctions that bar the defendant from taking action against nonparties as "universal injunctions," "global injunctions," or "defendant-oriented injunctions." Despite its potential to confuse, this Article uses the term "nationwide injunction" because it is the name that courts repeatedly use when issuing this type of injunction.

The Article focuses on the use of nationwide injunctions against the federal executive branch to enjoin implementation of federal laws and policies, because that is the context in which they have most frequently been issued and has been the focus of most scholarly criticism. . . .

II

. . . . The text of Article III does not spell out the scope of the judiciary's equitable powers, but tradition and precedent suggest that broad remedial injunctions are constitutionally permissible, and in some cases essential, as a means of enabling the courts to check the political branches. . . .

The first sentence of Article III of the U.S. Constitution declares that "[t]he judicial Power of the United States, shall be vested in one Supreme Court, and in such inferior courts as the Congress may from time to time ordain and establish." The "judicial Power" includes the power to issue both legal and equitable remedies, but the text of Article III does not spell out the scope of those remedies.

Federal courts' equitable powers derive from traditional equity, which serves as both a source of, and limit on, courts' exercise of that power. Tradition provides little clarity in this instance, however. No rule has ever barred courts from issuing injunctions controlling a defendant's conduct vis-à-vis nonparties. To the contrary, the "bill of peace," which allowed courts to issue remedies to individuals closely connected and similarly situated to the plaintiff, suggests that, in traditional equity courts could grant injunctions that applied to nonparties, albeit in a more circumscribed context than the broad nationwide injunctions issued today. Accordingly, the historical practice supports the conclusion that courts have always had the authority to issue equitable relief that encompasses nonparties.

In any case, federal courts' equitable authority should keep pace with the expansion of the political branches' role in enacting laws and implementing policies with nationwide effect. . . .

Some scholars argue that Article III's "case or controversy" requirement limits not only who has standing to sue, but also the scope of federal courts' power to order equitable relief. . . .

Even under this narrow view of courts' equitable power, however, courts can issue injunctions that apply to nonparties as long as they are crafted in terms of providing complete relief to the plaintiff. For example, in a school desegregation case, the only way to alleviate the plaintiff's injury is to require the defendant to allow *all* nonwhite students in the jurisdiction to attend the school; an order requiring the defendant to admit only the plaintiff would not address the injury. Likewise, in the litigation challenging the Department of Justice's policy of withholding funding from so-called "sanctuary cities," the Seventh Circuit upheld the nationwide injunction because funds were distributed nationwide from a single pool of money, and thus "conditions imposed on one can impact the amounts received by others." Accordingly, that court concluded "piecemeal relief is ineffective to redress the injury, and only nationwide relief can provide proper and complete relief." In these cases, the defendant is required to take action affecting parties other than the plaintiff for the purpose of addressing the *plaintiff's* injury, which is consistent with the view that courts cannot order equitable relief beyond that needed to provide a remedy to the plaintiff. . . .

Courts regularly issue remedies broader than required to address the injury that gave plaintiff standing to sue. For example, federal judges sometimes issue prophylactic injunctions that go beyond the plaintiff's "actual injury." The Supreme Court upheld such a prophylactic injunction in *Hutto v. Finney*, which prohibited a prison from *ever* putting prisoners into solitary confinement for more than thirty days, even though this practice did not violate the Eighth Amendment in every case. The Court explained that because the defendant prison had not complied with the district court's earlier orders, and because the conditions as a whole in the isolation cells amounted to cruel and unusual punishment, the district court was "justified in entering a comprehensive order to insure against the risk of inadequate compliance." . . .

The class action device further demonstrates that courts have the constitutional authority to enjoin defendants from taking action affecting nonparties. Under Federal Rule of Civil Procedure 23, a few named individuals can bring a lawsuit on behalf of all similarly situated individuals across the nation as long as they satisfy the four class certification requirements listed in Rule 23(a), as well as Rule 23(b)(2)'s requirement that the "party opposing the class has acted . . . on grounds that apply generally to the class, so that final injunctive relief . . . is appropriate respecting the class as a whole."

Rule 23(a)'s requirements are primarily intended to protect the rights of absent class members, not the defendants. They require the court to find that the class is sufficiently numerous to justify a class action, that the named plaintiffs' claims are similar to the absent class members that they seek to represent, and that named plaintiffs will be adequate representatives of the class. As long as those requirements are met, and the party opposing the class "has acted or refused to act on grounds that apply generally to the class," a court can issue injunctive relief that applies to *everyone* within the class, whether that person was named in the lawsuit, appeared in court, or even knew a class action had been brought on his or her behalf.

Class actions are premised on the quasi-fiction that absent class members are parties to the suit, but absent class members appear no differently situated from the nonparties who benefit from nationwide injunctions. Absent class members, like nonparties affected by a nationwide injunction, have never appeared before a court, may not even be aware of the lawsuit, and never have to demonstrate that they have a "case" or "controversy." . . .

Critics of nationwide injunctions point out that granting such relief is in tension with the existence of class actions. Why require plaintiffs to go to the trouble of certifying a class if they can get nationwide injunctive relief without doing so? The point is valid as a matter of policy, but it does not address the constitutional question. If class actions are constitutionally permissible, then it would seem that Article III does not prevent federal courts from ordering defendants to cease taking action as it affects individuals who would not have had standing to sue. . . .

At its core, the debate over nationwide injunctions is really a debate about the role of the federal courts in the constitutional structure. Are courts primarily intended to resolve disputes between the parties, or do they also declare the meaning of federal law for everyone? To what degree are courts intended to serve as a check on the political branches, and should their authority expand in lockstep with that of Congress and the President? The reaction to nationwide injunctions turns, in large part, on these larger questions about the place of the courts in our system of government.

Federal courts serve a dual function: They exist to resolve disputes between the parties before them and also to declare the meaning of law for everyone. Scholars dispute the degree to which law declaration is merely incidental to dispute resolution, rather than an independent and significant aspect of the judicial power. The tension between these two models can be seen in a range of doctrines and their exceptions: the prohibition against advisory opinions (dispute resolution), countered by the common practice of giving alternative grounds for decisions (law declaration); the rule against judicial issue creation (dispute resolution), and the many exceptions to that rule (law declaration); the requirement of standing (dispute resolution), with exceptions for associational standing, the "one good plaintiff" rule, and for moot cases that are capable of repetition yet evading judicial review (law declaration). The debate over nationwide injunctions is closely related to these larger questions about the judicial role.

Those opposed to nationwide injunctions tend to see courts as primarily resolvers of individual disputes. These scholars either reject the law declaration model completely or view the courts' power to declare the meaning of the law as incidental to their dispute resolution role. [Professor] Bray perceives judges' increased use of nationwide injunctions as reflecting a shift in their perception of their role vis-à-vis unconstitutional statutes—one that mirrors the shift from dispute resolution to law declaration. He argues that traditionally, judges viewed their rulings not as invalidating unconstitutional laws but as refusing to apply them in the cases before them. . . .

In other words, those scholars who view courts as primarily serving to resolve individual disputes generally reject nationwide injunctions as overreaching, while those who believe that a significant aspect of the judicial function is law declaration generally view such injunctions more favorably. That is not to say that proponents of the dispute resolution model will inevitably reject all nationwide injunctions, or that those in the law declaration camp will put no limits on judicial power to issue such injunctions. But scholars' underlying assumptions about the judicial role are likely to shape their responses to this form of equitable relief.

Attitudes towards nationwide injunctions also turn on one's view of the courts as a check on the political branches. If courts are limited to deciding individual cases and lack the power to issue broader injunctions, then they lose a significant tool with which to curb abuses of power by the other branches.

Nationwide injunctions are an essential means by which courts can halt unconstitutional or illegal federal policies that may cause irreparable harm to thousands or millions of people. The United States must obey judgments in individual cases in which it is a defendant, but it is not bound to follow either district or circuit court precedent in future cases. The executive can, and often does, act strategically to avoid generating either circuit or Supreme Court precedent, such as by choosing not to appeal and mooting cases in which plaintiffs seek to do so. The political branches can announce a new federal policy at the eleventh hour, when it is difficult for most of the affected individuals to quickly file suit. Class certification may be impossible or time consuming and difficult to obtain. The executive can be expected to fight class certification by mooting claims by named plaintiffs or challenging whether the named class members are adequate representatives. Absent nationwide injunctions, all of these strategies can be used to avoid judicial decisions affecting more than a few individuals at a time—unless courts have the power to issue nationwide injunctions.

Of course, district court judges can err, mistakenly halting an executive program that a higher court ultimately determines is lawful. But when they do, they will quickly be reversed—albeit after a delay of a few days, or at most weeks, that may temporarily frustrate implementation of federal policy. When district courts are presented with a legal challenge to an illegal executive policy that goes into effect immediately, however, a nationwide injunction by a lower federal court may be the only realistic way to prevent the political branches from overstepping their bounds. The stakes are high either way, but the trade-off is clear: Eliminating nationwide injunctions takes away the risk that lower courts will mistakenly halt implementation of perfectly legal federal policies, but it also creates the risk that the federal government will deprive thousands or millions of their rights during the months or years it can take before the Supreme Court can resolve the matter. . . .

III

Although federal courts have the constitutional authority to issue nationwide injunctions, such broad injunctions are not justified in every case. Nationwide injunctions come with both costs and benefits that courts should consider carefully before issuing them. Such injunctions are an appropriate remedy in three categories of cases: when they are the only method of providing the plaintiff with complete relief; when they are the only means of preventing irreparable injury to individuals similarly situated to plaintiffs; and when they are the only practical remedy because a more limited injunction would be chaotic to administer and would impose significant costs on the courts or others. In cases in which nationwide injunctions can serve one or more of these goals, the benefits of such an injunction may outweigh the costs.

The Supreme Court has explained that "injunctive relief should be no more burdensome to the defendant than necessary to provide complete relief to the plaintiffs." Implicit in that statement is the assumption that injunctions should be broad enough to provide such relief. In some cases, an injunction that enforces rights of individuals who are not parties to the lawsuit is required to achieve that goal. School desegregation cases provide a paradigmatic example. If an African American plaintiff challenges a segregated public school system, granting an injunction requiring the defendant school system to admit the plaintiff only, and no other African American child, would not alleviate the plaintiff's injury. Challenges to policies that cross state lines—such as regulations concerning clean air and water, as well as some immigration policies—also require broad injunctions. In such cases, the "very nature of the rights appellants seek to vindicate requires that the decree run to the benefit not only of appellants but also for all persons similarly situated."

Recent cases challenging federal immigration laws and policies illustrate the need for nationwide injunctions to relieve the injuries suffered by the plaintiffs in those cases. In the challenge to the second iteration of President Trump's travel ban, the state of Hawaii claimed that the travel ban injured "its residents, its employers, its educational institutions, and its sovereignty," and in particular prevented it from recruiting students and faculty to attend its University. An individual plaintiff, a Muslim imam, was injured because the ban barred a close relative from an affected country from visiting him and his family in Hawaii, and also because he claimed the ban denigrated his religion. The Hawaii District Court issued a nationwide injunction against enforcement of portions of the travel ban, and the Ninth Circuit affirmed the injunction to the extent it covered entry of nationals from the six designated countries. Although the Supreme Court narrowed the injunction to "foreign nationals who have a credible claim of a bona fide relationship with a person or entity in the United States," it kept in place an injunction prohibiting the government from applying the executive order's ban on entry to nonparties. . . .

The injunction's broad scope was essential to protect the plaintiffs' interests. As Hawaii explained, restrictions on the entry of foreign nationals would impede the University's ability to recruit these noncitizens to be students or faculty and would discourage many from applying for admission or job openings or accepting an offer. Nor would an injunction specific to Hawaii be feasible in the immigration context, because the United States does not restrict travel among the fifty states by a noncitizen lawfully residing in one of them. . . .

This same logic supported a Texas District Court's decision to issue a nationwide injunction banning implementation of President Obama's 2014 initiative granting deferred action to undocumented immigrant parents of

U.S. citizens and lawful permanent residents. Although twenty-six states filed suit, the district court found that only Texas had standing to bring the lawsuit based on Texas's claim that it would be forced to provide these new recipients of deferred action with state-subsidized driver's licenses. Nonetheless, the Fifth Circuit affirmed the district court's nationwide injunction after Texas argued that recipients of deferred action in other states could travel to Texas, take up residence, and then apply for driver's licenses—thereby causing Texas the same injury.

The obligation to provide complete relief to the plaintiff also justifies nationwide injunctions in cases involving issues that cross state lines—such as pollution of the air or water, tainted food, or defective products. For example, in *Northwest Environmental Advocates v. EPA*, several regional and national environmental and conservation organizations sued the EPA, challenging under the Clean Water Act a federal regulation exempting ships from the requirement to obtain a permit before discharging ballast water. The groups claimed that the exemption for ballast waters injured their "members' recreational, aesthetic, scientific, educational, conservational, and economic interests in the natural resources of [the] waters [of the United States]," but they did not seek class certification or identify potentially injured members in every state that would be affected by the regulation. After finding the regulation violated the Clean Water Act, the Court vacated the regulation containing the exemption under the APA's requirement that a court "hold unlawful and set aside" agency action found to be "not in accordance with law."

Neither the plaintiffs nor the defendant suggested that the court enter a geographically limited injunction, and for good reason. The environmental harm from discharge of ballast waters could not be easily contained geographically, and thus prohibiting ballast water discharge in some regions of the United States but not others would not have alleviated the plaintiffs' injury. As this case illustrates, it would be difficult to craft injunctive relief limited to the plaintiff alone, or to a single geographic region, in cases involving easily dispersed or mobile items, such as cases concerning endangered species or the safety of food or medical devices. . . .

Nationwide injunctions are at times the only way to prevent irreparable injury to individuals who cannot easily or quickly join in litigation. For example, in cases challenging a new obstacle to casting a ballot issued on the eve of an election, or an exemption allowing industry to begin drilling or logging in a previously protected area, or an immigration policy that will immediately change immigration status, a large group of individuals can face imminent and irreparable injury and yet be incapable of quickly bringing their individual cases before courts.

The first iteration of the travel ban litigation is a salient recent example of the problem. Millions of people were affected by the executive order banning travel into the United States by the nationals of seven predominantly Muslim countries, as well as halting the entry of all refugees. The order went into effect upon issuance, barring entry even by those who had already obtained visas and were en route to the United States at the time the order was issued. A number of lawsuits were filed within hours and days of the executive order's implementation on behalf of individuals, entities, and states affected by the travel ban.

Most of the thousands of individuals affected by the travel ban lacked the capacity to file suit quickly, however. By definition, all were outside of the United States, all were noncitizens, and most did not have access to lawyers familiar with the U.S. immigration system. In any case, the judicial system would not have had the capacity to provide thousands of plaintiffs with a quick resolution of their claims for relief on an individual, case-by-case basis. Requiring all of the affected noncitizens to remain outside the United States unless and until they are able to file individual lawsuits and obtain a judicial remedy would delay their entry into the United States for months or years, often causing them irreparable injury. . . .

Immigration is just one area in which a change in government policy might injure thousands or millions of individuals who lack the ability to file suit quickly themselves. New restrictions on state voting laws enacted on the eve of an election, or an exemption allowing emission of air or water pollutants, can also have immediate, harmful effects on thousands of people, most of whom will not be able to file suit. Typically, the U.S. Supreme Court will take months or years to address the issue, and its ruling would therefore come years too late for those who had lost the right to vote, or who had suffered the ill effects of breathing polluted air or drinking contaminated water. . . .

Nationwide injunctions are sometimes the only practicable method of providing relief and can avoid the cost and confusion of piecemeal injunctions. . . .

Again, the recent litigation challenging executive immigration policies illustrates the point. Hawaii sought to enjoin President Trump's travel ban on the ground that prohibiting entry into the United States by foreign nationals would harm its economy, university, and individuals living within the state. As already explained, a geographically limited injunction would not have alleviated Hawaii's injuries. But in any case, a geographically limited injunction would have been both ineffective and extraordinarily confusing to the thousands of people required to implement and obey it.

We know this for a fact, because a district court in Massachusetts issued just such a geographically limited injunction a few days after the travel ban went into effect. That court ordered Customs and Border Protection officials to "notify airlines that have flights arriving at Logan Airport . . . that individuals on these flights will not be detained or returned based solely on the basis of the Executive Order." The order was confusing not only for the federal immigration officials required to follow it, but also for the foreign officials and airline personnel who determine who is permitted to board airplanes headed to the United States. In the confusion that followed, some foreign nationals were permitted to enter the United States through Boston's Logan Airport, but many others were barred from doing so. And some immigrants switched their flights to fly into Logan Airport and then traveled by train, bus, car, or domestic flight to their original destination—rendering the geographic limit on the injunction pointless. . . .

The APA appears to authorize nationwide injunctions in cases challenging federal agency action. Under 5 U.S.C. § 706(2), courts are required to "hold unlawful and set aside" agency action it finds to be invalid—language that suggests that when a court finds a rule was promulgated in violation of the procedures laid out in the APA, or is contrary to an agency's governing statute, then the rule can no longer apply to *anyone*. Indeed, that is how the D.C. Circuit has long interpreted it. . . .

Finally, a related benefit of nationwide injunctions is that they avoid duplicative litigation that would needlessly sap the resources of litigants and courts. . . .

But nationwide injunctions are not justified in every case challenging a national policy—a fact that some courts have failed to appreciate.

For example, a district court judge in Texas issued a nationwide injunction barring the Obama administration's transgender bathroom policy on the ground that a "nationwide injunction is necessary because the alleged violation extends nationwide." A district court in Illinois gave the same reason to support of its nationwide injunction barring implementation of the Trump administration's policy of restricting funding to sanctuary cities. Similarly, a number of courts have argued that nationwide injunctions are essential to protect the uniform application of federal law. In most contexts, however, neither the fact that a federal law or policy extends nationwide (as most do), nor uniformity provides an adequate rationale for nationwide injunctions.

To the contrary, our federal judicial system is intentionally designed to allow lower courts to reach different conclusions about the meaning of federal law—conflicts in interpretation that remain unless and until the Supreme Court chooses to resolve the split. Plaintiffs usually have a choice of state or federal court when asserting a federal claim, and often can select among various federal district courts as well. District court decisions have no precedential value, and federal courts of appeals are free to diverge from the decisions of other circuits. Occasionally Congress chooses to promote uniformity over percolation by requiring that certain categories of cases be brought in a single forum, but those areas of law are the exception. For the most part, Congress has structured the federal judiciary to prioritize percolation over the uniform, nationwide interpretation of federal law. Accordingly, federal courts cannot justify nationwide injunctions on the ground that it is essential to achieve immediate uniformity in the interpretation of federal law. . . .

IV

In addition to the benefits described in Part III, nationwide injunctions also come with significant costs—costs that district courts have too often failed to consider. Nationwide injunctions promote forum shopping, politicize the judiciary, allow a single district court judge to control policy for the nation, prevent the percolation of federal law, can lead to conflicting injunctions, and put pressure on the Supreme Court to quickly resolve cases that are often in an embryonic stage with a poorly developed evidentiary record. These are costs that should be taken into account by courts before issuing such injunctions. . . .

Forum shopping, and the politicization of the judiciary that inevitably accompanies it, is a valid concern, but abolishing nationwide injunctions is both an over- and under-inclusive response to that problem. Forum shopping is not limited to cases involving nationwide injunctions. . . .

If forum shopping generally is a problem, Congress could amend venue statutes to restrict the number of courts in which a case could be filed without eliminating nationwide injunctions. If forum shopping is particularly problematic in the context of nationwide injunctions because it allows an outlier judge to halt a federal policy nationwide, Congress could channel cases seeking nationwide injunctions into a single forum. Indeed, pending legislation proposes doing just that. The Assigning Proper Placement of Executive Action Lawsuits Act (APPEAL Act) would give the federal district courts in Washington, D.C. exclusive original jurisdiction over all lawsuits challenging an executive order, action, or memorandum. Other options to prevent forum shopping include assigning a judge by lottery and requiring that nationwide injunctions be issued only by three-judge district courts with the right to take an immediate appeal to the U.S. Supreme Court. . . .

Nationwide injunctions can also stymie the development of the law and the percolation of legal issues in the lower courts. . . .

[But] a nationwide injunction issued by one court need not always stop other courts from weighing in on the matter. For example, although district courts issued nationwide injunctions against the travel ban, both the Fourth and Ninth Circuit reviewed those decisions and issued their own opinions in those cases. Likewise, although nationwide injunctions have barred the executive from withholding funds from so-called "sanctuary cities," different federal courts continue to address the issue.

In some cases, however, a nationwide injunction by one court could put an end to all litigation. For example, if a court enjoins an agency from commencing enforcement actions, and such actions are the only way in which a legal issue gets before a court, then no other court will be able to weigh in. Accordingly, courts should consider whether a broad nationwide injunction would prevent the law from percolating in the other circuits, and that cost should inform a court's decision whether to enter such an injunction. . . .

Critics of nationwide injunctions argue that they are inconsistent with the structure of our federal judicial system, and in particular with the nonexistent precedential value of district court opinions and the limited precedential effect of decisions by the federal courts of appeals. . . . Finally, critics contend that nationwide injunctions are at odds with the existence of class actions under Federal Rule of Civil Procedure 23(b)(2) because they enable a court to provide classwide relief without first certifying a class.

Clearly, there are tensions between these doctrines and nationwide injunctions. But as any student in a Federal Courts class well knows, tensions abound in the structure and operation of the federal court system, which must incorporate competing goals into a system that has developed organically over time. The federal judicial system balances the advantages of uniform interpretation of federal law against federalism, regional autonomy, and the benefits of percolation. Individuals' due process rights are in uneasy tension with various methods of aggregating similarly-situated litigants' claims. Finality, efficiency, and speedy resolution of disputes must be weighed against fairness and accuracy. These tensions are inevitable and are not limited to cases involving nationwide injunctions. . . .

V

Although this Article defends nationwide injunctions, it is not an unqualified defense. . . .

The best practice is for a federal district court to establish procedures to ensure that it has all the relevant information about the costs and benefits of the proposed scope of an injunction before issuing it. The court should hold a hearing at which the parties to the litigation, as well as interested third parties, can present evidence and make arguments about the proper scope of the remedy. The court should then issue a written ruling addressing the costs and benefits of an injunction in the case at hand that will provide a guide to the appellate courts, which may be asked to review the scope of the injunctive relief. . . .

Admittedly, however, nationwide injunctions give a single district court judge unusual power to control federal policy for the nation, and forum shopping exacerbates the problem. Accordingly, broad discretion to grant nationwide injunctions may raise more concerns than broad discretion to resolve binary cases. If so, however, the better solution is to prevent forum shopping in cases in which parties seek a nationwide injunction—such as by directing such cases to a particular court, or randomly assigning them to an appropriate court—rather than to eliminate nationwide injunctions completely. . . .

[F]or those who perceive the federal judiciary as a check on the political branches, nationwide injunctions are an essential tool. Without nationwide injunctions, the federal courts would be powerless to protect thousands or millions of people from potential illegal or unconstitutional government policies—policies that can be applied with minimal notice or process, and to many who lack the ability to bring their individual cases before the courts. Indeed, the recent surge in nationwide injunctions could be seen as a symptom of the real problem—the executive branch's increasingly common practice of unilaterally making major policy changes outside of the legislative process.

TEST YOUR KNOWLEDGE: To assess your understanding of the material in this chapter, **click here** to take a quiz.

The Constitution of the United States

We the People of the United States, in Order to form a more perfect Union, establish Justice, insure domestic Tranquility, provide for the common defence, promote the general Welfare, and secure the Blessings of Liberty to ourselves and our Posterity, do ordain and establish this Constitution for the United States of America.

Article I

Section 1. All legislative Powers herein granted shall be vested in a Congress of the United States, which shall consist of a Senate and House of Representatives.

Section 2. The House of Representatives shall be composed of Members chosen every second Year by the People of the several States, and the Electors in each State shall have the Qualifications requisite for Electors of the most numerous Branch of the State Legislature.

No Person shall be a Representative who shall not have attained to the Age of twenty five Years, and been seven Years a Citizen of the United States, and who shall not, when elected, be an Inhabitant of that State in which he shall be chosen.

Representatives and direct Taxes shall be apportioned among the several States which may be included within this Union, according to their respective Numbers, which shall be determined by adding to the whole Number of free Persons, including those bound to Service for a Term of Years, and excluding Indians not taxed, three fifths of all other Persons. The actual Enumeration shall be made within three Years after the first Meeting of the Congress of the United States, and within every subsequent Term of ten Years, in such Manner as they shall by Law direct. The Number of Representatives shall not exceed one for every thirty Thousand, but each State shall have at Least one Representative; and until such enumeration shall be made, the State of New Hampshire shall be entitled to chuse three, Massachusetts eight, Rhode-Island and Providence Plantations one, Connecticut five, New-York six, New Jersey four, Pennsylvania eight, Delaware one, Maryland six, Virginia ten, North Carolina five, South Carolina five, and Georgia three.

When vacancies happen in the Representation from any State, the Executive Authority thereof shall issue Writs of Election to fill such Vacancies.

The House of Representatives shall chuse their Speaker and other Officers; and shall have the sole Power of Impeachment.

Section 3. The Senate of the United States shall be composed of two Senators from each State, chosen by the Legislature thereof, for six Years; and each Senator shall have one Vote.

Immediately after they shall be assembled in Consequence of the first Election, they shall be divided as equally as may be into three Classes. The Seats of the Senators of the first Class shall be vacated at the Expiration of the second Year, of the second Class at the Expiration of the fourth Year, and of the third Class at the Expiration of the sixth Year, so that one third may be chosen every second Year; and if Vacancies happen by Resignation, or otherwise, during the Recess of the Legislature of any State, the Executive thereof may make temporary Appointments until the next Meeting of the Legislature, which shall then fill such Vacancies.

No Person shall be a Senator who shall not have attained to the Age of thirty Years, and been nine Years a Citizen of the United States, and who shall not, when elected, be an Inhabitant of that State for which he shall be chosen.

The Vice President of the United States shall be President of the Senate, but shall have no Vote, unless they be equally divided.

The Senate shall chuse their other Officers, and also a President pro tempore, in the Absence of the Vice President, or when he shall exercise the Office of President of the United States.

The Senate shall have the sole Power to try all Impeachments. When sitting for that Purpose, they shall be on Oath or Affirmation. When the President of the United States is tried, the Chief Justice shall preside: And no Person shall be convicted without the Concurrence of two thirds of the Members present.

Judgment in Cases of Impeachment shall not extend further than to removal from Office, and disqualification to hold and enjoy any Office of honor, Trust or Profit under the United States: but the Party convicted shall nevertheless be liable and subject to Indictment, Trial, Judgment and Punishment, according to Law.

Section 4. The Times, Places and Manner of holding Elections for Senators and Representatives, shall be prescribed in each State by the Legislature thereof; but the Congress may at any time by Law make or alter such Regulations, except as to the Places of chusing Senators.

The Congress shall assemble at least once in every Year, and such Meeting shall be on the first Monday in December, unless they shall by Law appoint a different Day.

Section 5. Each House shall be the Judge of the Elections, Returns and Qualifications of its own Members, and a Majority of each shall constitute a Quorum to do Business; but a smaller Number may adjourn from day to day, and may be authorized to compel the Attendance of absent Members, in such Manner, and under such Penalties as each House may provide.

Each House may determine the Rules of its Proceedings, punish its Members for disorderly Behaviour, and, with the Concurrence of two thirds, expel a Member.

Each House shall keep a Journal of its Proceedings, and from time to time publish the same, excepting such Parts as may in their Judgment require Secrecy; and the Yeas and Nays of the Members of either House on any question shall, at the Desire of one fifth of those Present, be entered on the Journal.

Neither House, during the Session of Congress, shall, without the Consent of the other, adjourn for more than three days, nor to any other Place than that in which the two Houses shall be sitting.

Section 6. The Senators and Representatives shall receive a Compensation for their Services, to be ascertained by Law, and paid out of the Treasury of the United States. They shall in all Cases, except Treason, Felony and Breach of the Peace, be privileged from Arrest during their Attendance at the Session of their respective Houses, and in going to and returning from the same; and for any Speech or Debate in either House, they shall not be questioned in any other Place.

No Senator or Representative shall, during the Time for which he was elected, be appointed to any civil Office under the Authority of the United States, which shall have been created, or the Emoluments whereof shall have been encreased during such time; and no Person holding any Office under the United States, shall be a Member of either House during his Continuance in Office.

Section 7. All Bills for raising Revenue shall originate in the House of Representatives; but the Senate may propose or concur with Amendments as on other Bills.

Every Bill which shall have passed the House of Representatives and the Senate, shall, before it become a Law, be presented to the President of the United States; If he approve he shall sign it, but if not he shall return it, with his Objections to that House in which it shall have originated, who shall enter the Objections at large on their Journal, and proceed to reconsider it. If after such Reconsideration two thirds of that House shall agree to pass the Bill, it shall be sent, together with the Objections, to the other House, by which it shall likewise be reconsidered, and if approved by two thirds of that House, it shall become a Law. But in all such Cases the Votes of both Houses shall be determined by yeas and Nays, and the Names of the Persons voting for and against the Bill shall be entered on the Journal of each House respectively. If any Bill shall not be returned by the President within ten Days (Sundays excepted) after it shall have been presented to him, the Same shall be a Law, in like Manner as if he had signed it, unless the Congress by their Adjournment prevent its Return, in which Case it shall not be a Law.

Every Order, Resolution, or Vote to which the Concurrence of the Senate and House of Representatives may be necessary (except on a question of Adjournment) shall be presented to the President of the United States; and before the Same shall take Effect, shall be approved by him, or being disapproved by him, shall be repassed by two thirds of the Senate and House of Representatives, according to the Rules and Limitations prescribed in the Case of a Bill.

Section 8. The Congress shall have Power To lay and collect Taxes, Duties, Imposts and Excises, to pay the Debts and provide for the common Defence and general Welfare of the United States; but all Duties, Imposts and Excises shall be uniform throughout the United States;

To borrow Money on the credit of the United States;

To regulate Commerce with foreign Nations, and among the several States, and with the Indian Tribes;

To establish an uniform Rule of Naturalization, and uniform Laws on the subject of Bankruptcies throughout the United States;

To coin Money, regulate the Value thereof, and of foreign Coin, and fix the Standard of Weights and Measures;

To provide for the Punishment of counterfeiting the Securities and current Coin of the United States;

To establish Post Offices and post Roads;

To promote the Progress of Science and useful Arts, by securing for limited Times to Authors and Inventors the exclusive Right to their respective Writings and Discoveries;

To constitute Tribunals inferior to the supreme Court;

To define and punish Piracies and Felonies committed on the high Seas, and Offences against the Law of Nations;

To declare War, grant Letters of Marque and Reprisal, and make Rules concerning Captures on Land and Water;

To raise and support Armies, but no Appropriation of Money to that Use shall be for a longer Term than two Years;

To provide and maintain a Navy;

To make Rules for the Government and Regulation of the land and naval Forces;

To provide for calling forth the Militia to execute the Laws of the Union, suppress Insurrections and repel Invasions;

To provide for organizing, arming, and disciplining, the Militia, and for governing such Part of them as may be employed in the Service of the United States, reserving to the States respectively, the Appointment of the Officers, and the Authority of training the Militia according to the discipline prescribed by Congress;

To exercise exclusive Legislation in all Cases whatsoever, over such District (not exceeding ten Miles square) as may, by Cession of particular States, and the Acceptance of Congress, become the Seat of the Government of the United States, and to exercise like Authority over all Places purchased by the Consent of the Legislature of the State in which the Same shall be, for the Erection of Forts, Magazines, Arsenals, dock-Yards, and other needful Buildings;—And

To make all Laws which shall be necessary and proper for carrying into Execution the foregoing Powers, and all other Powers vested by this Constitution in the Government of the United States, or in any Department or Officer thereof.

Section 9. The Migration or Importation of such Persons as any of the States now existing shall think proper to admit, shall not be prohibited by the Congress prior to the Year one thousand eight hundred and eight, but a Tax or duty may be imposed on such Importation, not exceeding ten dollars for each Person.

The Privilege of the Writ of Habeas Corpus shall not be suspended, unless when in Cases of Rebellion or Invasion the public Safety may require it.

No Bill of Attainder or ex post facto Law shall be passed.

No Capitation, or other direct, Tax shall be laid, unless in Proportion to the Census or enumeration herein before directed to be taken.

No Tax or Duty shall be laid on Articles exported from any State.

No Preference shall be given by any Regulation of Commerce or Revenue to the Ports of one State over those of another: nor shall Vessels bound to, or from, one State, be obliged to enter, clear, or pay Duties in another.

No Money shall be drawn from the Treasury, but in Consequence of Appropriations made by Law; and a regular Statement and Account of the Receipts and Expenditures of all public Money shall be published from time to time.

No Title of Nobility shall be granted by the United States: And no Person holding any Office of Profit or Trust under them, shall, without the Consent of the Congress, accept of any present, Emolument, Office, or Title, of any kind whatever, from any King, Prince, or foreign State.

Section 10. No State shall enter into any Treaty, Alliance, or Confederation; grant Letters of Marque and Reprisal; coin Money; emit Bills of Credit; make any Thing but gold and silver Coin a Tender in Payment of Debts; pass any Bill of Attainder, ex post facto Law, or Law impairing the Obligation of Contracts, or grant any Title of Nobility.

No State shall, without the Consent of the Congress, lay any Imposts or Duties on Imports or Exports, except what may be absolutely necessary for executing its inspection Laws: and the net Produce of all Duties and Imposts, laid by any State on Imports or Exports, shall be for the Use of the Treasury of the United States; and all such Laws shall be subject to the Revision and Controul of the Congress.

No State shall, without the Consent of Congress, lay any Duty of Tonnage, keep Troops, or Ships of War in time of Peace, enter into any Agreement or Compact with another State, or with a foreign Power, or engage in War, unless actually invaded, or in such imminent Danger as will not admit of delay.

Article II

Section 1. The executive Power shall be vested in a President of the United States of America. He shall hold his Office during the Term of four Years, and, together with the Vice President, chosen for the same Term, be elected, as follows

Each State shall appoint, in such Manner as the Legislature thereof may direct, a Number of Electors, equal to the whole Number of Senators and Representatives to which the State may be entitled in the Congress: but no Senator or Representative, or Person holding an Office of Trust or Profit under the United States, shall be appointed an Elector.

The Electors shall meet in their respective States, and vote by Ballot for two Persons, of whom one at least shall not be an Inhabitant of the same State with themselves. And they shall make a List of all the Persons voted for, and of the Number of Votes for each; which List they shall sign and certify, and transmit sealed to the Seat of the Government of the United States, directed to the President of the Senate. The President of the Senate shall, in the Presence of the Senate and House of Representatives, open all the Certificates, and the Votes shall then be counted. The Person having the greatest Number of Votes shall be the President, if such Number be a Majority of the whole Number of

Electors appointed; and if there be more than one who have such Majority, and have an equal Number of Votes, then the House of Representatives shall immediately chuse by Ballot one of them for President; and if no Person have a Majority, then from the five highest on the List the said House shall in like Manner chuse the President. But in chusing the President, the Votes shall be taken by States, the Representation from each State having one Vote; A quorum for this Purpose shall consist of a Member or Members from two thirds of the States, and a Majority of all the States shall be necessary to a Choice. In every Case, after the Choice of the President, the Person having the greatest Number of Votes of the Electors shall be the Vice President. But if there should remain two or more who have equal Votes, the Senate shall chuse from them by Ballot the Vice President.

The Congress may determine the Time of chusing the Electors, and the Day on which they shall give their Votes; which Day shall be the same throughout the United States.

No Person except a natural born Citizen, or a Citizen of the United States, at the time of the Adoption of this Constitution, shall be eligible to the Office of President; neither shall any Person be eligible to that Office who shall not have attained to the Age of thirty five Years, and been fourteen Years a Resident within the United States.

In Case of the Removal of the President from Office, or of his Death, Resignation, or Inability to discharge the Powers and Duties of the said Office, the Same shall devolve on the Vice President, and the Congress may by Law provide for the Case of Removal, Death, Resignation or Inability, both of the President and Vice President, declaring what Officer shall then act as President, and such Officer shall act accordingly, until the Disability be removed, or a President shall be elected.

The President shall, at stated Times, receive for his Services, a Compensation, which shall neither be encreased nor diminished during the Period for which he shall have been elected, and he shall not receive within that Period any other Emolument from the United States, or any of them.

Before he enter on the Execution of his Office, he shall take the following Oath or Affirmation:—"I do solemnly swear (or affirm) that I will faithfully execute the Office of President of the United States, and will to the best of my Ability, preserve, protect and defend the Constitution of the United States."

Section 2. The President shall be Commander in Chief of the Army and Navy of the United States, and of the Militia of the several States, when called into the actual Service of the United States; he may require the Opinion, in writing, of the principal Officer in each of the executive Departments, upon any Subject relating to the Duties of their respective Offices, and he shall have Power to grant Reprieves and Pardons for Offences against the United States, except in Cases of Impeachment.

He shall have Power, by and with the Advice and Consent of the Senate, to make Treaties, provided two thirds of the Senators present concur; and he shall nominate, and by and with the Advice and Consent of the Senate, shall appoint Ambassadors, other public Ministers and Consuls, Judges of the supreme Court, and all other Officers of the United States, whose Appointments are not herein otherwise provided for, and which shall be established by Law: but the Congress may by Law vest the Appointment of such inferior Officers, as they think proper, in the President alone, in the Courts of Law, or in the Heads of Departments.

The President shall have Power to fill up all Vacancies that may happen during the Recess of the Senate, by granting Commissions which shall expire at the End of their next Session.

Section 3. He shall from time to time give to the Congress Information of the State of the Union, and recommend to their Consideration such Measures as he shall judge necessary and expedient; he may, on extraordinary Occasions, convene both Houses, or either of them, and in Case of Disagreement between them, with Respect to the Time of Adjournment, he may adjourn them to such Time as he shall think proper; he shall receive Ambassadors and other public Ministers; he shall take Care that the Laws be faithfully executed, and shall Commission all the Officers of the United States.

Section 4. The President, Vice President and all civil Officers of the United States, shall be removed from Office on Impeachment for, and Conviction of, Treason, Bribery, or other high Crimes and Misdemeanors.

Article III

Section 1. The judicial Power of the United States, shall be vested in one supreme Court, and in such inferior Courts as the Congress may from time to time ordain and establish. The Judges, both of the supreme and inferior Courts, shall hold their Offices during good Behaviour, and shall, at stated Times, receive for their Services, a Compensation, which shall not be diminished during their Continuance in Office.

Section 2. The judicial Power shall extend to all Cases, in Law and Equity, arising under this Constitution, the Laws of the United States, and Treaties made, or which shall be made, under their Authority;—to all Cases affecting Ambassadors, other public Ministers and Consuls;—to all Cases of admiralty and maritime Jurisdiction;—to Controversies to which the United States shall be a Party;—to Controversies between two or more States;—between a State and Citizens of another State,—between Citizens of different States,—between Citizens of the same State claiming Lands under Grants of different States, and between a State, or the Citizens thereof, and foreign States, Citizens or Subjects.

In all Cases affecting Ambassadors, other public Ministers and Consuls, and those in which a State shall be Party, the supreme Court shall have original Jurisdiction. In all the other Cases before mentioned, the supreme Court shall have appellate Jurisdiction, both as to Law and Fact, with such Exceptions, and under such Regulations as the Congress shall make.

The Trial of all Crimes, except in Cases of Impeachment, shall be by Jury; and such Trial shall be held in the State where the said Crimes shall have been committed; but when not committed within any State, the Trial shall be at such Place or Places as the Congress may by Law have directed.

Section 3. Treason against the United States, shall consist only in levying War against them, or in adhering to their Enemies, giving them Aid and Comfort. No Person shall be convicted of Treason unless on the Testimony of two Witnesses to the same overt Act, or on Confession in open Court.

The Congress shall have Power to declare the Punishment of Treason, but no Attainder of Treason shall work Corruption of Blood, or Forfeiture except during the Life of the Person attainted.

Article IV

Section 1. Full Faith and Credit shall be given in each State to the public Acts, Records, and judicial Proceedings of every other State. And the Congress may by general Laws prescribe the Manner in which such Acts, Records and Proceedings shall be proved, and the Effect thereof.

Section 2. The Citizens of each State shall be entitled to all Privileges and Immunities of Citizens in the several States.

A Person charged in any State with Treason, Felony, or other Crime, who shall flee from Justice, and be found in another State, shall on Demand of the executive Authority of the State from which he fled, be delivered up, to be removed to the State having Jurisdiction of the Crime.

No Person held to Service or Labour in one State, under the Laws thereof, escaping into another, shall, in Consequence of any Law or Regulation therein, be discharged from such Service or Labour, but shall be delivered up on Claim of the Party to whom such Service or Labour may be due.

Section 3. New States may be admitted by the Congress into this Union; but no new State shall be formed or erected within the Jurisdiction of any other State; nor any State be formed by the Junction of two or more States, or Parts of States, without the Consent of the Legislatures of the States concerned as well as of the Congress.

The Congress shall have Power to dispose of and make all needful Rules and Regulations respecting the Territory or other Property belonging to the United States; and nothing in this Constitution shall be so construed as to Prejudice any Claims of the United States, or of any particular State.

Section 4. The United States shall guarantee to every State in this Union a Republican Form of Government, and shall protect each of them against Invasion; and on Application of the Legislature, or of the Executive (when the Legislature cannot be convened), against domestic Violence.

Article V

The Congress, whenever two thirds of both Houses shall deem it necessary, shall propose Amendments to this Constitution, or, on the Application of the Legislatures of two thirds of the several States, shall call a Convention for proposing Amendments, which, in either Case, shall be valid to all Intents and Purposes, as Part of this Constitution, when ratified by the Legislatures of three fourths of the several States, or by Conventions in three fourths thereof, as the one or the other Mode of Ratification may be proposed by the Congress; Provided that no Amendment which may be made prior to the Year One thousand eight hundred and eight shall in any Manner affect the first and fourth

Clauses in the Ninth Section of the first Article; and that no State, without its Consent, shall be deprived of its equal Suffrage in the Senate.

Article VI

All Debts contracted and Engagements entered into, before the Adoption of this Constitution, shall be as valid against the United States under this Constitution, as under the Confederation.

This Constitution, and the Laws of the United States which shall be made in Pursuance thereof; and all Treaties made, or which shall be made, under the Authority of the United States, shall be the supreme Law of the Land; and the Judges in every State shall be bound thereby, any Thing in the Constitution or Laws of any State to the Contrary notwithstanding.

The Senators and Representatives before mentioned, and the Members of the several State Legislatures, and all executive and judicial Officers, both of the United States and of the several States, shall be bound by Oath or Affirmation, to support this Constitution; but no religious Test shall ever be required as a Qualification to any Office or public Trust under the United States.

Article VII

The Ratification of the Conventions of nine States, shall be sufficient for the Establishment of this Constitution between the States so ratifying the Same.

Amendment I

Congress shall make no law respecting an establishment of religion, or prohibiting the free exercise thereof; or abridging the freedom of speech, or of the press; or the right of the people peaceably to assemble, and to petition the Government for a redress of grievances.

Amendment II

A well regulated Militia, being necessary to the security of a free State, the right of the people to keep and bear Arms, shall not be infringed.

Amendment III

No Soldier shall, in time of peace be quartered in any house, without the consent of the Owner, nor in time of war, but in a manner to be prescribed by law.

Amendment IV

The right of the people to be secure in their persons, houses, papers, and effects, against unreasonable searches and seizures, shall not be violated, and no Warrants shall issue, but upon probable cause, supported by Oath or affirmation, and particularly describing the place to be searched, and the persons or things to be seized.

Amendment V

No person shall be held to answer for a capital, or otherwise infamous crime, unless on a presentment or indictment of a Grand Jury, except in cases arising in the land or naval forces, or in the Militia, when in actual service in time of War or public danger; nor shall any person be subject for the same offence to be twice put in jeopardy of life or limb; nor shall be compelled in any criminal case to be a witness against himself, nor be deprived of life, liberty, or property, without due process of law; nor shall private property be taken for public use, without just compensation.

Amendment VI

In all criminal prosecutions, the accused shall enjoy the right to a speedy and public trial, by an impartial jury of the State and district wherein the crime shall have been committed, which district shall have been previously ascertained by law, and to be informed of the nature and cause of the accusation; to be confronted with the witnesses against him; to have compulsory process for obtaining witnesses in his favor, and to have the Assistance of Counsel for his defence.

Amendment VII

In Suits at common law, where the value in controversy shall exceed twenty dollars, the right of trial by jury shall be preserved, and no fact tried by a jury, shall be otherwise re-examined in any Court of the United States, than according to the rules of the common law.

Amendment VIII

Excessive bail shall not be required, nor excessive fines imposed, nor cruel and unusual punishments inflicted.

Amendment IX

The enumeration in the Constitution, of certain rights, shall not be construed to deny or disparage others retained by the people.

Amendment X

The powers not delegated to the United States by the Constitution, nor prohibited by it to the States, are reserved to the States respectively, or to the people.

Amendment XI

The Judicial power of the United States shall not be construed to extend to any suit in law or equity, commenced or prosecuted against one of the United States by Citizens of another State, or by Citizens or Subjects of any Foreign State.

Amendment XII

The Electors shall meet in their respective states and vote by ballot for President and Vice-President, one of whom, at least, shall not be an inhabitant of the same state with themselves; they shall name in their ballots the person voted for as President, and in distinct ballots the person voted for as Vice-President, and they shall make distinct lists of all persons voted for as President, and of all persons voted for as Vice-President, and of the number of votes for each, which lists they shall sign and certify, and transmit sealed to the seat of the government of the United States, directed to the President of the Senate;—the President of the Senate shall, in the presence of the Senate and House of Representatives, open all the certificates and the votes shall then be counted;—The person having the greatest number of votes for President, shall be the President, if such number be a majority of the whole number of Electors appointed; and if no person have such majority, then from the persons having the highest numbers not exceeding three on the list of those voted for as President, the House of Representatives shall choose immediately, by ballot, the President. But in choosing the President, the votes shall be taken by states, the representation from each state having one vote; a quorum for this purpose shall consist of a member or members from two-thirds of the states, and a majority of all the states shall be necessary to a choice. And if the House of Representatives shall not choose a President whenever the right of choice shall devolve upon them, before the fourth day of March next following, then the Vice-President shall act as President, as in case of the death or other constitutional disability of the President.—The person having the greatest number of votes as Vice-President, shall be the Vice-President, if such number be a majority of the whole number of Electors appointed, and if no person have a majority, then from the two highest numbers on the list, the Senate shall choose the Vice-President; a quorum for the purpose shall consist of two-thirds of the whole number of Senators, and a majority of the whole number shall be necessary to a choice. But no person constitutionally ineligible to the office of President shall be eligible to that of Vice-President of the United States.

Amendment XIII

Section 1. Neither slavery nor involuntary servitude, except as a punishment for crime whereof the party shall have been duly convicted, shall exist within the United States, or any place subject to their jurisdiction.

Section 2. Congress shall have power to enforce this article by appropriate legislation.

Amendment XIV

Section 1. All persons born or naturalized in the United States, and subject to the jurisdiction thereof, are citizens of the United States and of the State wherein they reside. No State shall make or enforce any law which shall abridge the privileges or immunities of citizens of the United States; nor shall any State deprive any person of life, liberty, or property, without due process of law; nor deny to any person within its jurisdiction the equal protection of the laws.

Section 2. Representatives shall be apportioned among the several States according to their respective numbers, counting the whole number of persons in each State, excluding Indians not taxed. But when the right to vote at any election for the choice of electors for President and Vice-President of the United States, Representatives in Congress, the Executive and Judicial officers of a State, or the members of the Legislature thereof, is denied to any of the male inhabitants of such State, being twenty-one years of age, and citizens of the United States, or in any way abridged, except for participation in rebellion, or other crime, the basis of representation therein shall be reduced in the proportion which the number of such male citizens shall bear to the whole number of male citizens twenty-one years of age in such State.

Section 3. No person shall be a Senator or Representative in Congress, or elector of President and Vice-President, or hold any office, civil or military, under the United States, or under any State, who, having previously taken an oath, as a member of Congress, or as an officer of the United States, or as a member of any State legislature, or as an executive or judicial officer of any State, to support the Constitution of the United States, shall have engaged in insurrection or rebellion against the same, or given aid or comfort to the enemies thereof. But Congress may by a vote of two-thirds of each House, remove such disability.

Section 4. The validity of the public debt of the United States, authorized by law, including debts incurred for payment of pensions and bounties for services in suppressing insurrection or rebellion, shall not be questioned. But neither the United States nor any State shall assume or pay any debt or obligation incurred in aid of insurrection or rebellion against the United States, or any claim for the loss or emancipation of any slave; but all such debts, obligations and claims shall be held illegal and void.

Section 5. The Congress shall have the power to enforce, by appropriate legislation, the provisions of this article.

Amendment XV

Section 1. The right of citizens of the United States to vote shall not be denied or abridged by the United States or by any State on account of race, color, or previous condition of servitude.

Section 2. The Congress shall have the power to enforce this article by appropriate legislation.

Amendment XVI

The Congress shall have power to lay and collect taxes on incomes, from whatever source derived, without apportionment among the several States, and without regard to any census or enumeration.

Amendment XVII

The Senate of the United States shall be composed of two Senators from each State, elected by the people thereof, for six years; and each Senator shall have one vote. The electors in each State shall have the qualifications requisite for electors of the most numerous branch of the State legislatures.

When vacancies happen in the representation of any State in the Senate, the executive authority of such State shall issue writs of election to fill such vacancies: Provided, That the legislature of any State may empower the executive thereof to make temporary appointments until the people fill the vacancies by election as the legislature may direct.

This amendment shall not be so construed as to affect the election or term of any Senator chosen before it becomes valid as part of the Constitution.

Amendment XVIII

Section 1. After one year from the ratification of this article the manufacture, sale, or transportation of intoxicating liquors within, the importation thereof into, or the exportation thereof from the United States and all territory subject to the jurisdiction thereof for beverage purposes is hereby prohibited.

Section 2. The Congress and the several States shall have concurrent power to enforce this article by appropriate legislation.

Section 3. This article shall be inoperative unless it shall have been ratified as an amendment to the Constitution by the legislatures of the several States, as provided in the Constitution, within seven years from the date of the submission hereof to the States by the Congress.

Amendment XIX

The right of citizens of the United States to vote shall not be denied or abridged by the United States or by any State on account of sex.

Congress shall have power to enforce this article by appropriate legislation.

Amendment XX

Section 1. The terms of the President and the Vice President shall end at noon on the 20th day of January, and the terms of Senators and Representatives at noon on the 3d day of January, of the years in which such terms would have ended if this article had not been ratified; and the terms of their successors shall then begin.

Section 2. The Congress shall assemble at least once in every year, and such meeting shall begin at noon on the 3d day of January, unless they shall by law appoint a different day.

Section 3. If, at the time fixed for the beginning of the term of the President, the President elect shall have died, the Vice President elect shall become President. If a President shall not have been chosen before the time fixed for the beginning of his term, or if the President elect shall have failed to qualify, then the Vice President elect shall act as President until a President shall have qualified; and the Congress may by law provide for the case wherein neither a President elect nor a Vice President elect shall have qualified, declaring who shall then act as President, or the manner in which one who is to act shall be selected, and such person shall act accordingly until a President or Vice President shall have qualified.

Section 4. The Congress may by law provide for the case of the death of any of the persons from whom the House of Representatives may choose a President whenever the right of choice shall have devolved upon them, and for the case of the death of any of the persons from whom the Senate may choose a Vice President whenever the right of choice shall have devolved upon them.

Section 5. Sections 1 and 2 shall take effect on the 15th day of October following the ratification of this article.

Section 6. This article shall be inoperative unless it shall have been ratified as an amendment to the Constitution by the legislatures of three-fourths of the several States within seven years from the date of its submission.

Amendment XXI

Section 1. The eighteenth article of amendment to the Constitution of the United States is hereby repealed.

Section 2. The transportation or importation into any State, Territory, or possession of the United States for delivery or use therein of intoxicating liquors, in violation of the laws thereof, is hereby prohibited.

Section 3. This article shall be inoperative unless it shall have been ratified as an amendment to the Constitution by conventions in the several States, as provided in the Constitution, within seven years from the date of the submission hereof to the States by the Congress.

Amendment XXII

Section 1. No person shall be elected to the office of the President more than twice, and no person who has held the office of President, or acted as

President, for more than two years of a term to which some other person was elected President shall be elected to the office of the President more than once. But this Article shall not apply to any person holding the office of President when this Article was proposed by the Congress, and shall not prevent any person who may be holding the office of President, or acting as President, during the term within which this Article becomes operative from holding the office of President or acting as President during the remainder of such term.

Section 2. This article shall be inoperative unless it shall have been ratified as an amendment to the Constitution by the legislatures of three-fourths of the several States within seven years from the date of its submission to the States by the Congress.

Amendment XXIII

Section 1. The District constituting the seat of Government of the United States shall appoint in such manner as the Congress may direct:

A number of electors of President and Vice President equal to the whole number of Senators and Representatives in Congress to which the District would be entitled if it were a State, but in no event more than the least populous State; they shall be in addition to those appointed by the States, but they shall be considered, for the purposes of the election of President and Vice President, to be electors appointed by a State; and they shall meet in the District and perform such duties as provided by the twelfth article of amendment.

Section 2. The Congress shall have power to enforce this article by appropriate legislation.

Amendment XXIV

Section 1. The right of citizens of the United States to vote in any primary or other election for President or Vice President, for electors for President or Vice President, or for Senator or Representative in Congress, shall not be denied or abridged by the United States or any State by reason of failure to pay any poll tax or other tax.

Section 2. The Congress shall have power to enforce this article by appropriate legislation.

Amendment XXV

Section 1. In case of the removal of the President from office or of his death or resignation, the Vice President shall become President.

Section 2. Whenever there is a vacancy in the office of the Vice President, the President shall nominate a Vice President who shall take office upon confirmation by a majority vote of both Houses of Congress.

Section 3. Whenever the President transmits to the President pro tempore of the Senate and the Speaker of the House of Representatives his written declaration that he is unable to discharge the powers and duties of his office, and until he transmits to them a written declaration to the contrary, such powers and duties shall be discharged by the Vice President as Acting President.

Section 4. Whenever the Vice President and a majority of either the principal officers of the executive departments or of such other body as Congress may by law provide, transmit to the President pro tempore of the Senate and the Speaker of the House of Representatives their written declaration that the President is unable to discharge the powers and duties of his office, the Vice President shall immediately assume the powers and duties of the office as Acting President.

Thereafter, when the President transmits to the President pro tempore of the Senate and the Speaker of the House of Representatives his written declaration that no inability exists, he shall resume the powers and duties of his office unless the Vice President and a majority of either the principal officers of the executive department or of such other body as Congress may by law provide, transmit within four days to the President pro tempore of the Senate and the Speaker of the House of Representatives their written declaration that the President is unable to discharge the powers and duties of his office. Thereupon Congress shall decide the issue, assembling within forty-eight hours for that purpose if not in session. If the Congress, within twenty-one days after receipt of the latter written declaration, or, if Congress is not in session, within twenty-one days after Congress is required to assemble, determines by two-thirds vote of both Houses that the President is unable to discharge the powers and duties of his office, the Vice President shall continue to discharge the same as Acting President; otherwise, the President shall resume the powers and duties of his office.

Amendment XXVI

Section 1. The right of citizens of the United States, who are eighteen years of age or older, to vote shall not be denied or abridged by the United States or by any State on account of age.

Section 2. The Congress shall have power to enforce this article by appropriate legislation.

Amendment XXVII

No law, varying the compensation for the services of the Senators and Representatives, shall take effect, until an election of Representatives shall have intervened.

The Administrative Procedure Act

Title 5, U.S. Code, Chapter 5
Administrative Procedure

§ 551. Definitions.

For the purpose of this subchapter—

(1) "agency" means each authority of the Government of the United States, whether or not it is within or subject to review by another agency, but does not include—

(A) the Congress;

(B) the courts of the United States;

(C) the governments of the territories or possessions of the United States;

(D) the government of the District of Columbia;

or except as to the requirements of section 552 of this title—

(E) agencies composed of representatives of the parties or of representatives of organizations of the parties to the disputes determined by them;

(F) courts martial and military commissions;

(G) military authority exercised in the field in time of war or in occupied territory; or

(H) functions conferred by sections 1738, 1739, 1743, and 1744 of title 12; subchapter II of chapter 471 of title 49; or sections 1884, 1891–1902, and former section 1641(b)(2), of title 50, appendix;

(2) "person" includes an individual, partnership, corporation, association, or public or private organization other than an agency;

(3) "party" includes a person or agency named or admitted as a party, or properly seeking and entitled as of right to be admitted as a party, in an agency proceeding, and a person or agency admitted by an agency as a party for limited purposes;

(4) "rule" means the whole or a part of an agency statement of general or particular applicability and future effect designed to implement, interpret, or prescribe law or policy or describing the organization, procedure, or practice requirements of an agency and includes the approval or prescription for the future of rates, wages, corporate or financial structures or reorganizations thereof, prices, facilities, appliances, services or allowances therefor or of valuations, costs, or accounting, or practices bearing on any of the foregoing;

(5) "rule making" means agency process for formulating, amending, or repealing a rule;

(6) "order" means the whole or a part of a final disposition, whether affirmative, negative, injunctive, or declaratory in form, of an agency in a matter other than rule making but including licensing;

(7) "adjudication" means agency process for the formulation of an order;

(8) "license" includes the whole or a part of an agency permit, certificate, approval, registration, charter, membership, statutory exemption or other form of permission;

(9) "licensing" includes agency process respecting the grant, renewal, denial, revocation, suspension, annulment, withdrawal, limitation, amendment, modification, or conditioning of a license;

(10) "sanction" includes the whole or a part of an agency—

(A) prohibition, requirement, limitation, or other condition affecting the freedom of a person;

(B) withholding of relief;

(C) imposition of penalty or fine;

(D) destruction, taking, seizure, or withholding of property;

(E) assessment of damages, reimbursement, restitution, compensation, costs, charges, or fees;

(F) requirement, revocation, or suspension of a license; or

(G) taking other compulsory or restrictive action;

(11) "relief" includes the whole or a part of an agency—

(A) grant of money, assistance, license, authority, exemption, exception, privilege, or remedy;

(B) recognition of a claim, right, immunity, privilege, exemption, or exception; or

(C) taking of other action on the application or petition of, and beneficial to, a person;

(12) "agency proceeding" means an agency process as defined by paragraphs (5), (7), and (9) of this section;

(13) "agency action" includes the whole or a part of an agency rule, order, license, sanction, relief, or the equivalent or denial thereof, or failure to act; and

(14) "ex parte communication" means an oral or written communication not on the public record with respect to which reasonable prior notice to all parties is not given, but it shall not include requests for status reports on any matter or proceeding covered by this subchapter.

[§ 552, which codifies the Freedom of Information Act, § 552a, "Records maintained on individuals," and § 552b, "Open meetings," are omitted.—Ed.]

§ 553. Rule making.

(a) This section applies, according to the provisions thereof, except to the extent that there is involved—

(1) a military or foreign affairs function of the United States; or

(2) a matter relating to agency management or personnel or to public property, loans, grants, benefits, or contracts.

(b) General notice of proposed rule making shall be published in the Federal Register, unless persons subject thereto are named and either personally served or otherwise have actual notice thereof in accordance with law. The notice shall include—

(1) a statement of the time, place, and nature of public rule making proceedings;

(2) reference to the legal authority under which the rule is proposed; and

(3) either the terms or substance of the proposed rule or a description of the subjects and issues involved.

Except when notice or hearing is required by statute, this subsection does not apply—

(A) to interpretative rules, general statements of policy, or rules of agency organization, procedure, or practice; or

(B) when the agency for good cause finds (and incorporates the finding and a brief statement of reasons therefor in the rules issued) that notice and public procedure thereon are impracticable, unnecessary, or contrary to the public interest.

(c) After notice required by this section, the agency shall give interested persons an opportunity to participate in the rule making through submission of written data, views, or arguments with or without opportunity for oral presentation. After consideration of the relevant matter presented, the agency shall incorporate in the rules adopted a concise general statement of their basis and purpose. When rules are required by statute to be made on the record after opportunity for an agency hearing, sections 556 and 557 of this title apply instead of this subsection.

(d) The required publication or service of a substantive rule shall be made not less than 30 days before its effective date, except—

(1) a substantive rule which grants or recognizes an exemption or relieves a restriction;

(2) interpretative rules and statements of policy; or

(3)   as otherwise provided by the agency for good cause found and published with the rule.

(e)   Each agency shall give an interested person the right to petition for the issuance, amendment, or repeal of a rule.

§ 554. Adjudications.

(a)   This section applies, according to the provisions thereof, in every case of adjudication required by statute to be determined on the record after opportunity for an agency hearing, except to the extent that there is involved—

(1)   a matter subject to a subsequent trial of the law and the facts de novo in a court;

(2)   the selection or tenure of an employee, except a [1] administrative law judge appointed under section 3105 of this title;

(3)   proceedings in which decisions rest solely on inspections, tests, or elections;

(4)   the conduct of military or foreign affairs functions;

(5)   cases in which an agency is acting as an agent for a court; or

(6)   the certification of worker representatives.

(b)   Persons entitled to notice of an agency hearing shall be timely informed of—

(1)   the time, place, and nature of the hearing;

(2)   the legal authority and jurisdiction under which the hearing is to be held; and

(3)   the matters of fact and law asserted.

When private persons are the moving parties, other parties to the proceeding shall give prompt notice of issues controverted in fact or law; and in other instances agencies may by rule require responsive pleading. In fixing the time and place for hearings, due regard shall be had for the convenience and necessity of the parties or their representatives.

(c)   The agency shall give all interested parties opportunity for—

(1)   the submission and consideration of facts, arguments, offers of settlement, or proposals of adjustment when time, the nature of the proceeding, and the public interest permit; and

(2)   to the extent that the parties are unable so to determine a controversy by consent, hearing and decision on notice and in accordance with sections 556 and 557 of this title.

(d)   The employee who presides at the reception of evidence pursuant to section 556 of this title shall make the recommended decision or initial decision required by section 557 of this title, unless he becomes unavailable to the agency. Except to the extent required for the disposition of ex parte matters as authorized by law, such an employee may not—

(1)   consult a person or party on a fact in issue, unless on notice and opportunity for all parties to participate; or

(2)   be responsible to or subject to the supervision or direction of an employee or agent engaged in the performance of investigative or prosecuting functions for an agency.

An employee or agent engaged in the performance of investigative or prosecuting functions for an agency in a case may not, in that or a factually related case, participate or advise in the decision, recommended decision, or agency review pursuant to section 557 of this title, except as witness or counsel in public proceedings. This subsection does not apply—

(A)   in determining applications for initial licenses;

(B)   to proceedings involving the validity or application of rates, facilities, or practices of public utilities or carriers; or

(C)   to the agency or a member or members of the body comprising the agency.

(e)   The agency, with like effect as in the case of other orders, and in its sound discretion, may issue a declaratory order to terminate a controversy or remove uncertainty.

§ 555. Ancillary matters.

(a)   This section applies, according to the provisions thereof, except as otherwise provided by this subchapter.

(b)   A person compelled to appear in person before an agency or representative thereof is entitled to be accompanied, represented, and advised by counsel or, if permitted by the agency, by other qualified representative. A party is entitled to appear in person or by or with counsel or other duly qualified representative in an agency proceeding. So far as the orderly conduct of public business permits, an interested person may appear before an agency or its responsible employees for the presentation, adjustment, or determination of an issue, request, or controversy in a proceeding, whether interlocutory, summary, or otherwise, or in connection with an agency function. With due regard for the convenience and necessity of the parties or their representatives and within a reasonable time, each agency shall proceed to conclude a matter presented to it. This subsection does not grant or deny a person who is not a lawyer the right to appear for or represent others before an agency or in an agency proceeding.

(c)   Process, requirement of a report, inspection, or other investigative act or demand may not be issued, made, or enforced except as authorized by law. A person compelled to submit data or evidence is entitled to retain or, on payment of lawfully prescribed costs, procure a copy or transcript thereof, except that in a nonpublic investigatory proceeding the witness may for good cause be limited to inspection of the official transcript of his testimony.

(d)   Agency subpoenas authorized by law shall be issued to a party on request and, when required by rules of procedure, on a statement or showing of general relevance and reasonable scope of the evidence sought. On contest, the court shall sustain the subpoena or similar process or demand to the extent that it is found to be in accordance with law. In a proceeding for enforcement, the court shall issue an order requiring the appearance of the witness or the production of the evidence or data within a reasonable time under penalty of punishment for contempt in case of contumacious failure to comply.

(e)   Prompt notice shall be given of the denial in whole or in part of a written application, petition, or other request of an interested person made in connection with any agency proceeding. Except in affirming a prior denial or when the denial is self-explanatory, the notice shall be accompanied by a brief statement of the grounds for denial.

§ 556. Hearings; presiding employees; powers and duties; burden of proof; evidence; record as basis of decision.

(a)   This section applies, according to the provisions thereof, to hearings required by section 553 or 554 of this title to be conducted in accordance with this section.

(b)   There shall preside at the taking of evidence—

     (1)   the agency;

     (2)   one or more members of the body which comprises the agency; or

     (3)   one or more administrative law judges appointed under section 3105 of this title.

This subchapter does not supersede the conduct of specified classes of proceedings, in whole or in part, by or before boards or other employees specially provided for by or designated under statute. The functions of presiding employees and of employees participating in decisions in accordance with section 557 of this title shall be conducted in an impartial manner. A presiding or participating employee may at any time disqualify himself. On the filing in good faith of a timely and sufficient affidavit of personal bias or other disqualification of a presiding or participating employee, the agency shall determine the matter as a part of the record and decision in the case.

(c)   Subject to published rules of the agency and within its powers, employees presiding at hearings may—

     (1)   administer oaths and affirmations;

     (2)   issue subpoenas authorized by law;

     (3)   rule on offers of proof and receive relevant evidence;

     (4)   take depositions or have depositions taken when the ends of justice would be served;

     (5)   regulate the course of the hearing;

     (6)   hold conferences for the settlement or simplification of the issues by consent of the parties or by the use of alternative means of dispute resolution as provided in subchapter IV of this chapter;

(7) inform the parties as to the availability of one or more alternative means of dispute resolution, and encourage use of such methods;

(8) require the attendance at any conference held pursuant to paragraph (6) of at least one representative of each party who has authority to negotiate concerning resolution of issues in controversy;

(9) dispose of procedural requests or similar matters;

(10) make or recommend decisions in accordance with section 557 of this title; and

(11) take other action authorized by agency rule consistent with this subchapter.

(d) Except as otherwise provided by statute, the proponent of a rule or order has the burden of proof. Any oral or documentary evidence may be received, but the agency as a matter of policy shall provide for the exclusion of irrelevant, immaterial, or unduly repetitious evidence. A sanction may not be imposed or rule or order issued except on consideration of the whole record or those parts thereof cited by a party and supported by and in accordance with the reliable, probative, and substantial evidence. The agency may, to the extent consistent with the interests of justice and the policy of the underlying statutes administered by the agency, consider a violation of section 557(d) of this title sufficient grounds for a decision adverse to a party who has knowingly committed such violation or knowingly caused such violation to occur. A party is entitled to present his case or defense by oral or documentary evidence, to submit rebuttal evidence, and to conduct such cross-examination as may be required for a full and true disclosure of the facts. In rule making or determining claims for money or benefits or applications for initial licenses an agency may, when a party will not be prejudiced thereby, adopt procedures for the submission of all or part of the evidence in written form.

(e) The transcript of testimony and exhibits, together with all papers and requests filed in the proceeding, constitutes the exclusive record for decision in accordance with section 557 of this title and, on payment of lawfully prescribed costs, shall be made available to the parties. When an agency decision rests on official notice of a material fact not appearing in the evidence in the record, a party is entitled, on timely request, to an opportunity to show the contrary.

§ 557. Initial decisions; conclusiveness; review by agency; submissions by parties; contents of decisions; record.

(a)   This section applies, according to the provisions thereof, when a hearing is required to be conducted in accordance with section 556 of this title.

(b)   When the agency did not preside at the reception of the evidence, the presiding employee or, in cases not subject to section 554(d) of this title, an employee qualified to preside at hearings pursuant to section 556 of this title, shall initially decide the case unless the agency requires, either in specific cases or by general rule, the entire record to be certified to it for decision. When the presiding employee makes an initial decision, that decision then becomes the decision of the agency without further proceedings unless there is an appeal to, or review on motion of, the agency within time provided by rule. On appeal from or review of the initial decision, the agency has all the powers which it would have in making the initial decision except as it may limit the issues on notice or by rule. When the agency makes the decision without having presided at the reception of the evidence, the presiding employee or an employee qualified to preside at hearings pursuant to section 556 of this title shall first recommend a decision, except that in rule making or determining applications for initial licenses—

(1)   instead thereof the agency may issue a tentative decision or one of its responsible employees may recommend a decision; or

(2)   this procedure may be omitted in a case in which the agency finds on the record that due and timely execution of its functions imperatively and unavoidably so requires.

(c)   Before a recommended, initial, or tentative decision, or a decision on agency review of the decision of subordinate employees, the parties are entitled to a reasonable opportunity to submit for the consideration of the employees participating in the decisions—

(1)   proposed findings and conclusions; or

(2)   exceptions to the decisions or recommended decisions of subordinate employees or to tentative agency decisions; and

(3)   supporting reasons for the exceptions or proposed findings or conclusions.

The record shall show the ruling on each finding, conclusion, or exception presented. All decisions, including initial, recommended, and tentative decisions, are a part of the record and shall include a statement of—

(A) findings and conclusions, and the reasons or basis therefor, on all the material issues of fact, law, or discretion presented on the record; and

(B) the appropriate rule, order, sanction, relief, or denial thereof.

(d)

(1) In any agency proceeding which is subject to subsection (a) of this section, except to the extent required for the disposition of ex parte matters as authorized by law—

(A) no interested person outside the agency shall make or knowingly cause to be made to any member of the body comprising the agency, administrative law judge, or other employee who is or may reasonably be expected to be involved in the decisional process of the proceeding, an ex parte communication relevant to the merits of the proceeding;

(B) no member of the body comprising the agency, administrative law judge, or other employee who is or may reasonably be expected to be involved in the decisional process of the proceeding, shall make or knowingly cause to be made to any interested person outside the agency an ex parte communication relevant to the merits of the proceeding;

(C) a member of the body comprising the agency, administrative law judge, or other employee who is or may reasonably be expected to be involved in the decisional process of such proceeding who receives, or who makes or knowingly causes to be made, a communication prohibited by this subsection shall place on the public record of the proceeding:

(i) all such written communications;

(ii) memoranda stating the substance of all such oral communications; and

(iii) all written responses, and memoranda stating the substance of all oral responses, to the materials described in clauses (i) and (ii) of this subparagraph;

(D) upon receipt of a communication knowingly made or knowingly caused to be made by a party in violation of this subsection, the agency, administrative law judge, or other employee presiding at the hearing may, to the extent consistent with the interests of justice and the policy of the underlying statutes, require the party to show cause why his claim or interest in the proceeding should not be dismissed, denied, disregarded, or otherwise adversely affected on account of such violation; and

(E) the prohibitions of this subsection shall apply beginning at such time as the agency may designate, but in no case shall they begin to apply later than the time at which a proceeding is noticed for hearing unless the person responsible for the communication has knowledge that it will be noticed, in which case the prohibitions shall apply beginning at the time of his acquisition of such knowledge.

(2) This subsection does not constitute authority to withhold information from Congress.

§ 558. Imposition of sanctions; determination of applications for licenses; suspension, revocation, and expiration of licenses.

(a) This section applies, according to the provisions thereof, to the exercise of a power or authority.

(b) A sanction may not be imposed or a substantive rule or order issued except within jurisdiction delegated to the agency and as authorized by law.

(c) When application is made for a license required by law, the agency, with due regard for the rights and privileges of all the interested parties or adversely affected persons and within a reasonable time, shall set and complete proceedings required to be conducted in accordance with sections 556 and 557 of this title or other proceedings required by law and shall make its decision. Except in cases of willfulness or those in which public health, interest, or safety requires otherwise, the withdrawal, suspension, revocation, or annulment of a license is lawful only if, before the institution of agency proceedings therefor, the licensee has been given—

(1)   notice by the agency in writing of the facts or conduct which may warrant the action; and

(2)   opportunity to demonstrate or achieve compliance with all lawful requirements.

When the licensee has made timely and sufficient application for a renewal or a new license in accordance with agency rules, a license with reference to an activity of a continuing nature does not expire until the application has been finally determined by the agency.

§ 559. Effect on other laws; effect of subsequent statute.

This subchapter, chapter 7, and sections 1305, 3105, 3344, 4301(2)(E), 5372, and 7521 of this title, and the provisions of section 5335(a)(B) of this title that relate to administrative law judges, do not limit or repeal additional requirements imposed by statute or otherwise recognized by law. Except as otherwise required by law, requirements or privileges relating to evidence or procedure apply equally to agencies and persons. Each agency is granted the authority necessary to comply with the requirements of this subchapter through the issuance of rules or otherwise. Subsequent statute may not be held to supersede or modify this subchapter, chapter 7, sections 1305, 3105, 3344, 4301(2)(E), 5372, or 7521 of this title, or the provisions of section 5335(a)(B) of this title that relate to administrative law judges, except to the extent that it does so expressly.

Title 5, U.S. Code, Chapter 7
Judicial Review

§ 701. Application; definitions.

(a)   This chapter applies, according to the provisions thereof, except to the extent that—

(1)   statutes preclude judicial review; or

(2)   agency action is committed to agency discretion by law.

(b)   For the purpose of this chapter—

(1)   "agency" means each authority of the Government of the United States, whether or not it is within or subject to review by another agency, but does not include—

(A)   the Congress;

(B)   the courts of the United States;

(C)   the governments of the territories or possessions of the United States;

(D)   the government of the District of Columbia;

(E)   agencies composed of representatives of the parties or of representatives of organizations of the parties to the disputes determined by them;

(F)   courts martial and military commissions;

(G)   military authority exercised in the field in time of war or in occupied territory; or

(H)   functions conferred by sections 1738, 1739, 1743, and 1744 of title 12; subchapter II of chapter 471 of title 49; or sections 1884, 1891–1902, and former section 1641(b)(2), of title 50, appendix; and

(2)   "person", "rule", "order", "license", "sanction", "relief", and "agency action" have the meanings given them by section 551 of this title.

§ 702. Right of review.

A person suffering legal wrong because of agency action, or adversely affected or aggrieved by agency action within the meaning of a relevant statute, is entitled to judicial review thereof. An action in a court of the United States seeking relief other than money damages and stating a claim that an agency or an officer or employee thereof acted or failed to act in an official capacity or under color of legal authority shall not be dismissed nor relief therein be denied on the ground that it is against the United States or that the United States is an indispensable party. The United States may be named as a defendant in any such action, and a judgment or decree may be entered against the United States: Provided, That any mandatory or injunctive decree shall specify the Federal officer or officers (by name or by title), and their successors in office, personally responsible for compliance. Nothing herein (1) affects other limitations on judicial review or the power or duty of the court to dismiss any action or deny relief on any other appropriate legal or equitable ground; or (2) confers authority to grant relief if any other statute that grants consent to suit expressly or impliedly forbids the relief which is sought.

§ 703. Form and venue of proceeding.

The form of proceeding for judicial review is the special statutory review proceeding relevant to the subject matter in a court specified by statute or, in the absence or inadequacy thereof, any applicable form of legal action, including actions for declaratory judgments or writs of prohibitory or mandatory injunction or habeas corpus, in a court of competent jurisdiction. If no special statutory review proceeding is applicable, the action for judicial review may be brought against the United States, the agency by its official title, or the appropriate officer. Except to the extent that prior, adequate, and exclusive opportunity for judicial review is provided by law, agency action is subject to judicial review in civil or criminal proceedings for judicial enforcement.

§ 704. Actions reviewable.

Agency action made reviewable by statute and final agency action for which there is no other adequate remedy in a court are subject to judicial review. A preliminary, procedural, or intermediate agency action or ruling not directly reviewable is subject to review on the review of the final agency action. Except as otherwise expressly required by statute, agency action otherwise final is final for the purposes of this section whether or not there has been presented or determined an application for a declaratory order, for any form of reconsideration, or, unless the agency otherwise requires by rule and provides that the action meanwhile is inoperative, for an appeal to superior agency authority.

§ 705. Relief pending review.

When an agency finds that justice so requires, it may postpone the effective date of action taken by it, pending judicial review. On such conditions as may be required and to the extent necessary to prevent irreparable injury, the reviewing court, including the court to which a case may be taken on appeal from or on application for certiorari or other writ to a reviewing court, may issue all necessary and appropriate process to postpone the effective date of an agency action or to preserve status or rights pending conclusion of the review proceedings.

§ 706. Scope of review.

To the extent necessary to decision and when presented, the reviewing court shall decide all relevant questions of law, interpret constitutional and statutory provisions, and determine the meaning or applicability of the terms of an agency action. The reviewing court shall—

(1)   compel agency action unlawfully withheld or unreasonably delayed; and

(2)   hold unlawful and set aside agency action, findings, and conclusions found to be—

    (A)   arbitrary, capricious, an abuse of discretion, or otherwise not in accordance with law;

    (B)   contrary to constitutional right, power, privilege, or immunity;

    (C)   in excess of statutory jurisdiction, authority, or limitations, or short of statutory right;

    (D)   without observance of procedure required by law;

    (E)   unsupported by substantial evidence in a case subject to sections 556 and 557 of this title or otherwise reviewed on the record of an agency hearing provided by statute; or

    (F)   unwarranted by the facts to the extent that the facts are subject to trial de novo by the reviewing court.

In making the foregoing determinations, the court shall review the whole record or those parts of it cited by a party, and due account shall be taken of the rule of prejudicial error.

Steamboat Act of 1852

10 Stat. 61 (Aug. 30, 1852)

Be it enacted by the Senate and House of Representatives of the United States of America in Congress assembled, That no license, register, or enrolment, under the provisions of this or the act to which this is an amendment, shall be granted, or other papers issued by any collector, to any vessel propelled in whole or in part by steam, and carrying passengers, until he shall have satisfactory evidence that all the provisions of this act have been fully complied with; and if any such vessel shall be navigated, with passengers on board, without complying with the terms of this act, the owners thereof and the vessel itself shall be subject to the penalties contained in the second section of the act to which this is an amendment.

Sec. 2. *And be it further enacted,* That it shall be the duty of the inspectors of the hulls of steamers, and the inspectors of boilers and engines, appointed under the provisions of this act, to examine and see that suitable and safe provisions are made throughout such vessel to guard against loss or danger from fire; and no license or other papers, on any application, shall be granted, if the provisions of this act for preventing fires are not complied with, or if any combustible material liable to take fire from heated iron, or any other heat generated on board of such vessels in and about the boilers, pipes, or machinery, shall be placed at less than eighteen inches distant from such heated metal or other substance likely to cause ignition, unless a column of air or water intervenes between such heated surfaced and any wood or other combustible material so exposed, sufficient at all times, and under all circumstances, to prevent ignition; and further, when wood is so exposed to ignition, as an additional preventive, it shall be shielded by some incombustible material in such manner as to leave the air to circulate freely between such material and the wood. *Provided, however,* That when the structure of such steamers is such, or the arrangement of the boilers or machinery is such that the requirements aforesaid cannot, without serious inconvenience or sacrifice, be complied with, inspectors may vary therefrom, if in their judgment it can be done with safety.

Sec. 3. *And be it further enacted,* That every vessel so propelled by steam, and carrying passengers, shall have not less than three double-acting forcing pumps, with chamber at least four inches in diameter, two to be worked by hand and one by steam, if steam can be employed, otherwise by hand; one whereof shall be placed near the stern, one near the stem, and one amidship; each having a suitable, well-fitted hose, of at least two thirds the length of the vessel, kept at all times in perfect order and ready for immediate use; each of which pumps shall also be supplied with water by a pipe connected therewith, and passing through the side of the vessel, so low as to be at all times in the water when she is afloat: *Provided,* That, in steamers not exceeding two hundred tons measurement, two of said pumps may be dispensed with; and in steamers of over two hundred tons, and not exceeding five hundred tons measurement, one of said pumps may be dispensed with.

Sec. 4. *And be it further enacted,* That every such vessel, carrying passengers, shall have at least two good and suitable boats, supplied with oars, in good condition at all times for service, one of which boats shall be a life-boat made of metal, fire-proof, and in all respects a good, substantial, safe sea boat, capable of sustaining, inside and outside, fifty persons, with life-lines attached to the gunwale, at suitable distances. And every such vessel of more than five hundred tons, and not exceeding eight hundred tons measurement, shall have three life-boats; and every such vessel of more than eight hundred tons, and not exceeding fifteen hundred tons measurement, shall have four life-boats; and every such vessel of more than fifteen hundred tons measurement, shall have six life-boats—all of which boats shall be well furnished with oars and other necessary apparatus: *Provided, however,* The inspectors are hereby authorized to exempt steamers navigating rivers only, from the obligation to carry, of the life-boats herein provided for, more than one, the same being of suitable dimensions, made of metal and furnished with all necessary apparatus for use and safety—such steamers having other suitable provisions for the preservation of life in case of fire or other disaster.

Sec. 5. And be it further enacted, That every such vessel, carrying passengers, shall also be provided with a good life-preserver, made of suitable material, or float well adapted to the purpose, for each and every passenger, which life-preservers and floats shall always be kept in convenient and accessible places in such vessel, and in readiness for the use of the passengers; and every such vessel shall also keep twenty fire-buckets and five axes; and there shall be kept on board every such vessel exceeding five hundred tons measurement, buckets and axes after the rate of their tonnage, as follows: on every vessel of six hundred tons measurement, five buckets and one axe for each one hundred tons measurement, decreasing this proportion as the tonnage of the vessel increases, so that any such vessel of thirty-five hundred tons, and all such vessels exceeding the same shall not be required to keep but three buckets for each one hundred tons of measurement, and but one axe for every five buckets.

Sec. 6. *And be it further enacted,* That every such vessel carrying passengers on the main or lower deck, shall be provided with sufficient means convenient to such passengers for their escape to the upper deck in case of fire or other accident endangering life.

Sec. 7. *And be it further enacted,* That no loose hemp shall be carried on board any such vessel; nor shall baled hemp be carried on the deck or guards thereof, unless the bales are compactly pressed and well covered with bagging, or a similar fabric; nor shall gunpowder, oil of turpentine, oil of vitriol, camphene, or other explosive burning fluids or materials which ignite by friction, be carried on board any such vessel, as freight, except in cases of special license for that purpose, as hereinafter provided; and all such articles kept on board as stores, shall be secured in metallic vessels: and every person who shall knowingly violate any of the provisions of this section, shall pay a penalty of one hundred dollars for each offence, to be recovered by action of debt in any court of competent jurisdiction.

Sec. 8. And be it further enacted, That hereafter all gunpowder, oil of turpentine, oil of vitriol, camphene, or other explosive burning fluids, and materials which ignite by friction, when packed or put up for shipment on board of any such vessel, shall be securely packed or put up separately from each other and from all other articles, and the package, box, cask, or vessel containing the same, shall be distinctly marked on the outside with the name or description of the articles contained therein; and every person who shall pack or put up, or cause to be packed or put up for shipment on board of any such vessel, any gunpowder, oil of turpentine, oil of vitriol, camphene, or other explosive burning fluids, or materials which ignite by friction, otherwise than as aforesaid, or shall ship the same, unless packed and marked as aforesaid, on board of any steam-vessel carrying passengers, shall be deemed guilty of a misdemeanor, and punished by a fine not exceeding one thousand dollars, or imprisonment not exceeding eighteen months, or both.

SEC. 9. *And be it further enacted,* That instead of the existing provisions of law for the inspection of steamers and their equipment, and instead of the present system of pilotage of such vessels, and the present mode of employing engineers on board the same, the following regulations shall be observed, to wit: The collector or other chief officer of the customs, together with the supervising inspector for the district, and the judge of the district court of the United States for the district in each of the following collection districts, namely, New Orleans and St. Louis, on the Mississippi River; Louisville, Cincinnati, Wheeling, and Pittsburg, on the Ohio River; Buffalo and Cleveland, on Lake Erie; Detroit, upon Detroit River; Nashville, upon the Cumberland River; Chicago, on Lake Michigan; Oswego, on Lack Ontario; Burlington, in Vermont; Galveston, in Texas; Mobile, in Alabama; Savannah, in Georgia; Charleston, in South Carolina; Norfolk, in Virginia; Baltimore, in Maryland; Philadelphia, in Pennsylvania; New York, in New York; New London, in Connecticut; Boston, in Massachusetts; Portland, in Maine; and San Francisco, in California—shall designate two inspectors, of good character and suitable qualifications to perform the services required of them by this act within the respective districts for which they shall be appointed, one of whom, from his practical knowledge of ship-building, and the uses of steam in navigation, shall be fully competent to make a reliable estimate of the strength, seaworthiness, and other qualities of the hulls of steamers and their equipment, deemed essential to safety of life, when such vessels are employed in the carriage of passengers, to be called the Inspector of Hulls; the other of whom, from his knowledge and experience of the duties of an engineer employed in navigating vessels by steam, and also in the construction and use of boilers, and the machinery and appurtenances therewith connected, shall be able to form a reliable opinion of the quality of the material, the strength, form, workmanship, and suitableness of such boilers and machinery to be employed in the carriage of passengers, without hazard to life, from imperfections in the material, workmanship, or arrangement of any part of such apparatus for steaming, to be called the Inspector of Boilers; and these two persons thus designated, if approved by the Secretary of Treasury, shall be, from the time of such designation, inspectors, empowered and required to perform the duties herein specified, to wit:

First. Upon application in writing by the master or owner, they shall, once in every year at least, carefully inspect the hull of each steamer belonging to their respective districts and employed in the carriage of passengers, and shall satisfy themselves that every such vessel so submitted to their inspection is of a structure suitable for the service in which she is to be employed, has suitable accommodations for her crew and passengers, and is in a condition to warrant the belief that she may be used in navigation as a steamer, with safety to life, and that all the requirements of law in regard to fire, boats, pumps, hose, life-preservers, floats, and other things, are faithfully complied with; and if they deem it expedient, they may direct the vessel to be put in motion, and may adopt any other suitable means to test her sufficiency and that of her equipment.

Second. They shall also inspect the boilers of such steamers before the same shall be used, and once in every year thereafter, subjecting them to a hydrostatic pressure, the limit to which, not exceeding one hundred and sixty-five pounds to the square inch for high pressure boilers, may be prescribed by the owner or the master, and shall satisfy themselves by examination and experimental trials, that the boilers are well made of good and suitable material; that the openings for the passage of water and steam respectively, and all pipes and tubes exposed to heat are of proper dimensions, and free from obstruction; that the spaces between the flues are sufficient, and that the fire line of the furnace is below the prescribed water-line of the boilers; and that such boilers and the machinery and the appurtenances may be safely employed in the service proposed in the written application, without peril to life; and shall also satisfy themselves that the safety-valves are of suitable dimensions, sufficient in number, well arranged, and in good working order, (one of which may, if necessary in the opinion of the inspectors, to secure safety, be taken wholly from the control of all persons engaged in navigating such vessel;) that there is a suitable number of gauge-cocks properly inserted, and a suitable water-gauge and steam-gauge indicating the height of the water and the pressure of the steam; that in or upon the outside flue of each outside high-pressure boiler, there is placed in a suitable manner alloyed metals, fusible by the heat of the boiler when raised to the highest working pressure allowed, and that in or upon the top of the flues of all other high-pressure boilers in the steamer, such alloyed metals are placed, as aforesaid, fusing at ten pounds greater pressure than said metals on the outside boilers, thereby, in each case, letting steam escape; and that adequate and certain provision is made for an ample supply of water to feed the boilers at all times, whether such vessel is in motion or not; so that, in high-pressure boilers, the water shall not be less than four inches above the flue: *Provided, however,* in steamers hereafter supplied with new high-pressure boilers, if the alloy fuses on the outer boilers at a pressure of ten pounds exceeding the working pressure allowed, and at twenty pounds above said pressure on the inner boilers, it shall be a sufficient compliance with this act.

Third. That in subjecting to the hydrostatic test aforesaid, boilers called and usually known under the designation of high-pressure boilers, the inspectors shall assume one hundred and ten pounds to the square inch as the maximum pressure allowable as a working power for a new boiler forty-two inches in diameter, made of inspected iron plates at least one fourth an inch thick, in the best manner, and of the quality herein required, and shall rate the working power of all high-pressure boilers, whether of greater or less diameter, old or new, according to their strength compared with this standard: and in all cases the test applied shall exceed the working power allowed, in the ratio of one hundred an sixty-five to one hundred and ten, and no high-pressure boilers hereafter made shall be rated above this standard: and in subjecting to the test aforesaid, that class of boilers usually designated and known as low-pressure boilers, the said inspectors shall allow as a working power of each new boiler a pressure of only three fourths the number of pounds to the square inch to which it shall have been subjected by the hydrostatic test and found to be sufficient therefor, using the water in such tests at a temperature not exceeding sixty degrees Fahrenheit; but should such inspectors be of the opinion, that said boiler by reason of its construction or material will not safely allow so high a working pressure, they may, for reasons to be stated specifically in their certificate, fix the working pressure of said boiler at less than three-fourths of said test pressure, and no lower-pressure boiler hereafter made shall be rated in its working pressure above the aforesaid standard: and provided that the same rules shall be observed in regard to boilers heretofore made, unless the proportion between such boilers and the cylinders or some other cause renders it manifest that its application would be unjust, in which case the inspectors may depart from these rules, if it can be done with safety; but in no case shall the working pressure allowed exceed the hydrostatic test, and no valve under any circumstances shall be loaded or so managed in any way as to subject a boiler to a greater pressure than the amount allowed by the inspectors, nor shall any boiler or pipe be approved which is made in whole or in part of bad material, or is unsafe in its form, or dangerous from defective workmanship, age, use, or any other cause.

Fourth. That when the inspection in detail is completed, and the inspectors approve of the vessel and her equipment throughout, they. shall make and subscribe a certificate to the collector of the district, substantially as follows:—

State of _____ District of _____ Application having been made in writing by _____ to the subscribers, inspectors for said district, to examine the steamer _____ of _____ whereof _____ are owners, and _____ is master, we having performed that service, now, on this ___ day of A. D. ____ do certify, that she was built in the year   , is in all respects staunch, seaworthy, and in good condition for navigation, having suitable means of escape in case of accident from the main to the upper deck, that she is provided with (here insert the number of state-rooms, the number of berths therein, the number of other permanent berths for cabin passengers, the number of berths for deck or other classes of passengers, the number of passengers of each class for whom she has suitable accommodations, and in case of steamers sailing to or from any European port or to or from any port on the Atlantic or the Pacific, a distance of one thousand miles or upwards, the number of each she is permitted to carry,—and in case of a steamer sailing to any other port, a distance of five hundred miles or upwards, the number of deck passengers she is permitted to carry, also the number of boilers, and the form, dimensions, and material of which each boiler is made, the thickness of the metal, and when made—if made after this act takes effect, and of iron, whether they are such in all respects as the act requires, whether each boiler has been tried by hydrostatic test, the amount of pressure to the square inch in pounds applied to it, whether the amount allowed as the maximum working power was determined by the rule prescribed by this act, if not, the reason for a departure from it; also the number of safety valves required, their capacity, the load prescribed for each valve, how many are left in the control of the persons navigating the vessel, whether one is withdrawn, and the manner of securing it against interference, also the number and dimensions of supply pipes, and whether they and the other means provided are sufficient at all times and under all circumstances, when in good order, to keep the water up four inches at least above the top of the flue; also the number and dimensions of the steam-pipes, the number and kind of engines, the dimensions of their cylinders, the number and capacity of the forcing-pumps, and how worked, the number and kind of gauge-cocks, water and steam gauges, where situate[d], and how secured; also the manner of using alloyed metals, and the pressure at which they are known by the inspectors to fuse; the equipments for the extinguishment of fires, including hose, fire-buckets, and axes; the provisions for saving life in case of accident, including boats, life-preservers, and substitutes therefor, where kept, and all other provisions made on board for the security of the lives of passengers.) And we further certify, that the equipment of the vessel throughout, including pipes, pumps, and other means to keep the water up to the point aforesaid, hose, boats, life-preservers, and other things, is in conformity with the provisions of law; and that we declare it to be our deliberate conviction, founded upon the inspection which we have made, that the vessel may be employed as a steamer upon the waters named in the application, without peril to life, from any imperfection of form, materials, workmanship, or arrangement of the several parts, or from age or use. And we further certify, that said vessel is to run within the following limits, to wit: from _____ to _____ and back, touching at intermediate places.

And which certificate shall be verified by the oaths of the inspectors signing it, before a person competent by law to administer oaths. And in case the said inspectors do not grant a certificate of approval, they shall state, in writing, and sign the same, their reasons for their disapproval.

Fifth. Upon the application of the master or owner of any steamer employed in the carriage of passengers, for a license to carry gunpowder, oil of turpentine, oil of vitriol, camphene, or other explosive burning fluids, and materials which ignite by friction, or either of them, the inspectors shall examine such vessel, and if they find that she is provided with chests or safes composed of metal, or entirely lined therewith, or one or more apartments thoroughly lined with metal at a secure distance from any fire, they may grant a certificate to that effect, authorizing such vessel to carry as freight any of the articles aforesaid, those of each description to be secured in such chest, safe, or apartment, containing no other article, and carried at a distance from any fire to be specified in the certificate: Provided, That any such certificate may be revoked or annulled at any time by the inspectors, upon proof that either of the said articles have been carried on board said vessel, at a place or in a manner not authorized by such certificate, or that any of the provisions of this act in relation thereto have been violated.

Sixth. The said inspectors shall keep a regular record of certificates of inspections of vessels, their boilers, engines, and machinery, whether of approval or disapproval, and when recorded, the original shall be delivered to the collector of the district; they shall keep a like record of certificates, authorizing gunpowder, oil of turpentine, oil of vitriol, camphene, or other explosive burning fluids and materials which ignite by friction, or either of them, to be carried as freight, by any such vessel; and when recorded deliver the originals to said collector; they shall keep a like record of all licenses to pilots and engineers, and all revocations thereof, and shall from time to time report to the supervising inspector of their respective districts, in writing, their decisions on all applications for such licenses, or proceedings for the revocation thereof, and all testimony received by them in such proceedings.

Seventh. The inspectors shall license and classify all engineers and pilots of steamers carrying passengers.

Eighth: Whenever any person claiming to be qualified to perform the duty of engineer upon steamers carrying passengers, shall apply for a certificate, the Board of Inspectors shall examine the applicant, and the proofs which he produces in support of his claim; and if, upon full consideration, they are satisfied that his character, habits of life, knowledge, and experience in the duties of an engineer, are all such as to authorize the belief that the applicant is a suitable and safe person to be intrusted with the powers and duties of such a station, they shall give him a certificate to that effect, for one year, signed by them, in which certificate they shall state the time of the examination, and shall assign the appointee to the appropriate class of engineers.

Ninth. Whenever any person claiming to be a skilful pilot for any such vessel shall offer himself for a license, the said board shall make diligent inquiry as to his character and merits; and if satisfied that he possesses the requisite skill, and is trustworthy and faithful, they shall give him a certificate to that effect, licensing him for one year to be a pilot of any such vessels within the limit prescribed in the certificate; but the license of any such engineer or pilot may be revoked upon proof of negligence, unskilfulness, or inattention to the duties of the station: *Provided,* however, If in cases of refusal to license engineers or pilots, and in cases of the revocation of any license by the local board of inspectors, any engineer or pilot deeming himself wronged by such refusal or revocation, may, within thirty days after notice thereof, on application to a supervising inspector, have his case examined anew by such supervising inspector, upon producing a certified copy of the reasons assigned by the local board for their doings in the premises; and such supervising inspector may revoke the decision of such local board of inspectors and licenses such pilot or engineer; and like proceedings, upon the same conditions may be had by the master or owner of any such vessel, or of any steamboat-boiler, for which the said local board shall have refused, upon inspection, to give a certificate of approval, or shall have notified such master or owner of any repairs necessary after such certificate has been granted.

Tenth. It shall be unlawful for any person to employ, or any person to serve as engineer or pilot, on any such vessel, who is not licensed by the inspectors; and any one so offending shall forfeit one hundred dollars for each offence: *Provided, however,* That if a vessel leaves her port with a complement of engineers and pilots and on her voyage is deprived of their services, or the services of any of them, without the consent, fault, or collusion of the mater, owner, or any one interested in the vessel, the deficiency may be temporarily supplied, until others, licensed, can be obtained.

Eleventh. In addition to the annual inspection, it shall be the duty of said board to examine, seasonably, steamers arriving and departing, so often as to enable them to detect any neglect to comply with the requirement of law, and also any defects or imperfections becoming apparent after the inspection aforesaid, and tending to render the navigation of the vessel unsafe, which service may be performed by one of the board; and if he shall discover an omission to comply with the law or that repairs have become necessary to make the vessel safe, he shall at once notify the master, stating in the notice what is required; and if the master deems the requirements unreasonable or unnecessary, he may take the opinion of the board thereon, and if dissatisfied with the decision of such board may apply for a reexamination of the case to the supervising inspector as is hereinbefore provided; and if he shall refuse or neglect to comply with the requirements of the local board, and shall, contrary thereto, and while the same remains unreversed by the supervising inspector, employ the vessel by navigating her, the master and owner shall be liable for any damage to the passengers and their baggage which shall occur from any defects so as aforesaid stated in said notice, which shall be in writing, and all inspections and orders shall be promptly made by the inspectors; and where it can be safely done in their judgment, they shall permit repairs to be made where those interested can most conveniently do them; and no inspectors of one district shall modify or annul the doings of the inspectors of another district, in regard to repairs, unless there is a change in the state of things demanding more repairs than were thought necessary when the order was made; nor shall the inspectors of one district appoint a person coming from another, if such person has been rejected for unfitness or want of qualifications.

Twelfth. The said board, when thereto requested, shall inspect steamers belonging to districts where no such board is established; and if a certificate of approval is not granted, no other inspection shall be made by the same or any other board, until the objections made by the inspectors are removed; and if any vessel shall be navigated after a board of inspectors have refused to make the collector a certificate of approval, she shall be liable to the same penalties as if she had been run without a license: *Provided, however,* That nothing herein contained shall impair the right of the inspectors to permit such vessel to go to another port for repairs, if, in their opinion, it is safe so to do.

Thirteenth. The said board of inspectors shall have power to summon before them witnesses, and to compel their attendance by the same process as in courts of law; and after reasonable time given to the alleged delinquent, at the time and place of investigation, to examine said witnesses under oath, touching the performance of their duties by engineers and pilots of any such vessel; and if it shall appear satisfactorily that any such engineer or pilot is incompetent, or that life has been placed in peril by reason of such incompetency, or by negligence or misconduct on the part of any such person, the board shall immediately suspend or revoke his license, and report their doings to the chief officer of the customs; and the said chief officer of the customs shall pay out of the revenues herein provided such sums to any witness so summoned under the provisions of this act, for his actual travel and attendance, as shall be officially certified, by an inspector hearing the case, upon the back of the summons, not exceeding the rates allowed to a witness for travel and attendance in the Circuit and District Courts of the United States.

Fourteenth. That the said board shall report promptly all their doings to the chief officer of the customs, as well as all omissions or refusals to comply with the provisions of law on the part of any owner or master of any such vessel, propelled in whole or in part by steam, carrying passenger.

Fifteenth. That it shall at all times be the duty of all engineers and pilots licensed under this act, and all mates, to assist the inspectors in the examination of any such vessels to which any such engineer, mate, or pilot belongs, and to point out all defects and imperfections in the hull or apparatus for steaming, and also to make known to them at the earliest opportunity, all accidents occasioning serious injury to the vessel or her equipment, whereby life may be in danger, and in default thereof the license of any such engineer or pilot shall be revoked.

SEC. 10. *And be it further enacted,* That in those cases where the number of passengers is limited by the inspector's certificate, it shall not be lawful to take on board of any steamer a greater number of passengers than is certified by the inspectors in the certificate; and the master and owners, or either of them, shall be liable, to any person suing for the same, to forfeit the amount of passage money and ten dollars for each passenger beyond the number allowed. And moreover, in all cases of an express or implied undertaking to transport passengers, or to supply them with food and lodging, from place to place, and suitable provision is not made of a full and adequate supply of good and wholesome food and water, and of suitable lodging for all such passengers, or where barges, or other craft, impeding the progress, are taken in tow, for a distance exceeding five hundred miles, without previous and seasonable notice to such passengers, in all such cases the owners and the vessel shall be liable to refund all the money paid for the passage, and to pay also the damage sustained by such default or delay: *Provided, however,* That if in any such case a satisfactory bond is given to the marshal for the benefit of the plaintiff, to secure the satisfaction of such judgment as he may recover, the vessel shall be released.

SEC. 11. *And be it further enacted,* That if the master of a steamer or any other person, whether acting under orders or not, shall intentionally load or obstruct, or cause to be loaded or obstructed, in any way or manner, the safety valve or valves of a boiler, or shall employ any other means or device whereby the boiler shall be subjected to a greater pressure than the amount allowed by the certificate of the inspectors, or shall be exposed to a greater pressure, or shall intentionally derange or hinder the operation of any machinery or device employed to denote the state of the water or steam in any boiler, or to give warning of approaching danger, it shall, in any such case, be a misdemeanor, and any and every person concerned therein, directly or indirectly, shall forfeit two hundred dollars, and may at the discretion of the court, be in addition thereto imprisoned not exceeding eighteen months.

SEC. 12. *And be it further enacted,* That if at any time there be a deficiency of water in a boiler, by suffering it to fall below three inches above the flue as prescribed in this act, unless the same happens through inevitable accident, the master, if it be by his order, assent, or connivance, and also the engineer, or other person, whose duty it is to keep up the supply, shall be guilty of an offence for which they shall severally be fined one hundred dollars each; and if an explosion or collapse happens in consequence of such deficiency, they, or any of them, may be further punished by imprisonment, for a period of not less than six nor more than eighteenth months.

SEC. 13. *And be it further enacted,* That hereafter all boilers of steamboats made of iron shall be constructed of plates which have been stamped according to the provisions of this act.

SEC. 14. *And be it further enacted,* That it shall be the duty of such inspectors to ascertain the quality of the material of which the boiler-plates of any such boiler so submitted to their inspection are made; and to satisfy themselves by any suitable means, whether the mode of manufacturing has been such as to produce iron equal to good iron made with charcoal, such as in their judgment may be used for generating steam-power without hazard to life; and no such boiler shall be approved which is made of unsuitable material, or of which the manufacture is imperfect, or is not in their opinion, of suitable strength, or whose plates are less than one fourth of an inch in thickness, for a high-pressure boiler of forty-two inches in diameter, and in that proportion of strength according to the maximum of working pressure allowed for high-pressure boilers of greater or less diameter, or which is made of any but wrought iron of a quality equal to good iron made with charcoal.

SEC. 15. *And be it further enacted,* That all plates of boiler-iron shall be distinctly and permanently stamped in such manner as the Secretary of the Treasury shall prescribe, and if practicable, in such place or places that the mark shall be left visible after the plates are worked into boilers; with the name of the manufacturer, the quality of the iron, and whether or not hammered, and the place where the same is manufactured.

SEC. 16. *And be it further enacted,* That it shall be unlawful to use in such vessel for generating steam for power, a boiler, or steam-pipe connecting the boilers made after the passage of this act, of any iron unless it has been stamped by the manufacturer as herein provided; and if any person shall make for use in any such vessel, a boiler of iron not so stamped, intended to generate steam for power, he shall, for any such offence, forfeit five hundred dollars, to be recovered in an action of debt by any person suing for the same; and any person using or causing to be used in any such vessel such a boiler to generate steam for power, shall forfeit a like sum for each offence.

Sec. 17. *And be it further enacted,* That if any person shall counterfeit the marks and stamps required by this act, or shall falsely stamp any boiler-iron, and be convicted thereof, he shall be fined not exceeding five hundred dollars and imprisoned not exceeding two years. And if any person or persons shall stamp or mark plates with the name or marks of another with intent to mislead, deceive, or defraud, such person or persons shall be liable to any one injured thereby, for all damage occasioned by such fraud or deception.

Sec. 18. *And be it further enacted,* That in order to carry this act fully into execution, the President of the United States shall, with the advice of the Senate, appoint nine supervising inspectors, who shall be selected for their knowledge, skill, and experience in the uses of steam for navigation, and who are competent judges not only of the character of vessels but of all parts of the machinery employed in steaming, who shall assemble together at such places as they may agree upon once in each year at least, for joint consultation and the establishment of rules and regulations for their own conduct and that of the several boards of inspectors within the districts, and also to assign to each of the said nine inspectors the limits of territory within which he shall perform his duties. And the said supervising inspectors shall each be paid for his services after the rate of fifteen hundred dollars a year, and in addition thereto, his actual reasonable traveling expenses, incurred in the necessary performance of his duty when away from the principal port in his district, and certified and sworn to by him under such instructions as shall be given by the Secretary of the Treasury, who is hereby authorized to pay such salaries, and also such travelling expenses, and the actual reasonable expenses (both to them and other inspectors) of transporting from place to place the instruments used in inspections, which expenses shall be proved to his satisfaction.

Sec. 19. *And be it further enacted,* That the supervising inspectors shall watch over all parts of the territory assigned them, shall visit, confer with, and examine into the doings of the several boards of inspectors, and shall, whenever they think it expedient, visit such vessels, licensed, and examine into their condition, for the purpose of ascertaining whether the provisions of this act have been observed and complied with, both by the board of inspectors and the master and owners; and it shall be the duty of all masters, engineers, and pilots of such vessels, to answer all reasonable inquiries and to give all the information in their power, in regard to any such vessel so visited, and her machinery for steaming, and the manner of managing both.

Sec. 20. *And be it further enacted*, That whenever a supervising inspector ascertains to his satisfaction that the master, engineer, pilot, or owner of any such vessel fail to perform their duties according to the provisions of this act, he shall report the facts in writing to the board in the district where the vessel belongs, and, if need be, cause the negligent or offending parties to be prosecuted; and if he has good reason to believe there has been, through negligence, or from any other cause, a failure of the board who inspected the vessel to do its duty, he shall report the facts in writing to the Secretary of the Treasury, who shall cause immediate investigation into the truth of the complaint, and if he deems the cause sufficient, shall remove the delinquent.

Sec. 21. *And be it further enacted*, That it shall be the duty of such supervising inspectors to see that the said several boards within their respective collection districts execute their duties faithfully, promptly, and, as far as possible, uniformly, in all places, by following out the provisions of this act, according to the true intent and meaning thereof; and they shall, as far as practicable by their established rules, harmonize differences of opinion when they exist in different boards.

Sec. 22. *And be it further enacted*, That the said supervising inspectors shall also visit collection districts in which there are no boards of inspectors, if there be any where steamers are owned or employed, and each one shall have full power to inspect any such steamer or boilers of each steamer in any such district, or in any other district where, from distance or other cause, it is inconvenient to resort to the local board, and to grant certificates of approval according to the provisions of this act, and to do and perform in such districts all the duties imposed upon boards in the districts where they exist: *Provided,* That no supervising or other inspector shall be deemed competent to inspect in any case where he is directly or indirectly personally interested, or is associated in business with any person who is so interested, but in all such cases the duty shall be performed by disinterested inspectors, and inspection made in violation of this rule shall be void and of no effect.

Sec. 23. *And be it further enacted,* That it shall be the duty of each of the collectors or other chief officer of the customs for the districts aforesaid, except San Francisco, to make known without delay, to the collectors of all the said districts, except San Francisco, the names of all persons licensed as engineers or pilots for such vessels, and the names of all persons from whom upon application, licenses have been withheld, and the names of all whose licenses have been revoked or suspended, and also the names of all such vessels which neglect or refuse to make such repairs as may be ordered under the provisions of this act, and the names of all for which license has been, on application, refused.

Sec. 24. *And be it further enacted,* That it shall be the duty of the collectors or other chief officers of the customs and of the inspectors aforesaid, within the said several districts, to enforce the provisions of law against all such steamers arriving and departing; and upon proof that any collector or other chief officer of the customs, or inspector, has negligently or intentionally omitted his duty in this particular, such delinquent shall be removed from office, and shall also be subject to a penalty of one hundred dollars for each offence, to be sued for in an action of debt before any court of competent jurisdiction.

Sec. 25. *And be it further enacted,* That the collector or other chief officer of the customs, shall retain on file all original certificates of the inspectors required by this act to be delivered to him, and shall give to the master or owner of the vessel therein named, two certified copies thereof, one of which shall be placed by such master or owner in some conspicuous place in the vessel, where it will be most likely to be observed by passengers and others, and there kept at all times; the other shall be retained by such master or owner as evidence of the authority thereby conferred; and if any person shall receive or carry any passenger on board any steamer not having a certified copy of the certificate of approval as required by this act, placed and kept as aforesaid; or who shall receive or carry any gunpowder, oil of turpentine, oil of vitriol, camphene, or other explosive burning fluids, or materials which ignite by friction, as freight, on board any steamer carrying passengers, not having a certificate authorizing the same, and a certified copy thereof placed and kept as aforesaid; or who shall stow or carry any of said articles, at a place or in a manner not authorized by such certificate, shall forfeit and pay for each offence one hundred dollars, to be recovered by action of debt in any court of competent jurisdiction.

Sec. 26. *And be it further enacted,* That every inspector who shall willfully certify falsely touching any such vessel propelled in whole or in part by steam, and carrying passengers, her hull, accommodations, boilers, engines, machinery, or their appurtenances, or any of her equipments, or any matter or thing contained in any certificate signed and sworn to by him, shall on conviction thereof, be punished by fine not exceeding five hundred dollars, or imprisonment not exceeding six months, or both.

SEC. 27. *And be it further enacted,* That if any such vessel carrying passengers, having a license and certificate, as required by this act, shall be navigated without having her hull, accommodations, boilers, engines, machinery, and their appurtenances, and all equipments, in all things conformable to such certificate, the master or commander by whom she shall be so navigated, having knowledge of such defect, shall be punished by fine not exceeding one hundred dollars, or imprisonment not exceeding two months, or both: *Provided,* That such master or commander shall not be liable for loss or deficiency occasioned by the dangers of navigation, if such loss or deficiency shall be supplied as soon as practicable.

SEC. 28. *And be it further enacted,* That on any such steamers navigating rivers only, when from darkness, fog, or other cause, the pilot on watch shall be of opinion that the navigation is unsafe, or from accident to, or derangement of the machinery of the boat, the engineer on watch shall be of the opinion that the further navigation of the vessel is unsafe, the vessel shall be brought to anchor, or moored, as soon as it prudently can be done: *Provided,* That if the person in command shall, after being so admonished by either of such officers, elect to pursue such voyage, he may do the same; but in such case both he and the owner of such steamer shall be answerable for all damages which shall arise to the person of any passenger and his baggage from said causes in so pursuing the voyage, and no degree of care or diligence shall in such case be held to justify or excuse the person in command, or said owners.

SEC. 29. *And be it further enacted,* That it shall be the duty of the supervising inspectors to establish such rules and regulations to be observed by all such vessels in passing each other, as they shall from time to time deem necessary for safety; two printed copies of which rules and regulations, signed by said inspectors, shall be furnished to each of such vessels, and shall at all times be kept up in conspicuous places on such vessels, which rules shall be observed both night and day. Should any pilot, engineer, or master of any such vessel neglect or willfully refuse to observe the foregoing regulations, any delinquent so neglecting or refusing, shall be liable to a penalty of thirty dollars, and to all damage done to any passenger, in his person or baggage, by such neglect or refusal; and no such vessel shall be justified in coming into collision with another if it can be avoided.

Sec. 30. *And be it further enacted,* That whenever damage is sustained by any passenger or his baggage, from explosion, fire, collision, or other cause, the master and the owner of such vessel, or either of them, and the vessel, shall be liable to each and every person so injured, to the full amount of damage, if it happens through any neglect to comply with the provisions of law herein prescribed, or through known defects or imperfections of the steaming apparatus, or of the hull; and any person sustaining loss or injury through the carelessness, negligence, or willful misconduct of an engineer or pilot, or their neglect or refusal to obey the provisions of law herein prescribed as to navigating such steamers, may sue such engineer or pilot, and recover damages for any such injury caused as aforesaid by any such engineer or pilot.

Sec. 31. *And be it further enacted,* That before issuing the annual license to any such steamer, the collector or other chief officer of the customs for the port or district, shall demand and receive from the owner or owners of the steamer, as a compensation for the inspections and examinations made for the year, the following sums, in addition to the fees for issuing enrolments and licenses, now allowed by law, according to the tonnage of the vessel, to wit: for each vessel of a thousand tons and over, thirty-five dollars; for each of five hundred tons and over, but less than one thousand tons, thirty dollars; and for each under five hundred tons and over one hundred and twenty-five tons, twenty-five dollars; and for each under one hundred and twenty-five tons, twenty dollars, at the time of obtaining registry, and once in each year thereafter, pay according to the rate of tonnage before mentioned, the sum of money herein fixed. And each engineer and pilot licensed as herein provided, shall pay for the first certificate granted by any inspector or inspectors, the sum of five dollars, and for each subsequent certificate one dollar, to such inspector or inspectors, to be accounted for and paid over to the collector or other chief officer of the customs; and the sums derived from all sources above specified shall be quarterly accounted for and paid over to the United States in the same manner as other revenue.

Sec. 32. *And be it further enacted,* That each inspector shall keep an accurate account of every such steamer boarded by him during the year, and of all his official acts and doings which in the form of a report he shall communicate to the collector or other chief officer of the customs, on the first days of May and November, in each year.

Sec. 33. *And be it further enacted,* That the inspectors in the following districts shall each be allowed annually, the following compensation, to be paid under the direction of the Secretary of the Treasury, in the manner officers of the revenue are paid, to wit:

For the district of Portland, in Maine, three hundred dollars.

For the district of Boston and Charlestown, in Massachusetts, eight hundred dollars.

For the district of New London, in Connecticut, three hundred dollars.

For the district of New York, two thousand dollars.

For the district of Philadelphia, in Pennsylvania, one thousand dollars.

For the district of Baltimore, in Maryland, one thousand dollars.

For the district of Norfolk, in Virginia, three hundred dollars.

For the district of Charleston, in South Carolina, four hundred dollars.

For the district of Savannah, in Georgia, four hundred dollars.

For the district of Mobile, in Alabama, one thousand dollars.

For the district of New Orleans, or in which New Orleans is the port of entry, in Louisiana, two thousand dollars.

For the district of Galveston, in Texas, three hundred dollars.

For the district of St. Louis, in Missouri, fifteen hundred dollars.

For the district of Nashville, in Tennessee, four hundred dollars.

For the district of Cincinnati, Ohio, fifteen hundred dollars.

For the district of Wheeling, Virginia, five hundred dollars.

For the district of Pittsburgh, Pennsylvania, fifteen hundred dollars.

For the district of Chicago, Illinois, five hundred dollars.

For the district of Detroit, Michigan, eight hundred dollars.

For the district of Cleveland, Ohio, five hundred dollars.

For the district of Buffalo, New York, twelve hundred dollars.

For the district of Oswego, or of which Oswego is the port of entry, New York, three hundred dollars.

For the district of Vermont, two hundred dollars.

For the district of San Francisco, California, fifteen hundred dollars.

Sec. 34. *And be it further enacted,* That the Secretary of the Treasury shall provide the inspectors with a suitable number of instruments, of uniform construction, so as to give uniform results to test the strength of boilers.

Sec. 35. *And be it further enacted,* That it shall be the duty of the master of any such steamer to cause to be kept a correct list of all the passengers received and delivered from day to day, noting the places where received and where landed, which record shall be open to the inspection of the inspectors and officers of the customs at all times; and in case of default, through negligence or design, the said master shall forfeit one hundred dollars, which penalty, as well as that for excess of passengers, shall be a lien upon the vessel: *Provided,* however, A bond may, as provided for in other cases, be given to secure the satisfaction of the judgment.

Sec. 36. *And be it further enacted,* That every master or commander of any such steamer, shall keep on board of such steamer, at least two copies of this act to be furnished to him by the Secretary of the Treasury; and if the master or commander neglects or refuses so to do, or shall unreasonably refuse to exhibit a copy of the same to any passenger who shall ask it, he shall forfeit twenty dollars.

Sec. 37. *And be it further enacted,* That any inspector who shall, upon any pretence, receive any fee or reward for his services rendered under this act, except what is herein allowed to him, shall forfeit his office; and if found guilty, on indictment, be otherwise punished, according to the aggravation of the offence, by fine not exceeding five hundred dollars, or imprisonment not exceeding six months, or both.

Sec. 38. *And be it further enacted,* That all engineers and pilots of any such vessel shall, before entering upon their duties, make solemn oath before one of the inspectors herein provided for, to be recorded with the certificate, that he will faithfully and honestly, according to his best skill and judgment, perform all the duties required of him by this act, without concealment or reservation; and if such engineer, pilot, or any witness summoned under this act as a witness, shall, when under examination on oath, knowingly and intentionally falsify the truth, such person shall be deemed guilty of perjury, and if convicted be punished accordingly.

SEC. 39. *And be it further enacted,* That the supervising inspectors appointed under the provisions of this act, shall, within their respective districts, under the direction of the Secretary of the Treasury, take the examination, or receive the statements in writing, of persons of practical knowledge and experience in the navigation of steam-vessels, the construction and use of boilers, engines, machinery, and equipments, touching the form, material, and construction of engines and their appurtenances; the causes of the explosion of boilers and collapse of flues and the means of prevention; the kind and description of safety-valves, water and steam gauges or indicators; equipments for the extinguishment of fires, and for the preservation of life in case of accident, on board of such vessels, and all other means in use or proper to be adopted, for the better security of the lives of persons on board vessels propelled in whole or in part by steam; the advantages and disadvantages of the different descriptions of boilers, engines, and their appurtenances, safety-valves, water and steam-gauges or indicators, equipments for the prevention or extinguishment of fires, and the preservation of life in case of accident, in use on board such vessels; whether any, and what further legislation is necessary or proper for the better security of the lives of persons on board such steam-vessels; which examination and statements so taken and received shall be transmitted to the Secretary of the Treasury, at such time as he shall prescribe.

SEC. 40. *And be it further enacted,* That it shall be the duty of the Secretary of the Treasury to cause such interrogatories to be prepared and published as in his opinion may be proper to elicit the information contemplated by the preceding section, and upon the receipt of the examination and statements taken by the inspectors shall report the same to Congress, together with the recommendation of such further provisions as he may deem proper to be made for the better security of the lives of person on board steam-vessels.

SEC. 41. *And be it further enacted,* That all penalties imposed by this act may be recovered in an action of debt by any person who will sue therefor in any court of the United States.

Sec. 42. *And be it further enacted,* That this act shall not apply to public vessels of the United States or vessels of other countries; nor to steamers used as ferry-boats, tug-boats, towing-boats, nor to steamers not exceeding one hundred and fifty tons burthen and used in whole or in part for navigating canals. The inspection and certificate required by this act shall in all cases of ocean steamers constructed under contract with the United States for the purpose, if desired, of being converted into War Steamers, be made by a Chief Engineer of the Navy, to be detailed for that service by the Secretary of the Navy, and he shall report both to said Secretary and to the supervising inspector of the district where he shall make any inspection.

Sec. 43. *And be it further enacted,* That all such parts of this act as authorize the appointment and qualification of inspectors, and the licensing of engineers and pilots, shall take effect upon the passage thereof, and that all other parts of this act shall go into effect at the times and places as follows: in the districts of New Orleans, St. Louis, Louisville, Cincinnati, Wheeling, Pittsburgh, Nashville, Mobile, and Galveston, on the first day of January next, and in all other districts on the first day of March next.

Sec. 44. *And be it further enacted,* That all parts of laws heretofore made, which are suspended by or are inconsistent with this act, are hereby repealed.

Interstate Commerce Act of 1887

24 Stat. 379 (Feb. 4, 1887)

Be it enacted by the Senate and House of Representatives of the United States of America in Congress assembled, That the provisions of this act shall apply to any common carrier or carriers engaged in the transportation of passengers or property wholly by railroad, or partly by railroad and partly by water when both are used, under a common control, management, or arrangement, for a continuous carriage or shipment, from one State or Territory of the United States, or the District of Columbia, to any other State or Territory of the United States, or the District of Columbia, or from any place in the United States to an adjacent foreign country, or from any place in the United States through a foreign country to any other place in the United States, and also to the transportation in like manner of property shipped from any place in the United States to a foreign country and carried from such place to a port of transshipment, or shipped from a foreign country to any place in the United States and carried to such place from a port of entry either in the United States or an adjacent foreign country: *Provided, however,* That the provisions of this act shall not apply to the transportation of passengers or property, or to the receiving, delivering, storage, or handling of property, wholly within one State, and not shipped to or from a foreign country from or to any State or Territory as aforesaid.

The term "railroad" as used in this act shall include all bridges and ferries used or operated in connection with any railroad, and also all the road in use by any corporation operating a railroad, whether owned or operated under a contract, agreement, or lease; and the term "transportation" shall include all instrumentalities of shipment or carriage.

All charges made for any service rendered or to be rendered in the transportation of passengers or property as aforesaid, or in connection therewith, or for the receiving, delivering, storage, or handling of such property, shall be reasonable and just; and every unjust and unreasonable charge for such service is prohibited and declared to be unlawful.

Sec. 2. That if any common carrier subject to the provisions of this act shall, directly or indirectly, by any special rate, rebate, drawback, or other device, charge, demand, collect, or receive from any person or persons a greater or less compensation for any service rendered, or to be rendered, in the transportation of passengers or property, subject to the provisions of this act, than it charges, demands, collects, or receives from any other person or persons for doing for him or them a like and contemporaneous service in the transportation of a like kind of traffic under substantially similar circumstances and conditions, such common carrier shall be deemed guilty of unjust discrimination, which is hereby prohibited and declared to be unlawful.

Sec. 3. That it shall be unlawful for any common carrier subject to the provisions of this act to make or give any undue or unreasonable preference or advantage to any particular person, company, firm, corporation, or locality, or any particular description of traffic, in any respect whatsoever, or to subject any particular person, company, firm, corporation, or locality, or any particular description of traffic, to any undue or unreasonable prejudice or disadvantage in any respect whatsoever.

Every common carrier subject to the provisions of this act shall, according to their respective powers, afford all reasonable, proper, and equal facilities for the interchange of traffic between their respective lines, and for the receiving, forwarding, and delivering of passengers and property to and from their several lines and those connecting therewith, and shall not discriminate in their rates and charges between such connecting lines; but this shall not be construed as requiring any such common carrier to give the use of its tracks or terminal facilities to another carrier engaged in like business.

Sec. 4. That it shall be unlawful for any common carrier subject to the provisions of this act to charge or receive any greater compensation in the aggregate for the transportation of passengers or of like kind of property, under substantially similar circumstances and conditions, for a shorter than for a longer distance over the same line, in the same direction, the shorter being included within the longer distance; but this shall not be construed as authorizing any common carrier within the terms of this act to charge and receive as great compensation for a shorter as for a longer distance: *Provided, however,* That upon application to the Commission appointed under the provisions of this act, such common carrier may, in special cases, after investigation by the Commission, be authorized to charge less for longer than for shorter distances for the transportation of passengers or property; and the Commission may from time to time prescribe the extent to which such designated common carrier may be relieved from the operation of this section of this act.

SEC. 5. That it shall be unlawful for any common carrier subject to the provisions of this act to enter into any contract, agreement, or combination with any other common carrier or carriers for the pooling of freights of different and competing railroads, or to divide between them the aggregate or net proceeds of the earnings of such railroads, or any portion thereof; and in any case of an agreement for the pooling of freights as aforesaid, each day of its continuance shall be deemed a separate offense.

SEC. 6. That every common carrier subject to the provisions of this act shall print and keep for public inspection schedules showing the rates and fares and charges for the transportation of passengers and property which any such common carrier has established and which are in force at the time upon its railroad, as defined by the first section of this act. The schedules printed as aforesaid by any such common carrier shall plainly state the places upon its railroad between which property and passengers will be carried, and shall contain the classification of freight in force upon such railroad, and shall also state separately the terminal charges and any rules or regulations which in any wise change, affect, or determine any part or the aggregate of such aforesaid rates and fares and charges. Such schedules shall be plainly printed in large type, of at least the size of ordinary pica, and copies for the use of the public shall be kept in every depot or station upon any such railroad, in such places and in such form that they can be conveniently inspected.

Any common carrier subject to the provisions of this act receiving freight in the United States to be carried through a foreign country to any place in the United States shall also in like manner print and keep for public inspection, at every depot where such freight is received for shipment, schedules showing the through rates established and charged by such common carrier to all points in the United States beyond the foreign country to which it accepts freight for shipment; and any freight shipped from the United States through a foreign country into the United States, the through rate o[f] which shall not have been made public as required by this act, shall, before it is admitted into the United States from said foreign country, be subject to customs duties as if said freight were of foreign production; and any law in conflict with this section is hereby repealed.

No advance shall be made in the rates, fares, and charges which have been established and published as aforesaid by any common carrier in compliance with the requirements of this section, except after ten days' public notice, which shall plainly state the changes proposed to be made in the schedule then in force, and the time when the increased rates, fares, or charges will go into effect; and the proposed changes shall be shown by printing new schedules, or shall be plainly indicated upon the schedules in force at the time and kept for public inspection. Reductions in such published rates, fares, or charges may be made without previous public notice; but whenever any such reduction is made, notice of the same shall immediately be publicly posted and the changes made shall immediately be made public by printing new schedules, or shall immediately be plainly indicated upon the schedules at the time in force and kept for public inspection.

And when any such common carrier shall have established and published its rates, fares, and charges in compliance with the provisions of this section, it shall be unlawful for such common carrier to charge, demand, collect, or receive from any person or persons a greater or less compensation for the transportation of passengers or property, or for any services in connection therewith, than is specified in such published schedule of rates, fares, and charges as may at the time be in force.

Every common carrier subject to the provisions of this act shall file with the Commission hereinafter provided for copies of its schedules of rates, fares, and charges which have been established and published in compliance with the requirements of this section, and shall promptly notify said Commission of all changes made in the same. Every such common carrier shall also file with said Commission copies of all contracts, agreements, or arrangements with other common carriers in relation to any traffic affected by the provisions of this act to which it may be a party. And in cases where passengers and freight pass over continuous lines or routes operated by more than one common carrier, and the several common carriers operating such lines or routes establish joint tariffs of rates or fares or charges for such continuous lines or routes, copies of such joint tariffs shall also, in like manner, be filed with said Commission. Such joint rates, fares, and charges on such continuous lines so filed as aforesaid shall be made public by such common carriers when directed by said Commission, in so far as may, in the judgment of the Commission, be deemed practicable; and said Commission shall from time to time prescribe the measure of publicity which shall be given to such rates, fares, and charges, or to such part of them as it may deem it practicable for such common carriers to publish, and the places in which they shall be published but no common carrier party to any such joint tariff shall be liable for the failure of any other common carrier party thereto to observe and adhere to the rates, fares, or charges thus made and published.

If any such common carrier shall neglect or refuse to file or publish its schedules or tariffs of rates, fares, and charges as provided in this section, or any part of the same, such common carrier shall, in addition to other penalties herein prescribed, be subject to a writ of mandamus, to be issued by any circuit court of the United States in the judicial district wherein the principal office of said common carrier is situated or wherein such offense may be committed, and if such common carrier be a foreign corporation, in the judicial circuit wherein such common carrier accepts traffic and has an agent to perform such service, to compel compliance with the aforesaid provisions of this section; and such writ shall issue in the name of the people of the United States, at the relation of the Commissioners appointed under the provisions of this act; and failure to comply with its requirements shall be punishable as and for a contempt; and the said Commissioners, as complainants, may also apply, in any such circuit court of the United States, for a writ of injunction against such common carrier, to restrain such common carrier from receiving or transporting property among the several States and Territories of the United States, or between the United States and adjacent foreign countries, or between ports of transshipment and of entry and the several States and Territories of the United States, as mentioned in the first section of this act, until such common carrier shall have complied with the aforesaid provisions of this section of this act.

Sec. 7. That it shall be unlawful for any common carrier subject to the provisions of this act to enter into any combination, contract, or agreement, expressed or implied, to prevent, by change of time schedule, carriage in different cars, or by other means or devices, the carriage of freights from being continuous from the place of shipment to the place of destination; and no break of bulk, stoppage, or interruption made by such common carrier shall prevent the carriage of freights from being and being treated as one continuous carriage from the place of shipment to the place of destination, unless such break, stoppage, or interruption was made in good faith for some necessary purpose, and without any intent to avoid or unnecessarily interrupt such continuous carriage or to evade any of the provisions of this act.

Sec. 8. That in case any common carrier subject to the provisions of this act shall do, cause to be done, or permit to be done any act, matter, or thing in this act prohibited or declared to be unlawful, or shall omit to do any act, matter, or thing in this act required to be done, such common carrier shall be liable to the person or persons injured thereby for the full amount of damages sustained in consequence of any such violation of the provisions of this act, together with a reasonable counsel or attorney's fee, to be fixed by the court in every case of recovery, which attorney's fee shall be taxed and collected as part of the costs in the case.

Sec. 9. That any person or persons claiming to be damaged by any common carrier subject to the provisions of this act may either make complaint to the Commission as hereinafter provided for, or may bring suit in his or their own behalf for the recovery of the damages for which such common carrier may be liable under the provisions of this act, in any district or circuit court of the United States of competent jurisdiction; but such person or persons shall not have the right to pursue both of said remedies, and must in each case elect which one of the two methods of procedure herein provided for he or they will adopt. In any such action brought for the recovery of damages the court before which the same shall be pending may compel any director, officer, receiver, trustee, or agent of the corporation or company defendant in such suit to attend, appear, and testify in such case, and may compel the production of the books and papers of such corporation or company party to any suit; the claim that any such testimony or evidence may tend to criminate the person giving such evidence shall not excuse such witness from testifying but such evidence or testimony shall not be used against such person on the trial of any criminal proceeding.

Sec. 10. That any common carrier subject to the provisions of this act, or, whenever such common carrier is a corporation, any director or office thereof, or any receiver, trustee, lessee, agent, or person acting for or employed by such corporation, who, alone or with any other corporation, company, person, or party, shall willfully do or cause to be done, or shall willingly suffer or permit to be done, any act, matter, or thing in this act prohibited or declared to be unlawful, or who shall aid or abet therein, or shall willfully omit or fail to do any act, matter, or thing in this act required to be done, or shall cause or willingly suffer or permit any act, matter, or thing so directed or required by this act to be done not to be so done, or shall aid or abet any such omission or failure, or shall be guilty of any infraction of this act, or shall aid or abet therein, shall be deemed guilty of a misdemeanor, and shall, upon conviction thereof in any district court of the United States within the jurisdiction of which such offense was committed, be subject to a fine of not to exceed five thousand dollars for each offense.

SEC. 11. That a Commission is hereby created and established to be known as the Inter-State Commerce Commission, which shall be composed of five Commissioners, who shall be appointed by the President, by and with the advice and consent of the Senate. The Commissioners first appointed under this act shall continue in office for the term of two, three, four, five, and six years, respectively, from the first day of January, anno Domini eighteen hundred and eighty-seven, the term of each to be designated by the President; but their successors shall be appointed for terms of six years, except that any person chosen to fill a vacancy shall be appointed only for the unexpired term of the Commissioner whom he shall succeed. Any Commissioner may be removed by the President for inefficiency, neglect of duty, or malfeasance in office. Not more than three of the Commissioners shall be appointed from the same political party. No person in the employ of or holding any official relation to any common carrier subject to the provisions of this act, or owning stock or bonds thereof, or who is in any manner pecuniarily interested therein, shall enter upon the duties of or hold such office. Said Commissioners shall not engage in any other business, vocation, or employment. No vacancy in the Commission shall impair the right of the remaining Commissioners to exercise all the powers of the Commission.

SEC. 12. That the Commission hereby created shall have authority to inquire into the management of the business of all common carriers subject to the provisions of this act, and shall keep itself informed as to the manner and method in which the same is conducted, and shall have the right to obtain from such common carriers full and complete information necessary to enable the Commission to perform the duties and carry out the objects for which it was created; and for the purposes of this at the Commission shall have power to require the attendance and testimony of witnesses and the production of all books, papers, tariffs, contracts, agreements, and documents relating to any matter under investigation, and to that end may invoke the aid of any court of the United States in requiring the attendance and testimony of witnesses and the production of books, papers, and documents under the provisions of this section.

And any of the circuit courts of the United States within the jurisdiction of which such inquiry is carried on may, in case of contumacy or refusal to obey a subpoena issued to any common carrier subject to the provisions of this act, or other person, issue an order requiring such common carrier or other person to appear before said Commission (and produce books and papers if so ordered) and give evidence touching the matter in question; and any failure to obey such order of the court may be punished by such court as a contempt thereof. The claim that any such testimony or evidence may tend to criminate the person giving such evidence shall not excuse such witness from testifying; but such evidence or testimony shall not be used against such person on the trial of any criminal proceeding.

SEC. 13. The any person, firm, corporation, or association, or any mercantile, agricultural, or manufacturing society, or any body politic or municipal organization complaining of anything done or omitted to be done by any common carrier subject to the provisions of this act in contravention of the provisions thereof, may apply to said Commission by petition, which shall briefly state the facts; whereupon a statement of the charges thus made shall be forwarded by the Commission to such common carrier, who shall be called upon to satisfy the complaint or to answer the same in writing within a reasonable time, to be specified by the Commission. If such common carrier, within the time specified, shall make reparation for the injury alleged to have been done, said carrier shall be relieved of liability to the complainant only for the particular violation of law thus complained of. If such carrier shall not satisfy the complaint within the time specified, or there shall appear to be any reasonable ground for investigating said complaint, it shall be the duty of the Commission to investigate the matters complained of in such manner and by such means as it shall deem proper.

Said Commission shall in like manner investigate any complaint forwarded by the railroad commissioner or railroad commission of any State or Territory, at the request of such commissioner or commission, and may institute any inquiry on its own motion in the same manner and to the same effect as though complaint had been made.

No complaint shall at any time be dismissed because of the absence of direct damage to the complainant.

Sec. 14. That whenever an investigation shall be made by said Commission, it shall be its duty to make a report in writing in respect thereto, which shall include the findings of fact upon which the conclusions of the Commission are based, together with its recommendation as to what reparation, if any, should be made by the common carrier to any party or parties who may be found to have been injured; and such findings so made shall thereafter, in all judicial proceedings, be deemed prima facie evidence as to each and every fact found.

All reports of investigations made by the Commission shall be entered of record, and a copy thereof shall be furnished to the party who may have complained, and to any common carrier that may have been complained of.

Sec. 15. That if in any case in which an investigation shall be made by said Commission it shall be made to appear to the satisfaction of the Commission, either by the testimony of witnesses or other evidence, that anything has been done or omitted to be done in violation of the provisions of this act, or of any law cognizable by said Commission, by any common carrier, or that any injury or damage has been sustained by the party or parties complaining, or by other parties aggrieved in consequence of any such violation, it shall be the duty of the Commission to forthwith cause a copy of its report in respect thereto to be delivered to such common carrier, together with a notice to said common carrier to cease and desist from such violation, or to make reparation for the injury so found to have been done, or both, within a reasonable time, to be specified by the Commission; and if, within the time specified, it shall be made to appear to the Commission that such common carrier has ceased from such violation of law, and has made reparation for the injury found to have been done, in compliance with the report and notice of the Commission, or to the satisfaction of the party complaining, a statement to that effect shall be entered of record by the Commission, and the said common carrier shall thereupon be relieved from further liability or penalty for such particular violation of law.

Sec. 16. That whenever any common carrier, as defined in and subject to the provisions of this act, shall violate or refuse or neglect to obey any lawful order or requirement of the Commission in this act named, it shall be the duty of the Commission, and lawful for any company or person interested in such order or requirement, to apply, in a summary way, be petition, to the circuit court of the United States sitting in equity in the judicial district in which the common carrier complained of has its principal office, or in which the violation or disobedience of such order or requirement shall happen, alleging such violation or disobedience, as the case may be; and the said court shall have power to hear and determine the matter, on such short notice to the common carrier complained of as the court shall deem reasonable; and such notice may be served on such common carrier, his or its officers, agents, or servants, in such manner as the court shall direct; and said court shall proceed to hear and determine the matter speedily as a court of equity, and without the formal pleadings and proceedings applicable to ordinary suits in equity, but in such manner as to do justice in the premises; and to this end such court shall have power, if it think fit, to direct and prosecute, in such mode and by such persons as it may appoint, all such inquiries as the court may think needful to enable it to form a just judgment in the matter of such petition; and on such hearing the report of said Commission shall be prima facie evidence of the matters therein stated; and if it be made to appear to such court, on such hearing or on report of any such person or persons, that the lawful order or requirement of said Commission drawn in question has been violated or disobeyed, it shall be lawful for such court to issue a writ of injunction or other proper process, mandatory or otherwise, to restrain such common carrier from further continuing such violation or disobedience of such order or requirement of said Commission, and enjoining obedience to the same; and in case of any disobedience of any such writ of injunction or other proper process, mandatory or otherwise, it shall be lawful for such court to issue writs of attachment, or any other process of said court incident or applicable to writs of injunction or other proper process, mandatory or otherwise, against such common carrier, and if a corporation, against one or more of the directors, officers, or agents of the same, or against any owner, lessee, trustee, receiver, or other person failing to obey such writ of injunction or other proper process, mandatory or otherwise; and said court may, if it shall think fit, make an order directing such common carrier or other person so disobeying such writ of injunction or other proper process, mandatory or otherwise, to pay such sum or money not exceeding for each carrier or person in default the sum of five hundred dollars for every day after a day to be named in the order that such carrier or other person shall fail to obey such injunction or other proper process, mandatory or otherwise; and such moneys shall be payable as the court shall direct, either to the party complaining, or into court to abide the ultimate decision of the court, or into the Treasury; and payment thereof may, without prejudice to any other mode of recovering the same, be enforced by attachment or order in the nature of a writ of execution, in like manner as if the same had been recovered by a final decree in personam in such court. When the subject in dispute shall be of the value of two thousand dollars or more, either party to such proceeding before said court may appeal to the Supreme Court of the United States, under the same regulations now provided by law in respect of security for such appeal; but such appeal shall not operate to stay or supersede the order of the court or the execution of any writ or process thereon; and such court may, in every such matter, order the payment of such costs and counsel fees as shall be deemed reasonable. Whenever any such petition shall be filed or presented by the Commission it shall be the duty of the district attorney, under the direction of the Attorney General of the United States, to prosecute the same; and the costs and expenses of such prosecution shall be paid out of the appropriation for the expenses of the courts of the United States. For the purposes of this act, excepting its penal provisions, the circuit courts of the United States shall be deemed to be always in session.

Sec. 17. That the Commission may conduct its proceedings in such manner as will best conduce to the proper dispatch of business and to the ends of justice. A majority of the Commission shall constitute a quorum for the transaction of business, but no Commissioner shall participate in any hearing or proceeding in which he has any pecuniary interest. Said Commission may, from time to time, make or amend such general rules or orders as may be requisite for the order and regulation of proceedings before it, including forms of notices and the service thereof, which shall conform, as nearly as may be, to those in use in the courts of the United States. Any party may appear before said Commission and be heard, in person or by attorney. Every vote and official act of the Commission shall be entered of record, and its proceedings shall be public upon the request of either party interested. Said Commission shall have an official seal, which shall be judicially noticed. Either of the members of the Commission may administer oaths and affirmations.

Sec. 18. That each Commissioner shall receive an annual salary of seven thousand five hundred dollars, payable in the same manner as the salaries of judges of the courts of the United States. The Commission shall appoint a secretary, who shall receive an annual salary of three thousand five hundred dollars, payable in like manner. The Commission shall have authority to employ and fix the compensation of such other employees as it may find necessary to the proper performance of its duties, subject to the approval of the Secretary of the Interior.

The Commission shall be furnished by the Secretary of the Interior with suitable offices and all necessary office supplies. Witnesses summoned before the Commission shall be paid the same fees and mileage that are paid witnesses in the courts of the United States.

All of the expenses of the Commission, including all necessary expenses for transportation incurred by the Commissioners, or by their employees under their orders, in making any investigation in any other places than in the city of Washington, shall be allowed and paid, on the presentation of itemized vouchers therefor approved by the chairman of the Commission and the Secretary of the Interior.

Sec. 19. That the principal office of the Commission shall be in the city of Washington, where its general sessions shall be held; but whenever the convenience of the public or of the parties may be promoted or delay or expense prevented thereby, the Commission may hold special sessions in any part of the United States. It may, by one or more of the Commissioners, prosecute any inquiry necessary to its duties, in any part of the United States, into any matter or question of fact pertaining to the business of any common carrier subject to the provisions of this act.

Sec. 20. That the Commission is hereby authorized to require annual reports from all common carriers subject to the provisions of this act, to fix the time and prescribe the manner in which such reports shall be made, and to require from such carriers specific answers to all questions upon which the Commission may need information. Such annual reports shall show in detail the amount of capital stock issued, the amounts paid therefor, and the manner of payment for the same; that dividends paid, the surplus fund, if any, and the number of stockholders; the funded and floating debts and the interest paid thereon; the cost and value of the carrier's property, franchises, and equipment; the number of employees and the salaries paid each class; the amounts expended for improvements each year, how expended, and the character of such improvements; the earnings and receipts from each branch of business and from all sources; the operating and other expenses; the balances of profit and loss; and a complete exhibit of the financial operations of the carrier each year, including an annual balance-sheet. Such reports shall also contain such information in relation to rates or regulations concerning fares or freights, or agreements, arrangements, or contracts with other common carriers, as the Commission may require; and the said Commission may, within its discretion, for the purpose of enabling it the better to carry out the purposes of this act, prescribe (if in the opinion of the Commission it is practicable to prescribe such uniformity and methods of keeping accounts) a period of time within with all common carriers subject to the provisions of this act shall have, as near as may be, a uniform system of accounts, and the manner in which such accounts shall be kept.

Sec. 21. That the Commission shall, on or before the first day of December in each year, make a report to the Secretary of the Interior, which shall be by him transmitted to Congress, and copies of which shall be distributed as are the other reports issued from the Interior Department. This report shall contain such information and data collected by the Commission as may be considered of value in the determination of questions connected with the regulation of commerce, together with such recommendations as to additional legislation relating thereto as the Commission may deem necessary.

Sec. 22. That nothing in this act shall apply to the carriage, storage, or handling of property free or at reduced rates for the United States, State, or municipal governments, or for charitable purposes, or to or from fairs and expositions for exhibition thereat, or the issuance of mileage, excursion, or commutation passenger tickets; nothing in this act shall be construed to prohibit any common carrier from giving reduced rates to ministers of religion; nothing in this act shall be construed to prevent railroads from giving free carriage to their own officers and employees, or to prevent the principal officers of any railroad company or companies from exchanging passes or tickets with other railroad companies for their officers and employees; and nothing in this act contained shall in any way abridge or alter the remedies now existing at common law or by statute, but the provisions of this act are in addition to such remedies: *Provided,* That no pending litigation shall in any way be affected by this act.

Sec. 23. That the sum of one hundred thousand dollars is hereby appropriated for the use and purposes of this act for the fiscal year ending June thirtieth, anno Domini eighteen hundred and eighty-eight, and the intervening time anterior thereto.

Sec. 24. That the provisions of sections eleven and eighteen of this act, relating to the appointment and organization of the Commission herein provided for, shall take effect immediately, and the remaining provisions of this act shall take effect sixty days after its passage.

Index